THE RACE AND MEDIA READER

The Race and Media Reader provides a wide-ranging introduction to major issues and debates surrounding the role that the media plays in ongoing struggles around race and racism in the United States today. The essays collected here come from a wide variety of disciplinary, theoretical, and methodological perspectives, and focus on a broad range of media practices, racial and ethnic populations, and historical moments. These readings, curated by Gilbert Rodman, offer an intersectional approach to thinking about media and the politics of race, arguing that media representations of specific racial/ethnic identities need to be understood within the broader social, cultural, and economic contexts in which they circulate. With concise introductory notes by Rodman, these selections ask readers to take a critical stance on the media's role as one of the most powerful institutions involved in the creation and maintenance of problematic racial hierarchies, and to consider ways of thinking and acting that might bring us closer to a world where racism no longer exists.

Gilbert B. Rodman is an Associate Professor of Communication Studies at the University of Minnesota, where his research focuses on critical media studies, cultural studies, popular culture, communication technologies, intellectual property, and the politics of race and ethnicity.

D1601901

THE RACE AND MEDIA READER

Edited by
GILBERT B. RODMAN

Routledge
Taylor & Francis Group

NEW YORK AND LONDON

First published 2014
by Routledge
711 Third Avenue, New York, NY 10017

and by Routledge
2 Park Square, Milton Park, Abingdon, Oxon OX14 4RN

Routledge is an imprint of the Taylor & Francis Group, an informa business

Library of Congress Cataloging-in-Publication Data

The race and media reader / edited by Gilbert B. Rodman.
    pages cm
  Includes bibliographical references and index.
  1. Minorities in mass media.   2. Race relations in mass media.   3. Racism in mass media.   4. Mass media and race relations.   I. Rodman, Gilbert B., 1965– editor of compilation.
P94.5.M55R32   2013
302.2308—dc23   2013014460

ISBN: 978-0-415-80158-4 (hbk)
ISBN: 978-0-415-80159-1 (pbk)

Typeset in Amasis
by Apex CoVantage, LLC

Printed and bound by CPI Group (UK) Ltd, Croydon, CR0 4YY

CONTENTS

ACKNOWLEDGMENTS

Thanks very much to Matt Byrnie for getting this project off the ground, and to Erica Wetter and Margo Irvin for helping to bring it back to earth again after a long flight. Many thanks as well to all the students who have wrestled with these issues in my classes over the past twenty years or so. This is a stronger collection—and I am a wiser teacher—for their questions and insights, their hopefulness and honesty, and their boldness and courage.

INTRODUCTION: TEACHING/LEARNING ABOUT RACE

Racial prejudice and institutional racism remain major problems in the United States today. Whatever advances have been made over the years with respect to racial politics, the United States remains a nation deeply divided along racial fault lines, and race continues to matter tremendously when it comes to the distribution of education, jobs, housing, health care, justice, and political power. These injustices are perpetuated across a wide range of major institutions: political, economic, social, cultural, educational, religious, and otherwise. One of the most important such institutions, though, is "the media."[1] Put simply, "race" is a set of cultural and historical fictions that we tell ourselves over and over again on a daily basis—fictions that help to produce and maintain a hierarchical racial formation—and the media remains one of the primary sets of institutions where such stories circulate.

When I teach my undergraduate course on race and media, I try to underscore just how widespread such narratives are by giving my students a simple exercise. I put them into small groups and ask them to imagine that they've just met someone for the first time. Then I ask them to create a list of all the clues they might use—short of actually asking the other person directly—to figure out their new acquaintance's race. Two things invariably happen next.

First, my students always compile a *very* long list of possible clues. We fill the blackboard with dozens of physical traits, linguistic quirks, cultural practices, occupational characteristics, and other things that might allow my students to figure out someone's race. To be sure, some of their suggestions are more unreliable (or, perhaps, more subtle) than others, and some of them do a better job of eliminating certain possibilities than they do in pinning down the right one. But my students never struggle to come up with multiple litmus tests that might help them solve the riddle at hand. In this respect, the narratives of race are incredibly easy to recognize and acknowledge.

Second, this exercise always makes my students *profoundly* uncomfortable. Regardless of their own racial/ethnic backgrounds, they recognize very quickly that most (if not all) of the potential distinguishing traits on their lists are rooted in highly dubious stereotypes. They know perfectly well, for example, that not all dishwashers are Latino/a and that not all lawyers are white. At the same time, however, they know that there are significant patterns in how different types of labor are distributed across different racial and ethnic populations. They may not like that those patterns are real. They may not actively want to use these sorts of stereotypes in their daily lives. But this exercise helps to remind my students that such stereotypes still actively (albeit often unconsciously) shape the "common sense" ways that my students move through the world. In this respect, the narratives of race are often exceptionally difficult to acknowledge—especially insofar as they remind my students that the world is not a simple meritocracy and that many of them often benefit substantially from such inequities.

There are several other important lessons about race and media that this exercise helps to convey to my students. For example, the fluency with which my students can spontaneously generate long lists of significant (if imperfect) markers of racial difference demonstrates just how well trained they are in the largely unspoken "rules" of racial and ethnic identification. It's not a coincidence that, in nearly twenty years of using this exercise, the only students who have ever had obvious trouble contributing to the list-making process have been international students who had been in the country for less than a year. For everyone else—even nonnatives—living in the United States for any length of time is enough to impart an implicit, yet quite powerful, understanding of the existing racial order. We are socialized—early and often—to see racial and ethnic difference and to mentally place the people we encounter into (what we assume to be) their "proper" racial and ethnic categories on a daily basis.

The lists that my students construct also help to reveal how thoroughly our understanding of race—both individually and collectively—is shaped by mediated narratives and representations. Students (especially, though by no means exclusively, white students) who have had little to no actual life experience with racial and ethnic populations different from their own have nonetheless amassed a sizable body of knowledge (flawed though it often is) about those communities: what they look like, how they talk, what they eat, how they dress, what kind of music they like, what kind of jobs they have, and so on. When I ask my students how they "know" so much about a particular racial or ethnic group (even if they recognize, as they sometimes do, that much of their knowledge is actually wrong), they invariably cite television programs, newspaper stories, movies, video games, and other mass media texts as their primary sources of such information. In many cases (again, most often for white students), those media representations actually trump real life experiences, insofar as students will frequently identify their friends of other races as exceptions to the rule (i.e., the dominant media narrative) when it comes to what those racial populations are "really" like.

Additionally, this exercise helps to demonstrate that our fluency in recognizing racial differences is actually a culturally and historically grounded phenomenon, rather than simply the "natural" by-product of recognizing "obvious" differences. Partially, this is because so many of the distinguishing characteristics that my students come up with are clearly rooted in culture, rather than nature. There's nothing genetic, after all, about a taste for hip-hop or country music. More crucially, though, this exercise makes it easier to recognize other equally visible traits and characteristics that could be used to place the people around us into distinct identity categories of one sort or another yet somehow manage not to result in the sort of hierarchical social and political order that exists around race.

Handedness, for example, is a real distinction that exists between people that is very easy to spot in everyday public life: simply pay attention to which hand someone favors as they write, or eat, or press buttons, or pick up objects (and so on), and it's usually obvious if they are right- or left-handed. Yet despite the ease with which we can distinguish "lefties" from "righties," even in a crowd of total strangers, this is not a skill that most of us have honed very well, largely because handedness isn't a form of identity that matters in the same way that race does. Though southpaws may claim that the world is still biased against them in noticeable ways—scissors don't work properly, coffee mugs face backwards, and so on—they also generally recognize that these are not forms of discrimination that dramatically affect their chances to succeed in the world. There are no ghettos where left-handed people reside in disproportionate numbers because the economy and the housing market discriminate against them. Left-handers are not disproportionately stopped by the police, convicted of crimes, or sentenced to death. They are not routinely denied admission to college or turned down for jobs and promotions. Nor are they consistently portrayed in the mainstream media—either in fictional or nonfictional contexts—as more lazy, stupid, immoral, dishonest, sexually "loose" (and so on) than right-handers.

In contrast, all of those inequities (and many more) *do* exist in significant ways when it comes to different racial and ethnic identities. We typically don't pay attention to handedness in the way that we pay attention to race, because our social order doesn't systematically disadvantage lefties in the way that it does people of color. Put simply, race is a form of difference that makes a huge difference when it comes to one's opportunities for success and happiness—and this is a byproduct of political, cultural, and historical circumstances, rather than the "natural" order of things.

One final lesson that arises out of this exercise involves the complicated ways that racial identity is both a personal, private, and individual phenomenon (you are who/what you understand yourself to be) and a social, cultural, and mediated phenomenon (you are who/what other people understand you to be). After my students and I spend a while discussing the various issues described above, I always ask them to use their finely honed skills at placing people into their "proper" racial categories to figure out what *my* racial and ethnic identity actually is. Their answers to this question always vary wildly—and are almost always wrong. It is, in many respects, an unfair question to pose, since even someone with a finely tuned sense of subtle racial cues may find it difficult to look past my pink skin and pick up on the full "truth" that I am part black, part white, and part Native American.[2] While I generally think of (and refer to) myself as "mixed," this act of self-labeling provides no guarantees for how other people categorize me. It's been my experience that most (though by no means all) strangers and new acquaintances see the color of my skin and read me as white (at least insofar as they let on), even though that's not how I have ever identified myself. Moreover, the process of "outing" myself as "mixed" still frequently leads people (especially those who have deeply internalized the "one-drop" rule of racial identity) to decide that I'm really black. The complicated story of my own racial identity (and its fraught relationship with the dominant narratives of how race is supposed to function) is by no means unique, of course. The world is filled with people whose family trees are just as jumbled as mine. But telling my story to my students helps to underscore the fact that our racial identities are *not* simply roles that we perform from within based on our own knowledge of who/what we "really" are: they're just as much roles that are routinely, repeatedly, and automatically imposed on us by other people (and, of course, we do precisely the same to them).

* * * * *

The goal of this reader is to provide an introductory survey of some of the major issues and debates about the role that the media plays in the ongoing struggles around race and racism in the United States today. One of the major principles I used in selecting specific authors and essays for this volume was to insist that the various chapters focus on questions of *racism*, rather than just race. Put simply, race only matters enough to make it the focal point of a university course because it remains an issue that is politically charged, fraught, and deadly serious. To teach race without teaching racism is to pretend that the world is somehow a level playing field or that race is nothing more than a matter of incidental curiosity, rather than one of the primary mechanisms by which US society is sorted, separated, and structured into the high and the low, the rich and the poor, the powerful and the weak, the central and the marginal. The essays collected here come from a wide variety of disciplinary, theoretical, and methodological perspectives. They focus on a broad range of media practices, racial and ethnic populations, and historical moments. But they all treat race as a fundamentally political phenomenon that matters deeply when it comes to how the world is organized.

As a topic, "race and media" covers an exceptionally large and diverse territory, and no single volume can possibly do justice to the full range of scholarship and criticism encompassed by such a label. The first draft of the table of contents for this volume was almost twice as long as that for the book you now hold in your hands—and, even then, I had already passed over dozens of other worthy essays in whittling that preliminary lineup of readings down to a not-quite-manageable size. I wish this collection could be longer and more exhaustive in its coverage than it is, but the economics of publishing militate against 700-page anthologies.

The clustering and ordering of these essays is both purposeful and (almost) arbitrary. While I've placed the individual pieces into thematic sections that speak to major analytic concerns with respect to the study of race and media, many—perhaps even most—of the essays collected herein speak across more than one of these themes. Kembrew McLeod's essay on sampling and hip-hop, for instance, has just as much to say about issues of race and technology as it does about the politics of appropriation. Grant Farred's analysis of the challenges that Yao Ming poses, as a Chinese national, to the NBA's "post-racial" branding strategies could fit just as easily in the section on globalization as it does in the section on institutions. And so on. As is the case with race itself, the attempt to craft neat, discrete identifying categories—and then to impose those categories onto a world that is inevitably much messier than that—is inherently flawed.

It is also worth remembering that while racism is certainly not a problem that is unique to the United States, racial formations (see chapter 2) also vary significantly across both geopolitical borders and historical contexts—enough so as to place sharp limitations on how well specific analyses of race and racism travel across either space or time. While some of the readings collected here come from (and speak to) racial formations elsewhere around the world, the full range of global variations with respect to race and racism is far beyond the scope of this project.

I'd like to close this introduction with a warning that I always give to my students at the start of my course on race and media: there are no easy answers to the problem of racism in any of the essays collected here. There's a recurring tendency in US culture to try and reframe difficult issues so as to make them seem much cleaner and easier than they really are and to offer up simple solutions that do more to wish the problem away than to actually resolve it. The classic sitcom episode about racism, for instance, tends to reduce the subject to nothing more than a

matter of easily correctable personal prejudices and pretends that most racial conflicts can be solved in twenty-two minutes (leaving time for commercials) with a few simple clichés ("What we learned today, children, is that people who look different from us on the outside are really just like us on the inside."). It's sweet. It's happy. It gets us to the next commercial break without upsetting the sponsors. But if racism were truly that simple, it would have disappeared ages ago, and there would be no need for anyone to teach (or learn) about how racism works.

Notes

1. In colloquial usage, "the media" is an exceptionally loose and baggy term. It encompasses everything from blockbuster Hollywood films seen by tens of millions of people to pirate radio stations with audiences that (on a good day) number in the hundreds, from dance-pop divas with massive promotional machines behind them to independent blogger-journalists who rely solely on word of mouth to attract readers. In many—perhaps even most—contexts, when people talk about "the media," what they *really* mean is "the mainstream media": i.e., the various institutions that occupy (and, in many ways, create) the ostensible center of the culture, most of which are wholly owned subsidiaries of the handful of multinational conglomerates that control the majority of the world's media outlets. This volume uses the term in its much broader sense, to include the full range of media outlets: big and small, powerful and weak, central and marginal, dominant and oppositional.

2. To be clear, this description is itself a problematic fiction, since it depends on the false notion that race is a simple genetic trait that is passed on from parents to their children. To the extent that this form of bad science lies at the root of how race is most commonly understood in the United States, however, mapping out my heritage with these types of fractions is the "proper" way to try and fit my racial identity into the standard narratives of how race works.

SECTION I

CONCEPTS AND DEFINITIONS

Before we can attempt to have any sort of constructive discussion about contemporary racial politics, we need to have a clear sense of the key concepts at the core of the subject. Too often, attempts at such conversations flounder because the various parties involved are working with very different assumptions about what the most basic terms of the debate actually mean. This section of the reader helps to lay the definitional foundations that can (hopefully) forestall that sort of confusion and that will help to make the various arguments found in the subsequent sections of the book more intelligible.

The quotation marks in the title of the American Anthropological Association's (AAA) statement on "race" underscore the simple, yet all too often unrecognized, fact that this thing we call "race" is a cultural and historical construct, rather than a natural, biological, or scientific phenomenon. The common sense understanding of race in the United States is that it is genetic: something that we each inherit from our parents and that lies at the natural core of who we really are. The AAA's statement is a succinct refutation of that supposed truth and a forthright claim that the various race-related behaviors, traits, and tendencies that we (stereo)typically ascribe to the "natural" differences between the races are actually rooted in cultural practices. To be clear, this insight doesn't mean that race isn't real or that its impact on the world is somehow imaginary. On the contrary, there are plenty of major concepts that are obviously and entirely cultural, rather than natural, phenomena yet that still help to shape and structure our society in significant ways. Like "justice," "democracy," "freedom," "love" (and so on), the concept of "race" still does very powerful work in the world around us. To recognize that "race" (and the work that it does) had to be invented, however, is a crucial step toward trying to reinvent it, and thus remake the world around us in more just and egalitarian ways.

Michael Omi and Howard Winant's essay introduces the concept of "racial formation": a model for understanding race as a structural and institutional phenomenon (rather than just a simple category of personal identity) that functions as "a fundamental *organizing principle* of social relationships." This is a crucial insight for helping us understand how race and (even more importantly) racism work: that is, the recognition that race isn't a form of identity that accidentally matches up with significant social and political hierarchies, as much as it is one of the primary mechanisms used to produce and reinforce such hierarchies in the first place.

In everyday usage—at both the individual level of personal conversations and the more public level of mainstream media discourse—many people invoke the concept of "racism" as if it were a simple synonym for "prejudice." To say that someone is racist is typically just another way of claiming that he or she harbors some sort of unwarranted negative bias toward people of other races. Beverly Daniel Tatum's essay presents a strong—and absolutely vital—case for thinking of these two concepts as related, but not at all equivalent. The distinction that she draws between prejudice (i.e., a form of individual bigotry that is equally accessible to everyone) and racism (i.e., a hierarchical system of power and privilege that routinely works to the disadvantage of people of color) is essential to understanding the very different ways that the racial order functions for whites than it does for people of color.

Peggy McIntosh's short essay—an oft-cited classic—offers a succinct summary of how white privilege consistently provides a plethora of social, cultural, and economic benefits to white people, even when (or, perhaps, *especially* when) they aren't even aware that they're receiving such perks. The relative invisibility of this process is absolutely crucial here, as it helps to explain how racism routinely shapes the world around us in ways that maintain a hierarchical social order structured around racial differences.

Finally, Stuart Hall's essay offers a productive distinction between what he calls "overt" and "covert" forms of racism. He also provides a brief analysis of an attempt to produce a documentary television program with an antiracist agenda for the British Broadcasting Corporation (BBC), and the difficult— perhaps even irresolvable—debates that ensued about how best to craft "good" (i.e., politically progressive) media representations of race and racism. The questions and challenges raised by those debates serve as a helpful segue into the next section of this reader.

1.
STATEMENT ON "RACE"
American Anthropological Association

> *The following statement was adopted by the Execu-*
> *tive Board of the American Anthropological Asso-*
> *ciation, acting on a draft prepared by a committee*
> *of representative American anthropologists. It does*
> *not reflect a consensus of all members of the AAA,*
> *as individuals vary in their approaches to the study*
> *of "race." We believe that it represents generally the*
> *contemporary thinking and scholarly positions of*
> *a majority of anthropologists. (May 17, 1998)*

In the United States both scholars and the general public have been conditioned to viewing human races as natural and separate divisions within the human species based on visible physical differences. With the vast expansion of scientific knowledge in this century, however, it has become clear that human populations are not unambiguous, clearly demarcated, biologically distinct groups. Evidence from the analysis of genetics (e.g., DNA) indicates that most physical variation, about 94%, lies *within* so-called racial groups. Conventional geographic "racial" groupings differ from one another only in about 6% of their genes. This means that there is greater variation within "racial" groups than between them. In neighboring populations there is much overlapping of genes and their phenotypic (physical) expressions. Throughout history whenever different groups have come into contact, they have interbred. The continued sharing of genetic materials has maintained all of humankind as a single species.

Physical variations in any given trait tend to occur gradually rather than abruptly over geographic areas. And because physical traits are inherited independently of one another, knowing the range of one trait does not predict the presence of others. For example, skin color varies largely from light in the temperate areas in the north to dark in the tropical areas in the south; its intensity is not related to nose shape or hair texture. Dark skin may be associated with frizzy or kinky hair or curly or wavy or straight hair, all of which are found among different indigenous peoples in tropical regions. These facts render any attempt to establish lines of division among biological populations both arbitrary and subjective.

Historical research has shown that the idea of "race" has always carried more meanings than mere physical differences; indeed, physical variations in the human species have no meaning except the social ones that humans put on them. Today scholars in many fields argue that "race" as it is understood in the United States of America was a social mechanism invented during the 18th century to refer to those populations brought together in colonial America: the English and other European settlers, the conquered Indian peoples, and those peoples of Africa brought in to provide slave labor.

From its inception, this modern concept of "race" was modeled after an ancient theorem of the Great Chain of Being, which posited natural categories on a hierarchy established by God or nature. Thus "race" was a mode of classification linked specifically to peoples in the colonial situation. It subsumed a growing ideology of inequality devised to rationalize European attitudes and treatment of the conquered and enslaved peoples. Proponents of slavery in particular during the 19th century used "race" to justify the retention of slavery. The ideology magnified the differences among Europeans, Africans, and Indians, established a rigid hierarchy of socially exclusive categories, underscored and bolstered unequal rank and status differences, and provided the rationalization that the inequality was natural or God-given. The different physical traits of African-Americans and Indians became markers or symbols of their status differences.

As they were constructing US society, leaders among European-Americans fabricated the cultural/behavioral characteristics associated with each "race," linking superior traits with Europeans and negative and inferior ones to blacks and Indians. Numerous arbitrary and fictitious beliefs about the different peoples were institutionalized and deeply embedded in American thought.

Early in the 19th century the growing fields of science began to reflect the public consciousness about human differences. Differences among the "racial" categories were projected to their greatest extreme when the argument was posed that Africans, Indians, and Europeans were separate species, with Africans the least human and closer taxonomically to apes.

Ultimately "race" as an ideology about human differences was subsequently spread to other areas of the world. It became a strategy for dividing, ranking, and controlling colonized people used by colonial powers everywhere. But it was not limited to the colonial situation. In the latter part of the 19th century it was employed by Europeans to rank one another and to justify social, economic, and political inequalities among their peoples. During World War II, the Nazis under Adolf Hitler enjoined the expanded ideology of "race" and "racial" differences and took them to a logical end: the extermination of 11 million people of "inferior races" (e.g., Jews, Gypsies, Africans, homosexuals, and so forth) and other unspeakable brutalities of the Holocaust.

"Race" thus evolved as a worldview, a body of prejudgments that distorts our ideas about human differences and group behavior. Racial beliefs constitute myths about the diversity in the human species and about the abilities and behavior of people homogenized into "racial" categories. The myths fused behavior and physical features together in the public mind, impeding our comprehension of both biological variations and cultural behavior, implying that both are genetically determined. Racial myths bear no relationship to the reality of human capabilities or behavior. Scientists today find that reliance on such folk beliefs about human differences in research has led to countless errors.

At the end of the 20th century, we now understand that human cultural behavior is learned, conditioned into infants beginning at birth, and always subject to modification. No human is born with a built-in culture or language. Our temperaments, dispositions, and personalities, regardless of genetic propensities, are developed within sets of meanings and values that we call "culture." Studies of infant and early childhood learning and behavior attest to the reality of our cultures in forming who we are.

It is a basic tenet of anthropological knowledge that all normal human beings have the capacity to learn any cultural behavior. The American experience with immigrants from hundreds of different language and cultural backgrounds who have acquired some version of American culture traits and behavior is the clearest evidence of this fact. Moreover, people of all physical variations have learned different cultural behaviors and continue to do so as modern transportation moves millions of immigrants around the world.

How people have been accepted and treated within the context of a given society or culture has a direct impact on how they perform in that society. The "racial" worldview was invented to assign some groups to perpetual low status, while others were permitted access to privilege, power, and wealth. The tragedy in the United States has been that the policies and practices stemming from this worldview succeeded all too well in constructing unequal populations among Europeans, Native Americans, and peoples of African descent. Given what we know about the capacity of normal humans to achieve and function within any culture, we conclude that present-day inequalities between so-called "racial" groups are not consequences of their biological inheritance but products of historical and contemporary social, economic, educational, and political circumstances.

2.
RACIAL FORMATION
Michael Omi and Howard Winant

In 1982–83, Susie Guillory Phipps unsuccessfully sued the Louisiana Bureau of Vital Records to change her racial classification from black to white. The descendant of an 18th-century white planter and a black slave, Phipps was designated "black" in her birth certificate in accordance with a 1970 state law which declared anyone with at least 1/32nd "Negro blood" to be black.

The Phipps case raised intriguing questions about the concept of race, its meaning in contemporary society, and its use (and abuse) in public policy. Assistant Attorney General Ron Davis defended the law by pointing out that some type of racial classification was necessary to comply with federal record-keeping requirements and to facilitate programs for the prevention of genetic diseases. Phipps's attorney, Brian Begue, argued that the assignment of racial categories on birth certificates was unconstitutional and that the 1/32nd designation was inaccurate. He called on a retired Tulane University professor who cited research indicating that most Louisiana whites have at least 1/20th "Negro" ancestry.

In the end, Phipps lost. The court upheld the state's right to classify and quantify racial identity.[1]

Phipps's problematic racial identity, and her effort to resolve it through state action, is in many ways a parable of America's unsolved racial dilemma. It illustrates the difficulties of defining race and assigning individuals or groups to racial categories. It shows how the racial legacies of the past—slavery and bigotry—continue to shape the present. It reveals both the deep involvement of the state in the organization and interpretation of race, and the inadequacy of state institutions to carry out these functions. It demonstrates how deeply Americans both as individuals and as a civilization are shaped, and indeed haunted, by race.

Having lived her whole life thinking that she was white, Phipps suddenly discovers that by legal definition she is not. In US society, such an event is indeed catastrophic.[2] But if she is not white, of what race is she? The *state* claims that she is black, based on its rules of classification,[3] and another state agency, the court, upholds this judgment. But despite these classificatory standards which have imposed an either-or logic on racial identity, Phipps will not in fact "change color." Unlike what would have happened during slavery times if one's claim to whiteness was successfully challenged, we can assume that despite the outcome of her legal challenge, Phipps will remain in most of the social relationships she had occupied before the trial. Her socialization, her familial and friendship networks, her cultural orientation, will not change. She will simply have to wrestle with her newly acquired "hybridized" condition. She will have to confront the "Other" within.

The designation of racial categories and the determination of racial identity is no simple task. For centuries, this question has precipitated intense debates and conflicts, particularly in the US—disputes over natural and legal rights, over the distribution of resources, and indeed, over who shall live and who shall die.

A crucial dimension of the Phipps case is that it illustrates the inadequacy of claims that race is a mere matter of variations in human physiognomy, that it is simply a matter of skin color. But if race cannot be understood in this manner, how *can* it be understood? We cannot fully hope to address this topic—no less than the meaning of race, its role in society, and the forces which shape it—in one chapter, nor indeed in one book. Our goal in this chapter, however, is far from modest: we wish to offer at least the outlines of a theory of race and racism.

What Is Race?

There is a continuous temptation to think of race as an *essence,* as something fixed, concrete, and objective. And there is also an opposite temptation: to imagine race as a mere *illusion,* a purely ideological construct which some ideal non-racist social order would eliminate. It is necessary to challenge both these positions, to disrupt and reframe the rigid and bipolar manner in which they are posed and debated, and to transcend the presumably irreconcilable relationship between them.

The effort must be made to understand race as an unstable and "decentered" complex of social meanings constantly being transformed by political struggle. With this in mind, let us propose a definition: *race is a concept which signifies and symbolizes social conflicts and interests by referring to different types of human bodies.* Although the concept of race invokes biologically based human characteristics (so-called "phenotypes"), selection of these particular human features for purposes of racial signification is always and necessarily a social and historical process. In contrast to the other major distinction of this type, that of gender, there is no biological basis for distinguishing among human groups along the lines of race.[4] Indeed, the categories employed to differentiate among human groups along racial lines reveal themselves, upon serious examination, to be at best imprecise, and at worst completely arbitrary.

If the concept of race is so nebulous, can we not dispense with it? Can we not "do without" race, at least in the "enlightened" present? This question has

been posed often, and with greater frequency in recent years.[5] An affirmative answer would of course present obvious practical difficulties: it is rather difficult to jettison widely held beliefs, beliefs which moreover are central to everyone's identity and understanding of the social world. So the attempt to banish the concept as an archaism is at best counterintuitive. But a deeper difficulty, we believe, is inherent in the very formulation of this schema, in its way of posing race as a *problem,* a misconception left over from the past, and suitable now only for the dustbin of history.

A more effective starting point is the recognition that despite its uncertainties and contradictions, the concept of race continues to play a fundamental role in structuring and representing the social world. The task for theory is to explain this situation. It is to avoid both the utopian framework which sees race as an illusion we can somehow "get beyond," and also the essentialist formulation which sees race as something objective and fixed, a biological datum.[6] Thus we should think of race as an element of social structure rather than as an irregularity within it; we should see race as a dimension of human representation rather than an illusion. These perspectives inform the theoretical approach we call racial formation.

Racial Formation

We define *racial formation* as the sociohistorical process by which racial categories are created, inhabited, transformed, and destroyed. Our attempt to elaborate a theory of racial formation will proceed in two steps. First, we argue that racial formation is a process of historically situated *projects* in which human bodies and social structures are represented and organized. Next we link racial formation to the evolution of hegemony, the way in which society is organized and ruled. Such an approach, we believe, can facilitate understanding of a whole range of contemporary controversies and dilemmas involving race, including the nature of racism, the relationship of race to other forms of differences, inequalities, and oppression such as sexism and nationalism, and the dilemmas of racial identity today.

From a racial formation perspective, race is a matter of both social structure and cultural representation. Too often, the attempt is made to understand race simply or primarily in terms of only one of these two analytical dimensions.[7] For example, efforts to explain racial inequality as a purely social structural phenomenon are unable to account for the origins, patterning, and transformation of racial difference.

Conversely, many examinations of racial difference—understood as a matter of cultural attributes *à la* ethnicity theory, or as a society-wide signification system, *à la* some poststructuralist accounts—cannot comprehend such structural phenomena as racial stratification in the labor market or patterns of residential segregation.

An alternative approach is to think of racial formation processes as occurring through a linkage between structure and representation. Racial *projects* do the ideological "work" of making these links. *A racial project is simultaneously an interpretation, representation, or explanation of racial dynamics, and an effort to reorganize and redistribute resources along particular racial lines.* Racial projects connect what race *means* in a particular discursive practice and the ways in which both social structures and everyday experiences are racially *organized,* based upon that meaning. Let us consider this proposition, first in terms of large-scale or macro-level social processes, and then in terms of other dimensions of the racial formation process.

Racial Formation as a Macro-Level Social Process

To *interpret the meaning of race is to frame it social structurally.* Consider for example, this statement by Charles Murray on welfare reform:

My proposal for dealing with the racial issue in social welfare is to repeal every bit of legislation and reverse every court decision that in any way requires, recommends, or awards differential treatment according to race, and thereby put us back onto the track that we left in 1965. We may argue about the appropriate limits of government intervention in trying to enforce the ideal, but at

least it should be possible to identify the ideal: Race is not a morally admissible reason for treating one person differently from another. Period.[8]

Here there is a partial but significant analysis of the meaning of race: it is not a morally valid basis upon which to treat people "differently from one another." We may notice someone's race, but we cannot act upon that awareness. We must act in a "color-blind" fashion. This analysis of the meaning of race is immediately linked to a specific conception of the role of race in the social structure: it can play no part in government action, save in "the enforcement of the ideal." No state policy can legitimately require, recommend, or award different status according to race. This example can be classified as a particular type of racial project in the present-day United States—a "neoconservative" one.

Conversely, *to recognize the racial dimension in social structure is to interpret the meaning of race.* Consider the following statement by the late Supreme Court Justice Thurgood Marshall on minority "set-aside" programs:

A profound difference separates governmental actions that themselves are racist, and governmental actions that seek to remedy the effects of prior racism or to prevent neutral government activity from perpetuating the effects of such racism.[9]

Here the focus is on the racial dimensions of *social structure*—in this case of state activity and policy. The argument is that state actions in the past and present have treated people in very different ways according to their race, and thus the government cannot retreat from its policy responsibilities in this area. It cannot suddenly declare itself "color-blind" without in fact perpetuating the same type of differential, racist treatment.[10] Thus, race continues to signify difference and structure inequality. Here, racialized social structure is immediately linked to an interpretation of the meaning of race. This example too can be classified as a particular type of racial project in the present-day United States—a "liberal" one.

To be sure, such political labels as "neoconserva-tive" or "liberal" cannot fully capture the complexity of racial projects, for these are always multiply de-termined, politically contested, and deeply shaped by their historical context. Thus, encapsulated within the neoconservative example cited here are certain egalitarian commitments which derive from a previ-ous historical context in which they played a very different role, and which are rearticulated in neocon-servative racial discourse precisely to oppose a more open-ended, more capacious conception of the meaning of equality. Similarly, in the liberal example, Justice Marshall recognizes that the contemporary state, which was formerly the architect of segrega-tion and the chief enforcer of racial difference, has a tendency to reproduce those patterns of inequality in a new guise. Thus he admonishes it (in dissent, signif-icantly) to fulfill its responsibilities to uphold a robust conception of equality. These particular instances, then, demonstrate how racial projects are always concretely framed, and thus are always contested and unstable. The social structures they uphold or at-tack, and the representations of race they articulate, are never invented out of the air, but exist in a definite historical context, having descended from previous conflicts. This contestation appears to be permanent in respect to race.

These two examples of contemporary racial projects are drawn from mainstream political de-bate; they may be characterized as center-right and center-left expressions of contemporary racial politics.[11] We can, however, expand the discussion of racial formation processes far beyond these fa-miliar examples. In fact, we can identify racial proj-ects in at least three other analytical dimensions: first, the political spectrum can be broadened to in-clude radical projects, on both the left and right, as well as along other political axes. Second, analysis of racial projects can take place not only at the macro-level of racial policy-making, state activity, and collective action, but also at the micro-level of everyday experience. Third, the concept of racial projects can be applied across historical time, to identify racial formation dynamics in the past. We shall now offer examples of each of these types of racial projects.

The Political Spectrum of Racial Formation

We have encountered examples of a neoconserva-tive racial project, in which the significance of race is denied, leading to a "color-blind" racial politics and "hands off" policy orientation; and of a "liberal" racial project, in which the significance of race is affirmed, leading to an egalitarian and "activist" state policy. But these by no means exhaust the political possibilities. Other racial projects can be readily identified on the contemporary US scene. For example, "far right" proj-ects, which uphold biologistic and racist views of dif-ference, explicitly argue for white supremacist policies. "New right" projects overtly claim to hold "color-blind" views, but covertly manipulate racial fears in order to achieve political gains.[12] On the left, "radical demo-cratic" projects invoke notions of racial "difference" in combination with egalitarian politics and policy.

Further variations can also be noted. For example, "nationalist" projects, both conservative and radical, stress the incompatibility of racially defined group identity with the legacy of white supremacy, and there-fore advocate a social structural solution of separation, either complete or partial.[13] As we saw in Chapter 3, nationalist currents represent a profound legacy of the centuries of racial absolutism that initially defined the meaning of race in the US Nationalist concerns con-tinue to influence racial debate in the form of Afrocen-trism and other expressions of identity politics.

Taking the range of politically organized racial projects as a whole, we can "map" the current pattern of racial formation at the level of the public sphere, the "macro-level" in which public debate and mobili-zation takes place.[14] But important as this is, the ter-rain on which racial formation occurs is broader yet.

Racial Formation as Everyday Experience

At the micro-social level, racial projects also link signification and structure, not so much as efforts to shape policy or define large-scale meaning, but as the applications of "common sense." To see racial projects operating at the level of everyday life, we have only to examine the many ways in which, often unconsciously, we "notice" race.

One of the first things we notice about people when we meet them (along with their sex) is their race. We utilize race to provide clues about *who* a person is. This fact is made painfully obvious when we encounter someone whom we cannot conveniently racially categorize—someone who is, for example, racially "mixed" or of an ethnic/racial group we are not familiar with. Such an encounter becomes a source of discomfort and momentarily a crisis of racial meaning.

Our ability to interpret racial meanings depends on preconceived notions of a racialized social structure. Comments such as, "Funny, you don't look black," betray an underlying image of what black should be. We expect people to act out their apparent racial identities; indeed we become disoriented when they do not. The black banker harassed by police while walking in casual clothes through his own well-off neighborhood, the Latino or white kid rapping in perfect Afro patois, the unending *faux pas* committed by whites who assume that the non-whites they encounter are servants or tradespeople, the belief that non-white colleagues are less qualified persons hired to fulfill affirmative action guidelines, indeed the whole gamut of racial stereotypes—that "white men can't jump," that Asians can't dance, etc., etc.—all testify to the way a racialized social structure shapes racial experience and conditions meaning. Analysis of such stereotypes reveals the always present, already active link between our view of the social structure—its demography, its laws, its customs, its threats—and our conception of what race means.

Conversely, our ongoing interpretation of our experience in racial terms shapes our relations to the institutions and organizations through which we are imbedded in social structure. Thus we expect differences in skin color, or other racially coded characteristics, to explain social differences. Temperament, sexuality, intelligence, athletic ability, aesthetic preferences, and so on are presumed to be fixed and discernible from the palpable mark of race. Such diverse questions as our confidence and trust in others (for example, clerks or salespeople, media figures, neighbors), our sexual preferences and romantic images, our tastes in music, films, dance, or sports, and our very ways of talking, walking, eating, and dreaming become racially coded simply because we live in a society where racial awareness is so pervasive. Thus in ways too comprehensive even to monitor consciously, and despite periodic calls—neoconservative and otherwise—for us to ignore race and adopt "color-blind" racial attitudes, skin color "differences" continue to rationalize distinct treatment of racially identified individuals and groups.

To summarize the argument so far: the theory of racial formation suggests that society is suffused with racial projects, large and small, to which all are subjected. This racial "subjection" is quintessentially ideological. Everybody learns some combination, some version, of the rules of racial classification, and of her own racial identity, often without obvious teaching or conscious inculcation. Thus are we inserted in a comprehensively racialized social structure. Race becomes "common sense"—a way of comprehending, explaining, and acting in the world. A vast web of racial projects mediates between the discursive or representational means in which race is identified and signified on the one hand, and the institutional and organizational forms in which it is routinized and standardized on the other. These projects are the heart of the racial formation process.

Under such circumstances, it is not possible to represent race discursively without simultaneously locating it, explicitly or implicitly, in a social structural (and historical) context. Nor is it possible to organize, maintain, or transform social structures without simultaneously engaging, once more either explicitly or implicitly, in racial signification. Racial formation, therefore, is a kind of synthesis, an outcome, of the interaction of racial projects on a society-wide level. These projects are, of course, vastly different in scope and effect. They include large-scale public action, state activities, and interpretations of racial conditions in artistic, journalistic, or academic fora,[15] as well as the seemingly infinite number of racial judgments and practices we carry out at the level of individual experience.

Since racial formation is always historically situated, our understanding of the significance of race, and of the way race structures society, has changed enormously over time. The processes of racial formation we encounter today, the racial projects large and small which structure US society in so many ways, are merely the present-day outcomes of a complex historical evolution. The contemporary racial order remains transient. By knowing something of how it evolved, we can perhaps better discern where it is heading. We therefore turn next to a historical survey of the racial formation process, and the conflicts and debates it has engendered.

The Evolution of Modern Racial Awareness

The identification of distinctive human groups, and their association with differences in physical appearance, goes back to prehistory, and can be found in the earliest documents—in the Bible, for example, or in Herodotus. But the emergence of a modern conception of race does not occur until the rise of Europe and the arrival of Europeans in the Americas. Even the hostility and suspicion with which Christian Europe viewed its two significant non-Christian "Others"—the Muslims and the Jews—cannot be viewed as more than a rehearsal for racial formation, since these antagonisms, for all their bloodletting and chauvinism, were always and everywhere religiously interpreted.[16]

It was only when European explorers reached the Western Hemisphere, when the oceanic seal separating the "old" and the "new" worlds was breached, that the distinctions and categorizations fundamental to a racialized social structure, and to a discourse of race, began to appear. The European explorers were the advance guard of merchant capitalism, which sought new openings for trade. What they found exceeded their wildest dreams, for never before and never again in human history has an opportunity for the appropriation of wealth remotely approached that presented by the "discovery."[17]

But the Europeans also "discovered" people, people who looked and acted differently. These "natives" challenged their "discoverers'" pre-existing conceptions of the origins and possibilities of the human species.[18] The representation and interpretation of the meaning of the indigenous peoples' existence became a crucial matter, one which would affect the outcome of the enterprise of conquest. For the

"discovery" raised disturbing questions as to whether *all* could be considered part of the same "family of man," and more practically, the extent to which native peoples could be exploited and enslaved. Thus religious debates flared over the attempt to reconcile the various Christian metaphysics with the existence of peoples who were more "different" than any whom Europe had previously known.[19]

In practice, of course, the seizure of territories and goods, the introduction of slavery through the *encomienda* and other forms of coerced native labor, and then through the organization of the African slave trade—not to mention the practice of outright extermination—all presupposed a worldview which distinguished Europeans, as children of God, full-fledged human beings, etc., from "Others." Given the dimensions and the ineluctability of the European onslaught, given the conquerors' determination to appropriate both labor and goods, and given the presence of an axiomatic and unquestioned Christianity among them, the ferocious division of society into Europeans and "Others" soon coalesced. This was true despite the famous 16th-century theological and philosophical debates about the identity of indigenous peoples.[20]

Indeed debates about the nature of the "Others" reached their practical limits with a certain dispatch. Plainly, they would never touch the essential: nothing, after all, would induce the Europeans to pack up and go home. We cannot examine here the early controversies over the status of American souls. We simply wish to emphasize that the "discovery" signalled a break from the previous proto-racial awareness by which Europe contemplated its "Others" in a relatively disorganized fashion. In other words, the "conquest of America" was not simply an epochal historical event—however unparalleled in its importance. It was also the advent of a consolidated social structure of exploitation, appropriation, domination. Its representation, first in religious terms, but soon enough in scientific and political ones, initiated modern racial awareness.

The conquest, therefore, was the first—and given the dramatic nature of the case, perhaps the greatest—racial formation project. Its significance was by no means limited to the Western Hemisphere, for it began the work of constituting Europe as the metropole, the center, of a group of empires which could take, as Marx would later write, "the globe for a theater."[21] It represented this new imperial structure as a struggle between civilization and barbarism, and implicated in this representation all the great European philosophies, literary traditions, and social theories of the modern age.[22] In short, just as the noise of the "big bang" still resonates through the universe, so the overdetermined construction of world "civilization" as a product of the rise of Europe and the subjugation of the rest of us, still defines the race concept.

From Religion to Science

After the initial depredations of conquest, religious justifications for racial difference gradually gave way to scientific ones. By the time of the Enlightenment, a general awareness of race was pervasive, and most of the great philosophers of Europe, such as Hegel, Kant, Hume, and Locke, had issued virulently racist opinions.

The problem posed by race during the late 18th century was markedly different than it had been in the age of "discovery," expropriation, and slaughter. The social structures in which race operated were no longer primarily those of military conquest and plunder, nor of the establishment of thin beachheads of colonization on the edge of what had once seemed a limitless wilderness. Now the issues were much more complicated: nation-building, establishment of national economies in the world trading system, resistance to the arbitrary authority of monarchs, and the assertion of the "natural rights" of "man," including the right of revolution.[23] In such a situation, racially organized exploitation, in the form of slavery, the expansion of colonies, and the continuing expulsion of native peoples, was both necessary and newly difficult to justify.

The invocation of scientific criteria to demonstrate the "natural" basis of racial hierarchy was both a logical consequence of the rise of this form of knowledge, and an attempt to provide a more subtle and nuanced account of human complexity in the new, "enlightened" age. Spurred on by the classificatory scheme of living organisms devised by Linnaeus

in *Systema Naturae* (1735), many scholars in the 18th and 19th centuries dedicated themselves to the identification and ranking of variations in humankind. Race was conceived as a *biological* concept, a matter of species. Voltaire wrote that "the negro race is a species of men (sic) as different from ours . . . as the breed of spaniels is from that of greyhounds," and in a formulation echoing down from his century to our own, declared that:

> If their understanding is not of a different nature from ours . . ., it is at least greatly inferior. They are not capable of any great application or association of ideas, and seem formed neither for the advantages nor the abuses of philosophy.[24]

Jefferson, the preeminent exponent of the Enlightenment doctrine of "the rights of man" on North American shores, echoed these sentiments:

> In general their existence appears to participate more of sensation than reflection. . . . [I]n memory they are equal to whites, in reason much inferior . . . [and] in imagination they are dull, tasteless, and anomalous. . . . I advance it therefore . . . that the blacks, whether originally a different race, or made distinct by time and circumstances, are inferior to the whites. . . . Will not a lover of natural history, then, one who views the gradations in all the animals with the eye of philosophy, excuse an effort to keep those in the department of Man (sic) as distinct as nature has formed them?[25]

Such claims of species distinctiveness among humans justified the inequitable allocation of political and social rights, while still upholding the doctrine of "the rights of man." The quest to obtain a precise scientific definition of race sustained debates which continue to rage today. Yet despite efforts ranging from Dr. Samuel Morton's studies of cranial capacity[26] to contemporary attempts to base racial classification on shared gene pools,[27] the concept of race has defied biological definition.

In the 19th century, Count Joseph Arthur de Gobineau drew upon the most respected scientific studies of his day to compose his four-volume *Essay on the Inequality of Races* (1853–1855).[28] He not only greatly influenced the racial thinking of the period, but his themes would be echoed in the racist ideologies of the next one hundred years: beliefs that superior races produced superior cultures and that racial intermixtures resulted in the degradation of the superior racial stock. These ideas found expression, for instance, in the eugenics movement launched by Darwin's cousin, Francis Galton, which had an immense impact on scientific and sociopolitical thought in Europe and the United States[29] In the wake of civil war and emancipation, and with immigration from southern and Eastern Europe as well as East Asia running high, the United States was particularly fertile ground for notions such as social darwinism and eugenics.

Attempts to discern the *scientific meaning* of race continue to the present day. For instance, an essay by Arthur Jensen which argued that hereditary factors shape intelligence not only revived the "nature or nurture" controversy, but also raised highly volatile questions about racial equality itself.[30] All such attempts seek to remove the concept of race from the historical context in which it arose and developed. They employ an *essentialist* approach which suggests instead that the truth of race is a matter of innate characteristics, of which skin color and other physical attributes provide only the most obvious, and in some respects most superficial, indicators.

From Science to Politics

It has taken scholars more than a century to reject biologistic notions of race in favor of an approach which regards race as a *social* concept. This trend has been slow and uneven, and even today remains somewhat embattled, but its overall direction seems clear. At the turn of the century Max Weber discounted biological explanations for racial conflict and instead highlighted the social and political factors which engendered such conflict.[31] W. E. B. Du Bois argued for a sociopolitical definition of race by identifying "the color line" as "the problem of the 20th century."[32] Pioneering cultural anthropologist Franz Boas rejected attempts to link racial identifications and cultural traits, labelling as pseudoscientific any assumption of a continuum of "higher" and "lower"

cultural groups.[33] Other early exponents of social, as opposed to biological, views of race included Robert E. Park, founder of the "Chicago school" of sociology, and Alain Leroy Locke, philosopher and theorist of the Harlem Renaissance.[34]

Perhaps more important than these and subsequent intellectual efforts, however, were the political struggles of racially defined groups themselves. Waged all around the globe under a variety of banners such as anticolonialism and civil rights, these battles to challenge various structural and cultural racisms have been a major feature of 20th-century politics. The racial horrors of the 20th century—colonial slaughter and apartheid, the genocide of the holocaust, and the massive bloodlettings required to end these evils—have also indelibly marked the theme of race as a political issue *par excellence.*

As a result of prior efforts and struggles, we have now reached the point of fairly general agreement that race is not a biologically given but rather a socially constructed way of differentiating human beings. While a tremendous achievement, the transcendence of biologistic conceptions of race does not provide any reprieve from the dilemmas of racial injustice and conflict, nor from controversies over the significance of race in the present. Views of race as socially constructed simply recognize the fact that these conflicts and controversies are now more properly framed on the terrain of politics. By privileging politics in the analysis which follows we do not mean to suggest that race has been displaced as a concern of scientific inquiry, or that struggles over cultural representation are no longer important. We do argue, however, that race is now a preeminently political phenomenon. Such an assertion invites examination of the evolving role of racial politics in the United States. This is the subject to which we now turn.

Dictatorship, Democracy, Hegemony

For most of its existence both as European colony and as an independent nation, the United States was a *racial dictatorship*. From 1607 to 1865—258 years—most non-whites were firmly eliminated from the sphere of politics.[35] After the Civil War there was the brief egalitarian experiment of Reconstruction which terminated ignominiously in 1877. In its wake followed almost a century of legally sanctioned segregation and denial of the vote, nearly absolute in the South and much of the Southwest, less effective in the North and far West, but formidable in any case.[36] These barriers fell only in the mid-1960s, a mere quarter-century ago. Nor did the successes of the black movement and its allies mean that all obstacles to their political participation had now been abolished. Patterns of racial inequality have proven, unfortunately, to be quite stubborn and persistent.

It is important, therefore, to recognize that in many respects, racial dictatorship is the norm against which all US politics must be measured. The centuries of racial dictatorship have had three very large consequences: first, they defined "American" identity as white, as the negation of racialized "otherness"—at first largely African and indigenous, later Latin American and Asian as well.[37] This negation took shape in both law and custom, in public institutions and in forms of cultural representation. It became the archetype of hegemonic rule in the United States. It was the successor to the conquest as the "master" racial project.

Second, racial dictatorship organized (albeit sometimes in an incoherent and contradictory fashion) the "color line" rendering it the fundamental division in US society. The dictatorship elaborated, articulated, and drove racial divisions not only through institutions, but also through psyches, extending up to our own time the racial obsessions of the conquest and slavery periods.

Third, racial dictatorship consolidated the oppositional racial consciousness and organization originally framed by marronage[38] and slave revolts, by indigenous resistance, and by nationalisms of various sorts. Just as the conquest created the "native" where once there had been Pequot, Iroquois, or Tutelo, so too it created the "black" where once there had been Asante or Ovimbundu, Yoruba or Bakongo.

The transition from a racial dictatorship to a racial democracy has been a slow, painful, and contentious one; it remains far from complete. A recognition of the abiding presence of racial dictatorship, we contend, is crucial for the development of a theory of racial formation in the United States. It is also crucial to the task of relating racial formation to the broader context of political practice, organization, and change.

In this context, a key question arises: in what way is racial formation related to politics as a whole? How, for example, does race articulate with other axes of oppression and difference—most importantly class and gender—along which politics is organized today?

The answer, we believe, lies in the concept of *hegemony.* Antonio Gramsci—the Italian communist who placed this concept at the center of his life's work—understood it as the conditions necessary, in a given society, for the achievement and consolidation of rule. He argued that hegemony was always constituted by a combination of coercion and consent. Although rule can be obtained by force, it cannot be secured and maintained, especially in modern society, without the element of consent. Gramsci conceived of consent as far more than merely the legitimation of authority. In his view, consent extended to the incorporation by the ruling group of many of the key interests of subordinated groups, often to the explicit disadvantage of the rulers themselves.[39] Gramsci's treatment of hegemony went even farther: he argued that in order to consolidate their hegemony, ruling groups must elaborate and maintain a popular system of ideas and practices—through education, the media, religion, folk wisdom, etc.—which he called "common sense." It is through its production and its adherence to this "common sense," this ideology (in the broadest sense of the term), that a society gives its consent to the way in which it is ruled.[40]

These provocative concepts can be extended and applied to an understanding of racial rule. In the Americas, the conquest represented the violent introduction of a new form of rule whose relationship with those it subjugated was almost entirely coercive. In the United States the origins of racial division, and of racial signification and identity formation, lie in a system of rule which was extremely dictatorial. The mass murders and expulsions of indigenous people, and the enslavement of Africans, surely evoked and inspired little consent in their founding moments.

Over time, however, the balance of coercion and consent began to change. It is possible to locate the origins of hegemony right within the heart of racial dictatorship, for the effort to possess the oppressor's tools—religion and philosophy in this case—was crucial to emancipation (the effort to possess one-self). As Ralph Ellison reminds us, "The slaves often took the essence of the aristocratic ideal (as they took Christianity) with far more seriousness than their masters."[41] In their language, in their religion with its focus on the Exodus theme and on Jesus's tribulations, in their music with its figuring of suffering, resistance, perseverance, and transcendence, in their interrogation of a political philosophy which sought perpetually to rationalize their bondage in a supposedly "free" society, the slaves incorporated elements of racial rule into their thought and practice, turning them against their original bearers.

Racial rule can be understood as a slow and uneven historical process which has moved from dictatorship to democracy, from domination to hegemony. In this transition, hegemonic forms of racial rule—those based on consent—eventually came to supplant those based on coercion. Of course, before this assertion can be accepted, it must be qualified in important ways. By no means has the United States established racial democracy at the end of the century, and by no means is coercion a thing of the past. But the sheer complexity of the racial questions US society confronts today, the welter of competing racial projects and contradictory racial experiences which Americans undergo, suggests that hegemony is a useful and appropriate term with which to characterize contemporary racial rule.

Our key theoretical notion of racial projects helps to extend and broaden the question of rule. Projects are the building blocks not just of racial formation, but of hegemony in general. Hegemony operates by simultaneously structuring and signifying. As in the case of racial opposition, gender- or class-based conflict today links structural inequity and injustice on the one hand, and identifies and represents its subjects on the other. The success of modern-day feminism, for example, has depended on its ability to reinterpret gender as a matter of both injustice and identity/difference.

Today, political opposition necessarily takes shape on the terrain of hegemony. Far from ruling principally through exclusion and coercion (though again, these are hardly absent) hegemony operates by including its subjects, incorporating its opposition. *Pace* both Marxists and liberals, there is no longer any universal or privileged region of political action or discourse.[42] Race, class, and gender all represent potential antagonisms whose significance is no longer given, if it ever was.

Thus race, class, and gender (as well as sexual orientation) constitute "regions" of hegemony, areas in which certain political projects can take shape. They share certain obvious attributes in that they are all "socially constructed," and they all consist of a field of projects whose common feature is their linkage of social structure and signification.

Going beyond this, it is crucial to emphasize that race, class, and gender, are not fixed and discrete categories, and that such "regions" are by no means autonomous. They overlap, intersect, and fuse with each other in countless ways. Such mutual determinations have been illustrated by Patricia Hill Collins's survey and theoretical synthesis of the themes and issues of black feminist thought.[43] They are also evident in Evelyn Nakano Glenn's work on the historical and contemporary racialization of domestic and service work.[44] In many respects, race is gendered and gender is racialized. In institutional and everyday life, any clear demarcation of specific forms of oppression and difference is constantly being disrupted.

There are no clear boundaries between these "regions" of hegemony, so political conflicts will often invoke some or all these themes simultaneously. Hegemony is tentative, incomplete, and "messy." For example, the 1991 Hill-Thomas hearings, with their intertwined themes of race and gender inequality, and their frequent genuflections before the altar of hard work and upward mobility, managed to synthesize various race, gender, and class projects in a particularly explosive combination.[45]

What distinguishes political opposition today—racial or otherwise—is its insistence on identifying itself and speaking for itself, its determined demand for the transformation of the social structure, its refusal of the "common sense" understandings which the hegemonic order imposes. Nowhere is this refusal of "common sense" more needed, or more imperilled, than in our understanding of racism.

What Is Racism?

Since the ambiguous triumph of the civil rights movement in the mid-1960s, clarity about what racism means has been eroding. The concept entered the lexicon of "common sense" only in the 1960s. Before that, although the term had surfaced occasionally,[46] the problem of racial injustice and inequality was generally understood in a more limited fashion, as a matter of prejudiced attitudes or bigotry on the one hand,[47] and discriminatory practices on the other.[48] Solutions, it was believed, would therefore involve the overcoming of such attitudes, the achievement of tolerance, the acceptance of "brotherhood," etc., and the passage of laws which prohibited discrimination with respect to access to public accommodations, jobs, education, etc. The early civil rights movement explicitly reflected such views. In its espousal of integration and its quest for a "beloved community" it sought to overcome racial prejudice. In its litigation activities and agitation for civil rights legislation it sought to challenge discriminatory practices.

The later 1960s, however, signalled a sharp break with this vision. The emergence of the slogan "black power" (and soon after, of "brown power," "red power," and "yellow power"), the wave of riots that swept the urban ghettos from 1964 to 1968, and the founding of radical movement organizations of nationalist and Marxist orientation, coincided with the recognition that racial inequality and injustice had much deeper roots. They were not simply the product of prejudice, nor was discrimination only a matter of intentionally informed action. Rather, prejudice was an almost unavoidable outcome of patterns of socialization which were "bred in the bone," affecting not only whites but even minorities themselves.[49] Discrimination, far from manifesting itself only (or even principally) through individual actions or conscious policies, was a structural feature of US society, the product of centuries of systematic exclusion, exploitation, and disregard of racially defined minorities.[50] It was this combination of relationships—prejudice, discrimination, and institutional inequality—which defined the concept of racism at the end of the 1960s.

Such a synthesis was better able to confront the political realities of the period. Its emphasis on the structural dimensions of racism allowed it to address the intransigence which racial injustice and inequality continued to exhibit, even after discrimination had supposedly been outlawed[51] and bigoted expression stigmatized. But such an approach also had clear limitations. As Robert Miles has argued, it tended to "inflate" the concept of racism to a point at which it lost precision.[52] If the "institutional" component of racism were so pervasive and deeply rooted, it became difficult to see how the democratization of US society could be achieved, and difficult to explain what progress had been made. The result was a levelling critique which denied any distinction between the Jim Crow era (or even the whole *longue durée* of racial dictatorship since the conquest) and the present. Similarly, if the prejudice component of racism were so deeply inbred, it became difficult to account for the evident hybridity and inter-penetration that characterizes civil society in the United States as evidenced by the shaping of popular culture, language, and style, for example. The result of the "inflation" of the concept of racism was thus a deep pessimism about any efforts to overcome racial barriers, in the workplace, the community, or any other sphere of lived experience. An overly comprehensive view of racism, then, potentially served as a self-fulfilling prophecy.

Yet the alternative view—which surfaced with a vengeance in the 1970s—urging a return to the conception of racism held before the movement's "radical turn," was equally inadequate. This was the neoconservative perspective, which deliberately restricted its attention to injury done to the individual as opposed to the group, and to advocacy of a color-blind racial policy.[53] Such an approach reduced race to ethnicity,[54] and almost entirely neglected the continuing organization of social inequality and oppression along racial lines. Worse yet, it tended to rationalize racial injustice as a supposedly natural outcome of group attributes in competition.[55]

The distinct, and contested, meanings of racism which have been advanced over the past three decades have contributed to an overall crisis of meaning for the concept today. Today, the absence of a clear "common sense" understanding of what racism means has become a significant obstacle to efforts aimed at challenging it. Bob Blauner has noted that in classroom discussions of racism, white and non-white students tend to talk past one another. Whites tend to locate racism in color consciousness and find its absence color-blindness. In so doing, they see the affirmation of difference and racial identity among racially defined minority students as racist. Non-white students, by contrast, see racism as a system of power, and correspondingly argue that blacks, for example, cannot be racist because they lack power. Blauner concludes that there are two "languages" of race, one in which members of racial minorities, especially blacks, see the centrality of race in history and everyday experience, and another in which whites see race as "a peripheral, nonessential reality."[56]

Given this crisis of meaning, and in the absence of any "common sense" understanding, does the concept of racism retain any validity? If so, what view of racism should we adopt? Is a more coherent theoretical approach possible? We believe it is.

We employ racial formation theory to reformulate the concept of racism. Our approach recognizes that racism, like race, has changed over time. It is obvious that the attitudes, practices, and institutions of the epochs of slavery, say, or of Jim Crow, no longer exist today. Employing a similar logic, it is reasonable to question whether concepts of racism which developed in the early days of the post-civil rights era, when the limitations of both moderate reform and militant racial radicalism of various types had not yet been encountered, remain adequate to explain circumstances and conflicts a quarter-century later.

Racial formation theory allows us to differentiate between race and racism. The two concepts should not be used interchangeably. We have argued that race has no fixed meaning, but is constructed and transformed sociohistorically through competing political projects, through the necessary and ineluctable link between the structural and cultural dimensions of race in the United States. This emphasis on projects allows us to refocus our understanding of racism as well, for racism can now be seen as characterizing some, but not all, racial projects.

A racial project can be defined as *racist* if and only if it *creates or reproduces structures of domination based on essentialist*[57] *categories of race.* Such a definition

recognizes the importance of locating racism within a fluid and contested history of racially based social structures and discourses. Thus there can be no timeless and absolute standard for what constitutes racism, for social structures change and discourses are subject to rearticulation. Our definition therefore focuses instead on the "work" essentialism does for domination, and the "need" domination displays to essentialize the subordinated.

Further, it is important to distinguish racial awareness from racial essentialism. To attribute merits, allocate values or resources to, and/or represent individuals or groups on the basis of racial identity should not be considered racist in and of itself. Such projects may in fact be quite benign.

Consider the following examples: first, the statement, "Many Asian Americans are highly entrepreneurial"; second, the organization of an association of, say, black accountants.

The first racial project, in our view, signifies or represents a racial category ("Asian Americans") and locates that representation within the social structure of the contemporary United States (in regard to business, class issues, socialization, etc.). The second racial project is organizational or social structural, and therefore must engage in racial signification. Black accountants, the organizers might maintain, have certain common experiences, can offer each other certain support, etc. Neither of these racial projects is essentialist, and neither can fairly be labelled racist. Of course, racial representations may be biased or misinterpret their subjects, just as racially based organizational efforts may be unfair or unjustifiably exclusive. If such were the case, if for instance in our first example the statement in question were "Asian Americans are naturally entrepreneurial," this would by our criterion be racist. Similarly, if the effort to organize black accountants had as its rationale the raiding of clients from white accountants, it would by our criterion be racist as well.

Similarly, to allocate values or resources—let us say, academic scholarships—on the basis of racial categories is not racist. Scholarships are awarded on a preferential basis to Rotarians, children of insurance company employees, and residents of the Pittsburgh metropolitan area. Why then should they not also be offered, in particular cases, to Chicanos or Native Americans?

In order to identify a social project as racist, one must in our view demonstrate a link between essentialist representations of race and social structures of domination. Such a link might be revealed in efforts to protect dominant interests, framed in racial terms, from democratizing racial initiatives.[58] But it might also consist of efforts simply to reverse the roles of racially dominant and racially subordinate.[59] There is nothing inherently white about racism.[60]

Obviously a key problem with essentialism is its denial, or flattening, of differences within a particular racially defined group. Members of subordinate racial groups, when faced with racist practices such as exclusion or discrimination, are frequently forced to band together in order to defend their interests (if not, in some instances, their very lives). Such "strategic essentialism" should not, however, be simply equated with the essentialism practiced by dominant groups, nor should it prevent the interrogation of internal group differences.[61]

Without question, any abstract concept of racism is severely put to the test by the untidy world of reality. To illustrate our discussion, we analyze the following examples, chosen from current racial issues because of their complexity and the rancorous debates they have engendered:

- Is the allocation of employment opportunities through programs restricted to racially defined minorities, so-called "preferential treatment" or affirmative action policies, racist? Do such policies practice "racism in reverse"? We think not, with certain qualifications. Although such programs necessarily employ racial criteria in assessing eligibility, they do not generally essentialize race, because they seek to overcome specific socially and historically constructed inequalities.[62] Criteria of effectiveness and feasibility, therefore, must be considered in evaluating such programs. They must balance egalitarian and context-specific objectives, such as academic potential or job-related qualifications. It should be acknowledged that such programs often do have deleterious consequences for whites who are not personally the source of the discriminatory practices the programs seek to overcome. In this case, compensatory measures should be enacted to vitiate the charge of "reverse discrimination."[63]

- Is all racism the same, or is there a distinction between white and non-white versions of racism? We have little patience with the argument that racism is solely a white problem, or even a "white disease."[64] The idea that non-whites cannot act in a racist manner, since they do not possess "power," is another variant of this formulation.[65]

For many years now, racism has operated in a more complex fashion than this, sometimes taking such forms as self-hatred or self-aggrandizement at the expense of more vulnerable members of racially subordinate groups.[66] Whites can at times be the victims of racism—by other whites or non-whites—as is the case with anti-Jewish and anti-Arab prejudice. Furthermore, unless one is prepared to argue that there has been no transformation of the US racial order over the years, and that racism consequently has remained unchanged—an essentialist position *par excellence*—it is difficult to contend that racially defined minorities have attained no power or influence, especially in recent years.

Having said this, we still do not consider that all racism is the same. This is because of the crucial importance we place in situating various "racisms" within the dominant hegemonic discourse about race. We have little doubt that the rantings of a Louis Farrakhan or Leonard Jeffries—to pick two currently demonized black ideologues—meet the criteria we have set out for judging a discourse to be racist. But if we compare Jeffries, for example, with a white racist such as Tom Metzger of the White Aryan Resistance, we find the latter's racial project to be far more menacing than the former's. Metzger's views are far more easily associated with an essentializing (and once very powerful) legacy: that of white supremacy and racial dictatorship in the United States, and fascism in the world at large. Jeffries's project has far fewer examples with which to associate: no more than some ancient African empires and the (usually far less bigoted) radical phase of the black power movement.[67] Thus black supremacy may be an instance of racism, just as its advocacy may be offensive, but it can hardly constitute the threat that white supremacy has represented in the United States nor can it be so easily absorbed and rearticulated in the dominant hegemonic discourse on race as white supremacy can. All racisms, all racist political projects, are not the same.

- Is the redrawing—or gerrymandering—of adjacent electoral districts to incorporate large numbers of racially defined minority voters in one, and largely white voters in the other, racist? Do such policies amount to "segregation" of the electorate? Certainly this alternative is preferable to the pre-Voting Rights Act practice of simply denying racial minorities the franchise. But does it achieve the Act's purpose of fostering electoral equality across and within racial lines? In our view such practices, in which the post-1990 redistricting process engaged rather widely—are vulnerable to charges of essentialism. They often operate through "racial lumping," tend to freeze rather than overcome racial inequalities, and frequently subvert or defuse political processes through which racially defined groups could otherwise negotiate their differences and interests. They worsen rather than ameliorate the denial of effective representation to those whom they could not effectively redistrict— since no redrawing of electoral boundaries is perfect, those who get stuck on the "wrong side" of the line are particularly disempowered. Thus we think such policies merit the designation of "tokenism"—a relatively mild form of racism—which they have received.[68]

Parallel to the debates on the concept of race, recent academic and political controversies about the nature of racism have centered on whether it is primarily an ideological or structural phenomenon. Proponents of the former position argue that racism is first and foremost a matter of beliefs and attitudes, doctrines and discourse, which only then give rise to unequal and unjust practices and structures.[69] Advocates of the latter view see racism as primarily a matter of economic stratification, residential segregation, and other institutionalized forms of inequality which then give rise to ideologies of privilege.[70]

From the standpoint of racial formation, these debates are fundamentally misguided. They frame the problem of racism in a rigid "either-or" manner. We believe it is crucial to disrupt the fixity of these positions by simultaneously arguing that ideological beliefs have structural consequences, and that social structures give rise to beliefs. Racial ideology and social structure, therefore, mutually shape the nature of racism in a complex, dialectical, and overdetermined manner.

Even those racist projects which at first glance appear chiefly ideological turn out upon closer examination to have significant institutional and social structural dimensions. For example, what we have called "far right" projects appear at first glance to be centrally ideological. They are rooted in biologistic doctrine, after all. The same seems to hold for certain conservative black nationalist projects which have deep commitments to biologism.[71] But the unending stream of racist assaults initiated by the far right, the apparently increasing presence of skinheads in high schools, the proliferation of neo-Nazi computer bulletin boards, and the appearance of racist talk shows on cable access channels, all suggest that the organizational manifestations of the far right racial projects exist and will endure.[72] Perhaps less threatening but still quite worrisome is the diffusion of doctrines of black superiority through some (though by no means all) university-based African American Studies departments and student organizations, surely a serious institutional or structural development.

By contrast, even those racisms which at first glance appear to be chiefly structural upon closer examination reveal a deeply ideological component. For example, since the racial right abandoned its explicit advocacy of segregation, it has not seemed to uphold—in the main—an ideologically racist project, but more primarily a structurally racist one. Yet this very transformation required tremendous efforts of ideological production. It demanded the rearticulation of civil rights doctrines of equality in suitably conservative form, and indeed the defense of continuing large-scale racial inequality as an outcome preferable to (what its advocates have seen as) the threat to democracy that affirmative action, busing, and large-scale "race-specific" social spending would entail.[73] Even more tellingly, this project took shape through a deeply manipulative coding of subtextual appeals to white racism, notably in a series of political campaigns for high office which have occurred over recent decades. The retreat of social policy from any practical commitment to racial justice, and the relentless reproduction and divulgation of this theme at the level of everyday life—where whites are now "fed up" with all the "special treatment" received by non-whites, etc.—constitutes the hegemonic racial project at this time. It therefore exhibits an unabashed structural racism all the more brazen because on the ideological or signification level, it adheres to a principle of "treating everyone alike."

In summary, the racism of today is no longer a virtual monolith, as was the racism of yore. Today, racial hegemony is "messy." The complexity of the present situation is the product of a vast historical legacy of structural inequality and invidious racial representation, which has been confronted during the post-World War II period with an opposition more serious and effective than any it had faced before. As we will survey in the chapters to follow, the result is a deeply ambiguous and contradictory spectrum of racial projects, unremittingly conflictual racial politics, and confused and ambivalent racial identities of all sorts. We begin this discussion by addressing racial politics and the state.

Notes

1. *San Francisco Chronicle,* 14 September 1982, 19 May 1983. Ironically, the 1970 Louisiana law was enacted to supersede an old Jim Crow statute which relied on the idea of "common report" in determining an infant's race. Following Phipps' unsuccessful attempt to change her classification and have the law declared unconstitutional, a legislative effort arose which culminated in the repeal of the law. See *San Francisco Chronicle,* 23 June 1983.

2. Compare the Phipps case to Andrew Hacker's well-known "parable" in which a white person is informed by a mysterious official that "the organization he represents has made a mistake" and that ". . . [a]ccording to their records . . ., you were to have been born black: to another set of parents, far from where you were raised." How much compensation, Hacker's official asks, would "you" require to undo the damage of this unfortunate error? See Hacker, *Two Nations: Black and White, Separate, Hostile, Unequal* (New York: Charles Scribner's Sons, 1992), pp. 31–32.

3. On the evolution of Louisiana's racial classification system, see Virginia Dominguez, *White By Definition: Social Classification in Creole Louisiana* (New Brunswick: Rutgers University Press, 1986).

4. This is not to suggest that gender is a biological category while race is not. Gender, like race, is a social construct. However, the biological division of humans into sexes—two at least, and possibly intermediate ones as well—is not in dispute. This provides a basis for argument over gender divisions—how "natural," etc.—which does not exist with regard to race. To ground an argument for the "natural" existence of race, one must resort to philosophical anthropology.

5. "The truth is that there are no races, there is nothing in the world that can do all we ask race to do for us. . . . The evil that is done is done by the concept, and by easy—yet impossible—assumptions as to its application." (Kwame Anthony Appiah, *In My Father's House: Africa in the Philosophy of Culture* [New York: Oxford University Press, 1992].) Appiah's eloquent and learned book fails, in our view, to dispense with the race concept, despite its anguished attempt to do so; this indeed is the source of its author's anguish. We agree with him as to the non-objective character of race, but fail to see how this recognition justifies its abandonment. This argument is developed below.

6. We understand essentialism as *belief in real, true human, essences, existing outside or impervious to social and historical context.* We draw this definition, with some small modifications, from Diana Fuss, *Essentially Speaking: Feminism, Nature, & Difference* (New York: Routledge, 1989), p. xi.

7. Michael Omi and Howard Winant, "On the Theoretical Status of the Concept of Race" in Warren Crichlow and Cameron McCarthy, eds., *Race, Identity, and Representation in Education* (New York: Routledge, 1993).

8. Charles Murray, *Losing Ground: American Social Policy, 1950–1980* (New York: Basic Books, 1984), p. 223.

9. Justice Thurgood Marshall, dissenting in *City of Richmond v. J.A. Croson Co.*, 488 U.S. 469 (1989).

10. See, for example, Derrick Bell, "Remembrances of Racism Past: Getting Past the Civil Rights Decline," in Herbert Hill and James E. Jones, Jr., eds., *Race in America: The Struggle for Equality* (Madison: The University of Wisconsin Press, 1993) pp. 75–76; Gertrude Ezorsky, *Racism and Justice: The Case for Affirmative Action* (Ithaca: Cornell University Press, 1991) pp. 109–111; David Kairys, *With Liberty and Justice for Some: A Critique of the Conservative Supreme Court* (New York: The New Press, 1993), pp. 138–41.

11. Howard Winant has developed a tentative "map" of the system of racial hegemony in the U.S. circa 1990, which focuses on the spectrum of racial projects running from the political right to the political left. See Winant, "Where Culture Meets Structure: Race in the 1990s," in idem, *Racial Conditions: Politics, Theory, Comparisons* (Minneapolis: University of Minnesota Press, 1994).

12. A familiar example is use of racial "code words." Recall George Bush's manipulations of racial fear in the 1988 "Willie Horton" ads, or Jesse Helms's use of the coded term "quota" in his 1990 campaign against Harvey Gantt.

13. From this perspective, far right racial projects can also be interpreted as "nationalist." See Ronald Walters, "White Racial Nationalism in the United States," *Without Prejudice* Vol. 1, no. 1 (Fall 1987).

14. To be sure, any effort to divide racial formation patterns according to social structural location—"macro" vs. "micro," for example—is necessarily an analytic device. In the concrete, there is no such dividing line. See Winant, "Where Culture Meets Structure."

15. We are not unaware, for example, that publishing this work is in itself a racial project.

16. Antisemitism only began to be racialized in the 18th century, as George L. Mosse clearly shows in his important *Toward the Final Solution: A History of European Racism* (New York: Howard Fertig, 1978).

17. As Marx put it:

    The discovery of gold and silver in America, the extirpation, enslavement, and entombment in mines of the aboriginal population, the beginning of the conquest and looting of the East Indies, the turning of Africa into a warren for the commercial hunting of blackskins, signalized the rosy dawn of the era of capitalist production. These idyllic proceedings are the chief momenta of primitive accumulation. (Karl Marx, *Capital,* Vol. I [New York: International Publishers, 1967], p. 751.)

    David E. Stannard argues that the wholesale slaughter perpetrated upon the native peoples of the Western hemisphere is unequalled in history, even in our own bloody century. See his *American Holocaust: Columbus and the Conquest of the New World* (New York: Oxford University Press, 1992).

18. Winthrop Jordan provides a detailed account of the sources of European attitudes about color and race in *White Over Black: American Attitudes Toward the Negro, 1550–1812* (New York: Norton, 1977 [1968]), pp. 3–43.

19. In a famous instance, a 1550 debate in Valladolid pitted the philosopher and translator of Aristotle, Ginés de Sepúlveda, against the Dominican Bishop of the Mexican state of Chiapas, Bartolomé de Las Casas. Discussing the native peoples, Sepúlveda argued that:

    In wisdom, skill, virtue and humanity, these people are as inferior to the Spaniards as children are to adults and women to men; there is as great a difference between them as there is between savagery and forbearance, between violence and moderation, almost—I am inclined to say, as between monkeys and men (Sepúlveda, *Democrates Alter,* quoted in Tsvetan Todorov, *The Conquest of America: The Question of the Other* [New York: Harper and Row, 1984], p. 153).

    In contrast, Las Casas defended the humanity and equality of the native peoples, both in terms of their way of life—which he idealized as one of innocence, gentleness, and generosity—and in terms of their readiness for conversion to Catholicism, which for him as for Sepúlveda was the true and universal religion (Las Casas, "Letter to the Council of the Indies," quoted ibid, p. 163). William E. Connolly interrogates the linkages proposed by Todorov between early Spanish colonialism and contemporary conceptions of identity and difference in *Identity/Difference: Democratic Negotiations of Political Paradox* (Ithaca: Cornell University Press, 1991), pp. 40–48.

20. In Virginia, for example, it took about two decades after the establishment of European colonies to extirpate the indigenous people of the greater vicinity; fifty years after the establishment of the first colonies, the elaboration of slave codes establishing race as *prima facie* evidence for enslaved status was well under way. See Jordan, *White Over Black.*

21. Marx, *Capital,* p. 751.

22. Edward W. Said, *Culture and Imperialism* (New York: Alfred A. Knopf, 1993).

23. David Brion Davis, *The Problem of Slavery in The Age of Revolution* (Ithaca: Cornell University Press, 1975).

24. Quoted in Thomas F. Gossett, *Race: The History of an Idea in America* (New York: Schocken Books, 1965) p. 45.

25. Thomas Jefferson, *Notes on Virginia* [1787], in Merrill D. Peterson, *Writings of Thomas Jefferson* (New York: The Library of America, 1984), pp. 264–66, 270. Thanks to Kimberly Benston for drawing our attention to this passage.

26. Proslavery physician Samuel George Morton (1799–1851) compiled a collection of 800 crania from all parts of the world which formed the sample for his studies of race. Assuming that the larger the size of the cranium translated into greater intelligence, Morton established a relationship between race and skull capacity. Gossett reports that "In 1849, one of his studies included the following results: the English skulls in his collection proved to be the largest, with an average cranial capacity of 96 cubic inches. The Americans and Germans were rather poor seconds, both with cranial capacities of 90 cubic inches. At the bottom of the list were the Negroes with 83 cubic inches, the Chinese with 82, and the Indians with 79." Gossett, *Race*, p. 74. More recently, Steven Jay Gould has reexamined Morton's data, and shown that his research data were deeply, though unconsciously, manipulated to agree with his "a priori conviction about racial ranking." (Gould, *The Mismeasure of Man* [New York: W. W. Norton, 1981], pp. 50–69).

27. Definitions of race founded upon a common pool of genes have not held up when confronted by scientific research which suggests that the differences *within* a given human population are every bit as great as those *between* populations. See L. L. Cavalli-Sforza, "The Genetics of Human Populations," *Scientific American* (September 1974), pp. 81–89.

28. A fascinating summary critique of Gobineau is provided in Tsvetan Todorov, *On Human Diversity: Nationalism, Racism, and Exoticism in French Thought,* trans. Catherine Porter (Cambridge, MA: Harvard University Press, 1993), esp. pp. 129–40.

29. Two recent histories of eugenics are Allen Chase, *The Legacy of Malthus* (New York: Knopf, 1977); Daniel J. Kevles, *In the Name of Eugenics: Genetics and the Uses of Human Heredity* (New York: Knopf, 1985).

30. Arthur Jensen, "How Much Can We Boost IQ and Scholastic Achievement?" *Harvard Educational Review* 39 (1969), pp. 1–123.

31. See Weber, *Economy and Society,* Vol. I (Berkeley: University of California Press, 1978), pp. 385–87; Ernst Moritz Manasse, "Max Weber on Race," *Social Research,* Vol. 14 (1947), pp. 191–221.

32. Du Bois, *The Souls of Black Folk* (New York: Penguin, 1989 [1903]), p. 13. Du Bois himself wrestled heavily with the conflict between a fully socio-historical conception of race, and the more essentialized and deterministic vision he encountered as a student in Berlin. In "The Conservation of Races" (1897) we can see his first mature effort to resolve this conflict in a vision which combined racial solidarity and a commitment to social equality. See Du Bois, "The Conservation of Races," in Dan S. Green and Edwin D. Driver, eds., *W. E. B. Du Bois On Sociology and the Black Community* (Chicago: University of Chicago Press, 1978), pp. 238–49; Manning Marable, *W.E.B. Du Bois: Black Radical Democrat* (Boston: Twayne, 1986), pp. 35–38. For a contrary, and we believe incorrect reading, see Appiah, *In My Father's House,* pp. 28–46.

33. A good collection of Boas's work is George W. Stocking, ed., *The Shaping of American Anthropology, 1883–1911: A Franz Boas Reader* (Chicago: University of Chicago Press, 1974).

34. Robert E. Park's *Race and Culture* (Glencoe, IL: Free Press, 1950) can still provide insight; see also Stanford H. Lyman, *Militarism, Imperialism, and Racial Accommodation: An Analysis and Interpretation of the Early Writings of Robert E. Park* (Fayetteville: University of Arkansas Press, 1992); Locke's views are concisely expressed in Alain Leroy Locke, *Race Contacts and Interracial Relations,* ed. Jeffrey C. Stewart (Washington, DC: Howard University Press, 1992), originally a series of lectures given at Howard University.

35. Japanese, for example, could not become naturalized citizens until passage of the 1952 McCarran-Walter Act. It took over 160 years, since the passage of the Law of 1790, to allow all "races" to be eligible for naturalization.

36. Especially when we recall that until around 1960, the majority of blacks, the largest racially defined minority group, lived in the South.

37. Toni Morrison, *Playing in the Dark: Whiteness and the Literary Imagination* (Cambridge, MA: Harvard University Press, 1992); Richard Drinnon, *Facing West: The Metaphysics of Indian-Hating and Empire-Building* (Minneapolis: University of Minnesota Press, 1980); Michael Paul Rogin, *Fathers and Children: Andrew Jackson and the Subjugation of the American Indian* (New York: Knopf, 1975).

38. This term refers to the practice, widespread throughout the Americas, whereby runaway slaves formed communities in remote areas, such as swamps, mountains, or forests, often in alliance with dispossessed indigenous peoples.

39. Antonio Gramsci, *Selections from the Prison Notebooks,* edited and translated by Quintin Hoare and Geoffrey Nowell Smith (New York: International Publishers, 1971), p. 182.

40. Anne Showstack Sassoon, *Gramsci's Politics*, 2nd ed. (London: Hutchinson, 1987); Sue Golding, *Gramsci's Democratic Theory: Contributions to Post-Liberal Democracy* (Toronto: University of Toronto Press, 1992).

41. Ralph Ellison, *Shadow and Act* (New York: New American Library, 1966), p. xiv.

42. Chantal Mouffe makes a related argument in "Radical Democracy: Modern or Postmodern?" in Andrew Ross, ed., *Universal Abandon: The Politics of Postmodernism* (Minneapolis: University of Minnesota Press, 1988).

43. Patricia Hill Collins, *Black Feminist Thought: Knowledge, Consciousness, and the Politics of Empowerment* (New York and London: Routledge, 1991).

44. Evelyn Nakano Glenn, "From Servitude to Service Work: Historical Continuities in the Racial Division of Paid Reproductive Labor," *Signs: Journal of Women in Culture & Society*, Vol. 18, no. 1 (Autumn 1992).

45. Toni Morrison, ed., *Race-ing Justice, En-gendering Power: Essays on Anita Hill, Clarence Thomas, and the Construction of Social Reality* (New York: Pantheon, 1992).

46. For example, in Magnus Hirschfeld's prescient book, *Racism* (London: Victor Gollancz, 1938).

47. This was the framework, employed in the crucial study of Myrdal and his associates; see Gunnar Myrdal, *An American Dilemma: The Negro Problem and Modern Democracy*, 20th Anniversary Edition (New York: Harper and Row, 1962 [1944]). See also the articles by Thomas F. Pettigrew and George Fredrickson in Pettigrew et al., *Prejudice: Selections from The Harvard Encyclopedia of American Ethnic Groups* (Cambridge, MA: The Belknap Press of Harvard University, 1982).

48. On discrimination, see Frederickson in ibid. In an early essay which explicitly sought to modify the framework of the Myrdal study, Robert K. Merton recognized that prejudice and discrimination need not coincide, and indeed could combine in a variety of ways. See Merton, "Discrimination and the American Creed," in R. M. McIver, ed., *Discrimination and National Welfare* (New York: Harper and Row, 1949).

49. Gordon W. Allport, *The Nature of Prejudice* (Cambridge, MA: Addison-Wesley, 1954) remains a classic work in the field; see also Philomena Essed, *Understanding Everyday Racism: An Interdisciplinary Theory* (Newbury Park, CA: Sage, 1991). A good overview of black attitudes toward black identities is provided in William E. Cross, Jr., *Shades of Black: Diversity in African-American Identity* (Philadelphia: Temple University Press, 1991).

50. Stokely Carmichael and Charles V. Hamilton first popularized the notion of "institutional" forms of discrimination in *Black Power: The Politics of Liberation in America* (New York: Vintage, 1967), although the basic concept certainly predated that work. Indeed, President Lyndon Johnson made a similar argument in his 1965 speech at Howard University:

> But freedom is not enough. You do not wipe away the scars of centuries by saying: Now you are free to go where you want, do as you desire, and choose the leaders you please.
>
> You do not take a person who, for years, has been hobbled by chains and liberate him (sic), bring him up to the starting line of a race and then say, "You are free to compete with all the others," and still justly believe that you have been completely fair.
>
> Thus it is not enough just to open the gates of opportunity. All our citizens must have the opportunity to walk through those gates.
>
> This is the next and more profound stage of the battle for civil rights. We seek not just freedom but opportunity—not just legal equity but human ability—not just equality as a right but equality as a fact and as a result. (Lyndon B. Johnson, "To Fulfill These Rights," reprinted in Lee Rainwater and William L. Yancey, *The Moynihan Report and the Politics of Controversy* [Cambridge, MA: MIT Press, 1967, p. 125].)

This speech, delivered at Howard University on June 4, 1965, was written in part by Daniel Patrick Moynihan. A more systematic treatment of the institutional racism approach is David T. Wellman, *Portraits of White Racism* (New York: Cambridge University Press, 1977).

51. From the vantage point of the 1990s, it is possible to question whether discrimination was ever effectively outlawed. The federal retreat from the agenda of integration began almost immediately after the passage of civil rights legislation, and has culminated today in a series of Supreme Court decisions making violation of these laws almost impossible to prove. See Ezorsky, *Racism and Justice;* Kairys, *With Liberty and Justice for Some*. As we write, the Supreme Court has further restricted antidiscrimination laws in the case of *St. Mary's Honor Center v. Hicks*. See Linda Greenhouse, "Justices Increase Workers' Burden in Job-Bias Cases," *The New York Times*, 26 June 1993, p. 1.

52. Robert Miles, *Racism* (New York and London: Routledge, 1989), esp. chap. 2.

53. The *locus classicus* of this position is Nathan Glazer, *Affirmative Discrimination: Ethnic Inequality and Public Policy*, 2nd ed. (New York: Basic Books, 1978); for more recent formulations, see Murray, *Losing Ground;* Arthur M. Schlesinger, *The Disuniting of America: Reflections on a Multicultural Society* (New York: W. W. Norton, 1992).

54. See Chapter 1.
55. Thomas Sowell, for example, has argued that one's "human capital" is to a large extent culturally determined. Therefore the state cannot create a false equality which runs counter to the magnitude and persistence of cultural differences. Such attempts at social engineering are likely to produce negative and unintended results: "If social processes are transmitting real differences—in productivity, reliability, cleanliness, sobriety, peacefulness [!]—then attempts to impose politically a very different set of beliefs will necessarily backfire. . . ." (Thomas Sowell, *The Economics and Politics of Race: An International Perspective* [New York: Quill, 1983], p. 252).
56. Bob Blauner, "Racism, Race, and Ethnicity: Some Reflections on the Language of Race" [unpublished manuscript, 1991].
57. Essentialism, it will be recalled, is understood as belief in real, true human essences, existing outside or impervious to social and historical context.
58. An example would be the "singling out" of members of racially defined minority groups for harsh treatment by authorities, as when police harass and beat randomly chosen ghetto youth, a practice they do not pursue with white suburban youth.
59. For example, the biologistic theories found in Michael Anderson Bradley, *The Iceman Inheritance: Prehistoric Sources of Western Man's Racism, Sexism and Aggression* (Toronto: Dorset, 1978), and in Frances Cress Welsing, *The Isis (Yssis) Papers* (Chicago: Third World Press, 1991).
60. "These remarks should not be interpreted as simply an effort to move the gaze of African-American studies to a different site. I do not want to alter one hierarchy in order to institute another. It is true that I do not want to encourage those totalizing approaches to African-American scholarship which have no drive other than the exchange of dominations—dominant Eurocentric scholarship replaced by dominant Afrocentric scholarship. More interesting is what makes intellectual domination possible; how knowledge is transformed from invasion and conquest to revelation and choice; what ignites and informs the literary imagination, and what forces help establish the parameters of criticism." (Toni Morrison, *Playing in the Dark*, p. 8.)
61. Lisa Lowe states: "The concept of 'strategic essentialism' suggests that it is possible to utilize specific signifiers of ethnic identity, such as Asian American, for the purpose of contesting and disrupting the discourses that exclude Asian Americans, while simultaneously revealing the internal contradictions and slippages of Asian Americans so as to insure that such essentialisms will not be reproduced and proliferated by the very apparatuses we seek to disempower." Lisa Lowe, "Heterogeneity, Hybridity, Multiplicity: Marking Asian American Differences," *Diaspora*, Vol. 1, no. 1 (Spring 1991), p. 39.
62. This view supports Supreme Court decisions taken in the late 1960s and early 1970s, for example in *Griggs v. Duke Power*, 401 U.S. 424 (1971). We agree with Kairys that only ". . . [F]or that brief period in our history, it could accurately be said that governmental discrimination was prohibited by law" (Kairys, *With Liberty and Justice For Some*, p. 144).
63. This analysis draws on Ezorsky, *Racism and Justice*.
64. See for example, Judy H. Katz, *White Awareness: Handbook for Anti-Racism Training* (Norman: University of Oklahoma Press, 1978).
65. The formula "racism equals prejudice plus power" is frequently invoked by our students to argue that only whites can be racist. We have been able to uncover little written analysis to support this view (apart from Katz, ibid., p. 10), but consider that it is itself an example of the essentializing approach we have identified as central to racism. In the modern world, "power" cannot be reified as a thing which some possess and others don't, but instead constitutes a relational field. The minority student who boldly asserts in class that minorities cannot be racist is surely not entirely powerless. In all but the most absolutist of regimes, resistance to rule itself implies power.
66. To pick but one example among many: writing before the successes of the civil rights movement, E. Franklin Frazier bitterly castigated the collaboration of black elites with white supremacy. See Frazier, *Black Bourgeoisie: The Rise of a New Middle Class in the United States* (New York: The Free Press, 1957).
67. Interestingly, what they share most centrally seems to be their antisemitism.
68. Having made a similar argument, Lani Guinier, Clinton's nominee to head the Justice Department's Civil Rights Division was savagely attacked and her nomination ultimately blocked. See Guinier, "The Triumph of Tokenism: The Voting Rights Act and the Theory of Black Electoral Success," *Michigan Law Review* (March 1991). We discuss these events in greater detail in this book's Epilogue, below.
69. See Miles, *Racism*, p. 77. Much of the current debate over the advisability and legality of banning racist hate speech seems to us to adopt the dubious position that racism is primarily an ideological phenomenon. See Mari J. Matsuda et al., *Words That Wound: Critical Race Theory, Assaultive Speech, and the First Amendment* (Boulder, CO: Westview Press, 1993).

70. Or ideologies which mask privilege by falsely claiming that inequality and injustice have been eliminated. See Wellman, *Portraits of White Racism.*

71. Racial teachings of the Nation of Islam, for example, maintain that whites are the product of a failed experiment by a mad scientist.

72. Elinor Langer, "The American Neo-Nazi Movement Today," *The Nation,* July 16/23, 1990.

73. Such arguments can be found in Nathan Glazer, *Affirmative Discrimination,* Charles Murray, *Losing Ground,* and Arthur M. Schlesinger, Jr., *The Disuniting of America,* among others.

3.
DEFINING RACISM

"Can We Talk?"

Beverly Daniel Tatum

Early in my teaching career, a White student I knew asked me what I would be teaching the following semester. I mentioned that I would be teaching a course on racism. She replied, with some surprise in her voice, "Oh, is there still racism?" I assured her that indeed there was and suggested that she sign up for my course. Fifteen years later, after exhaustive media coverage of events such as the Rodney King beating, the Charles Stuart and Susan Smith cases, the O. J. Simpson trial, the appeal to racial prejudices in electoral politics, and the bitter debates about affirmative action and welfare reform, it seems hard to imagine that anyone would still be unaware of the reality of racism in our society. But in fact, in almost every audience I address, there is someone who will suggest that racism is a thing of the past. There is always someone who hasn't noticed the stereotypical images of people of color in the media, who hasn't observed the housing discrimination in their community, who hasn't read the newspaper articles about documented racial bias in lending practices among well-known banks, who isn't aware of the racial tracking pattern at the local school, who hasn't seen the reports of rising incidents of racially motivated hate crimes in America—in short, someone who hasn't been paying attention to issues of race. But if you are paying attention, the legacy of racism is not hard to see, and we are all affected by it.

The impact of racism begins early. Even in our preschool years, we are exposed to misinformation about people different from ourselves. Many of us grew up in neighborhoods where we had limited opportunities to interact with people different from our own families. When I ask my college students, "How many of you grew up in neighborhoods where most of the people were from the same racial group as your own?" almost every hand goes up. There is still a great deal of social segregation in our communities. Consequently, most of the early information we receive about "others"—people racially, religiously, or socioeconomically different from ourselves—does not come as the result of firsthand experience. The secondhand information we do receive has often been distorted, shaped by cultural stereotypes, and left incomplete.

Some examples will highlight this process. Several years ago one of my students conducted a research project investigating preschoolers' conceptions of Native Americans.[1] Using children at a local day care center as her participants, she asked these three- and four-year-olds to draw a picture of a Native American. Most children were stumped by her request. They didn't know what a Native American was. But when she rephrased the question and asked them to draw a picture of an Indian, they readily complied. Almost every picture included one central feature: feathers. In fact, many of them also included a weapon—a knife or tomahawk—and depicted the person in violent or aggressive terms. Though this group of children, almost all of whom were White, did not live near a large Native American population and probably had had little if any personal interaction with American Indians, they all had internalized an image of what Indians were like. How did they know? Cartoon images, in particular the Disney movie *Peter Pan,* were cited by the children as their number-one source of information. At the age of three, these children already had a set of stereotypes in place. Though I would not describe three-year-olds as prejudiced, the stereotypes to which they have been exposed become the foundation for the adult prejudices so many of us have.

Sometimes the assumptions we make about others come not from what we have been told or what we have seen on television or in books, but rather from what we have *not* been told. The distortion of historical information about people of color leads young people (and older people, too) to make assumptions that may go unchallenged for a long time. Consider this conversation between two White students following a discussion about the cultural transmission of racism:

"Yeah, I just found out that Cleopatra was actually a Black woman."

"What?"

The first student went on to explain her newly learned information. The second student exclaimed in disbelief, "That can't be true. Cleopatra was beautiful!"

What had this young woman learned about who in our society is considered beautiful and who is not? Had she conjured up images of Elizabeth Taylor when she thought of Cleopatra? The new information her classmate had shared and her own deeply ingrained assumptions about who is beautiful and who is not were too incongruous to allow her to assimilate the information at that moment.

Omitted information can have similar effects. For example, another young woman, preparing to be a high school English teacher, expressed her dismay that she had never learned about any Black authors in any of her English courses. How was she to teach about them to her future students when she hadn't learned about them herself? A White male student in the class responded to this discussion with frustration in his response journal, writing "It's not my fault that Blacks don't write books." Had one of his elementary, high school, or college teachers ever told

him that there were no Black writers? Probably not. Yet because he had never been exposed to Black authors, he had drawn his own conclusion that there were none.

Stereotypes, omissions, and distortions all contribute to the development of prejudice. *Prejudice* is a preconceived judgment or opinion, usually based on limited information. I assume that we all have prejudices, not because we want them, but simply because we are so continually exposed to misinformation about others. Though I have often heard students or workshop participants describe someone as not having "a prejudiced bone in his body," I usually suggest that they look again. Prejudice is one of the inescapable consequences of living in a racist society. Cultural racism—the cultural images and messages that affirm the assumed superiority of Whites and the assumed inferiority of people of color—is like smog in the air. Sometimes it is so thick it is visible, other times it is less apparent, but always, day in and day out, we are breathing it in. None of us would introduce ourselves as "smog-breathers" (and most of us don't want to be described as prejudiced), but if we live in a smoggy place, how can we avoid breathing the air? If we live in an environment in which we are bombarded with stereotypical images in the media, are frequently exposed to the ethnic jokes of friends and family members, and are rarely informed of the accomplishments of oppressed groups, we will develop the negative categorizations of those groups that form the basis of prejudice.

People of color as well as Whites develop these categorizations. Even a member of the stereotyped group may internalize the stereotypical categories about his or her own group to some degree. In fact, this process happens so frequently that it has a name, *internalized oppression.* Some of the consequences of believing the distorted messages about one's own group will be discussed in subsequent chapters.

Certainly some people are more prejudiced than others, actively embracing and perpetuating negative and hateful images of those who are different from themselves. When we claim to be free of prejudice, perhaps what we are really saying is that we are not hate-mongers. But none of us is completely innocent. Prejudice is an integral part of our socialization, and it is not our fault. Just as the preschoolers my student interviewed are not to blame for the negative messages they internalized, we are not at fault for the stereotypes, distortions, and omissions that shaped our thinking as we grew up.

To say that it is not our fault does not relieve us of responsibility, however. We may not have polluted the air, but we need to take responsibility, along with others, for cleaning it up. Each of us needs to look at our own behavior. Am I perpetuating and reinforcing the negative messages so pervasive in our culture, or am I seeking to challenge them? If I have not been exposed to positive images of marginalized groups, am I seeking them out, expanding my own knowledge base for myself and my children? Am I acknowledging and examining my own prejudices, my own rigid categorizations of others, thereby minimizing the adverse impact they might have on my interactions with those I have categorized? Unless we engage in these and other conscious acts of reflection and reeducation, we easily repeat the process with our children. We teach what we were taught. The unexamined prejudices of the parents are passed on to the children. It is not our fault, but it is our responsibility to interrupt this cycle.

Racism: A System of Advantage Based on Race

Many people use the terms *prejudice* and *racism* interchangeably. I do not, and I think it is important to make a distinction. In his book *Portraits of White Racism,* David Wellman argues convincingly that limiting our understanding of racism to prejudice does not offer a sufficient explanation for the persistence of racism. He defines racism as a "system of advantage based on race."[2] In illustrating this definition, he provides example after example of how Whites defend their racial advantage—access to better schools, housing, jobs—even when they do not embrace overtly prejudicial thinking. Racism cannot be fully explained as an expression of prejudice alone.

This definition of racism is useful because it allows us to see that racism, like other forms of oppression, is not only a personal ideology based on racial prejudice, but a *system* involving cultural messages and institutional policies and practices, as well as the beliefs and actions of individuals. In the context of the United States, this system clearly operates to the advantage of Whites and to the disadvantage of people of color. Another related definition of racism, commonly used by antiracist educators and consultants, is "prejudice plus power." Racial prejudice when combined with social power—access to social, cultural, and economic resources and decision-making—leads to the institutionalization of racist policies and practices. While I think this definition also captures the idea that racism is more than individual beliefs and attitudes, I prefer Wellman's definition because the idea of systematic advantage and disadvantage is critical to an understanding of how racism operates in American society.

In addition, I find that many of my White students and workshop participants do not feel powerful. Defining racism as prejudice plus power has little personal relevance. For some, their response to this definition is the following: "I'm not really prejudiced, and I have no power, so racism has nothing to do with me." However, most White people, if they are really being honest with themselves, can see that there are advantages to being White in the United States. Despite the current rhetoric about affirmative action and "reverse racism," every social indicator, from salary to life expectancy, reveals the advantages of being White.[3]

The systematic advantages of being White are often referred to as White privilege. In a now well-known article, "White Privilege: Unpacking the Invisible Knapsack," Peggy McIntosh, a White feminist scholar, identified a long list of societal privileges that she received simply because she was White.[4] She did not ask for them, and it is important to note that she hadn't always noticed that she was receiving them. They included major and minor advantages. Of course she enjoyed greater access to jobs and housing. But she also was able to shop in department stores without being followed by suspicious salespeople, and could always find appropriate hair care products and makeup in any drugstore. She could send her child to school confident that the teacher would not discriminate against him on the basis of race. She could also be late for meetings, and talk with her mouth full, fairly confident that these behaviors would not be attributed to the fact that she was White. She could express an opinion in a meeting or in print and not have it labeled the "White" viewpoint. In other words, she was more often than not viewed as an individual, rather than as a member of a racial group.

This article rings true for most White readers, many of whom may have never considered the benefits of being White. It's one thing to have enough awareness of racism to describe the ways that people of color are disadvantaged by it. But this new understanding of racism is more elusive. In very concrete terms, it means that if a person of color is the victim of housing discrimination, the apartment that would otherwise have been rented to that person of color is still available for a White person. The White tenant is, knowingly or unknowingly, the beneficiary of racism, a system of advantage based on race. The unsuspecting tenant is not to blame for the prior discrimination, but she benefits from it anyway.

For many Whites, this new awareness of the benefits of a racist system elicits considerable pain, often accompanied by feelings of anger and guilt. These uncomfortable emotions can hinder further discussion. We all like to think that we deserve the good things we have received, and that others, too, get what they deserve. Social psychologists call this tendency a "belief in a just world."[5] Racism directly contradicts such notions of justice.

Understanding racism as a system of advantage based on race is antithetical to traditional notions of an American meritocracy. For those who have internalized this myth, this definition generates considerable discomfort. It is more comfortable simply to think of racism as a particular form of prejudice. Notions of power or privilege do not have to be addressed when our understanding of racism is constructed in that way.

The discomfort generated when a systemic definition of racism is introduced is usually quite visible in the workshops I lead. Someone in the group is usually quick to point out that this is not the definition you will find in most dictionaries. I reply, "Who wrote the dictionary?" I am not being facetious with this response. Whose interests are served by a "prejudice only" definition of racism? It is important to understand that the system of advantage is perpetuated when we do not acknowledge its existence.

Racism: For Whites Only?

Frequently someone will say, "You keep talking about White people. People of color can be racist, too." I once asked a White teacher what it would mean to her if a student or parent of color accused her of being racist. She said she would feel as though she had been punched in the stomach or called a "low-life scum." She is not alone in this feeling. The word *racist* holds a lot of emotional power. For many White people, to be called racist is the ultimate insult. The idea that this term might only be applied to Whites becomes highly problematic for after all, can't people of color be "low-life scum" too?

Of course, people of any racial group can hold hateful attitudes and behave in racially discriminatory and bigoted ways. We can all cite examples of horrible hate crimes which have been perpetrated by people of color as well as Whites. Hateful behavior is hateful behavior no matter who does it. But when I am asked, "Can people of color be racist?" I reply, "The answer depends on your definition of racism." If one defines racism as racial prejudice, the answer is yes. People of color can and do have racial prejudices. However, if one defines racism as a system of advantage based on race, the answer is no. People of color are not racist because they do not systematically benefit from racism. And equally important, there is no systematic cultural and institutional support or sanction for the racial bigotry of people of color. In my view, reserving the term *racist* only for behaviors committed by Whites in the context of a White-dominated society is a way of acknowledging the ever-present power differential afforded Whites by the culture and institutions that make up the system of advantage and continue to reinforce notions of White superiority. (Using the same logic, I reserve the word *sexist* for men. Though women can and do have gender-based prejudices, only men systematically benefit from sexism.)

Despite my best efforts to explain my thinking on this point, there are some who will be troubled, perhaps even incensed, by my response. To call the racially motivated acts of a person of color acts of racial bigotry and to describe similar acts committed by Whites as racist will make no sense to some people, including some people of color. To those, I will respectfully say, "We can agree to disagree." At moments like these, it is not agreement that is essential, but clarity. Even if you don't like the definition of racism I am using, hopefully you are now clear about what it is. If I also understand how you are using the term, our conversation can continue—despite our disagreement.

Another provocative question I'm often asked is "Are you saying all Whites are racist?" When asked this question, I again remember that White teacher's response, and I am conscious that perhaps the question I am really being asked is, "Are you saying all Whites are bad people?" The answer to that question is of course not. However, all White people, intentionally or unintentionally, do benefit from racism. A more relevant question is what are White people as individuals doing to interrupt racism? For many White people, the image of a racist is a hood-wearing Klan member or a name-calling Archie Bunker figure. These images represent what might be called *active racism,* blatant, intentional acts of racial bigotry and discrimination. *Passive racism* is more subtle and can be seen in the collusion of laughing when a racist joke is told, of letting exclusionary hiring practices go unchallenged, of accepting as appropriate the omissions of people of color from the curriculum, and of avoiding difficult race-related issues. Because racism is so ingrained in the fabric of American institutions, it is easily self-perpetuating.[6] All that is required to maintain it is business as usual.

I sometimes visualize the ongoing cycle of racism as a moving walkway at the airport. Active racist behavior is equivalent to walking fast on the conveyor belt. The person engaged in active racist behavior has identified with the ideology of White supremacy and is moving with it. Passive racist behavior is equivalent to standing still on the walkway. No overt effort is being made, but the conveyor belt moves the bystanders along to the same destination as those who are actively walking. Some of the bystanders may feel the motion of the conveyor belt, see the active

racists ahead of them, and choose to turn around, unwilling to go to the same destination as the White supremacists. But unless they are walking actively in the opposite direction at a speed faster than the conveyor belt—unless they are actively antiracist—they will find themselves carried along with the others.

So, not all Whites are actively racist. Many are passively racist. Some, though not enough, are actively antiracist. The relevant question is not whether all Whites are racist, but how we can move more White people from a position of active or passive racism to one of active antiracism? The task of interrupting racism is obviously not the task of Whites alone. But the fact of White privilege means that Whites have greater access to the societal institutions in need of transformation. To whom much is given, much is required.

It is important to acknowledge that while all Whites benefit from racism, they do not all benefit equally. Other factors, such as socioeconomic status, gender, age, religious affiliation, sexual orientation and mental and physical ability, also play a role in our access to social influence and power. A White woman on welfare is not privileged to the same extent as a wealthy White heterosexual man. In her case, the systematic disadvantages of sexism and classism intersect with her White privilege, but the privilege is still there. This point was brought home to me in a 1994 study conducted by a Mount Holyoke graduate student, Phyllis Wentworth.[7] Wentworth interviewed a group of female college students, who were both older than their peers and were the first members of their families to attend college, about the pathways that lead them to college. All of the women interviewed were White, from working-class backgrounds, from families where women were expected to graduate from high school and get married or get a job. Several had experienced abusive relationships and other personal difficulties prior to coming to college. Yet their experiences were punctuated by "good luck" stories of apartments obtained without a deposit, good jobs offered without experience or extensive reference checks, and encouragement provided by willing mentors. While the women acknowledged their good fortune, none of them discussed their Whiteness. They had not considered the possibility that being White had worked in their favor and helped give them the benefit of the doubt at critical junctures. This study clearly showed that even under difficult circumstances, White privilege was still operating.

It is also true that not all people of color are equally targeted by racism. We all have multiple identities that shape our experience. I can describe myself as a light-skinned, well-educated, heterosexual, able-bodied, Christian African American woman raised in a middle-class suburb. As an African American woman, I am systematically disadvantaged by race and by gender, but I systematically receive benefits in the other categories, which then mediate my experience of racism and sexism. When one is targeted by multiple isms—racism, sexism, classism, heterosexism, ableism, anti-Semitism, ageism—in whatever combination, the effect is intensified. The particular combination of racism and classism in many communities of color is life-threatening. Nonetheless, when I, the middle class Black mother of two sons, read another story about a Black man's unlucky encounter with a White police officer's deadly force, I am reminded that racism by itself can kill.

The Cost of Racism

Several years ago, a white male student in my psychology of racism course wrote in his journal at the end of the semester that he had learned a lot about racism and now understood in a way he never had before just how advantaged he was. He also commented that he didn't think he would do anything to try to change the situation. After all, the system was working in his favor. Fortunately, his response was not typical. Most of my students leave my course with the desire (and an action plan) to interrupt the cycle of racism. However, this young man's response does raise an important question. Why should Whites who are advantaged by racism *want* to end that system of advantage? What are the *costs* of that system to them?

A *Money* magazine article called "Race and Money" chronicled the many ways the American economy was hindered by institutional racism.[8] Whether one looks at productivity lowered by racial tensions in the workplace, or real estate equity lost

through housing discrimination, or the tax revenue lost in underemployed communities of color, or the high cost of warehousing human talent in prison, the economic costs of racism are real and measurable.

As a psychologist, I often hear about the less easily measured costs. When I ask White men and women how racism hurts them, they frequently talk about their fears of people of color, the social incompetence they feel in racially mixed situations, the alienation they have experienced between parents and children when a child marries into a family of color, and the interracial friendships they had as children that were lost in adolescence or young adulthood without their ever understanding why. White people are paying a significant price for the system of advantage. The cost is not as high for whites as it is for people of color, but a price is being paid.[9] Wendell Berry, a white writer raised in Kentucky, captures this psychic pain in the opening pages of his book, *The Hidden Wound:*

> If white people have suffered less obviously from racism than black people, they have nevertheless suffered greatly; the cost has been greater perhaps than we can yet know. If the white man has inflicted the wound of racism upon black men, the cost has been that he would receive the mirror image of that wound into himself. As the master, or as a member of the dominant race, he has felt little compulsion to acknowledge it or speak of it; the more painful it has grown the more deeply he has hidden it within himself. But the wound is there, and it is a profound disorder, as great a damage in his mind as it is in his society.[10]

The dismantling of racism is in the best interests of everyone.

A Word about Language

Throughout this chapter I have used the term *White* to refer to Americans of European descent. In another era, I might have used the term *Caucasian.* I have used the term *people of color* to refer to those groups in America that are and have been historically targeted by racism. This includes people of African descent, people of Asian descent, people of Latin American descent, and indigenous peoples (sometimes referred to as Native Americans or American Indians).[11] Many people refer to these groups collectively as non-Whites. This term is particularly offensive because it defines groups of people in terms of what they are not. (Do we call women "non-men?") I also avoid using the term *minorities* because it represents another kind of distortion of information which we need to correct. So-called minorities represent the majority of the world's population. While the term *people of color* is inclusive, it is not perfect. As a workshop participant once said, White people have color, too. Perhaps it would be more accurate to say "people of more color," though I am not ready to make that change. Perhaps fellow psychologist Linda James Myers is on the right track. She refers to two groups of people, those of acknowledged African descent and those of unacknowledged African descent, reminding us that we can all trace the roots of our common humanity to Africa.

I refer to people of acknowledged African descent as Black. I know that *African American* is also a commonly used term, and I often refer to myself and other Black people born and raised in America in that way. Perhaps because I am a child of the 1960s "Black and beautiful" era, I still prefer *Black*. The term is more inclusive than *African American,* because there are Black people in the United States who are not African American—Afro-Caribbeans, for example—yet are targeted by racism, and are identified as Black.

When referring to other groups of color, I try to use the terms that the people themselves want to be called. In some cases, there is no clear consensus. For example, some people of Latin American ancestry prefer *Latino,* while others prefer *Hispanic* or, if of Mexican descent, *Chicano.*[12] The terms *Latino* and *Hispanic* are used interchangeably here. Similarly, there are regional variations in the use of the terms *Native American, American Indian,* and *Indian.* American Indian and *Native people* are now more widely used than *Native American,* and the language used here reflects that. People of Asian descent include Pacific Islanders, and that is reflected in the terms *Asian/Pacific Islanders* and *Asian Pacific Americans.*

However, when quoting others I use whichever terms they use.

My dilemma about the language to use reflects the fact that race is a social construction.[13] Despite myths to the contrary, biologists tell us that the only meaningful racial categorization is that of human. Van den Berghe defines race as "a group that is socially defined but on the basis of *physical* criteria," including skin color and facial features.[14]

Racial identity development, a central focus of this book, usually refers to the process of defining for oneself the personal significance and social meaning of belonging to a particular racial group. The terms *racial identity* and *ethnic identity* are often used synonymously, though a distinction can be made between the two. An ethnic group is a socially defined group based on *cultural* criteria, such as language, customs, and shared history. An individual might identify as a member of an ethnic group (Irish or Italian, for example) but might not think of himself in racial terms (as White). On the other hand, one may recognize the personal significance of racial group membership (identifying as Black, for instance) but may not consider ethnic identity (such as West Indian) as particularly meaningful.

Both racial and ethnic categories are socially constructed, and social definitions of these categories have changed over time. For example, in his book *Ethnic Identity: The Transformation of White America,* Richard Alba points out that the high rates of intermarriage and the dissolution of other social boundaries among European ethnic groups in the United States have reduced the significance of ethnic identity for these groups. In their place, he argues, a new ethnic identity is emerging, that of European American.[15]

Throughout this book, I refer primarily to racial identity. It is important, however, to acknowledge that ethnic identity and racial identity sometimes intersect. For example, dark-skinned Puerto Ricans may identify culturally as Puerto Rican and yet be categorized racially by others as Black on the basis of physical appearance. In the case of either racial or ethnic identity, these identities remain most salient to individuals of racial or ethnic groups that have been historically disadvantaged or marginalized.

The language we use to categorize one another racially is imperfect. These categories are still evolving as the current debate over Census classifications indicates.[16] The original creation of racial categories was in the service of oppression. Some may argue that to continue to use them is to continue that oppression. I respect that argument. Yet it is difficult to talk about what is essentially a flawed and problematic social construct without using language that is itself problematic. We have to be able to talk about it in order to change it. So this is the language I choose.

Notes

1. C. O'Toole, "The effect of the media and multicultural education on children's perceptions of Native Americans" (senior thesis, Department of Psychology and Education, Mount Holyoke College, South Hadley, MA, May 1990).

2. For an extended discussion of this point, see David Wellman, *Portraits of White racism* (Cambridge: Cambridge University Press, 1977), ch. 1.

3. For specific statistical information, see R. Farley, "The common destiny of Blacks and Whites: Observations about the social and economic status of the races," pp. 197–233 in H. Hill and J.E. Jones, Jr. (Eds.), *Race in America: The struggle for equality* (Madison: University of Wisconsin Press, 1993).

4. P. McIntosh, "White privilege: Unpacking the invisible knapsack," *Peace and Freedom* (July/August 1989): 10–12.

5. For further discussion of the concept of "belief in a just world," see M. J. Lerner, "Social psychology of justice and interpersonal attraction," in T. Huston (Ed.), *Foundations of interpersonal attraction* (New York: Academic Press, 1974).

6. For a brief historical overview of the institutionalization of racism and sexism in our legal system, see "Part V: How it happened: Race and gender issues in U.S. law," in P.S. Rothenberg (Ed.), *Race, class, and gender in the United States: An integrated study,* 3d ed. (New York: St. Martin's Press, 1995).

7. P.A. Wentworth, "The identity development of nontraditionally aged first-generation women college students: An exploratory study" (master's thesis, Department of Psychology and Education, Mount Holyoke College, South Hadley, MA, 1994).

8. W.L. Updegrave, "Race and money," *Money* (December 1989): 152–72.

9. For further discussion of the impact of racism on Whites, see B. Bowser and R. G. Hunt (Eds.), *Impacts of racism on White Americans* (Thousand Oaks, CA: Sage, 1981); P. Kivel, *Uprooting racism: How White people can work for racial justice* (Philadelphia: New Society Publishers, 1996); and J. Barndt, *Dismantling racism: The continuing challenge to White America* (Minneapolis: Augsburg Press, 1991).

10. W. Berry, *The hidden wound* (San Francisco: North Point Press, 1989), pp. 3–4.

11. It is important to note here that these groups are not necessarily mutually exclusive. For example, people of Latin American descent may have European, African, and Native American ancestors. The politics of racial categorization has served to create artificial boundaries between groups with shared ancestry.

12. It is difficult to know which is the preferred term to use because different subgroups have different preferences. According to Amado Padilla, younger U.S.-born university-educated individuals of Mexican ancestry prefer *Chicano(a)* to *Mexican American* or *Hispanic.* On the other hand, *Latino* is preferred by others of Mexican ancestry or other Latin American origin. Those of Cuban ancestry may prefer *Cuban American* to *Latino,* whereas recent immigrants from Central America would rather be identified by their nationality (e.g., *Guatematecos* or *Salvadoreños).* A. Padilla (Ed.), *Hispanic psychology* (Thousand Oaks, CA: Sage, 1995).

13. For an expanded discussion of the social construction of race, see M. Omi and H. Winant, *Racial formation in the United States,* 2d ed. (New York: Routledge, 1994).

14. P.L. Van den Berghe, *Race and racism* (New York: Wiley, 1967).

15. See R. Alba, *Ethnic identity: The transformation of White America* (New Haven: Yale University Press, 1990).

16. For a discussion of the census classification debate and the history of racial classification in the United States, see L. Wright, "One drop of blood," *The New Yorker* (July 25, 1994): 46–55.

4.
WHITE PRIVILEGE
Unpacking the Invisible Knapsack
Peggy McIntosh

Through work to bring materials from Women's Studies into the rest of the curriculum, I have often noticed men's unwillingness to grant that they are over-privileged, even though they may grant that women are disadvantaged. They may say they will work to improve women's status, in the society, the university, or the curriculum, but they can't or won't support the idea of lessening men's. Denials which amount to taboos surround the subject of advantages which men gain from women's disadvantages. These denials protect male privilege from being fully acknowledged, lessened or ended.

Thinking through unacknowledged male privilege as a phenomenon, I realized that, since hierarchies in our society are interlocking, there was most likely a phenomenon of white privilege that was similarly denied and protected. As a white person, I realized I had been taught about racism as something that puts others at a disadvantage, but had been taught not to see one of its corollary aspects, white privilege, which puts me at an advantage.

I think whites are carefully taught not to recognize white privilege, as males are taught not to recognize male privilege. So I have begun in an untutored way to ask what it is like to have white privilege. I have come to see white privilege as an invisible package of unearned assets that I can count on cashing in each day, but about which I was "meant" to remain oblivious. White privilege is like an invisible weightless knapsack of special provisions, maps, passports, codebooks, visas, clothes, tools and blank checks.

Describing white privilege makes one newly accountable. As we in Women's Studies work to reveal male privilege and ask men to give up some of their power, so one who writes about white privilege must ask, "Having described it, what will I do to lessen or end it?"

After I realized the extent to which men work from a base of unacknowledged privilege, I understood that much of their oppressiveness was unconscious. Then I remembered the frequent charges from women of color that white women whom they encounter are oppressive. I began to understand why we are justly seen as oppressive, even when we don't see ourselves that way. I began to count the ways in which I enjoy unearned skin privilege and have been conditioned into oblivion about its existence.

My schooling gave me no training in seeing myself as an oppressor, as an unfairly advantaged person, or as a participant in a damaged culture. I was taught to see myself as an individual whose moral state depended on her individual moral will. My schooling followed the pattern my colleague Elizabeth Minnich has pointed out: whites are taught to think of their lives as morally neutral, normative, and average, and also ideal, so that when we work to benefit others, this is seen as work which will allow "them" to be more like "us."

I decided to try to work on myself at least by identifying some of the daily effects of white privilege in my life. I have chosen those conditions which I think in my case *attach somewhat more to skin-color privilege* than to class, religion, ethnic status, or geographic location, though of course all these other factors are intricately intertwined. As far as I can see, my African American co-workers, friends, and acquaintances with whom I come into daily or frequent contact in this particular time, place and line of work cannot count on most of these conditions.

1. I can if I wish arrange to be in the company of people of my race most of the time.
2. If I should need to move, I can be pretty sure of renting or purchasing housing in an area which I can afford and in which I would want to live.
3. I can be pretty sure that my neighbors in such a location will be neutral or pleasant to me.
4. I can go shopping alone most of the time, pretty well assured that I will not be followed or harassed.
5. I can turn on the television or open to the front page of the paper and see people of my race widely represented.
6. When I am told about our national heritage or about "civilization," I am shown that people of my color made it what it is.
7. I can be sure that my children will be given curricular materials that testify to the existence of their race.
8. If I want to, I can be pretty sure of finding a publisher for this piece on white privilege.
9. I can go into a music shop and count on finding the music of my race represented, into a supermarket and find the staple foods that fit with my cultural traditions, into a hairdresser's shop and find someone who can cut my hair.
10. Whether I use checks, credit cards or cash, I can count on my skin color not to work against the appearance of financial reliability.
11. I can arrange to protect my children most of the time from people who might not like them.
12. I can swear, or dress in second-hand clothes, or not answer letters, without having people attribute these choices to the bad morals, the poverty, or the illiteracy of my race.

13. I can speak in public to a powerful male group without putting my race on trial.
14. I can do well in a challenging situation without being called a credit to my race.
15. I am never asked to speak for all the people of my racial group.
16. I can remain oblivious of the language and customs of persons of color who constitute the world's majority without feeling in my culture any penalty for such oblivion.
17. I can criticize our government and talk about how much I fear its policies and behavior without being seen as a cultural outsider.
18. I can be pretty sure that if I ask to talk to "the person in charge," I will be facing a person of my race.
19. If a traffic cop pulls me over or if the IRS audits my tax return, I can be sure I haven't been singled out because of my race.
20. I can easily buy posters, postcards, picture books, greeting cards, dolls, toys, and children's magazines featuring people of my race.
21. I can go home from most meetings of organizations I belong to feeling somewhat tied in, rather than isolated, out-of-place, outnumbered, unheard, held at a distance, or feared.
22. I can take a job with an affirmative action employer without having co-workers on the job suspect that I got it because of race.
23. I can choose public accommodations without fearing that people of my race cannot get in or will be mistreated in the places I have chosen.
24. I can be sure that if I need legal or medical help, my race will not work against me.
25. If my day, week, or year is going badly, I need not ask of each negative episode or situation whether it has racial overtones.
26. I can choose blemish cover or bandages in "flesh" color and have them more or less match my skin.

I repeatedly forgot each of the realizations on this list until I wrote it down. For me, white privilege has turned out to be an elusive and fugitive subject. The pressure to avoid it is great, for in facing it I must give up the myth of meritocracy. If these things are true, this is not such a free country; one's life is not what one makes it; many doors open for certain people through no virtues of their own.

In unpacking this invisible knapsack of white privilege, I have listed conditions of daily experience that I once took for granted. Nor did I think of any of these prerequisites as bad for the holder. I now think that we need a more finely differentiated taxonomy of privilege, for some of these varieties are only what one would want for everyone in a just society, and others give license to be ignorant, oblivious, arrogant and destructive.

I see a pattern running through the matrix of white privilege, a pattern of assumptions that were passed on to me as a white person. There was one main piece of cultural turf; it was my own turf, and I was among those who could control the turf. *My skin color was an asset for any move I was educated to want to make.* I could think of myself as belonging in major ways and of making social systems work for me. I could freely disparage, fear, neglect, or be oblivious to anything outside of the dominant cultural forms. Being of the main culture, I could also criticize it fairly freely.

In proportion as my racial group was being made confident, comfortable, and oblivious, other groups were likely being made inconfident, uncomfortable, and alienated. Whiteness protected me from many kinds of hostility, distress and violence, which I was being subtly trained to visit, in turn, upon people of color.

For this reason, the word "privilege" now seems to me misleading. We usually think of privilege as being a favored state, whether earned or conferred by birth or luck. Yet some of the conditions I have described here work systematically to overempower certain groups. Such privilege simply *confers dominance* because of one's race or sex.

I want, then, to distinguish between earned strength and unearned power conferred systemically. Power from unearned privilege can look like strength when it is in fact permission to escape or to dominate. But not all of the privileges on my list are inevitably damaging. Some, like the expectation that neighbors will be decent to you, or that your race will not count against you in court, should be the norm in a just society. Others, like the privilege to ignore less powerful people, distort the humanity of the holders as well as the ignored groups.

We might at least start by distinguishing between positive advantages, which we can work to spread, and negative types of advantage, which unless rejected will always reinforce our present hierarchies. For example, the feeling that one belongs within the human circle, as Native Americans say, should not be seen as privilege for a few. Ideally it is an *unearned entitlement.* At present, since only a few have it, it is an *unearned advantage* for them. This paper results from a process of coming to see that some of the power that I originally saw as attendant on being a human being in the United States consisted in unearned advantage and conferred dominance.

I have met very few men who are truly distressed about systemic, unearned male advantage and conferred dominance. And so one question for me and others like me is whether we will be like them, or whether we will get truly distressed, even outraged, about unearned race advantage and conferred dominance, and, if so, what will we do to lessen them. In any case, we need to do more work in identifying how they actually affect our daily lives. Many, perhaps most, of our white students in the U.S. think that racism doesn't affect them because they are not people of color, they do not see "whiteness" as a racial identity. In addition, since race and sex are not the only advantaging systems at work, we need similarly to examine the daily experience of having age advantage, or ethnic advantage, or physical ability, or advantage related to nationality, religion, or sexual orientation.

Difficulties and dangers surrounding the task of finding parallels are many. Since racism, sexism, and heterosexism are not the same, the advantages associated with them should not be seen as the same. In addition, it is hard to disentangle aspects of unearned advantage which rest more on social class, economic class, race, religion, sex, and ethnic identity than on other factors. Still, all of the oppressions are interlocking, as the Combahee River Collective Statement of 1977 continues to remind us eloquently.

One factor seems clear about all of the interlocking oppressions. They take both active forms, which we can see, and embedded forms, which as a member of the dominant group one is taught not to see. In my class and place, I did not see myself as a racist because I was taught to recognize racism only in individual acts of meanness by members of my group, never in invisible systems conferring unsought racial dominance on my group from birth.

Disapproving of the systems won't be enough to change them. I was taught to think that racism could end if white individuals changed their attitudes. But a "white" skin in the United States opens many doors for whites whether or not we approve of the way dominance has been conferred on us. Individual acts can palliate, but cannot end, these problems.

To redesign social systems, we need first to acknowledge their colossal unseen dimensions. The silences and denials surrounding privilege are the key political tool here. They keep the thinking about equality or equity incomplete, protecting unearned advantage and conferred dominance by making these taboo subjects. Most talk by whites about equal opportunity seems to me now to be about equal opportunity to try to get into a position of dominance while denying that *systems* of dominance exist.

It seems to me that obliviousness about white advantage, like obliviousness about male advantage, is kept strongly inculturated in the United States so as to maintain the myth of meritocracy, the myth that democratic choice is equally available to all. Keeping most people unaware that freedom of confident action is there for just a small number of people props up those in power and serves to keep power in the hands of the same groups that have most of it already.

Although systemic change takes many decades, there are pressing questions for me and I imagine for some others like me if we raise our daily consciousness on the perquisites of being light-skinned. What will we do with such knowledge? As we know from watching men, it is an open question whether we will choose to use unearned advantage to weaken hidden systems of advantage, and whether we will use any of our arbitrarily awarded power to try to reconstruct power systems on a broader base.[1]

Note

1. This is an authorized excerpt of McIntosh's original white privilege article, "White Privilege and Male Privilege: A Personal Account of Coming to See Correspondences through Work in Women's Studies," Working Paper 189 (1988), Wellesley Centers for Women, Wellesley College, MA.

5.
THE WHITES OF THEIR EYES
Racist Ideologies and the Media
Stuart Hall

In this essay I want to address two, related, issues. The first concerns the way the media—sometimes deliberately, sometimes unconsciously—define and construct the question of race in such a way as to reproduce the ideologies of racism. The second is concerned with the very difficult problems of strategy and tactics which arise when the left attempts to intervene in the media construction of race, so as to undermine, deconstruct and question the unquestioned racist assumptions on which so much of media practice is grounded.

We need to think about both these questions together: the often complex and subtle ways in which the ideologies of racism are sustained in our culture; and the equally difficult question as to how to challenge them in the practice of ideological struggle. Both form the basis of a wider anti-racist strategy which—I argue here—neglects the ideological dimensions at our peril.

For very complex reasons, a sort of racist 'common sense' has become pervasive in our society. And the media frequently work from this common sense, taking it as their base-line without questioning it. We need, urgently, to consider ways in which, *in addition* to the urgent and necessary political task of blocking the path to power of the openly organized racist and right-extremist organizations, we can also begin to construct an anti-racist common sense. This task of making anti-racist ideas popular is and must be part of a wider democratic struggle which engages, not so much the hard-line extremists of the right, or

even the small numbers of the committed and converted, but the great body of common sense, in the population as a whole, and amongst working people especially, on which the struggle to build up an anti-racist popular bloc will ultimately depend.

Questions of strategy and tactics are not easy, especially when what is at issue is the winning of popular positions in the struggle against racism. There are few short cuts or ready-made recipes. It does not follow that, because our hearts are in the right place, we will win the struggle for 'hearts and minds.' And even the best analysis of the current situation provides few absolute guide-lines as to what we should do in a particular situation. Neither passionate left-wing convictions nor the immutable laws of history can ever replace the difficult questions of political calculation on which the outcome of particular struggles ultimately turns. This essay is written in the firm conviction that we need to be better prepared, both in our analysis of how racist ideologies become 'popular', and in what are the appropriate strategies for combatting them. Both, in their turn, depend on a more open, less closed and 'finalist' debate of positions among people on the left committed to the anti-racist struggle. In discussing the second aspect, I will draw on some recent experiences of attempts to intervene politically in the area of racism and the mass media.

In 1979, the Campaign Against Racism In The Media (CARM) won the opportunity to make a programme putting its case in the BBC's 'access television' slot, *Open Door*. The programme, *It Ain't Half Racist, Mum*, was transmitted twice, in February and March of that year, in the usual corners of the schedule reserved for clearly labelled 'minority programmes'. The programme produced a significant response. It was widely reviewed; CARM received over 600 letters, the great majority of them favourable; the programme also triggered off an internal storm within the BBC and an appeal by one distinguished programme presenter, Robin Day, to the BBC Appeals Tribunal on the grounds that his performance in a debate on Immigration (which he chaired) had been misrepresented in the programme. Since then, the programme has been widely used by a variety of anti-racist groups and in schools and colleges, as a way of triggering off a discussion of racism and the media, though the BBC has kept an extremely tight grip on the programme's distribution and has been something less than helpful in promoting it.

The CARM group, composed largely of anti-racist media workers, worked for some time preparing and discussing the approach to the programme, viewing extracts and bargaining with the reluctant broadcasters to allow the extracts we wanted to criticize being used in the programme (many, including ITN and BBC News, refused). I was invited, at a fairly late stage in the process, to help prepare a script and to present the programme jointly with Maggie Steed. *It Ain't Half Racist, Mum* has been well received on the whole, by the left and anti-racist groups. It has also been severely criticized, on several occasions, by Carl Gardner and Margaret Henry, original members of the CARM team, who thought the programme seriously misdirected and leaky with missed opportunities.[1] This experience provides us with a useful opportunity to reconsider both the general issue of racism and the media, and the even more serious and knotty problem of strategies of left interventions in mainstream television programming.

In 1980 I was invited by Alan Horrox and his small team in the Thames Television Schools department to help prepare and script a series of four programmes on the media and social problems, to be transmitted for schools as the second 'Viewpoint' series in Thames's *English Programme*. The first 'Viewpoint' series had also been concerned with

representations of social issues on television, and contained the excellent and much-shown double programme on sexual stereotypes, *Superman And The Bride*. It had also proved highly controversial and ran into trouble with the Independent Broadcasting Authority (IBA) who would not agree to repeat the series, despite its highly favourable reception, until a number of changes had been made. The IBA especially required changes to those parts which made the links between programming policy and television company ownership; and to the style of presentation which, in its view, did not sufficiently clearly acknowledge that this was only *one* of many possible 'viewpoints' on the subjects treated. (The vast majority of unsigned and unauthored programmes transmitted nightly are, presumably, viewed only through the universal all-seeing, neutral, balanced and impartial 'eye' of God.)

The making of the second 'Viewpoint' series was, therefore, something of a tricky exercise. One of the programmes we made also covered the handling and presentation of race in the media, though from a different point of view from that adopted in the CARM programme. This programme, *The Whites Of Their Eyes*, has also been transmitted twice in the usual ITV School programme schedule, moving up to attract 30% of the school viewing audience. This was for a different audience from that which we aimed for in the CARM programme. It was intended for an audience, in a controlled viewing situation, in schools, viewed with a teacher, and allowing for considerable follow-up work in the classroom (a special 'project' booklet for the series was produced for classroom use by Andrew Bethel).

The CARM programme, on the other hand, aimed at the general viewing public, or that part of it still able to keep its eyes open late at night or on a sleepy Sunday. Together, these programmes form the background to this article.

Before discussing these programmes in more detail, however, we might usefully begin by defining some of the terms of the argument. 'Racism and the media' touches directly the problem of *ideology*, since the media's main sphere of operations is the production and transformation of ideologies. An intervention in the media's construction of race is an intervention in the *ideological* terrain of struggle. Much murky water has flowed under the bridge provided by this concept of ideology in recent years; and this is not the place to develop the theoretical argument. I am using the term to refer to those images, concepts and premises which provide the frameworks through which we represent, interpret, understand and 'make sense' of some aspect of social existence. Language and ideology are not the same—since the same linguistic term ('democracy' for example, or 'freedom') can be deployed within different ideological discourses. But language, broadly conceived, is by definition the principal medium in which we find different ideological discourses elaborated.

Three important things need to be said about ideology in order to make what follows intelligible. First, ideologies do not consist of isolated and separate concepts, but in the articulation of different elements into a distinctive set or chain of meanings. In liberal ideology, 'freedom' is connected (articulated) with individualism and the free market; in socialist ideology, 'freedom' is a collective condition, dependent on, not counterposed to, 'equality of condition', as it is in liberal ideology. The same concept is differently positioned within the logic of different ideological discourses. One of the ways in which ideological struggle takes place and ideologies are transformed is by articulating the elements differently, thereby producing a different meaning: breaking the chain in which they are currently fixed (e.g. 'democratic' = the 'Free' West) and establishing a new articulation (e.g. 'democratic' = deepening the democratic content of political life). This 'breaking of the chain' is not, of course, confined to the head: it takes place through social practice and political struggle.

Second, ideological statements are made by individuals: but ideologies are not the product of individual consciousness or intention. Rather we formulate our intentions *within ideology*. They pre-date individuals, and form part of the determinate social formations and conditions into which individuals are born. We have to 'speak through' the ideologies which are active in our society and which provide us with the means of 'making sense' of social relations and our place in them. The transformation of ideologies is thus a collective process and practice, not an individual one. Largely, the processes work *unconsciously*, rather than by conscious intention. Ideologies produce different forms of social consciousness, rather than being produced by them. They work most effectively when we are not aware that how we formulate and construct a statement about the world is underpinned by ideological premises; when our formations seem to be simply descriptive statements about how things are (i.e. must be), or of what we can 'take-for-granted'. 'Little boys like playing rough games; little girls, however, are full of sugar and spice' is predicated on a whole set of ideological premises, though it seems to be an aphorism which is grounded, not in how masculinity and femininity have been historically and culturally constructed in society, but in Nature itself. Ideologies tend to disappear from view into the taken-for-granted 'naturalized' world of common sense. Since (like gender) race appears to be 'given' by Nature, racism is one of the most profoundly 'naturalized' of existing ideologies.

Third, ideologies 'work' by constructing for their subjects (individual and collective) positions of identification and knowledge which allow them to 'utter' ideological truths as if they were their authentic authors. This is not because they emanate from our innermost, authentic and unified experience, but because we find ourselves mirrored in the positions at the centre of the discourses from which the statements we formulate 'make sense'. Thus the same 'subjects' (e.g. economic classes or ethnic groups) can be differently constructed in different ideologies. When Mrs Thatcher says, 'We can't afford to pay ourselves higher wages without earning them through higher productivity', she is attempting to construct at the centre of her discourse an identification for workers who will cease to see themselves as opposed or *antagonistic to* the needs of capital, and begin to see themselves in terms of the *identity of interests* between themselves and capital. Again, this is not only in the head. Redundancies are a powerful material way of influencing 'hearts and minds'.

Ideologies therefore work by the transformation of discourses (the disarticulation and re-articulation of ideological elements) and the transformation (the fracturing and recomposition) of subjects-for-action. How we 'see' ourselves and our social relations *matters*, because it enters into and informs our actions and practices. Ideologies are therefore a site of a distinct type of social struggle. This site does not exist on its own, separate from other relations, since ideas are not free-floating in people's heads. The ideological construction of black people as a 'problem population' and the police practice of containment in the black communities mutually reinforce and support one another. Nevertheless, ideology is a practice. It has its own specific way of working. And it is generated, produced and reproduced in specific settings (sites)—especially, in the apparatuses of ideological production which 'produce' social meanings and distribute them throughout society, like the media. It is therefore the site of a particular kind of struggle, which cannot be simply reduced to or incorporated into some other level of struggle—for example, the economic class struggle, which is sometimes held to govern or determine it. It is the struggle over what Lenin once called 'ideological social relations', which have their own tempo and specificity. It is located in specific practices. Ideological struggle, like any other form of struggle, therefore represents an intervention in an existing field of practices and institutions; those which sustain the dominant discourses of meaning of society.

The classic definition of ideology tends to regard it as a dependent sphere, which simply reflects 'in ideas' what is happening elsewhere, for example, in the mode of production, without any determinacy or effectivity of its own. This is a reductive and economistic conception. Of course, the formation and distribution of ideologies have determinate conditions, some of which are established outside of ideology itself. Messers Murdoch and Trafalgar House command (through *The Times, Sunday Times* and the *Express* group) the resources of institutionalized ideological power in ways which no section of the left could currently aspire to. Nevertheless, ideologies are not fixed forever in the place assigned to them by 'the economic': their elements, as Laclau has argued,[2] have 'no necessary class belongingness'. For instance, 'democracy' belongs *both* to ruling-class ideology, where it means the Western system of parliamentary regimes, *and* to the ideologies of the left, where it means or refers to 'popular power', against the ruling

power bloc. Of course, though the heads of small shopkeepers are not necessarily filled exclusively with 'petty-bourgeois thoughts,' certain ideological discourses *do* have or have acquired, historically, well-defined connections with certain class places. (It is easier for a small shopkeeper, than for an assembly line-worker in British Leyland, to think of his or her interests as equivalent to those of an independent self-employed small capitalist.) These 'traces,' as Gramsci called them, and historical connexions—the terrain of past articulations—are peculiarly resistant to change and transformation: just as it is exceedingly hard, given the history of imperialism, to disinter the idea of 'the British people' from its nationalistic connotation.

New forms of ideological struggle can bring old 'traces' to life, thus Thatcherism has revivified liberal political economy. Even in such well-secured cases, transformations *are* possible ('the people' coming to represent, not the 'nation, unified under the ruling class', but the *common* people *versus* the ruling class—an antagonistic relation rather than an equivalent and unifying one). The corollary of this is that there is no fixed, given and necessary form of ideological consciousness, dictated exclusively by class position. A third of the British working class has regularly seen itself, in terms of how it votes, as 'rightfully subordinate to those who are naturally born to rule over others'. The famous working-class deference Tory vote shows they do not necessarily see themselves as their class position would lead us to suppose: e.g. as the 'majority exploited class which ought to supplant the class which rules over us'.

At the last (1979) election, Mrs Thatcher clearly had some success in getting skilled and organized workers to *equate* (articulate together) their own opposition to incomes policies, wage control and the demand for a 'return to collective bargaining', with her own, very different, conception of 'letting market forces decide wage levels'. Just as the working class is not impervious to reactionary or social-democratic ideas, so it is not *a priori* impervious to racist ideas. The whole history of Labour socialism and reformism is a refutation of the idealistic hope (rooted in economism) that the economic position of the working class will make it inevitable that it thinks only progressive, antiracist or revolutionary ideas. Instead, what we have seen over the past two decades is the undoubted penetration of racist ideas and practices, not only into sections of the working class, but into the very organizations and institutions of the labour movement itself.

Let us look, then, a little more closely at the apparatuses which generate and circulate ideologies. In modern societies, the different media are especially important sites for the production, reproduction and transformation of ideologies. Ideologies are, of course, worked on in many places in society, and not only in the head. The fact of unemployment, as the Thatcher government knows only too well, is, among other things, an extremely effective ideological instrument for converting or constraining workers to moderate their wage claims. But institutions like the media are peculiarly central to the matter since they are, by definition, part of the dominant means of *ideological* production. What they 'produce' is, precisely, representations of the social world, images, descriptions, explanations and frames for understanding how the world is and why it works as it is said and shown to work. And, amongst other kinds of ideological labour, the media construct for us a definition of what *race* is, what meaning the imagery of race carries, and what the 'problem of race' is understood to be. They help to classify out the world in terms of the categories of race.

The media are not only a powerful source of ideas about race. They are also one place where these ideas are articulated, worked on, transformed and elaborated. We have said 'ideas' and 'ideologies' in the plural. For it would be wrong and misleading to see the media as uniformly and conspiratorially harnessed to a single, racist conception of the world. Liberal and humane ideas about 'good relations' between the races, based on open-mindedness and tolerance, operate inside the world of the media—among, for example, many television journalists and newspapers like the *Guardian*—alongside the more explicit racism of other journalists and newspapers like the *Express* or the *Mail*. In some respects, the line which separates the latter from the extreme right on policies such as, for example, guided repatriation for blacks, is very thin indeed.

It would be simple and convenient if all the media were simply the ventriloquists of a unified and racist 'ruling class' conception of the world. But neither a unifiedly conspiratorial media nor indeed a unified racist 'ruling class' exist in anything like that simple way. I don't insist on complexity for its own sake. But if critics of the media subscribe to too simple or reductive a view of their operations, this inevitably lacks credibility and weakens the case they are making because the theories and critiques don't square with reality. They only begin to account for the real operation of racism in society by a process of gross abstraction and simplification.

More important, the task of a critical theory is to produce as accurate a knowledge of complex social processes as the complexity of their functioning requires. It is not its task to console the left by producing simple but satisfying myths, distinguished only by their super-left wing credentials. (If the laws and tendencies of the capitalist mode of production can be stated in a simplified form because they are essentially simple and reducible, why on earth did Marx go on about them for so long—three uncompleted volumes, no less?) Most important of all, these differences and complexities have real *effects*, which ought to enter into any serious political calculation about how their tendencies might be resisted or turned. We know, for example, that the broadcasting institutions are not 'independent and autonomous' of the state in the way suggested in the official wisdom. But if we neglect to ask why the question of 'independence' and the media's 'relative autonomy' are so important to their functioning, and simply reduce them to what we think of as their essential nature—pure instruments of ruling-class or racist ideology—we will not be able to deconstruct the credibility and legitimacy which they, in fact, carry (which depends, precisely, on the fact that 'autonomy' is not a pure piece of deception). Moreover, we will have an over-incorporated conception of the world, where the state is conceived, not as a necessarily contradictory formation, but as a simple, transparent instrumentality. This view might flatter the super-radical conscience, but it has no place in it for the concept of class struggle, and defines no practical terrain on which such struggles could be conducted. (Why it has passed so long for 'Marxism' is a mystery.) So we must attend to the complexities of the ways in which race and racism are constructed in the media in order to be able to bring about change.

Another important distinction is between what we might call 'overt' racism and 'inferential' racism. By *overt* racism, I mean those many occasions when open and favourable coverage is given to arguments, positions and spokespersons who are in the business of elaborating an openly racist argument or advancing a racist policy or view. Many such occasions exist; they have become more frequent in recent years—more often in the press, which has become openly partisan to extremist right-wing arguments, than in television, where the regulations of 'balance', 'impartiality and neutrality' operate.

By *inferential* racism I mean those apparently naturalized representations of events and situations relating to race, whether 'factual' or 'fictional', which have racist premises and propositions inscribed in them as a set of *unquestioned assumptions*. These enable racist statements to be formulated without ever bringing into awareness the racist predicates on which the statements are grounded.

Both types of racism are to be found, in different combinations, in the British media. Open or overt racism is, of course, politically dangerous as well as socially offensive. The open partisanship of sections of the popular press on this front is an extremely serious development. It is not only that they circulate and popularise openly racist policies and ideas, and translate them into the vivid populist vernacular (e.g. in the tabloids, with their large working-class readership); it is the very fact that such things can now be openly said and advocated which *legitimates* their public expression and increases the threshold of the public acceptability of racism. Racism becomes 'acceptable'—and thus, not too long after, 'true'—just common sense: what everyone knows and is openly saying. But *inferential racism* is more widespread—and in many ways, more insidious, because it is largely *invisible* even to those who formulate the world in its terms.

An example of *this* type of racist ideology is the sort of television programme which deals with some 'problem' in race relations. It is probably made by a good and honest liberal broadcaster, who hopes to do some good in the world for 'race relations' and

who maintains a scrupulous balance and neutrality when questioning people interviewed for the programme. The programme will end with a homily on how, if only the 'extremists' on *either side* would go away, 'normal blacks and whites' would be better able to get on with learning to live in harmony together. Yet every word and image of such programmes are impregnated with unconscious racism because they are all predicated on the unstated and unrecognized assumption that the *blacks* are the *source of the problem*. Yet virtually the whole of 'social problem' television about race and immigration—often made, no doubt, by well-intentioned and liberal-minded broadcasters—is precisely predicated on racist premises of this kind. This was the criticism we made in the CARM programme, *It Ain't Half Racist, Mum*, and it was the one which most cut the broadcasters to their professional quick. It undermined their professional credentials by suggesting that they had been partisan where they are supposed to be balanced and impartial. It was an affront to the liberal consensus and self-image which prevails within broadcasting. Both responses were, in fact, founded on the profound misunderstanding that racism is, by definition, mutually exclusive of the liberal consensus—whereas, in inferential racism, the two can quite easily cohabit—and on the assumption that if the television discourse could be shown to be racist, it must be because the individual broadcasters were intentionally and deliberately racist. In fact, an ideological discourse does *not* depend on the conscious intentions of those who formulate statements within it.

How, then, is race and its 'problems' constructed on British television? This is a complex topic in its own right, and I can only illustrate its dimensions briefly here by referring to some of the themes developed in the two programmes I was involved in. One of the things we tried to show in *The Whites Of Their Eyes* was the rich vocabulary and syntax of race on which the media have to draw. Racism has a long and distinguished history in British culture. It is grounded in the relations of slavery, colonial conquest, economic exploitation and imperialism in which the European races have stood in relation to the 'native peoples' of the colonized and exploited periphery.

Three characteristics provided the discursive and power-coordinates of the discourses in which these relations were historically constructed. (1) Their imagery and themes were polarized around fixed relations of subordination and domination. (2) Their stereotypes were grouped around the poles of 'superior' and 'inferior' natural species. (3) Both were displaced from the 'language' of history into the language of Nature. Natural physical signs and racial characteristics became the unalterable signifiers of inferiority. Subordinate ethnic groups and classes appeared, not as the objects of particular historical relations (the slave trade, European colonization, the active underdevelopment of the 'underdeveloped' societies), but as the given qualities of an inferior *breed*. Relations, secured by economic, social, political and military domination were transformed and 'naturalized' into an order of *rank*, ascribed by Nature. Thus, Edward Long, an acute English observer of Jamaica in the period of slavery wrote (in his *History of Jamaica*, 1774)—much in the way the Elizabethans might have spoken of 'the Great Chain Of Being'—of 'Three ranks of men [sic], (white, mulatto and black), dependent on each other, and rising in a proper climax of subordination, in which the whites hold the highest place.'

One thing we wanted to illustrate in the programme was the 'forgotten' degree to which, in the period of slavery and imperialism, popular literature is saturated with these fixed, negative attributes of the colonized races. We find them in the diaries, observations and accounts, the notebooks, ethnographic records and commentaries of visitors, explorers, missionaries and administrators in Africa, India, the Far East and the Americas. And also something else: the 'absent' but imperializing 'white eye'; the unmarked position from which all these 'observations' are made and from which, alone, they make sense. This is the history of slavery and conquest, written, seen, drawn and photographed by The Winners. They cannot be *read* and made sense of from any other position. The 'white eye' is always outside the frame—but seeing and positioning everything within it.

Some of the most telling sequences we used were from early film of the British Raj in India—the source of endless radio 'reminiscences' and television

historical show-pieces today. The assumption of effortless superiority structures every image—even the portioning in the frame: the foregrounding of colonial life (tea-time on the plantation), the background of native bearers. . . . In the later stages of High Imperialism, this discourse proliferates through the new media of popular culture and information—newspapers and journals, cartoons, drawings and advertisements, and the popular novel. Recent critics of the literature of imperialism have argued that, if we simply extend our definition of nineteenth century fiction from one branch of 'serious fiction' to embrace popular literature, we will find a second, powerful strand of the English literary imagination to set beside the *domestic* novel: the male-dominated world of imperial adventure, which takes *empire*, rather than *Middlemarch*, as its microcosm. I remember a graduate student, working on the construction of race in popular literature and culture at the end of the Nineteenth Century, coming to me in despair—racism was so *ubiquitous*, and at the same time, so *unconscious*—simply assumed to be the case—that it was impossible to get any critical purchase on it. In this period, the very idea of *adventure* became synonymous with the demonstration of the moral, social and physical mastery of the colonizers over the colonized.

Later, this concept of 'adventure'—one of the principal categories of modern *entertainment*—moved straight off the printed page into the literature of crime and espionage, children's books, the great Hollywood extravaganzas and comics. There, with recurring persistence, they still remain. Many of these older versions have had their edge somewhat blunted by time. They have been distanced from us, apparently, by our superior wisdom and liberalism. But they still reappear on the television screen, especially in the form of 'old movies' (some 'old movies', of course, continue to be made). But we can grasp their recurring resonance better if we identify some of the base-images of the 'grammar of race'.

There is, for example, the familiar *slave-figure*: dependable, loving in a simple, childlike way—the devoted 'Mammy' with the rolling eyes, or the faithful field-hand or retainer, attached and devoted to 'his' Master. The best-known extravaganza of all—*Gone With The Wind*—contains rich variants of both. The 'slave-figure' is by no means limited to films and programmes *about* slavery. Some 'Injuns' and many Asians have come on to the screen in this disguise. A deep and unconscious ambivalence pervades this stereotype. Devoted and childlike, the 'slave' is also unreliable, unpredictable and undependable—capable of 'turning nasty', or of plotting in a treacherous way, secretive, cunning, cut-throat once his or her Master's or Mistress's back is turned: and inexplicably given to running way into the bush at the slightest opportunity. The whites can never be sure that this childish simpleton—'Sambo'—is not mocking his master's white manners behind his hand, even when giving an exaggerated caricature of white refinement.

Another base-image is that of the 'native'. The good side of this figure is portrayed in a certain primitive nobility and simple dignity. The bad side is portrayed in terms of cheating and cunning, and, further out, savagery and barbarism. Popular culture is still full today of countless savage and restless 'natives', and sound-tracks constantly repeat the threatening sound of drumming in the night, the hint of primitive rites and cults. Cannibals, whirling dervishes, Indian tribesmen, garishly got up, are constantly threatening to over-run the screen. They are likely to appear at any moment out of the darkness to decapitate the beautiful heroine, kidnap the children, burn the encampment or threatening to boil, cook and eat the innocent explorer or colonial administrator and his lady-wife. These 'natives' always move as an anonymous collective mass—in tribes or hordes. And against them is always counterposed the isolated white figure, alone 'out there', confronting his Destiny or shouldering his Burden in the 'heart of darkness', displaying coolness under fire and an unshakeable authority—exerting mastery over the rebellious natives or quelling the threatened uprising with a single glance of his steel-blue eyes.

A third variant is that of the 'clown' or 'entertainer'. This captures the 'innate' humour, as well as the physical grace of the licensed entertainer—putting on a show for The Others. It is never quite clear whether we are laughing with or at this figure: admiring the physical and rhythmic grace, the open expressivity and emotionality of the 'entertainer', or put off by the 'clown's' stupidity.

One noticeable fact about all these images is their deep *ambivalence*—the double vision of the white eye through which they are seen. The primitive nobility of the ageing tribesman or chief, and the native's rhythmic grace always contain both a nostalgia for an innocence lost forever to the civilized, and the threat of civilization being over-run or undermined by the recurrence of savagery, which is always lurking just below the surface; or by an untutored sexuality, threatening to 'break out'. Both are aspects—the good and the bad sides—of *primitivism*. In these images, 'primitivism' is defined by the fixed proximity of such people to Nature.

Is all this so far away as we sometimes suppose from the representation of race which fill the screens today? These *particular* versions may have faded. But their *traces* are still to be observed, reworked in many of the modern and up-dated images. And though they may appear to carry a different meaning, they are often still constructed on a very ancient grammar. Today's restless native hordes are still alive and well and living as guerrilla armies and freedom fighters in the Angola, Zimbabwe or Namibian 'bush'. Blacks are still the most frightening, cunning and glamorous crooks (and policemen) in New York cop series. They are the fleet-footed, crazy-talking under-men who connect Starsky and Hutch to the drug-saturated ghetto. The scheming villains and their giant-sized bully boys in the world of James Bond and his progeny are still, unusually, recruited from 'out there' in Jamaica, where savagery lingers on. The sexually-available 'slave-girl' is alive and kicking, smouldering away on some exotic TV set or on the covers of paperbacks, though she is now the centre of a special admiration, covered in a sequinned gown and supported by a white chorus line. Primitivism, savagery, guile and unreliability—all 'just below the surface'—can still be identified in the faces of black political leaders around the world, cunningly plotting the overthrow of 'civilization': Mr Mugabe, for example, up to the point where he happened to win both a war and an election and became, temporarily at any rate, the best (because the most politically credible) friend Britain had left in that last outpost of the Edwardian dream.

The 'Old Country'—white version—is still often the subject of nostalgic documentaries: 'Old Rhodesia', whose reliable servants, as was only to be expected, plotted treason in the outhouse and silently stole away to join ZAPU in the bush . . . Tribal Man in green khaki. Black stand-up comics still ape their ambiguous incorporation into British entertainment by being the first to tell a racist joke. No Royal Tour is complete without its troupe of swaying bodies, or its mounted tribesmen, paying homage. Blacks are such 'good movers', so *rhythmic*, so *natural*. And the dependent peoples, who couldn't manage for a day without the protection and know-how of their white masters, reappear as the starving victims of the Third World, passive and waiting for the technology or the Aid to arrive, objects of our pity or of a *Blue Peter* appeal. They are not represented as the subjects of a continuing exploitation or dependency, or the global division of wealth and labour. They are the Victims of Fate.

These modern, glossed and up-dated images seem to have put the old world of Sambo behind them. Many of them, indeed, are the focus of a secret, illicit, pleasurable-but-taboo admiration. Many have a more active and energetic quality—some black athletes, for example, and of course the entertainers. But the connotations and echoes which they carry reverberate back a very long way. They continue to shape the ways whites see blacks today— even when the white adventurer sailing up the jungle stream is not *Sanders Of The River*, but historical drama-reconstructions of Stanley and Livingstone; and the intention is to show, not the savagery, but the serenity of African village life—ways of an ancient people 'unchanged even down to modern times' (in other words, still preserved in economic backwardness and frozen in history for our anthropological eye by forces unknown to them and, apparently, unshowable on the screen).

'Adventure' is one way in which we *encounter* race without having to *confront* the racism of the perspectives in use. Another, even more complex one is 'entertainment.' In television, there is a strong counter-position between 'serious,' informational television, which we watch because it is good for us, and 'entertainment,' which we watch because it is pleasurable. And the purest form of pleasure in entertainment television is *comedy*. By definition, comedy is a licensed zone, disconnected from the serious. It's all 'good, clean fun.' In the area of fun and pleasure it is forbidden to pose a serious question, partly because it seems so puritanical and destroys the pleasure by switching registers. Yet race is one of the most significant themes in situation comedies—from the early Alf Garnett to *Mind Your Language, On The Buses, Love Thy Neighbour* and *It Ain't Half Hot, Mum*. These are defended on good 'anti-racist' grounds: the appearance of blacks, alongside whites, in situation comedies, it is argued, will help to naturalize and normalize their presence in British society. And no doubt, in some examples, it does function in this way. But, if you examine these fun occasions more closely, you will often find, as we did in our two programmes, that the comedies do not simply include blacks: they are *about race*. That is, the same old categories of racially-defined characteristics and qualities, and the same relations of superior and inferior, provide the pivots on which the jokes actually turn, the tension-points which move and motivate the situations in situation comedies. The comic register in which they are set, however, protects and defends viewers from acknowledging their incipient racism. It creates disavowal.

This is even more so with the television stand-up comics, whose repertoire in recent years has come to be dominated, in about equal parts, by sexist and racist jokes. It's sometimes said, again in their defence, that this must be a sign of black acceptability. But it *may* just be that racism has become more normal: it's hard to tell. It's also said that the best tellers of anti-Jewish jokes are Jews themselves, just as blacks tell the best 'white' jokes against themselves. But this is to argue as if jokes exist in a vacuum separate from the contexts and situations of their telling. Jewish jokes told by Jews among themselves are part of the self-awareness of the community. They are unlikely to function by 'putting down' the race, because both teller and audience belong on equal terms to the same group. Telling racist jokes across the racial line, in conditions where relations of racial inferiority and superiority prevail, reinforces *the difference* and reproduces the unequal relations because, in those situations, the point of the joke depends on the existence of racism. Thus they reproduce the categories and relations of racism, even while normalizing them through laughter. The stated good intentions of the joke-makers do not resolve the problem here, because they are not in control of the circumstances—conditions of continuing racism—in which their joke discourse will be read and heard. The time *may* come when blacks and whites can tell jokes about each other in ways which do not reproduce the racial categories of the world in which they are told. The time, in Britain, is certainly *not yet arrived*.

Two others arenas which we tried to illustrate in both programmes related to the 'harder' end of television production—news and current affairs. This is where race is constructed as *problem* and the site of *conflict* and debate. There have been good examples of programmes where blacks have not exclusively appeared as the source of the 'problem' (ATV's *Breaking Point* is one example) and where they have not been exclusively saddled with being the aggressive agent in conflict (the London Weekend Television *London Programme* and the Southall Defence Committee's *Open Door* programme on the Southall events are examples). But the general tendency of the run of programmes in this area is to see blacks—especially the mere fact of their existence (their 'numbers')—as constituting a problem for English white society. They appear as law-breakers, prone to crime; as 'trouble'; as the collective agent of civil disorder.

In the numerous incidents where black communities have reacted to racist provocation (as at Southall) or to police harassment and provocation (as in Bristol), the media have tended to assume that 'right' lay on the side of the law, and have fallen into the language of 'riot' and 'race warfare' which simply feeds existing stereotypes and prejudices. The precipitating conditions of conflict are usually *absent*—the scandalous provocation of a National Front march through one of the biggest black areas, Southall, and the saturation police raiding of the last refuge for black youth which triggered off Bristol—to take only two recent examples. They are either missing, or introduced so late in the process of signification, that they fail to dislodge the dominant definition of these events. So they testify, once again, to the disruptive nature of black and Asian people *as such*.

The analysis of the media coverage of Southall contained in the NCCL Unofficial Committee of Inquiry *Report*,[3] for example, shows how rapidly, in both the television and press, the official definitions of the police—Sir David McNee's statement on the evening of 23 April, and the ubiquitous James Jardine, speaking for the Police Federation on the succeeding day—provided the media with the authoritative definition of the event. These, in turn, shaped and focused what the media reported and how it explained what transpired. In taking their cue from these authoritative sources, the media reproduced an account of the event which, with certain significant exceptions, translated the conflict between racism and anti-racism into (a) a contest between Asians and the police, and (b) a contest between two kinds of extremism—the so-called '*fascism*' of left and right alike.

This had the effect of downgrading the two problems at the centre of the Southall affair—the growth of and growing legitimacy of the extreme right and its blatantly provocative anti-black politics of the street; and the racism and brutality of the police. Both issues had to be *forced* on to the agenda of the media by a militant and organized protest. Most press reports of Southall were so obsessed by embroidering the lurid details of 'roaming hoardes of coloured youths' chasing young whites 'with a carving knife'—a touch straight out of *Sanders Of The River*, though so far uncorroborated—that they failed even to mention the death of Blair Peach. This is selective or tunnel-vision with a vengeance.

A good example of how the real causes of racial conflict can be absorbed and transformed by the framework which the media employ can be found in the *Nationwide* coverage of Southall on the day following the events. Two interlocking frameworks of explanation governed this programme. In the first, conflict is seen in the conspiratorial terms of far-left against extreme-right—the Anti-Nazi League against the National Front. This is the classic logic of television, where the medium identifies itself with the moderate, consensual, middle-road, Average viewer, and sets off, in contrast, extremism on both sides, which it then equates with each other. In this particular exercise in 'balance', fascism and anti-fascism are represented as *the same*—both equally *bad,* because the Middle Way enshrines the Common Good under all circumstances. This balancing exercise provided an opportunity for Martin Webster of the National Front to gain access to the screen, to help set the terms of the debate, and to spread his smears across the screen under the freedom of the airwaves: 'Well,' he said, 'let's talk about Trotskyists, extreme Communists of various sorts, raving Marxists and other assorted left wing cranks.' Good knockabout stuff. Then, after a linking passage—'Southall, the day after'—to the second framework: rioting Asians *vs* the police. 'I watched television as well last night,' Mr Jardine argued, 'and I certainly didn't see any police throwing bricks . . . So don't start making those arguments.' The growth of organized political racism and the circumstances which have precipitated it were simply not visible to *Nationwide* as an alternative way of setting up the problem.

In the CARM programme *It Ain't Half Racist, Mum,* we tried to illustrate the inferential logic at work in another area of programming: the BBC's 'Great Debate' on Immigration. It was not necessary here to start with any preconceived notions, least of all speculation as to the personal views on race by the broadcasters involved—though one can't expect either the BBC hierarchy or Robin Day to believe that. You have simply to look at the programme with one set of questions in mind: Here is a problem, defined as 'the problem of immigration'. What is it? How is it defined and constructed through the programme? What logic governs its definition? And where does that logic derive from? I believe the answers are clear. The problem of immigration is that 'there are too many blacks over here', to put it crudely. It is *defined* in terms of *numbers of blacks* and what to do about them. The *logic* of the argument is 'immigrants = blacks = too many of them = send them home'. That is a racist logic. And it comes from a chain of reasoning whose representative, in respectable public debate and in person, on this occasion, was Enoch Powell. Powellism set the agenda for the media. Every time (and on many more occasions than the five or six we show in the programme) the presenter wanted to define the base-line of the programme which others should address, Mr Powell's views were indicated

as representing it. And every time anyone strayed from the 'logic' to question the underlying premiss, it was back to 'as Mr Powell would say . . . ' that they were drawn.

It certainly does not follow (and I know of no evidence to suggest) that Robin Day subscribes to this line or agrees with Mr Powell on anything to do with race. I know absolutely nothing about his views on race and immigration. And we made no judgement on his views, which are irrelevant to the argument. If the media function in a systematically racist manner, it is not because they are run and organized exclusively by active racists; this is a category mistake. This would be equivalent to saying that you could change the character of the capitalist state by replacing its personnel. Whereas the media, like the state, have a *structure*, a set of *practices* which are *not* reducible to the individuals who staff them. What defines how the media function is the result of a set of complex, often contradictory, social relations; not the personal inclinations of its members. What is significant is not that they produce a racist ideology, from some single-minded and unified conception of the world, but that they are so powerfully constrained—'spoken by'—a particular set of ideological discourses. The power of this discourse is its capacity to constrain a very great variety of individuals: racist, anti-racist, liberals, radicals, conservatives, anarchists, know-nothings and silent majoritarians.

What we said, however, about the *discourse* of problem television was true, despite the hurt feelings of particular individuals, and demonstrably so. The premiss on which the Great Immigration Debate was built and the chain of reasoning it predicated was a racist one. The evidence for this is in what was said and how it was formulated—how the argument unfolded. If you establish the topic as 'the numbers of blacks are too high' or '*they* are breeding too fast', the opposition is obliged or constrained to argue that 'the numbers are not as high as they are represented to be'. This view is opposed to the first two: but it is also imprisoned by the same logic—the logic of the 'numbers game'. Liberals, anti-racists, indeed raging revolutionaries can contribute 'freely' to this debate, and indeed are often obliged to do so, so as not to let the case go by default: without breaking for a moment the chain of assumptions which holds the racist proposition in place. However, changing the terms of the argument, questioning the assumptions and starting points, breaking the logic—this is a quite different, longer, more difficult task.

One element of the struggle, then, is to try to start the debate about race somewhere else. But this depends on making visible what is usually invisible: the assumptions on which current practices depend. You have to expose, in order to deconstruct. This is certainly not the *only* kind of intervention—and one of the problems with the discussion of strategy on the left is exactly the left's inflexibility: the assumption that there is only one key to the door. That, at any rate, was the main (though not the only) reason why the group involved in making the final version of the CARM programme decided not to go for the all-out, over-arching résumé of the anti-racist case, in twenty-five minutes, but instead to adapt to the given terrain (we don't choose our own battle-grounds), and take a very specific target. In short, to do a programme *about* the media and racism, *on* the media, *against* the media.

This, however, is one of the main criticisms levelled at the CARM programme by its critics: that it was too confined to and preoccupied with exposing the media, and didn't make the general anti-racist case. About this opinions can and do genuinely differ, though the critics—I'm afraid—preferred to attribute these differences, not to the genuine problems of political calculation, but to 'bad faith' on our part (see for example, Gardner and Henry, op. cit.). I did think that the limited opportunity provided by *Open Door*, with all its problems (out-of-prime-viewing scheduling, low budgets, little time in the studio, restricted access to equipment, etc.) should best be used to hammer a particular target: to make the media, for once, speak 'against' the media's dominant practice, and thus reveal something about how they normally function. This means limiting the topics covered, going for a narrow-gauge approach rather than a scatter-fire programme covering the history and causes of racism *in general*. It may have been the wrong choice. It wasn't necessarily because we lost our 'left-wing' nerve—as I think is the main, and familiar, imputation.

A second line of criticism is about the audience aimed for. Gardner and Henry, for example, criticize CARM for going for the 'general audience', which, they argue, is to adopt the traditional media view of the audience as an undifferentiated, passive mass. They would have preferred the programme to 'equip the black, left-wing and anti-racist movements with the tools and knowledge about the workings of television racism' (op. cit., p. 75). Again, a genuine matter of disagreement. Another view (the one I took) is that black, left-wing and anti-racist groups, already active in the anti-racist struggle, are the last people who need to be instructed about how media racism works—least of all in a twenty-five minute programme on a public TV channel. Such organized activists have far more effective, internal channels for such purposes. What such groups face is the stark fact of a growing racist common sense and the lack of 'access' to the means to engage with this type of popular consciousness. But I'm afraid that, to enter the struggle on this *popular* level is a quite different order of political task from that of confirming the already-confirmed views of the converted. It means struggling over the muddy and confused middle-ground: the ground where Powellism, Thatcherism and the National Front have, in recent years, made such remarkable headway.

I suspect that, behind this criticism lies a much deeper debate about political strategy which these critics did not openly engage: the left confronts very sharp alternatives now between the broadening and deepening of democratic struggle, pressing on with 'class-against-class' confrontations as if nothing had happened to left-vanguardism since the heroic days of May 1968—although the whole terrain of popular struggle has shifted decisively against the left offensive. Ultimately, then, the debates about strategies turn on the analysis of political conjunctures. And it is *this* which should be openly debated—rather than caricatured into an eternal conflict between the 'true' and the 'false' left.

Not only the 'middle ground' but liberal consciousness itself must be an object of struggle—if what we intend is the winning of positions in a protracted war of position. Indeed, if the CARM programme had a 'target audience', I would unhesitatingly define it, not as the casual or confirmed racist (who are unlikely to be converted by twenty-five minutes on BBC 2) but precisely the *liberal consensus*. For the 'liberal consensus' is the linch-pin of what I called 'inferential racism'. It is what keeps active and organized racism in place. So this was one, at least, of the targets we aimed for. And, recognizing, from our analysis, that one kind of common sense is not displaced in an evening, we deliberately tried to think realistically about what the programme could and *could not* do. 'Pessimism of the intellect, optimism of the will': there is nothing worse, for the left, than mistaking a tiny skirmish for the final show-down. For, if optimistic voluntarism raises hearts and hopes for a little while, it is followed, as day follows night, by a corresponding gloom and pessimism. (Gramsci is excellent on the oscillations of high optimism and deep pessimism on the left in periods of rapidly shifting fortunes.) CARM's intervention could not be anything but a tiny movement in a long war of position, on the stony ground which television, regularly, delivers to the wrong side. Political calculation begins with defining the target of action, the limits of the terrain, an accurate assessment of the balance of forces and a correct estimation of the enemy's strength. Horses for courses.

The third major criticism was that the programme's style and form reproduced that of the standard formats of dominant television practice—trying to beat the professionals at their own game, rather than consciously breaking those frames. In fact, this is predicated on a much more complex, though largely unstated, argument that it is the forms rather than the content and premisses of ideological discourses which constitute their effectivity. Therefore, the main task is to 'deconstruct the forms of the television discourse'. 'We wanted the programme to be *offensive* . . .,' Gardner and Henry argued. This is a complicated issue, and a contentious one: by no means the simple either/or alternative in which it is presented. I myself thought we should go further in the direction of 'deconstruction' than the material constraints on programme production eventually allowed. So that is to concede one major weakness in the programme's conception. But after that, argument, not assertion, needs to take over.

Is it true that ideologies work exclusively by their forms? This position depends on an anti-realist aesthetic—a fashionable position in debates about ideology in the early 1970s. In its absolute form, it needed to be, and has been, quite effectively challenged and qualified. It represented at the time a certain justified 'formalist' reaction to the over-preoccupation with 'content' and 'realism' on the traditional left. But it was and is open to very serious criticism. For one thing, it was founded on a rather loony and quite a-historical view of the narrative and presentational forms in television. They were said *all* to belong to the same type of 'realism'—*the* realism of *the* realist text, was the phrase—which, apparently, was introduced in the fourteenth century and had persisted, more or less, right up to *Man Alive*. This highly specious account was sealed—quite incorrectly—with the signature of Brecht. In this absolutist form, the thesis has proved quite impossible to defend, and many of those who first proposed it have since either backed away from its excesses or fallen into an eloquent silence.

The view that lumps together the latest, banal, TV documentary and the TV drama documentary on the General Strike of 1926, *Days Of Hope*, is so historically naïve and simplistic, and so crude politically, as to give it the status of a blunderbuss in a war conducted by missile computers. This is not to deny the importance of form in the discussion of ideology. Nor is it to deny that programmes which simply reproduce the existing dominant forms of television do not sufficiently break the frames through which audiences locate and position themselves in relation to the knowledge which such programmes claim to provide. But the argument that *only* 'deconstructivist' texts are truly revolutionary is as one-sided a view as that which suggests that forms have no effect. Besides, it is to adopt a very formalistic conception of form, which, in fact, accepts the false dichotomy between 'form' and 'content' only; where the left has traditionally been concerned exclusively with the latter, this view was concerned only with the former. There were other calculations to be made. For example, that using the existing format of the typical programme which viewers are accustomed to, to identify with one kind of truth, one could undermine, precisely, the credibility of the media by showing that even this form could be used to state a different kind of truth.

A second consideration is this: if all the dominant television forms are 'realist' and realist narratives are bad, does it follow that all avant-garde or 'deconstructivist' narratives are good? This is also a rather loony position to take. The history of culture is littered with non-revolutionary 'avant-gardes': with 'avant-gardes' which are revolutionary in form only; even more, with 'avant-gardes' which are rapidly absorbed and incorporated into the dominant discourse, becoming the standard orthodoxies of the next generation. So, 'breaking and interrupting' the forms is no guarantee, in itself, that the dominant ideology cannot continue to be reproduced. This is the false trail along which some of the French theorists, like Julia Kristeva and the *Tel Quel* group, tried to drive us, by a species of polite intellectual terrorism, in the 1970s. In hindsight, the left was quite right to resist being hustled and blackmailed by these arguments.

This is no abstract debate, restricted to intellectuals of the left bank exclusively. It relates to political choices—harsh ones, to which there are no simple solutions, but which confront us every day. In any left bookshop today, one will find the imaginatively-designed, style-conscious, frame-breaking, interrogative avant-garde 'little journals' of the left: interrupting the 'dominant ideologies' in their form at every turn—and remorselessly restricted to a small, middle class, progressive audience. One will also find the traditionally-designed, ancient looking, crude aesthetics of the 'labour movement' journals (*Tribune*, the *Morning Star*, *Socialist Challenge*, for example)—remorselessly restricted to an equally small and committed audience. Neither appears to have resolved the extremely difficult problem of a truly revolutionary form *and* content, or the problem of political effectiveness—by which I mean the breakthrough to a mass audience. This is not simply a problem of the politics of popular communication on the left: a burning issue which no simple appeal to stylistic aggressiveness has yet been able to solve. If only the social division of labour could be overcome by a few new typographical or stylistic devices!

Actually, however, it would be wrong to end this piece with a simple defence of what was done, which simply mirrors by reversal the criticisms levelled. We knew we had an exceedingly rare opportunity—not something the left can afford to squander. We knew the programme could have been better, more effective—including using more effectively ideas we did or had to jettison. These are genuinely matters of debate and properly the subject of criticism. I want, instead, to draw a different lesson from this episode. It is the degree to which the left is unable to confront and argue through constructively the genuine problems of tactics and strategy of a popular anti-racist struggle. To be honest, what we know collectively about this would not fill the back of a postage stamp. Yet, we continue to conduct tactical debates and political calculation as if the answers were already fully inscribed in some new version of Lenin's *What Is To Be Done?* Our mode of political calculation is that of the taking of absolutist positions, the attribution of bad faith to those genuinely convinced otherwise—and thereby, the steady advance of the death-watch beetle of sectarian self-righteousness and fragmentation.

It somehow enhances our left-wing credentials to argue and debate as if there is some *theory* of political struggle, enshrined in the tablets of stone somewhere, which can be instantly translated into the one true 'correct' strategy. The fact that we continue to lose the key strategic engagements and, in the present period, have lost very decisive terrain indeed, does not dent, even for a moment, our total certainty that we are on the 'correct line'. My own view is that we hardly begin to know how to conduct a popular anti-racist struggle or how to bend the twig of racist common sense which currently dominates popular thinking. It is a lesson we had better learn pretty rapidly. The early interventions of the Anti-Nazi League in this area, at a very strategic, touch-and-go moment in the anti-racist struggle was one of the most effective and imaginative political interventions made in this period by groups other than the already-engaged groups of black activists. It is an experience we can and must build on—not by imitating and repeating it, but by matching it in imaginativeness. But even that leaves no room for complacency—as we watch the racist slogans raised on the soccer stands and listen to racist slogans inflect and infect the chanting of young working class people on the terraces. Face to face with this struggle for popular advantage, to fight on only one front, with only one weapon, to deploy only one strategy and to put all one's eggs into a single tactic is to set about winning the odd dramatic skirmish at the risk of losing the war.

Notes

1. Carl Gardner, 'Limited Access', *Time Out* (23 February 1979); 'It Ain't Half A Hot Potato Mum', *Time Out* (23 February 1979); and Carl Gardner (with Margaret Henry), 'Racism, Anti-Racism and Access Television', *Screen Education*, 31, Summer 1979.

2. Ernesto Laclau, *Politics and Ideology in Marxist Theory*, New Left Books, 1977.

3. *Southall: Report of the Unofficial Committee of Inquiry*, National Council of Civil Liberties, 1980.

SECTION II

REALITIES AND REPRESENTATIONS

One of the fundamental issues connected to the media's role in perpetuating racism revolves around questions of representation. There is a long tradition of scholarship dedicated to exposing the pervasive forms of bias and distortion inherent in mainstream media depictions of people of color. This is crucial work, and it needs to continue—but it's also not enough. Implicit in much of this work, after all, is the assumption that the problem of "bad" representations can be solved by eliminating them and replacing them with "good" ones. But, as the readings in this section demonstrate, the relationship between media representations and the politics of race is much more complicated than that.

Randy Ontiveros's essay helps to underscore one of the drawbacks of traditional studies of media representations: that is, that focusing on how specific racial/ethnic groups are depicted in media texts results in critical blind spots when it comes to populations that are not represented at all. Ontiveros analyzes the media "brownout" that existed around the Chicano civil rights movement of the 1950s and 1960s, and reveals how the mainstream media's historical tendency to limit its discussion of racial politics to black/white relations has frequently worked to the detriment of political struggles waged by other populations of color.

Juxtaposing the heroic cinematic depiction of Joe Clark (a black principal of an impoverished high school in Paterson, NJ) with unsavory (but true) details from Clark's actual career as an educator, George Lipsitz's essay breaks down the ways that popular media texts that *seem* to depict strong black characters can still ultimately promote a politically regressive racial agenda. Lipsitz also offers up a useful counter narrative— significantly, not the sort of narrative that Hollywood is prone to transforming into major feature films—of what a more progressive and uplifting approach to public education and race actually looks like.

An important part of the politics of representation is the question of who has the power to look (and, in so doing, to analyze and judge the objects of such a gaze) without being subject to comparable scrutiny in return. In the various racial formations that have existed in the United States, that sort of power has largely been reserved for whites. bell hooks's essay inverts that problematic directional gaze in productive and important ways, by examining some of the ways that black people have collectively imagined and represented whiteness.

Kathy Newman's essay focuses on black radio's efforts in the 1940s and 1950s to create a profitable consumer culture in black America, and how those efforts in turn helped (albeit accidentally) to lay the foundation for the use of consumer boycotts as a key tactic in the civil rights movement. At the core of Newman's argument is a recognition that the politics of any given set of media representations (in this case, mass-market radio advertising geared to black audiences) cannot simply be read off their surfaces.

Instead, such representations need to be understood within the broader social, cultural, political, and economic contexts in which they circulate.

The essay by Sut Jhally and Justin Lewis comes from a classic study of audience responses to *The Cosby Show*: a study that produced very depressing (but also very important) findings about the impact of "good" representations of people of color on racial attitudes. *Cosby* was ostensibly the perfect answer to decades of demands for positive, uplifting mainstream media representations of black Americans. Not only were the Huxtables a happy, well-adjusted family led by two very successful professionals, but the show was *the* most popular television series in the United States for years. But, as Jhally and Lewis discovered, it also served to reinforce many white viewers' beliefs that the United States really was a colorblind meritocracy, with the success of the fictional Huxtables somehow proving that real black people stuck in poverty were largely to blame for their own misfortunes.

Tricia Rose's essay provides an important example of how problematic media representations are often stitched together to produce a moral panic around racial "Others." Rose weaves together an analysis of actual violence at hip-hop public events, highly distorted (and panic-riddled) media representations of those events, and the impact that such representations have on how powerful economic and cultural institutions (in this case, insurance companies, concert promoters, and public policymakers) respond to the "threat" posed by people of color occupying public space.

6.
NO GOLDEN AGE

Television News and the Chicano Civil Rights Movement
Randy Ontiveros

On August 30, 1972, a small group of young Chicano and Chicana activists invaded Catalina Island. The action was part of what they called *la Marcha de la Reconquista*, a three-month-long "March of the Reconquest" aimed at drawing attention to discrimination against Mexican Americans and at protesting what organizers said was the US government's illegal takeover of Mexican land in 1848. Dressed in combat boots, khaki uniforms, and their signature headwear, these Brown Berets traveled twenty-six miles from the Los Angeles shore, raised a Mexican flag over the Avalon harbor, and reclaimed the popular tourist destination for Mexico. Local authorities initially allowed the militant group to stay, but after two weeks they decided they had had enough. On September 12 the police issued an order to leave the island, and the Berets complied. The Chicano invasion of Catalina was over.[1]

This largely forgotten moment in the history of Chicano/a activism is striking in that it captures something of the ambiguous position that Mexican Americans have long occupied within the imaginary of the United States, the uncertain "third space" of a population at once not-quite-native and not-quite-alien. Ascending the hillside in their military garb, the young radicals looked the part of Cuban-style invaders, and yet they gestured toward a time when the United States was the aggressor. Just as striking, though, is what the Catalina invasion reveals about the inadequacies of the mass media and of the network news in particular during a period celebrated by many as the "Golden Age" of television. In the first decades

after World War II the networks earned a reputation for quality journalism, particularly for their bold coverage of the black civil rights movement.[2] Yet they rarely reported on the Mexican American civil rights movement occurring simultaneously, and when they did cover events, it was often through a very narrow filter in which Chicanos and Chicanas were framed as threats to the integrity of the nation. Newsmakers ignored major stories such as the 1969 Chicano Youth Liberation Conference in Denver, among others.[3] Yet the Catalina story—a minor episode in the chronology of the Chicano movement by any measure—appeared on the August 31, 1972, edition of the *CBS Evening News*. In its framing of the incident, CBS tapped into viewers' fear that the country was under siege, while simultaneously offering an ideological assurance that government authorities were in control. At the end of that evening's broadcast Walter Cronkite reported that "a group of militant Mexican Americans" had "staged a peaceful invasion of Catalina Island."[4] Here was an opportunity for the network to inform its audience about the movement's complex goals, but instead Cronkite glossed over the protesters' motives, saying only that "they claim Mexico never ceded the island to the United States after the Mexican-American War in 1848."[5] He then fought back a dismissive grin as he noted that "everybody at least so far seems to be taking the invasion quite peacefully."[6]

CBS's unwillingness to engage with the politics surrounding this event is entirely consistent with most of the coverage of the Chicano movement during the 1960s and 1970s. To date no one has critically examined news footage of Mexican American activism in this era, perhaps because of the difficult nature of the television archive, or perhaps because we are only now beginning to understand where the Chicano movement fits into the mosaic of progressive social movements of the mid-twentieth century.[7] In the pages that follow I mine this footage for its patterns and its omissions as I argue that the network news had a substantive effect not only on how the Chicano civil rights movement unfolded, but also on how it has come to be remembered within the popular historical imagination of the 1960s and 1970s. Governed as they were by the black-white binary that has animated US history since the beginning, the corporate-owned networks largely ignored Mexican American activism during these decades, and when they did cover the movement, they tended to represent the Chicano movement not as a complex campaign for equality, but as one of several forces destroying America from within.

To unpack this argument I have divided the essay into three sections. The first section discusses the near "brownout"[8] on news related to Mexican Americans between the unveiling of television at the 1939 World's Fair in New York and the historic farmworker strike that began in 1965. I track the dynamics surrounding this brownout, arguing that it emerged from specific limitations within the news business and from a persistent cultural tendency to view Mexican Americans as interlopers in the nation's primordial conflict between black and white. In the second section of the essay I examine footage from the archives, beginning with the landmark coverage of César Chávez and continuing through the mid-1970s, when many prominent Chicano/a organizations collapsed and when coverage of civil rights activism all but stops. What one sees in this footage is a complex visual mechanics that situated Mexican American activists within a reductive filter that made them appear either as suffering saints or as dangerous radicals. In the mid-1960s Chávez became the template for the former as he strategically exploited TV's insatiable desire for hero figures. But by the end of the 1960s and into the 1970s, as demand for more sensational

television intensified and as Nixon remade the political landscape, reporting on the Chicano movement was increasingly dominated by images and narratives of public disorder. Often these segments were placed alongside similarly anxious segments about black radicalism, the war in Vietnam, or a purportedly out-of-control youth counterculture, so that the Chicano movement appeared on the screen as just one more threat to a vulnerable America defined by politicians and pundits not as the protesters out in the streets exercising their democratic rights, but as those sitting in their living rooms consuming television. The impact of this visual binary between suffering saint and dangerous radical was profound. Television undoubtedly helped the farmworker cause, but the networks' paper-thin coverage of the Chicano movement also ensured that (1) most viewers would see Mexican American activism not for its rich complexity but through a grossly oversimplified filter, if they saw it all, and (2) that this filter would contribute to the erasure of the Chicano movement from the dominant historical imagination. In the final section of the essay I offer a critical commentary on how this coverage of the Chicano movement fits within larger efforts by conservatives to discredit the progressive activism of the 1960s and 1970s and to transform the state from a guarantor of civil rights into a guarantor of capital accumulation through increasingly draconian law-and-order policies.

The mid-twentieth century has been celebrated in films such as *Good Night and Good Luck* (2005) and elsewhere as a golden age in TV news, but in studying footage of Chicano/a politics we find reason to reconsider this sentimental narrative. Certainly there were fleeting moments of insight in this period. However, due to the technical limitations of a twenty-three-minute program that relied increasingly on arresting visuals and the political limitations of a corporate-funded, government-regulated monopoly system, it was all too rare for newsmakers during the 1950s, '60s, and '70s to stray beyond shallow consensus viewpoints and to provide substantive background on the social movements that were remaking the social landscape of the United States. As we will see, these limitations and their effects still register today.

Early Television's Brownout

The network news made an inauspicious start at the dawn of the television age, with inaugural programs such as NBC's *Camel News Caravan* and CBS's *Television News with Douglas Edwards* functioning as little more than stale bulletin services.[9] Yet by 1965—the year that the National Farm Workers Association (later the United Farm Workers) declared its historic grape strike and the year sometimes cited as the beginning of the Chicano movement—television news had become a major institution in American society. As television critics have observed, the story that had facilitated this shift and made the evening news a nationwide authority was the struggle to end Jim Crow.[10] For more than a century, coverage of black civil rights activism had been the exclusive territory of black journalists, but when network producers went looking for a story that would demonstrate the power of television, they were drawn to the powerful scenes of white-on-black violence taking place in the South. As a result, events such as the murder of Emmitt Till, the integration of schools in Little Rock, and the 1963 March on Washington became major milestones in US media history. Sasha Torres argues convincingly that civil rights activists and network journalists had reached an unspoken agreement with each other.[11] Television provided the publicity that activists needed to resist the Bull Connors of the world. In exchange, Martin Luther King Jr. and others provided the compelling images that networks wanted so that they could manufacture a sense of seriousness and establish themselves as the official chroniclers of the nation's history.

Of course, black civil rights activism of this era changed more than just television. It had a deep and lasting impact on nearly every aspect of contemporary life, including Mexican American politics. F. Arturo Rosales, author of one of the definitive histories of the Chicano movement, has said that he was inspired to become an activist as he read newspaper coverage of the Birmingham bombings and other events while stationed at an air force base in Great Britain. I know of no written account of Mexican Americans watching Martin Luther King's 1963 "I Have a Dream Speech," but it is reasonable to

think that more than a few Chicanos and Chicanas were moved to action by what remains one of television's most influential moments.[12] Many young Mexican Americans became activists because of the work of King and other leaders, and some even became participants in the antisegregation struggle. Maria Varela, for example, worked in Alabama as a Student Nonviolent Coordinating Committee (SNCC) literacy tutor in preparation for the pivotal 1964 elections.[13] Elizabeth Sutherland Martínez, for her part, was director of SNCC's New York office and also a volunteer in Mississippi.[14]

Grassroots narratives like these are significant because they draw our attention to often-obscured intersections between black and Chicano/a activism during this period. They also challenge more recent efforts to use the exaggerated image of upwardly mobile Latinos/as as a counterpoint to the supposed intransigence of African Americans.[15] Yet even as we note connections between black and Chicano/a activism in the 1960s and 1970s we must be mindful of divergences as well, among them the fact that if television had been late in getting to the story of the black civil rights movement, it was even more dilatory when it came to stories involving Mexican Americans. Available records indicate that prior to the farmworker strike that began in 1965 there were only a handful of reports even remotely related to Chicano/as, most of them dealing rather predictably with alleged drug smuggling along the border, the controversial *bracero* program, or unauthorized immigration. There is one notable exception: the September 27, 1960, premier of ABC's *Bell and Howell Close Up!*, which, according to an archival summary, examined discrimination against blacks, Jews, Puerto Ricans, Japanese, Chicano/as, and Native Americans in selected communities across the United States.[16] Generally, though, television watchers in the 1940s, 1950s, and early 1960s were more likely to see news coverage of Mexicans in Mexico than of Mexicans in the United States. Corporate networks were eager to create new markets for their media commodities in Latin America, so they supported State Department outreach to nonaligned countries with coverage that largely followed official positions.[17] Mexicans in the United States did not have an embassy, of course, and they had not yet been targeted as a growth market for advertisers, which meant that by and large the networks saw nothing to report about them.

Mexican Americans thus were excluded from what Gaye Tuchman calls "the news net," that collection of wire services, bureaus, and other news-gathering practices that generate content and create in audiences a sense of what is newsworthy.[18] With its promise of "catching" all of the meaningful stories on any particular day, the news net makes an implicit claim to universality. Yet in the 1940s and 1950s (and even today) the major networks lacked reporters with experience in covering Chicano/a stories. There were few, if any, Mexican Americans working in establishment media outlets, and since the nation's educational institutions largely excluded Mexican American history from their curricula, the mostly white journalists who staffed the major news organizations would have had little exposure to Chicano/a issues as part of their formal education. These narrow institutional considerations were themselves bound up with broader cultural dynamics involving Mexican Americans, as large news organizations in the United States have tended to handle stories about the Southwest (where Mexican Americans have historically been concentrated) as regional items. This tendency exists in part because the nations journalistic and political institutions are headquartered in New York and Washington, D.C., respectively, but on a more fundamental level, it is a residue of longstanding colonial perceptions of what we today call the Southwest. Mary Pat Brady has shown how nineteenth- and early twentieth-century literature—including journalism—imagined the territories expropriated from Mexico as barren lands without human agency, thereby rendering long-established Indian and *mexicano* communities as invisible and clearing the way for the capitalist development of the region's tremendous natural resources.[19] I would argue that the inability of television producers to engage with postwar Mexican American politics brought this tradition of erasure into a new medium and a new context. (Their failure was reinforced, incidentally, by early TV westerns such as *The Cisco Kid,* which also signified Mexicanness on the small screen in highly restrictive ways.) Newsmakers intuited that the black civil rights movement would make for captivating television because the story they were telling could be sutured into the nation's psychosocial drama of black versus white, freedom versus slavery—a drama that as Toni Morrison argues is related only by indirection to the lives of African Americans.[20] Coverage of the black civil rights movement thus encouraged viewers to situate what they were seeing on the screen within the fantasy of US exceptionalism, to imagine a "more perfect union" unfolding before their very eyes. The Chicano movement, by contrast, did not offer similar narrative pleasures, for while African Americans through their persistent exclusion have been central to the founding mythologies of the United States, Mexican Americans have been detained at the border of the nation's racial imaginary, sometimes included but more often excluded from the stories and images that make up the dominant history of the United States.

The inability of the newsmakers to give meaningful coverage of Chicano/a politics in the early years of television represents a failure of the media industry, one that still has consequence. Not only did the networks do a disservice to their audiences by neglecting to inform them of a major story, but they also created the interpretive conditions for the Chicano movement to appear as if it came out of nowhere. Mexican American activism after World War II was similar to black politics of the same era in that soldiers and civilians alike were unwilling to tolerate a segregated status quo after participating in a conflict that had been fought in the name of democracy. Anticommunist policies were doing considerable damage to the progressive infrastructure that had been built up within Chicano/a communities during the Great Depression, but in the 1940s, 1950s, and 1960s groups such as the Community Service Organization, the League of United Latin American Citizens, the American G.I. Forum, la Asociación Nacional México-Americano, el Congreso del Pueblo de Habla Española, and the Mexican American Political Association all worked to maintain a protest tradition that went back to the nineteenth century.[21] Activists in these groups fought against the anti-union Taft-Hartley Act and in support of school desegregation, affordable housing, and equal employment opportunities. There were many defeats, but there were also important victories. In 1947 the federal courts ruled in *Westminster v. Mendez* that segregated "Mexican schools" were unconstitutional. It was a landmark case that later served as precedent in *Brown v. Board of Education*.[22] In 1949 activists made it possible for the decorated soldier Felix Longoria to be buried at Arlington National Cemetery after his family was denied use of whites-only facilities in Three Rivers, Texas.[23] The incident drew the attention of a young senator named Lyndon Baines Johnson and served as catalyst for the creation of the American G.I. Forum, a Mexican American civil rights organization that survives today. In 1954 the Supreme Court ruled in *Hernandez v. Texas* that the Fourteenth Amendment protected all racial minorities, and not just African Americans, as the law had previously said. The case would never have gone forward without the help of a nationwide fund-raising drive on Spanish-language radio and other Chicano/a communication networks to pay for legal expenses.[24]

Each weekday evening Walter Cronkite ended the broadcast with his signature sign-off: "And that's the way it is." The phrase was meant to assure viewers of the truth of what they had just seen, but in television's early years CBS and its rivals ignored the stories mentioned here, along with many others. This news brownout did not keep Mexican Americans from organizing, but it did have an impact. Chicano/a organizations of this era faced tremendous obstacles in establishing themselves and often had to shut down because they lacked the cultural and political capital that media attention sometimes delivers. The networks also became complicit in the construction of a narrative still powerful today, one that suggests that Mexican Americans have been quiescent for much of their history. The 1940s, 1950s, and early 1960s saw intense civil rights activism among Chicanos and Chicanas, but in part because of the network failure to cover this activism, it can appear in retrospect that Mexican Americans were not involved in politics until much later. The consequences of this myopia have been profound. Many Chicanos and Chicanas remain ignorant about an important chapter in their cultural history. Meanwhile, the general public still perceives Chicano/a activism as a new or at best sporadic phenomenon, rather than as a persistent narrative in US history tied to clear patterns of injustice.

Televising *el Movimiento*

In the previous pages we examined the scant coverage of Mexican American issues in the early years of television. The next section tracks the story of César Chávez and the California grape strike, the first that networks covered substantively. We will see that while the camera transformed Chávez into a global icon and advanced what had been an almost quixotic quest for farmworker justice, it also laid the foundation for a visual binary in which Mexican American activists appeared either as one-dimensional martyrs or as traitors. What got lost as a result of this binary was the ideological complexity and the moral urgency of progressive Chicano/a politics.

I begin with a brief history of the grape strike.[25] César Chávez had formed the National Farm Workers Association (NFWA) in 1962 after working for the Community Service Organization (CSO), a group that used Saul Alinsky's methods to increase Mexican American voter turnout. Frustrated by the CSO's unwillingness to organize farmworkers, Chávez formed the NFWA in the hopes of winning union protections for one of the nation's most exploited populations. In those early years Chávez did the nontelegenic work of driving up and down California's Central Valley, introducing himself to farmworkers, surveying their needs and opinions, and signing up members. He planned to do this tedious but essential groundwork for several years, but when Filipino farmworkers with the Agricultural Workers Organizing Committee declared a strike in 1965, Chávez realized he had an opportunity. Union leaders quickly organized a vote, and on September 16, 1965, the members of the NFWA decided to strike. Initially they received very little national media attention, but that changed in spring of 1966 when the television cameras arrived. Looking to pressure Governor Pat Brown into supporting the strike, union leadership organized a three-hundred-mile pilgrimage from Delano to Sacramento. Although there was internal disagreement about using religious iconography in a political campaign, scenes of humble farmworkers walking in the hot Central Valley sun made for good television.[26] Network coverage of the pilgrimage helped the farmworkers win their first major victory, a contract with winemaker and liquor distributor Schenley Industries.[27] It was the first time that workers in California's fields had won union recognition.

As the farmworkers pressed on, television coverage transformed Chávez into the only Chicano/a activist recognizable to a broad public, or what Todd Gitlin perceptively calls "a media-certified celebrity leader."[28] The attraction of the camera to Chávez was not an accident, though, as the leader had learned early in his career just how powerful a tool television could be. In 1959, during one of his first attempts to organize farmworkers, Chávez arranged for the local news in Oxnard, California to film as workers set fire to a steel drum full of referrals for jobs being given illegally to exploited Mexican *braceros*. Not long after, owners agreed to give preference to local labor and to raise wages from sixty-five cents to ninety cents an hour.[29] When the NFWA went on strike six years later, Chávez once again found creative ways to exploit the media. The 1966 pilgrimage described above is one example of how Chávez used television to stir public sympathy for a population rarely seen in dominant media. But by far the most prominent example of Chávez using the camera for the benefit of *la causa* was his fast in the spring of 1968. With tensions running high inside the organization and with grower negotiations at an impasse, Chávez felt he needed to do something dramatic to refocus his energies and the energies of the union.[30] Initially he told no one about the fast, but by the time it ended twenty-five days later it had become a national media event. Seated beside the senator and soon-to-be presidential candidate Robert Kennedy, Chávez took communion on March 10 in front of network cameras. The iconic footage was broadcast by NBC that night, just three months short of Kennedy's tragic assassination.[31]

Chávez's critics accused him of pandering to the camera, and for this reason he and his supporters insisted that the fast was not an effort to draw media attention.[32] Chávez was undoubtedly sincere in his religious convictions, but his actions were by all appearances the product of careful strategy.

Chávez seems to have understood that by performing the stereotypical role of "the humble Mexican," he could allay any fears that might arise from that other deeply rooted stereotype, the figure of the Latin revolutionary. He seemingly also understood television's fascination with martyr figures, a fascination first cathected through coverage of John F. Kennedy's assassination. Television was an increasingly crowded universe of people and events vying for screen time, but Chávez successfully drew media attention to the farmworker strike by transforming his body into a racialized spectacle of suffering, just as King, the Little Rock Nine, and many others had been doing in the South. Sasha Torres explains that images of racialized bodies enduring physical suffering made for powerful television fare because they demonstrated the new medium's ability to seemingly transport the isolated home viewer to the scene and to show there what appeared to be unfiltered reality. With activists such as Chávez giving apparently authentic performances of injury, viewers (primarily but not exclusively white) were able to indulge in a fantasy of cutting through the mythologies around race and grasping at long last the truth of what it meant to be black or brown.[33] To use Zora Neale Hurston's memorable phrase, television seemed to provide a window on "how it feels to be colored me," but without the risks of minoritized subjectivity.

Most white Americans in the mid-1960s knew far less about exploitation in the fields of California than they did about segregation in the South. In November of 1960, CBS had broadcast Edward R. Murrow's famous *Harvest of Shame,* but interestingly the program focused primarily on black farmworkers. Nevertheless, Chávez's media strategy gained extensive news coverage, more than any other single Mexican American activist, before or after. There was, as I mentioned, the groundbreaking coverage of the April 1966 pilgrimage to Sacramento, as well as the March 1968 footage of Chávez ending his fast. There was additional footage in the months that followed, including a brief NBC update on August 13, 1968, a May 1969 episode of the NBC program *Frank McGee Reports* dedicated to the strike, and a CBS segment on September 29, 1969, in which Chávez utilized the new strategy of winning public support by warning of the dangers that pesticides posed to consumers.[34] Coverage picked up even more in the first years of the next decade. According to the Vanderbilt Television News Archive, between 1970 and 1973 the three major networks broadcast almost fifty segments on the union and related a number of important developments: historic contracts in the summer of 1970, a lettuce strike announced that same year, the violent efforts by the Teamsters to sabotage the farmworkers' union, Chávez's arrest for refusing a court order to suspend the boycott, the union leader's involvement in the 1972 elections, the murder of farmworker Juan de la Cruz in 1973, and more. In later years there would be limited coverage of Chávez's 1988 fast against pesticides, as well as news of his death on April 23, 1993.[35] Never again, though, would Chávez enjoy the level of visibility he had in the late 1960s and early 1970s.

Television was inarguably an indispensible tool in the grape strike. Yet the invention of César Chávez as the first and perhaps only Chicano/a "civil rights subject" (to use Herman Gray's memorable phrase) came with considerable drawbacks.[36] First, it influenced leadership dynamics in often problematic ways. Television is a uniquely intimate medium in that it is watched mostly in private spaces, where it becomes a part of everyday life. Mobile media devices are transforming this intimacy in ways that are quite fascinating, but it remains the case that television viewers are drawn to characters who are paradoxically exceptional in their persona and common in their outlook. In other words, audiences identify most readily with figures they perceive as "average" but who still have a certain charisma.[37] (Think, for example, of ironic characters such as Lucille Ball, Cliff Huxtable, and Jerry Seinfeld, or of journalistic "everyman" figures such as Murrow.) Through this privileging of character, the television news tends to exacerbate what is always a danger in social movements, namely, the establishment of top-down leadership structures centered on a charismatic individual. We see this dynamic quite readily with the black civil rights movement, where the figure of Martin Luther King Jr. overshadows the countless others who brought down Jim Crow. In the Chicano/a context, the cameras helped make Chávez's considerable

magnetism a focal point of the entire struggle, even though (as he himself always insisted) the farmworkers were the soul of the union. As the strike went on, Chávez became so overwhelmed by publicity demands that he was increasingly unable to do the more important work of organizing.[38] This in itself was a problem, but even more problematic was the fact that television obscured the grassroots energy that powered the movement, particularly the work of the many women who served as organizers, administrators, child-care providers, negotiators, cooks, recruiters, and picketers. To give only the most prominent example, Dolores Huerta was as important to the United Farm Workers (UFW)[39] as Chávez himself, but cameras did not gravitate toward her because as a woman she did not fit the masculinist mode of the messiah come to deliver his people.[40] To be sure, television was not solely to blame for the autocratic structure that some say undid the UFW, but in building something of a cult of personality around Chávez, it played a key part.[41]

A second disadvantage to television's production of César Chávez as a synecdoche for the entire Chicano movement was the ensuing neglect of the movement's historical and ideological richness. The farmworkers' movement was just one of many elements that constituted what we have come to call the Chicano movement, and in fact the relationship between the UFW and other aspects of the movement was complicated because Chávez saw himself more as a labor leader than as a cultural defender. The grape strike presented journalists with an opportunity to inform their audience about the extent of Chicano/a activism in the 1960s and 1970s and to contextualize that activism within the political tradition described earlier. Journalists, however, rarely took this opportunity, both because they lacked airtime and because they lacked background. As a result, a viewer sitting in her living room watching coverage of the Chicano movement would likely get the impression that the events being reported had no history and thus no credibility. To give only one example, on June 3, 1969, ABC filed a brief report on a protest at the confirmation hearings of Supreme Court nominee Warren Burger by Reies López Tijerina.[42] Tijerina's admittedly theatrical effort to make a citizen's arrest of Burger was part of long-standing efforts to win recognition for Hispano communities in New Mexico that had been robbed of their land by the US judiciary system. However, since no historical background was given, Tijerina came across as a lunatic, and (worse) his cause was made to seem like a farce. This sort of coverage was not an isolated example. Chicano/a activism was often reported with little or no context, and as a result activists routinely appeared on the screen not as part of a larger tradition of political dissent, but as troublemakers and malcontents.[43]

We have thus arrived at the other pole in the television news binary under discussion: the production of narratives and images that positioned Mexican Americans as radicals while discursively linking the Chicano movement to other perceived threats, including black militancy, war unrest, the youth counterculture, and Latin-inflected communism. To put this framing in perspective, it is important to first note that while there was a contingent of Chicano/as open to violence, especially in self-defense, the Chicano movement was overwhelmingly peaceable.[44] Nevertheless, activities such as voter education and antipoverty programming do not televise well, which meant that apart from the grape strike and its iconic leader, the networks usually only ran stories that involved rioting, vandalism, and other forms of public disorder. A powerful media dialectic was thus crystallizing on the airwaves, one in which Chicano/a activists were represented either as suffering saints or (more often) as dangerous revolutionaries. On one side was the figure of César Chávez. On the other side were those violent, undifferentiated masses threatening to bring the American experiment to an end.

Once again there is a telling parallel to black activism. Herman Gray and Sasha Torres both argue that while the creation of "the civil rights subject" proved pivotal for racial progress, it also established a polarized vision of black personhood in which the only two images available to the TV-consuming public were the noble middle class citizen eager to realize the American dream and, on the other hand, the pathological subject—what Torres calls "the civil rights subject undone."[45] The sympathetic figure of King was replaced in the second half of the 1960s by unsympathetic figures such as Malcolm X, Huey Newton, Bobby Seale, and Angela Davis, leading eventually, Torres says, to "representations of blacks as crack addicts, homeless people, teenage mothers, gang-bangers, drug dealers, and children threatened by 'random' ghetto violence."[46]

Mexican Americans found themselves subject to the same reductive treatment and were even at times linked to this specter of black militancy. For example, on August 31, 1970, the *CBS Evening News* ran a segment on what it called "a nationwide menace" of violence against police officers.[47] Reporter John Laurence first describes a raid on a Philadelphia Black Panther headquarters following the murder of a Philadelphia cop. Commissioner Frank Rizzo then gives an on-camera interview in which he cites the shootout as evidence of America's decline: "It's just the society we live in today . . . the law only applies to the law-abiding and the police. We let idiots like this [nodding at the Panthers headquarters] survive under our form of government. Maybe we'll have to change it."[48] The irony is remarkable: here is the police chief of a major American city suggesting that the United States might have to end democratic governance if it wants to protect citizens from armed "idiots" with radical ideas. The Panthers, however, are not allowed an opportunity to respond. Instead, CBS producers cut to the story of four police officers in California who were ambushed in what Sergeant Lee Hayes thinks might be part of an imminent "revolution" being stirred up by "agitators that came out of this Chicano demonstration in Los Angeles."[49] Two days earlier a large antiwar rally in East L.A. called the Chicano Moratorium (discussed below) had devolved into a bloody confrontation with the police. Hayes links the Riverside shootout with this recent news item, asserting that rioters from L.A. "whipped our people up into doing it."[50] The sergeant gives no evidence, though, and Mexican Americans are again not allowed a response. Broadcasts such as this one fomented concern among many whites (and more than a handful of nonwhites) that the nation was being imperiled by recalcitrant minorities, since in stacking reports the newsmakers made it seem that black and Chicano/a activism represented a coordinated attack on the forces of law and order.

There were numerous other occasions in the late 1960s and early 1970s when Chicano/a activism was filtered through the prism of real or imagined violence. On April 28, 1970, ABC reporter Gregory Jackson warned viewers that "a Mexican American upheaval is gathering force in Southern Texas."[51] In this instance the implied comparison was not to the domestic threat of black radicalism, but rather to the foreign threat of Fidel Castro. Jackson reports that this insurgency in South Texas—a region long associated with civil unrest imported from Latin America—will be led by José Angel Gutiérrez, a man who "looks like an accountant, but talks like a revolutionary."[52] A similar report ran on June 15, 1971, but this time it was "two days of rioting and burning" in Albuquerque by Mexican Americans, "many of them high on marijuana and drink."[53] Associating Chicano/a activism now with countercultural deviancy, the segment quotes city officials as saying that "hippie outsiders were behind the chaos." Yet again the reporter gives no basis for such a claim. Two months later, on August 1, 1972, ABC updated viewers on the April hijacking of Frontier Airlines Flight 737 by Ricardo Chavez Ortiz.[54] Chavez Ortiz claimed he was acting on behalf of all Chicanos and Chicanas, and so reporter Dick Shoemaker traveled into East L.A. for a melodramatic exposé of the social conditions there. One could argue that at least the journalist attempted to educate viewers about the economic problems faced by many Mexican Americans, but the segment makes the barrio a site of pathology rather than the product of policymaking. Also, Shoemaker merely hints at Chavez's likely severe mental health problems, which made him a questionable spokesperson at best for the Chicano movement.

Reporting on Chicano/a activism in the late 1960s and early 1970s characteristically represented the Chicano movement as a menace, and not simply as a matter of story selection, but also in terms of framing. Despite network claims of objectivity, their limited coverage of Chicano/a activism was bent both aurally and visually toward the police interpretation of events over and against the perspectives of Mexican Americans. We can see this dynamic most clearly in television footage of the Chicano Moratorium, a major milestone of the Chicano movement.

On August 29, 1970, an estimated 25,000 mostly Mexican Americans assembled together in East Los Angeles to protest the Vietnam War.[55] The event had been planned for months as a peaceful assembly, but by the end of the day clashes with the police left more than 150 arrested, more than 60 injured, and 3 dead—including esteemed Chicano journalist Ruben Salazar. All three major networks gave at least passing coverage to the event, but the relatively extensive reporting by NBC stands out as an example of how TV journalism coverage oriented viewers toward the police point of view. The initial report that aired on August 30 begins with reporter Frank Bourgholtzer giving viewers an on-camera exposition of what had taken place the day before. Trouble began, he says, when some of the participants at the "spirited antiwar rally" were allegedly caught shoplifting at a local liquor store.[56] Emphasizing the effectiveness of law enforcement in dealing with this stereotypical barrio behavior, Bourgholtzer says that "the police quickly solved the problem at the Green Mill, but that small confrontation set off a chain of reactions that exploded into a wild and vicious riot."[57] By the time his recap has finished, the visuals have shifted from the reporter's direct address to footage of the riot. The viewer watches as police officers march in formation, first pushing against the crowd and then drawing back as rocks and other projectiles fly across the top half of the television screen. Amid this chaos one hears the voice of an angry protester who yells from off-screen: "You guys, don't forget you guys started this."[58] His comment is a powerful counternarrative to the official version of what happened that day, but it becomes lost in sounds and images edited through the lens of what Aaron Doyle calls a "law-and-order ideology" that sees aggressive policing as the only remedy for a society being destroyed from within by its underclasses.[59] Shooting from behind police lines so as to protect the crew and add drama, NBC cameras at the Chicano Moratorium give the viewer a police-eye perspective that allows viewers to look down the barrel of a gun and to imagine themselves as heroes in the unfolding social drama.

This law-and-order orientation of the riot footage is reinforced by those who appear on camera to interpret the event. As usual, Chicano/as were not given the opportunity to provide their accounts of what had unfolded that tragic day. Instead, Mexican Americans are visible only as an undifferentiated mass or briefly as injured suspects being reined in by the more powerful authorities. To be fair, the reporter gestures toward an alternative perspective by saying that the protest was motivated by "the unfairness evident in Vietnam casualty figures."[60] Yet Bourgholtzer's voice-over is overpowered by the accompanying images of chaos. Bureaucratic spokespersons, on the other hand, are allowed considerable screen time to give their perspective. In the follow-up report that aired on August 31, Chief Davis of the Los Angeles Police Department makes a startling claim:

> I would say they're [the protesters] definitely carrying out the orders of the Communist Party of the United States of America . . . more than ten months ago a decision was made to more or less give up on the black people, other than the Black Panther activity . . . the efforts [by Communists] have been concentrated in the Mexican American areas, and with this riot you'd say with some success.[61]

The official is not pressed by the reporter for evidence. Instead, as in other broadcasts, a white male authority is projected into living rooms as the voice of order—no matter how absurd his reasoning—while Chicano/a activists become associated with irrationality and violence.

To be sure, there were fleeting moments when TV journalism's binary of noble crusader or ignoble revolutionary seems to bend a bit, making visible the always incomplete process of hegemony. For example, in July of 1970 NBC aired a two-part special report on "the Mexican Americans." Set in San Antonio, the broadcast opens with an on-camera commentary by Mayor W. W. McAllister on "our citizens of Mexican descent." McAllister opines:

> They're very fine people. They're home loving. They love beauty. They love flowers. They love music. They love dancing. Perhaps they're not quite as, uh, let's say as ambitiously motivated as the Anglos are to get ahead financially, but they manage to get a lot out of life.[62]

Absurd remarks by authorities often go unquestioned in network journalism, but in this segment McAllister's paternalistic racism is challenged by Mariano Aguilar, a young Chicano who offers his own blunt assessment of McAllister's opinion: "Racism. The whole attitude. The Anglo community, the gringo community as we call it here, they believe that anybody who is not white Anglo-Saxon Protestant is culturally and physically inferior, so what the hell. So we've been dealing with this for two hundred years."[63] It is remarkable that Aguilar appears on screen at all, but even more remarkable is how the report is assembled. In most coverage of this period, Chicano/a bodies are filmed with a long shot or a medium-long shot, if they are recorded at all. In the NBC footage of the Chicano Moratorium, for example, protestors consistently appear at some distance away from the camera lens. The viewer is placed at a literal and figurative remove from Mexican American subjects and sees not their individuality but rather their collective pathologies. In this broadcast from San Antonio we see something different. Aguilar and two friends are sitting with reporter Jack Perkins at a table. The camera is positioned close to the three Chicanos and at eye level, and when Aguilar is speaking we get a close-up shot. Through these editorial decisions the viewer is invited to sit down with the young men while they share a beer and a cigarette and talk—without anger and with obvious insight—about their lives. Instead of screening Mexican American activism as deviance, NBC gives us a brief glimpse of the Chicano movement as a reasoned response to a long and painful history of racism in South Texas.

Regrettably, we know very little about Mexican American television watching during the 1960s and 1970s, but we do know that this particular broadcast had an impact on contemporaneous Chicano/a politics. Angered by McAllister's racist remarks, activists from Texas boycotted the San Antonio Savings Association, a bank then owned by the mayor.[64] Yet even this special report moves toward the saint/rebel binary, with the reporter warning of "a potentially explosive situation. There are those in San Antonio working to cool it, but there are also those plotting to make it explode."[65] The following night's broadcast considers at some length the threats that

Chicano/a activists might pose to whites. "Do they hate the gringo?" Perkins wonders.[66] "If they do," he continues, "why have the barrios—unlike the black ghettoes—never exploded?"[67] Perkins has no answer to these questions, but he does claim that "there are today young firebrands growing in the barrios, secret men in hidden places who are plotting violence."[68] These "hot radicals" may now be on the "fringes" of Mexican American politics, but Perkins concludes that without reform, even moderates will decide that violence is the only answer.[69] As in all traditions tied to marginalized subjectivity, Mexican American politics has always been marked by an uneasy tension between militancy and pacifism. Yet because of its need for dramatic narrative and accessible images, the network news in the 1960s and 1970s proved incapable of mining the complexities of Chicano movement activism. Instead it swung between two poles—the suffering saint on one hand and dangerous radical on the other—without ever giving viewers insight into how they themselves might be implicated in the story.

Television coverage of Chicano/a activism dropped off considerably toward the latter part of the 1970s. There were broadcasts such as the May 8, 1978, CBS report on rioting in Houston after the death of a Mexican American man while in police custody, as well as coverage on July 4, 1980, of Chicano/a reactions to the acquittal of two men in Arizona accused of torturing and killing three Mexican immigrants.[70] For the most part, though, coverage began to shift away from the binary that had dominated coverage in the earlier part of the decade. In its place was the emergence of Chicano/as (or "Hispanics" as they were increasingly called in government and advertising circles) as a constituency to be courted by politicians looking for votes and by corporations looking for markets. When it existed at all, nightly news coverage of Mexican Americans increasingly consisted of stories about elected officials making publicity visits to the barrios, or of soft news stories about the growing numbers of Hispanics and how they are changing America—as if the influence of Mexican Americans and other Latino/a populations on US history and culture was something new.[71] The only notable exception to this broad trend occurred in 1993 when students

demanding a Chicano/a studies program at UCLA went on a hunger strike. More recently, networks covered the momentous immigrants' rights marches of May 2006, but by then new media and grassroots independent reporting—"citizen journalism," as it is sometimes called—was already turning the evening news into a relic.

Corporate News and Movement Memory

Having glimpsed the evolution of TV coverage of the Chicano movement, we must ask why the networks shifted from largely sympathetic to largely unsympathetic representations of civil rights activism. The issue is complex, of course, but it has much to do with increased competition in the television industry. In the early 1960s, producers had sought images of political violence as a means of manufacturing a sense of journalistic seriousness. By the late 1960s, the situation had changed dramatically. Saturation coverage of Kennedy's assassination had persuaded most people of TV's power as chronicler of the nation's official history, so newsmakers were no longer as anxious to prove themselves.[72] Also, television sets had become furniture in almost every home, which meant that networks had to find new ways to attract audiences.[73] ABC, which for many years had run a distant third in the ratings chase, was airing sexier and more violent programming, motivating others to follow suit.[74] Executives who were once willing to broadcast the evening news at a loss because they believed it would contribute to the network's "prestige" were now ordering news divisions to contribute to the network's bottom line, and news producers responded by pursuing stories with high-impact images and unambiguous "good-versus-evil" narratives.[75] The Chicano movement was falling victim to the intensified tabloidization of TV news.

It cannot be emphasized enough that the institutional dynamics reshaping the television news dovetailed with larger currents in US politics, for, despite Richard Nixon's frequent protestations that the so-called liberal media had it out for him, the reframing of the civil rights movement that took place on TV screens at the end of the 1960s aligned well with Nixon's strategy of exploiting white paranoia about the

collapse of America.[76] Earlier I discussed how coverage of the black civil rights movement in the 1950s
played into nationalist fantasies about the march of
American democracy. Nixon turned this logic on its
head by claiming that progressive political struggles
such as the Chicano movement, feminism, the gay
and lesbian rights movements, the black power movement, and others were fundamentally un-American.
No longer was civil rights activism seen on the small
screen as part of a tradition of dissent. Instead it was
televised as a threat to the well-being of the "silent
majority," Nixon's famous code word for the white,
middle class, straight families that were increasingly
represented in popular media and by the political establishment as the "real" America. I am not arguing
that the networks were taking their marching orders
from the president; the relationship between political
power and cultural power is rarely that direct in a democracy. It is the case, however, that television has
historically been highly sensitive to executive power,
largely because it is FCC appointees who grant li-
censes to private interests seeking access to public
airwaves. A kind of symbiotic relationship emerged
in which the increasingly sensationalized programming of the networks—including the news—stirred
in viewers a sense of perpetual unease and thus reinforced Nixon's message that the nation itself was in
peril.[77] The result: Chicano/a activism of the 1960s
and 1970s became conflated with, and was ultimately
obscured by, the disparate social, political, and moral
threats that were reportedly endangering the American dream.

This symbiosis between televised representations
of civil rights and the Nixonian rhetoric of decline
was not a simple failure on the part of the networks
to honor the objective ideals of journalism. It was
instead a by-product of the ideological and practical
work that dominant media performs within a neo-
liberal economy in which the state serves as guarantor of the efficient movement of private capital
and citizens carry out their civic duty by shopping.
Corporate television journalism, then as now, was
structured around an assurance that the state would
protect viewers in troubled times. We saw this dynamic
operating quite clearly in coverage of the Chicano
Moratorium, as images of unruly minorities were

counterbalanced by an implicit promise that the "thin
blue line" of police officers seen on the screen would
ultimately restore order. In a period when global flows
of capital were reorganizing the state in fundamental
ways, nightly images of authorities apparently restoring order after events like the Chicano Moratorium
offered viewers a visual basis for the kind of confidence in governing institutions that is necessary for
the continued investment of capital by individual consumers and corporate investors. Sandwiched between
segments, the commercials are easily overlooked, but
they too played a part in shaping how the Chicano
movement was received during the sixties and seventies and how it has been incorporated within the
dominant historical memory. Advertisements, with
their implicit promise of abundance, made for a
sharp contrast with the images of political unrest, allowing viewers to detach themselves from the realm
of participatory politics and to identify instead with
the seemingly apolitical life of the commodity. There
is something profoundly strange in watching an up-
tempo commercial for Lanacane ("For itching problems anywhere, except your eyes") used as a lead-in
to scenes of rioting in Los Angeles, as NBC had done
with its coverage of the Chicano Moratorium.[78] Yet, if
the uncanniness of this jump went unnoticed by most
viewers, it was because they had been trained to make
careful distinctions between the imagined unruliness
of the street and the no-less-imagined safety of the
domestic sphere and its consumer logic. Political institutions in the United States were increasingly making the same distinction, responding not to activists
using public space to demand recognition of their
rights, but to private corporations. The result of this
ongoing process has been the consolidation of a neo-
liberalism that compels us to think that the market,
rather than collective action, is the best remedy for
social and political injustice.

The mid-twentieth century is often remembered
as the golden age of broadcast journalism, a time
when the television news was more than the alarm-
ist headlines, shallow reporting, kneejerk punditry,
and tabloid features that dominate today's media
landscape. This nostalgic narrative is compelling
because it allows us to hope that things might be
better, but the archive of TV coverage of Mexican

American politics suggests the need for a different story. There were moments of remarkable insight and courage, just as today there are examples to be found of network reporting that is informed and independent. However, in watching network reporting on the Chicano movement, one is not struck by the professional nature of journalism but by a lack of research and the frequent inability to get around narrow conventions of race and politics in the United States. It was not for a lack of alternatives. Print journalists such as Carey McWilliams and Stan Steiner had shown that it was possible to reflect intelligently on the Chicano movement as it unfolded. The networks, though, showed themselves largely incapable of recognizing the significance of postwar activism by Mexican Americans. The impact of this exclusion has been considerable. During the 1950s, 1960s, and 1970s, paper-thin coverage by newsmakers made it difficult for movement activists to gain the sympathy of members of the public, who, when they saw the Chicano movement at all, saw it as a threat or as a curiosity. Activists had some success in challenging the dominance of traditional media through the creation of an independent Chicano/a press, but there can be little doubt that the networks stood in the way of a meaningful democratic debate about the issues raised by Chicano/a activists. Moreover, because the network news established itself during these same decades as the official "first draft" of the nation's history, its insipid handling of Mexican American activism all but guaranteed that the movement would be inscribed only on the margins of US history. Given the power that television continues to have in shaping popular perceptions of the sixties, it is unsurprising that many people are limited in their knowledge of the Chicano movement to a hazy recollection of César Chávez, if they know anything at all.

If the news landscape looked the same today as it did during the 1960s and 1970s, it would be tempting to despair. Fortunately, the explosion of online media such as blogs, social networking sites, podcasts, and video-sharing sites is fast eroding the enormous influence that the networks have had over the reception of new social movements in the public sphere. Obviously the Internet is not a silver bullet. (The mere existence of digital media does not guarantee an informed public, let alone bring about social justice.) Still, the proliferation of news and opinion platforms means both that the networks are more accountable in terms of fact checking, and also that progressive activists—Chicanos and Chicanas included—can find alternatives to the narrow filtering that makes the evening news as pallid today as it was forty years ago. Ultimately, though, the most important lesson to be learned from network coverage of the Chicano movement in the 1960s and 1970s might be that media should not be allowed to define political priorities. In our image-oriented society, visibility is often equated with power. There are real limits, though, to defining what is meaningful as that which can be seen. We often imagine racism through its most spectacular forms: dead or damaged bodies, segregated facilities, or unbearable labor conditions. These are real enough, of course, but many forms of social injury are woven into the fabric of everyday life, and their very banality makes them hard to communicate through the surface of the television screen. Likewise, many of the things that progressive activists fight for do not televise well: the opportunity to do meaningful work, the freedom for communities and individuals to live where they choose, the right to control our own bodies, and the chance to learn. The archive of television news coverage of the Chicano civil rights activism teaches us a great deal about the cultural politics surrounding civil rights at a pivotal moment in US and world history. Its most important lesson, though, might be that what matters most in politics—as in life—often goes unrecorded.

Notes

My thanks to staff at the Vanderbilt Television News Archive, the Library of Congress, the Library of American Broadcasting, and the NBC News Archives for their invaluable assistance with this essay. Many thanks also to John Rowe, Inderpal Grewal, Laura Kang, Rafael Pérez-Torres, Ricardo Ortíz, Yolanda Padilla, Curtis Marez, Ricky T. Rodríguez, Elena Machado Sáez, Sarah Banet-Weiser, to the Minority Cultural Studies Group at the University of Maryland, and to my many wonderful colleagues, especially Kandice Chuh, David Wyatt, Peter Mallios, Kent Cartwright, Robert Levine, Sangeeta Ray, Mary Helen Washington, Ana Patricia Rodríguez, Zita Nunes, and Jonathan Auerbach.

1. For fuller accounts of this incident see Marguerite V. Marin, *Social Protest in an Urban Barrio: A Study of the Chicano Movement, 1966–1974* (Lanham, Md.: University Press of America, 1991), 165–69; Armando Navarro, *Mexican American Youth Organization: Avant-Garde of the Chicano Movement in Texas* (Austin: University of Texas Press, 1995), 65–66; Dial Torgerson, "Rumors Are Rife in Avalon Over Brown Beret Invasion," *Los Angeles Times*, August 31, 1972, sec. 1.

2. Sasha Torres, *Black, White, and in Color: Television and Black Civil Rights* (Princeton, N.J.: Princeton University Press, 2003); Gene Roberts and Hank Klibanoff, *The Race Beat: The Press, the Civil Rights Struggle, and the Awakening of a Nation* (New York: Knopf, 2006).

3. For more on the landmark Chicano Youth Liberation Conference, see Ernesto B. Vigil, *The Crusade for Justice: Chicano Militancy and the Government's War on Dissent* (Madison: University of Wisconsin Press, 1999). For general histories of the Chicano movement, see Rodolfo Acuña, *Occupied America: A History of Chicanos,* 7th ed. (Upper Saddle River, N.J.: Pearson Prentice Hall, 2011); George Mariscal, *Brown-Eyed Children of the Sun: Lessons from the Chicano Movement, 1965–1975* (Albuquerque: University of New Mexico Press, 2005); Carlos Munoz Jr., *Youth, Identity, Power: The Chicano Movement,* rev. ed. (New York: Verso, 2007); Francisco A. Rosales, *Chicano! The History of the Mexican American Civil Rights Movement* (Houston, Tex.: Arte Público Press, 1996).

4. *CBS Evening News,* CBS, August 31, 1972.

5. Ibid.

6. Ibid.

7. The television archive is problematic, as anyone who has spent time studying the medium can attest. Much of the programming of the 1940s and early 1950s is lost, and while things improved in the late 1950s after video-recording technology became available, even then preservation was spotty. To make matters worse, networks keep a tight grip on what they do have, despite the fact that their programming was transmitted on public airwaves. (Lawmakers could do a tremendous service to society if they required that broadcasters make their archives freely available for educational purposes as a condition of use.) In writing this essay, I consulted the Motion Picture, Broadcasting, and Recorded Sound Division at the Library of Congress, the Paley Center for Media, the UCLA Film and Television Archive, the Library of American Broadcasting, and the Vanderbilt Television News Archive, which has been recording the news every evening since August 5, 1968. Unless otherwise indicated, television broadcasts cited herein refer to material found in the Vanderbilt archive.

8. My thanks to the anonymous reader at *American Quarterly* who suggested this phrase and who made several other helpful suggestions.

9. Erik Barnouw, *Tube of Plenty: The Evolution of American Television,* 2d ed. (New York: Oxford University Press, 1990), 102–3.

10. Roberts and Klibanoff, *The Race Beat;* Torres, *Black, White, and in Color.*

11. Torres, *Black, White, and in Color,* 15. For a detailed analysis of how the national news intervened in racial politics at the local level, see Steven D. Classen, *Watching Jim Crow: The Struggles Over Mississippi TV, 1955–1969* (Durham, N.C.: Duke University Press, 2004).

12. Rosales, *Chicano!,* xiii. Sadly, we do not have many published reflections by Chicano/a activists on how they encountered African American civil rights activism and what it meant to them, although we do have general commentary on the subject. See Muñoz, *Youth, Identity, Power,* 66.

13. Maria Varela, "Time to Get Ready," January 6, 2007. I have a copy of this unpublished autobiographical essay in my possession.

14. Elizabeth Sutherland Martinez, *Letters from Mississippi* (New York: McGraw-Hill, 1965).

15. For an insightful study of the discourse of Latino upward mobility and its meanings for contemporary racial politics, see Arlene Dávila, *Latino Spin: Public Image and the Whitewashing of Race* (New York: New York University Press, 2008).

16. "Cast the First Stone," *Bell and Howell Close Up!,* ABC, September 27, 1960. The program is cited in Daniel Einstein, *Special Edition: A Guide to Network Television Documentary Series and Special News Reports, 1955–1979* (Metuchen, N.J.: Scarecrow, 1987), 95.

17. Michael Curtin, *Redeeming the Wasteland: Television Documentary and Cold War Politics* (New Brunswick, N.J.: Rutgers University Press, 1995), 60–91.

18. Gaye Tuchman, *Making News: A Study in the Construction of Reality* (New York: Free Press, 1978), 23.

19. Mary Pat Brady, *Extinct Lands, Temporal Geographies: Chicana Literature and the Urgency of Space* (Durham, N.C.: Duke University Press, 2002), 13–48.

20. Toni Morrison, *Playing in the Dark: Whiteness and the Literary Imagination* (Cambridge, Mass.: Harvard University Press, 1992), 6.

21. For more on Mexican American civil rights activism immediately before and after World War II, see Zaragosa Vargas, *Labor Rights Are Civil Rights: Mexican American Workers in Twentieth-Century America* (Princeton, N.J.: Princeton University Press, 2005); Mario T. García, *Memories of Chicano History: The Life and Narrative of*

Bert Corona (Berkeley: University of California Press, 1994); Mario T. García, *Mexican Americans: Leadership, Ideology, and Identity, 1930–1960* (New Haven, Conn.: Yale University Press, 1989); Vicki Ruíz, *Cannery Women, Cannery Lives: Mexican Women, Unionization, and the California Food Processing Industry, 1930–1950* (Albuquerque: University of New Mexico Press, 1987); Cynthia Orozco, *No Mexicans, Women, or Dogs Allowed: The Rise of the Mexican American Civil Rights Movement* (Austin: University of Texas Press, 2009). On social protest in the nineteenth century, see Kirsten Silva Gruesz, *Ambassadors of Culture: The Transamerican Origins of Latino Writing* (Princeton, N.J.: Princeton University Press, 2002).

22. Rosales, *Chicano!,* 104–5.
23. Patrick Carroll, *Felix Longoria's Wake: Bereavement, Racism, and the Rise of Mexican American Activism* (Austin: University of Texas Press, 2003).
24. Rosales, *Chicano!,* 108. See also the 2009 PBS documentary *A Class Apart,* which incidentally makes an excellent resource when teaching comparative racial formation and the law.
25. There is a large body of literature on César Chávez and the grape strike, including Jacques E. Levy, *Cesar Chavez: Autobiography of La Causa* (New York: Norton, 1975); Peter Matthiessen, *Sal Si Puedes (Escape If You Can): Cesar Chavez and the New American Revolution* (Berkeley: University of California Press, 2000); Margaret Eleanor Rose, "Women in the United Farm Workers: A Study of Chicana and Mexican Participation in a Labor Union, 1950–1980" (Ph.D. diss., University of California, Los Angeles, 1988); Susan Ferriss and Ricardo Sandoval, *The Fight in the Fields: Cesar Chavez and the Farmworkers Movement,* ed. Diana Hembree (New York: Harcourt Brace, 1997); Cesar Chavez, *An Organizer's Tale: Speeches,* ed. Ilan Stavans (New York: Penguin, 2008); Miriam Pawel, *The Union of Their Dreams: Power, Hope, and Struggle in Cesar Chavez's Farm Worker Movement* (New York: Bloomsbury Press, 2009).
26. Matthiessen, *Sal Si Puedes,* 127–28.
27. "Farmworkers Complete Their 300-Mile March from Delano to Sacramento, California," NBC, airdate unknown, http://nbcnewsarchives.com, Media ID#1070 BU96. The archive does not indicate when this report was aired, but the online description suggests that it was broadcast on the *Huntley-Brinkley Report* on Monday, April 11, 1966, one day after the conclusion of the march.
28. Todd Gitlin, *The Whole World Is Watching: Mass Media in the Making and Unmaking of the New Left,* 2d ed. (Berkeley: University of California Press, 2003), 3–4.

29. Ferriss and Sandoval, *The Fight in the Fields,* 58–60.
30. Levy, *Cesar Chavez,* 272.
31. NBC, March 10, 1968, http://nbcnewsarchives.com, Media ID 0186BURB.
32. Ferriss and Sandoval, *The Fight in the Fields,* 144.
33. Torres, *Black, White, and in Color,* 10. Torres borrows the phrase "the burden of liveness" from Jose Muñoz in order to name the imperative that television placed on blacks to give apparently authentic performances of minoritized suffering. She writes, "In the context of the civil rights movement, bearing 'the burden of liveness' required movement workers to produce arresting television images juxtaposing peaceful protest with physical suffering at the hands of violent segregationists." This is precisely what César Chávez did during his 1968 fast and repeatedly throughout his career, including in the 1988 fast that was to be one of his last major public protests.
34. According to one account, the United Farm Workers began using public concern about the safety of pesticides as a means of garnering support for the union in 1968. See Laura Pulido, *Environmentalism and Economic Justice: Two Chicano Struggles in the Southwest* (Tucson: University of Arizona Press, 1996), 85.
35. According to the Vanderbilt Television New Archive's searchable online database (http://tvnews.vanderbilt.edu/), Chávez's second high-profile fast was covered by ABC, CBS, and NBC on the evening of August 21, 1988. The labor leader's death was covered by all three networks on April 23, 1993, with additional coverage of his funeral on April 29.
36. Writing about the cultural politics of African American activism, Herman Gray uses the term "civil rights subjects" to describe "those black, largely middle-class benefactors who gained the most visibility as well as material and status rewards from the struggles and opportunities generated by the civil rights movement." Just as the television camera turned King into the face of the integration struggle, so too did the network news transform César Chávez into a Chicano civil rights subject, a public figure whose particular image came to represent Mexican Americans as a whole. See Herman Gray, "Remembering Civil Rights: Television, Memory, and the 1960s," in *The Revolution Wasn't Televised: Sixties Television and Social Conflict,* ed. Lynn Spigel and Michael Curtin (New York: Routledge, 1997), 353.
37. Todd Gitlin has commented on this phenomenon. Drawing on the work of Francesco Alberoni, he writes: "The modern person, lacking either roots in tradition or a powerfully present God, longs for contact with an idealized parent and identification with an idealized

self. But in a society formally committed to egalitarian values, he or she also wants to bring the idealized parent back down to human scale, to the scale of the *admirable.*" See Gitlin, *The Whole World Is Watching,* 147.

38. See Ferriss and Sandoval, *The Fight in the Fields,* 225–27.

39. In 1966 the National Farm Workers Association merged with the Agricultural Workers Organizing Committee to become the United Farm Workers.

40. For a groundbreaking collection of Dolores Huerta's writings, see Mario T. García, ed., *A Dolores Huerta Reader* (Albuquerque: University of New Mexico Press, 2008).

41. Ferriss and Sandoval, *The Fight in the Fields,* 225–27. See also Pawel, *The Union of Their Dreams.*

42. *ABC News,* ABC, June 3, 1969.

43. This failure was of course not limited to coverage of the Chicano movement. Television journalism is often criticized for its inability to give meaningful context to current events, which is one reason why public debate in the United States so frequently suffers from historical amnesia. Budget constraints, the need to cover multiple stories in a short time period, and above all the demand for high-impact visuals make it difficult for producers in the commercial news system to give anything but the most basic background. This reality proves particularly problematic in the case of a topic such as the Chicano movement, for research suggests that TV has the greatest influence on audience perception when viewers have little other exposure to the issue at hand. Since few viewers during the 1960s and 1970s were educated about Mexican American history, the mediocre coverage by the media may have proved especially influential. See Edwin Diamond, *The Tin Kazoo: Politics, Television, and the News* (Cambridge, Mass.: MIT Press, 1975). For a discussion of television's sway over uninformed audiences see Curtin, *Redeeming the Wasteland,* 195.

44. Armando Navarro claims that the more militant activists were often barrio youths who found in the Chicano movement an alternative to gang life. See Navarro, *Mexican American Youth Organization,* 60–61.

45. Torres, *Black, White, and in Color,* 89.

46. Ibid.

47. *CBS News,* CBS, August 31, 1970.

48. Ibid.

49. Ibid.

50. Ibid.

51. *ABC News,* ABC, April 28, 1970.

52. Ibid.

53. *NBC Nightly News,* NBC, June 15, 1971.

54. ABC News, ABC, August 1, 1972.

55. For information on this event and a thorough study of Chicano/a antiwar activism, see Lorena Oropeza, *¡Raza Sí! ¡Guerra No! Chicano Protest and Patriotism during the Viet Nam War Era* (Berkeley: University of California Press, 2005).

56. *NBC News,* NBC, August 30, 1970.

57. Ibid.

58. Ibid.

59. Aaron Doyle, *Arresting Images: Crime and Policing in Front of the Television Camera* (Toronto: University of Toronto Press, 2004), 38. For a deft commentary on how the Chicano Moratorium ignited "a Chicano public sphere over and against a national one," see Chon A. Noriega, *Shot in America: Television, the State, and the Rise of Chicano Cinema* (Minneapolis: University of Minnesota Press, 2000), xxix.

60. *NBC News,* NBC, August 30, 1970.

61. *NBC News,* NBC, August 31, 1970.

62. *NBC News,* NBC, July 6, 1970.

63. Ibid.

64. Navarro, *Mexican American Youth Organization,* 180–81.

65. *NBC News,* NBC, July 6, 1970.

66. Ibid.

67. Ibid. Perkins here articulates what Arlene Dávila argues is an ideologically driven contrast between African Americans as a troublesome minority and Latino/as as an exemplary one. In certain respects this comparison is not a new one: María Amparo Ruiz de Burton in her 1885 novel *The Squatter and the Don* relies on a narrative strategy of denigrating blackness in order to argue for the incorporation of the formerly Mexican citizens of the newly conquered US Southwest into a "white" America. However, as Dávila notes, this contrast is asserted with increasing frequency in order to deflect attention from the growing inequality produced over the last forty years by neoliberal policies. Just one month after Perkins made this remark on air, the barrio of East Los Angeles did indeed "explode" at the Chicano Moratorium, though more because of police aggression than because of Mexican American rage. See María Amparo Ruiz de Burton, *The Squatter and the Don* (New York: Modern Library, 2004).

68. *NBC News,* NBC, July 6, 1970.

69. Ibid.

70. *CBS Evening News,* CBS, May 8, 1978; *NBC News,* NBC, July 4, 1980.

71. Dávila makes this point when commenting on a May 2005 *Newsweek* article on the election of Los Angeles mayor Antonio Villaraigosa that was titled "How Hispanics Will Change America." She writes: "Are Latinos not part of that 'America' they are supposedly said to

change and affect? In other words, a Latino victory is celebrated, but the specter of foreignness remains, as Latinos are presented as a threat that could 'change our system.'" See Dávila, *Latino Spin,* p. 48.

72. Barnouw, *Tube of Plenty,* 332.

73. Lynn Spigel, *Make Room for TV: Television and the Family Ideal in Postwar America* (Chicago: University of Chicago Press, 1992), 1.

74. Barnouw, *Tube of Plenty,* 260–65.

75. Ibid., 346.

76. For a brilliant account of how Richard Nixon used white paranoia to rebuild the GOP, see Rick Perlstein, *Nixonland: The Rise of a President and the Fracturing of America* (New York: Scribner, 2008). For commentary on how television fit within this shifting political landscape, especially with respect to youth culture, see Aniko Bodroghkozy, *Groove Tube: Sixties Television and the Youth Rebellion* (Durham, N.C.: Duke University Press, 2001), 16.

77. The normative television viewer is often imagined as white, but evidence suggests that Mexican Americans were also influenced by network representations of the Chicano movement (and left politics more broadly) as menace. For example, Congressman Henry Gonzales of Texas garnered support from Anglos and from moderate Mexican Americans by contrasting himself with the supposed radicals seen on TV. On April 3, 1969, he gave what became in movement circles a notorious speech on the floor of Congress in which he denounced José Angel Gutiérrez and the volunteers of MAYO as "drawing fire from the deepest wellsprings of hate." Something similar happened in California when the struggle to incorporate East L.A. in the early 1970s was defeated by (among other things) fears that Chicano radicals would take over the machinery of city government. Such fears would likely not have had the traction they did had it not been for the paranoid perspective circulating even among Mexican American families that watched the evening news. For Congressman Gonzales's speech see "Race Hate," 91st Congress, 1st session, *Congressional Record* 115 (April 3, 1969): H 8590–8591. For more on the debate in East L.A. see Ernesto Chávez, *"¡Mi Raza Primero!" (My People First!): Nationalism, Identity, and Insurgency in the Chicano Movement in Los Angeles, 1966–1978* (Berkeley: University of California Press, 2002), 94–97.

78. *NBC News,* NBC, August 30, 1970.

7.

LEAN ON ME

Beyond Identity Politics

George Lipsitz

Once the victim's testimony is delivered, however, there is thereafter, forever, a witness somewhere: which is an irreducible inconvenience for the makers and shakers and accomplices of this world. These run together, in packs, and corroborate each other. They cannot bear the judgment in the eyes of the people whom they intend to hold in bondage forever, and who know more about them than their lovers.

—JAMES BALDWIN

In making the motion picture *Lean on Me* in 1989, director John Avildsen interrupted his *Karate Kid* series to turn his attention temporarily toward education. Defying skeptics who charged that he would probably keep making *Karate Kid* films until someone drove a stake through his heart, the director of *Rocky* presented a depiction of the adventures of an inner-city high school principal in a film that offered viewers a cross between *To Sir with Love* and *The Terminator.* Television and newspaper advertisements for *Lean on Me* boasted that the film told the story of a "real life" hero—Joe Clark, the African American principal of Eastside High School in Paterson, New Jersey. But Joe Clark is no hero. He exemplifies a new kind of cowardice, not a new kind of heroism. By celebrating his actions, this film expresses nothing that is new, just a very old and very destructive form of racism.

I have a personal connection to this film and to the situations it depicts. I grew up in Paterson and attended Eastside High School, graduating in 1964. Even then, Paterson was a dying industrial

city plagued by high rates of poverty and unemployment. Half my high school class dropped out before graduation; five of the minority and white working-class students who graduated were killed in the Vietnam War. During the summer after our graduation, frustrated and angry black youths staged a civil insurrection in Paterson, setting fire to ghetto buildings and assaulting police officers and civilians with rocks, bottles, and sniper fire. A feature story in the *New York Times* commenting on the disturbance described Paterson as "a burned out inferno of crippled factories and wasted lives."

Growing up in Paterson during those years offered a young person an education inside and outside of the classroom. In a school whose population was divided among whites, blacks, and Puerto Ricans, racial tensions permeated every interaction. We knew that no matter what group we belonged to, somebody hated us. People could get jumped, robbed, and maybe even killed simply for being in the wrong place at the wrong time. Yet we also learned to deal with differences, to make friends with people from all backgrounds, to recognize the things we had in common and the things that divided us.

Ten percent of my class went on to college, mostly those who came from comfortable middle-class homes like my own. We had known all our lives that we would get college educations. Regardless of how hard we worked or how well or poorly we performed as students, our parents' aspirations, intentions, and material support would see to it that we went to college somewhere. At the same time, most of our classmates knew that for them higher education was out of the question, that no matter how hard they worked or how well they performed in school, their futures almost certainly lay in low-wage jobs in Paterson's declining industrial sector. Soon, even those jobs disappeared. My classmates and I went to school in the same building and seemed to receive the same education, but there was a big difference between those whose class and race made it seem natural and necessary to take college prep courses, and those channeled into business and vocational tracks who faced, at best, a future of low-paid labor.

During the years that I attended Eastside, my father served as the principal of Central High, a school with an even larger minority population and dropout rate than Eastside's at that time. My father was a gentle and generous man who cared deeply about the students in his school. He could be a strict disciplinarian when he had to be, but he knew that a positive self-image and a sense of social connection could motivate students more effectively and more permanently than punishment. He befriended the students in his school who had behavior problems, learning their names and inquiring about their interests. He helped them with personal and family problems and worked tirelessly to help them secure employment so they could experience the responsibilities, respect, and sense of purpose that a job can bring to a young person. He turned the schools he ran into community centers, involved parents in the educational process, and fashioned after-school and evening programs that spoke to the broader needs of the neighborhood and the city.

My father and my mother had both attended Paterson's public schools in their childhood years. As children of immigrant parents they felt that they owed a great debt to the United States for many reasons, but most of all because of the education they received and the ways in which it encouraged, nurtured, and sustained their growth as critical, contemplative, and creative people and citizens. They knew that had their families remained in Europe, they would certainly have been sent to Hitler's concentration camps. That realization left them with a strong sense of social justice and an empathy for all oppressed people,

not just their fellow Jews. My mother and father became teachers to repay the debt they felt they owed to this country, to give to others the great gifts that they had received. After my father died from a heart attack at the age of forty-nine during my senior year in high school in 1964, my family remained involved in public education in Paterson. My sister and my mother both taught at Eastside at different times during the 1960s and 1970s and established reputations as the kind of demanding and dedicated instructors that students remember long after their school years have been completed. Over the years, I have learned a great deal from them about what it means to try to offer a quality education in an inner-city school. My father, my mother, my sister, and many of their colleagues and friends have devoted much of their lives to that effort. I know how hard a job they have, how much patience and love it takes to try to neutralize the effects of poverty and racism, even temporarily. I know as well that no amount of good intentions, no mastery of teaching techniques, and no degree of effort by individual educators can alter meaningfully the fundamentally unequal distribution of resources and opportunities in this society.

Neither the true history of Paterson's economic decline nor the actual conditions facing its educators appear in Lean on Me. Instead, the director of Rocky and The Karate Kid presents us with another kind of fairy tale, a story about how serious social problems can be solved simply by reciting rules, how challenges to public order by women and members of aggrieved racial minorities can be quelled by male heroes strong enough and determined enough to bully and intimidate their opponents. This glorification of a small-time demagogue and grandstander ignores the structural problems facing cities like Paterson, the realities of unequal funding for schools, and the health and nutrition problems of more and more children growing up in poverty.

Joe Clark rose to public prominence during the mid-1980s as part of a coordinated campaign by neoconservatives to hide from the consequences of their own actions in cutting social programs and educational opportunities during the Reagan years. A favorite of right-wing foundations and their educational spokesperson William Bennett, Clark blamed liberals and the civil rights movement for the sorry state of inner-city schools. He offered his own record as an administrator who ruled with an iron hand as a model for improving the schools without spending any more money on education. He called Reverend Jesse Jackson "a constipated maggot," and claimed that young black men were "barbarians who are out of control."[1] He became famous among conservatives because he patrolled Eastside High School carrying a baseball bat and a bullhorn, behavior that titillated neoconservative politicians and public relations flacks with the dream of enlisting blacks (whom they had already demonized as brutal) in a campaign of counterinsurgency against unruly inner-city minority youths. Although Clark has never developed any following in, or connection with, African American communities, his ability to enact white fantasies have made him a favorite among what James Baldwin called "the makers and shakers and accomplices of this world."

Lean on Me opens with a montage that portrays the predominately black students and staff of Eastside High School as lazy, licentious, boisterous, and brutal. With stereotypical caricatures that hearken back to nineteenth-century minstrel shows and D. W. Griffith's 1915 white supremacist film, *Birth of a Nation,* Avildsen raises the specter of out-of-control black bodies to set the stage for his authoritarian black hero. *Lean on Me* glamorizes the way Clark resorts to physical intimidation and verbal abuse to make teachers, parents, and students knuckle under to law and order as he defines them. The film attributes the demise of discipline in Eastside High School to the control over school policy won by black female parents and teachers as a result of the civil rights movement of the 1960s. Like *Birth of a Nation,* it summons up authoritarian patriarchal power as the necessary antidote to a broad range of misbehavior by blacks, ranging from lascivious attacks on white women to the laziness of public employees, from the uninhibited speech and body movements of black teenagers to brutal assaults on white authority figures and on "innocent" fellow blacks. Fusing elements of previous high school "disruption" films with the theme of the lone vigilante, Avildsen's motion picture displays no awareness of the aspirations,

experiences, or feelings of students, parents, and teachers, much less any acknowledgment of the actual social conditions they confront.

As principal of Eastside High School, Clark illegally expelled large numbers of students from school on the grounds that he viewed them as troublemakers. He fueled fights between teacher and parent factions and—most important for his cinematic image— roamed the halls of his school carrying a baseball bat in order to threaten unruly students. These actions won praise from neoconservative pundits, but they did nothing to solve the educational problems facing the school and its students. Clark failed to lower the dropout rate, to improve academic performance, or to raise scores on standardized tests. Instead, his incessant self-promotion exacted serious costs on the school, which eventually became clear even to his patrons in conservative foundations.

Clark took a "sick leave" from his $65,000 a year principal's job so that he could continue to collect his salary while he toured the country giving lectures to conservative groups at $7,000 per appearance. He was in Los Angeles preparing to appear on the Arsenio Hall show when a musical act hired for an Eastside High School assembly featured several G-string clad male dancers. Clark declared himself innocent of any failure to supervise his school, blaming the whole affair on "the essence of some kind of surreptitious act" and in the process offering his students a negative lesson in avoiding responsibility for one's actions.[2] He sought appointment to an unexpired term on the Board of Freeholders in Essex County (about ten miles from Paterson), explaining that he needed experience in an administrative office as preparation for running for national office; "I'm not going to be a Jesse Jackson," he declared, referring to questions about the civil rights leader's lack of administrative experience during his 1984 and 1988 campaigns for the presidency. Clark turned his leave of absence into an extended audition for more support from conservative foundations, avoiding the actual work of running a school so that he could pontificate about education and pursue more lucrative and less taxing employment as a full-time speaker.

When his year on leave expired, Clark retired from his post. He filed a workman's compensation claim against the Board of Education, charging that his endocarditis (deterioration of the aortic valve) had been caused by the board's lack of appreciation of his efforts. Clark vowed that the school district "will pay for the damage they inflicted upon my mortal soul."[3] Conservative foundations are not usually supportive of government workers who defy their superiors, expect taxpayers to support them during sick leaves while they rake in thousands of dollars lecturing about their favorite political causes, and then file highly dubious workman's compensation claims. Nevertheless, these foundations continued to embrace Clark because of his utility to their efforts to increase the possessive investment in whiteness.

The Joe Clark portrayed in *Lean on Me* gave white audiences one more chance to blame the victim, one more opportunity to believe that the anguish in African American ghettos stems from the underdeveloped character of the poor rather than from routine and systematic inequality in resources and opportunities. Since 1973, when President Nixon abandoned public housing and diverted War on Poverty funds into revenue-sharing schemes designed to lower local taxes on real estate, this country has been systematically exacerbating the crises facing the urban underclass. The value of grants given through the Aid to Dependent Children program fell by one-third from 1969 to 1985 when inflation is taken into account. The 1981 Deficit Reduction Act took away from the poor one dollar of benefits for every dollar earned. Critics charged that these policies would have disastrous effects on poor families and their children, and consequently on the nation's future. Time has shown these critics to be correct.

At the same time, federal policies have fueled a spending spree by and for the rich. Defense boondoggles, insider trading, unregulated speculative schemes, hostile takeovers, and profiteering from bad loans have wreaked havoc in the US economy over the past decades. Yet the taxpayer has always been there to pick up the tab, protecting the savings-and-loan bandits and other corporate looters from the consequences of their own actions. How does a country that has spent most of the past twenty years exploiting its poor children in order to feed the greed of the rich justify itself to itself? How do politicians and public relations flacks who promise to return us to family values explain their participation in the construction of a casino economy that brings an apocalypse on the installment plan to inner-city families? The answer to both questions is to blame the victims, to channel middle class fears into a sadistic and vindictive crusade that racializes the poor and then blames them for their powerlessness.

The neoconservatism of our time has not only widened the gap between rich and poor, between whites and communities of color, but it has also encouraged the growth of a vigilante mentality, as violent and sadistic as the crimes it purports to oppose. From Bernhard Goetz's shooting of four youths on a New York subway car to the Philadelphia Police Department's bombing of MOVE headquarters to the Los Angeles police roundups of fourteen-year-olds in the name of stopping gang violence, we seem to have convinced ourselves that once we have identified our enemies we no longer need to observe the due process of law. Most often invoked in the name of fighting criminality, this attitude instead elevates a criminal mentality to the front lines of social policy. It is an attitude rooted in resentment and fear, exploited by law-and-order politicians and the makers of vigilante films alike.

The problem with this attitude is that it only works as a way to treat someone else—none of us would allow ourselves to be treated in that fashion. Thus, Joe Clark's belittling and humiliating of his students won audience approval because audiences believed that such treatment would be legitimate and might work against the faceless "others" in the ghetto that have been created for us by the media. If they were to think of those students as their own children, they would never allow anyone to treat them in that fashion. Indeed, the conservative pundits who fawned over Clark did not line up to send their own children to Eastside High School. Yet, as we have seen over and over again, once the erosion of civil liberties and the diminution of human dignity gets started, it does not stop with its original victims. As Jesse Jackson warns, there is no way we can hold another person down in the dirt without climbing into the dirt ourselves.

In this context, it is not hard to see why there is a major motion picture about Joe Clark—an honor denied to Septima Clark, Reverend Buck Jones, Paul Robeson, Fannie Lou Hamer, Ella Baker, and other courageous fighters for the African American community. Hollywood does not believe that white American audiences want to see black heroes who love their own communities and struggle to win resources for them. In Hollywood, there is no room for adult blacks operating in their own interests, only for black sidekicks or terrified blacks in need of white protection. The prototypical example was Alan Parker's *Mississippi Burning,* which presented the 1964 civil rights struggle in Mississippi as if black people played only the role of passive victims. From *Birth of a Nation* to *Gone with the Wind,* from *Lean on Me* to *Driving Miss Daisy,* Hollywood has always preferred its faithful black servants. Joe Clark is only the latest in long line of smiling sycophants on- and off-screen, reassuring white America that it will never have to wake up to its racial record and face its responsibilities.

Yet *Lean on Me* adds a new and frightening aspect to this traditional scenario. Clark's purported heroism stems from no positive accomplishment. He does not help his own students nor does he serve as a role model for other educators. His sole function is to fuel the spite, resentment, and rage of the privileged. His mass-mediated image maintains the myth that counterinsurgency will prevail when justice does not, that schools can succeed by becoming prisons—or more precisely, that prisons are more important to society than schools. In keeping with the neoconservative contempt for public education, Clark brings the model of the military and the penitentiary to urban education. It does not matter to his admirers that such behavior cannot develop the intellectual and personal resources necessary for a lifetime of citizenship and work; what does matter is that it imposes a dictatorial and authoritarian model on the poor and presents people who have problems *as* problems.

Joe Clark is not the problem, nor does his perspective bear any relation to a solution. Once he has exhausted his usefulness to those in power he will be shoved aside, like so many before him. What will remain long after Joe Clark has been forgotten, however, are the problems of the inner-city schools, and the sadism in search of a story fueled by these kinds of images. As film viewers, we need to ask ourselves how our imaginations are being colonized, and for what ends. Perhaps one cannot really blame filmmakers for opportunistically exploiting the racial hatreds and social vindictiveness of the motion picture audience. Hollywood filmmakers are in business to make money, and they have never hidden their willingness to exploit the darkest recesses of the human character to turn a profit for their investors. But at least they could have given this execrable film an appropriate title. In its internal message and social mission, it is not so much *Lean on Me* as *Step on Them.*

None of this is to deny the crippling effects of crime in our society, most of all on the inner city and its inhabitants. Nor is it to assert the irrelevance of discipline, order, self-control, and character for any individual or group. It is only to argue against simplistic and self-serving diagnoses of deep and complex social problems. Locating the origins of white anxieties in the alleged character deficiencies of people from aggrieved racial groups evades an honest engagement with the materialism, selfishness, and predatory competitiveness of *all* social groups in the wake of the changes that neoconservative economics and politics have brought. Nearly every reputable scholarly study shows that unemployment, inferior educational opportunities, and social inequalities are directly linked to increases in crime. People of color have simply been the ones hardest hit by these structural transformations. Declining numbers of blue collar jobs, capital flight, discrimination by employers in the expanding retail sector of the economy, locating new businesses in suburban locations, residential segregation, and cutbacks in social programs and government employment have all contributed to increased rates of minority unemployment. For example, unemployment among African American youths quadrupled between 1961 and 1986, while white youth unemployment remained static.

It is understandable that fear of crime makes many people wish to respond with a strong show of force against lawbreakers. But force can create as well as restrain criminality. It can teach people that force is the accepted way of controlling others, especially if it is applied indiscriminately against whole populations. Studies show that exposure to boot-camp correctional facilities structured around humiliating disciplinary routines makes inmates more rather than less aggressive. Force is even more counterproductive when used against law-abiding citizens—the vast majority of people in poor and minority communities. Nearly 5 percent of African Americans report that they have been unjustly beaten by police officers, and African Americans are more than nine times as likely to die at the hands of police officers than are whites. Highly publicized cases in the 1990s like the Rodney King beating in Los Angeles and the killing of Jonny Gammage by police officers in Pittsburgh convince a large proportion of minority observers (and many who are not minorities as well) that a code of silence protects police officers from the consequences of their actions against members of aggrieved communities. Of the nearly 47,000 police brutality cases reported to the federal Department of Justice between 1986 and 1992 (not including complaints to municipal, county, and state agencies), only 15,000 were investigated, and only 128 led to prosecution of any kind. Most important, the most sophisticated social scientific studies show that while neither poverty nor racial discrimination alone *cause* crime, aggressive acts of violence are more likely to emanate from people under conditions of poverty, racial discrimination, and inequality. As Judith and Peter Blau observed nearly twenty years ago, "[A]ggressive acts of violence seem to result not so much from lack of advantages as from being taken advantage of."[4]

Fighting crime effectively entails addressing its constituent causes, not indulging in the counterproductive escapism, sermonizing, and muscle flexing advanced in films like *Lean on Me*. Yet while we are waiting for the broad structural solutions that we need, we still must address issues of individual morality, personal accountability, and disrespect for law and order. I propose that we start by strictly enforcing the laws that ban discrimination in housing and hiring, regulate environmental pollution and unsafe working conditions, and guarantee minimum wages, due process, and equal protection of the law to all citizens. In that vein, I suggest swift and certain punishment meted out against one individual who flaunted the

law brazenly, who deliberately obstructed justice, and who denied citizens the protections guaranteed to them in the Constitution. In his book *The Color Line,* the great historian John Hope Franklin describes the actions of this individual clearly. Appointed to a post in the Department of Education by the president of the United States, this person refused to investigate complaints about racial and gender discrimination, forcing the plaintiffs to ask that he be placed in contempt of court for his refusal to do what the law required him to do. When asked at a hearing if he was violating the time frames established for civil rights enforcement in *Adams v. Bell,* if he was violating them "on all occasions" and violating them directly on complaints "most of the time" or at least "half of the time," this bureaucrat answered, "That's right." When asked if "meanwhile you are violating a court order rather grievously, aren't you?" he answered yes.

On the strength of this record, this individual was promoted to chair the Equal Employment Opportunity Commission. In the first year at that job, the time needed to process complaints went from five months to nine months. The backlog of unanswered complaints went from 31,000 at the time of his appointment to 61,686 complaints four years later. This miserable performance earned him an appointment to a federal judgeship, where in one case, he refused to recuse himself from a dispute that involved the direct financial interests of his personal and professional patron, instead issuing a ruling that vacated a judgment of $10.4 million against his patron's family-owned business.[5] Perhaps readers can help me locate this malefactor and bring him to justice. His name is Clarence Thomas.

Clarence Thomas and Joe Clark prove that not all white supremacists are white, that white supremacist policies can be pursued by people from all backgrounds. This should come as no surprise; it is the way power works. No oppressed group in history has ever been immune to the opportunism of individuals who desire to distance themselves from the stigma associated with their oppression. At the same time, if not all white supremacists are white, all whites do not have to be white supremacists.

Just as Joe Clark's blackness did not prevent him from acting on behalf of white supremacy, a white scholar named George Rawick made his life's work exposing and attacking the possessive investment in whiteness. The narrator of Chester Himes's 1940s novel, *If He Hollers Let Him Go,* reflects on the range of identities open to white people when he ruminates on "how you could take two guys from the same place" and "one would carry his whiteness like a loaded stick, ready to bop everybody else in the head with it; and the other guy would just simply be white as if he didn't have anything to do with it and let it go at that."[6] Much of my education about the role whites can play in antiracist activity came from Rawick, an irascible and exasperating individual with many shortcomings and an assortment of personal problems who got one thing absolutely right. He was white man who knew where he stood in respect to racism. Through his activism and his scholarship he battled white supremacy, not solely out of sympathy for others but out of a sense of social justice and self-respect. The truths that appear in his scholarly writings will never make it onto the big screens of Hollywood, but they have something important to teach us about the role whites can play in fighting against white supremacy.

Born in Brooklyn in 1929, Rawick went to Erasmus Hall High School, where one of his acquaintances was Al Davis, who later became famous for his temper tantrums, paranoia, and indifference to public opinion as the owner of the Oakland Raiders football team. Many of Rawick's friends observed that he often displayed social skills similar to those of his high school classmate. He fought with everyone he knew at one time or another, even his best friends. He could be obstinate, irritating, and rude. He could also be flexible, considerate, and caring. He once described himself as a descendant of radical rabbis and gun-running gangsters, and his professional demeanor displayed evidence of both sensibilities.

Educated in and out of school by trade-union militants, Rawick attended Oberlin College in Ohio after graduating from high school in the mid-1940s. He traveled by train to Ohio, carrying with him radical pamphlets and wearing a zoot suit, fashionable by Brooklyn standards but an outfit that provoked considerable consternation in Ohio. Rawick went on to do graduate work at the University of Wisconsin and

the University of Chicago, but he remained committed to political work through his involvement with a variety of left-wing splinter groups. Rawick's doctoral research examined New Deal programs aimed at youth, but he became an expert on oral history when the civil rights movement erupted. He realized that his many years of study and critique of US capitalism had left him completely unprepared for the mass mobilization by African Americans and their allies, and consequently he felt compelled to explore other kinds of information and evidence. Moreover, he realized that his formal education had taught him little about the history of racism.

In 1964, C.L.R. James asked Rawick if any materials existed portraying slavery in the United States from the slaves' point of view. Because of his research on the New Deal, Rawick knew about the Works Progress Administration (WPA) slave narratives—transcriptions of interviews with elderly blacks conducted during the 1930s, probing their memories of slavery. His search led him to microfilm records in the Library of Congress, which provided the raw material for a seventeen-volume series that Rawick got Greenwood Press to publish along with an introductory volume of his own, *From Sundown to Sunup,* which explained the significance of the collection. In the first six chapters of his book, Rawick presents an extraordinary history and interpretation of the activity of slaves, demonstrating the dialectical interplay between accommodation and resistance that characterized their existence. The final two chapters lay out an argument about the causes, functions, and contradictions of white racism based on the centrality of slavery to the history of all people in the United States.

Rawick described how "racism took its strongest hold among those people who most thoroughly participated in the new, revolutionary developments of the modern world." He explained how coalitions between white and black workers foundered, not just because of the material advantages that racial segregation brought to whites, but because racism provided an outlet for all the repressed anguish and frustration that workers felt from the transformation from preindustrial to industrial society. He explained that white workers created a debased image of African Americans that filled real needs for them; blacks became a locus of both contempt and envy onto which whites projected their own repressed desires for pleasure and unrestrained free expression. Rawick showed how working-class racism never existed alone, how it emerged out of the hardships and self-hatred imposed on white workers by the humiliating subordinations of class.[7]

I first encountered Rawick in the late 1970s when I was finishing my own dissertation at the University of Wisconsin and working under his supervision as a teaching assistant at the University of Missouri–St. Louis. He suffered from a variety of ailments at the time, including diabetes, and his health was further damaged by his refusal to take proper medication or to attend to other measures necessary to protect his well-being. He was prone to mood shifts and long periods of depression. I saw him give some of the best and some of the worst lectures I ever heard during those two years. Once he placed the War of 1812 in the wrong century (not an easy mistake to make) and depicted it as a conflict between competing approaches to exterminating Native Americans (not necessarily a bad idea, but a nuance that had escaped many previous investigators and that conflicted with nearly all the available evidence). When he completed that lecture he approached me in the back of the hall and asked, "How crazy was that?" I had to admit it was pretty crazy.

When Rawick felt healthy, he came through with well-crafted, entertaining, carefully researched lectures replete with brilliant insights and observations. I noticed that these occasions often depended upon the makeup of his audience. When his listeners included white working-class students or African Americans of any background he seemed to have a special understanding of their lives, and to feel a special compulsion to reach them; he became a well-organized, scintillating lecturer capable of connecting the most complicated abstractions to vivid and unforgettable illustrative anecdotes. For me, his examples were always the best part, because they displayed a seemingly limitless understanding of, and empathy with, the joys and sorrows of working-class life.

George Rawick's lectures and the long conversations that always followed them provided me with an extraordinary education about social identities and social power. They made me aware of the power of conversation and the importance of the specific and the concrete, the legitimacy of personal stories as a way of understanding the world. From them I learned about a vast range of events and ideas, about the contours and contradictions of social movements ranging from the nineteenth-century Knights of Labor to the Missouri sharecroppers' strikes of the late 1930s, from the sectarian Left of the 1940s to the to the countercultures and antiwar mobilizations of the New Left of the 1960s. He told me about demonstrating against the Korean War in 1950 in New York with Bayard Rustin and David Dellinger, about picketing the US embassy during an antiwar demonstration in London in 1967 with Allen Ginsberg and Mick Jagger. It got to the point where I half expected him to come up with a personal memory of everyone he analyzed, including Terence Powderly and Karl Marx. He had an enormous network of friends and associates with whom he kept in constant touch. They comprised a "who's who" of radical politics; so much so that once when he was running out of money, he decided not to pay his phone bill because he reasoned that the FBI would not tolerate losing the opportunity to eavesdrop on his conversations and consequently would prevent the phone company from discontinuing his service. He could never prove it, but his continued access to telephone service seemed to indicate that he was correct.

Rawick understood that social struggle begins with who people really are, not who we would like them to be; that political contestation takes multiple and varied forms, ranging from religious rituals to popular culture; and that struggle on the factory floor has always been connected to and dependent on struggles in other sites—on plantations and Native American reservations, on street corners and country roads, in high-tech laboratories and libraries. Most important, he understood the connections between the possessive investment in whiteness and the contradictions of the social movements of his time.

Growing up in an ethnic, immigrant working-class neighborhood during the 1930s gave George Rawick firsthand experience with social movements. During that decade the Great Depression overwhelmed the resources of traditional ethnic organizations such as fraternal orders, burial societies, and credit circles that linked ethnic identities to economic interests. The collapse of ethnic institutions came at a time when chain stores and mass marketing created new communities of consumers, when automated production methods broke down skill monopolies among ethnic groups and encouraged the concentration of diverse groups of unskilled and semiskilled workers in common workplaces, and when the emergence of mass organizing drives by the Congress of Industrial Organization (CIO) drew young workers into what historian Lizabeth Cohen calls "a culture of unity."[8] Simultaneously, the popular front activities of the Communist Party, the cultural programs of the New Deal, and writings by ethnic activists and journalists including Louis Adamic, Langston Hughes, and Jack Conroy emphasized the multicultural origins of the United States. The culture of the 1930s glorified the "common man" and changed the reigning image of the immigrant from the unwanted alien banned by the 1924 Immigration Act into a redemptive outsider who had become American by choice and therefore personified the nation's true spirit. Fiorello La Guardia in New York and Anton Cermak in Chicago attained the office of mayor by pulling together interethnic electoral coalitions that celebrated their diversity. When Cermak's patrician opponent bragged about being part of a family that came over on the Mayflower and implied that his second-generation Czech immigrant opponent (nicknamed "Pushcart Tony") was unfit for high office, Cermak responded that his family might not have come over on the Mayflower, but they got here as fast as they could.[9]

The 1930s' "culture of unity" broke down ethnic antagonisms among European Americans and forged a common identity that grew out of mass mobilizations on factory floors and city streets. Participants in the social movements of the 1930s sought and secured real institutional resources to replace the exhausted and inadequate ethnic self-help structures that had let them down when the Depression came. The culture of unity won bargaining recognition for industrial workers in mass-production industries, but also social security pensions and survivors' benefits, federally subsidized home loans, National Labor Relations Board protection for collective bargaining, federal responsibility for welfare, and other direct social benefits. These resources from the state made European Americans less dependent upon separate ethnic identities, and they helped create the standard of living, the suburban neighborhoods, the workplace opportunities, and the educational subsidies that enabled the children and grandchildren of immigrants to become middle class and to blend together into a "white" identity. Earlier in this book I have pointed out at great length the disastrous consequences that ensued from the ways in which these gains excluded communities of color and created a possessive investment in whiteness, but the gains themselves, the collective struggle for them, and the institutions and resources they provided help explain how unity might be constructed among members of diverse groups.

Although the victories secured by the culture of unity disproportionately benefited whites, the coalitions of the 1930s did cut across color lines. As James Baldwin recalled in 1976, "[I]n a way, we were all niggers in the thirties. I do not know if that really made us more friendly with each other—at bottom, I doubt that, for more would remain of that friendliness today—but it was harder then, and riskier to attempt a separate peace, and benign neglect was not among our possibilities."[10] The perception that a separate peace was dangerous made all the difference in key campaigns in crucial industries for the CIO, as a temporary alliance across racial lines won unprecedented victories. Unfortunately, not all parts of the coalition reaped the fruits of victory to an equal degree.

The CIO needed the cooperation and participation of African American, Mexican American, and Asian American workers to organize mass-production industries, in part because the same discriminatory practices that relegated those groups to dirty, unpleasant jobs like foundry work also gave them key roles in production: if the foundry shuts down, the factory cannot run. Historians Robin D. G. Kelley and Vicki Ruiz (among others) present detailed descriptions of the importance of black workers to the organization of the CIO in Alabama and the centrality of Chicanas to organization in the canning industry on the West Coast.[11]

Yet postwar opportunities available to whites separated their interests from those of communities of color. In his provocative and enlightening book *Blackface/White Noise,* Michael Rogin presents an important anecdote that illuminates this general process. He describes a predominately Jewish group of war veterans who participated in a cooperative housing development in the Philadelphia suburb of Abington Township. That area had previously been restricted to white Christians by restrictive covenants, but under pressure from the veterans, the new development broke the local barriers against Jewish residency. Yet while experiencing ethnic inclusion, these same veterans practiced racial exclusion, appeasing the anxiety of their new Christian neighbors by agreeing not to open their development to blacks. "We wanted to let Negroes in—they're veterans too," an organizer of the cooperative confessed, "but we've been advised that mortgage investors, unfortunately, will not take Negroes in a mixed project." When some veterans and Jewish activists objected to this bargain, the cooperative's representative stood firm, explaining that "only after every possibility was exhausted did we reluctantly arrive at the conclusion that we must have a 'white' community if we were to have any at all."[12]

Rogin's anecdote encapsulates the process of ethnic inclusion by racial exclusion that transformed the "culture of unity" of the 1930s into the social democratic version of the possessive investment in whiteness during the 1940s, 1950s, and 1960s. Many white immigrants and their descendants developed especially powerful attachments to whiteness because of the ways in which various Americanization programs forced them to assimilate by surrendering all aspects of their own ethnic organization and identification. As Patricia Williams explains, "Sometimes I wonder how many of our present cultural clashes are the left-over traces of the immigrant wars of the last century and the beginning of this one, how much of our reemerging jingoism is the scar that marks the place where Italian kids were mocked for being too dark-skinned, where Jewish kids were taunted for being Jewish, where poor Irish rushed to hang lace curtains at the window as the first act of climbing the ladder up from social scorn, where Chinese kids were tortured for not speaking good English."[13]

Yet shared experiences in social movements of the 1930s and a lingering concern for social justice helped connect some whites to the civil rights movement of the 1950s and 1960s in ways that called whiteness into question. George Rawick was one of those whites. He later told an interviewer that the politics of the Old Left were destroyed by the suddenness of the civil rights movement's successes. "No one anticipated it," he remembered. "I was fundamentally a racist because I had not thought about it and was challenged by it. Somehow I was convinced that the problem was me and I had to resolve the contradiction."[14]

Reasoning that the fact of exploitation was more important than the identity of the victim, Rawick threw himself into antiracist work in the 1950s and 1960s in both his activism and his academic work. Because he had been part of labor and civil rights groups with black leaders, it was easier for him to envision antiracist coalitions based on what he called the self-activity—the things people do by and for themselves in the face of repressive power—and social analysis of people of color themselves, and to reject white paternalistic approaches, which all too often saw racism as a symptom of broader social problems rather than an issue in its own right. His experiences with the slave narratives and his careful reading of Du Bois gave him an advantage over other theorists of whiteness, because he drew upon the sophisticated version of "white studies" developed out of necessity by blacks.

Rawick wrote *From Sundown to Sunup* to reveal the connections between contemporary self-activity among African Americans and the rivers of resistance that could be traced back to the days of slavery. His book not only helped explain the self-activity of the civil rights movement, but also revealed the importance of work as a crucible for revolt, and illuminated the important lessons that could be learned by all workers from the forms of resistance undertaken by slaves to resist their subordination. He managed an incredibly difficult task—to write about oppression without obscuring resistance, and to write about resistance while acknowledging the terrible price that people pay for not having power. In his concluding chapters, he analyzed how and why racism functions in working-class life, how it enables individuals to externalize elements of self-hatred and self-loathing into contempt and fear of others.

Rawick thought his work was over when his introduction and the first seventeen volumes of the slave narratives came out, but during a speaking engagement at Tougaloo College outside Jackson, Mississippi, a friend suggested that they look in the Mississippi state archives to see if they contained any slave narratives not included in the Library of Congress collection. Five volumes emerged from the search in the Mississippi archives, and Rawick launched an inquiry into similar caches in other libraries and archives in Alabama, Missouri, Indiana, and Oklahoma. He immersed himself in the stories told by ordinary people about the ways in which broad structural forces made their presence felt in everyday life. Today libraries all over the country contain dozens of volumes of WPA-collected narratives listed under the title, *The American Slave: A Composite Autobiography.*

Rawick never sought recognition from the main credentialing institutions of our society. No professional honor would ever have pleased him as much as a good conversation with a young worker. A story he often told about himself illustrates the depth of his feeling. Shortly after *From Sundown to Sunup* was published, Rawick boarded a bus in Detroit. To his amazement and delight he noticed a young black worker carrying a copy of his book. At the next stop, two more passengers got on the bus, each carrying a copy of the book. Figuring that this was a trend, he tried to calculate how many thousands of copies the book was selling in Detroit if every busload of passengers represented three copies. When the next stop produced a fourth passenger, with a fourth copy of the book, he began composing remarks for the mass conference of revolutionary workers that he was sure would follow from the success of the book. It was only when he could no longer contain his curiosity and he asked one man carrying the book that Rawick found out he had stumbled onto a black history study group carrying that week's assigned reading. Rawick told the story with self-deprecating humor, but I have always found it significant that the possibility of rank-and-file workers picking up his book meant more to George than all the laudatory reviews and extensive academic sales—indeed, it would have meant more to him than a Pulitzer Prize or a National Book Award.

Rawick also kept himself alert for the hidden possibilities of struggle in even the most conventional arenas. He once lived across the hall from St. Louis Cardinals football players MacArthur Lane and Ernie McMillan. They became symbols for him of the working class, while their boss, Cardinals owner Bill Bidwill, came to represent management. Rawick could describe all the dynamics of the class struggle through the relationship between Bidwill and his players; for him it was another episode in the history of industrial capitalism. When Bidwill turned his factory into a runaway shop and moved the team to Phoenix, following so many other St. Louis industries to the Sun Belt, Rawick was ready with the appropriate critique of management for its squandering of social possibilities. Because of his stories, the whole history of the working class and its connections across racial lines became accessible and tangible to me in new ways; I began to see patterns for the first time.

Of course, Rawick's best gift to all of us has been his writing; not just the slave narratives and *From Sundown to Sunup,* but decades of articles like the important one on self-activity in an early issue of *Radical America* and several written under pseudonyms for obscure leftist journals. They all evidence Rawick's abiding faith in the ingenuity and perseverance of the working class. They express his delight in the symbolic victories with which people keep alive their hopes for a better future. Most of all, they show his capacity to listen to people, to take them seriously, and to fight alongside them rather than commanding or lecturing them into submission. Some people think that such writing is preaching to the already converted, but I think of it more as entertaining the troops, as showing us what we are capable of even under the most dire circumstances, and reminding us how many kindred spirits there have been and continue to be in this world. I know that the things that Rawick has taught me have informed everything I've written about the working class, and I'm sure that Robin D. G. Kelley, David Roediger, Peter Rachleff, Eileen Eagan, Margaret Creel Washington, Stan Weir, Katharine Corbett, Marty Glaberman, and many others would make similar testimonials. Of course that's just the tip of the iceberg; if every historian who lifted an idea from *Sundown to Sunup* had paid Rawick five cents, he would have had enough money to buy the Cardinal football team and move them back to St. Louis with MacArthur Lane as coach.

Hollywood will always prefer stories about the Joe Clarks of this world to stories about people like Fannie Lou Hamer. The true and useful history that George Rawick discovered in the WPA slave narratives will never eclipse the popular exposure given to the destructive lies told in *Birth of a Nation, Gone with the Wind,* or *Lean on Me.* Neoconservative foundations and mainstream media outlets will always try to hide the possessive investment in whiteness, its causes, and its consequences. The makers of *Rocky* and *The Karate Kid* cannot be expected to understand the WPA slave narratives and the lessons they hold about power and struggle for people from all backgrounds. Gil Scott-Heron used to say that the revolution will not be televised, and we should not expect it to appear in the form of high-budget motion pictures from major studios either. Yet revolutionary potential remains among white people willing to resist racism and to struggle openly against it.

After a series of devastating and paralyzing strokes, George Rawick died in 1990. I miss him very much and wish more people knew how important he was. But I would be a poor student if I did not focus on the main lesson that he tried to bring to our attention. Rawick taught us that fighting racism was everyone's business; that the self-activity of oppressed people holds the key to the emancipation of everybody. For all his personal problems he understood that white people have an important role to play in antiracist work. Whites cannot free themselves without acting against the poisonous pathologies of white supremacy—both referential and inferential. Anyone can make antiracist proclamations, but antiracist practices come only from coordinated, collective action. The rewards offered to people from all races to defend the possessive investment in whiteness are enormous, while the dangers of challenging it are all too evident. But in every era, people emerge to fight for something better. Identifying racism and fighting against it may preclude us from joining the ranks of the makers and shakers and accomplices of

this world, but at least it will enable us, in the words of Toni Cade Bambara, "to tell the truth and not get trapped."[15] As W.E.B. Du Bois observed many years ago about the possessive investment in whiteness in his own day, "Such discrimination is morally wrong, politically dangerous, industrially wasteful, and socially silly. It is the duty of whites to stop it, and to do so primarily for their own sakes."[16]

Notes

The epigraph is from Baldwin, *The Devil Finds Work* (New York: Dell, 1976), 134–135.

1. Jeffrey Page, "Joe Clark Faults Black Leaders," *Bergen Record,* November 15, 1989, sec. A.
2. Mike Kelly, "Time for the Boot," *Bergen Record,* November 14, 1989, sec. B.
3. Jeffrey Page, "Clark Asks Workers' Compensation," *Bergen Record,* September 6, 1990, sec. B.
4. Bernard D. Headley, "Black on Black Crime: The Myth or the Reality?" *Crime and Social Justice* 20 (n.d.), 53; Jesse Jackson, "A Bold Call to Action," in *Inside the LA. Riots,* ed. Don Hazen (New York: Institute for Alternative Journalism, 1992), 149.
5. John Hope Franklin, *The Color Line: Legacy for the Twenty-First Century* (Columbia: University of Missouri Press, 1993), 15, 16 (see chap. 1, n. 69); Jane Mayer and Jill Abramson, *Strange Justice: The Selling of Clarence Thomas* (New York: Plume, 1995), 163.
6. Chester Himes, *If He Hollers Let Him Go* (New York: Thunder's Mouth Press, 1986), 41.
7. In this summary of Rawick's work I draw upon David Roediger's characteristically insightful essay "Notes on Working Class Racism" in his indispensable collection *Towards the Abolition of Whiteness,* 61–68. I have also learned much from Paul Buhle's "Preface: Visions of Emancipation—Daniel De Leon, C.L.R. James, and George Rawick," in *Within the Shell of the Old: Essays on Workers' Self-Organization,* ed. Don Fitz and David Roediger (Chicago: Kerr, 1990), 1–4.
8. Lizabeth Cohen, *Making a New Deal* (Cambridge: Cambridge University Press, 1990), 323–361.
9. Roger Daniels, *Coming to America: A History of Immigration and Ethnicity in American Life* (New York: Harper, 1990), 282.
10. Baldwin, *The Devil Finds Work,* 29–30.
11. Vicki Ruiz, *Cannery Women/Cannery Lives: Mexican Women, Unionization, and the California Food Processing Industry, 1930–1950* (Albuquerque: University of New Mexico Press, 1987) (see chap. 3, n. 19); Robin D.G.

Kelley, *Hammer and Hoe: Alabama Communists during the Great Depression* (Chapel Hill: University of North Carolina Press, 1990), 138–151.

12. Michael Rogin, *Blackface/White Noise: Jewish Immigrants in the Hollywood Melting Pot* (Berkeley and Los Angeles: University of California Press, 1998), 253 (see chap. 5, n. 1).

13. Patricia J. Williams, *The Rooster's Egg: On the Persistence of Prejudice* (Cambridge: Harvard University Press, 1996), 65.

14. David Roediger, "Black Freedom and the WPA Slave Narratives: Dave Roediger Interviews George Rawick," in *Within the Shell of the Old: Essay on Workers' Self-Organization,* ed. Don Fitz and David Roediger (Chicago: Kerr, 1990), 10.

15. Toni Cade Bambara quoted in Darlene Clark Hine, Elsa Barkley Brown, and Rosalyn Terborg-Penn, eds., *Black Women in America: An Historical Encyclopedia* (Bloomington and Indianapolis: Indiana University Press, 1993), 80.

16. W.E.B. Du Bois quoted in Kevin Gaines, *Uplifting the Race: Black Leadership, Politics, and Culture in the Twentieth Century* (Chapel Hill, University of North Carolina Press, 1996), 175 (see chap. 3, n. 15).

8.
REPRESENTING WHITENESS
IN THE BLACK IMAGINATION
bell hooks

Although there has never been any official body of black people in the United States who have gathered as anthropologists and/or ethnographers whose central critical project is the study of whiteness, black folks have, from slavery on, shared with one another in conversations "special" knowledge of whiteness gleaned from close scrutiny of white people. Deemed special because it was not a way of knowing that has been recorded fully in written material, its purpose was to help black folks cope and survive in a white supremacist society. For years black domestic servants, working in white homes, acted as informants who brought knowledge back to segregated communities—details, facts, observations, psychoanalytic readings of the white "Other."

Sharing, in a similar way, the fascination with difference and the different that white people have collectively expressed openly (and at times vulgarly) as they have traveled around the world in pursuit of the Other and Otherness, black people, especially those living during the historical period of racial apartheid and legal segregation, have maintained steadfast and ongoing curiosity about the "ghosts," "the barbarians," these strange apparitions they were forced to serve. In the chapter on "Wildness" in *Shamanism, Colonialism, and The Wild Man,* Michael Taussig urges a stretching of our imagination and understanding of the Other to include inscriptions "on the edge of official history." Naming his critical project, identifying

the passion he brings to the quest to know more deeply *you who are not ourselves,* Taussig explains:

> I am trying to reproduce a mode of perception—a way of seeing through a way of talking—figuring the world through dialogue that comes alive with sudden transformative force in the crannies of everyday life's pauses and juxtapositions, as in the kitchens of the Putumayo or in the streets around the church in the Nina Maria. It is always a way of representing the world in the roundabout "speech" of the collage of things . . . It is a mode of perception that catches on the debris of history . . .

I, too, am in search of the debris of history, am wiping the dust from past conversations, to remember some of what was shared in the old days, when black folks had little intimate contact with whites, when we were much more open about the way we connected whiteness with the mysterious, the strange, the terrible. Of course, everything has changed. Now many black people live in the "bush of ghosts" and do not know themselves separate from whiteness, do not know this thing we call "difference." Though systems of domination, imperialism, colonialism, and racism, actively coerce black folks to internalize negative perceptions of blackness, to be self-hating, and many of us succumb, blacks who imitate whites (adopting their values, speech, habits of being, etc.) continue to regard whiteness with suspicion, fear, and even hatred. This contradictory longing to possess the reality of the Other, even though that reality is one that wounds and negates, is expressive of the desire to understand the mystery, to know intimately through imitation, as though such knowing worn like an amulet, a mask, will ward away the evil, the terror.

Searching the critical work of postcolonial critics, I found much writing that bespeaks the continued fascination with the way white minds, particularly the colonial imperialist traveler, perceive blackness, and very little expressed interest in representations of whiteness in the black imagination. Black cultural and social critics allude to such representations in their writing, yet only a few have dared to make explicit those perceptions of whiteness that they think will discomfort or antagonize readers. James Baldwin's collection of essays *Notes of A Native Son* (1955) explores these issues with a clarity and frankness that is no longer fashionable in a world where evocations of pluralism and diversity act to obscure differences arbitrarily imposed and maintained by white racist domination. Writing about being the first black person to visit a Swiss village with only white inhabitants, who had a yearly ritual of painting individuals black who were then positioned as slaves and bought, so that the villagers could celebrate their concern with converting the souls of the "natives," Baldwin responded:

> I thought of white men arriving for the first time in an African village, strangers there, as I am a stranger here, and tried to imagine the astounded populace touching their hair and marveling at the color of their skin. But there is a great difference between being the first white man to be seen by Africans and being the first black man to be seen by whites. The white man takes the astonishment as tribute, for he arrives to conquer and to convert the natives, whose inferiority in relation to himself is not even to be questioned, whereas I, without a thought of conquest, find myself among a people whose culture controls me, has even in a sense, created me, people who have cost me more in anguish and rage than they will ever know, who yet do not even know of my existence. The astonishment with which I might have greeted them, should they have stumbled into my African village a few hundred years ago, might have rejoiced their hearts. But the astonishment with which they greet me today can only poison mine. ("Stranger in the Village")

Addressing the way in which whiteness exists without knowledge of blackness even as it collectively asserts control, Baldwin links issues of recognition to the practice of imperialist racial domination.

My thinking about representations of whiteness in the black imagination has been stimulated by classroom discussions about the way in which the absence of recognition is a strategy that facilitates making a group "the Other." In these classrooms there have been heated debates among students when white students respond with disbelief, shock, and rage, as they listen to black students talk about whiteness, when they are compelled to hear observations, stereotypes, etc., that are offered as "data" gleaned from close scrutiny and study. Usually, white students respond with naive amazement that black people critically assess white people from a standpoint where "whiteness" is the privileged signifier. Their amazement that black people watch white people with a critical "ethnographic" gaze, is itself an expression of racism. Often their rage erupts because they believe that all ways of looking that highlight difference subvert the liberal conviction that it is the assertion of universal subjectivity (we are all just people) that will make racism disappear. They have a deep emotional investment in the myth of "sameness" even as their actions reflect the primacy of whiteness as a sign informing who they are and how they think. Many of them are shocked that black people think critically about whiteness because racist thinking perpetuates the fantasy that the Other who is subjugated, who is subhuman, lacks the ability to comprehend, to understand, to see the working of the powerful. Even though the majority of these students politically consider themselves liberals, who are anti-racist, they too unwittingly invest in the sense of whiteness as mystery.

In white supremacist society, white people can "safely" imagine that they are invisible to black people since the power they have historically asserted, and even now collectively assert over black people, accorded them the right to control the black gaze. As fantastic as it may seem, racist white people find it easy to imagine that black people cannot see them if within their desire they do not want to be seen by the dark Other. One mark of oppression was that black folks were compelled to assume the mantle of invisibility, to erase all traces of their subjectivity during slavery and the long years of racial apartheid, so that they could be better—less threatening—servants. An effective strategy of white supremacist terror and dehumanization during slavery centered around white control of the black gaze. Black slaves, and later manumitted servants, could be brutally punished for looking, for appearing to observe, the whites they were serving as only a subject can observe, or see. To be fully an object then was to lack the capacity to see or recognize reality. These looking relations were reinforced as whites cultivated the practice of denying the subjectivity of blacks (the better to dehumanize and oppress), of relegating them to the realm of the invisible. Growing up in a Kentucky household where black servants lived in the same dwelling with her white family who employed them, newspaper heiress Sallie Bingham recalls, in her autobiography *Passion and Prejudice* (1989), "Blacks, I realized, were simply invisible to most white people, except as a pair of hands offering a drink on a silver tray." Reduced to the machinery of bodily physical labor, black people learned to appear before whites as though they were zombies, cultivating the habit of casting the gaze downward so as not to appear uppity. To look directly was an assertion of subjectivity, equality. Safety resided in the pretense of invisibility.

Even though legal racial apartheid no longer is a norm in the United States, the habits of being cultivated to uphold and maintain institutionalized white supremacy linger. Since most white people do not have to "see" black people (constantly appearing on billboards, television, movies, in magazines, etc.) and they do not need to be ever on guard, observing black people, to be "safe," they can live as though black people are invisible and can imagine that they are also invisible to blacks. Some white people may even imagine there is no representation of whiteness in the black imagination, especially one that is based on concrete observation or mythic conjecture; they think they are seen by black folks only as they want

to appear. Ideologically, the rhetoric of white supremacy supplies a fantasy of whiteness. Described in Richard Dyer's (1988) essay "White," this fantasy makes whiteness synonymous with goodness:

> Power in contemporary society habitually passes itself off as embodied in the normal as opposed to the superior. This is common to all forms of power, but it works in a peculiarly seductive way with whiteness, because of the way it seems rooted, in common-sense thought, in things other than ethnic difference. . . . Thus it is said (even in liberal textbooks) that there are inevitable associations of white with light and therefore safety, and black with dark and therefore danger, and that this explains racism (whereas one might well argue about the safety of the cover of darkness, and the danger of exposure to the light); again, and with more justice, people point to the Judaeo-Christian use of white and black to symbolize good and evil, as carried still in such expressions as "a black mark," "white magic," "to blacken the character," and so on.

Socialized to believe the fantasy, that whiteness represents goodness and all that is benign and non-threatening, many white people assume this is the way black people conceptualize whiteness. They do not imagine that the way whiteness makes its presence felt in black life, most often as terrorizing imposition, a power that wounds, hurts, tortures, is a reality that disrupts the fantasy of whiteness as representing goodness.

Collectively, black people remain rather silent about representations of whiteness in the black imagination. As in the old days of racial segregation where black folks learned to "wear the mask," many of us pretend to be comfortable in the face of whiteness only to turn our backs and give expression to intense levels of discomfort. Especially talked about is the representation of whiteness as terrorizing. Without evoking a simplistic, essentialist "us and them" dichotomy that suggests black folks merely invert stereotypical racist interpretations, so that black becomes synonymous with goodness and white with evil, I want to focus on that representation of whiteness that is not formed in reaction to stereotypes but emerges as a response to the traumatic pain and anguish that remains a consequence of white racist domination, a psychic state that informs and shapes the way black folks "see" whiteness. Stereotypes black folks maintain about white folks are not the only representations of whiteness in the black imagination. They emerge primarily as responses to white stereotypes of blackness. Speaking about white stereotypes of blackness as engendering a trickle-down process, where there is the projection onto an Other of all that we deny about ourselves, Lorraine Hansberry in *To Be Young, Gifted, and Black* (1969) identifies particular stereotypes about white people that are commonly cited in black communities and urges us not to "celebrate this madness in any direction":

> Is it not "known" in the ghetto that white people, as an entity, are "dirty" (especially white women— who never seem to do their own cleaning); inherently "cruel" (the cold, fierce roots of Europe; who else could put all those people into ovens *scientifically*); "smart" (you really have to hand it to the m.f.'s); and anything *but* cold and passionless (because look who has had to live with little else than their passions in the guise of love and hatred all these centuries)? And so on.

Stereotypes, however inaccurate, are one form of representation. Like fictions, they are created to serve as substitutions, standing in for what is real. They are there not to tell it like it is but to invite and encourage pretense. They are a fantasy, a projection onto the Other that makes them less threatening. Stereotypes abound when there is distance. They are an invention, a pretense that one knows when the steps that would make real knowing possible cannot be taken—are not allowed.

Looking past stereotypes to consider various representations of whiteness in the black imagination, I appeal to memory, to my earliest recollections of ways these issues were raised in black life. Returning to memories of growing up in the social circumstances created by racial apartheid, to all black spaces on the edges of town, I re-inhabit a location where black folks associated whiteness with the terrible, the terrifying, the terrorizing. White people were

regarded as terrorists, especially those who dared to enter that segregated space of blackness. As a child I did not know any white people. They were strangers, rarely seen in our neighborhoods. The "official" white men who came across the tracks were there to sell products, Bibles, insurance. They terrorized by economic exploitation. What did I see in the gazes of those white men who crossed our thresholds that made me afraid, that made black children unable to speak? Did they understand at all how strange their whiteness appeared in our living rooms, how threatening? Did they journey across the tracks with the same "adventurous" spirit that other white men carried to Africa, Asia, to those mysterious places they would one day call the third world? Did they come to our houses to meet the Other face to face and enact the colonizer role, dominating us on our own turf? Their presence terrified me. Whatever their mission they looked too much like the unofficial white men who came to enact rituals of terror and torture. As a child, I did not know how to tell them apart, how to ask the "real white people to please stand up." The terror that I felt is one black people have shared. Whites learn about it secondhand. Confessing in *Soul Sister* (1969) that she too began to feel this terror after changing her skin to appear "black" and going to live in the South, Grace Halsell described her altered sense of whiteness:

> Caught in this climate of hate, I am totally terror-stricken, and I search my mind to know why I am fearful of my own people. Yet they no longer seem my people, but rather the "enemy" arrayed in large numbers against me in some hostile territory. . . . My wild heartbeat is a secondhand kind of terror. I know that I cannot possibly experience what *they*, the black people experience. . . .

Black folks raised in the North do not escape this sense of terror. In her autobiography, *Every Good-bye Ain't Gone* (1990), Itabari Njeri begins the narrative of her northern childhood with a memory of southern roots. Traveling south as an adult to investigate the murder of her grandfather by white youth who were drag racing and ran him down in the streets, killing him, Njeri recalls that for many years "the distant and accidental violence that took my grandfather's life could not compete with the psychological terror that begun to engulf my own." Ultimately, she begins to link that terror with the history of black people in the United States, seeing it as an imprint carried from the past to the present:

> As I grew older, my grandfather assumed mythic proportions in my imagination. Even in absence, he filled my room like music and watched over me when I was fearful. His fantasized presence diverted thoughts of my father's drunken rages. With age, my fantasizing ceased, the image of my grandfather faded. What lingered was the memory of his caress, the pain of something missing in my life, wrenched away by reckless white youths. I had a growing sense—the beginning of an inevitable comprehension—that this society deals blacks a disproportionate share of pain and denial.

Njeri's journey takes her through the pain and terror of the past, only the memories do not fade. They linger, as does the pain and bitterness: "Against a backdrop of personal loss, against the evidence of history that fills me with a knowledge of the hateful behavior of whites toward blacks, I see the people of Bainbridge. And I cannot trust them. I cannot absolve them." If it is possible to conquer terror through ritual reenactment, that is what Njeri does. She goes back to the scene of the crime, dares to face the enemy. It is this confrontation that forces the terror of history to loosen its grip.

To name that whiteness in the black imagination is often a representation of terror: one must face a palimpsest of written histories that erase and deny, that reinvent the past to make the present vision of racial harmony and pluralism more plausible. To bear the burden of memory one must willingly journey to places long uninhabited, searching the debris of history for traces of the unforgettable, all knowledge of which has been suppressed. Njeri laments in her Prelude that "nobody really knows us"; "So institutionalized is the ignorance of our history, our culture, our everyday existence that, often, we do not even know ourselves." Theorizing black experience, we seek to uncover, restore, as well as to deconstruct,

so that new paths, different journeys are possible. Indeed, Edward Said (1983) in "Traveling Theory" argues that theory can "threaten reification, as well as the entire bourgeoise system on which reification depends, with destruction." The call to theorize black experience is constantly challenged and subverted by conservative voices reluctant to move from fixed locations. Said reminds us:

> Theory, in fine, is won as the result of a process that begins when consciousness first experiences its own terrible ossification in the general reification of all things under capitalism; then when consciousness generalizes (or classes) itself as something opposed to other objects, and feels itself as contradiction to (or crisis within) objectification, there emerges a consciousness of change in the status quo; finally, moving toward freedom and fulfillment, consciousness looks ahead to complete self-realization, which is of course the revolutionary process stretching forward in time, perceivable now only as theory or projection.

Traveling, moving into the past, Njeri pieces together fragments. Who does she see staring into the face of a southern white man who was said to be the one? Does the terror in his face mirror the look of the unsuspected black man whose dying history does not name or record? Baldwin wrote that "people are trapped in history and history is trapped in them." There is then only the fantasy of escape, or the promise that what is lost will be found, rediscovered, returned. For black folks, reconstructing an archaeology of memory makes return possible, the journey to a place we can never call home even as we reinhabit it to make sense of present locations. Such journeying cannot be fully encompassed by conventional notions of travel.

Spinning off from Said's essay, James Clifford in "Notes on Travel and Theory" celebrates the idea of journeying, asserting that

> This sense of worldly, "mapped" movement is also why it may be worth holding on to the term "travel," despite its connotations of middle-class "literary," or recreational, journeying, spatial

practices long associated with male experiences and virtues. "Travel" suggests, at least, profane activity, following public routes and beaten tracks. How do different populations, classes, and genders travel? What kinds of knowledges, stories, and theories do they produce? A crucial research agenda opens up.

Reading this piece and listening to Clifford talk about theory and travel, I appreciated his efforts to expand the travel/theoretical frontier so that it might be more inclusive, even as I considered that to answer the questions he poses is to propose a deconstruction of the conventional sense of travel, and put alongside it, or in its place, a theory of the journey that would expose the extent to which holding on to the concept of "travel" as we know it is also a way to hold on to imperialism. For some individuals, clinging to the conventional sense of travel allows them to remain fascinated with imperialism, to write about it seductively, evoking what Renato Rosaldo (1989) aptly calls in *Culture and Truth* "imperialist nostalgia." Significantly, he reminds readers that "even politically progressive North American audiences have enjoyed the elegance of manners governing relations of dominance and subordination between the 'races.'" Theories of travel produced outside conventional borders might want the Journey to become the rubric within which travel as a starting point for discourse is associated with different headings—rites of passage, immigration, enforced migration, relocation, enslavement, homelessness. Travel is not a word that can be easily evoked to talk about the Middle Passage, the Trail of Tears, the landing of Chinese immigrants at Ellis Island, the forced relocation of Japanese-Americans, the plight of the homeless. Theorizing diverse journeying is crucial to our understanding of any politics of location. As Clifford asserts at the end of his essay: "Theory is always written from some 'where,' and that 'where' is less a place than itineraries: different, concrete histories of dwelling, immigration, exile, migration. These include the migration of third world intellectuals into the metropolitan universities, to pass through or to remain, changed by their travel but marked by places of origin, by peculiar allegiances and alienations."

Listening to Clifford "playfully" evoke a sense of travel, I felt such an evocation would always make it difficult for there to be recognition of an experience of travel that is not about play but is an encounter with terrorism. And it is crucial that we recognize that the hegemony of one experience of travel can make it impossible to articulate another experience and be heard. From certain standpoints, to travel is to encounter the terrorizing force of white supremacy. To tell my "travel" stories, I must name the movement from a racially segregated southern community, from a rural black Baptist origin, to prestigious white university settings, etc. I must be able to speak about what it is like to be leaving Italy after I have given a talk on racism and feminism, hosted by the parliament, only to stand for hours while I am interrogated by white officials who do not have to respond when I inquire as to why the questions they ask me are different from those they asked the white people in line before me. Thinking only that I must endure this public questioning, the stares of those around me, because my skin is black, I am startled when I am asked if I speak Arabic, when I am told that women like me receive presents from men without knowing what those presents are. Reminded of another time when I was strip-searched by French officials, who were stopping black people to make sure we were not illegal immigrants and/or terrorists, I think that one fantasy of whiteness is that the threatening Other is always a terrorist. This projection enables many white people to imagine there is no representation of whiteness as terror, as terrorizing. Yet it is this representation of whiteness in the black imagination, first learned in the narrow confines of the poor black rural community, that is sustained by my travels to many different locations.

To travel, I must always move through fear, confront terror. It helps to be able to link this individual experience to the collective journeying of black people, to the Middle Passage, to the mass migration of southern black folks to northern cities in the early part of the twentieth century. Michel Foucault posits memory as a site of resistance suggesting (as Jonathan Arac puts it in his introduction to *Postmodernism and Politics*) that the process of remembering can be a practice which "transforms history from a judgment on the past in the name of a present truth to a 'counter-memory' that combats our current modes of truth and justice, helping us to understand and change the present by placing it in a new relation to the past." It is useful when theorizing black experience to examine the way the concept of "terror" is linked to representations of whiteness.

In the absence of the reality of whiteness, I learned as a child that to be "safe" it was important to recognize the power of whiteness, even to fear it, and to avoid encountering it. There was nothing terrifying about the sharing of this knowledge as survival strategy; the terror was made real only when I journeyed from the black side of town to a predominately white area near my grandmother's house. I had to pass through this area to reach her place. Describing these journeys "across town" in the essay "Homeplace: A Site of Resistance" I remembered:

It was a movement away from the segregated blackness of our community into a poor white neighborhood. I remember the fear, being scared to walk to Baba's, our grandmother's house, because we would have to pass that terrifying whiteness—those white faces on the porches staring us down with hate. Even when empty or vacant those porches seemed to say *danger,* you do not belong here, you are not safe.

Oh! that feeling of safety, of arrival, of homecoming when we finally reached the edges of her yard, when we could see the soot black face of our grandfather, Daddy Gus, sitting in his chair on the porch, smell his cigar, and rest on his lap. Such a contrast, that feeling of arrival, of homecoming— this sweetness and the bitterness of that journey, that constant reminder of white power and control.

Even though it was a long time ago that I made this journey, associations of whiteness with terror and the terrorizing remain. Even though I live and move in spaces where I am surrounded by whiteness, surrounded, there is no comfort that makes the terrorism disappear. All black people in the United States, irrespective of their class status or politics, live with the possibility that they will be terrorized by whiteness.

This terror is most vividly described in fiction writing by black authors, particularly the recent novel by Toni Morrison (1987), *Beloved.* Baby Suggs, the black prophet, who is most vocal about representations of whiteness, dies because she suffers an absence of color. Surrounded by a lack, an empty space, taken over by whiteness, she remembers: "Those white things have taken all I had or dreamed and broke my heartstrings too. There is no bad luck in the world but white folks." If the mask of whiteness, the pretense, represents it as always benign, benevolent, then what this representation obscures is the representation of danger, the sense of threat. During the period of racial apartheid, still known by many folks as Jim Crow, it was more difficult for black people to internalize this pretense, hard for us not to know that the shapes under white sheets had a mission to threaten, to terrorize. That representation of whiteness, and its association with innocence, which engulfed and murdered Emmett Till was a sign; it was meant to torture with the reminder of possible future terror. In Morrison's *Beloved* the memory of terror is so deeply inscribed on the body of Sethe and in her consciousness, and the association of terror with whiteness is so intense, that she kills her young so that they will never know the terror. Explaining her actions to Paul D. she tells him that it is her job "to keep them away from what I know is terrible." Of course Sethe's attempt to end the historical anguish of black people only reproduces it in a different form. She conquers the terror through perverse reenactment, through resistance, using violence as a means of fleeing from a history that is a burden too great to bear. It is the telling of that history that makes possible political self-recovery.

In contemporary society, white and black people alike believe that racism no longer exists. This erasure, however mythic, diffuses the representation of whiteness as terror in the black imagination. It allows for assimilation and forgetfulness. The eagerness with which contemporary society does away with racism, replacing this recognition with evocations of pluralism and diversity that further mask reality, is a response to the terror, but it has also become a way to perpetuate the terror by providing a cover, a hiding place. Black people still feel the terror, still associate it with whiteness, but are rarely able to articulate the varied ways we are terrorized because it is easy to silence by accusations of reverse racism or by suggesting that black folks who talk about the ways we are terrorized by whites are merely evoking victimization to demand special treatment.

Attending a recent conference on cultural studies, I was reminded of the way in which the discourse of race is increasingly divorced from any recognition of the politics of racism. I went there because I was confident that I would be in the company of likeminded, progressive, "aware" intellectuals; instead, I was disturbed when the usual arrangements of white supremacist hierarchy were mirrored both in terms of who was speaking, of how bodies were arranged on the stage, of who was in the audience, of what voices were deemed worthy to speak and be heard. As the conference progressed I began to feel afraid. If progressive people, most of whom were white, could so blindly reproduce a version of the status quo and not "see" it, the thought of how racial politics would be played out "outside" this arena was horrifying. That feeling of terror that I had known so intimately in my childhood surfaced. Without even considering whether the audience was able to shift from the prevailing standpoint and hear another perspective, I talked openly about that sense of terror. Later, I heard stories of white women joking about how ludicrous it was for me (in their eyes I suppose I represent the "bad" tough black woman) to say I felt terrorized. Their inability to conceive that my terror, like that of Sethe's, is a response to the legacy of white domination and the contemporary expressions of white supremacy is an indication of how little this culture really understands the profound psychological impact of white racist domination.

At this same conference I bonded with a progressive black woman and white man who, like me, were troubled by the extent to which folks chose to ignore the way white supremacy was informing the structure of the conference. Talking with the black woman, I asked her: "What do you do, when you are tired of confronting white racism, tired of the day-to-day incidental acts of racial terrorism? I mean, how do you deal with coming home to a white person?" Laughing, she said, "Oh, you mean when I am suffering from White People Fatigue Syndrome. He gets that more than I do." After we finished our laughter, we talked about the way white people who shift locations, as her companion has done, begin to see the world differently. Understanding how racism works, he can see the way in which whiteness acts to terrorize without seeing himself as bad, or all white people as bad, and black people as good. Repudiating "us and them" dichotomies does not mean that we should *never* speak the ways observing the world from the standpoint of "whiteness" may indeed distort perception, impede understanding of the way racism works both in the larger world as well as the world of our intimate interactions. Calling for a shift in locations in "the intervention interview" published with the collection *The Post-Colonial Critic* (1990), Gayatri Spivak clarifies the radical possibilities that surface when positionality is problematized, explaining that "what we are asking for is that the hegemonic discourses, the holders of hegemonic discourse should de-hegemonize their position and themselves learn how to occupy the subject position of the other." Generally, this process of repositioning has the power to deconstruct practices of racism and make possible the disassociation of whiteness with terror in the black imagination. As critical intervention, it allows for the recognition that progressive white people who are anti-racist might be able to understand the way in which their cultural practice reinscribes white supremacy without promoting paralyzing guilt or denial. Without the capacity to inspire terror, whiteness no longer signifies the right to dominate. It truly becomes a benevolent absence. Baldwin ends his essay "Stranger in the Village" with the declaration: "This world is white no longer, and it will never be white again." Critically examining the association of whiteness as terror in the black imagination, deconstructing it, we both name racism's impact and help to break its hold. We decolonize our minds and our imaginations.

References

Arac, Jonathan (ed) (1986) *Postmodernism and Politics*. Minneapolis: University of Minnesota Press.

Baldwin, James (1955; rpt. 1984) *Notes of a Native Son*. Boston: Beacon Press.

Bingham, Sallie (1989) *Passion and Prejudice*. New York: Knopf.

Clifford, James (1989) "Notes on Travel and Theory," *Inscriptions* 5: pp. 177–188.

Dyer, Richard (1988) "White," *Screen, 29*(4), pp. 44–65.

Halsell, Grace (1969) *Soul Sister*. New York: World Publishing Co.

Hansberry, Lorraine (1969) *To Be Young, Gifted, and Black*. Englewood Cliffs, NJ: Prentice Hall.

hooks, bell (1990) "Homeplace: A Site of Resistance," in *Yearnings: Race, Gender, and Cultural Politics*. Boston: South End Press.

Morrison, Toni (1987) *Beloved*. New York: Knopf.

Njeri, Itaberi (1990) *Every Good-bye Ain't Gone*. New York: Random House.

Rosaldo, Renato (1989) *Culture and Truth: The Remaking of Social Analysis*. Boston: Beacon Press.

Said, Edward (1983) *The World, the Text, and the Critic*. Cambridge: Harvard University Press.

Spivak, Gayatri C. (1990) *The Post-Colonial Critic: Interviews, Strategies, Dialogues*. S. Harasym (ed). New York: Routledge.

Taussig, Michael (1987) *Shamanism, Colonialism, and the Wild Man: A Study in Terror and Healing*. Chicago: University of Chicago Press.

9.
THE FORGOTTEN FIFTEEN MILLION

Black Radio, Radicalism, and the Construction of the "Negro Market"
Kathy M. Newman

In 1949 *Sponsor* magazine used the following headline to grab the attention of national advertisers who had long ignored African American consumers—the "forgotten" fifteen million.

> *The forgotten 15,000,000: Ten billion a year Negro market is largely ignored by national advertisers.* When a segment of the over-all American population that is larger than the population of the entire Dominion of Canada is overlooked and under-developed by US national advertisers and their agencies, something would seem to be wrong. In the case of America's 15,000,000 Negroes, something very definitely is.[1]

With this article, *Sponsor* offered a new solution to an old problem in American advertising: the problem of racism versus the bottom line. To help advertisers overcome their racism toward the African American consumer, *Sponsor* used the success stories of radio stations that were already targeting the "Negro market." With testimonials from black radio stations all over the country, *Sponsor* argued that black radio could make black audiences into loyal listeners and loyal consumers.

Much of the evidence in *Sponsor*'s early features on the Negro market rested on the huge advertising success of one radio station in particular—WDIA, Memphis—the first radio station in the country to target all of its programming to African Americans. In its pioneer feature on the "forgotten 15,000,000," *Sponsor* reproduced one of WDIA's promotional brochures. With a picture of one of the black gospel groups promoted by the station, the brochure claimed

that WDIA was "Out Front Down South" and was "the top choice with more than ½ MILLION NEGROES." By 1957, less than ten years later, there were over six hundred radio stations targeting 30 to 100 percent of their programming to African Americans in cities all over the country, and national advertisers were beginning to take black consumers more seriously—at least the ones they could reach via the airwaves.

Although these black consumers have been forgotten since the 1940s, we have much to gain by remembering them in the 1990s. First of all, their story challenges the idea that postwar consumer culture was marked by the standardization of the consumer. Advertisers who targeted the Negro market sought to construct an explicitly "Negro" consumer. Through radio, marketers sought a lower-income/working-class audience, for whom television was not yet a primary form of mass entertainment. This fact forces us to reconsider an accepted wisdom about the 1950s: the notion that advertisers were only interested in a homogeneous, white, middle class market. Second, the story of the forgotten fifteen million challenges the accepted wisdom that African Americans were completely excluded from national advertising markets until the 1960s and 1970s. Their story shows us, instead, that African Americans were targeted by national advertising, through radio, starting in the 1940s.

These arguments draw from the pioneering social and cultural history of Robin Kelley, Robert Weems, and Lizabeth Cohen. They argue that there is a dialectic between consumer identity and political identity in the history of African American social movements. Robert Weems, in his pathbreaking *Desegregating the Dollar,* argues that after businesses recruited African American consumers in the 1930s and 1940s, African Americans used their economic power for political gain in the Civil Rights boycotts of the 1950s and 1960s. Focusing more on culture than politics, Robin Kelley shows that African American workers who participated in boycotts in the postwar era were conscious of their power as consumers, especially in their patronage of mass transit and downtown businesses: "Unlike in the workplace, where workers entered as disempowered producers dependent on wages for survival and beholden, ostensibly at least, to their superiors, working people entered public transportation as consumers—and with a sense of consumer entitlement."[2] In a similar vein, Lizabeth Cohen, writing about African American labor activism in Chicago in the 1920s and 1930s, argues that "participation in mainstream commercial life made blacks feel more independent and influential as a race."[3]

This argument—that participation in mainstream commercial life might have positive consequences for marginalized groups—is rarely made in progressive scholarship. A more emblematic response to consumer culture can be found in Manning Marable's account of marketing to African Americans in the twentieth century. Marable argues that "the impact of corporate America's massive exploitation of the Black consumer market has created a profoundly negative effect within Black culture and consciousness." He cites examples of companies that have used manipulative tactics to sell alcohol and tobacco to black consumers, such as Schieffelin's sponsoring of an advertisement for scotch with the testimony of Jesse Owens, and the Kool cigarettes sponsorship of the Kool Jazz Festivals. In these cases, Marable objects both to the nature of the products, alcohol and tobacco, and to the tactics used to sell them: black athletes and jazz music.[4]

But by focusing only on scotch and tobacco, and overlooking other products and other advertising venues, such as radio, Marable misses the fact that corporate sponsorship of black culture has offered African Americans access to mainstream consumer

culture and new outlets for black culture. Black radio pushed Schaefer beer, Philip Morris cigarettes, Nadinola skin lighteners, and Royal Crown hair products, but it also pushed Cadillacs, Quaker Oats, and GE appliances. Black radio provided news about the Ethiopian ambassador's visit to the United States and news about *Brown v. Board of Education.* Black radio offered rhythm and blues, gospel music, and homemaker shows. Black radio advocated higher education, recreation, and community service. Black radio supported voting rights, good health, and the "right to buy." Black radio, though it was a part of corporate America's exploitation of the black consumer, had some positive effects within black culture and black consciousness.

The Forgotten Fifteen Million

In 1947 an FCC report suggested that "a small segment of the listening audience carefully selected as a minority group, may, if it is loyally attached to the station, give it a unique fascination for advertisers." In 1947 television threatened to replace radio as the medium through which national advertisers could reach the broadest audience, and thus radio was looking for new and "narrower" markets. WDIA's success with programming for the Memphis black community—and *Sponsor's* reporting of it—helped to ensure that African Americans would be the one of the first audiences to be "carefully selected as a minority group" by independent radio stations throughout the country.[5] Although the postwar period is generally thought of as a period of mass standardization of products and consumers, the history of the Negro market shows that marketing in the postwar era was a diverse, heterogeneous, and complex process. The diversity of advertising-sponsored media allowed marketers to use a medium like television to reach what they called the "class" market while using radio and magazines to reach a "mass" audience, a "working-class" audience, and a variety of minority audiences.

As a result, the sociology of marketing for difference became an industry unto itself, with a specialized professional discourse that was published in textbooks and advertising trade magazines. *Sponsor* magazine and its annual feature on black radio, for example, were the innovations of a World War II veteran named Norman Glenn, who began monthly publication of the magazine in 1946. He decided to start his own trade magazine after working in the advertising department of *Broadcasting* magazine. He noticed that *Broadcasting* was geared toward only one-half of the economic equation of the broadcast industry—stations and managers—rather than the needs of the product sponsor. And it was the sponsor, Glenn realized, that paid for radio. So why not devote a trade magazine to the sponsor's point of view? The magazine became a hit: *Sponsor* was the primary journal for broadcast advertisers—on radio and television—for much of its twenty-year life span.

In the fall of 1949 *Sponsor* hailed the potential of the "forgotten fifteen million" African American consumers and singled out black radio as one of the best ways to tap their $10 billion-per-year income. The magazine estimated that there were radios in the homes of between 68 and 84 percent of southern African Americans, arguing that in spite of the many factors that separated blacks and whites, there was no such thing as "segregated ears."[6] Three years later *Sponsor* expanded its coverage into a nineteen-page feature on the growing black radio industry. Using the 1950 US Census, *Sponsor* showed that between 1940 and 1950, the number of African Americans living in urban centers increased by 46 percent, that the black median income rose by 192 percent (compared to 146 percent for whites), and that 91.5 percent of African Americans in the civilian labor force were employed. In a comparison of urban black consumer markets by size, the Memphis market ranked ninth, with African Americans making up nearly 50 percent of the city's total population.[7]

When *Time* magazine discovered the Negro market in 1954, the magazine seemed determined to show that cultivating the Negro market could lead to great social and economic change. In a story that featured the screening of an advertising film made by the Johnson Publishing Co., titled *The Secret of Selling the Negro, Time* reported that the economic rise of the African American "helped break down many segregation barriers."[8] *Time*'s Freudian slip—the film was originally titled *The Secret of Selling the Negro*

Market—is one of the many curious features of this article. But equally important is the fact that the article appeared in July 1954, just two months after the Supreme Court decision on *Brown v. the Board of Education*. Citing figures from Johnson's film and *Sponsor* magazine, *Time* made the connection between civil rights and the right to consume, concluding that the emergence of the Negro market was a good thing for the economy and for race relations: "Most retailers feel that even in Southern stores discrimination will disappear gradually, wiped out by the legal pressure against segregation and the economic rise of the South. Eventually, the Negro market will merge into and become indistinguishable from the overall market."[9] Therefore, at the same time that the Negro market was conceived of as a separate (and not necessarily equal) sphere, *Sponsor, Time,* and academics such as Joseph Johnson offered it as one route to integration. Between the courts and the democratic power of the dollar, they imagined, discrimination would disappear.

Even the *Pittsburgh Courier* reported that "many civic leaders below the Mason Dixon line are of the opinion that [Negro radio] will do more for lowering Jim Crow barriers than flowery oratory."[10] Black radio and its promise of the black consumer continued to draw praise throughout the mid-fifties: in 1956 Alex Haley coauthored a feature on black radio for *Harper's* with Albert Aberbanel, using much of the material provided by the previous five years of *Sponsor's* "Annual Negro Section":

"Negro radio" as it is popularly called, seems to have sprung up almost spontaneously, over night, all over the country. The surprising thing is that no one thought of it before, that for years talented Negroes knocked at closed doors, trying to get jobs in radio. . . . Almost all Negroes share a common desire for race progress, and the station and sponsors who make a special effort to attract them are showing an increased respect for Negroes as a people. Any discriminated-against minority group is also quick to take personal pride in the achievements of any of its members, so radio programs featuring Negroes offer excellent opportunities for listener identification. And finally, in segregated areas, such programs indirectly tell their listeners where they can go to shop without fear of being embarrassed.[11]

The irony here is palpable. Aberbanel and Haley described African Americans as a "discriminated-against minority" and as no more than "embarrassed" when they encountered discrimination in the marketplace. But understatement aside, these authors were not wrong in their basic premise: that the "Negro market" was founded on the double edge of segregation and race consciousness—especially in the South.

In 1957, a year when controversies over segregation and race consciousness drew the National Guard to Little Rock, Arkansas, *Time* returned to the subject of the Negro market—this time to report the successful sale of WDIA for $1 million. *Time* justified the "thumping price" with the argument that the Negro market was crucial to the national market: "The Negro market can make—or break—the sales programs of even the biggest advertisers. These 17.3 million customers are growing in power and influence . . . faster than the US average. Though Negro stations were unheard-of ten years ago, they prosper today in every sizable city in the South and in big cities up North."[12] But perhaps because of controversies around school desegregation, this article made no mention of the integrationist potential of black buying power. Rather, the tone of the article focused on racial and class difference, on the "cotton pickers" who took portable radios to the field to hear "Theo ('Bless My Bones') Wade" and musical shows like *Tan Town Coffee Club, Wheelin' on Beale,* and *Hallelujah Jubilee.*

This emergence of the Negro market in the 1950s—and the importance of radio—challenges the conventional wisdom that marketers in the 1950s were interested only in finding (and producing) a standard white middle class consumer. The rise of the Negro market shows that postwar marketing strategies were divided by media and by demographics, and that advertisers actively sought black consumers for national brands and products directed at the Negro market. Moreover, hair straighteners and skin lighteners were not the only products

that sponsored black radio stations. A close look at the first black radio station, WDIA, will challenge the conventional wisdom that African Americans were largely excluded from exposure to national advertising until the 1960s. The history of marketing at WDIA shows that African Americans were encouraged to join in mainstream consumer behavior: to buy cars, washing machines, and new homes—to chew Wrigley's gum, eat Wonder Bread, listen to Philco radios, and drink Seven-Up.[13]

Ask Mr. Sponsor: WDIA and the Production of the Negro Market

In the 1940s and 1950s, black consumers were recruited through an expanding nexus of black newspapers and periodicals, such as *Ebony* magazine. But radio was the most prevalent form of nationally sponsored mass culture in African American homes in the 1950s and early 1960s: more African Americans owned radios than owned televisions, subscribed to newspapers, or subscribed to magazines. Radio was so prevalent in black homes, in fact, that *Ebony* magazine bought time on black radio stations to increase its circulation. In the mid-1950s it was estimated that on average, 94 percent of all black homes had at least one radio set. Regionally this was broken down into two statistics: radio penetration was equal to 98 percent in the North, and over 80 percent in the South. And thus more African Americans were exposed to national advertising on the radio than through any other black medium in the 1950s.[14]

Because of prejudice against black consumers, advertisers interested in targeting the Negro market had only a handful of academic studies and trade magazines like *Sponsor* for market research on black consumers. Racism was one factor; lack of telephones in black homes was another. The national rating companies, such as "Hooper" (which dominated the ratings market in the 1930s and 1940s), relied on the "telephone coincidental method" to obtain program ratings. With this system, researchers called radio listeners and asked them what program they were listening to at the time of the telephone call. In the 1940s fewer than 50 percent of Americans owned telephones, and the percentage of African

Americans who owned telephones was much lower than the national average—especially in the South.

Thus radio station managers turned to *Sponsor* magazine's annual "Negro Radio" issue. *Sponsor* was the primary resource for advertisers interested in the Negro market, and WDIA was *Sponsor*'s most featured station. Thus the success of WDIA helped station managers around the country make the switch to black radio. And as the new black stations had success stories to share, their testimonials appeared in *Sponsor* magazine: black radio expanded at a rate of about one hundred new stations per year from 1949 to 1958. In the beginning, however, most of *Sponsor*'s advice on the Negro market was provided by Bert Ferguson, the white entrepreneur who was general manager and part owner of WDIA.

In 1948 Ferguson hired Nat D. Williams, a popular black high school teacher, to host the first show for black listeners in Memphis. Williams, who was also an entertainer and a nationally syndicated newspaper columnist in the Negro press, called his show *The Tan Town Jamboree*. To test the success of the show, Ferguson delivered pamphlets to the doorsteps of homes in black neighborhoods and asked listeners to write back with their comments on the new program. The response was overwhelming, and Ferguson began to expand WDIA's black programming. For the next eighteen months, he added black shows on an ad hoc basis until the station was completely converted from its previous format (though the news department, sales department, and general managers were staffed by whites until the 1960s). Williams helped to recruit a team of talented African American blues entertainers, comedians, teachers, and preachers to work as disc jockeys, and their shows ranged from gospel, blues, and rhythm and blues to sewing, agriculture, and homemaking.[15]

Early successes persuaded advertisers that WDIA was a good investment: General Home Service Co. was one of the first companies to sponsor the new programming: in the thirteen weeks that they sponsored fifteen-minute shows on WDIA, they sold 546 washers, "more than any other dealer had disposed of and almost as many as all the G.E. dealers in Memphis together had sold" in the same period.[16] In later years a station promotion in which listeners

were asked to collect and send in Carnation Milk labels brought 168,364 labels into the station; when the Pure Oil company gave away free rabbit-foot key chains bearing potentially winning "serial numbers" with each fill-up, the company went through 50,000 key chains in thirteen weeks; in another case, a Memphis used-car dealer doubled the number of cars he sold per month after buying advertising on WDIA.[17] In 1954 station owners increased the WDIA signal from 250 to 50,000 watts, and by 1955 WDIA carried more national advertising than any other black station in the country.[18]

What made WDIA so successful? Why were African Americans in Memphis and the surrounding tri-state area willing to buy the products WDIA advertised? This is an important question; the fact that black incomes were rising after World War II did not guarantee that African American consumers were going to buy more, or buy more luxury goods. As Colin Campbell has argued, it is important to distinguish between the "presence in a population of a new *ability* to buy inessentials and a new *willingness* to do so."[19] WDIA successfully channeled the purchasing habits of African Americans toward particular brands of essential food products, such as Lily White Flour, Southern Belle Sausage, and Carnation Canned Milk. And as for "inessentials," such as home appliances, remodeling services, travel, and automobiles, black radio stations advertised these products to a much larger audience than black periodicals such as *Ebony* magazine. And while black radio stations advertised many products that have been associated with the exploitation of black consumers, such as cigarettes, alcohol, skin lighteners and hair straighteners, black radio also advertised mainstream products associated with middle class life in America.

It was this balance between segregation on the one hand and a growing race consciousness on the other that *Sponsor* used to explain the buying habits of Memphis African Americans. *Sponsor* taught advertisers how segregation shaped (and therefore helped to predict) black consumption patterns. *Sponsor* used charts to show that the median income for African Americans was about half the median income for whites in 1950, but pointed out that because of racial segregation in the real estate, restaurant, and recreational markets, African Americans spent less of their income on rent, vacations, and dining out: "Negroes still extend a lower-than-average patronage to many restaurants, night clubs, theaters, hotels, and vacation spots and generally spend less for out-of-home recreation than whites, since they can't always be sure they won't be embarrassed."[20] "Embarrassment" is a troubling euphemism for racism, but *Sponsor*'s point was clear enough: if discrimination discouraged African Americans from going out, broadcasters could capitalize on this by advertising products that African Americans would want to use while entertaining at home.

At the same time, *Sponsor* pointed out, African Americans spent a *higher* percentage of their income on staple food and household goods, thus "pay[ing] more and buy[ing] more of the things that are nationally advertised."[21] WDIA research found that African Americans were buying 80 percent of the rice, 70 percent of the canned milk, and 65 percent of the flour in Memphis grocery stores.[22] Other black radio stations reported advertising success with items like upholstery, tract homes, and packaged drug products, noting that blacks entertained more in their homes, could not move "just anywhere," and could not access the same quality of medical care as whites.[23] While black radio may have helped African Americans to imagine themselves as consumers of a lifestyle previously reserved for whites, it seems unlikely that an advertising appeal so integrated with the logic and consequences of segregation could result in the Negro market becoming indistinguishable from the overall market, as *Time* had prophesied in 1954.

On the other hand, as Robin Kelley has argued, segregation has often gone hand-in-hand with a positive sense of African American "congregation."[24] Kelley borrows this idea from the historian Earl Lewis, who explained that the difference between congregation and segregation was a difference in choice. Congregation, Lewis wrote, "symbolized an act of free will, whereas segregation represented the imposition of another's will."[25] Kelley uses this idea to suggest that we can learn something about collective action by examining the collective pleasures displayed in the consumption of transportation, music, and athletics: "Knowing what happens in these spaces of pleasure can help us understand the solidarity black people have shown at political mass meetings, illuminate the bonds of fellowship we find in churches and voluntary associations, and unveil the *conflicts* across class and gender lines that shape and constrain these collective struggles" (47). Kelley is not naively optimistic; he uses Lewis's words to warn us that "congregation in a Jim Crow environment produced more space than power." But in this space, he argues, African Americans could "gather their cultural bearings" and turn race prejudice into race pride (45).

The Negro market was founded on this dialectic between race prejudice and race pride, within the new "space" provided by black radio. *Sponsor* acknowledged segregation as the major reason for the existence of a separate Negro market, but it also recognized that a growing race pride in the accomplishments of African American artists and entertainers was one of segregation's unwitting effects: "The great mass of US Negroes will continue as an identifiable group for a long, long time to come. As long as there is racial segregation or racial prejudice in this country, Negroes will continue to turn to their own news and entertainment media for everything from the interpretation of new legislation to the enjoyment of performing artists of their own race."[26] This quote suggests that if radio entrepreneurs and advertisers wanted to attract the Negro market to black radio, they needed to provide an African American "interpretation of new legislation" and feature black performers. It was not enough to know how much flour was purchased by black households in Memphis.

The most important factor in marketing to African Americans was the hiring of black disc jockeys. *Sponsor* argued that black listeners had more "confidence" in disc jockeys they could tell were black, and that racially specific listener identification had social, political, and commercial consequences: "Seldom can a Negro—particularly one who is getting more and more proud of his racial heritage as his status improves—find anything in the ordinary air show sponsored by a national advertiser with which he can identify himself. . . . Negro-appeal radio therefore is *the* radio in the increasingly race-conscious, race-proud world of millions of colored Americans."[27] Black disc jockeys were crucial to the sound of "race consciousness" on the radio. WDIA used its black staff for community outreach projects called the WDIA "goodwill" events. The WDIA staff volunteered its labor to host and perform in the station's first "Goodwill Revue" in 1949, and the funds raised were donated to a Christmas charity. In the same year, WDIA celebrated the radio debut of the "Teen Town Singers," a high school singing group. WDIA offered a $100 savings bond to local high school students for winning essays on the topic of "community life" and sponsored teen forums, an "I Speak for Democracy" contest, and an annual spelling bee.

The most famous of the WDIA disc jockeys, the blues singer B. B. King, remembers Bert Ferguson as a "fantastic person" who "believed in helping people." King called WDIA a "big learning center for people like myself." He remembers WDIA as a separate, safe space for the black staff members who worked there—an oasis, a place for black culture to flourish, and an interracial workplace in the segregated South:

> At that time the South was segregated. But we had a feeling, us blacks did, when we got into the radio station, it was almost like being in a foreign country, and going to your embassy. When you get there, you know this is home. . . . So when we got into WDIA we felt like we meant something. We felt that we were citizens. We felt we were appreciated. And we didn't have to say, "Yes, sir" or "Yes, ma'am" or "No, sir," or "No, ma'am," unless we felt that it was honor that was due to someone, not simply because we were black and they were white. Everybody worked by that, and when you walked back on the streets it was again like leaving the embassy, in that foreign country, until it really changed, and WDIA did a lot to change it.[28]

B. B. King's memory of WDIA as a "home embassy" in a foreign country resonates with Earl Lewis's notion of the "congregation" that can come out of "segregation." WDIA was a product of segregation, but it provided jobs for black performers and offered black culture, music, news, and entertainment to the Memphis black community.

WDIA never promoted community without simultaneously offering a vision for "good citizenship"

and "family values." The station news editor, Marie Wathen, and program director, Chris Spindel, developed many of the goodwill-instilling and audience-recruiting programs for the station in the early 1950s. Wathen initiated programs that counseled listeners on the "problems of marriage" and "family welfare." The 1952 license renewal application described the family welfare program as an "important educational service," designed to enjoin listeners "to live better, more productive, and happier lives."[29]

The station also campaigned against venereal disease and tuberculosis, offering free testing for both. Good citizenship also included voting: a record of public service announcements used for the month of July in 1952 includes spots for voter registration, the League of Women Voters, the Girl Scouts, the Elks Club, Civil Defense, AA, Farm Safety, three churches, a plug for the Red Sox (a Negro League baseball team), and the WDIA free movie program. This was another goodwill stunt aimed at the young: WDIA brought screens and speakers to neighborhoods where the kids were too poor to go to the movies in town, and the previews always included promotional films featuring the station's black disc jockey staff.[30]

By the mid-1950s, Ferguson and his staff had made WDIA into "not just a radio station but an advertising force."[31] Ferguson knew he was producing a loyal audience whose function was to consume the products advertised on the station. In 1957, after nearly ten years of experimenting with black radio, *Sponsor* agreed that the WDIA formula worked around the country, and that rhythm and blues, gospel music, black disc jockeys, community outreach, and goodwill projects were crucial to a black radio station's commercial success:

> Many of these elements add up to a strong sense of loyalty, a need for identification with the Negro community even though there is a concurrent struggle for acceptance in the non-Negro community. The best of the Negro radio stations and newspapers encourage this search for identification—and they sell their advertisers' products better for doing this. They encourage fund raising for a new Negro hospital or help distribute Salk vaccine in Negro areas. They provide

buses for handicapped Negro children or work to get better paving in Negro neighborhoods.[32]

Black disc jockeys, community involvement, and "goodwill" projects helped create a sense of black community identification, which in turn increased the sales of products advertised on black stations. Racial "identification" was essential to commercialization.

WDIA provided the Memphis black community with a "home embassy"—a new space for entertainment, information, music, citizenship, and "goodwill." WDIA also led to the increased participation of Memphis African Americans in the mainstream commercial life of the region. By the mid-1950s, the buying habits of the Memphis black community were noted by white and African American business owners alike: "In the last decade . . . the trend in buying power among these people [African Americans] has been sharply upward. This has been associated with the growing industrial importance of this area, an increase in the wages of the Negro, both in industry and in agriculture, and the general upward trend of income throughout the United States. This increased buying power has been keenly felt by the retail establishment of Memphis."[33] Likewise, as the buying power of African Americans increased, so did their sense of consumer entitlement. WDIA symbolized the link between consumption and culture: listeners knew that when they bought the products advertised on WDIA, they helped to keep the station in business. Without their consumption, WDIA would not have survived.

For WDIA and its black listeners, the relationship between commercialism and community was a dialectical one. WDIA did not "create" the black community—the black community existed long before the radio station. Instead, WDIA used existing community leaders—teachers, preachers, homemakers, and talented entertainers—to sell advertising. WDIA even used the idea of community—spelling bees, 4-H shows, neighborhood film screenings, Little League baseball teams, schools for handicapped children, and community fund-raisers—to sell advertising. But in the process WDIA gave the black community access to the sounds of mainstream consumer culture, new jobs in the field of mass media, exposure to national advertising, news of interest to the black

community, electronic mass culture created exclusively for a black audience, activities and social events that drew participants from black listeners throughout the Memphis region, and information about local products and retail outlets. WDIA used the black community for profit, but the black community profited, too.

Moreover, the impact of WDIA went far beyond Memphis. Louis Cantor argues in his book about WDIA that it "created the sound that changed America" because WDIA became the model for black radio stations throughout the country. WDIA proved that stations could make money selling products to black consumers, and as a result there was an explosion of black programs and stations over the course of the 1950s. In 1949 there was a handful of stations with programs for African Americans. In 1957 there were more than six hundred. In 1949 there were sixteen black disc jockeys. In 1957 there were more than one thousand. Black radio had become a commercial *and* a cultural force.

Black Radio Stations and the Color of Sound

Radio was the most prevalent form of nationally sponsored mass culture in African American homes in the postwar era. Black radio had an immediacy that helped create a new outlet for black community expression, but it was equally plagued by the ephemerality of radio sound. On the other hand, in spite of the ephemerality of radio sound, black radio had the power to unite, to unify, to bring together. Through stations like WDIA, radio helped to bind the African American community living in rural and urban neighborhoods in Memphis into a "regional family." Maurice "Hotrod" Hulbert, one of the most prominent disc jockeys at WDIA, remembers the first time he realized the power that black radio had to unite the black community:

I found out that the radio was a way to really help people. It had a power that I didn't know. There was a family that was burned out, burned out completely, [their house burned] completely to the ground. I asked for help [over the radio] and people began to bring in food, clothing, and

I had my first automobile, that I owned, a little Chevrolet, and I was going to different places and picking up furniture, picking up food, picking up money, and it ended up that . . . people were bringing them furniture out there in trucks, bringing them money, clothes, and they had more than they had when the house burned down. That showed me something about radio. People responded.[34]

According to Hulbert, it was after seeing the response of the black community to the needs of the family whose house burned down that WDIA started the annual tradition of the "Goodwill Review." WDIA proved to product sponsors that it could sell goods, but it also brought the black community together in a new space: the space provided by the airwaves.

Radio had another advantage over television and the printed media: the American race problem was generally defined as a problem of color rather than sound.[35] Television was replacing radio as the new broadcast medium, and as radio researcher Henry Bullock pointed out, African Americans were not pictured as members of this new, broad, audience—in programming or in advertisements. It was easier for them to find themselves represented on the radio: "Negroes choose radio over television because of the greater opportunities for self-identification offered by the former medium. Radio gives greater freedom to the imagination, freeing the Negro from the 'left-out' feeling that a visual medium imposes."[36] African Americans were "left out" of mainstream media visual representations at the same time that the "black" sound, in music and in disc jockey style and voice, was being transmitted and imitated across the radio dial—even on stations that targeted a white audience. In essence, "black" voices could be used to sell over the airwaves where anyone might hear them, whereas black models were only seen within the enclosed pages of the Negro press.

On the other hand, even if the vast majority of African Americans owned and used radios, not all of them appreciated programs directed toward a black audience. As another radio researcher named William L. Smith argued, some black listeners found black radio itself to be a form of segregation, full of "detrimental racial stereotype[s]," lacking in quality

and "too limited." Smith's study of black radio listeners in Columbus, Ohio, and Baton Rouge, Louisiana, found that even when 65 percent of the respondents in both areas listened to black radio, 60 percent of them preferred "general-appeal" programming.[37] As it turned out, finding the right sound, the right copy, and the right disc jockey for maximum black listener identification was hardly an exact science, especially since what it meant to sound authentically black was itself contested terrain.

This contest was most in evidence in the criticisms of black radio. A radio researcher named Henry Bullock found that middle and upper class African Americans in particular were resentful of black radio; in his research focus groups, they expressed their distaste for the medium.

> "I for one," complained a participant, "would like to stand on the housetop and castigate every radio station in Houston that keys its market towards the Negro." Another participant confirmed this, saying, "I'd like to give them a piece of my mind." Showing the force of the alienation inherent in this type of radio programming, still another advised: "Do like I do. Don't buy the product."[38]

This participant thought that a boycott of the products advertised on black radio stations might discourage the "segregation" of the airwaves. But there is a trace of irony in this listener's disdain: black radio was one of the first national media to advertise a middle class lifestyle for African Americans: luxury cars, suburban homes, remodeling services, and name-brand appliances.

The negative reaction of middle class listeners was linked not only to the minstrel implications of the clowning black disc jockey—many of the early black disc jockeys got their entertainment training on the minstrel circuit—but also to black radio's southern roots. *Sponsor* revealed its knowledge of this problem in the following case study of inappropriate ad copy:

> The WDAS, Philadelphia disk jockey didn't like the look of the copy. But he read it anyway. Within minutes, the Negro-appeal station's phones were ringing. Negro callers were furious. Station

manager Bob Klein started checking in a hurry and soon discovered what had gone wrong. A large super market, anxious to stimulate weekend sales in its meat department, had sent over some last-minute copy which went something like this: "Say, folks . . . want some good ol' Southern eating? Well, just get a load of some of these weekend meat specials just waitin' for you to come in and buy 'em."

Sponsor explained that the ad was for the lowest-priced meat cuts, like "pig knuckles," "ham hocks," "chitlins," and "kidneys." One listener who lived in the "swank Lincoln Drive area of Germantown" complained to the station that she "wouldn't feed that kind of stuff to my poodle." Bob Klein, WDAS station manager, understood that "good ol' Southern eating was exactly the kind of thing Negroes don't look back to with any fond remembrance."[39]

Sponsor understood that there were other things that middle class African Americans didn't want to be reminded of: the South was one; menial labor was another. *Sponsor* warned its readers about the mixed popularity of black actors in domestic positions: "Many Negro performers get a mixed reception from Negroes themselves—particularly those who appear in menial or subservient positions to white people. Negro tastes vary, just as whites' do; some stars are popular with one group of their own race, yet unpopular with another."[40] Phrases like "taste" and "class item" were frequently used in these articles to signal the class position of the listeners; these code words allowed *Sponsor* to hint at the class divisions within the black community without broadcasting the fact that in spite of black radio's popularity, the new medium drew its harshest critics from the black elite.

Though most of the time *Sponsor* tried to present an upscale image of the black radio audience, denying that the medium attracted "dollar-down" customers, some of its features highlighted "low-income" products. One national brand representative explained why his company chose black radio for its medicinal chewing gums, Feen-a-mint and Chooz: "Products of this type have traditionally shown more strength in lower-income, semiskilled, or unskilled occupational groups. Since this is in the main

true of the Negro group, as it is also true of certain white groups regionally, we feel the Negro market is one which should be shown attention."[41] This kind of confession was rare for a *Sponsor* feature. The magazine published an annual issue on black radio to combat the advertising world's negative view of the Negro market as a lower-income market. But in this same issue, *Sponsor* quoted a report published by the BBDO advertising agency, which suggested that black radio had "a greater appeal to the masses of lower income."[42] In 1957, because of the new prominence of television in middle class markets, radio had a "greater appeal to the masses of lower income" regardless of race. Radio was now a demographically specific medium, with programming for teens, religious groups, lower-income housewives, and "working-class" listeners—both on and off the job.

But the appeal of black radio to working-class listeners was not simply a matter of "taste." It was also a matter of material circumstances. Radios were cheaper than televisions, newspapers, and magazines and thus easier for lower-income listeners to afford. Black radio was also a vital resource in areas in which African American literacy rates were low. Moreover, radio was popular among working-class listeners because black employment patterns often constrained leisure time. According to Henry Bullock, "a far lesser proportion of Negroes have leisure time to be more responsive to eye-absorbing (as contrasted with ear-absorbing) channels of entertainment."[43] Radio programming offered news and entertainment in a form that could be enjoyed not only as an alternative to work but as an accompaniment to it.

Sponsor showed its audience how to maximize this advantage, explaining that if stations targeted African Americans who worked for white employers, advertisers could get two markets for the price of one. The following example came from WRMA in Montgomery, Alabama:

Advertisers are missing a large Negro audience with double purchasing power during the hours from 9:00 a.m. to 3:00 p.m. Negro maids (there are 15,000 in this area) tune to this station while they are working in white homes. Many of them do some of the small-item grocery buying for the white family, such as bread, milk, coffee, tea, sugar, etc. Negro maids are the ones who actually *use* floor wax, furniture polish, glass cleaner, laundry starch, detergents, and soaps. They use them in their homes, too. If the maid suggests one brand over another, the white housewife will usually comply.[44]

As another *Sponsor* article put it, by making a direct pitch to black domestics, an advertiser could "sell both whites and Negroes."[45] But in order to "sell" them both, the African American domestic worker had to perform a disturbing double labor: she waxed the floor on the one hand, and sold floor wax to her white employer on the other.

Other testimonials, like one from WHOD in Pittsburgh, explained why employers and advertisers alike might have seen radio in the workplace as a good thing: "Early morning time is unusually good in Negro Radio due to the high percentage of factory workers in the Pittsburgh area who start on an 8:00 am shift. These same workers tune in during the day at their place of employment. We have talked with many employers who *like* their employees to listen to our shows while they work. Fast rhythm music means fast work tempo."[46] In this situation, black radio served the needs of capital on both ends, providing music to drive a "fast work tempo" in the factory, and advertisements to sell goods to the African American workers.

On the other hand, some black radio stations were aware of the class and taste differences among their listeners, offering different kinds of programming to appeal to these different groups. The results of a study that KBWR, San Francisco, did of the 150,000 black residents in the Bay Area showed that the station's black programming attracted a high percentage of *all* the area's black residents: "Radio is the only medium that penetrates this vast audience in widely separated areas. A personal survey showed that 96% of the interviewees are acquainted with our Sepia Serenade programs. Some 63% prefer to listen in the morning, 91% in the afternoon, 48% in the evening, and 65% on Sunday."[47] These statistics suggest that KBWR achieved phenomenal cross-class appeal. KBWR's survey also raises the possibility that black

stations attracted audiences that varied by class, time of day, gender, and region. A black station in Chattanooga was most successful with singers, orchestras, and popular music; in Hollywood, the black station relied primarily on rhythm and blues; in Nashville, the black station used gospel shows and food talk shows to attract women listeners in the midmorning, and rhythm and blues shows in the early morning and late afternoon to attract a male audience.[48]

Black radio did not please everyone. For some black listeners, especially in the middle classes, black radio was more about "segregation" than "congregation." But throughout the 1950s, black radio still contributed to African Americans' sense of consumer power in four ways: it integrated black working-class and lower-income consumers, especially, into the mainstream of American consumer culture; it provided a cross-class space (similar to black churches and black lodges) for the expression of racial pride and identification; it provoked some black listeners, especially those in the middle classes, to consider the consumer realm as a realm for protest; and it sparked national interest in the phenomenon of the "Negro market," which made boycotting for civil rights an increasingly effective tactic. Black listeners who resented black radio, such as those quoted earlier, were quick to suggest the boycott as a remedy for the forms of commercialization that they resented. On a grander scale, as the nation began to take black consumers more seriously, the boycott became a more effective tactic for political activism. Black radio made the "Negro market" into a national reality.

Conclusion

The relationship between the emergence of the Negro market and the high incidence of African American boycotting during the Civil Rights movement is unique in the history of advertising and activism. No minority group in the history of broadcasting has ever been as self-consciously recruited, or as actively discriminated against, as the African American audience commodity. Nor has any group in American history used the consumer boycott to the same extent— or with the same success—as African Americans did during the Civil Rights movement.

But the relationship is suggestive: before there could be a "revolt" of the Negro market there had to *be* a market, and no other medium directed to the black community had as much advertising from national advertisers as black radio in the 1950s. Radio advertisements—and community programming—assured African Americans that they had consumer power. When they used that consumer power to exert *political* pressure on southern businesses and northern lunch counters, the nation was shocked. So, perhaps, were some of the very advertisers that used stations like WDIA to "sell" the Negro market.

In the act of remembering this story, the story of the "forgotten fifteen million," we are forced to rethink a number of conventional wisdoms about advertising, African Americans, and activism in the 1950s. This story shows us that advertisers sought to recruit, and create, a heterogeneous population of consumers in the postwar era. This story shows us that African Americans were exposed to national advertising before the 1960s. And finally this story shows us that participation in the marketplace, for African Americans, had some positive consequences for black culture and black consciousness. After a decade of black radio, and a decade of black consumption of national products, consumer activism became a central tactic in a national struggle for African American civil rights. Boycotting would have been a less effective strategy—especially in terms of publicity—had black radio not created a national context for, and awareness of, a national Negro market.

Even Martin Luther King Jr., in a 1967 address to the black National Association of Radio Announcers (NARA), acknowledged the social, political, and cultural impact of black radio. While he stressed the role of the announcer in the black community, he also recognized black radio as a cultural "bridge" between blacks and whites: "I have come to appreciate the role which the radio announcer plays in the life of our people; for better or for worse, you are opinion makers in the community. . . . The masses of Americans who have been deprived of educational opportunity are almost totally dependent on radio as their means of relating to the society at large. . . . In a real sense, you have paved the way for social and political change by creating a powerful cultural bridge between black and

white."[49] Black radio, with its white-teen spin-offs, did "create the sound that changed America." But before black radio crossed over, it offered the black community the sounds of national advertising and postwar consumption. It changed America by turning "segregation" into "congregation." It changed America by providing a "home embassy" in the segregated South and the urban North. It changed America by remembering the "forgotten fifteen million"—so that today we can do the same.

Notes

1. "The Forgotten 15,000,000," *Sponsor*, 10 October 1949, 24. *Sponsor* magazine was the first trade magazine to promote the Negro market in an annual feature.
2. Robin Kelley, *Race Rebels: Culture, Politics, and the Black Working Class* (New York: Free Press, 1994), 61. Like Kelley, Dana Frank argues that the political tactics associated with consumer power, such as the boycotts, were often linked to labor struggles, especially strikes. Dana Frank, *Purchasing Power: Consumer Organizing, Gender, and the Seattle Labor Movement, 1919–1929* (New York: Cambridge University Press, 1994). Robert Weems has written the only synthetic history of black consumer activism, *Desegregating the Dollar: African American Consumerism in the Twentieth Century* (New York: New York University Press, 1998). See also Andor Skotnes, "'Buy Where You Can Work': Boycotting for Jobs in African-American Baltimore, 1933–1934," *Journal of Social History* (summer 1994): 735–61. For the best overview of black radio, see William Barlow, *Voice Over: The Making of Black Radio* (Philadelphia: Temple University Press, 1998). An excellent history of WDIA also exists: Louis Cantor, *Wheelin' on Beale: How WDIA-Memphis Became the Nation's First All-Black Radio Station and Created the Sound That Changed America* (New York: Pharos Books, 1992), 41–55.
3. Lizabeth Cohen, *Making a New Deal: Industrial Workers in Chicago, 1919–1939* (Cambridge: Cambridge University Press, 1990), 154. Lizabeth Cohen has been kind enough to share with me some materials from her book, *A Consumer's Republic: The Politics of Mass Consumption in Postwar America* (New York: Alfred A. Knopf, 2003).
4. Manning Marable, *How Capitalism Underdeveloped Black America: Problems in Race, Political Economy, and Society* (Boston: South End Press, 1983), 161–63. With this critique, Marable echoes the critique of David Caplovitz, who shows how lower-income communities have long been inundated by alcohol advertising, tobacco advertising, and sleazy credit schemes. David

Caplovitz, *The Poor Pay More: Consumer Practices of Low-Income Families* (New York: Free Press, 1963).

5. Peter Fornatale and Joshua E. Mills, *Radio in the TV Age* (Woodstock, N.Y.: Overlook Press, 1980), 15.

6. "The Forgotten 15,000,000," 25.

7. "The Negro Market: $15,000,000,000 to Spend," *Sponsor,* 28 July 1952, 31; Joseph T. Johnson, *The Potential Negro Market* (New York: Pageant Press, 1952).

8. "The Negro Market: How to Tap $15 Billion in Sales," *Time,* 5 July 1954, 70.

9. Ibid.

10. Article from the *Pittsburgh Courier,* quoted in Cantor, *Wheelin' on Beale,* 170.

11. Albert Abarbanel and Alex Haley, "A New Audience for Radio," *Harper's,* February 1956, 57–59. See also J. Fred MacDonald, *Don't Touch That Dial! Radio Programming in American Life, 1920–1960* (Chicago: Nelson-Hall, 1979). The black press confirms this as well—in 1947, one year before WDIA began experimenting with black-appeal programming, *Opportunity* lamented the state of black acceptance into the industry: "Up to now little has happened in radio to ennoble the medium in the eyes of the Negro, and it must be conceded, if somewhat reluctantly, that despite hope and fervent prayer, not very much more is likely to happen in the foreseeable future" ("On Stage . . . " *Opportunity,* July–September, 1947, 167).

12. "Biggest Negro Station," *Time,* 11 November 1957, 50.

13. "Negro Radio's Clients," *Sponsor,* 26 September 1959, 40–42.

14. "4th Annual Negro Section," *Sponsor,* 19 September 1955, 116. "*Ebony* magazine, for instance, runs a monthly saturation campaign in two dozen major Negro markets that begins some three days prior to publication and continues through the date it hits the stands" (133).

15. This summary is drawn from "Breaking the Color Barrier," chap. 3 of Cantor's *Wheelin' on Beale,* 41–55.

16. "Negro Results: Rich Yield for All Types of Clients," *Sponsor,* 28 July 1952, 38–39.

17. "The Carnation Story," WDIA promotional brochure, WDIA collection, Center for Southern Folklore; "Case Histories: Stations Report Sales and Audience Results," *Sponsor,* 28 September 1957, 41; "Negro Radio Results: Documented 'Case Histories' in Story Below Dramatize the Sales Power of Negro-Slanted Air Medium during 1955 Season," *Sponsor,* 19 September 1955, 141.

18. "Negro Radio: Over 600 Stations Strong Today—Negro-Slanted Shows Are Aired in 39 of 48 States, Cover 3.5 Million Negro Homes," *Sponsor,* 19 September 1955, 148.

19. Colin Campbell, *The Romantic Ethic and the Spirit of Modern Consumerism* (Oxford: Basil Blackwell, 1989), 18.

20. "The Negro Market: $15 Billion Annually—U.S. Negroes Buy Top-Quality, Brand-Name Goods of All Types. But You Must Know Where, When, and Why," *Sponsor,* 24 August 1953, 66.

21. "The Negro Market: $15 Billion Annually," 67.

22. Cantor, *Wheelin' on Beale,* 145.

23. "Negro Radio Results," *Sponsor,* 20 September 1954, 53, 155, 157.

24. Kelley, *Race Rebels,* 45. Frances Fox Piven and Richard A. Cloward refer to this phenomenon in similar terms, noting that the possibilities for black organizing by midcentury were enhanced by the cadre of black business and cultural leaders sustained by black patronage. They argue that this base was built up during the economic modernization of the South and also resulted from African American economic, political, and cultural "separation and concentration." Frances Fox Piven and Richard A. Cloward, *Poor People's Movements: Why They Succeed, How They Fail* (New York: Vintage Books, 1977), 204–5.

25. Kelley, *Race Rebels,* 45.

26. "The Negro Market: $15,000,000,000 to Spend," *Sponsor,* 28 July 1952, 30.

27. Joseph Wootton, "a Negro himself," and black-appeal station representative, quoted in "Negro Radio: Keystone of Community Life," *Sponsor,* 24 August 1953, 68.

28. B. B. King, taped interview, aired on WDUQ, Pittsburgh, 15 February 1998.

29. Exhibit "E," Additional Program Data, application for renewal of license, 1952, WDIA collection, Center for Southern Folklore.

30. Cantor, *Wheelin' on Beale,* 235.

31. "The Carnation Story," WDIA promotional brochure, WDIA collection, Center for Southern Folklore.

32. "The Negro Market: Why Buyers Are Looking Twice," *Sponsor,* 28 September 1957, 33.

33. Paul Hardman Sisco, "The Retail Function of Memphis" (Ph.D. diss., University of Chicago, 1954), 31.

34. Maurice Hulbert, interview, aired on WDUQ, Pittsburgh, 15 February 1998.

35. A potent example: the radio show *"Amos 'n' Andy"* boasted millions of black and white listeners in the 1930s and 1940s but suffered a backlash from black audiences and skittish advertisers when it crossed over to television. Although both the radio and the TV show had their fans and critics, the criticism leveled against the TV show was much stronger, and more effective, than the criticisms of the radio show that preceded it. Melvin

Ely, *The Adventures of Amos 'n' Andy: A Social History of an American Phenomenon* (New York: Free Press, 1991).

36. Henry Allen Bullock, "Consumer Motivations in Black and White—II," *Harvard Business Review* 39, no. 4 (July–August 1961): 117. Throughout this study, he quotes from his book-length study of the Houston Negro Market, *Pathways to the Houston Negro Market* (Ann Arbor: Edwards Brothers, 1957).

37. William L. Smith, "A Comparison of the Attitudes of Negro Respondents in Columbus, Ohio, and Baton Rouge, Louisiana, toward Negro-Appeal Radio Programs Being Broadcast in Those Areas" (M.A. thesis, Ohio State University, 1957), 93–94.

38. Henry Allen Bullock, "Consumer Motivations in Black and White—I," *Harvard Business Review* 39, no. 3 (May–June 1961): 90.

39. "Tips on Selling via Negro Radio," *Sponsor,* 20 September 1954, 144.

40. "The Forgotten 15,000,000," 54.

41. Agency Analysis: Admen Tell Why and How They Buy Negro Radio," *Sponsor,* 28 September 1957, 39.

42. "The Negro Market: Why Buyers Are Looking Twice," 33.

43. Bullock, "Consumer Motivations in Black and White—II," 116.

44. "Tips on Selling via Negro Radio," 148.

45. "The Forgotten 15,000,000," 55.

46. "Tips on Selling via Negro Radio," 148.

47. "Tips on How to Get Most Out of Negro Radio," 78.

48. "Tips on Selling via Negro Radio," 148.

49. William Barlow, "Commercial and Noncommercial Radio," in *Split Image: African Americans in the Mass Media,* ed. William Barlow and Jannette L. Dates (Washington, D.C.: Howard University Press, 1990), 225.

References

Barlow, William. *Voice Over: The Making of Black Radio.* Philadelphia: Temple University Press, 1999.

Barlow, William, and Jannette L. Dates, eds. *Split Image: African Americans in the Mass Media.* Washington, D.C.: Howard University Press, 1990.

"Biggest Negro Station." *Time,* 11 November 1957, 50.

Bullock, Henry Allen. "Consumer Motivations in Black and White—I." *Harvard Business Review* 39, no. 3 (May–June 1961): 89–124.

———. "Consumer Motivations in Black and White—II." *Harvard Business Review* 39, no. 4 (July–August 1961): 112–33.

Campbell, Colin. *The Romantic Ethic and the Spirit of Modern Consumerism.* Oxford: Basil Blackwell, 1989.

Cantor, Louis. *Wheelin' on Beale: How WDIA-Memphis Became the Nation's First All-Black Radio Station and Created the Sound That Changed America.* New York: Pharos Books, 1992.

Caplovitz, David. *The Poor Pay More: Consumer Practices of Low-Income Families.* New York: Free Press, 1963.

Cohen, Lizabeth. *A Consumers' Republic: The Politics of Mass Consumption in Postwar America.* New York: Alfred A. Knopf, 2003.

———. *Making a New Deal: Industrial Workers in Chicago, 1919–1939.* Cambridge: Cambridge University Press, 1990.

Ely, Melvin. *The Adventures of Amos 'n' Andy: A Social History of an American Phenomenon.* New York: Free Press, 1991.

Fortnatale, Peter, and Joshua E. Mills. *Radio in the TV Age.* Woodstock, N.Y.: Overlook Press, 1980.

Frank, Dana. *Purchasing Power: Consumer Organizing, Gender, and the Seattle Labor Movement, 1919–1929.* New York: Cambridge University Press, 1994.

Kelley, Robin. *Race Rebels: Culture, Politics, and the Black Working Class.* New York: Free Press, 1994.

MacDonald, J. Fred. *Radio Programming in American Life, 1920–1960.* Chicago: Nelson-Hall, 1979.

Marable, Manning. *How Capitalism Underdeveloped Black America: Problems in Race, Political Economy, and Society.* Boston: South End Press, 1983.

"On Stage . . . " *Opportunity,* July–September 1947, 167.

Piven, Frances Fox, and Richard A. Cloward. *Poor People's Movements: Why They Succeed, How They Fail.* New York: Vintage Books, 1977.

Sisco, Paul Hardman. "The Retail Function of Memphis." Ph.D. diss., University of Chicago, 1954.

Skotnes, Andor. "'Buy Where You Can Work': Boycotting for Jobs in African-American Baltimore, 1933–1934." *Journal of Social History* (summer 1994): 735–61.

Smith, William L. "A Comparison of the Attitudes of Negro Respondents in Columbus, Ohio, and Baton Rouge, Louisiana, toward Negro-Appeal Radio Programs Being Broadcast in those Areas." M.A. thesis, Ohio State University, 1957.

Sponsor Magazine, 1945–1968.

WDIA collection, Center for Southern Folklore, Memphis, Tennessee.

Weems, Robert E. *Desegregating the Dollar: African American Consumerism in the Twentieth Century.* New York: New York University Press, 1998.

10.
WHITE RESPONSES
The Emergence of "Enlightened" Racism
Sut Jhally and Justin Lewis

In the previous chapter we suggested that the presence of upper middle class black people on television created the impression among white TV viewers that anyone, regardless of race, color, or creed, could "make it" in the modern United States. We now come to the most disturbing aspect of this misconception.

The Insidious Return of Racism

Although *The Cosby Show* and others like it seem to persuade some white viewers that black doctors and lawyers have become almost commonplace, most white respondents realized that the Huxtables were, in fact, unusual black people. The role of television in this sense is more complicated than it first appears. Our evidence suggests that shows like *The Cosby Show* cultivate, for white viewers, a curious contradiction: the Huxtables' presence on TV finally proves that "anyone can make it"; yet most people know that the vast majority of black people are not like the Huxtables:

> He's not representing what most blacks are. He's not even representing what most whites are—but especially, he's not representing what most blacks are.

> They [the black people the respondent sees every day] are all lower income and have that jive talk, so that I hardly understand them, whereas this . . .

> [Father and daughter discussing whether class would make a difference] Money would be a big issue

at that point. . . . *The house is the biggest part of the show. It's a gorgeous, big house. . . . Do you know how much a house in New York goes for, Dad? You know how many typical black families live in those homes?*

Despite their statements about how real, average, or regular the Huxtable family is, most white viewers realized that the Huxtables were not a typical black family. Many observed that they were far less typical than the more working class characters in black sitcoms like *The Jeffersons* or *Good Times*:

> It's not a typical black family though. . . . *[The]* Jeffersons *is typical.*

> [Other black shows] are directed more to blacks. . . . That show [The Jeffersons] tries to grasp as a family, you know, any black family type of thing.

> The only show that I've watched on a daily basis was Good Times. It was so much more realistic than The Cosby Show. They were poor, which is easier to make for a black situation considering what the average layman perceives of black people.

This contradiction, despite some of the liberal ideas that inform it, leads to a decidedly illiberal conclusion. The only way to explain the failure of most black people to achieve what the Huxtables have achieved is to see most black people as intrinsically lazy or stupid. Few white respondents actually articulated such a nakedly racist attitude, preferring to suppress (publicly, at least) the logical outcome of this contradiction. We can see, nevertheless, that the absence of an awareness of the role of class in sustaining racial inequalities means that this racist conclusion is kept simmering (consciously or unconsciously) beneath the surface. Our study would seem to confirm the fears of Henry Louis Gates (1989: 40):

> As long as *all* blacks were represented in demeaning or peripheral roles, it was possible to believe that American racism was, as it were, indiscriminate. The social vision of "Cosby," however, reflecting the minuscule integration of blacks into the upper middle class, reassuringly throws the blame for black poverty back onto the impoverished.

The Cosby Show, by demonstrating the opportunity for African Americans to be successful, implicates the majority of black people who have, by the Huxtable criterion, failed.

The show's emphasis on education, for all its good intentions, simply compounds this impression. The Huxtables' children are constantly urged by their parents to recognize the importance of educational achievement and to try hard to get good grades. This provides the viewer with an explanation for the comparative failure of most other black people: if they had only tried harder in school, maybe they would have succeeded. As Bill Cosby says of the Huxtables, "This is an American family—an *American* family—and if you want to live like they do, and you're willing to work, the opportunity is there."

The lesson was not lost on most white respondents. Although they happily welcomed the Huxtables into their homes, careful examination of their discussions made it clear that this welcome would not be extended to all black people. What shows like *The Cosby Show* allow, we discovered, was a new and insidious form of racism. The Huxtables proved that black people can succeed; yet in doing so they also prove the inferiority of black people in general (who have, in comparison with whites, failed).

In his study of television news, Robert Entman makes a similar point. He highlights the contradiction between the black people who appear on the news as stories and the increasing number of black anchors and reporters who tell those stories. He suggests that black people in news stories are mainly linked with crime and special interest politics. Entman (1990: 342–343) writes:

> These images would feed the first two components of modern racism, anti-black affect and resistance to blacks' political demands. On the other hand, the positive dimension of the news, the presence of black anchors and other authority figures, may simultaneously engender an impression that racial discrimination is no longer a problem, bolstering the third component of modern racism, an impression that blacks are not inferior and undesirable, working against *old-fashioned racism* [our emphasis].

In other words, there is a distinction to be made between the crude racism of old and its new, more insidious, and apparently enlightened forms. We shall, in this chapter, explore the origin and character of this duplicitous attitude.

Definitions of Black: Color versus Culture

We are used to thinking of racism as an attitude that is crude in its simplicity. The racist discriminates between people purely on the basis of race or color. Although it would be foolish to assume that this kind of prejudice is a thing of the past, we must acknowledge that racism today clothes itself more respectably, allowing a deep-rooted racism to appear to be open-mindedly liberal.

It is easy to forget that race and racial difference involve a great deal more than the categories of physiognomy and skin pigmentation. The differences between a black person and a white person in the United States are deeply rooted in their distinct and separate racial histories, histories encapsulating a host of material and cultural distinctions that render the experience of being black quite different from the experience of being white. Race, in other words, is a social as well as a physical construction.

Racial discrimination, throughout its infamous history, has usually been predicated on a series of perceived symbolic links between skin color and culture. To colonialists, slave owners, and promoters of apartheid, such discrimination meant a straightforward denunciation of black culture as uncivilized, inferior, or threatening. Despite their manifest crudity, these racist attitudes have never been as simple or homogeneous as they sometimes appear. From colonialism onward, the racist discourses within white societies have borne contradictory assumptions about the relation between nature and nurture. Black people have been seen as simultaneously within the reaches of white society and beyond it. The black person's soul was therefore treated, on the one hand, as a changeable commodity open to the influences of missionary zeal and, on the other, as the heart of darkness, inherently irredeemable.

Once placed in the industrial melting pots of the late twentieth century, black people struggling for achievement in an oppressive white world disentangled many of the associations between race and culture. The successes of some black people, against the odds, in a predominantly white environment have made notions of biological determinism decidedly less fashionable. Even limited black success makes white claims to racial superiority difficult to sustain. Although the notion of white racial superiority has certainly not disappeared, it is less common now than ideas of racial equality. But this does not mean the end of racism. Far from it. As an instrument of repression, racism now takes more subtle forms.

In most Western countries, particularly in the United States, the idea that white people and black people are irrevocably tied to discrete cultures has been seriously compromised by the promise of social mobility: the idea that anyone, regardless of race, creed, or class, can change their class. The principle of social mobility is now enshrined within legal structures that, although not guaranteeing racial equality, at least give the idea of equal rights a certain amount of credibility.

Racism is, however, capricious, and it has adapted to this discursive climate by absorbing a number of contradictions. The history of racism, we have demonstrated, is now embedded in an iniquitous capitalist system, where economic rather than racial laws ensure widespread racial segregation and disadvantage.

These, in turn, encourage white people, looking around them at the comparative prosperity of whites over blacks, to believe in an imagined cultural superiority and simultaneously to give credence to the idea that we are only what we become.

These beliefs lead to an attitude that separates blackness from the color that defines it. Blackness becomes a cultural notion associated with African Americans, but, from a white perspective, not irredeemably so. It is the same perspective adopted by nineteenth-century missionaries: blackness is seen as a condition from which black people can be liberated.

How is such an apparently archaic attitude sustained in the modern United States? The answer returns us, once again, to the national failure to come to terms with the harsh realities of class barriers. The phenomenon of racism, unlike inequality of wealth and opportunity, is understood not as a consequence of social structures but as the collective sum of individual opinions. If white people as individuals, the thinking goes, stop discriminating against black people, then racial equality is suddenly possible.

We have, we hope, revealed the naïveté of this position. Yet it persists not only among the gullible but throughout mainstream opinion in the United States. Accordingly if, as our study suggests, most white people believe such racism is a thing of the past, then how can we explain the failure of black people, as a group, to achieve parity with white people? In the absence of a class analysis, the answer is to see most black people as culturally inferior. This classless logic says that if most black people fail when there are no individuals discriminating against them, then there must be something wrong with them.

Bill Cosby, whether as himself or as Dr. Heathcliff Huxtable, is easily assimilated into this ideology. He is, as Mark Crispin Miller (1986) argues, visible "proof" of the meritocratic mythology that fuels the American dream, a black person who has achieved success beyond the confines of a racially defined culture. He has, in this sense, escaped from the shackles of his racial origins. It is as if racial disadvantage is something that black people are born with rather than something imposed upon them.

This is racism masquerading as liberalism. White people are willing to accept that black and white people can be equal, and their enjoyment of *The Cosby Show* is testimony to this. They can accept the Huxtables as people who are "just like us." Beneath this progressive attitude, however, lies an implicit and unstated rejection of the majority of black people, who are not like the Huxtables and, by implication, not "like us."

How does this apparently liberal racism manifest itself among the white groups in our audience study? The answer, we shall suggest, reveals a great deal about the ambivalent way many white people *really* feel about black people.

The Black and White *Cosby Show*

One criticism that black people have made of *The Cosby Show* is that the Huxtable family behaves, as Gates has put it, "just like white people." Although this statement is more complex than it sounds at first, it raises an interesting possibility. Perhaps white people do not actually see the Huxtables as a black family at all. Perhaps they see them as white—or as some shade of gray in between.

We discovered that many white people do not view the Huxtables as only black. Just as people were able to see *The Cosby Show* as both realistic and unrealistic, most members of our white audience saw the Huxtable family as simultaneously black *and* white. Before we describe this ambiguous perception in more detail, it is useful to clarify what it means.

Most white people—certainly those who watch *The Cosby Show*—no longer see skin color as a barrier to liking someone or treating them as an equal. Unimpeded by such all-encompassing prejudice, they are able to discriminate between black people, some of whom have succeeded, some of whom have not. However, they quietly (and perhaps unconsciously) retain the association of blackness as an indicator of cultural inferiority, albeit one from which African Americans, if they are talented enough or hard working enough, can escape. This position is arrived at not through malice but through a failure to adequately recognize the disadvantaged position black people occupy in the class structure. This failure is extremely significant because, without such a recognition, there is no nonracist way to resolve the disparity between

the Huxtables (and other successful black TV characters) and the majority of comparatively unsuccessful black people. Television, we have suggested, is culpable, albeit unwittingly, at every stage in this process.

This argument explains why many white viewers express considerable ambivalence about issues of race on *The Cosby Show*. The Huxtables are, on the one hand, undeniably black, proving the just nature of the brave, new, nonracist world. They are, on the other, unlike most other black people because they fit neatly into the privileged middle class world of television. Because this world has traditionally been the preserve of white people, the Huxtables' entry into it does indeed make them appear to be "just like white people." It is hardly surprising, in this context, if many of the whites' responses were confused: the Huxtables represent the compromise between black and white culture that is unconsciously seen as a prerequisite of black success.

The degree to which the color was seen to fade from the show varied. Some respondents insisted that, as one person put it, "You can't notice it [the Huxtables' race] at all." This statement is itself revealing. It does not refer to variations in skin tone; rather, it demonstrates the perception of blackness as a function of culture (in its general sense) rather than skin color. Their color is, after all, no more or less noticeable than is that of any other group of African Americans. It is their culture, the way they speak and behave, that makes their color less noticeable.

Respondents were asked whether they felt *The Cosby Show* would be very different if the characters were white rather than black. As we pointed out in Chapter 3, a number of respondents felt that the Huxtables' assimilation into a white televisual world was complete enough to say, as these respondents did:

> *If they were carrying off the thing the same way, you know, really making a satire of life the way they're doing it, average everyday things that happen every day, then I don't think it would be that much different, you know. Because what they do is they really carry it off and say these are the things that can happen to anybody, I don't care if you're white, black, pink, yellow, or green, this happens to everybody in*

everyday life. That's what they do. They just satirize everything that happens in normal life.

I don't think it would be all that different; they seem to come across . . . I think it is generic enough so that anyone could watch it and appreciate it. Like they acknowledge their own heritage and they happen to be black.

I think at the beginning you would notice it more because it is an all-black show and it was something different. . . . I don't think it makes a difference if they are black or white if it's funny.

You can't [notice color], really! I mean, it wouldn't be any different if they were white.

I would imagine there's some kind of subtlety there that I'm missing, that I'm not picking up on right away. It would have to be different, I would think; but I can't see in what capacity. . . . They don't seem to make any reference to their race.

This last comment is particularly interesting. The respondent feels sure that there must be some difference, yet she is unable to detect anything identifiably "black" about the Huxtables.

There is an underlying tension beneath these apparently liberal statements. The fact that "you just think of them as people," praise for which *The Cosby Show* is singled out, does not prove that race is no longer an issue. Quite the contrary: these particular black people are unusual because they have *transcended* their racial origin and, in so doing, have become normal.

The notion of "average," "everyday," or "generic" that these respondents refer to, although it appears to be ethnically neutral, is actually racially specific. The statement that they are "just like any other family" or "just like us" is specific to the Huxtables; it does not refer to black people in general. As one respondent put it:

I like the fact that they're black and they present a whole other side of what you tend to think black families are like.

The Huxtables may be thought to be normal or average, but they are unlike most black families. The everyday world of the Huxtables is the everyday,

generic world of white television. One respondent made this point directly:

What they're trying to do here is portray a black family in a white family atmosphere.

Most other group members preferred to make this point by implication, referring to a notion of "normality" that is clearly white. So, for example, when one respondent suggested that, unlike most black TV characters, "they just act like people," he was implying a separation between ordinary people and black people. So, unlike most black people, as another respondent put it:

You can just identify with this family, even if they're a different race.

Similarly, one group member stated:

I have Jewish friends, that are so good, that I don't know they're Jewish. . . . There is no constant reminder that this is a black family.

He was implying that being white Anglo-Saxon is the norm from which others deviate.

These responses are ambiguous rather than color-blind. The respondents knew that they were watching a black family but "forgot" in the face of its familiarity. "You lose track of it," said one woman, "because it's so average." Another respondent described how the Huxtables' race "just sort of drifted" out of her mind while watching. This forgetfulness is simply a way of sustaining two contradictory interpretations of the same thing. The Huxtables are, in this sense, both black and white. This working class white woman, when asked if she was aware of the Huxtables' race, replied:

Not at all. But at the same time they don't neglect the black pride which I think is a hard thing to do; and I think they've done it successfully. They've done shows on Martin Luther King and on going down to Washington to do Civil Rights marches when they get together with the grandparents . . . but they do it in a way that's not [too conspicuous or threatening].

Other respondents replied to the same question in the same way:

> *It depends on what they are talking about. Again, what issue they are dealing with. If they are dealing with something that pertains to black people in particular, I'm aware of it; but if they are not, it really, I don't think it really comes to mind.*

> *Yes and no. You're aware because at points they make you aware, but you could lose track of it because it's so average.*

> *Their attributes are white—in comparison to* Good Times *or something like that. . . . I'd say it's fifty-fifty, sometimes their culture and attitudes, the things they say, bring you back to the fact that this is an entirely black cast, so I'd say 50 percent of the time I notice, 50 percent I don't.*

> *There's something in Clair's voice. There's something in Clair's voice that is not white American.*

Now You See It, Now You Don't

What makes these ambivalent responses particularly interesting is their particularity to *The Cosby Show.* These respondents were not usually so ambiguous about race. They share a common definition of what blackness is, and they recognize it when they see it. This perception manifested itself when respondents were asked to talk about other, more traditional black TV sitcoms, shows like *Good Times, The Jeffersons, 227,* and *Amen.* While most respondents were able to link these shows under the general category of "black sitcoms," they did not, significantly, include *The Cosby Show* in this category (only one person in the entire white sample made such a link). As one respondent put it, "I think [those shows] are totally different." The difference being that those shows, unlike *The Cosby Show,* involve what is identified as "black humor" in a "black setting."

The black shows that are seen to signify blackness more strongly are, accordingly, compared unfavorably to *The Cosby Show.* These other black sitcoms were often denigrated by white groups for being "slapstick," "loud," "full of yelling and screaming," "stereotypical," and more "black in style and humor":

> *I don't like them, to be honest with you. They're sarcastic, they're loud, they yell, there's no, they just criticize each other openly.*

> *I think they are more stereotypical black shows than* Cosby. *I don't think* Cosby *is stereotypical black. . . . I mean they really don't make much point to the fact that they're black. And certainly don't do black stereotypical things like* Good Times *used to do. But I think* Amen, 227, *are more that way. They talk the slick black accent, and they work on the mannerisms, and I think they make a conscious effort to act that way like they are catering to the black race in that show. Whereas* Cosby, *you know, definitely doesn't do that. He's upper middle class and he's not black stereotypical. There's a difference in the tone of those shows, completely.*

> *I think there's a lot of black families out there that are similar to the Cosbys that they're not such a stereotype black. You know, talking like the black slang or that kind of stuff, . . . being portrayed as intelligent, white-collar workers and that kind of thing. I should think, from a black perspective,* The Cosby Show *is more complimentary to blacks than some of the other shows. You know, the 227, the older woman hanging out of the window watching the neighbors walk by and stuff like that, which is reality in a lot of situations but in terms of. . . . It just seems to be heavy into black stereotyping.*

> Cosby *is much better. . . . The actors are much better, a lot funnier, more stuff you can relate to; they're a lot funnier than the other two. . . . Like Amen, the daughter who dates the priest, or whatever he is, you know she's just not realistic, from my point of view anyway. With 227 and Jackie, I don't relate to her or care for her at all as an actress, and she's hardly a realistic person. You can get involved in* The Cosby Show *and feel that you understand it, you're a part of it and can relate to it; while on these other shows there's not even usually a whole plot, it's just kind of there.*

> *If you look at* Good Times, *it's a majority of black. It was very racist the going over the white. The "whitey" down the street, you know.*

> *They [the Huxtables] don't base any humor on black and white kind of thing yet; they let it be known*

that they are a black family, etc., etc. But the Jeffer-sons actually made many, many jokes on black-white interaction.

I couldn't picture doing some of those things they did [on Good Times*] or being so desperate for a new refrigerator.*

I don't watch that much TV so I don't watch that many; but I've seen one of them with a black cast and they weren't as funny. Atypical of whatever happens in life and all that.

It's slapstick. It's too noisy for me . . . and I don't remember much about the family, or the interactions, or relationships. Except the slapstick and the volume of it. I'd usually miss half the dialogue. It was all extraneous.

I remember that it [The Jeffersons*] was a little bit more slapstick, a little bit more . . . stereotypical. Much more stereotypical. They were more concerned with racial issues, blatant racial issues. There was a couple in the building who were mixed race. And it was much more interested in class, and the difference between class, middle class versus working class. So it was a much different show.*

Running through these statements is a clear dislike of the kind of blackness these other sitcoms repre-sent. The use of the term *stereotypical* by these re-spondents is interesting in this respect. Normally the term *stereotypical* implies a critical awareness that the stereotype is, in some important way, misleading. This was not necessarily the case with members of our white groups. On the contrary, a vague awareness of media stereotypes was combined with an equally vague assumption that perhaps these stereotypes were, after all, accurate. So, for example, a show that "seems to be heavy into black stereotyping" may also be "reality in a lot of situations." What makes these shows stereotypical for these white viewers is partly that they are seen as unambiguously black. They remind the viewer of racial issues that *The Cosby Show* allows them to forget. So they are "much more stereotypical" partly because "they were more con-cerned with racial issues, blatant racial issues." These programs are seen as "black humor" for black people;

as one respondent says: "Like they are catering to the black race in that show." This perception is not im-partial: the blackness on display here is seen by these respondents, almost universally, as negative.

One respondent made an unusual attempt to pur-sue the question of stereotyping in relation to news coverage, but even she went on to acknowledge that it was difficult for her to make a critical judgment:

You know how they show, in a courtroom, when they accuse someone, and they would probably always be black. And then the white tend to be left out, I think, in terms of crime. And I don't know, is that re-ally what's happening? Or is it just the way the media are reporting it? You have no way of knowing. I have no way of knowing.

In other words, in the absence of other information, we have to accept the stereotypical image as the most plausible one. As a consequence, there was, for the white respondents, only a tiny discursive space between an awareness of TV stereotypes of black people and acceptance of those stereotypes. To con-demn other black shows for being stereotypical was, therefore, close to condemning them for being too black. *The Cosby Show,* as a corollary to this, is less stereotypical and therefore less black.

Some white respondents (particularly in the up-per middle class groups) expressed their dislike for these stereotypical shows by not watching them at all:

Do you want to know the truth? I tried once, and I couldn't relate to any of it. I don't even know which one I had on. It did not hold my attention at all, and I never turned them back on.

Those who did watch one of these shows appeared to do so without much enthusiasm, particularly when they were compared to the "calm, thought-out" *Cosby Show.* A typical complaint was that they were "less easy to relate to." "They're just not like our fam-ily." Just as the absence of race on *The Cosby Show* allows the inclusion of white viewers, the cultural presence of race on other shows serves to alienate the same white viewers. One woman suggested that she was aware of race when watching other black sitcoms, "But you don't think about it with *The Cosby Show*. . . . It doesn't even cross my mind." Or, as another respondent put it, although other black sitcoms exploit identifiably "black humor," with *The Cosby Show* "you just think of them as people."

What do these responses to the Huxtable household signify? In the first instance, it appears that *The Cosby Show* has an appeal among white audiences that other black shows do not. These respondents, as we described in Chapters 2 and 3, had few problems relating to or identifying with the Huxtable family. This identification allows them the enjoyment of taking part vicariously in the pleasant lives of the Huxtables "because," as one respondent observed, *The Cosby Show* "relates mostly to usual, regular families and stuff, and their regular problems, and stuff like that."

Would these viewers enjoy the show as much if its blackness was overtly signified? Moreover, is the absence of any discussion or acknowledgment of racism on *The Cosby Show* a prerequisite for these viewers' enjoyment and participation (as viewers)? The answers to these questions reveal the limits of the apparently liberal perception that the Huxtables are less obviously black because they are, for these white viewers, "just like us." On the whole, these respondents want to be reminded neither that the Huxtables are black nor, still less, of the existence of any form of racism.

A number of respondents were aware, when prompted, that black issues were either introduced with the greatest delicacy or entirely absent from *The Cosby Show*. One respondent suggested that, having been accepted by a wide audience, the Huxtables were able to make gentle references to their race:

> The early shows, to the best of my recollection, were devoid [of reminders they were black]. They could have been anybody. They didn't have to be black. It was only after the show maintained its popularity for a while that they—I interpret—that they had the ability to keep reminding people that they were black. . . . Suddenly they would be speaking in a black idiom. . . . It's just to put a little bit blacker face on what was until then just happened to be a very good comedy, about realistic people who were played by black people.

Although a couple of the more self-consciously liberal respondents were critical of the show's failure to go beyond such gentle reminders, most felt that this restraint was positive. Although one respondent did suggest that *The Cosby Show* had now established enough credibility (among white people) to deal with racial issues, she remained unenthusiastic about the prospect:

> They don't want to deal with the issue of interracial. . . . Life is tough enough anyways, and then to get into interracials. . . . I think if the Cosbys did it, though, I don't think they would have any problems. I think it would be all right, you know; people have a lot of trust in them.

Most other respondents rejected the idea much more unequivocally. Some expressed this by saying that they watched the show to enjoy it, not to be preached at; others stated that the introduction of black issues would be "alienating" and that the show would "lose a lot" if it dealt with racism, with the ominous consequence that they would "probably lose the white audience they have":

> I think they'd get a lot of mixed publicity for the show. And it would start to alienate some people.

> I don't think they want to get into those provocative things . . . you know, controversial subjects which raise race, gayness, grievances, losses, yeah, that stuff. I suppose they think there's enough of that anyway. Let's keep this nice and easy.

> I think it was intentional on The Cosby Show; they want them, they don't want them to be a racially oriented show. They want it to be just another family.

> It's the only show I can ever remember where a black family was shown, and they were upper middle class, professional family, having situations that were familiar to most people—well, familiar to that type of person. And race is never an issue.

> I think it's low. It would diminish their show. I wouldn't want to see them, you know, doing the black and white thing. Yeah, I don't like that. I really don't think they need to do that.

Other respondents expressed a similar sentiment in relation to Bill Cosby's support for black causes and politicians. Such support made them distinctly uneasy:

> But why did Bill Cosby go after this [Tawana Brawley case]? There are plenty of children on the streets of New York that have been raped. And why is he not, as a parent, going after these? . . . Excuse me, but does he also support Jesse Jackson? That really upsets me, about Bill Cosby. . . . So in terms of principles and stuff, I really question Cosby. . . . But then I have to question Bill Cosby's philosophy and principles and everything, if he can stand behind someone like Jesse Jackson. I don't see Bill Cosby in the pure sense that I saw him years ago.

> Then you read about him giving money to the Negro College Fund and you wonder, you don't want to watch a show that's against you, you know . . . against the white race.

Bill Cosby is, in these responses, removed from the comfortable sanctity of *The Cosby Show* and placed in a context that emphasizes his blackness. Our respondents reflect here the accuracy of TV producer Norman Lear's assessment of white viewers when he says: "I don't think there's any question that white America is uncomfortable with victimization, or however you want to term the black experience, that which makes you feel guilty, feel uncomfortable" (quoted in Riggs, 1991).

To introduce black issues would transform the Huxtables from a celebrated Everyfamily into a *black* family, an identity these respondents would prefer to avoid. One respondent illustrated this perspective thus:

> My speculation is that they're trying to present a family who's just a normal American family. And that, as white people don't talk about racial issues all the time, or confront them, or deal with them, then neither would this family. They're trying to get the point across that it's not an all-consuming issue in their lives.

To be "normal" here means, as we have seen, to be part of the dominant culture, which is white and, on television, middle or upper middle class. Class is therefore seen as a signifier of race: to be working class and black is seen as being *more* black.

One manifestation of this entangling of perceptions of class and race occurred during a discussion with an upper middle class white group. The group, having complained that the Huxtables, as working professionals, could not possibly cope without some form of domestic help, were asked if such a character should be introduced into the show. Their response was equivocal because, for them, the presence of class differences automatically signaled *racial* tensions:

> A loaded issue. If they bring in help, what's the color going to be? Are they going to be treated as a second-class citizen? . . . It would take some courage because it makes it trickier.

Questions of class are not seen as generally difficult; they are "tricky" in this case only because the Huxtables are black. The Huxtables' perceived universality is, therefore, partly a function of their privileged class position.

This reaction to class differences is compounded by the nature of contemporary television. The middle class world of television is one without struggle. To admit a black family to this world without disrupting it, the family must, like white TV characters, rise to this social position effortlessly. As far as most viewers in the study were concerned, to include class or racial issues would have made *The Cosby Show* seem less "normal" and ironically, less "realistic."

We can see, in this respect, how television has created a form of doublethink in which it becomes necessary for black characters to deny the realities that distinguish black experience in order to appear credible and realistic.

The general resistance of most white viewers in our study to the possibility of transforming the Huxtables into a blue-collar family suggests that this perception is widespread. The Huxtables, having risen to the comfortable upper middle class world, have, for many white viewers, thereby disentangled themselves from their racial origin. They did not want to see the show, as one respondent put it, "stoop down to another cultural level." To be a blue-collar family, in the media world, would emphasize their "blackness"; as professionals, contrarily, they merge into the "normal" white world of TV. Social mobility, in this sense, becomes a form of sanctity from more unpleasant reminders of racial difference.

Biology versus Culture

The significance of this ambiguity about the Huxtables' race becomes a little clearer when we examine the responses of whites who did *not* articulate it. For these viewers, the Huxtables' race, their blackness, formed a nonnegotiable part of the show. Although such responses were less common among white viewers than some variation of the more colorblind response, they took a number of different tones ranging from progressive to reactionary. These differences originated in quite different attitudes toward black people and race relations.

Viewers who held a number of overtly racist assumptions or were antagonistic in some way toward *all* black people seemed unable to ignore the Huxtables' color. This inability made it difficult for them to identify with the show, and watching it was less enjoyable. Such responses in this study were present only in glimpses. The reactions noted by one interviewer while recruiting participants suggested that some people with strongly held racist views would dislike *The Cosby Show* simply because it was black. One person, refusing to take part in the study, remarked that the show was "stupid, stupid, stupid." Because the respondents were only people who watched *The Cosby Show,* we were less likely to hear this kind of response. Whenever an overtly racist judgment was made, it was fairly blatant. One interview group, for example, was interrupted toward the end of the session by friends, who castigated *The Cosby Show* for being "too black":

> The show is too black. . . . It's too black, centered around the black race.

A more subtle articulation of this reaction came from a viewer who, unlike all the other white interviewees, put *The Cosby Show* in the same category as other black shows. Though he enjoyed some aspects of these shows, he criticized them for excluding white people from their casts. In an inverse version of the discourse of racial stereotyping (used by most black respondents), he argued that the only white people who appeared on the show were "fat and stupid"— this being evidence of what he saw as *The Cosby Show's* pro-black, anti-white position.

The differences between this kind of reading and the more ambiguous view of *The Cosby Show's* race is instructive. The more overtly racist viewer is less able to distinguish between blackness as a physical and a cultural category. It is more difficult for those expressing a more overt form of racism to forget that the Huxtables are black because skin color is seen to bear an inevitable cultural message. It is a discourse of biological determinism that can only work to amplify the signifier "black." The ability of other respondents to disentangle the physical from the cultural is, by the same token, a prerequisite for their apparently enlightened failure to identify *The Cosby Show* as a black show.

A few respondents articulated racial awareness in quite a different way. These people also rejected the idea that the Huxtables could be white but saw their "blackness" as enjoyable. This idea, though perhaps deeply felt, was expressed only tentatively. As one woman put it, "It wouldn't be as funny if it was white. . . . They have a way about them—I don't know what it is." The inexplicable appeal of the Huxtables' blackness—the idea that the show would lose an ineffable something if it became white—was, for some respondents, clearly more difficult to articulate than the idea that "you forget that they're black." If nothing else, this tells something about the nature of the dominant white culture, and, in particular, what that culture allows white people, or makes it easy for white people, to say about black people. It is easier, in other words, to celebrate the absence of blackness than its presence.

Only the viewers who were most positive about *The Cosby Show* as a *black* show were able to offer any explanation. One referred to her enjoyment of black culture, while another felt it was more "fun" and "colorful" because it was a black show ("Black moms are cooler"). These people tended to be the most progressive in their racial attitudes, and they usually had considerable experience of black people in their own lives.

The Consequences of Classlessness

There is a sense in which *The Cosby Show* does appear, for a number of white viewers, to cultivate a liberal attitude toward black people and racial equality. The lapses into moments of color-blindness that characterized so many white responses is, in this sense, a major step forward. The series does, as Dyson suggests, allow white North Americans "to view black folks as *human beings.*" *The Cosby Show* proves that black people can be just like white people or, as one respondent put it, "that black people are just like us." The inevitabilities of crude racism have been disentangled; the color of someone's skin can, indeed, signify nothing.

Before we hurl our hats into the air proclaiming *The Cosby Show* to be the vision of the racially tolerant society to come, we should reflect that this victory in race relations is a rather hollow one, achieved at an extremely high price. For many white respondents, the Huxtables' class position distinguishes them from other black people, making it possible for white audiences to disentangle them from preconceived (white) notions of black culture (they're "upper middle class," not "black"). The Huxtables, in this sense, look like most white families on television. If it is necessary for black people to become upper middle class to be spared the prejudice of whites, then it is a price most cannot afford to pay. The acceptance of the Huxtables as an Everyfamily did not dislodge the generally negative associations white viewers have of "black culture," attitudes quickly articulated when other black TV sitcoms were discussed. *The Cosby Show* caters to a need for familiarity, and, in this sense, the price it pays for acceptance is that the Huxtables do appear "just like white people."

For many white respondents in our study, the Huxtables' achievement of the American dream leads them to a world where race no longer matters. This attitude enables white viewers to combine an impeccably liberal attitude toward race with a deep-rooted suspicion of black people.

They are, on the one hand, able to welcome a black family into their homes; they can feel an empathy with them and identify with their problems and experiences. They will, at the same time, distinguish between the Huxtables and most other black people, and their welcome is clearly only extended as far as the Huxtables. If *The Cosby Show* were about a working class family, it would be an unpleasant reminder of the class-based inequalities that support our racially divided society. *The Cosby Show* thus allows white people the luxury of being both liberal and intolerant. They reject bigotry based upon skin color, yet they are wary of most (working class) black people. Color difference is okay, cultural difference is not.

This tells us something about the nature of modern racism. The blackness that many white people fear or regard as inferior is no longer simply a function of skin pigmentation; blackness is seen, instead, as the cultural category that appears to bind most black people to certain class positions, to stunt their capacity for upward mobility. As we have suggested, in a culture that makes it difficult to talk in terms of social and class barriers, this neoracism is the only way to explain why the Huxtables have made it in a United States where most black people have not.

At the same time, *The Cosby Show* panders to the limits of white liberalism, allowing white audiences the sanctimonious pleasure of viewing the world through rose-tinted spectacles. Although we disagree with Shelby Steele's general analysis of race, we concur with his description of the relationship between *The Cosby Show* and white audiences when he says:

> The success of this handsome, affluent black family points to the fair-mindedness of whites who, out of their essential goodness, changed society so that black families like the Huxtables could succeed. Whites can watch *The Cosby Show* and feel complimented on a job well done. . . . On Thursday nights, Cosby, like a priest, absolves his white viewers, forgives and forgets the sins of the past (Steele, 1990: 11).

References

Entman, Robert. 1990. "Modern Racism and the Images of Blacks in Local Television News." *Critical Studies in Mass Communication* 7 (no. 4, December).

Gates, Henry Louis. 1989. "TV's Black World Turns—But Stays Unreal." *New York Times*, November 12.

Miller, Mark Crispin. 1986. "Deride and Conquer." In *Watching Television: A Pantheon Guide to Popular Culture*, edited by Todd Gitlin. New York: Pantheon.

Riggs, Marlon. 1991. *Color Adjustment* (a film produced, directed, and written by Marlon Riggs). San Francisco: California Newsreel.

Steele, Shelby. 1990. *The Content of Our Character*. New York: Harper Perennial.

11.
"FEAR OF A BLACK PLANET"

Rap Music and Black Cultural Politics in the 1990s

Tricia Rose

Introduction

Popular wisdom regarding rap's (or Hip Hop's) political development sustains that rap music was not always political. It began as an apolitical "party music" with limited social relevance. For many observers, the advent of the group Public Enemy (PE) marked the emergence of rap as a political cultural form; PE as a point of enlightenment, as it were. The success of their "A Nation of Millions" (1988), ushered in a new rap aesthetic: gold chains are out, African medallions in; pride in oneself is pride in Black unity. Rap fans still believe in the power of "boomin' systems" and "gettin' funky," but they have attended to PE rapper Chuck D's advice to "move somethin'" and "own somethin'," too.

Clearly, Public Enemy marked a significant break in rap's dominant discursive terrain. Prior to the emergence of group members Chuck D, Flavor Flav, Terminator X, Professor Griff, and the Sl-Ws, party-oriented funkateers like Run-DMC, The Fat Boys, and Whodini dominated the commercial rap scene. Even Run-DMC's frustrated and renunciatory 1983 hit "It's Like That" is a far cry from Public Enemy's resistive and emancipatory 1989 anthem "Fight the Power." Lyrically, rap's thematic territory has grown more complex and direct. Public Enemy's success opened the door to more politically and racially explicit material, some of which has made important interventions while other material seems dedicated solely to its potential sales value.

While a shift in rap's political articulations did take place, confining the definition of the cultural politics of rap to lyrical content addresses only the most obvious and explicit facet of the politics of Black cultural expression. To dismiss rappers who do not choose so-called "political" subjects as "having no politically resistive meaning" requires ignoring the complex web of institutional policing to which all rappers are subject.

Rap's cultural politics lies not only in its lyrical expression but in the nature and character of its journey through the institutional and discursive territories of popular culture. As is the case for cultural production generally, the politics of rap music involves the contestation over public space, expressive meaning, interpretation, and cultural capital. In short, it is not just what one says, it is where one can say it, how others react to what one says, and whether one has the means with which to command public space. Cultural politics is not simply poetic politics, it is the struggle over context, meaning, and public space.

> [Cultural politics is] the complex process by which the whole domain in which people search to create meaning about their everyday lives is subject to politicization and struggle. . . . The central issue of such a cultural politics is the exercise of power in both institutional and ideological forms and the manner in which "cultural practices" relate to this context. (Angus & Jhally, 1989, p. 2)

Ideological power and resistance is exercised through signs and language. As Angus and Jhally point out, critical links exist between institutional and ideological power. Popular pleasure involves territorial struggles and Black pleasure involves a particularly thorny struggle. If a Black teenage performer can draw 10,000 Black, Brown, and White teenagers into a major urban arena and they leave shouting "My Addidas!," a significant moment in the politics of Black cultural production has occurred. Run-DMC's cry, "My Addidas!," is the chorus for a rap that describes the style, attitude, and demeanor of a "B-boy" (Hip Hop fan). "My Addidas!" celebrates Hip Hop style and street attitude: shoelaces untied, (shoe) tongues raised up, and sneakers clean as a whistle. Yet, sneakers are understood to be the shoe of choice for athletes, teenagers, and street criminals. Black teenage males sporting sneakers and other Hip Hop gear are perceived as criminal equivalents. Loud, public celebration of an object that signifies one's alien status is an act of defiance and self-possession.

My central concern here is the exercise of institutional and ideological power over Hip Hop and the manner in which the Hip Hop community (e.g., fans and artists) relate and respond to this context. More specifically, I will try to untangle the complex relationships between the political economy of rap and the sociologically based crime discourse that frames it. This involves a close examination of the large venue's resistance to rap and the media interpretations of rap concerts and incidents of "violence" that have occurred at them.[1] As exercises of institutional and ideological power are often experienced personally as well as collectively, I have constructed a collage of cultural politics in which the experience of being "resisted by venues" and the dominant discursive explanations for such resistance are conterminous.

Show-Stoppers

Picture this: Thousands of young Black folks milled around waiting to get into the large arena. The big rap summer tour was in town, and it was a prime night for one to show one's stuff. The pre-show show was in full effect. Folks were dressed in the latest "fly gear": bicycle shorts, high-top sneakers, chunk jewelry, baggy pants, and polka-dotted tops. The hair styles were a fashion show in themselves: high-top fade designs, dreads, corkscrews, and braids. Crews of young women were checking out the brothers; posses of brothers were scoping out the sisters, each comparing styles among themselves. Some wide-eyed pre-teenyboppers were soaking in the teenage energy, thrilled to be out with the older kids.

As the lines for entering the arena began to form, dozens of mostly White private security guards dressed in red polyester v-neck sweaters and grey work pants began corralling the crowd through security checkpoints. The free-floating spirit started to sour, and a sense of hostility mixed with humiliation crystalized. Men and women were lined up separately in preparation for the weapons search. Coed groups dispersed and people moved toward their respective search lines. Each person had to submit to a full-body pat-down and a pocketbook, knapsack, and soul search. Generally, however, it appeared that the men were being treated with less respect and more hostility.

As I approached the female security guards, fear began to well up inside me. What if, I wondered to myself, they find something I was not allowed to bring inside? What is prohibited, anyway? I stopped to think: "All I have in my small purse is my wallet, eyeglasses, keys, and a notepad, nothing 'dangerous.'" The female security guard patted me down and scanned my body with an electronic scanner while anxiously keeping an eye on the other sisters in line to make sure no one slipped past her. She opened my purse and fumbled through it, pulling out a nail file. She stared at me as if to say, "Why did you bring this in here?" I did not answer her right away, hoping she would drop the file back into my purse and let me go through. She continued to stare at me, trying to size me up to see if I was there to cause trouble. By now, however, my attitude had turned foul; my childlike enthusiasm to see my favorite rappers had all but fizzled out. I did not know the file was in my purse, but the guard's accusatory posture rendered such innocent excuses moot. Finally, I replied tersely: "It's a nail file, what's the problem?" The guard handed it back to me, satisfied (I supposed) that I did not intend to use it as a weapon, and I proceeded into the arena. As I passed her, I thought bitterly to myself: "This arena is a public place and I am entitled to come here and bring a nail file if I want to." Yet, my words rang hollow in my head; the language of entitlement could not erase my sense of alienation. I felt harassed and unwanted: "This arena isn't mine, it is hostile, alien territory." An unspoken message hung in the air: "You're not wanted here, let's get this over with and then we'll just send you all back where you came from." By this point, I was glad I had brought the nail file. I mused: "At least if one of those guards harasses me I'll have something to fight back with."

I recount this incident for several reasons. First, incidents similar to it continue to take place when rap concerts are held. A hostile tenor, if not one of actual verbal abuse, is a regular part of the rap fan's contact with arena security and police. Second, I want to provide a depiction of the high-level anxiety and antagonism that confronts young Black rap fans who are often merely tolerated and regarded with heightened suspicion and hostility by concert security forces. Imagine now the level of frustration that might possibly well up in a young Black teenaged boy or girl faced with this kind of social antagonism on a consistent basis. Large arenas and other hostile institutions that treat young African Americans with suspicion and fear are themselves often the subject of rappers' lyrics. Indeed, Hip Hop artists articulate a range of counter-reactions to the range of institutional policing faced by many young African Americans:

I've been wonderin' why
Peoples livin' in fear
Of my shade
(Or my hi-top fade)
I'm not the one runnin'
But they got me on the run
Treat me like I have a gun. (Public Enemy, 1990)

Here we go, yo
I'm a Negro wit an ego, so
Don't tell me what I'm doin' is illegal, no
I resort to violence only when provoked
Contrary to rumors I ain't no joke. (Salt 'n Pepa,
   1990)

Fuck the police, comin' straight from the
   underground
A young nigga got it bad 'cause I'm brown
And not the other color, so police think
They have the authority
To kill the minority. (NWA, 1988)

Young African Americans are positioned in fundamentally antagonistic relationships to the institutions that most prominently frame and constrain their lives. The public school system, the police, and the popular media perceive and construct them as a dangerous internal element in urban America—an element that if allowed to roam about freely will threaten the social order, an element that must be policed. The social construction of rap and rap-related violence is fundamentally linked to the social discourse on Black containment and fears of a Black planet. In this light arena security forces are the metaphorical foot-soldiers in the war to contain African Americans' public presence and public pleasure. The paramilitary posture of concert guards is a surface manifestation of a complex network of ideological and economic processes that attempt to justify the policing of rap music, Black youth, and African Americans generally.

It is this ideological position regarding Black youth that frames media and institutional attacks on rap and separates resistance to rap from attacks sustained by rock-and-roll artists. Black expression is by no means the only expression under attack. Popular White expressions, especially heavy metal rock music has recently sustained increased sanction and assaults by politically and economically powerful organizations such as the Parent's Music Resource Center (PMRC), American Family Association (AFA), and Focus on the Family (FF). These organizations are not fringe groups; they are supported by major corporations, national school associations, and local police and municipal officials.[2] However, critical differences exist between the nature of the attacks made against Black youth expression and White youth expression. The terms of the assaults on rap music, for example, are part of a long-standing sociologically based discourse that positions Black influences as a cultural threat to American society.[3] Consequently, rappers, their fans, and Black youth in general are constructed as co-conspirators in the spread of Black aesthetic and discursive influence. Heavy metal rock music may be viewed as a threat to the fiber of American society by the anti-rock organizations, but the fans (e.g., "our children") are depicted as *victims* of its influence. Unlike heavy metal's victims, the majority of rap's fans are the youngest representatives of a Black presence whose cultural difference is an ongoing internal threat to America's cultural development. These differences between the ideological nature of sanctions against rap and heavy metal are of critical importance because they articulate the ways in which racial discourses deeply inform social control efforts in the United States.

According to Haring (1989), "venue availability [for rap tours] is down 33% because buildings are limiting rap shows."[4] The apparent genesis of arena owners' "growing concern" is the September 10, 1988, Nassau (NY) Coliseum rap show when the stabbing death of 19-year-old Julio Fuentes focused national attention on rap concert-related "violence." As Haring notes:

> In the wake of that incident, TransAmerica [a major insurance company] cancelled blanket insurance coverage for shows produced by G Street Express in Washington D.C., the show's promoter. Although G Street has since obtained coverage, the fallout of that cancellation has cast a pall over rap shows, resulting in many venues imposing stringent conditions or refusing to host the shows at all. (p. 80)

That the experience was frightening and dangerous for those involved is incontestable; however, the incident was not the first to result in an arena death, nor was it the largest or most threatening. During the same weekend of the Fuentes stabbing, 1,500 people were hurt when a "crowd without tickets tried to pull down fences" during singer Michael Jackson's performance in Liverpool, England (Associated Press, 1988). Yet, the Associated Press article made no mention of insurance company cancellations, no similar pall was cast over Jackson's music or musical genre, nor was any particular group held accountable for the incident. What sparked the venue owners' panic

in the Nassau event was a preexisting anxiety regarding rap's core audience, namely Black working-class youth. The growing popularity of rap music and the media's interpretation of the incident fed directly into those anxieties. The Nassau incident and the social control discourse that frames it provides justification for a wide range of efforts to contain the Black teen presence while shielding these practices behind naturalized concerns over public safety.

The pall cast over rap shows was primarily facilitated by New York media coverage of the incident. The *New York Post* headline, "Rampaging Teen Gang Slays 'Rap' Fan" (Pelleck & Sussman, 1988) fed easily into White fears that Black teens need only a spark to start an uncontrollable urban forest fire. Fear of Black anger, lawlessness, and amorality were affirmed by the media's interpretation and description of this incident. Venue owners all over the country were anxious to learn about what happened that night in Nassau County, and press interpretations were a critical aid in constructing the event's official transcript. According to Haring (1989), Norm Smith, assistant general manager for the San Diego Sports Arena, "attributes the venue's caution to the influence of discussions building management has had with other arenas regarding problems at rap shows" (p. 80). These discussions between venue managers and owners are framed by incident reports that are documented by venue security staff and local police as well as next-day media coverage. Such self-referential reports are woven together into a hegemonic interpretation of arena "violence." According to the *New York Times* coverage of the Nassau incident, the stabbing was a byproduct of a "robbery spree" conducted by a dozen or so young men (Marriott, 1988); Fuentes was apparently stabbed while attempting to retrieve his girlfriend's stolen jewelry. Marriott notes that of the 10,000 concertgoers, this dirty dozen was solely responsible for the incident. While the race of the perpetrators was not mentioned in the text, a photo of a handcuffed Black male (sporting a Beverly Hills Polo Club sweatshirt!) and mention of the assailants' Bedford-Stuyvesant residences stereotypically positioned them as members of the inner-city Black poor. This portrait of wanton Black male aggressiveness was framed by an enlarged inset quote which read: "A detective said the thieves 'were in a frenzy, like sharks feeding.'" By contrast, my own conversations with people who attended the event revealed that many concertgoers had no idea the incident even took place until they read the newspapers the next day.

Thus described as Black predators seeking blood for sustenance, the twelve Black youth who were stealing jewelry for money were viciously dehumanized. Poor youths who commit street crimes do so to attain consumer goods. In a society in which quality and quantity of amassed consumer goods is equated with status and prowess, it should not be surprising that some of these teenagers, who have accurately assessed their unlikely chances for economic mobility, steal such goods from other people.[5] The *Times* article not only mischaracterized their motives but also set a tone of uncontrolled widespread violence in describing the entire concert. The event was framed exclusively by the perspective of the police; no quotes were included from other concert patrons or anyone other than Nassau County Police Commissioner Rozzi and a Detective Nolan. In the Nassau Coliseum case, police reports and media coverage form a solitary text binding racist depictions of Blacks as animals to ostensibly objective, statistically based police documentation, thus rendering any other interpretation of the so-called night of rampage irrelevant. Ultimately, this reporting provides venue owners with perfect justification to significantly curtail or ban rap performances at their arenas. As Haring reports, according to the Nassau Coliseum's director of marketing Hilary Hartung, no rap shows have been held at the coliseum since the September 1988 stabbing incident. Hartung "suspects it's by mutual choice" and claims the following:

> The venue looks at every concert individually. We check with all arenas before a concert comes here to check incident reports for damage or unruly crowds. It could be [a] heavy metal concert or [a] rap concert. (p. 80)

The social construction of "violence," that is, when and how particular acts are defined as violent, is part of a larger process of labeling social phenomena.[6] Rap-related violence is one facet of the contemporary urban crisis that purportedly consists of a rampant drug "culture" and "wilding" gangs of Black and Hispanic youth. When the (New York City) *Daily News* headline reads, "L.I. [Long Island] Rap-Slayer Sought" (Kruggel & Roga, 1988) or a *Newsweek* story is dubbed "The Rap Attitude" (Gates, 1990), these labels are important because they assign a particular meaning to a phenomenon (or event) and locate it within a larger context. Labels are critical to the process of interpretation because they provide a context for social behavior. As Hall (1978) points out in *Policing the Crisis,* once a label is assigned, "thereafter the use of the label is likely to mobilize this whole referential context, with all its associated meaning and connotations" (p. 19). The question then is not "Is there really violence at rap concerts?" but rather "How are these crimes contextualized and labeled?" In what already existing categories, for example, was the pivotal Nassau Coliseum incident framed? Further, whose interests do these interpretive strategies serve, and what are the repercussions?

Venue owners may have the final word on booking decisions but they are not the only site of institutional gate keeping. Another major power broker, the insurance industry, can refuse to insure an act approved by venue management. By way of explanation, to gain access to a venue, a touring band or group first hires a booking agent to negotiate the act's fee. The booking agent then hires a concert promoter who "purchases" the group's show and presents the show to both the insurance company and the venue managers. If an insurance company will not insure a show because they believe it represents an unprofitable risk, then the venue owner will not book the show. Moreover, the insurance company and the venue owner reserve the right to charge whatever insurance or permit fees they deem reasonable on a case-by-case basis. For example, Three Rivers Stadium in Pittsburgh (PA) recently tripled its normal $20,000 permit fee for the group The Grateful Dead. Those insurance companies that will insure rap concerts have raised their minimum coverage from about $500,000 to almost $5 million worth of coverage per show (Rose, 1990). Accordingly, several major arenas have made it almost impossible to book a rap show, and others have flatly refused to book rap acts at all.

During my interview with Richard Walters, a booking agent with the Famous Talent Agency (a major booking agency that books many prominent rap acts), I asked him if booking agents had responded to venue bans on rap music by leveling charges of racial discrimination against venue owners. His answer was stunning:

> These facilities are privately owned, [owners] can do anything they want. You say to them: "You won't let us in because you're discriminating against Black kids." They say to you, "Fuck you, who cares? Do whatever you got to do, but you're not coming in here. You, I don't need you, I don't want you. Don't come, don't bother me. I will book hockey, ice shows, basketball, country music and graduations. I still do all kinds of things 360 days out of the year. But I don't need you. I don't need fighting, shootings and stabbings." Why do they care? They have their image to maintain. (Rose, 1990)

Walter's imaginary conversation is a brutally candid description both of the scope of power venue owners have over access to large public urban spaces and the racially exclusionary silent code that governs booking policies. It is also an explicit articulation of the aura created by the red-and-grey suited arena security guard who inquired about the purpose of my nail file. Given this scenario, the unfortunate death of Julio Fuentes was not seen as cause for despair over the unnecessary loss of life; rather, it became the source of an image problem for venue owners and a sign of invasion by an unwanted element with little political or social leverage.

Because rap has an especially strong urban following, freezing rap out of major metropolitan arenas has a dramatic impact on rap artists' profits and ability to reach their fan base via live performance. Rap groups such as Public Enemy and others rely heavily on live performance settings to address current social issues, media miscoverage, and other issues that especially concern Black America. Because Black youth are constructed as a permanent threat to social order, large public gatherings of them are viewed as dangerous events. Black youth, who are highly conscious of their alienated and marginalized lives, will continue to be hostile toward those institutions and environments that reaffirm this aspect of their reality.

The presence of a predominantly Black audience in a 15,000-person capacity arena, communicating with major Black cultural icons whose music, lyrics, and attitudes illuminate and affirm Black fears and grievances provokes within the larger society a fear of the consolidation of Black rage. For venue owners and insurance companies, broken chairs, injury claims, or Black fatalities apparently are not important in and of themselves; however, they are important in that they symbolize a loss of control which might involve challenges to the current social configuration. Such incidents suggest the possibility that Black rage can be directed at the people and institutions that support the containment and oppression of Black people. As rapper Ice Cube (1990) forebodes in his rap, "The Nigga You Love to Hate": "Just think if niggas decided to retaliate?"

Venue resistance to rap music is driven both by economic calculations and the hegemonic media interpretation of rap's fans, music, and concert-related violence. The relationship between real acts of violence, police incident reports, economic calculations, and media accounts is complex and interactive. Further, it has most often worked to reproduce readings of rap concert violence as examples of Black cultural disorder and sickness. This matrix masks the source of discursive and institutional power by directing attention away from blatant and active forces of discrimination and fueling racially motivated control efforts by the police and discriminatory insurance and booking policies. Media accounts of these rap-related incidents solidify these hegemonic interpretations of Black criminality. Gilroy's (1987) study of race and class in Britain, *There Ain't No Black in the Union Jack,* devotes considerable attention to deconstructing dominant images of Black criminality. Gilroy reveals several ideological similarities between dominant media and police interpretations of race and crime in the United States and Britain. His interpretation of the construction of Black criminality in Britain is appropriate here:

... distinctions between the actual crimes which Blacks commit and the symbolism with which the representation of these crimes has become endowed is highly significant. ... The manner in which anxiety about Black crime has provided hubs for the wheels of popular racism is an extraordinary process which is connected with the day to day struggle of police to maintain order and control at street level, and at a different point, to the political conflicts which mark Britain's move towards more authoritarian modes of government intervention and social regulation. (p. 110)

Deconstructing the media's ideological perspective on Black crime does not suggest that "real" acts of violence by and against Black youth do not take place. However, these real acts are not accessible to the public without critical mediation by hegemonic discourses. Angus and Jhally (1989) describe this dynamic in more general terms:

... the distinction between "images" and "real life" can no longer be regarded as tenable. Social representations constitute social identities. The real is always mediated through images. (p. 6)

Consequently, real violence is always/already positioned as part of the prevailing images of Black violence and within the larger discourse on the Black urban threat. While violence at rap concerts can be interpreted as a visible instance of Black-on-Black crime, because it takes place in a White-dominated "safety zone" (i.e., public arena) it is widely interpreted as a loss of control on home territory. When rap concert-related violence takes place outside the invisible fence that surrounds poor Black communities, it raises the threat factor.

The rap community is aware that the "violence at rap concerts" label is being used to contain Black mobility and rap music, not to diminish violence against Blacks. Rappers have re-articulated a longstanding awareness among African Americans that crimes against Blacks (especially Black-on-Black crimes), do not carry equal moral weight or political imperative. Ice Cube's (1990) "Endangered Species"

captures a familiar reading of state-sanctioned violence against young Black males:

Every cop killer ignored
They just send another nigger to the morgue
A point scored
They could give a fuck about us
They'd rather find us with guns and white
    powder ...
Now kill ten of me to get the job correct.
To serve, protect and break a nigga's neck.

Since the Nassau Coliseum incident, "violence" at rap concerts has continued to take place, and the media's assumed links between rap and disorder have grown more facile. The media's repetition of rap-related violence and the urban problematic that it conjures is not limited to the crime blotters: it also informs live performance critiques. In either circumstance the assumption made is that the significance of rap is its aesthetic and spatial disruptions, not its musical innovation and expressive capacity.[7] Consequently, the dominant media critiques of rap's aesthetic are conditioned by the omnipresent fears of Black influence—again, fears of a Black (aesthetic) planet.

In a particularly hostile Los Angeles Times review of Public Enemy's 1990 summer tour stop at the San Diego Sports Arena, newspaper critic John D'Agostino (1990) articulates a complex microcosm of social anxieties concerning Black youth, Black aesthetics, and rap music. D'Agostino's extensive next-day review column, entitled "Rap Concert Fails to Sizzle in San Diego," features a prominent caption: "Although it included a brawl, the Sports Arena concert seemed to lack steam and could not keep the under-sized capacity audience energized" (p. F-l). In the opening sentence D'Agostino confesses that "rap is not a critic's music; it is a disciple's music." This confession hints at its author's cultural illiteracy and is itself sufficient to render his subsequent critique irrelevant; yet D'Agostino continues, offering a description of the event which completely contradicts the article's title and caption. Despite the caption's suggestion of a slow and less than exciting event, the article's opening paragraph presents the audience as mindless and dangerous fanatics, mesmerized by rap's rhythms:

> For almost five hours, devotees of the Afros, Queen Latifah, Kid 'n Play, Digital Underground, Big Daddy Kane and headliners Public Enemy were jerked into spasmodic movement by what seemed little more than intermittent segments of a single rhythmic continuum. It was hypnotic in the way of sensory deprivation, a mind- and body-numbing marathon of monotony whose deafening, pre-recorded drum and bass tracks and roving klieg lights frequently turned the audience of 6,500 into a single-minded moveable beast. Funk meets Nuremberg Rally. (p. F-5)

Apparently, rap music is completely unintelligible to D'Agostino; moreover, his inability to interpret the sounds frightens him. This reading of the concert event, which makes explicit his fear and ignorance, condemns rap on precisely the grounds that make it compelling. For example, because the reviewer cannot explain why a series of bass or drum tracks moved the crowd, the audience seemed "jerked into spasmodic movement" suggestive of an "automatic" or "involuntary" response. The coded familiarity of the rhythms and "hooks" that rap samples from other Black music (especially funk and soul music) carries with it the power of Black collective memory. These sounds are cultural markers, and responses to them are in a sense "automatic" because they immediately conjure collective Black experience, past and present (Lipsitz, 1990). D'Agostino, while he senses the rhythmic continuum, interprets it as "monotonous" and "mind- and body-numbing." The very pulse that fortified the audience in San Diego, left him feeling sensorially deprived; the rhythms that empowered and stimulated the crowd numbed him, body and mind. D'Agostino's subsequent description of the music as capable of moving the crowd as a "single-minded, moveable beast" further amplifies his confusion and anxiety regarding the power and meaning of the drums in Black musical culture. What he perceives as monotonous percussive rhythms is frightening to him precisely because that same pulse energized and

empowered the mostly Black, youthful audience. Unable to negotiate the relationship between his fear of the audience and of the wall of sound that supported their pleasure yet pushed him to the margins, D'Agostino interprets Black pleasure as dangerous and automatic.

The sense of community rap facilitates (Pratt, 1989) and its privileging of Black aesthetics and cultural codes (Snead, 1986) displaces critics like D'Agostino and the hegemonic ideology to which they subscribe. By linking funk (rap) music to a Nazi rally, D'Agostino ultimately depicts Black youth as an aggressive, dangerous, fascist element whose behavior is sick, inexplicable, and orchestrated by rappers (whom he likens to hatemongering rally organizers). Rap, he suggests, is thus not even a disciples' music but rather a soundtrack for the celebration of Black fascist domination. Once this construction of Black fascism is in place, D'Agostino devotes the bulk of his review to the performances, describing them as "juvenile," "puerile," and, in the case of Public Enemy, an act that "relies on the controversy to maintain interest." In mid-review he describes a brawl that followed Digital Underground's performance:

> After the house lights were brought up following DU's exit, a fight broke out in front of the stage. Security guards, members of various rappers' entourages, and fans joined in the fray that grew to mob size and then pushed into a corner of the floor at one side of the stage. People rushed the area from all parts of the arena, but the scrapers were so tightly balled together that few serious punches could be thrown, and, in a few minutes, a tussle that threatened to become a small scale riot instead lost steam. (p. F-5)

My own mezzanine-level, stage-side seat afforded me a clear view of the stage at this concert. To me this tussle appeared nothing more than a small-scale scuffle. Fans did not rush from all areas, as D'Agostino purports, to participate in the fight, which was easily contained in fewer than five minutes. Indeed, few people even responded to the fight except to watch silently until the fracas fizzled out. Out of

6,500 people a group of 30, who were quickly surrounded by security guards, falls significantly short
of a "mob." The melee that "threatened to become
a small scale riot" was apparently only threatening in
the reviewer's colonial imagination.

D'Agostino concludes by suggesting that rap is
fizzling out, that juvenile antics and staged controversy no longer hold audiences' attention and therefore signify the death of rap music. What happened
to the "single-minded, moveable beast" that reared
its ugly head in his introduction? How did Black fascism dissolve into harmless puerility in fewer than
five hours? D'Agostino had to make that move; his
distaste for rap music, coupled with his fear of Black
youth, left him little alternative but to slay the single-
minded beast by literally disconnecting its power
source. Ultimately, his review sustains a fear of Black
energy and passion while it simultaneously attempts
to allay this fear by suggesting that rap is dying. The
purported imminent death of rap music, however,
is a myth that deliberately misconstrues Black rage
as mere juvenile rebellion yet retains the necessary
specter of Black violence to justify the social repression of rap music and Black youth alike. The concert
that D'Agostino claims "failed to sizzle" was, in fact,
too hot to handle.

Navigating the minefield of mass media misrepresentation and institutional policing has leavened
rap's expressive potential. Media coverage regarding
rap-related violence has had a significant impact on
rappers' musical and lyrical content and presentation.
The most explicit response to this has been the Hip
Hop music industry-based Stop The Violence movement (STV), which was organized in direct response
to the Nassau Coliseum incident. In the words of
STV's primary organizer, Nelson George (1990), "it
was time for rappers to define the problems and defend themselves" (p. 12). Thus, STV attempted to redefine the interpretation and meaning of rap-related
violence and discourage Black-on-Black crime.

> The goals of the STV [were] for the rappers to
> raise public awareness of black on black crime
> and point out its real causes and social costs; to
> raise funds for a charitable organization already
> dealing with the problems of illiteracy and crime

in the inner city; [and] to show that rap music is
a viable tool for stimulating reading and writing
skills among inner-city kids. (George, 1990, p. 12)

In January 1990 STV released a 12-inch single
entitled "Self-Destruction" featuring several prominent rappers "dropping science" on the cost of
Black-on-Black crime to African Americans, the
desire for unity in the African American community,
and the media's stereotypical depiction of rap fans
as criminals:

> Well, today's topic, self-destruction,
> it really ain't the rap audience that's buggin'
> it's one or two suckas, ignorant brothers,
> tryin' to rob and steal from one another.
> You get caught in the mid.
> So to crush that stereotype, here's what we did.
> We got ourselves together so that you can unite,
> and fight for what's right;
> not negative, 'cause the way we live is positive.
> We don't kill our relatives.

In addition to producing the all-star single and its
accompanying music video and organizing several
public marches, STV published a photoessay volume on the STV movement (George, 1990). *Stop
The Violence: Overcoming Self-Destruction* offers a
history of the STV, pages of Black crime statistics,
and teens' testimonials on their experiences with
Black-on-Black violence. The book targets young,
urban African Americans to "educate and reform"
them and help them avoid self-destructive behaviors.
It was cosponsored by the National Urban League,
which also serves as the beneficiary of all monies
raised as a result of STV's efforts.

Unfortunately, in its reform-oriented response
STV did not redefine the problem; instead, it accepted the sociologically based terms laid out in the dominant media's coverage. Uncritically employing the
labels "Black-on-Black crime" and "self-destruction,"
STV's resulting self-help agenda fits comfortably into
the discourse of social pathology that has long been
used to explain rap-related violence. The movement's
marginal attempts to position these acts of violence
and crimes as symptoms of economic inequality are

insufficient to compensate for the logic of cultural pathology that dominates its ideology. Pages of statistics documenting the number of Blacks killed by other Blacks reinforce the dominant construction of Black pathology while discussion of the economic, social, and institutional violence to which Blacks are subjected remain neutralized. Economically oppressed Black communities must contend with scarce and substandard housing and health services, minimal municipal services (as described in PE's rap, "911 is a Joke"), police harassment and brutality, and economic, racial, and sexual discrimination. These conditions are fundamentally linked to the "Black-on-Black crime" phenomena and to constructions of social violence.

The STV agenda should have retained a dialectical tension between Black self-destructive behavior and the immense institutional forces that foster such behaviors. Cries in the lyrics of "Self-Destruction" for Blacks to avoid walking the destructive path that has been laid out for them, to keep themselves in check, and to love themselves over-emphasize the autonomy of Black agency in the face of massive societal counterforces. An inherent dialectical tension exists between the desire to preserve personal agency and free will (e.g., "fight the power," "overcoming *self*-destruction") and the necessary acknowledgment of the structural forces that constrain agency (e.g., institutional racism, White supremacy, class oppression). The illusion that exercising Black agency can be severed from the racist and discriminatory context within which agency takes place ignores this dialectical tension. Once severed from social context, agency is easily translated into cultural pathology which blames the victim for his or her behavior and, therefore, his or her circumstances. This discursive tension is a critical element in contemporary Black cultural politics. The forces that constrain Black agency must be acknowledged while the spirit and reality of Black free will preserved. Agency and oppression must be acknowledged and addressed jointly, otherwise the incapacity to overcome self-destructive behavior is erroneously viewed as being disconnected to structures of oppression and easily equated with cultural pathology. STV did not successfully negotiate this tension, but it did garner significant financial

resources and managed to mobilize a critical mass of Hip Hop representatives to speak out on behalf of social control in the name of Black free will.

The institutional policing of rap music is a complex and interactive process that has had a significant impact on rap's content, image, and reception. The Nassau Coliseum incident, which necessarily includes the social construction of the incident, the pre-existing discourse on Black urban crime, and fears of rap's political and social power served as catalysts for explicit and sanctioned efforts to contain rap's influence and public presence. That pivotal incident in New York allowed an already suspicious public to blame rap for encouraging urban violence, placed the Hip Hop community on the defensive, and effectively refocused attention *away* from the systemic reasons for such violence.

Rap music is fundamentally linked to larger social constructions of Black culture as an internal threat to dominant American culture and social order. According to hooks (1990), rap's capacity as a form of testimony and an articulation of the young, Black, urban critical voice has profound potential as a language of liberation and social protest. Contestation over the meaning and significance of rap music, controversies regarding its ability to occupy public space, and struggles to retain its expressive freedom constitute critical aspects of contemporary Black cultural politics.

During the centuries-long period of Western slavery, elaborate rules and laws were designed to control slave populations. Constraining the mobility of slaves, especially at night and in groups, was of special concern because slave owners reasoned that revolts could be organized by Blacks who moved too freely and without surveillance (Davis, 1966). Whites were rightfully confident that Blacks had good reason to escape, revolt, and retaliate. Contemporary laws and practices that curtail and constrain Black mobility in urban America function in much the same way and for similar reasons. Likewise, large groups of today's African Americans, especially teenagers, represent a modern threat to the social order of oppression. Albeit more sophisticated and more difficult to trace, contemporary policing of African Americans resonates with the legacy of slavery.

Rap's poetic voice is deeply political in content and spirit, but its hidden struggle—that of access to public space and community resources and the interpretation of Black expression—constitutes rap's hidden politics. Hegemonic discourses have rendered these institutional aspects of Black cultural politics invisible. Political interpretations of rap's explosive and resistive lyrics are critical to understanding contemporary Black cultural politics, yet they reflect only a part of the battle. Rap's hidden politics must also be revealed; otherwise, whether or not we "believe the hype" will not make any difference.

Notes

1. Venues are clubs, theaters, and other performance spaces. I am concerned specifically with large venues, e.g., the Capital Center (near Washington, DC), Nassau (NY) Coliseum, and Madison Square Garden (New York City). Also, note that I am particularly interested in accounts of rap music in major newspapers; music periodicals are not the focus here.
2. See *Rock and Roll Confidential* (RRC), especially their special pamphlet, "You've Got a Right To Rock: Don't Let Them Take It Away" (1990). This pamphlet is a detailed documentation of the censorship movements and their institutional bases and attacks. *RRC* is edited by David Marsh and can be subscribed to by writing to *RRC*, Dept. 7, Box 341305, Los Angeles, CA 90034.
3. Attacks on earlier popular Black expressions such as jazz and rock-and-roll were grounded in fears that White youth were deriving too much pleasure from Black expressions, and that these primitive, alien expressions were dangerous to young people's moral development (see Chapple & Garofalo, 1979; Erenberg, 1981; Jones, 1963; Ogren, 1989; Lipsitz, 1990).
4. Obviously, Haring is referring to building owners. In my research on venues, writers and venue representatives consistently refer to the buildings as the point of power and not their owners. This language serves to render invisible the powerful people who control public space access and make discriminatory bureaucratic decisions.
5. See Messerschmidt (1986) for an important critique of the race, gender, and class factors in street crime reportage (see especially pp. 54–58).
6. See Messerschmidt (1986), especially Chapter Three, "Powerless Men and Street Crime." In it, Messerschmidt

notes that: "Public perception of what serious violent crime is—and who the violent criminals are—is determined first by what the state defines as violent and the types of violence it overlooks. . . . The criminal law defines only certain kinds of violence as criminal—namely, one-on-one forms of murder, assault, and robbery, which are the types of violence young marginalized minority males primarily engage in. The criminal law excludes certain types of avoidable killings, injuries and thefts engaged in by powerful white males, such as maintaining hazardous working conditions or producing unsafe products" (p. 52).
7. Jon Pareles and Peter Watrous, two prominent popular music critics for the *New York Times,* have made noteworthy attempts to offer complex and interesting critiques of rap music. In many cases, however, a significant number of letters to the editor have appeared complaining about the appearance and content of their reviews and articles.

References

Angus, I., & Jhally, S. (1989). Introduction. In I. Angus & S. Jhally (Eds.), *Cultural politics in contemporary America* (pp. 1–14). New York: Routledge, Chapman & Hall.
Associated Press. (1988, September 12). 1500 hurt at Jackson concert. *New York Post,* p. 9.
Chapple, S., & Garofalo, R. (1979). *Rock 'n roll is here to pay.* Chicago: Nelson Hall.
D'Agostino, J. (1990, August 28). Concert fails to sizzle in San Diego. *Los Angeles Times* (San Diego edition), pp. F-l, F-5.
Davis, D. B. (1966). *The problem of slavery in western culture.* Ithaca: Cornell University Press.
Erenberg, L. A. (1981). *Steppin' out: New York night life and the transformation of American culture, 1890–1930.* Chicago: University of Chicago Press.
Gates, D. (1990, March 19). The rap attitude. *Newsweek,* pp. 56–63.
George, N. (Ed.). (1990). *Stop the violence: Overcoming self-destruction.* New York: Pantheon.
Gilroy, P. (1987). *There ain't no black in the Union Jack.* London: Hutchinson.
Hall, S. (1978). *Policing the crisis.* New York: Macmillan.
Haring, B. (1989, December 16). Many doors still closed to rap tours. *Billboard,* p. 1.
hooks, b. (1990). *Yearning: Race, gender and cultural politics.* Boston: South End.
Ice Cube. (1990). *Amerikka's Most Wanted.* Priority Records.
Jones, L. (1963). *Blues people.* New York: Morrow Quill.

Kruggel, M., & Roga, J. (1988, September 12). L.I. rap-slayer sought. *New York Daily News*, p. 3.

Lipsitz, G. (1990). *Time passages: Collective memory and American popular culture*. Minneapolis: University of Minnesota Press.

Marriott, M. (1988, September 19). 9 charged, 4 with murder, in robbery spree at L.I. rap concert. *New York Times*, p. B-3.

Messerschmidt, J. W. (1986). Capitalism, patriarchy and crime: Toward a socialist feminist criminology. Totowa, NJ: Roman & Littlefield.

NWA. (1988). *Straight outta Compton*. Priority Records.

Ogren, K. J. (1989). *The jazz revolution: Twenties America and the meaning of jazz*. New York: Oxford University Press.

Pelleck, C. J., & Sussman, C. (1988, September 12). Rampaging teen gang slays 'rap' fan. *New York Post*, p. 9.

Pratt, R. (1989). Popular music, free space, and the quest for community. *Journal of Popular Music and Society, 13*(4), 59–76.

Public Enemy. (1988). *It takes a nation of millions to hold us back*. Def Jam Records.

Public Enemy. (1990). *Fear of a Black Planet*. Columbia Records.

Rose, T. (1990). [Interview with Richard Walters of Famous Talent Agency.]

Snead, J. A. (1986). On repetition in Black culture. In H. L. Gates (Ed.), *Race, writing and difference*. Chicago: University of Chicago Press.

Salt 'n Pepa. (1990). *Blacks' magic*. Next Plateau Records.

AUTHENTICITIES AND APPROPRIATIONS

Cultural creativity and innovation can come from many different places. One of the most common of these arises when people from different cultures come into close and extended contact, and their respective cultural practices and traditions start to influence one another. In some cases, these cultural intersections can safely be characterized as simple exchanges between relatively equal partners. In other cases, however, particularly when the cultures involved are marked by racial difference and a hierarchical power relationship, such cultural "borrowings" are often—though not always—more akin to "theft" than to "love." The essays in this section explore the thorny politics of how such cultural influences work (or, in some cases, fail to work) across racial lines.

Kembrew McLeod's essay intervenes in the ongoing debates about the ethics and politics of digital sampling, especially as that practice is used in the production of hip-hop music. McLeod situates sampling in the context of the oral traditions of black US culture and does so in ways that effectively undermine any efforts to dismiss sampling as examples of "uncreative" or "unethical" forms of cultural theft.

Drawing on a seemingly disparate range of examples from a broad historical swath of both art and music, Arthur Jafa's essay explores a vital distinction between cross-racial cultural influences that can reasonably be understood as forms of respectful homage and those that are more akin to racist appropriations. It also includes a brief autobiographical lesson about the complicated ways that cultural influences can work across racial lines, even in spite of the ways that one might expect an encounter between particular media texts and particular audiences to play out.

My own essay on the moral panic surrounding Eminem explores the way that cross-racial cultural borrowing—especially when it involves white artists with a visibly deep respect for and commitment to a black aesthetic—can be profoundly threatening to the stability of the dominant racial hierarchy. In particular, it looks at the ways that cultural norms around racial identity and performance are routinely wielded as punitive weapons to punish "race traitors" and to maintain a clear cultural and political separation between different racial and ethnic populations.

Karen Shimakawa's essay examines a set of prerecorded audio walking tours that are designed so as to guide their predominantly white tourist-audiences through "exotic" ethnic neighborhoods in New York City. Shimakawa unpacks the ways that the particular markers of racial/ethnic "authenticity" (as constructed by and for whites) that are invoked in these recordings reinforce the privileged normativity of traditional middle class whiteness, and how the tours in question trade in highly dubious racial/ethnic stereotypes. At the same time, however, she recognizes that these recordings also offer the more progressive possibility of pulling white tourist-audiences out of their comfortable (and largely unconscious) ways of inhabiting public space, and into a more expansive understanding of the fraught relationships that exist between racially marked bodies and the urban landscape.

Liz Bird's chapter revolves around a novel—and revelatory—approach to studying media audiences. Putting together focus groups of television viewers and asking them to collectively create a proposal for a new television series, Bird's study demonstrates the subtle ways that media representations infiltrate white audiences' collective understandings of other racial groups and become the major touchstones for defining "authentic" examples of those groups' norms, practices, and beliefs.

There are no real Klingons—except, of course, for the small community of *Star Trek* fans who have willfully adopted (and, in some cases, invented) Klingon cultural practices for themselves. Peter Chvany's examination of this particular subset of *Trek* fans is an especially useful example of how fictional representations of race and ethnicity can help to throw significant light on the artificial nature of the real thing. The notion that "Klingon" might serve as a legitimate example of a "real" ethnicity seems, on the surface, to be laughable—except that, as Chvany's argument makes plain, "authentic" ethnicity is itself a semantically slippery concept, and *Trek* fans roleplaying as Klingons are not as far removed as we might typically think from the fictions of race and ethnicity that we perform and witness every day.

12.
COPYRIGHT, AUTHORSHIP, AND AFRICAN AMERICAN CULTURE

Kembrew McLeod

African-American culture comes out of a primarily oral culture. Black American slaves, not allowed to read, continued the oral traditions of the various African cultures from which they came.[1] While I do not collapse the nuances and differences that exist within African-American culture into a neat, essentialized whole, I nevertheless maintain that prominent elements of African-American culture engage in an intertextual mode of cultural production.

I have selected two extended examples—one shorter (oral folk preaching) and the other quite long (hip-hop music)—that illustrate contradictions that occur when the intertextual practices of African-American cultural production become articulated with intellectual property law. The intertextual practices that characterize many aspects of African-American culture conflict with a particular way of understanding authorship and ownership that originated in Western Enlightenment and Romanticist thought, and these differences have resulted in significant consequences.

Originality, Plagiarism and African-American Oral Folk Preaching

Plagiarism is inescapably intertwined with copyright (both concepts came into being around the same time) and, moreover, these concepts are bound up in the capitalist relations that began to emerge in Europe during seventeenth century.[2] During this time, there was a push to view texts as commercial products and the author as the manufacturer of those texts, a process which Scollon argues represents the "economic/ideological system which arose at the time of the Enlightenment."[3] Scollon concludes, "The traditional view of plagiarism constitutes, in fact, an ideological position which privileges a concept of the person established within the European Enlightenment."[4]

This particular concept of the person, in part, provides the basis for a model of communication that dominated communication studies from its early stages (e.g., there is a message that originates from a singular individual, the sender, and this message gets transmitted to a receiver). Numerous studies have demonstrated that this is a culturally situated model that is connected to a particular historical time and social group. Therefore, the simple conceptualization of a speaker or writer rooted in Enlightenment thought is not a tenable concept, because "real life" is more complex.[5] Scollon concludes:

A closer analysis of the concept of plagiarism shows that, in fact, it disguises these complexities by masking them in the idea that . . . [people] . . . speak and write as unified biological persons who always represent themselves in a straightforward and sincere way. . . . In other words, the concept of plagiarism is a shorthand compilation of a rather hefty set of assumptions about who should or should not have the right to use discourse to create individual, autonomous voices in a society. In yet other words, the concept of plagiarism is fully embedded within a social, political, and cultural matrix that cannot be meaningfully separated from its interpretation.[6]

For example, those who do not have the right to "use discourse to create individual, autonomous voices" are those who engage in discursive tactics that do not conform to these conceptualizations of originality and authorship.

The invention of the printing press not only is directly connected with capitalism, copyright and plagiarism, it was instrumental in facilitating the shift from oral to written manuscript, then to print culture in Europe. Print culture resulted in attempts to close down intertextuality by emphasizing Romantic notions of "originality" and "creativity," and at this time there came into being the notion that words can be privately owned. Put simply, Ong states, "Typography had made the word into a commodity."[7]

This newly conceptualized "private ownership of words," as Ong labels it, provided a philosophical basis for the emergence of copyright laws that followed the invention of the printing press, which unambiguously tied up the newly formed concept of plagiarism with commodity capitalism.[8] Bettig echoes these arguments when he states that there is a direct connection between the rise of typography, capitalism and the commodification of literary and artistic domains.[9] The thread that ties these concepts together is copyright law, and plagiarism provides the deeply resonating moral underpinnings for this economically grounded legal construction.

Plagiarism and African-American Oral Folk Preaching

Martin Luther King Jr. not only borrowed words and ideas in his graduate school work, but also in many of the documented speeches he gave throughout his life. We can either view this as an intellectual shortcoming or use this understanding as a springboard to construct more complex notions of how other cultures understand the role and use of knowledge. Both Scollon[10] and Johannesen[11] emphasize that their critiques of the tenets that underlie plagiarism should not be read as an endorsement of a uniformly relativistic view of plagiarism, and I agree with their

cautions. Nevertheless, they argue that King's borrowings of words and ideas can be understood in light of their critiques, and they believe that we should not view plagiarism in the one dimensional way that dominates the academy.[12] "I use the oratory of Martin Luther King, Jr.," Johannessen writes, "as illustrative of discourse that, while reflective of multiple cultural and intellectual influences, was shaped significantly by a cultural tradition that approved of the unattributed borrowing of ideas and held words and ideas to be communal resources."[13]

In 1985 Coretta Scott King—Martin Luther King Jr.'s widow—appointed Stanford University historian Clayborne Carson to head the King Papers Project, which was dedicated to preserving, annotating and publishing King's writings from his early years as a student up through the time of his death in 1968.[14] In a front-page story published on November 9, 1990, the *Wall Street Journal* disclosed that the King Papers Project's researchers had found, in Carson's words at a press conference called after the *Journal* published its story, "a pattern of appropriation, of textual appropriation."[15] The *New York Times* and other major US newspapers (the *Washington Post,* the *Boston Globe,* etc.) placed the story on their front pages, and it was extensively covered during 1990 in regional newspapers, national magazines, and on radio and television.

The *Boston Globe*'s coverage of the controversy was typical, beginning with the sentence,

"Researchers at Stanford University said yesterday they have discovered numerous instances of plagiarism in Rev. Martin Luther King, Jr.'s writings as a graduate student, and Boston University has started an investigation of whether King's use of others' material without giving credit violated the integrity of the doctoral degree he received there."[16]

The *New York Times* and other newspapers that picked up the story quoted Carson as saying, "By the strictest definition of plagiarism—that is, any appropriation of words or ideas—there are instances of plagiarism in these papers."[17]

One theme within many of the stories published in newspapers was that this discovery may, as *New York*

Times writer Anthony De Palma stated, "tarnish the myth of the man."[18] Many writers also emphasized that King was well aware of the principles of citation, expressing bewilderment over why Dr. King appropriated the words and ideas of others without giving proper credit.

This confusion was intensified by the fact that Dr. King apparently did not attempt to conceal his appropriations. First, he paid tribute to the man from whom he borrowed material that appeared on the fifth page of his dissertation; also, King cited this person's work in the bibliography and he sporadically footnoted that work as well.[19] Second, the *New York Times* reported that King "not only retained his graduate school papers, but also deposited them in an archive at Boston University where they would become available to scholars."[20] Another story quoted a researcher as saying, "Why didn't he know better?" and "Why did he do it? Was he so insecure that he thought this was the only way to get by?"[21]

Why did he do it? I cannot answer that question any more definitively than can other scholars and pundits who have weighed in on the matter, partially because King neither spoke of this issue to any known living person nor did he leave any evidence of his intentions. I want to argue, nevertheless, that perhaps the reason why King never spoke of this to anyone is because he did not think it an issue. That is, the practices that led him to appropriate the words and ideas of others were so much a part of the cultural tradition that King grew up in that he did not see what he did to be a problem.

That he did not try to hide what he did is perhaps the most significant indicator that he did not believe he was wrong when he borrowed the words and ideas of others without proper, consistent attribution in his doctoral dissertation and graduate school class papers. As stated above, King deposited his graduate papers in the Boston University archives; moreover, he often referred to the scholars whose words he borrowed—not exactly the best strategy for a knowing, calculating plagiarist to employ.[22]

Rather than turning to some of the more sensational explanations the media reported ("Was he so insecure that he thought this was the only way to get by?"), I here make a point that, with minor exceptions, the media overwhelmingly failed to consider—the

fact that King's "motives" were perhaps nothing more than the unconscious habits resulting from years of enculturation within the black folk-preaching tradition of which he, his father, and grandfather were a part. Keith D. Miller argues:

Legally forbidden to read and write, slaves had created a highly oral religious culture that treated songs and sermons as shared wealth, not private property. During and after slavery, African-American folk preachers gained stature by merging their identities with earlier, authoritative bearers of the Word. In this context, striking originality might have seemed self-centered or otherwise suspect. While growing up, King absorbed this tradition, hearing religious themes and metaphors that originated during slavery.[23]

Because earlier black folk preachers usually could not write down their sermons, they borrowed sermons and traded with other preachers, working from the assumption that language is created by everyone and that it could not be considered private property.[24] Miller gives the example of two sermons King heard as a child, "The Eagle Stirs Her Nest" and "Dry Bones in the Valley," which date back to the end of slavery and continue to be heard in black churches today.[25] "A large community shares those two sermons," Miller[26] continues, "for only with the arrival of print have people come to view language as private property to be copyrighted, packaged, and sold as a commodity."[27] Moreover, the imitation of important and long-standing pulpit texts and preaching styles was a fully accepted method of apprenticeship among the black folk preachers from whom King learned.[28]

Reagon discusses the notion of apprenticeship in the two traditions in which King was immersed: Western-based academia and the black folk pulpit. She states that Western-based academia stresses the importance of developing one's thesis by drawing on a thoroughly identified database cultivated by other scholars who came before, and that this process is given the highest status within the Western academy.[29] This is, Reagon argues, "keyed to the ownership, possession, private-property ethos that drives so much of Western cultural nationalism."[30]

In beginning to study a practice within an area of African-American culture such as the black folk ministry, one is primarily an imitator, and the phase that marks the passage from apprentice to master is when one is seen as finding his or her "voice."

Reagon states, "Within African American culture, there is a very high standard placed on the moment when one not only makes a solid statement of the song or the sermon, but the offering is given in one's own signature."[31] This "signature" is marked by an original "sound," "style," "rhythm" or "voice"—a conceptualization that differs considerably from many fields of Western academic culture that define originality within the parameters of the analysis of the data and what one does with it based on that analysis, or both. Reagon writes,

> "The academic process looks at the documentation: Did she or he reveal every step made through the documentation and is the trail of the search clearly outlined? Living within a society where style and voice are not perceived as signature—are not understood as data—makes survival challenging."[32]

Garrow asserts that explaining King's "transgressions" in graduate school vis-à-vis the cultural tradition from which he emerged does disservice to his intellect.[33] But this is not true, because King was obviously smart enough to be able to discern the differences between the standards and ethics of academia and the black folk preaching tradition that grounded him. King—like many African Americans (and other minority groups) who straddle between two cultures—found a way to negotiate a hybrid system when, in Miller's[34] words, he "ventured outside the universe of African-American orality to negotiate his way through the unfamiliar terrain of intellectualized print culture."[35]

Speaking of this negotiated hybrid system, Reagon argues that those who "straddle" construct a new network of rules and practices that are an amalgamation of the differing systems they take part in.[36] "Therefore no system," Reagon writes, "neither the one of our birth nor the one we adopt through mastery, is sacred. Both systems become instruments or tools."[37] By "straddling," King learned to synthesize

effectively these cultural traditions in ways that allowed him to make sense of the world and, further, to help make sense of the world for others. One of King's greatest attributes was his ability to integrate—articulate—seemingly disparate ideologies and ideas so that, for instance, he could rearticulate many of the key notions that white America held dear in a way that made whites understand the necessity of the black freedom struggle.[38] Miller states:

> Resisting his professors' rules about language and many notions of the Great White Thinkers, King crafted highly imaginative, persuasive discourse through the folk procedures of voice merging and self-making. Reanimating the slaves' world view, he prodded John F. Kennedy and most of white America to listen for the first time to the slaves' time-honored cry for racial equality.[39]

This is important because, Miller argues, "King's borrowing gives us an additional reason to reconsider intertextuality, collaboration, the rhetoric of protest, orality and literacy, the social context of invention, and our sacrosanct notion of language as private property."[40] It is important to note that many of the above-mentioned concepts *directly* apply to hip-hop music—intertextuality, the rhetoric of protest, orality and literacy, the social context of invention, as well as (to slightly modify the wording above) the sacrosanct notion of *music* as private property. Because hip-hop has forced itself to the center of mainstream American culture, this self-consciously rebellious musical culture based in the experiences and modes of cultural production that many African Americans share provides a significant, contemporary example of these issues.

Hip-hop is significant because it has become a massive money-making industry that is based on a form of cultural production that flies in the face of particular Western notions of originality and authorship in much the same way King's black folk pulpit style did. Because hip-hop digitally samples and recontextualizes fragments of copyrighted sound recordings, it was an easy target for intellectual property infringement lawsuits in its early commercially successful days (and, of course, it continues to be). By looking at the way in which hip-hop evolved and was transformed by these new legal and economic relations, we can gain a better understanding of how race, intellectual property law, cultural production and a variety of other elements come to be articulated.

Hip-Hop, Sampling and Copyright Law

Tricia Rose claims that Ong's notion of a postliterate orality is a useful one to apply to hip-hop's mode of cultural production.[41] Both digital sampling and rapping create a technological and cultural form of literacy that incorporates the intertextual referencing of varying elements, both the language-based and the more amorphously aural. Similarly, Schumacher discusses how technology, especially in hip-hop, is now very much a part of musical production.[42] Digital sampling creates new modes of production, all while drawing on older modes—in this case, the cultural traditions discussed by Rose.[43] This is another notion of authorship, Schumacher argues, a notion that is not seen as equal in the eyes of the law because it does not conform to Enlightenment and Romantic notions of originality and authorship.[44]

Schumacher goes further than Rose in his critique of what he considers the fundamental basis of intellectual property law. He argues that intellectual property law is, first, a *property law* and that the author should be seen as a historical construct, and that further, these notions of originality and authorship are deeply embedded in capitalist relations. Copyright is a culturally bound law that could not deal with the collision of a particular form of cultural production rooted in the European practice of composing and notating music and the more improvisatory African-American tradition of jazz. Just as copyright law did not know how to deal with jazz artists' appropriation of certain phrases and whole choruses from popular songs, copyright law still has not come to terms with sampling.[45]

"The Sound of (Hip-Hop) Music": A Brief History

Rap music, as it is popularly known, is but one element of a larger cultural movement called hip-hop. "When I say the word 'hip-hop,'" explains Richie "Crazy Legs" Colon, an early participant in hip-hop

culture, "I'm including every element—the graf[fiti], the dance, the music, everything, the rapping."[46] It is important to understand hip-hop music as being directly tied to a historical social movement that developed in the South Bronx during the mid-1970s because many have dehistoricized the development of hip-hop by, for instance, tracing the roots of "rap music" to the vocal delivery style of Bob Dylan or by other similar comparisons.

Hip-hop culture, broadly speaking, incorporates four prominent elements: "breaking" (or breakdancing), "tagging" or "bombing" (marking the walls of buildings and subways with graffiti), "DJ"-ing (collaging the best fragments of records by using two turntables), and "MC"-ing (more commonly referred to as "rapping").[47] The significance of breakdancing and graffiti should not be downplayed, but it is obvious that DJs and MCs have become hip-hop's most noticeable and persistent components; therefore, I will focus primarily on them.

The key figure in the development of hip-hop music was the DJ.[48] During the early to mid-1970s, DJs simply spun popular records that kept the party alive and people dancing, existing more in the mold of radio and club DJs. In the early days of hip-hop there were a number of DJs who had strong followings in each of their districts throughout the Bronx. These DJs rarely had access to large clubs; the primary venues were block parties, schools and parks (where, as legend has it, they would plug their sound systems into lampposts and play until the police broke up the gathering).

The most popular of these early DJs was Jamaican immigrant Kool DJ Herc, who is credited with two new musical methods that, Rose argues, separated hip-hop music from other popular musics and provided the groundwork for further innovation.[49] The first was Herc's habit of isolating the fragments of songs that were the most popular with dancers and segueing them into one long musical collage. These song fragments were composed of the percussion breaks within the songs and came to be known as "breakbeats." Early DJ pioneer Afrika Bambaataa recalls Kool Herc's DJ style:

> Now he took the music of Mandrill like "Fence-walk," certain disco records that had funky

percussion breaks like The Incredible Bongo Band when they came out with "Apache" and he just kept that beat *going.* It might be that certain part of the record that everybody waits for—they just let their inner self go and get wild.[50]

Kool Herc told me:

"I quickly realized that those breakbeats were making the crowd go crazy, so I just started digging deeper and deeper into my record collection, ya know? As long as I kept the beat going with the best parts of those records, everybody would keep dancing. And the culture just evolved from that."[51]

Other DJs built on the collaged breakbeat method and began expanding on the possibilities that two turntables could offer. One of the first DJs to pick up on the breakbeat technique was Grandmaster Flash, who went further than Kool Herc in his turntable wizardry.[52]

With two turntables Flash was able, in his own words, to

"take small parts of records and, at first, keep it on time, no tricks, keep it on time. I'm talking about very short beats, maybe 40 seconds, keeping it going for about five minutes, depending on how popular that particular record was."[53]

Flash continues:

"After that, I mastered punch phasing—taking certain parts of a record where there's a vocal or drum slap or a horn. I would throw it out and bring it back, keeping the other turntable playing. If this record had a horn in it before the break came down I would go—BAM, BAM, BAM-BAM—just to try this on the crowd."[54]

Another technique credited to Grandmaster Flash is "scratching."[55]

Kool Herc is credited with a second important innovation—the development of the live MC.[56] During parties he began "dropping rhymes" or shouting simple phrases that were popular in the streets like

"rock on my mellow," "to the beat y'all," or "you don't stop" on top of the breakbeats he played.[57] Herc borrowed this rhythmic form of talking (called "toasting") from the microphone personalities who deejayed in his native Jamaica, and he is recognized as the person who brought this style to New York.[58] Early on, when Herc began concentrating more on mixing breakbeats, he enlisted the help of his friend Coke La Rock to take over the duties of the MC (Master of Ceremonies). The MC was responsible for exciting the dancers and giving the party a live feel, functioning as an agent of crowd control—and thus diffusing tensions that might arise from rival groups in the crowd.[59]

When Grandmaster Flash realized that people were paying too much attention to what he was doing (instead of dancing) he saw the importance of having live MC accompaniment.[60] Along with Melle Mel, Scorpio, Kidd Creole, and Raheem and Cowboy, Flash formed Grandmaster Flash and the Furious Five.[61] This group, along with many other groups of MCs and DJs—such as Grand Wizard Theodore and the Fantastic Five, DJ Breakout and the Funky Four, Cold Crush Brothers, and the Treacherous Three—fought for microphone supremacy in local parks and clubs.[62]

Until July 1979, when the Sugarhill Gang released "Rapper's Delight," hip-hop was strictly an underground phenomenon that had not been documented beyond the numerous bootleg tapes of live performances that circulated throughout the city.[63] The release of "Rapper's Delight" forever changed hip-hop music's (and hip-hop culture's) relationship with the music industry. It also changed the way hip-hop music sounded for a majority of listeners, because mass record distribution was the only way most consumers could hear this new musical form.

The Sugarhill Gang was not a part of the South Bronx hip-hop scene that had developed in the 1970s; the group was put together by Sugarhill Records owners Sylvia and Joe Robinson.[64] The Sugarhill Gang had no street credibility and was not known to anyone involved in the Bronx hip-hop scene, but this did not stop them from having a huge hit—selling over 2 million records worldwide.[65] Grandmaster Flash recalled hearing "Rapper's Delight" back in 1979, stating: "What is this? I heard this record on the radio almost every 10 minutes on almost every station that

I switched to. They said it was these boys out of Jersey."[66] At another time he said: "I'm saying to myself, I don't know of anybody else from here to Long Island that's doing this. Why don't I know of this group called the Sugarhill who?"[67]

Because I'm interested in the development of hip-hop's sound—its production techniques—I argue that the first 20 years of *recorded* hip-hop can be divided into five relatively distinct though still somewhat overlapping phases, beginning with the Sugarhill era and carrying through to the late 1990s. These particular phases are *not* mutually exclusive; *neither are they the only potential way of organizing hip-hop's history.* For my purposes, however, it is a useful framework for analyzing the evolution of hip-hop's musical production. Tuff City Records owner Aaron Fuchs identifies four major periods in recorded hip-hop during a discussion of sampling in a *Billboard* article he authored, something that provides the basis for my organizational scheme.

The first period (about 1979–1983) featured the live funk band sound of the Sugarhill era, which came to be known as "old school" when a new wave of rappers entered the hip-hop arena with their stripped down, "hardcore" sound. This "hardcore" sound that dominated the second period (about 1983–1987) was characterized, according to Fuchs,[68] by a predominance of "electronic drums and synthesizers."[69] The proliferation of the use of digital samplers created a third distinctive period (about 1986–1992), during which time samples (digitally recorded fragments of preexisting sounds) of old funk, rock, soul, jazz and reggae records became a prominent part of much hip-hop music.

Fuchs, writing in 1992, argued that as sampling moved into its third or fourth year of popularity, it was superseded by the incorporation of live instrumentation that was often sampled and inserted in a hip-hop production.[70] This phase constitutes the fourth period of recorded hip-hop music (about 1992–1996) which, to some extent, has been complemented by a resurgence in sampling but with an emphasis on only one or two obvious recognizable hooks. This is typical of the most recent period of recorded hip-hop, about 1996–2001. Again, this is not the only way of organizing hip-hop's aural history as it exists on record, and the specific dates can

be argued, but this rough organizational scheme is appropriate for this analysis.

"Rapper's Delight" changed the way hip-hop sounded. Before this single was released, hip-hop performances were almost uniformly comprised of the DJ spinning and manipulating records while the MC rapped on top of the music.[71] "Rapper's Delight" featured a live band that provided the background music over which the MCs could rap, and its sound was radically different from the hip-hop music that was performed in the parks and clubs by DJs and MCs when the Sugarhill Gang's hit song was recorded. One similarity the backing track of this record shared with its hip-hop predecessors is the fact that it appropriated its music from an existing song. The Sugarhill Records live house band lifted the background track of the popular disco song "Good Times," by Chic, using the bass line and chords as its instrumental foundation. This appropriation set a precedent for a controversy that still brews today because it prompted a lawsuit by Nile Rogers, the song's cowriter.[72]

Because these studio musicians essentially performed the role of the DJ on record, it is unsurprising that "Rapper's Delight" wasn't the only early hip-hop song to borrow from previous hits. The Funky Four Plus One's "Rappin' and Rockin' the House" (released shortly after "Rapper's Delight") essentially took its backing track from Cheryl Lynn's "Got To Be Real." Similarly, numerous hip-hop songs appropriated the Tom Tom Club's "Genius of Love," such as Grandmaster Flash and the Furious Five's "It's Nasty" and Dr. Jeckyll & Mr. Hyde's "Genius Rap," which featured those rappers rhyming on top of the Tom Tom Club's instrumental track.

The live funk band sound dominated the first few years of recorded hip-hop until Run-DMC released their debut single in 1983 and, after this release, musicians were largely replaced by the DJ/producer on hip-hop records.[73] In light of this, the live funk band sound can be seen as an anomaly, a relatively short-lived trend that used traditional instruments in an attempt to translate hip-hop onto record before samplers became affordable. It was soon superseded by the extremely influential sound ushered in by Run-DMC, which more closely resembled the way hip-hop sounded in the days before it was committed to vinyl, with its emphasis on just the beats and rhymes.

Run-DMC stripped down their music to simple drum machine beats, sparse keyboard embellishments, bass, scratch sounds, and the occasional live rock guitar, helping to redefine the sound of hip-hop music for the next few years. In addition, Run-DMC was possibly the first group to overtly employ a DJ cutting up records on a hip-hop release (on their song "Peter Piper"), which also had a huge influence.[74] Toop claims that after the release of this record, "thousands of records based on scratchy samples have followed in the wake of 'Peter Piper.'"[75] He continues, "By parading the fact that they use stolen fragments of ancient vinyl, all these tracks have emphasized the importance of this disregard for recording studio conventions."[76]

The use of samplers revolutionized the way hip-hop was recorded, making them a quintessential production tool in hip-hop, allowing hip-hop artists to expand on the techniques used in hip-hop's early stages. One important factor contributing to the rise of sampling in hip-hop—which during the mid-1980s was still a relatively underground genre that had small recording budgets—was the drop in the cost of digital samplers. When samplers were first introduced in the market they cost upwards of $50,000, but by the mid-1980s they were relatively affordable, costing as little as $2,000.[77]

Digital samplers became a primary tool in hip-hop music-making because it allowed DJs/producers to piece together breakbeats and sounds in a similar (but more sophisticated) way than the early DJs did. Sampling is a way of paying homage to older artists; it is also a kind of musical archeology, an archaeology that is significant when it is applied to black music which, as a result of music industry fostered conditions, has a notoriously short shelf life.[78] From the early days of the music industry up through today, many popular jazz, funk, soul, rhythm and blues and hip-hop albums go out of print quickly, much faster than their rock and pop counterparts. This is partially what Stetsasonic's Daddy-O is talking about when he raps in "Talkin' All That Jazz": "Tell the truth James Brown was old 'til Eric B came out with 'I Got Soul'/ Hiphop brings back old R&B/ If we would not people could have forgot."[79]

This song was written as a response to the attacks on sampling that came from older members of both the black and white music communities. It was specifically a reply that Daddy-O penned after hearing R&B songwriter Mtume blast what he called "Memorex music."[80] Daddy-O further explained his position on sampling by saying: "Sampling's not a lazy man's way. We learn a lot from sampling; it's like school for us."[81] Another Stetsasonic member, Prince Paul, has played a significant role as a hip-hop producer in pushing the boundaries of what can be done with sampling (he produced the first three De La Soul albums, among other hip-hop classics).

After the introduction of sampling in hip-hop music, virtually every hip-hop record used this technique. By the early 1990s, James Brown had been sampled on an estimated 2,000 records.[82] Similarly, Parliament-Funkadelic's music has provided a source for innumerable samples that has been used in hip-hop songs. An illustration of how pervasive the sampling of the P-Funk catalog has been lies in a lawsuit filed by a publishing company that owns some of Parliament-Funkadelic's songs. The suit extensively lists virtually every record label that released hip-hop records as well as dozens of hip-hop stars.[83]

Within what I have identified as the fourth period of recorded hip-hop, however, live instrumentation increasingly dominated the way hip-hop records were produced. Rapper and producer Dr. Dre, whose album *The Chronic* was released in 1992, epitomizes the use of live production techniques in hip-hop. Speaking about *The Chronic* before it was released, hip-hop producer Sir Jinx said:

> "It's gonna revolutionize, just change everything, because he didn't use samples. He might have used one or two or three, but as of a whole album, no. And that's gonna change up everything, because that's showing that we don't need the samples."[84]

This was no hollow boast; *The Chronic* went on to sell millions of records, becoming one of the biggest and most influential hip-hop records of the decade.

Like any major trend in hip-hop music (as well as pop music), many emulators followed suit by incorporating live instrumentation into their records. The decline in the use of samples taken directly from records and the increased use of "traditional" musicians in recorded hip-hop during the early to mid-1990s was, in part, a result of the enforcement of copyright law in this area. The contradiction between hip-hop music's intertextual mode of musical production and the economic and legal restrictions of copyright law created significant obstacles that dissuaded producers from sampling as freely as they had in the past. Before I further address those issues, I will outline a history of the development of hip-hop as it relates to the marketplace.

The Business of Hip-Hop

In the time since the late 1970s, hip-hop rose from an underground phenomenon confined to the black and Hispanic neighborhoods of the South Bronx to a billion-dollar industry. Today it pervades nearly every facet of popular culture: TV shows, commercials and movies feature hip-hop performers (Will Smith, LL Cool J, and Queen Latifah have all starred in successful TV sitcoms, movies, or both). The pop charts are dominated by hip-hop and hip-hop-influenced music, and hip-hop fashion styles have come to dominate the dress of young blacks and whites throughout America.

I'm not willing to claim that hip-hop music never was a commodity (though when it was being performed for free in local parks it came close), but I nevertheless agree with Rose when she argued,

"What is more important about the shift in hip-hop's orientation is not its movement from pre-commodity to commodity but the shift in control over the scope and direction of the profit-making process, out of the hands of local black and hispanic entrepreneurs and into the hands of larger white-owned, multinational businesses."[85]

Put another way, the means of production shifted from the community that developed this music to the corporations that control the distribution of most hip-hop records that are purchased each year.

During the 1970s hip-hop was a performance-oriented medium confined to the South Bronx, where

"B-Boys" (short for "Break-Boys," who danced to the breakbeats the DJs spun) competitively "battled" each other in breakdance competitions. Little Rodney Cee, then of the hip-hop group The Funky Four Plus One, gave a description of the environment that dominated hip-hop at the time.

An uptown group would battle a downtown group. What I mean by battle is that they could come and they would say, "Okay. Us four are better than your four," and we would go at it. We would pick one and we would dance against each other. We'd do one move and they'd do a move and the crowd liked it. That's where the competition came in. This is before any records, before any money was made. This was from our hearts.[86]

Another early hip-hop pioneer, DJ Lovebug, echoed these somewhat romanticized sentiments: "Back in the day, we used to push refrigerator-size speakers through the blocks . . . It was just for the love of it. We wasn't gettin' no money at all."[87] In the early days of hip-hop, DJs such as Kool Herc, Grandmaster Flash and Afrika Bambaataa often played for free in outdoor parks, house parties and community centers because of a lack of other venues. Soon, Grandmaster Flash's popularity surpassed that of Kool Herc's and Flash began to play for paying customers at numerous high schools and small clubs. By 1977, Flash's following had grown to the point where he was playing in clubs to crowds numbering more than 3,000.[88]

Before the mega success of the "Rapper's Delight" single, many (including Grandmaster Flash) believed that this new style's popularity would not translate into significant record sales. "I didn't think that somebody else would want to hear a record re-recorded onto another record with talking on it," Grandmaster Flash said, "I didn't think it would reach the masses like that."[89] Flash recalls an incident that took place in 1977 when he was approached by a small record label:

"Let me bring you into the studio," said one of the owners. "Do exactly what you guys do at a party, but let's go into a recording studio."

"It wouldn't work," said Flash. "Who would wanna spend $4.99?" He was charging a dollar or two for the shows in school gymnasiums and community centers at housing projects. "Nobody would want to buy the record." The idea was killed. "I regret that," says Flash. "Coulda been the first."[90]

Instead, the Sugarhill Gang were the first to release a hip-hop record. The release and subsequent popularity of this record—it became the biggest selling 12-inch single in history—was a watershed event in the commercialization of hip-hop because, before this record's release, the only way in which hip-hop was heard was in the clubs and via homemade cassettes of live performances, which were traded extensively within the New York boroughs.[91] Jazzy Jay (another early hip-hop participant) boasted, "I mean, we had tapes that went platinum before we was even involved with the music industry,"[92] and Grandmaster Flash claimed to have sold his taped performances at "a buck a minute."[93]

After the commercial success of "Rapper's Delight," many of the MCs and DJs who were popular on the club circuit began signing primarily to independent record labels. While hip-hop continued to gain new fans and grow in popularity through the early 1980s, it never achieved a sustained success on the level of "Rappers Delight" until the mid- to late 1980s.[94] This largely grassroots-fueled momentum helped provoke an intense, short-lived media infatuation with hip-hop culture (that singled out and highlighted the elements of rapping and breakdancing) during the early 1980s. Soon after, a deluge of movies that featured breakdancing and rapping such as *Flashdance, Wild Style, Beat Street, Breakin'* (plus a sequel), and *Krush Groove* were produced and released. Although many people in the mainstream music industry treated hip-hop as a passing fad, hip-hop's popularity continued to increase throughout the 1980s, a trend that intensified into the late 1990s.

Soon to be a major player in what would become the hip-hop music industry, Def Jam Records was cofounded in 1984 by Russell Simmons, the brother of Run-DMC's Run.[95] By 1985, Simmons' label had released a string of 12-inch singles that sold over 250,000 each, an unprecedented number at the time, launching the careers of LL Cool J and The Beastie Boys. Simmons' business partner, Rick Rubin, produced the debut albums of soon-to-be multiplatinum artists LL Cool J, The Beastie Boys and Public Enemy. He also had a hand in producing Run-DMC's *Raising Hell,* the first hip-hop album to go platinum.[96] After starting the company with a $5,000 investment, Simmons and Rubin signed a $1 million distribution deal in 1985 with the giant corporate record label CBS, starting a trend that other independent labels would follow.

The evolution of Def Jam reflects many of the business-related trends within hip-hop, and it supports Nelson George's argument in *The Death of Rhythm & Blues* that major labels inevitably absorb the most vital black-owned labels if they prove profitable. By the late 1980s, Simmons and Rubin had parted ways, and Simmons became the sole owner of the operation until 1996. That year, Simmons sold 50% of Def Jam (a company that started as a grassroots label that he cofounded with a $5,000 investment) to the major label PolyGram for $33 million.[97]

In 1998, the German beverage giant Seagram purchased PolyGram, and in 1999 the company bought Universal Music, reducing the number of US major labels from six to five (the AOL/Time-Warner merger with EMI/Capitol in 2000 would further reduce the number of major labels to four). Around this time, Seagram paid Def Jam a reported $100 million for the remaining shares of the hip-hop label it did not already own, completely dissolving Def Jam into the corporate structure of the Universal Music Group. Motown Records followed a quite similar path, and by 2000 both Motown and Def Jam—two of the twentieth century's most important and culturally significant black owned record labels—became reduced to the mere arms of a corporate behemoth. In regard to business practices, the story of Def Jam is in many ways the story of hip-hop.[98]

While Run-DMC was considered the first hip-hop group to attract a predominantly white rock audience, The Beastie Boys (the first white hip-hop group of note) were the first rappers to top the *Billboard* album charts—a sign that hip-hop had finally infiltrated the white suburbs of America.[99] This was another significant moment in the evolution of hip-hop, a wake-up call to the major labels that hip-hop was becoming a very profitable genre. These major labels, which had the distinct advantage of access to large amounts of capital and better distribution, moved quickly to sign new artists and, in a field dominated by small independent labels, many major labels began to absorb these smaller labels either through distribution deals (such as CBS's relationship with Def Jam Records or RCA's relationship with Jive Records) or by purchasing the independents outright (as Warner Brothers did with the small but profitable Tommy Boy and Sleeping Bag labels).[100]

In 1988, annual hip-hop record sales reached $100 million, which accounted for 2% of the music industry's sales. The next year *Billboard* (the music industry's trade journal) added hip-hop charts to its magazine and MTV debuted *Yo! MTV Raps*, which quickly became the network's highest rated show.[101] By 1992, hip-hop was estimated as generating $400 million annually, roughly 5% of the music industry's annual income, and in 1995 CNN reported that hip-hop's annual sales had risen to 8% of the music industry's annual income.[102]

Within a decade, hip-hop's popularity and annual sales skyrocketed, a success that triggered a notable side effect, namely, a proliferation of lawsuits involving copyright infringement.[103] The deluge of lawsuits began in 1986, when 1960s and 1970s funk artist Jimmy Castor sued Def Jam and the Beastie Boys for their appropriation of the phrase "Yo, Leroy" from Castor's 1977 record "The Return of Leroy (Part I)."[104] Other important legal actions include the $1.7 million suit brought against De La Soul for their use of a Turtles song fragment in their 1989 album *Three Feet High and Rising*.[105] Also, Vanilla Ice was sued for using the bass hook from a David Bowie and Queen song as the foundation for his hit song "Ice Ice Baby," a dispute that was settled after Vanilla Ice agreed to share publishing royalties with the sampled artists.[106] The list of sampling copyright infringement lawsuits is extensive and includes lawsuits brought against Tag Team, MC Hammer, Jazzy Jeff and the Fresh Prince, Tone Loc and dozens of others.[107]

While many suits have been filed, most have been settled out of court because the expense involved in fully litigating a copyright infringement case is massive.[108] As a result, the music industry has been anxiously awaiting a legal precedent to be set so that many of the muddy issues surrounding sampling may be cleared.[109] In one example that breaks from this trend of settling out of court, the Supreme Court ruled in favor of rappers 2 Live Crew after the group was sued for reworking Roy Orbison's hit "Pretty Woman" in a lewd and arguably humorous fashion, sampling Orbison's original drum beat and bass line.[110]

2 Live Crew's lawyers argued that the song was a parody and it should be protected as such, while Orbison's publishing company's lawyers claimed that the song violated their client's copyrights to the original song. The court voted unanimously that the commercial nature of the song did not disqualify it from potentially being "fair use," and the court returned the case down to a lower court with expanded guidelines concerning "fair use."[111] While the case attracted a great amount of attention and celebration in some circles, the court's ruling did not significantly affect the way *sampling* is legally defined because most rappers and hip-hop producers do not use samples in a way that a parody defense could convincingly be used.

The only other major case that has reached a verdict stage is Gilbert O'Sullivan's suit against Biz Markie, in which Markie used a 20-second sample from O'Sullivan's most popular song, the 1973 hit "Alone Again (Naturally)."[112] Immediately after the suit was filed, the album that contained the contested song was ordered off the shelf, and it became the focus of extensive media attention.[113] Judge Duffy, who presided over the case, handed down a strongly worded ruling that not only found the defendant guilty of copyright infringement, but also invoked the Seventh Commandment when suggesting Markie be subject to criminal prosecution for "stealing."[114] In the ruling, Duffy wrote:

> "Thou shalt not steal" has been an admonition followed since the dawn of civilization. Unfortunately, in the modern world of business this admonition is not always followed. Indeed, the defendants in this action for copyright infringement would have this court believe that stealing

is rampant in the music business and, for that reason, their conduct here should be excused. The conduct of the defendants herein, however, violates not only the Seventh Commandment, but also the copyright laws of this country.[115]

This ruling sent Shockwaves through the music industry, which immediately took notice of the possibility of criminal prosecution.[116] For those looking for some sort of precedent to be set, entertainment lawyer Stewart Levy argued, "This isn't the seminal case everyone wanted."[117] It is important to note that the ruling did not provide any guidelines for dealing with cases of sampling that were less substantial and easy to recognize (Markie used a sizable chunk of the original song's chorus), and there remain almost as many gray areas in the law after the case as before.[118]

As a result, this highly charged legal climate has put many in the music industry on edge. With virtually every major record label releasing hip-hop records and almost every record company owning the rights to records being sampled, this industry has a great interest in how samples are used. Most companies have taken defensive measures to guard against both copyright infringement lawsuits against them and the unauthorized sampling of records they own.

For instance, as early as 1990 it was one executive's job at PolyGram (which owns the rights to most James Brown recordings) to periodically listen to new releases on other labels for the Soul Brother #1's trademark scream.[119] Many companies developed entire departments devoted to this practice; in the early 1990s EMI Music Publishing had a staff of six people whose sole job was to listen to new releases that may have contained samples of its property.[120] By the end of the 1990s, these types of departments existed and greatly expanded in virtually all major publishing and record companies.

On the other side of the coin, record companies that distribute hip-hop records became increasingly interested in making sure that all samples that appear on a forthcoming release are "cleared," particularly after the Biz Markie ruling.[121] "That was the turning point for people clearing stuff," states Hope Carr, the owner of a sample-clearing company.[122] "Clearing"

a sample involves licensing the use of a song fragment from its copyright owner(s) and working out a financial agreement that often involves a flat fee and/or some percentage of the new song's royalties. Businesses called "sample clearance houses" were established in the early 1990s and thrived as labels and artists increasingly employed them in order to avoid legal problems that may arise from sampling.[123] Put simply, today's hip-hop artists face an increasing array of complex legalities that their counter-parts in the earlier periods most likely never even considered.

Institutional Pressures on Hip-Hop Music Production

Detractors have labeled sampling "groove robbing,"[124] and they have argued that it is a form of aural plagiarism or it is just plain "stealing."[125] For instance, one entertainment lawyer diplomatically said, "It may be flattering to have the underlying works used for sampling purposes, but it's still taking," while another lawyer who represented an artist who had been sampled stated that it "is a euphemism in the music industry for what anyone else would call pickpocketing."[126] Mark Volman, a member of the 1960s rock band The Turtles that the hip-hop group De La Soul sampled, said, "Sampling is just a longer term for theft . . . Anybody who can honestly say sampling is some sort of creativity has never done anything creative."[127]

These characterizations of sampling as "theft," "pickpocketing" and being devoid of creativity are situated within a cultural tradition that conceives of originality and authorship in a radically different way. This reaction is not surprising considering mainstream America's lack of understanding regarding the intertextual modes of cultural production that produced African American folk preaching, blues and hip-hop.

Copyright lawyer Ken Anderson argues, "A jazz musician, for example, can quote from dozens of songs as he free-associates their musical implication, and those artistic references to the past are considered part of the art form, not a copyright infringement." A performance by a legendary jazz musician illustrates Anderson's point. "When Sonny Rollins played a rare solo saxophone concert at the Museum of Modern Art in 1985," Brown[128] states, "he quoted dozens, perhaps hundreds of songs from Tin Pan Alley to be-bop, honking some and crooning others, free-associating their musical and nostalgic implications, making them his own."[129] This intertextual mode of cultural production, which is akin to "voice-merging" in oral folk preaching traditions, is also echoed in the sampling methods used by hip-hop artists.

As sampling evolved within the musical practices of hip-hop, it grew more complex, and producers became more adept at deconstructing and reconfiguring small musical fragments in ways that sounded completely new. One example among many is the Beastie Boys' song "Sounds of Science," which incorporates the drum track, bass line, ambient sounds and guitar riffs from four very well-known Beatles songs in a way that makes the original sources almost impossible to recognize. In many cases the process of sampling is extremely complex, with a variety of different musical elements such as the bass drum, hi-hat, snare drum, and other drum sounds being layered beneath a bass line, keyboard sound, vocal snippet, guitar and other noises.

Many times these samples are drawn from numerous sources. Public Enemy coproducer Bill Stephney explained that many hip-hop producers use many recording tracks running simultaneously to create a single rhythm track:

"These kids will have six tracks of drum programs all at the same time. This is where sampling gets kind of crazy. You may get a kid who puts a kick from one record on one track, a kick from another record on another track, a Linn kick on a third track, and a TR-808 kick on a fourth—all to make one kick!"[130]

From the simple breakbeats created by DJs with two turntables in the mid-1970s to the dense and edgy sound collages of Public Enemy in the late 1980s and early 1990s, it is clear that existing but reconfigured recordings have provided the backbone of hip-hop music. But when hip-hop became a multimillion-dollar industry, numerous lawsuits were filed and, as a result of this, hip-hop artists found it increasingly difficult to operate the way their predecessors did. Labels reacted by creating a complex system of business and legal networks that include the above-mentioned sample clearance houses. The sample clearance practices that arose in the wake of industrywide copyright infringement lawsuits are often very expensive, and the financial burden is completely absorbed by the hip-hop artist, producer, or both, who pay for the costs out of his or her future royalties.[131]

When clearing a sample taken from a record, two types of fees must be paid: *publishing* fees and *master recording* (or *mechanical*) fees. The publishing fee, which is paid to the company or individual owning a particular song, often consists of a flexible and somewhat arbitrary formula that calculates a statutory royalty rate set by Congress.[132] This formula takes into account the sampled artist's popularity, the popularity of the artist that is sampling, and the time length of the sample used.[133] To obtain a license to use an original song's master recording (for example, a bass line from Chic's "Good Times" or James Brown's well-known scream), many times one must pay a one-time flat fee, which can often be very expensive—ranging from an estimated $2,000 to $7,000, with an additional two to four cents on every unit sold. A brief sample might require as much as a 50% stake in the new song's publishing, if it is allowed to be used at all.[134]

As I discussed in chapter 1, intellectual property law can be used ideologically. Producer Marley Marl says that because of hip-hop's graphic and confrontational reputation, "some artists won't give me permission to sample their music."[135] Similarly, Anita Baker will not allow any of her songs to be sampled by hip-hop artists, and James Brown forbids the sampling of his music in hip-hop songs about violence and drugs. Brown's special assistant states, "He really doesn't want to be involved in any kind of rap that demoralizes any segment of society."[136]

A director of a sample clearance house estimated that the clearance fees for the average hip-hop album totaled about $30,000 in the early 1990s, and those rates have risen throughout the 1990s.[137] Often, the cost can be much more. For instance, after De La

Soul was sued for copyright infringement, they took pains to clear the 50-plus samples that appeared on their follow-up album, *De La Soul is Dead,* which cost over $100,000 in clearance and legal fees. Sometimes it can cost that much for a single sample, as is the case with 2 Live Crew, who had to pay roughly $100,000 to lift a section of dialogue from Stanley Kubrick's *Full Metal Jacket*.[138]

This is an extremely large amount of money, especially when it is added to the cost of recording, promotion, music videos, etc.[139] The peril in paying such high fees is that often a great amount of money can be spent on records that achieve relatively little success (the vast majority of all records released in a given year fail commercially).[140] Hope Carr gives an example of this: "Say MCA quotes $4,000 on the master side and $2,000 on the publishing side . . . If you're some poor schmuck trying to put out the record yourself, you can't afford that—that's more than you're likely to earn on it."[141]

Tommy Boy record executive Daniel Hoffman says, "It's a legal and administrative hassle and it costs us a lot of money."[142] Chris Lighty, a hip-hop management company executive, states, "It's very hard to find these [copyright owners] and very expensive legally. You can spend between $5,000 and $10,000 just trying to obtain a license and still come up dry."[143] In reference to Lighty's comments about "coming up dry," he discusses a case in which a production team assumed that the licensing of a sample was imminent, so they completed and mastered the album only to find that the license was rejected. The production team had to reenter the studio to remaster the album, deleting the song with the unauthorized sample in the process because, Lighty states, "We decided it was expensive to remaster, but not as expensive as getting sued."[144]

The Beastie Boys' 1989 album *Paul's Boutique* contains a dizzying array of hundreds of samples from 1960s, 1970s and 1980s songs woven together, some that are extremely obscure and brief, and some slightly longer and more recognizable. (This album contains their song "Sounds of Science," which was discussed in the previous section.) Alan Light, an editor at *SPIN* and *Vibe,* comments on this album in relation to the current cost of sampling, "You could never make that record today. It would be *way* too expensive. You could

still use recognizable samples in 1989 and not have to pay millions and millions of dollars for them."[145]

A *Billboard* article describes the process of making sample-based music within the context of a highly charged legal environment and a nervous record company that has no desire to lose a substantial chunk of money (as did Warner Brothers in the above-mentioned Biz Markie case):

"When a project starts, we send a letter to the producer outlining all sorts of things that he needs to know about sampling to make a record with us," [PolyGram VP of business affairs] Hoffman says. "This includes keeping track of each song that was sampled." Additionally, PolyGram has begun asking for tapes of the original song, so that its legal department can evaluate "how extensive the sample is," Hoffman says. As the album nears completion, PolyGram follows up the original letter with a different letter to the artist, reminding the act that it is his or her responsibility to clear any samples. Additionally, if any remixes are done, the remixer gets a letter similar to the missive sent to the original producer.[146]

This highlights the complexities surrounding the practice of sampling within hip-hop after the music had become a high-profile, commercially successful genre. At the time that article was written (in 1992), the legal and bureaucratic procedures surrounding sampling were already in place and they became more fixed as the decade wore on.

By the mid-1990s, a large number of popular hip-hop artists who dominated the rap and pop charts used live musicians on their records—something that was virtually unheard of in the second half of the 1980s.[147] Interestingly, even when these artists were using recognizable instrumental phrases, these were often played by hired studio musicians who were instructed to make it sound like the original recording; this happened on Dr. Dre's *The Chronic.* This seemingly odd and circuitous music-making process is, in actuality, a rational course of action for a producer who wants to sidestep the often expensive *mechanical* royalty fee (though he or she still has to pay for the *publishing* fee).

For example, Naughty By Nature's Treach states that while samples were used on their debut album, over half of the album consisted of live instrumentation.[148] Treach told me that the use of live instrumentation was partially a stylistic decision but that it also had a lot to do with the cost of mechanical royalty licensing fees, especially in light of the cost of securing the right to use a Jackson 5 sample for their hit, "OPP."[149] Leading hip-hop magazine *The Source* reported that Redman's 1996 album *Muddy Waters* was a stylistic departure from his previous funky, sample-heavy outings. "With the soaring price of samples," *The Source* states, "Redman says he made a deliberate decision to do less sampling."[150] During an interview with me, Redman complained:

"They was taking me to the cleaners, fuckin' publishers. They wanted me to pay, like twenty G's [$20,000] for one sample, on top of all the other samples, and the video budget and the promotion. That means I won't see a fucking paycheck and my kids don't eat, you know what I'm saying?"[151]

Fugees member Wyclef says that his use of live instrumentation is primarily an aesthetic choice, because, in addition to being a hip-hop producer and MC, he is a talented multi-instrumentalist. Wyclef, who has both sampled other people's records and used live instruments to closely mimic records, told me that copyright has played a part, on a subconscious level, at least, in his use of instruments. He stated, "Yeah, it's a way of getting around that mechanical fee, so that has something to do with it. Licensing is expensive."[152]

While artistic innovation and individual vision were involved in the proliferation of live instrumentation during the 1990s, other circumstances also played a part. One major factor is the high cost of clearing samples, a practice that has become necessary as a result of the highly charged legal climate that exists in the music industry today. Hip-hop producers such as Marley Marl bring in live musicians to recreate a sample to bypass paying for the more expensive mechanical royalty fee.[153] Francesca Spero, a manager of hip-hop producers and musicians, tells a story she feels is representative of situations many hip-hop producers and artists found themselves:

[This] producer, who was to become famous for his contribution to hip-hop, is still an avid sampler. He samples not because he has to, but because he loves the flavor it gives his music and because it is part of his musical heritage and culture. Due to the legal climate surrounding sampling, more and more he is working with live musicians and sampling his own live drum sounds. But this is not his favorite thing. He started on two turntables in a local park, working the crowd. This is where sampling began, and it explains why sampling is his culture.[154]

By 1993, many hip-hop artists were steering clear of what some called the "sample hell" brought on by this restrictive legal environment.[155] Both David Landis and Sheila Rule, writers who have covered hip-hop trends and sampling cases, argue that this highly charged legal climate, together with the large expenses surrounding sampling, helped push hip-hop in the direction of live instrumentation.[156] Ken Anderson, an entertainment lawyer who defends hip-hop artists, argued that the evolution of hip-hop should not be "dictated by business concerns," and he expressed worries over the use of live music in hip-hop for "legal reasons."[157] For instance, when Public Enemy wanted to sample a bit of Buffalo Springfield's "For What It's Worth," the group discovered that it would be cheaper for them to have the song's original vocalist Stephen Stills sing the part of the song they were going to sample.[158]

Despite the powerful institutional pressures manifested by intellectual property law described above, hip-hop artists did not react in a uniform way, though they have largely responded in three particular ways. *First,* as I stated in the previous pages, by the early to mid-1990s many hip-hop artists incorporated live instrumentation into their music, either wholesale or by hiring studio musicians to imitate familiar riffs that are then sampled to avoid costly mechanical fees. *Second,* hip-hop artists who have the financial backing of large record labels can afford to sample significant sections of previously recorded songs in their own recordings. Because of the expensive flat fees, producers tend to shy away from collaging numerous samples. Artists and producers (such as Puff Daddy) favor using only one or two recognizable hooks or melodies. This is representative of the fifth, most recent, period of recorded hip-hop.

Third, artists have pushed themselves to more cleverly alter the unauthorized samples in their songs through effects such as reverb, flange, phasing, etc. The member of Cypress Hill who produces the group's instrumental tracks, DJ Muggs, states: "I don't worry much about copyrights. Yeah, I haven't been able to license some samples in the past, but the trick is to really fuck it up so that you don't even have to ask for permission."[159] Sample clearance business owner Hope Carr says that because the licensing fees are so high, "more people are doing songs without samples or trying to make songs where the samples are so obscure you don't hear them."[160]

Q-bert—a member of the turntablist crew Invisibl Skratch Piklz—said that copyright laws make "it more of a challenge for us because you really have to flip the sound. You really have to work it to make that sound so that it's not theirs anymore." He added, "That's what also makes it more beautiful as well. It makes you want to change that sound because if you just *use it* then it's theirs and that's stealing." He then says somewhat cryptically, "So if you can make it *not theirs*, it's yours."[161]

Mixmaster Mike—a fellow Invisibl Skratch Piklz member and full-time member of the Beastie Boys— agreed, saying that he included some unauthorized samples, sounds, and scratches from movies and records on his 1998 solo album, *Anti-Theft Device.* "I didn't clear all of them because it would be too expensive and a pain in the ass, tracking down all the movie studios and publishers and record companies from the records and films I used," Mike said. "Anyway, I feel like I flipped the sound so that it became mine. I just flipped the sound and made it hella fresh."[162]

Others still work within the sample clearance system, but apply the same philosophy by sampling more obscure artists. Underground hip-hop artist Voodo says that the artists he samples—often largely unknown 1960s and 1970s jazz-funk artists—do not charge high flat fees in the way more popular artists do. Voodo states:

That's probably the reason why my sound is the way it is. For some reason I've been able to clear every sample that I've ever used. Every sample, even though it still cost a lot, it was still clearable. It was like $2,000 or $3,000 for the actual use of the sample and $3,000 for the mechanical, you know, it gets deep! Certain artists aren't that much. . . . I *dare not* sample a Sade song or an Anita Baker song because they don't clear, well Sade will clear it, but you have to pay a grip. We're talking 50 G's [$50,000] or something stupid. . . . You've got to be more selective with the stuff you sample."[163]

Voodo strongly identifies the practice of sampling as an essential element of hip-hop culture. The fact that he and other artists feel so strongly about sampling emphasizes that it is certainly not seen as a mere tool or technique, but a profoundly resonating practice that is deeply imbedded in their culture. Voodo states:

I'm hip-hop to the death and I'll sample to the death. That's what it's about. If I stop sampling just on the premise that it's too expensive for me not wanting to pay a certain amount for the publishing or a percentage—if that's the case then I'm not doing my job as a B-Boy. My point is that hip-hop is a sampling thing. No doubt. I don't want to stop sampling. Hell no.[164]

The case of hip-hop and sampling is illustrative of what Coombe means when she writes that intellectual property law is both *prohibitive* and *productive.* It would be too simplistic to view the effects of intellectual property law as only closing down cultural production and meaning, something that is certainly not the case with hip-hop. True, artists' ability to freely sample has been severely limited, which many (including myself) argue has been to the detriment of this musical and cultural form. But it is just as interesting to look at *how* artists respond to these structural limitations.

Although intellectual property law has been prohibitive, it has also been productive in that artists have been forced to confront these parameters and to come up with creative ways of dealing with the restrictions imposed by the enforcement of copyright law. Again, they have done so by disguising their samples to the point that these samples are, potentially, unrecognizable to the artist who recorded the original song, or by hiring studio musicians to mimic a sound, thereby getting around paying the mechanical royalty fees.

Albums released in the late 1980s, such as Public Enemy's *It Takes a Nation of Millions to Hold Us Back* and the Beastie Boys' *Paul's Boutique*—albums that incorporated hundreds of samples in a dizzying aural collage—are virtually impossible to release today if they are to be distributed through mainstream channels. Despite that limitation, there is one significant distribution network where this can occur: the Internet. DJ Spooky points out that copyright law "is going to be utterly bypassed by technology."[165] He explains, "The only thing is that the mass distribution of this music will have to go online. The RIAA [Recording Industry Association of America], they are able to intercede on physical pressing plants, but not the online areas." In fact, however, the music industry *can* intercede on web sites, and has forced the closing down of many web sites that infringe on copyrighted musical works. I will return to this point in the final chapter.

Conclusion

Throughout most of the music's evolution, hip-hop used existing music as the foundation on which its musical bed was constructed, and in the time before the mid- to late 1980s, it did so in a relatively unfettered way. It is not coincidental that the first copyright infringement lawsuit that involved hip-hop was brought against the first rappers to land a number-one pop record on the *Billboard* charts. This suit set off a flurry of legal activity that still exists in the music industry. The application of copyright law in this area made it increasingly difficult for hip-hop artists to engage freely in the intertextual modes of musical production in the same way that they and their predecessors had.

Nevertheless, sampling did not die. Even if many song publishing companies and songwriters themselves do not respect sampling as a method of musical production, they tolerate the practice because, in part, it earns them money in exchange for

very little effort. The intertextual mode of cultural production that informs sampling may lend itself, as some have argued, to an anticapitalist ethic (with its communal, nonproprietary assumptions concerning culture), but capitalism has been remarkably adaptable when it encounters potentially resistive ideologies and practices.

Despite the fact that certain musicians do not like to have their music sampled, sampling has not disappeared from the contemporary music industry because it is another way of making money from a work that may be no longer generating income for the company. This is something that would have been inconceivable before hip-hop introduced this new mode of cultural production to the music industry. In light of this, it is not surprising that old song publishing catalogs—particularly of 1960s and 1970s funk and soul artists—are being purchased with the primary intention of licensing songs to hip-hop artists.[166]

Hip-hop's commercial explosion can also be seen as representing a shift in the means of production out of the hands of the local community and into the hands of corporations. Even though high-profile artists such as Puff Daddy have been given their own boutique labels, it is still the major labels that call the shots, and none of these labels favor a system that encourages, or approves of, unauthorized sampling. Therefore, even if artists are ideologically opposed to copyright restrictions, there is little or nothing they can do to change the situation, particularly because virtually all artist contracts have record company-enforced stipulations and rules regarding sampling.

Most top-selling hip-hop artists are signed to (or are distributed by) major labels, which release albums by artists who sample and which own the copyrights to albums that others sample. It is this interconnectedness that has led to the establishment of sample-clearing houses, businesses that secure licensing agreements for hip-hop artists who want to legitimately release a record that incorporates elements of another aural text. The cost of licensing, especially the cost of directly sampling a performance on another record, is often quite high, and it can cost as much as $100,000 to clear a single sample. This is one primary reason why hip-hop producers often hire musicians to recreate a musical phrase in order to only pay the less expensive publishing royalty fee. It is, in part, the exorbitant cost of licensing and legal fees that has led an artistic community whose *modus operandi* hinged on the borrowing of recorded music to essentially turn its central productive practice on its head.

A contemporary example of the way intellectual property law attempts to define where a text begins and where it ends is the way songwriting credits are assigned on many hip-hop albums. Mase, the Puff Daddy protégé who later quit rap and found God, included a song on his second album that listed *nine* people on the songwriting credits—six of whom never set foot in the studio when Mase recorded the song "Stay Out of My Way."[167] The interesting thing about the Mase song is that it sampled Madonna's 1990 song "Justify My Love" (written by Madonna, Lenny Kravitz and I. Chavez), which in turn sampled Public Enemy's 1988 song "Security of the First World" (written by J. Boxley, Chuck D and Eric Sadler).

The Madonna song does not credit Public Enemy in the liner notes of the album on which "Justify My Love" appears, in part because Public Enemy did not pursue the matter, and also because this type of crediting wasn't commonplace in 1990. But the liner notes of the Mase album, released 9 years later, coassigned both songwriting credit and sampling credit to Public Enemy, despite the fact that only the Madonna song was sampled in Mase's song. Throughout the 1980s it was extremely rare for hip-hop albums to include sampling credits or to assign partial songwriting credit to an artist who was sampled, but today this clear demarcation of the boundaries within a song is common.

Copyright law emerged out of the desire of seventeenth- and eighteenth-century printing houses to prevent pirates from reprinting what the houses considered to be their property. Despite the rhetoric that surrounds copyright law, from its very inception copyright has existed primarily to protect companies that control the means of production, and in most cases copyright law facilitates a transferal of artistic property from artists to larger entities. This is very true of the contemporary music industry. Because record companies are also defined as authors, they have the power to sue artists who appropriate their property even when the songwriters are ambivalent about being sampled.

In addition, Public Enemy was forced to remove from its web site digital audio files of their own songs that their old record company, Def Jam, had refused to release commercially. Chuck D and the rest of the group felt strongly that the songs should get to their fans, so they posted them for free; but because Def Jam owned the copyrights to the songs, the company was able to exert legal pressure to get the group to remove the tracks from the Internet. This helped fuel more antagonism between Public Enemy and its longtime label, with Chuck D characterizing the group's problems as a battle to control the products of the group's labor. It is the *ownership* of the means of production that facilitates record companies' ability to assert *authorship* and therefore control the context in which its property appears.

After Chuck D made much noise, Def Jam (which began as an independent label but is now fully owned by the world's largest record company) eventually released them from their contract, after which the group released their next album in MP3 form for $6. Such radical moves are not surprising, especially coming from a man who bragged about illegally sampling on a track released 10 years earlier, titled "Caught, Can I Get a Witness," from their classic album *It Takes a Nation of Millions to Hold Us Back*. (This is the same Public Enemy album that contained "Security of the First World," the song sampled on "Justify My Love".) Chuck D raps: "Caught, now in court 'cause I stole a beat/This is a sampling sport . . . I found this mineral that I call a beat/I paid zero."[168]

This discussion of hip-hop highlights the complexities of engaging in creative endeavors while under contractual agreements with intellectual property lawyers and record executives. The musical practices that currently shape the way hip-hop is produced represent a very interesting articulation of artistic innovation, formalized bureaucratic business practices, intellectual property law and cultural traditions that grew out of African-American culture. In spite of the institutional pressures imposed on hip-hop artists, sampling has not stopped. Artists adapted, though they certainly navigated within limiting parameters completely unknown to their forebears.

Notes

1. Miller, K. D. (1993, January 20). Redefining plagiarism: Martin Luther King's use of an oral tradition. *Chronicle of Higher Education, 39, 20,* A60.
2. Scollon, R. (1995). Plagiarism and ideology: Identity in intercultural discourse. *Language in Society, 24,* pp. 1–28.
3. Ibid., pp. 24–25.
4. Ibid., p. 3.
5. Ibid.
6. Ibid., p. 23.
7. Ong, W. (1982). *Orality and literacy.* New York: Routledge, p. 131.
8. Ibid., p. 131.
9. Bettig, R. V. (1996). *Copyrighting culture: The political economy of intellectual property.* Boulder, CO: Westview Press.
10. Scollon, R. (1995). Plagiarism and ideology: Identity in intercultural discourse. *Language in Society, 24,* 1–28.
11. Johannesen, R. L. (1995). The ethics of plagiarism reconsidered: The oratory of Martin Luther King, Jr. *Southern Communication Journal 60, 3,* 185–194.
12. Ibid.
13. Ibid., p. 186.
14. De Palma, B. (1990, November 10). Plagiarism seen by scholars in King's Ph.D. dissertation. *New York Times,* p. 1.
15. Ibid.
16. Radin, C. A. (1990, November 10). Researchers cite plagiarism by King. *Boston Globe,* p. 1.
17. De Palma, B. (1990, November 10). Plagiarism seen by scholars in King's Ph.D. dissertation. *New York Times,* p. 1.
18. Ibid., p. 1.
19. Ball, I. (1990, November 10). Luther King 'borrowed ideas.' *Daily Telegraph,* p. 11.
20. De Palma, B. (1990, November 10). Plagiarism seen by scholars in King's Ph.D. dissertation. *New York Times,* p. 1.
21. Ball, I. (1990, November 10). Luther King 'borrowed ideas.' *The Daily Telegraph,* p. 11.
22. De Palma, B. (1990, November 10). Plagiarism seen by scholars in King's Ph.D. dissertation. *New York Times,* p. 1.
23. Miller, K. D. (1993, January 20). Redefining plagiarism: Martin Luther King's use of an oral tradition. *Chronicle of Higher Education, 39, 20,* p. A60.
24. Miller, K. D. (1991, June). Martin Luther King, Jr. and the black folk pulpit. *Journal of American History, 78, 1,* 120–123.
25. Ibid.
26. Ibid.
27. Ibid., p. 121.
28. Garrow, D. J. (1991, June). King's plagiarism: Imitation, insecurity, and transformation. *Journal of American History, 78, 1,* 86–92.
29. Reagon, B. J. (1991, June). "Nobody knows the trouble I see"; or, "by and by I'm gonna lay down my heavy load." *Journal of American History, 78, 1,* 111–119.
30. Ibid., p. 117.
31. Ibid., p. 118.
32. Ibid.
33. Garrow, D. J. (1991, June). King's plagiarism: Imitation, insecurity, and transformation. *Journal of American History, 78, 1,* 86–92.
34. Miller, K. D. (1991, June). Martin Luther King, Jr. and the black folk pulpit. *Journal of American History, 78, 1,* 120–123.
35. Ibid., p. 121.
36. Reagon, B. J. (1991, June). "Nobody knows the trouble I see"; or, "by and by I'm gonna lay down my heavy load." *Journal of American History, 78, 1,* 111–119.
37. Ibid., p. 115.
38. Johannesen, R. L. (1995). The ethics of plagiarism reconsidered: The oratory of Martin Luther King, Jr. *Southern Communication Journal, 60, 3,* 185–194.
39. Miller, K. D. (1991, June). Martin Luther King, Jr. and the black folk pulpit. *Journal of American History, 78, 1,* 120–123, p. 123.
40. Miller, K. D. (1987, April). Keith Miller responds. *College English, 49,* 478–480, p. 480.
41. Ong, W. (1982). *Orality and literacy.* New York: Routledge; Rose, T. (1994). *Black noise: Hip-hop music and Black culture in contemporary America.* Hanover, CT: Wesleyan University Press.
42. Schumacher, T. G. (1995). "This is a sampling sport": Digital sampling, rap music and the law in cultural production. *Media, Culture & Society, 17,* 253–273.
43. Rose, T. (1994). *Black noise: Hip-hop music and black culture in contemporary America.* Hanover, CT: Wesleyan University Press.
44. Schumacher, T. G. (1995). "This is a sampling sport": Digital sampling, rap music and the law in cultural production. *Media, Culture & Society, 17,* 253–273.
45. Cutler, C. (1995). Plunderphonics. In R. Sakolsky & F. W. Ho (Eds.), *Sounding Off! Music as subversion/resistance/revolution* (pp. 67–86). Brooklyn: Autonomedia.
46. Fernando, S. H. Jr. (1994). *The new beats: Exploring the music, culture, and attitudes of hip-hop.* New York: Doubleday.
47. Rose, T. (1994). *Black noise: Hip-hop music and black culture in contemporary America.* Hanover, CT: Wesleyan University Press.
48. Beadle, J. J. (1993). *Will pop eat itself? Pop music in the soundbite era.* London: Faber and Faber.
49. Rose, T. (1994). *Black noise: Hip-hop music and black culture in contemporary America.* Hanover, CT: Wesleyan University Press.

50. Toop, D. (1991). *Rap attack 2: African hip-hop to global hip-hop.* London: Serpent's Tail, p. 60.

51. Kool Herc, personal correspondence, November 13, 1998.

52. George, N. (1998). *Hip-hop America.* New York: Viking.

53. Toop, D. (1991). *Rap attack 2: African hip-hop to global hip-hop.* London: Serpent's Tail, pp. 63–66.

54. Ibid., p. 65.

55. Rose, T. (1994). *Black noise: Hip-hop music and black culture in contemporary America.* Hanover, CT: Wesleyan University Press.

56. Ibid.

57. Toop, D. (1991). *Rap attack 2: African hip-hop to global hip-hop.* London: Serpent's Tail, p. 69.

58. Samuels, D. (1991, November 11). The hip-hop on hip-hop: The 'black music' that isn't either. *New Republic,* 24.

59. Fernando, S.H. Jr. (1994). *The new beats: Exploring the music, culture, and attitudes of hip-hop.* New York: Doubleday.

60. Caston, K. (1994, March 25). Hip-hop's roots: The old school. *Dallas Morning News,* p. 42.

61. Williams, S. (1994). *Message from the street: The best of Grandmaster Flash, Melle Mel & the Furious Five* [CD]. Los Angeles: Rhino.

62. Fernando, S.H. Jr. (1994). *The new beats: Exploring the music, culture, and attitudes of hip-hop.* New York: Doubleday.

63. Toop, D. (1991). *Rap attack 2: African hip-hop to global hip-hop.* London: Serpent's Tail, p. 69.

64. Fernando, S. H. Jr. (1994). *The new beats: Exploring the music, culture, and attitudes of hip-hop.* New York: Doubleday.

65. Ibid.

66. Berman, E. (1993, December 23). The godfathers of hip-hop. *Rolling Stone,* 137.

67. Toop, D. (1992). *The Sugar Hill story* [CD]. New York: Sequel Records.

68. Fuchs, A. (1992, May 23). What's in a hip-hop drum beat?; Plenty if you own the original master. *Billboard,* 4.

69. Ibid.

70. Ibid.

71. Marcus, G. (1991). *Dead Elvis: A chronicle of a cultural obsession.* New York: Doubleday.

72. George, N. (1998). *Hip-hop America.* New York: Viking.

73. Brown, G. (1990). *The information game: Ethical issues in a microchip world.* New York: Humanities Press.

74. Toop, D. (1991). *Rap attack 2: African hip-hop to global hip-hop.* London: Serpent's Tail.

75. Ibid., pp. 162–163.

76. Ibid., p. 163.

77. Snowden, D. (1989, August 6). Sampling: A creative tool or license to steal? *Los Angeles Times,* Calendar, p. 61; Brown, J. H. (1990, November). "They don't make music the way they used to": The legal implications of "sampling" in contemporary music. *Wisconsin Law Review,* 1941–1990.

78. Rose, T. (1994). *Black noise: Hip-hop music and black culture in contemporary America.* Hanover, CT: Wesleyan University Press.

79. Stetsasonic. (1988). *In Full Gear.* [CD]. New York: Tommy Boy.

80. George, N. (1998). *Hip-hop America.* New York: Viking, p. 89.

81. Rose, T. (1994). *Black noise: Hip-hop music and black culture in contemporary America.* Hanover, CT: Wesleyan University Press.

82. Culture Vulture. (1992, April 26). *Newsday,* 3; Snider, E. (1992, August 23). He's back and he's proud. *St. Petersburg Times,* p. 18.

83. Hochman, S. & Phillips, C. (1992, September 13). Pop eye. *Los Angeles Times,* Calendar, p. 69.

84. Fernando, S. H, Jr. (1994). *The new beats: Exploring the music, culture, and attitudes of hip-hop.* New York: Doubleday, p. 237.

85. Rose, T. (1994). *Black noise: Hip-hop music and black culture in contemporary America.* Hanover, CT: Wesleyan University Press, p. 40.

86. Toop, D. (1995). *Ocean of sound: Aether talk, ambient sound and imaginary worlds.* New York: Serpent's Tail, p. 71.

87. Berman, E. (1993, December 23). The godfathers of hip-hop. *Rolling Stone,* p. 139.

88. Toop, D. (1991). *Rap attack 2: African hip-hop to global hip-hop.* London: Serpent's Tail.

89. Norris, C. (1994, May/June). Needle phreaks: The planet's best DJs find a new groove. *Option, 56,* 53.

90. Berman, E. (1993, December 23). The godfathers of hip-hop. *Rolling Stone,* p. 142.

91. Toop, D. (1991). *Rap attack 2: African hip-hop to global hip-hop.* London: Serpent's Tail.

92. Fernando, S.H. Jr. (1994). *The new beats: Exploring the music, culture, and attitudes of hip-hop.* New York: Doubleday, p. 12.

93. Toop, D. (1991). *Rap attack 2: African hip-hop to global hip-hop.* London: Serpent's Tail, p. 78.

94. Marcus, J. (1995). Don't stop that funky beat: The essentiality of digital sampling to hip-hop music. In Negativland (Ed.), *Fair use: The story of the letter u and the numeral 2* (pp. 205–212). Concord, CA: Seeland.

95. Cox, M. (1984, December 4). Hip-hop Music. *Wall Street Journal,* p. 1.

96. Fernando, S. H. Jr. (1994). *The new beats: Exploring the music, culture, and attitudes of hip-hop.* New York: Doubleday.

97. Simpson, J. C. (1992, May 7). The impresario of hip-hop. *Time,* 69; Rawsthorn, A. (1994, November 17). Poly-Gram kicks into rap groove with RAL/Def Jam move. *Financial Times,* 28; Trapp, R. (1994, November 17). PolyGram raps up hip-hop label in $33 million deal. *Independent,* p. 36.

98. Seagram reportedly buys Def Jam. (1999, February 26). SonicNet. [Online] Available: http://www.sonicnet.com

99. Lloyd, R. (1987, February 22). The Beasties' hip-hop bonanza: Selling & setting records. *Washington Post,* p. F1.

100. Silverman, E. R. (1989, May 29). Hip-hop goes the way of rock 'n' roll: Record moguls snap up labels. *Crain's New York Business,* 3.

101. Ibid.; Samuels, D. (1991, November 11). The hip-hop on hip-hop: The 'black music' that isn't either. *New Republic,* 24.

102. Vaughn, C. (1992, December). Simmons' rush for profits. *Black Enterprise,* 67; Hip-hop. [Broadcast] (1995, June 14). *CNN.*

103. McAdams, J. (1993, January 30). Clearing House: EMI Music uses sampling committee. *Billboard,* 1.

104. Snowden, D. (1989, August 6). Sampling: A creative tool or license to steal? *Los Angeles Times,* Calendar, p. 61.

105. Snider, E. (1992, August 23). He's back and he's proud. *St. Petersburg Times,* p. 18; Pop eye: Sampling wars. (1989, July 23). *Los Angeles Times,* Calendar, p. 73.

106. Garcia, G. (1990, June 3). Play it again sampler. *Time,* p. 69.

107. Ruling expands 'sampling' case law. (1998, July 10). *New York Law Journal,* p. 5; UK remixers win settlement in sample case. (1998, May 16). *Music Week,* p. S1; Russell, D. (1992, January 4). Judge clips Biz Markie on sampling issue. *Billboard,* 1.

108. Gordon, S. R. & Sanders, H. J. (1989, September 10). Stolen tunes [Letter to the Editor]. *New York Times,* p. B7.

109. Brown, G. (1990). *The information game: Ethical issues in a microchip world.* New York: Humanities Press; Marcus, J. (1995). Don't stop that funky beat: The essentiality of digital sampling to hip-hop music. In Negativland (Ed.), *Fair use: The story of the letter u and the numeral 2* (pp. 205–212). Concord, CA: Seeland.

110. Biskupic, J. (1994, March 8). Court hands parody. *Washington Post,* p. A1.

111. (1994). *Campbell v. Acuff-Rose Music, Inc.,* 114 S. Ct. 1164 (U.S.S.C.); Graham, G. (1994, March 8). Rappers win copyright suit. *Financial Times,* p. 6.

112. Philips, C. (1992, January 1). Songwriter wins large settlement in hip-hop suit. *Los Angeles Times,* p. F1.

113. Cox, M. (1991, December 20). Hip-hop album is ordered off shelves for lifting another record's music. *Wall Street Journal,* p. B6.

114. Landis, D. (1992, January 16). Court fights over hip-hop music. *USA Today,* p. 2D; Soocher, S. (1992, May 1). As sampling suits proliferate, legal guidelines are emerging. *New York Law Journal,* p. 5.

115. New York judge orders record recall in first-ever sampling decision. (1992, January 27). [Online] *Entertainment Litigation Reporter.* Available: Lexis-Nexus.

116. Brown, G. (1990). *The information game: Ethical issues in a microchip world.* New York: Humanities Press.

117. Sugarman, R. G. & Salvo, J. P. (1992, March 16). Sampling litigation in the limelight. *New York Law Journal,* 1; Soocher, S. (1992, May 1). As sampling suits proliferate, legal guidelines are emerging. *New York Law Journal,* 5.

118. Goldberg, D. & Bernstein, R. J. (1993, January 15). Reflections on sampling. *New York Law Journal,* 3.

119. Tomsho, R. (1990, November 5). As sampling revolutionizes recording, debate grows over aesthetics, copyrights. *Wall Street Journal,* p. B1.

120. Brown, G. (1990). *The information game: Ethical issues in a microchip world.* New York: Humanities Press.

121. Soocher, S. (1992, May 1). As sampling suits proliferate, legal guidelines are emerging. *New York Law Journal,* 5.

122. Fernando, S. H. Jr. (1994). *The new beats: Exploring the music, culture, and attitudes of hip-hop.* New York: Doubleday.

123. Rule, S. (1992, April 21). Record companies are challenging 'sampling' in hip-hop. *New York Times,* p. C13.

124. Henken, J. (1988, October 16). Sounding off by the numbers: Making music the MIDI way. *Los Angeles Times,* Calendar, p. 66.

125. Goldberg, D. & Bernstein, R. J. (1993, January 15). Reflections on sampling. *New York Law Journal,* 3.

126. Soocher, S. (1989, February 13). License to sample. *National Law Journal,* 1–5; Harrington, R. (1991, December 25). The groove robbers' judgement: Order on 'sampling' songs may be rap landmark. *Washington Post,* p. D1.

127. Hochman, S. (1991, December 18). Judge raps practice of 'sampling.' *Los Angeles Times,* p. F1.

128. Brown, G. (1990). *The information game: Ethical issues in a microchip world.* New York: Humanities Press.

129. Ibid., p. 1948.

130. Rose, T. (1994). *Black noise: Hip-hop music and black culture in contemporary America.* Hanover, CT: Wesleyan University Press.

131. Documents that accompany sound masters. (1995, September). *Entertainment Law & Finance, 10, 6,* 7; Pedroso, A.I. (1994, April). Tips for music producer agreements. *Entertainment Law & Finance, 11, 1,* 3.

132. Fernando, S.H. Jr. (1994). *The new beats: Exploring the music, culture, and attitudes of hip-hop.* New York: Doubleday.

133. A new spin on music sampling: A case for fair play. (1992). *Harvard Law Review, 105,* 726–739; Finell, J.G. (1992, May 22). How a musicologist views digital sampling issue. *New York Law Journal,* 5.

134. Taraska, J. (1998, November 14). Sampling remains prevalent despite legal uncertainties. *Billboard,* 12.

135. Shiver, Jr., J. (1994, April 11). Digital double trouble: From rap music to medical formulas, little seems safe from duplication. *Los Angeles Times,* p. A1.

136. Jones, C. (1996, December 22). Haven't I heard that 'whoop' (or 'hoop') somewhere before? *New York Times,* p. B44.

137. Fernando, S.H. Jr. (1994). *The new beats: Exploring the music, culture, and attitudes of hip-hop.* New York: Doubleday.

138. Browne, D. (1992, January 24). Settling the bill: Digital sampling in the music industry. *Entertainment Weekly, 102,* 54.

139. Spero, F. (1992, December 5). Sample greed is hurting hip-hop business. *Billboard,* 7.

140. A new spin on music sampling: A case for fair play. (1992). *Harvard Law Review, 105,* 726–739.

141. Taraska, J. (1998, November 14). Sampling remains prevalent despite legal uncertainties. *Billboard,* 12.

142. Browne, D. (1992, January 24). Settling the bill: Digital sampling in the music industry. *Entertainment Weekly, 102,* 54.

143. Russell, D. (1992, January 4). Judge clips Biz Markie on sampling issue. *Billboard,* 1.

144. Ibid.

145. Hofmann, J.G. (Producer). (1999, March 12). *Beastiography.* New York: MTV.

146. Morris, C. (1992, May 23). Sampling safeguards follow suit. *Billboard,* 1.

147. Hunt, D. (1993, June 29). Liberating hip-hop with jazz sound: Freestyle Fellowship adds riffs to rhymes. *Los Angeles Times,* Calendar, p. 1; Hill, B. (1995, March 26). A grass-roots movement: Live performances build Philly band's support. *Washington Post,* p. G1; Gettelman, P. (1994, March 4). US3 breaks the sound barrier; the group's blend of hip-hop and jazz takes the blue note label to new heights. *Billboard,* p. 6;

Guilliatt, R. (1993, January 31). Pop music: Jazz and hip-hop take the plunge. *Los Angeles Times,* Calendar, p. 3.

148. Landis, D. (1992, January 16). Court fights over hip-hop music. *USA Today,* 2D.

149. Treach, personal correspondence, January 30, 1998.

150. Brodeur, S. (1996, December). Seeing red: The funkadelic Redman continues to bring the outer limits back to the underground. *Source,* 85–88.

151. Redman, personal correspondence, December 5, 1997.

152. Wyclef, personal correspondence, February 27, 1998.

153. Fernando, S.H. Jr. (1994). *The new beats: Exploring the music, culture, and attitudes of hip-hop.* New York: Doubleday.

154. Spero, F. (1992, December 5). Sample greed is hurting hip-hop business. *Billboard,* 7.

155. Buchsbaum, H. (1993, September 17). The law in your life: Hip-hop musicians and copyright law. *Scholastic Update,* 12.

156. Landis, D. (1992, January 16). Court fights over hip-hop music. *USA Today,* 2D; Rule, S. (1992, April 24). Drumbeat heat: Record companies are challenging 'sampling' in hip-hop music. *Houston Chronicle,* p. 4.

157. Rule, S. (1992, April 24). Drumbeat heat: Record companies are challenging 'sampling' in hip-hop music. *Houston Chronicle,* p. 4.

158. Taraska, J. (1998, November 14). Sampling remains prevalent despite legal uncertainties. *Billboard,* 12.

159. DJ Muggs, personal correspondence, February 12, 1998.

160. Jones, C. (1996, December 22). Haven't I heard that 'whoop' (or 'hoop') somewhere before? *New York Times,* B44.

161. Q-Bert, personal correspondence, May 29, 1997.

162. Mike D, personal correspondence, April 13, 1998.

163. Voodo, personal correspondence, June 2, 1997.

164. Ibid.

165. DJ Spooky, personal correspondence, October 7, 1999.

166. Jones, C. (1996, December 22). Haven't I heard that 'whoop' (or 'hoop') somewhere before? *New York Times,* p. B44.

167. Mase. (1999). Stay out of my way. On *Double up* [CD]. New York: Bad Boy.

168. Public Enemy. (1988). Security of the first world. On *It takes a nation of millions to hold us back* [CD]. New York: Def Jam.

13.
MY BLACK DEATH
Arthur Jafa

There were two major instances in which black aesthetics radically redirected Western art practice in the twentieth century. The first is the advent of African "art" in Europe. Europeans were confronted with artifacts that were essentially alien; i.e., they were the products of radically different assumptions about how one apprehends and responds to the world. There was little understanding of the cultural context that generated these artifacts, how their forms were arrived at or how their structures of meaning operated, what they might mean to their makers.

The second instance occurred with the emergence of jazz, yet another alien artifact but one decidedly more familiar (due to its domestic origins). In the first instance—the arrival of African sculptural artifacts in Europe—you get the artifact without its creators in tow. But with the arrival of jazz, the impact isn't solely the result of the music, the artifact in this instance, but it also results from the manifest being of its creators, the way they spoke and behaved, the way they dressed, their idiomatic manner of occupying (and penetrating) space, their individual styles and philosophies, and the consensual articulations of the aesthetic and generative processes of the music. The repercussions of these two instances of cultural insurgency are near unquantifiable in magnitude, but a few things seem clear.

Picasso's *Demoiselles d'Avignon* (and hence modernism) is the direct result of his confrontation with African artifacts. His invention of Cubism was provoked by his inquiry into the spacial implications of these artifacts. This is a commonly accepted line. To be more precise, Cubism is the direct transposition of these spacial implications onto the practice of Western painting. At the time Western painting (despite Cézanne's violent cage rattling) had become trapped by the limitations (and distortions) of Western Renaissance perspective (single "fixed" vantage/vanishing point), itself a conflation of the logic of Western egocentricism (the sun revolves around the Earth) into a system of ordering space and time. African artifacts provided an alternative system with which to order space and time.

Cubism's utilization of multiple "fixed" vantages, rather than the single "fixed" vantage of Western Renaissance perspective, betrays a limited comprehension of the logic of multiple "dynamic" vantages apparent in the forms of African artifacts, a logic shared by post-Einsteinian views of space/time. Robert Farris Thompson has described in *African Art in Motion* how many of the artifacts in the possession of European artists like Picasso were never intended to be (i.e., were not designed to be) seen on a pedestal, in a fixed position. These sculptural artifacts moved around the viewer, as much as, if not more than, the viewer moved around the artifact. This is a radical alternative to the Western paradigm in which the subject has agency while the object has none.

Picasso, as quoted by André Malraux, said:

"People are always talking about the influence the Negroes had on me. What about it? We all loved the fetishes. Van Gogh said his generation had Japanese art—we have the Negroes. Their forms have no more influence on me than on Matisse, or on Derain. But for Matisse and Derain, the masks were sculpture—no more than that. When Matisse showed me his first Negro head, he talked about Egyptian art. But when I went to the Musée de l'Homme, the masks were not just sculpture. They were magical objects. . . . I understand what their sculptures did for the Negroes. . . . They were weapons—to keep people from being ruled by spirits, to help them free themselves. Tools. *Les Demoiselles d'Avignon* must have come that day, not because of the forms, but because it was my first canvas of exorcism!"

Another crucial aspect of Picasso's confrontation with black aesthetics has only recently come to light. Ostensibly an investigation of Picasso's utilization of photography, one can only smile in wonder at the publication of *Picasso and Photography: The Dark Mirror* (Baldasari, 1998). The book reveals that Picasso possessed some forty photographs taken by Edmond Fortier, a Dakar-based photographer who was the most prolific publisher of postcards from French West Africa beginning in 1900–01. The photographs, supposedly "studies," are of African women, generally bare-breasted and often with arms raised over the head or folded behind the back. (I suspect the appearance of these clearly suppressed materials is a result of the Picasso Museum's desperate need to feed its publishing wing.)

This book reveals, in rather explicit comparative detail, how Picasso used these photographs as the basis for the development of *Les Demoiselles d'Avignon*. The standard argument is that *Demoiselles* represented "the invention of colored forms that no longer intended to imitate the external world but only to signify it. The canvas ceased to be a mirror—however deforming—of the visible, in order to become a plastic language (*écriture*)." In fact, as these materials make evident, Picasso's work imitates not only the African artifacts to which he had access, but the very bodies, by way of Fortier's "objective" representations, from which these embodiments of black being were derived. Picasso's combined access

to African artifacts and Fortier's photographs made explicit the presence of the highly conceptual formal system employed by these artifacts. The implications of this would seem to demand some major reconsiderations of the conceptual origins and parameters of modernism: how black bodies activate space, or the volumetric intensity of black bodies, of cities; and the attraction of the entropic; modernism as a substrand of black aesthetics; the black body as the premier anti-entropic figure of the twentieth century. The trauma provoked by the introduction of the black body into white space is profound.

Our notion of the "abstract" arises from a simple refusal of, or resistance to, the ontological fact of black being (and its material dimension, the black body), what I've described as "the inconceivability of the black body to the white imagination." Simply put, representations of the black body, as rendered by traditional African artifacts, were rejected (by whites) as instances of verisimilitude and instead received as "highly stylized" or "abstract." Europeans preferred to understand these artifacts as creative distortions rather than accept the existence of human beings that looked so radically different in appearance from them. This radical difference of appearance functions, in the Western mind-set, as the sign of a radically different (alien) ontology, which of course threatened the Eurocentric belief in itself as the defining model of humanity. This, in turn, has provoked the ongoing struggle against the acceptance of the "other," and its full humanity.

Duchamp was initially as content as Picasso, and others, to explore the space/time implications of African artifacts. But inevitably, Duchamp, smarter than anyone else around, became deeply interested in how African artifacts *behaved* rather than simply how they looked (their gaze). Duchamp peeped that these artifacts were, in fact, not art but instruments whose functionality had been arrested, and that much of their power was derived from their radically alienated, and de facto transgressive, relationship to the context in which they found themselves. Consequently, Duchamp's urinal was engendered by his desire to model a work after the contextual dissonance provoked by the placement of these (black) artifacts in (white) museums. And it's no accident that

Duchamp chose the urinal, a white artifact which contains and channels dark matter, or shit, the stuff of black being. Surrealism can be understood as an investigation of the psychic frisson produced by the juxtaposition of incongruent objects (a cow and an ironing board), the paradigmatic example being "the black body in white space."

In similar fashion, Jackson Pollock ('s practice) couldn't have been without jazz. It's indisputable that Pollock was very good at what he did, but the problem arose, inevitably, because he didn't know what he was doing. His genius, and I think it was genius, resided in his ability to transpose jazz's improvisational flow and trajection, an essentially alien aesthetic methodology, onto the practice of painting. Western painting, which up until the twentieth century had been primarily mimetic, i.e., primarily preoccupied with capturing the appearance of the physical universe, realized with Pollock a radically new, and fully implemented, paradigm. This new paradigm privileged the performance of processional formations, and constituent significations, at the expense of the mimetic impulse.

Pollock's method, often spoken of in terms of gesture and choreography, consists largely of improvised dance as a means of getting paint down onto the canvas. Lee Krasner has related that Pollock would listen to jazz continually, and obsessively, while he painted. This is particularly significant given the absence of a mimetic subject in Pollock's work. (The works to which I am referring, clearly those on which his reputation lies, are those which dispense with even the vestiges of, generally psychoanalytically read, iconographies.) Were Pollock painting a mountain or an apple, the music to which he painted would be of questionable relevance or significance, but because Pollock's paintings are pictures of his process of getting the paint onto the canvas, of the physically located rhythmic perturbations of the paint's application, the music which animated his movements while simultaneously providing the aesthetic model for his action becomes extremely significant.

Why black music? It's clear that one of the defining factors which contributed to the development and power of black American music, and other musics of the Diafra (the black Diaspora), was a sort of

contextual displacement equivalent to HIV's leap of the species barrier. By this I'm suggesting that with the Middle Passage, African music, like HIV (which hypothetically existed for some time in a species of monkey found in Central Africa), found itself freed from its natal ecology—with its attendant checks and balances, its natural predation—and thus freed, expanded exponentially, in the process mutating from African music(s) into black music(s).

(In the 1930s the USDA, in an effort to combat soil erosion, introduced kudzu, a Japanese vine, to Mississippi. By 1955, having escaped its original planting, kudzu had become "the vine that ate the South." Today, it infests over 250,000 acres of land in Mississippi, costing over $20 million a year to combat. Similarly, "Plague of Europeans" David Killingray '73)

It's somewhat paradoxical that in a context which radically circumscribed the mobility of the black body, black musical expressivity found itself both formally unbound and pressed into service in a manner which, classically, it would not have had to serve. Black musical expressivity not only survived the Middle Passage but, free of the class strictures of its natal context (which had limited its avenues of articulation and calcified its content) and unconstrained by a need to speak the experiences of a ruling class, evolved new forms with which to embody new experiences. A black music evolved equal to the unprecedented existential drama and complexity of the circumstance in which black people (Africans) found themselves.

Is it an accident that Mondrian was the first major European artist to recognize Pollock's work as some new shit?

(Vinyl recordings became black in sublimated response to the separation of the black voice from the black body, a separation which solved the conundrum of how to bring black music into white spaces minus the black bodies, i.e., black beings, which, by their very nature as musically productive entities, were assertive and thus troubling to whites.)

Pollock's crisis was precipitated by his inability to access the signification inherent in the methodology (jazz improvisational flow and trajection) he had so powerfully appropriated and implemented in his work. Classically, jazz improvisation is first and fore-most signified self-determination. This actually pre-cedes its function as musical gesture. For the black artist to stand before an audience, often white, and to publicly demonstrate her decision-making capacity, her agency, rather than the replication of another's agency, i.e., the composers, was a profoundly radical and dissonant gesture (akin in contemporary terms to the catalytic effect of hip-hop sampling and/or Sher-rie Levine's practice in their respective discourses). This signification of one's "self-determination" is in turn premised on one's "self-possession." There is no "self-determination" without "self-possession." And, "self-possession" is *the* existential issue for black Americans.

For Pollock—a white man and as such assumed to be self-determined and self-possessed—the dem-onstration of such reads as little more than ubiquitous white masculinist privilege (jacking off, the primary critique of the following generations of abstract ex-pressionists). Pollock, unable to access his work's signification, its structures of meaning, found himself vulnerable to critiques that the work was essentially without meaning. It's significant that Pollock's last productive period, and certainly his healthiest, ends, so the story goes, with the first viewing of Hans Na-muth's famous film of Pollock painting, projected in the kitchen for Pollock and his friends. Apparently Pollock got up when the film ended, walked over to the liquor cabinet, and proceeded to drink himself into a violent stupor, thus ending over two years of sobriety, a sobriety which he never recovered.

"When I am painting, I'm not aware of what I'm doing." Pollock saw himself dancing around, a white being behaving, embarrassingly, like a black being (like a nigger), thus destroying the fragile state of grace, of disembodied (white) being, under which he'd created his most powerful works.

(The classic cartoons showing monkeys making abstract paintings spoke to the sublimated realization that Pollock's practice was in large measure black.)

Pollock, feeling like a charlatan, reintroduces figu-ration in his late works. This pathetic attempt to inject the work with meaning, a meaning which he himself

could access, signals a total aesthetic collapse. So tragically, having failed at legitimately investing the work with meaning, Pollock kills himself.

Was Jackson Pollock white trash? Pollock's par-ticular genius was possible precisely because of his alienation. In that his alienation allowed him an atypi-cal relationship to the culture of black America. This is similar to the relationship which Elvis had to black American music, and which Picasso, in a much more covert fashion, had to African art. (Elvis's black satu-ration and white trash status is mirrored by Picasso's status as a Spaniard, un/moored, in Paris.) In each of these instances, and despite the seemingly inevi-table denial that occurred once influence became an issue, the breakthrough nature of the work achieved was made possible by an initially humble, and thus by definition nonsupremacist, relationship to the cata-lytic artifact at hand. Just as Beethoven was humble in the face of the body of work that had preceded him, these artists were each students of the work under whose influence they had fallen, students in a fashion which white supremacy would typically make unlikely.

(John Cage spent his entire career avoiding the term "improvisation," saturated as it was with black meaning.)

This is a story I've told a number of times. I worked on Stanley Kubrick's *Eyes Wide Shut* as sec-ond unit director of photography for approximately a year and a half. We'd occasionally receive calls from Stanley while we were shooting. Lisa, the second unit director, would relay his instructions and add, typi-cally, that Stanley said to "keep up the good work." A couple of times Lisa tried to hand me the phone so that Stanley could speak to me. Each time I waved her away, saying I'd speak to him later, ostensibly be-cause I was too involved in shooting.

A little before the film was set for release, I'm hanging out in Germany and I get a call from Lisa. She asks if I'm available to shoot in New York the following week. We agree on a date and I make ar-rangements to return to New York. A few days later, I'm boarding a plane for New York, I look over and see the cover of *USA Today:* "Filmmaker Stanley Ku-brick dead at 70." I'd spoken to Lisa not five hours earlier. I figure it to be a hoax, but I get to New York and it's confirmed: Stanley had passed suddenly and the shoot was canceled.

Over the next several days, I got extremely depressed. I'd never spoken to Kubrick. I wondered why, in over a year of working on the film, I'd never been available to speak to him. I realized that there'd been too much that I'd wanted to say. I'd, unconsciously, been waiting for the film's completion in the hope that I'd be able to have a real conversation with him. I'd wanted to tell him that he'd changed my life, and that I'd surely been, as a black, preadolescent inhabitant of the Mississippi Delta, the farthest thing imagined when he'd envisioned who the audience for *2001: A Space Odyssey* might be.

Two years after its initial release in '68, the film finally reached my hometown, Clarksdale, Mississippi. It played a drive-in theater on the outskirts of town, three nights only, Friday, Saturday, and Sunday. I barely slept that week. My father had promised to take me but by Sunday something had come up. So, a year later, I'm ten, the film finally plays at a movie theater proper. Recently opened, the West End Cinema is located in a part of town that's exclusively white. Clarksdale was essentially segregated at this point.

That Saturday my parents dropped me off at the twelve-thirty matinee. There's clearly no big demand, over two years after its release, for *2001: A Space Odyssey* in Clarksdale, Mississippi. The theater's empty except for me and two couples, both white. The lights go down, the movie begins, and it's like being buried alive. I'd never experienced anything like it before. It quite literally blew my mind. And to say that I couldn't make heads or tails of the movie is an understatement. (And even now, I'm still searching for an art experience capable of matching the effect this film had on me, its ability to simultaneously alienate and ravish. And in this fashion, the film had provided me with a model for how powerful art could be.)

There's no dialogue for the first twenty-five minutes of the film. There's little exposition. When people finally speak, they speak in hypnotic, sedated tones. And dramatically speaking, very little seems to happen during the first two thirds of the movie. The disembodied computer, HAL, displays decidedly more emotion than any of the flesh-and-blood characters. The few dispassionate exchanges between characters are punctuated by extended sequences containing little or no additional dialogue.

By the time the film reaches its intermission, I'm alone in the theater, the other moviegoers having abandoned it at some earlier point.

After the intermission, the film becomes, relatively speaking, more narratively compelling, in that things happen, yet the characters display the same narcotized, somnambulistic tone, now completely at odds with the dire circumstances in which they find themselves. (Anyone familiar with psychoanalysis will recognize the mute, vaguely conspiratorial affect of the analyst.) By the time the spaceship reaches its destination, Jupiter, only a single crew member has survived. He proceeds to launch himself down to the planet's surface in pursuit of the origin of the enigmatic black monolith uncovered on the moon's surface earlier. From this point onward, the film ceases to be narrative in any conventional Hollywood sense. Whereas the preceding parts of the film are characterized by various lacks—lack of color, lack of action, lack of apparent emotional consequence (save HAL's mournful end)—and whereas before we were stuck in a universe of arrested causality, an addict's nod, the film's finale, the descent and its aftermath, seems to dispense with causality altogether, except in the most primal sense, cinema's persistence of vision. The descent is a headlong rush composed of an extended, and unprecedented, barrage of chromatically over-saturated, spacially distorted, and elliptically sequenced imagery, all interspersed with shots of the astronaut's increasingly hysterical and emotionally overwrought grimaces (a bad trip, the result of some nightmarishly potent, and unexpected, combination of LSD and speed). This is all abruptly terminated by a shift to a very European, very white hotel room in which Bowman, still in spacesuit, observes himself aging progressively 'til the point of death (attended only by the black monolith), and his rebirth as the luminously white starchild, at which point the film ends.

There's of course an inescapably troubling, particularly for a young black kid in the early seventies, racial dimension of the film. First, there is the absolute whiteness of the context (both figuratively and literally). All of the characters are Caucasian and they are, in their demeanor, both archetypically and atavistically white. This is a whiteness that's sterile, creepy, and ultimately seductive (I'd guess Kubrick's background, a Bronx Jew, is relevant here). The interiors they occupy seem devoid of any artifacts that might be read as anything other than the products of an extremely Eurocentric worldview. And second, there is the absence of both black people and/or any apparent sign of blackness. This absence is misleading. Ultimately, I came to recognize the film's highly repressed and anxiety-ridden preoccupation with blackness. And given the times, how could it have been otherwise?

2001's obsession with/suppression of blackness is atypical of the genre only with respect to the elegance of its construction. And who could possibly fully disentangle the clusterfuck of racism (and sexism) that's typical of classic science fiction and its retarded offspring, science fiction films? *2001* is about fear of genetic annihilation, fear of blackness. (Black rage, Black Power, Black Panthers, black planet, black dick, etc.) White phallic objects (starships) move through all-encompassing blackness (space) from one white point (stars) to another. This fear of space, this horror vacui, is a fear of contamination, a contamination of white being by black being which, by the very nature of the self-imposed fragile ontological construction of white being, equals the annihilation of white being.

2001 begins in Africa. The black monolith functions as a catalytic artifact in that it provokes man's evolutionary leap forward from its earlier, primitive (apelike) state. (The initial design of the monolith was in the form of a black pyramid, a clear sign of black civilization.) There's the implication that the monolith generates man's increased capacity rather than simply stimulates some latent ability. This evolutionary leap sets in motion developments which culminate with man's discovery of a second black monolith on the moon's surface. *2001*'s astronauts travel through space in pursuit of (in fact at the directive of) a signal which issues forth from this advanced and clearly more evolved black sentient entity.

(Have you noticed that *2001*'s monolith, Darth Vader's uniform/flesh, and H.R. Giger's alien are all composed of the same black substance?)

2001's white/star child is engendered by a black sentient body, subliminally, and desperately, positing the possibility of pure white being issuing forth from all-encompassing dark matter. A manifestation of white fear of genetic annihilation by the (black) other. This anxiety is played out over and over in numerous science fiction films. For example, in *Alien* all the characters (excepting the white-blooded science officer), male and female alike, are sexually assaulted by the alien and impregnated with black beings. The alien is in fact a six-foot-eight Sudanese, "Bolaji" (never, to my knowledge, given a last name), wearing H.R. Giger's Esu-Elegba–derived jet-black monster suit with penis-tipped head. Yaphet Kotto (ur-Negro signifier if there ever were one) plays the only black member of the doomed crew. And during the initial confrontation, coming face-to-face with the alien, he recognizes it as the bad nigger it clearly is. His pragmatism suggests that he stands the best chance of surviving this encounter, but predictably, he meets his end attempting to prevent the alien from ravaging the helpless white woman. Coming to her rescue, he tells her to move away, but she's frozen (by the alien's magnificence), so, his pragmatism (one could say his sanity) having abandoned him, he moves to get between them. The alien swats him away with his big black tail, grabs him (bringing him face-to-face), and pokes a hole in his head with his chops (teeth). Casting him aside, the alien shifts its attention back to his victim of choice. She stands, breathing heavily, transfixed as the alien slides its tail between her legs. We cut away (but continue to hear her suspiciously ecstatic moans).

In *Star Wars*, Darth Vader/Dark Invader (black body/black voice, in fact the voice of Jack Johnson, James Earl Jones, clearly a blood despite subsequent revisions) is transformed by the Force's "Darkside" (black body engenders a white child, a skywalker no less). And the film's finale, a rush down the Death Star's corridors, to destroy the engendering black womb, Vader's crib, is a diminished and more overtly nihilistic replay of Bowman's Jupiter fall down the corridors of light, a rush to Death. Star. Child.

Why had I been so attracted to *2001*? Apollo generation, the first moon landing had just gone down a few years prior, and I was fairly obsessed with spaceships. I'd followed the progress of the film in magazines like *Popular Mechanics. 2001* was the first novel I'd ever bought, though I confess not to having read it until after seeing the film. That got me in the theater.

The film's slow, glacial pageantry impressed the altarboy in me, exposing me to what I'd identify now as a minimalist sensibility, a sensibility to which, I believe, I was predisposed by the flatness and austerity of the Delta, by the landscape's beauty and trance dimensions. This exposure dovetailed with a number of other things.

There was my then nascent melancholy and the beginning recognition of a certain sort of categorical constraint, dictated by my blackness, and yet completely at odds with (1) the boundless possibility conveyed to those of my generation by television, and (2) the emancipatory fallout of the Black Power movement. My family's move from the moderately progressive Tupelo to the essentially segregated Clarksdale, situated at the Delta's epicenter, had a cathartic impact, as did a continual and enmeshing confrontation with the extreme deprivations of the region and its abject pleasures. An exposure to the transfixing, and for me unprecedented, blackness of its inhabitants, their arresting beauty and dense corporeal being, the inescapable duality of absence and presence, the inevitable embrace, as a nascent black man, of a certain temperamental cool (a flattened affect), simply put is the dark matter of black being. These all begged certain questions, at the time inarticulate and unformed, to which years later my introduction to Miles Davis provided an answer. Where do I/we enter into these discourses on beauty and being (the answer of course being wherever and however we choose to).

The film ends, I get up in a daze and walk out into the lobby. And even now, thirty years later, I remember exactly, in crystalline detail, what the lobby looked like, the angle the sun shafted through the space, the lint hovering overhead, the drag of the carpet. I looked over and saw the manager, white and older, quietly reading his paper in the otherwise empty lobby. And the thing is, at this point in my life I didn't have unchaperoned interactions with white people, young or old. He was sitting in the ticket booth with the door open so I walked over to him and said, "Excuse me, sir, I've just come out of the movie, could you tell me what it was about?" He looked down at me over his paper, paused a moment, and said, "Son, I've been looking at it all week and haven't got a clue." And that's the last thing I remember. I don't remember how I got home, what other conversations I might have had, nothing. But that brief interaction I've never forgotten. The film had completely leveled our differences, race, class, age. So that for that moment, in the presence of this monumental work, we were equal.

a black hagakure.

a dream of death and the continual dissipation of dense black being (power and consciousness) osiris dismembered (diafra) and a part can't come together (can't remember) though the parts no longer fit, and this not fitting, this growth after dismemberment, keeps us (men and women) harder coming strong (anti entropic beasts) falling together even as we fall apart

would limit the number of blacks that can gather, a boon for Christ, one a bitch two a threat three an insurrection, no getting together coming together no drums rising up so churches, funerals, simple gatherings and places become reunions become rememberance be luciferian (fire, light) be revolution.

to the central conundrum of black being (the double bind of our ontological existence) lie in the fact that common misery both defines and limits who we are. such that our efforts to eliminate those forces which constrain also functions to dissipate much of which gives us our specificity, our uniqueness, our flavor and that by destroying the binds that define we will cease to be, but this is the good death (cachoeira) and to be embraced.

14.
RACE . . . AND OTHER FOUR LETTER WORDS
Eminem and the Cultural Politics of Authenticity
Gilbert B. Rodman

End of the world: best rapper's white, best golfer's black.

—comedian Chris Rock

Gaps

Describing the work on race and racism done at the Centre for Contemporary Cultural Studies at the University of Birmingham in the 1970s, Hall (1992) wrote:

> We had to develop a methodology that taught us to attend, not only to what people said about race but . . . to what people could not say about race. It was the silences that told us something; it was what wasn't there. It was what was invisible, what couldn't be put into frame, what was apparently unsayable that we needed to attend to. (p. 15)

As Hall explained it, those at the Birmingham School took this particular turn because they came to recognize that analyzing media texts to identify and critique the ways that people of color were routinely misrepresented, stereotyped, and demonized was simply not an effective way to struggle against racism. The problem here was *not* that media representations didn't matter in the United Kingdom then—or that they don't matter in the United States today. On the contrary, people of color continue to be regularly depicted as dangerous criminals who threaten to destroy the existing social order; as exotic primitives to be feared, despised, and controlled; as helpless children dependent on charity from the technologically superior West; and as fetishized objects readily available for White appropriation—and as long as images like these remain in heavy circulation, it's vital that cultural critics continue to identify and critique them.

But it's also not enough. Implicit in the focus on "bad" representations, after all, is the notion that enough "good" representations will solve the problem. Perhaps the clearest example of the fundamental flaw in this philosophy can be found in *The Cosby Show.* Although *Cosby* presented a far more uplifting public image of Black people than had previously been the norm on US television, those "kinder, gentler" fictions didn't translate very well into better living conditions for *real* Black people. In fact, the widespread popularity of *Cosby* may actually have made it easier for large segments of White America to believe that the Huxtables' upscale lifestyle was more representative of Black America than was really the case, which, in turn, suggested that there was no longer a socioeconomic gap of any real significance between White and Black America—or, more perniciously, that if such disparities *did* exist, it was because poor Blacks had "failed" to live up to the impossibly picturesque example of Cliff and Claire and their designer-sweater-wearing children. What's ultimately at issue here is not the (in)accuracy of *Cosby's* representations of Black America—after all, it's not as if sitcoms about White families provide us with consistently faithful reflections of White America either—but rather what is *not* represented. In the absence of a range of images of Black people at least as broad and varied as the standard prime-time depictions of Whites, *any* single program, no matter how positive or enlightened or uplifting, carries a representational burden that it can't possibly bear in full.[1]

Following Hall, then, I want to suggest that racism, as it currently lives and breathes in the United States, depends at least as much on the gaps in contemporary public discourse on race as it does on flawed media representations of people of color. There are, of course, more of these silences than I can do justice to in this essay, and so I won't say as much here as I might about how the "national conversation" on race (such as it is) frequently uses racially coded language (*crime, welfare, the inner city*, etc.) that studiously avoids explicit references to *race*; or how diligently that discourse steers clear of addressing the actual question of *racism*; or how, when racism *is* actually acknowledged, it's too often reduced to a matter of individual prejudice and bigotry, rather than recognized as a set of systematic and institutional discriminatory practices.[2] As important as these silences are, my concern here is a different sort of gap in mainstream US discourses on race: the one that transforms the common, pervasive, and age-old phenomenon of racial blending (in its multiple and various forms) into something invisible, aberrant, and novel.

For instance, the notion that race is a historical invention (rather than a biological fact)—and the corollary notion that racial categories are fluid and variable—is neither recent news nor an especially controversial idea among scientists and scholars who study race.[3] Nonetheless, even in reputable mainstream media discourse, this well-established fact can be treated as if it were a still untested theory—or, at best, an unresolved question.[4] Similarly, men and women from "different" racial groups have come together (even if such unions have not always been characterized by mutual consent) to produce "mixed race" babies for centuries. Yet it wasn't until the 2000 census that the US government officially recognized that "check one box only" is an awkward instruction for many people to follow when asked to identify their race.

The phenomenon of cultural exchange between "different" racial populations also has a long and tangled history, but such exchanges are still often treated as if they were a dangerous new phenomenon. This is especially true in cases where the borrowing that takes place is recognizably more about love than theft[5]: where Whites take up Black styles, forms, and/or genres, not to claim them as their own nor to transform them into something "universal" (and thus something dehistoricized, decontextualized, and deracinated), but in ways that suggest genuine respect for—and even deference toward—Black culture. Jafa (2003) mapped out a historical trajectory of such reverent borrowing that encompasses the influence of African sculpture and photography on Pablo Picasso's invention of cubism, improvisational jazz on Jackson Pollock's abstract painting, and rhythm and blues (R&B) on Elvis Presley's early brand of rockabilly:

> In each of these instances, and despite the seemingly inevitable denial that occurred once influence became an issue, the breakthrough nature of the work achieved was made possible by an initially humble, and thus by definition nonsupremacist, relationship to the catalytic artifact at hand. Just as Beethoven was humble in the face of the body of work that had preceded him, these artists were each students of the work under whose influence they had fallen, students in a fashion which white supremacy would typically make unlikely. (p. 250)

The "seemingly inevitable denial" that Jafa mentioned is the discursive move that tries to reclaim the art in question as a fundamentally White phenomenon that can be embraced by the dominant culture without any acknowledgment of the aesthetic and cultural miscegenation that originally gave rise to it.[6]

This article focuses on a contemporary example of reverential cultural borrowing: hip-hop superstar Eminem and the public controversies that swirl around him. As a White man working in a musical idiom dominated by Black aesthetic sensibilities—and who does so without trying to evade or denigrate the Black gatekeepers who are the genre's primary critical arbitrators—Eminem poses a significant threat to the culture's broader fiction that this *thing* we call "race" is a fixed set of natural, discrete, and nonoverlapping categories. And it's *this* facet of Eminem's stardom—his public performances of cultural miscegenation—that is the unacknowledged issue hidden at the core of the various moral panics around him.

Norm

Why is it that the only forms of popular culture that apparently have some sort of direct effect on audiences are the *dangerous* ones? No one seems to believe that more Meg Ryan movies will transform the United States into a land of sweetly perky romantics, yet the sort of virtual violence depicted in *The Matrix* could be cited as an "obvious" inspiration for the very real violence that took place at Columbine in 1999. Few people seem willing to claim that popular computer games like *The Sims* will produce a world of brilliant and creative social planners, but it's almost a given that graphically violent games like *Mortal Kombat* will generate armies of murderous superpredator teens bent on terror and mayhem. *The Cosby Show* (as noted earlier) was unable to usher in an era of racial harmony and tolerance, but edgy cartoons such as *South Park* will supposedly turn otherwise angelic, well-adjusted children into foul-mouthed, misbehaving delinquents. And in spite of several decades of pop songs extolling the virtues of peace, love, and understanding, we're not a visibly kinder, gentler, more tolerant people . . . but we can safely blame Eminem's brutal, homophobic, misogynist raps for corrupting our youth, poisoning our culture, and unraveling the moral fabric of the nation.

Or so the story goes. I make these comparisons not to argue that we should be unconcerned with the content of our mass media fare nor to suggest that Eminem's music plays an entirely benign role in contemporary US culture. It would be going too far, after all, to claim that popular music has no recognizable impact on social values, or to suggest that, behind his foul-mouthed, criminally psychotic facade, Eminem is really just a misunderstood, lovable little ragamuffin. Rather, I raise the question of Eminem's allegedly

harmful influence precisely because the broader discourse around him is far too saturated with overtones of controversy for me to safely ignore the issue. In this climate, any public statement about Eminem is implicitly obligated to focus on his multiple offenses against good taste, common decency, and fundamental moral values.[7] Commentators who "fail" to emphasize such issues—especially those that dare to suggest that Eminem might actually have talent worthy of praise—are themselves subject to stringent critique for ignoring the "real" (and, apparently, the only) story.[8] I don't want to dismiss the moral concerns of Eminem's detractors out of hand, but I also think that, too often, they manage to ignore what's genuinely novel (and important) about Eminem. In the midst of the moral panic that surrounds Eminem, however, it's rhetorically difficult to get to those other questions without first addressing the agendas set by the dominant discourse.

Most of the public debate about Eminem over the past several years has focused on the offensive, antisocial, irresponsible, dangerous, violent, misogynistic, and/or homophobic nature of his lyrics—and there's plenty of grist to be found for this particular mill. Listen to Eminem's first three major label releases and—among other things—you'll hear him insult his fans, drive with a fifth of vodka in his belly, assault his high school English teacher, encourage children to mutilate themselves, kidnap and kill his producer, shoot cashiers during armed robberies, rape his mother, and (at least twice) murder his wife with sadistic brutality. In the hyper-masculine world of Eminem's music, women are invariably "sluts" and "bitches" and "hos," and men he disapproves of are routinely derided as "pussies" and "faggots." It's not surprising, then, that Eminem has been roundly condemned from the right as a despoiler of common decency and morality, and from the left as an obnoxious promoter of a culture of violence that terrorizes women and gays.[9]

Nonetheless, I want to suggest that what matters about the controversy surrounding Eminem is not what it reveals, but what it conceals. To be sure, there are real and important issues at stake in the public furor over Eminem, especially around questions of misogyny and homophobia. Cultural criticism, however, is not—or at least shouldn't be—an all-or-nothing game, where *any* aesthetic or political flaw necessarily renders a particular work wholly irredeemable, in spite of what laudable qualities it might possess (and, of course, the reverse is equally true). Eminem's music contains more than its fair share of misogynistic and homophobic lyrics, but simply to reduce it to these (as many critics do) doesn't help to explain Eminem. It merely invokes a platitude or a sound bite to explain him *away.*

Much of the moral panic here involves a disturbing sort of scapegoating, where Eminem is made into a bogeyman for social ills that are far larger and far older than any damage that he might have been able to do in a mere 5 years or so of musical stardom. Reading Eminem's critics (from both the left and the right), one gets the impression that he has single-handedly opened up a previously untapped well of bigotry and violence, and that the very novelty and uniqueness of his brand of poison has somehow overwhelmed the aura of peace-loving tolerance that otherwise characterizes the day-to-day life of US culture.

The major complaints lodged against Eminem are the latest in a long history of complaints about the excesses of the mass media. And it would be easy to respond to this very traditional sort of condemnation of the dangers of popular culture with the very traditional litany of rebuttals: that is, to note that mass media effects are rarely as direct or powerful as the "violent lyrics produce violent crime" equation implies, or that the social ills in question arise from an impossibly tangled knot of multiple causes, or that audiences may be using all this "dangerous" media fare to channel their *pre*-existing antisocial attitudes into relatively harmless fantasies. Whatever merits there might be in such rhetorical strategies (all of which can be found in popular defenses of Eminem's music),[10] they ultimately don't do much to change the basic question at hand ("Does Eminem's music pose a threat to public health and safety?"). They merely answer that question in the negative, while leaving the original "moral panic" frame intact.

And that frame desperately needs to be broken. Part of the nature of a moral panic, after all, is that it presents an exaggerated threat to the social order

as a way to draw attention away from genuine cracks and flaws in that order.[11] In the case at hand, it's worth noting that mainstream US culture is already rife with misogyny and homophobia, and was so long before Eminem was born: enough so that his hyper-masculine lyrical excesses may actually be the *least* transgressive, *most* normative thing about him. This doesn't get Eminem off the hook when it comes to his particular renditions of these problematic cultural norms—not at all—but it does suggest that the real stakes in this particular discursive struggle are not those visible on the surface: that Eminem is being taken to task for transgressions that are too disturbing, too unsettling, and too threatening to mainstream US culture to be openly acknowledged. And so what I want to do for the rest of this essay is to tease out some of *those* silences in the public debates about Eminem: silences that, to my ears anyway, scream out for attention quite loudly.

Role

A significant portion of the case against Eminem revolves around the question of his status as a role model for his (supposedly) youthful audience.[12] He doesn't just depict antisocial violence in his music, the argument goes, he personifies it in compelling fashion through the use of first-person narratives. News stories about domestic violence, for instance, are safe (in part) because they're presented with a sufficiently distanced tone so as not to glorify the brutality involved. Eminem, on the other hand, gives us the story from the batterer's point of view—and does so with a wildly manic glee—that sends the message that it's perfectly okay for men to beat, torture, and kill their wives. Such, at least, is the major rap against Eminem: that his music is simply far too real in its violence and hatred to actually work as safe entertainment.

Buried not very far beneath the surface of this critique, however, is a dicey set of assumptions about the relationship between art and reality. When it comes to the aesthetics and politics of popular music, one of the trickiest words that a songwriter/vocalist can utter is "I." In some cases, the use of first-person address is a straightforward form of autobiographical witnessing, whereas in other cases, it's clearly a temporary adoption and performance of a fictional persona. Taken as an abstract question of form and style, it's relatively easy to recognize that the lines between the autobiographical and the fictional "I" are often hopelessly blurred. True stories, after all, must still be dramatized and performed in their telling, and purely fictional tales often involve honest expressions of their interpreters' experiences and personalities.

When one gets down to specific cases, however, many of those nuances wither away. Tellingly, they often do so in ways that afford already-valorized forms of musical expression more artistic license than other, "lesser" musical genres enjoy. In this respect, mainstream rock, folk, and country musicians have much more liberty to use the first person to utter violently aggressive, sexually provocative, and/or politically strident words than do artists working in genres like dance or rap. Which means—not coincidentally—that the artists most frequently denied the right to use the fictional "I" tend to be women and/or people of color.

For example, John Lennon—while still a lovable mop-top, no less—could sing "I'd rather see you dead, little girl, than to be with another man" ("Run for Your Life").[13] Johnny Cash could boast that he'd "shot a man in Reno just to watch him die" ("Folsom Prison Blues"). Bob Shane (of the Kingston Trio) could stab a woman to death for unspecified reasons and regret nothing other than that he was caught before he could escape to Tennessee ("Tom Dooley"). Eric Clapton could gun down a sheriff in the street without audible remorse or regret ("I Shot the Sheriff"). And Bruce Springsteen could undertake a murderous rampage across Nebraska in which he killed "ten innocent people" with a sawed-off shotgun ("Nebraska").

All of these musical crimes were generally understood to be acceptable forms of dramatic musical fiction—or, at least, none of them sparked any significant wave of moral outrage from the public at large—and all demonstrate quite clearly what Foucault (1969/1999) called "the author function":

Everyone knows that, in a novel offered as a narrator's account, neither the first-person pronoun

nor the present indicative refers exactly to the writer or to the moment in which he [sic] writes but, rather, to an alter ego whose distance from the author varies, often changing in the course of the work. It would be just as wrong to equate the author with the real writer as to equate him [sic] with the fictitious speaker; the author function is carried out and operates in the scission itself, in this division and this distance. (p. 215)

The musicians cited above are all understood to be "authors" in Foucault's sense of the term (even when, as in Clapton's case, they're singing other people's songs), and so their most violent musical narratives are readily interpreted as artistic fictions.

Musicians who "fail" to be White, straight, economically privileged, and/or male, however, are frequently and forcefully denied comparable artistic license, even when (or perhaps *especially* when) they're working within artistically valorized musical genres such as rock. For instance, when Madonna or Prince sing about sexual escapades in the first person, they're made into poster children for why compact discs (CDs) need parental warning labels—with "critics" such as Tipper Gore leading the charge to police the musical soundscape.[14] When Alanis Morissette hurls bitter musical invective at a duplicitous ex-lover ("You Oughta Know"), rock critics are quick to accuse her of being an "angry woman" and a "man hater"—whereas male rock stars who offer venomous musical kiss-offs to former girlfriends (e.g., Bob Dylan, Elvis Costello) are lauded as visionary poets. When Ice-T or NWA use music to narrate revenge fantasies about firing back at criminally violent police officers, they're met with public outrage forceful enough to cancel national concert tours and expunge the offending songs from already released albums—and in Ice-T's case, the backlash's racism is underscored by the public framing of his offending song ("Cop Killer") as an example of (everything that's wrong with) gangsta rap, even though it came from an album released by his speed metal band, Body Count. In cases like these, the possibility that these musicians are invoking the fictional "I" is one that the dominant public discourse largely refuses to recognize or accept. "Common sense," it seems, tells us that John Lennon didn't *really* want to kill his first wife when he wrote "Run For Your Life," but that "Cop Killer" *must* be taken as a literal expression of the truth about Ice-T's felonious desires.

Part of Eminem's musical brilliance, then, is his ability to recognize this double standard and to use the tension between the fictional and the autobiographical "I" to fuel his art. His first three nationally released albums—1999's *The Slim Shady LP*, 2000's *The Marshall Mathers LP*, and 2002's *The Eminem Show*—find him self-consciously sliding back and forth between (a) his "real life" identity as Marshall Mathers (who he describes as "just a regular guy"), (b) his professional alter ego, Eminem (the self-assured, swaggering rap star), and (c) the fictional character, Slim Shady (the evil trickster persona that *Eminem* [rather than Marshall] sometimes adopts). For example, in "Role Model" (from *Slim*), Eminem complains that his critics can't see through the fictions he's constructed and that the villainous demon they're railing against (Shady) doesn't really exist. In "Stan" (from *Marshall*), Shady explains—with great sensitivity, no less—to an overzealous fan that the violence and venom found in Eminem's music is "just clowning." And in "Without Me" (from *Eminem*), Marshall notes that his fans (and perhaps even his critics) clearly prefer Shady to him. As Carson (2002) described it

> so obsessed with identity that he's got three of them, he uses his alter egos' turf fights to create an arresting conundrum: perspective without distance. Juggling scenarios to flash on not only his reactions but his perceptions about his reaction, even as he baits you about *your* reactions, he analyzes himself by dramatizing himself, and the effect is prismatic because nothing is ever resolved. At one level, a line like "How the fuck can I be white? I don't even exist" ["Role Model"] . . . is just another deft reminder that "Eminem" is a persona. But when it comes sideswiping out of the racket, it can sound downright, um, existential—an inversion of the central conceit of Ralph Ellison's *Invisible Man*. (p. 88)

Given the frequency with which Eminem's music involves first-person narratives, cynical observers have wondered whether Eminem is simply too egotistical to rap about anything other than himself. But this fairly common reading of Eminem's art—and of rap in general—points to a fundamental failure to recognize the historical connection between the deliberately over-the-top lyrical posturing of hip-hop and the longstanding oral traditions of boasting, toasting, and playing the dozens found in African American culture: oral traditions that themselves weave together authentic self-expression and performative hyperbole in ways sophisticated enough to make the "I" being invoked by the speaker impossible to parse neatly.

When push comes to shove, then, whether Eminem really means what he says in his songs is, quite literally, an example of the canonical loaded question: "Have you stopped beating your wife yet?" Without wanting to dismiss Eminem's real-life outbursts of physical violence (which are a separate issue altogether), I think that a better question to ask is this: Why do so many people find it so extraordinarily difficult to envision Eminem (and other rappers) as someone who might have enough creativity, intelligence, and artistry to fashion and perform a convincing fictional persona? To be sure, such a rethinking of Eminem's art doesn't have to result in either respect or approval: One can, after all, still be disturbed and offended by fiction. For that matter, many critics are simply unable to recognize what Eminem does as *art* in the first place, apparently assuming that *art* and *abrasiveness* are mutually exclusive categories.[15]

Nonetheless, at the root of the widespread, collective inability to see Eminem as an *author*, as an *artist*, as a *performer*, we find a cultural bias at least as disturbing as the goriest of his musical fantasies: a bias that rests on the prejudicial notion that "some people" are wholly incapable of higher thinking and artistic creativity—and that their ability to create "fiction" is limited to making minor modifications to their otherwise unvarnished personal experiences. In this case, those "some people" are rappers—which is, in turn, a thinly disguised code for "African Americans" in general. Here, then, is another one of those problematic discursive silences, where criticizing rap or hip-hop becomes a way to utter sweeping condemnations of Black people and Black culture without ever having to explicitly frame such commentary in racial terms.

To be sure, this particular slippage is partially enabled by the discourses of authenticity that play a crucial role in rap aesthetics and hip-hop culture. Critically successful rappers, after all, typically have to establish that they have an "authentic" connection to "street life" and/or "the hood," and they will often justify the violent themes, drag references, and profane language in their music as honest reflections of the real-life environments from whence they came. At the same time, however, the dominant aesthetics of rock, folk, and country *also* depend heavily on questions of "authenticity," but they manage to do so without any serious expectations that the "authenticity" of the musicians in question must be read as "autobiography."

Quite the contrary, as a rock star like Bruce Springsteen can use his small-town, working-class upbringing as a license to compose authentic *fictions* about that culture. The authenticity of a song like "The River" (to take but one example) clearly doesn't depend on the lyrics' faithfulness to Springsteen's personal experience. We know full well that the rock star who we hear on the radio and see on MTV didn't get his high school girlfriend pregnant and wind up trapped in a life of chronic unemployment, melancholic depression, and shattered dreams. In cases like Springsteen's—that is, those typically found in rock, folk, and country contexts—even when one's authenticity is unmistakably connected to biographical facts, that connection actually authorizes musicians to adopt dramatic personae and invent *fictional* scenarios, and the "truth" of those fictions is rarely measured by their proximity to real events.

Perhaps more crucially, we need to remember that authenticity must always be *performed* to be recognized and accepted as such. It's not enough for Springsteen's fans and critics simply to know that he comes from a working-class background. In order to maintain his status as an "authentic" working-class icon, he must continue to dress and talk and perform in ways consistent with mythical standards of "working-class-ness" long after his own daily life has ceased to resemble the lives he sings about. There's a pernicious double standard at work here that affords White musicians the freedom to separate their authenticity from their real lives, a freedom that Black artists rarely enjoy. Of

course, as a White man, Eminem seems an odd person to fall victim to such a bias . . . but that actually leads directly into the next part of my argument.

Race

Is Eminem the Elvis of rap: a White man who makes Black music credibly, creatively, and compellingly? Or—alternately—is Eminem . . . the Elvis of rap: a White man who's unfairly achieved fame and fortune by making Black music, while Black artists with equal (if not greater) talent languish in poverty and obscurity?[16]

Obviously, I've rigged the question so that the answer is inescapable—Eminem *is* the Elvis of rap—but then the question of racial identity as it relates to Eminem's music (which has dogged his career from the start) has been a rigged one all along. After all, no matter what answer one decides upon, to take the question's basic premise at face value is to start from an essentialist (and highly problematic) assumption: namely, that the musical terrain can be neatly divided up into nonoverlapping territories that match up perfectly with the "natural" racial and ethnic categories used to identify people. Black people make Black music, White people make White music—and one dare not cross these lines lightly.

Lest there be any confusion, let me make it clear that my critique of these assumptions is not simply an argument for music as some sort of "colorblind" sphere of cultural activity. On the contrary, questions of race and racial politics are absolutely crucial to understanding *any and every* major form of US popular music since the rise of minstrelsy. Where essentialist models of musical culture run aground is in failing to recognize that the history of US popular music involves an extended series of intermingled and creolized styles that have nonetheless been mythologized as if they were racially pure forms. Jazz, for instance, commonly gets pegged as "Black music" despite the fact that early jazz drew heavily on the instrumental structures of European military marching bands. Similarly, rock has come to be widely understood as "White music" despite the central roles that the blues, R&B, and Black gospel all played in its birth.

Insofar as they help to shape the musical terrain in significant fashion, these racialized ways of categorizing music are very real—and very powerful—but they are not simply natural facts. Rather, they are culturally constructed *articulations*: processes by which otherwise unrelated cultural phenomena—practices, beliefs, texts, social groups, and so on—come to be linked together in a meaningful and *seemingly* natural way.[17] Although it may still make sense to talk about rap as "Black music," it does so only if we acknowledge that such a label bespeaks not some sort of essential blackness at the music's core, but broad and tangled patterns of musical performance, distribution, and consumption that *historically* have been *associated with* African Americans.

Given this, there's no inherent reason why a White man like Eminem can't still be a critically acclaimed rapper, but we can still ask meaningful questions about the relationship of Eminem's music to the broader terrain of US racial politics. In the end, however, the actual questions that critics have asked about Eminem's racial authenticity tell us more about the racism of the culture in which Eminem operates than they do about Eminem himself. As was the case with Elvis before him, questions about Eminem's racial authenticity perpetuate the larger culture's tendency to reduce all racial politics to the level of the (stable, coherent, essentialized) individual. Framing the issue as one of "what's a White man doing making Black music?" helps to deflect attention away from the racism of the culture industry and allows us to duck difficult—yet significant—questions about institutionalized racism and popular music that deserve to be addressed more openly and directly. For instance:

- Why *does Billboard* still segregate its charts along racial and ethnic lines, carving out separate categories for "R&B/Hip-Hop" and "Latin" music in ways that implicitly proclaim the "Hot 100/200" charts to be the province of White America?
- Why *do* rap acts have to pay higher insurance premiums for their concert tours—often high enough to prevent many rappers from touring at all—even when actual incidents of violence

and property damage at hip-hop shows are no more common or severe than those at rock or country concerts?[18]
- Why *can't* a genre with as large a fan base as rap—according to the Recording Industry Association of American (RIAA), it's been the second best-selling music in the United States (behind rock) every year since 1999[19]—manage to get radio airplay in proportion to its popularity, even in major urban markets?

If we're going to treat racism in the music industry with the seriousness that we should, *these* structural and institutional issues are the sorts of questions we should focus on first. After all, if the musical terrain is racially segregated to such an extent that a White rapper (or a Black rocker) constitutes a noteworthy transgression—and it is—it's only because the larger institutional forces in play actively work to maintain the tight articulations between specific racial communities and musical genres.

Questions about Eminem's racial authenticity also make it easier for critics to simply ignore *what* he says entirely—from his most violent and disturbing narratives to his most trenchant and insightful sociopolitical commentaries—by simply denying him the moral right to speak at all (at least in his chosen genre/idiom). Focusing on whether Eminem should make "Black music" does little to address questions of racial politics and racism meaningfully. Instead, depending on how one answers the "should he or shouldn't he?" question, such a focus underscores one of two problematic ideas: (a) the essentialist/segregationist notion that Black and White music, Black and White culture, Black and White people should each keep to their own kind, or (b) the naive, "color-blind" myth that race is simply irrelevant to popular music and is thus something that we can ignore completely. Either way, such arguments amount to a form of magical thinking: that is, they attempt to deal with very real—and very complicated—questions of the relationship between race and culture by reducing them to pithy sound bites that transform race into a nonissue.[20]

Perhaps most crucially, though, questions about Eminem's racial authenticity mask a more subtle, but no less disturbing, agenda—one that's about maintaining rigid lines between the races when it comes to behaviors, attitudes, and politics: lines that Eminem violates deliberately, forcefully, repeatedly, and threateningly. And *these* are forceful threats that Eminem *should* follow through on more fully.

Bête

Race *is* at the heart of the Eminem uproar—but not in the way that it's typically framed. The problem with Eminem isn't that he's just another White man ripping off Black culture—he's not the new Vanilla Ice—it's that he manages to perform "Blackness" and "Whiteness" *simultaneously*, blending the two in ways that erase precisely the same racial boundaries that White America has worked the hardest to maintain over the past several centuries.

Perhaps the easiest road into this piece of my argument goes through Miami and draws on another controversial rap act: 2 Live Crew. When their 1989 album, *As Nasty As They Wanna Be*, first went gold (i.e., sold 500,000 copies), there was no public outcry, no lawsuits, no obscenity trials, no moralistic hand-wringing over what havoc this "dangerous" music was wreaking upon its audiences, because the bulk of those sales were in predominantly Black and Latin inner city markets. Where 2 Live Crew ran into a buzz saw of controversy was when they started to "cross over" to White audiences in significant ways. It's no coincidence that their infamous obscenity trial took place not in Dade County (i.e., Miami, the urban market that the band called home and the site of their strongest fan base), but in Broward County (i.e., the much Whiter, much richer, much more suburban county just north of Miami). As has long been the case, White America has only really cared about the allegedly dangerous effects of popular culture when its own children were the ones purportedly in harm's way. "Hip hop," as Eminem sagely reminds us, "was never a problem in Harlem, only in Boston, after it bothered the fathers of daughters starting to blossom" ("White America").

The moral panic over Eminem and his music is much the same phenomenon, only on a larger and more threatening scale. Eminem, after all, has reached

a loftier level of stardom than 2 Live Crew ever dreamed of, and so his cultural and political impact (real or imagined) is of a much higher magnitude. 2 Live Crew faded back into the woodwork pretty quickly after the flap over *Nasty* died down. Eminem, on the other hand, is already one of the top-100-selling artists of all time, with more than 27 million units sold as of March 2006.[21] More important than sheer sales figures, however, is the perceived source of Eminem's threat. His music hasn't "crossed over" from Black to White: It's come *from within* White America, publicly giving the lie to the conceit that there's a neat and immutable line that separates White from Black—with all the dark, dirty, dangerous stuff allegedly living on the "other" side of that line.

Put another way, the vision of itself that mainstream White America works overtime to perpetuate is a vision largely devoid of hate, violence, and prejudice.[22] White America generally ignores or dismisses such attitudes, behaviors, and practices when they manifest themselves in its own ranks, while actively projecting them onto a broad range of marginalized Others: Black bodies, brown bodies, lower class bodies, foreign bodies, and so on. At best (if you can call it that), when White America has to face its own warts and blemishes, it tries to find ways to explain them away as exceptions, as aberrations, as deviations . . . *anything* but as a common and pervasive aspect of White America's normal condition.

And Eminem clearly knows all this. For instance, he begins "The Real Slim Shady" with a sneering line—"Y'all act like you never seen a white person before"—that calls his race-baiting critics to task for their inability to understand that someone could walk and talk and rap and act the way that he does and still be White. Even more bluntly, on "The Way I Am," he rails against White folks intent on trying to fix his racial identity in ways that allow *them* to maintain *their* illusions about the stability of race:

I'm so sick and tired/ of being admired/ that I wish that I/ would just die or get fired/ and dropped from my label/ let's stop with the fables/ I'm not gonna be able/ to top on "My Name Is"/ and pigeonholed into some poppy sensation/ to cop me rotation/ at rock and roll stations/ and

I just do not got the patience/ to deal with these cocky Caucasians/ who think I'm some wigger who just tries to be black/ 'cause I talk with an ac/ cent and grab on my balls/ so they al/ ways keep asking the same fuckin' questions./ What school did I go to?/ What 'hood I grew up in?/ The why, the who what, when, the where and the how/ till I'm grabbing my hair and I'm tearing it out.

To be sure, Eminem is not the first artist to blur these lines—not by a long shot—but the manner in which he does so is rare for someone at his level of public visibility. Unlike Vanilla Ice, for instance, Eminem's investment in hip-hop comes across as the sort of genuine passion of a lifelong fan, rather than as a temporary mask that can be (and, in Ice's case, was) removed at the end of the show. Unlike the Beastie Boys, Eminem comes across as someone who cares as much (if not more) about maintaining the overall integrity of hip-hop culture as he does about his commercial success. As Rux (2003) put it, "Eminem may have been born *white* but he was socialized as *black*, in the proverbial hood—and the music of the proverbial hood in America for the last twenty-five years has been hip-hop music" (p. 21).[23]

Historically speaking, this sort of deviance from the heart of Whiteness has been met in three different ways. The race traitor in question has been reassimilated, rendered invisible, and/or excommunicated. And so Eminem's *real* crime may simply be that he's too popular to be ignored, too brash to be pulled back into the bosom of unthreatening Whiteness, and so he must be branded as a demon, a deviant, a monster, a *bête noire*—who's all the more *bête* for "failing" to be *noire*—and then the demon must be cast out, lest his racially blurred performance come to be accepted as a viable option for other members of the White club.

A crucial aspect of this threat to hegemonic Whiteness is the way that Eminem's unwavering self-presentation as "White trash" works to unsettle the dominant cultural mythology that equates Whiteness with middle-class prosperity. If Rux (2003) was right to claim that Eminem was "socialized as Black," to a large extent, it's because of the strong correlation between race and class in US culture. The Blackness in

Eminem's background that Rux pointed to is rooted in the fact that Eminem's childhood poverty placed him in the disproportionately Black " 'hood" of inner city Detroit. And so it's significant that a number of Eminem's detractors play "the race card" to steer the broader conversation away from the sort of cross-racial, *class-based* alliances that Eminem's popularity suggests might be possible.

This practice was especially pronounced with respect to *8 Mile* (Grazer, Hanson, & Iovine, 2002), Eminem's first foray into Hollywood acting, where a number of critics complained that the film took unfair swipes at the Black bourgeoisie. For example, writing about the film in *The New Republic*, Driver (2002) complained that

> far from untethering hip-hop from race, Eminem's class bait-and-switch simply replaces the fact of blackness—i.e., skin color—with an idea of blackness that equates being black with being poor, angry, and uneducated. Eminem is perpetuating precisely the idea that animated Norman Mailer's 1957 essay "The White Negro." . . . Eminem would likely object to Mailer's racist posturing, particularly in light of his steadfast refusal to utter the word "nigger" in any context. "That word," he says, "is not even in my vocabulary." Unfortunately, judging from the evidence, neither is the term "black middle class." (p. 42)

Somewhat more gracefully—at least insofar as he doesn't repeat Driver's curious error of implicitly treating Eminem as the film's author—but still problematically, Grundmann (2003) wrote that

> despite its honorable intentions, the film ends up exploiting the social reality of the inner city black people it portrays. It turns them into profitable spectacle, while remaining silent on the causes of their oppression. At the same time, the film is openly hostile toward the *Ebony* magazine set, which it juxtaposes with Rabbit's white working-class identity. (p. 35)

Insofar as (a) the film's principal villains *are* Black and middle class, (b) their class position *is* the pivotal

distinction that marks them as threats to the community, and (c) the *real* Black middle class is hardly the
principal force working to keep the *real* working class
down, there's some merit to these critiques . . . and
yet it's a perversely narrow-minded and—to be blunt
about it—suburban way to read a film that (a) defies Hollywood convention by centering its story on
working-class people, (b) refuses to cater to the still
far too common stereotypes that portray poor people as thugs and criminals, (c) avoids the trap of representing the middle class as primarily White and/
or idyllically benign, and (d) depicts strong examples
of working-class solidarity across racial lines. In the
eyes of critics worried about the film's open hostility
"towards the *Ebony* magazine set," cross-racial alliances are apparently a laudable and welcome goal
when it comes to the middle class, but undesirable,
disturbing, and threatening when it happens amongst
the lumpen proletariat. The sort of critiques that
Driver (2003) and Grundmann (2003) offered might
be more compelling if the film's narrative presented
an unambiguous vision of class mobility for Whites
at the expense of cross-racial friendships. Tellingly,
however, *8 Mile* ends on a much more subtle note.
Rabbit (Eminem) wins the big rap battle against the
middle-class Black poser, but he doesn't ride off
into the sunset with a new recording contract in his
pocket and guaranteed stardom before him while his
Black posse remains stuck in the ghetto. Instead, he
leaves the club where he's just scored his big triumph
so that he can go back *to finish his shift* at the factory where he makes his living. This isn't the triumph
of White exceptionalism over the Black bourgeoisie:
it's a surprisingly honest (for Hollywood, anyway)
acknowledgment that having aesthetic talent doesn't
guarantee that one will have financial success. More
important, it's an ending that leaves Eminem's character firmly embedded in the same community
where he grew up.

Rage

Part of what makes *8 Mile* such an interesting film
is the way it negotiates a relatively nuanced understanding of the intersections of race and class in US
culture. In moving toward my conclusion, though,

I want to focus on a slightly different class-related
question—one that turns the harsh glare of the spotlight (or is that a *search*light?) back on *us* as cultural
critics: namely, the perceived impropriety of what
are popularly (if not entirely properly) understood
to be lower class forms of expression, and the concurrent inability of much of the professional managerial class (including us academics) to accept that
smart, insightful, and valuable thoughts can come
out of "coarse," "inarticulate," and "obscenity-laced"
mouths.

And Eminem's is an unabashedly coarse mouth.
*Fuck, shit, piss, cum, tits, cock, dick, balls, asshole, cunt,
pussy, ho, bitch, slut, faggot, jack-off, cocksucker, motherfucker.* All these—and much, much more—are main-
stays in Eminem's lyrical lexicon. Significantly, the
one time-honored example of linguistic crudity that
Eminem emphatically and self-consciously *won't* use
is "nigger," but that isolated gesture of political sensitivity, no matter how sincere it is, doesn't manage
to save Eminem from being roundly castigated—and
dismissed out of hand—for the unrepentant crude-
ness with which he expresses himself otherwise.

I'm not the first critic (by any means) to point
to the role that class prejudices play with respect to
whose speech we value and whose we don't. hooks
has written on multiple occasions (1994, 2000) about
her undergraduate years at Stanford, and how her
"failure" to conform to bourgeois standards of classroom decorum—standards that she'd never encountered growing up in rural Kentucky—marked her as
a "bad" student, in spite of her articulateness and
intelligence. Kipnis's (1992, 1999) work on *Hustler*
pointed to the ways in which politically progressive
critics who would otherwise applaud the magazine's
stinging jabs at big business and big government
nonetheless manage to dismiss *Hustler's*, political
commentary because of the "low class" nature of
the magazine's satire. And Berlant (1996) argued that
dominant US media representations of political protest promote a nefarious double standard in which
"political emotions like anxiety, rage, and aggression
turn out to be feelings only privileged people are justified in having" (p. 408). Poor folks and women and
people of color, she argued, must play the role of
"the well-behaved oppressed" (p. 408) if they have

any hopes of having their political voices heard (much less taken seriously).

Eminem, of course, may never have read hooks or Kipnis or Berlant (or the like)—but that's actually part of my point. His intelligence and wit and keen sense of the political terrain may not derive from the sort of "book learning" that we tend to value in academic settings, but his intellect is no less real for that. Nor is it less insightful simply because it comes in a package that includes four-letter words and unchecked rage. I don't think it's a coincidence, though, that so many critiques of Eminem's music focus on the foulness of his language—and I suspect that at least some of the controversy around him would go away if only he could make his points in more polite and genteel fashion.

But why should he? Especially when many of his sociopolitical critiques *are* angry ones—and often justifiably so. I don't want to simply romanticize Eminem as some sort of organic intellectual or working-class hero—that would be precisely the sort of patronizing elitism that I'm trying to guard against here—but I *do* want to suggest that, as cultural critics, *we* could stand to be more self-reflective about our own class position and biases, and about how readily we dismiss potentially valuable cultural criticism simply because it comes from someone who says "motherfucker" in public without flinching.

And there *is* thoughtful—and even progressive—cultural commentary to be found in Eminem's music: from pointed quips about a litigation-happy culture[24] to extended rants against President Bush's war on terror,[25] from biting critiques of racism in the music industry[26] to scathing indictments of the classism that made Columbine a "national tragedy" when daily violence in inner city schools can't make the news at all.[27] Although no one's likely to confuse Eminem with Public Enemy anytime soon—political statements remain a sidebar for him, rather than his primary agenda—he's also a more multifaceted and politically engaged artist than his detractors seem able or willing to recognize.

None of this is meant to draw some sort of magical shield around Eminem and his music, nor do I want to suggest that he's not fair game for criticism himself. He clearly understands that language is a powerful tool—and a powerful weapon: "I guess words are a motherfucker./ They can be great./ Or they can degrade./ Or, even worse,/ they can teach hate" ("Sing for the Moment"). And so the sensitivity that he shows when it comes to avoiding "the N-word" is something he could conceivably apply to his unabashed use of the word "faggot" as a general term of insult. And one might hope that someone who displays the sort of intelligence that Eminem does in his rhymes could also recognize that if he *really* wants to provide a better life for his daughter, as he so frequently claims, he might want to reconsider his tendency to portray women as bitches and sluts who (at best) are nothing more than "good fucks."[28]

That being said, I don't want to argue for some sort of simple trade-off here, where we'll agree to forgive Eminem for the violent misogyny of, say, "Kill You" or "'97 Bonnie and Clyde" because the penetrating and insightful sociopolitical critique found in, say, "What I Am" or "Square Dance" makes up for his more disturbing narratives. But I'm even more leery of the reverse trade-off that it seems we may be too eager to make: the one where we let our distaste for Eminem's most disturbing messages simply trump the valuable contributions he *does* have to make to a broader set of conversations about race, class, media, and politics.

Arguably, a large part of what scares many people about Eminem is that they look at him and see bits of themselves that they'd prefer not to acknowledge. After all, it's not as if he single-handedly invented misogyny or homophobia or violent fantasies out of thin air. Those were all present in US culture in significant ways long before Eminem was born, and it's the rare person raised in such a culture who can legitimately claim to be completely free of all such failings. But part of what I think that we—as cultural critics—should value about Eminem is precisely that we can look at him and see bits of ourselves that we *should* acknowledge. And if we happen *not* to be particularly proud of some of those facets of ourselves, that's fine. But, in such a scenario, we should go about the difficult task of working to change those unsavory aspects of our personalities and lifestyles, rather than simply pretending they're not there and/or projecting them onto Other, more marginalized people.

Put another way, when it comes to current public discourses around both race (in general) and Eminem (more specifically), too many scholars and critics (i.e., people like us) fail to adequately acknowledge their own roles—however passive or implicit those might be—in shaping and maintaining some of the more disturbing forms of racial hierarchy and disenfranchisement. I think it's perfectly fine for cultural critics to hold Eminem's feet to the fire for his more egregious lyrical excesses but only if they—*we*—are also self-reflexive enough to do so in ways that aren't ultimately about trying to protect *our* positions of privilege at the expense of others.

A good example of what this sort of nuanced criticism looks like comes from *Ms.*, in which Morgan (1999) carefully registered her concerns with the misogynist aspects of Eminem's music, but then, in terms that resonate strongly with Hall's (1992) admonition to attend to "the silences" in the discourse, she deliberately refused to join the chorus of voices demanding Eminem's censure. "At best," she wrote, "hip-hop is a mirror that unflinchingly reflects truths we would all much rather ignore. . . . A knee-jerk reaction to violent hip-hop is often a case of kill the messenger. In the end, it's silence—not lyrics—that poses the most danger" (p. 96). When it comes to Eminem, there are many such silences that deserve to be filled with productive noise, but let me point to three of the biggest.

With respect to gender and sexuality, the silence we most need to shatter is the one that pretends that Eminem's degradation of gays and women is abnormal. After all, the "clean" versions of Eminem's albums that Kmart and Wal-Mart (those stalwart retail institutions of middle America) were willing to sell didn't delete the misogyny and homophobia: just the drug references and profanities. Mainstream US culture has a *long* way to go before it can hold Eminem's feet to the fire on this front without hypocrisy.

With respect to class, the silence that Eminem's highly visible "White trash" pride should help dispel is the one around White poverty. Although people of color still remain far more likely to be poor than Whites are, the vast majority (68%) of the people living below the poverty line are White. That's certainly not the face of poverty one is typically shown by the

mainstream media, however, which prefers to pretend that Whiteness and affluence go hand in hand.

With respect to race, the silence that Eminem is best positioned to help us break is the powerful taboo against miscegenation: cultural, metaphorical, or otherwise. Given the ongoing apoplexy and fear that have dominated the mainstream discourse on "the browning of America," there's a lot of value to be learned from a figure who manages to blur the lines between Black and White music, Black and White culture, Black and White performance with ease, with talent, and—perhaps most important—with a large dose of humility about his Whiteness.

And if, as a culture, we can't break those silences, then we're in very deep trouble indeed.

Coda

In an earlier draft of this essay, that last sentence served as my closing thought. But then, suddenly, the ground on which I was working shifted beneath me: not quite so dramatically that I needed to start over from scratch, but enough so that I couldn't just pretend that the changes in the terrain hadn't happened. This is one of the occupational hazards of studying contemporary culture (popular or otherwise). It's a constantly moving target, which makes it difficult (if not impossible) to pin one's objects of study down with any descriptive or critical finality. In the case at hand, the shift in the terrain resulted from the fall 2004 release of Eminem's fourth major-label album, *Encore*, and the unprecedented lack of controversy that it inspired.[29] In the face of apparent public indifference to Eminem's latest efforts to push middle America's moral panic buttons, I had to wonder what had happened to hip-hop's most controversial superstar. Was the moral panic over? Had Eminem finally won over his former detractors? Or had he simply lost his edge?

Encore was clearly a commercial success—it sold more than 4 million copies and, even though it wasn't officially released until November, it was still one of the 100 best-selling albums of 2004—but as both an aesthetic endeavor and a public provocation, it failed. Badly. The most generous critics routinely described the album using adjectives like "spotty," "uneven," and "inconsistent," and the only public controversy involving Eminem since its release—the presence of his phone number in Paris Hilton's hacked cell-phone address book—found him playing an incidental and supporting role in someone else's drama, rather than his more accustomed role as an instigator and gadfly.

In many ways, though, *Encore*'s failure is potentially more interesting than any of Eminem's previous successes, as it helps to demonstrate the extent to which his career actually *is* fueled by a considerable artistic talent. Although his detractors often prefer to understand Eminem as completely talentless—or, perhaps more generously, as someone who wastes his talent on unworthy, amoral endeavors—the double-edged failure of *Encore* underscores how tightly his skills as an auteur and a provocateur are intertwined with one another. Horror stories such as "'97 Bonnie and Clyde" and "Kim" bothered people as viscerally as they did not simply because of the violent misogyny visible on their surfaces, but because they are compelling and powerful works of art.[30] *Encore*, on the other hand, fails as art largely because it doesn't try very hard to get under its listeners' skin—and where it does make an effort to provoke, it largely fails because Eminem sounds like he's just going through the motions.

More crucially for my purposes, though, *Encore*'s shortcomings demonstrate how much his artistry depends on the race-blurring aspects of his musical performance. Explaining what distinguishes Eminem from most other White rappers, Carson (2002) wrote that those other artists "deracinate" the music by

> keeping the beats but redefining the attitude as frat-boy acting out. What makes Eminem more challenging is that he's audibly assimilated hip-hop as *culture*. His nasal pugnacity is unmistakably the sound of a White kid for whom this music was so formative that he never heard it as someone else's property. (p. 88)

Encore ultimately falls apart because Eminem seems to have drifted away from his culturally miscegenated roots and toward a sort of frat-boy prankster aesthetic that was largely absent in his earlier work. Where once he had used music to feud with worthy public targets like censorious politicians and corporate

bigwigs (or even compellingly dramatic private targets like his mother and his ex-wife), now he's picking on the likes of Michael Jackson and Triumph the Insult Comic Dog. And where once he wielded his profanity-filled pen like a keenly honed sword, now he's building entire tracks around the slap-happy adolescent joys of farts, belches, and retching.

The major exception to this downslide—and the song that critics commonly cited as one of the few tracks that helped to elevate the album from "muddled" to "uneven"—is "Mosh." Released as the album's second single, just prior to Election Day in the United States, the song is interesting enough musically, even if it doesn't quite live up to the best of Eminem's previous efforts. It lacks the playfulness and catchy beats of "The Real Slim Shady"; it doesn't flow as smoothly or effortlessly as "The Way I Am"; it doesn't have the same thrilling, in-your-face edginess that characterizes "White America," but it's also something Eminem has never given us before: a full-fledged protest song. "Fuck Bush," Eminem proclaims, "until they bring our troops home," with the rest of the song—and the video that accompanies it—explicitly beckoning the nation to come together and vote "this monster, this coward that we have empowered" out of office. As noted earlier, Eminem's music has never been completely apolitical, but it has also never made politics its central theme as directly or insistently as "Mosh" does.

"Mosh" doesn't manage to save *Encore* (any more than it managed to help defeat Bush), but as a rhetorical gambit, it's pointed enough to suggest that Eminem might, in his own way, be the Madonna of his generation: a controversial—and seemingly dismissible—pop star who turns out to be a much more outspoken figure when it comes to political issues than most observers (fans included) would have imagined possible. One early believer in Eminem's potential for politically progressive musical agitation was Carson (2002):

> Right now, dissing his would-be censors aside, our hero's political acumen is roughly on a par with Daffy Duck's. But with his flair for topicality, a few more skids in the Dow could turn him as belligerent as Public Enemy's Chuck D, and wouldn't *that* be interesting? (p. 90)

And though most of *Encore* sounds more like "Daffy Duck" than anything Eminem had ever released before, the forceful pugnacity of "Mosh" provides reason to believe—or at least hope—that Eminem might someday really turn out to be "our hero" after all.

Acknowledgments

Many friends and colleagues—far too many to list here, though they all have my thanks—offered helpful comments on previous versions of this essay. My special thanks, however, go out to Charles Acland, Marcy Chvasta, Stacy Holman Jones, Michael LeVan, and Margaret Werry.

Notes

1. For more on the racial politics of *The Cosby Show*, see Dyson (1993, pp. 78–87), Gray (1995, pp. 79–84), Jhally and Lewis (1992).
2. There are many sources for more detailed arguments about these particular discursive silences and evasions, but some of the best are hooks (2000), McIntosh (1988/1998), Tatum (1999), and Williams (1997).
3. A small portion of this literature includes Berger (1999), Dyer (1997), Frankenberg (1993), Gilroy (2000), Ignatiev (1995), Ignatiev and Garvey (1996), Lipsitz (1998), Omi and Winant (1986), Roediger (1994), Tatum (1999), and Williams (1997).
4. For example, see Begley (1995), Henig (2004), and Wade (2004).
5. And, of course, here I'm borrowing (with love) the phrase *Love and Theft* that Eric Lott (1995) used as the title of his groundbreaking book on blackface minstrelsy.
6. Also see Boyd (2003, pp. 122–127) for a nuanced discussion of the differences between *imitation* and *influence* with respect to White artists working in Black idioms.
7. As Smith (2002) sardonically noted, "Every article ever published on Eminem can be paraphrased thus: Mother, Libel, Guns, Homosexuals, Drugs, Own Daughter, Wife, Rape, Trunk of Car, Youth of America, Tattoos, Prison, Gangsta, White Trash" (p. 96).
8. For instance, both Boehlert (2000/2001) and Hoyt (2000) complained that critics simply have routinely dismissed and/or glossed over Eminem's most offensive lyrics, even as the public controversy raging around Eminem remains the perennial focus of much of what's been written about him in the mainstream press over the past several years.

9. For example, see Boehlert (2000/2001), Brown (2000), DeCurtis (2000), Farley (2000), Frere-Jones (2001/2002), and Hoyt (2000).
10. For example, see Carson (2002), Croal (2000), Doherty (2000), Kim (2001), Morgan (1999), Rux (2003), Smith (2002), and Tyrangiel (2002).
11. Sociologist Stan Cohen described a moral panic as

   a condition, episode, person or group of persons emerges to become defined as a threat to societal values and interests; its nature is presented in a stylized and stereo typical fashion by the mass media; the moral barricades are manned [sic] by editors, bishops, politicians and other right-thinking people; socially accredited experts pronounce their diagnoses and solutions; ways of coping are evolved or (more often) resorted to; the condition then disappears, submerges or deteriorates and becomes more visible. Sometimes the object of the panic is quite novel and at other times it is something which has been in existence long enough, but suddenly appears in the limelight. Sometimes the panic is passed over and is forgotten, except in folklore and collective memory; at other times it has more serious and long-lasting repercussions and might produce such changes as those in legal and social policy or even in the way society conceives itself. (quoted in Hall, Crichter, Jefferson, Clarke, & Roberts, 1978, pp. 16–17)

   In extending and updating the notion of the "moral panic" as a category of social analysis, McRobbie (1994) noted

   that at root the moral panic is about instilling fear in people and, in so doing, encouraging them to try and turn away from the complexity and the visible social problems of everyday life and either to retreat into a 'fortress mentality'—a feeling of hopelessness, political powerlessness and paralysis—or to adopt a gung-ho 'something must be done about it' attitude. The moral panic is also frequently a means of attempting to discipline the young through terrifying their parents. This remains a powerful emotional strategy. (p. 199)

12. As far as I can tell, Eminem's detractors have simply assumed that his primary audience consists of minors, but I've yet to see any hard data offered in support of this claim. This is a time-honored, if not exactly honest, rhetorical device when it comes to moralistic condemnations of popular culture. Framing the issue as one of "protecting children" not only carries more affective weight than "protecting young adults," but it also implicitly absolves the critics invoking such rhetoric from the need to actually pay attention to what real audiences

have to say about their media choices. I don't doubt that Eminem's fan base includes a significant number of minors, but the claim that Eminem's audience is mostly children needs to be backed up with something more than the knee-jerk assumption that popular culture (or, more narrowly, hip-hop) is "just for kids."

13. Lennon quite possibly borrowed this line from Elvis Presley's version of "Baby, Let's Play House."

14. Gore's self-proclaimed fandom for artists such as the Rolling Stones—who didn't exactly make sexually prim music in their heyday—only serves to underscore the fact that there was something more than just sexually provocative lyrics at stake in her attacks on what she called "porn rock."

15. Novelist Zadie Smith (2002) rebutted this attitude by noting that:

Salvador Dali was an asshole. So was John Milton. Eminem's life and opinions are not his art. His art is his art. Sometimes people with bad problems make good art. The interesting question is this: When the problems go, does the art go, too? Oh, and if that word "art" is still bothering you in the context of a white-trash rapper from Detroit, here's a quick useful definition of an artist: someone with an expressive talent most of us do not have. (p. 98)

16. For a more extended discussion of the racial politics of Elvis's stardom, see Rodman (1994).

17. For an extended definition of *articulation* as the term is most commonly used in cultural studies, see Hall (1986).

18. For a more extended discussion of this practice, see Rose (1991).

19. See RIAA (2003).

20. See Garon (1996) for an especially cogent version of this argument with respect to the blues.

21. See RIAA (2006).

22. For more extended versions of this argument, see Goad (1997), hooks (1994, 2000), Lott (1995), and Williams (1997).

23. Also see Boyd (2003, pp. 127–129).

24. "They say music can alter moods and talk to you/ but can it load a gun up for you and cock it too?/ Well, if it can, then the next time you assault a dude/ just tell the judge that it was my fault/ and I'll get sued." ("Sing for the Moment")

25. "The bogey monster of rap,/ yeah, the man's back/ with a plan to am/ bush this Bush administration,/ mush the Senate's face in,/ push this generation/ of kids to stand and fight/ for the right to say something you might not like/ . . . All this terror—America demands action./ Next thing you know you got Uncle

Sam's ass askin'/ to join their army or what you'll do for their navy./ You're just a baby gettin' recruited at eighteen./ You're on a plane now eatin' their food and their baked beans./ I'm twenty-eight—they gonna take you 'fore they take me." ("Square Dance")

26. "Look at these eyes, baby blue, baby just like yourself,/ if they were brown, Shady lose, Shady sits on the shelf./ But Shady's cute, Shady knew Shady's dimples would help/ make ladies swoon baby, ooh baby! Look at my sales./ Let's do the math: if I was black I would've sold half./ I ain't have to graduate from Lincoln High School to know that." ("White America")

27. "And all of this controversy circles me/ and it seems like the media immediately/ points a finger at me./ So I point one back at 'em/ but not the index or pinky/ or the ring or the thumb/ it's the one you put up/ when you don't give a fuck/ when you won't just put up/ with the bullshit they pull/ 'cause they full of shit too./ When a dude's gettin' bullied/ and shoots up his school/ and they blame it on Marilyn/ and the heroin./ Where were the parents at?/ And look where it's at:/ middle America./ *Now* it's a tragedy. *Now* it's so sad to see./ An upper class city/ havin' this happen./ Then attack Eminem 'cause I rap this way." ("The Way I Am")

28. For example, one of the anonymous reviewers of this essay seemed willing to accept my general argument concerning the racial politics underlying the moral panic around Eminem but still expressed discomfort at the lack of an unequivocal condemnation of Eminem's sexism and homophobia. Given that the version of this essay read by reviewers already refused to whitewash (pun fully intended) Eminem's more unsavory lyrics, it's hard not to read such a critique as an example of what Williams (1997) called "battling biases": a form of analytical paralysis in which progressive outrage at one form of political injustice is blindly used to reinforce the less-than-progressive status quo along a different axis. "Upon occasion," Williams noted, "the ploughshare of feminism can be beaten into a sword of class prejudice" (p. 32). The recognition that Eminem's music is more complicated than a straightforward expression of patriarchal privilege doesn't require us to erase Eminem's sexism and homophobia from critical discussions of his public personae. At most, it might require us to inject a bit of productive nuance to our understanding of Eminem's sexual politics. Kipnis's (1999) commentary on the tangled class–gender politics of *Hustler*, for instance, could just as easily be used to describe the misogynistic aspects of Eminem's music: "Doesn't this reek of disenfranchisement rather than any certainty of male power over women?

The fantasy life here is animated by a cultural disempowerment in relation to a sexual caste system and a social class system" (p. 151). Such an analysis doesn't let Eminem's violent sexism off the hook—any more than Kipnis simply ignored *Hustler's* objectification of women—but it also refuses to pretend that our analysis of Eminem's music and stardom can safely be reduced to a single strand of identity politics.

29. Michael Jackson complained that the video for the album's first single, "Just Lose It," was defamatory insofar as it included a satirical swipe at Jackson with respect to the still-pending child molestation charges against him. This "controversy," however, died down almost as quickly as it surfaced.

30. Tori Amos's cover of " '97 Bonnie and Clyde" may be the clearest illustration of the artistry inherent in Eminem's song. In the context of an album (*Strange Little Girls*) where she covers a dozen songs written by men that explicitly construct powerful visions of masculinity, Amos's performance of Eminem's musical fantasy is simultaneously a critical (feminist?) appropriation of the narrative and an absolutely eery embodiment of it.

References

Begley, S. (1995, February 13). Three is not enough: Surprising new lessons from the controversial science of race. *Newsweek, 125,* 67–69.

Berger, M. (1999). *White lies: Race and the myths of whiteness.* New York: Farrar, Strauss & Giroux.

Berlant, L. (1996). The face of America and the state of emergency. In C. Nelson and D. P. Gaonkar (Eds.), *Disciplinarity and dissent in cultural studies* (pp. 397–439). New York: Routledge.

Boehlert, E. (2001). Invisible man: Eminem. In N. Hornby & B. Schafer (Eds.), *Da Capo best music writing 2001: The year's finest writing on rock, pop, jazz, country, & more* (pp. 119–127). Cambridge, MA: Da Capo Press. (Reprinted from Salon.com, June 7, 2000, http://salon.com)

Boyd, T. (2003). *The new H.N.I.C: The death of civil rights and the reign of hip hop.* New York: New York University Press.

Brown, E. (2000, June 26/July 3). Classless clown. *New York, 33,* 153.

Carson, T. (2002, December). This land is his land. *Esquire, 138,* 86, 88, 90, 94.

Croal, N. (2000, May 29). Slim Shady sounds off. *Newsweek, 135,* 62–64.

DeCurtis, A. (2000, August 3). Eminem's hate rhymes. *Rolling Stone, 846,* 17–18, 21.

Doherty, B. (2000, December). Bum rap: Lynne Cheney vs. Slim Shady. *Reason, 32,* 56–57.

Driver, J. (2002, November 25). Class act. *The New Republic, 227,* 42.

Dyer, R. (1997). *White.* New York: Routledge.

Dyson, M. E. (1993). *Reflecting black: African American cultural criticism.* Minneapolis: University of Minnesota Press.

Farley, C. J. (2000, May 29). A whiter shade of pale. *Time, 155,* 73.

Foucault, M. (1999). What is an author? (J. V. Harari, Trans.). In J. D. Faubion (Ed.), *Aesthetics, method, and epistemology: Essential works of Foucault, 1954–1984* (Vol. II, pp. 205–222). New York: The New Press. (Original work published 1969)

Frankenberg, R. (1993). *White women, race matters: The social construction of whiteness.* Minneapolis: University of Minnesota Press.

Frere-Jones, S. (2002). Haiku for Eminem. In J. Lethem & P. Bresnick (Eds.), *Da Capo best music writing 2002: The year's finest writing on rock, pop, jazz, country, & more* (pp. 138–140). Cambridge, MA: Da Capo Press. (Reprinted from *The Chicago Reader,* May 24, 2001)

Garon, P. (1996). White blues. In N. Ignatiev & J. Garvey (Eds.), *Race traitor* (pp. 167–175). New York: Routledge.

Gilroy, P. (2000). *Against race: Imagining political culture beyond the color line.* Cambridge, MA: Harvard University Press.

Goad, J. (1997). *The redneck manifesto: How hillbillies, hicks, and white trash became America's scapegoats.* New York: Touchstone.

Gray, H. (1995). *Watching race: Television and the struggle for "blackness."* Minneapolis: University of Minnesota Press.

Grazer, B. (Producer), Hanson, C. (Producer/Director), & Iovine, J. (Producer). (2002). *8 Mile* [Motion picture]. United States: Universal Studios.

Grundmann, R. (2003, Spring). White man's burden: Eminem's movie debut in *8 Mile. Cineaste, 28,* 30–35.

Hall, S. (1986). On postmodernism and articulation: An interview with Stuart Hall. *Journal of Communication Inquiry, 10*(2), 45–60.

Hall, S. (1992). Race, culture, and communications: Looking backward and forward at cultural studies. *Rethinking Marxism, 5*(1), 10–18.

Hall, S., Crichter, C., Jefferson, T., Clarke, J., & Roberts, B. (1978). *Policing the crisis: Mugging, the state, and law and order.* New York: Holmes & Meier.

Henig, R. M. (2004, October 10). The genome in black and white (and gray). *The New York Times Magazine,* 46–51.

hooks, b. (1994). *Teaching to transgress: Education as the practice of freedom.* New York: Routledge.

hooks, b. (2000). *Where we stand: Class matters.* New York: Routledge.

Hoyt, M. (2000, September/October). An Eminem exposé: Where are the critics? *Columbia Journalism Review, 39,* 67.

Ignatiev, N. (1995). *How the Irish became white.* New York: Routledge.

Ignatiev, N., & Garvey, J. (Eds.). (1996). *Race traitor.* New York: Routledge.

Jafa, A. (2003). My black death. In G. Tate (Ed.), *Everything but the burden: What white people are taking from black culture* (pp. 244–257). New York: Harlem Moon.

Jhally, S., & Lewis, J. (1992). *Enlightened racism:* The Cosby Show, *audiences, and the myth of the American Dream.* Boulder, CO: Westview.

Kim, R. (2001, March 5). Eminem—bad rap? *The Nation, 272,* 4–5.

Kipnis, L. (1992). (Male) desire and (female) disgust: Reading *Hustler.* In L. Grossberg, C. Nelson, P. Treichler, L. Baughman, & J.M. Wise (Eds.), *Cultural studies* (pp. 373–391). New York: Routledge.

Kipnis, L. (1999). *Bound and gagged: Pornography and the politics of fantasy in America.* Durham, NC: Duke University Press.

Lipsitz, G. (1998). *The possessive investment in whiteness: How white people profit from identity politics.* Philadelphia: Temple University Press.

Lott, E. (1995). *Love and theft: Blackface minstrelsy and the American working class.* New York: Oxford University Press.

McIntosh, P. (1998). White privilege: Unpacking the invisible knapsack. In P.S. Rothenberg (Ed.), *Race, class, and gender in the United States: An integrated study* (4th ed., pp. 163–169). New York: St. Martin's.

McRobbie, A. (1994). The moral panic in the age of the postmodern mass media. In *Postmodernism and popular culture* (pp. 198–219). New York: Routledge.

Morgan, J. (1999, August/September). White noise. *Ms., 9,* 96.

Omi, M., & Winant, H. (1986). *Racial formation in the United States: From the 1960s to the 1980s.* New York: Routledge.

Recording Industry Association of America. (2003). *2003 consumer profile.* Retrieved April 10, 2006, from http://www.riaa.com/news/marketingdata/pdf/2003consumer profile.pdf

Recording Industry Association of America. (2006). *Gold & platinum top artists.* Retrieved April 10, 2006, from http://www.riaa.com/gp/bestsellers/topartists.asp

Rodman, G.B. (1994). A hero to most?: Elvis, myth, and the politics of race. *Cultural Studies, 8,* 457–483.

Roediger, D.R. (1994). *Towards the abolition of whiteness.* New York: Verso.

Rose, T. (1991). "Fear of a black planet": Rap music and black cultural politics in the 1990s. *Journal of Negro Education, 60,* 276–290.

Rux, C.H. (2003). Eminem: The new white Negro. In G. Tate (Ed.), *Everything but the burden: What white people are taking from black culture* (pp. 15–38). New York: Harlem Moon.

Smith, Z. (2002, November). The Zen of Eminem. *Vibe, 10,* 90–98.

Tatum, B.D. (1999). *"Why are all the black kids sitting together in the cafeteria?" and other conversations about race.* New York: Basic Books.

Tyrangiel, J. (2002, June 3). The three faces of Eminem. *Time, 159,* 66–67.

Wade, N. (2004, November 14). Race-based medicine continued . . . . *The New York Times,* section 4, p. 12.

Williams, P.J. (1997). *Seeing a color-blind future: The paradox of race.* New York: Noonday.

15.
MIND YOURSELF

On Soundwalking, Race and Gender

Karen Shimakawa

Be Ready for the Unexpected, as You Do in the Real World[1]

Soundwalk's tag-line—'Audio tours for people who don't normally take audio tours'—sums up their objective neatly: the company aims to offer auditors/ walkers the chance—literally—to step outside their normalised bodily experiences of the world. A series of audio files available as compact disks or mp3 downloads, Soundwalk's tours of neighbourhoods in New York City, Paris and elsewhere have proved immensely popular and profitable for their creators (founders Stephan Crasneanscki and Michel Sitruk and sound designer Dug Winningham). Purchasers of the CD versions receive information on getting to the starting point, as well as on the narrator and sound/music samples; this information is available to downloaders via the website. Although both versions offer a schematic, annotated map of the route, these maps are not referred to in the course of the walks; all the walker/listener needs to do is get to the starting point and press PLAY.

Beginning in 2002, Oversampling, Inc. (Soundwalk's parent company) has released more than 15 walking tours of New York City neighbourhoods, including walks in Times Square, Chinatown and three interest-specific walks in the Bronx ('Hip-Hop', 'Graffiti' and 'Yankees') as well as tours of several Paris neighbourhoods (including St Germain des Prés and Palais Royal). Each audio tour uses binaural recording[2] simulating ambient sounds (traffic, pedestrians, music from passing cars, etc.) that correspond to the sites specified in each tour. In contrast to more experimental projects like the conceptual sound artist Janet Cardiff's *Her Long Black Hair* (a 2005 audio walk through New York's Central Park sponsored by the Public Art Fund), Soundwalk markets itself (via its own website, Amazon.com, and other travel-related retail outlets, as well as the Museum of Modern Art gift shop), explicitly appealing to tourists.[3]

The narrator is typically presented as a neighbourhood 'insider' who promises to take the walker/ listener on a gritty, hipper, more 'real' tour of the neighbourhood, rather than the sanitised versions typically marketed to outsiders. Each lays some 'authentic' claim to their neighbourhood: Jazzy Jay (co-founder of Def Jam Records) leads us through the Bronx 'Hip-Hop Walk', for example, pointing out the sites of his childhood in addition to the culturally significant landmarks (James Monroe High School, alma mater of many early graffiti and rap luminaries); Vinny Vella (Jimmy Petrille on 'The Sopranos') takes us to a park in Little Italy where he fed pigeons as a kid; and Johnny Solitto, novelist and former stockbroker, takes us to his old office at Goldman Sachs on the 'Wall Street' soundwalk. As these examples suggest, the narrators of the New York soundwalks are almost exclusively male—the two exceptions are Pearl Gluck, the narrator of the 'Hasidic Williamsburg: Women' soundwalk (discussed below) and Ivy (no surname provided), the alto-voiced, punky androgyne gallery owner who leads us through the Meatpacking District.[4] By and large, the gender/sex of the narrator goes unremarked, and the walker/listener is structured as gender-neutral. The exceptions, however, are striking in their aggressive (if implicit, in the case of the Chinatown soundwalk) attempts to discipline the walker/listener into normatively gendered embodiments.

What is the appeal of these tours? Certainly, the authentic/exotic soundtrack flourishes on each tour suggest that a heavy dose of voyeurism and fetishisation is at work here: resonating gongs, plinking pipas and thumping Asian pop music accompany you on the Chinatown walk; police sirens, bass-heavy backbeats and cars backfiring (*or are those gun shots?*) pepper the Bronx walks; and sitars and street beggars serenade you as you float down the Ganges in Varanasi. However, a summary dismissal of these works on the basis of fetishisation is, I think, too easy (or perhaps just incomplete) in trying to understand how they work, and it belies the more complicated content and *conflicted effects* of these tours; in this chapter, I shall consider the affective work these tours do in attempting to draw us into these 'exotic' sites and somatic spaces via specifically gendered bodily performances. To be clear: I am not suggesting that these tours do *not* exoticise, fetishise or objectify the (imagined) residents of these neighbourhoods—they clearly do, and are often quite explicit about such voyeuristic aims—but I want also to ask how we might think about their productivity: not only *how do they fail to deliver on their promises?* but also *what might they deliver instead?*

Brian Massumi's examination of the *biogram*[5] offers us a way of answering these questions, by refocusing the question of bodily *identity* in terms of asking how bodies and subjectivities are produced—constantly, dynamically, multiply/contradictorily, *in motion* and *in space*. In keeping with his project to revise notions of 'identity' previously conceived in terms of (static) *positionalities* in favour of a more dynamic, processual model, Massumi argues for a version of identity in which 'positionality is an emergent quality of movement' (Massumi, *Parables for the Virtual*, p. 8). This approach poses difficulties, however, since the very

recognition of an identity names a seemingly static *position* that is fictional to the extent it purports to describe a quality or characteristic whose meaning is stable over time: likening consciousness to Zeno's philosophical arrow, 'the transition from bow to target is not decomposable into constituent points. . . . It is only after the arrow hits it[s] mark that its real trajectory may be plotted. The points or positions really appear *retrospectively*, working backward from the movement's end. . . . *A thing is when it isn't doing*' (Massumi, *Parables for the Virtual*, p. 6; emphasis in the original). The body's identity is never stable or permanent, he suggests, and to the extent that we link a fixed, historical category of identity to it we engage in an act of retrospection/reconstruction of a moment past. How, then, to account for identities—raced, gendered, sexed, etc.—as produced, experienced and communicated and made functional in the present?

Focusing on the sense/act of *proprioception* (a mode of sensing/moving the body self-referentially, that is, by 'displacements of the parts of the body relative to each other', p. 179) as a counter or partner to the more familiar mode of *cognitive mapping* (exo-referential orientation of the body based on the abstract grid of Euclidian space), Massumi posits the biogram as that unit by which we move ourselves, *experienced as selves*, through space/time.[6] Experienced most spectacularly and self-consciously by so-called 'synesthetes' (a diagnostic label for individuals who record memories across the conventional boundaries of discrete senses), '[t]he biogram is a literal, graphically-diaphanous event-perception', writes Massumi, one that, he suggests, operates on a less pathologised level for embodied subjects more generally: 'It is what is portended when you remember seeing space in time' (p. 188). In other words, the biogram is one of the ways we carry or move through our pasts in/with our bodies, how 'identity' is experienced and reproduced temporally and spatially.

In illustrating his concept, Massumi relates the case of synesthete S., whose biograms 'came in "walks"'. He would store biograms as 'objects' deposited at a particular turn along a meandering walk. There they would remain as mnemonic landmarks that would come into sight as approached. Massumi continues:

> The walks themselves were biograms of a configurational kind. They were composed of a number of synesthetic objects stored in vicinity to one another. They had to be re-accessed in order, following the proprioceptive twists and turns of the walk . . . To find a memory, S. would have to enter the right geography and then move ahead proprioceptively.
>
> (Massumi, Parables for the Virtual, p. 193)

Soundwalks operate in much the same way as S.'s biograms. Walkers are directed along a specified route, laid out proprioceptively: we are not instructed to follow a paper map (although one is made available to the walker via the CD packaging or as a website download), but rather directed via paratactic directions such as 'turn right at the next traffic light and walk along the blue wall', etc. Along the way, we are told what to look at (and how to see it); we are instructed to visit particular stores and restaurants and told what to purchase/eat; and at various sites we are given contextual information (provided by the narrator and community 'experts') that imbue these sites with histories and meanings. In other words, having been given the 'right geography', walkers are presented with (what is purported to be) the narrator's prior sense-memories—following these mnemonic landmarks, we are invited to collect and cash in the sensory deposits presumably left there for us by the narrator.

Massumi does not address the specificity of the biogram; the body that moves through space in order to enact or inhabit its identity remains, for him, 'the body' (or occasionally 'you'). Presumably this is in keeping with his focus on the body that precedes or evades (if only temporarily) the constraints of static (gendered or raced) identity, his interest in Zeno's arrow perpetually caught in mid-flight, before its (identity) trajectory can be mapped. But what if the synesthete's route is plotted along a gendered and/or raced grid? The soundwalks I discuss below proleptically attempt to envisage/produce gendered, raced bodies in motion, bodies that can become gendered and raced *through* motion. It is an interesting (and, I believe, well-intentioned), if impossible, project: can you learn something of the other's experience by *literally* walking a mile in her shoes? In this cartography I would like to examine two sets of soundwalks, both of which take the form of 'ethnic' tourism: the Hasidic Williamsburg (male and female) walks and the Chinatown walk. Along with the Little Italy walk and (in different and less explicitly marked ways) the Bronx Hip-Hop and Graffiti walks, these tours make ethnic ventriloquism and/or voyeurism an explicit selling point.[7] It seems almost needless to argue that these tours fail to deliver on their promises of full identification/embodiment of the other's biogram; I want to suggest, however, that by looking more closely at the means by which that promise is made, and the various reasons for their failure, we might begin to see the potential for political work that such failure makes possible.

That's My Name, That's Your Name, because Today We're One

Perhaps the most explicit and extensive in their insistence on the walker/listener's adoption of the narrators' biograms, the Hasidic Williamsburg Soundwalks offer the walker/listener the chance to be (or masquerade as) a Hasidic woman or man for an hour as she/he tours this Brooklyn neighbourhood known as a long-standing ethnic enclave first established by Hasidic Jews fleeing European persecution in the nineteenth and early twentieth centuries. Walkers are repeatedly instructed on how to be(have like) a 'good Jewish girl' or to 'blend in, like a real Jew', and we are given explicit instructions on how we may achieve this transformation.[8]

Unlike other Soundwalks, the Hasidic Williamsburg walks begin with instructions on what (not) to wear: 'In order to experience our community there's a way to dress,' Joseph Pierkarski (the men's narrator) begins, 'and that is modestly.' Pearl Gluck is more detailed in her sartorial prescriptions for women: 'So here's the bad news,' she warns. 'It's also the good news. You're actually gonna look like a good girl for one day. You gotta wear a long skirt, you gotta keep those elbows covered, and keep those collarbones nice and protected from the eyes of the opposite sex.' After giving a rationale for these restrictions ('what [the Hasidic men] should be thinking about when they're walking their streets is their Torah, the given word of God, not you') she then orders us to 'get up, make sure your sleeves are long enough, your skirt is long enough, and your collar's high enough' before we leave the (women's side of the) restaurant where we first 'met' Pearl. The biogrammatical function of clothing features prominently throughout both walks: one of the first stops on Joseph's tour is a dry goods store where male walkers are instructed to purchase a yarmulke, a transaction whose completion prompts Joseph to tell us approvingly, 'Now you're going to be a Jew like everybody else.' Correlatively, Pearl walks us past Tip Top Wigs, but 'you're not going in there,' she tells us, 'since I'm not married, and you're me, you don't need to cover your hair.'

Having adopted the appropriate costume for this biogram, we are thereby better positioned (literally) to perform another biogrammatic task: to *move/behave* as a Hasidic women or man. 'You gotta follow my rhythm,' Pearl tells us. 'Don't walk around and be precious, don't be super-friendly, and don't walk around and be disrespectful,' she warns, 'just be here, in the community, like you belong. Like I belong.' Joseph is even more detailed: 'what I want you to do is follow me. And I also want you to listen to my footsteps as I walk. One, two, three, actually, let's do the Yiddish [counts in Yiddish in rhythm to his footsteps].' Later, he instructs us, 'Of course, I don't want you talking to any women. . . . Also, when you see two women walking on the street, try not to walk between them.' Following their directions, the inference goes, will give us some glimpse into the lived, bodily experience of *being* a Hasidic woman or man as they might move through the streets of Williamsburg.

Having (presumably) mastered our narrators' movements, we are led to various locations in the neighbourhood, through which we are given an illustrated history of Williamsburg and of the Ba'al shem tov movement, delivered by Joseph, Pearl, various rabbis and community members. But even these more educational moments ('let me tell you about us') are punctuated with jarringly biogrammatic, identificatory injunctions: as we're about to enter the

first temple on the men's route, Joseph instructs us, 'if anybody asks, you're Jewish. Because I'm sure at one point in someone's life and history, in your family tree, somebody was Jewish. So, for the sake of this trip right now, you are Jewish. Are you ready?' We are not told the stakes of failure—is it a requirement that one be Jewish to enter this part of the synagogue?—but we are praised afterwards by a (*relieved?*) Joseph: 'You were great. You've been initiated.' Pearl's route does not enter the ground floor of the synagogue (where women are prohibited) but the subject of sex segregation does prompt a different sort of invitation to experience embodied Hasidic identity. As we pass the synagogue where Joseph's walker was initiated, she tells us, 'It's at this point you're going to lose your man if you're with one. It doesn't matter. I say find a nice Jewish boy. Listen, I'm not one for clichés, but they *really* please their women. It's not a cliché—it's the law. Every month man's gotta please his wife, no matter what. So I say, let the guy go, and keep looking [*laughs*].' In a tour otherwise dominated by descriptions and explanations of Hasidic female sexuality and the centrality of the reproduction of heteronormative familial structures, Pearl invites us (as non-Hasidic women) to imagine we live their sexual lives. Elsewhere Pearl and other commentators explain the conventions of traditional courtship, expectations regarding reproduction and child-rearing, sexual practices and prohibitions; here, though, we are positioned *as* the partner of a Hasidic Jewish man within that culture.[9]

For the most part, Joseph's movement instructions do not emphasise gender/sex differentiation; it is assumed (as is clear in his invitation into the synagogue) that the walker/listener is male and that his blocking applies (only) to men. Pearl's instructions, as indicated above, are more overtly and explicitly about gender differentiation—and these instructions primarily come in the form of prohibitions. 'Don't look directly into the eyes of the men,' she tells us. 'Don't make too much noise. Don't bother the men,' she says as we enter a bookshop. Where Joseph invites us to walk fast (having posited a brisk pace as a specifically masculine gesture) and, at one point, 'listen to this music with me [a sprightly klezmer piece] and dance across the bridge', Pearl's companion is repeatedly cautioned to restrain her movements, to stay out of certain buildings (the synagogues) and to refrain from purchasing certain items (men's clothing).

The Williamsburg walks consistently ask the walker to *be* a Hasidic woman or Hasidic man by accessing Joseph's and Pearl's biograms; while there are moments in which our failure to do so is marked and we are addressed as outsiders, these tours seem to emphasise the possibility of success: we are given detailed and direct instructions on how to elicit the biograms, with the promise that the involuntary nature of biogrammatic movement will take things from there—that we will, as Joseph promises, 'experience what it's like to be a Hasidic Jew'. My experiences of taking the women's walk, and listening to the men's walk, however, were far from the biogrammatically transporting experience the narrators seem to promise: the high collars and long sleeves felt restricting (especially during the walk I took on a humid late July afternoon); the injunction to avoid eye contact made interactions with people on the street feel somewhat uncomfortable (*is this person looking at me/wanting to initiate a conversation/glaring at me for transgressing or trespassing?*); and the walk past the synagogues (one of which is quite beautiful and well known) made me keenly aware of the fact that the men's walk *did* go through these buildings. Male walkers I queried almost universally opted *not* to dance across the overpass 'with Joseph', despite the klezmer soundtrack, and many opted not to purchase or wear a yarmulke (and refrained from entering the synagogues). Both my experience and those of other walkers was generally that of feeling firmly, and in some cases staunchly, *outside* the Hasidic male or female biogram into which we were so insistently inserted. What then to make of these purposeful refusals/deviations from the prescripted biograms?

This Is Chinatown, Baby . . .
Are You Scared Yet?

The Chinatown soundwalk was one of the first created, the one that garnered widespread media coverage, and continues to be one of their best sellers (now in its fourth revision). Following the standard

'boiler-plate' liability waiver (read by a female performer in heavily accented English), we are invited to a restaurant at the edge of Chinatown; after a few seconds of ambient restaurant noise, we hear, 'Hi, is this seat taken?' and we 'meet' our narrator Jami Gong, who begins by assuring us of his qualifications for the job: 'These are *my* streets,' he tells us confidently. 'These are *my* people. So listen to me carefully, and I will take care of you.' As in the Williamsburg walks, there is an invitation to inhabit the narrator's (imagined) body/identity: 'Be one with me,' he instructs us, and later we are told to 'get ready to see, to smell, to touch, and to be Chinese', as if offering a mystical transubstantiation into the exotic other's body.

This extended introduction orients the walker/listener in relation to the narrator, and to the space through which she/he is to be moved/moving. There are two appeals being made: on the one hand, the promise that we should 'get ready to . . . *be* Chinese', an offer of mystical transubstantiation into the exotic other's body; on the other hand, though, we are informed that this body-snatch will be, as in the best scary movies, dangerously incomplete: 'I will bring you into places where you are not supposed to go,' Jami warns us, and so we are dependent on an authentic, native informant who can claim ownership over '*my* streets . . . *my* people' to 'take care of [us]'. This dynamic tension between *being* and *needing* the other is sustained throughout the walk, and contributes to the spectacularity of the 'failure' of transubstantiation as well as the opening up of new possibilities.

For the most part, the walk follows the second strategy: we are plunged into a strange, dangerous and otherwise impenetrable Other-world and our only hope of survival is Jami. There are numerous 'educational' interludes throughout (voiced both by Jami, providing a history of Chinese migration to the United States, for example; as well as by priests, academics and shop proprietors, who provide historical and cultural contexts on some of the sites visited) that resemble the content of more mainstream tours; however, the most written-about (and evidently the most viscerally effective) episodes are less info-taining in the traditional sense: an early version of the tour walked us up to the screen door of a sweatshop to peer in on the women at their sewing machines and cutting tables; Jami tells us that at one time, his mother laboured here.[10] Later we are instructed to walk past another building where 'rumour has it that it was and still is an opium den . . . don't even try to get inside . . . I warn you, they do not appreciate your attention. Remember, this is Chinatown—you don't mess with this kind of business. Keep on walking.' We *are* instructed to enter another building, but discreetly, and to look through the crack in the door of a third floor apartment where, it is promised, 'there is an old man playing cards'. Jami tells us that 'This is Mr Lam. He is a big boss . . . He used to be head of the biggest triad in Chinatown, the Ghost Shadows. Not too long ago, they retired him.' After informing us that we are spying on a former crime boss, Jami abandons us for our descent back to the street where he tells us he'll be waiting ('be careful on your way back,' he warns us), and suddenly we are left 'alone' to make our way back into the daylight. In these seemingly perilous encounters[11] (and the peril is enhanced greatly through SFX— gunshots, women moaning in pain and/or ecstasy, hawkers aggressively selling phone cards) we are presented with a textbook stereotype of Chinatown: at turns threatening and alluring in its otherness, (over-) sexed and gendered as, if not overtly female, then *penetrable* (albeit at some risk). 'This is not New York,' a Chinese woman coos seductively in our ear, 'This is not even America. This is Chinatown, baby . . . are you scared yet?'

The use of a woman's voice, as counterpoint to Jami's, is a tactic employed throughout the walk. Whereas Jami (speaking with the mildly inflected accent of a second-generation Chinese American) stakes an ownership claim to Chinatown, the woman whose voice we hear in the disclaimer seems to occupy a very different relationship to us, and even to Chinatown itself. Her voice surfaces periodically among the ambient sounds behind Jami: the ecstatic moans in Mr Lam's stairwell; fragments of a Chinese folksong in the background; fevered, shallow breaths as we traverse a dark and 'scary' underpass. Jami may *own* Chinatown; this woman evidently *embodies* it—and *that* embodiment is emphatically exterior, if not altogether *exotic*: we are invited, under Jami's supervision, to consume it/her. It is in part through this stark aural/aesthetic/spatial juxtaposition, in fact, that we are invited to identify bodily with Jami in terms of race *and* gender.

Chinatown—A World within a World within a World [*Repeat/Fade*]

And yet . . . when I take this or other soundwalks, a curious thing happens: I go slightly numb. That is not quite it: my senses are hijacked. Everything *draws in* a bit: touch (the jostling of other pedestrians, ambient temperature, etc.), sight, even smell and taste— all are subordinated to what Jami (in the Chinatown example) tells me to feel, hear, smell and taste.[12] The woman's voice is—for lack of a better term— disorienting: isolated and sited (for the most part) very locally (often behind and to the side of the listener), her voice frequently startled me, as I repeatedly mistook it on the recording for an external, 'real' voice intruding on my tour. Other walkers report similar experiences: when I assigned these walks to my class, several students reported turning to look for someone over their shoulder, experiencing sudden or fleeting geographic vertigo—becoming aware, suddenly, that they did not know where they were (in the cartographic sense), even in neighbourhoods with which they were otherwise very familiar; several others reported nearly being struck by cars, having fallen out of sync with the beautiful, organically choreographed dance between pedestrians and cars that characterises New York City traffic. It is a process not unrelated, I think, to those Department of Transportation statistics linking cell phone usage with increased incidences of car accidents, but I would argue that it is different too: the voice of the narrator in your ear is in some sense *with you* in the space your body occupies—you actually *need* that voice to move you through that space safely, and to tell you how to occupy and apprehend that space. It is obvious, perhaps: you do what the recording tells you to do—you have, after all, purchased it for that very purpose.

Yet what is most palpable for me as I take this tour, as with the Hasidic Williamsburg walk, is the way the tour *fails* to interpellate the walker/listener fully into that exotic/erotic sound—and landscape. If part of the promise is to enable us to '*be* Chinese' (or, I would argue, to be a Chinese-American man as Jami is), and to attempt to put us somatically into that body/identity, the dangerous thrill of submission to Jami's instructions (which are frequently cast as vaguely risky) puts us more firmly in our own bodies, even as it places that body's safety in the authentic native's care. What I am suggesting is that by trying to promise *both simultaneously*, the soundwalk succeeds at doing neither, and instead puts the walker/listener *somewhere else*: we are not Jami, but nor are we allowed to be comfortably in our own skins, either. The normal/normative way in which we typically move through the world as unselfconscious agents is temporarily disrupted; that we fail to assume (what we imagine to be) Jami's biogram seamlessly or comfortably only heightens our awareness that we are no longer seamlessly or comfortably located in our *own* biograms.

Is there something productive to be made of this failed attempt? Judith Halberstam has argued for a consideration of failure as an 'alternative to the violent triumphalism that victory implies . . . . Failure, as a practice, recognizes that alternatives are embedded already in the dominant and that power is never total or consistent; indeed, failure can exploit the unpredictability of ideology and its indeterminate qualities.'[13] What might be made of the indeterminacy of this *somewhere else* body produced in/through the soundwalk? Following the neurological literature on this phenomenon, Massumi notes that 'biograms are described as having an odd status: they are "*involuntary and elicited*"' (*Parables for the Virtual*, p. 189; emphasis in original, footnote omitted). One chooses to move one's body and attention in a particular direction proprioceptively; what follows, however, in terms of sense experience of that movement, is 'peripersonal [and] autonom[ous]' (Massumi, *Parables for the Virtual*, p. 189). One interesting consequence of this incongruity is that it leaves open the possibility for 'mistakes'—an error or mis-step in the act of elicitation (failing or refusing to take up the mnemonic clue, for example, means the sense-memory will not be accessed); conversely, even an accidental or unscripted encounter with the object of elicitation can evoke the sense-memory unintentionally. In other words, biograms are, on the one hand, one of the ways our

bodies become sites of embedded identities and histories; and, on the other, there is some play in the joints between bodies, their emplacements, history and identity.

'In the circus of synesthesia', writes Massumi, 'you never really know what act will follow. The rabbit might turn into a dove and fly away' (*Parables for the Virtual*, p. 191). That this '*be*[ing] Chinese', which Jami promises never occurs, does not entirely negate its effectiveness in presenting the walker with a new/altered biogram: discomfort (or even fear) may signal another kind of newness, an out-of-body-ness that is neither wholly me nor wholly Jami. The synthesis of Chineseness, hetero-masculinity and ownership/self-sovereignty is, in dominant culture, a novel premise. And while it may not be fully realised in the course of the walk, perhaps the discomfort of having consciously to negotiate gendered, raced embodiment in the face of that failure is productive: the work of social identity-formation laid bare as differential, relational and as *work*. Perhaps we might see this as a potentially profound (if subtle) exercise in re-subjectification: the walker willingly commits herself to another subject's biogram—a (failed) act of faith and fictionalisation that she nonetheless performs *with/in her body*. It is this submission to bodily vulnerability, I would argue, that distinguishes the 'failures' of the Chinatown walk from those of the Williamsburg walks and opens the walker (willingly or otherwise) to new possibilities, rather than to the biogrammatic re-trenching that results when we simply balk at Joseph's and Pearl's exhortations to *be* their narrators.

'Reaccessing the biogram', suggests Massumi, 'and pulling a determinate strand of organized experience, is to reapproach the point where the materiality of the body *minds itself*' (*Parables for the Virtual*, p. 190). To the extent that we are engaged in the project of analysing or critiquing regimes of hierarchy and oppression based on (perceived) identifications, then, perhaps a *conscious* engagement with our and others' biograms holds the possibility of eliciting or (re-) producing specific pasts by their emplacements of the body. What if the Chinatown soundwalk actually (if unintentionally) pulls new or different strands of experience? What, then, might the body mind[ing] itself be, or be becoming?

Notes

1. 'Disclaimer', http://www.soundwalk.com/disc.php (excerpt). Accessed 12 October 2006. The full text of the disclaimer is also included as the first track of all Soundwalk audio tours.
2. Binaural recording utilises a particular arrangement of microphones in the recording process resulting in audio recordings that, when played back on stereo headphones, simulate 360-degree sound spatialisation.
3. In addition to the neighbourhood walks, Soundwalk is in partnership with various corporate sponsors to produce specialised products, such as their collaboration with Puma ('Train Away' running guides to New York, London, Berlin and Paris), a mobile phone download project with France Télécom, and an audio tour of the Louvre coordinated with the content (and release date) of the film version of *The Da Vinci Code*. The centrepieces of the company upon which these corporate projects build, however, are the neighbourhood walking tours. Rave reviews in *Wired* (1 September 2002), *New York Times* (1 September 2003) and elsewhere have fuelled this success and the company continues to produce new walks at a rate of several a year, while releasing updated versions of current walks.
4. The four Paris walks, in contrast, are narrated (in sultry, dulcet tones) by four young (judging by their photographs), beautiful and very *femme* European actresses; and while each professes an affection for/familiarity with her respective neighbourhood, their qualifications appears to lie elsewhere: perhaps in keeping with the (stereotypical) Parisian theme, their walks are moody and reflective, laced with tales of love and (hetero-)sex, heartbreak and betrayal. Another notable exception is the 'Varanasi: City of Light' soundwalk, which is narrated by Robert Svoboda, US-based author and 'expert' on Ayurvedic medicine. Packaged as a glossy, art photograph-filled hardcover book and CD, this soundwalk appears to be aimed at the armchair traveller, which might explain the choice of a similarly situated 'outsider' as narrator.
5. *Parables for the Virtual: Movement, Affect, Sensation* (Durham, NC: Duke University Press, 2002).
6. Massumi's construction of the biogram is intended as a neologism deriving from the term 'diagram' as it is deployed in recent architectural theory: 'Synesthetic forms . . . are lived diagrams based on already lived experience, revived to orient further experience. Lived and relived: biograms might be a better word for them than

"diagrams" ' (Massumi, *Parables for the Virtual*, pp. 186–7). Massumi does not appear to be referencing the term as it has been used in earlier evolutionary psychology and anthropology or, more recently, molecular biodynamics.
7. The Varanasi, India soundwalk is similarly explicit in its appeal to racial/ethnic exoticism; that walk, however, was conceived as primarily targeting an 'armchair' audience rather than contemplating its use by actual travellers and as such, its invocation of an 'other' biogram is arguably different. In addition, the narrator for this walk, unlike those of most of the others, is already an (albeit very knowledgeable) 'outsider': Dr Robert Svoboda, an American expert on Ayurvedic medicine.
8. As discussed in more detail below, the implied addressee is presumably non-Hasidic, and arguably non-Jewish.
9. To be fair, there are many other instances in each of these tours—perhaps the majority—in which the walker is not expected or imagined to attain full identification with the narrator. Some of the most interesting moments occur when the walker cannot, or will not, take up the biogrammatic deposit left for her/him. Both Pearl and Joseph address the walker in Yiddish, but Pearl soon remembers: 'Oh wait. You don't speak Yiddish.' Later she tries to teach us a phrase, but gives up in exasperation: 'Nah, not like that. You know what, scratch that.' Similarly, Joseph gives us an extended description of the walking habits of Hasidic men and women respectively: 'Look at the men . . . they're always walking so fast, like they're always running somewhere . . . But check out the women: the women, on the other hand, are a lot slower.' It's clear in his anthropological stance that we are being positioned as outsider-observers; in these instances he does not invite us to move like our Hasidic counterparts, only to study them from a distance.
10. This stop was eliminated from the tour after the first edition.
11. Although I am arguing that this 'scary' appeal predominates throughout the tour, it is not the only characterisation of Chinatown in it: other stops on the tour include a community senior centre, a bustling, 100-year-old tea house, a Buddhist temple, a herbalist, etc.
12. Most of the soundwalks, including the Williamsburg and Chinatown walks, include stops at restaurants or delicatessens, where the narrator usually tells us what to order.
13. Judith Halberstam, 'Notes on Failure', unpublished manuscript.

16.
IMAGINING INDIANS
Negotiating Identity in a Media World
S. Elizabeth Bird

Introduction: The Indian as a Cultural Icon

It's one of the most celebrated images of the American Indian.[1] A tight close-up of a middle-aged man, his stoic face speaking for the suffering of generations, watches the despoilment of his ancestral lands by the heedless pollution of the White man. The depth of his agony is revealed by the single tear forming in the corner of his eye. This 1972 public service advertisement, targeting environmental pollution, became an American popular icon, solidifying the environmentally-conscious, spiritual "noble savage" as the prevailing archetype of the Indian. The actor who posed for the shot, "Iron Eyes" Cody, seemed to personify that archetype in his professional and personal life.

More than twenty years later, when Cody died, his personal identity began to unravel, as it emerged that his real name was Espera (or Oscar) DeCorti, an Italian-American with no Indian ancestry. He had lived out his life as a kind of "going native" fantasy, marrying an Indian woman, adopting Indian children, and acting as an Indian spokesman. He was only the latest in a line of Indian "wannabes" that included Englishman Archie Belaney ("Grey Owl"), and "Cherokee" Chief Long Lance, who was raised as a southern Black or "colored" man (Francis 1992). Indeed, many of the "Indians" who most caught the public imagination turned out to possess not a drop of Native blood.

Into this anecdote are packed many of the elements that make the role of the American Indian in popular culture so distinctive, not only in the United States, but also elsewhere. The original inhabitants of the Americas were decimated in what amounted to genocide in the eighteenth and nineteenth centuries, and they are still one of the most disadvantaged groups in the country, suffering from high levels of poverty, unemployment, and sickness.[2] At various times in the past, and even today, they have been stereotyped as savages, cannibals, sexual predators, and shiftless, drunken losers (Berkhofer 1979). Yet at the same time, they have been exalted as noble and spiritual—the true symbol of America, and the source of wisdom for a culture that has gone astray. White people have been "playing Indian" for a century or more, and they still do, meeting on weekends all over the United States and Europe, to dress in Indian regalia and act out Indian rituals (DeLoria 1999). Indian shamans, real and spurious, have become rich from teaching White people supposed Indian lore, and initiating them into rituals like sweat lodges (Whitt 1995). According to mainstream culture, "real" Indians are wise, calm, spiritual—and living in a kind of mythical nether-world. If a football team chose a grinning Black stereotype as its symbol, and called itself the "Coons," there would be uproar. Yet the Washington Redskins continue to use their cartoonish mascot—after all, who is to be offended, since there aren't any real Indians around anymore? (Davis 1993)

It's hardly surprising then, that images of Indians in contemporary popular culture are limited and one-dimensional, with a heavy overlay of romanticism. There is now a substantial body of literature that documents the representation of American Indians in popular literature, television, film, and so on, extending to representation in text books (e.g., Ashley and Jarratt-Ziemski 1999; Berkhofer 1979; Bird 1996, 1999; Churchill 1994; Francis 1992). American Indians are popular not only in the United States and Canada, but also in Europe, where Indian hobbyist groups are widespread (DeLoria 1999), and where novelists like Karl May in Germany established a tradition of "going-Indian" romanticism. Contemporary Indian life is rarely represented, and occasional recent films, such as the Indian-directed *Smoke Signals,* a funny and honest portrayal of modern reservation life, cannot compete with the long-established narrative resonance achieved with such blockbusters of noble savagery as *Dances with Wolves.*

Taken as a whole, this intertextual melange of imagery suggests that American Indians as symbols are a potent presence in North American and European cultural narratives, while one wonders whether these narratives speak in any way to Indians themselves. As cultural studies scholars have long argued, we cannot presume to read the cultural meaning of anything through textual analysis alone. Yet very few scholars have studied audience response to American Indian representation, from the standpoint of either Indian or non-Indian audiences. Hanson and Rouse (1987), having acknowledged the consistency of the noble savage imagery in contemporary culture, write, "far less certain is the precise connection between the familiar caricature of the generic Indian and the more complex set of beliefs and attitudes that individuals actually had concerning Native Americans" (p. 57). My purpose in this study was to explore this connection, extending the discussion not only to how White audiences respond to representations of Indians, but also how Indians respond to, and imagine representations of themselves. Hanson and Rouse (1987), using a social scientific survey of students' attitudes toward Indians, conclude that their (mostly white) respondents' perceptions tend to be positive, rejecting the older stereotypes of war-like, primitive people, and claiming to value the contributions of diverse Indian

cultures. They paint a picture of a rather open-minded population, who value diversity (a message they were probably used to receiving in the sociology and anthropology classes from which they were recruited). Their respondents rated television and movies as their most important source of information about Indians.

Yet Hanson and Rouse's data also point to the acceptance of stereotypes. For instance, the students associated Indians with rural and traditional lifestyles, and tended to think of them as living in the past. Respondents agreed that Indians tend to be "submissive" and "withdrawn," even as they disagreed that Indians were "lazy," "weak," "undependable," or "unpatriotic," all of which might have described popular perceptions in the nineteenth century.

I believe this study shows that by the late twentieth century, college students knew how to give an appropriate response to a survey on racial attitudes, and few are likely to offer strongly pejorative comments. Indeed, it shows both the strengths of survey research—its ability to paint a broad picture using a large, representative sample—and its weaknesses—its inability to penetrate beneath surface attitudes. Although these students rejected the old Western stereotypes, they appear to have internalized the more contemporary stereotype, without seeing it in any way as derogatory. Prevailing American attitudes would not favor "submissive" and "withdrawn" as positive descriptions of most Americans, yet it seems unlikely that these students meant these terms as negative. Rather, they accepted the stoicism and laconicism of Indians as part of the "noble savage" paradigm. While Hanson and Rouse read their results as indicating a breakdown of stereotypes, I believe they merely suggest a shifting to a "positive" stereotype that reflects a self-conscious "political correctness."

Support for this view comes from my earlier research that compared Indian and White responses to *Dr. Quinn, Medicine Woman,* an Old West television series that featured Cheyenne characters (Bird 1996). This research had been based on focus groups with Indian and White viewers, who were asked to view episodes of the program privately, and then discuss them in an open-ended format. Group members were asked to discuss the Cheyenne characters in much the same general terms as other characters (that is, they were not asked questions about whether the representations were "positive" or "negative"). My conclusion was that the largely stereotypical presentation of Indians (stoic, non-emotional, spiritual, and so on) was accepted as authentic and essentially unremarkable by White audiences, while Indian viewers found it inauthentic, irritating, and one-dimensional. A typical contrast was in response to an episode in which the main Cheyenne character is unjustly imprisoned by the Army. He refuses to protest, even facing a mock firing squad without showing emotion. A White woman remarked approvingly on this: "Indians are like that. You know, they can be very intense emotionally but able to suppress it and not show it" (Bird, 253). Indian viewers were especially angered by this story, arguing that "his manhood was suppressed," and the character was not allowed to show normal emotions. "He just . . . put his head down, made him look pitiful. That kind of pissed me off" (Bird, 256). Similarly, Shiveley, in comparing male Indian and Anglo responses to a classic Western, *The Searchers,* found that while both groups enjoyed the film, the Anglo viewers also thought it was authentic in its portrayal of the Old West, while the Indian men rejected the dehumanizing they saw as central to the imagery, and did not perceive its historical representation as in any way authentic.

Thus, I suggest that while contemporary perceptions of American Indians are not generally "negative," in the sense of Indians being classified as savage, demonic, lazy, or drunk, they are still narrow, and ultimately objectifying. Hanson and Rouse's students may have known the right things to say about Indians and their cultural contributions, but their perceptions of Indians are still framed in a particular way, with media as central agents. As Thompson (1990) puts it, a central role of media is the "public circulation of symbolic forms" (p. 219), and the Indian is undoubtedly a potent symbolic construction in America and elsewhere. Many Americans, and almost all Europeans, have little direct contact with Indians, and so popular depictions are especially important. Indians themselves simply do not find symbolic representations that resonate in any way with their own experiences and identity.

Ethnography and Response

Both my study and Shively's work were based on analysis of qualitative focus groups with Indians and non-Indian people, and both pointed to the importance of qualitative, open-ended methodologies in drawing a more subtle picture of audience response. Both studies fit within the tradition of "audience response" studies, focusing on a specific text, and they begin to get at the way that media representations connect with people's sense of identity, in a similar (though less extensive) way as studies like Bobo's (1995) on Black women reading the film *The Color Purple.* As defined by Woodward (1997), "Identity gives us an idea of who we are and of how we relate to others and to the world in which we live. Identity marks the ways in which we are the same as others who share that position, and the ways in which we are different from those who do not" (pp. 1–2). For instance, a central character in *Dr. Quinn* was Sully, a glamourous, long-haired loner who has lived with the Cheyenne and "knows their ways." White viewers, especially women, liked him, seeing in him an ideal hero: "He stands up for the women and . . . the blacks . . . and the American Indians and . . . he's always doing the right stuff," commented one (Bird, 255). Sully unproblematically fits with a White sense of identity related to the West and the Frontier, in which the role of the good White man is to relate to and speak for the oppressed, but ultimately to guide them gently toward the inevitable progress of civilization. He comes from a long line of border-crossing mountain men, traced back to early pioneer narratives and the novels of James Fenimore Cooper, and he became a staple in the Western narratives of Europe, such as the still-popular German novels of Karl May. He is the personification of the "going native" fantasy that fuels Indian hobbyists and role-players (Baird 1996). For all its mainstream resonance, this is a narrative that violates Indians' own sense of identity. They recognized the theme: "I can't think of one movie that there hasn't been this White guy that has somehow been part of their culture" (Bird, 255). But they resented it strongly: "Here's another White person fixing the Indians" (p. 255), "I know a lot of old stories . . . I can't ever recall one where anyone talked about a long-haired, light-skinned, hairy guy that helped my tribe" (p. 256).

Discussing the relationship between identity and media representations, Woodward (1997) writes, "Representation as a cultural process establishes individual and collective identities, and symbolic systems provide possible answers to the questions: who am I?; what could I be?; who do I want to be?" (p. 14). For Whites and Indians, the experience of watching the *Dr. Quinn* Indians and wannabes, or "classic" movies like *The Searchers,* is diametrically opposed—Whites' identity is validated and authenticated, while Indian identity is denied and erased. Indian participants in my study spoke about how media representation is so rooted in mainstream representations that it may be impossible for conventional media to provide the kind of narratives that speak to Indian identity. An Ojibwa participant spoke of the need to transcend conventional media forms and reinvent identity: "I think what's coming up now is virtual reality experience rather than just one dimension. We're going to have something more than T.V., where . . . our people will win the game" (Bird, 259).

Creating a New Media Experience

The earlier studies suggest that Indian people do believe media representations are important, both for their sense of personal identity and as literal mediators through which relationships between themselves and people of other ethnicities are filtered. The daily experience of American Indians is that White people constantly see them through the lens provided by the media. Ojibwa writer Jim Northrup writes about traveling to New York City in the aftermath of *Dances with Wolves,* and finding himself treated as a minor celebrity and curiosity, because of his Indian appearance. "One cab driver took a $10 bill out of his wallet for us to autograph. I signed as Kevin Costner [the star *of Dances*], and I believe my wife used the name Pocahontas" (Northrup 1995). The film *Smoke Signals,* based on the writing of Sherman Alexie, a Coeur D'Alene Indian, and scripted by him, includes a sequence in which the two young central characters take a long bus trip from Washington State to the Southwest. The more confident Victor instructs his nerdy, bespectacled friend Thomas how to look like a "real Indian," exhorting him to let his long hair flow free, "look stoic," and "look like you've just come back from hunting a buffalo." Thomas protests that they are from a tribe of fishermen not hunters, but Victor knows that the popular image of Indians is a generic Plains Indian buffalo hunter: "This isn't *Dances with Salmon,* you know!" At a rest stop, Thomas attempts to change his image, with limited success. However, reality sets in when the pair realize their seats have been taken by two surly, mildly racist white men, and they must move or risk a confrontation. The message is clear—mainstream society loves the Indian in his proper, mythical place, but in real life, Indians are still second-class citizens.

Beyond Reception Study: Mediated Indian Identities

With these points in mind, I devised a study that I hoped would offer a more subtle and nuanced understanding both of White perceptions of Indians, and of how Indians might re-imagine the role of media in representing themselves. Working in Duluth, Minnesota, I recruited 10 groups, each with four participants (although 2 groups ended up with three, due to last-minute drop-outs). Two groups consisted of White women, two of White men, two of Indian men, and two of Indian women, while one comprised Indian and White women, and another Indian and White men. Since the task involved a group planning exercise with minimal direction and supervision, I decided it would be most effective if the members already knew each other; usually one individual was contacted, and he or she was then asked to recruit three friends/acquaintances. No formal attempt at randomness was made, although I wished to avoid a sample only of traditional-aged students. Some Indian participants were recruited through the city's American Indian Cultural Center, others through programs at the University of Minnesota, Duluth's School of Medicine, which actively recruits Indian students. The result was a pool of 38 participants, ranging in age from 17 to 58, with an average age of 30. Each participant was compensated with a check for $50.

The groups were told that their mission was to design a fictional television series they would want to watch regularly.[3] It could be any genre (sitcom, drama and so on), and could be set anywhere, at any time period. The program should include a cast of characters, both major and minor, and the group had to decide who they were and how they related to each other. Their goal was to design the program in as much detail as they could, providing a history of the characters, developing a detailed story for the first episode, and outlining some of the events and storylines that would happen over the next six weeks. At the end of the estimated two hours, they were to summarize their decisions on forms provided. The sessions were also audiotaped, and the transcripts analyzed. The only restriction was that at least one character should be White, one American Indian, and one a woman, although none of these had to be a leading character. I hoped to avoid focusing the group's attention too heavily on the issue of Indian characterization; the groups were simply told that the project was a creative experiment. After full instructions, coffee, and soft drinks were provided, I withdrew while the groups talked. My decision not to interact with the participants was deliberate; as far as possible I wished for this to be an "ethnographic encounter" among themselves, and not between myself and them, thus minimizing the possibility of my agenda becoming a central focus. In fact, my research assistant recruited and set up some of the groups completely independently, so that I never met some of the participants.

Clearly, this is not an "audience response study" in the familiar sense; there is no media text to view, and no viewers watching and decoding. This choice emerges out of a growing dissatisfaction among audience researchers about the limitations of response studies, as discussed in Chapter 1. In a media-saturated culture, it is no longer possible to separate out the "effects" of particular media (if it ever was), and the goal must be to reach a more holistic, anthropological understanding of how people's world views are patterned by the media, and how the media are inserted into their daily lives. As Drotner (1994) argues, for media ethnographers this implies a move away from the specific reception studies: "In empirical terms the context of investigation is widened to include areas beyond the immediate situation of reception . . . media ethnographers apply a variety of methods in order to better grasp the dynamics of mediated meaning-making . . . as part of everyday life" (p. 345).

Creating the Series

Most of the groups began in varying degrees of despair, discussing how impossible the task was, and wondering about the point of the exercise. One participant commented, "Did you see the *Seinfeld*, this is kinda funny, Seinfeld writing a pilot for his own show. That's what I kind of feel like right now." However, all eventually got down to the task at hand, and produced a variety of creative ideas (the $50 payment proved crucial, turning the exercise into a "job" that had to be done properly, rather than a frivolous activity!). Several groups began with drama, but almost all ended up creating comedies or "comedy-dramas," often discussing how humor can deal with serious issues and connect people who may not have much in common, a point echoing Drotner's (1994) observation that when she asked young people to create their own videos, "humour . . . was the genre everybody could agree upon" (p. 353).

In the end, each group transcript averaged over 40 pages, providing a wealth of ethnographic detail about how people actually integrate generic conventions, stereotypes, and their everyday experience in a mediated world. All groups talked at length about their need to have programming to which they related, and which spoke to them, and all drew to varying degrees on both their own experiences and their "media literacy"—their enculturated grasp of standard televisual generic forms, especially those they liked best. While there was much to be gleaned from the exercise, I will focus here on the implications of the American Indian characterization, and how talk about it helped shed light on internalized perceptions of Indian identity.

In analyzing and drawing conclusions from the data, I am aware of the need to remain cautious.

Perhaps most crucially, there is the danger of essentializing the responses—of assuming that everything people say or do is because they are one ethnicity or another, rather than because of other aspects of their individual identities. We all inhabit many interlocking identities, connected with our gender, class, personal history, age, and any number of other factors. For instance, in the mixed male group an older man tended to set the agenda for the three younger participants; it was hard to determine if the rather hostile attitude of one of the other participants was because he felt marginalized as an Indian, because he resented the confidence of the older man—or maybe he was just in a bad mood. As a researcher, I can listen to the tapes, pay attention to tone of voice, and study the words, but must always be aware of the numerous complexities of the social interaction I have set in motion, as well as the fact that this moment is embedded in a much broader cultural context. It was impossible, for instance, to find groups of people whose level of existing acquaintanceship was the same; some groups comprised people who already knew each other very well, others were acquainted mostly through such contexts as college classes, and in two groups at least some of the members were meeting for the first time. These factors clearly affected the nature of the conversations that developed, and in presenting my analysis, I have tried to incorporate this as far as I can. There are certainly times I would like to be able to retreat into the techniques of the social scientist, devising ways to control all the messy "variables" that interfere with certainty!

Nevertheless, it is well-established that, especially for people of color, ethnicity is indeed a dominating factor in self-identity, and certainly plays into their interaction with media representation. For White people, on the other hand, whiteness is essentially taken for granted, and accepted as the norm, while most of the Indian participants made it clear that for them, their ethnicity is something of which they are aware all the time, comprising one crucial lens through which they view the world, including the media. So while I am sure many factors played into the groups' interaction, there nevertheless emerged a consistency in the discourse about "Indianness," and

it was that consistency that convinced me of the appropriateness of my conclusions.

Whites Represent Indians

In analyzing the White groups, I was interested in how their own creations would connect to earlier work, in which White audiences appeared to have naturalized familiar stereotypes, and did not appear very interested in the development of Indian characters. To a great extent, that turned out to be true. The first White group comprised four women: a 58-year-old office worker, a 35-year-old administrator, a 32-year-old university admissions worker, and a 42-year-old secretary. Although not all close friends, they all knew each other, and the group dynamic was lively and cordial, with all four participants actively contributing. Their favorite shows were all sitcoms: *Frasier, The Nanny, Friends,* and *Wings,* respectively. Significantly, they began by talking about their favorites, and formulating how "their" show would fit in this genre. Soon, they settled on the idea of a twenty-something husband-and-wife team (Scott and Jennifer) running a connected hairdressing salon and body shop (car repair garage). The show is called *Dents and Tangles.* Tired of big city life, they have moved home to Duluth to start their business. The action will focus around their struggles to make it, amid an array of supporting characters. They develop detailed character sketches of the characters. For instance, Jennifer is described in writing thus: "27 years old, BBA degree, cosmetology background. Excited to start her own business and establish herself as a manager. Her relationship with Glenn (Scott's dad) will be complicated, as she and Scott see themselves as equals professionally. She's very stylish." Seven characters are given this kind of detailed description, both in the group's written summaries and their taped conversation.

At various moments, someone reminds the group that an Indian character is needed. One suggests, "maybe an Indian girl could be one of the best stylists and have her be really flashy and beautiful," citing *Pocahontas* as an example. Later, the same woman mentions Marilyn, a character in the popular series *Northern Exposure,* set in Alaska and featuring several

Native characters: "She was good, her heritage came through and she was really very quietly intelligent." Another agrees: "That was the first thing that clipped into my mind was *Northern Exposure*." It was quickly decided that Marilyn could be exported from that series intact: "We could have her make some one-line saying at the end of the show . . . And in some episodes you could have her say something and leave the shop in the middle of the show, say something rather, um . . . prophetic, as though she knew what the outcome of the situation was going to be." The final written description of Marilyn read: "early 40s? (no one's sure). Goes to Jennifer once every six weeks for a quarter inch cut, never anything different. Very soft-spoken, wise, prophetic."

All in all, this group's result was revealing. The discussion of "Marilyn" was cursory compared to the detailed development of other characters, and the group relied entirely on an already-existing media character, while all other character descriptions emerged through dialogue about personal experience and knowledge. *Northern Exposure*'s Marilyn was unusually well-developed (although still sketchy compared to the Whites; Taylor, 1996), yet the version imported to *Dents and Tangles* was one-dimensionally stereotypical—wise, spiritual, silent. In discussing the events that would ensue in the first few episodes, the group detailed the escapades of even the minor characters, except for Marilyn, as someone occasionally remembers and says something like, "Oh yes, then Marilyn comes in, says something wise, and all that." It's hardly a stretch to imagine professional TV programmers developing their characters in much the same way.

The second White female group consisted of a 30-year-old community organizer, a 36-year-old secretary, a 37-year-old community organizer, and a 38-year-old "homemaker/mom." All were regular television watchers, whose favorite programs were *Northern Exposure, ER,* and the female-oriented sitcoms *Grace under Fire* and *Roseanne.* They all knew each other quite well, and shared a perspective that supported progressive social ideas and community change. Their shared understanding and familiarity led to an easy rapport and an atmosphere in which everyone contributed. Reflecting their combined preferences,

they developed a contemporary "comedy/drama" called *Mesabi North,* featuring the everyday lives of a mixed group of people in a Duluth apartment building. This group set out to make the situation "funky," featuring an eclectic mix of types. With much laughter, they seem to be gently satirizing the tendency in American shows to showcase a "diverse" cast. This immediately leads them into the need to have an Indian character, who at first will be the apartment owner/manager:

M: She's Native American, she's trans-gender . . . She's our main character right now.
S: She's a vegetarian. She's into Earth stuff, you know keeping the environment clean.
M: That's where that funky smell comes from.
S: She's got some funky smells coming from her apartment, incense you know.
G: Hippie stuff.
S: Crystals, all the crystals and all the rocks around her.

Soon they decide that this central character will be White, but "How about . . . there was an American Indian elder living in the building?" This is met with approval: "sort of like a mother, spiritual advisor?" The group goes on to describe a range of deliberately stereotyped characters—a single, Latina mother, a gay couple, a lesbian couple, a Hmong immigrant family, and so on. They assert that the humor will emerge from the interaction among them: "and then also a better understanding of different lifestyles . . . maybe," commented one. The end result is that virtually all the characters are stereotypical. Even given that, the group provides much more detail for some characters; the gay male couple is quite fully realized, with details of occupations, hobbies, and personal appearance, as the group refer often to their own gay friends. They have more trouble with the Indian woman, as they grope for appropriate descriptions:

S: Selma's our Native American Elder Women.
M: Yup, elder lady . . .
S: What's Selma's last name? She don't need a last name, we just go by Selma.

M: It could be like Selma Morning Star.

L: I like Selma Morning Star.

M: Make her last name sound more Native American . . . Black-feather . . . or . . .

S: Sunbear.

M: Blackhawk . . . or . . .

S: Brownbear, Selma Brownbear.

M: Or Redbird.

L: Selma Blackbear. Or how 'bout Redbird?

M: She has beadwork classes and she sells her beadwork at the pow-wows in the summer.

G: Not just beadwork. She does it all.

S: Weaving and basketmaking and makes rugs . . .

In the plot outlines for the first few weeks, Selma gets little mention, after one episode in which other tenants think she is smoking pot (she is actually burning sage in a ritual). Once again, the group has drawn heavily on existing symbolic forms to create their character, and then cannot think what to do with her.

Both White male groups were slightly younger than the women. The first comprised a 25-year-old jeweler, who favored the sitcom *In Living Color,* a 25-year-old graphic artist, and a 23-year-old student, both of whose favorite program was *Friends.* The three were friends, who socialize together frequently, and their conversation is free-flowing and uninhibited. They name their program *Crazy Horse Casino,* setting it in a conservative Southern community, where a couple is trying to open a casino. At one point, the group gets into a long digression about the enormous (and presumably shady) profits made by Indian casinos. This group was probably the least engaged of any group, constantly having to return to task, while drinking whisky (not provided by me!). Their characterization is weak, and they are immediately flummoxed by the need to include an Indian character. Before they settle on the casino idea, they cast around for possibilities. One suggests a Western: "I mean, how are we going to incorporate all three characters in something else?" Certainly, if one were to look at the kinds of popular media texts that do incorporate a White person, a woman, and an Indian, that would seem a fair question. However, these young men agree that they are not familiar enough with the genre, and move on to a sitcom. First they

suggest a White couple adopting an Indian child; their next attempt, drawing on one of the member's experience in the jewelry business, is also strikingly stereotypical:

K: OK, how 'bout the setting is a jewelry store in like, downtown Duluth, and they have to deal with all the drunk Indians that come in.

J: Hey . . . the one could be a recurring character.

K: There you go.

However, they decide this is also going nowhere, and move on. After several false starts, they decide on a male Indian, married to a White woman, who opens a casino in the South. One asks whether an Indian casino "would be too racially stereotyped," to which another replies, "who cares?" and the third adds, "It's our show, dang right."

Drawing on more stereotypes that Indian casino profits probably derive from White expertise or Mob connections, one suggests: "How 'bout, the thing that's really pissing him off is the wife runs it and he's the Indian guy. So he's gotta stay home and take care of this little kid. Or he's like a janitor or something." They go on to discuss the humor involved in having the Indian try to hide his ancestry while running an Indian casino, settling on his name as Todd Crazy Horse. They continue to explore various characteristics for Todd, having him sexually involved with several casino employees, while his wife fumes, and taking direction from the Mob. They talk often about "dialog between Todd and Mary Beth which would outline humorous conflict resulting from his heritage," but cannot come up with specifics. In the end, it is clear they have no idea how to develop the character, although they do a much more coherent job with his wife and other supporting characters.

The second White male group included a 25-year-old cook, a 24-year-old student, and a 27-year-old "unemployed graduate student," whose favorite programs were *Seinfeld,* the fantasy drama *Hercules,* and *Friends.* They did not know each other, but were mutual friends of my graduate assistant (a fact I did not learn until after the completion of the interviews). They began by spending about 15 minutes getting to know each other by discussing mutual friends, hobbies, jobs, and favorite TV shows, discovering many commonalities, and working amiably and collaboratively. They quickly agreed on a sitcom, and discussed how they disliked the kind of planned diversity that characterizes many such shows:

J: I think they have over-killed that in a lot of the shows these days. Just decided that it must have this ethnic background, this kind of show . . .

H: I just don't like it when it is so obvious, because then it's like it's just the opposite. And then it's just like so fake then.

Between them they developed a rather rich scenario for their sitcom, *The Other Lebanon,* centered around a bar in a Colorado town, originally settled by nineteenth century Lebanese immigrants. Conflicts emerge between the locals and "rich, yuppie ski resort people," who are becoming increasingly numerous. This group was explicitly determined not to be stereotypical, and introduced some interesting characters, such as a highly-educated bartender and a female garage owner, both of whom are given a wealth of detail. The bartender, for instance, is described as "a kind of a helper with community counselor person. His character is not too witty . . . I don't want another *Cheers* or anything. He's caring, he listens, and he doesn't drink on the job or anything, but when he does drink he really lets loose and you get to see him do that once in a while. That'll be in the third week . . . that'll be a real shocker." Later more details are added, such as "six years of college in philosophy" and "it could follow as far as him deciding in life what he wanted to do while he's a bartender. That could be more serious, you know, being in touch with himself . . . "

They tried hard with the Indian character, beginning with a false start in which they visualized a group of students as the main characters: "But um, there'd be a chaperone, and build off of the image of the wise American Indian, somebody that's kind of calm." This was rejected as clichéd, and the group settled on their character: "There's an Indian women, she's a musician, a good musician, she plays rock music, to traditional Irish, to Patsy Cline . . . She owns a profitable, kind of alternative movie theater . . . things

you wouldn't see . . . She's not a shaman or anything." However, once established, the group found it difficult to know what to do with her, only mentioning her once again, to reiterate that she would defy expectations in terms of her musical repertoire. Meanwhile, their other characters and scenarios were described carefully and thoroughly, and the group mapped out detailed events in four episodes, never mentioning the Indian woman after the first episode. The most striking thing about this group was that, even with their determination not to stereotype, they essentially found themselves unable to draw on cultural knowledge that would help them imagine a fully-developed Indian character.

Indians Represent Themselves

The White groups were clearly most comfortable with stories and characters that fit both their own lives and the mainstream media genres they experience every day, genres that take the White experience for granted. Minority viewers often have to read against the grain, and view representations through a lens that places ethnic identity in the forefront. Lind (1996), following Cohen (1991) and others, stresses the importance of "relevance" in audience interpretations of media—the fact that cultural identity is a crucial framing device through which people view media imagery. American Indians, like other minorities, spend their lives acutely aware of their ethnicity, and of media representations of it. In my *Dr. Quinn* study, for example, White focus groups rarely initiated discussion of Indian representation, taking it for granted. I usually had to raise it as a topic, something that never happened with the Indian groups, who always raised it almost immediately.

So it was not surprising that the groups in this study all took the opportunity to create a program that explicitly explored issues of Indian identity and life. The first male Indian group included four pre-medical students, aged 33, 20, 27, and 32. They listed their favorite shows as *ER,* the mostly Black sitcom *Fresh Prince of Bel Air, Seinfeld,* and *Star Trek: Next Generation.* The group members did not know each other especially well, having come into the Duluth program from Nebraska, Texas, Maryland, and

Minnesota. Nevertheless, their rapport was strong, and their conversation was exceptionally fluent and good-humored, drawing especially on their common cultural experiences as minorities. Their comedy, *Red Earth,* evolves through a series of ideas that all involve people as outsiders, beginning with one participant describing his own life: "Coming from a reservation, becoming urbanized . . . and going back to the reservation . . . Being accepted in your traditional beliefs versus the societal beliefs . . . I actually wrote a story on my own a long time ago . . . I called it *The Glass Culture.*" Others then discuss having a White female doctor trying to be accepted on a reservation, or an Indian doctor trying to fit into suburban America. To this is added a story about an Indian student's struggle to become accepted as a doctor.

This prompts reflection from other group members, as they talk about the differences among minority experiences: "Even if you are a minority, the Black struggle is hard to relate to the Native American struggle . . . You got a Black . . . brought over here from another country. What is their stake in this? . . . But what can you tell a Native American? I have to be here, that's all. Struggle's totally different . . . nobody has a stake in this country but us." Initially, the group is concerned that they keep the program accessible, not alienating the mainstream by focusing only on Indians, but gradually the ideas become more and more "theirs." The next scenario is a rewrite of history, in which the Indians fight back, forming a majority, with "casinos all over America . . . Indians buy back all the land, and kick the intruders out." This iteration was called *Return of the Buffalo*—"one of the Indian prophecies, when the Buffalo get replenished the wars will start and then the Indians will take the land back." In another development, "It'd be real funny if some aliens came to the planet and said, 'all Native Americans stay here, and all non-Native Americans get out.'"

C: And then you'd have everybody in the world trying to find out who they married back in there. Yes, I'm 1/2,000ths. I need to be over here, and then you have a little line that says, "tribal papers". . .

S: . . . and you ask them what kind of Native American and they'll say Cherokee. Cause every White person I talk to says, "yeah, I got some Indian in me." What kind? "Oh, Cherokee."

C: I mean you gotta have a show that Native Americans take over something . . . even the apes took over . . . God, *Planet of the Apes.* We can have *Planet of the Indians* . . . We could have *Rain Man* . . . Anytime he sees a White person he just pees on them.

M: It's called *Red Earth.*

The idea of an Indian/alien takeover takes hold, with "buffalo being teleported down here . . . Just like *Independence Day* . . . all you see is a dark cloud." The mother ship, in the form of a giant teepee, invades Washington, D.C., using buffalo dung as bombs, and forcing a meeting with the White, female President ("so we take care of the woman and the Anglo in one"). Later they adapt the idea, positing a Native American planet which is exploring distant lands, the first being Earth. They send a scout (George, who takes his name off the Washington Monument) to Earth, and he has to adapt and make contact. No one believes his story, and he ends up in the jail, the "nuthouse," or the "drunk tank." Ideas flow thick and fast as his survival skills are tested:

C: He spends his night on the town. He's running round these White people with hatchets . . . You can see George Scout stripping the bones . . .

S: George goes driving.

R: George searches for a mate.

S: See George in Central Park roasting . . .

S: His ass . . .

C: A human being on a stick . . .

M: Want some White meat?

R: Man, White people be complaining about this show. Scare the shit out of that grad student [*my research assistant*].

C: He'll say, "Is this what they really think about me? They look at me like I'm food!"

R: George starts selling drugs for extra money.

S: Starts selling drugs out of the Washington monument.

Eventually George meets, but eats the President, then goes home to Red Earth, and "everybody's pissed at him because he's changed." Although they now know "the Earth is an evil place," the invasion proceeds. Observes one participant: "suddenly it's become a dark satire."

The second Indian male group included two brothers—a 41-year-old video producer and social worker and a 46-year-old counselor—a 39-year-old unemployed man and a 36-year-old cook. Their favorite TV choices were sports, *Northern Exposure*, news, and the classic sitcom *M*A*S*H*. They all lived and worked in Duluth, and had known each other for some time, so their rapport was easy and the conversation fluent. They created a drama "with comedy" called *School Days*, set in the 1960s in an Oklahoma Indian boarding school.[4] Like the first group, their discussion gained an increasingly strong Indian identity as the time progressed. They began with a stereotyped scenario of a White couple who go to an Indian elder for enlightenment, reasoning that this was the kind of story that would appeal to the mainstream viewer. Gradually the seeker of truth evolves into Joe, an Indian man who has lost his sense of identity in a White world, and the elder is his grandfather, who counsels him. As this happens, we learn through flashbacks about his life growing up in the oppressive boarding school (something two of the participants had experienced). As one participant says, "this Indian . . . is being tormented by the matrons of the boarding school for trying to hold on to his ways . . . But he goes on to become well educated and graduates from the boarding school, maintaining his identity all the way through. No matter what they put him through. A lot of it's never told . . . That our people have success stories."

They envisage the young man visiting home, having been taught not to speak Ojibwa at the school: "He knows the language but he doesn't dare speak it . . . and then maybe he kinda hides it from his grandpa that he's being locked into a room or that he's being punished for singing or for praying or using the medicines." The series would humorously explore relationships among students as they defy the authorities, while also featuring compassionate teachers and friendships among students and staff. Remembering that a White character is required, the group creates Miss December, the school principal. "Everything she

talks, everything she says is demeaning . . . she's a cold-hearted bitch." The group saw humour as crucial, and media as a key to reducing prejudice:

> Prejudice is based on . . . you don't have the knowledge . . . The thing we battle the most is stereotypes . . . No matter how successful we are, we're just an Indian or we're just a Black, or we're just a Mexican. So you turn that into humor . . . You turn that whole thing around and what you're doing while you're laughin', while you're learnin', is you're correcting stereotypes, and learnin' how to laugh at them, together.

The Indian female groups also tackled the issue of identity directly. The first group were all students, aged 17, 18, 19, and 21, whose favorite shows were *Fresh Prince* (2), news, and *Seinfeld*. All were from different Minnesota towns, except one, a Navajo from New Mexico, and although they were acquaintances from college, they did not know each other particularly well. Nevertheless, the similarities in their ages, and their common experiences, led to a friendly, easy rapport in which everyone contributed. Opting immediately for a comedy, they began by laughing about a reservation setting "with everyone going around saying 'How!'" Tossing ideas around, they mention the White "wannabe"—"you know there's always one non-Native always just hangs around the Indians." They move on to visualize an Indian school, not unlike the previous group's, with a cast of Indian students and a mean, sadistic White teacher. Then one member suggests they "make it about something that you would never even think of an Indian being—how 'bout a car salesman?" The group runs with this, playing with stereotypes of Indian reservation life all the way. They name the series *Rez Rider*, a common term for the kind of beaten-up car found on reservations, deliberately contrasting that with the super-car that was the star of the old series *Knight Rider*. Their star is Melvin Two Hairs, an Indian "car dealer to the stars" in the exclusive Los Angeles suburb of Brentwood. He sells expensive foreign cars, and the humor revolves around the reservation lifestyle he maintains in the ritzy neighborhood. His "company car" is "Rusty," the Rez Rider, which is described as a character itself: "the typical rusted, taped-up, reservation ride." They create the car in rapid dialogue:

D: You know, you have maybe a flashlight for a head light . . .

M: . . . and you can only get out on one side. And you have to open it from the outside.

L: You have a plastic window in the back . . .

T: . . . Duct-taped seats, powder compact for rear view mirror . . .

D: You know, you have all your bumper stickers from the powwow just holding your fender up . . .

L: "Red power."

D: And you know, like his muffler is being held up by an old belt. Then the antenna is the clothes hanger. You ever seen that?

L: And you don't even have reverse. You gotta get out and push it.

D: A truck, one of those little bitty ones, that can only fit one person . . . somebody heavy, like totally hogs the seat. And everybody has to ride in the back, and it only gets to go up to 45 miles an hour . . . and oh . . . he's gotta have that one-eyed, three-legged dog sitting right there in the passenger seat.

Melvin is married to Ruthie, and they have "hellion" five-year-old twins, "like little rez kids who, when they see people they're sneaking up on them . . . and they're all dirty. All crusty." The requisite White character is Mrs. Dubois, a rich, sophisticated widow who keeps buying cars from Melvin, and being shocked by his reservation ways. One day Ruthie serves dinner:

D: And instead of having a whole, expensive dinner, it's fry bread, mutton and beans.

L: And some commod. orange juice [government commodities given to reservations].

T: Oh, and then they have that big block of butter. And the wrapper's still on it: "For Reservation."

Nevertheless, Mrs. Dubois is a classic "wannabe," constantly hoping Melvin will teach her about Indian lore and tradition. The message coming from the group is that Whites need a dose of reality when it comes to Indians—and the squalor of reservation life, even as comedy, is that reality, not the spiritual savage.

The second Indian female group included a 27-year-old social services secretary, a student who did not give her age, a 34-year-old human services case manager, and a 29-year-old educator. All were local, living and working in the Duluth area, and had known each other for some time. Their favorite programs were *ER* (2), *Star Trek Deep Space Nine,* and *Star Trek Voyager,* and they began their discussion by talking about the need for more "wholesome" and "family-oriented" TV programming, particularly decrying "sex-obsessed" comedies like *Friends.* They decided to create an issues-based comedy-drama called *Migizi Way.* Like the other Indian groups, they quickly decide to explore stereotypes, beginning with commentary on the sad state of Indian representation in TV:

B: There are very few television shows that portray Native Americans as Native Americans. Like, *Northern Exposure* had some guy that was non-Indian portraying an Indian.

I: Which one was that?

B: Um . . . I can't think of what his name was on the show . . . He helped Maurice, and he worked at the store.

M: Ed . . .

B: That's it.

M: He wasn't an Indian?

B: He wasn't an Indian.

I: Ed's not an Indian.

B: He had to dye his hair black every week to keep it black, blond as . . .

I: Ohhh, I'm so disillusioned.

B: He was Scandinavian, blond as they can come.

I: I'm so disappointed, I didn't know that.

Briefly, they consider a show set "on the rez," but decide against it: "I don't think anyone wants to watch life on the rez. It's too close to reality. They don't want to watch drunken Indians stagger about the streets." Instead, they decide they "would like to see a show that did what *Cosby* did for Blacks . . . Have some role models . . . " They choose a present-day setting: "We don't need any more historical, romantic Indian pictures. We want reality here." Again, they debate whether "reality" is what they really want: "get the rez humor out there . . . that's funny. But just how much of the real life rez do you want to expose?" One points out that "reality" isn't all negative: "I mean Native Americans: some are doctors, some are nurses, and some. . . . I mean I know a doctor, a nurse that's Native American. So it's not like it can't be done."

Just as the White groups had to find a role for the "token Indian," this group debated the required White character:

I: Yeah . . . how 'bout, eh, why does one have to be white? We can have a token white person.
M: Let's have a drunk white person.
B: No, no, that wouldn't be nice.
I: How 'bout the redneck white person, comes in, that you'd have to deal with once in a while to educate him . . . that Jeff guy . . . Foxworth, that's it. [*Jeff Foxworthy, a popular "redneck" comedian*]
M: We'd have him come in . . .
I: Yeah, and he's not a malicious person.
M: He's just a total moron.
I: He doesn't know, that's all.

They go on to talk about the value of "guest-starring people like Native Americans that are stars, like Billy Mills . . . actually showing real life characters that are Native American, that are role models." They develop a promising scenario about an Indian clinic, drawing on their own experiences, saying it would be more "real" than shows like *ER.* They discuss the possible need for a strong male character, since most of the discussion has reflected their experiences as single mothers:

I: The other thing is, I have a hard time finding, looking for a strong male role model figure. Should we have him as a mythical figure? You know, as a shadow?
B: Kinda like the white buffalo.
I: A mythical figure . . . is there any? Is that a reality? . . . A strong male Native American. Do you know any?

T: No.
I: So we can make one up.
B: So it would be mythical.
I: It is mythical, right.
B: That's the saddest state of affairs.

Eventually, like the other groups' stories, their scenario grapples with Indian people's movement between two worlds. In their tale, Mary Migizi, a 35-year-old Indian woman, returns to a reservation in Minnesota, about to give birth to her fourth child. Migizi means "bald eagle" in Ojibwa; the group deliberately chose the combination of English and Ojibwa words for their character's name, after debating whether to name her Mary Eagle. Her husband has just been killed in a drunk-driving accident, and she had been making a living as a writer/illustrator in the White world. Now she returns to her life with her husband's family, and over the next few episodes, experiences a kind of rebirth herself, as she rediscovers her cultural identity. Episodes would feature Mary's struggles with bureaucracy; for instance, her husband was an enrolled tribal member, while she has to fight to prove to authorities that she is a "real" Indian. The token White character is Steve, a good looking publisher who is excruciatingly "politically correct"; he is "always asking if saying this would be offensive."

Indians and Whites Together

Only two groups included both Indian and White participants, and these each produced an interesting and rather different group dynamic. The male group included two Indian students, aged 19 and 20, whose favorite TV shows were *Friends, Seinfeld,* and "news"; and "cartoons," *Seinfeld,* and the Discovery Channel respectively. The White members were a 37-year-old student, who enjoyed *Seinfeld, ER,* and "news"; and a 23-year-old student who liked *Cheers, Seinfeld,* and *M*A*S*H.*

The group began amiably, with one member suggesting that the shared appeal of *Seinfeld* might make a good starting point, and agreeing that humor was the key. It was not long, however, before a little tension emerged. Most of the first few minutes is a dialogue between the two White men; the older man (T) then asks one of the Indian students, "What are you thinking, D?" He replies: "Yeah, comedy . . . but maybe something a little bit, kinda realistic." T replies that he only watches comedies; "I don't watch things like *NYPD Blue*." D counters with "Why do you watch comedies?" as the other Indian (W) mentions that he does not watch "that stuff" (serious drama) either. D, addressing T in a rather challenging way, asks, "Are those even realistic?" W seems to be trying to defuse the situation: "Ah, I'd imagine some are. They're different from our culture." D continues to address T: "Do you like to see your blood, guts, sex, all that? Do you like that?" The younger White man, J, makes a joke about trying to work all that into a comedy, and the group gets down to that task, again with the two White men doing most of the talking, and suggesting various scenarios for an ensemble show. Tension emerges again as the issue of ethnicity arises:

T(White):	We could have a White woman, and an American Indian . . . um . . . a White woman and an American Indian and an African-American and . . .
W(Indian):	Why?
T:	You know, just to add some diversity, and then we can just add the whole array of ethnicities, like a Hispanic landlord, or something like that.
W:	Or Asian.
T:	Yeah, or Asian, we could bring them all into this.
D (Indian, *sarcastically*):	Or maybe you could have a blind guy who doesn't know the difference between colors.

The two White men try to ignore the sarcasm, but the conversation struggles on uncomfortably as they try to address the issue of ethnicity:

J (White):	That'd be a good idea. Because that would emphasize the, kind of, almost like a . . . you can tell their ethnicity without even seeing

them or something, based on their behavior, or at least, that's where the jokes would lie. Not to make fun of, but to, eh, I guess make fun of it, it's a comedy.

T (White):	Yeah. Or we could do, eh, we could have a comedy, you know, like you were talking about, poking fun at some cultural stereotypes or something. You know. Unless that's a real sensitive issue to anybody here.
D (Indian):	Or poking fun at the White majority population. That'd be good.
T (White):	Yeah. And you know, like um . . . you know, I think a lot, you know, is that kind of a sensitive, is that a sensitive area, what eh, um, do you guys have . . . Are there, what are like some of the stereotypes you feel about White people that we can poke fun at?
D (Indian):	I don't know.
J (White):	It doesn't have to be all based on that but . . . you could just look at normal things that, uh, I guess normal things . . .
T (White):	That people make fun of each other.
J (White):	Than to slant them each way.
D (Indian):	Just to be humorous.
T (White):	Unless that's, you know . . . That's one area we can poke humor at. You know, we can switch gears completely and focus on something else, you know . . . that's kinda on a cutting edge type thing, I mean, and it could be kinda sensitive. Um, you know, we can switch gears completely and do some other type of humor.
J (White):	I think the best humor is from poking fun at characters . . . like *Seinfeld*, you poke fun at Kramer because of what he does or George because he's such a weasel . . . But sometimes these ethnic things get in there a little bit, it's not that major.
D (Indian):	Soup Nazi and . . . That's funny. The irony is funny, too.

The halting, cautious tone of the dialogue, peppered with frequent hesitations, is markedly different from the free-flowing discourse of the homogeneous groups. While it is apparent that in particular the personalities of D and T do not mesh well, it's also clear that their different worldviews are closely linked to their sense of ethnic identity. Left to themselves, I suspect that T and J, the two white men, would move into the kind of comfortable interplay that other White groups demonstrated, probably articulating the taken-for-granted whiteness of the other groups. The presence of the two Indian men prevents this, and seems to frustrate them. In turn, the two Indian men seem to want to address their sense of disempowerment, as the other Indian groups did, but express their resistance for the most part in sarcastic, conversation-derailing comments (D) or silence (W). Significantly, of the 13,900 words included in the entire session's transcript, 9,500 are spoken by T and J, while the two Indian men account for 4,400, a ratio of over 2:1.

The topic of ethnicity surfaces a few more times, as the group grapples with the need to include a "quota," as D puts it. Again, we see some irritation, as T tries to get them settled on the ethnicities of the "two guys and a girl" who will be main characters. There is some sentiment for the location being Colorado:

T (White):   Let's say, eh, guys that, from all over, that wound up converging for whatever reason, I mean, then they have their apartment there. How's that sound?

D (Indian):   Like White trash, trailer park type.

T (White):   Is that what you want? You want that?... Well, be sensitive here, don't go, try not to be getting too offensive ... just make it eh, you know a character, you know, just a character . . . we'll let the ethnicities . . . be just something aside. I mean . . . the show is the primary focus, the ethnicities are just coincidental, you know, and it doesn't have to be a White trash trailer park or anything like that,

cause I think, you know that carries some eh, you know, that's getting kind of offensive. Yeah, baggage and what not . . .

W (Indian):   I get you.

T (White):   So . . .

D (Indian):   I thought it was humorous.

T and J try to lead a discussion of the characters. Unlike any other group, it is suggested that each individual takes ownership of a character, "playing" them, in a way. T presses D on "his" character, an Indian male D named "Wookie," trying to get him to flesh out the character:

D: I guess he came from around here and he's out there soul searching.

T: OK, so he's from Duluth originally, you getting this J? . . . How old is he?

D: Eh, 22, 23.

T: OK, how long has he been out in Colorado?

D: Not too long.

T: A year, two years?

D: OK, right.

T: Um, is there anything . . . about this character that's kind of . . . humorous?

D: I don't know. Is there?

T: It's your character, I don't know . . . So, you want to think about it for a while, OK?

D: Sure.

They move on to J's character, Sonja, a Scandinavian girl. J begins describing her as a typical blonde, blue-eyed beauty, but then defensively checks himself:

J: . . . But I mean, good looking in the Norwegian hair, um, blue eyes, and that doesn't always constitute someone's good looking.

D: But it does for you.

J: No, actually not, it's not a given by any means, by me.

D: You like fat sows?

The discussion limps on, as various members of the group tackle one character or another. Everyone studiously avoids mentioning ethnicity as any kind of defining characteristic; it is simply agreed that two characters will be Indian males. J voices frustration at how unsatisfactory all the characters seem to be, provoking comments from the two Indian men:

D: The essence of a person, I mean, how do you capture it on TV?

W: Yeah, that's what I'm saying. How could you do it unless you get real characters?

T: Well, like, so you want to add more to your character?

D: Well, what else, what do we do? Maybe to everybody, how do we, how do you capture a person?

W: How do you make it seem like they really do exist?

Everyone seems to be aware that something is not quite working. Finally, everyone responds to D's deliberately off-the-wall suggestion that Wookie is a tattoo and body-piercing artist, who pierces Gil (the other Indian man's) scrotum, and causes infection. At last this is something all the men can relate to, and they engage in a long, animated debate about what would happen to a man's "sac" following this mishap, especially when his parents were coming to visit. This is followed by more discussion about the various characters, and the creation of vignettes involving Sonia as a veterinarian specializing in disturbed animals, or Stan as a frustrated chef. By the end of the session, the group has a set of essentially disconnected characters and some humorous, if also disconnected incidents, and the four part on apparently friendly terms. The lesson they all seemed to learn was that questions of ethnic identity are best avoided, in the interests of cordial relationships.

The female group was more successful in producing a coherent setting, plot-line, and cast of characters, although their show was not as fully-realized as most of the homogeneous groups. Their discussion was dramatically more cordial and collaborative than the men's. The group consisted of two Indian students, ages 19 and 23, from North Dakota and New Mexico respectively, both in Duluth for the College of Medicine summer program. The White participants were also students, aged 37 and 24, and not in the medical program. As a group, they did not know each other well before the meeting; in fact this was one of the two groups in which some members were meeting for the first time, having been brought together by mutual acquaintances. The group spent quite some time (almost 15 minutes) on "getting acquainted" conversation, discussing their favorite TV shows, and the qualities they look for in them. Finally, V, one of the two Indian women, suggests that they go around the table and introduce the type of show each would like to see. Comedies are suggested; when V speaks, she introduces the idea of a more "realistic" program:

V: I guess this is my dream, maybe something about maybe how people see each other by what color they are rather than the inside. I mean, that goes from like if they're big on the outside . . . and most of the nicer people are big, and people just judge people on that . . . I know I would want—maybe just because of my background—I know I would . . . watch.

This idea is taken up with enthusiasm, and it is quickly agreed that the setting will be a college campus, and that the focus will be on how minorities find acceptance hard. Unlike the male group, the women take on the issue head-on, and seem to agree to learn from each other:

P (White): Talking about Duluth, I was saying how I thought all the people were friendly and real nice . . . and this friend of mine I was talking to, um, was a minority and she looked at me really funny and I said, "Oh, isn't that how you've experienced Duluth," and she said, "no, not at all, the people are really, um, covertly prejudiced, you know." They don't necessarily come right out and say anything, but it's the underlying way they treat you and everything.

V (Indian):   I agree.

P: I've heard a lot of people say that about Minnesota in general.

V: I heard there was a lot of nice people... but um, coming from New Mexico where there's a large Hispanic and Native American population it was just so different. I mean, to this day um, like when we go to the mall, we just don't get service, we just don't. People just don't even say hi. That's a real big pain.

P: Up here or in New Mexico?

V: Up here.

D (White):   Really?

S (Indian):   Absolutely... I came originally from a reservation in North Dakota, and I've been around, I mean I'm attending college in Minnesota—Concordia—and I've experienced it all, with just no service. I mean, here I am, I smile and try to um, push away those stereotypes, I do my best to inform people that don't know about our culture... I mean, it's out there.

P: I dated some minorities when I was younger and just the things that my own family members would say to me... or people would stare at you sometimes... I just think that it's really awful for people to judge people... So that would be... do you guys want to do that?

S: Sure.

All four women began a spirited and friendly discussion of their own experiences of stereotyping and discrimination, making clear attempts to relate to each other, such as in P's story of leaving the blonde, blue-eyed world of Scandinavian Minnesota:

P (White):   I remember one time I went to New York, and a lot of people have dark hair and so I like really stuck out like

a thumb. It was just kinda different, because you're like used to being in an area where you kinda blend in, and all of a sudden... It didn't bother me... I just noticed it, because some of my friends said something to me.

S (Indian):   Would it have bothered you, I don't mean to be... I'm just saying hypothetically, what if somebody did say to you, "you have to have these," would it have occurred to you, I'm away from home, I'm in a different environment... What would you have done if they called you, "hey you blondie, go back to your own..."

P: ... like we talked about in this class, how impossible it would be to really put yourself in the other person's shoes because you just don't realize how much White privilege there is everywhere?

They talk about humor, and its potential to hurt, in detailed, personal stories:

S: I went to summer school to finish my first year... I was lonely and I was away from home and things and I'd get my mail and I overheard this conversation. This girl was taking a summer school class, they were studying Indians... I overheard It... um, they were literally mocking us, and it hurt me, it hurt me. As it is I was homesick... and they were saying things like, "What's the first thing you think of when you think of an Indian?" And he was saying savage Indian and hysterically laughing. And I was thinking... I have to be strong... that made me think that people literally think things are funny, but they don't think about it. Later... I approached them, and said how it had hurt me and things, and they literally switched around the story and they said they didn't mean any disrespect . . .

P:　　　　Good for you.

Every so often, the group works to apply these personal anecdotes to their TV scenario, as in an exchange about the sensitive issue of roommate allocation:

D:　　　　We could do a show, just on that, or on the roommate thing.

P:　　　　So who do we want for characters?

D:　　　　Well, we could have two women, I mean, one a Native American and one a White woman, and being roommates and just kind of trying to understand each other and deal with first year of college. That takes care of our characters that we need.

V:　　　　Or we could start the show with a student orientation and then you know, people are checking in with the dorm or whatever. And then go from there. Walking around, looking for a room or something.

P:　　　　And walking past a room and then maybe a minority in the room and thinking oh, my gosh.

S:　　　　And thinking, I hope that's not my roommate.

D:　　　　So, those are the thoughts running through the person's head. OK.

They discuss in detail the kind of town the college should be in, and raise various general scenarios that might be addressed, such as dating, interaction with professors, freshman orientation, and so on. Naming the Indian character provokes discussion, with suggestions that it might be a name that doesn't sound obviously Indian:

P (Indian):　Maybe like Lisa or . . . Lisa Johnson, Thompson, or . . .

S (Indian):　My friend's name is May, but her full name is Maymingwa.

P (White):　OK, Native American female's name. How do you spell that?

S (Indian):　I don't even know how to spell it. Means butterfly.

D (White):　Oh, it does?

P (White):　That's pretty.

The group discusses which reservation May comes from, and what her academic and professional goals are, before moving on to her White roommate:

V (Indian):　Ok, her name is Sara Smith.

S (Indian):　Geeze, I don't know.

P (White):　What's her background?

V (Indian):　Are we going to make her snooty or . . . really wealthy?

S (Indian):　I don't know, I don't want to be stereotyping . . .

P (White):　Would say successful . . . successful family who owns a local business in town.

D (White):　Sure, there you go . . . So her name is well known.

More details are provided for both Sara and May, who will butt heads and have preconceptions about each other, but will eventually learn to value their friendship. At one point, they briefly discuss how to identify the two characters:

V:　　　　Do you prefer to be called Anglo or Caucasian, or it doesn't matter? White?

D:　　　　Doesn't matter . . . I never thought of myself as anything really.

P:　　　　What do you guys prefer?

V:　　　　Personally it doesn't matter. I mean, Indian is fine, Native American or American Indian.

S:　　　　As long as they have respect. The main word.

This group was considerably more successful than the male mixed group. They produced a detailed setting on the college campus, calling the program

Rainbow Ties. Their two main characters were well-conceived, and both drew on the Indian and White members' personal experiences. Potential plots were rather weak and briefly described: "Then there'd be things about dating . . ." Most of their conversation consisted of personal narratives, which in themselves were very revealing about their experiences with ethnic diversity, and the kind of stereotypes that emerge in everyday life. While both mixed groups did not know their fellow members well, they each addressed this differently. The male group seemed consciously to avoid the obvious ethnic differences, producing stilted and sometimes hostile debate. The female group embraced the difference from the beginning, and through their discussion, they worked hard to see each other's point of view, exhibiting the collaborative style so often noted in female interaction (see chapter 3). They used the final 20 minutes or so to learn more about each other, not in terms of ethnicity, but rather in terms of personal history, career plans and so on, and parted on very friendly terms. Their TV program was less developed than most of the homogeneous groups, but that may be largely because of the need to establish a personal relationship; those groups that already knew each other well were exactly those who "got down to business" the fastest. For me, the very fact that we could not put together inter-ethnic groups of close friends was in itself revealing and a little discouraging.

Conclusion: Negotiating Identity in a Media World

We know that television does not mirror reality (nor do people want it to), but that it refracts back a sense of reality that speaks to people in different ways. *Seinfeld* became the most popular TV show in America, not because it literally resembled the lives of its White, urban fans, but because it created a sense of recognition among them. *Seinfeld* never developed an audience among African-Americans, and it did not succeed in Britain, either. And for the mainstream American majority, there are countless opportunities to recognize themselves, and the genres that tell the familiar tales. As Livingstone (1999) writes, "Media cultures provide not only interpretive frameworks, but also sources of pleasure and resources for identity-formation which ensure that individuals . . . have a complex identity of which part includes their participatory relations with particular media forms" (p. 100).

The program scenarios created by the White participants in this study told tales that with varying degrees of creativity, felt quite familiar, reflecting their own taste for mainstream sitcoms. The main players were people like them, and they pulled from a wide cultural repertoire in which people like them might interact. They had difficulty placing their required Indian characters in their scenarios, and they were largely unable to develop their personalities. They drew heavily on media-generated stereotypes of nobility and stoicism; even when they consciously attempted to subvert those stereotypes, they did not know how to "write" the characters. This is particularly striking when one remembers that northern Minnesota, where the study was done, has a fairly significant Indian population, unlike many regions in the United States. As the Indian groups' discussion indicated (and in fact as the current occupations and career plans of the Indian participants showed), Indian people are to be found everywhere in the region, in any number of settings, yet to many White people they are apparently invisible.

For the Indian participants, the media world is clearly one they must negotiate. Although some did like popular sitcoms, the range of their favorite TV programs was quite different, with news and sport getting mentions, and appreciation for fish-out-of-water sitcoms like *Fresh Prince*. Several appreciated the *Star Trek* series, in which cultures often collide. Their scenarios spoke vividly about how it feels to be an outsider, and they revel in the chance for Indians to be the stars, and the winners. Their White characters, although often unsympathetic, and certainly at times stereotypical, are drawn from the personal experience of living as an Indian in a White world, and not so much from media images. The same can be said for their Indian main players—they are acutely aware of the prevailing Indian media stereotypes, and reject them angrily, in a way that speaks volumes about being marginalized in a world of alien media imagery.

I conceived this study as an attempt to extend the study of media reception in creative directions, striving for what Ang (1996) calls "an ethnographic *mode of understanding*" (p. 72, italics in original). One way to do this is to move away from confronting specific texts, finding ways to "back into" the question, as I have tried to do here. This study was not about how specific "audiences" respond to specific images, but rather was an attempt to explore how people construct their notions of reality by using imaginative tools that are largely given to them through mediated images. If White groups were largely unable to imagine Indians in non-stereotypical ways, it is not simply because they have watched *Dances with Wolves*. It is more because their cultural tool-kit contains only a limited array of possibilities, which have worked together over time and across media to produce a recognizable cultural "script" about Indians. *Dances with Wolves* contributes to that script; so do *Dr. Quinn*, Indian dolls, toy tomahawks—you name it. For most White Americans, to live in a media world is to live with a smorgasbord of images that reflect back themselves, and offer pleasurable tools for identity formation. American Indians, like many other minorities, do not see themselves, except as expressed through a cultural script they do not recognize, and which they reject with both humor and anger.

Notes

1. While the designation "Native American" is also widely used, I will use "American Indian," which is preferred in Minnesota.
2. Latest data show that in spite of revenue derived from gambling operations in some states, the overall living conditions for American Indians have declined, with unemployment over 50 percent on many reservations (Associated Press 2000).
3. I am indebted to Renee Botta and Carolyn Bronstein for sharing an unpublished paper using a similar methodology. In quoting transcripts, I do not attribute statements, except when quoting group exchanges, when initials are used to distinguish contributors.
4. Thousands of Indian children were forcibly removed from their families and educated in government-funded boarding schools, from the nineteenth century into the second half of the twentieth, with the goal of "cultural assimilation."

References

Ang, I. (1996). *Living Room Wars: Rethinking Media Audiences for a Postmodern World*. New York: Routledge.

Ashley, J., and K. Jarratt-Ziemski. (1999). Superficiality and Bias: The (Mis)Treatment of Native Americans in U.S. Government Textbooks. *The American Indian Quarterly* 23(3–4): 49–62.

Associated Press. (2000). Casino Revenues Haven't Helped Most Indians. *St. Petersburg Times,* Sept. 3: A17.

Baird, R. (1996). Going Indian: Discovery, Adoption, and Renaming toward a "True American," from *Deerslayer* to *Dances with Wolves*. In *Dressing in Feathers: The Construction of the Indian in American Popular Culture,* edited by S.E. Bird. Boulder, CO: Westview Press.

Berkhofer, R. (1979). *The White Man's Indian*. New York: Vintage Books.

Bird, S.E. (1996). Not My Fantasy: The Persistence of Indian Imagery in *Dr. Quinn, Medicine Woman*. In *Dressing in Feathers: The Construction of the Indian in American Popular Culture,* edited by S.E. Bird. Boulder, CO: Westview Press.

Bird, S.E. (1999). "Gendered Representation of American Indians in Popular Media." *Journal of Communication* 49: 3, 61–83.

Bobo, J. (1995). *Black Women as Cultural Readers*. New York: Columbia University Press.

Churchill, W. (1994). *Indians Are Us: Culture and Genocide in Native North America*. Monroe, ME: Common Courage Press.

Cohen, J. (1991). The "Relevance" of Cultural Identity in Audiences' Interpretations of Mass Media. *Critical Studies in Mass Communication* 5: 442–54.

Davis, L. (1993). Protest Against the Use of Native American Mascots: A Challenge to Traditional American Identity. *Journal of Sport and Social Issues* 17(1): 9–22.

DeLoria, P. (1999). *Playing Indian*. New Haven: Yale University Press.

Drotner, K. (1994). Ethnographic Enigmas: The "Everyday" in Recent Media Studies. *Cultural Studies* 8(2): 341–57.

Francis, D. (1992). *The Imaginary Indian: The Image of the Indian in Canadian Culture*. Vancouver: Arsenal Pulp Press.

Hanson, J.R., and L.P. Rouse. (1987). Dimensions of Native American Stereotyping. *American Indian Culture and Research Journal* 11(4): 33–58.

Lind, R. (1996). Diverse Interpretations: The "Relevance" of Race in the Construction of Meaning in, and the Evaluation of, a Television News Story. *Howard Journal of Communication* 7: 53–74.

Livingstone, S. (1999). Imaginary Spaces: Television, Technology, and Everyday Consciousness. In *Television and*

Common Knowledge, edited by J. Gripsrud. London: Routledge.

Northrup, J. (1995). Indian Issues Column. *Duluth News Tribune*, July 26: 7A.

Shiveley, J. (1992). Cowboys and Indians: Perceptions of Western Films among American Indians and Anglos. *American Sociological Review* 57: 725–734.

Taylor, A. (1996). Cultural Heritage in Northern Exposure. In *Dressing in Feathers: The Construction of the Indian in American Popular Culture*, edited by S.E. Bird. Boulder, CO: Westview Press.

Thompson, L. (1990). *Ideology and Modern Culture: Critical Social Theory in the Era of Mass Communication*. Cambridge, UK: Polity Press.

Whitt, L. (1995). Cultural Imperialism and the Marketing of Native America. *American Indian Culture and Research Journal* 19: 1–32.

Woodward, K. (1997). *Identity and Difference*. London: Sage.

17.
"DO WE LOOK LIKE FERENGI CAPITALISTS TO YOU?"

Star Trek's *Klingons as Emergent Virtual American Ethnics*

Peter A. Chvany

The Imperial Klingon Forces, a nonprofit *Star Trek* fan club that advertised itself on the Internet recently, can be reached in care of a residential address at an apartment in Grand Forks, North Dakota.[1]

The prospect of Klingon warriors overrunning the United States from a secret base near Grand Forks probably fails to strike terror into the heart. I am aware of no recent calls for Klingon self-determination, repatriation, or insurgency. *Star Trek* fans, even those as much attracted to the shows' violent warrior races and explosive interstellar conflicts as to its messages of humanist tolerance, are not widely noted for their actual violence. And as a friend to whom I outlined this article reminded me, one obvious problem with treating Klingons as an American "ethnic" group is that they are fictional. Anyone who calls him- or herself a Klingon—and many do—does so in limited contexts, at *Star Trek* conventions or within the discursive subspace of an Internet/Usenet newsgroup. The "real" ethnic identity of such individuals always proves to be something else. Like National Guardsmen, rather than the Michigan Militia, Klingons are warriors late at night, on weekends, or in moments stolen at the terminal on the job. They can distinguish a fantasy identity (and politics) from their real lives, even if to other *Trek* fans the militaristic rhetoric of some sectors of Klingon fandom comes across as "quasi-ss style."[2]

Yet at the 1994 annual symposium sponsored by Education for Public Inquiry and International Citizenship (EPIIC), an undergraduate research program at Tufts University, Benedict Anderson noted that several competing factions in the bloody Bosnian ethnic crisis were buying arms with money raised through Internet solicitations. These appeals successfully targeted American and Canadian "ethnics" who identified with one or another Bosnian group attempting to "cleanse" the others, or to resist such cleansing. In North American terms, Anderson implied, the amounts raised were trivial: a few million dollars here and there. But those North American dollars, contributed by interest groups whose connections to the contested homeland were primarily emotional and nostalgic, and who were not at risk when the ordnance they funded did its work, had considerably more buying power on the European market, in "the homeland," than they had back "home" in North America. Anderson's study, *Imagined Communities,* had argued that the New World nation-states of the nineteenth century—and by extension, modern ideologies of nation and nationalism—were narrative byproducts, indeed fictions, of modern print capitalism. Now he extended his argument into the perilous techno-politico-cultural territory of the late twentieth century, where ideas of "the nation," "homeland," "kinship," "true faith," and "blood ties" are as effective and deadly as ever, maybe more so, despite—or because of?—the notorious uncertainties of "postmodern" identity categories. The Internet, that new frontier whose transformative potential had begun to seem a matter of market hype, figured in Anderson's discussion as a very real site of emergent political struggle, a multimedia late-capitalist textual space through which resurgent nationalisms create and disseminate their community self-conceptions, effectively defying both the liberal ideology of harmonious pluralism and the supposed impossibility, in the postmodern era, of taking simply defined ethnic identities seriously any more.

I call Klingons-who likewise throng the Internet—"American ethnics" with this serious set of stakes in mind. I court what Renan called the "grave mistake" of confusing ethnicity with nation, and of attributing to a mere "ethnographic" group the sovereignty of "really existing peoples," in order to investigate the productive lessons of deliberate ethnic misreading.[3] If Klingons are not an ethnic group, as seems obvious, then what are ethnicity's criteria? If it is a self-elected denomination, as we assume when we respect the polite custom of calling each ethnic group what *it* asks us to call it, then would we take *Star Trek* fans in leather armor, latex ridged-forehead masks, and long scraggly wigs seriously if they began to wear their regalia in public, or on the job, and demanded recognition? Would we politely serve them our best imitation *qagh*?[4] Is ethnic nationalism primarily a modern phenomenon that arises as a result of, or in reaction to, the growth of modern capitalist nation-states, as Anderson and many others argue? Or should we follow Anthony Smith's tactic of crossculturally investigating the historical underpinnings of ethnic differentiation, in a belief that while *nationalism* is "a wholly modern phenomenon," it "incorporates several features of pre-modern *ethnie* and owes much to the general model of ethnicity which has survived in many areas until the dawn of the 'modern era'"?[5] Are ethnic groups best understood as having recognizable, distinct, unique cultures with their own cultural contents, or should ethnicity be regarded as one of the cultural discourses that polices the borders of "otherness," borders defined by the differences between one group and another, not the unique identity of either group alone?

I argue that ethnicity is a socially structured performance of contradictory ideological fictions.

I propose that we look at Klingons as "ethnics" precisely because their group identity *is* fictional and has a traceable history of recent origin, yet is nonetheless the object of debate, ongoing revision, and (re)construction. The shifting, seemingly accidental character of Klingon "identity" sheds light on contemporary popular and theoretical debates about ethnicity as a category of social difference. Like a mathematical "limiting case" that reveals the behavior of a function under non-routine conditions, Klingons test commonsense assumptions about the nature of ethnicity. They exist outside ethnicity as people ordinarily experience it, since they exist outside reality entirely. Yet emergent Klingons are not *purely* fictional: they appear in living bodies at *Star Trek* conventions, hold Internet discussions, have a language and culture, and participate in the same political and cultural processes as other ethnic groups do—perhaps doubly so, since they participate both "in character" and "out of character." As emergent, marginal, and virtual ethnics (in the sense both of the "virtual" space of the Internet and of the physical sciences—"virtual" photons form the image in a mirror), Klingons allow us insight into the processes by which ethnic fictions acquire their peculiar form of reality in the daily lives of real people. I will discuss how and why the fictionality of those ethnic fictions, the staginess of their performances, gives way to belief in their reality, to conviction, to "identity." Klingon ethnicity is a new American ethnicity; the more interesting question is: where does it fit in the existing, complex scheme of American identities? Who are these emergent American ethnics? Are they truly new at all, or an old group in new clothing?

Ethnic Notions: Klingons on Screen

Literary critic Werner Sollors provides one of several recent reminders that ethnicity, around the world but perhaps especially in the United States, is an "ambiguous and elusive" term. Its slipperiness relates both to its use as a "safety valve" deflecting Americans (and people elsewhere) from discussing better-defined but more troublesome issues (race, power relations, class, gender, sexuality) and to the real contradictions of US and world cultural diversity.[6]

Sollors attempts to make sense of US ethnic confusions by refraining ethnicity in terms of conflicting languages of "consent and descent" that have been employed by groups from around the globe who "consented to become . . . Americans" but wished to preserve distinct descent-based heritages.[7] This approach leads him into difficulty in discussing groups who did *not* so consent (Native Americans, African slaves, conquered Mexicans), and occasionally betrays an urge to simplify ethnic contradictions rather than accounting fully for their complexity. But it has the value of highlighting experiential and cultural similarities across group faultlines and of foregrounding the relational quality of ethnic construction, the fact that one must first compare ethnicities to contrast them.

In America, the idea of ethnicity can refer to the "national" origins of people who immigrated primarily from Europe after the mid-nineteenth century: Irish Americans, Italian Americans, Polish Americans, and so on. Tellingly, earlier Germans, "Dutch," and Scots are generally considered part of the dominant "Anglo" "majority," even if they arrived relatively recently.[8] Ethnicity can also refer to religious groups, such as Jewish Americans, who may be identified (or self-identify) more with their traditions than with their nation of origin.

The idea of "ethnicity" is less commonly ascribed when the difference from the supposed norm is a matter of "race," as with Americans of African or indigenous descent. On the other hand, the Modern Language Association-affiliated Society for the Study of the Multi-Ethnic Literature of the United States (MELUS) tends to generalize the term to such "racial" groups. The case of Asian Americans is still less clear. The long-standing, starkly dualistic, "black or white" quality of "race" relations in the United States leads even many contemporary "multiculturalist" scholars to forget that American society never was only a matter of black and white. Asians have clearly faced devastating oppression, but some historians and critics find that oppression's character difficult to judge while the difference between "race" and "ethnicity" remains murky.[9] Chicanos and other people of Hispanic descent often suffer similar theoretical neglect. Like the category "Asian," the category "Hispanic" obscures some sharp internal differences—cultural, linguistic, or historical—by concentrating on one or two similarities such as language, or by ignorantly

conflating disparate groups.[10] Yet "ethnicity" and "race" *can* function synonymously: Sollors reminds us that "before the rise of the word 'ethnicity,' the word 'race' was widely used. . . . The National Socialist genocide in the name of 'race' is what gave the word a bad name and supported the substitution."[11]

Once "ethnics" come to the attention of "mainstream" Americans, concerns about their status often focus on issues of language, which is regarded by many as a primary site of acculturation or resistance—witness the debate in the mid-1990s over "Ebonics" in Oakland, California. Finally, despite the position taken by critics like Sollors who see "race" as a special category of "ethnicity" rather than the other way around, the obvious bodily differences of physical appearance so dear to racist thinking often play a key role in ethnic differentiation even when race is otherwise believed not to be a factor.

Klingons, insofar as they exist, qualify as "ethnic" on all of these counts. Their appearance, especially since the first of the *Star Trek* films in 1979, marks them as non-"white," indeed nonhuman: their bony forehead ridges betoken both a beloved *Trek* tactic of inexpensive alien-making and a routine *Trek* conflation of cultural differences with visible, physical ones.[12] But even in the less high-budgeted original show, Klingons bore signs of racialized body typing. They were universally goateed and mustachioed, at a time when facial hair was most obviously associated with the Beats, and the Beats with jazz and black culture. They sported dark makeup: the color of a Klingon soldier glimpsed briefly in the early episode "Errand of Mercy" varies obviously from "blackface" to "whiteneck," and many other Klingon faces are smudgy, as if the bootblack were melting in the studio lights. And they were played, in two of three starring appearances in the first series, by actors of "ethnic" heritage known for playing "ethnic" roles: John Colicos as Kor in "Errand of Mercy," Michael Ansara as Kang in "Day of the Dove." The exception was William Campbell as Koloth in "The Trouble with Tribbles." Not coincidentally, this was the episode in which Klingons were least threatening, most humorous, and yet most strongly marked by a bodily difference that "told." The episode's Klingon spy who "passes" as a (somewhat swarthy) human aide-de-camp is discovered because tribbles, creatures that coo for all humans and some Vulcans, squawk when brought near him, as they do around all Klingons. Internet *Star Trek* fans claim that when Colicos "was called to play the part of Kor . . . the Cold War was going on, and the general thought was that of the Russians versus US. He suggested to the makeup artist to make him a futuristic Mongol."[13]

In more recent years, with the casting of African American actor Michael Dorn as the continuing Klingon character Worf, the racialized representation of the Klingons took a turn toward the domestic black Other rather than the swarthy foreigner. Klingons had become allies, rather than enemies, of the show's "United Federation of Planets," and the orphaned Worf had been raised on earth by (Russian Jewish) foster parents. The show's resulting "playing in the dark" did not lead to simplistic "black" stereotypes: Klingons also acquired a warrior code reminiscent of samurai *bushido* and ritual swords that might be variants on Middle Eastern scimitars.[14] Like Mr. Spock before him, or his contemporary crewmate Data—the android who wished to become human—Worf offered screenwriters an opportunity to investigate "human nature" by contrasting human crew members with nonhuman others, who usually proved "human" at heart. Such contrasts were all the more dramatically powerful the more nuanced the nonhuman Other in question.[15] But stereotypical ideas about blackness nevertheless affected the ethnic construction of Klingon nature in important ways. Although several guest Klingons were played by white actors (for example, entertainer John Tesh in "The Icarus Factor," or Worf's mate, played by Suzie Plakson), black actors were considered for Worf "mainly to simplify the application of the dark Klingon makeup."[16] The original series' Klingon darkness had thus passed into the realm of natural fact; or, to restate Hollywood's curious racist logic, the best actor for a once-"Mongolian" part is a black man. Dorn's commanding presence also seemed responsible for encouraging the show's production staff to imagine Klingons as sexually potent, emotionally demonstrative, physically threatening (but fully in control of their physicality), and in touch with a genuine, uncomplicated "masculine" identity and spirituality,

even when they were female—attributes that had not been routinely combined in earlier representations of Klingons but that *are* routine components of the white imagination of African Americans, especially black men. A *TV Guide* article on guest Klingon James Worthy, the black basketball star, commented at length on his "stealthy moves, leonine grace, and . . . reputation as a gentle soul," traits all paradoxically appropriate to his transformation into the "surly, ferocious Klingon named Koral."[17] The paradox betrays a standard white racist longing for a perceived black authenticity, an erotic admiration of black bodies, and a complex fear of and attraction to cathartic black violence.[18]

But because even the white dominant cultural imagination is contradictory and multivalent, because Klingon ethnic construction had a prior history not limited to "the black image in the white mind,"[19] and because the extended histories and personnel changes of series television and serial film production lend themselves to the creation of formal and narrative counterdiscourses, there have been other notable (if problematic) aspects of Klingon "ethnicity." The sixth *Star Trek* feature film, *The Undiscovered Country,* extended the old clichéd analogy between the Klingon Empire and the Soviet Union by imagining the Empire beset by energy crises and pollution, and open to both perestroika and détente with the Federation. In the same film, audiences were treated to Klingons with a wide range of skin tones, including Christopher Plummer's Orientalized General Chang, David Warner's relatively light-skinned Chancellor Gorkon, Dorn as Worf's grandfather, and background characters who ranged from off-white to dark black. Whether this increase in Klingon diversity indicated a renewed awareness in Hollywood of *Soviet* or *American* multiethnic complexity is less telling than the differentiation itself. Its offhanded pluralism played against its bizarre assumption that a Klingon named "Chang" might look vaguely "Asiatic" and enjoy tormenting our heroes by quoting Shakespeare while launching torpedoes at them. Was the audience expected to laugh at the stereotyping or with it, or accept it unconsciously, or all of the above? Meanwhile, casual dialogue in one 1988 *Next Generation* television episode hinted that some

Klingons—or screenwriters—considered their difference from humans a matter of religion, asking Worf to join their insurrection against Federation "infidels" and Klingons who had too willingly acculturated to human norms. The Klingon rebels represented this mistake as a relinquishment of "birthright" in the biblical language of Jacob and Esau, but countered it with language reminiscent of the American popular conception of Islamic jihads ("Heart of Glory").[20] Later dramatizations of Klingon ritual and religion examined quasi-Buddhist (or Sufi? Hindu? Catholic?) meditation practices and starvation-induced visionary experiences. The Klingon culture-hero Emperor Kahless was resurrected in clone form like a postmodern Arthur ("Rightful Heir"), an allusion further strengthened late in 1995 when Worf and Kor (now an old ridge-headed man rather than a young blackfaced future-Mongol) went in search of Kahless's thousand-years-lost sword on an episode of *Deep Space Nine*. Thus throughout *Star Trek*'s history, Klingons have been markedly different from the Federation/human norm, despite the complex web of specific differences they have signified. But even in being different their culture has paralleled real human cultures at every turn.

Ethnic Notions: Klingons in the Virtual Real World

Perhaps the most interesting factor in the representation of Klingon "ethnicity," however, is the Klingon language. Developed to add verisimilitude to the opening sequence of the first feature film (so that Klingons fleeing a menacing interstellar cloud entity could be translated in subtitles, like other non-English-speakers), Klingon became unexpectedly realistic when Paramount hired an academic linguist, Marc Okrand, to create something suitable. Okrand took the task seriously, attracting the attention not only of *Trek* fans but of other linguists. Thus at present, Klingon represents one of the most visible *Trek* subcultures. The Klingon Language Institute, for example, is licensed by Paramount; publishes a quarterly journal, *HolQeD* ("Language Science"), which is registered with the Library of Congress and abstracted in the Modern Language Association International

Bibliography; boasts an international membership; sponsors a language course through the mails; and is translating the Bible and *Hamlet* into Klingon. But the Klingon Language Institute is only the tip of a Klingon chuchHuD. Because Okrand's *Klingon Dictionary* is available in the extensive *Star Trek* sections of most chain bookstores, Usenet newsgroups devoted to fan culture, Klingon or otherwise, now feature a small but noticeable number of bilingual or wholly Klingon postings.

The Klingon Dictionary cheekily suggests that to study a language, even a created one, *is* to study a recognizable and distinct "culture," promising that one can "learn to speak Klingon like a native" even as the indicia (dis)claim that "this book is a work of fiction."[21] The text contains many in-jokes, like the fact that the word for the pesky "tribble" is pronounced "yick." But the introduction also employs sophisticated mock-sociological discussions of ethnic differentiation for comic effect, for example noting that "the word for *forehead* . . . is different in almost every dialect," presumably because Klingons' forehead ridges vary greatly.[22] Such moments, though intentionally amusing, repackage certain real-world ideologies of ethnicity in apparent seriousness. For example, the differences among the many Klingon dialects are said to have imperial stakes, since upon succession "the new emperor's dialect becomes the official dialect. . . . Klingons who do not speak [it] are considered either stupid or subversive."[23] In effect, political discrimination on the basis of a simultaneously linguistic and bodily difference—if the dialect and the forehead *do* go together—is so fundamental to "human nature" that Okrand imagines it applies universally to aliens as well.[24]

Science fiction fans who dislike *Star Trek* often point to such assumptions as evidence of the franchise's failure of imagination: *Trek*'s aliens never really think in nonhuman ways. *Trek* fans, on the other hand, proceed in their Internet postings to create an imagined Klingon community largely in accordance with such assumptions. Bison, a fan who wrote recently on the newsgroup alt.shared-reality.startrek.klingon (a space for collaborative fan fiction writing), referred to another fan's created character as a "halfbreed."[25] On the one hand, this remark alluded to fan debates about the smooth-foreheaded Klingons of the original series: they can be regarded as Klingon-human "fusion" hybrids bred by the Empire for use as intermediaries in dealings with the Federation, or overlooked as reflecting real-world budgetary constraints and thus without relevance to the series' internal chronology.[26] But Bison also echoed terrestrial attitudes about "mulattos" and other people of "mixed" descent, who are often believed to be unsure of their identity and to experience automatic rejection by both "parent" groups. The other fan's Klingon-Vulcan hybrid character "would never be accepted" by real Klingons, Bison opined. "Besides," he or she went on, "Klingons and Vulcans cannot procreate but Klingons and Romulans can."[27] This last remark illustrates the powerful certainty fans can bring to bear on topics that, properly speaking, no one can really have a definitive answer to. Since Vulcans and Romulans are pointedly defined in *Star Trek* as closely genetically related, one might expect Klingon interbreeding with either race to amount to the same thing.[28] But Bison believes otherwise and renders a definitive judgment that other fans must somehow respond to. Such certainty illustrates how contemporary real-world ideologies about ethnicity can powerfully constrain the fan imagination of topics which are supposedly marked by science fiction's limitless possibilities. Likewise, an FAQ for the international Klingon Assault Group (a "frequently-asked-questions" document many newsgroups post periodically to help acquaint new users with key terms and procedures) echoes the language of much contemporary "ethnic" writing when it remarks that "the first step" in joining the organization "is to determine whether you have the KLINGON SPIRIT in your heart and soul." Such language represents Klingon identity in terms of an authentic, interior feeling even as it goes on to explain that "your ship's Genetics Engineer [i.e., a sponsoring fan] can assist you in creating or purchasing facial appliances for the ridges"—which is as clear and conscious a statement of the material nuts-and-bolts mechanics of Klingon ethnic "construction" as any academic theorist could labor to uncover.[29] The coexistence of what cultural critics call "essentialist" and "constructionist" perspectives in such statements—the tension between

Klingonness as "being" and as "becoming"—should not be a surprise by itself. Critic Diana Fuss, among others, has commented on how even radically anti-essentialist theories such as "deconstruction" often depend on displaced, repressed, or unexamined essentialisms.[30] But key questions remain. Is it only because Klingon identity is so *obviously* "constructed" that fans think about it in "constructionist" terms? How important is the idea of a Klingon "heart and soul" to these fans? Would they define "real" ethnicities as *only* matters of heart and soul, and not of historical construction and "shared-reality"?

Often, the implicit answer seems to be yes. On the other hand, many fans regard their meaning-making and role-playing activities with a mixture of playfulness and skepticism that allows them to challenge the ideological content not only of "canonical" *Star Trek* product, but of other fans' discourses and, self-reflexively, of their own. To be interested in Klingons might signal a kind of resistance to cultural authority all by itself, since the series' Klingons are uneasy allies at best, and frequently "the enemy"; where Klingon fan culture is concerned, everyone chooses to be an outsider to some degree. Ael t'Arrilaiu, pseudonymous author of an FAQ for the alt.shared-reality.startrek.klingon group, defines her character with coy anti-essentialist self-consciousness as "Half Rihannsu [Romulan], Mostly Jewish, touch of Klingon Blood." She cautions those who would create interesting characters for others to interact with to "Get real? Er, as real as Trek can be."[31] Ael describes herself as a Romulan double agent who admires Klingons and works secretly to promote their Empire. At the same time, she cautions neophyte writers not to react "personally" to other fans who write in character, advising that "if someone offends you" the best course is to "try and make peace."[32] This is not the most obviously "Klingon" of sentiments, but it is repeated by Trekkan in the FAQ for the Klingon Assault Group. Although KAG members enjoy "go[ing] to fan conventions and intimidat[ing] other species," they also "help charities with food and blood drives" and stress "communication, cooperation and participation" rather than the no-holds-barred Klingon aggressiveness depicted on television.[33] A recent fan discussion on the alt.startrek.klingon newsgroup that raised the question of whether "Klingons were basically Russians in space, and Romulans were essentially Chinese" ended by having compared Klingons to Arabs, Vikings, Japanese, Soviets, feudal Europeans, and African Americans; Romulans to ancient Romans (or Greeks) and Japanese; Vulcans to Chinese, Arabs, Romans, and Greeks; Cardassians to Nazi Germans or Israelis (depending on whether the Bajorans they once oppressed are read as Jews or Palestinians); Ferengi to Arabs and Jews.[34] The obvious point—which at least one fan made—is that in all this, the heroic Federation stands in for the American view of itself. But if this is true then why do many Americans (and some fans outside the United States) want to be Klingons? If there is an "ethnic identity" under construction here, it is being negotiated in a number of different ways. Fans' interests and desires neither vary so much that they can be called purely "individual," nor fall into such neat categories that they can be pigeonholed as "racist," "ethnocentric," or even strictly "American."

On the other hand, while there are dedicated *Star Trek* watchers of all races and ethnicities, the active "fan" community *is* predominantly made up of "white" folks. The list of non-US countries that post to Klingon newsgroups tends to confirm this: Northern European or European-colonized locations like the United Kingdom, Canada, Finland, Germany, the Netherlands, Sweden, and Australia predominate. As critic Daniel Bernardi has noted, between the 1960s and the 1990s *Star Trek* has moved from "a liberal humanist project that is inconsistent and contradictory" to an equally inconsistent but noticeably less liberal "backlash trajectory . . . drawing heavily on the discourse of whiteness and the politics of neoconservatism."[35] How much fan whiteness matters—and what whiteness itself is, ethnically speaking—are thus key concerns. How should we regard an emergent ethnicity that emerges from a social space so strongly bounded by prior ethnic and political realities?

Like Ferengi Capitalists? Klingon Ethnicity and Whiteness

In "DissemiNation," postcolonial theorist Homi K. Bhabha discusses a split, in the production of nationhood through narrative, between "the continuist, accumulative temporality of the pedagogical, and the repetitious, recursive strategy of the performative."[36] We might restate Bhabha's remarks as a comment on the fact that while nations and ethnic groups typically conceive of their existence as a linear progression through historical time, individuals acquire and experience their own ethnicity in the day-to-day performance of ethnic ritual and life. Bhabha's point may help explain why Klingon identity is so powerfully clear to *Star Trek* fans. Fans often write as if that identity were well-understood and stable, though their own activities challenge and transform it. They often see it as invested with profound and clear significance despite its fictionality, its complexity, and its lack of historical depth. Klingons, as an imagined community, are not particularly numerous and have "traditions" only some thirty years old. Yet this is nearly the age the United States had reached as a nation by the date of the Louisiana Purchase, roughly the age of the contemporary concept of Chicano/a ethnic identity (as distinguished from older, less politically-charged ideas of "Mexicans" or "Mexican Americans"), and roughly my own biographical age. This is time enough for repetitious, recursive performances of even a wholly "fictitious" identity to take on an experiential "reality." Many people watch television programs as often as their forebears attended church; given reruns, perhaps more so. Television creates a shared media culture; ethnicity is a cultural process: thus there is a potentially "ethnicity-generating" character to watching television. The question becomes: how does TV-mediated ethnicity relate to the construction and performance of better-known ethnic identities?

In some ways, the relationship is quite direct. French sociologist Pierre Bourdieu has analyzed the processes by which individuals gain a *sens pratique,* a preconscious "feel for the game" of cultural norms. People take corresponding "dispositions" within a cultural "field"—sets of behaviors that feel natural and inevitable, because they are learned in the course of intensely personal life-histories, but which often prove to be strikingly alike for individuals in similar race, class, or gender positions within the larger society. These dispositions can extend to the way people perform and transform the norms of a culture not in actual existence. For example, actor Michael Dorn has attributed his success in gaining the part of Worf to his prior fannish familiarity with the codes of Klingon conduct. On auditioning, Dorn notes, "I did not wear makeup . . . but I took on the psychological guise of a Klingon. I walked into Paramount in character. No jokes. No laughing with the other actors. I sat by myself waiting for my interview. When my turn came, I walked in, didn't smile, did the reading, thanked them, and walked right out."[37] In Bourdieu's terms, Dorn had the right disposition for the part, a combination of inner feelings and outer mannerisms. But he had acquired that disposition without the benefit of growing up Klingon or belonging to a real community. His knowledge came solely from TV and film.

Curiously, however, Dorn emphasized Klingon traits that were not predominant in John Colicos's inaugural urbane-barbarian turn as Kor, William Campbell's cheery Koloth, or Christopher Lloyd's wisecracking Kruge of *Star Trek III: The Search for Spock*.[38] The prior Klingon interpretations closest to Dorn's were Michael Ansara's Kang—a commander under highly unusual stresses—and Mark Lenard's stoic starship captain of the brief opening moments of *Star Trek: The Motion Picture*. But Dorn substantially revised even these portrayals. Like Bison, he had a fannish certainty about Klingon identity and ran with it, bodying forth a complex character in part because he threw aside the wider range of Klingon personae that had been available. His interpretation might make sense *only* for Worf, the orphan, "the only Klingon in Starfleet": an alien military officer who tries to fit in among humans who believe his race to be overly emotional and violent, who practices strict self-control—much like a black actor trying to fit into a predominantly white entertainment industry that holds similar beliefs about African Americans. But Dorn's performance has become the template for later actors and fans.[39] Such paradigm shifts occasionally overtake even real-world ethnic dispositions: consider the sudden hatlessness of American men after John F. Kennedy's hatless inaugural. And thus such dispositions amount to considerably more than "walking the walk and talking

the talk." They remind us that walking and talking are complex, socially-conditioned, learned activities, however obvious and natural they later come to seem. Belief and behavior systems that are originally "ideological" categories, like class membership or ethnicity, naturalize themselves through socially learned individual performance. "Culture turn[s] into nature," and what feels most personal can also be a clear mark of one's group identity. The opposition between individual and group itself is revealed as frequently false.[40]

Similarly, Okrand's *Klingon Dictionary* provides a guide to the pronunciation of Klingon consonants. The text's claim that "the Klingon government . . . has accepted English as the lingua franca" shows why I call Klingons "American" ethnics: the American insistence that the world speak our language is here universalized.[41] But Okrand also frequently warns that "gh" or "H," "q" or "Q" are "not like anything in English" and can only be approximated by sounds from German or Yiddish, or Mexican Spanish or Aztec. And no matter how hard they try, the text claims, "very few non-Klingons speak Klingon without an accent."[42]

These statements are reminiscent of Bourdieu's discussions of class-marked speech habits and the power of social distinctions to shape individual behavior.[43] Linguists like Okrand have shown that the range of sounds produceable by the human speech apparatus is greater than the range of sounds used in any single language or dialect. But the study of multilingual persons shows that past a certain developmental age, most people have difficulty hearing, and learning to properly produce, sounds not recognized as significant in either their "native tongue" or their regional or class dialect. This limitation can be partially overcome by long, hard practice, as actors learn. But that fact in turn suggests that one's own speaking voice, ordinarily counted among the most personal and immutable bodily facts, is likewise the result of early learning and practice, during which the codes of the social environment become internalized and alternative possibilities are excluded.[44] To return to Bhabha's point: behavioral markers of class, nation, or ethnicity, whatever their real or imaginary history, are also a matter of repetition, recursively reproducing that history as lived experience. Internet Klingon fans frequently query each other about the availability of videotapes illustrating combat techniques for the Klingon *batlh'etlh,* the "honor sword." Practicing the *batlh'etlh*—tapes *are* available—may be practicing a martial arts fiction. But it is through precisely such bodily performances that ordinary "ethnic" habits are acquired and become indistinguishable from one's own most genuine persona.

While such a line of argument suggests that Klingon ethnicity is a real quality worth talking about, listing behaviors that characterize Klingons as "ethnics" ignores a cardinal insight of recent anthropological and theoretical studies of ethnicity: that ethnicity is often determined not by the racial, religious, linguistic, or cultural content of each ethnic group but by *relations* among groups, and by the *value* placed upon perceived ethnic differences. As Thomas Hylland Eriksen puts it: "only in so far as cultural differences are perceived as being important, and are made socially relevant, do social relationships have an ethnic element. . . . Ethnicity refers both to aspects of gain and loss in interaction, and to aspects of meaning in the creation of identity. In this way it has a political, organisational aspect as well as a symbolic one."[45] Given this perspective, the ethnic character of Klingon culture becomes less obvious. The crucial issue is not that Klingon ethnicity is "fictional," since every ethnicity is fictional in much the same way, but that we must reinsert Klingon ethnicity in the web of relationships of its social surroundings.

Star Trek is largely a product of the dominant culture. Thus its fans tend to affiliate themselves with the dominant-culture understanding of which groups qualify as "ethnic" and what "being ethnic" means. This tendency powerfully influences fannish activity, whatever a fan's individual position with respect to US society. Thus Klingons are neither understood as an ethnic group by the majority culture nor, as participants in that culture, do Klingons understand *themselves* as ethnics. The nonidentification of Klingons as a group is more a matter of *Star Trek* fans' own self-conception than of the invisibility and hostility often visited upon other, better-defined marginalized groups. If there is any widely identified social

subgroup Klingons belong to, it is "Trekkers."[46] This group *is* often stigmatized in the popular imagination for overindulging in escapist pop-culture pursuits. But Trekkers themselves remain mainstream. Witness the parade of *Trek*-related popular magazine covers, the eight films, the five television series, and the culture industry of both "canonical" (i.e., Paramount-sponsored) and gray-market fan paraphernalia. Trekkers are not a "colonized" people *as* Trekkers. They are not systematically "dichotomized" by the mutual processes of insider/outsider differentiation noted by sociologists of ethnicity. The differences from the mainstream that remain are "undercommunicated" in everyday interactions: no one much cares if you dress like a Klingon in the privacy of your own home, or even at a convention, though other hotel guests are apt to stare.[47] Once you take off the costume, no one can tell you from a mere mortal.[48] The resulting lack of a sense of major stakes in interactions between fans and non-fans makes Trekkers, or Klingons, only an "emergent" ethnicity; ethnicity is not quite ethnic when its boundaries are so vague and the stakes so low.

Furthermore, ethnic borders are difficult to cross despite the internal "dispositional" changes which can and do take place within any given ethnicity—recall how Michael Dorn's dispositional changes to Klingon behavior only made Klingons seem more like who Dorn himself was, a black man among a mostly white crew. The prior ethnic context from which Klingon fans emerge is again crucial. So who are the Trekkers, ethnically speaking? Do they have an ethnic identity of their own, or not? Though there are certainly African American, Asian American, and Chicano *Trek* fans, as well as non-men, non-straights, non-Americans, differently abled people, and so on, the science fiction audience is noticeably whiter on average, speaking strictly of skin color, than the population at large. Having investigated the nature of ethnicity, its status as something fictional that nonetheless has powerful social effects, we are in a position to understand that fan whiteness is not merely a coincidental or easily changeable aspect of *Trek* culture. Whiteness as a *cultural* space, not merely a pigmentation, marks many of the assumptions and activities of the fan community.

Henry Jenkins, an academic and fan who has studied "media fandom" in an openly "ethnographic" manner, but also as an insider, understands media fans not as passive consumers of mass culture but as "textual poachers" who employ complex reading and revising strategies to transform their experiences into acts of cultural production and pop reconstruction.[49] Fans, according to Jenkins, "raid mass culture, claiming its materials for their own use, reworking them as the basis for their own cultural creations and social interactions. . . . Unimpressed by institutional authority and expertise, the fans assert their own right to form interpretations, to offer evaluations, and to construct cultural canons. . . . [T]hey often are highly educated, articulate people who come from the middle classes."[50]

As a long-time *Star Trek* fan, I can't help but agree with Jenkins's assertions. But what group can afford to raid mass culture with such confidence, or to be "unimpressed by institutional authority," which is for many other groups an overwhelming consideration? Klingon fan activity represents a triple "investment"— a psychological commitment to representations of Klingon bodies and culture, the "dressing-up" activity of Klingon identity-construction (perhaps similar to the intense labor of "drag" performance), and the investment of time and money serious fan pursuits require. Thus, acting Klingon requires prior access to capital, whether the "cultural" or the ordinary economic kind.[51] Middle class white Americans, *or* those committed to pursuing that group's dreams of economic autonomy and a de-ethnicized, "assimilated" cultural life, remain more likely on average to possess such advantages. Klingon fandom is not just something engaged in mostly by white fans: it is a choice of interests much more available to those already in possession of, or seeking, "white" middle-class social identity.

In this light, claiming Klingon identity is a less unproblematically positive gesture of anti-mainstream activity. While fans' textual poaching should indeed be read as politically progressive in its refusal to bow to Paramount's corporate control of the *Star Trek* canon, there is nonetheless something politically suspicious about mostly white fans mimicking the performance of a black actor who played an alien

who was under considerable pressure to assimilate back into a human (i.e., white) cultural norm. Acting Klingon expresses an acknowledgment of the empty compromises of identifying with the dominant culture. But at the same time it provides relatively advantaged members of society a claim to marginalization without relinquishing their relatively greater access to power. Writing on the political significance of drag in gay male culture, Carol-Anne Tyler has investigated a similarly problematic double bind. Male appropriation of behaviors and styles that the dominant culture codes as "feminine" can both signal a positive identification with women by marginalized gay men and reflect continuing male privilege to appropriate from the disempowered. Such double binds do not tell us that all men (or whites, or straights) are "in power" so much as they caution us against believing that any group is as disempowered as it is sometimes comforting to believe. What counts is the complex and shifting structure of each relationship between people or groups, rather than an absolute hierarchy.

Klingon fans, whose rhetoric of spiritualism and masculinity recalls the "men's movement," are indeed reminiscent of the genuinely self-questioning but still privileged white men's movement participants discussed in Fred Pfeil's recent study *White Guys*. They tell us as much about middle class self-doubt and political disengagement as about the creation of a culture that could function as a genuine alternative to dominant culture, as many fans believe it already does. Pfeil finds that both the emotional attractions of the men's movement and its political limitations correspond to those of a broad range of alternative cultural movements. A common characteristic of all these groups is "the extent to which political identities are conceived . . . first and foremost as *cultural* identities."[52] Such groups show a "tendency to leap over history for myth, the polity for the tribe." Pfeil believes this tendency reveals an underlying "inability to understand social relations and social change in terms of historically and structurally constituted relations of power."[53] Such movements, that is, respond to a growing awareness of contradictions in late capitalist society which make it desirable to work out new relationships among social groups and even to transform society at large. But they persistently mis-recognize the solutions to these crises as needing to arise primarily, even exclusively, from the creation of new "cultures" or the recovery of fanciful precapital-ist "identities," which may have been genuine in the past but can now only be put into play as market-ing niches. As a result, "alternative" cultures end up creating commodities that big business sells back to them at a substantial markup. Similarly, if you've ever priced a good "working phaser" at a *Star Trek* con-vention, the feeling that your love of imaginative play has been turned into a weapon against your pock-etbook (probably by another fan who shares your passions) is a familiar one. It does not necessarily prevent you from cooperating in your own impover-ishment by buying one; the urge to acquire the ma-terial trappings of one's cultural difference, however little different one really is in one's daily behavior, has itself been successfully promoted by contemporary mainstream society.[54]

In applying such critiques to Klingon fan culture I do not accuse *Star Trek* fans of falling prey to "false consciousness"—at least not more so than anyone else. Few who know me well would miss the irony in my posing as a disinterested critic of *Trek* fan culture rather than a very deeply "invested" fan. But irony is certainly also at work in Trekkan's FAQ for the Klin-gon Assault Group, which proudly declares that the organization charges no membership dues—after all, "do we look like Ferengi Capitalists to you?"—but notes that members must "create or purchase their own Uniforms," and that ship quartermasters "often can sell Uniforms to ship members at a substantial discount."[55] A kind of pyramid scheme haunts such remarks. But *no one* in contemporary society is entirely free of such profit motives; no one can be secure while failing to think in terms of personal ben-efit, even the academic critic who writes his fannish experience into his professional work. But clearly, one need not look like a Ferengi to act like a capi-talist. Nor will donning Klingon garb and profess-ing warrior virtues, by itself, replace one's white or middle-class social role with something significantly different. Failing to understand how one's activities take place within the constraints of contemporary market forces and ethnic realities, even when the

activities seem most freely and "individually" chosen, or most in accordance with some deeply felt "heri-tage," means relinquishing paramount opportunities for transforming the situation. One lesson of fandom may be that groups with primarily culturalist aims are more likely to make people *feel* better than to make the world better: not a pointless gain, but arguably not a lasting one either.

So whither Klingon—or white—"ethnicity"? Isn't it at least significant that *Star Trek* fans, white or otherwise, are rethinking the terms of whiteness itself? Surely it is. But in what direction is the domi-nant culture around those fans moving, and does fan activity resist that culture's pressures and refuse its enticements, or merely find friendlier accommoda-tions with them? Another science fiction text of the early 1990s is considerably less confident than the *Star Trek* franchise and its fans about the wisdom of searching for ever-more-fragmented cultural "identi-ties." In his novel *Nimbus,* published in 1993, science fiction author Alexander Jablokov uses the biblical story of the Gileadites and Ephraimites, who could distinguish each other because they pronounced the word "shibboleth" differently, to outline the manipula-tion of ethnic identity in a postindustrial future where "artificial ethnic groups" could be created by pros-thetic mental modification, high-tech brain surgery. "Tie their [ethnic] identity to simple speech accents," one character tells another, "and let all the other arti-ficial ethnic groups identify them that way, and have an emotional reaction. . . . We can fiddle with Ruma-nian pronunciation and create five different groups within the city of Kishinyov in a matter of weeks."[56] In Jablokov's universe, such ethnic conflicts *have* in-deed been promoted, during a series of wars at the turn of the twenty-first century. The breakdown of society into smaller and smaller groups, which Pfeil identifies as a hallmark of the culturalist response to high-tech postmodernism, has accelerated, in Jablo-kov's universe, to the point where a group called the Messengers manifests its difference from main-stream humanity not only by communicating in a privately developed language, but by outfitting their foreheads with surgically-implanted skull ridges to mimic a supposed descent from Neanderthals. They might almost be Klingons—or Klingon fans taking the next step in making their fannish identity real. But at the same time, in Jablokov's vision of the future, the obscure imperatives of profit wreak their usual havoc on what's left of human freedoms. The number of ethnic conflicts around the world, and the intensity of ethnic conflict, has increased. But money is still being merrily made by those who have the power to cheerlead and profit from such disasters. Cultural fragmentation benefits those in power far more than it does those who see such fragmentation as a form of resistance.

In short, Jablokov's future looks a great deal like the times in which he wrote about it. As Benedict Anderson has noted, the era of high-tech ethnic conflict, and high-stakes profitmaking from it, is *now.* Without committing the science-fictional sin of believing that Jablokov's grimly clever predictions will inevitably materialize, we should notice that what he imagines as necessary for the construction of artificial ethnicities is a set of technological refinements on processes *already* at work: cybernetic devices to program the human brain to believe in concepts it can already program *itself* for, bodily modifications already implicit in gender-change operations, facelifts, and the burgeoning "cultures" of body art and body piercing. The time when Klingon fans might willingly elect to undergo such modifications in order to improve their performance of a lifestyle that promises relief from postmodern stresses, that promises to make them not-white without subjecting them to the discrimination faced by people "of color," may not be far off. Surely such moves would meet with the usual anti-Trekkie derision. But whether this would be anything other than so many pots calling kettles "black" as they practiced their own ethnic self-delusions is, given the fact that we are only fantasizing here, impossible to determine.

Notes

1. The title of my essay is quoted from Trekkan's KAG FAQ (Klingon Assault Group Frequently Asked Questions) postings (Online posting, Newsgroup alt.startrek.klingon, posted 2 January 1996, accessed 4 January 1996 and "Re: KAG FAQ," Online posting, Newsgroup alt.startrek.klingon, posted 3 January 1996, accessed 4 January 1996). Author has not responded to request

for permission to cite. Internet newsgroup postings for which I have secured express authorial permission to cite are annotated in the notes accordingly. I have attempted to contact all Internet authors and have given those who responded an opportunity to comment on this article. Thanks for assistance in preparing this essay are due Henry Jenkins, who validated the study of *Star Trek* fan culture and pointed the way; Dr. Lawrence M. Schoen of the Klingon Language Institute, and Elliott McEldowney for alerting me to its existence; Shannon Jackson and J. Martin Favor, for suggesting the use of performance theory in the study of ethnicity; and Susan Gorman, Dan Shaw, Kim Hébert, Greg Howard, Min Song, Kathleen Gillespie, Juliet Cooke, Jed Shumsky, and my parents and siblings, who have been listening to my theories about Klingons for years, when not offering their own.

2. SkullBuddy, "Re: What Is KAG . . . ?" (Online posting, Newsgroup alt.startrek.klingon., posted 2 January 1996, accessed 4 January 1996). Author has not responded to request for permission to cite.

3. Ernest Renan, "What Is a Nation?," trans. Martin Thom, in *Nation and Narration,* ed. Homi K. Bhabha (New York: Routledge, 1990), 8.

4. According to *The Klingon Dictionary, qagh* is a "serpent worm (as food)," a delicacy portrayed on *Star Trek: The Next Generation* as best eaten live (Marc Okrand, *The Klingon Dictionary: English/Klingon, Klingon/English,* rev. ed. [New York: Pocket Books, 1992], 183). *Star Trek's* fascination with the Klingons' diet as a classic sign of their racial/cultural difference owes a clear debt to ethnology; it may likewise signify a race-and-class-marked transgression of social "distinctions" (in Pierre Bourdieu's sense) that mark Klingons as (often gleefully) déclassé, arid, unassimilated.

5. Anthony D. Smith, *The Ethnic Origins of Nations* (Cambridge: Blackwell, 1986), 18.

6. Werner Sollors, *Beyond Ethnicity: Consent and Descent in American Culture* (New York: Oxford University Press, 1986), 5.

7. Ibid., 6, 7.

8. Of course even this definition of "the majority" may reflect a dominant-culture perspective. German Americans, we should recall, sometimes faced severe ethnic discrimination during the world wars. "Scots" were identical to "Anglo-Saxons" for Thomas Dixon, the Scottish American author of *The Clansman* (1905)—but Dixon was a virulent negrophobe whose word should perhaps not be taken as gospel. Historian Leonard Pitt notes that the upper-class Mexican Vallejo brothers, captured by troops of the 1846 "Bear Flag

Rebellion" initiated by US adventurers in California, regarded a black prison guard as both an "Anglo" and a "blackguard" in the colloquial sense, for daring to "use the word 'greaser' in addressing two men of the 'purest blood of Europe!' " (Leonard Pitt, *The Decline of the Californios: A Social History of the Spanish-Speaking Californians, 1846–1890* [Berkeley: University of California Press, 1966], 27). Mexican social codes, though not race-blind, drew different distinctions from those of the United States: the Vallejos also moved in social circles with Pío Pico, a Californian territorial governor whose grandmother was a "mulatta" and who himself was dark-skinned (Robert L. Carlton, "Blacks in San Diego County: A Social Profile, 1850–1880," *Journal of San Diego History* 21[4] [1975]: 11). The question of whose codes applied to Pico and the Vallejos, and when, is thus not simple. Similarly, contemporary Chicano/a critics have highlighted the ludicrousness of representing Mexicans as "foreigners" to the vast US territory wrested from Mexico. Thus it is unasked questions of who constitutes "the majority" and who "the outsiders" that often constitute the crux of ethnic conflict.

9. Theodore Allen has opened a useful way out of such disabling impasses by suggesting a focus on oppression first and the forms it takes second. He goes on to make a provisional distinction between "racial" and "national" oppression according to whether oppressors suppress or cultivate differences within an oppressed group. See *The Invention of the White Race* (New York: Verso, 1994).

10. For a brief discussion of contemporary conflicts over the naming of communities of Spanish descent in the United States, see Ramón Gutiérrez and Genaro Padilla, "Introduction," in *Recovering the U.S. Hispanic Literary Heritage,* eds. Ramón Gutiérrez and Genaro Padilla (Houston: Arte Público, 1993), especially 17–18.

11. Sollors, *Beyond Ethnicity,* 38.

12. Many of *Trek*'s alien races since the 1980s are distinguished by similar facial "appliances," which create a more thorough visual estrangement than the pointed ears of the Vulcan Mr. Spock or the antennae and blue makeup of the original show's Andorians. Bajorans, featured prominently on *Deep Space Nine,* have only a set of ridges across the bridge of the nose, whereas "Morn," a regular at the same show's interstellar casino, sports an elaborate head appliance which conceals all but the actor's eyes. Meanwhile, on *Voyager,* the visible sign of Commander Chakotay's Native American heritage is a large tattoo across his left temple. The major races discussed in the remainder of this article are summarized as follows:

Race	Physical Features	Cultural Features
Klingons	forehead ridges	warlike
Vulcans	pointy ears	logical, stoic
Romulans	pointy ears	emotional, stoic
Ferengi	big ears, bumpy heads	greedy capitalists
Cardassians	gray skin, neck tendons	military state
Bajorans	nose ridges	mystics

13. Todd Hansen, "Re: Klingons = Russians?," Online posting, Newsgroup alt.startrek.klingon, posted 5 December 1995, accessed 4 January 1996. Author has given permission to cite.

14. See Toni Morrison, *Playing in the Dark: Whiteness and the Literary Imagination* (Cambridge, MA: Harvard University Press, 1992).

15. Science fictional play with differences that turn out to be estranged similarities is a hallmark of the genre and by no means limited to *Star Trek.* But each incarnation of *Star Trek* has exerted tremendous narrative pressure on its nonhumans to humanize, perhaps revealing a specifically American preoccupation with normalizing and regulating social difference and assimilating pluralities (though other ideological pressures are certainly at play as well). Thus the assimilationist "melting pot" paradigm usually takes precedence over the pluralist "salad bowl," despite *Trek*'s widely lauded (and lately deplored, by some vocal Internet critics of *Voyager*'s white female captain and black Vulcan security officer) multiculturalism. The wider field of science fiction is relatively less preoccupied with this theme. Narratives abound in which alienness is preferable to "humanity," or in which human nature undergoes radical change, or in which alien and human remain irreducibly different (though not necessarily antagonistically so).

16. Larry Nemecek, *The "Star Trek: The Next Generation" Companion,* rev. ed. (New York: Pocket Books, 1995), 20.

17. Deborah Starr Seibel, "Klingon for a Day," *TV Guide,* (Oct. 16, 1993): 30.

18. By contrast, the visibly "black" men of recent *Star Trek* productions have been more obviously conceived in an overcautious, polite attempt *not* to play any "race cards." La Forge of *The Next Generation* evinced callow asexuality and even helpless victimizability (as in "The Mind's Eye" and the film *Generations*). *Deep Space Nine*'s Sisko, the station's commander and the show's nominal star, until the last few seasons of the series' run faded into the ensemble. His increasing prominence since the 1995–96 season went hand in hand not only with his character's promotion to captain but with a change

of appearance toward the character the actor (Avery Brooks) portrayed on *Spenser for Hire:* the mysterious black sidekick Hawk, who played out white private eye Spenser's aggressive impulses. My black male students have commented on the contradictions of white liberal politics apparent in such facts, noting ruefully that while two "brothers" were stars on *The Next Generation,* one pulled double minority duty as a blind man, one was concealed behind an alien mask.

19. See George Fredrickson's classic study *The Black Image in the White Mind: The Debate on Afro-American Character and Destiny, 1817–1914* (Hanover, NH: Wesleyan University Press, 1971).

20. A later two-part episode explicitly *titled* "Birthright" renewed the implicit connection between Worf and Data, nonhumans whose emotional struggles best revealed the American understanding of "human nature." Interestingly, both characters' problems seemed to lie in the masculine subjectivity of men who lack father figures, and thus male traditions and role models, in a Hollywood renarration of the "men's movement." For comparison, when Dr. Crusher attended the funeral of her grandmother she wandered into a gothic romance in which a ghostly and lascivious alien life form attempted to seduce her, as it had several centuries' worth of her maternal line ("Sub Rosa"); *Star Trek*'s vision of a "women's" tradition?

21. Okrand, *The Klingon Dictionary,* 1, 4.

22. Ibid.

23. Ibid.

24. The role of physical appearance in motivating ethnic and racial oppression remains debated; for some strong refutations of its importance, see Allen's *Invention of the White Race,* or George Fredrickson, *White Supremacy* (New York: Oxford University Press, 1981). Both studies cite the different racial histories of the United States and the Caribbean as evidence disproving claims that the races "naturally" find each other distasteful.

25. Bison, "SB EPSILON: PERSONEL [*sic*] BIO: Barok Vorkithic," Online posting, Newsgroup alt.shared-reality.startrek. klingon, posted 12 November 1995, accessed 13 November 1995. Author has not responded to request for permission to cite.

26. The *Deep Space Nine* episode "Trials and Tribble-ations" (1996) raised this issue only so that Worf could brusquely dismiss it as something Klingons do not discuss with outsiders.

27. Bison, "Barok Vorkithic."

28. The original-series episode "Balance of Terror" established this relationship to highlight the pitfalls of racism: a crewman who believed that the Vulcan Mr. Spock might be a traitor, when the *Enterprise* crew discovered that Romulans looked like Vulcans, was later saved from death by Spock during a battle with a Romulan vessel.

29. Trekkan, KAG FAQ.

30. See Diana Fuss, *Essentially Speaking* (New York: Routledge, 1989).

31. Ael t'Arrilaiu [Heidi Wessman], "A.SR.S.K FAQ ver 1.0," Online posting, Newsgroup alt.shared-reality.startrek. klingon, posted 2 December 1995, accessed 7 December 1995.) Author has given permission to cite.

32. Ael t'Arrilaiu [Heidi Wessman], "UPDATED A.SR.S.K FAQ (ver. 2.0)," Online posting, Newsgroup alt.shared-reality.startrek.klingon, posted 2 December 1995, accessed 6 December 1995.) Author has given permission to cite.

33. Trekkan, KAG FAQ.

34. See note 12 for a description of the various alien races. Dan Joyce, "Klingons = Russians?," Online posting, Newsgroup alt.startrek.klingon, posted 5 December 1995, accessed 4 January 1996. Author has given permission to cite.

35. Daniel Leonard Bernardi, "The Wrath of Whiteness: The Meaning of Race in the Generation of Star Trek." Ph.D. dissertation, University of California, Los Angeles, 1995, 28, 29. This dissertation was published under the title *"Star Trek" and History: Race-Ing toward a White Future* (New Brunswick, NJ: Rutgers University Press, 1998).

36. Homi K. Bhabha, "DissemiNation: Time, Narrative, and the Margins of the Modern Nation," in *Nation and Narration,* ed. Homi K. Bhabha (New York: Routledge, 1990), 297.

37. Nemecek, *The "Star Trek: The Next Generation" Companion,* 20. At a convention I attended in Denver in late 1988, Dorn reported that he was excited when his agent told him that Paramount wanted to cast a Klingon: his agent did not know what Paramount was talking about, but Dorn put him at ease because he felt he knew exactly what to give them.

38. Campbell's appearance as a Klingon commander is especially interesting since he had, a season earlier, appeared as the bratty infant alien superbeing Trelane ("The Squire of Gothos"), who manifested himself as a kind of twenty-third-century Liberace—not the image one now has of a Klingon warrior, but nevertheless somewhat present in Koloth's easy banter.

39. Leah R. Vande Berg, "Liminality: Worf as Metonymic Signifier of Racial, Cultural, and National Differences," in *Enterprise Zones: Critical Positions on Star Trek,* ed. Taylor Harrison, Sarah Projansky, Kent A. Ono, and Elyce Rae Helford, (Boulder, CO: Westview Press, 1996), 51–68.

40. Pierre Bourdieu, *Distinction: A Social Critique of the Judgement of Taste,* trans. Richard Nice (Cambridge, MA: Harvard University Press, 1984), 190.

41. Okrand, *The Klingon Dictionary,* 10. As critic Leah R. Vande Berg has noted, "cultural imperialism—and not multiculturalism—is the dominant discursive position affirmed" in the *Trek* universe (Vande Berg, "Liminality," 65).

42. Okrand, *The Klingon Dictionary,* 14, 13.

43. See Bourdieu, *Distinction,* 190–93, for one discussion of the various ways class tastes become "embodied."

44. In other words, while it is true that all people from Boston are individuals, and that not all have "Boston accents," it is also true that many Bostonians have very strong Boston accents, not because of their ethnicity or their genes but because the Bostonian speech environment (which crosses race, class, and gender lines) is so influential.

45. Thomas Hylland Eriksen, *Ethnicity and Nationalism: Anthropological Perspectives* (London: Pluto, 1993), 12.

46. Fans generally prefer "Trekkers" to "Trekkies" since it does not sound like a diminutive or like "groupies" (for further discussion of this point see John Tulloch and Henry Jenkins, *Science Fiction Audiences: Watching "Doctor Who" and "Star Trek"* [New York: Routledge, 1995], 11); given the logic of English grammar it also positively suggests someone engaged in an activity—worker, builder, swimmer, Trekker—rather than a passive recipient of mass culture. Fan resistance to the "Trekkie" label is obviously reminiscent of conflicts between "insider" and "outsider" labels for other marginal groups. As a fan somewhat suspicious of fans' keen sensitivity to outsider criticism, cavalierly dismissive as it often is, I often refer to myself as a Trekkie, perhaps like progressive gay and lesbian activists who have appropriated the term "queer" as a positive marker, but perhaps also like African Americans who use the word "nigger."

47. Eriksen, *Ethnicity and Nationalism,* 27, 21.

48. The case of the *Whitewater* juror who wore her Starfleet uniform to court remains unique, as far as I know, and has excited considerable debate in fan circles. Many *Trek* fans side with the mainstream and believe that her bringing fiction into reality in such a way was distasteful. This fact suggests that we will not be seeing Klingons outside fan space anytime soon.

49. Henry Jenkins, *Textual Poachers: Television Fans and Participatory Culture* (New York: Routledge, 1992), 1.

50. Ibid., 18.

51. Here I am extending some remarks Bourdieu makes on the dual investment involved in the way individuals acquire cultural competence: "It is in no way suggested that the corresponding behavior is guided by rational calculation. . . . Culture is the site, par excellence, of misrecognition, because, in generating strategies adapted to the objective chances of profit of which it is the product, the sense of investment secures profits which do not need to be pursued as profits" (*Distinction,* 85–86).

It would, of course, be unwise to push the analogy of Klingon performance with "drag" too far without knowing whether fans in their warrior dress are ever physically attacked in the way transvestite and transgendered people often are. Given the "look" of Klingon costuming, the more appropriate parallel would clearly be with leather/biker cultures: the performance is of a "masculine" rather than a "feminine" role. On the other hand, my (outsider's) impression of the leather image is that it usually lacks a "camp" dimension that *Trek* costuming can probably not help provoking in a non-Trekker audience, while camp *is* associated with transvestism to some degree.

52. Fred Pfeil, *White Guys: Studies in Postmodern Domination and Difference* (New York: Verso, 1995), 210.

53. Ibid., 225.

54. This is a good example, in a *Star Trek* context, of what the Italian Marxist thinker Antonio Gramsci called "hegemony": the process by which dominant culture entices willing obedience rather than compelling it from the unwilling.

55. Trekkan, KAG FAQ.

56. Alexander Jablokov, *Nimbus* (New York: Avon, 1993), 160.

SECTION IV

TECHNOLOGIES AND INSTITUTIONS

The media rarely (if ever) operates as a completely isolated or autonomous force in the world. Its activities inevitably intersect with those of other powerful institutions in ways that reflect a complicated network of influences and tensions, alliances and oppositions. This section explores a variety of ways that the media's interests connect and/or collide with those of other significant institutions (government agencies, elite cultural gatekeepers, technological/industrial standards, etc.) around the politics of race.

There's an old saying that "the camera never lies," which speaks to the widespread cultural assumption that the various technologies involved in photography (cameras, film, lighting, etc.) merely capture and reproduce the natural world as it really is. Richard Dyer's essay, however, reveals not only that the camera routinely "lies" when it comes to race, but that the technological apparatuses in question were deliberately and self-consciously designed so as to favor white subjects over those of other races. Much as problematic racial hierarchies are embedded into the very foundation of other major institutions (education, the family, the law, etc.), they are also inscribed into the industrial standards of media technologies.

One of the most important political issues for any marginalized population (racial or otherwise) is the struggle over that group's systematic exclusion from the dominant culture's elite institutions. With respect to race in the United States, people of color have routinely been un(der)represented in history books, art museums, the literary canon (and so on) in ways that make it appear as if all the truly important contributions to the culture have come from whites. Herman Gray's essay offers a nuanced analysis of one major breakthrough for black America on this front: Wynton Marsalis's installation as the first artistic director for the Lincoln Center's jazz program. Gray celebrates the political significance of Marsalis's appointment as a long overdue recognition of jazz as an aesthetically important musical genre, while also recognizing the problematic ways that this honor simultaneously reinforces the ongoing marginalization of other equally valuable black cultural practices.

People and institutions in positions of relative privilege will often invoke the notion of "colorblindness" as a dubious rhetorical gambit aimed at maintaining a sharply hierarchical racial order. Because race shouldn't matter, the argument goes, we should actively ignore its existence: a move that, not surprisingly, works against efforts to call attention to systematic forms of institutional racism. Grant Farred's essay looks at how the "post-racial," colorblind marketing philosophy of the National Basketball Association was effectively shattered by the on-court success of Yao Ming, a Chinese national who played center for the Houston Rockets. Farred maps out the complicated (and convoluted) ways that Yao simultaneously helped fulfill the league's desire to expand its presence (and profitability) into new global markets, while also exposing the league's claim to have "transcended" race for the "colorblind" lie that it actually was.

Dwight McBride's pointedly polemical essay looks at a different form of racialized institutional branding: the fashion aesthetic cultivated by clothier Abercrombie & Fitch and its forceful celebration of an exceptionally well-to-do—and exceptionally white—leisure-oriented lifestyle. McBride's analysis articulates the ways that Abercrombie & Fitch's efforts to promote and sharpen its brand manifested themselves across a broad range of the corporation's business practices, including its public advertising and marketing campaigns, its employee training manuals, and its discriminatory hiring practices.

In 1995, Hurricane Katrina made landfall on the US Gulf Coast, flooding the city of New Orleans and leaving tens of thousands of people—mostly poor blacks left unaccounted for in the city's evacuation plans—stranded and homeless. Michael Eric Dyson's essay examines the way that this "natural" disaster—one of the most devastating in US history—was not natural at all. While the hurricane in and of itself was beyond human control, a variety of intersecting institutional forces—from racist urban planning to stereotypical media representations, from overindustrialization of the Louisiana wetlands to a woefully inadequate and undermaintained levee system—combined to magnify the massive loss of life and livelihood that the storm brought to impoverished people of color in New Orleans.

George Lipsitz's essay examines the moral panic over hip-hop music as it manifested in a series of mid-1990s congressional hearings about the music and its alleged role in the spread of urban drug use, gang-related violence, and deteriorating city centers. At the core of Lipsitz's argument is the recognition that these hearings effectively made scapegoats of impoverished black youth by casting them as the root cause of social and economic problems for which they were actually the primary victims, while drawing attention away from the disastrous corporate and government policies—policies related to housing, education, law enforcement, and economic (dis)investment—that were the more salient causes of the social ills in question.

Carol Stabile's essay comes from a larger book project that maps out the history of crime journalism in the United States as an institution singularly dedicated to maintaining a tightly structured social order in which noble white men are understood to be the worthy protectors of vulnerable, virtuous white women against the ever-present threat of violent black men. The real world, of course, is nowhere near as simple or predictable as this narrative makes it out to be, and real crimes "fail" to fit this androcentric, white supremacist frame on a regular basis—and yet, as Stabile's research demonstrates, mainstream journalism sticks to this narrative with astonishing persistence. Crimes that fit this frame are reported faithfully—and even sensationalized—while crimes that fail to do so go largely uncovered.

18.
THE LIGHT OF THE WORLD
Richard Dyer

A television company is about to shoot a panel discussion before a studio audience. The producer, from the control room, is discussing with the floor manager in the studio how the audience looks in his monitor. The producer says something about the number of black people at the front of the audience. 'You're worried there are not too many whites obviously there?', asks the floor manager. No, says the producer, it's nothing like that, a mere technical matter, a question of lighting—'it just looks a bit down.'

This exchange occurred in the preparation of a programme about the street fighting that took place in Handsworth, Birmingham, in September 1985, fighting that was largely understood to be about race and which was the most vivid and controversial of many such incidents throughout Britain that year. The exchange was recorded by the Black Audio Film Collective and included in their film *Handsworth Songs* (1987),[1] which explores the cultural construction of 'race riots'. That construction is embedded in part in the professional common sense of media production, two items of which are registered in this exchange.

One item, which is less germane to the subject of this chapter, is that of 'balance'. The floor manager cannot at first understand what the producer is getting at. Is it perhaps the racial composition of the audience in numerical and representative terms? The topic of the programme has been constructed as race riots, and to have 'balance' one has to think in terms of sides and ensure that equal numbers on each side are represented. This lies behind the floor manager's remark about there perhaps not being 'enough white people obviously there', and the producer understands what he is getting at. However, it is not what concerns him or us here, whereas the second notion at play in the exchange goes straight to the heart of the matter.

For the producer it is a purely aesthetic matter. The image looks 'down': dull, dingy, lacking sparkle. There is no reason to presume he is saying this because he finds black people dislikeable or uninteresting. He is, in the terms of professional common sense, right: shoot the scene in the usual way with the usual technology with that audience and it will look 'down'. The corollary is that if you do it the usual way with a white audience, it will look 'up', bright, sparkling. What I want to explore in this chapter is how this comes to be and what it signifies.

What is at issue is an aesthetic technology. The producer is making a statement about the formal quality, the look, of a setup. The technology he is using and the habitual ways of using it both produce a look that assumes, privileges and constructs an image of white people.

All technologies are at once technical in the most limited sense (to do with their material properties and functioning) and also always social (economic, cultural, ideological). Cultural historians sometimes ride roughshod over the former,

unwilling to accept the stubborn resistance of matter, the sheer time and effort expended in the trial
and error processes of technological discovery, the
internal dynamics of technical knowledge. Yet the
technically minded can also underestimate, or even
entirely discount, the role of the social in technology. Why a technology is even explored, why that
exploration is funded, what is actually done with
the result (out of all the possible things that could
be done with it), these are not determined by purely
technical considerations. Given tools and media do
set limitations to what can be done with them, but
these are very broad; in the immediacy and instan-
taneity of using technologies we don't stop to consider them culturally, we just use them as we know
how—but the history, the social inscription, is there
all the same.

Several writers have traced the interplay of
factors involved in the development of the photographic media (e.g. Altman 1984, Coleman 1985,
Neale 1985, Williams 1974) and this chapter is part
of that endeavour. I am trying to add two things, in
addition to the specificity of a focus on light. The
first is a sense of the racial character of technologies, supplementing the emphasis on class and gender in previous work. Thus just as perspective as an
artistic technique has been argued to be implicated
in an individualistic world view that privileges both
men and the bourgeoisie, so I want to argue that
photography and cinema, as media of light, at the
very least lend themselves to privileging white people. Second, I also want to insist on the aesthetic,
on the technological construction of beauty and
pleasure, as well as on the representation of the
world. Much historical work on media technology is
concerned with how media construct images of the
world. This is generally too sophisticatedly conceptualised to be concerned with anything so vulgar as
whether a medium represents the world accurately
(though in practice, and properly, this lingers as an
issue) but is concerned with how an ideology—a
way of seeing the world that serves particular social interests—is implicated in the mode of representation. I have no quarrel with this as such, but I
do want to recognise that cultural media are only
sometimes concerned with reality and are at least

as much concerned with ideals and indulgence, that
are themselves socially constructed. It is important
to understand this too and, indeed, to understand
how representation is actually implicated in inspira-
tions and pleasures.

The aesthetic technology at issue in this chapter
is light and lighting. This is fundamental to all photographic media; why this is so and what it involves are
discussed in the next section ('Light and the Photographic Media'). Mainstream cinema (above all,
Hollywood) developed a particular style of lighting
that may be called 'movie lighting', and this will be
described in the same section. Both the technology
of lighting and the specific mode of movie lighting
have racial implications. The third section of the
chapter ('Lighting for whiteness') discusses these in
historical and current practice, looking at the way
the aesthetic technology of light has a tendency to
assume, privilege and construct an idea of the white
person. [. . .]

Light and the Photographic Media

Photography and film are media of light. Writing
about them frequently asserts this. Consider these
titles, chosen from what comes to hand as I write:
'Painting with Light' (Milner 1930, about film lighting),
Painting in Light (Alton 1949, about cinematography),
Printed Light (Ward and Stevenson 1986, about early
photography), *Narration in Light* (Wilson 1986, about
point of view in film and not dealing specifically with
light at all); or these statements:

> Lighting is the very essence of the motion pic-
> ture. Figuratively it is the palette of the art direc-
> tor and occupies the same relation as pigment
> does to painting. It is the medium.
>
> (Ihnen and Atwater 1925: 27)

> As writers work with words, and directors with
> players, [the cameraman] works with a more elu-
> sive medium: light.
>
> (Hoadley 1939: 52)

> [P]hotography is building with light; light is the
> medium, a medium of infinite plasticity.
>
> (De Maré 1970: 55)

Basically, the visual part of the illusion we call the motion picture is nothing but the accurate control of light.

(Handley 1967: 120)

Films are light.

(Federico Fellini, quoted in Malkiewicz 1986: 1)

Such titles and statements are not metaphors: photography and film really are technologies of light. A photographic image is the product of the effect of light on a chemically prepared surface (the stock); a single frame of a projected film is one such surface with light shining through it on to a screen. No light, no photos or films.

The apparatus of light does not only concern stock and projection. Schematically, the following are involved.

- The light thrown at the subject of the image, in this sense the *lighting*. This may simply be the available light in the location, be it natural or artificial, which may be assisted (e.g. by reflectors and other kinds of bouncing) or controlled (e.g. by filtering sunlight though muslin or glass). It may equally involve a wide array of kinds of lighting apparatus, produced by a variety of means, using various lenses, reflectors and so on, all with different qualities of light.
- The properties of the *subject*. Objects (including people) reflect and absorb light differently, as well as being of different colours.
- The *stock*. Different kinds of stock are sensitive to different kinds and intensities of light.
- *Exposure*. The length of time the photographic stock is exposed to the light and the size of the aperture through which light passes both affect how light is registered on the stock and therefore how it looks when developed and projected.
- The *development* of the stock, during which many adjustments and transformations in light qualities can be achieved.
- *Projection*. Different kinds of projectors produce different qualities of light, and of course film seen on video is different again.

All these elements are in play in the history and practice of the photographic media, including film. A change in stock to register certain colour and textural qualities entails changes in, say, lighting and make-up, which in turn call for modifications in developing procedures and eventually the stock itself. The introduction of sound and colour were particularly intense periods of such alteration, but the technology has never stayed still.[2] Nor was this a purely internal, technical history, since it is entwined with issues of economics, fashion, social pressure and aesthetics.

The history of light technology, even if we just confine ourselves now to film, is highly intricate. Yet through it one can see operating a fairly consistent sense of what light in film should be, which acted as both benchmark and goal for most innovations and variations. This is embodied in a style of lighting developed by the 1920s[3] which became and remains so widespread that it can be referred to as, for instance, 'cinema lighting' (Coutard 1966: 9) or the 'film look' (Malkiewicz 1986: 100). I shall call it 'movie lighting' and will draw examples principally from Hollywood films, since by the 1920s they had come to dominate and set standards for most other film production.

Although this lighting style involves all the elements described above as contributing to the medium's technology of light, it is most easily described in relation to the light thrown at the subject, 'lighting' in this sense. Its guiding principal is controlled visibility. At a very basic level, movie lighting wants to ensure that what is important in a shot is clearly visible to the audience. This may seem laboriously elementary but, on the one hand, simply shooting in available light may not achieve this (as all casual photographers know) and, on the other, what constitutes importance in a shot is not a given, but a matter of the film-makers' choices. It may certainly not be story clarity in any obvious sense. In a mystery film, it may be important that the audience cannot see something. In a star vehicle, seeing the star to best advantage may outweigh other narrative considerations. In a drama in which no character is supposed to take precedence over the others in the audience's sympathies, equal visibility for all concerned may be required, something that is quite hard to achieve (given the way natural, and normal domestic, light fall). It is in relation to such problems of film expression that the elaborately controlled method of movie lighting evolved.

Movie lighting nearly always considers people to be the most important element in a shot. In practice, this means lighting people so that they are clearly separated from their surroundings, and do not appear to merge with the scenery. Most often, lighting is set up in two stages, once for the overall setting, once for the people in it, with the latter referred to as the 'figure lighting'. It is common in movies for there to be a perceptible difference between the figure lighting in a long or medium shot and that in a close-up. This is so even in films as early as *Hearts of the World* (USA 1918) and *Way Down East* (USA 1920) (both directed by D. W. Griffith), where the full panoply of light technology was not yet in place. In the former, there is a scene where the heroine (Lillian Gish) is menaced by a German officer (Eric von Stroheim). The lighting in the shots of them together is an even, overall illumination. However, in the close-ups of her, cringing from his advances against a wall, she is lit slightly from below, with no light on the wall—the light catches her wide eyes and the whiteness of her face is emphasised by the contrast with the darkness of the wall. Such a change in light for expressive purposes between mid and close shots is unnaturalistic but wholly within the convention of movie lighting. In *Way Down East*, when the hero and heroine (Robert Harron and Lillian Gish) first meet, the long and medium shots of them are taken in unassisted sunlight, with only the placing of the performers ensuring that at least each face is visible. However, the close-ups of Harron and Gish use a variety of techniques (soft focus, gauzes, placement against plain white backgrounds, side lighting) to make them special; editing in combination with lighting makes them stand out, as befits both their role as the lovers and their star status. Both these examples also construct the characteristic glow of white women, contrasted especially in the first case with a dark masculine desire that, under the pressure of war propaganda, would also have been felt as racially other.

Figure lighting is the main concern of this chapter, since what is at issue is the image of people. Movie figure lighting ensures the proper visibility of each performer (according to the needs of narration, star status and so on) by a use of several lights, classically in a three-point system consisting of a primary light (the *key*), giving general illumination of the figure, a second, softer light (the *fill*), eliminating some of the shadows created by the key and other set lighting, and *backlighting*, which serves to keep the figure separate from the background as well as creating, when wanted, the rim and halo effects of heroic and glamour lighting.

In practice, movie lighting is a good deal more complex and flexible than this. Three lights for figure lighting is minimal and the picture is always complicated by the infinite range of placements possible for all three positions and by their relationship to other lighting in the scene and to all the other elements that constitute light in film. Nor was the pattern of lighting fixed in the 1920s to remain utterly unchanged ever since. Hollywood, the paradigm of movie style, was influenced by, for instance, both 1920s German ('expressionist') lighting styles, with their much greater emphasis on chiaroscuro effects cutting across the figure (as in, especially, film noir and the horror film), and the bright, bounced, overall white light of the French new wave, less concerned with picking out the figures in a hierarchy of importance.[4] Yet such influences modified movie lighting rather than displacing it, and I have been struck while writing this chapter how extraordinarily pervasive the style remains, in ordinary television as much as in contemporary art cinema and still overwhelmingly in Hollywood movies.

The film *Mauvais sang* (France 1986),[5] for instance, is lit in a bright, hyper-realist style, combining yellowish tungsten with white quartz light; light sources visible on screen often appear to be the source for the lighting overall, characters often step into or out of light without reference to either dialogue or narrative; in short, *Mauvais sang* has a very modern, contemporary look, quite different from classic Hollywood. Yet on inspection many of the norms of movie lighting are in place. Take a scene in which the central character, Alex, visits two men, Marc and Hans. The room he finds them in is lit by fluorescent lighting hung over a billiard table. At first glance, one takes this to be the whole source of lighting for the scene, but in fact lighting at a 45° angle from above screen left illuminates the tops of the men's heads. A woman, Anna, is introduced into the scene and there are shots of her and Alex, establishing his interest in her. Both are shot in head and shoulders close-up, but cropped at the top and placed slightly to one side of the image, unconventional framing by movie norms. In her case, the framing cuts off the very top of her head, though much of her hair is visible. There is a relatively strong, warm light on her face from screen left (slightly to the front of her face), a less strong light from screen right, creating highlights as well as eliminating the shadows from her neck (shadows cast by the main light), and some light catching what we can see of her hair. As with movie figure lighting, this has little to do with the visible light source in the scene. Lighting so clearly from sides and top is different from the characteristic positions of movie lighting, yet it is none the less a form of three-point lighting. Alex also has the key and fill, more fully to one side and the other of his head, but, as the top of his head is cropped at his brow, it is hard to tell whether he is lit from above. The difference in the lighting between Anna and Alex is gender-related: she is more glowingly and he more harshly lit. The blending of the three-point lighting in her case creates a softer, more unified look; the greater (relative) severity of the lighting on him creates a degree of contrast. Such gender differentiation also has to do with whiteness: she inhabits (albeit principally in his perception) a space of transcendence, whereas he is a body seeking transcendence.

Even in a smart, postmodern film like *Mauvais sang*, the basic qualities of movie lighting remain: ensured visibility, figures lit quasi-independently of setting, and codes that are gendered and white-related. This is even more evidently true of contemporary Hollywood and television, and not only drama[6] but quiz and chat shows and even documentary and news. Indeed, as I have been writing this, I have become riveted by watching light catch the hair and ensure the outlined contours (without going so far as haloing or rimming) of newscasters and TV weather reporters. The sense of the normality of this is still pervasive. A current 'leisure know-how' guide on how to *Make Better Home Videos*, the kind of basic, common-sense, 'no point of view' paperback you can buy in a supermarket, offers exactly the same three-point lighting plan as simply how to light a person (Owen 1993: 104–7).

This chapter focuses on movie figure lighting, and above all face lighting. This is principally because my concern is with how images of (white) people are constructed, but it is also in line with photographic and film practices themselves. The face is seen as both the most important thing in an image and also, as a consequence, the control on the visual quality of everything else. At the point of shooting, a standard photography manual recommends use of an exposure meter: 'Take a reading off the most important part of your subject, e.g. face or person' (and uses a white face in illustration) (Greenhill *et al.* 1977: 48). At the point of development, Raoul Coutard observes of colour film: 'As the film stock is unstable, the laboratories need something to use as a fixed point from which to work in re-establishing the true colours; and what they work from are the actors' faces' (Coutard 1966: 11). At the point of reception, I well recall the advice that first-time purchasers of colour television were given about how to adjust their sets: get the people's faces right and everything else would fall into place. This is good advice, as long as you take the white face as the norm and don't mind non-white faces looking odd.

Movie lighting of the face is at the heart of ordinary production. The next section looks at its relation to whiteness in general terms before tracing the source of this and its implications in the historical development of a culture of light.

Lighting for Whiteness

The photographic media and, *a fortiori*, movie lighting assume, privilege and construct whiteness. The apparatus was developed with white people in mind and habitual use and instruction continue in the same vein, so much so that photographing non-white people is typically construed as a problem.

All technologies work within material parameters that cannot be wished away. Human skin does have different colours which reflect light differently. Methods of calculating this differ, but the degree of difference registered is roughly the same; Mill-erson (1972: 31), discussing colour television, gives light skin 43 per cent light reflectance and dark skin 29 per cent; Malkiewicz (1986: 53) states that 'a Caucasian face has about 35 percent reflectance but a black face reflects less than 16 percent'. This creates problems if shooting very light and very dark people in the same frame. Writing in *Scientific American* in 1921, Frederick Mills, 'electrical illuminating engineer at the Lasky Studios', noted that

> when there are two persons in [a] scene, possibly a star and a leading player, if one has a dark make-up and the other a light, much care must be exercised in so regulating the light that it neither 'burns up' the light make-up nor is of insufficient strength to light up the dark make-up.
>
> (1921: 148)

The problem is memorably attested in a racial context in school photos where either the black pupils' faces look like blobs or the white pupils have theirs bleached out.

The technology at one's disposal also sets limits. The chemistry of different stocks registers shades and colours differently. Cameras offer varying degrees of flexibility with regard to exposure (affecting their ability to take a wide lightness/darkness range). Different kinds of lighting have different colours and degrees of warmth, with concomitant effects on different skins. However, what is at one's disposal is not all that could exist. Stocks, cameras and lighting were developed taking the white face as the touchstone. The resultant apparatus came to be seen as fixed and inevitable, existing independently of the fact that it was humanly constructed. It may be—certainly was—true that photo and film apparatuses have seemed to work better with light-skinned peoples, but that is because they were made that way, not because they could be no other way.

All this is complicated still further by the habitual practices and uses of the apparatus. Certain exposures and lighting set-ups, as well as make-ups and developing processes, have become established as normal. They are constituted as the way to use the medium. Anything else becomes a departure from

the norm, or even a problem. In practice, such normality is white.

The question of the relationship between the variously coloured human subject and the apparatus of photography is not simply one of accuracy. This is certainly how it is most commonly discussed, in accounts of innovation or advice to photographers and film-makers. There are indeed parameters to be recognised. If someone took a photo of me and made it look as if I had olive skin and black hair, I should be grateful but have to acknowledge that it was inaccurate. However, we also find acceptable considerable departures from how we 'really' look in what we regard as accurate photos, and this must be all the more so with photography of people whom we don't know, such as celebrities, stars and models. In the history of photography and film, getting the right image meant getting the one which conformed to prevalent ideas of humanity. This included ideas of whiteness, of what colour—what range of hue—white people wanted white people to be.

The rest of this section is concerned with the way the aesthetic technology of photography and film is involved in the production of images of whiteness. I look first at the assumption of whiteness as norm at different moments of technical innovation in film history, before looking at examples of that assumption in standard technical guides to the photographic media. The section ends with a discussion of how lighting privileges white people in the image and begins to open up the analysis of the construction of whiteness through light.

Innovation in the photographic media has generally taken the human face as its touchstone, and the white face as the norm of that. The very early experimenters did not take the face as subject at all, but once they and their followers turned to portraits, and especially once photographic portraiture replaced painted portraits in popularity (from the 1840s on), the issue of the 'right' technology (apparatus, consumables, practice) focused on the face and, given the clientele, the white face. Experiment with, for instance, the chemistry of photographic stock, aperture size, length of development and artificial light all proceeded on the assumption that what had to be got right was the look of the white face. This is where the big money lay, in the everyday practices of professional portraiture and amateur snapshots. By the time of film (some sixty years after the first photographs), technologies and practices were already well established. Film borrowed these, gradually and selectively, carrying forward the assumptions that had gone into them. In turn, film history involves many refinements, variations and innovations, always keeping the white face central as a touchstone and occasionally revealing this quite explicitly, when it is not implicit within such terms as 'beauty', 'glamour' and 'truthfulness'. Let me provide some instances of this.

The interactions of film stock, lighting and make-up illustrate the assumption of the white face at various points in film history. Film stock repeatedly failed to get the whiteness of the white face. The earliest stock, orthochromatic, was insensitive to red and yellow, rendering both colours dark. Charles Handley, looking back in 1954, noted that with orthochromatic stock, 'even a reasonably light-red object would photograph black' (1967: 121). White skin is reasonably light-red. Fashion in make-up also had to be guarded against, as noted in one of the standard manuals of the era, Carl Louis Gregory's *Condensed Course in Motion Picture Photography* (1920):

> Be very sparing in the use of lip rouge. Remember that red photographs black and that a heavy application of rouge shows an unnaturally black mouth on the screen.
>
> (316)

Yellow also posed problems. One derived from theatrical practices of make-up, against which Gregory inveighs in a passage of remarkable racial resonance:

> Another myth that numerous actors entertain is the yellow grease-paint theory. Nobody can explain why a performer should make-up in chinese yellow. . . . The objections to yellow are that it is non-actinic and if the actor happens to step out of the rays of the arcs for a moment or if he is shaded from the distinct force of the light by another actor, his face photographs BLACK instantly.
>
> (ibid.: 317; emphasis in original)

The solution to these problems was a 'dreadful white make-up' (actress Geraldine Farrar, interviewed in Brownlow 1968: 418) worn under carbon arc lights so hot that they made the make-up run, involving endless retouching. This was unpleasant for performers and exacerbated by fine dust and ultraviolet light from the arcs, making the eyes swollen and pink (so-called 'Klieg eyes' after the Kliegl company which was the main supplier of arc lights at the time (Salt 1983: 136)). These eyes filmed big and dark, in other words, not very 'white', and involved the performers in endless 'trooping down to the infirmary' (Brownlow 1968: 418), constantly interrupting shooting for their well-being and to avoid the (racially) wrong look.

It would have been possible to use incandescent tungsten light instead of carbon arcs; this would have been easier to handle, cheaper (requiring fewer people to operate and using less power) and pleasanter to work with (much less hot). It would also have suited one of the qualities of orthochromatic stock, its preference for subtly modulated lighting rather than high contrast of the kind created by arcs. But incandescent tungsten light has a lot of red and yellow in it and thus tends to bring out those colours in all subjects, including white faces, with consequent blacking effect on orthochromatic stock. This was a reason for sticking with arcs, for all the expense and discomfort.

The insensitivity of orthochromatic stock to yellow also made fair hair look dark 'unless you specially lit it' (cinematographer Charles Rosher, interviewed in Brownlow 1968: 262). Gregory similarly advised:

> Yellow blonde hair photographs dark . . . the more loosely [it] is arranged the lighter it photographs, and different methods of studio lighting also affect the photographic values of hair.
>
> (1920: 317)

One of the principal benefits of the introduction of backlighting, in addition to keeping the performer clearly separate from the background, was that it ensured that blonde hair looked blonde:

> The use of backlighting on blonde hair was not only spectacular but *necessary*—it was the only

way filmmakers could get blonde hair to look light-coloured on the yellow-insensitive ortho-chromatic stock.

(Bordwell *et al.* 1985: 226; my emphasis)

Backlighting became part of the basic vocabulary of movie lighting. As the cinematographer Joseph Walker put it in his memoirs:

We found [backlighting] necessary to keep the actors from blending into the background. [It] also adds a halo of highlights to the hair and bril-liance to the scene.

(Walker and Walker 1984: 218)

From 1926, the introduction of panchromatic stock, more sensitive to yellow, helped with some of the problems of ensuring white people looked properly white, as well as permitting the use of incandescent tungsten, but posed its own problems of make-up. It was still not so sensitive to red, but much more to blue. Max Factor recognised this problem, develop-ing a make-up that would 'add to the face sufficient blue coloration in proportion to red . . . in order to prevent excessive absorption of light by the face' (Factor 1937: 54); faces that absorb light 'excessively' are of course dark ones.

Colour brought with it a new set of problems, explored in Brian Winston's article on the invention of 'colour film that more readily photographs Cauca-sians than other human types' (1985: 106). Winston argues that at each stage the search for a colour film stock (including the development process, crucial to the subtractive systems that have proved most workable) was guided by how it rendered white flesh tones. Not long after the introduction of colour in the mid-1930s, the cinematographer Joseph Valentine commented that 'perhaps the most important single factor in dramatic cinematography is the relation between the colour sensitivity of an emulsion and the reproduction of pleasing flesh tones' (1939: 54). Winston looks at one such example of the search for 'pleasing flesh tones' in researches undertaken by Kodak in the early 1950s. A series of prints of 'a young lady' were prepared and submitted to a panel, and a report observed:

Optimum reproduction of skin colour is not 'exact' reproduction . . . 'exact reproduction' is rejected almost unanimously as 'beefy'. On the other hand, when the print of highest acceptance is masked and compared with the original sub-ject, it seems quite pale.

(David L. MacAdam 1951, quoted in Winston 1985: 120)

As noted above, white skin is taken as a norm but what that means in terms of colour is determined not by how it is but by how, as Winston puts it, it is 'preferred—a whiter shade of white' (ibid.: 121). Characteristically too, it is a woman's skin which provides the litmus test.

Colour film was a possibility from 1896 (when R. W. Paul showed his hand-tinted prints), with Tech-nicolor, the 'first entirely successful colour process used in the cinema', available from 1917 (Coe 1981: 112–39). Yet it did not become anything like a norm until the 1950s, for a complex of economic, tech-nological and aesthetic reasons (cf. Kindem 1979), among which was a sense that colour film was not realistic. As Gorham Kindem suggests, this may have been partly due to a real limitation of the processes adopted from the late 1920s, in that they 'could not reproduce all the colours of the visible spectrum' (1979: 35) but it also had to do with an early associa-tion with musicals and spectacle. The way Kindem elaborates this point is racially suggestive:

While flesh tones, the most important index of accuracy and consistency, might be carefully con-trolled through heavy make-up, practically dictat-ing the overall colour appearance, it is quite likely that other colours in the set or location had to be sacrificed and appeared unnatural or 'gaudy'.

(ibid.)

As noted elsewhere, accurate flesh tones are again the key issue in innovation. The tones involved here are evidently white, for it was lighting the compensa-tory heavy make-up with sufficient force to ensure a properly white look that was liable to make every-thing else excessively bright and 'gaudy'. Kindem re-lates a resistance to such an excess of colour with growing pessimism and cynicism through the 1930s as the weight of the Depression took a hold, to which black and white seemed more appropriate. Yet this seems to emphasise the gangster and social problem films of the 1930s over and above the comedies, musicals, fantasies and adventure films (think screwball, Fred and Ginger, Tarzan) that were, all the same, made in black and white. May it not be that what was not acceptable was escapism that was visually too loud and busy, because excess colour, and the very word 'gaudy', was associated with, indeed, coloured people?

A last example of the operation of the white face as a control on media technology comes from professional television production in the USA.[7] In the late 1970s the WGBH Educational Foundation and the 3M Corporation developed a special television signal, to be recorded on videotape, for the purpose of evaluating tapes. This signal, known as 'skin', was of a pale orange colour and was intended to duplicate the appearance on a television set of white skin. The process of scanning was known as 'skinning'. Operatives would watch the blank pale orange screen produced by tapes prerecorded with the 'skin' signal, making notes whenever a visible defect appeared. The fewer defects, the greater the value of the tape (reckoned in several hundreds of dollars) and thus when and by whom it was used. The whole process centred on blank images representing nothing, and yet founded in the most explicit way on a particular human flesh colour.

The assumption that the normal face is a white face runs through most published advice given on photo- and cinematography.[8] This is carried above all by illustrations which invariably use a white face, except on those rare occasions when they are discussing the 'problem' of dark-skinned people. Kodak announces on the tide page of its *How to Take Good Pictures* (1984) that it is 'The world's best-selling photography book', but all the photo examples therein imply an all-white world (with one picture of two very pink Japanese women); similarly, Willard Morgan's *Encyclopedia of Photography* (1963), billed as 'The complete photographer: the Comprehensive Guide and Reference for All Photographers' shows lack of racial completeness and comprehensiveness

in its illustrative examples as well as its text (even under such entries as 'Lighting in Portraiture' (Lewis Tulchin 2116–2127), 'Portrait Photography' (Edward Weston 2952–2955), 'Portraiture—Elementary Techniques' (Morris Germain 2955–2965), 'Portraiture Outdoors' (Dale Rooks 2965–2973) or 'Portraiture with the Speedlamp' (Editorial Staff 2973–2977)). Fifteen years after *John Hedgecoe's Complete Photography Course* (1979), *John Hedgecoe's New Book of Photography* (1994) is neither any more complete or new as far as race is concerned (Hedgecoe is both a bestseller and Professor of Photographic Art at the Royal College of Art in London, in other words a highly authoritative source). Even when non-white subjects are used, it is rarely randomly, to illustrate a general technical point. The only non-white subject in Lucien Lorelle's *The Colour Book of Photography* (1955) is a black woman in what is for this book a highly stylised composition. The caption reads:

> Special lighting effects are possible with coloured lamps . . . and light sources included in the picture. Exposure becomes more tricky, and should be based on a meter reading of a key highlight such as the dress.

The photo is presented as an example of an unusual use of colour, to which the model's 'colourfulness' is unwittingly appropriate. The advice to take the exposure meter reading from the dress is itself unusual: with white subjects, it is their skin that is determinant. In Lucille Khornah's *The Nude in Black and White* (1993), nine out of seventy-four illustrations feature non-white subjects—six with parts of the body painted in zebra stripes and two making an aesthetic contrast of black and white skins, all cases which play on skin colour. Only one illustration, a black mother and child, does not seem to be making a point out of the non-white subjects' colour. Some more recent guidebooks randomly do include non-white subjects,[9] but even now there is no danger of excesses of political correctness.

The texts that the illustrations accompany make the same assumption that the human subject is white. Cassell's *Cyclopaedia of Photography* (1911) is clearly destined for a world in which there are only fair faces, whose colour it is important to capture even when nature is not on one's side: 'A common defect in amateur portraits taken out of doors is the dark appearance of the sitters' faces' (Jones 1911: 428).

The most recent edition of the *Focal Encyclopedia of Photography* does at least have the grace to be upfront about the matter in the entry on 'Skin Tone':

> When used as a standard for quality control purposes, it is assumed, unless stated otherwise, that the typical subject is Caucasian with a skin reflectance of approximately 36%.
>
> (Stroebel and Richard 1993: 722)

In all this, inventors, commentators and advice-givers are not to be found stating that, if you want to capture the look of the white face correctly, you need to do so and so. They never refer to the white face as such, for to do so would immediately signal its particularity. It is rather in describing facial and skin qualities that the unpremeditated assumption of a white face is apparent. Josef von Sternberg (1955–6: 109) affirms that 'the skin should reflect and not blot light', something more readily achieved with white skin. Gerald Millerson, discussing the relative light reflectance of skin tones (1972: 35), compares 'light' skin with 'bronzed', as if dark skin is, as it is for a white norm, only sun induced. A much more racially explicit example is provided in Eric De Maré's *Photography*, a much reissued Penguin book 'designed to help and stimulate the amateur photographer' (blurb to the 1970 edition). De Maré discusses the problems of light when shooting out of doors and, inevitably, takes a young (white) woman as the subject:

> [W]e consider her complexion to be at all times of a delicious, peachy pink but, exposing on a sunny day without correction filter to adjust the blue cast from the sky, we shall be *shocked* to find that the colour film has recorded the skin as having a slight indigo tint.
>
> (1970: 295; my emphasis)

The words 'indigo' and 'tint' were widely used with a racial, even racist, meaning in British English.

A major theme in instructional writing is the elimination of shadow. This is taken as a self-evidently and absolutely desirable goal in all but those cases where the aim is a sort of 'arty' expressivity. This obsession with getting rid of shadows established itself early. Victor Fournel, writing in 1858 about contemporary portrait photography practices, noted the already elaborate apparatus to hand to eliminate shadows, observing that 'what frightens the middle classes above everything else are the model's shadows: they can only see in them a blackness which darkens [*rembrunit*] and saddens the figure' (quoted in Rouillé and Marbot 1986: 15).

Shadows on the face are one of the major *Faults in Photography* in Kurt Fritsche's 1966 book; nearly all the advice on lighting in Eugene Hanson's ideologically riveting *Glamour Guide: How to Photograph Girls* (1950) is on avoidance of shadows. In a pair of illustrations to *Photography in Colour with Kodak Films* (Bomback 1957), the superiority of eliminated shadows is affirmed by having the model smile slightly more in the less shadowed versions and adding effects of backlighting, thus emphasising the upbeat quality of the image. As the argument in Chapter 2 might lead one to expect, in all these—and nearly all other—examples, the model (a properly ambiguous term) is a woman, already white and in the light, not struggling towards whiteness and the light.

Elimination of shadow is partly determined by the desire for visibility. The camera lens cannot see into shadows as flexibly as can the human eye and fill lighting compensates for this. Yet even this imperative to see, and to see women, suggests a concern with the visible that has marked the white era, while shadows cut across the association of white people with the light that is explored later in this chapter.

The white-centricity of the aesthetic technology of the photographic media is rarely recognised, except when the topic of photographing non-white faces is addressed. This is habitually conceptualised in terms of non-white subjects entailing a departure from usual practice or constituting a problem. An account of the making of *The Color Purple* (1985) speaks of the 'unique photographic problems that occur when shooting a film with basically an all black cast' and goes on to detail the procedures the cinematographer, Allen Daviau, used to deal with these 'problems', in particular 'having the set interiors and set decorations darker than *normal*' (my emphasis)[10] (Harrell 1986: 54). Cicely Tyson recalled her experience of filming *The Blue Bird* in Russia in 1976, where there was little experience of filming black people. A white woman had been used during the lighting set-ups:

> They light everything for her and then I'm expected to go through the same paces with the same lighting. . . . Naturally, my black skin disappears on the screen. You can't see me at all.
>
> (quoted in Medved 1984: 128–9)

The Moscow crew (at the white centre of the multiracial USSR) assumed that there were just 'faces', which meant that they assumed a universal white face, which in turn obliged Tyson to make a fuss and become constituted as an exception or problem. In 1994, in an interview in the magazine *US* (November: 102), the African-American actor Joe Morton (whose films include *The Brother from Another Planet*, *Terminator 2* and *Speed*) was still having to consider the way he is filmed a problem:

> For black actors, if you're not lit correctly, your skin tone can look very odd. You shouldn't be lit with certain shades of green and yellow. And, lots of black men have broad noses, and that can be exaggerated.

Such examples are not confined to mainstream Hollywood productions. Basil Wright, a leading figure in British documentary in the 1930s, gives an account of shooting in the West Indies and the difficulties of having to film at midday, with the brilliance of the sun which 'kill[ed] all detail'.

> The crux of this *problem* was encountered when negro types [i.e. the normal inhabitants] had to be shot. With bright direct sunlight coming from overhead, it was almost impossible to get a good quality negative and yet retain the negro features. Rubbing the face and arms of the subject with butter or oil only brought up a few highlights,

even when aided by reflectors. Finally the problem was solved by staging scenes *in the shade* and using reflectors only.

> (Wright 1933: 227; first emphasis mine)

Here, what is more evidently at issue is a still rather inflexible technology, developed and adjusted for the white face; Wright's solution however is very similar to that of Daviau for *The Color Purple* fifty years later.

In Kris Malkiewicz's book *Film Lighting*, based on interviews with Hollywood cinematographers and gaffers, four of the interviewees discuss the question of lighting for black people (Malkiewicz 1986: 141). They come up with a variety of solutions: 'taking light off the white person' if there are people of different colour in shot (John Alonzo), putting 'some lotion on the [black person's] skin to create reflective quality' (Conrad Hall), using 'an orange light' (Michael D. Margulies). James Plannette is robust: 'The only thing that black people need is more light. It is as simple as that.' Even this formulation implies doing something special for black people, departing from a white norm. Some of the others (lotion, orange light) imply that the 'problem' is inherent in the technology, not just its conventional use.

Elsewhere, Ernest Dickerson, Spike Lee's regular cinematographer, indicates (1988: 70) the importance of choices made at every level of light technology when filming black subjects: lighting (use of 'warmer' light, with 'bastard amber' gels, tungsten lights on dimmers 'so they [can] be dialed down to warmer temperatures', and gold instead of silver reflectors), the subject (use of reflective make-up, 'a light sheen from skin moisturizer'), exposure (basing it on 'reflected readings on Black people with a spot meter'), stock ('Eastman Kodak's 5247 with its tight grain and increased color saturation') and development (using 'printing lights in the high thirties and low forties' to ensure that 'blacks will hold up to the release prints'). Dickerson is explaining his choices against his observation that 'many cinematographers cite *problems* photographing black people because of the need to use more light on them' (my emphasis). Much of his language indicates that he is involved in correcting a white bias in the most widely available and used technology: lights are warmer (than an implied cold norm), they are dialled down (from a usual cooler temperature), they are gold not silver, and the stock has more colour saturation. The whiteness implied here is not just a norm (silver not gold) but also redolent of aspects of the conceptualisation of whiteness discussed in previous chapters: coldness and the absence of colour.

The practice of taking the white face as the norm, with deleterious consequences for non-white performers (unless they are consciously taken into account), is evident in films which not only have stars of different colours but also apparently intend to treat them equally. This may be out of a liberal impulse (Sidney Poitier with Tony Curtis in *The Defiant Ones* (1958)), an expression of star power (Eddie Murphy with Nick Nolte in *48 Hours* (1982)) or identification of a box office trend (the Danny Glover–Mel Gibson *Lethal Weapon* series (1987–92)). However, it is rare that the black actor is in fact lit equally. Such films betray the assumption of the white face built into the habitual uses of the technology and have the effect of privileging the white man; they also contribute to specific perceptions of whiteness. Let me take two examples. The first, *In the Heat of the Night* (1967), makes the white man not only more visible but also more individualised. The second, *Rising Sun* (1993), goes further in privileging and constructing an idea of the white man.

The Sidney Poitier character, Virgil Tibbs, in *In the Heat* is emblematic of the Northern, educated, middle class black man. His adversary, but fellow cop, Bill Gillespie (Rod Steiger) is, on the contrary, a contradictory character. Tibbs is identified with his home turf (Philadelphia), whereas Gillespie, on whose turf (Sparta, Mississippi) the action unfolds, is in fact from another town and not really accepted by the local force: he is in a certain way more dislocated than Tibbs. He is unthinkingly bigoted but without the obsessive racism of the (white) rest of the town and police. He has a failed marriage in his past. He is an elaborated character, not a representative figure. Much of this is conveyed by dialogue and the two performers' different acting styles: Poitier's stillness and implied intensity, Steiger's busy, exteriorised method acting. It is also conveyed by lighting.

Poitier tends to be posed in profile or near silhouette, emphasising his emblematic presence; Steiger is more often shot face on, in, rather than against the light. Poitier is thus given considerable moral and intellectual authority, but little opportunity to display the workings of individuality on the face. In one scene, Tibbs (Poitier) and Gillespie (Steiger) are sitting talking together in the latter's home. There is a degree of *rapprochement* between them, with each revealing something of himself to the other. In the establishing shot, Poitier is screen left, sitting back in a reclining chair facing screen right, and Steiger is screen right, lying on a couch. The only visible light source is a large table lamp behind Poitier. Poitier is thus profiled and semi-silhouetted, while the light falls full on Steiger's face. As the scene proceeds, most of the shots are close-ups. The table lamp casts both their faces in half light, but this is far more marked with Poitier, whereas Steiger is given some additional fill light, removing most of the shadow from the side of his face away from the lamp. The set-ups for the shots of Poitier remain more or less side-on to camera but, after a few similar shots of Steiger, the camera takes up a frontal position for him, with backlighting and a stronger fill. As a result, not only is Steiger more fully visible to us, but he can display a range of modulations of expression that indicate the character's complex turmoil of feelings and reminiscences. Poitier, by contrast, remains the emblematic, unindividualised, albeit admirable, black man.

Rising Sun[11] is an expensive film involving an experienced director (Philip Kaufman) and often quite elaborate and attractive lighting set-ups (cinematographer Michael Chapman). It has two major stars in it, the black star (Wesley Snipes) having at the time of the film's appearance at least as much cinema box office clout as the white star (Sean Connery). And it is a film that knows about race: a thriller pivoting on questions of American-Japanese antagonisms, it both gives Snipes and Connery, as the detectives on the case, some (black–white) racially conscious dialogue and includes an African-American ghetto sequence to make a point about the Snipes character's roots. In other words, this is a film that has no reason not to light its central male pair so that each comes off equally well (which means, of course, not, in technical terms, lighting them the same). In separate shots they are indeed lit differently, enhancing the character and beauty of their faces to equal effect. Yet in shots featuring both of them, Connery is advantaged. A clear example occurs early on when Snipes and Connery are interviewing a security guard in a building where a corpse has been found. The guard is the most important character in the scene in terms of narrative (what has he seen?) and emotion (he is clearly holding something back for fear of losing his job); Snipes and Connery, as the stars and the investigators, have a different kind of importance, but one is not more important than the other. However, the lighting suggests otherwise. The guard is black. The scene is mostly shot with Connery standing between the guard (screen left) and Snipes (right). The light falls on Connery and is good for his colouring. His equal partner (Snipes) and the crucial witness (the guard), on the other hand, are shrouded in darkness.[12]

This example is caused by the assumption of the white face as a norm (get Connery right and the rest will fall into place); it has the effect of privileging the white performer. It also reproduces a particular construction of whiteness. The light catches Connery's temples, while Snipes and the guard are in darkness. Connery is literally but also figuratively enlightened: the light emphasises his forehead, or, in effect, his brain. Elsewhere, in two-shots where some kind of intermediate light setting has been chosen, not ideal for either star, Snipes' skin shines whereas Connery's disappears in the light—the surface of Snipes' flesh is evident, his corporeality, whereas Connery's flesh is dissolved into the light.

The historical construction of whiteness through light, of which *Rising Sun* is a late product, is the subject of the rest of this chapter. Before moving to that, however, I should like to look at one last recent example, which suggests both that it is not technically impossible to film black people with the same effect as for whites but that it is culturally extremely difficult.

A Few Good Men (1992) concerns two marines on trial for the murder of another. One, Lance Corporal Dawson (Wolfgang Bodison), is African-American, a point to which the film makes neither explicit nor implicit reference. At one point in the trial, it is revealed that Dawson once disobeyed an order (itself a central issue to the marine ethics on which the case turns) by taking food to a marine who was being harshly punished for a trivial mistake by being imprisoned without food; this is a turning point, because it establishes Dawson's high moral character. The shot, of him listening to his attorney Lieutenant Kaffee (Tom Cruise) drawing attention to the moral significance of his disobedience, has strong, hard side and top lighting. Dawson's (Bodison's) hair is shaved at the sides but cut to a flat top. This gives it a relatively open texture which catches the light, creating a glow atop his head, striking in a generally darkly lit scene. His fellow, white, defendant is also in the shot, but his haircut has a rounder shape and the top lighting is less full on his head, though he still benefits from the quasi-halo effect. The lighting on Dawson is more conspicuous, partly because he is the one at issue in narrative terms, but also because there is somewhat more contrast between his bright hair and dark face and because it is so unusual to see an African-American shot like this. It shows that the latter is technically possible, yet not only is the lighting unusually hard and directed, it is also called forth at an expressly ethical moment— white performers benefit habitually from such light at the head, there does not have to be a strong moral point being made.

At the end of the film, Dawson is acquitted of the murder but still dishonourably discharged: the death was the accidental result of obeying an order to rough up a weak and awkward recruit. Dawson realises that he should have disobeyed the order in accordance with a greater moral imperative. The final shot of him is taken at the door to the trial room, as Kaffee/Cruise is telling him that he does have honour because of this realisation. There is no top lighting and Dawson stands before the dark wood of the door; despite the moral accolade, there is no longer any virtuous light at his head. The film cuts back to Tom Cruise, himself dark-haired but lustrous and tinged with light from above. His character has been much more morally ambiguous throughout, and even at this point his triumph is as much a career success as a sign of moral growth, yet now the white hero has the light no longer accorded the black character.

Indeed, the recognition of the latter's virtue is given to Kaffee/Cruise, who tells him that he has honour, since he (Dawson) doesn't know it for himself: the white man, with that touch of light about his head, knows and names virtue in the black man, who now blends in with the darkness of the world.

Movie lighting in effect discriminates on the basis of race. As the rest of this chapter will argue, such discrimination has much to do with the conceptualisation of whiteness. There is also a rather different level at which movie lighting's discrimination may be said to operate. What is at issue here is not how white is shown and seen, so much as the assumptions at work in the way that movie lighting disposes people in space. Movie lighting relates people to each other and to setting according to notions of the human that have historically excluded non-white people.

Movie lighting focuses on the individual. Each person has lighting tailored to his or her personality (character, star image, actorly attributes). Each important person, that is. At a minimum, in a culture in which whites are the important people, in which those who have, rather than are, servants, occupy centre stage, one would expect movie lighting to discriminate against non-white people in terms of visibility, individualisation and centrality. I want however to push the argument a bit further. Movie lighting valorises the notion of the unique and special character of the individual, of the individuality of the individual. It is at the least arguable that white society has found it hard to see non-white people as individuals; the very notion of the individual, of the freely developing, autonomous human person, is only applicable to those who are seen to be free and autonomous, who are not slaves or subject peoples. Movie lighting discriminates against non-white people because it is used in a cinema and a culture that finds it hard to recognise them as appropriate subjects for such lighting, that is, as individuals.

Further, movie lighting hierarchises. It indicates who is important and who is not. It is not just that in white racist society, those who are not white will be lit to be at the bottom of the hierarchy, but that the very process of hierarchisation is an exercise of power. Other and non-white societies have hierarchies, of course; it is not innate to white nature. However, hierarchy, the aspirational structure, is one of the forms that power has taken in the era of white Western society.

Movie lighting also separates the individual, not only from all other individuals, but from her/his environment. The sense of separation from the environment, of the world as the object of a disembodied human gaze and control, runs deep in white culture. The prime reason for introducing backlighting in film was to ensure that the figures were distinguished from their ground, to make them stand out from each other and their setting. This was regarded as an obvious necessity, so clearly part of how to see life that it was an unquestionable imperative. Yet it expresses a view of humanity pioneered by white culture; it lies behind its highly successful technology and the terrible price the environment now pays for this.

People who are not white can and are lit to be individualised, arranged hierarchically and kept separate from their environment. But this is only to indicate the triumph of white culture and its readiness to allow some people in, some non-white people to be in this sense white. Yet not only is there still a high degree of control over who gets let in, but, as I want to argue in the rest of this chapter, the technology and culture of light is so constructed as to be both fundamental to the construction of the human image and yet felt to be uniquely appropriate to those who are white.

Notes

1. I'm grateful to Ann Gray for bringing this example to my attention.
2. Overviews of this history can be found in Handley 1967, Salt 1983 and Revault d'Allones 1991.
3. Salt (1983) finds examples as far back as 1909 and traces its variants through the 1910s, suggesting that it probably only became established as a norm around 1917–19.
4. In his study of lighting in film, Fabrice Revault d'Allones distinguishes movie or 'classical' lighting (which can be more highly wrought to the point of becoming 'baroque') from what he terms 'modernist' lighting. The latter does not seek to control meaning or to hierarchise elements in the image; nor does light itself carry meaning (of, for example, darkness being sinister). He takes the example of the film *Thérèse* (France 1986), about the life of a young nun:

Thérèse may die, but the lighting is the same as when she danced; she may turn out to be a saint, but she looks no more and no less radiant than before: the lighting resists dramatisation and symbolisation, subjectivisation and psychologisation.

(Revault d'Allones 1991: 10)

Revault d'Allones finds this kind of lighting in the work of individual directors at various points in the history of the cinema, but sees it as characteristic of only a brief period of cinema, around the French new wave in the 1960s. In its indifference to (racial) difference, such lighting will reproduce the privileging of the white face discussed in this chapter.

5. Director Léos Carax; photographer Jean-Yves Escoffier.
6. It is remorselessly true of the lighting in *The Jewel in the Crown*, for instance, discussed in Chapter 5.
7. I am grateful to William Spurlin of the Visual and Environmental Studies Department at Harvard University for telling me of this, explaining it and commenting on drafts of this paragraph.
8. This observation is based on analysis of a random cross-section of such books published this century. See Appendix at end of chapter.
9. See Appendix at end of chapter.
10. Film stock registers contrasts less subtly than the human eye, which tends, faced with real life, to compensate for excessive lightness or darkness; a black face against a light background, of set or costume, creates a strong contrast; adequately lighting a black performer's face in such circumstances (that is, directing more light at it than one would at a white person's face) risks bleaching out the sets and costumes.
11. Note that this figure, though illustrating the general point made in this paragraph, is a production still from a different scene to that discussed here.
12. José Arroyo notes Snipes coming off badly through lighting in a more recent vehicle for him (*Money Train* 1995): 'whenever there's a white person in the frame, discerning Snipes' features becomes a matter of eyestrain' (1996: 47).

Appendix: Instruction Manuals

The following manuals on photography, film and video were consulted for this chapter.

1892   Brothers, A. *Photography: its History, Processes, Apparatus and Materials*, London: C. Griffin.

c.1910   *Comment obtenir de Bonnes Photographies*, Paris: Kodak, Société Anonyme Française.

1911   Jones, Bernard E. *Cassell's Cyclopaedia of Photography*, London: Cassell.

1912   Talbot, Frederick A. *Moving Pictures: How They Are Made and Worked*, Philadelphia: J. B. Lippincott.

1920   Gregory, Carl Louis (ed.) *A Condensed Course in Motion Picture Photography*, New York: New York Institute of Photography.

c.1924   McKay, Herbert C. *Motion Picture Photography for the Amateur*, New York: Falk.

1929   Wheeler, Owen *Amateur Cinematography*, New York: Pitman.

1936   Deschin, Jacob *New Ways in Photography*, New York: Whittlesey House.

1939   Barton, Fred B. *Photography as a Hobby*, New York: Harper & Brothers.

1948   Archer, Fred *Fred Archer on Portraiture*, San Francisco: Camera Craft Publishing Co.

1950   Hanson, Eugene M. *Glamour Guide: How to Photograph Girls*, American Photographic Publishing Co. (no place given).

1955   Lorelle, Lucien *The Colour Book of Photography*, London: Focal Press. (Translation of *Traité pratique de la prise de vue en couleurs*, Paris: Publications Photo-Cinéma Paul Montel, n.d.)

1957   Bomback, Edward S. *Photography in Colour with Kodak Films*, London: Fountain Press.

1957   De Maré, Eric *Photography*, Harmondsworth: Penguin (reprinted at least five times up to 1970).

1963   Morgan, Willard B. (ed.) *The Encyclopedia of Photography*, New York: Greystoke Press.

1966   Fritsche, Kurt *Das Grosse Fotofehlerbuch*, Leipzig: VEB Fotokinoverlag. (Published in translation as *Faults in Photography: Causes and Corrections*, London/New York: Focal Press, 1968.)

1972   Millerson, Gerald *The Technique of Lighting for Television and Motion Pictures*, London: Focal Press.

1977   Greenhill, Richard, Murray Margaret, and Spence Jo, *Photography*, London: Macdonald Educational.

1979   Hedgecoe, John *John Hedgecoe's Complete Photography Course*, New York: Simon & Schuster.

1981   Craven, John and Wasley, John *Young Photographer*, East Ardsley: E P Publishing.

1984   Kodak *How to Take Good Pictures*, London: Collins. (A revised edition of *The World's Bestselling Photography Book.*)

1985   Busselle, Michael *The Manual of Male Photography*, London: Century Hutchinson.

1987   Haines, George *Go Photography*, London: Hamlyn. (Reprinted as *Learn Photography*, London: Dean, 1992.)

1988   Blaker, Alfred E. *Photography: Art and Technique*, Stoneham, MA: Butterworth.

1990   Cheshire, David *The Book of Video Photography*, New York: Knopf.

1990   Spillman, Ron *The Complete Photographer*, Surbiton: Fountain Press.

1992   Langford, Michael *Learn Photography in a Weekend*, London: Dorling Kindersley.

1992   Thomas, Philip *Photography in a Week*, London: Hodder & Stoughton.

1993   Khornak, Lucille *The Nude in Black and White*, New York: Amphoto.

1993   Freeman, Michael *Collins Photographer's Handbook*, London: HarperCollins.

1993   Owen, David *Make Better Home Videos*, Slough: Foulsham.

1993   Freeman, Michael *Collins Complete Guide to Photography*, London: HarperCollins.

1993   Freeman, Michael *Amphoto Guide to Photography*, New York: Amphoto.

1993   Stroebel, Leslie and Zakia, Richard (eds) *The Focal Encyclopedia of Photography* (3rd edn), Boston: Focal Press.

1994   Hedgecoe, John *John Hedgecoe's New Book of Photography*, New York: Dorling Kindersley.

1994   London, Barbara and Upton, John *Photography*, New York: HarperCollins (fifth edn).

This list was arrived at by consulting the relevant sections of bookshops and both university and public libraries, and also checking shelves at, for example, supermarkets, airports, railway stations. It

is in this sense random. As a result, the works constitute a cross-section including publications from specialist presses, leading houses and small publishers, relatively technical as well as introductory and simplifying texts, and general as well as focused (children, the nude) books. Only Buselle (1985), Freeman (1993) (*Collins Complete Guide*), Greenhill *et al.* (1977), Khornak (1993), Langford (1992) and London and Upton (1994) use non-white subjects in illustration.

References

Altman, Rick (1984) 'Towards a Theory of the History of Representational Technologies', Iris 2(2): 111–24.

Alton, John (1949) *Painting with Light*, New York: Macmillan.

Arroyo, José (1996) '*Money Train*', Sight and Sound 6(6) NS: 46–47.

Bordwell, David, Staiger, Janet and Thompson, Kristin (1985) *The Classical Hollywood Cinema: Film Style and Mode of Production to 1960*, New York: Columbia University Press.

Brownlow, Kevin (1968) *The Parade's Gone By*, London: Seeker & Warburg.

Coe, Brian (1981) *The History of Movie Photography*, London: Ash & Grant.

Coleman, A. D. (1985) 'Lentil Soup', Et cetera Spring: 19–31.

Coutard, Raoul (1966) 'Light of Day', Sight and Sound 35(1): 9–11.

De Maré, Eric (1970) *Photography*, Harmondsworth: Penguin. (First published 1957.)

Factor, M. (1937) 'Standardization of Motion Picture Make-up', *Journal of the Society of Motion Picture Engineers* 28(1): 52–62.

Greenhill, Richard, Murray, Margaret and Spence, Jo (1977) *Photography*, London: Macdonald.

Grover, Jan Zita (1995) 'Visible Lesions: Images of the PWA' in Creekmur, Corey K. and Doty, Alex (eds), *Out in Culture: Gay, Lesbian, and Queer Essays on Popular Culture*, Durham: Duke University Press, 355–81.

Handley, C. W. (1967) 'History of Motion-Picture Studio Lighting' in Fielding 1967: 120–24. (First published in the *Journal of the Society of Motion Picture and Television Engineers*, October 1954.)

Harrell, Al (1986) 'The Look of *The Color Purple*', *American Cinematographer* February: 51–56.

Hoadley, Ray (1939) *How They Make a Motion Picture*, New York: Thomas Y. Crowell.

Ihen, Wiard B. and Atwater, D. W. (1925) 'The Artistic Utilization of Light in the Photography of Motion Pictures',

Transactions of the Society of Motion Picture Engineers 21: 21–37.

Jones, Bernard E. (1911) *Cassell's Cyclopaedia of Photography*, London: Cassell.

Kindem, Gorham A. (1979) 'Hollywood's Conversion to Color: The Technological, Economic and Aesthetic Factors', *Journal of the University Film Association* 31(2): 29–36.

Malkiewicz, Kris (1986) *Film Lighting*, New York: Prentice-Hall.

Medved, Harry and Michael (1984) *The Hollywood Hall of Shame: The Most Expensive Flops in Movie History*, New York: Putnam.

Millerson, Gerald (1972) *The Technique of Lighting for Television and Motion Pictures*, London: Focal Press.

Mills, Frederick S. (1921) 'Film Lighting as a Fine Art: Explaining Why the Fireplace Glows and Why Films Stars Wear Halos', *Scientific American* 124: 148, 157–58.

Milner, Victor (1930) 'Painting with Light' in Hall, Hal (ed.) *Cinematographic Annual* 1: 91–108.

Neale, Steve (1985) *Cinema and Technology: Image, Sound, Colour*, London: Macmillan/British Film Institute.

O'Dea, William T. (1958) *The Social History of Lighting*, London: Routledge & Kegan Paul.

Owen, David (1993) *Make Better Home Videos*, Slough: Foulsham.

Revault d'Allonnes, Fabrice (1991) *La Lumière au cinéma*, Paris: Seuil/Cahiers du cinéma.

Rouillé, André and Marbot, Bernard (1986) *Le Corps et son image: photographies du dix-neuvième siècle*, Paris: Contrejour.

Salt, Barry (1983) *Film Style and Technology: History and Analysis*, London: Starword.

Sternberg, Josef von (1955–6) 'More Light', *Sight and Sound* 25(2): 70–75, 109–10.

Stroebel, Leslie and Zakia, Richard (eds) (1993) *The Focal Encyclopedia of Photography* (3rd edn), Boston: Focal Press.

Valentine, Joseph (1939) 'Make-up and Set Painting Aid New Film', *American Cinematographer* February: 54–56, 85.

Vincendeau, Ginette (1992) 'The Old and the New: Brigitte Bardot in 1950s France', *Paragraph* 15: 73–96.

Wagatsuma, Hiroshi (1967) 'The Social Perception of Skin Color in Japan', *Daedalus* 96(2): 407–43.

Walker, Joseph B. and Walker, Juanita (1984) *The Light on Her Face*, Hollywood: ASC Press.

Ward, John and Stevenson, Sara (1986) *Printed Light*, Edinburgh: HMSO.

Ware, Vron (1992) *Beyond the Pale: White Women, Racism and History*, London: Verso.

Warner, Marina (1976) *Alone of All Her Sex: The Myth and the Cult of the Virgin Mary*, London: Weidenfeld & Nicolson.

Warner, Marina (1994) *From the Beast to the Blonde*, London: Chatto & Windus.

Westmore, Frank and Davidson, Muriel (1976) *The Westmores of Hollywood*, London: W. H. Allen.

Williams, Raymond (1974) *Television: Technology and Cultural Form*, London: Fontana.

Wilson, George (1986) *Narration in Light: Studies in Cinematic Point of View*, Baltimore: Johns Hopkins University Press.

Wilton, Tamsin (1995) *Immortal, Invisible: Lesbians and the Moving Image*, London: Routledge.

Winston, Brian (1985) 'A Whole Technology of Dyeing: A Note on Ideology and the Apparatus of the Chromatic Moving Image', *Daedalus* 114(4): 105–23.

Wright, Basil (1933) 'Shooting in the Tropics', *Cinema Quarterly* 1(4): 227–28.

Young, Lola (1996) *Fear of the Dark: 'Race', Gender and Sexuality in the Cinema*, London: Routledge.

19.
JAZZ TRADITION, INSTITUTIONAL FORMATION, AND CULTURAL PRACTICE
Herman S. Gray

In 1991, Lincoln Center for the Performing Arts in New York City inaugurated its jazz program and installed its first artistic director, trumpet virtuoso Wynton Marsalis. This historic move, carried out by a major American cultural institution, signaled the emergence of a new period of visibility and legitimacy for jazz in the national culture. Lincoln Center's decision provides a reference point for exploring the operation of cultural politics—issues of aesthetics, race, and institutional formation—within a dominant cultural organization.[1] Moreover, it is an opportunity for reflecting on the sometimes tenuous and misunderstood relationship between the sociology of culture and cultural studies as analytic strategies for making sense of contemporary culture.

Marsalis's centrality here is by no means coincidental. Indeed, given his leadership of the generation of jazz musicians often referred to in the jazz press as "the young lions," his musical formation in New Orleans, his formal training at Tanglewood and the Juilliard School of Music, and his unparalleled recognition and achievements (e.g., Grammy Awards in both jazz music and classical music), Marsalis's role is perhaps singular. I mean, then, to highlight the media's representation of Marsalis, as well as his own use of media and Lincoln Center as platforms, in order to make sense of his impact as a musician and cultural advocate. In other words, I examine the tactical moves, social conditions, and cultural politics of the renewed attention to jazz as a cultural practice in the context of the media representations, debates, and polemics surrounding Marsalis and the legitimation and recognition of jazz by major cultural institutions like Lincoln Center.

While I develop the cultural politics of Marsalis and his work at Lincoln Center more thoroughly, I also gesture toward an alternative cultural approach to the practice of jazz. The set of productive practices and aesthetic approaches associated with Marsalis and Lincoln Center I shall refer to as a *canonical project*. The alternative, a view of aesthetics and productive practices that I locate in the metaphor of *the road and the street*, approaches the jazz tradition as a site for expansion and reinvention. I explicitly mark the social, cultural, and political boundaries of these practices, since they draw on distinct (though sometimes shared) technical vocabularies, cultural assumptions, aesthetic conceptions, and social investments in African American music traditions.

At the level of cultural and aesthetic politics, these distinctive approaches and practices enact different, but important, oppositional possibilities. Thus, while I place these practices in dialogue with each other, I also want to suggest that in the end they involve different ways of seeing the music in particular and (African American) cultural politics in general. I deliberately set into analytic (and political) tension, then, these cultural projects and the cultural politics—aesthetic and institutional—that they enact.

The growing media attention and public interest in jazz—the critical debate over its direction; the installation of Lincoln Center jazz program; the proliferation of philanthropic, public, and corporate financial support; and the growth of research and training opportunities in conservatories, institutes, and universities—signal a significant advance in the institutional recognition and legitimation of jazz.[2] This recognition and legitimation are especially striking when seen from the perspective of the sociology of culture that foregrounds the organizational, structural, and social relationships within and through which such recognition is achieved. In short, I view the activities and debates surrounding Marsalis and his canonical project at Lincoln Center as an effective (and largely successful) struggle for institutional space and recognition within contemporary culture. This effective struggle for institutional recognition and legitimacy is all the more significant when considered from the long view of the historic relationship between jazz and a dominant cultural institution like Lincoln Center, which, as the *Los Angeles Times* described it, is an "institution that has looked down its nose at jazz for decades."[3] Similarly, cultural studies help to clarify the cultural politics involved by alerting us to the racial, aesthetic, and discursive constructions and struggles that also lie at the center of this process.

Wynton Marsalis and his supporters are absolutely central to understanding this move toward institutional recognition and legitimation. In his varied roles as media personality, recording artist, cultural advocate, arts administrator, composer, and performer, one can tease out elements of his aesthetic and cultural project, as well as the institutional strategies for realizing them. Marsalis's vision and the cultural politics that underwrite it are pivotal for grasping the significance of the cultural struggles surrounding jazz since 1990. His effective, though no doubt polemical, directorship of the Lincoln Center program is a useful entree to this instance of contemporary cultural struggle.

Installing the Canon

Wynton Marsalis is one of the most accomplished, celebrated, and rewarded musicians of his generation.[4] Indeed, so prolific and celebrated is Marsalis that there have even been the inevitable comparisons

in the press to Leonard Bernstein.[5] Marsalis works in a variety of venues (jazz clubs, concerts, and festivals), media and educational settings (workshops, universities, radio, and television), and performance contexts (modern dance, ballet, opera, quintet, big band, and orchestra). His collaborations in related art fields include work with cellist Yo-Yo Ma, choreographers Garth Fegan, Peter Martins, and Twyla Tharp, as well as opera diva Kathleen Battle. His Grammy Awards, lucrative recording contracts, television and radio series, and directorship at Lincoln Center ensure a busy and demanding schedule.[6]

It is not just Marsalis's public visibility, commercial success, and professional achievements that I want to highlight here, but rather how the *figure* of Marsalis, in critical and popular discourse, may be read as an example of an oppositional cultural strategy by African Americans engaged in struggles for institutional legitimacy and recognition.[7] Marsalis himself, in fact, has used the social space of cultural performance and the institutional space of Lincoln Center as platforms from which to issue certain pronouncements about his vision of the music, culture, and tradition. Anchored by a modernist vision of aesthetics, a purist suspicion of the dangers of commercialism, and a deep commitment to racial pride, his is a cultural project—a canonical project, to be precise—which aims for institutional recognition, codification, and legitimation.

From his highly visible and influential public platform, Marsalis articulates a cultural, social, and aesthetic vision which aims to canonize jazz and to ensure it a significant place of cultural recognition and legitimacy for his and future generations.[8]

Aesthetic Modernism and Anticommercialism

One of Marsalis's most impressive qualities is his ability to forcefully articulate his aesthetic approach to jazz. Tony Scherman observes that "many disagree with him but few musicians or critics have what Marsalis can claim: a thought-out unified view, a cosmology, and aesthetic."[9] Marsalis's aesthetic approach to jazz involves a complex understanding of the music's contemporary cultural context, its historical formation and tradition, its technical elements, and the significance of its key innovators. Socially, Marsalis's aesthetic is founded on what he calls jazz's essence,

> Some of the essential traits of jazz are things that have nothing to do with music. . . . First comes the concept of playing. You take a theme, an idea, and you play with it. Just like you play with a ball . . . so you have the spirit of playing. Next is the desire to play with other people. That means learning to respect individuality . . . playing jazz means learning how to reconcile differences, even when they're opposites. . . . Jazz teaches you how to have a dialogue with integrity. . . . Good manners are important and spirituality . . . the soul of the music comes out of that. You have to want to make somebody feel good with what you play. Many so-called cutting edge forms assault the listener. But that's not the identity of jazz. The identity of jazz is to present itself with some soul to people.[10]

These characteristics form one part of Marsalis's view of jazz as a modern form. This social understanding is very much organized around his conception of the American character and his belief in the possibilities of American democracy. For Marsalis, jazz expresses a modern impulse. It "means a group of people coming together and playing without prepared music. It means negotiating your personality against the personality or with the personality of another musician with no controls over what the other musician is going to play. That's modern to me. That never existed until the twentieth century."[11]

Musically, Marsalis stresses conventional musical elements that characterize and hence distinguish jazz. These include blues, swing, collective improvisation, syncopation, call and response, vocal effects, and worldliness. So central are these constitutive elements to Marsalis's particular musical approach to jazz that it is worth quoting him directly and at length on each element:

> *Blues.* Blues gives the jazz musician an unsentimental view of the world. Blues is adult secular music, the first adult secular music

America produced. It has optimism that's not naive. You accept tragedy and move forward. . . . Blues is down home sophistication. . . . Blues is such a fundamental form that it's loaded with complex information. It has a sexual meaning, the ebb and flow of sexual passion; disappointment, happiness, joy, and sorrow. It has a whole religious connotation too, that joy and lift. . . . And blues gives you a way to combine dissonance and consonance.

> *Swing.* Swing means constant coordination, but in an environment that's difficult enough to challenge your equilibrium. In jazz somebody's playing on every beat. . . . That's what makes swinging in jazz a challenge. On every beat there's the possibility of the rhythm falling apart. You have the constant danger of not swinging. Swing isn't rigid. Somebody might take the swing in a new direction, and you have to be ready to go that way. You're constantly trying to coordinate with something that's shifting and changing. . . . A lot of what Afro-Americans did in music was refine things that already existed. Afro-Americans didn't invent it, but they refined it to another level and put another type of American twist to it.

> *Collective improvisation.* People getting together and making up music as a group.

> *Syncopation.* A syncopated approach to rhythm means you're always prepared to do the unexpected, always ready to find your equilibrium. . . . In jazz you're improvising within a form. You challenge that form with rhythms and harmonies. . . . It's all connected to the notion of playing. You set parameters and then you mess with them.

> *Call and Response.* Statement, then counterstatement and confirmation. . . . In jazz, the call and response is spontaneous. You invent it. Players call and respond freely, all the time. You have two types of call and response in jazz. The first is concurrent. . . . That's the most fascinating call and response, the simultaneous type. That's true collective improvisation. . . . The big bands made call and response sequential—that's the second

type—and orchestrated it. In big band music, the soloist played and then the ensemble responded with an arranged phrase.

Vocal Effects. There's achieving vocal effects on instruments, vocal effects that come, for the most part, from the Negro tradition, down home tradition. Southern shouts and moans, those slides and growls and crises and screams.

Worldliness. There is a spirit of worldliness in jazz. You can hear how jazz is connected to other musics from around the world. Folk musics specifically, but also classical tradition. . . . Ellington is the prime example. . . . He was trying to apply the sound of jazz, not by imitating other people's music but by understanding how its elements fit jazz; jazz music is not provincial.[12]

For Marsalis, then, jazz is the expression of the highest ideals of the black cultural (as opposed to racial) imagination. Jazz emerged out of a traceable past, structured by a formal set of elements, and practiced by a recognizable group of composers and performers. In other words, jazz is characterized by a complex set of social values, a sophisticated tradition of recognizable texts and practitioners, and a systematic means of reproduction. Recognizing these qualities, jazz, according to Marsalis, must be formally studied, systematically codified, and practiced through performance, education, and institutional recognition. It must be supported as well through an informed and critical public discourse.

Marsalis's aesthetic approach to jazz forms the basis upon which he identifies a particular corpus of styles, players, compositions, and standards by which the music is measured and judged. Within the jazz formation, he draws a rather sharp distinction between what he calls jazz and the avant-garde, particularly with respect to the seminal contributions of artists like Cecil Taylor and Ornette Coleman. Marsalis is especially forceful about this distinction: "I've talked to Ornette about his notion of free jazz. I think it's chaos. Maybe it's not, but that's what I think it is. Chaos is always out there; it's something you can get from any fifty kids in a band room."[13] While he is

quick to note that the family of players loosely known as the avant-garde do not call their music jazz, his view applies particularly to post-Coltrane stylistic developments in jazz; for example, the work of the World Saxophone Quartet and the Art Ensemble of Chicago.

I've listened to it (the avant-garde), I've played with the musicians, I was at the first concert the World Saxophone Quartet gave. I played on bills with the Art Ensemble of Chicago. It's not interesting to me to play like that. If I've rejected it, it's not out of ignorance of it. I don't know any people who like it. It doesn't resonate with anything I've experienced in the world. No food I've eaten, no sports I've played, no women I've known. I don't even like Coltrane's later stuff, to be honest. I don't listen to it like I do "A Love Supreme." It was with the type of things that that late period Coltrane did that jazz *destroyed its relationship to the public. That avant-garde conception of music, that's loud and self-absorbed—nobody's interested in hearing that on a regular basis.* I don't care how much publicity it gets. The public is not going to want to hear people play like that.[14]

Since, for Marsalis, jazz must be supported by a critical and informed discourse, in addition to avant-garde musicians and composers, he directs some of his most unforgiving criticism towards critics, journalists, and music industry personnel who in his estimation profoundly misunderstand and misrepresent the music. "Jazz commentary," he observes,

is too often shaped by a rebellion against what is considered the limitations of the middle-class. The commentators mistakenly believe that by willfully sliding down the intellectual, spiritual, economic, or social ladder, they will find freedom down where the jazz musicians (i.e., "real" people) lie. Jazz musicians, however, are searching for freedom of ascendance. This is why they practice. Musicians . . . are rebelling against the idea that they should be excluded from choosing what they want to do or think, against being forced into someone else's mold, whether it be the social agendas of the conservative establishment or the new fake liberal-establishment of which many well-meaning jazz observers are part.[15]

Along these same lines, Marsalis has more recently observed that "in jazz it is always necessary to be able to swing consistently and at different tempos. You cannot develop jazz by not playing it, not swinging or playing the blues. Today's jazz criticism celebrates as innovation forms of music that don't address the fundamentals of the music. But no one will create a new style of jazz by evading its inherent difficulties."[16]

It is in the deployment of his aesthetic vision against critical excesses and misrepresentations that one begins to get a glimmer of Marsalis's cultural politics; as early as 1988, in the editorial pages of the *New York Times,* and in his own volume, *Sweet Swing Blues on the Road,* Marsalis intervened directly in the public discourse about jazz.[17] These interventions are key, for in them Marsalis offers a corrective to what he sees as misrepresentations of jazz; the objective for Marsalis is, of course, to restore to musicians the authority of judgments and representation of the music and thus reestablish levels of competence, musicianship, and artistic integrity. This is how Marsalis put the matter:

> "Right now we're trying to get back to people playing at a competent level of musicianship. Another battle is for musicians to be recognized as authorities on music. That's never happened in jazz. And we're battling for the recognition of the ritual aspects of jazz, of the fact that jazz music is not like European classical music."[18]

Marsalis's attempt to distinguish jazz from what he regards as excessive (and damaging) confusion between European classical music and the jazz avant-garde is perhaps matched only by his contempt—aesthetic and technical—for the corrosive effects of commercialism on jazz. As such, he has consistently distanced and distinguished jazz from commercial forms like pop, rock, and hip-hop. His aesthetic modernism is complemented, then, by contempt for commercial contamination that threatens the purity, nobility, and integrity of jazz through confusion and

mimicry. "Jazz is not entertainment," Marsalis once quipped early in his career.[19] This sentiment captures Marsalis's contempt for the corrupting influences of commercialism on jazz. And he does not mince words to express his feelings about contemporary popular music: "*popular tunes are sad pieces of one-chord shit. Today's pop tunes are sad.* Turn on the radio and try to find a pop tune to play with your band. You can't do it. The melodies are static, the chord changes are just the same senseless stuff repeated over and over again."[20]

Jazz needs to be "protected," as it were, from these leveling influences, because in a culture driven by profit and record sales, confusion, misrepresentation, and, worse for Marsalis, a misuse of the term *jazz* can easily result. Again, Marsalis puts the matter forcefully and directly: "Anything is jazz; everything is jazz. Quincy Jones' shit is jazz, David Sanborn . . . that's not to cut down Quincy or David. I love funk, it's hip. No problem to it. *The thing is, if it'll sell records to call that stuff jazz, they'll call it jazz.* They call Miles' stuff jazz. That stuff is not jazz, man. Just because someone played jazz at one time, that doesn't mean they're still playing it."[21]

In a rather ironic twist, Marsalis suggests that while commercialism contributes to the social diminution and loss of cultural respect and legitimacy for the music (in the eyes of some), popular music benefits, aesthetically and culturally, from its association with jazz. This is how Marsalis explains it in his 1988 *New York Times* editorial: "I recently completed a tour of jazz festivals in Europe in which only two out of ten bands were jazz bands. The promoters of these festivals readily admit most of the music isn't jazz, but refuse to rename these events . . . seeking the aesthetic elevation that jazz offers."[22] In the same editorial he observed, "to many people, any kind of popular music can now be lumped with jazz. As a result audiences too often come to jazz with generalized misconceptions about what it is and what it is supposed to be. *Too often, what is represented as jazz isn't jazz at all. Despite attempts by writers and record companies and promoters and educators and even musicians to blur the lines for commercial purposes, rock isn't jazz and new age isn't jazz and neither are pop or third stream.* There may be much that is good in all of them, but they ain't jazz."[23] Such confusion and misrepresentation, when combined with the relentless commercial imperatives to sell records and at all costs to turn out hits, is, for Marsalis, at the heart of the matter. This situation, which generates misconceptions, misunderstandings, and appropriations of jazz, is what seems to trouble Marsalis most.

Racial Nationalism and American Democracy

A similar kind of protectionist stance defines Marsalis's conception of the role of African Americans in relationship to jazz. While certainly not limited to it, this conception begins with and is perhaps most evident in his defense of both jazz and African Americans against the persistent and destructive racial myths that still permeate many of the critical and popular conceptions about jazz and its practitioners. Marsalis confronted this myth directly in the editorial pages of the *New York Times*. "The myth of the noble savage in jazz," he asserts, "which was born early and stubbornly refuses to die, despite all the evidence to the contrary, regards jazz as merely as a product of noble savages—*music produced by untutored, unbuttoned semiliterates—for whom history does not exist.*"[24] For Marsalis, jazz critics and the misinformed commentary they produce are partly responsible for the perpetuation of this myth:

> "This myth was invented by early jazz writers who, in attempting to escape their American prejudice, turned out a whole world of new clichés based on the myth of the innate ability of early jazz musicians. Because of these writers' lack of understanding of the mechanics of music, they thought there weren't any mechanics. It is the 'they all can sing, they all have rhythm' syndrome."[25]

In contrast to the "semiliterate unbuttoned" image of the music that the myth of the noble savage presents, Linda Williams, writing in the *Wall Street Journal,* describes Marsalis as "a show business rarity: a black performer who has built up a big mass-market audience while taking a black nationalist approach to his art."[26] Williams suggests that, for Marsalis, "jazz is much more than entertainment: *It is an important expression of the 20th century Black experience in America. 'Jazz is,'* he recently wrote, '*the nobility of the race put into sound; the sensuousness of romance in our dialect; it is the picture of the people in all their glory.'* "[27]

Given the history, social climate, and deep cultural roots of the myths that Marsalis has taken on, one can begin to see the crucial role of racial (and, for some, black nationalist) politics within his larger cultural and aesthetic project. Indeed, as counter-discourse, Marsalis attacks this poisonous cultural assault on black people and jazz from a position carefully crafted from his own cultural formation in the black South, his intellectual mentoring by Stanley Crouch and Albert Murray, and his considerable command of musical history, aesthetics, and mechanics:

> My generation finds itself wedged between two opposing traditions. One is the tradition we know in such wonderful detail from the enormous recorded legacy that tells anyone who will listen that jazz broke the rules of European conventions and created rules of its own that were so specific, so thorough, and so demanding that a great art resulted. This art has had such universal appeal and application that it has changed the conventions of American music as well as those of the world at large.[28]

As with his conception of aesthetics and his position on the commercial corruption threatening jazz, Marsalis's racial politics are the source of considerable controversy. He has publicly debated jazz critic James Lincoln Collier on jazz criticism (especially Collier's writing about Duke Ellington). He has attracted bitter and often heated criticism from neo-conservative, liberal, even progressive cultural critics like Terry Teachout, Peter Watrous, and Gene Santoro. Neoconservative Teachout has even charged Marsalis with reverse racism, owing to Marsalis's hiring practices, booking policies, and his choices of repertory and commissions in the jazz program at Lincoln Center. While Treachout uses Marsalis's directorship of the program at Lincoln Center to attack Marsalis's intellectual mentors—Stanley Crouch and Albert Murray—his most vehement criticisms are directed toward Marsalis.[29] And while criticisms of Marsalis's choices in programming, orchestra personnel, and musical styles have come from musicians and critics alike, Treachout's is by far the most venomous in its disdain for the way that race in his view underwrites Marsalis's tenure as director. This criticism of Marsalis stems from Treachout's view of jazz as politically neutral, color-blind space of cultural and social practice, a space where, in his estimation, race should not, indeed cannot matter. Treachout suggests, for example, that "so far as can be determined, jazz was 'invented' around the turn of the 20th century by New Orleans blacks of widely varying musical education and ethnic background. . . . *But whites were playing jazz within a decade of its initial appearance, and began making important contributions to its stylistic development shortly thereafter. Until fairly recently, most musicians and scholars agreed that jazz long ago ceased to be a uniquely black idiom and became multicultural in the truest, least politicized sense of the word.*"[30]

Having established his view of jazz's historic multiculturalism, Treachout singles out Marsalis's Lincoln Center program for its race-based hiring policies and commissions. "Under Marsalis and Crouch," Treachout writes, "Jazz at Lincoln Center presents only programs about black musicians; whites are allowed to play with the Lincoln Center Jazz Orchestra, but the historic contributions of earlier white players, composers, and arrangers are systematically ignored, and contemporary white composers are not commissioned to write original pieces for the full orchestra. This policy is so egregiously race-conscious that it has even been attacked by admirers of Wynton Marsalis."[31] Treachout's essay is peppered throughout with direct attacks not just on Marsalis's guidance of the Lincoln Center jazz program, but Marsalis's character, politics, and musicianship. For instance,

Marsalis is unapologetic about such matters [his controversial leadership at Lincoln Center] and apparently he can afford to be. At thirty-three, in addition to having performed and recorded much of the classical trumpet literature, he is the most famous jazz musician in America. . . . Interestingly, not all of these achievements hold equally well under scrutiny. Technically speaking, Marsalis is a virtuoso by any conceivable standard . . . but his

jazz playing is felt by many to be cold and ironically enough derivative.

And,

Marsalis takes seriously, his job as an unappointed spokesman for Albert Murray's and Stanley Crouch's version of the jazz tradition. . . . He has been quick to criticize other musicians, notably, Miles Davis and Sonny Rollins, for "selling out" to commercial music. And he is adamant in defending his conduct as artistic director of Jazz at Lincoln Center.

And finally,

Although he uses white players both in the Lincoln Center Jazz Orchestra and in his own group, *it is widely believed that he harbors a general disdain for white musicians,* and the belief seems to be borne out by the facts.[32]

With passing digs at the generation of so-called "young lions" spawned by the success of Marsalis, Treachout details how racial politics in jazz operates: how privileging blackness in jazz works to the advantage of black players, in recording contracts, bookings, and appearances; how it contributes to the misrepresentation of social relations in the music (color-blind multiculturalism); and, perhaps most importantly, how it disadvantages white players. In the end, for Treachout, Marsalis is the most visible, successful, and hence egregious demonstration of the presence of reverse racism in jazz. He notes, bitterly, that

one can easily multiply such examples to show how reverse racism has become, if not universal, then potentially legitimate in jazz and indeed, how it has insinuated itself throughout the jazz community. . . . The new reverse racism in jazz is not, of course, an isolated phenomena. It has arisen at a time when such government policies as quota-based affirmative action have made race-consciousness a pervasive feature of American society. In the absence of these policies . . . it is unlikely that public institutions like Lincoln

Center and the Smithsonian Institution would lend the prestige of their names to artistic enterprises run on racialist lines, or submit meekly to cynical politicians playing the race card. . . . But that is just what makes the current epidemic in the jazz world so disturbing, and its implication so far-reaching.[33]

Marsalis's aesthetic and racial politics make for some strange bedfellows, indeed. White neoconservative idealists who celebrate the color-blind, multicultural aspects of jazz, mainstream critics, and in some cases black radical avant-garde players have for different reasons challenged Marsalis's heady pronouncements and his leadership of the Lincoln Center program. On the other hand, Marsalis has also brought together neoconservative African American cultural critics and intellectuals, young black performers, and largely liberal middle-class (white) audiences under a banner of a challenging but accessible middlebrow music, racial pride, and affirmation of American democracy and culture.

Marsalis's racial politics aim to establish the centrality of black presence and contributions to the American experience. Where Treachout sees (and aspires to) color blindness, Marsalis sees (and rejects) racial and cultural invisibility that is sustained by the continuing salience of racism in all aspects of American life and culture. Check out this 1994 exchange between Marsalis and an interviewer:

Q: How closely is jazz bound up with the experience of African Americans?

Marsalis: It is inseparable—in its inception. They created it. But why has who created it become more important than what was created? It has transcended its inception . . .

Q: One wonders if there will ever be a jazz innovator, someone on the level of Ellington who is white?

Marsalis: There might not, but it's not important. It doesn't make a difference. It is of no significance . . . why is it even an issue? That's the thing you have to examine.

Q: OK, why is it?

Marsalis: Because in our time racism still carries more weight than musical fact. Duke Ellington didn't have enough white in him? He's an American. He's from Washington, DC.

Q: People probably assume that it's important to you to say that all great innovators in jazz have been black.

Marsalis: I don't have to say it. I just say Louis Armstrong. I don't say black Louis Armstrong. I mean "what about pride in humanity?" Ellington's achievement is his achievement. It's a human achievement. Because, remember, the Afro-American experience is American experience. *Whenever the Negro is successful at something, there has to be an excuse made up for the why. The best way to do this is to make his achievement seem like something only he can do, for some racially derived reason*—which removes the direct competition and exchange that actually exists.[34]

And in the more controlled context of his own book, *Sweet Swing Blues on the Road,* Marsalis put the matter (the relationship between jazz and black folk) this way:

As Crouch says, "They invented it." People who invent something are always best at doing it, at least until other folk figure out what it is. If you celebrate less accomplished musicians because you share a superficial bond, you cheat yourself. Anyway if you ask most black Americans today who is their favorite jazz musician, they will name some instrumental pop musician. So much for race. The younger musicians of any racial group today swing in spite of their race, not because of it.[35]

Regardless of the venue or the occasion, in the final analysis Marsalis's view of the relationship between race and jazz is a complex amalgamation of deep belief in the possibility of American democracy, a celebration of African American contributions to American culture, and a critique of racism. An individualist ethic drives both his creative spirit and his sense of possibility for realizing his project in the institutional space of Lincoln Center.

Institutional Revolution

If nothing else, Marsalis has certainly used his position as artistic director of the Lincoln Center jazz program as a platform to bring together and realize a broader cultural project: to establish a jazz canon and create a space for its institutional legitimacy within a premier cultural institution. The conflicts over the realization of that project are as much generational as aesthetic and political. Peter Watrous, jazz critic for the *New York Times*, characterizes the conflicts this way:

> In many ways the fight is over not only the direction of jazz at Lincoln Center, which has been an exceptional advocate of younger musicians, but also the direction of jazz: Who has the right to represent it? What will its future be? How will its history be written? And despite the critics' prescriptive sound and fury, it's a fight that is over. The musicians, who commanded the bandstand, have won.[36]

If one accepts Watrous's critical appraisal, and I am strongly inclined to do so on the broader issue of cultural politics, then it is necessary to turn once again to Marsalis. For most critical observers agree he is *the* pivotal figure around which important institutional spaces have been opened and significant legitimation of and interest in the music realized. How Marsalis initially sought to realize this vision was set out in his 1988 *New York Times* editorial (well before his directorship of the Lincoln Center program was announced), where he wrote,

> We designed a Classical Jazz Series this year that deals with the music of Duke Ellington, Tadd Dameron, and Max Roach, as well as evenings given over to singers and instrumentalists interpreting standard songs. This series focuses on two things: the *compositions of major writers and the quality of improvisation.* . . . While enjoyment and entertainment are paramount matters in the Classical Jazz Series, it should be clear that we also see a need to *help promote understandings of what happens in jazz.* An important part of the

series, therefore, are program notes by Stanley Crouch, which seek *to explain the intent of the musicians as well as the meaning of the art.* . . . We feel that the proper presentation of notes, song titles and even small discographies will help audiences better understand the essential elements of the music and thereby enjoy the music even more. . . . Classical Jazz at Lincoln Center—whether celebrating the work of individual artists or using improvisational talents of masters . . . is intent on helping to give jazz, its artists and its products their deserved place in American culture. I also feel that the Classical Jazz Series gives Lincoln Center additional reason to regard itself as a center of world culture.[37]

Since 1988, through the Classical Series, commissioned works, collaborations, media and education, performance, and critical engagement with the discourse on jazz, Marsalis has used the institutional space and international reputation of Lincoln Center quite effectively—namely to increase the visibility and legitimacy of jazz.[38] For Marsalis, the recognition of a jazz canon by cultural institutions like Lincoln Center not only ensures the music's survival and legitimation in the society's dominant cultural institutions, but provides him with a prominent public forum from which to engage in political struggles over culture.

The effectiveness of Marsalis's cultural project cannot be ascribed solely to him, in isolation from the social, economic, and cultural transformations that have occurred in jazz since about 1990. Despite his effective intervention into the discursive debates on jazz, there have been notable developments in the political economy of the recording industry, corporate sponsorship of jazz festivals and performance venues, media coverage, education and training, and research on jazz. Many of the performance venues—notably small independent jazz clubs—have been replaced by corporate sponsorship, national franchises, megafestivals, and multicity tours.[39] Remaining local independent venues have to regularly book "name" talent to attract large and affluent-enough audiences in order to make their operations profitable. Although clubs and local performance venues long associated with jazz continue to turn over at a rapid pace, new forms of public cultural and financial support for the music have appeared in the form of foundation support, juried competitions, degree programs, research programs, and repertory programs at colleges and universities. Programs like those at Lincoln Center, the Kennedy Center, and Carnegie Hall are complemented by performance competitions like the Thelonious Monk Institute and research archives like the Institute for Jazz Studies at Rutgers University, the Center for Black Music Research in Chicago, the Smithsonian Institution, and the American Research Center.[40]

As for recorded music, the compact disk of course has replaced the vinyl LP as the standard format in which recorded music is presented. Through various distribution arrangements and marketing strategies between record companies and major corporations, jazz is effectively reaching new markets. Notable examples are arrangements between Blue Note Records and Starbucks Coffee, as well as those between cigarette manufacturers, liquor companies, car manufacturers, and jazz festivals.[41] Music videos, television commercials, and special campaigns (e.g., the United States Postal Service's commemorative stamp series on jazz legends) also have become an important means through which the music gains exposure. And, of course, public television and cable television (e.g., Bravo, Black Entertainment Television) have become important media outlets for showcasing jazz. For the most part, public and college radio remain the primary radio outlets for jazz, particularly since commercial outlets in major urban areas like New York, Los Angeles, and the San Francisco Bay Area no longer exist.

Audiences for jazz—both those who purchase the music on compact disk and those who attend concerts and clubs—are increasingly educated, affluent, young, and very often white.[42] To be sure Marsalis and his "young lion" associates have also helped stimulate interests in jazz on the part of black middle-class youth, some of whom, ironically, are also drawn to those commercial forms that Marsalis fears most for their insidious effects on the music—rap, acid jazz, house, jungle music, dance hall, and reggae. These styles have brought young people to jazz by

way of a search for new stylistic possibilities, as well as a familiarity with earlier players and styles within the jazz tradition.[43]

The popular and critical coverage of jazz, much of which is aimed at young affluent consumers, is limited to a small but energetic jazz press, including publications like *Down Beat, Jazz Times,* and *Jazz Is.* In the press, popular coverage of the music is limited largely to major metropolitan dailies like the *New York Times* and the *Los Angeles Times.* A growing body of independent films (e.g., *A Great Day in Harlem*), biographies, and scholarly monographs have begun to emerge as well.[44]

The Road and the Street

I want to propose that Marsalis's canonical project at Lincoln Center, while an expression of one form of resistant black culture, is also fundamentally conservative. Musicians and critics alike view this as a project that constructs a classical canon by formalizing it into static texts and confining it to museums, conservatories, and cultural institutions.[45] In fact, drawing on the insights of Amiri Baraka and African American literature, Nathaniel Mackey argues that such projects move jazz from a "verb" to a "noun."[46] In its "high modernist" tone and aesthetic assumptions, Marsalis's pronouncements on the aesthetic dangers and commercial corruption of popular music joins long-standing cultural debates about the relationship of high culture to popular culture and the contaminating effects of the latter on the former.[47] In Marsalis's cultural universe, the move to locate the corrosive effects of the popular arts on the jazz canon is, no doubt, a powerful political move.

In a climate of neoconservative assault on the arts and culture, Marsalis's cultural project is especially appealing precisely because it is built on crucial assumptions about the value of "culture" (and morality) in the still unrealized potential of American democracy. Politically, this scheme accepts a (traditional) view of the erosion of culture and values (which are under assault) and links it to powerful agencies of legitimation and recognition that aim to fix the limits of culture and protect it from the corrupting forces of the market, commerce, and untutored tastes. I find this position and its aesthetics culturally and politically conventional and elitist, the way that traditionalists (both radical and conservative) have always been on the question of popular culture. This vision relies on discourses and institutions of legitimation and power, a discerning and informed public, a critical community of judgment and evaluation, and powerful institutions to value and signal as important the conventions, technical rules, literatures, practitioners, and tradition on which a canon is constructed.[48]

Conservative or not, I do recognize, and even applaud, the strategic and effective interventions of Marsalis. Not so much as a capitulation to Marsalis's aesthetic and cultural politics, but to acknowledge the sheer complexity of the position and the effective results that Marsalis has staked out and enacted at Lincoln Center.

Where Marsalis mobilizes his rhetorical positions and institutional tactics around the need to canonize jazz, to ensure it institutional legitimacy in the broader American cultural landscape, when examined from within the politics of African American music a different set of cultural practices and political possibilities emerge. There *is* another approach to the jazz tradition. Indeed, when one considers the tradition itself and the productive practices and social conditions that shaped it, one finds many of the corruptive influences that Marsalis and his intellectual mentors fear most for their baneful effects on the music—popularity, dance, mass marketing, and the influence of popular styles.

While I can only gesture toward this other approach to the tradition—an approach which I characterize as the sensibility of the road and the street—I do so in order to make a point about the study of cultural practices and to foreground the politics at work in a different approach to jazz as a site of cultural struggle. By indicating an alternative to what I have called a "canonization project," I do not mean to suggest that the sensibilities and practices of a road-and-street aesthetic do not exist in Marsalis's own project. In fact, in *Sweet Swing Blues on the Road*, Marsalis writes quite robustly about the centrality of the road to his own formation and continuing practice as a jazz musician. I do, however, mean to underscore the fact that the locations and conditions

of production where jazz maintains its *motion and movement, innovation and expansion,* continue in those cultural spaces outside canonical discourses and institutional practices of legitimation.

I take the metaphor of the road and the street from the great territory bands of the 1930s and 1940s. The road (as opposed to, for instance, the "tour") was an expression used by musicians to describe life on the road—the experience of traveling from community to community, town to town, city to city to perform. The music, social relations, and cultural styles which defined urban black communities in the 1940s and 1950s were, as cultural historian Robin D. G. Kelley brilliantly details, the basis for the formation among many working-class blacks of political consciousness and cultural understanding of blackness.[49] Kelley argues that it was black popular forms and cultural styles found in the streets and clubs of black urban America that gave shape and expression to the cultural and political consciousness of blacks.

On the road, musicians perfected their skills, discovered new musical influences and players, made friends, and constructed communities that extended beyond the immediate confines of geography. Encounters on the road allowed musicians and bands to sharpen their acts, pick up new talent, modify their books, and gauge the response to their music. The literal road and the street, then, were places where musicians borrowed and mixed styles and experimented with new possibilities. In the process, they created music that was dynamic, dialogic, and fashioned out of the experiences and needs of everyday life. While I have no desire to re-create this literal "road and street," I do want to shift the discussion from this literal and historical road and street to a metaphorical one.

Although very much rooted in a jazz tradition, the metaphorical road and street of jazz as a cultural practice depends on a different conception of and relationship to the tradition. It requires a conception rooted in constant change and transformation, where tradition is not simply abstracted, codified, and preserved in critical judgments, cultural institutions, and repertory performance. In this image of jazz as a cultural practice, the music lives and breathes, as it were, in the active creations and experiences of changing performance and encounters with contemporary ideas, styles, influences, and performance possibilities, including those in popular and commercial culture. This difference in conception and approach represents far more than a semantic disagreement or conceptual dispute over how the music is represented. The point of the tradition in this view of jazz practice (including its canonical manifestations) is to change it, to reinvent it, to emphasize its "verbal" character, as Mackey puts it.[50]

In contrast to the aim of building a canonical tradition in order to ensure a place of legitimacy and recognition by dominant cultural institutions, an entire cohort of Marsalis's contemporaries—Don Byron, Gerri Allen, Steve Coleman, Cassandra Wilson, Graham Haynes, Courtney Pine, Kenny Garrett, and Branford Marsalis—continually draw from a range of stylistic influences which challenge and stretch the tradition. These musicians, like many of their predecessors, keep jazz moving through its engagement with popular forms, new technologies, and commercial routes of circulation. Instead of protecting the jazz tradition from the corrupting influences of popular and commercial forms like reggae, rap, rhythm and blues, dance hall (as well as Native American, South Asian, and African forms), this cohort of contemporary musicians expands the jazz tradition by reworking it through metaphorical encounters in the literal street. With an emphatic stress on the verbal rather than nominal dimension of the music, these musicians are engaged in a dynamic reinvention and dialogic rewriting of the tradition.

Jazz and Cultural Politics

I want to conclude, then, by highlighting the analytic and political implications of these two distinct, but related, cultural practices. These two kinds of practice operate simultaneously, very often existing side by side, within the same social, economic, and discursive space. And yet I think it is fair to say that, culturally, the distinct political effects and possibilities of each are quite different. Those practices that gain a measure of institutional recognition and legitimacy are privileged in terms of visibility, funding, and reproduction. I believe that this very move also results

in the marginalization and displacement of practices (and musicians) that do not enjoy a similar recognition and legitimacy. They point in different ways to different modalities and registers, different aesthetic possibilities, and cultural strategies that challenge, even rearrange, dominant conceptions and judgments of the music.

Marsalis and his supporters effectively consolidated and institutionalized a specific conception of jazz within a dominant cultural institution like Lincoln Center for the Performing Arts. Moreover, the program at Lincoln Center is emblematic of the legitimation of jazz that rests on powerful social and cultural assumptions about the value of art (in this case, "real jazz") as one important source for the inculcation of core American values—morality, integrity, and responsibility. Like the treatments of baseball and the Civil War, this narrative of jazz as both the expression and realization of what is quintessentially American is at the heart of Ken Burns's PBS documentary on the history of jazz.[51] With Wynton Marsalis as one of the central consultants and on-camera experts (jazz critic and Marsalis associate Stanley Crouch serves as another, as does the writer Albert Murray) in the documentary, PBS's *Jazz* and the installation of a jazz department at Lincoln Center is, I would argue, *the* final discursive move in the canonization of this specific narrative of jazz in the American cultural imagination. It is also crucial to the representation of late-twentieth-century American society and, in Burns's view (if the documentary is any indication), the culmination of the long march toward racial equality, a march that celebrates cultural diversity as one of the signal achievements of American democracy.[52]

I highlight the importance of these cultural moves by Marsalis and Ken Burns, not because I agree with their aesthetic position or the cultural politics on which they rest, but because I think they illustrate the complexity and significance of various kinds of black cultural moves, especially their political impact in the wider cultural and social arena of American culture.

Popular and critical discourses as well as significant financial support and interest have congealed around Marsalis's notion of jazz, its key texts, and exemplars. Culturally, this has resulted in the creation of a significant social and cultural space for jazz in popular discourse, the marketplace, and cultural institutions. In the context of ongoing wars about culture, values, and art, this is surely a significant accomplishment. And as the polemic surrounding Marsalis's tenure at Lincoln Center indicates, the continuing political struggles over how jazz is constructed, represented, and positioned does matter.

Notes

*   My thanks to the following friends, colleagues, and students who generously encouraged, read, and commented on various drafts of this chapter: Dwight Andrews, Leonard Brown, Russell Ellis, Stephen Feld, Janet Francendese, Rosa Linda Fregoso, Lisa Guererro, Saidiya Hartman, Robin D.G. Kelley, Elizabeth Long, Tommy Lott, Bill Lowe, Ronald Redono, David Scott, Sterling Stuckey, Lisa Thompson, Robert Thompson, David Wellman, Deborah Woo, and Richard Yarborough. Special thanks also to my research assistant, Cindy Lui, who helped me track down press accounts of Marsalis and the Lincoln Center program.

1. On these and similar themes, see Bernard Gendron, "Moldy Figs and Modernists: Jazz at War (1942–46)," in *Jazz among the Discourses,* ed. Krin Gabbard (Durham, N.C.: Duke University Press, 1995), 31–57; Steven Elworth, "Jazz in Crisis, 1948–1958: Ideology and Representation," in *Jazz among the Discourses,* ed. Krin Gabbard (Durham, N.C.: Duke University Press, 1995), 57–76.

2. "Jazz: A Special Section," *New York Times Magazine,* 25 June 1995, 29–40; Gene Santoro, "All That Jazz," *Nation,* 8 January 1996, 34–36; Peter Watrous, "Old Jazz Is Out, New Jazz Is Older," *New York Times,* 31 March 1994; Linda Williams, "A Young Musician Trumpets a Revival of Traditional Jazz," *Wall Street Journal,* 24 September 1986.

3. Richard Guilliatt, "The Young Lions Roar," *Los Angeles Times,* 13 September 1992.

4. Jervis Anderson, "Medium Cool," *New Yorker,* 12 December 1994, 69–83; Richard Guilliatt, "Eminence Jazz," *San Jose Mercury News,* 11 June 1993; "Jazz: A Special Section," *New York Times Magazine;* Gene Santoro, "Young Man with a Horn," *Nation,* 1 March 1993, 280–84; Williams, "A Young Musician."

5. Alex Ross, "Asking Some Good, Hard Truths about Music," *New York Times,* 12 November 1995.

6. For more recent developments in Marsalis's career see, David Hajdu, "Wynton's Blues," *Atlantic Monthly,* March 2003, 43–58.

7. Other notable examples of the effective use of similar strategies in important cultural sites include highly visible figures in theater, film, and African American studies.

8. Frank Conroy, "Stop Nit-Picking a Genius," *New York Times Magazine,* 25 June 1995, 28–31, 48, 54, 70; Wynton Marsalis, "What Jazz Is—and Isn't," editorial, *New York Times,* 31 July 1988; Wynton Marsalis, *Sweet Swing Blues on the Road* (New York: W. W. Norton, 1994).

9. Tony Scherman, "What Is Jazz?" *American Heritage,* October 1995, 66 ff.

10. Ibid.

11. Ibid.

12. Ibid.; quotations are from various places in the article.

13. Ibid.

14. Ibid.; my emphasis.

15. Marsalis, "What Jazz Is," 24.

16. Marsalis, *Sweet Swing Blues on the Road,* 141.

17. Marsalis, "What Jazz Is" and *Sweet Swing Blues on the Road.*

18. Scherman, "What Is Jazz?" 66 ff.

19. Quoted in Williams, "A Young Musician," 1.

20. James A. Liska, "Wynton and Branford: A Common Understanding," *Down Beat,* February 1994, 42 ff.; my emphasis.

21. Ibid.; my emphasis.

22. Marsalis, "What Jazz Is," 21; my emphasis.

23. Ibid.; my emphasis.

24. Ibid.; my emphasis.

25. Ibid.

26. Williams, "A Young Musician," 1.

27. Ibid.; my emphasis.

28. Marsalis, "What Jazz Is," 21.

29. Stanley Crouch is an essayist and jazz critic and Albert Murray is a novelist, biographer, and jazz writer.

30. Terry Treachout, "The Color of Jazz," *Commentary,* September 1995, 50 ff.; my emphasis.

31. Ibid.; Crouch serves as artistic advisor to Marsalis in the jazz program at Lincoln Center.

32. Ibid.; my emphasis.

33. Ibid.; my emphasis.

34. Scherman, "What Is Jazz?" 66 ff.; my emphasis.

35. Marsalis, *Sweet Swing Blues on the Road,* 142–43.

36. Watrous, "Old Jazz Is Out," C11.

37. Marsalis, "What Jazz Is," 24; my emphasis.

38. For more on this, see Santoro, "All That Jazz," 34; Ross, "Asking Some Good, Hard Truths," J3; Watrous, "Old Jazz Is Out."

39. See Santoro, "All That Jazz"; Peter Watrous, "Is There a Mid-Life Crisis at the JVC Festival?" *New York Times,* Arts and Leisure Section, 8 July 1995, 13.

40. Santoro, "All That Jazz."

41. Ibid.; Starbucks also owns a West Coast chain of up-scale music retailers, Hear Music.

42. Williams, "A Young Musician."

43. George Lipsitz, *Dangerous Crossroads: Popular Music, Postmodernism, and the Poetics of Place* (London: Verso, 1994); Santoro, "All That Jazz."

44. See Krin Gabbard, ed., *Jazz among the Discourses* (Durham, N.C.: Duke University Press, 1995); Santoro, "All That Jazz."

45. For example, Nathaniel Mackey, "Other: From Noun to Verb," in *Jazz among the Discourses,* ed. Krin Gabbard (Durham, N.C.: Duke University Press, 1995), 76–100; Santoro, "Young Man with a Horn"; Watrous, "Old Jazz Is Out."

46. Mackey, "Other: From Noun to Verb."

47. Patrick Brantlinger, *Bread and Circuses: Theories of Mass Culture and Social Decay* (Ithaca, N.Y.: Cornell University Press, 1983); Max Horkheimer and Theodor Adorno, "The Culture Industry: Enlightenment as Mass Deception," in *Dialectic of Enlightenment,* ed. Max Horkheimer and Theodor Adorno, trans. John Cumming (New York: Seabury Press, 1944; reprint, 1972), 120–67.

48. For more on how these operations work in jazz and rock, see Santoro, "All That Jazz"; Williams, "A Young Musician"; Robert Walser, *Running with the Devil: Power, Gender, and Madness in Heavy Metal Music* (Hanover, N.H.: University Press of New England, 1993).

49. Robin D. G. Kelley, "The Riddle of the Zoot Suit: Malcolm Little and Black Cultural Politics during World War II," in *Race Rebels: Culture, Politics, and the Black Working Class,* ed. Robin D. G. Kelley (New York: Free Press, 1994), 35–55.

50. Mackey, "Other: From Noun to Verb."

51. Krin Gabbard, "Ken Burns's 'Jazz': Beautiful Music, but Missing a Beat," *Chronicle of Higher Education,* 15 December 2000, B18–19; see also Ben Ratliff, "Fixing, for Now, the Image of Jazz," *New York Times,* 7 January 2001, sec. 2, 32–33; and "A Roundtable on Ken Burns's *Jazz,*" moderated by Geoffrey Jacques, *Journal of Popular Music Studies* 13, no. 2 (Fall 2001): 207–27.

52. See Gabbard, *Jazz among the Discourses.*

20.
PHANTOM CALLS
Race and the Globalization of the NBA [selections]
Grant Farred

Introduction

> A phantom speaks. What does this mean?
>
> Jacques Derrida,
> *Archive Fever: A Freudian Impression*

In Game Five of the 2004–05 National Basketball Association playoffs, the Houston Rockets' star Chinese center, Yao Ming, was called for a series of fouls against the Dallas Mavericks. Yao seemed perplexed by the calls, a little upset, even, but his coach Jeff Van Gundy was beside himself with anger. After the game, which the Rockets lost despite a solid effort from Yao, a livid Van Gundy accused the referees of making "phantom calls" against Yao. Van Gundy's statements set off a furor, not only within NBA circles but far beyond them. The controversy extended from Houston, Texas, to Shanghai, China—Yao's hometown—incorporating within its arc explosive issues of race, ethnicity, nationalism, and the workings of early twenty-first-century global capitalism.

In as much, however, as there is something strange about Yao's capacity to raise these issues, there is also, paradoxically, something historically appropriate about a Chinese player revealing the Phantoms that lurk in the American socio-political psyche. After all, basketball arrived in China decades before any Texan imagined a professional franchise in Houston: In fact, while the Chinese star Yao was drafted by the Houston Rockets in June 2002, the game had arrived in China not long after its invention in 1891.

The NBA may well be a globalized league today, but basketball was a sport global in its reach almost from the moment of its late-nineteenth century inception.

Basketball was founded by Canadian-born James Naismith in New England in the winter of 1891. The sport was popular from the start, from the moment that Naismith hung two peach baskets at the end of a makeshift "court" at the Young Men's Christian Association (YMCA) in Springfield, Massachusetts. Naismith was not trying to create a new game—sports historian Peter Bjarkman calls it "America's most native game"—he was simply trying to provide indoor exercise for gridiron players when it was too cold to go outside. Little did Naismith know that within a few years, basketball would reach the Far East. Yao's arrival in the NBA, however, could be attributed less to Naismith than to the evangelical politics of the YMCA (leaving aside, momentarily, the NBA's decades-old desire to expand its market to China). It was Christian missionaries, trained in the skills of basketball in precisely the kind of gym where Naismith routinely held court, who exported the Canadian's game to China. Armed with no literature other than the Bible and a booklet entitled "The Thirteen Rules of Basketball," professing a muscular Christianity among a colonized people deeply insecure about their own physiological prowess, the YMCA missionaries tried to recruit souls while teaching the natives a game they themselves had as yet barely mastered.

If the late-nineteenth century missionary politics of the YMCA explains Yao's twenty-first century arrival in the NBA, his status as minority can only be explained by mapping briefly the racial and socio-economic history of US basketball in the twentieth century. Professional basketball in America was not always the lucrative, glamorous enterprise it is today; its roots are much more humble, demonstrating a history filled with struggles to survive economically. While Yao entered the globalized, supposedly post-racial NBA, still dominated by the aura of Michael Jordan, the previous century had been marked by the struggles of the league's dominant minority—African Americans. Black players had fought racial discrimination to secure their right to participate as equals in not only basketball, but all American sport. The road from Springfield to Shanghai, from the African-American Michael Jordan to the Asian Yao Ming, runs not only from the YMCA through state-run Chinese basketball to the NBA, but also through the historic event of Jackie Robinson and the integration of American baseball.

As basketball was establishing itself in Asia, the "game spread like wildfire" in the United States, according to Bjarkman in *The History of the NBA*. Early in the twentieth century, basketball was adopted by American colleges while barnstorming leagues became a staple of the American entertainment industry. In fact, basketball games often took place in ball-rooms, providing the warm-up acts for dancing or big band music. It was from one such venue, the Renaissance Casino Ballroom, that the all-black New York Renaissance (the "Rens") took their name. For decades after its creation, however, basketball remained a haphazard enterprise—franchises came and went, all too quickly, leagues starting and folding, sometimes equally quickly. During that period, basketball wended its way through the American heartland, reaching such small Midwestern towns as Sheboygan and Oshkosh.

It was only after World War II that professional basketball began to come into its own. And even that early incarnation of the NBA—with its small audiences in small cities such as Syracuse and Fort Wayne, paltry salaries, and flat profits—is galaxies removed from what it would become in the 1980s and '90s. Energized by the "Magic" Johnson–Larry Bird rivalry, and then electrified by the unimagined brilliance of

Michael Jordan, the NBA would have been largely unrecognizable to those athletes who competed in the league's formative years. After Magic and Bird entered the NBA in 1979, the league produced a style of basketball that enthralled fans (and players), literally, across the globe. It made NBA stars household names (with Jordan undeniably on top, although with room for others) from Chicago to Kingston to Kinshasa. (This list includes the tough, competitive star centers Moses Malone and Patrick Ewing who would later, in different capacities, work with Yao.)

This was a far cry from the NBA's founding in 1949, established out of the merger between the Basketball Association of America (BAA) and the National Basketball League (NBL). Its first Commissioner, Maurice Podoloff, was—fittingly—a Canadian. In addition to administering the new league, Podoloff's other great accomplishment was overseeing its racial integration. Although African Americans had been playing basketball since its inception, boasting well-known professional franchises such as the Rens and the Harlem Globetrotters (who were actually from Chicago), in its first year the NBA was segregated.

Because basketball is not "America's game" (that honor, alas, goes to baseball), its integration was neither as spectacular as Jackie Robinson's introduction into the Major Leagues nor as memorialized as the event of a lone black man taking the field for the Brooklyn Dodgers in that 1947 game against the Boston Braves. And yet, even that signal moment in American cultural life, as the San Francisco Giants' star outfielder Barry Bonds argued just a few years ago, is a socio-political landmark now lost to most players, fans, and administrators. Today, many players have no idea as to who Jackie Robinson is or what he meant to the game.

Even more disregarded and little known is the story of basketball's integration. It is a legacy that has disappeared into the mists of cultural time and is recalled now only by sports historians and old-time African-American players like Wayne Embry (the center for the Cincinnati Royals from the late-1950s through the mid-1960s). But on April 25, 1950, Boston drafted the NBA's first black player—Charles Cooper, out of Duquesne University—early in the second round of the draft. In the ninth round,

Washington selected Earl Lloyd out of West Virginia State; and, finally, New York bought out the contract of Nat "Sweetwater" Clifton from its neighbors, the Harlem Globetrotters. There is, in Embry's polemically sub-titled autobiography, *The Inside Game: Race, Power, and Politics in the NBA*, an unmistakable pride in the recollection of that historic moment.

It is for this reason that, despite the discrepancy between the cultural significance afforded them, these moments of sports integration are so inextricably linked. It was Jackie Robinson's breaking the color barrier that made Cooper's, Lloyd's and Clifton's careers in the NBA possible—and, Embry knew, his own. An old-school player, bruising and combative as the Royals' undersized (6'8") center, Embry represents a generation of professional African-American athletes (in both basketball and baseball) who understood, both because of their historical proximity to and their coming-of-age in the Civil Rights era, the magnitude of their colleagues' achievements. After Robinson took the field for the Brooklyn Dodgers, professional basketball had little choice but to follow suit. The integration of the NBA in 1950 meant, inevitably, the collapse of history-filled professional black franchises, as Washington, Boston, and New York began to raid them for their talent. Of those outfits, it is only the Globetrotters who have survived in any sustainable form, and then only as a minstrel sideshow to the NBA—an all-too-colorful incarnation of their once splendid, barnstorming, and highly competitive selves. Also disappearing quickly, though not as quickly as the integration narrative, are recollections of the NBA before its Magic-Bird-Jordan days. Consigned to the dustbin of basketball history are players and teams foundational to the current league. Players such as the original "big man," George Mikan. At 6'10", Mikan, a "Goliath in canvas sneakers," was professional basketball's first "big man," dominating both the NBL and the NBA, winning a handful of championships in each. A graduate of DePaul University, Mikan anchored the NBA's first dynasty, the Minneapolis Lakers, winning four championships in the period between 1950 and 1955.

Mikan's success with the Lakers was quickly eclipsed, however, by the rise of arguably the greatest dynasty in the NBA: the Boston Celtics. The utter domination of Bill Russell's Celtics from 1957 to 1969 was such that those years in basketball history earned a singular sobriquet: the "Celtic Mystique." Coached until 1966 by the cigar-puffing Red Auerbach, the Celtics swept all before them during that glorious era. Also of no small historical significance was the decision by Auerbach to appoint, in the summer of 1966, Bill Russell as player-coach, making Russell the first black coach in the history of the NBA. With the likes of Bob Cousy, John Havlicek, Tom Heinsohn, and Sam Jones starring, the Celtics were the envy of all other teams. The most memorable aspect of that era, of course, is the rivalry between Russell and Wilt Chamberlain, the latter a flamboyant center for Philadelphia and then the Los Angeles Lakers. But Wilt—such an offensive force that he once scored 100 points in a single game—lost every time to Russell's Celtics.

Were it not for how ESPN's *Sportscenter* has valorized the dunk, Julius Erving's days as the star attraction in the American Basketball Association in the early 1970s would long since have been allowed to fade entirely from public memory. Under similar threat are Lew Alcindor's (later Kareem Abdul-Jabbar) brilliant college career and the elegance—capped by his signature "baby sky hook," a shot deemed "indefensible" by his opponents—he brought to the center position in his time with the Bucks and the Lakers. Those days are now the stuff of the ESPN archives and nostalgia.

And, finally, the scandal of rampant drug use in the NBA from the mid-1970s to the early 1980s is now nothing but a faintly odorous whiff, cleansed by the tough administration of Commissioner David Stern. The drug allegations were not uninformed by how "black" the league had become in the decades since its founding. A lawyer, Stern is credited with saving the NBA from disrepute, ignominy, lost TV revenues, and a propensity for self-destruction. So precipitously had the status of the NBA declined that the 1980 finals between Los Angeles and Philadelphia was only shown on tape delay, after midnight, on CBS. Stern is, of course, fortunate to have taken up the Commissioner's job at the right time. He became Commissioner in 1983, the year before Jordan entered the NBA and just as the league was recovering from the "lost decade" of the 1970s. The NBA was on the road to improved health courtesy of the bi-coastal, barely disguised racial rivalry between Magic and Bird.

This contest pitted the putatively "white" Celtics (actually filled with black players and headed by a black coach) versus the "black" Lakers (coached by Pat Riley, a white graduate of the University of Kentucky, where Coach Adolph Rupp had believed firmly in the virtues of segregation). Flashy, highly stylized in their on- and off-court moves, and led by the ever-smiling Magic, with Abdul-Jabbar his stalwart center, the Lakers were the progenitors of NBA hype and cool. For all their importance in resurrecting the NBA's fortunes, however, Magic and Bird were doing little more than playing a bi-racial John the Baptist to the True (black) Savior.

The phenomenon that was, and in some ways still is, Michael Jordan, was of course absolutely central to the NBA's revitalization. Jordan alone was responsible for the league's growth and, from the late-1980s, its expansion into a global enterprise. If the Celtics-Lakers rivalry had provided the NBA with a new cultural and economic foundation, it was Jordan who opened it to a whole new cultural and economic stratosphere. His Airness gave the NBA access to the whole world. According to Walter LaFeber, it was "his success in the global market that set Jordan apart" (80). Jordan made the NBA global; he played in the NBA but he belonged to the world. Jordan not only belonged to the moment of transformation from a national to a global league, he was its grandest fulfillment. His Airness made possible the infinite international growth of the NBA. His career was emblematic of the explosive growth of neo-liberal capitalism from the 1980s on.

This was the decade of Reagan. To borrow a phrase from Gordon Gecko, the character in *Wall Street*, it was the decade in which "greed" was "good," in which it was imagined that capital could proliferate endlessly. It was a "me-first," acquisitive ethos that Jordan and the NBA understood perfectly. It also took that mantra to heart as the league secured its standing as a prime-time cultural event and set its sights on expansion, both nationally and internationally. For Stern, the world was nothing but a market to

be cornered, a series of places where the NBA could sell its products and itself as consumable merchandise. With Europe already providing a steady stream of players, Stern took aim at the rest of the world. Early in his tenure, the Commissioner expressed his interest in China, already in the mid-1980s promising to be the biggest market of all. Jordan joined the Chicago Bulls in 1984 as an almost-post-Cold-War world was beginning to take shape. This was a world in which the flows of global capital and its capacity to proliferate his image enabled Jordan to transcend his North Carolina roots and his Chicago Bulls affiliation. *He* was *Michael Jordan*; the Bulls, at best, his supporting cast, at worst, merely the platform for his greatness. Most saliently, the Sternian ethos allowed him to transcend American society itself. By the end of his career in 2003, Jordan was one of the most recognized American athletes in the world.

Jordan was the athlete who single-handedly changed—well, with the help of Nike, McDonalds, Wheaties, Hanes, and his innumerable other endorsements— the way capital and sport interact. Over the course of some two decades, Jordan was the pivotal figure in a triangulated commercial marriage, a ménage-a-trois composed of the NBA, the media, and his own iconic presence, that spawned millions of dollars for all concerned. Basketball quickly became one of the most lucrative sports in the world, making billions of dollars every year for franchises, players, coaches, media networks, advertisers, and sponsors from Beijing to Barcelona to Buenos Aires. Jordan's rise as a global icon has been like Manna from Heaven for the NBA.

Basketball has a long "international" history, but the post-Jordan NBA is the game's first real global force. By the 04–05 season, the NBA could boast that its teams featured 81 international players from 35 countries. Representatives from Argentina to Turkey, from Croatia to Slovenia, from the Congo to Spain, filled its ranks. The globalization of the NBA is most obviously demonstrated in the annual draft day proceedings. Whereas in 1994 only four foreign players were drafted, this number had increased to 10 just five years later.

In June 2005, 18 foreign-born players were selected, including Australia's Andrew Bogut, who was taken by the Milwaukee Bucks as the number one pick. The expansion of US culture and capital into every corner of the basketball-playing world has succeeded in globalizing the NBA. In return, of course, the world is increasingly being NBA'ed: from one continent to another, basketball products, sneakers, replica outfits, baseball hats, and all kinds of paraphernalia have become highly desired consumable objects; all, of course, with the attendant hip-hop culture in tow—the eye-catching tattoos, the hairstyles, the "street" language, and the flashy jewelry. Moreover, basketball is beginning to displace once-dominant traditional sports. In the Anglophone Caribbean, administrators worry for the future of cricket, as young Jamaicans and Trinidadians begin to have hoop dreams; in China, the days of football's (soccer's) hegemony are passing as the sport takes second place while basketball courts sprout up like mushrooms in Shanghai and Beijing.

What the NBA did not expect in the wake of its internationalization, however, were the ways in which the post-Jordan globalization era would unexpectedly resurrect one of the ghosts that His Airness' benign presence had supposedly laid to rest: the Phantom of race. The Phantom is that unspeakable aspect of the political that is feared because of its capacity to disrupt the "normal" functioning of a society; the Phantom is feared because its presence not only haunts the body politic, but is palpably present even when its disorderly propensities are not at work. The Phantom, in literary terms, resembles the ghost of the dead king in *Hamlet*, and the historic aftereffects of slavery in Ralph Ellison's *Invisible Man*, and the murdered child in Toni Morrison's *Beloved*. They all give the living nary a moment's peace. In the post-Jordan NBA, race functions as a socio-political force. It compels, often in unexpected ways, a re-engagement with the effects of a segregated, discriminatory, and inequitable past. Rendered momentarily inactive by the Jordanesque discourse of post-racialism, it returns now to recall the ghosts of Clifton et al.

The Phantom is a threat because it resides in the self's relationship with the others who so closely resemble it—those to whom the self is bonded, like Russell to Wilt, Bird to Magic, Yao to his Chinese alterego, Wang. Antagonists, opponents, countrymen: the

ghosts of others are lodged deep in the psyche of the self. It is for this reason that the Phantom is always only a crisis, an event, an evocation, removed from reactivation and rearticulation. Increasingly, as the NBA draft has become more international, so has the Phantom of race reemerged, reanimating that divisive aspect of the NBA's past that the Jordan era was supposed to have buried. "The foreign invasion," writes *Newsweek* journalist Brook Larmer, "naturally, has its critics, from those who moan about the NBA's eagerness to exploit overseas markets to those who say it is part of a 'pearl drops' strategy to whiten a league whose players are mostly black—and whose fans and corporate sponsors who are mainly white" (2005a, 70).

The "racist" undergirdings of the "pearl drop strategy," however, offer an anachronistic racial dichotomy. This is because, in the post-Jordan era, race emerges in an internationalized NBA not only in a strictly bounded, black versus white sense. In the "phantom calls," race is conceived as a concatenation of political effects. It demands the linking together of different histories, continents, economies, cultures—American, African-American, Asian—in their always complicated relation to basketball, discourses about the body in public, and the nation itself. *Phantom Calls* explores the difficult, contorted, and fluid interplay of blackness, whiteness, and Asian-ness in relation to Yao Ming and the racial politics of the NBA. The focus in this pamphlet is on how these tensions, perceptions, and articulations of race mutate in their relationships to each other. In the terms suggested here, race can only be thought, in this moment of largely unhindered capital flows, as a phantasmatically complex logic. Race and racism are composed, in uneven degrees, of globalization, ethnicity, a complicated anti-Americanism, the reemergence of earlier, resolute and still efficacious articulations of (African-American) racial consciousness, and difficult translations from one national context to another.

In this era of globalization, the Phantom of race is articulated not through the body of the NBA's black (African-American) majority, but in the event of the minority athlete, who is not white but Asian. "Asian-ness" has often located Asian Americans outside of African-American blackness, which is to say, "above"

African Americans in the racial economy. While Asians have never been fully absorbed into the paradigm of whiteness, they enjoy a proximity to whiteness as a "model minority" that is forever beyond the reach of African Americans. There are, in fact, cultural moments and modalities that make Asians and Asian Americans, sometimes temporarily, sometimes more permanently, indistinct from whites and whiteness.

It is this linking together of historical forces that preoccupies *Phantom Calls* here—how the effects of race emanate from the political locale that is the NBA, a space in which the once dominant black vs. white racial dialectic has now transmuted into the post-racial era that is proving to be anything but post-racial. Indeed, the politics of the NBA is once again fraught with the ghostly presence of race, now refracted through the Asian body. It is striking that what is revealed through the event of Yao is the politically familiar. What is familiar to the American political landscape is made available and re-encountered through what is putatively strange: the body of the Chinese athlete. Except, of course, that the "strange" Asian body has for over a Naismithian century been conceptually intimate with, if physically removed from, American basketball. In this respect, Yao is less the stranger amongst us than a distant athletic relative "returned," from afar, to bring to life repressed political and cultural Phantoms.

Articulated through the event of Yao, race emerges in *Phantom Calls* not only as a critique of globalization, but refigured as a discourse about the body and cultural history of the (Chinese) nation in the era of neo-liberalization. Yao evokes a series of dialectics between China and the West. Embedded in this dialectic is the ghostly discourse of physiological inferiority: the historical sense that Asia has been, that it can still be, overwhelmed by the stronger, "superior," Western body (with an especial anxiety about the athletic prowess of the black body). This unease is revealed by Yao as he reflects upon his own singularity as an NBA player. From the moment he was chosen as the number one pick by the Houston Rockets in 2002, Yao understood how he would have to bear the burden of cultural and historical over-representation for Asians and Asian Americans: "diving, gymnastics,

table tennis. We've always been good at those sports. Not basketball. It's a Western sport, and we've never been good at it. So it means much more to China to have a star in basketball, because it says that in at least one way we can compete with the West. That's something China has not believed in a long time."

What is confronted in China is a unique historical phenomenon. It represents the coming-into-dominance of the neo-liberal Asian nation that is struggling, as much in full view of the world as privately, with the process of transition; a process for which it has been critiqued both internationally and locally. China is coming to terms with the changes that have taken place since the Cultural Revolution—the adoption of a market economy under Communist Party (CP) rule, a single party domination that has seen many challenges to its authority, especially the event of Tiananmen Square in June 1989. China manifests itself as fully located in a moment of intense contradictions: a neo-liberal capitalist economy overseen by a CP that favors "open markets" but not, in Karl Popper's terms, an "open society." China is now "capitalist" without being democratic, a nominally socialist society without anything remotely like a planned economy. Deeply suspicious of the West, it has in the past decade become the biggest beneficiary of direct foreign investment by Western capital. Whereas it was, during the Cultural Revolution, strongly opposed to organized sport (because it glorified the individual), it has since its readmission to the Olympic movement in 1979 aggressively pursued medals. China has been investing large amounts of money in the national sports system, an athletic model inherited from its old socialist comrades, the Soviet Union.

[. . .]

Speaking For

There was nothing in between
no mediating look or word
to conceal his wretchedness—or hers.

Milan Kundera, *Life is Elsewhere*

Race and racism, however, especially as they reference African Americans in relation to the event of Yao, are strange phenomena. Exactly how complicated and tendentious they are to speak is evident in the truncations, gaps, and silences that abound in Van Gundy's denunciations of the referees. By claiming prejudicial officiating against Yao, Van Gundy raises a specter that is disruptive to the post-racial, globalized representation of the NBA. Van Gundy's call compels more, however, than a globalized perspective, the recognition that the NBA now belongs in the world, with all its specialized, skilled gastarbeiters hailing from all over the world—even, of course, as the NBA is still primarily a US corporation. Van Gundy's silence about the local begins as a critique of the local and the ways in which that local both can and cannot accommodate Yao as a political subject. By positioning Yao as the symbolic victim of the American racial phantasmatic and his refusal to name race or racism, by "mediating" Yao, in Kundera's sense, Van Gundy makes possible a discussion about the condition of racial politics as it pertains to African-American players in the NBA. Van Gundy provokes one racialized question more than any other: Is Yao the target of "phantom calls" because he is not black? The condition of the NBA in its post-racial formation is such that the preponderance of African-American players has made it a cultural space that is "out of joint" with the rest of American society. Within the peculiar racial dynamic that is the NBA, the black player— at least since the demise of Bird's figuratively white Celtics in the late-1980s—is hegemonic and looks likely to be so for a good while yet. Because of his remove from and occasional antipathy to blackness, the Asian player can, in Van Gundy's unspoken racial economy, be cast as the racial minority.

Through Yao's protection by his white coach, the Asian athlete is not only represented metaphorically but subsumed into a collective, racially complicated, and victimized, proximate "whiteness." It is a whiteness produced out of his profession's complex racial logic. At the very least, Yao is situated outside of blackness, giving him access to a sui generis position in the NBA: the foreign player who is not white but is afforded the status of minority because he is not black. Because of the supposed evolution of the NBA into a post-racial black league, that space where blackness predominates so that it need not be (historically) named, African-American players do not have

access to the discourse of "discrimination." The putative majority cannot be victimized by itself. Having borne the brunt of racism in the NBA's early years, African Americans are now protected from it. However, as the event of Ron Artest in November 2004 demonstrated, black bodies continue to be vulnerable in NBA arenas. After committing an intentional foul against the Detroit Pistons in their home arena in Auburn Hills, the Indiana Pacers' Artest was involved in a scuffle with the Pistons' center, Wallace. A fracas ensued and Artest ended up supine on the scorer's table. Momentarily at rest, Artest was attacked by Pistons fans, the most vituperative of whom were overwhelmingly white and drunk. That event, for which Artest was fined $5 million and suspended for an unprecedented 73 games by the Commissioner, revealed that despite their hegemony African-American players are still located as "black"—which is to say recidivist—in moments of crisis. Revealed in the comparison between Yao and Artest is a signal difference, the difference between how the Phantom operates for the black and the Asian player: the black body is vulnerable to a physical, potentially career-ending white violence, while the Asian body is subject to a symbolic violence, the "bias" of the referee. The difference, that is, between the end of a lucrative NBA career and a bad call. However what is also drawn into question here are the geographical and conceptual parameters of "blackness": does it incorporate into its majoritarian position France's black guard Tony Parker or Haiti's Eric Dalembert? Is Dikembe Mutombo of the Democratic Republic of the Congo afforded the same protection as the US Virgin Islands' Tim Duncan? Are all blacknesses equal? Wasn't Ewing the African American and Olajuwon the African in the 1980s and '90s even though they both played on the 1992 American Dream Team at the Barcelona Olympics?

Following Jacques Rancière's thinking, Yao can be understood as a subject outside the "dominant categories of identification and classification." He is also, as we shall discuss later, a harbinger of the very process that will disarticulate what Rancière names the "established order" of economic things, in this instance, the disruption of the American "established order." However, where the event of the fouls may make Yao most efficacious as a distinctly racialized NBA player is in his capacity to highlight the historic "wrongs" and to draw into question the phantasmatic "equality" that is the post-racial NBA. In Rancière's terms, Yao inadvertently "created a common locus of dispute"—he makes race an issue in the NBA through his belonging that is not, and can never be, a full belonging. Not only is he a minority in the NBA, he is also outside of the dominant conception of what an NBA center should be.

It is Yao's antithetical relationship to the Phantom that explicates why Van Gundy's is, because of the conundrum of blackness, a racially and tactically complicated position. He cannot name the Phantom that is "racism" because to do so would be to imply that African-American players get, as it were, the calls; it would suggest they are not the victims of bad refereeing decisions in the same calculated way that Yao is. If Van Gundy charged NBA referees with racism, he would risk not only widespread public ire (of a very different kind), but also potentially alienate his own African-American players. How kindly would his star African-American guard, Tracy McGrady, take to being accused of inoculation from bad refereeing decisions because of his race? In order for Van Gundy to allege injustice he has to be aware of the parameters delineated by the Phantom. Van Gundy, especially because his whiteness makes his insinuations about racism suspect, is delimited by the presence of race. The most the coach can do is suggest that a particular mutation of racism is at work against Yao. Van Gundy has to rely on insinuation and nuance to do the work of political critique because he is himself disabled by his own racial location. Because he is not black, Yao does not have the same historic access to protection from racism; because the NBA has a racially complicated past that is not entirely passed, it has to insist upon itself as a post-racial, globalized enterprise that has transcended the inequities of its locality. The peculiar history of racism is everywhere and this is precisely why it cannot be spoken, even as it is strategically and rhetorically operative.

Americans in the NBA now routinely compete with and against other nationalities. However, Yao Ming represents a complication of this phenomenon. As the first foreign player who did not attend a US

college to be taken at number one in the draft, he arrived in the NBA surrounded by an entirely different kind of hype than that which greeted the selection of an American high school graduate such as LeBron James. Moreover, the barely-ex Shanghai Shark was soon the target of an ethnically offensive remark by Shaquille O'Neal, the league's dominant player. Asked about playing against Yao on Fox Sports Network's *The Best Damn Sports Show Period*, Shaq shot back: "Tell Yao Ming: ching-chong-yang-wah-ah-soh."

Even before the Shaq brouhaha, Yao entered the NBA as an ethnicized and racialized subject. For his part, Yao seems fully aware of the dominance of African Americans in the NBA, and of the role allotted to him in this racial drama. Yao did not respond to Shaq's ethnic taunting, dismissing it as nothing but typical NBA "trash talk." Asian-American cultural critics, on the other hand, were livid at O'Neal's disrespect to Yao—and by extension, to them. One of these commentators, Irwin Tang, invited Shaq to a "throw-down" in Chinatown. Commenting on the expectations symbolically imposed upon him by Asian Americans, Yao responded with a noticeable remove: "I sometimes think [Asian Americans] cheered for me when I came to the NBA not just because I was Chinese, but because they wanted me to be better than American players. It was as if they wanted me to punish US players for something other Americans had done to them. Maybe that was supposed to make them feel good, as though I was getting something back for them." Yao is, as we'll see, happy to bear the burden of over-representation for China. He will, however, have no truck with those whom he labels the "banana people": "People in China call American-born Chinese ABCs and say that they are 'banana people'—yellow on the outside, white on the inside." As much as Yao rejects the "banana people," distancing himself from and refusing to own the Asian-American experience, the ways in which Van Gundy represents him as a model citizen of the NBA allows Yao to be momentarily interpolated into a certain kind of Asian-American "model minority" discourse.

In Van Gundy's estimation, Yao is "very easy to officiate, because no matter what you do, he's just going to walk to the other end . . . He's not going to make a stand. He's not going to get a technical foul.

He's not going to kick a ball in the stands. And I applaud him for that. But he's also being taken advantage of for his kindness and his respect, and he's not being given the respect back." Van Gundy is representing Yao as the exemplary immigrant, the player who does not question authority, who plays by the rules even if the "law" is not always synonymous with justice; Yao's "discipline" is explicitly counterposed here to the "theatrical indiscipline" of other (African-American) players—those who "make a stand," "kick balls into the stands," or who refuse to "walk quietly to the other end" of the court. (Van Gundy's description of Yao recalls how Jackie Robinson would never vent his anger over racist taunts, in part because it was not his demeanor but also because Branch Rickey, the Dodgers' owner, warned Robinson against it. For his legendary restraint, Robinson was deemed by many to be, in the paternalistic jargon of the day, a "credit to his race.")

Again, Van Gundy raises the specter of race without actually using the term. Relying on the explicit comparison between those who respect the law and those who flout it, Van Gundy is able to mobilize the stereotype of the undisciplined African-American player—the Wallaces, the Iversons: black players known for the regularity with which they test, and occasionally transgress, the limits of the law. While Van Gundy will not directly address race, critics such as Larmer are prepared to identify the ghost: the threat of blackness. "To many observers, especially white fans watching the game from their suburban living rooms, Yao seemed the perfect antidote to the NBA's ills: a clean-cut, 1950s-style player who exuded humility rather than hubris." In the dying moment of the post-racial NBA dream, what is there for a white suburban fan to do but reach back nostalgically to the prelapsarian age? For the post-War innocence of the 1950s, when the league was a white league, symbolically if not literally, where authority was respected and the players, unlike their black contemporaries, knew their place? When humility—not hubris, and tattoos, cornrows, flashy jewelry, and incessant trash-talking—was the order of the day?

In the thwarted desire for the return to that historic moment, there is also the articulation of Yao as an "honorary white" player in the NBA. With the undisputed domination of African-American players in the NBA, white US players, to say nothing of white US stars, have become increasingly rare. Not quite an endangered species, but the sightings are few and far between. Into this racialized void has stepped, occasionally, the foreign player. Especially, we might add, the nondescript but effective white European recruit—the Pau Gasols (Spain), the Zydrunas Ilgauskases (Lithuania). By the end of the 1980s, Bird, Kevin McHale, Chris Mullin, and the ageless John Stockton were the nation's white stars. They were complemented by the likes of Smits and Schrempf.

Today, however, the only white "stars" are foreigners, such as the German Dirk Nowitzki and the South African-born, Canadian-raised, Steve Nash. These players have to bear the burden of white overrepresentation, a task for which they, to their credit, appear to have little appetite. These foreigners reject white America's ideological imposition, in part, perhaps, because in a globalized league they each, like Yao, already have a nationalist burden to bear. Mexico's Eduardo Najera or Croatia's Toni Kukoc might or might not want to publicly accept the burden of national overrepresentation, but they are reminded regularly, and often not by Americans, of their "foreignness" in the NBA. It is not unusual, in the various arenas where they play, to see Turkish flags waved in honor of "Hedo" Turkoglu or a Serbian and Montenegrin section urging on Vlade Divac; when Steve Nash of the Phoenix Suns returns to Canada to play the Toronto Raptors, affiliations become really twisted. Who do the Canadian fans root for? "Their" (South African-born) star or "their" team (comprised as it is entirely of Americans, from the coaches to the players, except for Belize's Milt Palacio)? The immigrant communities in North America might each lay claim to "their" star, much like Asian Americans have symbolically named Yao as "theirs," but there is nothing simple about the politics of affiliation in the global NBA, especially not for white European or South American players who are simultaneously athletic icons for the absent nation and, potentially, for the white American fantasy of an athletic prowess that can trump African-American hegemony in the league. (Black players from Haiti or the Congo bear only, in this regard, a single national burden. They can never stand in for, or as, the "Great White Basketball Hope.") All the while, of course, several of these "international" players are massively enamored of the culture—particularly the love for hip-hop music, the stylized dressing, and the tattoos—of black self-representation. Where does the foreign nation end and the immersion in a racialized Americanization begin? Can anyone play in the NBA and not become, to some extent, "American?" How are the "primary" allegiances to nation complicated by the condition of being a high-end gastarbeiter?

Devoid of tattoos, seemingly incapable of trash-talking, Yao is the very incarnation of humility. As a mode of athletic being, humility is grounded in the subsumption of the individual—the suppression of the colloquial ego—into the team project. The individual accomplishment, the logic of humility goes, matters only in so far as it serves the cause of the collective good. Recognized by journalists and fans alike as the consummate team player, Yao attributes his "self-diminishing" ethic to his basketball training in China: "Individual talent is everything in the NBA; that is different from China, where everything starts with teamwork" (Larmer, 2005b). This narrative of self-sacrifice, of the subordination of the self, is what has made Yao such a white-fan favorite and corporate darling. Surrounded by his ego-driven African-American peers, Yao appears to give himself up willingly. Except, of course, that he is no different from them in his consciousness about his individual statistics (points scored, rebounds snagged, and so on), and attempts to secure a huge sneaker contract (Reebok) and other endorsements. Add to this his racial mutability and Yao is strategically positioned as the ultimate team player while simultaneously transcending it—by virtue of his height, his national origin, his dramatic entrance into the league, and, of course, his "humility."

Yao's racial mutability is especially important in the absence of a Great White Basketball Hope. If a white player can't be found, an Asian will just have to do. Yao may insist upon his Chinese-ness, but the limitations of his racialized agency are such that he can be made to represent desires and fill longstanding cultural and ideological vacancies that are far removed from his own. Yao's physiological Asian-ness

does not preclude his ability to represent a symbolic whiteness. It is not only nature that abhors a vacuum but that white America cannot conceive of itself as an infinite athletic lack. Yao's is, in this politically charged way, not simply an "honorary whiteness" but a vitally necessary and strategic one too. Yao may conceive of himself as the inveterate team player, except that he could not have anticipated how many teams would lay claim to him as a member: the Sharks, the Rockets, the Chinese national side, Team White America, as well as China and Team Asia-America. To say nothing, of course, about the grand designs of Team Yao, the marketing machine that drives his branding.

In all his conformity to the team ethic, then, Yao evokes the condition of the model minority, the very discourse he so abhors. Yao instantiates, in the terms of Chinese cultural critic, Rey Chow, the "Protestant Ethnic." He is representative of the Asian immigrant who buys into the Puritan concept of hard work, self-sacrifice, and the honor in labor in order to secure a piece of the American Dream—which in Yao's case means a substantial share of NBA-generated American capital. However, there are crucial ways in which the designation "model minority" might be conceptually inaccurate and inadequate to describe Yao's condition. Because he was already a star, even if it was only in the CBA, he does not really conform to the trajectory of the model minority. A true model minority would owe everything to the United States, especially in the case of the political or economic refugee. For this model minority, its cultural, economic, and political achievements are a repudiation of the place of origin, that geo-political location that is not only oppressive but has also repressed the aesthetic potentiality of its erstwhile citizens. For the conventional narrative of the model minority, the immigrant-made-good, the US is the site of infinite possibility.

With Yao this trajectory does not apply. Because his propensity for labor and his skills derive from outside the US, the value added from his work ethic can be claimed by China. In this respect, Yao can more properly be conceived of as a variation on the classic Chinese "returnee": that Chinese subject educated and trained in the US but ultimately in service to the Chinese nation. The returnee's role has been crucial to China's economic boom because of its skills, capital, access to technology and *guanxi* ("connections")—all vital to funding and sustaining China's massive economic growth; many enterprises in China owe their existence to returnee capital and expertise. In this configuration of the Chinese subject, Yao might best be understood as the "returnee-in-(advanced)-training," with the added bonus of the economic and cultural capital he is already responsible for making available to China. As part of the condition of his release from the Sharks, Yao agreed—what choice did he have, really?—to turn part of his NBA salary and his earnings from endorsements over to the CBA.

As the returnee rather than the model minority, Yao performs the kind of self-exclusion—repeatedly marking himself as Chinese, not as "Asian-American" or, worse, "American"—that is unimaginable to the model minority, for whom inclusion into America is the paramount psychological, cultural, and political concern. It is Yao's returnee status that motivates his steadfast refusal to become a "banana person." Even as he is ethnically slurred by Shaq, his physical and racial alter-ego, he will not take refuge in the bosom of the resident ethnics: those who presume to make a claim upon him culturally and politically, those who see him as constitutively of them without ever accounting for or understanding how immensely powerful Chinese sovereignty is, as a national identity, for Yao. The "returnee" keeps in place a sharp distinction between himself and the model minority.

However, Yao performs, as it were, the model minority discourse on the court even as he distances himself from it rhetorically. In his "soft," "non-physical" style of play, Yao raises the historical specter of the feminized male Asian body. His aversion to the combative nature of "playing inside," where "big men" such as Shaq, Duncan, and Wallace make their living, exacerbates his reputation as a player lacking toughness, physically and mentally. That "softness" (sometimes more perception than reality because Yao is, sometimes, capable of asserting himself, even if it isn't in a Shaq-like way), counterposes the feminized "yellow" body to that of his hypermasculinized black opponent. Even in Houston Rockets ranks, there is the sense that Yao does not get calls, or, alternatively,

is often called against, because his "style" of play is not combative enough. In the summer of 2005, for the first time, Yao, instead of returning to China and playing with the national team (though he did do a little of that), remained in Houston. The reason? To work out against renowned NBA bruiser, the long since retired but still up-for-a-scrap Moses Malone. The old stalwart's task was to toughen Yao up.

There is no euphemism for this: Yao is being asked to play against type—to become more like a black center. His Asian-ness, those outside skills, feminized him in the rough-and-tumble of the NBA inside, and this made him vulnerable to bad calls by the referee. Moreover, it is precisely his "model" behavior, his refusal to contest calls or make his displeasure public (which he perceived to be helping his team), that makes him a liability for his teammates. Yao's soft skills were not sufficient. He had to assume a physicality distinct and removed from his own. He had to de-Asianize himself in order to maximize his value to the team; he had to, as it were, become black in order to really become a member of his team. Anything other than that condemned him to a pseudo-effectiveness, a difference that made him stand outside.

By employing Malone, Van Gundy was acknowledging that in order for Yao to get the calls, to "get respect," he has to physically and culturally reconstruct himself; Chinese summer team workouts with CBA-caliber players simply would not do. Midway through the 2005–06 season, Yao's toughness was still a work in progress. Young centers, such as Eddy Curry of the New York Knicks, shoved him aside or drove on him relentlessly because Yao's is a body they do not fear. In fact, players such as Curry, to say nothing of veterans such as Shaq or Wallace, are often intent on initiating physical contact with Yao, confident that it is a battle the Chinese center cannot win.

The body of the athlete, which has a long history of standing as the body of the nation, is simultaneously reduced and magnified in the Yao event. In its micro-articulation (Asian-American), it is asked to refute the myth of the feminized ethnic by challenging—and redressing the historic wrongs endured—those "American" bodies that have dismissed the physicality of the Asian male. As a representative of the

Chinese nation, Yao is expected to remain a national subject even as his basketball heritage seems difficult to unlearn and continues to disadvantage him in the NBA. According to CBA official Li Yuanwei, "I am not concerned that by playing in the NBA Yao Ming will develop a personality offensive to Chinese people." Which is, of course, by virtue of its denial, already an admission of concern. In his representation of the "Chinese people," Yao will not become an NBA—which is to say, "African-American"—player. He will not trash talk, he will not develop an "offensive personality," in more senses than one, and, to his detriment, he will not become more "physical." Paradoxically, in remaining Chinese, Yao highlights the limitations of the CBA and the shortcomings of its players. He also, inadvertently, brings together the issues of physicality and aesthetics: is it Yao's body or his style that works against him?

Yao's "inadequate" body is expected to do triple duty when it's struggling to perform sufficiently for its smallest unit: the team, the Houston Rockets. For Yao, the national body—the Chinese national team—might be a site of respite from the demands of Asian-America, Asia, and, to a lesser extent, the Rockets. Little wonder then that Yao, in a purely physical sense, might take such pride in playing for the Chinese national team. There, at the very least, his body—his away from the basket style, his good passing and his "soft" hands, and his reputed lack of physicality—is adequate; there, his body is not called into question; there, the nation sees itself as splendid and not shoved around by the likes of Shaq, Wallace, and Jermaine O'Neal.

It's telling, however, how Yao used race to negotiate his location within the global through the ideology of the sovereign local. Even as he is familiar with the racialized history embedded in the vernacular speech of the African-American popular, for Yao race is an experience always vitiated by his Chinese-ness. "I know what 'nigger' means," he's said, "and I know that it's a bad word. When I first joined the Rockets, my teammates thought they heard Colin [Colin Pine, his translator] and me using it all the time. There is a word in Chinese that sounds a lot like it, but it doesn't mean the same thing. It really sounds like 'NAY-guh' and it means 'that' or 'that one' in Mandarin." Yao can translate race and racism into its local terms, but he will not transplant it from the globality of US discourse to the sovereignty of China. He will not allow for the mutation of "NAY-guh" into "nigger." Politics and economics, the site of sovereignty and the site of labor, have to be kept strictly apart. Never the twain shall meet. The Chinese nation militates against the universalization of US-style racism.

However, much as Yao—in ways that are very different from Jordan and Barkley—disavows race, he cannot be insulated from its workings. He is racialized in relation to his coach, by his coach's deliberate racial vocabulary (punctuated as it is by Van Gundy's telling silences), and his opponents (most publicly Shaq). Yao is, against his will, compelled into race and, in the process, serves as an unlikely progenitor of a new discourse of race. It is the sovereign national, participating in the flows of global capital, who internationalizes race while, inadvertently, deconstructing and exposing the myth of the NBA as a post-racial cultural practice. At the moment that he discriminates between "nigger" and "NAY-guh," at the moment that his coach protests "bias" not "racism," Yao is inducted into a discourse of race that makes race an issue that mediates, with an urgency utterly foreign to Kundera's landscapes, Houston and Shanghai. "NAY-guh" may not mean "nigger," but the globalized reverberations of the latter may overwhelm the linguistic difference articulated by the former.

References

Bjarkman, Peter C. *The History of the NBA*. New York: Random House Value Pub., 1992.

Larmer, Brook. "How the Game Travels." *Foreign Policy* (September/October 2005a): 70.

Larmer, Brook. *Operation Yao Ming: The Chinese Sports Empire, American Big Business, and the Making of an NBA Superstar*. New York: Gotham Books, 2005b.

LaFeber, Walter. *Michael Jordan and the New Global Capitalism*. New York: W.W. Norton, 1999.

21.
WHY I HATE ABERCROMBIE & FITCH
Dwight A. McBride

The astronomical growth in the wealth and cultural influence of multinational corporations over the last fifteen years can arguably be traced back to a single, seemingly innocuous idea developed by management theorists in the mid-1980s: that successful corporations must primarily produce brands, as opposed to products.

> —Naomi Klein, *No Logo*

The company's [Abercrombie & Fitch's] success depends on the teenager's basic psychological yearning to belong. (Remember, the Columbine shootings happened at a school some reportedly called "Abercrombie High.") And that means more than just selling the right kinds of clothes.

> —Lauren Goldstein, "The Alpha Teenager"

Although [Bruce] Weber has drawn upon a style and even content pioneered by [George] Quaintance, he has not fulfilled the promise of the earlier artist. Weber has little compunction about appropriating a style of clearly gay male sensibility, marketing it, but making small but significant changes that deny and repress its historical conditions and antecedents.

This is not all that surprising, for Bear Pond is little more than Bruce Weber advertising, a new form of reactionary art. If the earlier Weber photos were used (explicitly) to sell Mr. Klein's briefs these later photos are peddling

a new—post Ronald Reagan, Ed Meese, and Bowers v. Hardwick—version of (gay) male eroticism. . . . Unable to deny the existence of (gay) male sexuality Weber has de-sexualized it and reduced it to obscured indicators and marketed it as free sexual expression.

> —Michael Bronski, "Blatant Male Pulchritude: The Art of George Quaintance and Bruce Weber's *Bear Pond*"

My interest—a polite way of labeling it perhaps—in Abercrombie & Fitch began quite a few years back. It was a rather ordinary weekend night much like countless others where friends and I were out having drinks at a bar (which bar is not important to the story, as will soon become apparent). For the first time, I noticed that easily one-third of the men in the bar were wearing some item of clothing or another that sported the label of "Abercrombie & Fitch," "A&F," or just plain "Abercrombie." I asked one of my friends, "What is Abercrombie & Fitch?" And it was with that—at the time—rather innocent question that my intellectual and political sojourn with Abercrombie began. Once I saw it, I literally could not stop seeing it in any number of the gay spaces that I frequented. Whether I was at home in Chicago or traveling in New York City, Los Angeles, Houston, or Atlanta, in any mainstream gay venue there was sure to be a hefty showing of Abercrombie wear among the men frequenting these establishments. Even at the time of this writing (in the summer of 2003), the trend has only lessened slightly among white men in the US urban gay male scene. Since this label has managed to capture the imagination (to say nothing of the wallets) of young, middle-to-upper-middle-class, white gay men (well at least mostly young—there are some men who are far beyond anything resembling Abercrombie's purported target age demographic of eighteen through twenty-two wearing this stuff; and occasionally one does see gay men of color sporting the brand, though not many), I recognized this trend as a phenomenon about which it might be worth finding out more.

What is it about Abercrombie—especially with its particular practice of explicitly branding its products—that seems to have a lock on this particular population? What is it about the "brand" that they identify with so strongly? What kind of statement are the men sporting this brand in this sexually charged, gay marketplace of desire making to their would-be observers or potential . . . interlocutors? And why is it that the men of color in these same spaces have not taken to this brand with equal fervor? What about the men of color who have? The central question, put somewhat more broadly, might be: what is it that Abercrombie is selling that gay white men seem so desperate to buy in legion?

Let me be extremely clear from the outset that my quarrel with Abercrombie is not of the Corrine Wood variety (she is a former lieutenant governor of Illinois), whose conservative diatribe against the "indecency" of the company's advertising could once be found at her state-sanctioned Web site. Nor is my beef with the company and its marketing strategy to be confused with that of the American Decency Association (ADA). Indeed, I hope never in my life to be associated with anything taking a principled stance on "decency." Quite a lot of that already seems to be going on in the United States these days without much help from the likes of me. If anything, ours is a country that could stand to loosen its puritanical belt a bit and adopt more of a live-and-let-live policy when it comes to human pleasures. Dare I say that we need more of a public discussion about pleasure, a better way of talking without shame in the United States about it—where we seek it out, how it is a great common denominator, how we all (conservatives and liberals alike) want and need it?

Such an open dialogue about pleasure might carry us far toward understanding some of the realities of our society, which are currently labeled "vices" and therefore banished from the realm of any "rational" discussion by "decent" people. Upon closer inspection, perhaps some of these so-called vices might be better understood as extensions of our humanity rather than deviations from some idealized form of it. Such a radical approach to conceiving of our humanity, our existence as sexual beings, might go far toward altering the circumstances of those recently much-discussed brothers on the "down low," for example, who have been newly "discovered" in the pages of the *New York Times Magazine* and elsewhere. For I remain convinced that the primary solution to the conditions that lead people to participate in unsafe sexual practices, young gay teens to commit suicide, and cultures of violence to produce and even sanction gay bashings and the like, resides in a loosening of the stranglehold that a puritanical, uncompassionate, intolerant morality (too often masking itself as Christian) has on the neck of our society. So let me set aside the concerns of readers who might lump this critique with those who have cast their lot with the decency police against Abercrombie. My concerns here, I am afraid, go far beyond anything quite so facile or pedestrian.

I begin first with a brief history of the company and the label of Abercrombie & Fitch itself. Second, I want to spend some time discussing the "A&F look," especially as it is exemplified in the *A&F Quarterly*—the sexy quarterly catalog/magazine that has been the source of much controversy among the decency police, the source of great interest among its young target audience and gay men, and the source of capital for serious collectors of the volumes, which sell in some cases for as much as seventy-five dollars on eBay. This last fact my research assistant and I discovered when we began to collect them for the purposes of this book. Third, I consider some aspects of the corporate culture of Abercrombie as it is represented by its stores, managers, and brand reps (as the clerks are called in Abercrombie-speak). This might help provide some insight into the current class action lawsuit that Abercrombie is facing (at the time of this writing) on discrimination charges in their hiring practices.

And, finally, I hope to refer back to these points in my analysis of how "Abercrombie" functions as an idea, in order to justify the title claim of this essay in putting forth why it is I hate Abercrombie & Fitch.

The label "Abercrombie & Fitch" dates back to 1892, when David T. Abercrombie opened David T. Abercrombie & Co., a small shop and factory in downtown Manhattan. Abercrombie, born in Baltimore, was himself an engineer, prospector, and committed outdoorsman. His love for the great outdoors was his inspiration for founding Abercrombie & Co., dedicated to producing high-end gear for hunters, fishermen, campers, and explorers. Among his early clientele and devotees was Ezra Fitch, a lawyer who sought adventure hiking in the Adirondacks and fishing in the Catskills. He came to depend upon Abercrombie's goods to outfit him for his excursions. In 1900 Fitch approached Abercrombie about entering into a business partnership with him. By 1904 the shop had relocated to 314 Broadway and was incorporated under the name "Abercrombie & Fitch."

The partnership was uneasy almost from its inception. Both men were headstrong and embraced very different ideas about the company's future. Abercrombie was content to continue to do what they were already doing well—outfitting professional outdoorsmen. Fitch, on the other hand, wanted to expand the business so that they could sell the idea of the outdoors and its delights to the general public. In retrospect, this might have been one of the very earliest cases of big business ideology winning out over small. The result of these feuds was that Abercrombie resigned from the company in 1907.

After his resignation, the company did follow Fitch's vision for its future and expanded into one of the largest purveyors of outdoor gear in the country. Abercrombie & Fitch was no ordinary retail store either. Fitch brought an IKEA-like innovation to the selling and displaying of his goods: stock was displayed as if in use; tents were set up and equipped as if they were in the great outdoors; and the sales staff was made up not of professional salesmen, but of outdoorsmen as well.

By 1913 Abercrombie & Fitch had expanded its inventory once again to include sport clothing. The company maintains that it was the first store in New York to supply such clothing to both women and men. In 1917 Abercrombie & Fitch changed locations once again, this time to a twelve-story building at Madison Avenue and Forty-fifth Street. By this point it had become the largest sporting goods store in the world. At this location, Fitch took the display tactics for which the company was by this time famous to an entirely new level, constructing a log cabin on the roof (which he used as a townhouse), an armored rifle range in the basement, and a golf school in the building. By this time the merchandise the store carried had expanded once again to include such exotic items as hot air balloons, portable trampolines, and yachting pennants, to name but a sampling.

Abercrombie's reputation was so well established by this point that it was known as the outfitter of the rich, famous, and powerful. Abercrombie outfitted Teddy Roosevelt's trips to Africa and the Amazon as well as Robert Peary's famous trip to the North Pole. James Brady recently reminded us in *Advertising Age* that Hem and Wolfie (i.e., Ernest Hemingway and Winston Frederick Churchill Guest) also shopped there. In an article bearing the title "Abercrombie & Fitch Forgets Its Days of Hem and Wolfie," Brady recounts the "real man" glory days of Abercrombie & Fitch while bemoaning the A&F of our day, when the company takes out a double-truck ad in *Rolling Stone* featuring half-naked, boxer-wearing white boys on roller skates sporting backwards baseball caps. The masculine anxiety of that writer's article notwithstanding, he does refer us back to a relevant source in Lillian Ross's 1950 *New Yorker* profile of Hemingway, where one of Hem's shopping trips to Abercrombie is recounted. Other famous early A&F clientele included such notables as Amelia Earhart, Presidents William Howard Taft and John F. Kennedy, Katherine Hepburn, Greta Garbo, Clark Gable, and Cole Porter. And apparently during prohibition, A&F was also a place to buy hip flasks.

It is evident that even in its earliest incarnation, Abercrombie was closely allied with white men (and to a lesser extent white women) of means, the life of the leisure classes, and a Norman Rockwell-like image of life in the United States, for which they were famous even then. It is not surprising that the clothier we know today developed from a company with early roots in exploration, adventure, and cultural tourism, which catered to the white upper classes. The advertising from any of its early catalogs even adopts an innocent, idealistic Rockwellian aesthetic in many instances. It was not long after Abercrombie's resignation in 1907 that the company published its first catalog, which was more than 450 pages long. Some 50,000 copies were shipped to prospective customers around the world. So A&F's legacy of an unabashed consumer celebration of whiteness, and of an elite class of whiteness at that, in the face of a nation whose past and present are riddled with racist ideas, politics, and ideology, is not entirely new. Still, I believe the particular form it has taken in our time bears our careful consideration for the harm that it does to our ways of thinking about and imagining our current racial realities in this country, as well as for the seemingly elusive difficulty it poses in our attempts to understand what about it makes many of us so uneasy.

In 1928 Fitch retired from the business. The company continued to grow and expand well into the 1960s, opening stores in the Midwest and on the West Coast. In the late 1960s, however, the store fell on economic hard times—likely due to the rapid changes in American values associated with that era—and filed for bankruptcy in 1977. The company was bought by Houston, Texas-based Oshman's Sporting Goods. The business continued to decline until Abercrombie was acquired by the Limited, Inc., in 1988. The Limited tried to position the brand as a men's clothing line and later added a preppy women's line under the label as well. These efforts, too, failed, until the Abercrombie makeover began to take shape in earnest under the hand of Michael Jeffries, the current CEO of Abercrombie & Fitch, in 1992. Jeffries was no stranger to the retail world before his arrival at Abercrombie. He had done a stint at then-bankrupt retailer Paul Harris, Inc., had a hand at running his own chain (Alcott & Andrews), and a long run at Federated Department Stores, Inc. After assuming his post with Abercrombie, Jeffries hired his own team of fashion designers. He tapped superstar fashion photographer Bruce Weber (widely known for his Calvin Klein, Ralph Lauren, and Karl Lagerfeld ads) for the playful coed shots on the walls of Abercrombie stores. Weber would go on, of course, to become the photographer for the infamous *A&F Quarterly* as well. The *A&F Quarterly* was launched in 1997 to, as one commentator puts it, "glamorize the hedonistic collegiate lifestyle on which the company built its irreverent brand image." Even the words of the commentator here are extraordinary for how "collegiate" and "irreverent" are conflated in the image of Abercrombie. Indeed, it is testimony to part of A&F's genius that it successfully produced a false radicalism by hitching its label to a "collegiate" lifestyle that is inevitably and overwhelming white and upper middle class. Whatever the case, what we do know is that Abercrombie has been a financial success since 1994, only two years after Jeffries took over and reorganized the brand with his own variety of lifestyle marketing, to which they remain thoroughly committed. In 1998, the year following the launching of the *A&F Quarterly*, Abercrombie spun off from the Limited to become once again an independent, publicly traded company.

Abercrombie & Fitch has devised a very clear marketing and advertising strategy that celebrates whiteness—a particularly privileged and leisure-class whiteness—and makes use of it as a "lifestyle" that it can commodify to sell otherwise extremely dull, uninspiring, and ordinary clothing. I am not, by the way, the first commentator to recognize this fact about the clothes themselves. The danger of such a marketing scheme is that it depends upon the racist thinking of its consumer population in order to thrive. Anyone familiar with the rise of the company and its label in recent years recognizes that it has done precisely that.

Abercrombie has worked hard to produce a brand strongly associated with a young, white, upper-class, leisure lifestyle. Nowhere is this more evident than in the *A&F Quarterly*. Since, however, I could not bring myself to ask for, only to be denied, permission to use photographs from those pages in this book, or to participate in a vicious cycle of perpetuating the lure of those images by repeating them here, I leave it to my reader to seek them out, as they relate to this analysis. They are readily available online and in any number of media venues. Instead, I would like to consider in some detail a document where the A&F

look gets perhaps it clearest articulation: the *Abercrombie Look Book: Guidelines for Brand Representatives of Abercrombie & Fitch* (revised August 1996).

Affectionately known in the everyday corporate parlance of Abercrombie as the *Look Book,* this pocket-size (3.5 x 5.5–inch and approximately 30-page-long) book devotes equal time to images and text. The book contains twelve images—all photographs of model brand representatives, save one sketch (which we will come to later). Four of the eleven photos (including the cover) are group shots; the remaining ones feature individual models. Of the group shots, two include the one African American model (or even visible person of color) in these pages, while all of the rest of the photos are of male and female models who appear to be white. All of the models also appear to be solidly within Abercrombie's stated target age group of eighteen through twenty-two, and they all appear in the photographs smiling and often in various states of repose. The book divides neatly into five sections: an introductory section, which addresses the relationship between the brand representative and the A&F look; a section entitled "Our Past," which gives a brief history of the company; a section called "Our Present"; followed by an "Our Future" section; and then finally the longest section (making up more than half the book) on "The A&F Look" (with subsections titled "Discipline," "Personal Appearance," and "Exceptions"). I provide such detail so that the reader will have an image of this book as an object, as well as a sense of its formal content.

The *Look Book* begins thus:

> Exhibiting the "A&F Look" is a tremendously important part of the overall experience at the Abercrombie & Fitch Stores. We are selling an experience for our customer; an energized store environment creates an atmosphere that people want to experience again and again. The combination of our Brand Representatives' style and our Stores Visual Presentation has brought brand recognition across the country.
>
> Our people in the store are an inspiration to the customer. The customer sees the natural Abercrombie style and wants to be like the Brand Representative . . .
>
> Our Brand is natural, classic and current, with an emphasis on style. This is what a Brand Representative must be; this is what a Brand Representative must represent in order to fulfill the conditions of employment. [Emphases appear as they do in the *Look Book.*]

The book continues in much the same vein, touting the virtues of the ideal brand representative. In the approximately seventeen pages of text in the book, the word "natural," for example, appears as a descriptor no fewer than fourteen times. In this regard, it is closely followed by its companion terms "American" and "classic" to account for what the book identifies alternately as the "A&F look" and the "A&F style." Such words in the context not only of Abercrombie, but in the context of US culture more broadly, are often understood for the coded ways of delineating the whiteness that they represent. Indeed, most of us carry in our imagination a very specific image that we readily access when such monikers as "natural, classic, American" are used. That image is not likely of the Native American, who has far more historic claim to such signifiers than those whom we have learned to associate with them. This fact, I think, speaks volumes about the incredible and abiding ideological feat that we encounter in the whiteness of the idea of "America" and of "the American."

Indeed, citizenship in the United States touches upon matters of social identity, including race and gender. While the dominant rhetoric of our national identity presents a color-blind, "united-we-stand," Horatio Alger narrative of upward mobility, in reality, citizenship is raced, gendered, and classed, and the original texts that define citizenship and national identity in the United States reflect this reality. UC-Berkeley ethnic studies professor Evelyn Nakano Glenn touches upon one aspect of American ideological citizenship when she discusses the importance of whiteness and autonomy in contrast with non-whiteness, subservience, and dependence:

> Since the earliest days of the nation, the idea of whiteness has been closely tied to notions of independence and self-control necessary for republican government. This conception of whiteness

developed in concert with the conquest and colonization of non-Western societies by Europeans. Imagining non-European "others" as dependent and lacking the capacity for self-governance helped rationalize the takeover of their lands, resources and labor (Glenn 18).

Glenn goes on to emphasize early in her essay that it is not just whiteness but masculine whiteness that "was being constructed in the discourse on citizenship." Colonization is a key aspect of this ideology of masculine whiteness, according to Glenn:

> Imagining non-European "others" as dependent and lacking the capacity for self-governance helped rationalize the takeover of their lands, resources and labor. In North America, the extermination and forced removal of Indians and the enslavement of blacks by European settlers therefore seemed justified. This formulation was transferred to other racialized groups, such as the Chinese, Japanese and Filipinos, who were brought to the U.S. in the late nineteenth and early twentieth centuries as low wage laborers. Often working under coercive conditions of indenture or contract labor, they were treated as "unfree labor" and denied the right to become naturalized citizens (18).

A commitment to masculine whiteness, with its emphasis on territoriality, exploitation of resources, and the perception of other non-whites as dependent and lacking in political and mental capacity, is part of the master narrative that formed an important foundation for our ideas of American citizenship. Indeed, we have come to a point in our history where any real variation on what we might mean when we say "American" or "America" is scarcely thinkable. The ideological work of equating American with whites and America with whiteness has been thoroughly achieved. Viewed in this way, Abercrombie's early beginnings as an outfitter of upper-class explorers, adventurers, and outdoorsmen may perhaps be more relevant to our understanding and appreciation of the label's appeal than we first imagined.

The *Look Book* is noteworthy for some of the contradictions it raises as well. For example, the A&F dress code delineates its commitment to whiteness even in terms of what it deems acceptable in the way of appearance. The investment here in whiteness is also an investment in class. Recall the earlier mention in the introduction to this book of the whiteness of capital. Consider the following guidelines:

- For men and women, a neatly combed, attractive, natural, classic hairstyle is acceptable.
- Any type of "fade" cut (more scalp is visible than hair) for men is unacceptable.
- Shaving of the head or any portion of the head or eyebrow for men or women is unacceptable.
- Dreadlocks are unacceptable for men and women.

It is also in this section of the *Look Book* that we are presented with the only sketch that appears in the book. It is a combination sketch of seven heads and faces, which carries the caption "Some Acceptable Hairstyles." Included in these drawings is an African American man with a neatly cut natural (a very short afro cut). There is also among these faces a man who appears much older than the A&F target age group. In fact, this is the only place in the book where an older person is ever pictured. Indeed, it would also be unusual to find older adults working as brand representatives in their stores or being featured as models in the *A&F Quarterly*.

What is interesting to note about the acceptable hairstyles is what is out and what is in. In the mid-90s, when this edition of the *Look Book* was published, the fade was a popular hairstyle for African American men. I confess, somewhat reluctantly, that I had one myself. Also, since shaved heads are excluded, this also would put a mounting segment (at the time) of African American men out of the running along with the odd white skinhead. Finally, dreadlocks, while considered by some to be among the most "natural" of hairstyles available to African Americans, are out. Indeed dreads, as they are often referred to, are even somewhat controversial within African American communities for their association with, among other things, Rastafarianism. So other than as a commitment to a white aesthetic, the exclusion of dreads (even in terms of A&F's own commitment to the "natural" look) seems curious.

On jewelry, the *Look Book* offers the following:

Jewelry must be simple and classic. A ring may be worn on any finger except the thumb. Gold chains are not acceptable for men. Women may wear a thin, short delicate silver necklace. Ankle bracelets are unacceptable. Dressy (e.g., gold-banded or diamond) watches are also unacceptable; watches should be understated and cool (e.g., leather straps or stainless steel). No more than two earrings in each ear can be worn at a time for women. Only one in one ear for men. Earrings should be no larger than a dime, and large dangling or large hoop earrings are unacceptable. . . . No other pierced jewelry is appropriate (e.g., nose rings, pierced lips, etc.).

Thumb rings signify alternative lifestyles at best and queer at worst. No gold chains for men? Who has been overidentified or even stereotyped with these in the popular imagination more than black men—from Mr. to any number of rap artists, and "ballers" more generally? In either case, the signifier "gold chain" demarcates potential employees of A&F in coded ways along race and class lines. A similar case can be made with regard to the reference to "large dangling or large hoop earrings." Here, too, Abercrombie codes for race and class without actually having to name it.

Still, of all of the dress code rules, the most amusing one to me has to be the following: "Brand Representatives are required to wear appropriate undergarments at all times." Is Abercrombie afraid that their brand representatives might actually be sexualized? The image of male genitalia flopping about in cargo shorts or, alternatively, of an 18–22-year-old version of the now infamous Sharon Stone leg-crossing scene in the film *Basic Instinct* (1992) comes to mind. Call me crazy, but there is just something about a company that flies in the face of such propriety in the pages of the *A&F Quarterly*—wherein no one seems to wear underwear or much else for that matter—being concerned about the appropriateness of the undergarments of its employees that strikes me as the height of hilarity and hypocrisy.

If the frequent use of such coded monikers in the *Look Book* were not enough to convince us that the A&F look is styled on a celebration of racial and cultural whiteness, consider that the *A&F Quarterly* is chock full of images of young white men and women (mostly men) with very little in the way of representation of people of color. Consider that criticism of Abercrombie's chosen photographer, Bruce Weber, draws him as (in)famous for his unabashed celebration of the white male nude. Recall the release by A&F in April 2003 of that inflammatory line of "Asian" themed T-shirts, which were hotly protested by the Asian American community among others. One of the shirts featured two stereotypical Chinese men drawn with exaggeratedly slanted eyes, donning pointed hats, and holding a banner between them that read: "Two Wongs Can Make It White." A spokesperson for A&F, when asked to respond to the controversy raised by the T-shirts, said, "We thought it would add humor." The line was pulled by the company soon after they were released. Consider also the variety of social engineering that goes into producing a virtually all-white sales staff in A&F stores. As one former assistant manager of one of Abercrombie's larger stores in the Midwest informed me, all the brand reps in his store were white, and all of the people who worked in the stockroom were black. Stockroom employees (in the larger stores where they employ such staff separately from brand reps) are less visible and are often assigned to work overnight shifts restocking the store.

Many people have asked me while I was working on this project—no doubt many will continue to do so—what's the big deal? Why pick on Abercrombie? They are doing no more or no less than Ralph Lauren or Banana Republic. I have said to those people and continue to say that such a simple equation is not only untrue, but denies the specificity of the particular brand of evil that Abercrombie is involved in capitalizing on. Ralph Lauren does, to be sure, commodity a particular upper-class American lifestyle.

Banana Republic has a history of a similar marketing scheme. However, A&F successfully crystallizes a racism that is only rumbling beneath the surface of other stores' advertising. Also, Ralph Lauren attempts to market and sell that lifestyle to everyone equally. That is, the underlying ethos of Ralph Lauren is not unlike the ideology of the American dream itself: you, too, can have this if you work for it.

Ralph Lauren "diversified" its ad campaigns in the 1990s. To demonstrate that fact, among other things, Ralph Lauren in 1993 took on Tyson Beckford, a black model of Jamaican and Chinese parentage, to represent its Polo Sport line exclusively. True, this diversity was of the variety of CNN diversity: news is read by white and Asian reporters, while black reporters do sports and entertainment and occasionally "substitute" for white news reporters. In the same vein, Beckford was engaged to model for Ralph Lauren's "sport" line and not its "blue label" (i.e., blue blood) line of suits, formal wear, and elegant apparel. Still, Beckford's own rags-to-riches story made for good press for a company clearly working its own variety of the diversity angle, which was a popular marketing strategy among hip retailers in the 1990s. Beckford represents perhaps the most notable example of this. He grew up in Jamaica and in Rochester, New York. As a youth he was involved in gangs, drugs, and was on his way down the road toward a life of crime, when an editor of the hip-hop magazine the *Source* discovered him. Not long thereafter, it would be Bruce Weber who would introduce Beckford to Ralph Lauren—whose signing of Beckford sent his modeling career into the stratosphere. Beckford himself has recognized that he would likely be dead or in jail had he not been taken up by that editor from the *Source*. There has been speculation about the veracity of Beckford's narrative of class ascension. Regardless, its construction generated good press for Ralph Lauren.

I should note, too, that neither Banana Republic nor Ralph Lauren participate in the kind of social engineering in terms of their store employees that A&F does. The employees of Banana Republic represent diverse racial backgrounds, while the sales associates at Ralph Lauren tend to represent an older model of the suit-wearing salesman in an upscale shop. The

latter, in addition to the Polo stores, also sells its line in fine department stores, where they have no direct control over choosing sales associates to represent the line. An added bit of anecdotal information with regard to Banana Republic also comes in the form of the person of Eduardo Gonzalez—one of the named litigants in the pending class action employment discrimination lawsuit against A&F. The class action complaint notes that Gonzalez, who was not hired as a brand representative at Abercrombie, was offered a job at Banana Republic:

> Indeed, immediately following his Abercrombie interview, he crossed the hall within the same mall to apply for a job at Banana Republic, a similar retail clothing store that competes directly with Abercrombie for customers and employees. An employee of Banana Republic asked Mr. Gonzalez if he was interested in applying to work as a manager. He applied to work as a sales associate, and is still employed by Banana Republic in that capacity.

If, as I suggest in chapter 6, images tend more often to follow and demonstrate where we are as a society rather than play the role of leading us to new places, then the particular brand of a socially engineered whitewashed world being advertised, branded, and sold to US consumers by Abercrombie should give us pause. Movie lovers may recall the song "Tomorrow Belongs to Me" from the film version of *Cabaret*. The song begins, like the lyrics, in a pastoral mode. The camera is tight on the face of the beautiful, young, blond, boy soprano. The scene is comforting, indeed beautiful. With each successive verse, however, the camera begins to pull back and to show more and more and more of the boy's body . . . donning a Hitler-youth uniform. His face becomes increasingly emphatic and angry. By the time we get to the fourth verse of the tune, the others in the crowd have joined in the song with a seriousness of purpose that can only be described as frightening:

> *The sun on the meadow is summery warm*
> *The stag in the forest runs free*
> *But gathered together to greet the storm*
> *Tomorrow belongs to me*

The branch on the linden is leafy and green
The Rhine gives its gold to the sea
But somewhere a glory awaits unseen
Tomorrow belongs to me

The babe in his cradle is closing his eyes
The blossom embraces the bee
But soon says the whisper, arise, arise
Tomorrow belongs to me

Now Fatherland, Fatherland, show us the sign
Your children have waited to see
The morning will come
When the world is mine
Tomorrow belongs to me
Tomorrow belongs to me
Tomorrow belongs to me

The number concludes with the final verse above being repeated twice more in a chilling, thunderous unity, as the crowd of townspeople gathered at the picnic joins in.

Some may call a comparison such as the one I am drawing here hyperbole. Others might say that I am overstating Abercrombie's case and undervaluing the realities of the Holocaust. Neither is my intention. I do, however, believe fervently in what Hannah Arendt in *Eichmann in Jerusalem* once called "the banality of evil." I am convinced that a version of it is what is at work in the politics of race in US society today, and that Abercrombie's marketing and branding practices represent only a symptom of that larger concern. Indeed, according to Edward Herman, "Arendt's thesis [in *Eichmann in Jerusalem*] was that people who carry out unspeakable crimes, like Eichmann, a top administrator in the machinery of the Nazi death camps, may not be crazy fanatics at all, but rather ordinary individuals who simply accept the premises of their state and participate in any ongoing enterprise with the energy of good bureaucrats." In the words of another philosopher-commentator on the "banality of evil": "Clichés, stock phrases, adherence to conventional, standardized codes of expression and conduct have the socially recognized function of protecting us against reality." This statement well describes the corporate culture of Abercrombie and the quasi-cultish devotion they seem to inspire.

There are those, no doubt, reading these pages who will find that it takes far too much of a liberal leap of faith to appreciate the argument I pose here against Abercrombie & Fitch. There are those who will not grasp, or who will feign confusion about grasping, the coded nature of the whiteness that A&F so clearly employs. It is for those readers that I include the more practical, everyday, anecdotal evidence that follows. The purview of such hard-boiled evidence (that which is usually associated with the "simple truth," a term whose discussion began this book) can usually be found in the area of the law.

As a system, the law deals in bodies, experience (rendered through testimony), and revels in the making of distinctions. The law is no place for nuances, ambiguities, subtleties, and, even at times, the vagaries so often associated with theoretical, academic discussion—and with the humanities in general. The law represents yet another realm in which the "simple truth" carries the day. Indeed, before the law, human complexity, the complexity of identities, the complexities of sexuality and desire, the complexities of social and economic circumstances, the complexities of institutional and corporate cultures and the unspoken codes by which they operate, the complexities of deep-seated racism, sexism, heterosexism, elitism, and so much more, all become flattened, cognizable, weighable, and therefore able to be adjudicated. I suppose this is why my sentiments about the law have always been conflicted. On the one hand, I have long admired the law's simplicity and the definitive clarity with which it makes claims and decides cases; on the other, I have bemoaned the law's inability to address concerns of specificity, to deal compassionately with human frailty, and to account in its judgment for the ambiguity and complexity of circumstances. Like most systems, the law is, of course, not simple. Its ways have evolved through crooks and turns—and not always ones that we would associate with justice and the good—that have brought it to this place in its history and development. It did not spring fully formed and perfect as if from the head of Zeus. As such, the law has evolved its own biases for what constitutes evidence, how evidence can and should be presented, what cases can come before the law, and how precedent drives the law's machinery. So even though I personally do not hold the truth of the law above other ways of creating and recognizing truth, I present the following here because I know that among the readers of this book will be those who do.

On June 17, 2003, a class action lawsuit was filed against Abercrombie & Fitch in the United Stated District Court of San Francisco, California, alleging discrimination in its hiring practices. Specifically, the complaint alleges that A&F discriminates against people of color, including Latinos, Asian Americans, and African Americans, in the hiring, job assignment, compensation, termination, and other terms and conditions of employment. There are nine named litigants in the complaint who filed on behalf of the class they represent: Eduardo Gonzalez, Anthony Ocampo, Encarnacion Gutierrez, Johan Montoya, Juancarlos Gomez-Montejano, Jennifer Lu, Austin Chu, Ivy Nguyen, and Angeline Wu. These litigants are represented by counsel from the Mexican American Legal Defense and Educational Fund; the Asian Pacific American Legal Center; the NAACP Legal Defense and Educational Fund; and the law firm of Lieff, Cabraser, Heimann & Bernstein. In August 2003 I had the privilege of meeting Anthony Ocampo, one of the named litigants in the lawsuit, over dinner in Chicago. Though I am not at liberty to discuss the particulars related to our dinner conversation that evening about the pending case, I do want to say what an impressive, brave, and astute—even if a bit shy—young man Ocampo is. With that, let me share some thoughts about the complaint itself (as a matter of public record), which I think further illuminates much of what I have been presenting up to this point about Abercrombie & Fitch.

What follows first are some representative points from the "Introductory Statement" portion of the complaint:

- Defendant Abercrombie & Fitch . . . is a national retail clothing seller that discriminates against minority individuals, including Latinos, Asian Americans, and African Americans . . . on the basis of race, color, and/or national origin, with respect to hiring, firing, job assignment, compensation and other terms and conditions of employment by enforcing a nationwide corporate policy of preferring white employees for sales positions, desirable job assignments, and favorable work scheduled in its stores throughout the United States.

- Abercrombie implements its discriminatory employment policies and practices in part through a detailed and rigorous "Appearance Policy," which requires that all Brand Representatives must exhibit the "A&F Look." The "A&F Look" is a virtually all-white image that Abercrombie uses not only to market its clothing, but also to implement its discriminatory employment policies and practices.

- When people who do not fit the "A&F Look" inquire about employment, managers sometimes tell them that the store is not hiring, or may provide them with applications even though they have no intention of considering them for employment. If applicants who do not fit the "A&F Look" submit applications, managers and/or Brand Representatives acting at their direction sometimes throw them away without reviewing them.

- Abercrombie publishes and distributes to its employees a "Look Book" that explains the importance of the Appearance Policy and the "A&F Look," and that closely regulates the Brand Representatives' appearance. The Company requires its managers to hire and continue to employ only Brand Representatives who fit within the narrow confines of the "Look Book," resulting in a disproportionately white Brand Representative workforce.

- Each store prominently posts large photographs of models—virtually all of whom are white. In addition, the Company publishes and sells *A&F Quarterly,* a magazine/catalog featuring almost exclusively white models . . .

- The Company rigorously maintains the "A&F Look" by careful scrutiny and monitoring of its stores by regional and district managers and corporate representatives. These managers and corporate representatives visit stores frequently to ensure, among other things, that the store is properly implementing the Company's discriminatory employment policies and practices. These visits are referred to as "blitzes." When managers or corporate representatives discover that minority Brand Representatives have been hired, they have directed that these Brand Representatives be fired, moved to the stock room or overnight shift, or have their hours "zeroed out," which is the equivalent of termination.

- The Company also scrutinizes and enforces compliance with the "A&F Look" by requiring all stores to submit a picture of roughly 10 of their Brand Representatives who "fit the 'Look'" to headquarters each quarter. The corporate officials then select roughly 15 stores' pictures as exemplary models that perpetuate the Company's discriminatory employment practices. They then disseminate these pictures to the over 600 A&F stores. The Brand Representatives in the pictures are almost invariably white. This practice and policy, like the others described above, constitutes an official directive to give preference to white Brand Representatives and applicants, and to discriminate against minority Brand Representatives and applicants.

- The A&F image is not limited to appearance; the Company accomplishes its discriminatory employment policies or practices by defining its desired "classic" and "cool" workforce as exclusively white . . . Abercrombie also encourages the recruitment and hiring of members of specified overwhelmingly white intercollegiate sports. However, the Company does not encourage recruitment from fraternities, sororities, or sports teams with significant minority populations.

It will surely come as no surprise that my sympathies where Abercrombie is concerned are very much in line with those of this lawsuit. When I first started thinking about this work more than two years ago now, the more I discovered about the company and its marketing and employment practices, the more surprised I was that a suit had not been brought

against them sooner. Such naiveté on my part underestimated the resourcefulness of A&F's ingenuity and, indeed, the ingenuity of racist discourse in our time to mask itself in the form of coded language. Some of this language I have been discussing, and some is attested to in the excerpts from the legal complaint that I have presented. The creation of an "A&F Look," which almost invariably functions to produce an exclusively white staff of brand representatives in Abercrombie's stores, might be understood as an elaborately devised method by the company of forestalling the potential legal exposure of such an exclusionary employment policy. The formal workings of what we might call the "corporate culture" of A&F provide the infrastructure for maintaining and reproducing the discriminatory, virtually all-white A&F look.

The A&F former store managers, former assistant managers, and former and current brand representatives with whom I have spoken over the course of this project all tell eerily similar stories. All of the personnel with whom I had occasion to speak have been white men. They ranged in age from nineteen to twenty-six and were either in college or were college educated. Some were gay, some straight. All of them, almost without exception, expressed how they enjoyed working at the company when they first started there. They also expressed their discomfort with some of the "unspoken" rules of the company, which they cited as their reason for ultimately leaving the employ of A&F. The allure of the experience seemed to hold sway over these men even after they had left the company. The men with whom I conducted formal interviews all cited fond memories from the experience, even as they all were convinced that something about it never felt quite right to them.

Chance (not his actual name), a straight white man in his early twenties, spoke with me about his experience at one of the larger stores on the West Coast, where he was a brand representative. He would later move on to manage a store on the East Coast. On the matter of employment practices he said, "The hiring policy is insane." He went on to suggest that it was the common practice of the general manager (GM) at the store—who Chance describes as "Abercrombied out"—to say that he was not in the business of hiring "ugly people." Informal games between the men in the stores were encouraged by management, in which they would have contests to see who could get the most "hot high school girls' [phone] numbers." Chance related to me that on the day when the store picture that would be sent to A&F headquarters was to be taken, Leo (not his real name), "the only black guy in the store," was asked by the GM to "watch the front" while they were taking the picture.

David (not his real name), a white gay man in his early twenties, spoke with me about his experience at a smaller store in the Northeast, where he worked during his college years. He would go on to become a manager in training (MIT) and an assistant manager (AM) at a large store in another region of the country. David told me about the corporate practice of tying a "target school" (college or university) to all the stores. One of the things he started to notice when he became an MIT and later an AM was that the brand representatives in his store were almost exclusively white and that "everybody who worked in the stockroom was black." He tells the story of the one African American male employee that he had in his store when he became an AM. He said he was a good employee with a really positive attitude, but the district manager (DM) wanted us (David and the store manager) to get rid of him because he "did not fit the look." "He's not Abercrombie," the DM said to David and the store manager. The DM went on to say to them that "this person cannot be on the schedule anymore." David said that "not having the look" is reason enough to be fired or not hired in the first place. "Race as an issue is implied," David told me. He always understood that to be the case, even though it was unspoken. When I asked him what happened to the guy, David replied, rather matter-of-factly, that he was essentially fired by the manager. The process began with the employee first being "zeroed out" in terms of the hours he was scheduled to work; eventually he was fired. David said that this was a common practice. Instead of actually terminating people, you just stop scheduling them (or "zero them out") until they inevitably get the picture. I asked David why he left the company. He said that he got tired of the antagonistic relationships that sometimes exist

between DMs and store-level management, where he was always hearing: "you can't schedule him . . ." or (in fits of frustration or anger) "your staff is ugly." "I got sick of judging people like that," he said. "I'm going to be a teacher. . . . It's just not right." He told me that before leaving his job at A&F, he once expressed his discomfort with some of these company practices to his GM (a white woman). According to David, her reply was: "You'll eventually get over it. You'll learn to let go of your feelings and get over it." David said he still could not believe that a store manager told him that. It was then that he knew his days with the company were numbered.

Randy is a white gay man in his early twenties as well. He started out as a brand representative at a store in the South while he was in college. Later he became an AM in another region of the country. He shared with me some of his observations in those positions. He spoke with alarming candor. At first there appeared to me to be a manner of innocence about his way of reporting this information that seemed almost unconscious of the profound implications of his statements. The more I spoke with him, however, the more I came to see that this was in part his affect and was not a statement on his level of recognition of the gravity of what he was relating.

When Randy began with the company, he had not yet come out as a gay man. The store where he started working had an all-white staff. He recalls that the managers were "really cool," a fact he came to appreciate later when he would learn that this was not the case with most GMs and DMs in the company. He reports that, in the stores, employees were encouraged to "look Abercrombie" and to "speak Abercrombie or Crombie." When they recruited new brand reps, which they all were involved in doing, Randy said that they were very clear on what they were looking for: "all-American," in "good shape," "no facial or skin problems," "clean shaven," "not a lot of makeup for girls . . . natural," "fraternity or football player–looking guys." He went on to say that it used to be "a big deal to look for white people." He added that African Americans and Asian Americans "can be A&F if they act white, have white friends, and are very assimilated." Randy reports feeling pressure to hire people who looked A&F. Employees who recruited the wrong sort knew they would run the risk of reprisal from the GM or the DM. I asked him what happened to people who were "not Abercrombie" who came in to apply for jobs. He said they were never called. He reports one case that occurred when he was an AM in which a qualified fifty-year-old woman applied for a GM position. Her application was never given to the DM because the DM "would be pissed off at us for wasting his time." He reported another case of an MIT he worked with once who "wasn't very attractive." The regional manager (RM) informed the DM that she needed to go. Randy said that while she wasn't great at her job, had she been "nice-looking she would still have gotten promoted." He cited the case of another girl who had been an A&F model who came to work in the same store. She was, according to Randy, "horrible at her job and still got promoted." She was even eventually sent to the home office.

It was Randy who first informed me about the practice of grading at A&F. The DM would review the work schedules, every name on the schedules had to have a grade (A through F) next to it, which reflected how "good-looking" the employee was. When upper management (especially Michael Jeffries or David Lieno, directors of stores) would come to town for a "blitz" (a word whose associations with Nazi Germany one cannot help noticing), people who were not A's were asked to leave the store. A preponderance of B's or worse in a schedule could be grounds for dismissal of a GM. Brand representatives were never informed of the grade they had been assigned and remained, in most cases, unfamiliar with the practice, according to Randy. When I asked him why he left the company, he said he left "because they were bad to me." He added that they treat management horribly and don't compensate them well, paying them halftime for overtime worked, with base salaries for AMs in the mid-twenty-thousand-dollar range. Even so, they want you to "look like you have money . . . come from a good family."

Ultimately, I suppose my reasons for hating Abercrombie & Fitch are not so different from the reasons that I have no truck with gay Republicans. It is not surprising when one observes that the attitudes

of those sporting Abercrombie often seem to have a great deal in common with political conservatives as well. In both cases, you have a group of mostly whites (many of them social and economic climbers themselves—less often are they those who were actually born with money), who are desperate to belong to a fraternity that guarantees all the benefits and liberties of white privilege. Recall the earlier discussion in the introduction to this book about vacationing and "getting away from it all." In the case of gay Republicans, we are often dealing with a group of people who understand themselves—but for this critical difference that their sexuality makes—as in line to be the beneficiaries of their white birthright in the United States: to be and receive the mantle of whiteness and all the privileges it entails. Were it not but for their sexuality, they too could enjoy the same kind of mobility, belonging, non-discrimination, social respect and respectability, wider economic entrepreneurial opportunity, and, indeed, the right to discriminate against all those others who do not belong. After all, to borrow a well-known slogan from a surprisingly appropriate context, "membership has its privileges." This is seen most readily in the fiscal conservatism of many gay Republicans, who are typically not supporters of affirmative action, welfare, or any other variety of social programs designed to support the poor and people of color in the United States. And when one looks at the disproportionate numbers of blacks and Latinos who make up the poor in the United States, the poor and people of color are populations that in public discussion don't always require a great deal of delineation.

In my critique of white gay Republicans, I do not mean to suggest that the distinctions between them and white gay liberals are so vast as to avoid mentioning this latter group here as well. Indeed, when it comes to addressing questions about who has access to be able to make the rational choice of a mate in the gay marketplace of desire, the similarities between the two become much clearer, as I will discuss in the next chapter. But even at the philosophical and political levels, Republicanism and liberalism have far more in common than might at first meet the eye. In this regard, gay liberalism and gay Republicanism are no exception. Consider the recent June 2003

Supreme Court ruling in the Texas sodomy case. What many in the LGBT community have embraced as a radical step forward by a conservative court really represents a new challenge in the struggle for queer liberation. The decision of the High Court effectively protected gay sexuality by privatizing it. After all, the majority opinion is based on arguments centering on privacy rights. The effect of this move is that civil expressions of gayness may at the very least be in for some hard political times ahead, and at the very worst become effectively outlawed. For privatizing gayness does not necessarily pave the way to gay "marriage" or civil unions, open expression of one's sexual identity in the military, or any number of other radical potentials with which the court's decision is presently being endowed. The extent to which the decision has a "liberal" look to it, while simultaneously retaining the potential for stultifying conservative Republican ramifications, is the extent to which gay liberalism and gay Republicanism may not be so different from one another in terms of their radical potentialities.

Still, just as much as gay Republicans are desperate to belong to a tribe of privilege and cultural and social dominance, so are those who are a part of the cult of Abercrombie. The cultish ideology that drives the engine of Abercrombie is not unlike the ideology that led Disney's Little Mermaid, Ariel, after falling in love with the beautiful white prince, to give up her birth identity (even as a princess of the Mer-people) in exchange for her legs (and more importantly her vagina, not to put too fine a point on the matter), so that she can, in the words of her principle number in the movie-musical, be "part of that world" (the world of people). Abercrombie, through its strategy of marketing "the good white life" in what is already a deeply racist society, has convinced a US public—whites (some young and some not so young), some people of color, and gay men—that if we buy their label, we are really buying membership into a privileged fraternity that has eluded us all for so long, even if for such vastly different reasons. In order for such a marketing strategy to work, in all of the diverse ways that this one clearly does, the consumer must necessarily bring to his or her understanding of A&F, and what association

with the brand offers him or her, a fundamentally racist belief that this lifestyle—this young, white, natural, all-American, upper class lifestyle—being offered by the label is what we all either are, aspire to be, or are hopelessly alienated from ever being. Only when such a perspective as this is brought to the consumer's viewing of the *A&F Quarterly,* to the stores and the special brand of social engineering that takes place by the company to make them "good looking" (and by definition white), and to the very dull and uninspiring clothes themselves (absent the label), does any of this literally cohere or "make sense." The very sense-making, the deciphering of the codes that allow one to appreciate what it is that "Abercrombie" stands for and means in our culture, can only be accomplished when we bring a variety of racialist thinking to the experience.

Either way, when you evolve a way to commodify and market the fundamental tenets of racist thinking that have held sway in the United States from the earliest moments of its inception as a republic (a feat Abercrombie seems successfully to have achieved), this example shows us that you can attach the label (whatever it may be) to even the most uninspiring products (in this case clothes), and they will sell in legion. Surely we know that people are not buying "Abercrombie" for the clothes. The catalog itself isn't even about featuring those, after all. People buy "Abercrombie" to purchase membership into a lifestyle. Lisa Marsh, the fashion business writer for the *New York Post,* said that Abercrombie's "aggressive lifestyle marketing makes you feel like you're buying a polo shirt and getting the horse and summer house on Martha's Vineyard with it."

Were that the extent of what they were selling, I might have less of a problem with Abercrombie. But to brazenly evolve a way of playing on consumers' worst racially based fears and inadequacies born of a racist structure that defines everything from standards of beauty to access to having the house on Martha's Vineyard, goes beyond mere "lifestyle marketing." In my judgment, that crosses the line into a kind of racism whose desire—played out to its logical conclusion—is not unlike a variety of ethnic cleansing. Its desire to produce and play on the consumer's desire for a white, "good-looking" world where one can "get away from it all," and to sell that idea as the "good life" in the context of a racist society, only redeploys and reinscribes the fundamental logic of white supremacy which, at bottom, makes such a marketing strategy possible and even appealing in the first place. This says a great deal, perhaps, about the status of "race relations" in the United States. It says even more about the deep and abiding contradictions that can be accommodated in our public thinking about race today that would scarcely have been possible to imagine even in the late 1960s or 1970s. Another failing of the radicality of liberalism?

Perhaps. In any case, the same reasoning that makes Abercrombie palatable to a US public, is the same reasoning that makes claims of "reverse discrimination" palatable and possible in our society. And that, in the end, is why I hate Abercrombie and Fitch.

References

Arendt, Hannah. *Eichmann in Jerusalem: A Report on the Banality of Evil.* New York: Penguin Classics, 2006.

Glenn, Evelyn Nakano. *Unequal Freedom: How Race and Gender Shaped American Citizenship and Labor.* Cambridge, MA: Harvard University Press, 2004.

22.
UNNATURAL DISASTERS

Race and Poverty

Michael Eric Dyson

The barrage of images in newspapers and on television tested the nation's collective sense of reality. There were men and women wading chest-deep in water—when they weren't floating or drowning in the toxic whirlpool the streets of New Orleans had become. When the waters subsided, there were dead bodies strewn on curbsides and wrapped in blankets by fellow sufferers, who provided the perished their only dignity. There were unseemly collages of people silently dying from hunger and thirst—and of folk writhing in pain, or quickly collapsing under the weight of missed medicine for diabetes, high blood pressure, or heart trouble. Photo snaps and film shots captured legions of men and women huddling in groups or hugging corners, crying in wild-eyed desperation for help, for any help, from somebody, anybody, who would listen to their unanswered pleas. The filth and squalor of their confinement—defecating where they stood or sat, or, more likely, dropped, bathed in a brutal wash of dredge and sickening pollutants that choked the air with ungodly stench—grieved the camera lenses that recorded their plight.

Men, women, and children tore through deserted streets lined with empty stores, hunting for food and water and clothing for their bodies. They were hurried along by the steadily diminishing prospect of rescue by the government, by *their* government, whose only visible representatives were the police who came after them for looting. There were wailing infants clasping crying mothers who mouthed prayers for someone to please just save their babies.

There were folk stuffed in attics pleading for the cavalry to come. Many colors were present in this multicultural stew of suffering, but the dominant color was black. From the sight of it, this was the third world—a misnomer, to be sure, since people of color are two-thirds of the world's population. The suffering on screen created cognitive dissonance; it suggested that this must be somewhere in India, or the outskirts of Biafra. This surely couldn't be the United States of America—and how cruelly that term seemed to mock those poor citizens who felt disunited and disconnected and just plain dissed by their government. This couldn't be the richest and most powerful nation on the globe, leaving behind some of its poorest citizens to fend for themselves.

And yet it was. It was bad enough to witness the government's failure to respond to desperate cries of help scrawled on the tattered roofs of flooded homes. But Hurricane Katrina's violent winds and killing waters swept into the mainstream a stark realization: the poor had been abandoned by society and its institutions, and sometimes by their well-off brothers and sisters, long before the storm. We are immediately confronted with another unsavory truth: it is the exposure of the extremes, not their existence, that stumps our national sense of decency. We can abide the ugly presence of poverty so long as it doesn't interrupt the natural flow of things, doesn't rudely impinge on our daily lives or awareness. As long as poverty is a latent reality, a solemn social fact suppressed from prominence on our moral compass, we can find our bearings without fretting too much about its awkward persistence.

It's not as if it was news to most folk that poverty exists in the United States. Still, there was no shortage of eureka moments glistening with discovery and surprise in the aftermath of Katrina. Poverty's grinding malevolence is fed in part by social choices and public policy decisions that directly impact how many people are poor and how long they remain that way. To acknowledge that is to own up to our role in the misery of the poor—be it the politicians we vote for who cut programs aimed at helping the economically vulnerable; the narrative of bootstrap individualism we invoke to deflect the relevance of the considerable benefits we've received while bitterly complaining of the few breaks the poor might get; the religious myths we circulate that bring shame on the poor by chiding them for lacking the appropriate hunger to be prosperous; and the resentment of the alleged pathology of poor blacks—fueled more by stereotypes than by empirical support—that gives us license to dismiss or demonize them.

Our being surprised, and disgusted, by the poverty that Katrina revealed is a way of remaining deliberately naive about the poor while dodging the responsibility that knowledge of their lives would entail. We remain blissfully ignorant of their circumstances to avoid the brutal indictment of our consciences. When a disaster like Katrina strikes—a *natural* disaster not directly caused by human failure—it frees us to be aware of, and angered by, the catastrophe. After all, it doesn't directly implicate us; it was an act of God. Even when human hands get involved, our fingerprints are nowhere to be found. We're not responsible for the poor and black being left behind; the local, state, or federal government is at fault.

We are thus able to decry the circumstances of the poor while assuring ourselves that we had nothing to do with their plight. We can even take special delight in lambasting the source of their suffering—a source that is safely external to us. We are fine as long as we place time limits on the origins of the poor's plight—the moments we all spied on television after the storm, but not the numbing years during which we all looked the other way. Thus we fail to confront our complicity in their long-term suffering.

By being outraged, we appear compassionate. This permits us to continue to ignore the true roots of their condition, roots that branch into our worlds and are nourished on our political and religious beliefs.

There are 37 million people in poverty in our nation, 1.1 million of whom fell below the poverty line in 2004.[1] Some of the poorest folk in the nation, people in the Delta, have been largely ignored, rendered invisible, officially forgotten. FEMA left them dangling precipitously on rooftops and in attics because of bureaucratic bumbling. Homeland Security failed miserably in mobilizing resources to rescue Katrina survivors without food, water, or shelter. President Bush lighted on New Orleans only after Mayor Ray Nagin's profanity-laced radio-show diatribe blasting the federal government for its lethal inertia. Because the government took its time getting into New Orleans, Katrina took many lives. Hundreds of folk, especially the elderly, died while waiting for help. But the government and society had been failing to pay attention to the poor since long before one of the worst natural disasters in the nation's history swallowed the poor and spit them back up. The world saw just how much we hadn't seen; it witnessed our negligence up close in frightfully full color.

The hardest-hit regions in the Gulf States had already been drowning in extreme poverty: Mississippi is the poorest state in the nation, with Louisiana just behind it.[2] More than 90,000 people in each of the areas stormed by Katrina in Louisiana, Mississippi, and Alabama made less than $10,000 a year. Black folk in these areas were strapped by incomes that were 40 percent less than those earned by whites. Before the storm, New Orleans, with a 67.9 percent black population, had more than 103,000 poor people. That means the Crescent City had a poverty rate of 23 percent, 76 percent higher than the national average of 13.1 percent.[3] New Orleans's poverty rate ranked it seventh out of 290 large US counties.[4]

Although black folk make up 31.5 percent of Louisiana's population, their offspring account for 69 percent of the children in poverty. Though the national average for elders with disabilities is 39.6 percent, New Orleans hovers near 57 percent. The New Orleans median household income is $31,369, far beneath the national median of $44,684.[5] A full 9 percent of households in New Orleans didn't own or have access to a vehicle.[6] That means that nearly one in four citizens in New Orleans, and one in seven in the greater New Orleans metropolitan area, had no access to a car.[7]

In fact, New Orleans ranks fourth out of 297 metropolitan areas in the country in the proportion of households lacking access to cars.[8] The top three metropolitan spots are in the greater New York area, which has the most extensive public transportation system in the country. New Orleans ranks ninth among 140 big cities for the same category, a far higher ranking than cities with similar demographic profiles such as Detroit and Memphis.[9] Black households nationwide generally have far less access to cars than white households, a trend mirrored in New Orleans, where only 5 percent of non-Latino whites were without car access, while 27 percent of blacks in New Orleans were without cars.[10] Nationwide, 19 percent of blacks lack access to cars.[11]

And children and elderly folk are even more likely to live in households without access to cars. Children and the elderly made up 38 percent of the population in New Orleans, but they accounted for 48 percent of the households without access to cars in the city.[12] The poor and the near-poor made up the vast majority of those without car access in New Orleans, accounting for nearly 80 percent of the city's car-less population.[13] These facts make it painfully clear just why so many folk could not evacuate before Katrina struck. They weren't shiftless, stupid, or stubborn, as some have suggested (FEMA's Michael Brown blamed the poor for staying behind and drowning while discounting or ignoring the many obstacles to their successful exodus). They simply couldn't muster the resources to escape destruction, and, for many, death.

The most glaring feature of their circumstance suggests that Katrina's survivors lived in concentrated poverty—they lived in poor neighborhoods, attended poor schools, and had poorly paying jobs that reflected and reinforced a distressing pattern of rigid segregation.[14] Nearly 50,000 poor folk in New Orleans lived in areas where the poverty rate approached 40 percent. In fact, among the nation's fifty largest cities with poor black families jammed

into extremely poor neighborhoods, New Orleans ranked second. Those households living in concentrated poverty often earn barely more than $20,000 a year. In neighborhoods with concentrated poverty, only one in twelve adults has a college degree, most children are reared in single-parent families, and four in ten working-age adults, many of whom are disabled, have no jobs.[15] Nearly every major American city has several neighborhoods that are desperately poor and severely segregated. Cities like Cleveland, New York, Atlanta, and Los Angeles have economically distressed neighborhoods where more than 30 percent of their population's poor blacks live.[16]

Concentrated poverty is the product of decades of public policies and political measures that isolate black households in neighborhoods plagued by severe segregation and economic hardship. For instance, the federal government's decision to concentrate public housing in segregated inner-city neighborhoods fueled metropolitan expansion. It also cut the poor off from decent housing and educational and economic opportunities by keeping affordable housing for poor minorities out of surrounding suburbs. The effects of concentrated poverty have been amply documented: reduced private-sector investment and local job opportunities; higher prices for the poor in inner-city businesses; increased levels of crime; negative consequences on the mental and physical health of the poor; and the spatial dislocation of the poor spurred by the "black track" of middle-class households to the suburbs.[17]

In the antebellum and post-Civil War south, New Orleans brought together slaves, former slaves, free blacks, Creoles of color, and Cajuns and other whites in an ethnically diverse mélange that reflected the city's Spanish, French, and African roots and influences. Despite the bustling ethnic and racial interactions—driven in part by the unique "backyard" patterns, where blacks and whites lived near each other, a practice that had its roots in slavery—the city endured increasing segregation as suburbanization made New Orleans blacker in the latter half of the twentieth century.[18] In the case of New Orleans, patterns of extreme exodus from urban centers to suburban communities followed a national trend. As the city got blacker, it got poorer. In 1960, New Orleans was 37 percent black; in 1970, it was 43 percent black; by 1980, it was 55 percent black. In 1990 the city was 62 percent black, and by 2000 it was more than 67 percent black. As whites fled New Orleans, they turned to Jefferson Parish, which is 69.8 percent white and only 22.9 percent black; to St. Bernard Parish, which is 88.29 percent white with a paltry 7.62 percent black population; and to St. Tammany Parish, which is 87.02 percent white and 9.90 percent black. The black middle class sought refuge in Gentilly and New Orleans East, intensifying the suffering of a largely black and poor inner city.[19]

Perhaps most damaging for the young, concentrated poverty stifles the academic success of black children. A child's socioeconomic status, along with other influential factors like teacher/pupil ratio, teacher quality, curriculum materials, expenditures per student, and the age of the school building, greatly affects his/her academic success. Wealthier parents are able to send their children to better public schools and higher-quality private schools, which, in turn, clear the path for admission to prestigious colleges and universities.[20] New Orleans has a 40 percent illiteracy rate; over 50 percent of black ninth graders won't graduate in four years. Louisiana expends an average of $4,724 per student and has the third-lowest rank for teacher salaries in the nation.[21] The black dropout rates are high and nearly 50,000 students cut class every day.

When they are done with school, many young black males end up at Angola Prison, a correctional facility located on a former plantation where inmates still perform manual farm labor, and where 90 percent of them eventually die.[22] New Orleans's employment picture is equally gloomy, since industry long ago deserted the city, leaving in its place a service economy that caters to tourists and that thrives on low-paying, transient, and unstable jobs.[23]

If President Bush is serious about what he said in his first speech on national television in Katrina's aftermath, that the "deep, persistent poverty" of the Gulf Coast "has roots in a history of racial discrimination, which has cut off generations from the opportunity of America," and that we must "rise above the legacy of inequality," then he must foster public policy and legislation that help the poor to escape

their plight.[24] But can a self-proclaimed antigovernment president develop policy that actually improves people's lives? Bush would have to change his mind about slashing $35 billion from Medicaid, food stamps, and other social programs that help the poor combat such a vile legacy. The federal government also owes the black poor better schools. Bush's No Child Left Behind Act of 2001 promised to bolster the nation's crumbling educational infrastructure, but conservative politics have only exacerbated the problems: underperforming schools, low reading levels, and wide racial and class disparities. The schools that need money the most—those whose students are up against challenges like outdated curriculum materials and poor teacher/pupil ratios—have their funding cut when their test scores don't measure up. Oddly enough, Bush has also failed to sufficiently fund his own mandate, reinforcing class and educational inequality.

Bush also owes it to the poor to use the bully pulpit of the presidency to address the health crisis in black America. When Katrina swept waves of mostly poor and black folk into global view, it also graphically uncovered their poor health. More than 83,000 citizens, or 18.8 percent of the population in New Orleans, lacked health insurance (the national average is 15.5 percent); the numbers for black women doubled those for white women.[25] Nationally, there are nearly 40 million folk without health insurance, many of them black and poor. They resort to the emergency ward for health maintenance. Their survival is compromised because serious diseases are spotted later than need be. If President Bush is the compassionate conservative he says he is, then he must help fix a health care system that favors the wealthy and the solidly employed.

Concentrated poverty does more than undermine academic success and good health; since there is a strong relationship between education and employment, and quality of life, it keeps the poor from better-paying jobs that might interrupt a vicious cycle of poverty. In New Orleans, severe underemployment and unemployment, and unstable employment, gang up on the black poor. This circumstance is made worse by the densely populated communities and housing in which they live, the sheer social misery of much of postindustrial urban Southern life, and their dreadful infant-mortality and homicide rates—the disenfranchised turn more readily and violently on each other rather than striking against the inequality that puts them at each other's throats.

The Lower Ninth Ward is a perfectly bleak example of the concentrated poverty the city's poor black residents confront. The Lower Ninth Ward, also known as the Lower 9, is symptomatic of the geographical isolation on which concentrated poverty feeds. The Lower 9 "crouches behind a pile of dirt, separated by a big bend in America's biggest river and a thick canal and eons of tradition from the 'high-class people' up on the high ground over in the French Quarter."[26] The Lower Ninth was one of the last neighborhoods in the city to be developed. To its west lies the Industrial Canal; to the north are the Southern Railway railroad and Florida Avenue Canal; to the east lies the parish line; and the river traces its southern border.[27] The Lower 9 grew so slowly because it was isolated from the rest of the city and because it lacked adequate drainage systems.[28] The Lower 9 evolved from a cypress swamp to a series of plantations that extended from the river to the lake. Poor black folk in search of affordable housing—and Irish, German, and Italian immigrant workers too— fled to the area although risking disease and natural disaster.

The Lower 9's growth was so delayed that by 1950 half of it remained undeveloped. The dry docks of the Industrial Canal were the center of development at the time, while some activity trickled out to residential areas in the neighborhood's northern section. By the end of the decade, the second bridge between the city and the Lower 9, the Claiborne Avenue Bridge, was built across Industrial Canal at Claiborne Avenue.[29] During this time, retail development along St. Claude Avenue took off and corner stores became popular. By 1965, industrial and commercial enterprise thrived on the strip that ran along the Industrial Canal between Claiborne and Florida Avenues.[30]

In September of 1965, Hurricane Betsy visited its deadly fury on New Orleans, killing eighty-one people and covering 80 percent of the Lower 9 in water. The storm's surge rose to ten feet, overwhelming the eight-foot levee. As with Katrina, survivors waded through waist-deep water holding babies to escape Betsy's aftermath. Other victims awaited rescue from their rooftops. Critics maintain that Betsy's carnage fueled the decline of the Lower 9, especially since many residents didn't receive adequate loans or other financial aid to help rebuild the neighborhood. Many longtime residents fled, and several commercial and industrial businesses soon followed.

The area received assistance in the late sixties and early seventies from a federal program that targeted blighted neighborhoods to spark metropolitan development and revitalization—leading to the Lower Ninth Ward Neighborhood Council, Total Community Action's Lower Ninth Ward Head Start Program, the Lower Ninth Ward Housing Development Corporation, and the Lower Ninth Ward Health Clinic. The Lower 9 has many small businesses, barber and beauty shops, corner grocery stores called "superettes," eating spots, gasoline stations, day care centers, churches, and Laundromats called "washeterias."[31] Despite its rich cultural and racial pedigree—the Lower 9 is home to famed entertainer Fats Domino and features during Carnival some of the most exciting "second-line" parades, characterized by churning rhythms and kinetic, high-stepping funk grooves—the area has continued to struggle with persistent and concentrated poverty.[32]

Before Katrina, the Lower 9 was peopled with poor blacks who were the maids, bellhops, and busboys who looked after tourists on pleasure hunts and thrill quests in New Orleans. They are now the clerks, cops, and carpenters who are helping to revive and rebuild the city, along with the sculptors, painters, and musicians who are staples of the local scene.[33] The vast majority of the Lower 9's 20,000 residents were black, and more than a third of them, 36 percent, lived beneath the poverty line, nearly double the statewide poverty rate.[34] The Lower 9's residents were often victims of the complicated racial dynamics in New Orleans, where police brutality and retail and business profiling dogged them from outside their neighborhood, and where bigotry against poorer, often darker, blacks echoed within many African American communities. The faces of the Lower 9's residents—though forgotten by their government and overlooked by their fellow citizens—looked out from their watery wasteland and for a moment focused the eyes of the world on their desperate plight.

But it was not merely that we forgot to see or know the poor that forged the searing image of our national neglect and American amnesia. And neither was it the fact that Katrina exposed, to our horror and amazement, the bitter outlines of concentrated poverty that we have reason to be ashamed. It is not all about what we saw—which, after all, may be a perverse narcissism that makes *their* plight ultimately about *our* failure and what *we* must learn at their great expense. It is also about what *they,* the poor, saw in us, or didn't see there, especially the government that didn't find or feed them until it was late—too late for thousands of them. It is their surprise, not ours, that should most concern and inform us. Perhaps it is their anger, too, that is inspiring, since the outrage of the black survivors proved their tenacious loyalty to a country that hasn't often earned it.

As Michael Ignatieff argues, the poor blacks struggling to survive Katrina's backlash saw more clearly than most others "what the contract of American citizenship entails."[35] For Ignatieff, a contract of citizenship "defines the duties of care that public officials owe to the people of a democratic society." Ignatieff says that the "Constitution defines some parts of this contract, and statutes define other parts, but much of it is a tacit understanding that citizens have about what to expect from their government." Ignatieff contends that the contract's "basic term is protection: helping citizens to protect their families and possessions from forces beyond their control."[36] According to Ignatieff, when a woman at the convention center proclaimed "We are American," it was "she—not the governor, not the mayor, not the president—[who] understood that the catastrophe was a test of the bonds of citizenship and that the government had failed the test." Ignatieff explores the racial backdrop to the government's disregard of the poor while clarifying the demand of the poor that we honor a contract by which we claim to abide:

It may be astonishing that American citizens should have had to remind their fellow Americans of this, but let us not pretend we do not know

the reason. They were black, and for all that poor blacks have experienced and endured in this country, they had good reason to be surprised that they were treated not as citizens but as garbage. . . . Let us not be sentimental. The poor and dispossessed of New Orleans cannot afford to be sentimental. They know they live in an unjust and unfair society. . . . So it is not—as some commentators claimed—that the catastrophe laid bare the deep inequalities of American society. These inequalities may have been news to some, but they were not news to the displaced people in the convention center and elsewhere. What was bitter news to them was that their claims of citizenship mattered so little to the institutions charged with their protection.[37]

In his lucid explanation of the compelling bonds of citizenship, Ignatieff outlines detriments to the social contract that make us all less than what we ought to be. Ignatieff calls attention to the role of race in coloring perceptions on either side of the cultural and political divide about how we should have met our moral and civic obligations to the poor. The deeper we dig into the story of Katrina, the more we must accept culpability for the fact that the black citizens of the Big Easy—a tag given New Orleans by black musicians who easily found work in a city that looms large in the collective American imagination as the home of jazz, jambalaya, and Mardi Gras—were treated by the rest of us as garbage.

Notes

1. Jacques Amalric, "Crises in New Orleans Is History Repeating Itself," WatchingAmerica.com, September 8, 2005, http://www.watchingamerica.com/liberation000040.html.
2. "Who Are Katrina's Victims?" Center for American Progress, September 6, 2005, p. 1. www.americanprogress.org.
3. Ibid.
4. Alan Berube and Bruce Katz, "Katrina's Window: Confronting Concentrated Poverty Across America," Brookings Institution, October 2005, http://www.brookings.edu/metro/pubs/20051012_concentratedpoverty.htm.
5. "Who Are Katrina's Victims?" pp. 1–2.

6. Ibid., p. 2.
7. Alan Berube and Steven Raphael, "Access to Cars in New Orleans," Brookings Institution, September 15, 2005, http://www.brookings.edu/metro/20050915_katrinacarstables.pdf.
8. Ibid.
9. Ibid.
10. Ibid.
11. Ibid.
12. Ibid.
13. Ibid.
14. Berube and Katz, "Katrina's Window."
15. Ibid.
16. Ibid.
17. Ibid. I first used the term "black track" to describe a pattern of black out-migration that mimics patterns of earlier out-migration of white middle-class families to suburban communities. See Michael Eric Dyson, *Reflecting Black: African-American Cultural Criticism* (Minneapolis: University of Minnesota Press, 1993), p. 188.
18. As historian Lawrence N. Powell argues: "Because habitable land was so scarce, the population of New Orleans had to squeeze together, cheek-by-jowl—upper-class gents next door to or one street over from raw-boned stevedores, Irish next to German, black next to white, in a salt-and-pepper pattern that still baffles visitors to the city. New Orleans never had ethnically and racially pure enclaves until modern suburbanization began slotting the population into segregated subdivisions." Lawrence N. Powell, "New Orleans: An American Pompeii?" September 2005, p. 21. Paper in author's possession.
19. Anthony Fontenot, "How to Rebuild New Orleans" (compiled by Aaron Kinney and Page Rockwell), Salon.com, September 30, 2005, http://www.salon.com/news/feature/2005/09/30/rebuild_reaction.
20. "The Racial Wealth Gap Has Become a Huge Chasm that Severely Limits Black Access to Higher Education," *The Journal of Blacks in Higher Education*, 2005, pp. 23–25.
21. Jordan Flaherty, "Notes from Inside New Orleans," *New Orleans Independent Media Center*, September 2, 2005, http://neworleans.indymedia.org/news/2005/4043.php.
22. Ibid.
23. Ibid.
24. "Bush: 'We Will Do What It Takes'" (transcript of Bush speech from Jackson Square in the French Quarter of New Orleans), CNN.com, September 17, 2005, http://www.cnn.com/2005/POLITICS/09/15/bush.transcript/index.html.
25. "Who Are Katrina's Victims?" p. 2.
26. Manuel Roig-Franzia, "Once More, a Neighborhood Sees the Worst," *Washington Post*, September 8, 2005, p. A18.
27. "Lower Ninth Ward Neighborhood Snapshot," Greater New Orleans Community Data Center, October 10, 2002, http://www.gnocdc.org/orleans/8/22/snapshot.html.
28. Ibid.
29. Ibid.
30. Ibid.
31. Ibid.; Roig-Franzia, "Once More," p. A18.
32. Roig-Franzia, "Once More," p. A18; Ceci Connolly, "9th Ward: History, Yes, but a Future?; Race and Class Frame Debate on Rebuilding New Orleans District," *Washington Post*, October 3, 2005, p. A01.
33. Connolly, "9th Ward."
34. Ibid.; Roig-Franzia, "Once More."
35. Michael Ignatieff, "The Broken Contract," *The New York Times Magazine*, September 25, 2005, p. 15.
36. Ibid.
37. Ibid.

23.
THE HIP-HOP HEARINGS
The Hidden History of Deindustrialization
George Lipsitz

> The playing field of contemporary culture may be new but it is still not level.
>
> —Juan Flores, From Bomba to Hip-Hop: Puerto Rican Culture and Latino Identity

In an early moment in Toni Morrison's 1977 novel *Song of Solomon,* teenager Guitar Baines voices a complaint to two men in a barber shop: he reports that the owner of the local pool hall will not sell him a beer. One of the barbers, Railroad Tommy, feels little sympathy for him. Summoning up the rancor he feels from a lifetime of disappointments, slights, refusals, and resentments, the barber points his finger at the youth and asks, "Is that all? He wouldn't let you have a beer?"

Drawing on his own bitter experiences, Railroad Tommy then offers the youth named Guitar a litany of all the other things he is *not* going to get in life, all the luxuries that the barber witnessed during his years working as a Pullman porter but never secured for himself: a private coach with red velvet chairs, a special private toilet, a custom-made eight-foot bed, a valet, a cook, a traveling secretary to attend to personal needs, enough money in the bank to get a loan without collateral, timber to sell, a ship to sail, a train to run, military honors, a breakfast tray with a red rose and warm croissants and hot chocolate delivered to your bed in the morning, pheasant baked in coconut leaves, vintage fine wine, and the dessert of ice cream inside a warm cake known as baked Alaska.

Intimidated by Railroad Tommy's torrent of bitterness unleashed by the complaint about not being able to buy a beer, Guitar Baines tries to lighten up the mood. "No baked Alaska?" he exclaims in mock horror. "You breaking my heart!" Seizing on the young man's choice of words, Railroad Tommy replies, "Well, now. That's something you will have— a broken heart." As the merriment dies in his eyes, Railroad Tommy adds, "And folly. A whole lot of folly. You can count on it."[1]

The exchange that Morrison stages between Guitar Baines and Railroad Tommy presupposes generational differences. Guitar Baines wants immediate gratification and pleasure today. His complaint does not get him any sympathy from Railroad Tommy, however, because the barber knows that many more disappointments and frustrations lie ahead. Yet the youth cannot possibly know why his elder is so upset. A shared sorrow produces conflict rather than connection between the two characters, because they see things from different generational frames.

This illustrative anecdote encapsulates many of Morrison's descriptions and plot devices in *Song of Solomon.* The novel revolves around intergenerational inheritance and antagonism, around the ways in which the pursuit of property and pleasure can cause suffering to others. Yet in a society based on property rights, not owning property can be hell. The long fetch of history in the novel shows that racism is an impediment to inheriting assets that appreciate in value and can be passed down to subsequent generations for Blacks. Only the injuries suffered by one generation become inherited by the next, not monetary wealth and property. The young condemn their elders constantly for the poverty and powerlessness that seem to be their lot without knowing the history of how things got that way, while the elders know so much about that history they can scarcely begin to communicate it to their children.

At a key moment in the novel, however, Morrison's narrator identifies the importance of work, achievement, and success. Money as an end in itself is corrupt, but discipline, dedication, work, and achievement in any endeavor are important. The narrator describes the farm that the protagonist's grandfather built after his emancipation from slavery. His hard work created a home and a business that encouraged other blacks to think they could succeed too. His work "colored their lives like a paintbrush and spoke to them like a sermon," indicating that with discipline, determination, and work they could secure inclusion in a country whose history had been premised on their exclusion. "But they shot the top of his head off and ate his fine Georgia peaches," Morrison's narrator writes, explaining that jealous whites could not tolerate a success that would serve as a good example to other Blacks. "And even as boys these men began to die and were dying still," Morrison's narrator contends.[2] Cut off from their inheritance, denied the power of a good example, Blacks suffer the death of hope from the murder of Macon Dead Sr., and the injury continues across generations. They do not get a private coach with red velvet chairs, money in the bank, a ship to sail, or even baked Alaska. But they do inherit a whole lot of folly.

In 1994, Black youths across the United States encountered a whole lot of folly from an unexpected source, from some members of the Black Congressional Caucus. At a time of severe unemployment, systematic housing discrimination, educational inequality, and rampant police brutality, these representatives launched an inquiry into the lyrics of rap music. They responded to overwhelming structural problems in society with a moral panic—a publicity campaign designed to portray people *with* problems *as* problems. Moral panics about popular music have a long and dishonorable history. Adult anxiety about the behavior

and values of young people has often led to attempts to blame the music young people like for disturbing cultural changes. In the United States at different moments during the twentieth century, efforts to suppress and censor Dixieland jazz, swing, bebop, and rock 'n' roll have all served as occasions where antiyouth and anti-Black discourses have blended together. It should not have been surprising, then, that hip-hop would face the same fate. The moral panic over hip-hop in the early 1990s took a novel turn, however, when these African American elected officials decided to take leading roles in attributing youth crime, drug use, and social disintegration in their communities to the popularity of "gangsta rap" music.

US representative Cardiss Collins, of Illinois, a member of the Black Congressional Caucus, presided over hearings in 1994. Held in response to a request by C. Delores Tucker, of the National Political Congress of Black Women, the hearings revealed deep divisions among Blacks, not only about the lyrics of gangsta rap songs, but also about the problems confronting African Americans in general. Although the sponsors of the hearings, key witnesses, and committee members all insisted that their efforts were directed solely against the music that young people liked rather than against the youths themselves, the hearings and the circumstances that brought them into being in the first place offered clear evidence of a deep chasm across generational lines.

Many witnesses at the hearings claimed that gangsta rap lyrics encouraged disrespect for women and that they glorified and promoted crime. The music's defenders claimed that the critics were blaming the messengers for news they did not wish to face, that gangster rap reported, recorded, and registered social changes that young people had seen with their own eyes, that gangsta rap was one of the few sites in US society capable of telling the truth about the devastation caused by deindustrialization and disinvestment in inner-city communities, about the effects of economic restructuring, the failure to enforce civil rights laws, the pervasiveness of police brutality, and the evisceration of the social wage caused by tax cuts and shifts in government spending away from social services and toward military procurement. Largely absent from this debate was an appreciation of how arguments over song lyrics obscured the ways in which both neoconservative and neoliberal racial politics had driven a wedge between generations, not just among African Americans, but among young people and their elders in other groups as well.

Ostensibly a debate about culture and crime, about censorship and social behavior, the hearings about gangsta rap actually advanced the agenda of the enemies of the Black community by demonizing the victims of unjust social policies, by attacking the most public and visible manifestation of these problems in popular culture. Gangsta rap emerged in neoconservative and neoliberal cosmologies as the only plausible explanation for contemporary ruptures between genders and among generations and racial groups, because people in power refuse to take responsibility for their own actions, for the policies that have created the very problems they purport to decry. Their efforts to censor and suppress gangsta rap music have attempted to obscure the social causes and consequences of disturbing historical changes, rendering as individual and personal experiences that actually have broad-based collective origins and effects.

Invited to present her views as the first witness at the hearings, C. Delores Tucker invoked the moral authority of Martin Luther King Jr. on behalf of her cause. She alleged that if the martyred civil rights leader were alive today he

> "would be marching and demonstrating against the glamorization of violence and its corrupting influence, which has now become a part of our culture in the name of freedom. This freedom, freedom from responsibility and accountability, is not the kind of freedom that Dr. King, Medgar Evers, John Lewis, James Farmer, Rosa Parks and so many others risked their lives for."[3]

Tucker claimed that for four hundred years African Americans had maintained a sense of humanity and morality that enabled them to survive the middle passage, slavery, and other horrors. But by the 1990s, "our morality, which has been the last vestige of our strength, [was] being threatened" by "lyrics out of the mouths of our own children," in her view.[4] Describing gangsta rap as "pornographic smut," Tucker alleged that this music provokes our youths to violence, drug use, and mistreatment of women. "This explains why so many of our children are out of control and why we have more black males in jail than we have in college," she charged.[5]

Syndicated radio talk show host Joseph Madison also invoked the legacy of the civil rights movement in his testimony at the hip-hop hearings. "I was 23 years old when I became the executive director of the Detroit NAACP," Madison explained, establishing his credentials as an activist and an authority on the policies best suited to serve Black people. He told the committee, "When radio stations bombard the airwaves with these messages of hate, killing, and self-destruction, it will cause a conflict even within those families that may have taught other values." Citing the case of his own fourteen-year-old son, Madison told the committee that images of thugs and criminals projected by gangsta rap had turned his son from a young man who had been on the school honor roll and a star athlete into someone who began dressing like gangsta rappers, a youth who told his father in one conversation that he felt that time in jail would be preferable to the life he was leading in his middle-class home.[6]

Madison took pains to say that "this is not a confrontation with young people," but then his subsequent testimony proved otherwise. After detailing how he had "educated" his son that "the pants had to come off the hip and the shoe strings had to go back in, and the language had to be cleaned up and the fascination with guns had to end," he referred derisively to young rappers for saying that "the older generation, the black leaders have done absolutely nothing. The black politicians have done nothing for this generation." Madison answered that charge by taking it personally, asserting,

> "Well, we obviously have more opportunities than we had 30, 40, 50 years ago and it was because many of us sitting here today sacrificed and gave our lives to see to it that this young generation has at least the opportunity to do what they need to do. Have we completed it all? No. And there is a lot of work to do, but this is not because we do not love our young people. It is just the opposite."[7]

Although often completely unaware of even the most elementary facts about the lyrics, artists, and music they condemned, Tucker, Madison, and other witnesses at the hearings were not incorrect in their perception of a generation gap among African Americans. Nor were they completely off base in detecting a certain contempt and resentment among young Blacks about the civil rights movement and its record. Young people interviewed by a reporter for the *Pittsburgh Courier* about holiday celebrations commemorating Dr. King's birthday in 1996, for example, expressed this disdain clearly. "Ours is not the same kind of struggle," one explained. "We really don't know what it was like back then. All we know now is that the only thing that counts in this world is money, power, and material wealth." Another opined, "Dr. King believed in righteousness, but that's not something you can take to the bank or to the grocery store. To survive in this society today, you've got to be the firstest with the mostest."[8]

These young people clearly did not know enough about the civil rights movement, about Dr. King's Poor People's March, about his support for striking sanitation workers in Memphis at the moment when he was assassinated, or about the broad-based struggle for jobs, education, and housing that accompanied efforts to secure access to public accommodations. On the other hand, Tucker, Madison, and other critics of African American youth did not display enough knowledge about the circumstances facing young people in their time, about the ways in which every significant institution in the society has made it clear to young people of color that they do not count, that their parents are considered losers, and that their communities are largely places where no one would live unless they had no other choice. Gangsta rap has not caused this division, although it is an interesting and important symptom of it. The campaign to censor and suppress gangsta rap has, nonetheless, been enormously important, because it serves as a prototypical example of the ways in which conservative cultural and political mobilizations operate to obscure public understanding of who has power in our society and what they do with that power. It blames the victims and absolves the perpetrators.

During the 1980s, the number of children living in poverty in the United States increased by 2.2 million. Among European Americans, child poverty rose from 11.8 percent in 1979 to 14.8 percent in 1989. For Latinos, child poverty went from 28 percent to 32 percent. The portion of poor African American children increased from 41.2 percent to 43.7 percent during that decade. Neoconservative commentators blamed these increases in poverty on the mental and cultural deficiencies of minorities.[9] In fact, the fastest growing segments of the poverty population in this time period were young white families with children, families headed by married couples, and families headed by high school graduates.[10]

The effects of deindustrialization, however, exerted a particularly devastating impact on minorities, especially on entry-level workers beginning their careers. In 1979, 23 percent of male workers between the ages of eighteen and twenty-four received wages below the poverty line, but by 1990, that number rose to 43 percent. Only 6 percent of full-time workers between the ages of twenty-five and thirty-four received poverty-level wages in 1979, but 15 percent did so by 1990. The impact of these changes fell most harshly on communities of color. Between 1965 and 1990, Black family income fell by 50 percent, and Black youth unemployment quadrupled.[11] The share of low-income households headed by Blacks increased by one-third.[12] Fifty percent of Black males employed in durable-goods manufacturing in five Great Lakes states lost their jobs as a result of computer-based automation or capital flight between 1979 and 1984.[13] For many young people who came of age as witnesses to the era of deindustrialization, the "victories" of the civil rights generation seem insubstantial. They came to know the meaning of race through their experiences, from long periods of unemployment, sporadic work at entry-level low-wage jobs, pervasive housing discrimination, stark educational inequality, oppressive police brutality, and toxic levels of environmental pollution in their neighborhoods.

The economic conditions that inner-city youths faced in the 1980s and 1990s were inflected by both their generational and their racial identities. Adults of the civil rights generation witnessed enormous changes in the racial rulebook of US society in their lives, but continuing and cumulative discrimination in housing, employment, and education has worked to prevent them from acquiring assets that appreciate in value to a sufficient degree that they can be passed on to the next generation. As Melvin Oliver and Thomas Shapiro demonstrate clearly and definitively in *Black Wealth, White Wealth,* past and present discrimination in real estate and other forms of asset accumulation leaves Black parents far less able than white parents to pass on their class status to their children. Only slightly more than one-third of Black adults with upper-level white-collar jobs successfully transmit their class status to their children, while it is extremely rare for white children from that background to fall in class status. In addition, twice as many Black children as white children fall from upper-level white-collar backgrounds to lower-level blue-collar positions. For blue-collar families, the statistics are even starker. Almost 60 percent of whites from blue-collar backgrounds rise in class status, but only slightly more than one-third of Black children experience similar upward mobility. One half of Blacks from upper-blue-collar families wind up at the bottom of the occupational hierarchy. Fewer than 30 percent of Blacks from lower-white-collar families move into professional jobs, but more than 50 percent of whites from lower-white-collar families move up into the professions.[14]

Under these circumstances, one could well understand citizens, congressional committees, and mass media outlets engaging in anxious debate about infant mortality, child nutrition, and health care, about youth education and employment, about the routine and pervasive violations of fair housing and fair lending laws that leave people from different races with starkly different opportunities and life chances. These discussions did indeed take place, but they attracted far less attention and played much smaller roles in the popular political imagination than cultural controversies about mass media images and their purported influences and effects. The reasons for this imbalance are multiple and complex, but one aspect of the problem stems from the strategic utility of questions about the evils of commercial culture for people interested in suppressing social memory and silencing social theory at the grass roots. The controversy over gangsta rap is only the latest in a long line of historical moral panics about mass media and social relations, panics that have almost always stemmed from the same sources and produced the same results.

During the Great Depression of the 1930s, for example, motion picture censors took aim at gangster films because they made crime seem like a logical response to social conditions rather than a grievous violation of personal and public moral codes. As Jonathan Munby has shown, sound films enabled Edward G. Robinson and James Cagney to bring the actual speech of an ethnic urban underclass to a broad audience, and their tremendous popularity (many theaters had Robinson and Cagney "imitation" shows before screenings) disclosed a broad desire to register the suffering and express the resentments of those who suffered most from the Depression.[15]

Gangster films, however, defamed Italian, Irish, Greek, and other ethnic Americans by reinforcing the association between ethnic identity and urban crime, echoing the vicious hatreds that had been widely disseminated by nativists and eugenicists during the 1920s as reasons to curtail immigration. These views were implicitly conservative, because by grounding the plight of the lower classes in their biological makeup, they portrayed efforts at social reform as futile. Yet many viewers of gangster films drew directly opposite conclusions, identifying with the "gangsters" as symbols of their own desire for upward mobility, as emblems of suppressed ethnic and class anger, and as icons who escaped the humiliating stigma of ethnic and class subordination through daring action and stylish consumption.[16]

Aware of the oppositional potential of such narratives, some representatives of conservative Catholic groups participated in censorship efforts enthusiastically during the Great Depression. Because Anglo-Protestants drew on vicious and pervasive anti-Catholicism in pressing for an end to immigration, for the deportation of alleged subversives and criminals, for the prohibition of alcohol consumption, and for the censorship of popular music and film, some respectable Catholics felt defensive. It is not unusual for members of aggrieved communities who have been defamed as not only alien but also nonnormative to embrace rigorous restraints on themselves, performing normativity in the face of their enemies in hopes of disproving the stereotypes.[17] During the Great Depression, conservative Catholics supported censorship in the hope of proving themselves and their entire religious group to be normative, moral, clean, and decent. They viewed the "glorification" of the Irish, Italian, or Greek gangster as ammunition for their enemies. Consequently, they sought to disrupt the link that connected ethnic identity to criminal behavior. In the process, however, they helped Anglo-Protestants to mute collective memories and to suppress social analyses of the conditions that immigrant and ethnic communities confronted. Disconnected from social causality, the gangster became an individual aberration whose "deviance" could be addressed only by repressive state power or by individual psychological treatment rather than meliorative social reform.

Similarly, during the post-World War II period, the House Un-American Activities Committee (HUAC) held repeated hearings into alleged Communist subversion in Hollywood. Committee counsel repeatedly asked actors of Jewish ancestry to disclose their original names, as if Emmanuel Goldenberg became Edward G. Robinson or Morris Carnovsky became Chester Morris because of a secret Communist plot rather than in response to American anti-Semitism. Witnesses were asked to spell out their non–Anglo Saxon names, even though the committee (having sent them subpoenas) knew perfectly well how they were spelled. The spelling exercise was designed to emphasize the foreign (and often Jewish) ancestries of the witnesses. This enabled the committee to create the impression that challenges to capitalism did not, and could not, originate in America. As part of a larger conservative ideological assault, HUAC wanted to brand the New Deal itself as subversive, to portray its thought and culture as foreign to America, to misrepresent antifascism as procommunism. The premise that only something outside the United States could account for anticapitalist attitudes led an otherwise largely cooperative and compliant Clifford Odets to protest to the committee that he had not been radicalized by anything said to him by members of the Communist Party. Odets insisted on telling the committee about the domestic origins of his alienation,

recalling how his mother "worked in a stocking factory in Philadelphia at the age of eleven and died a broken woman . . . at the age of forty-eight."[18] Odets's efforts to bring historical memory and social analysis back into the discussion proved futile. The success of HUAC came not through any exposure of actual Communist influence in Hollywood but rather from the articulation and dissemination of the idea that analyses of unequal and unjust social relations in the United States stemmed from the malicious actions of nonnormative individuals rather than from honest observation of social conditions.

Attempts to silence, regulate, and even criminalize rap music in the United States during the 1990s followed this same trajectory. These attempts emerged most clearly through what Leola Johnson calls "one of the most sustained censorship drives in United States history."[19] By examining the origins and evolution of these censorship efforts, we can see how the hip-hop hearings blamed the messenger in order to occlude the clear connections between the fantasies circulated in gangsta rap and the harsh realities of societal conditions.

Assistant Director Milt Ahlerich of the Federal Bureau of Investigation sent a letter in 1989 to Priority Records in Los Angeles complaining about a song that he did not name but was obviously "F——the Police," on the label's album *Straight Outta Compton,* by the group N.W.A.[20] Hiding behind the passive voice to disguise the agency of the bureau, the FBI official described the song as something that had been brought to his attention, although he did not say by whom, how, or why. Protecting himself against charges of censorship, Ahlerich explained that he was writing the letter merely to share his thoughts and concerns with company executives. He did not indicate how frequently the assistant director of the FBI took time out from fighting crime to share his personal thoughts and concerns with music producers. Later in the letter, however, Ahlerich claimed directly that he was expressing "the FBI's position relative to this song and its message." Complaining that the song "encouraged violence and disrespect for the law enforcement officer," the letter went on to state, "We in the law enforcement community take exception to such action."[21] Ahlerich later admitted to reporters that the FBI had never before taken an official position on any piece of music, literature, or art, apparently forgetting the bureau's zealous but futile efforts to decipher the lyrics of "Louie Louie" by the Kingsmen, an episode probably known in crime-fighting annals as "the Great Louie Louie Scare of 1964."[22] Nor could the bureau admit that it was, at that very moment, engaged in a twelve-year struggle to keep "confidential" a sheet of paper containing the lyrics of John Lennon's 1971 song "John Sinclair," even though the lyrics had been publicly available for years, printed on the back of the jacket of Lennon's album *Some Time in New York City.*[23]

Ahlerich conceded in his letter that nobody in the bureau had actually purchased *Straight Outta Compton* or at least would admit to having purchased it. Thus, he could not explain exactly how the song came to his attention, except by citing unstipulated actions by "responsible fellow officers" whom he did not name.[24] Directly or indirectly, however, the bureau's letter about "F——the Police" encouraged officers around the country to take action, and they did. Taking time out from the efforts to enforce the law, officers around the country set up an informal "fax" network designed to prevent public appearances by N.W.A. Off-duty officers withheld concert security services from the group, making it impossible for promoters to secure insurance for N.W.A. appearances.[25] Police harassment jeopardized or canceled the group's shows in Washington, D.C., Chattanooga, Milwaukee, and Tyler (Texas). N.W.A. performed in Cincinnati only because members of the Cincinnati Bengals professional football team (including city council member Reggie Williams) spoke up on their behalf. When members of the group sang the first few lines of "F——the Police" in Detroit, officers rushed the stage, fought with arena security staff, and followed N.W.A. to their hotel, where they detained the group for fifteen minutes. "We just wanted to show the kids," one officer explained to a reporter, "that you can't say 'f——the police' in Detroit."[26] Of course, by saying that, he violated his own rule. Then again, what he probably meant to say was that *they* can't say those words in Detroit.

The crusade against hip-hop emerged within local politics in Florida one year later. A federal district court

judge in Fort Lauderdale agreed with a complaint by conservative activist Jack Thompson, ruling the rap album *As Nasty as They Wanna Be,* by 2 Live Crew, to be obscene. Two years earlier, Thompson had been a candidate for the position of prosecuting attorney in Dade County, Florida, on the Republican ticket against the incumbent (and later US attorney general) Janet Reno. At one campaign appearance, Thompson handed Reno a prepared statement and asked her to check the appropriate box. The statement read, "I, Janet Reno, am a ___ homosexual, ___ bisexual, ___ heterosexual." It continued, "If you do not respond . . . then you will be deemed to have checked one of the first two boxes." Luther Campbell, known as Luke Skywalker, the leader of 2 Live Crew, had supported Reno, conducting voter registration drives on her behalf during that race.[27] Six weeks after losing the election, Thompson wrote letters to Janet Reno and to Florida governor Bob Martinez demanding an investigation of 2 Live Crew for possible violation of state obscenity statutes and racketeering codes in conjunction with *As Nasty as They Wanna Be.*[28]

Two days after the federal court ruling declared *As Nasty as They Wanna Be* obscene, a Broward County sheriff arrested Charles Freeman, a twenty-eight-year-old Black man and the owner of a music store, for the crime of selling a record and tape version of *As Nasty as They Wanna Be* to an adult undercover deputy. Officers put Freeman in handcuffs and took him to the police station. He was subsequently convicted of a first-degree misdemeanor. Sheriff's deputies also arrested two members of 2 Live Crew later that week for singing lyrics from the album at an adults-only concert.[29] An appeals court later overturned the district court's ruling, declaring *As Nasty as They Wanna Be* not to be obscene. Thompson's efforts, however, did persuade the Musicland stores with 752 outlets and the Trans World Stores with 450 branches to drop 2 Live Crew's album from their inventories.[30] At the same time, US Marine Corps officials, with a zeal never previously detected in regard to the presence of "pornography" on military bases, announced that base stores in Yuma, Arizona; Beaufort, South Carolina; Jacksonville, North Carolina; and Oceanside, California, had removed the group's album from their shelves.[31]

The videotaped beating of Rodney King by members of the Los Angeles Police Department in March 1991 and the mass violence directed against persons and property when a Simi Valley jury found the accused officers not guilty on April 29, 1992, set the stage for the next wave of attacks against rap music. For many hip-hop artists, fans, and critics, the Los Angeles rebellion demonstrated the broad community consensus behind hip hop's claims of police misconduct. They believed that rap songs like N.W.A.'s "F——the Police" had been prophetic but ignored. For these observers, there was truth in the claim made by Ice Cube when he was still with N.W.A.: that rappers are "underground street reporters."[32]

In contrast, others saw the riots as a consequence of the views and attitudes popularized by rap music. In May 1992, then Democratic presidential candidate Bill Clinton scolded rap artist Sister Souljah for commenting that she understood the "logic" behind attacks on white people during the rebellion. Souljah noted that if Blacks could attack one another violently every day in the ghetto, it should not be surprising that they would lash out at whites during the riots. Clinton distorted her remarks, however, condemning her as if she were calling for attacks on white people. Less than a month later, a group calling itself the Combined Law Enforcement Association of Texas (CLEAT) denounced the song "Cop Killer," which had been released several weeks before the riots on Ice-T's successful album *Body Count,* recorded with his speed metal band. Even though "Cop Killer" is not a rap song, Ice-T's long history as a rap artist and his visibility in films as an actor playing roles about inner-city life led many critics of the song to refer to it as gangsta rap. CLEAT called for a boycott of all products by Time Warner, the conglomerate distributing *Body Count.* It demanded the removal of the song and album from stores.

Two days after CLEAT announced its campaign against "Cop Killer," Los Angeles City Council member Joan Milke Flores, a Republican, joined the Los Angeles Police Protective League and the Fraternal Order of Police in asking the city council to demand that Time Warner stop selling the song. Vice President Dan Quayle attacked Ice-T at a national convention of radio talk show hosts,

and President George H.W. Bush denounced the rap artist at a national police association conclave. Sixty members of Congress declared "Cop Killer" to be "vile and despicable." Oliver North's "Freedom Alliance" urged the governors of all fifty states to bring criminal charges against Time Warner for distributing the song, and North hired Jack Thompson to represent these concerns at Time Warner's annual stockholders meeting.[33] The National Association of Black Police officers, however, opposed the boycott of Time Warner and the attacks on "Cop Killer." They identified police brutality as the cause of much antipolice sentiment, and they proposed the creation of independent civilian review boards "to scrutinize the actions of our law enforcement officers" as a way of ending the provocations that cause artists such as Ice-T "to respond to actions of police brutality and abuse through their music." Their statement noted wryly that "many individuals of the law enforcement profession do not want anyone to scrutinize their actions, but want to scrutinize the actions of others."[34]

Time Warner initially stood behind the song on free speech grounds. Ice-T announced his resolve to defy the pressure against him and his song. As the complaints mounted, however, both the artist and his label caved in. In Greensboro, North Carolina, police officers delivered an ultimatum to the management of one retail store that, if it kept selling *Body Count,* the police would not respond to any emergency calls at the establishment. Managers removed the album from the store's inventory.[35] Time Warner severed relations with Paris, a Bay Area rapper best known for his political lyrics attacking capitalism and celebrating the history of Black activist groups like the Black Panther Party.[36] Police departments around the country began requesting the managers of their pension funds to divest themselves of Time Warner stock. Ice-T had difficulty securing performing and speaking engagements because of police harassment. By August, Ice-T announced his decision to remove "Cop Killer" from the *Body Count* album. Early in 1993, when Time Warner executives asked Ice-T to make changes on the cover of his new album, *Home Invasion,* the artist severed his ties with the company completely.[37]

Starting in 1993, African American individuals and groups joined the campaign against rap music. Calvin Butts, pastor of the Abyssinian Baptist Church in Harlem, (and later appointed president of the State University of New York College at Old Westbury by Republican governor George Pataki) condemned rap music from the pulpit before attempting to drive a steamroller over a pile of compact discs and cassette tapes.[38] Los Angeles attorney Eric Taylor charged that African Americans like himself had just begun to realize the dreams of Frederick Douglass, Malcolm X, and Martin Luther King Jr. when

"another movement was emerging within the same community that quickly began tearing away at epic civil rights advancements. It labeled many blacks who have endured systemic obstacles to take part in the American Dream as 'sell-outs.' Ironically this movement has found a voice, and to some, legitimacy in gangsta rap music."[39]

Detroit ministers James Holley and Wendell Anthony called for a boycott of rap music, decrying it as "immoral, racist, and decadent."[40] In October 1993, the National Urban League and the National Association for the Advancement of Colored People started to host youth forums attacking gangsta rap, and the National Political Congress of Black Women launched demonstrations at retail record outlets against the sale of "obscene" rap songs.[41] Early in 1994, Senator Carol Mosley Braun and Representative Cardiss Collins, both Democrats from Illinois, responded to entreaties by C. Delores Tucker, of the National Political Congress of Black Women, to hold legislative hearings about rap music. As Leola Johnson astutely notes, Mosley Braun and Collins shifted the focus of attacks on rap music away from its supposedly seditious stance toward the police and instead critiqued the music as obscene, misogynist, and threatening to decency within Black communities. Although the legislators denied any intention to promote censorship, they did remind record industry executives, not so subtly, of the power of Congress to pass laws affecting the industry's financial position, such as the Audio Home Recording Act, implying that some form of self-censorship would secure future cooperation from legislators.[42]

In her opening remarks to the hip-hop hearings, C. Delores Tucker testified on behalf of the National Political Congress of Black Women that rap music glamorizes violence, degrades women, exposes children to smut, incites violence, and seduces young people into lives of crime. She argued that freedom of speech was not an issue, because rap lyrics are obscene, and "it was never intended by the Founding Fathers of this Nation that First Amendment rights be for the protection of obscenities."[43] Unlike Representative Collins, who seemed to favor an improved parental advisory rating system for popular music, Tucker argued that rap music should be banned because of the harm that it does to Black communities.

Committee member Clifford Stearns, a Republican from Florida, cited Joe Madison's testimony at a later hearing but gave it a slightly different spin. Attempting to reconcile Tucker's and Madison's views on misogyny, pornography, and intergenerational tensions among Blacks with the broader conservative agenda embodied in the attacks on "F——the Police," *As Nasty as They Wanna Be,* and "Cop Killer," Stearns noted Madison's remarks about his son's expressed preference for jail over his middle-class home and existence. Stearns opined, "For this reason, I am greatly disturbed by the proliferation of a music, a style, and class, and type that advocates the killing of police officers, the denigration of women, and the need for violent revolution."[44] Madison's actual testimony merely claimed that rap music made his son wear the wrong clothes and wish to leave his middle-class home, not that it advocates the killing of police officers, the denigration of women, or the need for violent revolution, but evidently Stearns felt the need to freestyle his own "rap" on the material given him by Madison.

Conservative spokesperson and former "drug czar" and secretary of education William Bennett followed Stearns's logic in 1995 when he teamed up with C. Delores Tucker in a joint public attack on "hate and sexism in rock and rap music and its corporate sponsors."[45] At the same time, Kansas senator Bob Dole launched his campaign for the Republican presidential nomination with a spirited condemnation of motion picture violence and gangsta rap music.[46] The systematic and sustained attack on rap music by white conservatives and Black liberals, by the FBI and police officers' associations, by local prosecutors and state governors, by members of the House of Representatives and the Senate, by presidential candidates and presidents might indicate that rap music genuinely poses a threat to public decency and safety. Yet the bad faith, cynicism, and opportunism of rap's opponents reveal something less than sincere concern for public morality.

The FBI might have had more credibility in its complaints about N.W.A.'s "F——the Police" if it had had a better record in responding to the 47,000 cases of police brutality reported to the Department of Justice between 1986 and 1992, of which only 15,000 were investigated and only 128 were designated for prosecution.[47] Alabama governor Guy Hunt, one of the first public figures to attack Ice-T's "Cop Killer" in 1992, would have been a better spokesperson for law and order had he not looted his inaugural fund to pay his personal expenses, a felony offense for which he was convicted and sentenced to a $211,000 fine and ordered to perform a thousand hours of community service in 1993.[48]

Oliver North would have been a more convincing spokesperson for law and order in the campaign to punish Time Warner for "Cop Killer" had he not himself defied the law against covert aid to the Contras in Nicaragua as a White House aide in the Reagan administration, a crime for which he was convicted, before an appeals court overturned the verdict as a result of one of those legal technicalities that conservatives always complain about until they are the direct beneficiaries of them. Jack Thompson would have been a more convincing opponent of *As Nasty as They Wanna Be* had he not targeted an entertainer who supported his opponent in the previous election. Bob Dole would have been a more convincing crusader against motion picture and music violence had he not singled out only the products of firms whose executive officers donated money to Democrats while expressly exempting from his critique films by Arnold Schwarzenegger, a Republican whose *Terminator* films portrayed every bit as much fantasy violence against the police as any song by N.W.A. or Ice Cube.

Singer Dionne Warwick, a cochair of the National Political Congress of Black Women and a witness against gangsta rap at the hip-hop hearings, would have been a more credible defender of "our children" from the alleged damages done to them by commercial popular music if she were not also the official on-camera spokesperson for a "psychic friends hot line" that encouraged children and adults to spend three dollars a minute on a telephone service that connects callers to "psychics" who purport to have special insights into the future. Warwick's concern for the corrupting evils of gangsta rap might have been more persuasive had she not agreed to a plea bargain in a Florida courtroom on June 5, 2002, to enter a drug treatment program in return for having charges dropped against her for possession of eleven marijuana cigarettes in a lipstick container at the Miami International Airport a month earlier.[49] William Bennett, the author of the *Book of Virtues*, might have been a more convincing critic of the morality of other people had the *Washington Monthly* not reported that he had lost an estimated eight million dollars gambling at casinos, and if he had not opined on his syndicated radio program that aborting Black babies would eliminate most of the crime committed in the United States. Bennett noted that that he opposes such a solution, not because it is genocidal and racist, but because he opposes abortion. He never revealed any evidence for his assumption that Blacks commit most of the crime in the United States.[50]

Perhaps the chair of the National Political Congress of Black Women, C. Delores Tucker, would have had more credibility in her campaign against the immorality of rap music had she not been fired as Pennsylvania's commonwealth secretary in 1977 for running a private for-profit business at state expense, had she not used state employees to write speeches for which she received $66,931, had she and her husband not been found to owe close to $25,000 in real estate taxes in 1973 on twelve properties that they owned in the North Philadelphia ghetto, and had she not set up a meeting in August 1995 in which she proposed that Time Warner create a record distribution company for her and give her control over the highly profitable Death Row Records label. When executives from Death Row Records filed suit against her for trying to interfere with their contracts with Time Warner, Tucker explained to a reporter that "whatever they accuse me of doing, it would be worth it to protect children," a comment that Dave Marsh notes "is markedly different than 'not guilty.'"[51]

Bad faith, personal hypocrisy, and political opportunism have been important features of the campaign against rap music, but they do not explain why the campaign exists or why it has largely succeeded. Like most conservative mobilizations over the past three decades, the crusade against rap music identifies real problems in people's lives: hostility between men and women, disintegration of family and community networks, urban violence, intergenerational tensions, and the materialism, vulgarity, and scopophilia of much popular culture and advertising. But like most other "moral panic" crusades, the campaign against rap music takes these social realities out of historical context, hiding their causes and consequences by making them matters of personal and private morality. The crusade against rap music suppresses social memory by claiming that only culture counts, that history—in this case deindustrialization, economic restructuring, white backlash against the civil rights agenda, and neoconservative politics—has nothing to do with the social disintegration in our society. Criticizing rap music enables conservatives and their allies to run away from their own responsibility for today's social problems, to blame cultural responses to intolerable conditions *for* those conditions.

The attack on rap not only suppresses social memory; it also silences social theory. Because conservatives have a theological faith in the infallibility of "the market" to convert private greed into public good, they can explain systemic social breakdown only in terms of the deviant actions of individuals. As a result, Vice President Dan Quayle attributed the Los Angeles rebellion to "a poverty of values in the inner city," and Pat Buchanan and Bruce Herschensohn argued that a return to prayer in the schools would address the root causes of the riots. The attack on rap music grows logically from that denial of history and of social theory. If we have bad conditions, it must be because of bad people and their private decisions,

not because of the systematic structuring of privilege and advantage for a few as a result of the systematic exploitation of and disadvantage for the many, not because of economic restructuring, the role of low-wage labor and unemployment in the new transnational economy, disinvestment in social institutions and the social wage, and the abandoned enforcement of civil rights laws and principles.

Not only does rap music make a convenient target for this crusade, but it is also a practice and an institution offering an alternative to the suppression of social memory and social theory. Early in the Reagan years, a White House aide announced the administration's goal as "defunding the left," a phrase used routinely by Pat Robertson and others to explain the philosophical agenda uniting diverse activities from attacks on the NEA to campaigns for school vouchers. As much as any institution in our society, hip-hop culture and rap music have been repositories of social memory, from the basic musical techniques of sampling songs from the past to their lyrical concern for Black history, from their specificity in detailing the devastation of inner cities to their eloquence in expressing the feelings and experiences of people that mainstream media and institutions ignore.

Throughout the sustained censorship campaign against hip-hop, rap artists and their defenders have conceded that the music's lyrics are sometimes obscene, sometimes celebratory about violence, and sometimes sexist and misogynist. They have also pointed out, however, that critics often forget that rap lyrics use metaphors—that Ice-T's "Grand Larceny" is actually about "stealing" a show and that his "I'm Your Pusher" is actually an antidrug song celebrating "dope beats and lyrics" with "no beepers needed."[52] While acknowledging and often condemning obscene, violent, and misogynist lyrics, they contend that these features were incidental to the music's main purpose: telling the truth about the conditions experienced by young people, especially those in inner-city ghettos and barrios. "This is our voice," argued Vinnie Brown, of the group Naughty by Nature. "If it wasn't for rap, you would never know that these horrors are going on in the community."[53] Chuck D, of Public Enemy, explained, "Hip-hop is not exactly a music. It's damn near real life."[54]

Rap music has created a discursive space open to young people who have little access to any actual physical space. They have found themselves largely not wanted as workers, as students, as citizens, or even as consumers. Police officers, private security guards, and gang violence have constrained their access to public spaces, and politicians and the mass media have demonized them as criminals responsible for the poverty of their own neighborhoods. Through rap music, they tell the story as it appears to them. Bushwick Bill, of the rap group the Geto Boys, stressed the material dimensions of hip-hop as a response to ghetto conditions in his answer to Senator Dole's attack on violence in rap music.

"Dole, who opposes affirmative action, has now bashed rap, which is the number one form of jobs to be had for a lot of inner city youths, as even if you don't rap, engineer, or produce, you can get paid to put up posters, pass out fliers, distribute promotional tapes, work on music video sets, do security, promote a club, just all kinds of things you can get paid to do. Not only is Dole's attack another attempt to censor us because this is our creative art form talking about what's going on, but also rap has been a way to get out of the ghetto without violence or selling drugs."[55]

Television personality and *Soul Train* host Don Cornelius astutely described rap music fans as young people who realize that they have been given the worst of everything this society has to offer.

"They are people who nobody really has spent much money on or spent much concern on. They are part of a more or less forgotten community. Along come these young rappers with all of this negative commentary who are saying, 'we know that you are there, we know what your problems are, we not only know what they are, we are willing to dramatize and comment on these problems in our records.'"[56]

A study by the California legislature in 1982 revealed that deindustrialization, capital flight, and neoconservative economic restructuring in the late 1970s had produced a 50 percent rise in unemployment in South Central Los Angeles, while purchasing power there had dropped by one-third.[57] In Los Angeles at the time of the 1992 rebellion, the African American poverty rate reached 32.9 percent, Black unemployment hovered between 40 and 50 percent, and forty thousand teenagers (20 percent of the sixteen- to nineteen-year-olds) were both unemployed and out of school.[58] In one study, nearly 5 percent of all Blacks reported being unjustly beaten by the police. Civilian deaths resulting from police brutality have long been at least nine times more likely to happen to Blacks than to whites.[59] Contrary to C. Delores Tucker's claim that violence promoted by rap music is the source of "the greatest fear" in Black communities, rampant discrimination, environmental hazards, on-the-job injuries, inadequate access to medical care, police brutality, and hate crimes remain the sources of the greatest threats to Black people and to other exploited and aggrieved populations. Even in respect to violence, the definitive sociological study in the field shows that "socioeconomic inequality between races, as well as economic inequality generally, increases rates of criminal violence" and that "aggressive acts of violence seem to result not so much from lack of advantages as from being taken advantage of."[60] Thus, Black-on-Black crime would be lessened by policies producing greater equality and opportunity.

Rap music has chronicled the devastation of inner cities and the demise of jobs, services, and opportunities during twenty-five years of neoconservative contraction of the industrial economy and the welfare state. Moreover, rap artists and their defenders have understood that many of the attacks on rap have been aimed at obscuring these realities. Rap artist Michael Franti, formerly a member of Disposable Heroes of Hiphoprisy and later the leader of Spearhead, argued,

"Rap didn't start the phenomena of people killing each other or mistreating women in our community. Education and welfare cuts and a buildup of jails has more to do with it. . . . Nobody got mad when Eric Clapton sang 'I Shot the Sheriff.' You've got *The Terminator,* a whole movie about blowing cops to bits, and there's Arnold Schwarzenegger posing with George Bush. It's hypocrisy."[61]

Representative Maxine Waters, a Democrat from California, spoke bluntly about the attack on rap.

"Let's not kid ourselves. There are those who have a political agenda in seeking to distract people from other issues. Sometimes our friends, the conservatives, are having a field day. They have always believed blacks cause most of the crime in America. After all, they say, look at the inordinately high number of blacks in prisons and on death row. Now their evil propaganda stands virtually unopposed in today's public debate over rap music."[62]

In a similar vein, David Harleston, a music industry executive associated with a popular hip-hop label, Def Jam Recordings, claimed,

"It is increasingly apparent that certain opponents of hip-hop music are of the misguided view that if we do not hear about the issues raised and addressed in the music, then those issues will not exist. In fact, one could argue that efforts to suppress hip-hop artists are efforts to ignore unpleasant realities that exist in America's back yard. Such a view simply denies reality. Silencing the messenger will not extinguish the problem."[63]

Tricia Rose, author of *Black Noise,* the best book on hip-hop, described the 1994 hearings chaired by Senator Mosley Braun and Representative Collins as

"a form of empty moral grandstanding, a shameful attempt by politicians to earn political favors and ride the wave of public frenzy about crime while at the same time remaining unable and often unwilling to tackle the real problems that plague America's cities and their poorest black children."[64]

Members of the civil rights generation are not wrong to detect resentment of them within gangsta rap, but their interpretation of the causes of the chasm between them and inner-city youths is

misdirected. In a brilliant chapter on gangsta rap in his indispensable book *Race Rebels,* Robin D.G. Kelley argues that the use of the word *Nigga* by gangsta rappers, a word choice deeply offensive to many in the civil rights generation, is an attempt to speak to "a collective identity shaped by class consciousness, the character of inner-city space, police repression, poverty, and the constant threat of intraracial violence."[65] In short, this word choice is a form of what Kelley calls "ghettocentricity," a moral choice to identify with the poorest and most aggrieved part of the collective community while rejecting individual solutions predicated on a personal upward mobility premised on forgetting the suffering one leaves behind for others to face. Most important, it represents an unwillingness to disidentify with the poorest, most despised, and most aggrieved members of the black community.

As Michael Eric Dyson explains,

"Gangsta rap is largely an indictment of mainstream and bourgeois black institutions by young people who do not find conventional methods of addressing personal and social calamity useful. The leaders of those institutions often castigate the excessive and romanticized violence of this music without trying to understand what precipitated its rise in the first place. In so doing, they drive a greater wedge between themselves and the youth they so desperately want to help."[66]

These intergenerational tensions are not new; they are part of the price Black people have always paid for white supremacy in America. White parents may imagine that they command the loyalty of their children purely through moral suasion, but like other forms of whiteness, white parental authority is heavily subsidized by the state. Peggy Pascoe points out that antimiscegenation laws were aimed not so much at banning interracial relationships or even interracial sex as at preventing the passing of property across racial lines. Black parents, conversely, find their authority routinely undermined by public and private policies designed to impede the accumulation of assets and intergenerational transfers of wealth within Black families. A character in James Baldwin's 1968 novel, *Tell Me How Long This Train's Been Gone,* articulates the implications of these policies for many Black youths in an eloquent soliloquy:

"I was very nearly lost because my elders, through no fault of their own, had betrayed me. Perhaps I loved my father, but I did not want to live his life. I did not want to become like him, he was the living example of defeat. He could not correct me. None of my elders could correct me because I was appalled by their lives. I was old enough to understand how their lives had happened, but rage and pity are not love, and the determination to outwit one's situation means that one has no models, only object lessons."[67]

In their desire to be seen, to wield the symbolic and material currency of American society, some rappers *do* rely on misogyny, abusive language, and eroticized brutality. How could it be otherwise, given the values, social relations, and reward structures of our society? But in a subculture that has made an art form out of talking back, the best rebukes of these rappers have come from within, from women rappers like Queen Latifah, M.C. Lyte, and Lauryn Hill, from politicized male rappers like Public Enemy and KRS-1. In addition, artists and intellectuals have utilized other media to provide important metacommentaries on hip-hop that evade the facile condemnations that dominated the hip-hop hearings. For example, rap artist Sister Souljah's book *No Disrespect* combines a moving memoir and a searing indictment of sexism, while Michael Eric Dyson's *Between God and Gangsta Rap* eloquently explores the ambivalence toward the genre felt by a man who is a father of a teenage son, an ordained Baptist minister, a university professor, and a knowledgeable and discerning fan of hip-hop.[68]

Government censorship and regulation or private mobilizations and moral panics cannot cure the ills that they misidentify and misattribute to rap music. But nurturing the social memory and social theory found in some rap music might lead us to a more mature and more responsible understanding of our problems and their solutions. Representative Maxine Waters, of California, whose district encompasses

many of the neighborhoods from which gangsta rap emerged, offered an example of precisely that kind of analysis in her testimony before the hip-hop hearings. Pointing out that hip-hop emerged from the bottom up, from children who created an art form in their garages and basements, Waters praised the success of rap artists in communicating their experiences to a wider world. "For decades, you and I and so many others have talked about the lives and the hopes of our people," she told the committee,

"pain and the hopelessness, the deprivation and abuse. Rap music is communicating that message like we never have. It is, indeed, as was described, the CNN of the community causing people from every sector, including black leadership, to listen and pay heed."[69]

Conceding that gangsta rap often contains lyrics that offend her, Waters related that she had grown up in a black community in St. Louis, where she heard obscene words many times before she ever heard them used by gangsta rappers, that she remembered them uttered by the most highly esteemed adults in church on Sunday morning. "I don't say to people, you should use them. I don't encourage them, but we had better stop pretending like we are hearing them for the first time."[70] Most important, Waters detailed her efforts to work with, rather than against, young rap artists, bringing them to Washington to meet with the Black Congressional Caucus and the Black Women's Forum and sponsoring a program, L.A. 17 to 30, designed to attract ghetto youths into vocational training as well as high school and community college courses and to place them in gainful employment.

The silencing of social memory and the suppression of grass roots social theory within hip-hop are not a matter of concern for African Americans exclusively. They are a process that harms our whole society. For in erasing history from public debate, we unduly constrain our understanding of the present. The demonization of black people in general and of inner-city youth in particular often proceeds through an argument that claims that poverty does not cause crime, that Depression-era Americans endured hardships nobly, and that the problems facing aggrieved racial minorities today stem solely from the internal moral and cultural failings of those groups. But in the 1930s, when white people were among the poorest parts of the population, many of today's dynamics prevailed. The humiliating subordinations and indignities of poverty ripped families apart then as they do now. Despair and rage over inequality provoked criminal behavior then as they do now, and they gave rise to popular preferences for sadistic and vengeful representations of social life then, the same as now. C. L. R. James shows in *American Civilization* that during the 1930s the gangster film, violent comic strips like Dick Tracy, and detective stories and motion pictures gave voice to popular desires for representation of what the Depression had done to them, for expression of the anger they felt—and feared. Writing about the plays of Clifford Odets during that decade, Robert Warshow later zeroed in on the intergenerational tensions between parents disappointed in their children and children who thought that their parents evaded the central fact of American life: "without a dollar you don't look the world in the eye." Warshow sees the young people in Odets's plays and the entire generation they depicted as internalizing cynicism but nonetheless engaging in the strongest subversion: "taking capitalism without sugar."[71] Young rap artists and their listeners tried taking capitalism without the sugar in the late 1980s and early 1990s. More than anything, they sought an art that refused to lie, that refused to run from the hard facts and harsh realities of their time.

William Drayton, who played Flavor Flav, the mischievous trickster in the rap group Public Enemy, used to wear a facsimile of a stopped alarm clock on his jacket, telling audiences, "We know what time it is." Part of the purpose of gangsta rap and all hip-hop has been to tell people what time it is. When Japanese troops occupied Singapore during World War II, they translated the names of all the streets into Japanese, imposed the Japanese calendar and year on the locals, and even mandated that standard time in Tokyo would prevail in the Singapore time zone. The Japanese military and colonial administrators understood the importance of imposing their own sense of what time it was on their victims and of

eliminating potentially alternative memories and histories. The attack on hip-hop in the 1990s sought to solidify the power of dominant groups by suppressing social memory in similar fashion.

The collective memory at the heart of hip-hop contains a material memory of the racial and generational dimensions of deindustrialization that would otherwise have remained hidden from history. It is not surprising that this kind of cultural expression attracts the wrath of powerful critics, but it is tragic that so many of them have been gullible enough to believe that battles over music censorship actually concern conflicts over music and morality rather than over power, privilege, and persecution. More than a decade after the hip-hop hearings, rap music remains a source of enormous profits for the music industry. The censorship campaigns of the 1980s and 1990s embodied in the hip-hop hearings did nothing to diminish the amount of misogyny and obscenity in the music's lyrics. These efforts did succeed, however, in frightening recording companies and radio stations away from politicized rap, away from songs with lyrics that critique dominant institutions in US society. With the notable exceptions of Lauryn Hill, Dead Prez, Mos Def, Talib Kweli, and a few others, most rap lyricists today place sexual pleasure and consumer purchases at the center of the social world. Censorship made sexism, misogyny, and materialism *more* prevalent in hip-hop rather than less. Only politicized answers to public problems have disappeared.

The sexism, misogyny, and materialism that govern hip-hop today help fuel corporate synergy and high profits for investors. Sean Combs, the performer known sequentially as Puff Daddy, P. Diddy, and then Diddy, has made singularly unimpressive contributions to hip-hop, but his celebrity status has enabled him to become chief executive officer and chairman of the board of directors of the Sean John clothing company. His firm outsources production to low-wage workers in impoverished parts of the world, such as Choloma, Honduras, where women and children who make Sean John sweatshirts that retail for more than fifty dollars receive less than twenty-five cents per shirt. The National Labor Committee, an antisweatshop activist group, reported that the managers of Southeast Textiles in Choloma refused to make contributions to an employee health plan, fired workers if they became pregnant, denied them water and bathroom breaks, and dismissed them if they complained. They also discovered that the 20 percent of the workshop not devoted to making clothes for Sean John produced clothing for Rocawear, a firm founded by hip-hop artist Jay-Z and producer Damon Dash.[72]

When former Run-DMC member Russell Simmons sold his Phat Fashions clothing line to the Kellwood Corporation in 2004 for $140 million, he proudly lauded hip-hop as "the best and most important brand-building force in America."[73] Unlike many contemporary entrepreneurs, Simmons has used his resources to promote many of the interests of the consumers who buy his products. He has sponsored voter registration drives, worked with hip-hop artist Wyclef Jean to organize rallies against budget cuts in education, and lobbied the state legislature against the harsh and repressive "Rockefeller Drug Laws" in New York State.[74] Yet Phat Farm subcontracts work to shops charged with violations of fair labor practices by the Garment Workers Center in Los Angeles and refuses to deal with SweatX, a unionized clothing company that pays fair wages and provides decent working conditions.[75]

Does Simmons's success show how powerful hip-hop is? Does it demonstrate that inner-city youths have built a multibillion dollar industry that helps shape important areas of American life? Does it offer hope that entrepreneurs dependent on the prestige from below, emanating from the style of inner-city youths, may actually help those youths as well? Or does it prove how weak hip-hop is? Does it show that it has been easily and fully co-opted into just another novel style, just another marketing opportunity? Does Russell Simmons's activism demonstrate how open the US political system is or how closed it has become? Does his political work express the unvoiced and unmet demands for justice of an ignored generation, or does it merely add marketing cachet to his product line and prove that no voices are heard in this society unless they represent the interests of capital?

The exploitation of workers in sweatshops does real harm to real people. It provides unfair gains and

unjust enrichments for investors and is dependent on the perpetuation of inequality, intimidation, and injustice. Yet the guardians of morality who found themselves sufficiently motivated to conduct congressional hearings and issue widespread condemnations of the words spoken on rap recordings in the early 1990s have not yet managed to utter a word of protest against hip hop's ties to sweatshop labor. They are interested in Russell Simmons's business and his celebrity status but have done next to nothing to provide the young people whose tastes have made Russell Simmons rich with jobs that pay decently, much less with meaningful participation in the key decisions that affect their lives.

Today's hip-hop artists and entrepreneurs can be as materialistic "as they wanna be" and even "as nasty as they wanna be" as long as it's all about a salary and not about reality. By the middle of the first decade of the twenty-first century, it has become clear that hip-hop plays a very different role in society from the one it played in the late 1980s. Despite all the good efforts by committed artists and activists at the local level, hip-hop is much more significant as a marketing category than as a cultural or political force. As twenty-five-year-old Allan Mashia argued at the National Urban League Influence Summit plenary session on hip-hop and social conscience in 2005, "What hip-hop is now is not what it was . . . hip-hop made you proud to be Black and inspired you to be positive and make something of yourself."[76] Of course, P. Diddy and Russell Simmons *have* made something of themselves but, like Macon Dead Jr. in *Song of Solomon,* only by exploiting others. The theft of inheritance perpetrated on Black people by discrimination and the dynamics of a system that allows inclusion only to those willing to police the boundaries of exclusion zealously against others stand behind the intergenerational bickering manifest during the hip-hop hearings—and behind many other kinds of folly as well.

Yet we need to remember that Railroad Tommy's pessimistic prediction is not the dominant message of *Song of Solomon.* At the end of the novel, Milkman Dead learns how to do the impossible, how to ride the air by surrendering to it. Like his grandfather who built a farm in the face of vigilante violence in the era of Reconstruction and like the hip-hop artists, activists, and intellectuals who have made an art form and a political praxis out of talking back, he learns that conscious action in the world makes all the difference, that for all our disappointments, resentments, and regrets, there is still important work to be done. The legendary hip-hop act Erik B. and Rakim claim, "It's not where you're from, it where you're at," as a way of inviting people from different backgrounds, neighborhoods, races, and countries to unite, to prove their worth through their artistry, initiative, and imagination. Toni Morrison's narrator in *Song of Solomon* makes the same appeal in a different way, describing how the work of Macon Dead Sr. led by example. In words that apply to the best works of hip-hop and the best activism of social movements, she writes:

> "You see?" the farm said to them. "See? See what you can do? Never mind you can't tell one letter from another, never mind you born a slave, never mind you lose your name, never mind your daddy dead, never mind nothing. Here, this here, is what a man can do if he puts his mind to it and his back in it. Stop sniveling," it said. "Stop picking around the edges of the world. Take advantage, and if you can't take advantage, take disadvantage. We live here. On this planet, in this nation, in this country right here. Nowhere else! We got a home in this rock, don't you see! Nobody starving in my home; nobody crying in my home, and I got a home, you got one too! Grab it. Grab this land! Take it, hold it, my brothers, make it, my brothers, shake it, squeeze it, turn it, twist it, beat it, kick it, kiss it, whip it, stomp it, dig it, plow it, seed it, reap it, rent it, buy it, sell it, own it, build it, multiply it, and pass it on—can you hear me? Pass it on!"[77]

Notes

1. Toni Morrison, *Song of Solomon* (New York: Alfred A. Knopf, 1977), 59–60.

2. Ibid., 237–38.

3. Subcommittee on Commerce, Consumer Protection, and Competitiveness of the Committee on Energy and Commerce, *Music Lyrics and Interstate Commerce*, H.R. hearing 112, 103rd Cong., 2nd sess., February 11, 1994, 5.

4. Ibid., 6.

5. Ibid., 5.

6. Subcommittee on Commerce, Consumer Protection, and Competitiveness of the Committee on Energy and Commerce, *Music Lyrics and Interstate Commerce*, February 11, 1994, 24.

7. Ibid., 31.

8. Reginold Bundy, "The Great Divide," *Pittsburgh Courier,* January 13, 1996, A1, A3.

9. On the alleged mental deficiencies of minorities, see Charles Murray and Richard Herrnstein, *The Bell Curve: Intelligence, Class Structure and American Life* (New York: Free Press, 1994). On their cultural deficiencies, see Dinesh D'Souza, *The End of Racism* (New York: Free Press, 1996).

10. Holly Sklar, *Chaos or Community: Seeking Solutions Not Scapegoats* (Boston: South End Press, 1995), 69.

11. Noel J. Kent, "A Stacked Deck," *Explorations in Ethnic Studies* 14, no. 1 (January 1991): 12,13; Richard Rothstein, "Musical Chairs as Economic Policy," in Don Hazen, ed., *Inside the L.A. Riots* (New York: Institute for Alternative Journalism, 1992), 143.

12. William Chafe, *The Unfinished Journey* (New York: Oxford University Press, 1986), 442; Kent, "A Stacked Deck," 11.

13. Richard Child Hill and Cynthia Negry, "Deindustrialization and Racial Minorities in the Great Lakes Region, USA," in D. Stanley Eitzen and Maxine Baca Zinn, eds., *The Reshaping of America: Social Consequences of the Changing Economy* (Englewood Cliffs, N.J.: Prentice-Hall, 1989), 168–78.

14. Melvin L. Oliver and Thomas M. Shapiro, *Black Wealth/White Wealth: A New Perspective on Racial Inequality* (New York: Routledge, 1995), 158.

15. For a detailed account of the extent and significance of censorship efforts aimed at the gangster film, see the brilliant dissertation by L. Jonathan Munby, "Screening Crime in the USA, 1929–1958: From Hays Code to HUAC: From Little Caesar to Touch of Evil," Ph.D. dissertation, University of Minnesota, 1995, especially 46–52.

16. In *Inventing the Public Enemy: The Gangster in American Culture, 1918–1934* (Chicago: University of Chicago Press, 1996), David E. Ruth presents an important discussion of gangster films that delineates the centrality of misogyny, material acquisitions, and style to that genre. This discussion holds some important parallels to the internal properties of the "gangster" image and ideal that emerges within gangsta rap as well.

17. See, for example, Nayan Shah, *Contagious Divides: Epidemics and Race in San Francisco's Chinatown* (Berkeley: University of California Press, 2001); Roderick Ferguson, *Aberrations in Black: Toward a Queer of Color Critique* (Minneapolis: University of Minnesota Press, 2004).

18. Brian Neve, *Film and Politics in America: A Social Tradition* (London: Routledge, 1992), 12.

19. Leola Johnson, "Silencing Gangsta Rap: Class and Race Agendas in the Campaign against Hardcore Rap Lyrics," *Temple Political and Civil Rights Law Review* 3, no. 19 (Fall 1993–Spring 1994): 25.

20. After leaving the bureau Milt Ahlerich became director of security for the National Football League, charged with the responsibility of keeping players from associating with criminals, illegal drugs, and steroids and engaging in sexual assaults and fights. The record, in this case, speaks for itself. The record of criminal activity by NFL players on his watch indicates that the zeal Ahlerich displayed in trying to suppress *imaginary* violence in gangsta rap did not carry over to effective policing of *actual* violence and other violations of the law by the athletes paid large sums of money by Ahlerich's millionaire employer-owners in the NFL.

21. Quoted in Houston A. Baker, "Handling 'Crisis': Great Books, Rap Music, and the End of Western Homogeneity" (Reflections on the Humanities in America), *Callaloo* 13 (1990): 177.

22. Dave Marsh, *Louie Louie: The History and Mythology of the World's Most Famous Rock 'n' Roll Song* (Ann Arbor: University of Michigan Press, 2004). See also Todd Snider's album *East Nashville Skyline*, Oh Boy Records OBR031, 2004.

23. Jon Wiener, *Gimme Some Truth: The John Lennon FBI Files* (Berkeley: University of California Press, 1999), 114.

24. Tricia Rose, *Black Noise: Rap Music and Black Culture in Contemporary America* (Hanover, N.H.: University Press of New England/Wesleyan University Press, 1994), 128.

25. Johnson, "Silencing Gangsta Rap," 29–30.

26. Dave March and Phyllis Pollack, "Wanted for Attitude," *Village Voice*, October 10, 1989, 33–37, quoted in Rose, *Black Noise*, 129.

27. Chuck Phillips, "The 'Batman' Who Took On Rap," *Los Angeles Times*, June 18, 1990, F1.

28. Chuck Phillips, "The Anatomy of a Crusade," *Los Angeles Times*, June 18, 1990, F4.

29. Associated Press, "Rap Group Members Arrested over 'Nasty' Lyrics," *St. Paul Pioneer Press*, June 11, 1990, 2.

30. Amy Binder, "Constructing Racial Rhetoric: Media Depictions of Harm in Heavy Metal and Rap Music," *American Sociological Review* 58 (December 1993): 753; Phillips, "The Anatomy of a Crusade," F4.

31. Chuck Phillips, "Boss Apparently OKs Crew's Use of 'U.S.A.,'" *Los Angeles Times*, June 26, 1990, F10.

32. Robin D.G. Kelley, *Race Rebels* (New York: Free Press, 1994), 190; Rose, *Black Noise*, 183.

33. Johnson, "Silencing Gangsta Rap," 31; Rose, *Black Noise*, 183.

34. Quoted in Johnson, "Silencing Gangsta Rap," 33.

35. Dave Marsh, "The Censorship Zone," *Rock & Rap Confidential* 100, August 1992, 5.

36. Ibid., 7.

37. Johnson, "Silencing Gangsta Rap," 33.

38. Rose, *Black Noise*, 184.

39. Eric Taylor, "Gangsta Rap Is Deferring the Dream," *Los Angeles Times*, March 7, 1994, F3.

40. Johnson, "Silencing Gangsta Rap," 34.

41. Ibid.

42. Subcommittee on Commerce, Consumer Protection, and Competitiveness, Committee on Energy and Commerce, *Music Lyrics and Interstate Commerce*, February 11, 1994, 4.

43. Ibid., 5–6.

44. Subcommittee on Commerce, Consumer Protection, and Competitiveness, Committee on Energy and Commerce, *Music Lyrics and Interstate Commerce*, H.R. hearing 112, 103rd Cong., 2nd sess., May 5, 1994, 75.

45. Marlene Cimons, "Outrage over Lyrics Unites Unlikely Pair," *Los Angeles Times*, July 5, 1995, A1.

46. Dave Marsh, "Cops 'n' Gangstas," *Nation*, June 26, 1995, 908.

47. Jesse Jackson, "A Call to Bold Action," in Hazen, ed., *Inside the L.A. Riots*, 149.

48. Marsh, "The Censorship Zone," 7.

49. Steve Eddy, "Warwick Blames Pot on Someone Else," *Orange County Register*, February 27, 2003, Show section, 2.

50. Joshua Green, "The Bookie of Virtue," *Washington Monthly*, June 2003.

51. Mark Landler, "Label Tied to Time Warner Sues a Critic of Rap Lyrics," *New York Times*, August 16, 1995, C5; Jeffrey Trachtenberg, "Interscope Records Sues Activist Critic, Alleging Distribution Pact Interference," *Wall Street Journal*, August 16, 1995, B8; Chuck Phillips, "Interscope Files Lawsuit against Rap Music Critic," *Los Angeles Times*, August 16, 1995, D1; Dave Marsh, "We Told You So," *Rock & Rap Confidential* 127, September 1995, 7.

52. Kelley, *Race Rebels*, 190.

53. Dave Marsh, "Doug and the Slugs," *Rock & Rap Confidential* 125, July 1995, 4.

54. Edna Gunderson, "Rap against Time Warner," *USA Today,* October 2, 1995, 4D.

55. Dave Marsh, "Cracked Rear View," *Rock & Rap Confidential* 125, July 1995, 2.

56. Subcommittee on Commerce, Consumer Protection, and Competitiveness of the Committee on Energy and Commerce, *Music Lyrics and Interstate Commerce,* February 11, 1994, 21.

57. Kelley, *Race Rebels,* 192.

58. Maxine Waters, "Testimony before the Senate Banking Committee," in Hazen, ed., *Inside the L.A. Riots,* 26.

59. Bernard D. Headley, "'Black on Black' Crime: The Myth and the Reality," *Crime and Social Justice* 20 (Fall–Winter 1983): 53.

60. Judith R. Blau and Peter M. Blau, "The Cost of Inequality: Metropolitan Structure and Violent Crime," *American Sociological Review* 47 (February 1982): 114, 126.

61. Gunderson, "Rap against Time Warner," 4D.

62. Subcommittee on Commerce, Consumer Protection, and Competitiveness of the Committee on Energy and Commerce, House of Representatives, February 11, 1994, 65.

63. Ibid., 38–39.

64. Tricia Rose, "Rap Music and the Demonization of Young Black Males," *USA Today Magazine,* May 1994, 35–36.

65. Kelley, *Race Rebels,* 210.

66. Michael Eric Dyson, *Between God and Gangsta Rap: Bearing Witness to Black Culture* (New York: Oxford University Press, 1996), 185.

67. James Baldwin, *Tell Me How Long This Train's Been Gone* (New York: Vintage, 1968), 204.

68. Sister Souljah, *No Disrespect* (New York: Times Books/Random House, 1994).

69. Subcommittee on Commerce, Consumer Protection, and Competitiveness of the Committee on Energy and Commerce, House of Representatives, May 5, 1994, 65–66.

70. Ibid., 65.

71. Robert Warshow, *The Immediate Experience* (New York: Atheneum, 1971), 64.

72. Lee Ballinger, "Sean 'P. Diddy' Combs and the Sweatshops: Making a Dollar out of 15 Cents," *Counterpunch,* October 31, 2003, 1; Earl Ofari Hutchinson, "P. Diddy and Hip Hop's Tattered Garments," *Hutchinson Report,* October 31, 2003, 1.

73. Susan Keith, "The Deal: Kellwood Buys Phat Fashions," *St. Louis Business Journal,* December 10, 2004, 1.

74. Tracie Rozhon, "Can Urban Fashion Be Def in Des Moines," *New York Times,* August 24, 2003, Business section, 9.

75. Ballinger, "Sean P. Diddy Combs and the Sweatshops," 1.

76. Amecia Taylor, "Mixing Hip-Hop and Social Conscientiousness," *Louisiana Weekly,* August 15–21, 2005, B5.

77. Morrison, *Song of Solomon,* 237–38.

24.
CRIMINALIZING BLACK CULTURE
Carol Stabile

In late October 1989, a middle-class white man named Charles Stuart dialed 911 from his car, which was parked in the predominantly African American neighborhood of Mission Hill in Boston, Massachusetts. His pregnant wife Carol had been shot in the head, he told dispatchers, by a black man who had carjacked them, and he had been shot in the stomach. News crews rushed to the scene where Carol Stuart lay dying, with her wounded husband bleeding next to her in the car. From the beginning, this was a story made for television.

Boston police immediately initiated an aggressive search of Mission Hill, suspending civil liberties and treating any black man in a jogging suit as a potential suspect. By 15 November, the police had come up with a suspect, William Bennett, who was then duly identified by Charles Stuart as the man who had carjacked the couple and fatally wounded his wife.[1] In a city that had become known for its racism after its violent response to attempts to desegregate Boston South High School in 1974–75, Charles Stuart's account of his wife's murder proved all too believable. Despite the fact that most women are murdered by intimates, that a white man would kill his pregnant wife was unthinkable. The racialized narrative Stuart offered police—one of black male violence against a white female victim—was a plausible one in the minds of whites. Although Boston police officials later claimed that Stuart had been a suspect all along, his story did not begin to fall apart until his brother Matthew identified him as the killer in late December.

Had the media been more critical of Stuart's story, and less predisposed to treat the words of a white victim as gospel, they might have reported that the Stuarts' marriage had been less than idyllic. Stuart had pressured his wife to get an abortion, he had taken out three life-insurance policies worth hundreds of thousands of dollars, and he had made repeated comments to family members about killing her.[2] Yet despite inconsistencies in his story—inconsistencies initially explained by reference to Stuart's own traumatic experience as a victim—it took the word of another white man to convince police and journalists that William Bennett was not the murderer.

When Stuart committed suicide in January 1990, there was no public discourse about a pathological culture of greed and consumption that might have motivated his crime. Whites as a racial group were not blamed in any way for the murder, his mother was not blamed for his behavior, and there was no scrutiny of his family and cultural background, the assumption being that family members had suffered enough. In place of identifying various pathologies that may have caused this crime, Stuart's murder of his pregnant wife was understood to be a shocking yet aberrant act, one that could not have been either anticipated or prevented and thus no cause for a moral panic or crusade.

The contrast between representations of this crime and any number of less heinous crimes committed by blacks could not be greater. Most obviously, a black suspect would never have elicited the sympathetic credulity extended to Stuart; nor would an alibi blaming a white man for the murder of a black woman have been at all believable to whites. Indeed, it is doubtful that the murder of a pregnant black woman would have attracted much media attention, particularly if the crime had occurred in an African American neighborhood. In the unlikely event that it had, certainly the media would have been more aggressive in investigating a husband's testimony, particularly when so much of it was inconsistent. Had Stuart been black, the crime would have been immediately inserted into a framework that held blacks as a group accountable for such violence, and black culture—particularly the behavior of black women—the explanation for any criminal acts perpetrated by African Americans.

The Stuart case was only one of a number of high-profile news stories featuring what Katheryn Russell (1998) calls "racial hoaxes" that proliferated in the late 1980s and 1990s.[3] A mere quarter of a century after the heyday of the Civil Rights Movement, racialized narratives shockingly similar to the lynch narratives of the late nineteenth century reasserted themselves with force and vigor and constructions of black villains and white victims quickly fell back into older, overtly racist narrative grooves. This chapter explicates the processes whereby such reversions were effected by tracking the gendered and raced narratives about crime created by institutions and individuals in the post-civil rights era. Focusing on high-profile crime news themes and cases, increasingly the only occasions in which media attention was directed to issues of race and racial disparities, the explanation for this shift begins with the scapegoating of black women and black culture that began to take shape in the 1960s and then turns to the myriad ways in which stories about criminals and victims worked to confirm the belief that if blacks were victims at all, then they were victims of their own culture. Black culture, and not white culture, was the cause of all the problems that civil rights activists had ascribed to white supremacy.

The Cult of True Womanhood, Sixties-Style

By the end of the 1960s, the historical threat that black men were said to pose to white womanhood had been mostly subsumed beneath narratives featuring violent, angry, and armed black men. Nevertheless, the link between black men and crime had expanded from an openly racist one based on fears of miscegenation (and a specific threat to white women) to a now generalized threat to society as a whole. Southern politicians continued to make reference to threats against white women, but this connection was not as easily or openly invoked in northern narratives about crime. In the north, the threat now invoked a discourse of fearful white people menaced by generalized black threats to their families and their property. But the older link between gender and race in crime narratives roiled just below the surface of these wider crime narratives, where it was to be all too easily invoked when the occasion warranted, particularly in high-profile family violence cases involving whites, like Charles Stuart's murder of his wife Carol.

Crime narratives of the post-civil rights era invoked an all too familiar cast of racist stereotypes, constructing scenarios that justified white fear and hatred, and creating a threat that was, like the early nineteenth-century threats used to provoke anti-black violence, mythic in its dimensions. Mass-mediated representations of black and white criminals and black and white victims gave new life to forms of institutionalized racism and reinvigorated an array of racist narrative practices that had lain dormant for a decade. Where the discourse of miscegenation, and its reliance on threatening black masculinity, dominated ideologies of race, gender, and crime in the decades that followed the Civil War, after the 1960s the focus lay not only on interracial unions and their threat to moral values, but increasingly on intraracial relations as well, on the ostensibly pathological nature of black culture, and the threat these posed to the moral or family values that were seen solely as the province of whiteness.

But there was one significant change. Across the nineteenth and twentieth centuries, women as a group were not subjected to the kind of systematic criminalization visited upon black men, mainly because ideologies of femininity and domesticity understood women as being inherently weaker than men, needy of protection, and hardly the powerful villains that protection scenarios required. For women to be constituted as a threat would have been to suggest that the forces of white androcentrism were neither as fully masculine nor as powerful as they understood themselves to be. As we have seen, the deeply seated misogyny that has been a thread in US threat constructions expressed itself in ways other than the criminalization of women (prostitutes being the somewhat unique exception): through protection scenarios that denied white women agency and black women presence, through the over-sexualized representations of black women, and through the distrust, suspicion, and occasionally open hatred with which women in general have been regarded. This is not to say, of course, that deviance in women was not punished, but rather that women— black or white—were not construed as the agents of moral panics in the same way that black men were. Women of all colors may have been despised and considered frail and unreliable, but until the 1960s they were not constructed as rationales for fear.

This narrative terrain was irrevocably changed by the events of the 1960s. Although today we tend to understand women's political organization in terms of the feminist movement that emerged after the Civil Rights Movement and the student anti-war movement, black women activists played a principal, if less historically acknowledged, role in the Civil Rights Movement. Activists like Ella Baker, Diane Nash, Rosa Parks, Ruby Doris Smith Robinson, and many others offered powerful examples of strong female leadership and political participation both before and after Betty Friedan called attention to the plight of white middle-class women.[4] Their participation, moreover, cut across the lines of class in ways that seldom occurred among white women. The pathologization and subsequent criminalization of black women, the first such widespread criminalization of women in US history, needs to be understood as the second arm of the racist reaction to the Civil Rights Movement and thus as a response to the political mobilization of which black women were a central part.

The criminalization of black women began in the 1960s, with a focus on black mothers receiving government assistance. Although US welfare policies have long found ways to exclude black people, women in particular, from receiving benefits, until the

1960s the discourse that justified these exclusions did not overtly suggest that black women should not receive benefits because of their criminal potential to exploit the system.[5] According to historian Rickie Solinger, as late as the 1950s,

a poor, resourceless mother, even an African-American one, particularly one with an illegitimate child, would generally have occupied a low, marginal status in the United States. Her status as a mother may have marked her as a slattern or a slut, but probably would have protected her from classification as an aggressor, a villain, an enemy of the people.

(2001: 142)

Solinger further points out that discourses that pathologized African American women for being "unnaturally strong and powerful in relation to their men" (2001: 155) were also a part of this earlier rhetorical terrain, but these were not yet part of a wider, national discourse about crime and the black family.

The nationalization of the discourse that identified the black family as the cause of crime, and black mothers as matriarchs of the crime wave, began to gather steam with the 1964 composition of what was purported to be a secret "internal memorandum" (Gresham 1989: 117). *The Negro Family: The Case for National Action* (hereafter referred to as the Moynihan Report) diagnosed "the deterioration of the fabric of negro society," which it saw as being caused by "the deterioration of the negro family" (1965). A key overseer of the transition from the war on poverty to the war on crime, Daniel Patrick Moynihan had served as an undersecretary of labor for the Kennedy and Johnson administrations, where he played an important role in formulating policy for the social programs that came to be known as the war on poverty. He left the Johnson administration in 1965 and later joined Richard Nixon's White House Staff as urban affairs advisor in 1968.

The Moynihan Report he authored in 1965 bears the imprimatur of this transition. Couched in liberal language about race, each section of the report begins by acknowledging the structural obstacles that racism placed in the path of black Americans, only to immediately undercut the power of the structural with an emphasis on the familial and the individual. The fourth chapter of the report, for example, begins by expressing admiration for the resilience of African Americans:

> That the Negro American has survived at all is extraordinary—a lesser people might simply have died out, as indeed others have. That the Negro community has not only survived, but in this political generation has entered national affairs as a moderate, humane, and constructive national force is the highest testament to the healing powers of the democratic ideal and the creative vitality of the Negro people.
>
> (1965)

Moynihan immediately added, "it may not be supposed that the Negro American community has not paid a fearful price for the incredible mistreatment to which it has been subjected over the past three centuries." In the report, this price lies in the "fundamental fact of Negro American family life," which is "the often reversed roles of husband and wife."

Like the psychoanalytic theory from which the Moynihan Report heavily borrowed, the family that it discussed was abstracted from its wider social and cultural milieu. The report criticized the mass media for creating "an image of the American family as a highly standardized phenomenon," but then immediately reified that image by suggesting that departures from this standardized norm were mainly negative. Arguing throughout that "a number of immigrant groups were characterized by unusually strong family bonds; these groups have characteristically progressed more rapidly than others," the report implied that African American families lacked such "strong family bonds," and that the entirety of the problems facing African Americans in the post-war period could be attributed to a subsequent family disorganization, in which "a large proportion of negro children and youth have not undergone the socialization which only the family can provide." Using a rhetoric that has since become second nature to conservative politicians, pundits, and reporters, the report continued, "disorganized families . . . have not provided

the discipline and habits which are necessary for personality development." The report characterized black families as highly dysfunctional social units: disorganized, lacking in discipline and socialization, retarded in terms of personality development; and black culture, governed as it was by women and not men, as a pathological one, since culture was rightly the province of masculinity.[6]

The Moynihan Report saw family disorganization as the primary cause of unemployment and the rationale for the naturalized link between blacks and crime.

> It is probable that at present, a majority of the crimes against the person, such as rape, murder, and aggravated assault are committed by negroes. There is, of course, no absolute evidence; inference can only be made from arrest and prison population statistics. The data that follow unquestionably are biased against negroes, who are arraigned much more casually than are whites, but it may be doubted that the bias is great enough to affect the general proportions.

Again, this passage exemplifies the shifting terrain of discourses about race in the 1960s. Acknowledging problems associated with bias (particularly the fact that blacks have been historically policed, not to mention arrested, convicted, imprisoned, and executed, with much greater frequency than whites), the report then dismissed these biases, suggesting that they could not possibly be as great as they appeared.

Although the Moynihan Report drew on E. Franklin Frazier's 1939 *The Negro Family in the United States* and Gunnar Myrdal's classic *An American Dilemma: The Negro Problem and Modern Democracy* (1944), where these earlier discussions of black families understood their "pathology" to result from racism, the Moynihan Report adroitly transferred responsibility for the disadvantages blacks faced in US society from a collective responsibility to an individual, or personal responsibility.[7] "Family disorganization" was responsible for "a large amount of juvenile delinquency and adult crime among negroes" and this disorganization was understood to be a direct result of "the failure of the father to play the role in family life required by American society." But it did not stop there. The failure of black fathers was not understood to be an effect of racist violence or the structural disadvantages confronted by black men. Rather, it was the effect of a "matriarchal negro society," in which "mothers made sure that if one of their children had a chance for higher education the daughter was the one to pursue it" and in which historical factors had predicated against "the emergence of a strong father figure," thereby denying "the very essence of the male animal" which "from the bantam rooster to the four-star general, is to strut." That "negro families in the cities are more frequently headed by a woman than those in the country" was the root cause of the problem, according to the report, since women-headed households emasculated men by denying them the opportunity to fulfill their role as breadwinners.[8]

The Moynihan Report turned the very strength and resilience of black women in the face of awful adversity into the source of racial problems, and poverty into the effect not of discrimination, but of pathological family structure. As an institution, marriage had not granted to black women any of the ideological or economic privileges reserved for whites. Historically excluded from the cult of true womanhood which relegated proper women to the domestic sphere, African American women were once again pathologized for not measuring up to a white supremacist standard that excluded them. That "fifty-six percent of Negro women, age 25 to 64, are in the work force, against 42 percent of white women" was seen not as an effect of economic forces that since slavery had forced black women of all ages into full-time labor, that had forced them to work parallel shifts as laborers in the public and private spheres, but as evidence of their pathological strength and their symbolic castration of their husbands and sons. Ironically, sympathy was for the first time extended to black men, who had been victimized not by lynch mobs, the Ku Klux Klan, or white citizens' councils, but by black women.

The belief that women are by definition weak and in need of white male protection is the centerpiece of racialized androcentrism. Acknowledging black women's strength and resilience undermined the very foundations of that system. In addition, it hardly seems coincidental that in the 1960s, when white middle-class men were beginning to lose control over women's wages and property, and as white women were moving in greater numbers into the full-time workforce, white men began to argue that the very source of the problems faced by black Americans resided in black men's inability to effectively dominate women.[9] In order to strengthen what it described as "the Negro American family structure," the Moynihan Report concluded that the federal government must design programs that had "the effect, directly or indirectly, of enhancing the stability and resources of the Negro American family." Beyond this, and despite its subtitle—"The Case for National Action"—it had nothing to say.

The ostensibly secret Moynihan Report lay fallow until the following spring, when presidential assistant Bill Moyers suggested it to President Johnson as the basis for a major policy speech he delivered, ironically, at all-black Howard University. In the speech, Johnson spoke about the "special nature of negro poverty":

> Perhaps most important—its influence radiating to every part of life—is the breakdown of the negro family structure. For this, most of all, white America must accept responsibility. It flows from centuries of oppression and persecution of the negro man. It flows from the long years of degradation and discrimination, which have attacked his dignity and assaulted his ability to produce for his family.
>
> (1966)

Throughout the summer that followed Johnson's speech, the Moynihan Report was "leaked to selected journalists" (Gresham 1989: 118). But according to Jewell Handy Gresham, "the event that cemented" the impact of the Moynihan Report was the Watts uprising in August 1965 (which occurred less than two weeks after the August passage of the Voting Rights Act), when "in a mad scramble for instant wisdom, journalists turned to the black family report and drew on its conclusions as explanations for the violent civil disorders" (118).[10]

Where the Moynihan Report stigmatized black women for having usurped authority in the domestic sphere, wider social forces were conspiring to criminalize them for taking advantage of the paternal authority of the state. When the state sought to protect black women, this theme ran, they abused its assistance through deceit, connivance, and fraud. Although the soubriquet "welfare queen" was a rhetorical invention of the late 1970s, "widespread hostility to poor mothers receiving public assistance money" (Solinger 2001: 139) on the part of politicians began to emerge in the mid-1960s. In fact, beginning in 1965, "the complexion of the poor turned decidedly darker. From only 27% in 1964, the proportion of African Americans in [news] pictures of the poor increased to 49% and 53% in 1965 and 1966, and then to 72% in 1967" (Gilens, quoted in Solinger 2001: 143) and "widespread hostility to poor mothers receiving public assistance money" on the part of politicians began to emerge in the mid-1960s, as poor women were more and more frequently depicted as black (Solinger 2001: 139). These representations were successful in disseminating a wildly distorted understanding of race, gender, and class to politicians and middle-class viewers alike, neither of whom had contact with many actual poor people. According to political scientist Martin Gilens, when respondents were asked by a 1982 poll, "What percent of all the poor people in this country would you say are black?" their guess was 50 percent (1996: 595).[11]

This racist and sexist emphasis in public discourse was observable as early as 1964 in Ronald Reagan's preliminary attacks on poor black women. At their heart, Reagan's arguments suggested that poor African American women were whores who had sex and then children for ridiculously small sums of money. In 1964 Reagan told a story he was to repeat for years to come: about "a young woman who had come before" a judge "for a divorce. She had six children, was pregnant with her seventh . . . She wanted a divorce so that she could get an eighty dollar raise" (Solinger 2001: 140). In 1971, fortified by the Moynihan Report's linking of a "culture of dependency" with blackness, then Governor of California Ronald Reagan touted his government works projects as a solution to this problem of an inferentially black "dependency" (*NBC Evening News*, 26 February 1971).

Reagan revived these narratives throughout his political career, most dramatically during his 1976 presidential campaign, when he spoke incessantly about "welfare misuse," citing "the case of a Chicago woman who used 80 names to collect money on welfare" (*CBS Evening News*, 7 March 1977). Linda Taylor, an African American woman, was said to have

> eighty names, thirty addresses, twelve Social Security cards and is collecting veterans' benefits on four nonexisting deceased husbands . . . And she's collecting Social Security on her cards. She's got Medicaid, getting food stamps, and she is collecting welfare under each of her names. Her tax-free income alone is over $150,000.
>
> (quoted in Zucchino 1997: 65)

Although a Cook County grand jury only charged Taylor with the theft of $8000 from public welfare in 1976, this dramatically reduced figure was never reported on television news.[12]

In these ways, the Civil Rights Movement's demands for equality were transformed into demands on the part of a now black, undeserving, and female poor for "handouts" and entitlements. The difficulties and hardships of poverty exacerbated by racist ceilings on economic advancement were effectively transformed into a magical feudal economy—the welfare state—where queenly black matriarchs exploited the very system that had so altruistically attempted to help them. The resultant images of female welfare frauds thus reworked the racist ideologies about pathological black femininity and its social consequences presented in the 1965 Moynihan Report in order to instantiate a vision of the poor in the USA as predominantly black, female, and inherently corrupt.[13] Images of black welfare queens gave further support to arguments that, as victims of nothing more than their own isolated shortcomings, these families were patently undeserving of any federal intervention, save in the shape of punishment.

The Politics of Emboldenment

The election of Ronald Reagan in 1980 marked the culmination of the nationalization of what was, broadly speaking, a white supremacist understanding of the effects of racism on African American communities. Under the sign of the perennially paternal, jovial, and reasonable movie star, who evoked nothing so much as the paterfamilias of 1950s sitcom legend, the Reagan Administration pursued an agenda that was at its very core both misogynist and racist. Although the media was to consistently—and erroneously—proclaim broad popularity for Reagan's presidency and policies, his candidacy made clear where he stood on issues of gender (unlike Carter, he opposed the Equal Rights Amendment and supported efforts to overturn abortion rights) and race (he was a staunch supporter of the racist apartheid regime in South Africa).[14] And Reagan made support of the silent white majority of racists and segregationists now united—north and south—under the banner of states' rights visible from the very beginning of his candidacy. Lest his meaning be unclear, and at the urging of Trent Lott, Reagan made his first campaign speech in Philadelphia, Mississippi, where less than 20 years before, Cheney, Schwerner, and Goodman had been murdered by white supremacists.

Reagan's domestic policies consistently conjured up the specter of race to demonize poor people, although as Manning Marable points out,

> Reagan never used blatantly racist language, because he didn't have to. As sociologist Howard Winant astutely observed, the New Right's approach to the public discourse of race was characterized by an "authoritarian version of color-blindness," an opposition to any government policies designed to redress blacks' grievances or to compensate them for both the historical or contemporary effects of discrimination, and the subtle manipulation of whites' racial fears. The New Right discourse strove to protect white privilege and power by pretending that racial inequality no longer existed.
>
> (2003: 73)

In place of the massive social spending that the *Report of the National Advisory Commission on Civil Disorders* (1968) had recommended as a first step toward addressing racism, Reagan cut federal low-income housing programs by 84 percent, offering up a newly reformulated "war on drugs" as the solution to urban decay, homelessness, and despair.

Reagan made racism and racist explanations for social problems publicly acceptable again, albeit through a more sophisticated language of race hating and baiting than that of George Wallace. Where before the rise of Reaganism racists, fearful of criticism from those quarters that had been sensitized by the Civil Rights Movement, were publicly criticized or self-censored their speech, after Reaganism forms of racialized discourses about crime and welfare became acceptable once more, particularly in the media. Television's visual dimension, and politicians' more skillful use of this medium, enhanced these racialized discourses and contributed to enabling linkages between crime and blackness, since no one had to draw attention to the fact that suspects in crime cases were identifiably black.

As conservatives became increasingly emboldened by their ideological successes in criminalizing African Americans, and in converting black victims deserving of federal protection and intervention into black villains deserving only of prison, their discourses regularly appealed to older, more overtly racist images. In place of the more liberal discourse that characterized the Moynihan Report and the careful coding of the war on crime, by 1988 presidential candidate George Bush, Sr. ran a series of ads featuring William Horton, a convicted murderer, who had been released on furlough only to kidnap a white couple, raping the woman.[15] The ads suggested that Dukakis not only was "soft" on crime, but he favored a revolving door approach to prisons, going so far as to issue "weekend passes" to murderers. Here again, visual imagery foregrounded an unspoken link between race and crime: the ad featured brown and black inmates passing through a revolving door.

According to Susan Estrich, a professor of law who was then working for the Dukakis campaign, the Willie Horton ad campaign

> was very much an issue about race and racial fear . . . You can't find a stronger metaphor, intended or not, for racial hatred in this country than a black man raping a white woman. And

that's what the Willie Horton story was. I talked to people afterward, men and women. Women said they couldn't help it, but it scared the living daylights out of them . . . I talked to men who said they couldn't help it either, but when they saw the leaflets later and the ads and the like, they couldn't help but thinking about their wives and feeling scared and crazy.

(quoted in Anderson 1995: 207)

A flurry of news reports followed the ad, as well as protests by civil rights activists like Jesse Jackson. But the news discourse aided in putting Dukakis on the defensive by inserting the controversy into a "hard on crime" framework. *ABC News* began one of its nightly news reports with the following: "The question is 'Where does the Governor stand on crime and punishment and what are the facts of the celebrated Horton prison furlough case, which the Vice President likes to say is proof that his opponent is soft on crime?'" (*ABC Evening News*, 22 September 1988). The report then immediately cut to a newspaper photograph of Horton, while reporter Jackie Judd observed, "Willie Horton has become the symbol of everything that Bush finds wrong with Dukakis on law and order, crime and punishment."

The ads provided the Bush campaign with an enormous amount of free publicity, allowing them to speak for victims writ large. One clip showed George Bush, Sr. criticizing the Democrats because, "When it comes to the plights of the victims and their families, there is what one can only describe as an astounding lack of sensitivity, a lack of human compassion" (*NBC Evening News*, 7 October 1988). During the same time slot, *ABC News* featured a segment on Massachusetts' successful prison furlough program, including an interview with Horton's victims, Angela and Clifford Barnes, who were campaigning for the Republican Party and demanding an "apology from Dukakis" (*ABC Evening News*, 7 October 1988). In response to critics, another report quoted Bush's aides as saying that "they would have used the Horton case even if he wasn't black and it's ridiculous to suggest that talking about law and order is somehow anti-black because blacks are even more concerned about crime than whites" (*NBC Evening News*,

24 October 1988). In distinct contrast to the time allotted to the Bush campaign's offensive against Dukakis, the Democrats and Dukakis never responded to the ad on a network news program.

The contrast between conservative run-ups to the 1968 and 1988 elections is instructive. Where, in 1968, the final months of the presidential campaign were devoted to law and order and war on crime issues that contained a more cautious link between race and crime, by 1988, after the conservative revolution, the link between violence, prisons, and African American men had become a form of common sense. Far from the color-blindness that contemporary commentaries ascribed to Reaganism and the political discourse that followed from it, racialized discourses about crime became important campaign issues by manipulating racist fears. In 1988, GOP political strategist Lee Atwater unapologetically described the Willie Horton ads, and their overtly racist discourse about monstrous black men raping white women, as the Bush campaign's "silver bullet" (quoted in Anderson 1995: 223), suggesting that the campaign ads were responsible for Bush's presidential win in 1988.

The late 1980s also ushered in a whole new lexicon for a range of "black" crimes. Having criminalized African American women and men, attention turned in the last half of the 1980s to a generation of youthful "superpredators."[16] Black gangs gained increasing coverage beginning in 1986, a trend that deepened in the early 1990s. The welfare queen morphed into the "crack mother" bearing "crack babies" in 1988, "black-on-black crime" emerged as a media category in 1989, and the first mention of "drive-by shootings" on television news occurred on September 1990.

In the resurgent racism of the late 1980s and 1990s, even efforts to recall events of the 1960s and to remember the fallen heroes of the Civil Rights Movement, were framed in such a way as to deny their victimhood and to reinforce a framework of black pathology instead. To raise issues of race in the final years of the twentieth century was invariably to invoke the specter of black pathology and the link between crime and race, absolving white people of racism in the process. In this fashion, network television frequently used the occasion of newly national celebrations of Martin Luther King's birthday not to talk about the very white supremacy that had caused his death, but to raise the specter of black pathology, testifying to the ways in which any mention of race was to be connected to crime in the last years of the twentieth century. Although televised news routinely reported on the numerous celebrations of King's birth throughout the country, as the 1980s gave way to the 1990s, reports were increasingly less likely to discuss the fact that few of King's goals for racial equality had been met. Indeed, Bill Moyers, the very person who had first brought the Moynihan Report to President Johnson's attention, televised "The Vanishing Black Family—Crisis in Black America" (1986), a special report that featured what the program touted as an "intimate" look at the lives of black teenage welfare moms and criminal black youths, during the week of the first national celebration of King's birthday. The first reference to the new category of "black-on-black crime" was, sadly enough, during a segment on Martin Luther King's birthday. The segment opened with a reference to Dr. King's dream, then cut to "black-on-black crime" in New Orleans and a discussion of why blacks were "prone" to violence (*CBS Evening News*, 15 January 1989).[17]

Credible Witnesses

They were coming downtown from a world of crack, welfare, guns, knives, indifference and ignorance. They were coming from a land with no fathers . . . They were coming from the anarchic province of the poor. And driven by a collective fury, brimming with the rippling energies of youth, their minds teeming with the violent images of the streets and the movies, they had only one goal: to smash, hurt, rob, stomp, rape. The enemies were rich. The enemies were white.

(Pete Hamill, quoted in Hancock 2003)

Between 1969 and 1989, the time-honored tradition of stories involving black threats to white womanhood was thrown into temporary abeyance, as news themes established that black culture rather than white racism was the cause for racial disparities in

the USA. By the late 1980s, the tide had changed. The widespread publicity allotted to the Horton case marked the resurgence of a revivified racist discourse on threatening black masculinity and threatened white femininity. The Horton case legitimized the resurgence of the logic that underlay nineteenth-century lynching narratives: white people's testimony was not to be questioned, black people's testimony was not to be believed, and black victims were not to be represented. Having tested the racist waters, so to speak, and eliciting no public outcry on the part of politicians, social movements, or the media powerful enough to challenge their framework, the emboldened forces of white supremacy were given new voice.

Numerous cases from the late 1980s offer abundant evidence of the revival of the myth of the black male sexual predator. On the evening of 19 April 1989, Trisha Meili, a 28-year-old investment banker with the Wall Street firm of Salomon Brothers, was brutally beaten, raped, and left for dead in Central Park. Five Harlem teenagers were convicted of the crime, which also contributed a new racialized word, "wilding," to the media lexicon of crime.[18] Thirteen years after the teens were convicted, DNA evidence as well as convicted rapist Matias Reye's confession that he had raped and assaulted the jogger by himself and did not know any of the youths who had been charged, resulted in the dismissal of the case against those who had been convicted.[19] But at the time of the incident, news narratives spoke with one voice, as it were, about the criminality of these youths, never questioning law enforcement officials' accounts.

The media became obsessed with the case, in part because the woman known as the Central Park Jogger (Meili remained anonymous until the publication of her 2004 memoir) was one of theirs, in terms of both race and class. Like Helen Jewett, the jogger could have been one of their sisters, daughters, girlfriends, or wives, although unlike Jewett, the jogger had the benefit of being virtuous. What happened to her, reports repeated, could have happened to any one of them and even feminists were swift to argue that gender trumped race in understanding the nature of the crime and the need for prosecutorial zeal in punishing the teenaged perpetrators. Anne Murray, who in 1989 was police bureau chief for *The New York Post*, said that "she was conflicted about how the editors had played the original story. 'I knew the coverage would be very different if the victim weren't white'" (quoted in Hancock 2003). According to feminist Kimberlé Crenshaw, racism explained why the case was on the cover of newspapers and the lead story on televised news for weeks after the attack, not to mention the role that "racial intimidation" played in the interrogation of the youths (quoted in Little 2002b).

As Crenshaw also pointed out, had the jogger been a woman of color, her treatment at the hands of the media would have been quite different, a point made clear by a similar case that occurred during the same time period. On 2 May 1989, just a few short weeks after the Central Park Jogger was assaulted, a 39-year-old African American woman was dragged inside an abandoned building in the Crown Heights section of Brooklyn, robbed, raped, and sodomized by three men, and then thrown down a 50 foot air shaft. Like the jogger, her survival was in question in the days following the crime. Like the jogger, she would also bear the physical scars of the assault for the remainder of her life, although unlike the jogger, she recalled the brutal assault. The rape was reported on the 11 p.m. news the day after it occurred (McFadden 1989: 31; 1990: B1), leading to the identification of the assailants by another victim, but the story was never considered front-page news copy, appearing on page 31 in 1989 and on B1 in 1990.[20] The story never made the national network news.

On the face of it, and save for the race, age, and class position of the victims, the two cases were shockingly similar. Two unaccompanied women were brutally assaulted, raped, and left for dead in the spring of 1989. But in the eighteen months following the incident, the case of the Central Park Jogger elicited an astounding 344 articles in the *New York Times*, while the case of the Brooklyn rape victim resulted in only three, one of which was about the African American minister who was serving as spokesperson for her family (Goldman 1989: B1) and contained a single mention of the Brooklyn victim.[21] The Brooklyn rape was never inserted into the news frame that had emerged following the assault on the

jogger—one of predatory males attacking an innocent and vulnerable woman. The obvious reasons behind the disproportionate coverage had everything to do with the intertwining of race and class in late twentieth century New York City. Not only was the Central Park victim, as one newscast put it, a "noted investment banker" (*NBC Evening News*, 24 April 1989), with degrees from Wellesley College and from Yale University, the crime took place in the heart of Manhattan.[22] Moreover, the Central Park case had familiar, identifiable perpetrators of color and a worthy white female victim. Where the attack on the jogger featured a crime and a location that had deep resonance for reporters for mainstream media outlets like the *New York Times* and national broadcast news personnel, a black victim, assaulted by black men in Brooklyn, did not.

If, in the case of the Central Park Jogger, the media provided no criticism of law enforcement, this owed much to the credibility possessed by law enforcement officials. If black victims' testimony has long been seen as suspect and worthy of skepticism, the testimony of African Americans charged with crime has been even more so.[23] Certainly, law enforcement officials and the media were primed by the overall resurgence of racism in the 1980s to uncritically consume the very discourses they were producing. As Barbie Zelizer puts it, journalists are an interpretive community "that are united through their collective interpretations of key public events" (1993: 223). In the case of the Central Park Jogger, law enforcement officials and the media uncritically united around an interpretation of this event that reflected their acceptance of the wider racialized framework of law and order.

In the end, although the crimes themselves were centrally about gender—about the most excessive forms of misogynist violence enacted upon women's bodies, about the sense of entitlement to women's bodies that violent men are encouraged to have—this was not a story that the media or law enforcement were prepared to tell. Instead, the story of the jogger was not one of male violence against women, but of interracial violence and the threat men of color presented to white women. Invested in the frame of "wilding" that supported this version of events, police and media were reluctant to back off from it. Even though another rape had occurred in Central Park just two days before Meili was attacked (and that victim retained a full memory of the event), neither police nor journalists raised the possibility of a link between the two. Instead, as *New York Newsday* columnist Jim Dwyer later observed: "The story was like a centrifuge . . . Everyone was pinned into a position—the press, the police, the prosecution— and no one could press the stop button" (quoted in Hancock 2003).

However self-critical journalists were with the passage of time, a centrifuge larger than this single story continued to exert its influence long after the Central Park Jogger case. While men of color are not to be believed, other high-profile crimes from the late 1980s and early 1990s attest to the credulity with which the words of white men were greeted during the same period. Not only did the fundamental belief in black criminality affect the behaviors of the criminal justice system as a whole, further legitimizing the use of excessive force against black suspects by police and increasing rates of incarceration, it also gave white criminals convenient scapegoats for their crimes, particularly those committed against women.

The Charles Stuart case with which this chapter began was only one in a series of cases involving violent and greedy white men who attributed their crimes to amorphous and unidentifiable black predators. On 21 April 1992, Jesse Anderson and his wife Barbara were leaving a Milwaukee restaurant when, according to his account, they were attacked by two black men who stabbed Barbara at least 21 times in the face, head, and body. Barbara Anderson died of her wounds the following Thursday and for five days Milwaukee police stopped and detained black men in the area where the crime had occurred, before charging Jesse Anderson with the crime on 28 April 1992 (DeJonge 1992: 3A). A classically abusive husband, Anderson had a history of violence against his wife (the mother of the couple's three children). He had repeatedly expressed anger over his wife's weight gain, and had contacted his insurance company prior to the murder regarding Barbara's $250,000 life-insurance policy ("Weight-Gain Angle Cited in Slaying" 1992: 1B). Four years later,

in 1996, Robert Harris told Baltimore police a similar narrative. An armed African American man had shot him and his fiancée, Teresa McLeod, Harris told police. Although Harris confessed within two days (again, the motive was McLeod's $250,000 life insurance policy), Baltimore police initially and aggressively pursued black suspects.

Perhaps nowhere was the credibility attributed to white narratives about black crime more evident than in the case of Susan Smith, a case that of all of these "racial hoaxes" accrued the most national televised coverage. On 26 October 1994, Susan Smith appeared under the headline "carjacked kids" on national television to issue a tearful plea to the black man she claimed had stolen the car containing her two children (*NBC Evening News*). For the first three days, all network news programs reported the case as a "kidnapping/carjacking," invoking a new category of crime to describe what had happened. And although three days after the children had disappeared, South Carolina Sheriff Howard Wells described Smith as both "victim and suspect" (*NBC Evening News*, 29 October 1994) and *CBS Evening News* reported that Smith was being "queried," it was not until 1 November that the carjacking frame finally gave way to the headline "Missing Boys." On 3 November, the children's bodies were found in a nearby lake and Smith was arrested for their murder.

Of course, no one expects violence of white women, particularly toward their own offspring, and this partly accounted for the media's blind acceptance of Smith's story about the boys' disappearance, as well as their venomous response to her once it was revealed that she had lied. Yet as part of a larger interpretive community that has historically attributed its most vicious, culturally illegible crimes to African Americans, Smith understood that her story would at least initially ring true to both law enforcement and the media: that, in effect, the words of a white mother would have force, power, and credibility. These narratives underscore the wider manufacturing and acceptance of nationalized racialized narratives about crime in US society. Stuart, Anderson, Harris, and Smith acknowledged the power of these racialized narratives when they blamed their violent acts on African American men. Counting on the fact that these narratives would be believed and accepted by law enforcement and the media, each of them was aware that they were accorded a belief status not afforded to African Americans. Each of them, in essence, organized their crime narratives around the fundamental connection between blackness and crime and the fact that, as white people, their narratives about violence would be trusted in automatic and often unconscious ways.[24]

Rodney King and O.J. Simpson

"I didn't believe in his [O.J.'s] innocence. But like most black people I knew, I wasn't interested in talking to white people about it unless they had sorted themselves out around the issues. This country just doesn't have the tools for black and white people to have those kind of conversations."

(Linda Burnham, Black Women's Resource Center, quoted in Younge 2005: 17)

Two cases following from the twinned themes of pathological black female hegemony within the private sphere and black male threats to white women came to define race and crime issues in the 1990s. The first resulted from the widely distributed videotape of the beating of motorist Rodney King in March 1991 and the LA uprisings that followed after a verdict was handed down in the case of his beating in 1992. The second concerned the arrest of former football player O.J. Simpson for the murders of his ex-wife Nicole Brown Simpson and Ron Goldman on 12 June 1994.

Although on the surface, the beating of Rodney King appeared to have little to do with the time-honored theme of black men assaulting white women, his violent beating resulted at least in part from that volatile ideological mix of sex and race. On 3 March 1991, Tim and Melanie Singer, husband and wife members of the California Highway Patrol, noticed King's Hyundai driving behind them at a high speed. Turning around, they gave chase. When King pulled the car over, his two companions complied with the Singers' orders for the car's occupants to leave the vehicle and lie on the ground face down, but King initially refused to get out of the car. Finally

exiting the car, according to Melanie Singer's testimony, he "grabbed his right buttock with his right hand and he shook it at me" (Linder 2001). Officer Stacey Koon also testified that King "grabbed his butt with both hands and began to shake and gyrate his fanny in a sexually suggestive fashion . . . As King sexually gyrated, a mixture of fear and offense overcame Melanie. The fear was of a Mandingo sexual encounter" (quoted in Mercer 1994). Whether the brutality of the beating (King was struck 56 times by arresting officers, while at least 23 police officers looked on) directly resulted from the threat King's "sexually suggestive" gyrations seemingly posed to Melanie Singer was really beside the point. Koon believed that King's actions were sexual in nature, and on the basis of that belief he attributed fear and offense to Melanie Singer. Taking it one step further, Koon asserted that her fear was of "a Mandingo sexual encounter," a phrase which hopelessly muddled a popular culture reference to the 1975 film *Mandingo* (in which a black slave burns down the plantation and escapes with a blonde southern bombshell) and the historical fear of black male sexuality that accompanied this narrative.[25] The arresting officers used this description to frame the incident as a whole, and in so doing the fear a white male police officer ascribed to a white female police officer became the pretext for their violent assault on King. Her fear, to their thinking, was sufficient legitimation for their use of force. The parallel between this and lynching narratives was lost on mainstream journalists.

On 29 April 1992, a suburban Simi Valley jury, made up of eleven whites and one person of Filipino descent, found three officers not guilty of official misconduct, filing false police reports, excessive force, and assault with a deadly weapon. Los Angeles immediately erupted in the worst violence the city had seen since the 1965 Watts uprising. It was later estimated that between 50 and 60 people lost their lives, more than 4000 were injured, 12,000 people were arrested, and property damage was estimated at $1 billion. For residents of color who lived in a city that had not only had to deal with the crack epidemic of the early 1990s, with intensified surveillance conducted by a highly militarized police force, with endemic poverty, and with appallingly low employment rates for its African American residents, the verdict in the trial of the four officers proved simply too much to bear.[26]

The immediate causes for the violence were well known—namely, that after decades of racist police violence, members of the Los Angeles Police Department had finally been caught in the act and then, unbelievably, cleared of all charges. Despite the fact that an investigation resulting from the King beating, and led by Warren Christopher (later Secretary of State in the Clinton Administration), found widespread racism and sexism in the LAPD, the image that prevailed after the riots was not of a criminal justice system that shared the racism of the LAPD, but of a white man being dragged from the cab of his truck and brutally beaten by black youths (that Reginald Denny was rescued and driven to the hospital by two black men and two black women was not part of the story the media told). Echoing the media response to the Watts uprising in 1965, and in a move that could have been professionally scripted in nearby Hollywood, the media and politicians reinforced a frame that focused on lawless black youth and the single mothers and pathological family structure that were to blame for them, with Vice President Dan Quayle weighing in on the deleterious effects of single motherhood. A case that had begun with police brutality, attempts on the part of police officers to legitimize their actions by invoking the figure of the sexually menacing black male, and African American frustration with a criminal justice system that had two different standards for punishing violence when it came to blacks and whites, was subsequently transformed into a punitive narrative about single motherhood and black pathology.

The arrest and trial of former football player O.J. Simpson in 1994 needs to be understood within this narrative context of betrayal and anger, following as it did only two years after the Los Angeles uprising. Billed as the trial of the century in a century that had begun with the similarly billed Henry Thaw trial, the crime had all the makings of a high-profile serialized case. Simpson was a wealthy, famous black man. His ex-wife, Nicole, was white and had made at least one previous 911 call to report having been beaten by

Simpson (O.J., she sobbed to the operator, was going "to beat the shit out of me"). The crime itself was an especially vicious one: both victims had had their throats cut and had been stabbed repeatedly.

If the verdict in the trial of the four police officers in the Rodney King beating shocked and dismayed African Americans, the jury's decision in the O.J. Simpson trial was said to take whites by surprise, "exposing," as innumerable news reports and round-the-clock reporting at what journalists referred to as "Camp O.J." routinely reminded viewers, an interpretive polarization between blacks and whites—a deep rift between races in terms of attitudes toward the dismissal of charges against Simpson.[27] The media coverage pitted race (represented as solely the concern of African Americans) against gender (which apparently only white people cared about), thereby managing to gloss over, or in numerous cases ignore, the cultural, economic, and political context in which the trial took place. Whether Simpson was guilty or not, he was being tried by a criminal justice system with a long history of incarcerating and executing African Americans for crimes they had not committed; a criminal justice system that, as the example of police officer Mark Furman illustrated during the course of the trial (Simpson's defense introduced tapes of Furman repeatedly using the word "nigger" and making overtly racist comments), was structurally racist. For many, Simpson himself was no more than a symbol of a wider system that had always treated blacks and whites differently when it came to crime and crime victims. As one resident of South Central later put it, acknowledging a truism not addressed by the mainstream media, "If O.J. had killed his first wife, who was an African American woman, all this wouldn't have happened." And another man more cynically recalled that when the verdict came down, "We said, 'wow,' at least a black guy got away sometimes. Because there are a lot of people—a lot of black folks—there's a lot of dead black folks that nobody ever went to jail for" (Del Barco 2005).

The theme repeated in endless media coverage of the trial and the verdict focused on African American prosecuting attorney Johnnie Cochran's use of what the media described as the "race card" in his introduction of the evidence about Furman.

Assuming that race played no role in the police's handling of the Simpson case, the discourse of the "race card" suggested that Cochran was using Simpson's race as a ploy to beat the charges against him. Other than Cochran's introduction of race, this logic held that race had nothing to do with either the media attention to the case or the criminal justice system's investigation of the crimes. The rhetoric of the "race card" flew in the face of all evidence, as Cochran well knew, having won a series of landmark decisions about racist police misconduct in the 1980s. *Time* magazine's now infamous darkening of the image of Simpson used on the cover of their magazine was only one of the more egregious—and obvious—examples of the racialized framework through which the Simpson case was understood ("An American Tragedy" 1994). Just as mainstream media had sought to explain the LA uprising through a framework that displaced issues of racism by blaming black communities, so the media in the Simpson case argued that race was not a fundamental part of how the case was investigated and understood, but was an issue artificially and manipulatively introduced by black people. The elite male privilege and the violence against women that were fundamental parts of this privilege were read through a prism that refracted only blackness.

Race and gender combined in these national crime stories to reinforce the historically overdetermined ideologies governing white belief in black criminality. Although this white belief was temporarily challenged in the cases of Charles Stuart, Jesse Anderson, Robert Harris, and Susan Smith, it was never effectively confronted. In the case of the beating of Rodney King, the issue of gender—particularly as it was used by LAPD officers to "explain" their beating—was not scrutinized by the press and thus the brutality of the police officers themselves was widely attributed to King's violent behavior and not their interpretation of its sexualized dimensions. Gender only became a factor in later attempts to "analyze" the causes of the subsequent uprising, which in a system so entrenched in racialized androcentrism could not have possibly had to do with racism on the part of white society, but strictly involved pathologies and causes internal to a monolithic black culture.

A similar myopia ran throughout the O.J. Simpson case, where an older narrative about black masculinity effectively erased references to elite male privilege and the violence against women that was a cornerstone of it.

Gender and the War on Drugs

High-profile racial hoaxes and crime cases involving African Americans as both victims and perpetrators were only one strand of the racialized narratives about crime that abounded in the 1980s and 1990s. The credibility and sympathy extended to white crime victims and suspects also affected serialized coverage of the war on drugs, offering stark examples of racialized disparity not only in arrests and sentencing, but in the narrative frameworks used to explicate drug use and to depict users of illegal drugs. Representations of drug use were themselves both raced and gendered during this period, with coverage of the crack "epidemic" in the late 1980s and early 1990s a case in point.

Attention to crack, for example, focused squarely on black women, with the media consistently depicting female crack users as products of that now familiar culture of dependency, blaming their drug use on their shortcomings as individual human beings. In "On Streets Ruled by Crack, Families Die," reporter Gina Kolata described how crack cocaine was "rapidly accelerating the destruction of families in poor urban neighborhoods where mothers are becoming increasingly addicted and children are selling the drug in greater numbers than ever before" (1989: A1+). Kolata's article emphasized the behavioral problems associated with crack use, saying little or nothing about the effects of the drug itself or its production or distribution.[28] Scant sympathy was accorded to crack users; instead, journalists like Kolata concentrated on this culture of drug abuse, and "the unraveling family," in which ever younger children were enlisted in the trade. Invoking the image of the African American "crack mother" that became popular in the late 1980s, Kolata represented crack users as being predisposed to drug abuse, and thus as the agents of their own destruction.[29] In so doing, Kolata echoed the argument presented in an earlier *CBS News Special*—that "Drug abuse—not jobs, not the economy, not the issue of war and peace—drug abuse is the nation's leading overall concern right now" ("48 Hours on Crack Street," 2 September 1986).

Users of methamphetamine, increased use of which began in the early 1990s, were treated altogether differently by the media. In distinct contrast to black users of crack in urban settings, white users of crystal methamphetamine were featured as either victims of an all-powerful, addictive substance or an economic downturn. The social devastation caused by the introduction of crack into economically fragile areas remains undeniable, as those addicted to it lose sight of everything but their addiction. But methamphetamine is in many ways a more threatening drug, frequently used by those already predisposed to violence (particularly racist skinheads and other white supremacists). Unlike the euphoria of crack, methamphetamine causes paranoia and violence and induces symptoms similar to paranoid schizophrenia. Like alcohol, methamphetamine can cause users to become violent. In July 1995, a New Mexico man, high on methamphetamine and alcohol, beheaded his 14-year-old son and threw the severed head onto a crowded highway. Again in 1995, a San Diego man took a tank he had stolen from a National Guard armory for a joy ride on a freeway, threatening motorists and forcing the closure of the freeway. Since the mid-1990s, moreover, dozens of men, women, and children have died in the explosions common in improvised methamphetamine labs.

The utter contrast between coverage of black crack and white methamphetamine users appeared starkly in a 1996 *New York Times* front-page article entitled, "Good People Go Bad in Iowa, and a Drug Is Being Blamed" (Johnson 1996: A1+). In extensive and sympathetic detail, the article focused on the devastating social consequences of increasing availability of methamphetamine in the Midwest. Methamphetamine users, the article stated, were "good people" victimized by a terrible drug. Methamphetamine, rather than a culture of poverty or pathological individuals, was to blame for the tragedies ensuing from its use, along with increasing unemployment, straitened economic circumstances, and even "an intense Midwestern work ethic" that encouraged

reliance on this form of speed (Johnson 1996: A8). Reporting on methamphetamine linked individuals' use of it to their work ethic: one researcher consulted for an article described it as

> a drug of the times in that it's a drug for people who don't have enough time . . . You have the sense that it's moms trying to juggle jobs and three kids and day care, and women working as waitresses on their feet for 12 hours a day. And it's truck drivers, carpet layers, people who work long hours doing tedious, repetitive tasks.
>
> (Goldberg 1997: 16)

Where crack addicts were cast as people disposed to escape reality and responsibility—because of their essentially shiftless racialized natures, not because of the effects of racism, chronic poverty, and despair—white users were rural, hardworking members of the working class. Driven by circumstances to drug use, they found themselves hopeless captives to a powerful substance. The message was clear: white drug users were victims of their circumstances and therefore deserving of sympathy and rehabilitation; black drug addicts were social parasites, beyond redemption and worthy of nothing more than punishment.

Conclusion

By the late 1990s, the mainstream, national media rarely mentioned race without invoking the twinned themes of crime and black pathology. Far from encouraging white society to confront the legacy of racism, to understand the continued effects of racism and consequent economic exploitation on African American communities, these themes permitted white elites to wash their hands of the problems that continued to beset African Americans. Instead, these themes fully legitimized the mixture of fear and rage with which whites continued to regard African Americans. By the waning years of the century, US society had created a narrative of fear and denial that had entirely transformed the political challenges that the Civil Rights Movement had presented into a saga about African Americans' inherent criminality and racial shortcomings.

Typically, media scholars tend to think about the effects of media content on viewers in terms of "vulnerable" populations like children, but the extent to which the behavior of law enforcement officials and police officers was affected by the racialized war on crime and war on drug discourses in the media has yet to be studied. Judging by cases of police brutality in the 1990s, and the testimony of police officers, it would appear that widespread media representations of blacks as criminals encouraged a violence-prone, trigger-happy culture when it came to treatment of African Americans. Twelve-year-old Michael Ellerbee would not have been shot in the back and killed on Christmas Eve 2002 by two Pennsylvania State Police officers had he been white.

Although it is outside the scope of this book to provide an analysis of the effects of racialized crime coverage on police, it should be clear that the kind of media narratives discussed thus far had effects on the stories that victims, suspects, and police told about their actions—that, broadly speaking, the social construction of crime as blackness had all too material effects on a range of institutional practices. Skolnick and Fyfe have argued that "evidence from historical sources, observational studies of police— our own and others—and legal materials shows that contemporary police brutality is both historically and sociologically related to lynching and related vigilante activities" (1993: 24). A century after the coverage of lynching discussed in chapter 4, journalists continue to draw from an inventory of discourses that seeks to explain rather than condemn such violent behaviors.

National coverage of high-profile crimes involving African Americans as either suspects or victims and serialized coverage of the war on drugs combined to firmly rearticulate race with crime during the 1980s and 1990s. But alongside these highly visible, national, and mostly serialized narratives about race and gender, against the backdrop of escalating incarceration rates for African American women and men, a revolution of sorts was taking place in local television news. Unlike national news stories, whose serialized nature and visibility elicited some criticism of their racism, as we will see in the next chapter, these local, episodic crime stories not only supported the broader themes pursued by national news stories,

but in a more low-key, mundane fashion helped to represent crime as a key issue of political and cultural concern and as a constant source of white fear.

Notes

1. Before Stuart's suicide, suspect William Bennett was identified as "Willie" Bennett in a move that—consciously or unconsciously—linked him to Willie Horton. After Stuart's suicide, news reports identified him by his proper name, "William."
2. See Rome (2004: 64), Russell (1998: 70), and Theoharis and Woznica (1990) for more detailed analyses of the Stuart case.
3. Russell provides summary data on racial hoaxes between 1987 and 1996 (1998: 72–75).
4. Numerous biographies, autobiographies, and historical accounts provide rich source material for a study of the female leaders of the Civil Rights Movement. See Evers-Williams (1999), Fleming (1998) for a biography of Ruby Doris Smith Robinson, Lee (2000) on Fannie Lou Hamer, Ransby (2005) on Ella Baker, as well as Branch (1989, 1998), Garrow (1988), and Halberstam (1998) for just a few examples.
5. Abramowitz (1996), Gordon (1995), Katz (1993), Kessler-Harris (2003), Mink (1996), Quadagno (1994), Roberts (1998), and Solinger (2001) offer excellent analyses of poverty, women, race, and the welfare state. See Kelley (1997) on the demonization of black urban poor people.
6. See Ortner's "Is Female to Male as Nature is to Culture?" (1974) for an expansion of this point.
7. Kunzel's "White Neurosis, Black Pathology: Constructing Out-of-Wedlock Pregnancy in the Wartime and Postwar United States" (1994) provides an excellent analysis of the pathologization of black families by twentieth-century experts. Also, see Solinger (1992) on the racialization of single white motherhood in the post-war era.
8. This example abundantly illustrates how the misogyny of psychoanalysis became the alibi for racism. Thus does racialized androcentrism reproduce itself both in theory and practice.
9. Anthropologist Eleanor Leacock (1981) argued that this is the way that the imposition of patriarchy proceeds. In the case of the First Nation people she was studying, Jesuits first had to win the Montagnais to patriarchy— to a belief system in which women were the property of husbands and one that insisted that masculinity depended on men's ability to dominate women—before they could be effectively colonized. Some tactics of racialized androcentrism never go out of fashion.

10. When the National Advisory Commission on Civil Disorders (established by Lyndon Johnson in 1967) published the Kerner Commission Report, the report concluded that the causes for such urban uprisings lay in "deepening racial division," and that in place of "blind repression" the US needed "a compassionate, massive, and sustained" commitment to action (1968: 1–2) in order to reverse this movement. The Kerner Commission's analysis and recommendations—which included a scathing indictment of the role that the news media had played in framing events—proved popular to neither journalists nor politicians, both of whom favored the explanatory framework put forth in the Moynihan Report.

11. According to the US Bureau of the Census, 22.7 percent of African Americans were poor in 2001 (http://www.census.gov/Press-Release/www/2002/cb02-124.html, accessed 20 May 2003).

12. The first references to the term welfare queen appeared in broadcast and print coverage of Taylor (*CBS Evening News*, 18 March 1977; *New York Times*, 19 March 1977: 8). The welfare queen and the crack mother are part of a broader fabric of racist discourses about African American mothers. See Quadagno (1994), Roberts (1998), and Humphries (1999) for further analyses. Humphries, in particular, is concerned with moral panics and processes of criminalization.

13. The effects of these resilient racist stereotypes should not be underestimated. According to Martin Gilens, "the dimension of racial attitudes with the strongest effect on welfare views is the extent to which blacks are perceived as lazy, and this perception is a better predictor of welfare attitudes than such alternatives as economic self-interest, egalitarianism, and attributions of blame for poverty" (1996: 594).

14. Slightly over half of all registered voters voted in the 1980 presidential election. Of these, 50.75 percent of the popular vote went to Reagan, while 49.24 percent went to Jimmy Carter and all "others." See Schudson and King (1995: 124–41) on the construction of Reagan's popularity by beltway journalists, as well as Michael Rogin's 1987 classic, *Ronald Reagan, The Movie*.

15. Culverson (2002) analyzes the twinned use of Horton and the welfare queen in the 1988 presidential campaign, arguing that the two worked hand-in-hand to appeal to racist fears.

16. Annin (1996) offers a vivid illustration of the emerging discourse about "super-predators."

17. J. Edgar Hoover, who had strenuously lobbied to prevent King's birthday from becoming a holiday, would have been pleased with this sort of coverage.

18. Charges against four of the youths were dropped in 2003. Imprisoned rapist Matias Reyes testified that he had committed the crime alone. See Alluh (2002), Little (2002a), and Schanberg (2002). See Best (1999) on the emergence of new vocabularies for understanding crime, like "wilding" and "carjacking."

19. A violent serial rapist, Reyes (who was known for gouging out the eyes of his victims) was convicted in 1991 of four rapes and the murder of a pregnant woman and was linked to eight rapes in the seven-month period that included the night of 19 April 1989.

20. Journalists who did cover the story did not invest much effort in doing so. McFadden's 1990 article contains paragraphs lifted verbatim from his 1989 article.

21. In the 18 months following the rape, the Central Park Jogger case appeared in eleven national network news segments. The Brooklyn rape case did not make national network news.

22. One wonders what "noted" meant in this context, particularly during an era when investment bankers typically came to the attention of the mass media for their criminal behavior.

23. See Carter (1969) for a vivid historical example of the disparity attributed to racialized testimony in the case of the Scottsboro suspects.

24. Although in these cases white victims were revealed to be perpetrators, there is no way of determining how many white perpetrators' racial hoaxes have never been revealed.

25. As Kevin Alexander Gray notes, "Mandingo" also conjured an earlier meaning of the word: "Mandinkas were the fiercest warriors of Africa. After a Caribbean slave revolt in the 1800s, John C. Calhoun of South Carolina, the leading intellectual of the Southern gentry, invoked the specter of Mandingo slaughtering white masters as justification for their enslavement" (2004).

26. Two of the officers acquitted, Officer Laurence Powell and Sergeant Stacey Koon, were later tried and convicted on federal civil rights charges. See Davis (1992) for an account of the events that led to the uprising.

27. Revealingly, there was no similar discussion of an interpretive rift in the case of the dismissal of charges against the police officers in the King beating case.

28. See journalist Gary Webb's *Dark Alliance: The CIA, the Contras, and the Crack Cocaine Explosion*. According to him, "it is undeniable that a wildly successful conspiracy to import cocaine existed for many years . . . innumerable American citizens—most of them poor and black—paid an enormous price as a result" (1999: xiii).

29. See Reeves and Campbell (1994) and Humphries (1999) for detailed analyses of these media representations. See Bourgois (2003) for a rich ethnographic study of Puerto Rican crack users in East Harlem.

References

Abramowitz, M. (1996) *Regulating the Lives of Women: Social Welfare Policy From Colonial Times to the Present,* revised edition. Boston: South End Press.

Alluh, D. (2002) "Marked as the Enemy: Central Park Five Members Speak," *Village Voice,* 6–12 November.

"An American Tragedy." (1994) *Time,* 143(26), 27 June: 28–35.

Anderson, D.C. (1995) *Crime and the Politics of Hysteria: How the Willie Horton Story Changed American Justice.* New York: Random House.

Annin, P. (1996) "'Superpredators' Arrive: Should We Cage the New Breed of Vicious Kids?" *Newsweek,* 22 January: 57.

Best, J. (1999) *Random Violence: How We Talk About New Crimes and New Victims.* Berkeley: University of California Press.

Bourgois, P. (2003) *In Search of Respect: Selling Crack in el Barrio.* New York: Cambridge University Press.

Branch, T. (1989) *Parting the Waters: America in the King Years, 1963–65.* New York: Simon and Schuster.

Branch, T. (1998) *Pillar of Fire: America in the King Years, 1963–65.* New York: Simon and Schuster.

Carter, D.T. (1969) *Scottsboro: A Tragedy of the American South.* Baton Rouge: Louisiana State University.

Culverson, D. (2002) "The Welfare Queen and Willie Horton," in C.R. Mann and M.S. Katz (eds) *Images of Color, Images of Crime* (126–36), 2nd edition. Los Angeles: Roxbury Publishing Company.

Davis, M. (1992) "LA: The Fire This Time," *CovertAction,* 41 (Summer): 12–21.

DeJonge, J. (1992) "Victim's Husband May Be Charged," *Capital Times,* 27 April: 3A.

Del Barco, M. (2005) "O.J. Simpson Verdict Leaves Lasting Legacy," *All Things Considered,* National Public Radio, 3 October.

Evers-Williams, M. (1999) *Watch Me Fly: What I Learned on the Way to Becoming the Woman I Was Meant to Be.* New York: Little, Brown and Company.

Fleming, C.G. (1998) *Soon We Will Not Cry: The Liberation of Ruby Doris Smith Robinson.* New York: Rowman and Littlefield Publishers, Inc.

Frazier, E.F. (1939) *The Negro Family in the United States.* Chicago, IL: University of Chicago Press.

"48 Hours on Crack Street." (1986) *CBS News Special,* 2 September.

Garrow, D.J. (1988) *Bearing the Cross: Martin Luther King, Jr., and the Southern Christian Leadership Conference.* New York: Vintage.

Gilens, M. (1996) "'Race Coding' and White Opposition to Welfare," *The American Political Science Review,* 90(3) (September): 593–604.

Goldberg. C. (1997) "Way Out West and Under the Influence," *New York Times,* 16 March, Section 4: 16.

Goldman, A.L. (1989) "Minister's Job Is Advocacy for Blacks," *New York Times,* 17 July: B1.

Gordon, L. (1995) *Pitied But Not Entitled: Single Mothers and the History of Welfare.* Cambridge, MA: Harvard University Press.

Gray, K.A. (2004) "Segregation and Hypocrisy Forever: The Legacy of Strom Thurmond," *CounterPunch,* 8 March.

Gresham, J.H. (1989) "The Politics of Family in America," *The Nation,* 249(4) (24/31 July): 116–22.

Halberstam, D. (1998) *The Children.* New York: Random House.

Hancock, L. (2003) "Wolf Pack: The Press and the Central Park Jogger," *Columbia Journalism Review,* 1 (January/February).

Humphries, D. (1999) *Crack Mothers: Pregnancy, Drugs, and the Media.* Columbus: Ohio State University Press.

Johnson, D. (1996) "Good People Go Bad in Iowa, and a Drug Is Being Blamed," *New York Times,* 22 February, A1+.

Johnson, L.B. (1966) "To Fulfill These Rights: Commencement Address at Howard University, 4 June 1965," Public Papers of the Presidents of the United States: Lyndon B. Johnson, 1965, vol. II, entry 301, Washington, DC: Government Printing Office: 635–40. Online. Available: http://www.lbjlib.utexas.edu/johnson/archives.hom/speeches.hom/650604.asp (accessed 6 October 2005).

Katz, M.B. (ed.) (1993) *The "Underclass" Debate: Voices From History.* Princeton: Princeton University Press.

Kelley, R.D.G. (1997) *Yo' Mama's Disfunktional!: Fighting the Culture Wars in Urban America.* Boston: Beacon Press.

Kessler-Harris, A. (2003) *In Pursuit of Equity: Women, Men, and the Quest for Economic Citizenship in 20th-Century America.* New York: Oxford University Press.

Kolata, G. (1989) "On Streets Ruled by Crack, Families Die," *New York Times,* 11 August: A1+.

Kunzel, R.G. (1994) "White Neurosis, Black Pathology: Constructing Out-of-Wedlock Pregnancy in the Wartime and Postwar United States," in J. Meyerowitz (ed.) *Not June Cleaver: Women and Gender in Postwar America, 1945–1960* (304–34). Philadelphia: Temple University Press.

Leacock, E. (1981) *Myths of Male Dominance: Collected Papers on Women Cross Culturally.* New York: Monthly Review Press.

Lee, C.K. (2000) *For Freedom's Sake: The Life of Fannie Lou Hamer.* Urbana: University of Illinois Press.

Linder, D. (2001) "The Trials of Los Angeles Police Officers in Connection With the Beating of Rodney King," Online. Available: http://www.law.umkc.edu/faculty/projects/ftrials/lapd/lapdaccount.html (accessed 4 October 2005).

Little, R.G. (2002a) "Across 110th Street: Changed Lives Among Central Park Five Family Members," *Village Voice*, 6–12 November.

Little, R.G. (2002b) "Rage Before Race: How Feminists Faltered on the Central Park Jogger Case," *Village Voice*, 16–22 October.

Marable, M. (2003) *The Great Wells of Democracy: The Meaning of Race in American Life.* New York: Basic Books.

McFadden, R.D. (1989) "2 Brooklyn Rape Suspects Charged in 2nd Case," *New York Times*, 6 May: 31.

McFadden, R.D. (1990) "2 Men Get 6 to 18 Years for Rape in Brooklyn," *New York Times*, 2 October: B1.

Mercer, K. (1994) "Fear of a Black Penis—White Males' Perceptions of Black Males—Man Trouble," *ArtForum*, April.

Mink, G. (1996) *The Wages of Motherhood: Inequality in the Welfare State, 1917–1942.* Ithaca, NY: Cornell University Press.

Myrdal, G. (1944) *An American Dilemma: The Negro Problem and Modern Democracy.* New York: Harper.

National Advisory Commission on Civil Disorders. (1968) *Report of the National Advisory Commission on Civil Disorders (Kerner Commission Report).* Washington, DC: US Government Printing Office.

The Negro Family: The Case for National Action (1965) Washington, DC: Office of Policy Planning and Research, United States Department of Labor.

Ortner, S. (1974) "Is Female to Male as Nature is to Culture?" in M.Z. Rosaldo and L. Lamphere (eds.), *Woman, Culture, and Society.* Stanford, CA: Stanford University Press.

Quadagno, J. (1994) *The Color of Welfare: How Racism Undermined the War on Poverty.* New York: Oxford University Press.

Ransby, B. (2005) *Ella Baker and the Black Freedom Movement: A Radical Democratic Vision.* Chapel Hill: University of North Carolina Press.

Reeves, J.L. and R. Campbell. (1994) *Cracked Coverage: Television News, the Anti-Cocaine Crusade, and the Reagan Legacy.* Durham, NC: Duke University Press.

Roberts, D. (1998) *Killing the Black Body: Race, Reproduction, and the Meaning of Liberty.* New York: Vintage.

Rogin, M. (1987) *Ronald Reagan, the Movie and Other Episodes in Political Demonology.* Berkeley: University of California Press.

Rome, D. (2004) *Black Demons: The Media's Depiction of the African American Male Criminal Stereotype.* Westport, CT: Praeger.

Russell, K.K. (1998) *The Color of Crime: Racial Hoaxes, White Fear, Black Protectionism, Police Harassment, and Other Macroaggressions.* New York: New York University Press.

Schanberg, S. (2002) "A Journey Through the Tangled Case of the Central Park Jogger," *Village Voice*, 20-26 November.

Schudson, M. with E. King (1995) "The Illusion of Ronald Reagan's Popularity," in *The Power of News* (124–41). Cambridge, MA: Harvard University Press.

Skolnick, J.H. and J.J. Fyfe. (1993) *Above the Law: Police and the Excessive Use of Force.* New York: The Free Press.

Solinger, R. (1992) *Wake Up Little Susie: Single Pregnancy and Race Before Roe v. Wade.* New York: Routledge.

Solinger, R. (2001) *Beggars and Choosers: How the Politics of Choice Shapes Adoption, Abortion, and Welfare in the United States.* New York: Farrar, Straus, and Giroux.

Theoharis, J. and L. Woznica. (1990) "The Forgotten Victims: The Collision of Race, Gender, and Murder," *Was It Worth It?* (February).

"The Vanishing Black Family: Crisis in Black America." (1986) *CBS Special Report*, 25 January.

Webb, G. (1999) *Dark Alliance: The CIA, the Contras, and the Crack Cocaine Explosion.* New York: Seven Stories Press.

"Weight-Gain Angle Cited in Slaying." (1992) *Capital Times*, 6 August: 1B.

Younge, G. (2005) "Trial That Split America," *Guardian Weekly*, 14-20 October: 17+.

Zelizer, B. (1993) "Journalists as Interpretive Communities," *Critical Studies in Mass Communication*, 10: 219–37.

Zucchino, D. (1997) *Myth of the Welfare Queen: A Pulitzer-Prize Winning Journalist's Portrait of Women on the Line.* New York: Scribner.

SECTION V

IDENTITIES AND GLOBALIZATIONS

Race is not a form of identity that works in isolation. It intersects with other social-structuring forms of personal identity, such as gender and socioeconomic class and sexual orientation. It gets conflated with national identities and confounded by movements (sometimes voluntary, sometimes forced) of bodies across geopolitical borders. It even gets tangled up with itself, insofar as the dominant culture's primary narrative about how race works (e.g., as a biological, genetic phenomenon) fails to match up very well with actual biological behavior (insofar as people of "different" races can—and frequently do—produce babies together). This section of the book addresses a variety of ways that all of these sorts of intersections of identity pose particular challenges to our understanding of race and media.

Essentialism is an oft-used rhetorical and analytical strategy when it comes to identity politics, and it is invoked with comparable frequency and fervor by people on both the dominant and marginalized sides of these struggles. At its core, this approach to racial identity assumes that there is some natural and inevitable fit between particular racial groups and particular sets of traits and/or beliefs (e.g., that Chicanos will "naturally" favor Democratic politicians over Republicans). Stuart Hall's essay offers a powerful and detailed critique of such essentialist models of identity, in which he argues that any antiracist movement that hopes to be successful needs to conceive of the relationship between racial identity and politics in a far more nuanced and contextualized fashion than essentialism allows.

Carol Stabile's examination of the broadcast blacklists of the 1950s points to ways that the anticommunist witch hunts of the McCarthy era frequently served as powerful tools for stifling many other forms of social and political activism. Stabile's research draws attention to the fact that the first successfully excommunicated targets of the television blacklist were two women whose primary "sins" against the political norms of the moment involved their active roles, not in any obvious communist or socialist organizations, but in the civil rights movement.

Patricia Williams's essay examines the ways that dominant public discourse, mediated and otherwise, often masks its efforts to protect white power and privilege by pitting other forms of identity politics against those related to race. As this particular "game" is played in the United States, socioeconomic class and/or gender are commonly invoked as a way to avoid overt discussions of race while still presenting a (thinly) coded attack on racial "Others." The spectre of the "welfare queen," for instance, appears to be a race-neutral epithet, yet the dominant images of this common media trope are invariably people of color.

Gloria Anzaldúa offers us an important lesson about the ways that linguistic differences—whether between a national language and a putatively "foreign" tongue, or between the dominant and marginalized dialects of a single language—often serve as problematic litmus tests for situating people in their "proper" places in the racial formation. She notes as well that a comparable set of hierarchical sorting takes place with respect to cultural tastes, in which "ethnic" movies and music (for instance) are often denigrated (even by people who belong to the ethnic group in question) as less worthy or valuable than the mainstream media texts that emanate from the national centers of cultural power.

Sarah Sharma's essay offers important insights into how "brownness" has become a newly recognizable, heavily policed form of racialized identity. More specifically, Sharma examines the moral panic around "brown" taxi drivers in major metropolitan areas in the aftermath of the 9/11 attacks, where "brown" is a loose label that reflects the indiscriminate ways that the dominant culture perceives a broad swath of dark-skinned, putatively Muslim, ethnic populations as a singular, cohesive danger. In the eyes of the newly securitized state, and in the context of the "war on terror," to be mobile and "brown" is to present a serious threat to the dominant (read: white) culture's control of public space.

Henry Yu's essay examines how Tiger Woods's rise to global stardom as a golf *wunderkind* posed significant challenges to dominant cultural narratives of race. Woods's multiracial heritage made him a potentially powerful and racially flexible icon of multinational marketing (the black man who conquered a white sport, the Thai national hero who could help open the southeast Asian market up for golf, etc.), but also a thorny problem for mainstream media outlets that didn't quite know how to properly frame a celebrity whose racial identity straddled so many of the normative discrete categories.

Adrian Piper's essay offers a more personal meditation on the challenges of inhabiting a racial formation where who and what you understand yourself to be doesn't match up very well (if at all) with who and what the people and institutions around you claim you are. Piper offers no easy answers to the "problem" of her racial identity—largely because she understands (correctly) that the problem here is not her at all: it's the system of racial categorization that excludes and punishes category-straddlers such as herself.

25.
OLD AND NEW IDENTITIES, OLD AND NEW ETHNICITIES
Stuart Hall

In my previous talk, I tried to open out the questions about the local and the global from their somewhat closed, somewhat over-integrated, and somewhat over-systematized formulations. My argument was that we need to think about the processes which are now revealing themselves in terms of the local and the global, in those two spaces, but we also need to think of these as more contradictory formulations than we usually do. Unless we do, I was concerned that we are likely to be disabled in trying to think those ideas politically.

I was therefore attempting—certainly not to close out the questions of power and the questions of appropriation which I think are lodged at the very center of any notion of a shift between the dispositions of the local and the global in the emergence of a cultural politics on a world scale—but rather to conceptualize that within a more open-ended and contingent cultural politics.

At the end of the talk, however, I was obliged to ask if there is a politics, indeed, a counter-politics of the local. If there are new globals and new locals at work, who are the new subjects of this politics of position? What conceivable identities could they appear in? Can identity itself be re-thought and re-lived, in and through difference?

It is this question which is what I want to address here. I have called it "Old and New Identities, Old and New Ethnicities" and what I am going to do first is to return to the question of identity and try to look at some of the ways in which we are beginning to

re-conceptualize that within contemporary theoretical discourses. I shall then go back from that theoretical consideration to the ground of a cultural politics. Theory is always a detour on the way to something more important.

I return to the question of identity because the question of identity has returned to us; at any rate, it has returned to us in British politics and British cultural politics today. It has not returned in the same old place; it is not the traditional conception of identity. It is not going back to the old identity politics of the 1960s social movements. But it is, nevertheless, a kind of return to some of the ground which we used to think in that way. I will make a comment at the very end about what is the nature of this theoretical-political work which seems to lose things on the one side and then recover them in a different way from another side, and then have to think them out all over again just as soon as they get rid of them. What is this never-ending theoretical work which is constantly losing and regaining concepts? I talk about identity here as a point at which, on the one hand, a whole set of new theoretical discourses intersect and where, on the other, a whole new set of cultural practices emerge. I want to begin by trying, very briefly, to map some of those points of intersection theoretically, and then to look at some of their political consequences.

The old logics of identity are ones with which we are extremely familiar, either philosophically, or psychologically. Philosophically, the old logic of identity which many people have critiqued in the form of the old Cartesian subject was often thought in terms of the origin of being itself, the ground of action. Identity is the ground of action. And we have in more recent times a psychological discourse of the self which is very similar: a notion of the continuous, self-sufficient, developmental, unfolding, inner dialectic of selfhood. We are never quite there, but always on our way to it, and when we get there, we will at last know exactly who it is we are.

Now this logic of identity is very important in a whole range of political, theoretical and conceptual discourses. I am interested in it also as a kind of existential reality because I think the logic of the language of identity is extremely important to our own self-conceptions. It contains the notion of the true self, some real self inside there, hiding inside the husks of all the false selves that we present to the rest of the world. It is a kind of guarantee of authenticity. Not until we get really inside and hear what the true self has to say do we know what we are "really saying."

There is something guaranteed about that logic or discourse of identity. It gives us a sense of depth, out there, and in here. It is spatially organized. Much of our discourse of the inside and the outside, of the self and other, of the individual and society, of the subject and the object, are grounded in that particular logic of identity. And it helps us, I would say, to sleep well at night.

Increasingly, I think one of the main functions of concepts is that they give us a good night's rest. Because what they tell us is that there is a kind of stable, only very slowly-changing ground inside the hectic upsets, discontinuities and ruptures of history. Around us history is constantly breaking in unpredictable ways but we, somehow, go on being the same.

That logic of identity is, for good or ill, finished. It's at an end for a whole range of reasons. It's at an end in the first instance because of some of the great decenterings of modern thought. One could discuss this very elaborately—I could spend the rest of the time talking about it but I just want to slot the ideas into place very quickly by using some names as reference points.

It is not possible to hold to that logic of identity after Marx because although Marx does talk about man (he doesn't talk about women making history but perhaps they were slotted in, as the nineteenth century so often slotted women in under some other masculine title), about men and women making history but under conditions which are not of their own choosing. And having lodged either the individual or collective subject always within historical practices, we as individuals or as groups cannot be, and can never have been, the sole origin or authors of those practices. That is a profound historical decentering in terms of social practice.

If that was not strong enough, knocking us sideways as it were, Freud came knocking from underneath, like Hamlet's ghost, and said, "While you're being decentered from left to right like that, let me decenter you from below a bit, and remind you that this stable language of identity is also set from the psychic life about which you don't know very much, and can't know very much. And which you can't know very much by simply taking thought about it: the great continent of the unconscious which speaks most clearly when it's slipping rather than when it's saying what it means." This makes the self begin to seem a pretty fragile thing.

Now, buffeted on one side by Marx and upset from below by Freud, just as it opens its mouth to say, "Well, at least I speak so therefore I must *be* something," Saussure and linguistics comes along and says, "That's not true either, you know. Language was there before you. You can only say something by positioning yourself in the discourse. The tale tells the teller, the myth tells the myth-maker, etc. The enunciation is always from some subject who is positioned by and in discourse." That upsets that. Philosophically, one comes to the end of any kind of notion of a perfect transparent continuity between our language and something out there which can be called the real, or the truth, without any quotation marks.

These various upsets, these disturbances in the continuity of the notion of the subject, and the stability of identity, are indeed, what modernity is like. It is not, incidentally, modernity itself. That has an older, and longer history. But this is the beginning of modernity as trouble. Not modernity as enlightenment and progress, but modernity as a problem.

It is also upset by other enormous historical transformations which do not have, and cannot be given, a single name, but without which the story could not be told. In addition to the three or four that I have quoted, we could mention the relativisation of the Western narrative itself, the Western episteme, by the rise of other cultures to prominence, and fifthly, the displacement of the masculine gaze.

Now, the question of trying to come to terms with the notion of identity in the wake of those theoretical decenterings is an extremely problematic enterprise. But that is not all that has been disturbing the settled logic of identity. Because as I was saying earlier when I was talking about the relative decline, or erosion, the instability of the nation-state, of the self-sufficiency of national economies and consequently, of national identities as points of reference, there has simultaneously been a fragmentation and erosion of collective social identity.

I mean here the great collective social identities which we thought of as large-scale, all-encompassing, homogenous, as unified collective identities, which could be spoken about almost as if they were singular actors in their own right but which, indeed, placed, positioned, stabilized, and allowed us to understand and read, almost as a code, the imperatives of the individual self: the great collective social identities of class, of race, of nation, of gender, and of the West.

These collective social identities were formed in, and stabilized by, the huge, long-range historical processes which have produced the modern world, just as the theories and conceptualizations that I just referred to very briefly are what constituted modernity as a form of self-reflection. They were staged and stabilized by industrialization, by capitalism, by urbanization, by the formation of the world market, by the social and the sexual division of labor, by the great punctuation of civil and social life into the public and the private; by the dominance of the nation state, and by the identification between Westernization and the notion of modernity itself.

I spoke in my previous talk about the importance, to any sense of where we are placed in the world, of the national economy, the nation-state and of national cultural identities. Let me say a word here about the great class identities which have stabilized so much of our understanding of the immediate and not-so-immediate past.

Class was the main locator of social position, that which organized our understanding of the main grid and group relations between social groups. They linked us to material life through the economy itself. They provided the code through which we read one another. They provided the codes through which we understood each other's languages. They provided, of course, the notions of collective action itself, that which would unlock politics. Now as I tried to say previously, the great collective social identities rise and fall and it is almost as difficult to know whether they are more dangerous when they are falling than when they are rising.

These great collective social identities have not disappeared. Their purchase and efficacy in the real world that we all occupy is ever present. But the fact is that none of them is, any longer, in either the social, historical or epistemological place where they were in our conceptualizations of the world in the recent past. They cannot any longer be thought in the same homogenous form. We are as attentive to their inner differences, their inner contradictions, their segmentations and their fragmentations as we are to their already-completed homogeneity, their unity and so on.

They are not already-produced stabilities and totalities in the world. They do not operate like totalities. If they have a relationship to our identities, cultural and individual, they do not any longer have that suturing, structuring, or stabilizing force, so that we can know what we are simply by adding up the sum of our positions in relation to them. They do not give us the code of identity as I think they did in the past.

It is a moot point by anybody who takes this argument directly on the pulses, as to whether they ever functioned in that way. Perhaps they never functioned in that way. This may be, indeed, what the narrative of the West is like: the notion that we told of the story we told ourselves, about their functioning in that way. We know that the great homogenous function of the collective social class is extremely difficult for any good historian to actually lay his or her finger on. It keeps disappearing just over the horizon, like the organic community.

You know the story about the organic community? The organic community was just always in the childhood you have left behind. Raymond Williams has a wonderful essay on these people, a range of social critics who say you can measure the present in relation to the past, and you know the past because back then it was much more organic and integrated. When was "back then"? Well, when I was a child, there was always some adult saying, "When I was a child, it was much more integrated." And so, eventually, some of these great collectivities are rather like those people who have an activity of historical nostalgia going on in their retrospective reconstructions. We always reconstructed them more essentially, more homogenously, more unified, less contradictorily than they ever were, once you actually know anything about them.

That is one argument. Whatever the past was like, they may have all marched forth, unified and dictating history forward, for many decades in the past. They sure aren't doing it now.

Now as I have said, the question of how to begin to think questions of identity, either social or individual, not in the wake of their disappearance but in the wake of their erosion, of their fading, of their not having the kind of purchase and comprehensive explanatory power they had before, that is what it seems to me has gone. They used to be thought of—and it is a wonderfully gendered definition—as "master concepts," the "master concepts" of class.

It is not tolerable any longer to have a "master concept" like that. Once it loses its "master" status its explanatory reach weakens, becomes more problematic. We can think of some things in relation to questions of class, though always recognizing its real historical complexity. Yet there are certain other things it simply will not, or cannot, decipher or explain. And this brings us face to face with the increasing social diversity and plurality, the technologies of the self which characterize the modern world in which we live.

Well, we might say, where does this leave any discourse on social identity at all? Haven't I now abolished it from about as many sides as I could think of? As has been true in theoretical work over the last twenty years, the moment a concept disappears

through the left hand door, it returns through the right hand window, but not in quite the same place. There is a wonderful moment in Althusser's text where he says, "I can now abolish the notion of ideas." And he actually writes the word "ideas" and draws a line through it to convince himself we need never use the word again.

In exactly the same way, the old discourse of the subject was abolished, put in a deep container, concrete poured over it, with a half-life of a million years. We will never look at it again, when, bloody hell, in about five minutes, we are talking about subjectivity, and the subject in discourse, and it has come roaring back in. So it is not, I think, surprising that, having lost one sense of identity, we find we need it. Where are we to find it?

One of the places that we have to go to is certainly in the contemporary languages which have rediscovered but repositioned the notion of the subject, of subjectivity. That is, principally, and preeminently, the languages of feminism and of psychoanalysis.

I do not want to go through that argument but I want to say something about how one might begin to think questions of identity from this new set of theoretical spaces. And I have to do this programmatically. I have to state what I think, from this position, identity is and is not as a sort of protocol, although each one could take me a very long time.

It makes us aware that identities are never completed, never finished; that they are always as subjectivity itself is, in process. That itself is a pretty difficult task. Though we have always known it a little bit, we have always thought about ourselves as getting more like ourselves every day. But that is a sort of Hegelian notion, of going forward to meet that which we always were. I want to open that process up considerably. Identity is always in the process of formation.

Secondly, identity means, or connotes, the process of identification, of saying that this here is the same as that, or we are the same together, in this respect. But something we have learnt from the whole discussion of identification, in feminism and psychoanalysis, is the degree to which that structure of identification is always constructed through ambivalence. Always constructed through splitting. Splitting between that which one is, and that which is the other.

The attempt to expel the other to the other side of the universe is always compounded by the relationships of love and desire. This is a different language from the language of, as it were, the Others who are completely different from oneself.

This is the Other that belongs inside one. This is the Other that one can only know from the place from which one stands. This is the self as it is inscribed in the gaze of the Other. And this notion which breaks down the boundaries, between outside and inside, between those who belong and those who do not, between those whose histories have been written and those whose histories they have depended on but whose histories cannot be spoken. That the unspoken silence in-between that which can be spoken is the only way to reach for the whole history. There is no other history except to take the absences and the silences along with what can be spoken. Everything that can be spoken is on the ground of the enormous voices that have not, or cannot yet be heard.

This doubleness of discourse, this necessity of the Other to the self, this inscription of identity in the look of the other finds its articulation profoundly in the ranges of a given text. And I want to cite one which I am sure you know but won't remember necessarily, though it is a wonderful, majestic moment in Fanon's *Black Skin, White Masks,* when he describes himself as a young Antillean, face to face with the white Parisian child and her mother. And the child pulls the hand of the mother and says, "Look, Mama, a black man." And he said, "For the first time, I knew who I was. For the first time, I felt as if I had been simultaneously exploded in the gaze, in the violent gaze of the other, and at the same time, recomposed as another."

The notion that identity in that sense could be told as two histories, one over here, one over there, never having spoken to one another, never having anything to do with one another, when translated from the psychoanalytic to the historical terrain, is simply not tenable any longer in an increasingly globalized world. It is just not tenable any longer.

People like me who came to England in the 1950s have been there for centuries; symbolically, we have been there for centuries. I was coming home. I am the sugar at the bottom of the English cup of tea.

I am the sweet tooth, the sugar plantations that rotted generations of English children's teeth. There are thousands of others beside me that are, you know, the cup of tea itself. Because they don't grow it in Lancashire, you know. Not a single tea plantation exists within the United Kingdom. This is the symbolization of English identity—I mean, what does anybody in the world know about an English person except that they can't get through the day without a cup of tea?

Where does it come from? Ceylon—Sri Lanka, India. That is the outside history that is inside the history of the English. There is no English history without that other history. The notion that identity has to do with people that look the same, feel the same, call themselves the same, is nonsense. As a process, as a narrative, as a discourse, it is always told from the position of the Other.

What is more is that identity is always in part a narrative, always in part a kind of representation. It is always within representation. Identity is not something which is formed outside and then we tell stories about it. It is that which is narrated in one's own self. I will say something about that in terms of my own narration of identity in a moment—you know, that wonderful moment where Richard II says, "Come let us sit down and tell stories about the death of kings." Well, I am going to tell you a story and ask you to tell one about yourself.

We have the notion of identity as contradictory, as composed of more than one discourse, as composed always across the silences of the other, as written in and through ambivalence and desire. These are extremely important ways of trying to think an identity which is not a sealed or closed totality.

Now we have within theory some interesting ways of trying to think difference in this way. We have learnt quite a lot about sexual difference in feminist writers. And we have learnt a lot about questions of difference from people like Derrida. I do think that there are some important ways in which Derrida's use of the notion of the difference between "difference" and "differance," spelt with an "a," is significant. The "a," the anomalous "a" in Derrida's spelling of difference, which he uses as a kind of marker that sets up a disturbance in our settled understanding of translation of our concept of difference is very important, because that little "a," disturbing as it is, which you can hardly hear when spoken, sets the word in motion to new meanings yet without obscuring the trace of its other meanings in its past.

His sense of "differance," as one writer has put it, remains suspended between the two French verbs "to differ" and "to defer," both of which contribute to its textual force, neither of which can fully capture its meaning. Language depends on difference, as Saussure has shown: the structure of distinctive propositions which make up its economy. But where Derrida breaks new ground is in the extent to which "differ" shades into "defer."

Now this notion of a differance is not simply a set of binary, reversible oppositions; thinking sexual difference not simply in terms of the fixed opposition of male and female, but of all those anomalous sliding positions ever in process, in between which opens up the continent of sexuality to increasing points of disturbance. That is what the odyssey of difference now means in the sense in which I am trying to use it.

That is about difference, and you might ask the question, where does identity come in to this infinite postponement of meaning that is lodged in Derrida's notion of the trace of something which still retains its roots in one meaning while it is, as it were, moving to another, encapsulating another, with endless shiftings, slidings, of that signifier?

The truth is that Derrida does not help us as much as he might here in thinking about the relationship between identity and difference. And the appropriators of Derrida in America, especially in American philosophical and literary thought, help us even less. By taking Derrida's notion of differance, precisely right out of the tension between the two textual connotations, "defer" and "differ," and lodging it only in the endless play of difference, Derrida's politics is in that very moment uncoupled.

From that moment unrolls that enormous proliferation of extremely sophisticated, playful deconstruction which is a kind of endless academic game. Anybody can do it, and on and on it rolls. No signifier ever stops; no-one is ever responsible for any meaning; all traces are effaced. The moment anything is lodged, it is immediately erased. Everybody has a great time; they go to conferences and do it,

as it were. The very notion of the politics which requires the holding of the tension between that which is both placed and not stitched in place, by the word which is always in motion between positions, which requires us to think both positionality and movement, both together, not one and the other, not playing with difference, or "finding nights to rest under" identity, but living in the tension of identity and difference, is uncoupled.

We have then to go on thinking beyond that mere playfulness into the really hard game which the play of difference actually means to us historically. For if signification depends upon the endless repositioning of its differential terms, meaning in any specific instance depends on the contingent and arbitrary stop, the necessary break. It is a very simple point.

Language is part of an infinite semiosis of meaning. To say anything, I have got to shut up. I have to construct a single sentence. I know that the next sentence will open the infinite semiosis of meaning again, so I will take it back. So each stop is not a natural break. It does not say, "I'm about to end a sentence and that will be the truth." It understands that it is contingent. It is a positioning. It is the cut of ideology which, across the semiosis of language, constitutes meaning. But you have to get into that game or you will never say anything at all.

You think I'm joking. I know graduate students of mine who got into this theoretical fix in the seventies, one enormous French theoretician after another, throwing them aside, until they could not commit a single word to paper at all because to say anything was to open oneself to the endless sliding of the signifier. So if they said, what I think Derrida really, in—really—ooh—start again, yes, start again.

Meaning is in that sense a wager. You take a bet. Not a bet on truth, but a bet on saying something. You have to be positioned somewhere in order to speak. Even if you are positioned in order to unposition yourself, even if you want to take it back, you have to come into language to get out of it. There is no other way. That is the paradox of meaning.

To think it only in terms of difference and not in terms of the relational position between the suturing, the arbitrary, overdetermined cut of language which says something which is instantly opened again to the play of meaning; not to think of meaning always, in supplement, that there is always something left over, always something which goes on escaping the precision; the attempt of language to code, to make precise, to fix, to halt, etc.; not to think it in that way is to lose hold of the two necessary ends of the chain to which the new notion of identity has to be conceptualized.

Now I can turn to questions of politics. In this conception of an identity which has to be thought through difference, is there a general politics of the local to bring to bear against the great, over-riding, powerful, technologically-based, massively-invested unrolling of global processes which I was trying to describe in my previous talk which tend to mop up all differences, and occlude those differences? Which means, as it were, they are different—but it doesn't make any difference that they are different, they're just different.

No, there is no general politics. I have nothing in the kitbag. There is nothing I can pull out. But I have a little local politics to tell you about. It may be that all we have, in bringing the politics of the local to bear against the global, is a lot of little local politics. I do not know if that is true or not. But I would like to spend some time later talking about the cultural politics of the local, and of this new notion of identity. For it is in this new frame that identity has come back into cultural politics in Britain. The formation of the Black diasporas in the period of post-war migration in the fifties and sixties has transformed English social, economic and political life.

In the first generations, the majority of people had the same illusion that I did: that I was about to go back home. That may have been because everybody always asked me: when was I going back home? We did think that we were just going to get back on the boat; we were here for a temporary sojourn. By the seventies, it was perfectly clear that we were not there for a temporary sojourn. Some people were going to stay and then the politics of racism really emerged.

Now one of the main reactions against the politics of racism in Britain was what I would call "Identity Politics One," the first form of identity politics. It had to do with the constitution of some defensive collective identity against the practices of racist

society. It had to do with the fact that people were being blocked out of and refused an identity and identification within the majority nation, having to find some other roots on which to stand. Because people have to find some ground, some place, some position on which to stand. Blocked out of any access to an English or British identity, people had to try to discover who they were. This is the moment I defined in my previous talk. It is the crucial moment of the rediscovery or the search for roots.

In the course of the search for roots, one discovered not only where one came from, one began to speak the language of that which is home in the genuine sense, that other crucial moment which is the recovery of lost histories. The histories that have never been told about ourselves that we could not learn in schools, that were not in any books, and that we had to recover.

This is an enormous act of what I want to call imaginary political re-identification, re-territorialization and re-identification, without which a counter-politics could not have been constructed. I do not know an example of any group or category of the people of the margins, of the locals, who have been able to mobilize themselves, socially, culturally, economically, politically in the last twenty or twenty-five years who have not gone through some such series of moments in order to resist their exclusion, their marginalization. That is how and where the margins begin to speak. The margins begin to contest, the locals begin to come to representation.

The identity which that whole, enormous political space produced in Britain, as it did elsewhere, was the category Black. I want to say something about this category which we all now so take for granted. I will tell you some stories about it.

I was brought up in a lower middle class family in Jamaica. I left there in the early fifties to go and study in England. Until I left, though I suppose 98 per cent of the Jamaican population is either Black or colored in one way or another, I had never ever heard anybody either call themselves, or refer to anybody else as "Black." Never. I heard a thousand other words. My grandmother could differentiate about fifteen different shades between light brown and dark brown. When I left Jamaica, there was a beauty contest in which the different shades of women were graded according to different trees, so that there was Miss Mahogany, Miss Walnut, etc.

People think of Jamaica as a simple society. In fact, it had the most complicated color stratification system in the world. Talk about practical semioticians; anybody in my family could compute and calculate anybody's social status by grading the particular quality of their hair versus the particular quality of the family they came from and which street they lived in, including physiognomy, shading, etc. You could trade off one characteristic against another. Compared with that, the normal class stratification system is absolute child's play.

But the word "Black" was never uttered. Why? No Black people around? Lots of them, thousands and thousands of them. Black is not a question of pigmentation. The Black I'm talking about is a historical category, a political category, a cultural category. In our language, at certain historical moments, we have to use the signifier. We have to create an equivalence between how people look and what their histories are. Their histories are in the past, inscribed in their skins. But it is not because of their skins that they are Black in their heads.

I heard Black for the first time in the wake of the Civil Rights movement, in the wake of the decolonization and nationalistic struggles. Black was created as a political category in a certain historical moment. It was created as a consequence of certain symbolic and ideological struggles. We said, "You have spent five, six, seven hundred years elaborating the symbolism through which Black is a negative factor. Now I don't want another term. I want that term, that negative one, that's the one I want. I want a piece of that action. I want to take it out of the way in which it has been articulated in religious discourse, in ethnographic discourse, in literary discourse, in visual discourse. I want to pluck it out of its articulation and rearticulate it in a new way."

In that very struggle is a change of consciousness, a change of self-recognition, a new process of identification, the emergence into visibility of a new subject. A subject that was always there, but emerging, historically.

You know that story, but I do not know if you know the degree to which that story is true of other parts of the Americas. It happened in Jamaica in the 1970s. In the 1970s, for the first time, Black people recognized themselves as Black. It was the most profound cultural revolution in the Caribbean, much greater than any political revolution they have ever had. That cultural revolution in Jamaica has never been matched by anything as far-reaching as the politics. The politics has never caught up with it.

You probably know the moment when the leaders of both major political parties in Jamaica tried to grab hold of Bob Marley's hand. They were trying to put their hands on Black; Marley stood for Black, and they were trying to get a piece of the action. If only he would look in their direction he would have legitimated them. It was not politics legitimating culture, it was culture legitimating politics.

Indeed, the truth is I call myself all kinds of other things. When I went to England, I wouldn't have called myself an immigrant either, which is what we were all known as. It was not until I went back home in the early 1960s that my mother who, as a good middle-class colored Jamaican woman, hated all Black people, (you know, that is the truth) said to me, "I hope they don't think you're an immigrant over there."

And I said, "Well, I just migrated. I've just emigrated." At that very moment, I thought, that's exactly what I am. I've just left home—for good.

I went back to England and I became what I'd been named. I had been hailed as an immigrant. I had discovered who I was. I started to tell myself the story of my migration.

Then Black erupted and people said, "Well, you're from the Caribbean, in the midst of this, identifying with what's going on, the Black population in England. You're Black."

At that very moment, my son, who was two and a half, was learning the colors. I said to him, transmitting the message at last, "You're Black." And he said, "No. I'm brown." And I said, "Wrong referent. Mistaken concreteness, philosophical mistake. I'm not talking about your paintbox, I'm talking about your head." That is something different. The question of learning, learning to be Black. Learning to come into an identification.

What that moment allows to happen are things which were not there before. It is not that what one then does was hiding away inside as my true self. There wasn't any bit of that true self in there before that identity was learnt. Is that, then, the stable one, is that where we are? Is that where people are?

I will tell you something now about what has happened to that Black identity as a matter of cultural politics in Britain. That notion was extremely important in the anti-racist struggles of the 1970s: the notion that people of diverse societies and cultures would all come to Britain in the fifties and sixties as part of that huge wave of migration from the Caribbean, East Africa, the Asian subcontinent, Pakistan, Bangladesh, from different parts of India, and all identified themselves politically as Black.

What they said was, "We may be different actual color skins but vis-a-vis the social system, vis-a-vis the political system of racism, there is more that unites us than what divides us." People begin to ask, "Are you from Jamaica, are you from Trinidad, are you from Barbados?" You can just see the process of divide and rule. "No. Just address me as I am. I know you can't tell the difference so just call me Black. Try using that. We all look the same, you know. Certainly can't tell the difference. Just call me Black. Black identity." Antiracism in the seventies was only fought and only resisted in the community, in the localities, behind the slogan of a Black politics and the Black experience.

In that moment, the enemy was ethnicity. The enemy had to be what we called "multi-culturalism." Because multi-culturalism was precisely what I called previously "the exotic." The exotica of difference. Nobody would talk about racism but they were perfectly prepared to have "International Evenings," when we would all come and cook our native dishes, sing our own native songs and appear in our own native costume. It is true that some people, some ethnic minorities in Britain, do have indigenous, very beautiful indigenous forms of dress. I didn't. I had to rummage in the dressing-up box to find mine. I have been de-racinated for four hundred years. The last thing I am going to do is to dress up in some native Jamaican costume and appear in the spectacle of multi-culturalism.

Has the moment of the struggle organized around this constructed Black identity gone away? It certainly has not. So long as that society remains in its economic, political, cultural, and social relations in a racist way to the variety of Black and Third World peoples in its midst, and it continues to do so, that struggle remains.

Why then don't I just talk about a collective Black identity replacing the other identities? I can't do that either and I'll tell you why.

The truth is that in relation to certain things, the question of Black, in Britain, also has its silences. It had a certain way of silencing the very specific experiences of Asian people. Because though Asian people could identify, politically, in the struggle against racism, when they came to using their own culture as the resources of resistance, when they wanted to write out of their own experience and reflect on their own position, when they wanted to create, they naturally created within the histories of the languages, the cultural tradition, the positions of people who came from a variety of different historical backgrounds. And just as Black was the cutting edge of a politics vis-a-vis one kind of enemy, it could also, if not understood properly, provide a kind of silencing in relation to another. These are the costs, as well as the strengths, of trying to think of the notion of Black as an essentialism.

What is more, there were not only Asian people of color, but also Black people who did not identify with that collective identity. So that one was aware of the fact that always, as one advanced to meet the enemy, with a solid front, the differences were raging behind. Just shut the doors, and conduct a raging argument to get the troops together, to actually hit the other side.

A third way in which Black was silencing was to silence some of the other dimensions that were positioning individuals and groups in exactly the same way. To operate exclusively through an unreconstructed conception of Black was to reconstitute the authority of Black masculinity over Black women, about which, as I am sure you know, there was also, for a long time, an unbreakable silence about which the most militant Black men would not speak.

To organize across the discourses of Blackness and masculinity, of race and gender, and forget the way in which, at the same moment, Blacks in the underclass were being positioned in class terms, in similar work situations, exposed to the same deprivations of poor jobs and lack of promotion that certain members of the white working class suffered, was to leave out the critical dimension of positioning.

What then does one do with the powerful mobilizing identity of the Black experience and of the Black community? Blackness as a political identity in the light of the understanding of any identity is always complexly composed, always historically constructed. It is never in the same place but always positional. One always has to think about the negative consequences of the positionality. You cannot, as it were, reverse the discourses of any identity simply by turning them upside down. What is it like to live, by attempting to valorise and defeat the marginalization of the variety of Black subjects and to really begin to recover the lost histories of a variety of Black experiences, while at the same time recognizing the end of any essential Black subject?

That is the politics of living identity through difference. It is the politics of recognizing that all of us are composed of multiple social identities, not of one. That we are all complexly constructed through different categories, of different antagonisms, and these may have the effect of locating us socially in multiple positions of marginality and subordination, but which do not yet operate on us in exactly the same way. It is also to recognize that any counter-politics of the local which attempts to organize people through their diversity of identifications has to be a struggle which is conducted positionally. It is the beginning of anti-racism, anti-sexism, and anti-classicism as a war of positions, as the Gramscian notion of the war of position.

The notion of the struggles of the local as a war of positions is a very difficult kind of politics to get one's head around; none of us knows how to conduct it. None of us even knows whether it can be conducted. Some of us have had to say there is no other political game so we must find a way of playing this one.

Why is it difficult? It has no guarantees. Because identifications change and shift, they can be worked on by political and economic forces outside of us and they can be articulated in different ways. There is absolutely no political guarantee already inscribed in an identity. There is no reason on God's earth why the film is good because a Black person made it. There is absolutely no guarantee that all the politics will be right because a woman does it.

There are no political guarantees of that kind. It is not a free-floating open space because history has lodged on it the powerful, tendential organization of a past. We bear the traces of a past, the connections of the past. We cannot conduct this kind of cultural politics without returning to the past but it is never a return of a direct and literal kind. The past is not waiting for us back there to recoup our identities against. It is always retold, rediscovered, reinvented. It has to be narrativized. We go to our own pasts through history, through memory, through desire, not as a literal fact.

It is a very important example. Some work has been done, both in feminist history, in Black history, and in working class history recently, which recover the oral testimonies of people who, for a very long time, from the viewpoint of the canon and the authority of the historian, have not been considered to be history-makers at all. That is a very important moment. But it is not possible to use oral histories and testimonies as if they are just literally the truth. They have also to be read. They are also stories, positionings, narratives. You are bringing new narratives into play but you cannot mistake them for some "real," back there, by which history can be measured.

There is no guarantee of authenticity like that in history. One is ever afterwards in the narrativization of the self and of one's histories. Just as in trying to conduct cultural politics as a war of positions, one is always in the strategy of hegemony. Hegemony is not the same thing as incorporating everybody, of making everybody the same, though nine-tenths of the people who have marginally read Gramsci think that that is what he means. Gramsci uses the notion of hegemony precisely to counteract the notion of incorporation.

Hegemony is not the disappearance or destruction of difference. It is the construction of a collective will through difference. It is the articulation of differences which do not disappear. The subaltern class does not mistake itself for people who were born with silver spoons in their mouths. They know they are still second on the ladder, somewhere near the bottom. People are not cultural dopes. They are not waiting for the moment when, like an overnight conversion, false consciousness will fall from their eyes, the scales will fall away, and they will suddenly discover who they are.

They know something about who they are. If they engage in another project it is because it has interpolated them, hailed them, and established some point of identification with them. It has brought them into the historical project. And that notion of a politics which, as it were, increasingly is able to address people through the multiple identities which they have—understanding that those identities do not remain the same, that they are frequently contradictory, that they cross-cut one another, that they tend to locate us differently at different moments, conducting politics in the light of the contingent, in the face of the contingent—is the only political game that the locals have left at their disposal, in my view.

If they are waiting for a politics of manoeuvre, when all the locals, in every part of the world, will all stand up at the same moment and go in the same direction, and roll back the tide of the global, in one great historical activity, it is not going to happen. I do not believe it anymore; I think it is a dream. In order to conduct the politics really we have to live outside of the dream, to wake up, to grow up, to come into the world of contradiction. We have to come into the world of politics. There is no other space to stand in.

Out of that notion some of the most exciting cultural work is now being done in England. Third generation young Black men and women know they come from the Caribbean, know that they are Black, know that they are British. They want to speak from all three identities. They are not prepared to give up any one of them. They will contest the Thatcherite notion of Englishness, because they say this Englishness is Black. They will contest the notion of Blackness because they want to make a differentiation between people who are Black from one kind of society and people who are Black from another. Because they need to know that difference, that difference that makes a difference in how they write their

poetry, make their films, how they paint. It makes a difference. It is inscribed in their creative work. They need it as a resource. They are all those identities together. They are making astonishing cultural work, the most important work in the visual arts. Some of the most important work in film and photography and nearly all the most important work in popular music is coming from this new recognition of identity that I am speaking about.

Very little of that work is visible elsewhere but some of you have seen, though you may not have recognized, the outer edge of it. Some of you, for example, may have seen a film made by Stephen Freers and Hanif Kureishi, called *My Beautiful Laundrette*. This was originally made as a television film for local distribution only, and shown once at the Edinburgh Festival where it received an enormous reception. If you have seen *My Beautiful Laundrette* you will know that it is the most transgressive text there is. Anybody who is Black, who tries to identify it, runs across the fact that the central characters of this narrative are two gay men. What is more, anyone who wants to separate the identities into their two clearly separate points will discover that one of these Black gay men is white and one of these Black gay men is brown. Both of them are struggling in Thatcher's Britain. One of them has an uncle who is a Pakistani landlord who is throwing Black people out of the window.

This is a text that nobody likes. Everybody hates it. You go to it looking for what are called "positive images" and there are none. There aren't any positive images like that with whom one can, in a simple way, identify. Because as well as the politics—and there is certainly a politics in that and in Kureishi's other film, but it is not a politics which invites easy identification—it has a politics which is grounded on the complexity of identifications which are at work.

I will read you something which Hanif Kureishi said about the question of responding to his critics who said, "Why don't you tell us good stories about ourselves, as well as good/bad stories? Why are your stories mixed about ourselves?" He spoke about the difficult moral position of the writer from an oppressed or persecuted community and the relation of that writing to the rest of the society. He said it is a relatively new one in England but it will arise more and more as British writers with a colonial heritage and from a colonial or marginal past start to declare themselves.

"There is sometimes," he said, "too simple a demand for positive images. Positive images sometimes require cheering fictions—the writer as Public Relations Officer. And I'm glad to say that the more I looked at *My Beautiful Laundrette*, the less positive images I could see. If there is to be a serious attempt to understand present-day Britain with its mix of races and colors, its hysteria and despair, then writing about it has to be complex. It can't apologize, or idealize. It can't sentimentalize. It can't attempt to represent any one group as having the total, exclusive, essential monopoly on virtue.

"A jejune protest or parochial literature, be it black, gay or feminist, is in the long run no more politically effective than works which are merely public relations. What we need now, in this position, at this time, is imaginative writing that gives us a sense of the shifts and the difficulties within our society as a whole. ·

"If contemporary writing which emerges from oppressed groups ignores the central concerns and major conflicts of the larger society, and if these are willing simply to accept themselves as marginal or enclave literatures, they will automatically designate themselves as permanently minor, as a sub-genre. They must not allow themselves now to be rendered invisible and marginalized in this way by stepping outside of the maelstrom of contemporary history."

(Following the lecture, questions were put from the audience.)

I have been asked to say more about why I speak about the politics of the local. I did not talk about other attempts to construct an alternative politics of the global principally because I have been trying to trace through the question of ethnicity; the question of positioning, of placing, which is what the term ethnicity connotes for me in relation to issues of the local and the global. And also, because in many respects, I don't think that those attempts to put together an alternative politics of the global are, at the moment, very successful.

But the second part of the question is the more important one. Why do I only talk about what is local when the questions I seem to be addressing are, of course, very universal, global phenomena?

I do not make that distinction between the local and the global. I think there is always an interpretation of the two. The question is, what are the locations at which struggles might develop? It seems to me that a counter-politics which is pitched precisely and predominantly at the level of confronting the global forces that are trying to remake and recapture the world at the moment, and which are conducted simply at that level, are not making very much headway.

Yet where there does seem the ability to develop counter-movements, resistances, counter-politics, are places that are localized. I do not mean that what they are about are "local" but the places where they emerge as a political scenario are localized because they are separated from one another; they are not easy to connect up or articulate into a larger struggle. So, I use the local and the global as prisms for looking at the same thing. But they have pertinent appearances, points of appearance, scenarios in the different locations.

There is, for instance, ecologically, an attempt to establish a counter-politics of the planet as a single place and that, of course, is important. And if I had taken the question of ecology rather than ethnicity as the prism through which I spoke, the story would have been told very differently. I hinted at that in my first talk when I said that ecological consciousness was constituting the sense of the global, and this is not necessarily entirely in the keeping of the advanced West.

So there is more than one political game being played. This isn't the only game. But if you came at it through the question of where those who have moved into representation, into politics, as it were, through the political movements that have been very powerful and important in the post-war world, and especially in the last twenty years, it is precisely their inability to connect up into one global politics which seems to be their difficulty. But when you try to find whether they are able to resist, to mobilize, to say something different to globalism at a more local level, they seem to have more purchase on the historical present. That's the reason why I concentrated the story from that point of view. But it would be wrong to think that you either work at one or the other, that the two are not constantly interpenetrating each other.

What I tried to say in my first talk was that what we usually call the global, far from being something which, in a systematic fashion, rolls over everything, creating similarity, in fact works through particularity, negotiates particular spaces, particular ethnicities, works through mobilizing particular identities and so on. So there is always a dialectic, a continuous dialectic, between the local and the global.

I tried to identify those collective social identities in relation to certain historical processes. The other ones which have been talked about are very important structurings, such as inside/outside, normal/pathological, etc. But they seem to recur: there are ways in which the other identities are lived. You know if you are inside the class, then you belong. If you are outside, then there is something pathological, not normal or abnormal, or deviant about you.

So I think of those identities somewhat differently. I think of those as ways of categorizing who is inside and who is outside in any of the other social identities. I was trying to identify, historically, some of the major ones that I think exist. If you say who you are you could say where you came from; broadly speaking, what race you belong to, a nation state of which you are a citizen or subject; you have a class position, an established and relatively secure gender position. You knew where you fitted in the world. That is what I meant, whereas most of us now live with a sense of a much greater plurality, a sense of the unfinished character of each of those. It is not that they have disappeared but they do not stitch us in place, locate us, in the way they did in the past.

Regarding a second question, as to what shifted on us: it was politics. What shifted was our attempt to understand why the scenario of the revolutionary class subject never appeared. What happened to it?

There were a few moments when it appeared. When were those? When you go back historically and look at those moments, they were not on stage as they ought to have been either. 1917 is not the subject of the unitary, already-identified Russian working class, making the future. It was not that! The Chinese Revolution is not that either. Nor is the seventeenth century, the history of the already formed bourgeoisie taking the stage. Actually, they do not take the political stage for another 200 years.

So if it is a bourgeois revolution in a larger sense, it cannot be specified in terms of actual historical actors. So, we had a way of living with that for a very long time. It is coming. Of course, it is more complex than that but the basic grid is still ok.

But then, one asks oneself, what politics flows from thinking it never really happened like that, but one day it will? After a time, if you are really trying to be politically active, in that setting you have to say to yourself: that may be the wrong question. It may be that I am not actually doing something now because I think that something in the works, some God in the machine, some law of history which I do not understand, is going to make it all right.

It is hard to describe this moment. It is a moment like waking up. You suddenly realize you are relying on history to do what you cannot do for yourself. You make a bungle of politics but "History," with a capital "H," is going to fly out of somebody's mouth at five minutes to midnight and make it all right. Or "the Economy" is going to march on the stage and say, "You have got it all wrong, you know. You ought to be over there: you are in the proletariat. You ought to be thinking that." Sort us all out, you know. And we are waiting for that moment; waiting, waiting, waiting 200 years for it.

Maybe you are waiting for the wrong thing. Not that the insights of that story, that theory, that narrative were wrong; I am not trying to throw that over. I am trying to throw over the moment of the political guarantee that is lodged in that, because then you do not conduct politics contingently; you do not conduct it positionally. You think someone has prepared the positions for you.

This is a very practical issue. You go into the miners' strike, which the British went into in the early eighties, the only major industrial showdown with the Thatcher government, on the assumption that the industrial working class was unified behind you when it was not. And you did not conduct a politics which had the remotest chance of unifying it because you assumed it was already unified.

If you said it seven times, it would be unified. So the miners' leader said it seven times. "The might of the unified industrial working class is now in a head-to-head with Thatcher." It was not. It was the wrong politics. Not the wrong struggle, but the wrong politics, conducted in the wrong way, in the light of some hope that history was going to rescue this simpler story out of the more complex one.

If you lose enough battles that way, you just do not play that game anymore. You have to play it differently. You have to try and make some politics out of people who insist on remaining different. You are waiting for them all to be the same. Before you get them inside the same political movement you will be here till doomsday.

You have to make them out of the folks in this room, not out of something else called socialism or whatever it is. We made history out of figments. Suddenly you see that it is a kind of way of sleeping at night: "I made a botch of that. I lost that one." You know, the way the left constantly told itself that all its losses were victories. You know, I just won that although I lost it. Heroically, I lost it.

Just let us win one. Leave the heroism out of it. And just win a few. The next time I will be in a little bit ahead. Not two steps behind but feeling good in myself. That is a moment I am trying to describe existentially. It did not happen like that. It happened in a complicated set of ways. But you realize at a certain moment, you go through a kind of transparent barrier that has kept you in a place, from doing and thinking seriously, what you should have been thinking about. That is what it is like.

Question: Could you then say something about winning one? Could you say something about what prospect you see for rebuilding another politics, other than the one Arthur Scargill headed in the miners' struggle? And what prospect that has for breaking down that exclusivist, solidified, ego-identified consciousness?

SH: The prospects for that are not very good because the left is still stuffed with the old notion of identity, which is why I am thinking about it. It is still waiting for the old identities to return to the stage. It does not recognize that it is in a different political game which

is required to articulate, precisely, differences that cannot be encapsulated any longer and represented in that unified body. So, we do not know whether we can shift enough of that old thinking to begin to ask the question. What would a politics like that be like?

We know a little bit about it. I do think, without being romantic about it, that the period of the GLC (Greater London Council) in London was very prefigurative, but that it cannot be repeated elsewhere. It was the bringing together of groups and movements which remained the same, and yet retained their differences. Nobody who came into the GLC said, "I will forget I am an activist black group because I am now in the same room as a feminist group." What you heard there was the very opposite of what we now usually think of as the conversation of a collective political subject coming into existence.

We think of a nice, polite, consensual discussion; everybody agreeing. What you heard there was what democracy is really like: an absolutely, bloody-unending row. People hammering the table, insisting, "Do not ask me to line up behind your banner, because that just means forgetting who I am." That row, that sound of people actually negotiating their differences in the open, behind the collective program, is the sound I am waiting for.

I think it did something; it opened some possibilities. It showed that it was possible. It had exactly what politics always has, which is the test, that differences do not remain the same as a result of the articulation.

One group has to take on the agenda of the other. It has to transform itself in the course of coming into alliance, or some kind of formation with another. It has to learn something of the otherness which created the other constituency. It doesn't mistake itself that it becomes it but it has to take it on board. It has to struggle with it to establish some set of priorities.

That is the sound that one is waiting for but on the whole, that is not the sound one is hearing in the politics opposed to Thatcherism. One is hearing, "Let us go back to the old constituencies. Line up behind us. The old parties will come again." I do not believe it. I think Thatcherism is more deep-seated than that; it is actually shaking the ground from underneath the possibility of a return to that old form of politics. So if you ask me what the possibilities are, then the first stage of it is in our own ranks. It is quarrelling among ourselves about which direction to go before one begins to open that out.

But I do think that there are possibilities in that. I think the reason why, in spite of the fact that the GLC was never below 60–65 percent in the popularity ratings, Thatcherism nevertheless destroyed it, was because it understood its prefigurative role. It understood that if it could persist, and make some changes to the lives of a variety of different constituencies in that city, other peoples would begin to say, "Here is a different kind of model. Here is a different way to go." What would that mean on a more national scale? What would that mean in another part of the country where the constituencies are different?

I think Thatcherism understood that and it blew the GLC out of the water. It destroyed it by legislative fiat. That tells you how important they knew it actually was. Thatcherism's popularity and hegemonic reach precisely arises from the fact that it articulates differences. The numbers of people who are 100 percent with the project on all fronts are very small indeed. What Thatcherism is fantastic at is the skill of mobilizing the different minorities and playing one minority against another. It is in the game of articulating differences. It always tries to condense them within something it calls "the Thatcherite subject" but there is no such thing. That is a political representation. It is the condensation of a variety of different identities. It plays on difference, and through difference, all the time. It tries to represent that difference as the same. But do not be mistaken about it. I do not think that is so.

Conducting the counter-hegemonic politics which I have been trying to describe does not carry any guarantees that it will win. All that I am saying is that there is a difference between the politics of positionality I have been outlining and some unitary politics which is successful, which is Thatcherism. That is not the difference. The difference is between two politics of positionality; one well-conducted and one which is conducted very half-heartedly, and which is, indeed, not being conducted at all.

Thatcherism is hegemonic because it is able to address the identities of a variety of people who have never been in the same political camp before.

It does that in a very complex way by always attending, through its political, social, moral and economic program, to the cultural and ideological questions. Always mobilizing that which it represents as already there. It says "the majority of English people." "The majority of the British people."

It does not have yet a majority. It is summoning up the majority and telling you that it is already a majority. And in the majority are a variety of people, people from different classes, people from different genders, people from different occupations, people from different parts of the country. That's what the Thatcherite majority is.

Next time round it will not be exactly the same. It cannot reproduce itself. It is not the essential class subject. That is not the politics of Thatcherism. Indeed, far from it; my own view is that no-one understands Gramsci better than Mrs. Thatcher. She has never read it but she does know that politics nowadays is conducted through the articulation of different instances. She knows that politics is conducted on different fronts. You have to have a variety of programs, that you are always trying to build a collective will because no socio-economic position will simply give it to you.

Those things she knows. We read Gramsci till the cows come home and we do not know how to do it. She cannot get a little bit of it off the ground. It is called "instinctive Gramsci-ism." "Instinctive Gramsci-ism" is what is beating us, not the old collective class subject.

Question: This idea of multiple identities, which you represented in some kind of "pie-chart." You gave an example of people who are Caribbean, British and Black. Is there five or ten percent or something which can be called "Humanity?"

SH: I do not think that there is. I think that what we call "the global" is always composed of varieties of articulated particularities. I think the global is the self-presentation of the dominant particular. It is a way in which the dominant particular localizes and naturalizes itself and associates with it a variety of other minorities.

What I think it is dangerous to do is to identify the global with that sort of lowest common denominator stake which we all have in being human. In that sense, I am not a humanist. I do not think we can mobilize people simply through their common humanity. It may be that that day will come but I do not think we are there yet. Both the sources of the powerful, and the sources of the powerless, we both, always, go towards those universal moments through locating ourselves through some particularity. So I think of the global as something having more to do with the hegemonic sweep at which a certain configuration of local particularities try to dominate the whole scene, to mobilize the technology and to incorporate, in subaltern positions, a variety of more localized identities to construct the next historical project.

I am deliberately using Gramscian terms—construct the hegemonic project, the historical project, in which is lodged a variety of differences but which are all committed either in a dominant, or a subaltern position, to a single historical project, which is the project of globalization, of the kind I think you are talking about.

That is what is "universal." I think universal is always in quotation marks. It is the universalizing aspect, the universalizing project, the universalizing hope to be universal. It is like Mrs. Thatcher's "All the British people." It is a way of trying to say everybody is now inside this particular form of globalization. And at that very moment, there I am. I remain Marxist. At that very moment, whenever the discourse

declares itself to be closed is the moment when you know it is contradictory. You know, when it says, "Everything is inside my knapsack. I have just got hold of all of you. I have a bit of all of you now. You are inside the bag. Can I close it?" No.

Something is just about to open that out and present a problem. Hegemony, in that sense, is never completed. It is always trying to enclose more differences within itself. Not within itself. It doesn't want the differences to look exactly like it. But it wants the projects of its individual and smaller identities to be only possible if the larger one becomes possible. That is how Thatcherism locates smaller identities within itself. You want to have the traditional family? You cannot do it for yourself because it depends on larger political and economic things. If you want to do that, you must come inside my larger project. You must identify yourself with the larger things inside my project. That is how you become part of history. You become a little cog in the larger part of history.

Now that is a different game from saying, "I want everybody to be exactly a replica of me." It is a more complicated game. But there is a moment when it always declares itself to be universal and closed, and that is the moment of naturalization. That's the moment when it wants its boundaries to be coterminous with the truth, with the reality of history. And that is always the moment which, I think, escapes it. That's my hope. Something had better be escaping it.

26.
THE TYPHOID MARYS OF THE LEFT
Gender, Race, and the Broadcast Blacklist
Carol Stabile

The "colonists" need not be party members or even deliberate cooperators. It is sufficient if they advance Communist objectives with complete unconsciousness.[1]

In June 1950, an organization calling itself American Business Consultants self-published *Red Channels: The Report of Communist Influence in Radio and Television*, a slender volume that would become known as the bible of the broadcast blacklist. In New York City, the center of broadcast production, the publication of this volume received little attention, overshadowed as it was by the onset of the Korean War less than a week later. In the muggy weeks that followed, anti-communist activists including Heather McCullough (whose previous efforts had prevented musician Larry Adler and dancer Paul Draper from taking the stage in Greenwich, Connecticut because of their alleged Red connections) and government institutions like the FBI began to quietly lay the groundwork for the purge of progressives from broadcasting that would ensue.[2]

Scholarly accounts of gender, race, and television in the 1950s have mainly focused on the ideological content of programming that ultimately made it onto the air.[3] This research has played an important role in reckoning with the political and cultural legacies of 1950s television. But the focus on ideology and content has prevented us from fully understanding the repressive nature of anti-communist thought and action, both in terms of the powerful ways in which the broadcast blacklist made the production

of progressive themes and images impossible, and in terms of how the fear that followed from the blacklist repressed the memory that such alternatives had ever existed. Counter to the images of white suburban women we have inherited from the 1950s, the first two casualties of the broadcast blacklist were professional women who were politically active—white actor Jean Muir and African American musician Hazel Scott—and whose involvement in civil rights was considered evidence of their communist sympathies.

This essay builds on earlier research on gender and 1950s television not by analyzing the absence of strong women, people of color, immigrants, and working-class families from the televisual landscape, but by looking at the elimination of the very cultural workers writing, agitating, and fighting to broadcast these representations. By remembering the lives and work of women who, in the words of blacklistee Shirley Graham Du Bois, have been "wiped out of history,"[4] my intention is to provide a supplementary lens for understanding Cold War television content. Such a lens would restore agency to these women and their standpoints, while at the same time understanding the representations of gender and family that came to dominate the prime-time lineup not as the effect of consensus, but as the result of a bitter war over content waged by anti-communists and their allies.

Although it occurred at a formative moment in the history of television, the broadcast blacklist has received little scholarly attention in media studies.[5] The role that gender played in the blacklist has received even less. Indeed, until very recently women working in broadcasting in the first half of the twentieth century have remained dim and shadowy figures—footnotes to a history in which the only agents were white men. Yet as Michele Hilmes has pointed out, women worked in a variety of roles in radio and television in the 1930s and 1940s.[6] Bertha Brainard and Judith Waller worked in production during the early days of broadcasting; writer, producer, director, and actor Gertrude Berg was one of the most influential figures in the history of broadcasting; radio host Mary Margaret McBride enjoyed enormous popularity in the 1930s and 1940s. By 1950, moreover, women like writer and composer Shirley Graham, writer and actor Ruth Gordon, and novelist and screenplay writer Vera Caspary, who were then working in other media industries, began to pursue job opportunities in the new medium of television.

Many of the women working in or gravitating toward broadcasting held progressive and often feminist views about gender, race, and class.[7] As working mothers, for example, neither Gertrude Berg nor Hazel Scott saw anything unnatural in combining careers with raising children. White women like Vera Caspary and Jean Muir fought against racism both professionally and in their personal lives. Ruth Gordon and her husband Garson Kanin shared screenwriting credits for *Adam's Rib* (1949) and *Pat and Mike* (1952), romantic comedies starring Katherine Hepburn and Spencer Tracy that featured women in the kind of strong, non-traditional roles that would disappear after the blacklist.

Telling the stories of those affected by the broadcast blacklist has meant searching for biographical traces that did not appear either on television or in the mainstream press. With the exception of journalist Jack Gould, who wrote for the *New York Times*, newspaper journalists feared criticizing anti-communists, lest they draw attention to themselves. The blacklist, moreover, is one drama that television has refused to turn into a made-for-TV movie, since the picture it paints of the early years of the medium is so deeply disturbing. The black press, in contrast, and particularly the *Chicago Defender*, paid a great deal of attention to the lives and political work of women who would eventually be blacklisted. Vera Caspary wrote articles

for the *Defender* about the Scottsboro boys in the early 1930s; the political activism of both Muir and Scott was documented in its pages; and the novels and life of Shirley Graham Du Bois were a source of great pride for the *Defender*, well before her 1950 marriage to W. E. B. Du Bois. In addition to the black press, FBI files on blacklistees obtained through Freedom of Information Act requests provided insight into levels of government surveillance, as well as anti-communist attitudes toward progressive women and their work.[8] The following material is drawn from these sources, as well as the archived papers of those who suffered from the blacklist. Together, these offer a rich and still untapped repository of ideas and content that would never appear on the air.

The Smear Artists

This is the day for the professional gossip, the organized rumor monger, the smear artist with the spray gun.[9]

Conservative ideologues had some cause to be concerned about the possibility that progressive content might appear on the new medium of television. With its ability to reach large audiences, television had the potential to affect the course of civil rights, especially in the north where criticisms of southern racism would eventually find more receptive eyes and ears. As the images that began to appear on news programs (a form of television content less directly controllable than entertainment) in the 1950s would prove, desegregating the representational spectrum could effectively challenge white supremacist ideologies by publicizing the struggles of those engaged in civil rights activism. As Lynn Spigel has so persuasively shown, the consumption of such images in the home—that romanticized bulwark of anti-communist ideology—made the threat of a red takeover of television even more troubling.[10]

Within a year of its publication, *Red Channels* had become widely known as the bible of the blacklist. Distributed for free to advertisers, sponsors, and network executives, its contents were frequently erroneous (the authors later blamed this on the inaccuracy of public records). The book consisted of an introduction written by Vince Hartnett, a frustrated radio writer and prominent anti-communist, and a list of alphabetized names, which were accompanied by an inventory of Communist and Communist "front" organizations to which the named individuals either belonged or had lent their names. In many cases, the information was at least a decade old; in just as many cases, the evidence was simply a positive reference in the pages of the Communist Party newspaper, the *Daily Worker.* Although few of those listed in *Red Channels* were current members of the Communist Party, nearly all had been involved in either civil rights or immigrants' rights. In the words of FBI director J. Edgar Hoover, many of those listed fell into the category of "fellow travelers," those who "willingly or unwillingly," intentionally or inadvertently, helped "the Communist conspiracy."[11]

Anti-communists were just as concerned with stars as they were with those workers who actually had some control over content. Neither Jean Muir nor Hazel Scott, the first two casualties of the blacklist, were writers or producers who created content. As one contemporary writer put it, "as 'Mother Aldrich' on television or the radio" Jean Muir "would have no opportunity to say anything but the innocuous lines put in that harassed lady's mouth by the program's author."[12] But both women had used the prestige conferred upon them by their modest stardom to advocate for civil rights and thus had been "exploited" by "Red Fascism . . . at pro-Soviet rallies, meetings and conferences."[13] Their public records of civil rights activism caused their names to appear in the lists of progressive cultural workers prepared by anti-communist groups and organizations. That neither woman had an established broadcast following allowed anti-communists to ventriloquize a largely fictitious, outraged audience with impunity, since these stars had not been able to establish a base of fans that might protest their firings. It would be a full year, for instance, before red hunters felt confident enough to go after Philip Loeb, who played Gertrude Berg's husband in the popular sitcom *The Goldbergs*, a program that had received thousands of positive letters from fans over its twenty-year run.

Muir and Scott had another circumstance in common that underscores the specific vulnerability of professional women: both were married to prominent men who had their own troubled relationships to the anti-communist movement. Muir's husband was Henry Jaffe, lead attorney for the American Federation of Radio Artists (AFRA, later the American Federation of Radio and Television Artists), which was at the time fighting its own internal battles with anti-communists, particularly over the imposition of loyalty oaths. Similarly, Scott was married to New York congressman, Baptist minister, and activist Adam Clayton Powell Jr., a civil rights leader and the first African American congressman from New York. Powell was standing for reelection in 1950.

For "the headline-seeking super-patriots"[14] promoting the blacklist, the prominence of Muir and Scott's husbands not only guaranteed more bang for the buck in terms of publicity, but also increased the pressure on these women to concede to the demands of anti-communists that they confess, repent, and name names. The effects of the blacklist on their own careers were devastating, but the secondary effects of the blacklist on husbands and children were potent incentives for cooperation. As Joanna Rapf, daughter of blacklisted screenwriter Maurice Rapf, put it, blacklistees "were men and women of deeply held convictions and remarkable integrity who risked a great deal, including their families' security, to stand up for what they believed was right."[15] For blacklisted women with families, whose careers and aspirations were understood to be secondary to those of their husbands, the pressure to choose between their convictions and their families' security was crushing. Both Muir and Scott had to weigh the potential damage to their careers and families against the damage to their husbands' careers in evaluating their respective defense strategies.

In addition, in a postwar culture in which attitudes toward women were becoming increasingly conservative, Muir and Scott's political activism was understood to be a violation of gender norms. Anti-communist activist and white supremacist Elizabeth Dilling very clearly articulated the equation between women's rights and communism in the 1940s, vehemently asserting that she was not alone in finding "my greatest privilege and happiness in being a wife and mother and in watching over my own children;

most women share this God-given instinct." Dilling and other anti-communists understood "the Communist bait of offering women sex equality with men through free love, state orphanages and collectivized factory kitchens, not as *flattery* but as *robbery*."[16] Understood as devils or dupes (and it scarcely mattered which), professional women who had apparently accepted the "Communist bait . . . of sex equality" directly threatened the social order anti-communists were protecting.

A Controversial Personality

In her later years, Jean Muir claimed that she became an actor entirely by accident. Born Jean Muir Fullarton in Suffern, New York, in 1911, Muir studied French at the Sorbonne in the heady atmosphere of the late 1920s, at a point in time when, according to fellow blacklistee Shirley Graham, everybody was in Paris: "Langston Hughes and Countee Cullen, Alain Locke, Lloyd and Edna Thomas, and young Adam Powell," Hazel Scott's future husband.[17] After returning to the United States in 1930, Muir appeared in a string of Broadway shows, until being discovered by a Warner Brothers scout while starring in *Saint Wench* in 1933. In the years that followed, the tall, willowy Muir made over twenty B pictures for Warner Brothers, playing a string of sassy ingénues in films like *As the Earth Turns* (1934), *Desirable* (1935), *Gentlemen are Born* (1934), *The White Cockatoo* (1935), A *Midsummer Night's Dream* (1935), *The Lone Wolf Meets a Lady* (1940), and *The Constant Nymph* (1943).

Muir's career in film reflects only one dimension of a much more complex life. The story told about Muir at the time she was blacklisted—a story that has shaped subsequent accounts—hewed closely to her star image, as the aging blonde ingénue cast as sitcom mom. Muir's statements to the press after she was fired from *The Aldrich Family* were carefully crafted public relations messages that sought to capitalize on her star image and role as wife and mother, thereby minimizing the threatening nature of her political agency. In her prepared statements, she either did not recall any association with the organizations listed in *Red Channels* or claimed to have resigned from all of them. In her testimony before the House

Un-American Activities Committee (HUAC) in 1953, a despondent and unemployed Muir emphatically denied being a member of the Communist Party, but held firm to her commitment to three reasons for her political activity: she had indeed supported the Spanish Loyalists' fight against fascism; she respected and admired Franklin Delano Roosevelt; and she was unswerving in her commitment to addressing "the overwhelming problem of the colored citizens in our country."[18]

Although anti-communists publicly demonized Jean Muir's political activities as these related to the Communist Party, the fulcrum of Muir's political activities was civil rights.[19] The mainstream press largely overlooked Muir's civil rights work, but the *Chicago Defender*'s accounts of her activities re-orient her story. At first, the black press was skeptical about Muir's involvement in anti-racist politics. In 1941, the *Defender* somewhat derisively reported that "ofay actress Jean Muir, who has recently turned producer, is doing a master show, perennial classic, 'Uncle Tom's Cabin,' in the latter part of November . . . Entirely revised, Miss Muir is on the lookout for her colored cast."[20] But by the 1940s, convinced that her political commitment was legitimate, Langston Hughes wrote glowingly in the *Defender* about Muir's contributions to a National Association for the Advancement of Colored People (NAACP) testimonial for secretary Walter White in 1944 (White was a personal friend who frequently attended dinners at Muir's home). At this event, Muir praised "the fine work Walter White did in Hollywood in educating the movie industry to abandon its old stereotypes of Negro caricature." Muir also told the gathering that moviegoers should write to the studios when they saw a "picture with decent Negro roles in it" as well as when they saw "an abomination . . . like 'Cabin in the Sky,'"[21] ironically advocating for the very consumer protests that anti-communists mobilized to fatally damage her career in 1950.

Like many of those listed in the pages of *Red Channels*, Muir had been most active during World War II, sponsoring a "Salute to Negro Troops" in 1941, part of the Double V campaign being waged against US racism;[22] participating in a panel on "Propagandizing the Negro's Cause" at a conference on "The Status of the Negro in a Fighting Democracy" in 1942;[23] speaking at an NAACP Student Conference in 1943 on the topic of the "Negro and Motion Pictures";[24] and at a rally against "anti-Negro" programs in New York City that same year.[25] At several NAACP events, Muir shared the stage with Eleanor Roosevelt.[26] All of these activities were reported in the pages of the *Defender*, a newspaper that anti-Communist leaders like Elizabeth Dilling (based in Chicago) and J. Edgar Hoover (whose FBI had been monitoring the black press since the 1920s) were reading and cataloguing.

After moving back to New York City in 1937, Muir married attorney Henry Jaffe in 1940. She returned briefly to Hollywood during World War II, but settled permanently in New York at the end of the war, when the demands of her marriage and family made work in radio and television more attractive. Muir had roles in televised anthologies like *Philco Television Playhouse*, *Boris Karloff Presents*, and the *Actor's Studio* in the late 1940s, but her broadcasting break came in 1950, when she was cast to play Henry Aldrich's mother in the televised version of *The Aldrich Family*, a popular radio sitcom about an awkward teen. Muir's casting, announced in *Variety* during the spring of 1950, went uncontested by red hunters.

According to *Red Channels*, Muir was clearly a fellow traveler. Her name appeared in the book with nine listings next to it. Most of the information came from the HUAC's 1949 "Report on Congress of American Women," which patronizingly described the organization as "just another Communist hoax specifically designed to ensnare idealistically minded but politically gullible women."[27] According to *Red Channels*, in addition to supporting the Congress of American Women, Muir had a history of participation in organizations said to be Communist fronts, like the Southern Conference for Human Welfare (a defunct civil rights organization that had struggled to bring New Deal reforms to the South). She had also sponsored *The Negro Quarterly*, according to *Red Channels*, a short-lived publication that included writings by Langston Hughes, Ralph Ellison, Richard Wright, and Herbert Aptheker.

Muir had no warning of the approaching storm until late August 1950, when National Broadcasting Company (NBC) abruptly cancelled the final rehearsal of the sitcom, scheduled the day before the live taping. The next day, General Foods Corporation, the program's sponsor, issued a formal statement to the press, announcing they had fired Jean Muir because she was "'a controversial personality' whose presence on the show might adversely affect the sale of the advertiser's product"[28] and "provoke unfavorable criticism and even antagonism among sizable groups of consumers."[29] In a statement issued to the press, General Foods defended the firing: "One of the fundamental objectives of General Foods advertising is to create a favorable and receptive attitude toward its products among the largest possible number of consumers."[30] NBC and Young & Rubicam, the advertising agency representing General Foods, declined to comment on Muir's firing, but General Foods claimed it was responding to protests by outraged anti-communist consumers, neglecting to mention that they had received a scant twenty phone calls and two telegrams in protest—hardly a mandate, considering the thousands of letters established programs like *The Goldbergs* received from fans of shows soon to be tainted by the shadow of the blacklist.[31]

Unlike the mainstream press, which made no mention of Muir's civil rights work, the *Defender* drew a clear link between blacklisting and civil rights. Muir, was, the *Defender* noted, "among those Hollywood stars who consistently contended for better acting roles for Negroes in the films."[32] As another article put it, "it strikes us as more than coincidental that a large number of the 151 radio and television artists listed happened to be champions of full democracy for all Americans, whatever their race or religion."[33] Among those champions of full democracy was pianist and actor Hazel Scott, whose firing occurred with less fanfare than that of Muir; and whose civil rights activism was less easily obscured.

Guilt by Listing

In and of itself, the casting of former ingénue Muir as the mother in a family sitcom was hardly newsworthy. Anti-communists did not object to the content of *The Aldrich Family* and had no interest in seeing the popular sitcom itself cancelled. In contrast, the very presence of *The Hazel Scott Show* on the struggling DuMont network was guaranteed to offend the white supremacist sensibilities of anti-communist individuals and organizations.[34] For anti-communists like Elizabeth Dilling and J. Edgar Hoover, any form of race mixing was evidence of communist conspiracy. Those engaged in civil rights work were, in both Dilling and Hoover's estimation, inherently un-American insofar as they opposed the natural order anti-communists believed was reflected in segregation and white supremacy. As early as 1920, concerned about what he had been reading in black newspapers and publications, Hoover recommended to his superiors that "something must be done to the editors of these publications as they are beyond doubt exciting the negro elements of this country to riot and to the committing of outrages of *all sorts.*"[35]

Featuring black performers on a new medium aimed at white audiences was a virtual violation of segregation, allowing images of African Americans into previously inviolable white domestic spheres. While anti-communist forces could not openly censor or boycott television news, the color line in entertainment programming was very strictly policed in the early years of television, even in New York City.[36] Progressive variety show hosts (many of them Jewish men) who booked black performers found themselves at the center of conflicts.[37] Although black musicians appeared on television in the late 1940s and 1950s, as they had in the early days of radio, such appearances were occasions for recrimination, hand wringing, and much controversy among networks and sponsors who feared these representations (produced as they were by New York liberals) would alienate Southern viewers. Variety show host Eddie Cantor provoked sponsors first by featuring a young Sammy Davis Jr. on his show and then using his handkerchief to mop Davis' brow. Cantor, whose criticisms of Hitler and fascism in the 1930s had caused numerous sponsors to drop him from their programs, boldly responded to the racist outcry on the part of sponsors by booking Davis for the remainder of the season.[38] Milton Berle clashed with Texaco when it tried to prevent him from booking the Four Step Brothers, refusing to go on stage himself unless they were allowed to perform. Network executives, advertisers, and sponsors alike justified this censorship by arguing that the very presence of black performers would cause "controversy," a code word for potential boycotts that might jeopardize the sale of sponsors' products.[39]

At a point in time when variety shows were being censured for featuring African American men as guests, *The Hazel Scott Show* not only had the temerity to feature a black woman, but the black woman in question starred in her own show. Scott's variety show made history: it was the first television show to star an African American (Nat King Cole's equally short-lived variety show did not appear until 1956). The program premiered on July 2, 1950 to critical acclaim. *Variety* noted that "Hazel Scott has a neat little show in this modest package," its "most engaging element" being Scott herself.[40] The 15-minute variety show was very quietly cancelled just a few months later, on September 29, a little over a week after Scott had appeared voluntarily before the HUAC. Although largely forgotten today, the significance of this variety show would not have been lost on anti-communists in the early 1950s.

Born in Trinidad in 1920, Hazel Scott's parents—her father was a well-known scholar and her mother a musician—immigrated to New York City in 1924, settling in Harlem. A talented, Juilliard-educated musician and performer, whose performances combined classical music and jazz in a style described as "Bach-to-boogie," Scott was a fixture at Barney Josephson's wryly named Café Society, the first integrated nightclub in the United States, where she was mentored by Jazz greats Billie Holiday and Mary Lou Williams. At Café Society, Scott rubbed elbows with others who would become prominent anti-communist targets: Paul Draper, Lena Horne, Langston Hughes, Canada Lee, Paul Robeson, Zero Mostel, and Eleanor Roosevelt, among others. Scott also performed on Broadway, in the musical revue *Sing Out the News* in 1938 (which also featured future blacklistees Will Geer and Philip Loeb) and in the vaudevillian revival *Priorities of 1942* (co-starring Paul Draper).

Having watched as talented African American performers like Louis Armstrong, Hattie McDaniel, Butterfly McQueen, and Bill Robinson were cast in humiliating roles in Hollywood films, Scott resisted the gravitational pull of Hollywood. "From *Birth of* a Nation," she wrote, "to *Gone With the Wind*, from *Tennessee Johnson*'s to *My Old Kentucky Home*; from my beloved friend Bill Robinson to Butterfly Mc-Queen; from bad to worse and from degradation to dishonor—so went the story of the Black American in Hollywood."[41] Refusing to play the stereotypical roles to which black women were consigned in the motion picture industry, Scott turned down the first four roles offered to her—all of which cast her as a "singing maid."[42] When she did make the move to Hollywood, Scott wrote a set of demands intended to prevent such racist stereotyping into her film contracts. In the first place, she wanted final-cut privileges when it came to her musical numbers. She also demanded control over her wardrobe, which included the right to wear her own clothing if she deemed the studio's wardrobe unacceptable. Her break with Columbia Pictures' Harry Cohn, in fact, involved "a costume which she felt stereotyped blacks."[43]

As further protection against racist stereotyping, Scott also insisted that she appear in films under her own name and not as a character written and controlled by someone else: "as herself, seated at the piano just as she would be in a nightclub."[44] Scott exercised similar control over her live performances. When she toured, Scott had a clause in her contract advising that she would not perform in segregated venues. In 1948, upon taking the stage and discovering that black and white patrons were seated in separate areas, she refused to perform and was escorted from the city of Austin by Texas Rangers. "Why would anyone come to hear me, a Negro," she told *Time* Magazine, "and refuse to sit beside someone just like me?"[45] After being told by a waitress in a restaurant near Spokane, Washington, that she and "a companion, Mrs. Eunice Wolf" would not be served "because they were Negroes," Scott brought a successful suit against the restaurant in 1950.[46] According to historian Dwayne Mack, Scott's victory helped African Americans challenge racial discrimination in Spokane, as well as inspiring civil rights organizations "to pressure the Washington state legislature to enact the Public Accommodations Act" in 1953.[47]

An African American woman, an immigrant herself, the wife of the first black congressman from New York, and an outspoken critic of white supremacy,

Scott was an obvious target for anti-communists. Her groundbreaking lawsuit was evidence of the challenge she posed to the racial status quo that red hunters were protecting under the guise of fighting the red menace. Accustomed to speaking her mind and with no knowledge of the extent and influence of the anti-red networks arrayed against her, Scott decided to challenge her blacklisting by appealing directly to the HUAC in September 1950.

Petitioning the State

> Turning on Communism is not to become an "informer" in any evil sense. It is, rather, alerting one's self and one's neighbor to hideous despoilers of human dignity. Hatred of communism is like hatred of sin and error: a moral obligation.[48]

Muir and Scott fought against their respective blacklistings by following advice dispensed by professional blacklisters like Vince Hartnett and the authors of *Red Channels*.[49] *The Road Back*, a pamphlet published by AWARE, Inc., a blacklisting organization founded by Vince Hartnett (author of the introduction to *Red Channels*), provided a twelve-step program for those in "entertainment-communications" who wished to rehabilitate themselves after being blacklisted. *The Road Back* made it clear that only the most ardent public embrace of anti-communism would set those accused on the road back to ideological purity and employment.[50] Credible evidence of a conversion to the anti-communist cause included publicly endorsing anti-communism at union meetings, writing letters to the editors of major newspapers in support of anti-communism, and fully cooperating with the FBI, the HUAC, and local police authorities. In the eyes of anti-communists, only naming other communists guaranteed a definite break with the cultural left.[51]

Believing that cooperation with the FBI and the HUAC would be sufficient evidence to offer to sponsors, networks, and advertising agencies concerning her political purity, Muir first approached the FBI, only appearing before the HUAC as a last resort in 1953.[52] NAACP head Walter White called FBI director J. Edgar Hoover in September 1950 to see if the FBI would help to clear Muir's name. The message

White left with Hoover's assistant was twofold. First, he hinted that he had valuable information about "the plans of some people on the 'left' to use the negro race." After dropping an anti-communist tidbit White knew Hoover could not resist, White asked if the director would be able to meet with Muir and Jaffe to discuss "the case involving Miss Muir."[53]

Hoover refused to make any promises to Jaffe and Muir, repeatedly reminding his agents that while they would be happy to accept any evidence Muir might provide, "We of course should merely listen."[54] Told by General Foods that they needed "something concrete before they reinstate her to this particular show," Jaffe sought a letter on Muir's behalf "to the effect that the FBI files do not reveal any evidence of anything disloyal as to the subject."[55] Accompanied by Jaffe, Muir was subsequently interviewed by the New York City field office in mid-October 1950. Muir cited her positive war record as evidence of her loyalty, although the fact that the FBI memorandum placed the word "positive" in scare quotes throughout the memo indicates their suspicion about the validity of this claim. Indeed, subsequent FBI reports argued instead that Muir had been a member of the Communist Party, providing an array of testimony from confidential informants. One informant offered the following by way of evidence:

> The informant stated that she [Muir] despised General Douglas MacArthur, which the informant felt to be the same feeling of most Communist sympathizers. In addition, the subject referred to her children as "units," which the informant felt was an unusual description.[56]

After Hartnett alerted the FBI to Muir's impending appearance as a friendly witness before the HUAC, the New York field office interviewed Muir for a second time.[57] Once again accompanied by her husband, Muir "proudly admitted membership" in the Southern Conference for Human Welfare and defended her participation in the National Committee to Abolish the Poll Tax, stating "that she could see no subversive ramification concerning this committee."[58] Disapproving of Muir's pride in her activism, in the pages of the reports, the FBI countered each

of Muir's assertions with "evidence" that these organizations were actually Communist fronts—in the case of the Southern Conference for Human Welfare citing the Tenney Committee's finding that it was a Communist-front organization "for racial agitation" and "money collecting media."[59]

Muir was torn between her own needs and those of her husband. Many years later, Muir recalled that Jaffe "had to defend me and, at the same time, he had to conduct a law practice. He couldn't risk being called left wing."[60] Actor Madeline Gilford was more blunt. Jaffe made Muir "get a settlement" with NBC, Gilford recalled, that prevented her from taking legal action against the network. As her legal counsel, Jaffe probably influenced Muir's decision to ask the NAACP not to pursue a proposed boycott against General Foods.[61] According to Gilford, Jaffe persuaded Muir to testify before the HUAC in 1953 in a last-ditch effort to rehabilitate her political reputation, "another decision she deeply regretted."[62]

Muir did not name names in her testimony, but she did concede the enormity of communist influence and her responses to her interlocutors bear witness to her despair. At the time, Muir told a reporter, "All I want . . . is the right to work. My feeling is one of complete heart-sickness. I feel as though I had undergone an amputation."[63] Depressed and out of work, Muir struggled with alcoholism throughout the 1950s, finally divorcing Jaffe in 1960. She played a handful of roles on television and stage in the early 1960s and began teaching drama at Stephens College in 1968. As late as the mid-1960s, television networks were still preventing Muir from telling her side of the story: in a television interview in 1968, the names of the advertisers, sponsor, and network who had been responsible for firing her were "blooped" out of her account.[64]

In contrast, Scott's appearance before the HUAC in September 1950 was a study in self-determination and moxie. In a lengthy and carefully crafted message that she insisted on reading into the record in its entirety, she denied that she was "ever knowingly connected with the Communist Party or any of its front organizations." Scott conceded her support for Communist Party member Benjamin J. Davis' run for City Council, arguing that Davis was supported by socialists, a group that "has hated Communists longer and more fiercely than any other."[65] Such distinctions did not matter to the FBI, which had already made its mind up about Scott. According to them, Scott "had always been in the pro-Communist group in the entertainment field."[66]

In contrast to Muir's defeatism, Scott went on the offensive in her appearance before the HUAC, attacking *Red Channels's* strategies and integrity and describing herself as "one of the victims" of *Red Channels's* "technique of half-truth and guilt-by-listing."[67] She repeatedly excoriated the practices of *Counter Attack* and *Red Channels*, asking Virginia congressman Burr Harrison: "If any committee, an official committee, lists me as having two heads, does that make me have two heads, and does that give *Red Channels* the right to publish I have two heads?"[68] "A few self-appointed patriotic virgins, such as the gentlemen of *CounterAttack*" and their "cunningly contrived lies," Scott told the committee, amounted to little more than "the slanders of little and petty men." Prophetically, Scott warned her audience, such "vicious slanders" would kill "the years of preparation, sacrifice, and devotion" of American entertainers. As a result, she concluded, "Instead of a loyal troupe of patriotic, energetic citizens, ready to give their all for America, you will demoralize them and end up with a dejected, wronged group whose creative value has been destroyed."[69] Recognizing the need for additional pressure, Scott followed up her HUAC appearance with a call to "boycott networks or program sponsors which suspend entertainers listed by private publications as disloyal without proof or a hearing."[70]

Scott's listing in *Red Channels*, her refusal to disassociate herself from civil rights, and her principled and passionate performance before the HUAC seriously curtailed a promising career in broadcasting. Because Scott was not as dependent as Muir on film or broadcasting for her livelihood, she continued to perform in the United States and Europe, even getting sporadic bookings on television variety shows like *Cavalcade of Stars*. Still, the blacklist combined with her husband's infidelities in personally devastating ways: Scott suffered a nervous breakdown and attempted suicide in 1951, as well as in 1957.[71] Like Muir, Scott divorced her husband in 1960.

These first two cases set the stage for how future blacklistings would be handled. When General Foods and NBC were called to account for Muir's firing by the press, sponsor and network alike defended their decision by stating Muir's presence would anger audiences and jeopardize General Foods's ability to make profits. But sponsors and networks were not responding to the protests of individual or even organized consumers—they were responding to shadowy threats made by organized anti-communists, whose reach beyond their immediate constituencies was questionable. In fact, a Gallup survey conducted in October 1950 and commissioned by General Foods "showed less than 40 percent of the nation had ever heard of the Muir blacklisting and less than 3 percent could relate the name of General Foods or Jell-O with her name."[72] Moreover, when sponsors and networks rallied to the defense of more profitable, apolitical stars who had been identified as Communists, as they did in 1953 when it was revealed that Lucille Ball had once been a member of the Communist Party, no further protests ensued.[73] These anti-red networks were not, as sponsors and networks would have it, evidence of some populist backlash against progressive performers and ideas. Instead, they reflected an institutional consensus about the need to police the ideological boundaries of the new medium.

The relationship between broadcasting and anti-communism has been understood as a concessionary one insofar as the broadcast industry represented itself as giving in to the pressures of anti-communist organizations. Given the industry's treatment of women and African Americans, its union-busting and its conservatism, the relationship between networks and anti-communist forces might be described more accurately as collaborative. Networks were not fans of Gertrude Berg, whose pro-labor politics had cost them money on more than one occasion and whose New Deal liberalism and celebrations of Jewish identity made them uncomfortable. Nor did they want to feature any African American women on their programs, much less an elegant and eloquent advocate of race pride and civil rights like Hazel Scott. In addition, and as social psychologist Marie Jahoda later observed, one of the goals of the blacklist was to promote conformity by making political activism itself suspect and by creating a climate of fear and paranoia.[74] The message implicitly sent by these cases was that performers who used their celebrity statuses to promote progressive causes were and would be forever vulnerable, despite the fact that those who wore their conservative politics on their sleeves would be lionized and rewarded. Few dared argue that programs like *I Was a Communist for the FBI* or domestic sitcoms featuring happy white people in their native habitat of the suburbs were propaganda for fear of retribution from anti-communist institutions, organizations, and individuals. Ironically, shows attempting to even depict or feature people of color (the gardener in *Father Knows Best*, played by the talented Hispanic actor Natividad Vacío, was called Frank Smith), immigrants, and the working class, much less convey progressive messages about gender, were dismissed as heavy-handed instances of red propaganda.

The Third Violinists

When questioned about *Red Channels*'s expansive definition of what constituted a security threat, one of its authors, Kenneth Bierly, described what came to be known as "the third violinist theory." A communist sympathizer who played third violin in a radio orchestra, Bierly explained: "Is sitting next to the first violinist . . . and he is going into the radio station and he is talking to the engineer and he has friends who are news commentators, and so forth and so on."[75] Arthur Schlesinger Jr. put this logic more baldly, describing fellow travelers as "the typhoid Marys of the left, bearing the germs of infection even if not suffering obviously from the disease."[76]

Professional women who had been politically active in civil rights and who refused to conform to conservative ideologies of appropriate female behavior were the quintessential "typhoid Marys of the left." Their presence in the industry was a threat to the androcentric world of anti-communism and its investment in a white nuclear family rooted in female submission. Women who had been active in civil rights were even more threatening to this social order, challenging both sexism and racism through their rejection of white male authority. After the blacklist, open

political identifications and affiliations with people of color thus became professional liabilities. The cases of Muir and Scott, and the swiftness with which these two actors were dispatched, sent a chilling message to all cultural workers, in effect communicating that to even express solidarity with those affected by the blacklist was to jeopardize one's professional future.

In the lethal wake of *Red Channels*, writers remaining in the industry learned to self-censor content that might give red hunters any cause for suspicion. When writer Rod Serling was working on a script based on the lynching of African American teen Emmett Till, he understood that a black victim would not be acceptable to sponsors. Consequently, he "dropped the idea of a Negro victim and changed it to an old pawnbroker." But this change proved insufficient: "The southern location had to be changed. An unspecified location was not good enough; it had to be New England."[77] Similarly, writer Reginald Rose was told that the black family in his *Thunder on Sycamore Street*, a drama based on the real-life attempts of a black family to move into suburban Cicero, Illinois, "would have to be changed to 'something else.' A Negro as beleaguered protagonist of a television drama was declared unthinkable. It would, they said, appall southern viewers."[78] Writers who would survive the purge either quickly internalized the need to avoid anything that might be considered "controversial" or quietly left an industry that was becoming ever more hostile to progressive ideas.

In the minds of the red hunters, representing women as anything but docile, white, middle-class wives and mothers who obediently submitted to male authority and control was evidence of communist contamination. Many progressive women resisted the resulting imposition of control, but paid a heavy price for their convictions. Vera Caspary's battles with studio heads over the content of films and scripts were legendary. She "raged like a shrew" when given Otto Preminger's first draft of the script for *Laura*: "Couldn't Otto understand that a woman could be generous, find jobs, lend money to a man without thought of paying for his sexual services?"[79] Adrian Scott's moving and funny television script about a wife who goes on strike to get wages for domestic labor, walking out on her husband and small children, languished on producers' desks for nearly a decade before being permanently shelved.[80] Shirley Graham's novel about African American poet Phillis Wheatley (1949), written for young adults, was adapted and performed for radio, but she was blacklisted before additional novels on Pocahontas (1953); Jean Baptiste Pointe DeSable, the Haitian founder of Chicago (1962); and Frederick Douglass (1947) could be broadcast. Gertrude Berg fought for years to prevent her iconic Molly Goldberg from moving from her famous tenement at 1030 East Tremont Avenue in the Bronx (the ethnic markings and urban solidarity of which had signified leftist tendencies to anti-communists). After years of struggle, the blacklist finally forced Molly's move to the suburban town of Haverville, where she desperately attempted to conform to the suburban ideal by purchasing commodities in order to fill her new home and dieting in order to pathologize her size.

In the words of historian Ellen Schrecker, "it is possible that the main impact" of the red scare "may well be in what did not happen rather than in what did . . . the books that were never written and the movies that were never made."[81] In a similar vein, Mack notes that Scott's short-lived television show "provided a glimmer of hope for African American viewers," arguing that had the show survived, postwar representations of African Americans might have actually challenged the racist stereotypes that would persist. The blacklist chilled the speech of writers, producers, actors, and other broadcast workers interested in pushing the representational boundaries of the new medium, issuing a clear warning about the kinds of programming content the new medium would tolerate. Not only did the blacklist eliminate a generation of progressive-minded cultural workers from the industry, but the deafening silence that followed it expunged the very memory of those people and their ideas from popular culture.

As Berg put it in a 1956 interview: "You see, darling, don't bring up anything that will bother people. That's very important. Unions, politics, fund-raising, Zionism, socialism, intergroup relations. I don't stress them. And after all, aren't all such things secondary to daily family living?"[82] Writer and producer John

Markus later described the "Network's oversensitivity to special interest groups" as emerging during the blacklist era.[83] But Markus' claim is deceptive, ignoring as it does the fact that the blacklist institutionalized an "oversensitivity" to complaints lodged by conservative groups. "People" referred only to those on the conservative end of the political spectrum. It was, of course, perfectly acceptable to offend women, people of color, immigrants, lesbians and gay men, and thoughtful people as a whole. Thus the blacklist made it unacceptable to offend the finer sensibilities of racists, sexists, homophobes, anti-Semites, and other supporters of hatred and intolerance. The toxic blend of racism and misogyny that centrally informed the practices of anti-communists would be built into the very structure of the industry, so much so that sixty years later, the representations that progressive writers, producers, and actors fought for in the 1950s—of women who were not punished for their independence and autonomy, of proud people of color who were not criminals, of immigrants understood to be fully American—still rarely appear on network and cable television.[84]

Notes

1. *Red Channels: The Report of Communist Influence in Radio and Television* (New York: American Business Consultants, 1950), 5–6.
2. The traffic between the FBI, other governmental branches and agencies, and private anti-communist organizations constituted a complex anti-red network. The authors of *Red Channels* were former FBI agents, veterans of the Bureau's New York City Red Squad, who had access to classified information about progressive activities. The coalition that organized the first attacks on broadcasting included Theodore Kirkpatrick, of *CounterAttack* and *Red Channels*, who emphasized his legitimacy by citing his status as a former FBI agent, bragging about his close work "with the House Un-American Activities Committee" (Jack Gould, "'Red Purge' for Radio, Television Seen in Wake of Jean Muir Ouster," *New York Times*, August 30, 1950, 33). The author of *Red Channels*'s introduction, Vince Hartnett, corresponded frequently with the FBI, as did anti-communist and white supremacist Elizabeth Dilling. Hartnett, Dilling, and the American Legion all provided information to the House Un-American Activities Committee.

3. Charlotte Brunsdon and Lynn Spigel, *Feminist Television Criticism: A Reader* (London: Open University Press, 2007); Mary Beth Haralovich, "Sitcoms and Suburbs: Positioning the 1950s Homemaker," *Quarterly Review of Film and Television*, 1, no. 1 (May 1989): 61–83; Nina C. Leibman, *Living Room Lectures: The Fifties Family in Film and Television* (Austin: University of Texas Press, 1995); George Lipsitz, *Time Passages: Collective Memory and American Popular Culture* (Minneapolis: University of Minnesota Press, 2001); Elaine Tyler May, *Homeward Bound: American Families in the Cold War Era* (New York: Basic Books, 1990/2008); Lynn Spigel, *Make Room for TV: Television and the Family Ideal in Postwar America* (Chicago: University of Chicago Press, 1992); Lynn Spigel and Denise Mann, *Private Screenings: Television and the Female Consumer* (Durham, NC: Duke University Press, 1992); and Ella Taylor, *Prime-Time Families: Television Culture in Post-War America* (Berkeley and Los Angeles: University of California Press, 1991).

4. Shirley Graham Du Bois, "As a Man Thinketh in His Heart, So Is He," in *The Parish News: Church of the Holy Trinity* (Brooklyn, NY: Vol. LVII, No. 4, February 1954), *Shirley Graham Du Bois Papers* (Box 27, Folder 3), 1–5.

5. See Thomas Doherty, *Cold War, Cool Medium: Television, McCarthyism, and American Culture* (New York: Columbia University Press, 2003); David Everitt, *A Shadow of Red: Communism and the Blacklist* (Chicago: Ivan R., 2007); and Patrick McGilligan and Paul Buhle, *Tender Comrades: A Backstory of the Hollywood Blacklist* (Boston, MA: St. Martin's Press, 1999) for scholarship specifically on the broadcast blacklist. Mainly, accounts of the blacklist era appear in autobiographical and biographical writing about the era. See Norma Barzman, *The Red and the Blacklist: An Intimate Memoir of a Hollywood Expatriate* (New York: Nation Books, 2004); Howard Blue, *Words at War: World War II Era Radio Drama and the Postwar Broadcasting Industry Blacklist* (New York: The Scarecrow Press, 2002); Karen Chilton, *Hazel Scott: The Pioneering Journey of a Jazz Pianist from Café Society to Hollywood to HUAC* (Ann Arbor: University of Michigan Press, 2008); John Henry Faulk, *Fear on Trial* (Austin: University of Texas Press, 1983); Gerald Horne, *Race Woman: The Lives of Shirley Graham Du Bois* (New York: New York University Press, 2000); and Glenn D. Smith Jr., *"Something on My Own": Gertrude Berg and American Broadcasting, 1929–1956* (New York: Syracuse University Press, 2007) for some of these. There is a voluminous body of literature on the Hollywood blacklist.

6. Michele Hilmes, *Radio Voices: American Broadcasting, 1922–1952* (Minneapolis: University of Minnesota Press, 1997). See Chapter 4 in particular.

7. A good number of them also did not neatly conform to ideals of heterosexual monogamy. Unmarried writer and actor Ruth Gordon traveled to Paris in 1929 to have her son and later married Garson Kanin, a man who was 16 years her junior. After living with her partner openly for seven years, Vera Caspary finally married him at the age of 47. A number of the women also wrote about affairs with women in their fiction and memoirs, although none identified as lesbian.

8. Both Muir and Scott's FBI records are accessible at http://cstabile.wordpress.com/.

9. "Testimony of Hazel Scott Powell," *Hearing Before the Committee on Un-American Activities* (Washington, DC: Government Printing Office, September 22, 1950), 3619–20.

10. Spigel, *Make Room for TV.*

11. J. Edgar Hoover, *Masters of Deceit: The Story of Communism in America and How to Fight It* (New York: Henry Holt and Company, 1958), 89.

12. "Hysteria and Civil Liberties," *The Survey*, October 1950, 458–59.

13. *Red Channels*, 5.

14. "Testimony of Hazel Scott Powell," 3613.

15. Joanne Rapf, "In Focus: Children of the Blacklist," *Cinema Journal* 44, no. 4 (Summer 2005): 77. See additional accounts in Griffin Fariello, *Red Scare: Memories of the American Inquisition* (New York: W. W. Norton and Company, 1980); McGilligan and Buhle, *Tender Comrades*; and Rapf, *In Focus.*

16. Elizabeth Dilling, *The Roosevelt Red Record and its Background* (Kenilworth, IL: Chicago, The Author, 1936), 144, original emphases.

17. Qtd in Horne, *Race Woman*, 106.

18. "Investigation of Communist Activities New York Area—Part I," *Subcommittee of the Committee on Un-American Activities* (Washington, DC: Government Printing Office, June 15, 1953), 15.

19. Muir's subsequent testimony before the HUAC in 1953 contains a lengthy series of questions about a Hollywood cocktail party she attended in 1936, supposedly hosted by Communists.

20. Paul Rhome, "Around Boston," *Chicago Defender*, September 13, 1941, 21.

21. Langston Hughes, "Here to Yonder," *Chicago Defender*, June 10, 1944, 12.

22. "'Salute to Troops' Will be Big Affair in New York December 3," *Chicago Defender*, December 27, 1941, 19.

23. "Lincoln U., Pa. Conference Studies Status of Negro in a Democracy," *Chicago Defender*, May 10, 1942, 4.

24. "Hastie, Jean Muir to Talk at NAACP Student Meet," *Chicago Defender*, national edition, September 11, 1943, 13.

25. "5,000 At Bronx Rally Hit 'Hate,'" *Chicago Defender*, August 7, 1943, 20.
26. "Mrs. FDR Speaks at Testimonial for Walter White," *Chicago Defender*, June 3, 1944, 11; "White Color No Criterion of Superiority—Mrs. FDR," *Chicago Defender*, November 13, 1943, 3.
27. *Report on the Congress of American Women* (Committee on Un-American Activities: US House of Representatives, October 23, 1949).
28. Jack Gould, "'Aldrich' Show Drops Jean Muir; TV Actress Denies Communist Ties," *New York Times*, August 29, 1950, 1.
29. Everitt, A *Shadow of Red*, 60.
30. Gould, "'Aldrich' Show Drops Jean Muir; TV Actress Denies Communist Ties," 1.
31. Erik Barnouw, *The Golden Web: A History of Broadcasting in the United States, 1933–1953* (New York: Oxford University Press, 1968), 269; and Everitt, A *Shadow of Red*, 150.
32. "Hit Ban on Jean Muir," *Chicago Defender*, September 23, 1950, 21.
33. "Our Dingy Underwear is Changing Colors," *Chicago Defender*, September 23, 1950, 66.
34. In a suggestive parallel with the fledgling Fox Network in the late 1980s and early 1990s, the DuMont network took risks the established networks were reluctant to gamble on. In addition to *The Hazel Scott Show*, DuMont also featured *The Gallery of Madame Liu-Tsong* (1951), starring Chinese-American actor Anna May (Wong Lui-Tsong), who played the owner of a chain of art galleries caught up in webs of international intrigue and mystery. See Kristal Brent Zook, *Color by Fox: The Fox Network and the Revolution in Black Television* (New York: Oxford, 1999) for more on the "revolution" at Fox.
35. Qtd in Athan Theoharis and J. S. Cox, *The Boss: J. Edgar Hoover and the Great American Inquisition* (Philadelphia, PA: Temple University Press, 1998), 57.
36. See Steven Classen's *Watching Jim Crow: The Struggles over Mississippi Television, 1955–1969* (Durham, NC: Duke University Press, 2004) for examples of such policing in broadcasting in the US South.
37. In contrast, after a controversy following his booking of Paul Draper, Ed Sullivan worked closely with Theodore Kirkpatrick of *CounterAttack* and *Red Channels* to ensure that those who appeared on *Toast of the Town* had been politically vetted. See Merle Miller, *The Judges and the Judged* (Garden City, New York: Doubleday, 1952), 174.
38. The consistently brave Cantor was also alone in issuing a statement of public support for Jean Muir in 1950, calling her blacklisting "one of the most tragic things that ever happened in show business." See "Cantor Backs Miss Muir," *New York Times*, September 6, 1950.
39. Victor Navasky, *Naming Names* (New York: Hill and Wang, 1991), 85.
40. Chilton, *Hazel Scott*, 34.
41. Qtd in Chilton, *Hazel Scott*, 72.
42. Chilton, *Hazel Scott*, 73.
43. Donald Bogle, *Toms, Coons, Mulattoes, Mammies, and Bucks: An Interpretive History of Blacks in American Films* (New York: Continuum, 2001), 125.
44. Ibid., 122.
45. Qtd in Chilton, *Hazel Scott*, 138.
46. "Hazel Scott Attorneys Score in Initial Round," *Spokane Daily Chronicle*, April 17, 1950, 1.
47. Dwayne Mack, "Hazel Scott: A Career Curtailed," *Journal of African American History*, 91, no. 2 (Spring 2006): 160.
48. *The Road Back* (New York: Aware, Inc., 1955), 3.
49. The community of progressive cultural workers in New York City was a closely-knit one. It is likely that Muir and Scott knew one another, but aside from the *Chicago Defender*'s linking of the two cases, and the fact that each was connected with the NAACP, I could locate no evidence that they corresponded regarding their blacklistings.
50. *The Road Back*, 1.
51. Ibid., 3.
52. Both Muir and Scott had come to the attention of anti-communists before 1950. Muir's name had been referenced several times in HUAC investigations of Hollywood. Scott had been the 1944 target of a con involving a telegram purportedly sent by J. Edgar Hoover. The telegram claimed that its writer had information about "dope traffic around you" that is "hindering our war effort by passing drugs among our negro and white servicemen" (Hazel Scott Powell FBI Files, "Western Union Telegram," 1944).
53. Jean Muir FBI Files, "FBI Office Memorandum," 1950.
54. Ibid.
55. Ibid.
56. Jean Muir FBI Files, "FBI Report," 1951, 20.
57. Jean Muir FBI Files, "Air Tel," 1953.
58. "Investigation of Communist Activities New York Area—Part I," 5.
59. Ibid., 8. In 1955, the FBI discovered they had made an error. In the 1950 memorandum that accompanied Muir and Jaffe's request for a meeting, Special Agent Charles Michael Noone had erroneously cited evidence that an informant had seen Jean Muir's Communist Party membership book, when the informant in question had in fact testified that he had *not* seen Jean Muir's Communist Party membership book. "It

appears," Agent Belmont wrote without a trace of irony, that "Noone bears sole responsibility for error" (Jean Muir FBI Files, "Office Memorandum," 1955). Muir's file was subsequently "changed to indicate the subject's true full name, Jean Fullarton Jaffe" and "placed in a closed status" (Ibid., 1956, 1–4). No one outside the FBI was alerted to this error.

60. Smith, *"Something on My Own"*, 152.

61. Ibid., 152–3.

62. Ibid., 152.

63. "On the Air: Trial by Sponsor," *New Republic*, September 11, 1950, 22–23.

64. "A.B.C. Puts Off Jean Muir Blacklist Interview," *New York Times*, December 25, 1965, 29.

65. "Testimony of Hazel Scott," 3621.

66. Hazel Scott Powell FBI Files "Memorandum," April 22, 1954.

67. "Testimony of Hazel Scott Powell," 3620.

68. Ibid., 3617.

69. Ibid.

70. "Hazel Asks Boycott in Red Whirl," *Chicago Defender*, national edition, October 7, 1950, 21.

71. Chilton, *Hazel Scott*, 158, 176.

72. Smith, *"Something on My Own"*, 153.

73. See Susan M. Carini, "Love's Labors Almost Lost: Managing Crisis During the Reign of 'I Love Lucy,'" *Cinema Journal* 43, no. 1 (Autumn 2003): 44–62 for an excellent account of the attempt to blacklist Lucille Ball and the public relations coup that saved Ball's career.

74. Marie Jahoda, "Psychological Issues in Civil Liberties," *American Psychologist* 11, no. 5 (May 1956): 234–40.

75. Everitt, *A Shadow of Red*, 29.

76. Navasky, *Naming Names*, 54.

77. Erik Barnouw, *The Image Empire: A History of Broadcasting in the United States from 1953* (New York: Oxford University Press, 1970), 35.

78. Ibid., 34.

79. Vera Caspary, *The Secrets of Grown-Ups: An Autobiography* (New York: McGraw Hill, 1979), 209.

80. Adrian Scott, "Ellie," *Adrian and Joan Scott Papers* (Box 13, File Folder 5, n.d.). A member of the Hollywood Ten, Adrian Scott had served prison time for his refusal to testify about his political activities. "Ellie" was submitted under the name "Richard Sanville," one of the pseudonyms Scott used.

81. Ellen Schrecker, *The Age of McCarthyism* (Boston, MA: Bedford Books, 1994), 92.

82. David Zurawik, *The Jews of Prime Time* (Hanover, NH: Brandeis University Press), 45.

83. "From the Goldbergs to 2005: The Evolution of the Sitcom," *Museum of Television and Radio Satellite Seminar Series* (New York: Museum of TV and Radio, 2005).

84. Although it is not within the scope of this essay to address the blacklists' anti-immigrant elements, certainly one of the most intransigent effects of the blacklist has been a longstanding antipathy on the part of network television to featuring immigrants (exceptions include: comic figures from fictitious countries, as in *Perfect Strangers*'s Balki Bartokomous or *Taxi*'s Latka Gravas; or aliens as immigrants, as in *Mork and Mindy*, *Alien Nation*, or the remake of *V*).

Archival Resources

Adrian Scott and Joan LaCour Scott Papers. Laramie, WY: American Heritage Center, University of Wyoming.

Gertrude Berg Papers. Syracuse, NY: University of Syracuse Library.

Shirley Graham Du Bois Papers. Cambridge, MA: Schlesinger Library, Harvard University.

Vera Caspary Papers. Madison: Wisconsin Historical Society.

27.
THE DISTRIBUTION OF DISTRESS
Patricia J. Williams

Many years ago, I was standing in a so-called juice bar in Berkeley, California. A young man came in whom I had often seen begging in the neighborhood. A more bruised-looking human one could not imagine: he was missing several teeth, his clothes were in rags, his blond hair was matted, his eyes red-rimmed, his nails long and black and broken. On this particular morning he came into the juice bar and ordered some sort of protein drink from the well-scrubbed, patchouli-scented young woman behind the counter. It was obvious that his presence disturbed her, and when he took his drink and mumbled, "Thanks, little lady," she exploded.

"Don't you dare call me 'little lady'!" she snarled with a ferocity that turned heads. "I'm a *woman* and you'd better learn the difference!"

"Sorry," he whispered with his head bowed, like a dog that had been kicked, and he quite literally limped out of the store.

"Good riddance," the woman called after him.

This took place some fifteen years ago, but I have always remembered the interchange because it taught me a lot about the not so subliminal messages that can be wrapped in the expression of Virtue Aggrieved, in which antibias of one sort is used to further the agenda of bias of another kind.

In an abstract sense, I understood the resentment for girlish diminutives. Too often as a lawyer I have been in courtroom situations where coy terms of endearment were employed in such a way that "the little lady, God-bless-her" became a marginalizing

condescension, a precise condensation of "She thinks she's a lawyer, poor thing." Yet in this instance, gender power was clearly not the issue, but rather the emotional venting of a revulsion at this man's dirty and bedraggled presence. It wasn't just that he had called her a little lady; she seemed angry that he had dared address her at all.

If, upon occasion, the ploughshare of feminism can be beaten into a sword of class prejudice, no less can there be other examples of what I call battling biases, in which the impulse to antidiscrimination is defeated by the intrusion or substitution of a different object of enmity. This revolving door of revulsions is one of the trickiest mechanisms contributing to the enduring nature of prejudice; it is at heart, I suppose, a kind of traumatic reiteration of injurious encounters, preserving even as it transforms the overall history of rage.

I was in England several years ago when a young Asian man was severely beaten in East London by a young white man. I was gratified to see the immediate renunciation of racism that ensued in the media. It was a somewhat more sophisticated and heartfelt collective self-examination than sometimes occurs in the United States in the wake of such incidents, where, I fear, we are much more jaded about all forms of violence. Nevertheless, what intrigued me most about the media coverage of this assault was the unfortunate way in which class bias became a tool for the denunciation of racism.

"Racial, Ethnic, or Religious Prejudice Is Repugnant," screamed the headlines.

Hooray, I thought.

And then the full text: "It is repugnant, *particularly*"—and I'm embellishing here—"when committed by a miserable low-class cockney whose bestial nature knows no plummeted depth, etc. etc."

Oh dear, I thought.

In other words, the media not only defined anti-Asian and anti-immigrant animus as ignorance, as surely it is, but went on to define that ignorance as the property of a class, of "the" lower classes, implying even that a good Oxbridge education inevitably lifts one above that sort of thing. As surely it does not.

And therein lies a problem, I think. If race or ethnicity is not a synonym for either ignorance or foreignness, then neither should class be an explanatory trashbin for racial prejudice, domestic incivility, and a host of other social ills. If the last fifty years have taught us nothing else, it is that our "isms" are no less insidious when beautifully polished and terribly refined.

None of us is beyond some such pitfalls, and in certain contexts typecasting can even be a necessary and helpful way of explaining the social world. The hard task is to untangle the instances where the categoric helps us predict and prepare for the world from those instances where it verges on scapegoating, projection, and prejudice.

To restate the problem, I think that the persistence of racism, ethnic and religious intolerance, as well as gender and class bias, is dependent upon recirculating images in which the general and the particular duel each other endlessly.

"*En garde*, you heathenish son of an inferior category!"

"Brute!" comes the response. "I am inalienably endowed with the unique luminosity of my rational individualism; it is you who are the guttural eruption of an unspeakable subclassification . . ."

Thrust and parry, on and on, the play of race versus ethnicity versus class versus blood feud. One sword may be sharper or quicker, but neither's wound is ever healed.

Too often these tensions are resolved simply by concluding that stereotyping is just our lot as humans so let the consequences fall where they may. But stereotyping operates as habit, not immutable trait, a fluid project that rather too easily flows across the shifting ecology of human relations. And racism is a very old, very bad habit.

This malleability of prejudice is underscored by a little cultural comparison. If class bias has skewed discussions of racism in the British examples I have just described, it is rather more common in the United States for race to consume discussions of class altogether. While I don't want to overstate the cultural differences between the United States and the United Kingdom—there is enough similarity to conclude that race and class present a generally interlocking set of problems in both nations—the United States does deem itself classless with almost the same degree of self-congratulation that the United Kingdom prides itself on being largely free of a history of racial bias. Certainly these are good impulses and desirable civic sentiments, but I am always one to look closely at what is deemed beyond the pale. *It will never happen here . . .* The noblest denials are at least as interesting study as the highest ideals.

Consider: for a supposedly classless society, the United States nevertheless suffers the greatest gap of any industrialized nation between its richest and poorest citizens. And there can be no more dramatic and ironic class consciousness than the Dickensian characteristics ascribed to those in the so-called underclass, as opposed to the rest—what are we to call them, the *over*class? Those who are deemed to have class versus those who are so far beneath the usual indicia of even lower class that they are deemed to have no class at all.

If this is not viewed by most Americans as a problem of class stasis, it is perhaps because class denominations are so uniformly understood to be stand-ins for race. The very term *underclass* is a *euphemism* for blackness, class operating as euphemism in that we Americans are an upbeat kind of people and class is usually thought to be an easier problem than race.

Middle-classness, on the other hand, is so persistently a euphemism for whiteness, that middle-class black people are sometimes described as "honorary whites" or as those who have been deracinated in some vaguely political sense. More often than I like to remember, I have been told that my opinion about this or that couldn't possibly be relevant to "real," "authentic" black people. Why? Simply because I don't sound like a Hollywood stereotype of the way black people are "supposed" to talk. "Speaking white" or "Talking black." No in-between. Speaking as a black person while sounding like a white person has, I have found, engendered some complicated sense of betrayal. "*You're* not black! You're not *white*!" No one seems particularly interested in the substantive ideas being expressed; but everyone is caught up with the question of whether anyone should have to listen to a white-voiced black person.

It is in this way that we often talk about class and race such that we sometimes end up talking about neither, because we insist on talking about race as though it were class and class as though it were race, and it's hard to see very clearly when the waters are so muddied with all that simile and metaphor.

By the same token, America is usually deemed a society in which the accent with which one speaks Does Not Matter. That is largely true, but it is not so where black accents are concerned. While there is much made of regional variations—New Yorkers, Minnesotans, and Southerners are the butts of a certain level of cheap satire—an accent deemed "black" is the one with some substantial risk of evoking outright discrimination. In fact, the speech of real black people ranges from true dialects to myriad patois, to regional accents, to specific syntactical twists or usages of vocabulary. Yet language identified as black is habitually flattened into some singularized entity that in turn becomes synonymous with ignorance, slang, big lips and sloppy tongues, incoherent ideas, and very bad—terribly unruly!—linguistic acts. Black speech becomes a cipher for all the other stereotypes associated with racial discrimination; the refusal to understand becomes rationalized by the assumption of incomprehensibility.

My colleague Professor Mari Matsuda has studied cases involving accent discrimination. She writes of lawsuits whose transcripts revealed an interesting paradox. One case featured a speaker whose accent had been declared incomprehensible by his employer. Nevertheless, his recorded testimony, copied down with no difficulty by the court reporter, revealed a parlance more grammatically accurate, substantively coherent, and syntactically graceful than any other speaker in the courtroom, including the judge. This paradox has always been the subject of some interest among linguists and sociolinguists, the degree to which language is understood in a way that is intimately linked to relations among speakers.

"Good day," I say to you. Do you see me as a genial neighbor, as part of your day? If so, you may be generously disposed to return the geniality with a hearty "Hale fellow, well met."

"Good day," I say. Do you see me as an impudent upstart the very sound of whose voice is an unwelcome intrusion upon your good day? If so, the greeting becomes an act of aggression; woe betide the cheerful, innocent upstart.

"Shall we consider race?" I say to you. If you are disposed to like me, you might hear this as an invitation to a kind of conversation we have not shared before, a leap of faith into knowing more about each other.

"Shall we consider race?" I say. *Not* "Shall I batter you with guilt before we riot in the streets?" But only: "Shall we *consider* race?" Yet if I am that same upstart, the blood will have boiled up in your ears by now, and very shortly you will start to have tremors from the unreasonable audacity of my meddlesome presumption. Nothing I actually say will matter, for what matters is that I am out of place . . .

This dynamic, this vital ingredient of the willingness to hear, is apparent in the contradiction of lower-status speech being simultaneously understood yet not understood. Why is the sound of black voices, the shape of black bodies so overwhelmingly agreeable, so colorfully comprehensible in some contexts, particularly in the sports and entertainment industries, yet deemed so utterly incapable of effective communication or acceptable presence when it comes to finding a job as a construction worker?

This is an odd conundrum, to find the sight and the sound of oneself a red flag. And it is a kind of banner, one's face and one's tongue, a banner of family and affiliation—that rhythm and stress, the buoyance of one's mother's tongue; that plane of jaw, that prominence of brow, the property of one's father's face. What to make of those social pressures that would push the region of the body underground in order to allow the purity of one's inner soul to be more fully seen? When Martin Luther King, Jr., urged that we be judged by the content of our character, surely he meant that what we looked like should not matter. Yet just as surely that enterprise did not involve having to deny the entirely complicated symbolic character of one's physical manifestation. This is a hard point, I confess, and one fraught with risk of misunderstanding. The color of one's skin is a part of ourselves. It does not matter. It is precious, and yet it should not matter; it is important and yet it must not matter. It is simultaneously our greatest vanity and anxiety, and I am of the opinion, like Martin Luther King, that none of this should matter.

Yet let me consider the question of self-erasure. I've written elsewhere about my concern that various forms of biotechnological engineering have been turned to such purposes—from skin lighteners to cosmetic surgery to the market for sperm with blond hair and eggs with high IQs. Consider the boy I read about who had started some sort of computer magazine for children. A young man of eleven, celebrated as a computer whiz, whose family had emigrated from Puerto Rico, now living in New York. The article recounted how much he loved computers because, he said, nobody judged him for what he looked like, and he could speak without an accent. What to make of this freedom as disembodiment, this technologically purified mental communion as escape from the society of others, as neutralized social space. What a delicate project, this looking at each other, seeing yet not staring. Would we look so hard, judge so hard, be so hard—what would we look like?—if we existed unself-consciously in our bodies—sagging, grayhaired, young, old, black, white, balding and content?

Let me offer a more layered illustration of the way in which these issues of race and class interact, the markers of class distinction and bias in the United Kingdom emerging also in the United States as overlapping substantially with the category of race. A few years ago, I purchased a house. Because the house was in a different state than where I was located at the time, I obtained my mortgage by telephone. I am a prudent little squirrel when it comes to things financial, always tucking away sufficient stores of nuts for the winter, and so I meet all the criteria of a quite good credit risk. My loan was approved almost immediately.

A short time after, the contract came in the mail. Among the papers the bank forwarded were forms documenting compliance with what is called the Fair Housing Act. It is against the law to discriminate against black people in the housing market, and one of the pieces of legislation to that effect is the Fair Housing Act, a law that monitors lending practices to prevent banks from doing what is called "red-lining." Red-lining is a phenomenon whereby banks circle certain neighborhoods on the map and refuse to lend in those areas for reasons based on race. There are a number of variations on the theme. Black people cannot get loans to purchase homes in white areas; or black people cannot get start-up money for small businesses in black areas. The Fair Housing Act thus tracks the race of all banking customers to prevent such discrimination. Unfortunately, some banks also use the racial information disclosed on the Fair Housing forms to engage in precisely the discrimination the law seeks to prevent.

I should repeat that to this point my entire mortgage transaction had been conducted by telephone. I should also say that I speak what is considered in the States a very Received-Standard-English, regionally northeastern perhaps, but not marked as black. With my credit history, with my job as a law professor, and no doubt with my accent, I am not only middle-class but match the cultural stereotype of a good white person. It is thus perhaps that the loan officer of this bank, whom I had never met in person, had checked off a box on the Fair Housing form indicating that I *was* "white."

Race shouldn't matter, I suppose, but it seemed to in this case, and so I took a deep breath, crossed out "white," checked the box marked "black," and sent the contract back to the bank. That will teach them to presume too much, I thought. A done deal, I assumed.

Suddenly said deal came to a screeching halt. The bank wanted more money as a down payment, they wanted me to pay more points, they wanted to raise the rate of interest. Suddenly I found myself facing great resistance and much more debt.

What was most interesting about all this was that the reason the bank gave for its newfound recalcitrance was not race, heaven forbid—racism doesn't exist anymore, hadn't I heard? No, the reason they gave was that property values in that neighborhood were suddenly falling. They wanted more money to cover the increased risk.

Initially, I was surprised, confused. The house was in a neighborhood that was extremely stable; prices in the area had not gone down since World War II, only slowly, steadily up. I am an extremely careful shopper and I had uncovered absolutely no indication that prices were falling at all.

It took my real estate agent to make me see the light. "Don't you get it," he sighed. "This is what they always do."

And even though I work with this sort of thing all the time, I really hadn't gotten it: for of course, *I* was the reason the prices were in peril.

The bank was proceeding according to demographic data that show any time black people move into a neighborhood in the States, whites are overwhelmingly likely to move out. In droves. In panic. In concert. Pulling every imaginable resource with them, from school funding to garbage collection to social workers who don't want to work in black neighborhoods to police whose too frequent relation to black communities is a corrupted one of containment rather than protection.

It's called a tipping point, this thing that happens when black people move into white neighborhoods. The imagery is awfully catchy you must admit: the neighborhood just tipping right on over like a terrible accident, whoops! Like a pitcher I suppose. All that nice fresh wholesome milk spilling out, running away . . . leaving the dark, echoing, upended urn of the inner city.

This immense fear of "the black" next door is one reason the United States is so densely segregated. Only two percent of white people have a black neighbor, even though black people constitute approximately thirteen percent of the population. White people fear black people in big ways, in small ways, in financial ways, in utterly incomprehensible ways.

As for my mortgage, I threatened to sue and eventually procured the loan on the original terms. But what was fascinating to me about this whole incident was the way in which it so exemplified the new problems of the new rhetoric of racism. For starters, the new rhetoric of racism never mentions race. It wasn't race but risk with which the bank was concerned. Second, since financial risk is all about economics, my exclusion got reclassified as just a consideration of class, and there's no law against class discrimination, after all, for that would present a restraint on one of our most precious liberties, the freedom to contract or not. If public schools, trains, buses, swimming pools, and neighborhoods remain segregated, it's no longer a racial problem if someone who just happens to be white keeps hiking the price for someone who just accidentally and purely by the way happens to be black. White people set higher prices for the "right," the "choice" of self-segregation. If black people don't move in, it's just that they can't *afford* to. Black people pay higher prices for the attempt to integrate, even as the integration of oneself is a threat to one's investment by lowering its value.

By this measure of mortgage worthiness, the ingredient of blackness is cast not just as a social toll but as an actual tax. A fee, an extra contribution at the door, an admission charge for the higher costs of handling my dangerous propensities, my inherently unsavory properties. I was not judged based on my independent attributes or individual financial worth as a client; nor even was I judged by statistical profiles of what my group actually do. (For, in fact, anxiety-stricken, middle-class black people make grovelingly good cake-baking neighbors when not made to feel defensive by the unfortunate, historical welcome strategies of bombs, burnings, or abandon.)

Rather, I was being evaluated based on what an abstraction of White Society writ large thinks we— or I—do, and that imagined "doing" was treated and thus established as a self-fulfilling prophecy.

However rationalized, this form of discrimination is a burden: one's very existence becomes a lonely vacuum when so many in society not only devalue *me*, but devalue *themselves* and their homes for having me as part of the landscaped view from the quiet of their breakfast nook.

I know, I know, I exist in the world on my own terms surely. I am an individual and all that. But if I carry the bank's logic out with my individuality rather than my collectively imagined effect on property values as the subject of this type of irrational economic computation, then *I*, the charming and delightful Patricia J. Williams, become a bit like a car wash in your backyard. Only much worse in real price terms. I am more than a mere violation of the nice residential comfort zone in question; my blackness can rezone altogether by the mere fortuity of my relocation.

"Dumping district," cringes the nice, clean actuarial family next door; "there goes the neighborhood . . ." as whole geographic tracts slide into the chasm of impecuniousness and disgust. I am the economic equivalent of a medical waste disposal site, a toxic heap-o'-home.

In my brand-new house, I hover behind my brand-new kitchen curtains, wondering whether the very appearance of my self will endanger my collateral yet further. When Benetton ran an advertisement that darkened Queen Elizabeth II's skin to a nice rich brown, the *Sun* newspaper ran an article observing that this "obviously cheapens the monarchy." Will the presentation of my self so disperse the value of my own, my ownership, my property?

This is madness, I am sure, as I draw the curtain like a veil across my nose. In what order of things is it *rational* to thus hide and skulk?

It is an intolerable logic. An investment in my property compels a selling of myself.

I grew up in a white neighborhood where my mother's family had been the only black people for about fifty years. In the 1960s, Boston began to feel the effects of the great migration of Southern blacks to the north that came about as a result of the Civil Rights Movement. Two more black families moved into the neighborhood. There was a sudden churning, a chemical response, a collective roiling with streams of froth and jets of steam. We children heard all about it on the playground. The neighborhood was under siege. The blacks were coming. My schoolmates' parents were moving out *en masse*.

It was remarkable. The neighborhood was entirely black within about a year.

I am a risk pool. I am a car wash.

I was affected, I suppose, growing up with those children who frightened themselves by imagining what it would be like to touch black bodies, to kiss those wide unkissable lips, to draw the pure breath of life through that crude and forbidden expanse of nose; is it really possible that a gentle God—their God, dear God—would let a *human* heart reside within the wet charred thickness of black skin?

I am, they told me, a jumble of discarded parts: low-browed monkey bones and infected, softly pungent flesh.

In fact, my price on the market is a variable affair. If I were crushed and sorted into common elements, my salt and juice and calcinated bits are worth approximately five English pounds. Fresh from the kill, in contrast, my body parts, my lungs and liver, heart and healthy arteries, would fetch some forty thousand. There is no demand for the fruit of my womb, however; eggs fresh from their warm dark sanctuary are worthless on the open market. "Irish Egg Donor Sought," reads an ad in the little weekly newspaper that serves New York City's parent population. And in the weird economy of bloodlines, and with the insidious variability of prejudice, "Irish eggs" command a price of upwards of five thousand pounds.

This silent market in black worth is pervasive. When a certain brand of hiking boots became popular among young people in Harlem, the manufacturer pulled the product from inner-city stores, fearing that such a trend would "ruin" the image of their boot among the larger market of whites.

It's funny . . . even shoes.

Last year I had a funny experience in a shoe store. The salesman would bring me only one shoe, not two.

"I can't try on a pair?" I asked in disbelief.

"When you pay for a pair," he retorted. "What if there were a hundred of you," he continued. "How would we keep track?"

I was the only customer in the store, but there were a hundred of me in his head.

In our Anglo-American jurisprudence there is a general constraint limiting the right to sue to cases and controversies affecting the individual. As an individual, I could go to the great and ridiculous effort of suing for the minuscule amount at stake in waiting for the other shoe to drop from his hand; but as for the real claim, the group claim, the larger defamation to all those other hundreds of me . . . well, that will be a considerably tougher row to hoe.

I am one, I am many.

I am amiable, orderly, extremely honest, and a very good neighbor indeed. I am suspect profile, market cluster, actuarial monster, statistical being.

My particulars battle the generals.

"Typecasting!" I protest.

"Predictive indicator," assert the keepers of the gate.

"Prejudice!" I say.

"Precaution," they reply.

Hundreds, even thousands, of me hover in the breach.

28.
HOW TO TAME A WILD TONGUE
Gloria Anzaldúa

"We're going to have to control your tongue," the dentist says, pulling out all the metal from my mouth. Silver bits plop and tinkle into the basin. My mouth is a motherlode.

The dentist is cleaning out my roots. I get a whiff of the stench when I gasp. "I can't cap that tooth yet, you're still draining," he says.

"We're going to have to do something about your tongue," I hear the anger rising in his voice. My tongue keeps pushing out the wads of cotton, pushing back the drills, the long thin needles. "I've never seen anything as strong or as stubborn," he says. And I think, how do you tame a wild tongue, train it to be quiet, how do you bridle and saddle it? How do you make it lie down?

> "Who is to say that robbing a people of
> its language is less violent than war?"
> —Ray Gwyn Smith[1]

I remember being caught speaking Spanish at recess—that was good for three licks on the knuckles with a sharp ruler. I remember being sent to the corner of the classroom for "talking back" to the Anglo teacher when all I was trying to do was tell her how to pronounce my name. "If you want to be American, speak 'American.' If you don't like it, go back to Mexico where you belong."

"I want you to speak English. *Pa'hallar buen trabajo tienes que saber hablar el inglés bien. Qué vale toda tu educación si todavía hablas inglés con un* 'accent,'"

my mother would say, mortified that I spoke English like a Mexican. At Pan American University, I, and all Chicano students were required to take two speech classes. Their purpose: to get rid of our accents.

Attacks on one's form of expression with the intent to censor are a violation of the First Amendment. *El Anglo con cara de inocente nos arrancó la lengua.* Wild tongues can't be tamed, they can only be cut out.

Overcoming the Tradition of Silence

> *Ahogadas, escupimos el oscuro.*
> *Peleando con nuestra propia sombra*
> *el silencio nos sepulta.*

En boca cerrada no entran moscas. "Flies don't enter a closed mouth" is a saying I kept hearing when I was a child. *Ser habladora* was to be a gossip and a liar, to talk too much. *Muchachitas bien criadas,* well-bred girls don't answer back. *Es una falta de respeto* to talk back to one's mother or father. I remember one of the sins I'd recite to the priest in the confession box the few times I went to confession: talking back to my mother, *hablar pa' 'trás, repelar. Hocicona, repelona, chismosa,* having a big mouth, questioning, carrying tales are all signs of being *mal criada.* In my culture they are all words that are derogatory if applied to women—I've never heard them applied to men.

The first time I heard two women, a Puerto Rican and a Cuban, say the word *"nosotras,"* I was shocked.

I had not known the word existed. Chicanas use *nosotros* whether we're male or female. We are robbed of our female being by the masculine plural. Language is a male discourse.

> And our tongues have become
> dry　　the wilderness has
> dried out our tongues　　and
> we have forgotten speech.
> 　　　　—Irena Klepfisz[2]

Even our own people, other Spanish speakers *nos quieren poner candados en la boca.* They would hold us back with their bag of *reglas de academia.*

Oyé Como Ladra: El Lenguaje de la Frontera

> *Quien tiene boca se equivoca.*
> 　　　　—Mexican saying

"*Pocho,* cultural traitor, you're speaking the oppressor's language by speaking English, you're ruining the Spanish language," I have been accused by various Latinos and Latinas. Chicano Spanish is considered by the purist and by most Latinos deficient, a mutilation of Spanish.

But Chicano Spanish is a border tongue which developed naturally. Change, *evolución, enriquecimiento de palabras nuevas por invención o adopción* have created variants of Chicano Spanish, *un nuevo lenguaje. Un lenguaje que corresponde a un modo de vivir.* Chicano Spanish is not incorrect, it is a living language.

For a people who are neither Spanish nor live in a country in which Spanish is the first language; for a people who live in a country in which English is the reigning tongue but who are not Anglo; for a people who cannot entirely identify with either standard (formal, Castillian) Spanish nor standard English, what recourse is left to them but to create their own language? A language which they can connect their identity to, one capable of communicating the realities and values true to themselves—a language with terms that are neither *español ni inglés,* but both. We speak a patois, a forked tongue, a variation of two languages.

Chicano Spanish sprang out of the Chicanos' need to identify ourselves as a distinct people. We needed a language with which we could communicate with ourselves, a secret language. For some of us, language is a homeland closer than the Southwest—for many Chicanos today live in the Midwest and the East. And because we are a complex, heterogeneous people, we speak many languages. Some of the languages we speak are:

1. Standard English
2. Working class and slang English
3. Standard Spanish
4. Standard Mexican Spanish
5. North Mexican Spanish dialect
6. Chicano Spanish (Texas, New Mexico, Arizona and California have regional variations)
7. Tex-Mex
8. *Pachuco* (called *caló*)

My "home" tongues are the languages I speak with my sister and brothers, with my friends. They are the last five listed, with 6 and 7 being closest to my heart. From school, the media and job situations, I've picked up standard and working class English. From Mamagrande Locha and from reading Spanish and Mexican literature, I've picked up Standard Spanish and Standard Mexican Spanish. From *los recién llegados,* Mexican immigrants, and *braceros,* I learned the North Mexican dialect. With Mexicans I'll try to speak either Standard Mexican Spanish or the North Mexican dialect. From my parents and Chicanos living in the Valley, I picked up Chicano Texas Spanish, and I speak it with my mom, younger brother (who married a Mexican and who rarely mixes Spanish with English), aunts and older relatives.

With Chicanas from *Nuevo México* or *Arizona* I will speak Chicano Spanish a little, but often they don't understand what I'm saying. With most California Chicanas I speak entirely in English (unless I forget). When I first moved to San Francisco, I'd rattle off something in Spanish, unintentionally embarrassing them. Often it is only with another *Chicana tejana* that I can talk freely.

Words distorted by English are known as anglicisms or *pochismos.* The *pocho* is an anglicized Mexican or American of Mexican origin who speaks Spanish with an accent characteristic of North Americans and who distorts and reconstructs the language according to the influence of English.[3] Tex-Mex, or Spanglish, comes most naturally to me. I may switch back and forth from English to Spanish in the same sentence or in the same word. With my sister and my brother Nune and with Chicano *tejano* contemporaries I speak in Tex-Mex.

From kids and people my own age I picked up *Pachuco*. Pachuco (the language of the zoot suiters) is a language of rebellion, both against Standard Spanish and Standard English. It is a secret language. Adults of the culture and outsiders cannot understand it. It is made up of slang words from both English and Spanish. *Ruca* means girl or woman, *vato* means guy or dude, *chale* means no, *simón* means yes, *churo* is sure, talk is *periquiar, pigionear* means petting, *que gacho* means how nerdy, *ponte águila* means watch out, death is called *la pelona*. Through lack of practice and not having others who can speak it, I've lost most of the *Pachuco* tongue.

Chicano Spanish

Chicanos, after 250 years of Spanish/Anglo colonization have developed significant differences in the Spanish we speak. We collapse two adjacent vowels into a single syllable and sometimes shift the stress in certain words such as *maíz/maiz, cohete/cuete*. We leave out certain consonants when they appear between vowels, *lado/lao, mojado/mojao*. Chicanos from South Texas pronounced *f* as *j* as in *jue (fue)*. Chicanos use "archaisms," words that are no longer in the Spanish language, words that have been evolved out. We say *semos, truje, haiga, ansina*, and *naiden*. We retain the "archaic" *j*, as in *jalar*, that derives from an earlier *h*, (the French *halar* or the Germanic *halon* which was lost to standard Spanish in the 16th century), but which is still found in several regional dialects such as the one spoken in South Texas. (Due to geography, Chicanos from the Valley of South Texas were cut off linguistically from other Spanish speakers. We tend to use words that the Spaniards brought over from Medieval Spain. The majority of the Spanish colonizers in Mexico and the Southwest came from Extremadura—Hernán

Cortés was one of them—and Andalucía. Andalucians pronounce *ll* like a *y*, and their *d*'s tend to be absorbed by adjacent vowels: *tirado* becomes *tirao*. They brought *el lenguaje popular, dialectos y regionalismos.*[4])

Chicanos and other Spanish speakers also shift *ll* to *y* and *z* to *s*.[5] We leave out initial syllables, saying *tar* for *estar, toy* for *estoy, hora* for *ahora (cubanos* and *puertorriqueños* also leave out initial letters of some words). We also leave out the final syllable such as *pa* for *para*. The intervocalic *y*, the *ll* as in *tortilla, ella, botella,* gets replaced by *tortia* or *tortiya, ea, botea*. We add an additional syllable at the beginning of certain words: *atocar* for *tocar, agastar* for *gastar.* Sometimes we'll say *lavaste las vacijas,* other times *lavates* (substituting the *ates* verb endings for the *aste*).

We use anglicisms, words borrowed from English: *bola* from ball, *carpeta* from carpet, *máchina de lavar* (instead of *lavadora*) from washing machine. Tex-Mex argot, created by adding a Spanish sound at the beginning or end of an English word such as *cookiar* for cook, *watchar* for watch, *parkiar* for park, and *rapiar* for rape, is the result of the pressures on Spanish speakers to adapt to English.

We don't use the word *vosotros/as* or its accompanying verb form. We don't say *claro* (to mean yes), *imagínate,* or *me emociona,* unless we picked up Spanish from Latinas, out of a book, or in a classroom. Other Spanish-speaking groups are going through the same, or similar, development in their Spanish.

Linguistic Terrorism

Deslenguadas. Somos los del español deficiente. We are your linguistic nightmare, your linguistic aberration, your linguistic *mestizaje,* the subject of your *burla*. Because we speak with tongues of fire we are culturally crucified. Racially, culturally and linguistically *somos huérfanos*—we speak an orphan tongue.

Chicanas who grew up speaking Chicano Spanish have internalized the belief that we speak poor Spanish. It is illegitimate, a bastard language. And because we internalize how our language has been used against us by the dominant culture, we use our language differences against each other.

Chicana feminists often skirt around each other with suspicion and hesitation. For the longest time I couldn't figure it out. Then it dawned on me. To be close to another Chicana is like looking into the mirror. We are afraid of what we'll see there. *Pena.* Shame. Low estimation of self. In childhood we are told that our language is wrong. Repeated attacks on our native tongue diminish our sense of self. The attacks continue throughout our lives.

Chicanas feel uncomfortable talking in Spanish to Latinas, afraid of their censure. Their language was not outlawed in their countries. They had a whole lifetime of being immersed in their native tongue; generations, centuries in which Spanish was a first language, taught in school, heard on radio and TV, and read in the newspaper.

If a person, Chicana or Latina, has a low estimation of my native tongue, she also has a low estimation of me. Often with *mexicanas y latinas* we'll speak English as a neutral language. Even among Chicanas we tend to speak English at parties or conferences. Yet, at the same time, we're afraid the other will think we're *agringadas* because we don't speak Chicano Spanish. We oppress each other trying to out-Chicano each other, vying to be the "real" Chicanas, to speak like Chicanos. There is no one Chicano language just as there is no one Chicano experience. A monolingual Chicana whose first language is English or Spanish is just as much a Chicana as one who speaks several variants of Spanish. A Chicana from Michigan or Chicago or Detroit is just as much a Chicana as one from the Southwest. Chicano Spanish is as diverse linguistically as it is regionally.

By the end of this century, Spanish speakers will comprise the biggest minority group in the U.S., a country where students in high schools and colleges are encouraged to take French classes because French is considered more "cultured." But for a language to remain alive it must be used.[6] By the end of this century English, and not Spanish, will be the mother tongue of most Chicanos and Latinos.

So, if you want to really hurt me, talk badly about my language. Ethnic identity is twin skin to linguistic identity—I am my language. Until I can take pride in my language, I cannot take pride in myself. Until I can accept as legitimate Chicano Texas Spanish, Tex-Mex, and all the other languages I speak, I cannot accept the legitimacy of myself. Until I am free to write bilingually and to switch codes without having always to translate, while I still have to speak English or Spanish when I would rather speak Spanglish, and as long as I have to accommodate the English speakers rather than having them accommodate me, my tongue will be illegitimate.

I will no longer be made to feel ashamed of existing. I will have my voice: Indian, Spanish, white. I will have my serpent's tongue—my woman's voice, my sexual voice, my poet's voice. I will overcome the tradition of silence.

> My fingers
> move sly against your palm
> Like women everywhere, we speak in code. . . .
> —Melanie Kaye/Kantrowitz[7]

"Vistas," Corridos, y Comida: My Native Tongue

In the 1960s, I read my first Chicano novel. It was *City of Night* by John Rechy, a gay Texan, son of a Scottish father and a Mexican mother. For days I walked around in stunned amazement that a Chicano could write and could get published. When I read *I Am Joaquín*[8] I was surprised to see a bilingual book by a Chicano in print. When I saw poetry written in Tex-Mex for the first time, a feeling of pure joy flashed through me. I felt like we really existed as a people. In 1971, when I started teaching High School English to Chicano students, I tried to supplement the required texts with works by Chicanos, only to be reprimanded and forbidden to do so by the principal. He claimed that I was supposed to teach "American" and English literature. At the risk of being fired, I swore my students to secrecy and slipped in Chicano short stories, poems, a play. In graduate school, while working toward a Ph.D., I had to "argue" with one advisor after the other, semester after semester, before I was allowed to make Chicano literature an area of focus.

Even before I read books by Chicanos or Mexicans, it was the Mexican movies I saw at the drive-in—the Thursday night special of $1.00 a carload—that gave me a sense of belonging. *"Vámonos a las vistas,"* my mother would call out and we'd all—grandmother, brothers, sister and cousins—squeeze into the car. We'd wolf down cheese and bologna white bread sandwiches while watching Pedro Infante in melodramatic tear-jerkers like *Nosotros los pobres,* the first "real" Mexican movie (that was not an imitation of European movies). I remember seeing *Cuando los hijos se van* and surmising that all Mexican movies played up the love a mother has for her children and what ungrateful sons and daughters suffer when they are not devoted to their mothers. I remember the singing-type "westerns" of Jorge Negrete and Miguel Aceves Mejía. When watching Mexican movies, I felt a sense of homecoming as well as alienation. People who were to amount to something didn't go to Mexican movies, or *bailes* or tune their radios to *bolero, rancherita,* and *corrido* music.

The whole time I was growing up, there was *norteño* music sometimes called North Mexican border music, or Tex-Mex music, or Chicano music, or *cantina* (bar) music. I grew up listening to *conjuntos,* three- or four-piece bands made up of folk musicians playing guitar, *bajo sexto,* drums and button accordion, which Chicanos had borrowed from the German immigrants who had come to Central Texas and Mexico to farm and build breweries. In the Rio Grande Valley, Steve Jordan and Little Joe Hernández were popular, and Flaco Jiménez was the accordion king. The rhythms of Tex-Mex music are those of the polka, also adapted from the Germans, who in turn had borrowed the polka from the Czechs and Bohemians.

I remember the hot, sultry evenings when *corridos*—songs of love and death on the Texas-Mexican borderlands—reverberated out of cheap amplifiers from the local *cantinas* and wafted in through my bedroom window.

Corridos first became widely used along the South Texas/Mexican border during the early conflict between Chicanos and Anglos. The *corridos* are usually about Mexican heroes who do valiant deeds against the Anglo oppressors. Pancho Villa's song, *"La cucaracha,"* is the most famous one. *Corridos* of John F. Kennedy and his death are still very popular in the Valley. Older Chicanos remember Lydia

Mendoza, one of the great border *corrido* singers who was called *la Gloria de Tejas*. Her *"El tango negro,"* sung during the Great Depression, made her a singer of the people. The everpresent *corridos* narrated one hundred years of border history, bringing news of events as well as entertaining. These folk musicians and folk songs are our chief cultural mythmakers, and they made our hard lives seem bearable.

I grew up feeling ambivalent about our music. Country-western and rock-and-roll had more status. In the 50s and 60s, for the slightly educated and *agringado* Chicanos, there existed a sense of shame at being caught listening to our music. Yet I couldn't stop my feet from thumping to the music, could not stop humming the words, nor hide from myself the exhilaration I felt when I heard it.

There are more subtle ways that we internalize identification, especially in the forms of images and emotions. For me food and certain smells are tied to my identity, to my homeland. Woodsmoke curling up to an immense blue sky; woodsmoke perfuming my grandmother's clothes, her skin. The stench of cow manure and the yellow patches on the ground; the crack of a .22 rifle and the reek of cordite. Homemade white cheese sizzling in a pan, melting inside a folded *tortilla*. My sister Hilda's hot, spicy *menudo, chile colorado* making it deep red, pieces of *panza* and hominy floating on top. My brother Carito barbecuing *fajitas* in the backyard. Even now and 3,000 miles away, I can see my mother spicing the ground beef, pork and venison with *chile*. My mouth salivates at the thought of the hot steaming *tamales* I would be eating if I were home.

Si Le Preguntas a Mi Mamá, "¿Qué eres?"

> "Identity is the essential core of who we are as individuals, the conscious experience of the self inside."
>
> —Kaufman[9]

Nosotros los Chicanos straddle the borderlands. On one side of us, we are constantly exposed to the

Spanish of the Mexicans, on the other side we hear the Anglos' incessant clamoring so that we forget our language. Among ourselves we don't say *nosotros los americanos, o nosotros los españoles, o nosotros los hispanos.* We say *nosotros los mexicanos* (by *mexicanos* we do not mean citizens of Mexico; we do not mean a national identity, but a racial one). We distinguish between *mexicanos del otro lado* and *mexicanos de este lado.* Deep in our hearts we believe that being Mexican has nothing to do with which country one lives in. Being Mexican is a state of soul—not one of mind, not one of citizenship. Neither eagle nor serpent, but both. And like the ocean, neither animal respects borders.

> *Dime con quien andas y te diré quien eres.* (Tell me who your friends are and I'll tell you who you are.)
> —Mexican saying

Si le preguntas a mi mamá, "¿Qué eres?" te dirá, "Soy mexicana." My brothers and sister say the same. I sometimes will answer *"soy mexicana"* and at others will say *"soy Chicana" o "soy tejana."* But I identified as *"Raza"* before I ever identified as *"mexicana"* or "Chicana."

As a culture, we call ourselves Spanish when referring to ourselves as a linguistic group and when copping out. It is then that we forget our predominant Indian genes. We are 70 to 80% Indian.[10] We call ourselves Hispanic[11] or Spanish-American or Latin American or Latin when linking ourselves to other Spanish-speaking peoples of the Western hemisphere and when copping out. We call ourselves Mexican-American[12] to signify we are neither Mexican nor American, but more the noun "American" than the adjective "Mexican" (and when copping out).

Chicanos and other people of color suffer economically for not acculturating. This voluntary (yet forced) alienation makes for psychological conflict, a kind of dual identity—we don't identify with the Anglo-American cultural values and we don't totally identify with the Mexican cultural values. We are a synergy of two cultures with various degrees of Mexicanness or Angloness. I have so internalized the borderland conflict that sometimes I feel like one cancels out the other and we are zero, nothing, no one. *A veces no soy nada ni nadie. Pero hasta cuando no lo soy, lo soy.*

When not copping out, when we know we are more than nothing, we call ourselves Mexican, referring to race and ancestry; *mestizo* when affirming both our Indian and Spanish (but we hardly ever own our Black ancestry); Chicano when referring to a politically aware people born and/or raised in the U.S.; *Raza* when referring to Chicanos; *tejanos* when we are Chicanos from Texas.

Chicanos did not know we were a people until 1965 when César Chávez and the farmworkers united and *I Am Joaquín* was published and *la Raza Unida* party was formed in Texas. With that recognition, we became a distinct people. Something momentous happened to the Chicano soul—we became aware of our reality and acquired a name and a language (Chicano Spanish) that reflected that reality. Now that we had a name, some of the fragmented pieces began to fall together—who we were, what we were, how we had evolved. We began to get glimpses of what we might eventually become.

Yet the struggle of identities continues, the struggle of borders is our reality still. One day the inner struggle will cease and a true integration take place. In the meantime, *tenemos que hacerla lucha. ¿Quién está protegiendo los ranchos de mi gente? ¿Quién está tratando de cerrar la fisura entre la india y el blanco en nuestra sangre? El Chicano, sí, el Chicano que anda como un ladrón en su propia casa.*

Los Chicanos, how patient we seem, how very patient. There is the quiet of the Indian about us.[13] We know how to survive. When other races have given up their tongue, we've kept ours. We know what it is to live under the hammer blow of the dominant *norteamericano* culture. But more than we count the blows, we count the days the weeks the years the centuries the eons until the white laws and commerce and customs will rot in the deserts they've created, lie bleached. *Humildes* yet proud, *quietos* yet wild, *nosotros los mexicanos*-Chicanos will walk by the crumbling ashes as we go about our business. Stubborn, persevering, impenetrable as stone, yet possessing a malleability that renders us unbreakable, we, the *mestizas* and *mestizos*, will remain.

Notes

1. Ray Gwyn Smith, *Moorland is Cold Country*, unpublished book.

2. Irena Klepfisz, "*Di rayze aheym*/The Journey Home," in *The Tribe of Dina: A Jewish Women's Anthology*, Melanie Kaye/Kantrowitz and Irena Klepfisz, eds. (Montpelier, VT: Sinister Wisdom Books, 1986), 49.

3. R.C. Ortega, *Dialectología Del Barrio*, trans. Hortencia S. Alwan (Los Angeles, CA: R.C. Ortega Publisher & Bookseller, 1977), 132.

4. Eduardo Hernandéz-Chávez, Andrew D. Cohen, and Anthony F. Beltramo, *El Lenguaje de los Chicanos: Regional and Social Characteristics of Language Used By Mexican Americans* (Arlington, VA: Center for Applied Linguistics, 1975), 39.

5. Hernandéz-Chávez, xvii.

6. Irena Klepfisz, "Secular Jewish Identity: Yidishkayt in America," in *The Tribe of Dina*, Kaye/Kantrowitz and Klepfisz, eds., 43.

7. Melanie Kaye/Kantrowitz, "Sign," in *We Speak In Code: Poems and Other Writings* (Pittsburgh, PA: Motheroot Publications, Inc., 1980), 85.

8. Rodolfo Gonzales, *I Am Joaquín/Yo Soy Joaquín* (New York, NY: Bantam Books, 1972). It was first published in 1967.

9. Kaufman, 68.

10. Chávez, 88–90.

11. "Hispanic" is derived from *Hispanis* (*España,* a name given to the Iberian Peninsula in ancient times when it was a part of the Roman Empire) and is a term designated by the US government to make it easier to handle us on paper.

12. The Treaty of Guadalupe Hidalgo created the Mexican American in 1848.

13. Anglos, in order to alleviate their guilt for dispossessing the Chicano, stressed the Spanish part of us and perpetrated the myth of the Spanish Southwest. We have accepted the fiction that we are Hispanic, that is Spanish, in order to accommodate ourselves to the dominant culture and its abhorrence of Indians. Chavez, 88–91.

29.
TAXI CAB PUBLICS AND THE PRODUCTION OF *BROWN SPACE* AFTER 9/11

Sarah Sharma

We need to thank god for those people that do it, that do it everyday to fight those enemies who drive taxis during the day and kill at night. (Senator Conrad Burns, August 25, 2006)

Since 9/11 people treat me differently, when people are drunk they just say it outright 'do you know Osama, how come you look like Osama, go back home terrorist.' In the day time I've noticed that people give orders now. Like, they don't talk to me like I'm a human, they don't treat me like a human but like an animal, go here, go there, turn. (Sam, a Toronto city taxi driver, March 2007)

Republican Senator Conrad Burns (1989–2007) had no apology for his 'taxi as terrorist' statement made at a fundraiser in Belgrade, Montana. In fact, Laura Bush took center stage right after him telling the crowd Senator Burns was 'a wonderful leader for Montana.' Neither were there any significant accounts from the major news networks reporting that Burns, the longest running senator in Montana's history, was a fear mongering racist or classist. At best, he was presented as foolish in his choice of words. Senator Conrad Burns had merely stirred up some controversy in these difficult times by singling out taxi drivers. But Burns continued to make this statement, with slight variations, two more times that week. In a campaign stop in Butte, Montana he exclaimed, 'This campaign is about the next generation; it is if we have a safe world and a secure world where our kids can go to bed at night and not worry about a guy that drives a taxicab in the daytime and kills at night.' The 'campaign' maintained Burns was only pointing out that terrorists *could* be anywhere. A public statement issued in his defense by a campaign spokesperson read, 'The point is there are terrorists that live amongst us. Not only here, but in Britain and the entire world. Whether they are taxi drivers or investment bankers, the fact remains that this is a new type of enemy.' There has yet to be a single report of an investment banker pulled away from a spreadsheet to meet the same violent fate innocent taxi drivers have endured post-9/11.

In Toronto, New York City, Washington DC, San Antonio, Sydney, Melbourne, and London, taxi drivers are victims of 9/11 revenge attacks. This occurs on top of already arduous and poor working conditions of long hours, deteriorating health, alienation, and a hardly manageable income. Across these urban centers the majority of cab drivers are South Asian, Middle Eastern, Russian, or North African. The public face of the city taxi driver is unarguably brown. Acts of violence range from the drunken slur 'you look like Osama' to cab drivers pulled out of their cabs, dragged onto the sidewalk, and killed. In London seven days after 9/11 three men in their mid-twenties dragged an asylum seeking taxi driver from Afghanistan out of his vehicle, smashed a bottle over his head, and kicked his body until he was paralyzed. During the attack he was taunted with racial slurs implicating him to 9/11 (Dodd 2001 p. 2). In the San

Francisco Bay Area over a three month period in the fall of 2003 two Sikh taxi drivers were shot and killed (Jayadev 2003). This time it was turbans that had signified Taliban. In Melbourne 2004, The Victoria Taxi Directorate with the help of the Ministry of Labor introduced a new policy that would allow taxi drivers to conceal their name tags from their fares if they were feeling under threat (Masanauskas 2004). Like New York and Toronto over 60 percent of Melbourne taxi drivers are Muslim and face regular racial taunts regarding their apparent essentialist terrorist proclivities.

The taxi-terrorist rant is a popular one of Islamophobic bloggers and terrorist watch groups such as *Jihad Watch, Muslim Monitor* and *Dhimmi Watch*. The taxi-terrorist articulation is also uttered by conservative politicians and by right-wing news sources such as WorldNetDaily.com and *Investor's Business Daily*. While none are bastions of news credibility, the importance of these 'sources' lies in how such fantastical constructions temporarily fix and define the features, behaviors, and spatial practices of brown. While the culture and politics of the cities where drivers have endured this violence are tied to different immigration histories and socio-economic contexts, what binds them is that they are all urban centers where the majority of taxis are driven by a reserve labor force of immigrant populations from South Asia, the Middle East, and North Africa. The significance of the taxi-terrorist articulation is therefore not tied to a particular city or even the specific paths of migration of the driver. Instead the significance of the 'taxi-terrorist' lies in a very specific spatio-temporality after 9/11—living and laboring in civic space as a fear inducing brown body.

Senator Burns was not simply implying that terrorists could be anywhere, he was tapping into a latent public anxiety that *immigrant taxi drivers were everywhere*. As a vehicle that roams urban space and connects private space to public space, the taxi is an important site in public discussions between journalists, artists, bloggers, politicians, and urban planners over the politics of civic space. The taxi figures prominently in debates over who has the *right to the city* (Mitchell 2003). The yellow cab has for decades worked as an iconic image of the Manhattan streetscape. Across other major cities, the taxi links local space to global space as it transports between airports, hotels, shopping centers, and business districts. It services the elderly and the infirmed, the too drunk to drive, and those not wanting to walk alone. It is a public space of transit: moving capital, serving safety, giving tours, and providing local knowledge. The taxi is absolutely integral to the daily life of any urban fabric, but it also incites fear. As soon as the skyline became a target, it seems too that the yellow car on the ground became an icon that unsettled and disturbed.

Out of this dual construction of the taxi cab, I introduce the concept of *Brown Space* as a means of understanding the particular spatial politics of brown as an 'identificatory strategy' after 9/11 (Silva 2010). On the one hand, the taxi is configured as a roving terrorist cell while on the other hand continues to figure in the popular imaginary as a 'public sphere on wheels.' One imaginary of the taxi is rooted in the dark corners of the conservative right. Here, the taxi becomes *Brown Space*, a site where the knowledge of brown is produced and then disciplined. The other vision of the taxi is promulgated by architects, television producers, and journalists. Here, the taxi figures romantically and prominently within the urban fabric *but* the embodied taxi driver is strangely absent. The missing driver works to distinguish public space from *Brown Space*. In both instances, an idealized civic space is one without brown.

Brown is either subject to strategic elimination because of its all too visible presence or is discursively rendered invisible. That there are plans and attempts to eliminate brown, on the one hand, and a discursive eliding, on the other, means that the more usual tension between invisibility and visibility that plagues 'others' does not have the same material reality for the brown taxi driver in the post-9/11 urban fabric. The brown taxi driver is not Ralph Ellison's *Invisible Man* who is 'seen through' and 'seen past' as if they do not exist. The fact of the matter is that the brown taxi driver is now completely visible and cannot take advantage of invisibility or anonymity in the city. Further, the brown taxi driver is not invisible in the same way as the Latina nannies, dog-walkers, Mexican gardeners, and Sri Lankan cooks that Saskia

Sassen locates as globalizations' growing under class (Sassen 1998). It is specifically in the discourse of the taxi as public space, as we will see later, where the taxi driver is absent. It is not because their labor is invisible or because they really do go unseen but because this form of brown is simply too difficult to contend with. Such dangerous animations of public space, where labor and the material conditions in which one labors are ignored, provides fertile ground for the production of *Brown Space*.

Before contextualizing these two configurations of the taxi, I begin with a framework for theorizing *Brown Space*. I follow with a discussion of the lived reality of taxi driving after 9/11. This section is based on 10 interviews lasting approximately two hours with Toronto city taxi drivers between 2004 and 2006 regarding experiences with their fares and conditions of their labor.

Theorizing a Framework for *Brown Space*

Jody Berland in *New Keywords* avows, 'Space has become a generous source for metaphor: one maps one's view of the world, or strategies for changing it; one finds one's space, and seeks to understand where something or someone is coming from' (2005, p. 334). I invoke the term *Brown Space* to forefront both the transient nature of the identifier and the 'publicness' of Brown as an alternative to conceptualizing identity in terms of community, spaces of belonging, or media representation. *Brown Space* is produced by two simultaneous and mutually reinforcing processes. The first is the demarcation of *Brown Space* from normalized civic space. The second refers to the various means by which the malleable spectrum of brown temporally halts—marking the parameters of brown.

In the taxi, the knowledge of brown is produced by seemingly innocent interrogations such as 'where are you from' to brutal acts of physical violence. Alongside this, the new knowledge of brown circulates on internet sites and in news media quips and sound bites. These mechanics of power fix momentarily what *it is* to be brown, what objects, practices, and characteristics will *now* signify and be included in the grab-bag space of brown. In every reference of

taxi driver to terrorist, brown becomes a little more known—it is named, its attributes are described, and it is dressed and donned.

Kumarini Silva's conceptualizing of brown as an 'identificatory strategy' rather than an 'identity' is based on a Foucauldian approach to disciplinarity (Foucault 1977). I extend her reliance on Foucault to include the mutual processes of regulation (Foucault 2003) as it relates to the taxi. As Foucault argues, the state normalizes through the two poles of biopower—regulation and discipline—wherein the body is understood as a kind of machine. Regulation and discipline are bound together by a common purpose: control over the life force of the individual and the social body. This entails the optimization of the productive forces of life through individuating and totalizing techniques of power. This becomes especially significant in the taxi as it is also a space of labor where brown is defined (knowledge) and disciplined (power). The wage laboring immigrant is disciplined in various intersecting means and ways.

Violence against brown is often able to escape the charge of state racism since what we are witnessing in the policing of brown does not operate strictly within a biological framework of skin color or singular racialized identities. This is precisely why Burns was able to elude the label of racist. To recall, his statement was not meant to be about race, but instead the deracialized 'faceless enemies.' Faceless, then, we might want to declare is the 'new Brown.' The lack of a racialized essential identity does not indicate a post-racial society or a postmodern movement away from troublesome essentialisms, instead in this instance it is strategic and works to intensify racial violence. The net is cast to locate this other through an even wider range of signifying objects, practices, and ways of being in public. This admonition that *it could be anyone*, an investment banker or a taxi driver, has the effect of sanctioning the unparalleled violence directed towards the brown bodies that are deemed scary and suspect.

Racism is still implicit in the production of *Brown Space* according to the second tenet of Foucault's theory of biopower. While the first refers to the hierarchy of biological difference, the second entails the elimination of threats to the purity, health, and security of the state under imperatives of race war (2003, p. 255). Brown is problematized as a unified other. Foucault defines racism as 'a way of introducing a break into the domain of life that is under power's control: the break between what must live and what must die' (p. 254). Creating a hierarchy of races, even different categories of brown, is a way of 'fragmenting the field of the biological that power controls' (p. 256). Brown, because it refuses fragmented categories, is seen to pose a greater biological and physical threat to the public. It is imagined as an uncontainable quality—the parameters of what is brown (what may be a threat, can) extend (infinitely) to no end.

In this context, what we are witnessing is the emergence of *Brown Space* as a by-product of its constitutive outside—'social order' and normalized civic space. Thus, the conduct of brown becomes more important than its signifying skin. Laboring in civic space and being close to the public is understood in the case of the brown taxi driver as a form of conduct. In other words, brown is not just the other to normalized social order—but a particular type of brown is under extensive scrutiny after 9/11.

The work of knowing brown is regulatory and disciplinary working to produce what Jack Bratich points to as part of the 'New Normal', in this case here the new normalized civic space post-9/11. Brown is understood as an indistinguishable figure or, as Bratich terms, an 'invisible network' where terrorists lurk. As such, not knowing what brown is exactly becomes an important political weapon for the state (Bratich 2006). In fact, the normalized society works best when there are unknown unknowns running amok because it calls upon everyday citizens to know. Mark Andrejevic (2005) argues individuals in a risk society or era responsibilization are encouraged to internalize government strategies. The cab becomes vulnerable to what Andrejevic calls 'lateral surveillance', a type of surveillance that is not top-down but is enacted across the social strata. While Andrejevic is referencing peer-to-peer monitoring and social networking, this surveillance strategy is not by any means site specific. Moreover, the taxi occupies a particularly precarious position in the post-9/11 securitization of everyday life. As James Hay

and Mark Andrejevic point out in 'the new social security' (2006), 'transportation technologies serve not only as vectors of attack (and hence the focus of security campaigns) but also as means for coordinating a distributed defense against a de-centralized threat' (2006, p. 341). The intimate yet terrifying space of the cab is at once a vehicle for the circulation of people and capital, but it is now seen as a potential weapon. For the inquiring passenger the taxi-cab doubles as an interrogation room or holding cell. As a result, the public takes on the career of a spy accumulating knowledge about brown while sitting in the cab. The augmenting of the citizen as soldier, citizen as terrorist, and citizen as representative or worker of state security is part and parcel of an era of 'flexible warfare', as Hay and Andrejevic (2006) argue. Other deployments of this redoubling are discussed in detail in their 2006 special issue of *Cultural Studies* on *Homeland Insecurities*. Post-9/11 good citizens are invited to become *ad hoc* officers of homeland security. But specific to the brown taxi driver is the experience whereby these *ad hoc* citizen-officers determine and relay to the taxi driver verbally and physically what their current status is in civic space. In the present geopolitical climate some days it is the drivers from Somalia that get the brunt of the taunts and on other days it is anyone that remotely signifies.

Stuart Hall's (1996) formulation of a constitutive outside to identity is helpful here. Hall argues that processes of identification require what is left outside the constitutive outside to consolidate the process. As malleable as it might be (Silva), there *is* a locatable 'other' of brown. It is a carefully and strategically articulated other—one that represents social order, the future of civilization (American style freedom), and the health of the social body. And it is this orderliness, this other, that does the public and state policing. It is not just that there is a constitutive outside, but rather that this outside can better police brown by producing *Brown Space* while simultaneously maintaining a public ideal free from the threat of brown.

In a point of divergence from Stuart Hall, *Brown Space* does not quite correspond to his theorizing of diasporic space as a marked out space for a subcultural identity within a hegemonic order (Hall &

Jefferson 1976). The Toronto taxi drivers I interviewed identified particular areas where people from
their diasporic communities would take rest. Sikh
taxi drivers discussed one particular house close
to Toronto's International Airport where they took
their breaks. Another referred to a taxi stand north
of the city where Iranian taxi drivers would stand
around and stretch. While there are spaces of congregation for drivers demarcated by the communities
they identify with, *Brown Space* is defined externally.
Brown Space is not a gathering space. It is a space
that is activated via identificatory strategies that are
always external to it. *Brown Space* is identified and
created simultaneously. In the same moment it is
elicited, its contents and inhabitants are sorted, ordered, and managed. In other words, brown is not
a space of belonging, empowerment, or resistance.
Although it could clearly become this, as organizing
and protesting are a large part of the city taxi driver's
struggle. My intent is not to diminish this but instead
to focus on what this space internalizes. *Brown Space*
is distinct from practices of place that are made by
choice or affinity, including organizing.

In *Brown Space* the daily life of its inhabitants are
subject to a constant biopolitical reduction in value.
In other words, taxi drivers are not only exposed to
death but they are, as I will discuss later, denied inclusion in public space. The taxi, as a vehicle transporting citizens, is part of the vision of thriving public
space, yet the driver, as potential terrorist, becomes
sub-human, a monster, and a threat to be eradicated.
As Foucault argues in *Society Must Be Defended*, it
is within a normalizing society that race or racism
becomes the precondition that makes killing acceptable (2003, p. 256). Foucault does not mean to literally kill—but rather to be exposed to death, 'When I
say killing, I obviously don't mean murder: the fact
of exposing someone to death, increasing the risk
of death for some people, or quite simply, political
death, expulsion, rejection, and so on' (p. 256). This
exclusion or elimination also includes the restriction
of certain population's public presence through regulation and discipline. When the taxi is hailed in the
public domain as a terrorist, a simultaneous statement is implied regarding the acceptable use and
ideal composition of public space.

Hailing *Brown Space*

In urban centers various economic, regulatory, and
disciplinary mechanisms of control have previously
worked to manage the class and racial dimensions of
the cab's perceived social threats. In Toronto, the On-
tario Coalition for Poverty has been organizing with
the Toronto Coalition of Concerned Taxi Drivers for
the past five years to fight the extensive ticketing, random checks, and bi-law infractions that taxi drivers
face when they pull over to catch fares or park for a
few minutes to use a toilet. In New York City, for
example, the taxi has a well documented history of
regulation as a site of extensive immigrant labor well
before it was conceived of us a potential terrorist
threat. Biju Mathew in *Taxi! Cabs and Capitalism* in
New York City explains Giuliani's *Quality of Life* reforms as they targeted taxi drivers (Mathew 2005). In
fact, taxi drivers were first publicly declared 'taxi terrorists' well before September 11 by Mayor Rudy Giuliani in response to a one day taxi strike on May 13,
1998 in New York City. The taxi driver's job action
was provoked by Giuliani's reform which targeted the
conduct of taxi drivers during a time of urban renewal
and the return of the white middle class to the city.[1]
'Terrorist' was just one of the many labels Giuliani
used to refer to the drivers—they were also described
as rapists, racists, and uncivilized men who urinate in
the street. Mathew relays how the initiation of a NYPD
Taxi Unit and *Operation Refusal* was a means of 'dis-
ciplining and punishing' taxi driver's public conduct
(2005, p. 129). *Operation Refusal* referred to a policy by
Giuliani and the Taxi and Limousine Commission that
would automatically suspend taxi drivers who refused
service to any fare. According to Giuliani, South Asian
taxi drivers had been refusing African American fares.
This complicated issue of US race relations became
a means to fine and dismiss taxi drivers for other
imagined offenses. Matthew maintains that New York
City's urban renewal manipulated race relations as a
mode of managing class relations. In the post-9/11
urban fabric there emerges another opportunity to
control the acceptable publicness of brown and this
time it occurs via lateral control.

The taxi is unsettling as an intimate and mobile
space of human encounter driven by 'the foreigner.'

It becomes especially threatening because routes and paths cannot be predetermined. As *WorldNet-Daily*, a conservative Christian news service, covers, 'If they're (taxi-drivers) not suspects themselves, they pick up suspects at airports and take them to safe-houses here. It is a Jihadi Network' (May 11, 2007). This sentiment is also captured by statements made by a civilian soldier blogging in Luton, UK,

> They operate as an organized surveillance opera-tion because they can be anywhere at any time and no body bats an eye lid at them being out of place because they are taxis. It is very worrying really considering they know the streets of Dun-stable inside out, they know whose (*sic*) who and where they live so have the community locked down.[2]

Here, the taxi is understood as a vehicle that should be under constant surveillance as it might be out-surveilling the state. Furthermore, this blogger makes an explicit assumption about the racialization of space; 'nobody bats an eye lid at them being out of place.' The taxi is constructed as an uncontainable threat that moves with far too much freedom; con-necting spaces that should not be connected, such as mosques to airports. The taxi is read as infiltrating civic space and collecting tactical knowledge about it.

Significantly, the driving of a taxi arises in this dis-course as indication of suspect behavior, rather than the form of intensive labor that it is. The taxi driver's mobility is imagined as a cultural trait. Another blog-ger writes,

> If I was a terrorist, I would NOT communicate through the internet or mail or cell phone, I'd start a network through the taxi services. This is such a ripe culture due to their mobility, how clearly taxicab drivers see transportation patterns, know where people are going, know who is using taxis (*sic*) and which locations are most vulnerable. In the Muslim world, they are very good at handoff and messenger relay systems.[3]

Being mobile and adept at message relay becomes part of the Muslim's essential identity. Immigrant taxi drivers are not taxi drivers because of specific economic and immigration stipulations that restrict access to other forms of work or careers they are already qualified for. No, they are understood here as taxi drivers because they are essentially both a mo-bile people and innately terrorists. In other words, mobility and having too much access to the public becomes an unruly and deviant characteristic of brown that must be quelled.

Another way of quelling brown's presence is by marking out the conduct of brown as 'inappropriate.' This can be seen in the recent conservative conster-nation over the installment of footbaths to accom-modate drivers' long hours and religious needs at Kansas City airport. *WorldNetDaily* reported that po-lice in Kansas were concerned that footbaths would result in groups of Muslim men loitering on airport property (May 11, 2007). Kansas City airport officials responded by denying that the footbaths were explic-itly for the Muslim drivers. Their public statement does not however respond to the accusation that police were concerned about Muslim taxi loiterers. Of course somewhere in the conservative public dia-logue one could now expect a taxi terrorist link. *Inves-tor's Business Daily* claimed the footbaths were them-selves a sanctioning of terrorism. The last line of their article reads 'What's next, prayer rug cleaning, and box cutter dispensers' (*Investor's Business Daily* May 3, 2007). Celebrity news personalities, such as Dennis Miller and Bill O'Reilly, responded to the foot-bath discussions with commentary on 'appropriate' public conduct (May 10, 2007). The production of *Brown Space* does not always depend on a direct ter-rorist articulation. Miller and O'Reilly remain silent about the terrorist accusation and instead stake big-oted claims over the taxi driver's rights in civic space. Miller and O'Reilly demonize otherness in such a way that is directed towards ridding space of certain types of publicness, ones that the taxi driver's pres-ence might entail.

> Miller: Everybody's got to try to fit into the col-lective a little here. And all this bringing your little specialties into the overview is starting to get real boring with me. If you're a cabdriver, drive the guy who has hailed you at some point.

O'Reilly: All right. I think you're right on the enough is enough. And I think the point about, look, you're here, this is our country. Fit in. You want to wash your feet, do it at home like everyone else, except . . .

Miller: Amen. The last 10 cab rides I've had in New York the guy hadn't washed anything.

(The O'Reilly Show, May 10, 2007)

Any transformation in the use of public space by this particular laboring individual is met with concern. The Miller-O'Reilly discussion indicates another tactical maneuver common to demarcating appropriate conduct for certain populations; the private sphere is invoked as soon as the public becomes too public for the powers that be. Relegating activities to the 'private' sphere is an attempt to veil the racist and classed implications of marking out space in such a way.

This outright mobilizing of the private sphere as a means of managing racialized and classed distinctions is further evidenced by the fact that within the same space, the modern airport, there are plenty of indications that grooming in public is not only acceptable but invited. Travelers, pilots, and flight attendants are encouraged to get a pedicure at one of the many airport spas, take a hot shower in the VIP lounge provided by a trusted carrier, or even get a massage in the very public aisle-way kiosks. From pedicures to footbaths the line between brown space and public space is pretty firmly managed. The malleable spectrum of brown touches down at Kansas City airport and grabs up footbaths, brown people that loiter, dirty feet, the overwhelming desire for grooming in public, and body odor.

Taxis without Drivers: Public Space after *Brown Space*

The popular imaginary of the taxi driver treats the taxi as a public laboratory where the state of things might be assessed and diagnosed. *Taxi! A Social History of the New York City Cabdriver* (2008) provides a rich history based on memoirs and other popular cultural texts of the taxi drivers changing public character. The changing face of the taxi driver parallels

larger interrelated social changes such as immigration, class mobility, and geopolitics. A popular reality television show, *Taxi Cab Confessions*, is an exemplar of this notion of the taxi as a public sphere on the road. The cabs from various US urban centers are fitted with hidden cameras and a driver who asks pointed and personal questions. In general, the taxi is often romanticized and sometimes operates as a vehicle for a nostalgic public. The taxi continues to be upheld as an emblem of thriving public space—where people intersect, cross paths, and share in the life of a city. But it is a pacified space, devoid of brown.

In 2007 ABC Primetime aired an investigative expose 'Taxicab Confessions: Racism on the Road—What would you do if your cab driver was saying hateful and racist things?' The conclusion of the episode revealed that the riding publics in New Jersey and Georgia would not intervene in racist tirades from the drivers but often join in. The show featured two drivers—one black and one white. This racial binary simplifies race relations in the United States to a matter of stereotyping. The racial comments made by the drivers referred to Jews, Chinese, Arabs, and African-Americans. These were old binaries and essentialisms, not unimportant but a sort of well established racism that the public would no longer be shocked by. It was as if 9/11 had never happened and America could return to racism as usual, not this murky one that hardly even passes for racism. This feature on 'racism today', in failing to contend with the material realities of taxi drivers post-9/11, is indicative of how the dual strategic identification and denial of brown is not seen as a form of racism but as necessary and justifiable to the security of the social order.

In another popular use of the taxi as a mobile public, the taxi is promoted as a site at which consumer desire might be transformed. Taxis in Toronto, London, Sydney, and New York are increasingly equipped with interactive screens in the backseat providing coupons to customers if they partake in consumer trivia. External advertisements on the taxi transmit messages across the city to target audiences that are 'upper class and high spenders' who are otherwise 'media elusive.'[4] *Ubiquitous Media Corporation* brands their own initiative as the 'Intelligent Use of Space' with 'genuinely engaged drivers who will go the extra mile for the brand they are advertising.' Here, the taxi is understood as another public space to colonize and a spectacle to enhance through privatization and media saturation. The taxi driver is imagined in the service of commercial institutions rather than the public. It is no wonder then that the response to the media saturation of the taxi is met by Habermasian like laments of the structural transformation of the cab. Andrew Friedman, author of *The World is Flat*, writes of cab drivers on their cellphones, in an op-ed in the *New York Times* 'The Taxi Driver,' 'I guess the era of foreign correspondents quoting taxi drivers is over. The taxi driver is too busy to give you a quote' (Friedman 2006). It turns out that Friedman was perhaps more disgruntled over the fact that he could not concentrate on his own work with the cab driver talking on the phone:

> After the car started to roll, I saw he had a movie playing on the screen in the dashboard—on the flat panel that usually displays the GPS road map. I noticed this because between his talking on the phone and the movie, I could barely concentrate. I, alas, was in the back seat trying to finish a column on my laptop.

Similarly, there is an imagined loss of the neutral observer who used to provide political and social commentary but is now drowned out by externally guided media technologies. Either way, the taxi is imagined to contain the unaffected driver who will do the necessary work of moving bodies, messages, and information. In these imaginings, however, the driver becomes disembodied, declassed, and e-raced; made external to public space but in the service of the public.

The most notable expression of how the taxi is an idealized public space might have been at the 2007 International Automobile Show. The opening exhibition TAXI07 marked the 100th anniversary of the taxi in New York City. The Design Trust for Public Space displayed blueprints and models for future taxi interiors and exteriors, green-friendly taxis, green spaces for taxi drivers to park and take breaks, and

taxi waiting areas for passengers. The driving ethos behind the installation was the notion of the taxi as a 'moving public space.' The Design Trust states a political commitment to resist the neo-liberal governing of public space after 9/11. TAXI07 combined the input of urban planners, architects, artists, and activists, combing their visions for the future of the taxi and public space. But, significantly missing from the exhibition was a connection between public space and the daily lives of the drivers—the racism, labor conditions, robberies, and the increasing association of taxi drivers as suspect populations. What TAXI07 committed itself to was public acknowledgment of the taxi's fundamental role in cultivating and maintaining civic space. But it did so as if the taxi's relationship to public space had nothing to do with who sits in the front seat. Instead technological, architectural, and urban planning solutions were offered to the problems of public space, without acknowledging the racial, political, economic difference that are all extremely crucial to post-9/11 civic space.

Living and Laboring *Brown Space*

The daily lives of taxi drivers today attests to the harsh reality of living and laboring in *Brown Space*. The taxi's mobility, coupled with the fact that it is also a space of labor, means the taxi is resistant to forms of spatial ordering that have typically been associated with state racism or even other brown spaces— camps, ghettoes, detainment centers, prisons, farms, meat packing plants, and border interrogation rooms. In Foucault's terms, the ordering of racialized space makes intelligible the production of truth claims and knowledge about a given population. Because the taxi eludes this form of ordering, one effective way of ordering the taxi in public life occurs by way of backseat dialogue that slips easily into public interrogations. The interior space of the cab becomes subject to producing the truth of brown through interaction. When the state and its 'media lapdogs' (McChesney 2002) consistently maintain that the enemy lies amongst us and is a shadowy figure—murky and muddy as the color brown—they delegate to the public the work of finding and knowing this faceless figure. Again, referring back to Bratich (2006) and

Andrejevic (2005), lateral surveillance is carried out as a form of sanctioned behavior under the auspices of protecting of the nation.

A common backseat dialogue that works to fix the spectrum of brown begins by questioning the drivers' origins. According to the drivers, conversations that are not about the weather usually begin by the simple question, 'Where are you from?' Hamid, a Toronto city taxi driver of 15 years who moved from Iran explains:

> People have always asked me where I'm from. It is the first question you get when you are a driver. When I first came they wanted to know about the Gulf War, what kind of education I had, and if I was trying to get a real job. Sometimes they were really asking to make sure I wasn't going to try working, trying to take a job or something. Now (since 9/11) they want to know if I have some relationship or something to say about the whole thing (9/11).

Hamid's statement reveals that the spectrum of brown is contingent upon the specific conjuncture in which the questions 'where are you from' is asked. In Toronto, the question at one point could not be disarticulated from the conservative accusation that an immigrant workforce was 'taking all of the jobs.' Taxi drivers' daily lives are compounded by geopolitical forces beyond their control and structured by the harsh struggle to make a livable wage. When the spectrum of brown lands and fixes on taxi cab, it does so differently depending on what possible threat brown might pose to the social order at a given time. As of late, the question 'where are you from' begins a process of sorting through brown bodies to determine which ones are suspect terrorists.

The taxonomic process that goes into defining brown is evidenced in the disturbing practice of passengers profiling drivers before entering the cab. All of the drivers recounted incidences and spoke of this as a new and constant feature of their lives post-9/11. Adam, who moved to Toronto from Somalia in 1995, explains,

> People come up to the cab window and look in and look at the driver from the passenger side.

> If they think you look like suspicious—like if you have a beard or you are wearing a hat (a taqiya), turban, there is something with Arabic or even Hindi writing in the cab they look at it, look at you, then they just pretend that they had a question to ask you and then they walk to the next cab. No one used to stop and ask me questions before.

With Adam's example, we see that the spectrum of brown gathers the taqiya, the turban, beards, and Arabic and Hindi characters. Adam adds, 'I know some (drivers) have less things laying around the cab that would make people ask questions, they don't want to deal with this for a ride.' Similar to the strategy in Melbourne of hiding your name tag, in New York City it has become much more common for taxi drivers to place patriotic paraphernalia somewhere in their car to negate the potential for harassment. Driving with a sticker of an eagle or flag signifies their 'love of freedom' and therefore their normality in the United States. A taxi driver in Melbourne profiled in the *Herald Sun* explained how he speaks English as clearly as possible the instant someone enters the cab (December 16, 2004). Sikh taxi drivers find themselves in a terrible bind. Their turban is precisely the reason why many drive cabs in the first place. Other forms of labor would require them to cut their beards or request the removal of turbans.

Answering questions, providing information, and creating a 'comfortable ride' is already part of the immaterial labor of driving a cab. As Judy, one of approximately 10 women cab drivers in Toronto explains, 'I listen to public radio all day, read the newspaper every time I am waiting for a fare or on my break, and can discuss anything with my passengers. I meet people from all over and I can learn about places I've never been.' This relationship is mutual in the best of circumstances and the taxi does become a potential public space and site of political dialogue. But in some instances these interactions are understood by the driver as a significant part of good customer service. SB, another driver from Iran, explains, 'I'm not interested really in the stock market but I need to know these things because I drive these business people all day. Partly, I want them to know I

am paying attention and secondly I know it helps for my tips to provide a good conversation.'

Significantly, the drivers also revealed the cultivation of a similar disposition of silence in recounting instances of racist tirades and participation in otherwise intrusive dialogue. Silence, and remaining stoic, is justified in the name of customer service. As Abraham, a driver who moved to Toronto from Eritrea a few years ago states,

It is just part of the job. You answer the questions even if you aren't comfortable. You don't know what they will do, who they are, if you become angry, it might be more difficult, and you just want to get through the time, drop them off, and let it go.

In many ways Abraham's description of his interaction with passengers in these situations sounds much like the experience of entering another country or crossing a border with a visa. When Abraham is driving a fare, he has entered an interrogative space in part organized by particular economic relation of power. He enters this contract under the assumption that he has also lost the right to defend himself.

If as I have maintained, the browning of space is a biopolitical process, then the means of regulating such space in part operates through economic relations. As Foucault argues, 'Biopower was without question an indispensable element in the development of capitalism; the latter would not have been possible without the controlled insertion of bodies within the machinery of production to economic processes' (1977, p. 141). The taxi is a vital cog in this machinery, and as such, the driver's productive capacity must be optimized; tightening the structure and control over their lives. Yet, the taxi driver/terrorist is also imagined as a destructive force with the potential to disrupt the biopolitical order and civic space. We can see that passengers become one of the diffuse mechanisms independent of the state apparatus that maintain both the economic and biopolitical order. They work to sustain a *normalized* society (Dreyfus & Rabinow 1982). But this structural context is further maximized through self-monitoring

and the individual driver's observance of norms. The silence and the response to interrogative questions can be read as evidence of the taxi driver's employment of submissive technologies of the self. They must cultivate a strategic disposition to tolerate the symbolic violence and verbal abuse out of fear for their lives and perhaps more commonly their economic livelihood. It becomes in their best interest to maintain composure during these interactions—to just do their job, as David Miller suggested earlier.

When the spaces serviced by immigrant labor become suspicious by fact of browns' all-too-public presence, there occurs a double expulsion from public life—one step away from publicness and two steps back from any real form of political public expression or participation within civic space. Joseph Pugliese has argued that at work here is systematic movement or foreclosure where select subjects will literally fail to appear within the civic spaces of the nation (2006, p. 26). Unfortunately, given the international division of labor there is no way that brown will fail to appear in the civic spaces of the nation. They may not participate, but they will appear. But when brown fails to appear in the *imaginary* of these civic spaces, it should be recognized that special spaces are being created for it elsewhere—such as *Brown Space*.

In the case of the taxi, the *productive force* of brown laboring bodies is not what is subject to intervention in the policing of brown. They are an economic necessity for a thriving metropolis. Instead it is the public presence of brown as it labors that is subject to restrictions. What is happening and is most likely to continue, is a governing of appropriate conduct and practice in public space in a way that will continue to mark out *Brown Space* from a normalized public.

Welcome then, to *Brown Space*. The waters here are murky, muddy, and scary. *Brown Space* consists of geographically disparate places like Guantanamo Bay, airports, prison ships, Gurdwaras, mosques, train stations, and taxis. *Brown Space* is filled with a range of bodies who are 'unknown unknowns', faceless enemies, white Muslims, black Christians, taxi drivers in turbans, women in chadors, suicide bombers with 'measured English accents',[5] and young wayward boys who don rucksacks and puffy jackets while riding public transport. There is no respite in *Brown Space*. Nor can we take respite in the post-9/11 proclamations of a renewed public with the (a)voiding of brown.

Acknowledgements

This essay was first presented at the 2008 Crossroads in Cultural Studies Conference in Kingston, Jamaica. A big thanks to Kumarini Silva for her early encouragement in fall of 2006 to expand my work on the taxi and for her feedback and advice on earlier drafts over the last few years. More thanks go to two anonymous reviewers who provided engaging criticism and direction and another thank you to Jeremy Packer for his comments on earlier drafts.

Notes

1. For a good discussion of how these reforms effected black/white race relations in NYC see Torres (2003).
2. (Marx Darkside June 28, 2004) http://www.jihad-watch.org/archives/002351.php#c26846.
3. *Terrorist Internet Super Highway*, Tuesday, September 05, 2006 1:36 PM.
4. http://www.ubiq-cab.com.
5. Two of the 7/07 London suicide bombers were characterized as having 'measured', 'thick' English accents.

References

Andrejevic, M. (2005) 'The work of watching one another: lateral surveillance, risk, and governance', *Surveillance and Society*, vol. 2, no. 4, pp. 479–497.

Berland, J. (2005) 'Space', in *New Keywords: A Revised Vocabulary of Culture and Society*, eds T. Bennett, L. Grossberg & M. Morris, Oxford, Blackwell.

Bratich, J. (2006) 'Public secrecy and immanent security', *Cultural Studies*, vol. 20, no. 4–5, pp. 493–511.

Dodd, V. (2001) 'Attack on America race attack: Three held after assault leaves Afghan taxi driver paralysed: Police say victim was taunted over US atrocity', *The Guardian*, 18 September.

Dreyfus, H. & Rabinow, P. (1982) *Michel Foucault: Beyond Structuralism and Hermeneutics*, Chicago, The University of Chicago Press.

Foucault, M. (1977) *Discipline and Punish*, New York, Vintage.

Foucault, M. (2003) *Society Must Be Defended*, London, Picador.

Friedman, A. (2006) 'The taxi driver', *New York Times*, 1 November.

Hall, S. (1996) 'Introduction: Who needs identity?', in *Questions of Cultural Identity*, eds S. Hall & P. Du Gay, London, Sage Publications.

Hall, S. & Jefferson, T. (eds) (1976) *Resistance Through Ritual*, London, Hutchinson.

Hay, J. & Andrejevic, M. (2006) 'Toward an analytic of governmental experiments in these times: Homeland security as the new social security', *Cultural Studies*, vol. 20, no. 4–5, pp. 331–348.

Investor's Business Daily (2007) [online] Available at: http://www.ibdeditorials.com/IBDArticles.aspx?id=263084562923369 (accessed 11 May 2007).

Jayadev, R. (2003) 'Sikh cab drivers say racism, recession put them in crosshairs', *Pacific News Service*, 27 October.

McChesney, R. (2002) 'September 11 and the structural limitations of U.S. journalism', in *Journalism After September 11: When Trauma Shapes the News*, eds B. Zelizer & S. Allan, London, Routledge, pp. 91–100.

Masanauskas, J. (2004) 'Muslim cab drivers cop terror taunts', *Herald Sun*, 16 December.

Mathew, B. (2005) *Taxi! Cabs and Capitalism*, New York, New Press.

Mitchell, D. (2003) *The Right to the City: Social Justice and the Fight for Public Space*, New York, Guilford Press.

Pugliese, J. (2006) 'Asymmetries of terror: Visual regimes of racial profiling and the shooting of Jean Charles de Menezes in the context of the war in Iraq', *Borderlands e-journal*, vol 5, no. 1.

Sassen, S. (1998) *Globalization and its Discontents*, New York, New York Press.

The O'Reilly Show (2007) [online] Available at: http://www.foxnews.com/story/0,2933,271255,00.html (accessed 11 May 2007).

Torres, S. (2003) *Black, White, and in Color: Television and Black Civil Rights*, Princeton, NJ, Princeton University Press.

WorldNetDaily (2007) [online] Available at: http://www.worldnetdaily.com/news/article.asp?ARTICLE_ID=55641 (accessed 11 May 2007).

30.
HOW TIGER WOODS LOST HIS STRIPES

Post-Nationalist American Studies as a History of Race, Migration, and the Commodification of Culture

Henry Yu

As the summer waned in 1996, the world was treated to the coronation of a new public hero. Eldrick "Tiger" Woods, the twenty-year-old golf prodigy, captured his third straight amateur championship and then promptly declared his intention to turn professional. The story became a media sensation, transferring the material of sports page headlines to the front page of newspapers in a way usually reserved for World Series championships or athletes involved in sex and drug scandals. Television coverage chronicled every step of Tiger's life, debating his impact upon the sport, and wondering if he was worth the reported $40 million which Nike was going to pay him for an endorsement contract. The strange career of Tiger Woods said much about the current situation of race, ethnicity, and capitalism in the United States. It also spoke to the still relatively unexamined ways in which definitions of racial and cultural difference in the United States connect to the global market of consumption and production.

Woods's eagerly anticipated professional debut was hailed in August 1996 as a multicultural godsend to the sport of golf. As a child of multiracial heritage, Woods added color to a sport that traditionally appealed to those who were white and rich. A multicolored Tiger in hues of black and yellow would forever change the complexion of golf, attracting inner-city children to the game in the same way that Michael Jordan had for basketball. Nike's initial T.V. ad campaign emphasized the racial exclusivity that has marked golf in the United States, stating that there were golf courses at which Tiger Woods still could not play. A Tiger burning bright would change all of that, of course, with a blend of power, grace, skill, and sheer confidence that could not be denied. "Hello World," Tiger Woods announced in another T.V. spot, asking America and the world whether they were ready for the new partnership of Tiger and Nike. The answer to the challenge seemed to be a resounding yes. A year later, in October of 1997, a poll published in *USA Today* reported that Nike's campaign featuring Tiger Woods was by far the most popular advertising campaign of the year.[1]

In this essay, I would like to discuss Tiger Woods's commercial debut as a way of examining how race, ethnicity, and the mass market in the United States can no longer be understood (and perhaps was never properly understood) without the context of global capitalism that frames definitions of cultural and national difference. Notions of ethnic and cultural difference in the United States have always depended upon transnational connections and comparisons. The increasing awareness recently among scholars and the mass media of global perspectives has been marked by a hope that globalization will lead to a decrease in tribalism and ethnicity. Consequently, the practice of a "post-nationalist American Studies" might be construed as an act of self-immolation, erasing national identity formation by pointing towards a future without nations. For me, such a vision would be misguided and dangerously deluded. National formation, and the concurrent practices of cultural and racial differentiation, have always been transnational in character, and they have always called for a perspective that can link ethnic formation with processes that transcend national borders. A post-nationalist American Studies, therefore, should strive to place nation formation within transnational contexts of racial and cultural differentiation.

Tiger Woods's story exemplifies the crossroads between the commercialization of sport in the United States and the production of racial and cultural difference. Golf is perhaps the epitome of a commodification of leisure that characterizes the current global success of American capitalism, and like many of the multibillion dollar sports and entertainment industries (cultural productions such as movies, television, music, etc.), golf is marked by representations of racial and cultural hierarchies. Perhaps more than any other sport, golf stands for white male privilege and racial exclusion. Some of the fascination with Tiger Woods can be explained by how acts of conspicuous leisure and consumption have become essential to both racial and class distinction in the United States. For its very significance as a bastion of hierarchy, golf has also become a marker of the opposition to racial and class exclusion. Similar to how Jackie Robinson's entry into baseball symbolized for Americans more than just the eventual desegregation of baseball but also that of American society, Tiger Wood's entry into golf was heralded as the entry of multiculturalism into the highest reaches of country-club America.

The manner in which observers initially explained Tiger's potential appeal was very revealing. A *Los Angeles Times* article on Tuesday, August 27, 1996, the day after Woods turned pro, declared that Tiger had a "rich ethnic background," calculating that his father was "a quarter Native American, a quarter Chinese, and half African American," and that his mother was "half Thai, a quarter Chinese, and a quarter white." How did we arrive at these fractions of cultural identity? Did they mean that he practiced his multicultural heritage in such a fractured manner, eating chow mein one day out of four, soul food on one of the other days, and Thai barbecue chicken once a week? Obviously not. The exactness of the ethnic breakdown referred to the purported biological ancestry of Woods's parents and grandparents.

The awkward attempts to explain Tiger's racial classification showed the continuing bankruptcy of languages of race in the United States. The racial calculus employed by both print and television reporters to explain Tiger's heritage reminds us uncomfortably of the biological classifications used in the Old South. The law courts of Louisiana tried for much of the nineteenth and twentieth centuries to calculate a person's racial makeup in the same precise manner, classifying people as mulatto if they were half white and half black, a quadroon if they were a quarter black, an octoroon if an eighth, and so on. The assumption was that blood and race could be broken down into precise fractions, tying a person's present existence in a racially segregated society with a person's purported biological ancestry. The upshot was that a single drop of black blood made a person colored, and no amount of white blood could overwhelm that single drop to make a person pure again.[2]

What was disturbing about the reception of Tiger Woods is how little we have changed from that conception of biological identity. Within American conceptions of race, Tiger Woods is an African American. The intricate racial calculus that broke Tiger into all manner of stripes and hues was a farce not only in terms of its facile exactitude, but also in its false complexity. According to the calculations, Tiger Woods is more Asian American than African American (a quarter Chinese on the father's side, plus a quarter Chinese and a half Thai on the mother's side, for a total of one-half Asian in Tiger, versus only half African American on the father's side, for a total of one-quarter black in Tiger . . .).[3] But this is an empty equation because social usage, and the major market appeal of Tiger, classifies him as black. "How Tiger Woods lost his stripes" describes the process by which the complexities of human migration and intermingling in this country become understood in the simplifying classifications of race.[4]

In his trek from the sports page to the front page, Tiger Woods quickly became another example of a black man making it in America because of his athletic skill. Woods earned his success through his prodigious accomplishments, but his popular apotheosis as black male hero fits him into generic modes of understanding African American masculinity. The

strange way in which multinational sports corporations value minority sports stars is indicative of the
more general American craving for individual black
heroes to redeem its ugly history. Whether it is Jackie
Robinson, Michael Jordan, Colin Powell, or Tiger
Woods, we constantly fantasize that a single person
will save us from racial problems which are endemic
and built into the structure of US society.

Tiger Woods combined a number of standard
ways in which African American men are perceived
as safe and nonthreatening. His Green Beret father,
like Colin Powell, was a war hero, embodying the
safe black man who sacrifices himself for the nation. Tiger's father correctly channeled the violent
masculinity that popular imagery ascribes to African
American males, forsaking the alleged criminality
(drug dealing, drive-by shooting, gang-banging) that
is the negative twin of the figure of the black war
hero. Better yet, Tiger's father directed the dangerous, sexual desirability of his black masculinity not
toward white women, but toward the safe option of
a foreign, Asian war bride. Tiger himself, as the son
of a black veteran who applied military discipline to
create a black male sports hero, served to connect
the appeal of the safe black male body as sports star
to a lineage of the black male as military hero. In the
light of how popular culture has overdetermined the
meaning of his body, how could Tiger not have lost
his stripes? After all, classified as a black male, he
combined the social virtues of Michael Jordan with
those of Colin Powell.[5]

More than blackness, however, Tiger Woods was
seen to transcend racial division within his own body.
As the sports star progeny of the black male military hero and the Asian wife picked up in the United
States's foray into Vietnam, he added racial diversity
into his black body. Media imagery, though, could not
quite manage to represent this added complication.
When Tiger Woods won his first professional golf
tournament, and again when he won the prestigious
Masters, newspaper photographs overwhelmingly
showed him hugging his father. His mother Kultida
was either cropped from the frame or blocked by
the powerful imagery of the black American military
father triumphantly joined with his black American
sports star son. Along with the disappearing stripes

of Tiger's racial complexity, Thai American Kultida
Woods faded into black.

The attempt to see within Tiger Woods the embodiment of multiculturalism was a valiant attempt
to contain within a single body all of the ethnic diversity in the social body that multiculturalism claims
to represent. The awkwardness of description, and
its inevitable failure, resulted both from a flawed
conception of ethnic origins and from our inability
to leave behind an obsession with the idea that race
is a biological category represented by individuals.
It is possible to describe a person's racial history in
terms of fractions, because each of those fractions
was supposedly a whole person one or two generations before. Tiger Woods as a single body, however,
cannot express the fractions within—like almost all
children of supposed mixed heritage in this country,
his whole quickly becomes his darkest part.

Woods himself, as a child, attempting to rebut his
reduction by others to a state of blackness, came up
with the term "Cablinasian" (CAucasian + BLack +
INdian + ASIAN) to encapsulate his mixed makeup.
Mentioned briefly by the press, the term achieved
no currency or usage. Since the power of racial categories comes from their work of tying a number
of people together under a single description, a label such as Cablinasian that serves only to describe
Woods's own individual admixture has little use. Indeed, though Woods had found a name for his own
unique brand of pain, he might as well have used his
own name "Tiger" to label what was in the end a virtually singular racial description.

The confusion of tongues regarding how to
name Tiger's complex heritage is a direct result
of the confusion over race that continues to be-
devil this country. Multiculturalism in the form embraced by corporate America is no more than this
tired language with an added commodification of
ethnicity. We want racial and cultural categories to
be neatly represented by individuals, so that a multicultural Benetton or Calvin Klein advertisement
will have a number of visible people of color—an
African American, an Asian American, a Latino or
Latina—and an assortment of generic white people.
Multiculturalism is about different individuals getting
along, and this is the version which is being sold by

multinational corporations like Nike, in the hopes that all of these differing people will buy the same objects in a shared market of goods.[6] Nike's ad campaign showing young children of various visible minorities chanting the mantra of "I am Tiger Woods" ostensibly offered Tiger as the role model for multicultural America, but it also managed to call forth a world market ready to consume Nike's products. Like Nike's earlier slogan for basketball icon Michael Jordan, "I want to be like Mike," the phrase "I am Tiger Woods" could be translated by consumers as "My body is black and I am up and coming just like him," but more likely it meant "I want to wear what Tiger wears."

Tiger Woods serves as an example to introduce some issues concerning race and culture in an international perspective, particularly in terms of the interaction among ethnicity, national definition, and global capitalism. There has been a great deal of exciting scholarship in recent years exploring transnational perspectives, and my account is not meant to survey these works, but to sketch some suggestive issues which I see arising out of them. I want first to think about multicultural narratives as shorthand histories for international migration, and then to tie this to the perceived international appeal of Tiger's mixed ethnicity.

The awkward attempts to describe Woods's heritage bear the legacy of Old South notions of race, but they also arise from the late-nineteenth-century context of massive international labor migration.[7] Culture as a theory describing human difference can be linked to two particular historical developments of the nineteenth century: national formation and the rise of migrant labor to satisfy the expanding production that resulted from expanding capitalist development. The rise and triumph of the concept of culture at the beginning of the twentieth century supposedly eclipsed earlier biological definitions of race, but in some ways the idea of culture, and of multiculturalism, is little more than the grafting of nonbiological claims onto preexisting categories of race. Moreover, like the category of biological race, the culture concept erases history, suppressing into static categories the historical origins of how some people become defined as different.

Theories of biological race that arose in the nineteenth century emphasized belonging to some fictive category (for instance, Negroid, Mongoloid, Caucasoid) that collapsed racial type and geographical location. This mythic tie between race and spatial location called forth an epic history stretching back to prehistoric ancestors, tying racial difference to origins deep in time. We still operate with a version of this classificatory scheme when we identify some physical features as "Asian" (straight black hair) and others as "African" (brown skin) or "European" (light skin).[8] American Studies has acquired a central awareness of how racial theories that attributed variations in behavior and in physical and mental abilities to differences in racial type have for centuries served as justification for social oppression and hierarchy.

An anthropological conception of culture that came to the fore in the early twentieth century redefined variety in human behavior and practice as a consequence of social processes. Meant to eliminate any association of mental capacity with biological race, the theory of culture proved relatively successful as a way of attacking biological justifications for social hierarchy. The culture concept as it has been used in theories of multiculturalism, however, has mirrored the suppositions of racial theories about the centrality of biological ties to the past. Particularly in the way differences in behavior between people whose ancestors have come from Africa, Asia, or Europe have been explained as cultural in origin, cultural difference has paralleled the boundaries of earlier definitions of racial difference.

Created by anthropologists visiting exotic locales, culture as an intellectual concept has always been riven by the contradiction that it has come to be an *object* of description (the actual practices of various "cultures") at the same time that it has really only been the description of practices. Culture, as it was defined by early theorists such as Franz Boas, is transferred among physical human bodies through social means of communication. Embodied in social rituals and practices, culture was a way of life, reproduced by social groups that were bound together by such acts. As a set of descriptions, ethnographies were claimed by anthropologists to describe actual "cultures," but the differentiation between what was unique to one culture versus another always depended upon the perspective of Europeans or Americans implicitly comparing their objects of study to other ways of life (often, unwittingly, their own). Arising out of a systematic awareness of differences, the concept of culture is undermined when users forget its origin as a description. *Culture* as a word is continually used as if it were an object with causal powers ("Franz did that because his culture is German"), rather than a product of the very act of describing that is the way of life of anthropologists and those who see the world anthropologically ("Franz, in comparison with other people I have known, does things differently, and I make sense of that difference by describing those acts and linking them to my awareness that he and other people I have known who do things that way all come from Germany"). Unfortunately, in popular language such as that of multiculturalism, the word *culture* has come to have universal significance at the same time that it signifies less and less.

Despite the ability to perform cultural practices described as being the embodiment of some particular culture (for instance, "German culture"), we are constantly faced with examples of how cultural membership has very little to do with performance ability. Take, for instance, the examples of white American missionaries in Japan and Japanese immigrants in the United States during the nineteenth and twentieth centuries. There were a number of children of American missionaries to Japan who were born and raised in Japan, and came to be adept at speaking the local language and understanding and practicing local customs and ways of life. They knew how to use chopsticks; they wore "native" dress; they were allowed to play the same Japanese games as their childhood friends. Were they, by any definition, Japanese? Perhaps with a definition that is restricted to functional ability at performing cultural practices, but in any other sense they are anomalies, freaks of culture that serve to uphold the notion of culture as nonbiological ("they know what Japanese culture is") at the same time that they point to the not-so-hidden reliance of cultural differentiation on legal nationality and biological definitions of race.

Such a reliance is highlighted by the example of Japanese immigrants who came to the United States during the same period, parallel emigrés traveling in opposite directions. Children of theirs born in the United States were invariably raised in American schools, adept at American customs and the local language of English. They ate hamburgers and French fries; they wore Boy Scout uniforms and shouted the Pledge of Allegiance; they were allowed to play in American games with their childhood friends. Legal standards of national citizenship categorized them as American. But if internment of a whole people on the basis of ancestry during World War II means anything, questions of national loyalty, cultural performance, and racial biology have been so confused in US history that the maintenance of culture as a separate category of analysis gains little more payback than a perverse sense of irony. Japanese Americans, despite the possibility of being described as culturally similar to other Americans, were still treated as if they were racially different and nationally suspect.

Lest we think that such examples are anomalous or irrelevant today, we should consider Korean-born orphans adopted by "white" Americans in Minneapolis. How are the new parents to treat the "cultural" heritage of their children? Should they deny that the biological link has a cultural expression, and thus pretend that the children are like any white children? Such a utopian fantasy would be principled, idealistic, and most likely psychologically cruel, for there can be little doubt that the children will receive repeated and stark messages from other people that they are not white. To immerse the children in their "Korean heritage" might prove a practical defense against a debilitated sense of self-worth, but it would be a child-rearing also based on a specious link between culture and biology.

Cultural differentiations, like the biological notions of race that they purportedly replace, rely upon an historical narrative of population migration. No matter how much even the most astute observers believe that culture is a purely social phenomenon, divorced from biology, there are presumed links to histories of the physical migration of human bodies that lead to generalizations based upon physical type. On the whole, these links have practical functions, connecting individual human bodies to histories of population migration. Seeing a body, and being trained to perceive that it shares particular physical characteristics with those descended from individuals who live in Asia, allows fairly accurate suppositions about biological ancestors from somewhere in Asia.

But almost inevitably false assumptions are made concerning the cultural knowledge and practices of such a person, and the relation of culture to the body's biological origin. So children of American missionaries in China, never having set foot in the United States until the age of eighteen or nineteen, can get off a boat in San Francisco and instantly be American in the legal and cultural senses. The norm of American identity has been so equated historically with whiteness that the very term *white American* in most situations is repetitive and redundant. Americans of color require a modifying term such as African or Asian or Hispanic. The term *European American* has been invented to extend the logic of geographic origins for different races, but in the absence of any color modifier, the term *American* means white.

The children, grandchildren, and great-grandchildren of Chinese immigrants to the United States will always be seen as possessing Chinese culture, no matter how inept they are at what it means to be Chinese in China (and in America)—they will be asked whether they know how to translate Chinese characters, how to cook chow mein, and to discuss the takeover of Hong Kong. Orphans from Korea who grew up in Minneapolis with Scandinavian American parents, no matter how young they were when they were transported from South Korea, will always be linked to Korean culture—they will be allowed to discover their real culture or *re*discover their culture. At worst, and in a manner reminiscent of the internment of Japanese Americans, airport security officers or the FBI will suspect Arab Americans of being terrorists because of the way they spell their names, the clothes they wear, or the color of their skin. At the heart of all of these distinctions is not race as a biological category or culture as a nonbiological category, but a presumed history of population migrations.

Multiculturalism in the United States has had a long history of making transnational connections. If it really is because someone's grandfather came from Croatia and someone else's came from Canada that one is different from the other, then present cultural differences echo past national differences. Since there is an assumption that what makes someone different here in the United States is their link to some other place in the world, origins and biological heritage are all-important. Even when the differences are supposedly racial, they still presume a difference today arising from a difference in origin yesterday. Tiger Woods's formula of admixture, for instance, reveals a foundation in national, racial, and cultural difference. His Thai portion is national and/or cultural in origin. The Chinese would presumably be the same, with a hint of racial determinism (his Chinese grandparents were probably legally Thai in a national sense, with an indeterminately long history of living in Thailand). His African and Native American parts most certainly fixate on (some notion of) biological race with an assumption that there would be some accompanying cultural differences. His Caucasian (or white) heritage is racial and cultural in the same sense as his blackness, presuming an illusory tie to some mountains in Eastern Europe.

As an historical narrative defining the origins of difference, multiculturalism has linked the politics of the present to a biological genealogy of the individual body's past. This narrative has been a program for political empowerment, because it opposes the racial descriptions it mirrors, but in overturning the exclusion of those previously left out by promising their inclusion, multiculturalism as a political ideology has curiously reiterated the very "foreign" nature of those left out. Multiculturalism has valued those who were previously excluded by turning the terms of their exclusion into the terms of their inclusion. Embracing the foreign nature of ethnicity rather than sending foreigners packing, cultural pluralists have replaced nativism with exoticism.

Multiculturalism, like the narrative of biological race that it opposes, reveals the defining power of imperialism, when Europeans surveyed populations of the world and marked the boundaries between them. Long histories of continual population migration and movement were erased as bodies were given the attribute of "native"—mapping them into a "local" origin that was assigned to them by European knowledge.[9] Categorized by abstract identities such as race, nation, and culture, individuals and social groups all over the globe were defined and came to define themselves through such identifications.[10] The power of these identities for the last two centuries in creating imagined social and institutional ties is undeniable, but there is always the danger of missing the underlying demographic changes that lay at the base of such arbitrary ties.

There are myriad ways in which people are similar and different—male or female, position in a family, age, sexuality, height, shoe size, on and on. One of these ways is where one's grandparents came from, but if the reason someone has been treated differently in the United States is that their grandfather came from China, this tie is important less because of what was unique and native to China (both in the nineteenth century and now) and more because of how racial difference and animosity have been defined in North America; how, in other words, people in the United States have come to define "whiteness" by European origin and linked otherness in racial and cultural terms with non-European origin. Racial, cultural, and national categorization therefore have been inextricably linked in history, and in the most foundational sense these linkages have depended upon an awareness of population migration. Ultimately, however, these definitions of race and culture have not actually been about the migration histories of biological bodies; the definition of whiteness in opposition to other racial types, at its core, has been about the social privileges of not being considered colored. The strange conundrum of culture as a theory is that it assumes and then hides the same links between physical bodies and migration that biological theories of race did. In attempting to define more fairly in this way, we may end up reproducing the logic of justifying white privilege in the United States.

I Sing the Body Eclectic? Transnational Fractions and National Wholes

The fractional nature of the racial and cultural categories in Tiger Woods was as arbitrary as the classification of him as African American. The key factor that undermines Tiger Woods's racial formula is the fiction that somehow his ancestors were racially or culturally whole. When he was broken up into one-fourth Chinese, one-fourth Thai, one-fourth African American, one-eighth American Indian, and one-eighth Caucasian, the lowest common denominator of one-eighth leads to a three-generation history. Tracing a three-step genealogy of descent back to an original stage of pure individuals places us at the end of the nineteenth century. If we were to consider other striped, Tiger Woods–like bodies in a similar manner, they might be described as containing fractions like a sixteenth or even a thirty-second. But in any case the individuals who are imagined to live at the beginning point of the calculations are whole only because they have been assumed to originally exist in a shared moment of purity.

The timing of this moment of imagined purity is partly founded upon the coincidence of migration with national identity. The illusion of ethnic and racial wholeness of a grandparent's generation marks the importance of nineteenth-century nationalism in defining bodies. Emigrating from established or emergent nations, migrants during the nineteenth and early twentieth centuries had their bodies marked by nationality—Irish, Chinese, Japanese, Italian, German. That their bodies were whole in a national sense allowed for a consequent holistic definition of their racial and cultural origin.

Both race and culture as categories of belonging have often presupposed a biological genealogy of national origin. This view was legally enshrined in the 1924 National Origins legislation, when each nation was given a maximum quota for migrants to the United States. Every immigrant entering and every body already in the United States was defined by a national past. A migrant body was marked as a member of a single nation, and thus a national purity was conveyed regardless of a person's heterogeneous or complicated origins. Immigrants may have come from a place that did not exist as a political and legal nation, or they may have gone through numerous national entities before entering the United States, any of which could come to be defined as their "national origin." For instance, migrants from the area now known as South Korea were in the early part of the twentieth century counted as Japanese nationals. Virtually all Koreans understood that as a colonized and subject people they were not Japanese in a cultural or biological sense, but their legal status according to the National Origins Act meant that they had to have a national origin, and like other members of the nation of Japan, they were to be excluded from the United States on the basis of national categories.

Even with the supposed eclipse of biological notions of race in the twentieth century, we cling to definitions of national and cultural origin as a shorthand for describing biological origin. If you are a descendent of Asian immigrants to this country, for instance, you are forever being asked where you are originally from, regardless of whether you were born in Los Angeles, Denver, or New York. The confusion is not over whether an individual is American-born or not, since those asking are inevitably not satisfied with the answer of Los Angeles, Denver, or New York. What they are looking for is national origin, and therefore biological origin, even if the moment of origination is an act of migration undertaken by a grandparent. What they want to know is whether you are Japanese, Korean, Chinese, or Vietnamese (I suppose that they believe they can tell if you are from the Philippines, Polynesia, or India and therefore do not have to ask).[11]

The three-generation history of intermarriage that the one-eighth fractions ostensibly revealed actually described a family tree arbitrarily truncated. The hypothetically whole grandparents, given their own family genealogies of ancestry, would have themselves pointed to a past of intermingling population migrations. Further and further back in time, these genealogies would reveal that there has never been a set of racially whole individuals from which we have all descended. Whether in purportedly mixed or pure fashion, biological descent that invokes racially whole individuals in the past is an illusion.

With the possibility that future US Census surveys will no longer restrict individuals to single racial categories (allowing people to check more than one box for categories of racial belonging), perhaps American views of racial and cultural descent will finally leave the notion of pure, whole individuals behind. But this is doubtful. The new problem of complex logarithms and formulae to try to convert the new fractions of identity into whole numbers still results from the

same need to produce data that makes sense to demographers. How will all those who rely on population calculations from the US Census use totals that are not the sum of whole numbers of individuals, but crazy totals like 234,574.375 that themselves reflect the sum of a string of fractions such as three-fourths, an eighth, and a sixty-fourth? Or if we are to count partial blood as equivalent to being a full member of a race, we will create tallies that count Tiger Woods four times, as an African American, and again as an Asian American, and again as a white American, and again as a Native American, so that the sum of our parts will no longer add to the same whole number as our total population. The census could remain with the principle of the darkest blood winning out, forcing Tiger Woods to be black, or it could allow him to choose his own category of belonging. He could even choose to be white, even if it is highly unlikely anyone would let him get away with it.

If American understandings of culture still depend largely upon presumed biological origins, and in particular have been tied to nineteenth-century nation-states, what should a post-nationalist American Studies be doing? Since definitions of race and culture have always depended upon the idea that ethnic populations in the United States are somehow linked biologically and/or culturally to foreign populations somewhere else on the globe, is thinking about transnational connections really that new? The answer to both questions is that a post-nationalist perspective on American Studies should not aim to transcend national differentiation, but to reaffirm the need to make apparent the very reliance of narratives of American race, culture, and nation upon transnational phenomena.

More studies need to be done on the salience of transnational migration for American nationalism and on the presumptions of national identity which undergird notions of racial and cultural origin in the United States. Histories of diaspora that underemphasize the importance of nationalism in the attempt to highlight a continuity of shared cultural origin risk missing one of the foundational elements of transnational population migration—the state and all its legal powers of definition and coercion. Nationalist institutions and national identity in transnational perspective, therefore, must be primary concerns of post-nationalist study. At the same time, we need to put racial and cultural differentiation at the center of processes of production and commodification in the international economy.

A number of fine studies have been conducted under the rubric of Asian American Studies, for instance, that might serve as models for a post-nationalist American Studies. Like other work in Ethnic Studies, such as Chicano Studies, Border Studies, and works on the African Diaspora, Asian American Studies has often emphasized transnational perspectives that examine the multiple locations of diasporic migration. At its most fundamental level, an examination of one place as home and another as workplace can invoke the transnational connections of labor migration. For instance, Madeline Hsu examined how Cantonese, male migrant workers formed families even though fathers were on opposite sides of the Pacific from wives and children. These overseas families, despite long absences and a lack of shared residence to tie them together, became standard family practice in particular parts of southern China. Embodied in the practice of financial remittances from the father in the United States to the wife and children in China, Hsu's study of these functioning families serves as an example of how normative conceptions of family can evolve outside the geography of the nation form. Studies such as Hsu's show the porous nature of borders and the arbitrary nature of definitions of national difference; they do not, however, dissolve notions of national identity. Indeed, charting the history of these transnational families further reinforces how historically powerful national borders have been, even when they belied almost every facet of a person's lived experience. The migrants' sense of home (whether in China, where the wives and children resided, or in America, where the migrants resided), was still shaped by the policies of national inclusion and exclusion practiced within both nations.

A post-nationalist American Studies must see past unexamined national discourses such as those on the family that can discount or label as aberrations innumerable social practices. Susan Koshy's work on migrants from India in the United States and Britain shows how studying South Asian diasporic communities in a comparative fashion can reveal the marked differences in how nations treat immigrants and the consequences of these differences. In the realm of culture, Shu-mei Shih's analysis of Taiwanese-American director Ang Lee's reception in both Taiwan and the United States highlights the powerful effects of nationalism in a global economy of cultural production.[12]

There are examples as well from the Atlantic world, but being a scholar of Asian American Studies concerned with the long neglect of the Pacific world, I highlight scholarship on the Pacific. An example of a scholar who has used the insights of Asian American Studies to re-envision the history of the Atlantic world is Kariann Yokota, whose research on the early American republic as a postcolonial society uses many of the transnational perspectives of Asian American history to analyze white colonists at the end of the eighteenth century. Trying to prove their worth in a transatlantic world dominated by British culture, postcolonial Americans created definitions of whiteness that both celebrated and denigrated what was perceived to be native to the United States. Yokota's research suggests how concerns about the status of the new American nation in a transnational Atlantic world formed one of the foundations for a virulent racism among whites.[13]

Just as transnational perspectives on early Chinese immigrant families help us to understand the power of national definition in nineteenth-century life, so transnational perspectives on contemporary society will most likely reveal the continuing power of nationalism. As the public furor in 1996 over television celebrity Kathy Lee Gifford's line of children's clothing demonstrates, an awareness among many observers of the international connections in capitalism can lead not to a diminution of national identity, but to the reinforcement of it. When allegations were made that children's clothing sold under Kathy Lee Gifford's name was being made by child labor in Central America, a long-standing debate resurfaced about whether or not Americans should buy foreign-manufactured clothing. One answer to the incident was that clothing should be made by union labor in the United

States—"Buy American" and avoid the problems of oppressive labor conditions in foreign countries.

Besides avoiding the issue of how manufacturing production has been farmed out to low-wage regions around the globe and within the United States, such reactions echo the historical way in which low-wage competition has been racialized as foreign in order to draw the border between those within and without the nation.[14] Irish American labor agitator Dennis Kearney organized California workers in the 1870s by appealing to their solidarity as "whites" and as "Americans," in direct contrast to the "Chinese" and "foreign" workers who worked alongside them. That Kearney and the group of "whites" his appeal created were labor migrants to North America just as much as the Chinese was subsumed under the entwined categorizations of racial difference and of native versus foreigner. What connects the rhetorical construction of the "foreign" Chinese American worker in the 1870s to the "foreign" Central American worker in 1996 are the same processes of racialization and national exclusion. Asian American immigrant workers in the United States just happen to have embodied this classification of the perpetual foreigner, joining racial and national exclusion in a single body.

The xenophobic nationalism of "Buying American" is a duplicitous rhetoric of saving the other by saving ourselves. It says little about what should happen to workers in Honduras, Guatemala, Indonesia, and Malaysia—just that Americans should not buy products made by them. If it is terrible that foreigners should be made to work in oppressive situations, then the solution should be to buy products made in situations where fair labor practices can be guaranteed—these happen, of course, to be in the United States.

Transnational awareness is not the end of national identity, and in fact it has always been the root process for national awareness. The field of American Studies, which has as its subject American culture and society, has always necessitated transnational perspectives, whether it has practiced such analyses or not. What is needed in the future is a meaningful engagement with the issues of racial and cultural commodification in an international context.

The first step, however, in building something that might be labeled an institutional practice of post-nationalist American Studies is to be certain of why we might want to pursue such a practice and, in particular, who might be interested in the knowledge created. We must be careful to understand the ways in which academics in the United States have themselves come to understand and value exotic knowledge and cultural difference. If we are to achieve a post-nationalist American Studies, it cannot be founded on a lack of awareness of how intellectuals in the United States are themselves American and prize their bourgeois professional status.

The cosmopolitan perspective of many academics in the United States, so valuable as a critical viewpoint that distances them from the practices of American nationalism, should not be mistaken for some truly non-national point of view removed from the provincial national identities they critique. Embedded in a bourgeois world where they are allowed to produce cosmopolitan knowledge for each other's consumption, American intellectuals at times seem to live in a fantasy world of mystified intellectual and cultural production. Creating knowledge of the exotic and the unknown seemingly for the sake of Knowledge itself, or for the sake of a critique that is blind to their own class position and relationship to the world they describe, many academics lack a sense of the market in knowledge and status embodied by American institutions of higher education.[15] Or, if they are aware of their relations to the means of intellectual production, they are compelled by their own places in the institutional structure to continue to produce knowledge, albeit in an ironic mode, artfully distracting themselves from the utility of their actions and the privilege of their positions with the same sly smirk.

Perhaps more unsettling than labor organizers, who shout "Buy American" in response to the oppression of foreign workers, is the outlook of elites in the United States who link the exploitation of indigenous workers to the loss of their traditional cultures.[16] Narrated as a desire to protect native culture from eventual loss and extinction, this love of the exotic native reduces in the end to some version of "save the other for our own consumption." British and American imperial anthropologists earlier in this century rushed into the South Pacific alongside missionaries and gunboats in order to write descriptions of societies being changed by the very forces they themselves represented. Claiming that they were helping to save native cultures from extinction, the anthropologists produced ethnographies for the edification (and commodification) of British and American academies of higher learning. The anthropologists valued the exotic traditions of "disappearing" cultures—the people themselves were often disappearing due to disease and dislocation, but anthropologists' interest in the extinct nature of their "ways of life" had to do with their fascination in a culturally pure, traditional world that existed before white men arrived. The ways in which indigenous people were adapting, or not adapting, to changes were less interesting than the "lost" world they were trying to save.

There are perilous parallels between academic consumption of the exotic and commercial commodification. The marketing of the dream of a lack of intrusion on traditional culture, a sampling of exoticism without spoiling its pristine nature, still defines the views of much scholarship on ethnicity. The culture concept, as the product of a description of difference, has expired as a useful theory and acquired its greatest utility as a commodity. Imperial anthropology may be gone, but the act of producing ethnographic descriptions of the exotic in order to save them for knowledge from the despoliation of modernity still remains a scholarly agenda. Related to this process of exotic cultural consumption is a nationalist arrogance, which is often unself-conscious and held by people who otherwise think of themselves as lacking national identifications.

The dilettantism of American academic knowledge is founded upon a conjunction of class privilege and national power. What relation do university scholars have to the means of production? What privileged conditions in their own lives allow them the luxury of a cosmopolitan embrace of diverse local cultures? What fetishizing and collecting of "native" cultural products do they practice, and what allows them to indulge in such practices? Are they independently wealthy in the United States? Are US academics allowed to travel the world as alienated intellectuals because of the enormous diplomatic power of their national citizenship? How does their national identity, even as they act as critics of nationalism, grant them the capability of incorporating multicultural products and perspectives into their lives for their own display and benefit? How does a nationalist enterprise of incorporating knowledge in the interests of national power allow American intellectuals the fantasy of the creation of knowledge as an unquestioned good? Rooms full of "oriental" vases and hand-crafted products from Southeast Asia may fill scholars' rooms in upper middle class homes in the United States, but they have always had the luxury of being able to acquire them "outside" of the tourist market of mass consumption and production. The elitist fantasy is that such native crafts are outside of capitalism, as if their very value were not wholly dependent upon the opposition constructed between mass-produced artifacts and authentic, traditional products prized as different and thus valued.[17]

If the 1960s radical injunction to "think globally, act locally" succeeded in turning American insularity into an awareness of international context, perhaps it also signaled an embrace of the global to such an extent that the national lost significance or became important only as an enemy to be defeated. In some ways, the radical anti-Americanism of much radical dissent allowed for a critical view of American nationalism from a point outside of nationalist ideology, but it may also have deracinated the critic. Just as American children don't really believe in the link between the local and the global when they hear the mothers' cliché, "Eat your beans, because kids are starving in India," so American national power is often erased or forgotten when perspectives outside of the nation become central. A critical perspective situated outside and against nationalist ideology does not equate with being a starving Indian rather than a child of American abundance. Being an intellectual in the United States locates one's critical perspectives in specific class, institutional, and national positions. Neither disagreeing with national policy nor renouncing one's class status results in abandoning the comfortable and privileged position that American academics enjoy.

National Diversity and International Marketing

The processes of national and racial differentiation have contemporary resonance in a time when claims of a new globalism resound. The tying of what is ethnic here in the United States to what is native there in some other nation in the world is what makes Tiger Woods so appealing as a marketing force for corporations looking for global sales. Multinational corporations have already disaggregated every step of production and farmed each out to whatever specific locations in the world offer the cheapest production and labor costs. If the production side is no longer linked to singular nation-states, the consumption side perhaps never has been. The desire for international markets for goods is not a recent dream for capitalists—mercantilists three hundred years ago looked to national exports as a way of creating favorable balances of trade, and European and American manufacturers in the late nineteenth century fantasized about the vast China market long before companies like Nike dreamed about a billion pairs of Air Jordans being purchased by Chinese.

Understanding the perception of so many people that Tiger Woods had the potential for foreign marketing involves connecting international sales with an American-born, mixed racial or cultural body, and the narrative that allows that connection is a multicultural ideology that identifies the origins of his ethnic fractions with foreign nations. The potential of developing Asian markets for golf wear and athletic products is tied to the international appeal of Tiger's partial Asian heritage. Lost in the blackness of America's perception of Tiger, his Asian stripes can be earned on the global market, parlayed into increased sales for Nike in Southeast Asia and other growth markets for Nike's leisure products. If Michael Jordan has been the best ambassador for the international growth of basketball as a marketing vehicle, then Tiger Woods can be golf's equivalent, instantiating such global possibilities in his body. The image of Woods also serves to hide the idealization in golf of white male hierarchy by providing a nonwhite, multiracial body as a fantasy pinnacle.

There is a perverse irony in selling products back to the places where capital has gone to find cheap labor. Marketing golf in Thailand, Indonesia, and other Southeast Asian nations, such as Vietnam, evokes the ultimate capitalist dream of pouring relatively little capital into a location in order to produce products for export to places that will pay a healthy mark-up on production costs, and also recouping as much as possible from those very sites of production. Of course, it's not the women and children being paid thirteen cents an hour in Indonesia who will be able to play golf and buy Nike shoes. But even if it is local elites who make their portion of the profit from managing the cheap labor and creating the professional services and infrastructure for production, the dream remains of new markets springing up alongside labor sites.

Initial indications are that Nike's fantasy of Tiger Woods creating global markets is achieving mixed results. Jan Weisman's work on Thai perceptions of Tiger Woods suggests that the attempt to market Woods as a Thai hero was eagerly embraced by a number of sectors of Thai society. Upon his initial visit as a professional golfer in 1997, newspapers hailed him as native son, and the Thai prime minister met his entourage. Unfortunately, racial hierarchies in Thailand cut against Tiger's inclusion into an imagined Thai social body, and in particular his blackness made constructions of him as Thai difficult.

As in the United States, Tiger's African American military father became the defining characteristic of Tiger's mixed heritage, but within the historical context of US military presence in Thailand during the Vietnam war, Tiger's blackness also painted his mother with questionable moral stripes. Despite widespread efforts to portray Tiger's father as an elite Green Beret and thus different from the morally suspect GIs who had created a flourishing sex-trade industry in Thailand, Kultida Woods was trapped by the prejudices against Thai women who had sex with American soldiers, in particular black GIs. Though Woods's father was an elite officer, his mother was still marked with a low social status by such an association. Tiger Woods also did not act like a Thai national, neither speaking the language nor expressing the proper humility and devoutness of Thai

Buddhism. In the end, Woods's triumphant visit to Thailand succeeded in publicizing him as a sports superstar and marketing icon, but it failed to establish him as a native Thai.

More important than his inability (or unwillingness, since Tiger went out of his way to mark himself as American) to perform culture in a manner that would allow his inclusion, categories of color hierarchy threatened the extinction of Tiger's value as Thai. In a society which mirrored an American fetishization of white purity, Wood's Thai heritage was lost in his father's blackness. The globalization of American leisure products has also exported the commodity of whiteness. Weisman's fascinating research contains an analysis of how partial "white" heritage has been commodified in Thai beauty pageants. A recent Miss Universe from Thailand, for instance, was originally recruited to be a Miss Thailand contestant because of her perceived "white" physical features.[18]

The spreading awareness of global perspectives as somehow explaining changes in contemporary society has led to interesting narrative variations. In the recent book *Jihad vs. McWorld,* Benjamin R. Barber argues that the twin forces of global homogenization and ethnic tribalism are tearing the world apart.[19] Enabled by technological advances in communications and transportation, the bland plasticity and homogenization of capital is embodied in the international spread of McDonald's. Combined with the mass production of superficial images that conflate culture with advertising, a world has been created in which leisure, consumption, and happiness all fall within the range between sports and MTV.[20] Opposed to such globalization, but often partaking in the spread of capital, has been the politics of identity, fragmenting nations and fomenting fratricide and genocide. Globalism and tribalism, both destructive in their own way, each threaten to end democracy and free citizenship as we know it.

Of course, if racial differentiation is seen as a foundational element in the formation of national citizenship, then it is clear that democracy and free citizenship are, contrary to Barber's view, future goals that history teaches us have always been ideals built on racial and gender oppression. It might seem a trite point that American democracy, the globe's shining example of egalitarian society, was built upon the self-evident freedom of white men to rule everyone else,[21] but it points out how such narratives of nostalgic longing for a golden age of democracy are empty gestures. Barber may fancy himself a Cassandra warning of the decline of democracy in the face of globalism and ethnic fragmentation, but he resembles Chicken Little decrying a falling firmament that was never that heavenly.

Decline, however, might be preferable to narratives of progress and modernity that assume global capitalism is bringing a better and brighter world. Each and every day we are all becoming better people, closer to and more like each other, or so the story goes. The resistance to global tendencies from ethnic tribalism thus easily produces the idea that identities based on difference are somehow impeding the progress of global humanity. Whether racial, cultural, or national, an awareness of difference seems to buck the trend towards world peace and togetherness. The dream of Tiger Woods as the future thus resides in his embodiment of racial, cultural, and national fusion, allowing for the equation of "We are Tiger Woods" and "We are the world."

The classic tale of Western progress, with its concurrent descriptions of development and underdevelopment, has been almost the sole narrative of global history. There have also been a number of powerful explanations for the global connections of capitalist production and consumption that critique the dominance of the West—world systems theory and dependency theory being the foremost.[22] In the end, however, all of them are united in a shared belief that capitalism has become a global phenomenon, disagreeing only on when exactly this happened, and whether it is a desirable development. Whether the global spread of capitalism signals the progress of universal modernity or whether it encapsulates an oppressive Western system foisted upon the world, it is a global phenomenon nonetheless.[23] Whether we chase the spirit of capitalism, or decry the specter of commodification, we live in a world that has structured its life around production and consumption.

I have tried in this essay to suggest a number of different ways in which recognizing transnational connections can lead to interesting questions for a post-nationalist American Studies. Race and culture are not sociological categories, but definitions predicated upon historical narratives of identity. Definitions of what someone is now are tied biologically to a national origin in the past; these definitions were made in localized contexts, defining who belonged to a particular geographical locale and who else was a foreigner from somewhere else. But even though the distinctions were made in specific sites, they always invoked the international by imagining foreign nations with theoretically homogenous populations from which migrants originally came. Population migrations have always produced definitions of the difference between the local and the foreign, imagining a set of movements between here and somewhere else.

Racial and cultural differentiation has been at the center of such distinctions between the local and foreign. As languages that have served as shorthands for national origin and for who belonged and who did not, definitions of race and culture have always been based upon transnational comparisons and connections. Even in periods such as that between 1924 and 1965, when international immigration to the United States was virtually cut off, earlier transnational migrations were assumed in narratives of racial and cultural difference. Migration and the imagined comparisons between here and there that were linked to the movements of people and objects lie at the heart of American history. A post-nationalist American Studies that takes into account such a perspective, therefore, is a call for an examination of the importance of the transnational migrations that have defined racial and cultural differences in the United States. More than just recognizing the role of these migrations, however, we must also pay attention to the expansion of labor markets and capitalist production and consumption that have at times created these movements of people, and at other times have commodified the cultural differences they are seen to embody. In the end, I also contend that the position of the scholar must be considered, since the definitions and classifications that have resulted from the movements of history have marked us all, and to deny their relevance for the producers of knowledge only blinds us to the operations of power.

Notes

* Thanks to the members of the UCHRI research group and Hazel Carby, Michael Denning, Patricia Pessar, Andrés Resendez, Jace Weaver, and Bryan Wolf of the Race, Ethnicity, and Migration Program brown-bag colloquium at Yale for their helpful comments. Walter Johnson of NYU showed me an unpublished paper. Special acknowledgment to Kariann Yokota for her multiple, careful readings and large-scale additions to the subject matter and body of this essay, as well as numerous suggestions on the applicability of postcolonial theory to US history.

1. "Money" section report on popularity of Tiger Woods advertising campaign, *USA Today* (October 20, 1997); James K. Glassman, "A Dishonest Ad Campaign," *Washington Post* (Sept 17, 1996); Larry Dorman, "We'll Be Right Back, after This Hip and Distorted Commercial Break," *New York Times*, 145, sec. 8 (Sept 1, 1996; hype surrounding entrance into professional golfing world of twenty-year-old Tiger Woods); Robert Lipsyte, "Woods Suits Golf's Needs Perfectly," *New York Times*, 145, sec. 1 (Sept. 8, 1996); David Segal, "Golf's $60 Million Question: Can Tiger Woods Bring Riches to Sponsors, Minorities to Game?" *Washington Post* (August 31, 1996); Ellen Goodman, "Black (and White, Asian, Indian) like Me," *Washington Post* (April 15, 1995; golfer Tiger Woods is multiracial); Ellen Goodman, "Being More Than the Sum of Parts: When Tiger Woods Speaks of His Background as Multiracial, He Speaks for a Generation That Shuns Labels," *Los Angeles Times*, 114 (April 14, 1995); 'Tiger, Tiger, Burning Bright," *Los Angeles Times*, 113 (Sept 1, 1994; Tiger Woods wins U.S. Amateur Golf Championship).

2. Virginia Domínguez, *White by Definition: Social Classification in Creole Louisiana* (New Brunswick, NJ: Rutgers University Press, 1986).

3. Somewhat in jest, but further revealing the absurdity of such calculations, this is not even counting as Asian American the one-eighth American Indian coursing through his veins, a legacy of the original immigrants from Asia crossing over the Bering land bridge.

4. The phrase "how Tiger lost his stripes" was suggested to me by George Sánchez.

5. Thanks to Hazel Carby and Michael Denning for suggesting the importance of Tiger Woods's father as military hero, and the connections between such representations of safe black male bodies and the dangerous criminalized black male in popular culture. See Hazel Carby, *RACEMEN* (Cambridge: Harvard University Press, 1998).

6. On different types of multiculturalism, see David Palumbo-Liu's "Introduction," in *The Ethnic Canon:*

Histories, Institutions, and Interventions (Minneapolis: University of Minnesota Press, 1995). The marketing of diversity has been the subject of numerous newspaper articles, including the following: Patrick Lee, "As California's Ethnic Makeup Changes, Companies Are Facing New Challenges in Serving Diverse Customers," *Los Angeles Times,* 113 (Oct. 23, 1994); "So Long, Betty," *Christian Science Monitor,* 87 (Sept. 21, 1995); George White, "The Ethnic Side of Sears: Retailer Leads in Effort to Reach Diverse Markets," *Los Angeles Times,* 114 (Jan. 29, 1996); Walter C. Farrell, Jr., and James H. Johnson, Jr., "Toward Diversity, and Profits," *New York Times,* 146, sec. 3 (Jan. 12, 1997; workplace diversity makes both moral and economic sense).

7. There has been a good deal of interesting literature already on transnational movements of labor and how these diasporic movements have been at the heart of ethnic identity within the nation-states which arose at the same time. The United States was like many nations in the nineteenth century that derived part of their sense of national homogeneity from racializing and excluding diasporic labor from definitions of the national body.

8. Ashley Montagu, *Man's Most Dangerous Myth: The Fallacy of Race,* 5th ed. (New York: Oxford University Press, 1974).

9. Mary Louise Pratt, *Imperial Eyes: Travel Writing and Transculturation* (New York: Routledge, 1992); Margaret Hunt, "Racism, Imperialism, and the Traveler's Gaze in Eighteenth-Century *England,*" *Journal of British Studies* 32 (October 1993): 333–57.

10. Postcolonial scholarship, such as that of South Asian scholars on India and partition, has described how nations arose in the wake of decolonization, and the problems of ethnicity within states which were abstract entities created by colonial map-makers' fantasies of geographic and administrative order. A well-known example of this scholarship is Benedict Anderson's *Imagined Communities,* 2nd ed. (London: Verso, 1991), which includes an interpretation of the end of Dutch rule in the islands of the East Indies and the creation of the nation of Indonesia out of a myriad of diverse peoples, united by armed and political struggle, but also by an imagined unity that came out of a shared history of domination by Dutch colonizers. See also Jan Nederveen Pieterse and Bhikhu Parekh, eds., *The Decolonization of Imagination: Culture, Knowledge, and Power* (Atlantic Highlands, NJ: Zed Books, 1995); Arif Dirlik, ed., *The Postcolonial Aura: Third World Criticism in the Age of Global Capitalism* (Boulder: Westview Press, 1997), in particular the essay by Ann Stoler,

"'Mixed-bloods' and the Cultural Politics of European Identity in Colonial Southeast Asia," pp. 128–48; Arif Dirlik, *What's in a Rim? Critical Perspectives on the Pacific Region Idea* (Boulder: Westview Press, 1993), in particular the introduction, "Introducing the Pacific," and the essays by Alexander Woodside, "The Asia-Pacific Idea as a Mobilization Myth," pp. 13–28; Bruce Cumings, "Rimspeak: Or, the Discourse of the 'Pacific Rim,'" pp. 29–49; Neferti Xina M. Tadiar, "Sexual Economies in the Asia-Pacific Community," pp. 183–210; and Meredith Woo-Cumings, "Market Dependency in U.S.-East Asian Relations," pp. 135–57.

11. If a shared Asian American identity is formed for the most part from the experience of being treated as "Orientals" in a similar manner by other Americans, including being mistaken for each other, perhaps one of the largest reasons for the continued practice of excluding South Asians and most Filipinos and Pacific Islanders from a sense of identity with Asian Americans is that they are not mistaken for migrants from East Asia.

12. Madeline Hsu, "Between Diaspora and Native Place: Evolutions in the Relationship between Taishan County and Overseas Taishanese, 1849–1989"; Susan Koshy, "Category Crisis: South Asian Diasporic Negotiations of Racial Categories"; and Shu-mei Shih, "Globalization, Minoritization, and Ang Lee's Films"; all of these are unpublished papers given at the 1998 Association for Asian American Studies, Fifteenth Annual Conference, Honolulu, Hawaii. Hsu's and Koshy's research will be published in forthcoming books. See also Lisa Lowe, *Immigrant Acts: On Asian American Cultural Politics* (Durham, NC: Duke University Press, 1996).

13. Kariann Yokota's research appears in her doctoral dissertation in history, which is in progress at the University of California, Los Angeles.

14. Paul Ong, Edna Bonacich, and Lucie Cheng, eds., *The New Asian Immigration in Los Angeles and Global Restructuring* (Philadelphia: Temple University Press, 1994); Edna Bonacich et al., eds., *Global Production: The Apparel Industry in the Pacific Rim* (Philadelphia: Temple University Press, 1994); I. S. A. Baud, *Form of Production and Women's Labour: Gender Aspects of Industrialisation in India and Mexico* (Newbury Park: Sage, 1992); Michiel Scheffer, *Trading Places: Fashion, Retailers, and the Changing Geography of Clothing Production* (Utrecht: Department of Geography, 1992); Lisa Lowe and David Lloyd, eds., *The Politics of Culture in the Shadow of Capitalism* (Durham, NC: Duke University Press, 1998).

15. Anne McClintock, *Imperial Leather: Race, Gender, and Sexuality in the Colonial Contest* (New York: Routledge, 1995); Berth Lindfors, "Ethnological Show Business:

Footlighting the Dark Continent," in Rosemarie G. Thomson, ed., *Freakery: Cultural Spectacles of the Extraordinary Body* (New York: New York University Press, 1996), pp. 207–18. On Saartjie Baartman, the San woman exhibited in 1810–11 as the "Hottentot Venus," and on the previous topic, see Sander Gilman, "Black Bodies, White Bodies," *Critical Inquiry* 12 (1985): 204–42; *Exhibiting Cultures: The Poetics and Politics of Museum Display* (Washington, DC: Smithsonian, 1991); Johannes Fabian, *Time and the Other: How Anthropology Makes Its Object* (New York: Columbia University Press, 1983); Marianna Torgovnik, *Gone Primitive: Savage Intellects, Modern Lives* (Chicago: University of Chicago Press, 1990); Edward Said, *Culture and Imperialism* (New York: Random House, 1993); Ann Stoler, *Race and the Education of Desire: Foucault's History of Sexuality and the Colonial Order of Things* (Durham, NC: Duke University Press, 1995); on the disinterested knower, see Etienne Balibar, *Masses, Classes, and Ideas* (London: Verso, 1994); Robert Young, *White Mythologies: Writing History and the West* (New York: Routledge, 1990); Nicholas Canny and Anthony Pagden, eds., *Colonial Identity in the Atlantic World, 1500–1800* (Princeton: Princeton University Press, 1987).

16. Rob Wilson and Arif Dirlik, eds., *Asia/Pacific as Space of Cultural Production* (Durham, NC: Duke University Press, 1995).

17. Pierre Bourdieu, *Distinction* (Cambridge: Harvard University Press, 1984); James Clifford, "On Collecting Art and Culture," in *The Predicament of Culture* (Cambridge: Harvard University Press, 1988).

18. Jan Weisman, "Multiracial Amerasia Abroad: Thai Perceptions and Constructions of Tiger Woods," a paper given at the 1998 Association for Asian American Studies, Fifteenth Annual Conference, Honolulu, Hawaii. Weisman's research can be found in her 1998 doctoral dissertation in anthropology at the University of Washington.

19. Benjamin R. Barber, *Jihad vs. McWorld: How the Planet Is Both Falling Apart and Coming Together—and What This Means for Democracy* (New York: Times Books, 1995).

20. Fredric Jameson, *Postmodernism: Or, the Cultural Logic of Late Capitalism* (Durham, NC: Duke University Press, 1991).

21. For histories of the role of race in early American and Jacksonian democracy, see Edmund Morgan, *American Slavery, American Freedom: The Ordeal of Colonial Virginia* (New York: Norton, 1975); Alexander Saxton, *The Rise and Fall of the White Republic: Class Politics and Mass Culture in Nineteenth-Century America* (London: Verso, 1990); David Roediger, *The Wages of Whiteness: Race and the Making of the American Working Class* (London: Verso, 1991).

22. Patrick Wolfe, "Review Essay: History and Imperialism: A Century of Theory, from Marx to Postcolonialism," *American Historical Review* 102, no. 2 (April 1997): 388–420; Amy Kaplan and Donald Pease, eds., *Cultures of United States Imperialism* (Durham, NC: Duke University Press, 1993); John Tomlinson, *Cultural Imperialism: A Critical Introduction* (Baltimore: Johns Hopkins University Press, 1991); "Imperialism—A Useful Category of Historical Analysis?" *Forum in Radical History Review* 57 (1993). On modernization theory, see Walter W. Rostow, *The Stages of Economic Growth: A Non-Communist Manifesto* (Cambridge: Cambridge University Press, 1960); Partha Chatterjee, *Nationalist Thought and the Colonial World: A Derivative Discourse?* (Minneapolis: University of Minnesota Press, 1993), and *The Nation and Its Fragments: Colonial and Postcolonial Histories* (Princeton: Princeton University Press, 1993); Immanuel Wallerstein, *The Modern World-System,* vol. 1, *Capitalist Agriculture and the Origins of the European World-Economy in the Sixteenth Century* (New York: Academic Press, 1974), and vol. 2, *Mercantilism and the Consolidation of the European World-Economy, 1600–1750* (New York: Academic Press, 1980); see also his *The Capitalist World-Economy* (New York: Academic Press, 1989).

23. See Francis Fukuyama, *End of History and the Last Man* (New York: Free Press, 1992), for a prominent example of such a universal narrative of history and capitalism; on the foisting of capitalism on other societies, see Reinhold Wagnleitner, *Coca-Colonization and the Cold War,* trans. Diana Wolf (Chapel Hill: University of North Carolina Press, 1994). For a trenchant critique of the narratives of progress, see Dipesh Chakrabarty, "Postcoloniality and the Artifice of History: Who Speaks for 'Indian' Pasts?" *Representations* 37 (1992): 1–26.

31.
PASSING FOR WHITE, PASSING FOR BLACK
Adrian Piper

It was the new graduate student reception for my class, the first social event of my first semester in the best graduate department in my field in the country. I was full of myself, as we all were, full of pride at having made the final cut, full of arrogance at our newly recorded membership among the privileged few, the intellectual elite—this country's real aristocracy, my parents told me—full of confidence in our intellectual ability to prevail, to fashion original and powerful views about some topic we represented to ourselves only vaguely. I was a bit late and noticed that many turned to look at—no, scrutinize—me as I entered the room. I congratulated myself on having selected for wear my black velvet, bell-bottom pants suit (yes, it was that long ago) with the cream silk blouse and crimson vest. One of the secretaries who'd earlier helped me find an apartment came forward to greet me and proceeded to introduce me to various members of the faculty, eminent and honorable faculty, with names I knew from books I'd studied intensely and heard discussed with awe and reverence by my undergraduate teachers. To be in the presence of these men and attach faces to names was delirium enough. But actually to enter into casual social conversation with them took every bit of poise I had. As often happens in such situations, I went on automatic pilot. I don't remember what I said; I suppose I managed not to make a fool of myself. The most famous and highly respected member of the faculty observed me for a while from a distance and then came forward. Without introduction or preamble he said to me with a triumphant smirk, "Miss Piper, you're about as black as I am."

One of the benefits of automatic pilot in social situations is that insults take longer to make themselves felt. The meaning of the words simply don't register right away, particularly if the person who utters them is smiling. You reflexively respond to the social context and the smile rather than to the words. And so I automatically returned the smile and said something like, "Really? I hadn't known that about you"—something that sounded both innocent and impertinent, even though that was not what I felt. What I felt was numb, and then shocked and terrified, disoriented, as though I'd been awakened from a sweet dream of unconditional support and approval and plunged into a nightmare of jeering contempt. Later those feelings turned into wrenching grief and anger that one of my intellectual heroes had sullied himself in my presence and destroyed my illusion that these privileged surroundings were benevolent and safe; then guilt and remorse at having provided him the occasion for doing so.

Finally, there was the groundless shame of the inadvertent impostor, exposed to public ridicule or accusation. For this kind of shame, you don't actually need to have done anything wrong. All you need to do is care about others' image of you, and fail in your actions to reinforce their positive image of themselves. Their ridicule and accusations then function to both disown and degrade you from their status, to mark you not as having *done* wrong but as *being* wrong.

This turns you into something bogus relative to their criterion of worth, and false relative to their criterion of authenticity. Once exposed as a fraud of this kind, you can never regain your legitimacy. For the violated criterion of legitimacy implicitly presumes an absolute incompatibility between the person you appeared to be and the person you are now revealed to be; and no fraud has the authority to convince her accusers that they merely imagine an incompatibility where there is none in fact. The devaluation of status consequent on such exposure is, then, absolute, and the suspicion of fraudulence spreads to all areas of interaction.

> Mr. S. looked sternly at Mrs. P., and with an imperious air said, "You a colored woman? You're no negro. Where did you come from? If you're a negro, where are your free papers to show it?" . . . As he went away he looked at Mr. Hill and said, "She's no negro."
>
> —The Rev. H. Mattison, *Louisa Picquet,*
> *The Octoroon Slave and Concubine:*
> *A Tale of Southern Slave Life*

The accusation was one I had heard before, but more typically from other blacks. My family was one of the very last middle-class, light-skinned black families left in our Harlem neighborhood after most had fled to the suburbs; visibly black working-class kids my age yanked my braids and called me "paleface." Many of them thought I was white, and treated me accordingly. As an undergraduate in the late 1960s and early 1970s, I attended an urban university to which I walked daily through a primarily black working-class neighborhood. Once a black teenage youth called to me, "Hey, white girl! Give me a quarter!" I was feeling strong that day, so I retorted, "I'm not white and I don't have a quarter!" He answered skeptically, "You sure look white! You sure act white!" And I have sometimes met blacks socially who, as a condition of social acceptance of me, require me to prove my blackness by passing the Suffering Test: They recount at length their recent experiences of racism and then wait expectantly, skeptically, for me to match theirs with mine. Mistaking these situations for a different one in which an exchange of shared experiences is part of the bonding process,

I instinctively used to comply. But I stopped when I realized that I was in fact being put through a third degree. I would share some equally nightmarish experience along similar lines, and would then have it explained to me why that wasn't really so bad, why it wasn't the same thing at all, or why I was stupid for allowing it to happen to me. So the aim of these conversations clearly was not mutual support or commiseration. That came only after I managed to prove myself by passing the Suffering Test of blackness (if I did), usually by shouting down or destroying my acquaintance's objections with logic.

> The white kids would call me a Clorox coon baby and all kinds of names I don't want to repeat. And the black kids hated me. "Look at her," they'd say. "She think she white. She think she cute."
>
> —Elaine Perry, *Another Present Era*

These exchanges are extremely alienating and demoralizing, and make me feel humiliated to have presumed a sense of connectedness between us. They also give me insight into the way whites feel when they are made the circumstantial target of blacks' justified and deep-seated anger. Because the anger is justified, one instinctively feels guilty. But because the target is circumstantial and sometimes arbitrary, one's sense of fairness is violated. One feels both unjustly accused or harassed, and also remorseful and ashamed at having been the sort of person who could have provoked the accusation.

As is true for blacks' encounters with white racism, there are at least two directions in which one's reactions can take one here. One can react defensively and angrily, and distill the encounter into slow-burning fuel for one's racist stereotypes. Or one can detach oneself emotionally and distance oneself physically from the aggressors, from this perspective their personal flaws and failures of vision, insight, and sensitivity loom larger, making it easier to forgive them for their human imperfections but harder to relate to them as equals. Neither reaction is fully adequate to the situation, since the first projects exaggerated fantasies onto the aggressor, while the second diminishes his responsibility. I have experienced both, toward both blacks and whites. I believe that the perceptual and cognitive distortions that characterize any form of racism begin here, in the failure to see any act of racist aggression as a defensive response to one's own perceived attack on the aggressor's physical or psychological property, or conception of himself or of the world. Once you see this, you may feel helpless to be anything other than who you are, anything or anyone who could resolve the discord. But at least it restores a sense of balance and mutually flawed humanity to the interaction.

My maternal cousin, who resembles Michelle Pfeiffer, went through adolescence in the late 1960s and had a terrible time. She tried perming her hair into an Afro; it didn't prevent attacks and ridicule from her black peers for not being "black enough." She adopted a black working-class dialect that made her almost unintelligible to her very proper, very middle-class parents, and counted among her friends young people who criticized high scholastic achievers for "acting white." That is, she ran the same gauntlet I did, but of a more intense variety and at a much younger age. But she emerged intact, with a sharp and practical intellect, an endearing attachment to stating difficult truths bluntly, a dry sense of humor, and little tolerance for those blacks who, she feels, forgo the hard work of self-improvement and initiative for the imagined benefits of victim status. Now married to a wasp musician from Iowa, she is one tough cookie, leavened by the rejection she experienced from those with whom she has always proudly identified.

In my experience, these rejections almost always occur with blacks of working-class background who do not have extended personal experience with the very wide range of variation in skin color, hair texture, and facial features that in fact has always existed among African Americans, particularly in the middle class. Because light-skinned blacks often received some education or training apprenticeships during slavery, there tend to be more of us in the middle class now. Until my family moved out of Harlem when I was fourteen, my social contacts were almost exclusively with upper-middle-class white schoolmates and working-class black neighborhood playmates, both of whom made me feel equally alienated from both races. It wasn't until college and after that I reencountered the middle- and upper-middle-class

blacks who were as comfortable with my appearance as my family had been, and who made me feel as comfortable and accepted by them as my family had.

So Suffering Test exchanges almost never occur with middle-class blacks, who are more likely to protest, on the contrary, that "we always knew you were black!"—as though there were some mysterious and inchoate essence of blackness that only other blacks have the antennae to detect.

> "There are niggers who are as white as I am, but the taint of blood is there and we always exclude it."
> "How do you know it is there?" asked Dr. Gresham.
> "Oh, there are tricks of blood which always betray them. My eyes are more practiced than yours. I can always tell them."
> —Frances E. W. Harper, *Iola Leroy, or Shadows Uplifted*

When made by other blacks, these remarks function on some occasions to reassure me of my acceptance within the black community, and on others to rebuke me for pretending to indistinguishability from whiteness. But in either case they wrongly presuppose, as did my eminent professor's accusation, an essentializing stereotype into which all blacks must fit. In fact no blacks, and particularly no African American blacks, fit any such stereotype.

My eminent professor was one of only two whites I have ever met who questioned my designated racial identity to my face. The other was a white woman junior professor, relatively new to the department, who, when I went on the job market at the end of graduate school, summoned me to her office and grilled me as to why I identified myself as black and exactly what fraction of African ancestry I had. The implicit accusation behind both my professors' remarks was, of course, that I had fraudulently posed as black in order to take advantage of the department's commitment to affirmative action. It's an extraordinary idea, when you think about it: as though someone would willingly shoulder the stigma of being black in a racist society for the sake of a little extra professional consideration that guarantees nothing but suspicions of foul play and accusations of cheating. But it demonstrates just how irrationally far the suspicion of fraudulence can extend.

In fact I had always identified myself as black (or "colored" as we said before 1967). But fully comprehending what it meant to be black took a long time. My acculturation into the white upper-middle class started with nursery school when I was four, and was largely uneventful. For my primary and secondary schooling my parents sent me to a progressive prep school, one of the first to take the goal of integration seriously as more than an ideal. They gave me ballet lessons, piano lessons, art lessons, tennis lessons. In the 1950s and early 1960s they sent me to integrated summer camps where we sang "We Shall Overcome" around the campfire long before it became the theme song of the civil rights movement.

Of course there were occasional, usually veiled incidents, such as the time in preadolescence when the son of a prominent union leader (and my classmate) asked me to go steady and I began to receive phone calls from his mother, drunk, telling me how charming she thought it that her son was going out with a little colored girl. And the time the daughter of a well-known playwright, also a classmate, brought me home to her family and asked them to guess whether I was black or white, and shared a good laugh with them when they guessed wrong. But I was an only child in a family of four adults devoted to creating for me an environment in which my essential worth and competence never came into question. I used to think my parents sheltered me in this way because they believed, idealistically, that my education and achievements would then protect me from the effects of racism. I now know that they did so to provide me with an invincible armor of self-worth with which to fight it. It almost worked. I grew up not quite grasping the fact that my racial identity was a disadvantage. This lent heat to my emerging political conviction that of course it shouldn't be a disadvantage, for me or anyone else, and finally fueled my resolution not to allow it to be a disadvantage if I had anything at all to say about it.

I will live down the prejudice, I will crush it out . . . the thoughts of the ignorant and prejudiced will not concern me. . . . I will show to the world that

a man may spring from a race of slaves, yet far excel many of the boasted ruling race. —Charles W. Chesnutt, *Journals*

But the truth in my professors' accusations was that I had, in fact, resisted my parents' suggestion that, just this once, for admission to this most prestigious of graduate programs, I decline to identify my racial classification on the graduate admissions application, so that it could be said with certainty that I'd been admitted on the basis of merit alone. "But that would be passing," I protested. Although both of my parents had watched many of their relatives disappear permanently into the white community, passing for white was unthinkable within the branches of my father's and mother's families to which I belonged. That would have been a really, authentically shameful thing to do.

"It seems as if the prejudice pursues us through every avenue of life, and assigns us the lowest places. . . . And yet I am determined," said Iola, "to win for myself a place in the fields of labor. I have heard of a place in New England, and I mean to try for it, even if I only stay a few months."

"Well, if you will go, say nothing about your color."

"Uncle Robert, I see no necessity for proclaiming that fact on the house-top. Yet I am resolved that nothing shall tempt me to deny it. The best blood in my veins is African blood, and I am not ashamed of it."

—Harper, *Iola Leroy*

And besides, I reasoned to myself, to be admitted under the supposition that I was white would *not* be to be admitted on the basis of merit alone. Why undermine my chances of admission by sacrificing my one competitive advantage when I already lacked not only the traditionally acceptable race and gender attributes, but also alumni legacy status, an Ivy League undergraduate pedigree, the ability to pay full tuition or endow the university, war veteran status, professional sports potential, and a distinguished family name? I knew I could ace the program if I could just get my foot in the damn door.

Later, when I experienced the full force of the racism of the academy, one of my graduate advisors, who had remained a continuing source of support and advice after I took my first job, consoled me by informing me that the year I completed the program I had, in fact, tied one other student for the highest grade point average in my class. He was a private and dignified man of great integrity and subtle intellect, someone who I had always felt was quietly rooting for me. It was not until after his death that I began to appreciate what a compassionate and radical gesture he had made in telling me this. For by this time, I very much needed to be reminded that neither was I incompetent nor my work worthless, that I could achieve the potential I felt myself to have. My choice not to pass for white in order to gain entry to the academy, originally made out of naiveté, had resulted in more punishment than I would have imagined possible.

It wasn't only the overt sexual and racial harassment, each of which exacerbated the other, or the gratuitous snipes about my person, my lifestyle, or my work. What was even more insulting were the peculiar strategies deployed to make me feel accepted and understood despite the anomalies of my appearance, by individuals whose racism was so profound that this would have been an impossible task: the WASP colleague who attempted to establish rapport with me by making anti-Semitic jokes about the prevalence of Jews in the neighborhood of the university; the colleague who first inquired in detail into my marital status, and then attempted to demonstrate his understanding of my decision not to have children by speculating that I was probably concerned that they would turn out darker than I was; the colleague who consulted me on the analysis of envy and resentment, reasoning that since I was black I must know all about it; the colleague who, in my first department faculty meeting, made a speech to his colleagues discussing the research that proved that a person could be black without looking it.

These incidents and others like them had a peculiar cognitive feel to them, as though the individuals involved felt driven to make special efforts to situate me in their conceptual mapping of the world, not only by naming or indicating the niche in which they felt I belonged, but by seeking my verbal confirmation of it.

I have learned to detect advance warnings that these incidents are imminent. The person looks at me with a fixed stare, her tension level visibly rising. Like a thermostat, when the tension reaches a certain level, the mechanism switches on: out comes some comment or action, often of an offensive personal nature, that attempts to locate me within the rigid confines of her stereotype of black people. I have not experienced this phenomenon outside the academic context. Perhaps it's a degenerate form of hypothesis testing, an unfortunate side effect of the quest for knowledge.

> She walked away. . . . The man followed her
> and tapped her shoulder.
> "Listen, I'd really like to get to know you," he
> said, smiling. He paused, as if expecting thanks
> from her. She didn't say anything. Flustered, he
> said, "A friend of mine says you're black. I told him
> I had to get a close-up look and see for myself."
> —Perry, *Another Present Era*

The irony was that I could have taken an easier entry route into this privileged world. In fact, on my graduate admissions application I could have claimed alumni legacy status and the distinguished family name of my paternal great uncle, who not only had attended that university and sent his sons there, but had endowed one of its buildings and was commemorated with an auditorium in his name. I did not because he belonged to a branch of the family from which we had been estranged for decades, even before my grandfather—his brother—divorced my grandmother, moved to another part of the country, and started another family. My father wanted nothing more to do with my grandfather or any of his relatives. He rejected his inheritance and never discussed them while he was alive. For me to have invoked his uncle's name in order to gain a professional advantage would have been out of the question. But it would have nullified my eminent professor's need to tell me who and what he thought I was.

Recently I saw my great uncle's portrait on an airmail stamp honoring him as a captain of industry. He looked so much like family photos of my grandfather and father that I went out and bought two sheets worth of these stamps. He had my father's and grandfather's aquiline nose and their determined set of the chin. Looking at his face made me want to recover my father's estranged family, particularly my grandfather, for my own. I had a special lead: A few years previously in the South, I'd included a photo-text work containing a fictionalized narrative about my father's family—a history chock-full of romance and psychopathology—in an exhibition of my work. After seeing the show, a white woman with blue eyes, my father's transparent rosy skin and auburn-brown hair, and that dominant family nose walked up to me and told me that we were related. The next day she brought photographs of her family, and information about a relative who kept extensive genealogical records on every family member he could locate. I was very moved, and also astounded that a white person would voluntarily acknowledge blood relation to a black. She was so free and unconflicted about this, I just couldn't fathom it. We corresponded and exchanged family photos. And when I was ready to start delving in earnest, I contacted the relative she had mentioned for information about my grandfather, and initiated correspondence or communication with kin I hadn't known existed and who hadn't known that I existed, or that they or any part of their family was black. I embarked on this with great trepidation, anticipating with anxiety their reaction to the racial identity of these long-lost relatives, picturing in advance the withdrawal of warmth and interest, the quickly assumed impersonality and the suggestion that there must be some mistake.

> The dread that I might lose her took possession of me each time I sought to speak, and rendered it impossible for me to do so. That moral courage requires more than physical courage is no mere poetic fancy. I am sure I should have found it easier to take the place of a gladiator, no matter how fierce the Numidian lion, than to tell that slender girl that I had Negro blood in my veins.
> —James Weldon Johnson, *The Autobiography of an Ex-Coloured Man*

These fears were not unfounded. My father's sister had, in her youth, been the first black woman at a Seven Sisters undergraduate college and the first at an Ivy League medical school; had married into a white family who became socially, politically, and academically prominent; and then, after taking some family mementos my grandmother had given my father for me, had proceeded to sever all connections with her brothers and their families, even when the death of each of her siblings was imminent. She raised her children (now equally prominent socially and politically) as though they had no maternal relatives at all. We had all been so very proud of her achievements that her repudiation of us was devastating. Yet I frequently encounter mutual friends and colleagues in the circles in which we both travel, and I dread the day we might find ourselves in the same room at the same time. To read or hear about or see on television her or any member of her immediate family is a source of personal pain for all of us. I did not want to subject myself to that again with yet another set of relatives.

> Those who pass have a severe dilemma before they decide to do so, since a person must give up all family ties and loyalties to the black community in order to gain economic and other opportunities.
> —F. James Davis, *Who Is Black? One Nation's Definition*

Trying to forgive and understand those of my relatives who have chosen to pass for white has been one of the most difficult ethical challenges of my life, and I don't consider myself to have made very much progress. At the most superficial level, this decision can be understood in terms of a cost-benefit analysis: Obviously, they believe they will be happier in the white community than in the black one, all things considered. For me to make sense of this requires that I understand—or at least accept—their conception of happiness as involving higher social status, entrenchment within the white community and corresponding isolation from the black one, and greater access to the rights, liberties, and privileges the white community takes for granted. What is harder for me to grasp is how they could want these things enough to sacrifice the history, wisdom, connectedness, and moral solidarity with their family and community in order to get them. It seems to require so much severing and forgetting, so much disowning and distancing, not simply from one's shared past, but from one's former self—as though one had cauterized one's long-term memory at the moment of entry into the white community.

But there is, I think, more to it than that. Once you realize what is denied you as an African American simply because of your race, your sense of the unfairness of it may be so overwhelming that you may simply be incapable of accepting it. And if you are not inclined toward any form of overt political advocacy, passing in order to get the benefits you know you deserve may seem the only way to defy the system. Indeed, many of my more prominent relatives who are passing have chosen altruistic professions that benefit society on many fronts. They have chosen to use their assumed social status to make returns to the black community indirectly, in effect compensating for the personal advantages they have gained by rejecting their family.

Moreover, your sense of injustice may be compounded by the daily humiliation you experience as the result of identifying with those African Americans who, for demanding their rights, are punished and degraded as a warning to others. In these cases, the decision to pass may be more than the rejection of a black identity. It may be the rejection of a black identification that brings too much pain to be tolerated.

> All the while I understood that it was not discouragement or fear or search for a larger field of action and opportunity that was driving me out of the Negro race. I knew that it was shame, unbearable shame. Shame at being identified with a people that could with impunity be treated worse than animals.
>
> —Johnson, *The Autobiography of an Ex-Coloured Man*

The oppressive treatment of African Americans facilitates this distancing response by requiring every African American to draw a sharp distinction between the person he is and the person society perceives him to be—that is, between who he is as an individual, and the way he is designated and treated by others.

> The Negro's only salvation from complete despair lies in his belief, the old belief of his forefathers,

that these things are not directed against him personally, but against his race, his pigmentation. His mother or aunt or teacher long ago carefully prepared him, explaining that he as an individual can live in dignity, even though he as a Negro cannot.
>
> —John Howard Griffin, *Black Like Me*

This condition encourages a level of impersonality, a sense that white reactions to one have little or nothing to do with one as a person and an individual. Whites often mistake this impersonality for aloofness or unfriendliness. It is just one of the factors that make genuine intimacy between blacks and whites so difficult. Because I have occasionally encountered equally stereotypical treatment from other blacks and have felt compelled to draw the same distinction there between who I am and how I am perceived, my sense of impersonality pervades most social situations in which I find myself. Because I do not enjoy impersonal interactions with others, my solution is to limit my social interactions as far as possible to those in which this restraint is not required. So perhaps it is not entirely surprising that many white-looking individuals of African ancestry are able to jettison this doubly alienated and alienating social identity entirely, as irrelevant to the fully mature and complex individuals they know themselves to be. I take the fervent affirmation and embrace of black identity to be a countermeasure to, and thus evidence of, this alienation, rather than as incompatible with it. My family contains many instances of both attitudes.

There are no proper names mentioned in this account of my family. This is because in the African American community, we do not "out" people who are passing as white in the European-American community. Publicly to expose the African ancestry of someone who claims to have none is not done. There are many reasons for this, and different individuals cite different ones. For one thing, there is the vicarious enjoyment of watching one of our own infiltrate and achieve in a context largely defined by institutionalized attempts to exclude blacks from it. Then there is the question of self-respect: If someone wants to exit the African American community, there are few blacks who would consider it worth their while to prevent her. And then there is the possibility of retaliation: not merely the loss of credibility consequent on the denials by a putatively white person who, in virtue of his racial status, automatically has greater credibility than the black person who calls it into question, but perhaps more deliberate attempts to discredit or undermine the messenger of misfortune. There is also the instinctive impulse to protect the well-being of a fellow traveler embarked on a particularly dangerous and risky course. And finally—the most salient consideration for me, in thinking about those many members of my own family who have chosen to pass for white—a person who desires personal and social advantage and acceptance within the white community so much that she is willing to repudiate her family, past, history, and her personal connections within the African American community in order to get them is someone who is already in so much pain that it's just not possible to do something that you know is going to cause her any more.

Many colored Creoles protect others who are trying to pass, to the point of feigning ignorance of certain branches of their families. Elicited genealogies often seem strangely skewed. In the case of one very good informant, a year passed before he confided in me that his own mother's sister and her children had passed into the white community. With tears in his eyes, he described the painful experience of learning about his aunt's death on the obituary page of the *New Orleans Times-Picayune*. His cousin failed to inform the abandoned side of the family of the death, for fear that they might show up at the wake or the funeral and thereby destroy the image of whiteness. Total separation was necessary for secrecy.
—Virginia R. Domínguez, *White by Definition: Social Classification in Creole Louisiana*

She said: "It's funny about 'passing.' We disapprove of it and at the same time condone it. It excites our contempt and yet we rather admire it. We shy away from it with an odd kind of revulsion, but we protect it."

"Instinct of the race to survive and expand."

"Rot! Everything can't be explained by some general biological phrase."

"Absolutely everything can. Look at the so-called whites, who've left bastards all over the known earth. Same thing in them. Instinct of the race to survive and expand." —Nella Larsen, *Passing*

Those of my grandfather's estranged relatives who welcomed me into dialogue instead of freezing me out brought tears of gratitude and astonishment to my eyes. They seemed so kind and interested, so willing to help. At first I couldn't accept for what it was, their easy acceptance and willingness to help me puzzle out where exactly we each were located in our sprawling family tree. It is an ongoing endeavor, full of guesswork, false leads, blank spots, and mysteries. For just as white Americans are largely ignorant of their African—usually maternal—ancestry, we blacks are often ignorant of our European—usually paternal—ancestry. That's the way our slave-master forebears wanted it, and that's the way it is. Our names are systematically missing from the genealogies and public records of most white families, and crucial information—for example, the family name or name of the child's father—is often missing from our black ancestors' birth certificates, when they exist at all.

A realistic appreciation of the conditions which exist when women are the property of men makes the conclusion inevitable that there were many children born of mixed parentage.
—Joe Gray Taylor, *Negro Slavery in Louisiana*

Ownership of the female slave on the plantations generally came to include owning her sex life. Large numbers of white boys were socialized to associate physical and emotional pleasure with the black women who nursed and raised them, and then to deny any deep feelings for them. From other white males they learned to see black girls and women as legitimate objects of sexual desire. Rapes occurred, and many slave women were forced to submit regularly to white males or suffer harsh consequences. . . . As early as the time of the American Revolution there were plantation slaves who appeared to be completely white, as many of the founding fathers enslaved their own mixed children and grandchildren.

—Davis, *Who Is Black?*

So tracing the history of my family is detective work as well as historical research. To date, what I *think* I know is that our first European-American ancestor landed in Ipswich, Massachusetts, in 1620 from Sussex; another in Jamestown, Virginia, in 1675 from London; and another in Philadelphia, Pennsylvania, in 1751, from Hamburg. Yet another was the first in our family to graduate from my own graduate institution in 1778. My great-great-grandmother from Madagascar, by way of Louisiana, is the known African ancestor on my father's side, as my great-great-grandfather from the Ibo of Nigeria is the known African ancestor on my mother's, whose family has resided in Jamaica for three centuries.

I relate these facts and it doesn't seem to bother my newly discovered relatives. At first I had to wonder whether this ease of acceptance was not predicated on their mentally bracketing the implications of these facts and restricting their own immediate family ancestry to the European side. But when they remarked unselfconsciously on the family resemblances between us, I had to abandon that supposition. I still marvel at their enlightened and uncomplicated friendliness, and there is a part of me that still can't trust their acceptance of me. But that is a part of me I want neither to trust nor to accept in this context. I want to reserve my vigilance for its context of origin: the other white Americans I have encountered—even the bravest and most conscientious white scholars—for whom the suggestion that they might have significant African ancestry as the result of this country's long history of miscegenation is almost impossible to consider seriously.

She's heard the arguments, most astonishingly that, statistically, . . . the average white American is 6 percent black. Or, put another way, 95 percent of white Americans are 5 to 80 percent black. Her Aunt Tyler has told her stories about these whites researching their roots in the National Archives and finding they've got an African-American or

two in the family, some becoming so hysterical they have to be carried out by paramedics.

—Perry, *Another Present Era*

Estimates ranging up to 5 percent, and suggestions that up to one-fifth of the white population have some genes from black ancestors, are probably far too high. If these last figures were correct, the majority of Americans with some black ancestry would be known and counted as whites!

—Davis, *Who is Black?*

The detailed biological and genetic data can be gleaned from a careful review of *Genetic Abstracts* from about 1950 on. In response to my request for information about this, a white biological anthropologist once performed detailed calculations on the African admixture of five different genes, comparing British whites, American whites, and American blacks. The results ranged from 2 percent in one gene to 81.6 percent in another. About these results he commented, "I continue to believe five percent to be a reasonable estimate, but the matter is obviously complex. As you can see, it depends entirely on which genes you decide to use as racial 'markers' that are supposedly subject to little or no relevant selective pressure." Clearly, white resistance to the idea that most American whites have a significant percentage of African ancestry increases with the percentage suggested.

"Why, Doctor," said Dr. Latimer, "you Southerners began this absorption before the war. I understand that in one decade the mixed bloods rose from one-ninth to one-eighth of the population, and that as early as 1663 a law was passed in Maryland to prevent English women from intermarrying with slaves; and, even now, your laws against miscegenation presuppose that you apprehend danger from that source."

—Harper, *Iola Leroy*

(That legislators and judges paid increasing attention to the regulation and punishment of miscegenation at this time does not mean that interracial sex and marriage as social practices actually increased in frequency; the centrality of these practices to legal discourse was instead a sign that their relation to power was changing. The extent of uncoerced miscegenation before this period is a debated issue.)

—Eva Saks, "Representing Miscegenation Law," *Raritan*

The fact is, however, that the longer a person's family has lived in this country, the higher the probable percentage of African ancestry that person's family is likely to have—bad news for the DAR, I'm afraid. And the proximity to the continent of Africa of the country of origin from which one's forebears emigrated, as well as the colonization of a part of Africa by that country, are two further variables that increase the probability of African ancestry within that family. It would appear that only the Lapps of Norway are safe.

In Jamaica, my mother tells me, that everyone is of mixed ancestry is taken for granted. There are a few who vociferously proclaim themselves to be "Jamaican whites" having no African ancestry at all, but no one among the old and respected families takes them seriously. Indeed, they are assumed to be a bit unbalanced, and are regarded with amusement. In this country, by contrast, the fact of African ancestry among whites ranks up there with family incest, murder, and suicide as one of the bitterest and most difficult pills for white Americans to swallow.

"I had a friend who had two beautiful daughters whom he had educated in the North. They were cultured, and really belles in society. They were entirely ignorant of their lineage, but when their father died it was discovered that their mother had been a slave. It was a fearful blow. They would have faced poverty, but the knowledge of their tainted blood was more than they could bear."

—Harper, *Iola Leroy*

There was much apprehension about the unknown amount of black ancestry in the white population of the South, and this was fanned into an unreasoning fear of invisible blackness. For instance, white laundries and cleaners would not accommodate blacks because whites were afraid they would be "contaminated" by the clothing of invisible blacks.

—Davis, *Who Is Black?*

Suspicion is part of everyday life in Louisiana. Whites often grow up afraid to know their own genealogies. Many admit that as children they often stared at the skin below their fingernails and through a mirror at the white of their eyes to see if there was any "touch of the tarbrush." Not finding written records of birth, baptism, marriage, or death for any one ancestor exacerbates suspicions of foul play. Such a discovery brings glee to a political enemy or economic rival and may traumatize the individual concerned.

—Domínguez, *White by Definition*

A number of years ago I was doing research on a video installation on the subject of racial identity and miscegenation, and came across the Phipps case of Louisiana in the early 1980s. Susie Guillory Phipps had identified herself as white and, according to her own testimony (but not that of some of her black relatives), had believed that she was white, until she applied for a passport, when she discovered that she was identified on her birth records as black by virtue of having one thirty-second African ancestry. She brought suit against the state of Louisiana to have her racial classification changed. She lost the suit but effected the overthrow of the law identifying individuals as black if they had one thirty-second African ancestry, leaving on the books a prior law identifying an individual as black who had any African ancestry— the "one-drop" rule that uniquely characterizes the classification of blacks in the United States in fact even where no longer in law. So according to this long-standing convention of racial classification, a white who acknowledges any African ancestry implicitly acknowledges being black—a social condition, more than an identity, that no white person would voluntarily assume, even in imagination. This is one reason that whites, educated and uneducated alike, are so resistant to considering the probable extent of racial miscegenation.

This "one-drop" convention of classification of blacks is unique not only relative to the treatment of blacks in other countries but also unique relative to the treatment of other ethnic groups in this country. It goes without saying that no one, either white or black, is identified as, for example, English by virtue of having some small fraction of English ancestry. Nor is anyone free, as a matter of social convention, to do so by virtue of that fraction, although many whites do. But even in the case of other disadvantaged groups in this country, the convention is different. Whereas any proportion of African ancestry is sufficient to identify a person as black, an individual must have *at least* one-eighth Native American ancestry in order to identify legally as Native American.

Why the asymmetry of treatment? Clearly, the reason is economic. A legally certifiable Native American is entitled to financial benefits from the government, so obtaining this certification is difficult. A legally certifiable black person is *disentitled* to financial, social, and inheritance benefits from his white family of origin, so obtaining this certification is not just easy but automatic. Racial classification in this country functions to restrict the distribution of goods, entitlements, and status as narrowly as possible to those whose power is already entrenched. Of course this institutionalized disentitlement presupposes that two persons of different racial classifications cannot be biologically related, which is absurd.

This [one-drop] definition of who is black was crucial to maintaining the social system of white domination in which widespread miscegenation, not racial purity, prevailed. White womanhood was the highly charged emotional symbol, but the system protected white economic, political, legal, education and other institutional advantages for whites. . . . American slave owners wanted to keep all racially mixed children born to slave women under their control, for economic and sexual gains. . . . It was intolerable for white women to have mixed children, so the one-drop rule favored the sexual freedom of white males, protecting the double standard of sexual morality as well as slavery. . . . By defining all mixed children as black and compelling them to live in the black community,

the rule made possible the incredible myth among whites that miscegenation had not occurred, that the races had been kept pure in the South.

—Davis, *Who Is Black?*

But the issues of family entitlements and inheritance rights are not uppermost in the minds of most white Americans, who wince at the mere suggestion that they might have some fraction of African ancestry and therefore be, according to this country's entrenched convention of racial classification, black. The primary issue for them is not what they might have to give away by admitting that they are in fact black, but rather what they have to lose. What they have to lose, of course, is social status—and, insofar as their self-esteem is based on their social status as whites, self-esteem as well.

"I think," said Dr. Latrobe, proudly, "that we belong to the highest race on earth and the negro to the lowest."

"And yet," said Dr. Latimer, "you have consorted with them till you have bleached their faces to the whiteness of your own. Your children nestle in their bosoms; they are around you as body servants, and yet if one of them should attempt to associate with you your bitterest scorn and indignation would be visited upon them."

—Harper, *Iola Leroy*

No reflective and well-intentioned white person who is consciously concerned to end racism wants to admit to instinctively recoiling at the thought of being identified as black herself. But if you want to see such a white person do this, just peer at the person's facial features and tell her, in a complimentary tone of voice, that she looks as though she might have some black ancestry, and watch her reaction. It's not a test I or any black person finds particularly pleasant to apply (that is, unless one dislikes the person and wants to inflict pain deliberately), and having once done so inadvertently, I will never do it again. The ultimate test of a person's repudiation of racism is not what she can contemplate *doing* for or on behalf of black people, but whether she herself can contemplate calmly the likelihood of *being* black. If racial hatred has not manifested itself in any other context, it will do so here if it exists, in hatred of the self as identified with the other—that is, as self-hatred projected onto the other.

> Since Harry had come North he had learned to feel profound pity for the slave. But there is difference between looking on a man as an object of pity and protecting him as such, and being identified with him and forced to share his lot.
>
> —Harper, *Iola Leroy*

> Let me tell you how I'd get those white devil convicts and the guards, too, to do anything I wanted. I'd whisper to them, "If you don't, I'll start a rumor that you're really a light Negro just passing as white." That shows you what the white devil thinks about the black man. He'd rather die than be thought a Negro!
>
> —Malcolm X, *The Autobiography of Malcolm X*

When I was an undergraduate minoring in medieval and Renaissance musicology, I worked with a fellow music student—white—in the music library. I remember his reaction when I relayed to him an article I'd recently read arguing that Beethoven had African ancestry. Beethoven was one of his heroes, and his vehement derision was completely out of proportion to the scholarly worth of the hypothesis. But when I suggested that he wouldn't be so skeptical if the claim were that Beethoven had some Danish ancestry, he fell silent. In those days we were very conscious of covert racism, as our campus was exploding all around us because of it. More recently I premiered at a gallery a video installation exploring the issue of African ancestry among white Americans. A white male viewer commenced to kick the furniture, mutter audibly that he was white and was going to stay that way, and start a fistfight with my dealer. Either we are less conscious of covert racism twenty years later, or we care less to contain it.

Among politically committed and enlightened whites, the inability to acknowledge their probable African ancestry is the last outpost of racism. It is the litmus test that separates those who have the courage of their convictions from those who merely subscribe to them and that measures the depth of our dependence on a presumed superiority (of any kind, anything will do) to other human beings—anyone, anywhere—to bolster our fragile self-worth. Many blacks are equally unwilling to explore their white ancestry—approximately 25 percent on average for the majority of blacks—for this reason. For some, of course, acknowledgment of this fact evokes only bitter reminders of rape, disinheritance, enslavement, and exploitation, and their distaste is justifiable. But for others, it is the mere idea of blackness as an essentialized source of self-worth and self-affirmation that forecloses the acknowledgment of mixed ancestry. This, too, is understandable: Having struggled so long and hard to carve a sense of wholeness and value for ourselves out of our ancient connection with Africa after having been actively denied any in America, many of us are extremely resistant to once again casting ourselves into the same chaos of ethnic and psychological ambiguity that our diaspora to this country originally inflicted on us.

Thus blacks and whites alike seem to be unable to accord worth to others outside their in-group affiliations without feeling that they are taking it away from themselves. We may have the concept of intrinsic self-worth, but by and large we do not understand what it means. We need someone else whom we can regard as inferior, to whom we can compare ourselves favorably, and if no such individual or group exists, we invent one. For without this, we seem to have no basis, no standard of comparison, for conceiving of ourselves favorably at all. We seem, for example, truly unable to grasp or take seriously the alternative possibility of measuring ourselves or our performances against our own past novicehood at one end and our own future potential at the other. I think this is in part the result of our collective fear of memory as a nation, our profound unwillingness to confront the painful truths about our history and our origins, and in part the result of our individual fear of the memory of our own pasts—not only of our individual origins and the traumas of socialization we each suffered before we could control what was done to us, but the pasts of our own adult behavior—the painful truths of our own derelictions, betrayals, and failures to respect our individual ideals and convictions.

When I turned forty a few years ago, I gave my-self the present of rereading the personal journals I have been keeping since age eleven. I was astounded at the chasm between my present conception of my own past, which is being continually revised and updated to suit present circumstances, and the ac-tual past events, behavior, and emotions I recorded as faithfully as I could as they happened. My der-elictions, mistakes, and failures of responsibility are much more evident in those journals than they are in my present, sanitized, and virtually blameless image of my past behavior. It was quite a shock to encoun-ter in those pages the person I actually have been rather than the person I now conceive myself to have been. My memory is always under the control of the person I now want and strive to be, and so rarely un-der the control of the facts. If the personal facts of one's past are this difficult for other people to face too, then perhaps it is no wonder that we must cast about outside ourselves for someone to feel superior to, even though there are so many blunders and mis-deeds in our own personal histories that might serve that function.

For whites to acknowledge their blackness is, then, much the same as for men to acknowledge their femininity and for Christians to acknowledge their Ju-daic heritage. It is to reinternalize the external scape-goat through attention to which they have sought to escape their own sense of inferiority.

Now the white man leaned in the window, look-ing at the impenetrable face with its definite strain of white blood, the same blood which ran in his own veins, which had not only come to the negro through male descent while it had come to him from a woman, but had reached the negro a gen-eration sooner—a face composed, inscrutable, even a little haughty, shaped even in expression in the pattern of his great-grandfather McCaslin's face. . . . He thought, and not for the first time: *I am not only looking at a face older than mine and which has seen and winnowed more, but at a man most of whose blood was pure ten thousand years when my own anonymous beginnings became mixed enough to produce me.*

—William Faulkner, *Go Down, Moses*

I said . . . that the guilt of American whites in-cluded their knowledge that in hating Negroes, they were hating, they were rejecting, they were denying, their own blood.

—Malcolm X, *The Autobiography of Malcolm X*

It is to bring ourselves face to face with our obliter-ated collective past and to confront the continuities of responsibility that link the criminal acts of exter-mination and enslavement committed by our fore-fathers with our own personal crimes of avoidance, neglect, disengagement, passive complicity, and active exploitation of the inherited injustices from which we have profited. Uppermost among these is that covert sense of superiority a white person feels over a black person which buttresses his enjoyment of those unjust benefits as being no more or less than he deserves. To be deprived of that sense of superiority to the extent that acknowledgment of common ancestry would effect is clearly difficult for most white people. But to lose the social regard and respect that accompanies it is practically unbearable. I know—not only because of what I have read and observed of the pathology of racism in white people, but because I have often experienced the withdrawal of that social regard firsthand.

For most of my life I did not understand that I needed to identify my racial identity publicly and that if I did not I would be inevitably mistaken for white. I simply didn't think about it. But since I also made no special effort to hide my racial identity, I often experienced the shocked and/or hostile re-actions of whites who discovered it after the fact. I always knew when it had happened, even when the person declined to confront me directly: the startled look, the searching stare that would fix itself on my facial features, one by one, looking for the telltale "negroid" feature, the sudden, sometimes permanent withdrawal of good feeling or regular contact—all alerted me to what had transpired. Uh-oh, I would think to myself helplessly, and watch another blos-soming friendship wilt.

In thus travelling about through the country I was sometimes amused on arriving at some little railroad-station town to be taken for and treated as a white man, and six hours later, when it was learned that I was stopping at the house of the coloured preacher or school-teacher, to note the attitude of the whole town change.

—Johnson, *The Autobiography of an Ex-Coloured Man*

Sometimes this revelation would elicit a response of the most twisted and punitive sort: for example, from the colleague who glared at me and hissed, "Oh, so you want to be black, do you? Good! Then we'll treat you like one!" The ensuing harassment had a furious, retaliatory quality that I find difficult to understand even now: as though I'd delivered a deliberate and crushing insult to her self-esteem by choosing not to identify with her racial group.

> You feel lost, sick at heart before such unmasked hatred, not so much because it threatens you as because it shows humans in such an inhuman light. You see a kind of insanity, something so obscene the very obscenity of it (rather than its threat) terrifies you.
>
> —Griffin, *Black Like Me*

And I experienced that same groundless shame not only in response to those who accused me of passing for black but also in response to those who accused me of passing for white. This was the shame caused by people who conveyed to me that I was underhanded or manipulative, trying to hide something, pretending to be something I was not by not telling them I was black—like the art critic in the early 1970s who had treated me with the respect she gave emerging white women artists in the early days of second-wave feminism until my work turned to issues of racial identity; she then called me to verify that I was black, reproached me for not telling her, and finally disappeared from my professional life altogether. And there were the colleagues who discovered after hiring me for my first job that I was black, and revised their evaluations of my work accordingly. It was the groundless shame caused by people who, having discovered my racial identity, let me know that I was not comporting myself as befitted their conception of a black person: the grammar school teacher who called

my parents to inquire whether I was aware that I was black, and made a special effort to put me in my place by restricting me from participating in certain class activities and assigning me to remedial classes in anticipation of low achievement; and the graduate school classmate who complimented me on my English; and the potential employer who, having offered me a tenure-track job in an outstanding graduate department (which I declined) when he thought I was white, called me back much later after I'd received tenure and he'd found out I was black to offer me a two-year visiting position teaching undergraduates only, explaining to a colleague of mine that he was being pressured by his university administration to integrate his department. And the art critic who made elaborate suggestions in print about the kind of art it would be appropriate for someone with my concerns to make; and the colleague who journeyed from another university and interviewed me for four and a half hours in order to ascertain that I was smart enough to hold the position I had, and actually congratulated me afterwards on my performance. And there was the colleague who, when I begged to differ with his views, shouted (in a crowded restaurant) that if I wasn't going to take his advice, why was I wasting his time?

> I looked up to see the frowns of disapproval that can speak so plainly and so loudly without words. The Negro learns this silent language fluently. He knows by the white man's look of disapproval and petulance that he is being told to get on his way, that he is "stepping out of line."
>
> —Griffin, *Black Like Me*

When such contacts occurred, the interaction had to follow a strict pattern of interracial etiquette. The white person had to be clearly in charge at all times, and the black person clearly subordinate, so that each kept his or her place. It was a master-servant etiquette, in which blacks had to act out their inferior social position, much the way slaves had done. The black had to be deferential in tone and body language, . . . and never bring up a delicate topic or contradict the white. . . . This master-servant ritual had to be acted out carefully lest the black person be accused of "getting" out of his or her subordinate "place." Especially for violations of the etiquette, but also for challenges to other aspects of the system, blacks were warned, threatened, and finally subjected to extralegal violence.

—Davis, *Who Is Black?*

In a way this abbreviated history of occasions on which whites have tried to "put me in my place" upon discovering my racial identity was the legacy of my father who, despite his own similar experiences as a youth, refused to submit to such treatment. He grew up in a Southern city where his family was well known and highly respected. When he was thirteen, he went to a movie theater and bought a seat in the orchestra section. In the middle of the feature, the projectionist stopped the film and turned up the lights. The manager strode onto the stage and, in front of the entire audience, called out my father's name, loudly reprimanded him for sitting in the orchestra, and ordered him up to the balcony, where he "belonged." My father fled the theater, and, not long after, the South. My grandmother then sent him to a private prep school up North, but it was no better. In his senior year of high school, after having distinguished himself academically and in sports, he invited a white girl classmate on a date. She refused, and her parents complained to the principal, who publicly rebuked him. He was ostracized by his classmates for the rest of the year and made no effort to speak to any of them.

My mother, being upper-middle-class Jamaican, had no experience of this kind of thing. When she first got a job in this country in the 1930s, she chastised her white supervisor for failing to say, "Thank you," after she'd graciously brought him back a soda from her lunch hour. He was properly apologetic. And when her brother first came to this country, he sat in a restaurant in Manhattan for an hour waiting to be served, it simply not occurring to him that he was being ignored because of his color, until a waitress came up to him and said, "I can see you're not from these parts. We don't serve colored people here." My father, who had plenty of experiences of this sort, knew that I would have them, too. But he declined to accustom me to them in advance. He never hit me, disparaged me, or pulled rank in our frequent intellectual and

philosophical disagreements. Trained as a Jesuit and a lawyer, he argued for the joy of it, and felt proud rather than insulted when I made my point well. "Fresh," he'd murmur to my mother with mock annoyance, indicating me with his thumb, when I used his own assumptions to trounce him in argument. It is because of his refusal to prepare me for my subordinate role as a black woman in a racist and misogynistic society that my instinctive reaction to such insults is not resignation, depression, or passive aggression, but rather the disbelief, outrage, sense of injustice, and impulse to fight back actively that white males often exhibit as unexpected affronts to their dignity. Blacks who manifest these responses to white racism reveal their caregivers' generationally transmitted underground resistance to schooling them for victimhood.

A benefit and a disadvantage of looking white is that most people treat you as though you were white. And so, because of how you've been treated, you come to expect this sort of treatment, not perhaps realizing that you're being treated this way because people think you're white, but rather falsely supposing that you're being treated this way because people think you are a valuable person. So, for example, you come to expect a certain level of respect, a certain degree of attention to your voice and opinions, certain liberties of action and self-expression to which you falsely suppose yourself to be entitled because your voice, your opinion, and your conduct are valuable in themselves. To those who in fact believe (even though they would never voice this belief to themselves) that black people are not entitled to this degree of respect, attention, and liberty, the sight of a black person behaving as though she were can, indeed, look very much like arrogance. It may not occur to them that she simply does not realize that her blackness should make any difference.

Only one-sixteenth of her was black, and that sixteenth did not show. . . . Her complexion was very fair, with the rosy glow of vigorous health in the cheeks, . . . her eyes were brown and liquid, and she had a heavy suit of fine soft hair which was also brown. . . . She had an easy, independent carriage—when she was among her own caste— and a high and "sassy" way, withal; but of course she was meek and humble enough where white people were.

—Mark Twain, *Pudd'nhead Wilson*

But there may be more involved than this. I've been thinking about Ida B. Wells, who had the temerity to suggest in print that white males who worried about preserving the purity of Southern white womanhood were really worried about the sexual attraction of Southern white womanhood to handsome and virile black men; and Rosa Parks, who refused to move to the back of the bus; and Eartha Kitt, who scolded President Lyndon Johnson about the Vietnam War when he received her at a White House dinner; and Mrs. Alice Frazier, who gave the queen of England a big hug and invited her to stay for lunch when the queen came to tour Mrs. Frazier's housing project on a recent visit to the United States; and Congresswoman Maxine Waters, who, after the L.A. rebellion, showed up at the White House uninvited, and gave George Bush her unsolicited recommendations as to how he should handle the plight of the inner cities. I've also been thinking about the legions of African American women whose survival has depended on their submission to the intimate interpersonal roles, traditional for black women in this culture, of nursemaid, housekeeper, concubine, cleaning lady, cook; and what they have been required to witness of the whites they have served in those capacities. And I've been thinking about the many white people I've admired and respected, who have lost my admiration and respect by revealing in personal interactions a side of themselves that other whites rarely get a chance to see: the brand of racism that surfaces only in one-on-one or intimate interpersonal circumstances, the kind a white person lets you see because he doesn't care what you think and knows you are powerless to do anything about it.

When we shined their shoes we talked. The whites, especially the tourists, had no reticence before us, and no shame since we were Negroes. Some wanted to know where they could find girls, wanted us to get Negro girls for them. . . . Though not all, by any means, were so open about their purposes, all of them showed us how they felt

about the Negro, the idea that we were people of such low morality that nothing could offend us. . . . In these matters, the Negro has seen the backside of the white man too long to be shocked. He feels an indulgent superiority whenever he sees these evidences of the white man's frailty. This is one of the sources of his chafing at being considered inferior. He cannot understand how the white man can show the most demeaning aspects of his nature and at the same time delude himself into thinking he is inherently superior.

—Griffin, *Black Like Me*

It may indeed be that we African American women as a group have special difficulties in learning our place and observing the proprieties because of that particular side of white America to which, because of our traditional roles, we have had special access—a side of white America that hardly commands one's respect and could not possibly command one's deference.

To someone like myself, who was raised to think that my racial identity was, in fact, irrelevant to the way I should be treated, there are few revelations more painful than the experience of social metamorphosis that transforms former friends, colleagues, or teachers who have extended their trust, goodwill, and support into accusers or strangers who withdraw them when they discover that I am black. To look visibly black, or always to announce in advance that one is black is, I submit, never to experience this kind of camaraderie with white people—the relaxed, unguarded, but respectful camaraderie that white people reserve for those whom they believe are like them—those who can be trusted, who are intrinsically worthy of value, respect, and attention. Eddie Murphy portrays this in comic form in a wonderful routine in which he disguises himself in whiteface, then boards a bus on which there is only one visibly black passenger. As long as that passenger is on the bus, all of them sit silently and impersonally ignoring one another. But as soon as the visibly black passenger gets off, the other passengers get up and turn to one another, engaging in friendly banter, and the driver breaks open a bottle of champagne for a party. A joke, perhaps, but not entirely. A visibly black person may, in time, experience something very much like this unguarded friendship with a white person, if the black person has proven herself trustworthy and worthy of respect, or has been a friend since long before either was taught that vigilance between the races was appropriate. But I have only rarely met adult whites who have extended this degree of trust and acceptance at the outset to a new acquaintance they knew to be black. And to have extended it to someone who then *turns out* to be black is instinctively felt as a betrayal, a violation. It is as though one had been seduced into dropping one's drawers in the presence of the enemy. So a white person who accuses me of deceit for not having alerted her that I am black is not merely complaining that I have been hiding something about myself that is important for her to know. The complaint goes much deeper. It is that she has been lured under false pretenses into dropping her guard with me, into revealing certain intimacies and vulnerabilities that are simply unthinkable to expose in the presence of someone of another race (that's why it's important for her to know my race). She feels betrayed because I have failed to warn her to present the face she thinks she needs to present to someone who might choose to take advantage of the weaknesses that lie behind that public face. She may feel it merely a matter of luck that I have not taken advantage of those weaknesses already.

As the accused, I feel as though a trusted friend has just turned on me. I experience the social reality that previously defined our relationship as having metamorphosed into something ugly and threatening, in which the accusation is not that I have *done* something wrong, but that I *am* wrong for being who I am: for having aped the white person she thought I was, and for being the devalued black person she discovers I am. I feel a withdrawal of good will, a psychological distancing, a new wariness and suspicion, a care in choosing words, and—worst of all—a denial that anything has changed. This last injects an element of insensitivity—or bad faith—that makes our previous relationship extremely difficult to recapture. It forces me either to name unpleasant realities that the white person is clearly unable to confront or to comply with the fiction that there are no such realities, which renders our interactions systematically inauthentic. This is why I always feel discouraged when

well-intentioned white people deny to me that a person's race makes any difference to them, even though I understand that this is part of the public face whites instinctively believe they need to present; I know, firsthand, how white people behave toward me when they believe racial difference is absent. And there are very few white people who are able to behave that way toward me once they know it is present.

But there are risks that accompany that unguarded camaraderie among whites who believe they are among themselves, and ultimately those risks proved too much for me. I have found that often a concomitant of that unguarded camaraderie is explicit and unadorned verbal racism of a kind that is violently at odds with the gentility and cultivation of the social setting, and that would never appear if that setting were visibly integrated.

> I will tell you that, without any question, the *most* bitter anti-white diatribes that I have ever heard have come from "passing" Negroes, living as whites, among whites, exposed every day to what white people say among themselves regarding Negroes—things that a recognized Negro never would hear. Why, if there was a racial showdown, these Negroes "passing" within white circles would become the black side's most valuable "spy" and ally.
>
> —Malcolm X, *The Autobiography of Malcolm X*

I have heard an educated white woman refer to her husband's black physical education student as a "big, black buck"; I have heard university professors refer to black working-class music as "jungle music"; and I have heard a respected museum director refer to an actress as a "big, black momma." These remarks are different in kind from those uttered in expressions of black racism toward whites. When we are among ourselves we may vent our frustration by castigating whites as ignorant, stupid, dishonest, or vicious. That is, we deploy stereotyped white *attitudes* and *motives*. We do not, as these remarks do, dehumanize and animalize whites themselves. From these cases and others like them I have learned that the side of themselves some whites reveal when they believe themselves to be among themselves is just as demeaning as the side of themselves they reveal privately to blacks. This is, I suspect, the weakness whites rightly want concealed behind the public face; and the possibility that I might witness—or might have witnessed—it is the source of their anger at me for having "tricked" them. For part of the tragedy is that the racism I witness when their guard is down is often behavior they genuinely do not understand to be racist. So the revelation is not only of racism but of ignorance and insensitivity. The point of adopting the public face when whites are warned that a black person is among them is to suppress any nonneutral expression of the self that might be interpreted as racist.

Of course this brand of self-monitoring damage control cannot possibly work, since it cannot eliminate those very manifestations of racism that the person sees, rather, as neutral or innocuous. No one person can transcend the constraints of his own assumptions about what constitutes respectful behavior in order to identify and critique his own racism from an objective, "politically correct" standpoint when it appears. We need trusted others, before whom we can acknowledge our insufficiencies without fear of ridicule or retaliation, to do that for us, so as to genuinely extend our conceptions of ourselves and our understanding of what constitutes appropriate behavior toward another who is different. The fact of the matter is that if racism is present—which it is in *all* of us, black as well as white, who have been acculturated into this racist society—it will emerge despite our best efforts at concealment. The question should not be whether any individual is racist; that we all are to some extent should be a given. The question should be, rather, how we handle it once it appears. I believe our energy would be better spent on creating structured, personalized community forums for naming, confronting, owning, and resolving these feelings rather than trying to evade, deny, or suppress them. But there are many whites who believe that these matters are best left in silence, in the hope that they will die out of their own accord, and that we must focus on right actions, not the character or motivations behind them. To my way of thinking, this is a conceptual impossibility. But relative to this agenda, my involuntary snooping thwarts their good intentions.

My instinctive revulsion at these unsought revelations is undergirded by strong role modeling from my parents. I never heard my parents utter a prejudicial remark against any group. But my paternal grandmother was of that generation of very light-skinned, upper-middle class blacks who believed themselves superior both to whites and to darker-skinned blacks. When I was young I wore my hair in two long braids, but I recall my mother once braiding it into three or four, in a simplified cornrow style. When my grandmother visited, she took one look at my new hairstyle and immediately began berating my mother for making me look like a "little nigger pickaninny." When my father heard her say these words he silently grasped her by the shoulders, picked her up, put her outside the front door, and closed it firmly in her face. Having passed for white during the Great Depression to get a job, and during World War II to see combat, his exposure to and intolerance for racist language was so complete that no benefits were worth the offense to his sensibilities, and he saw to it that he never knowingly placed himself in that situation again.

> "Doctor, were I your wife, . . . mistaken for a white woman, I should hear things alleged against the race at which my blood would boil. No, Doctor, I am not willing to live under a shadow of concealment which I thoroughly hate as if the blood in my veins were an undetected crime of my soul."
> —Harper, *Iola Leroy*

My father is a very tough act to follow. But ultimately I did, because I had to. I finally came to the same point of finding these sudden and unwanted revelations intolerable. Although I valued the unguarded camaraderie and closeness I'd experienced with whites, it was ultimately not worth the risk that racist behavior might surface. I seem to have become more thin-skinned about this with age. But for years I'd wrestled with different ways of forestalling these unwanted discoveries. When I was younger I was too flustered to say anything (which still sometimes happens when my guard is down), and I would be left feeling compromised and cowardly for not standing up for myself. Or I'd express my objections in an abstract form, without making reference to my own racial identity, and watch the discussion degenerate into an academic squabble about the meaning of certain words, whether a certain epithet is really racist, the role of good intentions, whether to refer to someone as a "jungle bunny" might not be a backhanded compliment, and so forth. Or I'd express my objections in a personal form, using that most unfortunate moment to let the speaker know I was black, thus traumatizing myself and everyone else present and ruining the occasion. Finally I felt I had no choice but to do everything I could, either verbally or through trusted friends or through my work, to confront this matter head-on and issue advance warning to new white acquaintances, both actual and potential, that I identify myself as black—in effect, to "proclaim that fact from the house-top" (forgive me, Malcolm, for blowing my cover).

> "I tell Mr. Leroy," said Miss Delany, "that . . . he must put a label on himself, saying 'I am a colored man,' to prevent annoyance."
>
> —Harper, *Iola Leroy*

Of course, this method is not foolproof. Among its benefits is that it puts the burden of vigilance on the white person rather than on me—the same vigilance she exercises in the presence of a visibly black person (but even this doesn't always work: some whites simply can't take my avowed racial affiliation at face value, and react to what they see rather than what I say). And because my public avowal of my racial identity almost invariably elicits all the stereotypically racist behavior that visibly black people always confront, some blacks feel less of a need to administer the Suffering Test of blackness. Among the costs is that I've lost other white friends who are antagonized by what they see as my manipulating their liberal guilt or goodwill, or turning my racial identity into an exploitable profession, or advertising myself in an unseemly manner, or making a big to-do about nothing. They are among those who would prefer to leave the whole matter of race—and, by implication, the racism of their own behavior—shrouded in silence.

But I've learned that there is no "right" way of managing the issue of my racial identity, no way that will not offend or alienate someone, because my

designated racial identity itself exposes the very concept of racial classification as the offensive and irrational instrument of racism it is. We see this in the history of the classifying terms variously used to designate those brought as slaves to this country and their offspring: first "blacks," then "darkies," then "Negroes," then "colored people," then "blacks" again, then "Afro-Americans," then "people of color," now "African Americans." Why is it that we can't seem to get it right, once and for all? The reason, I think, is that it doesn't really matter what term we use to designate those who have inferior and disadvantaged status, because whatever term is used will eventually turn into a term of derision and disparagement by virtue of its reference to those who are derided and disparaged, and so will need to be discarded for an unsullied one. My personal favorite is "colored" because of its syntactical simplicity and aesthetic connotations. But cooking up new ways to classify those whom we degrade ultimately changes nothing but the vocabulary of degradation.

What joins me to other blacks, then, and other blacks to another, is not a set of shared physical characteristics, for there is none that all blacks share. Rather, it is the shared experience of being visually or cognitively *identified* as black by a white racist society, and the punitive and damaging effects of that identification. This is the shared experience the Suffering Test tries to, and often does, elicit.

But then, of course, I have white friends who fit the prevailing stereotype of a black person and have similar experiences, even though they insist they are "pure" white.

> It cannot be so embarrassing for a coloured man to be taken for white as for a white man to be taken for coloured; and I have heard of several cases of the latter kind.
>
> —Johnson, *The Autobiography of an Ex-Coloured Man*

The fact is that the racial categories that purport to designate any of us are too rigid and oversimplified to fit anyone accurately. But then, accuracy was never their purpose. Since we are almost all in fact racial hybrids, the "one drop" rule of black racial designation, if consistently applied, would either narrow the scope of ancestral legitimacy so far that it would exclude most of those so-called whites whose social power is most deeply entrenched, or widen it to include most of those who have been most severely disadvantaged by racism. Once we get clear about the subtleties of who in fact we are, we then may be better able to see just what our ancestral entitlements actually are, and whether or to what extent they may need to be supplemented with additional social and legal means for implementing a just distribution of rights and benefits for everyone. Not until that point, I think, when we have faced the full human and personal consequences of self-serving, historically entrenched social and legal conventions that in fact undermine the privileged interests they were designed to protect, will we be in a position to decide whether the very idea of racial classification is a viable one in the first place.

She really thought everyone would be like her some day, neither black nor white, but something in between. It might take decades or even centuries, but it would happen. And sooner than that, racism and the concept of race itself would become completely obsolete.

—Perry, *Another Present Era*

Yet it was not that Lucas made capital of his white or even his McCaslin blood, but the contrary. It was as if he were not only impervious to that blood, he was indifferent to it. He didn't even need to strive with it. He didn't even have to bother to defy it. He resisted it simply by being the composite of the two races which made him, simply by possessing it. Instead of being at once

the battleground and victim of the two strains, he was a vessel, durable, ancestryless, nonconductive, in which the toxin and its anti stalemated one another, seetheless, unrumored in the outside air.

—Faulkner, *Go Down, Moses*

These are frightening suggestions for those whose self-worth depends on their racial and social status within the white community. But no more frightening, really, than the thought of welcoming long-lost relatives back into the family fold and making adjustments for their well-being accordingly. One always has a choice as to whether to regard oneself as having lost something—status, if one's long-lost relatives are disreputable, or economic resources, if they are greedy; or as having gained something—status, if one's long-lost relatives are wise and interesting, or economic resources, if they are able-bodied and eager to work. Only for those whose self-worth strictly requires the exclusion of others viewed as inferior will these psychologically and emotionally difficult choices be impossible. This, I think, is part of why some whites feel so uneasy in my presence: Condescension or disregard seems inappropriate in light of my demeanor, whereas a hearty invitation into the exclusive inner circle seems equally inappropriate in light of my designated race. Someone who has no further social resources for dealing with other people besides condescension or disregard on the one hand and clubbish familiarity on the other is bound to feel at a loss when race provides no excuse for the former because of demeanor, whereas demeanor provides no excuse for the latter because of race. So no matter what I do or do not do about my racial identity, someone is bound to feel uncomfortable. But I have resolved that it is no longer going to be me.

SECTION VI

FUTURES AND SOLUTIONS?

While its specific forms and practices have varied over time, racism has been a powerful and pervasive force on the territory that is now the United States for over 500 years. And so it would be foolhardy and naive to believe that racism will simply wither away and die anytime soon. Nonetheless, one of the goals of this reader—and, more generally, of teaching courses on media and race at all—is to help promote ways of thinking and acting that might help bring us a little closer to a world where racism no longer exists. To be sure, this will not be an easy struggle, nor will it be a quick one. Power, after all, rarely (if ever) yields itself up willingly—and there are a lot of powerful forces and institutions invested in maintaining a sharply racialized social and political hierarchy. The struggle is also unlikely to be marked by consistent and inevitable forward progress. There will (hopefully) be moments when genuine advances are made, but there will almost certainly be other moments when significant ground is lost. None of the essays contained in this section pretend to offer easy answers to the Big Question that my students ask every semester—so what do we do about all this?—but they all offer valuable insights and suggestions for thinking about the best directions in which our future struggles might take us.

Derrick Bell's essay presents a fictional narrative in which the United States, as a nation, has to decide whether to willingly and knowingly trade away its entire black population to a group of space aliens. Fanciful as this thought experiment might seem, it poses an important set of questions for our understanding of the nation's deep collective investment in maintaining a hierarchical racial formation. How much does the United States actually value and/or want blacks (or any other racial/ethnic minority, for that matter)? How much (if at all) does Bell's hypothetical trade differ from previous moments in US history, when whites have treated people of color as nothing more than property to be bought and sold? Just how far have we come toward fully embracing the noble sentiment that all of us were created equal and are worthy and important members of the national community?

Lauren Berlant's essay doesn't offer its own prognosis for the future of race relations in the United States as much as it provides us with a sharp and nuanced analysis of how the dominant culture appears to imagine (with both hopefulness and fear) its own racialized future. Examining a broad cross section of media images and narratives about "the browning of America," Berlant notes the ways that mainstream media discourses have simultaneously courted the coming waves of racial and ethnic immigrants as the main source of hope for keeping the American dream alive, while also fearing those same "Others" as an overwhelming force who will radically transform who the "we" in "we, the people" actually are.

Michael Awkward's essay examines the national controversy that surrounded racially charged statements made by "shock jock" Don Imus during his national syndicated radio program in April 2007, and argues that Imus was transformed into a convenient, but ultimately undeserving, scapegoat by both black and white public figures. Awkward doesn't actually defend Imus or his words as much as he points to the curious and problematic way that Imus was made to stand in for a vast, unnamed host of more overtly racist figures and institutions. What lies at the root of this displaced anger is the nation's continuing reluctance (to put it mildly) to acknowledge the collective trauma inflicted by centuries of chattel slavery. Unless we, as a national community, can effectively come to grips with those psychic wounds, Awkward suggests we will continue to repeat the sort of ritualistic excoriation of individual figures, such as Imus, without ever addressing the more salient causes of our racial discord and mistrust.

Lori Harrison-Kahan offers a close and careful reading of what has been described as director Spike Lee's most apolitical film, *Inside Man*, and finds that it actually offers a subtle commentary on post-9/11 race relations in the United States. She argues that, appearances notwithstanding, the film's critique of contemporary racial politics is as sharp and pointed as that found in any of Lee's more obviously polemical films. Implicit in Harrison-Kahan's analysis is the suggestion that the post-9/11 reshaping of the racial formation in the United States has altered the ways that racial tensions and power dynamics are publicly expressed and that, as a result, those of us who study race and media will need to think in more subtle and nuanced ways about how the politics of race play out across the mediascape.

Finally, Catherine Squires's essay examines the ways that the growing visibility of openly multiracial public figures has shifted the dominant public discourse about how race works. Squires carefully and pointedly critiques the oft-heard sound-bite-sized claims that mixed-race people will magically solve racism by making us all one race. Instead, she argues that the increased (and long overdue) public awareness of multiracial identity needs to lead us to develop a kind of "racial courage" when it comes to how mainstream public discourse around race is conducted.

32.
RACIAL REALISM—AFTER WE'RE GONE

Prudent Speculations on America in a Post-Racial Epoch

Derrick Bell

It is time—as a currently popular colloquialism puts it—to "Get Real" about race and the persistence of racism in America. The very visible social and economic progress made by some African Americans can no longer obscure the increasingly dismal demographics that reflect the status of most of those whose forebears in this country were slaves. Statistics on poverty, unemployment, and income support the growing concern that the slow racial advances of the 1960s and 1970s have ended, and retrogression is well under way.

Perhaps Thomas Jefferson had it right after all. When musing on the future of Africans in this country, he expressed the view that blacks should be free, but he was certain that "the two races, equally free, cannot live in the same government."[1] Jefferson suspected that blacks, whether originally a distinct race, or made distinct by time and circumstances, are "inferior to the whites in the endowments both of body and mind."[2] Such differences prompted Jefferson to warn that "[i]f the legal barriers between the races were torn down, but no provision made for their separation, 'convulsions' would ensue, which would 'probably never end but in the extermination of the one or the other race.'"[3]

Jefferson's views were widely shared. In his summary of how the Constitution's framers came to include recognition and protection of human slavery in a document that was committed to the protection of individual liberties, Professor Staughton Lynd wrote: "Even the most liberal of the Founding Fathers were unable to imagine a society in which whites and Negroes would live together as fellow-citizens. Honor and intellectual consistency drove them to favor abolition; personal distaste, to fear it."[4]

In our era, the premier precedent of *Brown v. Board of Education* promised to be the twentieth century's Emancipation Proclamation. Both policies, however, served to advance the nation's foreign policy interests more than they provided actual aid to blacks. Nevertheless, both actions inspired blacks to push for long-denied freedoms. Alas, the late Alexander Bickel's dire prediction has proven correct. He warned that the *Brown* decision would not be reversed but "[could] be headed for—dread word—irrelevance."[5]

Given the current tenuous status of African Americans, the desperate condition of those on the bottom, and the growing resentment of the successes realized by those who are making gains despite the odds, one wonders how this country would respond to a crisis in which the sacrifice of the most basic rights of blacks would result in the accrual of substantial benefits to all whites? This primary issue is explored in a fictional story that could prove to be prophetic.

The Chronicle of the Space Traders

The first surprise was not their arrival—they had sent radio messages weeks before advising that they would land 1,000 space ships along the Atlantic coast on January 1, 2000. The surprise was the space ships themselves. Unlike the Star Wars variety, the great vessels, each the size of an aircraft carrier, resembled the square-shaped landing craft used to transport troops to beachhead invasion sites during World War II.

The great ships entered the earth's atmosphere in a spectacular fiery display that was visible throughout the western hemisphere. After an impressive, cross-continental "fly by," they landed in the waters just off the Atlantic coast. The lowered bows of the mammoth ships exposed cavernous holds that were huge, dark, and impenetrable.

Then came the second surprise. The welcoming delegation of government officials and members of the media covering the event could hear and understand the crew as they disembarked. They spoke English and sounded like the former President Ronald Reagan, whose recorded voice, in fact, they had dubbed into their computerized language translation system. The visitors, however, were invisible—at least they could not be seen by whites who were present or by television viewers to the special coverage that, despite howls of protest, had preempted football bowl games. American blacks were able to see them all too well. "They look like old South sheriffs, mean and ugly," some said. They were, according to others, "more like slave drivers and overseers." Particularly frantic reports claimed, "The visitors are dressed in white sheets and hoods like the Ku Klux Klan." In whatever guise they saw them, blacks all agreed that the visitors embodied the personification of racist evil.

The space visitors cut short the long-winded welcoming speeches, expressed no interest in parades and banquets, and made clear that their long journey was undertaken for one purpose, and one purpose only: trade. Here was the third surprise. The visitors had brought materials that they knew the United States needed desperately: gold to bail out the almost bankrupt federal, state, and local governments; special chemicals that would sanitize the almost uninhabitable environment; and a totally safe nuclear engine with fuel to relieve the nation's swiftly diminishing fossil fuel resources.

In return, the visitors wanted only one thing. This demand created more of a shock than a surprise. The visitors wanted to take back to their home star all African Americans (defined as all citizens whose birth certificates listed them as black). The proposition instantly reduced the welcoming delegation to a humbling disarray. The visitors seemed to expect this reaction. After emphasizing that acceptance of their offer was entirely voluntary and

would not be coerced, they withdrew to their ships. The Traders promised to give the nation a period of sixteen days to respond. The decision would be due on January 17, the national holiday commemorating Dr. Martin Luther King, Jr.'s birthday.

The Space Traders' proposition immediately dominated the country's attention. The President called the Congress into special session, and governors did the same for state legislatures that were not then meeting. Blacks were outraged. Individuals and their leaders cried in unison, "You have not seen them. Why don't you just say no?" Although for many whites the trade posed an embarrassing question, the Space Traders' offer proved to be an irresistible temptation. Decades of conservative, laissez-faire capitalism had taken their toll. The nation that had funded the reconstruction of the free world a half-century ago following World War II was now in a very difficult state. Massive debt had debilitated all functioning. The environment was in shambles, and crude oil and coal resources were almost exhausted.

In addition, the race problem had greatly worsened in the last decade. A relatively small group of blacks had survived the retrogression of civil rights protection that marked the 1990s. Perhaps twenty percent managed to make good in the increasingly technologically oriented society. But more than one-half of the group had sunk to an unacknowledged outcast status. They were confined in former inner-city areas that had been divorced from their political boundaries. High walls surrounded these areas, and entrance and exit were carefully controlled. No one even dreamed anymore that this mass of blacks and dark-complexioned Hispanics would ever "overcome."

Supposedly, United States officials tried in secret negotiations to get the Space Traders to exchange only those blacks locked in the inner cities, but the visitors made it clear that this was an all-or-nothing offer. During these talks, the Space Traders warned that they would withdraw their proposition unless the United States halted the flight of the growing numbers of blacks who—fearing the worst—were fleeing the country. In response, executive orders were issued and implemented, barring blacks from leaving the country until the Space Traders' proposition was fully debated and resolved. "It is your patriotic duty," blacks were told, "to allow this great issue to be resolved through the democratic process and in accordance with the rule of law."

Blacks and their white supporters challenged these procedures in the courts, but their suits were dismissed as "political questions" that must be determined by co-equal branches of government. Even so, forces that supported the proposition took seriously blacks' charges that if the nation accepted the Space Traders' proposition it would violate the Constitution's most basic protections. Acting swiftly, supporters began the necessary steps to convene a constitutional convention. In ten days of feverish work, the quickly assembled convention drafted and, by a substantial majority, passed an amendment that declared:

> Every citizen is subject at the call of Congress to selection for special service for periods necessary to protect domestic interests and international needs.

The amendment was scheduled for ratification by the states in a national referendum. If ratified, the amendment would validate previously drafted legislation that would induct all blacks into special service for transportation under the terms of the Space Traders' offer. In the brief but intense pre-election day campaign, pro-ratification groups' major argument had an appeal that surprised even those who made it. Their message was straightforward:

> The framers intended America to be a white country. The evidence of their intentions is present in the original Constitution. After more than 137 years of good faith efforts to build a healthy, stable interracial nation, we have concluded that our survival today—as the framers did in the beginning—requires that we sacrifice the rights of blacks in order to protect and further the interests of whites. The framers' example must be our guide. Patriotism and not pity must govern our decision. We should ratify the amendment and accept the Space Traders' proposition.

To their credit, many whites worked hard to defeat the amendment. Nevertheless, given the usual fate of minority rights when subjected to referenda or initiatives, the outcome was never really in doubt. The final vote tally confirmed the predictions. By a vote of seventy percent in favor—thirty percent opposed—Americans accepted the Space Traders' proposition. Expecting this result, government agencies had secretly made preparations to facilitate the transfer. Some blacks escaped, and many thousands lost their lives in futile efforts to resist the joint federal and state police teams responsible for the roundup, cataloguing, and transportation of blacks to the coast.

The dawn of the last Martin Luther King holiday that the nation would ever observe illuminated an extraordinary sight. The Space Traders had drawn their strange ships right up to the beaches, discharged their cargoes of gold, minerals, and machinery, and began loading long lines of silent black people. At the Traders' direction, the inductees were stripped of all but a single undergarment. Heads bowed, arms linked by chains, black people left the new world as their forebears had arrived.

And just as the forced importation of those African ancestors had made the nation's wealth and productivity possible, so their forced exodus saved the country from the need to pay the price of its greed-based excess. There might be other unforeseen costs of the trade, but, like their colonial predecessors, Americans facing the twenty-first century were willing to avoid those problems as long as possible.

Discussion

It is not a futile exercise to try to imagine what the country would be like in the days and weeks after the last space ship swooshed off and disappeared into deep space—beyond the reach of our most advanced electronic tracking equipment. How, one might ask, would the nation bear the guilt for its decision? Certainly, many white Americans would feel badly about the trade and the sacrifice of humans for economic well-being. But the country has a 200-year history of treating black lives as property. Genocide is an ugly, but no less accurate, description of what the nation did, and continues to do, to the American Indian. Ignoring the Treaty of Guadalupe Hidalgo was only the first of many betrayals by whites toward Americans of Spanish descent. At the time of writing, Japanese Americans who suffered detention during World War II and lost hard-earned property and status were still awaiting payment of the small compensation approved, but not yet funded, by Congress. The country manages to carry on despite the burden of guilt that these injustices impose against our own people. In all likelihood, the country would manage the Space Trader deal despite recriminations, rationalizations, and remorse. Quite soon, moreover, the nation could become preoccupied with problems of social unrest based on class rather than race.

The trade would solve the budget deficit, provide an unlimited energy source, and restore an unhealthy environment. The new resources, however, would not automatically correct the growing income disparities between blacks and whites as reflected in the growing income gap between upper and lower income families in the nation as a whole. According to the Center on Budget and Policy Priorities: "In 1985, 1986 and 1987, the poorest fifth of American families received only 4.6 percent of the national family income... ."[6] The poorest two-fifths of American families received 15.4 percent of the national family income in 1986 and 1987.[7] In contrast, "the richest fifth of all families received 43.7 percent of the national family income in 1986 and 1987, the highest percentage on record."[8] The top two-fifths of all families' share was 67.8 percent, which broke another record.[9] The poorest two-fifths of American families received a smaller share of the national family income in 1986 and 1987 than in any other year since the Census Bureau began collecting data in 1947.[10] Meanwhile, the richest two-fifths of American families received a larger share of the national income in 1987 than in any year since 1947.[11]

These statistics are shocking, but they are certainly not a secret. Even more shocking than the serious disparities in income is the relative silence of whites about economic gaps that should constitute a major political issue. Certainly, it is a matter of far more importance to voters than the need either to protect the American flag from "desecration" by protesters or to keep the "Willie Hortons" of the world from obtaining prison furloughs. Why the low level of interest about so critical a pocketbook issue? Why is there no political price to pay when our government bails out big businesses like savings and loans, Chrysler, Lockheed, and even New York City for mistakes, mismanagement, and thinly veiled theft that are the corporations' fault? Why is there no public outrage when thousands of farmers go under due to changes in economic conditions that are not their fault? Why does government remain on the sidelines as millions

of factory workers lose their livelihood because of owners' greed—not the workers' fault? Why is there no hue and cry at a tax structure that rewards builders who darken the skies with gigantic, expensive condominiums for the rich while the working class spend up to one-half of their minimum-wage incomes for marginal housing, and as our poor live on the streets?

The reasons are likely numerous and complex. One substantial factor, however, seems to be the unstated understanding by the mass of whites that they will accept large disparities in economic opportunity in comparison to other whites as long as they have a priority over blacks and other people of color for access to those opportunities. On any number of occasions in American history, whites have acquiesced in—when they were not pressuring for—policy decisions that subordinated the rights of blacks in order to further some other interest. One might well ask, what do the masses of working class and poor whites gain from this continued sacrifice of black rights that justifies such acquiescence when so often the policies limit whites' opportunities as well as those of blacks?

The answer is as unavoidable as it is disturbing. Even those whites who lack wealth and power are sustained in their sense of racial superiority by policy decisions that sacrifice black rights. The subordination of blacks seems to reassure whites of an unspoken, but no less certain, property right in their "whiteness." This right is recognized by courts and society as all property rights are upheld under a government created and sustained primarily for that purpose. With blacks gone, the property right in "whiteness" goes with them. How long will the masses of whites remain silent about their puny share of the nation's wealth?

The film *Resurgence* shows a poor southern white, mired in poverty, who nevertheless declares: "Every morning I wake up and thank God I'm white." But after we're gone, we can be fairly sure, this individual will not shout, "Thank God, I'm poor." What will he and millions like him shout when the reality of his real status hits him? How will the nation's leaders respond to discontent that has been building for so long and that has been so skillfully misdirected toward a group no longer here? It will be too late to call off the trade—too late to bring back African Americans to fill their traditional role. Indeed, even without an extraterrestrial trade mission, the hour is growing late for expecting that black people will always keep the hope of racial equality alive. For millions in what is now designated the underclass, that hope has already died in the devastation of their lives. The cost of this devastation is not limited to the ghetto. As manifestations of self-hate and despair turn to rage and retaliation against the oppressors, those costs will rise dramatically and frightfully.

When I ask audiences how Americans would vote on the Space Traders' offer, rather substantial majorities express the view that the offer would be accepted. That is a present day measure of an almost certain future decision—one that will be required whether or not we have trade-oriented visitors from outer space. The century-long cycles of racial progress and reform cannot continue, and should not. Those subordinated on the basis of color cannot continue forever in this status, and will not. Politics, the courts, and self-help have failed or proved to be inadequate. Perhaps the prospect of black people removed from the American landscape will bring a necessary reassessment of who has suffered most from our subordination.

Notes

1. Quoted in Staughton Lynd, *Slavery and the Founding Fathers,* in Black History 115, 129 (M. Drimmer ed., 1968) (citations omitted).
2. Robinson, Slavery in the Structure of American Politics, 1765–1820, at 91 (1971) (quoting Notes on the State of Virginia [Abernethy ed., 1964]).
3. *Id.* at 90.
4. Lynd, *supra* note 1, at 129.
5. Alexander Bickel, The Supreme Court and the Idea of Progress 151 (1978).
6. Center on Budget and Policy Priorities, Still Far from the Dream: Recent Developments in Black Income, Employment and Poverty 21 (Oct. 1988).
7. *Id.*
8. *Id.* at 22.
9. *Id.*
10. *Id.* at 21.
11. *Id.* at 22.

33.
THE FACE OF AMERICA AND THE STATE OF EMERGENCY
Lauren Berlant

When can I go
into the supermarket
and buy what I
need with my good looks?
                    —Allen Ginsberg, "America"

I. The Political is the Personal

"The tradition of the oppressed teaches us that the 'state of emergency' in which we live is not the exception but the rule. We must attain to a conception of history that is in keeping with this insight. Then we shall clearly realize that it is our task to bring about a real state of emergency."[1] When Walter Benjamin urges his cohort of critical intellectuals to foment a state of political counter-emergency, he responds not only to the outrage of Fascism in general, but to a particularly brutal mode of what we might call *hygienic governmentality*[2]: this involves a ruling bloc's dramatic attempt to maintain its hegemony by asserting that an abject population threatens the common good and must be rigorously governed and monitored by all sectors of society. Especially horrifying to Benjamin are the ways the ruling bloc solicits mass support for such "governing": by using abjected populations as exemplary of all obstacles to national life; by wielding images and narratives of a threatened "good life" that a putative "we" have known; by promising relief from the struggles of the present through a felicitous image of a national future; and by claiming that, because the stability of the core image is

the foundation of the narratives that characterize an intimate and secure national society, the nation must at all costs protect this image of a way of life, even against the happiness of some of its own citizens.

In the contemporary United States it is almost always the people at the bottom of the virtue/value scale—the adult poor, the non-white, the unmarried, the non-heterosexual, and the nonreproductive—who are said to be creating the crisis that is mobilizing the mainstream public sphere to fight the good fight on behalf of normal national culture, while those in power are left relatively immune. For example, while the public is incited to be scandalized by so-called "Welfare Queens," the refusal of many employers to recompense their workers with a living wage and decent workplace conditions engenders no scandal at all. Indeed, the exploitation of workers is encouraged and supported, while it is poor people who are vilified for their ill-gotten gains. The manufactured emergency on behalf of "core national values" advanced by people like William Bennett, magazines like the *National Review*, and organizations like FAIR (Federation for American Immigration Reform) masks a class war played out in ugly images and ridiculous stereotypes of racial and sexual identities and anti-normative cultures.[3] As Stephanie Coontz (1992) has argued, this core US culture has never actually existed, except as an ideal or a dogma. But the cultural politics of this image of the normal has concrete effects, both on ordinary identity and the national life the state apparatus claims to be representing.

In this essay I am going to tell a story about the transformation of the normative citizenship paradigm from a public form into the abstracted time and space of intimate privacy. I will start with a reading of the film *Forrest Gump* (Robert Zemeckis, 1994) and other scenes of mass politics and end with the film of Michael Jackson's song "Black or White" (John Landis, 1991). In between, and comprising the crux of this essay, I will be engaging another fictitious citizen: the new "Face of America" who, gracing the covers of *Time*, *Mirabella*, and the *National Review*, has been cast as an imaginary solution to the problems of immigration, multiculturalism, sexuality, gender, and (trans)national identity that haunt the US present tense.

This imaginary citizen or "woman" was invented in 1993 by *Time* magazine. She is a nameless, computer-generated heterosexual immigrant, and the figure of a future modal national population. Elsewhere (Berlant 1993, 1994), I have described the constriction of modal citizenship onto smaller and more powerless vehicles of human agency: fetuses and children. Joining this gallery of incipient citizens, the computer-generated female immigrant of our *Time* cannot act or speak on behalf of the citizenship she represents; she is more human than living Americans, yet less invested with qualities of personhood. With no capacity for agency, her value is also in her irrelevance to the concerns about achievement, intelligence, subjectivity, desire, demand, and courage that have recently sullied the image of the enfranchised American woman. Her pure isolation from lived history also responds to widespread debate about the value of working-class and proletarian immigrants to the American economy and American society. This essay will show how sectors of the mainstream public sphere link whatever positive value immigration has to the current obsessive desire for a revitalized national heterosexuality and a white, normal national culture.

Thus this is a story about official storytelling and the production of mass political experience[4]; it is also an opportunity to ask what it means that, since "68," the sphere of discipline and definition for proper citizenship in the United States has become progressively more private, more sexual and familial, and more

concerned with personal morality. How and why have other relations of power and sociality—those, for example, traversing local, national, and global economic institutions—become less central to adjudicating ethical citizenship in the United States?[5] How and why have so many pundits of the bourgeois public sphere (which includes the popular media, the official discourses and practices of policy-making, and the law) come to see commitments to economic, racial, gender, and sexual justice as embarrassing and sentimental holdovers from another time? And how might the privatization of citizenship help to devalue political identification itself for US citizens?

To begin to answer these questions, it might help first to see a bigger picture of the ways the spaces of national culture have recently changed, at least in the idealized self-descriptions of contemporary US official culture. Conservative attempts to restrict citizenship have so successfully transformed scenes of privacy into the main public spheres of nationality that, for example, there is nothing extraordinary about a public figure's characterization of sexual and reproductive "immorality" as a species of "un-American" activity that requires drastic hygienic regulation. This general shift has at least three important implications for the attempt to understand the cultural politics of citizenship in the official US present tense.

First, the transgressive logic of the feminist maxim "the personal is the political," which aimed radically to make the affects and acts of intimacy in everyday life the index of national/sexual politics and ethics, has now been reversed and redeployed on behalf of a staged crisis in the legitimacy of the most traditional, apolitical, sentimental patriarchal family values. Today, the primary guiding maxim might be "the political is the personal." Reversing the direction of the dictum's critique has resulted in an anti-political nationalist politics of sexuality whose concern is no longer what sex reveals about unethical power but what "abnormal" sex/reproduction/intimacy forms reveal about threats to the nation proper/the proper nation. As registered in the anti-gay-citizenship film *The Gay Agenda* (1993), the pro-gay response *One Nation Under God* (Teodoro Maniaci and Francine M. Rzeznik, 1994), and many pro-life pamphlets, the religious right calls the struggle to delegitimate gayness and return sexual identity to tacitness, privacy, and conjugal heterosexuality "The Second Civil War."[6] This general shift also informs the increasing personalization of politics, where "character" issues have come to dominate spaces of critique that might otherwise be occupied with ideological struggles about public life, and where the appearance of squeaky cleanness (read: independently wealthy conjugal heterosexuality) is marketed as an index of personal virtue (as in the recent cases of Michael Huffington in California and Mitt Romney in Massachusetts).

But personalizing citizenship as a scene of private acts involves more than designating and legislating sexual and familial practices as the main sites of civic ethics. Relevant here as well is an increasing tendency to designate political duty in terms of individual acts of consumption and accumulation. Two major economic platforms in the last twenty years bear this out: (1) the increasing emphasis on boycotts to enforce conservative sexual morality in the mass media (often on behalf of "our youth"); and (2) the staggering contention, by Presidents Reagan, Bush, and Clinton and their cohorts, that receiving federal welfare funds so morally corrupts individuals that they are responsible for the quotidian violence and decay of the inner city, and indeed more generally for the decline of the nation as a whole. This assertion refuses to account for many things racial, gendered, and economic, including the dramatic drop in employment opportunities and wages in the metropolitan industrial sector over the last twenty years, and the social devastation that has taken place precisely in those defunded areas; its logic of displacement onto the consumer reveals how the personal morality citizenship card being played by ruling blocs is central to the ideology of unimpaired entrepreneurial activity that is sanctified as free-market patriotism during and after the Reagan regime.[7]

The second effect of citizenship's privatization has to do with the relation of mass media to national culture. If individual practice in and around the family is one nodal point of postmodern national identity, another intimate sphere of public citizenship has been created as sentimental nationality's technological mirror and complement: the mass-mediated national public sphere. As I will elaborate shortly, activism performed in civic spaces has become designated as a demonized, deranged, unclean (a)social mob activity[8]; in contrast, every article about the Internet shows us that accessing and mastering national/global mass media forms has become widely construed as the *other* most evolved or developed scene and practice of being American. While at other moments in US history the mediations of mass culture have been seen as dangers to securing an ethical national life, the collective experiences of national mass culture now constitute a form of intimacy, like the family, whose national value is measured in its subjugation of embodied forms of public life.

Finally, there exists a dialectic between a privatized "normal" nation of heterosexual, reproductive family values and the public sphere of collective intimacy through which official mass nationality stays familiar, and I have suggested that these two domains now saturate what counts as mass community in the contemporary U.S. The compression of national life into these apparatuses of intimacy also advances the conservative desire to delegitimate the embodied public itself, both abstractly and in its concrete spatial forms. Michael Rogin has called this kind of wholesale deportation of certain embodied publics from national identity "American political demonology." This involves "the inflation, stigmatization, and dehumanization of political foes" by a cluster of populist, centrist, and right-wing politicians and thinkers (1987: xii). We see it happening in the right-wing and neoliberal loathing of a cluster of seemingly disparate national scenes: public urban spaces and populations; sexualities and affective existences that do not follow the privacy logic of the patriarchal family form; collectivities of the poor, whether of inner city gangs or workers at the bottom of the class structure; the most exploited (im)migrants; nonpaternal family forms; and racially-marked subjects who do not seem to aspire to or identify with the privacy/property norms of the ostensibly core national culture. The "American way of life" against which these deviancies are measured is, needless to say, a fantasy norm, but this fantasy generates images of collective decay monstrous and powerful enough to shift voting patterns and justify the terms of cruel legislation and juridical decree.

Persons categorized as degenerate typically enter the national register through stereotype, scandal, or unusually horrible death: otherwise their lives are not timely, not news of what counts as the national present. That is, they are part of the present but are inassimilable to the national in its pure form. The disfiguring marks of disqualified US citizenship are inscribed within the present tense by tactics ranging from the manufacture of scandal to strategies of throwaway representation, like jokes; and when collective contestation does happen, it is cast as a scene of silly and/or dangerous subrationality, superficiality, or hysteria.⁹ But my aim in this essay is not solely to explicate the ways public lives uncontained by the family form and mass mediation have become bad objects in the political public sphere. It is also to seek out and explore the moments of world-building optimism within the normalizing discourse of national privacy, to better understand what kinds of life are being supported by the privatization of US citizenship, and what kinds of good are being imagined in the ejection of entire populations from the national present and future.

II. On Being Normal, Average, Common, Ordinary, Standard, Typical, and Usual in Contemporary America¹⁰

One of the most popular vehicles celebrating citizenship's extraction from public life is the film *Forrest Gump*, which uses spectacles of the nation in crisis to express a nostalgic desire for official national culture, and which retells the story of recent US history as a story about the fragility of normal national personhood. Like the *Contract With America* that expresses the wish of the now mythic "angry white male" voter who feels that his destiny has been stolen from him by a coalition of feminists, people of color, and social radicals, *Forrest Gump* narrates the recent history of the United States using an image archive from contemporary rage at the radical movements of the 1960s and the culture of desire that borrowed their energy to challenge previously protected forms of American pro-family patriarchal pleasure and authority. To perform this act of rage as though it were a show of love, the film situates a

politically illiterate citizen in the place of civic virtue, and reinvents through him a revitalized, reproductive, private, and pre-political national heterosexuality. It is telling, here, that Forrest Gump is named after Nathan Bedford Forrest, founder of the Ku Klux Klan, and that an early film clip from of the Klan with Tom Hanks in Klan drag cites *Birth of a Nation* as *Forrest Gump*'s earliest cinematic progenitor. What does it suggest that these nostalgic, familial references to nationally-sanctioned racial violence are translated through someone incapable of knowing what they mean?

Forrest Gump follows the youth and middle age of an infantile citizen, a man who retains his innocence because he is five points shy of normal intelligence. We know he is such a statistical person because the principal of his school says so: to explain Forrest's horizon of life opportunity, the principal holds up a sign with statistics on it, which are clustered into the categories: Above Average, Normal, and Below Normal. Forrest has an IQ of 75, which would force him to attend what Mrs. Gump bitingly calls a "special" school: 80 is normal, and would give the child access to the standard pedagogical resources of the state. Forrest's mother refuses to submit to the rule of numbers, since she believes that people must make their own destinies. Therefore she fucks Forrest's way into normal culture by having sex with the principal of his school, her body in trade for five points of IQ and the privileged protections of normality.

Therein begins a simple story about gender, heterosexuality, and nationality that nonetheless articulates complicated ideas about how US citizens inhabit national history. First, *Forrest Gump* seeks to eradicate women from public life and nonreproductive sex from the ideal nation. As Mrs. Gump demonstrates, a virtuous woman does her business at home and organizes her life around caretaking, leaving the domestic sphere only to honor her child. Even more insidious than this 1950s style gender fantasy is the way the film sifts through the detritus of national history since the protest movements of the 1960s and their challenge to what constitutes a national public. First, the narrative replays the history of post-'68 America as a split between the evil of intention, which is defined as a female trait, and the virtue of shallowness, which is generally a male trait (except if the man has lusted after women, in which case his passions are figured both as violent to women and tainted by the cupidity/rapacity of feminine desire). Forrest Gump's "girl," Jenny Curran, inherits Mrs. Gump's horizon of historical possibility, organizing with her libidinous body a narrative of the corrupted national public sphere. Like Mrs. Gump, Jenny is there to have sex and to be sexually exploited, humiliated, and physically endangered in every intimate encounter she has with a man. Between 1971 and 1982 Jenny goes through each form of public, sensual degradation available in the *Time*-mediated version of American culture: the sexual and political revolution of the '60s, the drugs and disco culture of the '70s, and then, finally, the AIDS pandemic of the '80s. (Although the disease goes unnamed, Jenny seems to die of a special strain of AIDS that makes you more beautiful as your immune system collapses.) To add insult to history, the film seems to locate the bad seed of the '60s in the sexual abuse of Jenny by her alcoholic father. It is as though, for the family to be redeemed as a site of quasi-apolitical nation-formation, the pervasiveness of abuse has to be projected out onto the metropolitan public: Jenny's private trauma comes to stand not for the toxicity of familial privacy or patriarchal control of children, but for a *public* ill whose remedy seems bizarrely to require a return to the family, albeit a kinder, gentler, more antiseptic one. Before Jenny dies she is redeemed from her place as an abject sexual and historical subject via an act of reproductive sex with Forrest. The family is then fully redeemed by Forrest's single fatherhood of his eponymous son: symbolically eradicated from the nasty public world, women and friends are ultimately separated from the family form as well, absent the way public history is, except as animating memory.

In his random way, Forrest enters the national narrative too. But he encounters history without becoming historical, which in this film means being becoming dead, gravely wounded, or degenerate. Because he is mentally incapable of making plans or thinking conceptually, he follows rules and orders literally. Someone says "Run, Forrest," he runs; someone says "shrimp," he shrimps. This is why he can become an "All-American" football hero and why, in

the Army, Gump is considered a genius. This is why he can survive Vietnam while others around him fall and falter; why he endures when a hurricane obliterates every other shrimp boat in the south, (which produces "Bubba Gump," a financial empire made from shrimp and clothing tie-ins with the company logo); and why, when his friend Lt. Dan gambles on some "fruit" company called Apple, Gump is financially fixed for life. He takes risks but experiences nothing of their riskiness: a Vietnam with no Vietnamese, capitalism with no workers, and profit at a distance both from production and exploitation.[11] While Jenny deliberately seeks out the deteriorating political and aesthetic public culture of modern America, Gump notices nothing and excels at everything he decides to do. He is too stupid to be racist, sexist, and exploitative; this is his genius, and it is meant to be his virtue.

In addition to enjoying the patriarchal capitalist entitlements of American life as a man of football, war, and industry, and in addition to inventing the treasured and complexly linked national banalities "Have a Nice Day" and "Shit Happens," Gump makes three pilgrimages to the White House, where he meets Presidents Kennedy, Johnson, and Nixon. Each time he shakes a President's hand the President automatically inquires as to his well-being, a question that conventionally seeks a generic citizen's response, such as "Fine, Mr. President." But to Kennedy, Gump says "I gotta pee." With Johnson, Gump pulls down his pants to show the war wound on his "buttocks." With Nixon, he discusses his discomfort in Washington: Nixon transfers him to his favorite place, the Watergate Hotel, where Gump sees flashlights in the Democratic National Committee headquarters and calls Frank Wells. Forrest notices that Nixon soon resigns, but this event is as random to him as the white feather that floats in the film's framing shots. "For no particular reason," he keeps saying, these nice Presidents are shot, assaulted, or disgraced, along with George Wallace, John Lennon, Bobby Kennedy, Gerald Ford, and Ronald Reagan. No mention of Martin Luther King, Medgar Evers, or Malcolm X is made in *Forrest Gump*.

Gump narrates the story of his unearned and therefore virtuous celebrity to a series of people who sit on a park bench next to him in Savannah,

Georgia. They all assume he's stupid, partly because he repeats his mother's line "Stupid is as stupid does" so often it begins to make sense. But then the fact that this movie makes any sense at all is a tribute to two technologies of the gullible central to contemporary American life. First, the digital technology that makes it possible to insert Tom Hanks/Forrest Gump into nationally momentous newsreel footage from the past three decades. Using the technologies called "morphing" and bluescreen photography that enable computers to make impossible situations and imaginary bodies look realistic on film, *Forrest Gump* stages five national "historical" events.[12] In these moments the nation, often represented through the President's body, meets "the people," embodied by Gump, who has made a pilgrimage to Washington. Gump's clear anomalousness to the national norm, signalled in the explicit artificiality of Hanks' presence in the newsreel images, makes his successful infantile citizenship seem absurd, miraculous, or lucky; on the other hand, the narrative of his virtue makes him seem the ideal type of American. The technology's self-celebration in the film borrows the aura of Gump's virtuous incapacity to self-celebrate: the film seeks to make its audience want to rewrite recent US history into a world that might have sustained a Forrest Gump. To effect the audience's desire for his exemption from the traumas of history, the writers and director broadly ironize and parody an already wildly oversimple version of what constituted the 1960s and beyond: but the intensity of the visual and aural maneuvers the film makes suggests a utopian desire for one political revolution (the Reaganite one) to have already happened in the '60s, and another (the counter-culture's) never to have begun at all.

The second technology of the gullible, then, available in the film's revisionary historicism, is the right-wing cultural agenda of the Reagan revolution, whose effects are everywhere present. The ex-president is literally represented for a minute, in one of the film's many scenes of national trauma. But Reagan's centrality to the historical imaginary of *Forrest Gump* is signalled as powerfully by the *People* magazine his first interlocutor reads. This has Nancy Reagan on the cover, standing in both for her presidential husband and for the grotesqueness of feminine ambition.

Although it has the historical and technological opportunity, the film never shows Gump meeting, or even noticing, this President. Why should it? He *is* Reagan—Reagan, that is, as he sold himself, a person incapable of duplicity who operates according to a natural regime of justice and common sense in a national world that has little place for these virtues.[13]

With its claim to be without a political or sexual unconscious, and with its implied argument that to have an unconscious is to be an incompetent or dangerous American, *Forrest Gump* is a symptomatic product of the conservative national culture machine, with its desire to establish a simple, privacy-based model of normal America. This machine involves creating a sense of a traditional but also an urgently contemporary mass consent to an image/narrative archive of what a core national culture should look like: through an anti-political politics that claims to be protecting what it is promoting—a notion of citizenship preached in languages of moral, not political, accountability—the national culture industry seeks to stipulate that only certain kinds of people, practices, and property that are, at core, "American," deserve juridical and social legitimation. The modal normal American in this view sees her/his identity as something sustained in private, personal, intimate relations; in contrast, only the abjected, degraded, *lower* citizens of the United States will see themselves as sustained by public, coalitional, non-kin affiliations. *Forrest Gump* produces this political hierarchy too. For all its lightness and irony, there is something being wished-for when the film has Forrest "unconsciously" ridicule the Black Panthers and the left wing cultural and political imaginary, which is reduced to achieving the revolutionary liberation of the word "fuck" from the zone of "adult" language into public political discourse.[14] For all its idealization of Jenny Curran, the film is never more vicious about the desire to be and to have a public than when she leaves her terrible home to experiment in non-familial contexts. I have suggested that the crisis of the contemporary nation is registered in terms of threats to the imagined norm of privatized citizenship: *Gump* defines "normal" through the star's untraumatized survival of a traumatic national history, which effectively rewrites the traumas of mass unrest of the last few decades not as responses to systemic malaise, exploitation, or injustice, but as purely personal to the dead, the violent, and the violated.

Explicating this ejection of a non-conjugal and non-mass-mediated public life from the official/dominant present tense in the U.S. involves coordinating many different plateaus of privilege and experience. It also involves taking up Benjamin's challenge: to the state of emergency the official nation is now constantly staging about the ex-privilege of its elite representatives there must be a response, involving the creation of a state of counter-emergency. To do this will at least be to tell the story of a symbolic genocide within the U.S., a mass social death that takes place not just through the removal of entire populations from the future of national political life and resources, but also through cruel methods of representation in the mainstream public sphere and in the law. This is to say that the United States that the law recognizes is generated in representations of public opinion and custom; to take seriously the ordinary representations of the official public sphere is to enter a war of maneuver, an uncivil war that is currently raging everywhere around us.

III. Making Up Nations (1): Postmodern Mobocracy and Contemporary Protest

As anyone can see on the television news, a terrible state of political emergency exists on the streets of the contemporary U.S. There, ordinary conflicts among different publics about what the good life should entail are recast as menaces to national society, and images of political life "on the street" become evidence that a violent change threatens an idealized version of the national. Despite occasional attempts to caption images of public dissent respectfully, the typical modern T.V. news report represents the right and left through their most disorderly performances of resistance, to indicate that collective opposition is based not on principle, but on passions that are dangerous and destabilizing for the commonweal. Whether their acts are cast as naive, ridiculous, insipid, and shallow, or merely serious and unpragmatic, protesters are made to represent the frayed and fraying edges of national society.[15] Yet in news footage

of police activity during feminist, abortion, antiwar, civil rights, and Yippie demonstrations, we see that violent disorder is in fact rather more likely to come from the actions of police.[16] Michael Warner (1992) has argued that media sensationalism around collective public citizenship acts is partly driven by a desire to increase ratings and to whet the consuming public's appetite for mass disaster. More important than that, though, is the chilling effect such framing has on conceptions of political activism. Nonetheless politicians and the dominant press tend to ascribe the disorder to the resisters and, more insidiously, to the world they want to bring into being.

The double humiliation of protest in the mainstream media, making it both silly and dangerous, subtracts personhood from activists, making their very gestures of citizenship seem proof that their claims are illegitimate. This is especially germane in the portrayal of pro-life and gay collective actions. In contrast, political suffering is still palatable when expressed as a trauma or injury to a particular person. This narrowing in the means for making a legitimate claim on public sympathy has had a significant effect in a certain strain of US legal theory, where some are arguing that words and images can produce harms to a person as substantial as those made by physical acts of violence, such that violent and cruel talk should be actionable the way physical assault is (Matsuda 1993). But more than this, talk shows and other forms of gossip media have helped to make scenes of personal witnessing the only political testimony that counts. It is not that just everybody loves a good sob story. Trauma makes good storytelling and, as journalistic common sense constantly reminds us, it puts a "face" on an otherwise abstract issue.[17] Moreover, the sheer scale of the systematically brutal hierarchies that structure national capitalist culture can be overwhelming, leading to a kind of emotional and analytic paralysis in a public that cannot imagine a world without poverty or violence: here too, the facialization of US injustice makes it manageable and enables further deferral of considerations that might force structural transformations of public life. In the meantime, while the embodied activities of anonymous citizens have taken on the odor of the abject, the personal complaint form now bears a huge burden for vocalizing and embodying injustice in the United States.

Yet there *is* a kind of public and collective protest that the media honors. Take, for example, press reports of the 30th anniversary of Martin Luther King's March on Washington, and contrast them to reports on the gay and lesbian march on Washington on April 25, 1993. In 1963, the approach of King's march created panic and threats of racist counter-violence. But in retrospect, this event has been sanitized into a beautifully choreographed mass rationality, an auturist production of the eloquent, rhetorically masterful, and then martyred King. These solemn reports wax nostalgic for the days when protest was reasonable, and protestors were mainly men speaking decorously with their bodies, while asking for reasonable things like the ordinary necessities of life.[18]

This media legitimation of orderly national protest has a long history. The 1933 film *Gabriel Over the White House* (Gregory La Cava, 1933), for example, details with particular clarity the limited kind of citizenship activity a privacy-based mass democracy can bear, especially in times of economic crisis. Like other films of the depression,[19] *Gabriel* emplots the seeming fraudulence of the claim that democracy can exist in a capitalist society, by focusing on the "forgotten men" who had fought World War I for a United States that could not support them afterwards. To the "forgotten man" the depression broke a contract national-capitalism had made with national-patriotism: and the possibility of a legitimate *patriotic* class war among men was palpable everywhere in the U.S. In response to this decline in national-masculine prestige, the culture industry produced narratives that performed ways of sending rage into remission. I quote *Gabriel* at length to demonstrate Americans' longstanding ambivalence toward democracy's embodiment in collective struggle; but also to set up these images of collective dignity and sacrifice as the nostalgic horizon that official culture "remembers" in its scramble to codify the proprieties of mass national culture in the present tense.

Speaking on the radio during the depression is "John Bronson," leader of an army of unemployed men who are marching on their way to Washington from New York to find out whether the federal

nation feels accountable to their suffering. As Bronson speaks, the film shows the President having a treasure hunt in the Oval office with his nephew and then eating the marshmallow treasures he has hidden. They are not attending to the disembodied and dignified voice coming from the radio: this difficult task is left to the viewers who hear it while their eyes are distracted by the President's play:

People of America. This is John Bronson speaking, not for himself but for over a million men who are out of work who cannot earn money to buy food because those responsible for providing work have failed in their obligations. We ask no more than that which every citizen of the United States should be assured the right to live, the right to food in the mouths of our wives and children. Our underlying purpose is not revolutionary. We are not influenced by militant leaders. None of us are reds. We merely want work, and we believe this great United States of America under proper leadership can provide work for everybody. I have appealed to the President for an interview and the President says he will not deal with us because we are dangerous anarchists. We are not. We are citizens of America with full confidence in the American democracy, if it is properly administered. The people of America are hopelessly [speech drowned out by conversation between an African-American valet and the President about what coat the President will wear] . . . prosperous and happy. I ask your President now if he has ever read the Constitution of the United States as it was laid out by those great men that day in Philadelphia long ago, a document which guarantees the American people the rights of life, liberty, property, and the pursuit of happiness. All we ask are to be given those rights. This country is sound. The right man in the White House can bring us out of despair into prosperity again. We ask him at least to try.

Almost instantly after this speech Bronson is murdered, and enters the pantheon of anti-national patriotic martyrs (the "army of the unemployed" sings the almost eponymous "John Brown's Body" as it marches from city to city); but there is no violence by the workers. Indeed, becoming by executive order an official reserve army for American capital, they trade rage for wages the government pays them (the President eventually sets up utopian boot camps for the working poor, in support of the men's prestige in the family). As in the case of King's March on Washington, this suggests that the only way Americans can claim both rights and mass sympathy is to demonstrate not panic, anger, demand, and desire, but ethical serenity, hyperpatriotism, and proper deference. Political emotions like anxiety, rage, and aggression turn out to be the feelings only privileged people are justified in having. America's breach of its contract with its subordinated peoples becomes in this model of mass politics an opportunity for elites to feel sorry for themselves, and sympathy for the well-behaved oppressed: but the cruelty of sympathy, the costs it extracts in fixing abject suffering as the only condition of social membership, is measured in the vast expanse between the scene of feeling and the effects that policies exert.

This distortion of the origins and aims of disorder is not just due to the confusion of the moment, nor merely to the traditionally grotesque representation of public bodies made by political elites and editorial cartoonists. As a force in framing the contemporary conditions of national power, the misattribution of public disorder is a strategy to delegitimate anti-privacy citizenship politics, especially where they seek to unsettle the domains of white patriarchal nationalism. The mainstream press's representation of the serious carnival of women's liberation and antiwar activity of the early 1970s is not, after all, so far from the representation of sexual politics in mainstream places like *Newsweek* and *The Gay Agenda*, which features graphic descriptions of sexual display in gay pride parades and the March on Washington to equate negatively the spectacular modalities of the parade with the utopian national imaginary of Queers (see Berlant 1995). Accusations that political activists on parade are animals unable to assimilate to the rational norms of civic life are crucial weapons in the denationalization of these populations. There is no appreciation for the desire for continuity between everyday life and political activism behind these

serious carnivals: as in Marlon Riggs's *Tongues Untied* (1989), where the specific beauty and self-pleasure of protestors in parades is a form of sexual and political happiness, a part of the erotics of public personhood that queer politics imagines as central to the world of unhumiliated sexual personhood (at least for gay men) it means to bring forth in America: "Black men loving Black men is the Revolutionary Act."

Finally, John Grisham's *The Pelican Brief* (1992) and the film of it (Alan J. Pakula, 1993) summarize strikingly how the fear of mobocracy both constitutes and threatens to efface the popular spaces and animate bodies of adult citizens in the contemporary nation. The film opens outside of the Supreme Court in the middle of a demonstration. This, the first of four major street/mob scenes in the film, means to measure a crisis of national power brought on, or so it seems, by the people who insist on being represented by it. The opening shot of the protestors quotes the iconic images from the 1968 Democratic Convention in Chicago: wild-haired youths and police in helmets struggling to move, to hit, to fall, and to remain standing; loud, incoherent, angry voices.

The camera pulls back to reveal a disorderly mob, the faces in which are obscured by the sheer number of people and the placards that are being brandished. What is the protest about? I catalogue the signs and slogans: "abortion is murder"; uncaptioned pictures of aborted fetuses; "handgun control"; "no justice no peace"; "save our cities"; "AIDS cure now"; "Silence = Death"; "Come out come out wherever you are"; "gun control now"; "fur is death"; "pass gun control"; "execution is no solution"; "Death to Rosenberg" (this uncannily anticommunist sign actually refers to a liberal judge who is shortly thereafter assassinated for political reasons that are not at all linked to this cluster of protests). From this mélange of complaints we can conclude that in the contemporary United States collective social life is constituted within a sublime expanse of nationally-sanctioned violent death, a condition that the animated mob breaks down to its discrete evidences and testifies to by shouting out.

At the end of the film, the camera rests happily on the smiling face of Julia Roberts, who is watching Denzel Washington on television reporting that "she's just too good to be true." By this time we have entirely lost the trace of the opening protest. It turns out that there is nothing important about the scene, it is entirely gratuitous to the narrative. The activist judge is killed because he threatens the property privilege of a fat capitalist; this capitalist, Victor Mattiece, has contributed millions to the campaign of the film's vacuous Reagan-style president; in contrast, we never see the criminal in the flesh, only a newspaper photo of him. In short, citizens acting en masse seem to be protesting *the wrong things*, and to have irrelevant views about what kinds of corruption constrain their free citizenship.

Yet the logic of the book/film is more complex. We see that when the state imagines popular resistance, its paranoia invents mass political entities like the "underground army," an underdefined institution of faceless and random radicals (Grisham 1992, 47, 55). But when the state itself is reimagined here as a corrupt cabal of businessmen, lawyers, and politicians, the corruption is *personal* and does not rub off onto the institution, which apparently still works well when "good men" are in it. Likewise, Julia Roberts plays Darby Shaw, a sexy law student who writes the "Pelican Brief" not from a political motive, but out of love for her lover/law professor (whose mentor was Justice Rosenberg); Denzel Washington plays Gray Grantham, disinterested reporter for the *Washington Post*, out to get a story. Together they manage to create a non-subaltern-identified asexual, apolitical wedge of objective knowledge about the corrupt state: and in the end it is Roberts, with her guileless youth, her detached sexuality, her absolute privacy, her enormous smile, and her mass-mediated star aura, who becomes the horizon of the law's possibility and of a sanitized national fantasy, the new face of a remasculinized America where the boundaries are drawn in all the right places, and the personal is as vacuous as the political.[20]

IV. Making Up Nations (2): "The Idea is Reckless. . . . A Melding of Cultures"[21]

In contrast to the zone of privacy where stars, white people, and citizens who don't make waves with their bodies can imagine they reside, the immigrant to the United States has no privacy, no power to incorporate automatically the linguistic and cultural practices of normal national culture that lubricate life for those who can pass as members of the core society. This is the case whether or not the immigrant has "papers": indeed, the emphasis placed on *cultural* citizenship by books like Bennett's *The De-Valuing of America*, Brimelow's *Alien Nation*, and Henry's *In Defense of Elitism* suggests that acquiring the formal trappings of legitimate residence in the country is never sufficient to guarantee full acceptance by the nation.

These books argue that, where immigrants are concerned, the only viable model for nation-building is a process of "Americanization." I have suggested that, even for birthright citizens, the process of identifying with an "American way of life" increasingly involves moral pressure to identify with a small cluster of privatized normal identities: but what kinds of special pressure does this process involve for immigrants? What kinds of self-erasure, self-transformation, and assimilation are being imagined by those who worry that even the successful "naturalization" of immigrants will equal the denaturalization of the US nation? What does the project of making this incipient citizen "American" tell us about the ways national identity is being imagined and managed in the political public sphere?

When a periodical makes "special issue" out of a controversy, the controversy itself becomes a commodity whose value is in the intensity of identification and anxiety the journal can organize around it, and this is what is happening to immigration as a subject in the US mainstream. Captioning *Time*'s first "special issue" on immigration, *Immigrants: the Changing Face of America* (July 8, 1985), is a sentence that describes what kinds of boundaries get crossed and problems raised when the immigrant enters the United States: "Special Issue: Immigrants. They come from everywhere, for all kinds of reasons, and they are rapidly and permanently changing the face of America. They are altering the nation's racial makeup, its cities, its tastes, its entire perception of itself and its way of life" (1). The emphasis on time and space in this framing passage—"they" come from everywhere, "they" incite rapid change—suggests that there is something "special" about the contemporary immigrant to the U.S. that ought to create intensified anxieties about social change, even despite the widely held axiom that the U.S. is fundamentally "a nation of immigrants." The something that the force and velocity of immigrant cultural practices is radically changing is people's everyday lives in the nation, but that something is underspecified. We see in particular a change in the default reference of the category "race," and concurrently the city and its dominant "tastes." These unsettlements, in turn, have forced alterations in what had ostensibly been a stable national self-concept, based on common affinities and ways of life.

Of course, every crisis of immigration in US history has involved the claim that something essentially American is being threatened by alien cultural practices. In the 1985 *Time* Magazine variant on this national anxiety, however, immigrants to the United States are made stereotypical in newly ambivalent ways. *Time* first represents their challenge to the "us" and the "our" of its readership—everywhere implicitly native-born, white, male salaried citizens—through a cover that shows a classic huddled mass made up mostly of Latinos and Asians of all ages, with lined or worried faces. Their faces are in various stages of profile facing the reader's right, as though the "changing" face of America that the title declares is made visible in the dynamism of their rotation. In the present tense of a new national life, they are looking off toward the edge of the page at something unidentified: their future, America's future, the scene of their prospects contained in the magazine whose pages are about to be opened. The diverted gaze of the immigrants frees the reader from identification with them: the readers too, from their side of the border, are positioned to open the magazine and see their future prophesied and plotted.

I overread this cover story in part to set up a frame for thinking about the 1993 special issue of *Time* on immigration and national life, but also to look at how national publics are characterized and made in an age of mass mediation. *Time* presents its immigrants in segmented populations, which are defined in relation to the totality "Americans": "Hispanics," "Asians," and "Blacks" each get their own article. But *Time*'s task is not merely to document changes: to name a racial or ethnic population is to name for the

public a difficult problem it faces. Specifically, the issue responds to particular issues created by the 1965 Immigration and Nationality Act, which dissolved official preference given to European migration to the U.S. (26): while some section headings confirm that immigrants like "Asians" as a class and talented individuals like the Cuban poet Heberto Padilla contribute superbly to the core US national culture, alien cultures are mainly named because they seem to pose threats. For "Blacks" (said to be "left behind" by the wave of new races) and the rest of the US, "Hispanics" are the new "problem" population, so disturbing they get their own section and dominate several others, including "Business," "Policy," "The Border," "Religion," "Video," and "Behavior."

Yet the explicit rhetoric of the special issue is nothing if not optimistic: overall, the essays have a tinny and intense enthusiasm about immigration's effect on national life, and it is the ambivalent tone of voice they use to support optimism about the process of assimilation that is of interest here. An immigrant is defined by *Time* as a national alien who comes to America consciously willing to be exploited in exchange for an abstraction, "opportunity" (3, 57). But in lived terms opportunity is not abstract. If the immigrant's value is in her/his willingness to be economically exploited for freedom, *Time* also argues that the intense labor of mass assimilation into cultural literacy itself will further enrich the already existing indigenous "national culture" (33ff).

The American schoolroom has traditionally provided a hopeful glimpse of the nation's future, and some people still imagine it to be a Rockwellian scene of mostly pink-cheeked children spelling out the adventures of Dick and Jane. But come for a moment to the playground of the Franklin elementary school in Oakland, where black girls like to chant their jump-rope numbers in Chinese. "See you *mañana*," one student shouts with a Vietnamese accent. "Ciao!" cries another, who has never been anywhere near Italy. And let it be noted that the boy who won the National Spelling Bee in Washington last month was Balu Natarajan, 13, who was born in India, now lives in a suburb of Chicago, and speaks Tamil at home. "Milieu" was the word with which he defeated 167 other competitors. Let it also be noted that Hung Vu and Jean Nguyen in May became the first Vietnamese-born Americans to graduate from West Point. (29)

Like their parents, these child-immigrants are imagined as a heterogeneous population that lives mainly outside and on the streets of America. They compose a population whose tastes in food and art and whose creative knowledges ("Spanglish" is featured elsewhere, 81) are easily assimilable to the urges for commodity variation and self-improvement that already saturate the existing indigenous mass national "milieu." There are also *three* essays on elite immigrants who have freely brought "wealth," "brain power," and "culture" to enrich the land of opportunity that is the United States. Children and the elite: these good immigrants are good, in *Time*'s view, because they are the gift that keeps giving, willing to assimilate and to contribute difference and variation to American culture.

Meanwhile, in separate articles on immigrant women and children we see that worthy migration is a not only determined by intercultural influence and economic activity, but also by its utility as symbolic evidence for the ongoing power of American democratic ideals. That is, immigration discourse is a central technology for the reproduction of patriotic nationalism: not just because the immigrant is seen as without a nation or resources and thus is deserving of pity or contempt, but because the immigrant is defined as *someone who desires America* (82–3). Immigrant women especially are valued for having the courage to grasp freedom. But what is freedom for women? *Time* defines it not as liberation from oppressive states and economic systems, but as release from patriarchal family constraints, such that the free choice of love object is the pure image of freedom itself. Indeed, an explicit analogy is drawn between the intimacy form of consensual marriage and the value of American national culture:

Women migrate for the same reasons that men do: to survive, because money has become worthless at home, to find schooling and jobs. But they

also have reasons of their own. Single women may leave to escape the domination of their old-fashioned families, who want them to stay in the house and accept an arranged marriage . . . [for] home, like parentage, must be legitimized through love; otherwise, it is only a fact of geography or biology. Most immigrants to America found their love of their old homes betrayed. Whether Ireland starved them, or Nazi Germany persecuted them, or Viet Nam drove them into the sea, they did not really abandon their countries; their countries abandoned them. In America, they found the possibility of a new love, the chance to nurture new selves. . . . [Americanization] occurs when the immigrant learns his ultimate lesson: above all countries, America, if loved, returns love. (82; 100f)

I will return to the utopian rhetoric of national love anon. Although *Time* admits that there are other reasons people come to the U.S.—for example, as part of the increasingly global proletarian workforce (82)—its optimism about immigration is most powerfully linked not to the economic and cultural *effects* of immigration on the U.S. or its current and incipient citizens, but on the symbolic implications immigration has on national vanity: it is proof that the U.S. is a country worthy of being loved. This is, after all, the only imaginable context in which the United States can be coded as antipatriarchal: come to America and not only can you choose a lover and a specially personalized modern form of quotidian exploitation at work, but because you can and do choose them, they must be *prima facie* evidence that freedom and democracy exist in the U.S.

Meanwhile, for all its optimism about immigrant-American nation-formation, "The Changing Face of America" clearly emerges from a panic in national culture, and one motive for this issue is to substitute a new panic about change for an old one. Explicitly the issue responds to the kinds of nativist economic and cultural anxiety that helped shape the Immigration Reform and Control Act of 1986 and, more recently, California's Proposition 187. Three specific and self-contradictory worries predominate: the fear that immigrants, legal and illegal, absorb more resources than they produce, thus diverting the assets of national culture from legal citizens; the fear that immigrants, legal and illegal, are better capitalists than natal citizens, and thus extract more wealth and political prerogative than they by birthright should; and the fear that cities, once centers of cultural and economic capital, are becoming unlivable, as spatial boundaries between communities of the very poor, workers, and affluent residents have developed in a way that threatens the security of rich people and the authority of "the family."

The essay that most fully expresses this cluster of fears is the title essay, "The Changing Face of America," which provides a remarkable caption to the cover image. But what is striking about this essay, which equates "face" with place of national origin ("That guy is Indian, next to him is a Greek, next to him is a Thai," says one neighborhood tour guide, 26) is not the American xenophobia-style apprehension it expresses, acknowledges, and tries to manage. This panic of mistrust in the viability of a non-European-dominated "America" almost goes without saying in any contemporary mainstream discussion of the immigrant-effect: it is expressed in the chain of almost equivalent signs "immigrant," "alien," "minority," "illegal"; it is expressed in the ordinary phrase "wave of immigrants," which never quite explicitly details the specter of erosion and drowning it contains that has long haunted American concerns about the solidity of national economic and cultural property.

Instead, what distinguishes this special issue on immigration is the way it characterizes birthright American citizenship, and particularly how it codes the relationship between the animated corporeality of immigrant desire and the enervation of the native or assimilated American. The essay about America's changing face is illustrated by photographs of immigrants who have just landed within the hour at New York's Kennedy Airport. The photographs are not meant to tell stories about the immigrants' histories. Rather, *Time* claims that the captured image of the face in the picture records an immigrant's true feeling at the threshold, the feeling of anticipation that history is about to begin again, in the context of the new nation: "The moment of arrival stirs feelings of hope, anxiety, curiosity, pride. These emotions and many

others show in the faces on the following pages" (26). (These phrases caption a picture of a sleeping baby.) The immigrant portraits are like fetal sonograms or baby pictures. The specific bodies matter little. Their importance is in the ways they express how completely generic immigrant hopes and dreams might unfold from particular bodies: and they tell a secret story about a specific migrant's odds for survival—by which *Time* means successful Americanization.

The photographs of new immigrants are also made in an archaic style, often taking on the design of formal family daguerreotype portraits. Given *Time*'s explicit commitment, in this issue, to refurbishing Ellis Island, it is not surprising that these threshold images make the immigrants American ancestors before the process of living historically as an American has happened. What are the aims of this framing modality? First, to borrow the legitimating aura of American immigrants from past generations, with whom even Euro-Americans can still identify. Second, to signal without saying it that the "wave" is no mob, but actually a series of families, bringing their portable privacy to a land where privacy is protected. Third, the structure of generationality provides a strong model of natural change, evolutionary reproduction being the most unrevolutionary structure of collective transformation imaginable, even while worries about burgeoning new-ethnic populations (of color) seem to threaten the future of (white) modern nationality. Fourth, as Roland Barthes (1981) argues, the portrait photograph is a figure of displacement and a performance of loss or death: and as the immigrant has long been said to undergo a death and rebirth of identity in crossing the threshold to America, so too the picture might be said to record the "changing" over of the face as the subjects change the register of their existence.

Yet if death (of identities, identifications, national cultures) is everywhere in this issue of *Time*, and if these processes are linked complexly to the production of America, it is not simply the kind of death one associates with the iconic symbolics of national rebirth; nor its opposite, in the privileged classes' typical construction of ghetto violence and its specters as the end of America as "we" know it; nor in the standard depiction of an undervalued and exploited

underclass with a false image of the *class's* underval-
uation of "life"—although the special issue cues up
this cruel translation periodically in essays on the unlivable city. Mainly, "The Changing Face of America"
deploys images of national death to say something
extraordinary about the logics by which the American desire for property and privacy makes citizenship
itself a death-driven machine.

The essay on America's changing face captions
its photographs with a story about what happens
to the immigrant's sensuous body in the process
of becoming American: "America is a country that
endlessly reinvents itself, working the alchemy that
turns 'them' into 'us.' That is the American secret:
motion, new combinations, absorption. The process
is wasteful, dangerous, messy, sometimes tragic. It is
also inspiring." However the story, "in its ideal, is one
of earthly redemption," the magazine proclaims (24).
But the process of alchemy turns out to be virtually
vampiric.

> It was America, really, that got the prize: the enor-
> mous energy unleashed by the immigrant disloca-
> tions. Being utterly at risk, moving into a new and
> dangerous land, makes the immigrant alert and
> quick to learn. It livens reflexes, pumps adrena-
> line. . . . The immigrant who travels in both time
> and geographical space achieves a neat existen-
> tial alertness. The dimensions of time and space
> collaborate. America, a place, becomes a time:
> the future. . . . In this special issue, *Time* describes
> the newest Americans and addresses the myriad
> ways in which they are carrying on an honored
> tradition: contributing their bloodlines, their spirit
> and their energy to preserve the nation's vitality
> and uniqueness. (25)

The immigrant is full of vitality, and he/she provides
an energy of desire and labor that perpetually turns
America into itself. What then of the native citizen?
Throughout the text the problem of immigration
turns into the problem of abject America: it turns out
that to be an American citizen is to be anesthetized,
complacent, unimaginative. "There is nothing dead-
ened or smug about immigrants," the editors write.
In contrast, US citizenship is a form of annulment,

for the attainment of safety and freedom from the
anxiety for survival national-capitalism promises
turns out, again and again, to make old and new
citizens enervated, passive in the expectation that
at some point their constitutionally-promised "happiness" will be delivered to them. This passivity is
central to America's economic and cultural decline,
implies *Time*; the metaphysics of "success" leads to
the evacuation of ambition in the present tense, and
threatens the national future.[22]

Thus along with the problem of cultural transformation that immigration presents to the anxious
native public is a threatening, half-obscured question
of national identification and identity: in 1985 *Time*
proclaims the *new* immigrant as the only true American, while casting birthright and naturalized citizens
as subject to enervation, decay, and dissolution. The
very promise that lures persons to identify with their
native or assumed US national identity, the promise
of freedom unearned and privacy enjoyed, is cast as
an unmitigated economic disaster.

This is, perhaps, why "The Changing Face of
America" emphasizes the difference between the economic and the ideal United States: if masses of immigrants are necessary to provide the proletarian and
creative cultural energy for the nation's well-being,
the essential nation itself must be untouched by the
changing face of America, must be a theoretical nation where success is measured by civic abstractions
and moral obligations: "love" of "home" turns out to be
Time's foundation for democratic American morality;
American morality turns out to be the reality-effect
of national culture. If America is constituted meta-
physically, as an ethical space of faith or belief, then
intimacy with the principles of American democratic
culture—of property, privacy, and individuality—is
the only ground for the true practice of nationhood.
There are no immigrants or citizens there, in that zone
of abstraction, it is a dead space, dead to the fluctua-
tions of change. All the rest is just history.

V. Making Up Nations (3): Another *New* Face of America

When in 1993 *Time* revised its earlier construction of
the immigrant-effect, the magazine felt compelled to

do so not only because of the conflictual economic and cultural conditions of the present, but also because a new future was being assessed: it had just become common knowledge that "sometime during the second half of the 21st century the descendants of white Europeans, the arbiters of the core national culture for most of its existence, are likely to slip into minority status. . . . 'Without fully realizing it,' writes Martha Farnsworth Riche, director of policy studies at Washington's Population Reference Bureau."[23] The directionality of the earlier special issue on immigrants has reversed: whereas in the 1980s, the issue was immigration and the politics of assimilation (to Americanness), in the 1990s the issue seems to be the necessary adaptation all white Americans must make to the new multicultural citizenship norm, even the ones who don't live in New York, El Paso, and Los Angeles.

This special issue is thus a cultural *memento mori* for the white American statistical majority, but it is also a call to a mass action. But what kind of mass action? At the moment of its statistical decline, it becomes necessary to reinvent the image archive of the nation in a way that turns the loss of white cultural prestige into a gain for white cultural prestige. To perform this process of transfiguration, the cover of this issue is both more and less than a death mask; it is a new commercial stereotype advertising the future of national culture: "Take a good look at this woman. She was created by a computer from a mix of several races. What you see is a remarkable preview of The New Face of America."

The changes this special issue rings on the citizen-energy crisis of the earlier issue is indicated in the facelift the newer version gives to the faciality of the immigrant cover. Two particular domains of assimilation that have framed immigrant representation in the past are importantly altered here: in the threat and allure of the immigrant's body, and its relation to the ways assimilation is imagined, whether through generational change or the relation of labor and education to citizenship. What will count as full citizenship in the future which is also the now of the new? Whereas the earlier cover depicts multiple living ethnic-faced persons apparently involved with imagining their own future lives in America, the second

cover foregrounds a single, beautiful woman looking directly out of the page, at the reader, who is, in turn, invited to "Take a good look. . . ." The earlier faces were lined—texts of history written on the body; the new face of America reveals only the labor of a faint smile on a generically youthful face. The earlier faces are clearly artificial, standing in for a "wave" of face-types that Americans, in their national anxiety, have difficulty seeing as human; the second image looks like a photograph of an actually existing human being who could come from anywhere, but she is actually a Frankenstein monster composed from other "ethnic" human images, through a process of morphing. The new face of America involves a melding of different faces with the sutures erased and the proportions made perfect; she is a national fantasy from the present representing a post-historical—that is, post-white—future.

The "new face of America," then, has been manifestly individuated and gendered, specified and symbolized in the eight years between *Time*'s special issues. Moreover, the contexts for the immigrant image have also changed in the interval: in the '80's immigrants are public, collective, constructed by the activity of changing nations and subjectivities on the way to becoming American; in the second, the background to the new girl in the polis is merely a phenotypic index, a subject-effect. Behind her is a field of other immigrant faces, barely visible: the matrix of blurry faces, barely intelligible dots, is the dominant image of mass immigrant life in this *Time*, which is dedicated to disaggregating, categorizing, and managing the circulation and value of the contemporary immigrant population. The dots declare the immigrant a weak or faded sign, real only as an abstract racial type rather than as persons distinguished by movement through concrete and abstract spaces of any sort. As they recede behind the face of the future that is also called the "new face of America" in a kind of whirl of temporalizing, the immigrant dots are also already being forgotten.

The new American face also has a body. In the first issue the changing faces sit atop clothed bodies, because these persons are figured as social agents, capable of making history; in the second issue, the bodies are still and naked, hidden demurely behind the screen of the text, but available for erotic fantasy and consumption. This again raises images of the national fetal person, but differently than in its first incarnation. In 1985, the immigrants photographed *in situ* of their transition into the status "foreign national" were fetal-style because they were officially or wishfully caught as persons prior to their incorporation within the American national story: that is, the potential of their unfolding history was indistinguishable from their new identities as potential US citizens. In 1993, the new face of America has the corporeality of a fetus, a body without history, an abstraction that mimes the abstraction of the American promise that retains power *because* it is unlived.

In short, the cover situates American post-history in prelapsarian time. Appropriately, where the first issue describes the "possibility of finding a new love" in the national context as a matter of collectively inhabiting lawful national spaces or "homes," the latter text proclaims, early on, a kind of carnal "love" for the computer-generated cover girl's new face of America.[24]

But what of love's role in the technology of assimilation and nation-building? What is the labor of love, if not to lose sight of the labor of the immigrant in the blinding bright light of patriotic gratitude for the possibility that there will be, if "we" do not slip unawares into multiracial society, an intelligible national future after all? In the previous special issue, the female immigrant fleeing an archaic patriarchal family represented the limits of what immigration could do to alter America: to repeat, the narrative image of the woman in flight from intimate authoritarian structures translates into a figure of and desire for America, not the abject lived-in United States where suffering takes place and survival is decided locally, but abstract America, which foundationally authorizes an elastic language of love and happiness that incorporates and makes claim on any aspiring citizen's intimate desire, as long as the citizen is, in a deep way, "legal." Likewise, in 1993, an image of a sexualized cyborg gendered female explicitly bears the burden of mature and natural national love, which involves representing and effacing the transition the privileged classes of the United States must make to a new logic of national identity and narrative.

But love amounts even to more than this when it comes to revitalizing the national narrative: desiring to read the immigrant like the fetus and the child, whose histories, if the world is "moral," are supposed to unfold from a genetic/ethical kernel or rhizome, *Time* in 1993 installs the future citizen not in a family that has come from somewhere else, but in a couple form begotten by a desire to reproduce in private, that is to say, in a post-political domain of privacy authorized by national culture and law. It further illustrates this future through a series of photographic images, which are organized into a 7x7 square according to visible ethnicities now procreating in the U.S. The principles by which an American ethnic type is determined are very incoherent: "Middle Eastern," "Italian," "African," "Vietnamese," "Anglo-Saxon," "Chinese," "Hispanic." These images are organized on the page following the model of those multiplication squares children use to learn the multiplication tables: within these "reproduction squares" the images are morphed onto each other so that their future American "progeny" might be viewed in what is almost always its newly lightened form (66–67). The nationalist heterosexuality signified by this racial chain is suffused with nostalgia for the feeling of a stable and dominant collective identity: in the now of the American future *Time* sets forth, the loving heart is a closed-off border open only to what intimacy and intercourse produces, and even American strangers cannot enter the intimate national future, except by violence.[25]

Love of the new face embodies three feelings less hopeful than the ones I've been following so far: disappointment in and disavowal of the cultural and economic violence of the present tense; a counterinsurgent rage at what has been called "the new cultural politics of difference"; and an ambition for the nation's future (West 1990). Let me briefly address each of these. First, *Time* reinvents the "new" but not yet achieved or experienced American future in the context of a more conventional engagement with issues of immigrant practice, never hesitating to trot out the same old categories (illegals, immigrant high culture, transformed metropolitan life, etc.) and the same old defensive bromides (de Tocqueville and the *Federalist* papers are the real core of national identity that no immigrant culture can disturb). The ambition of the ex-privileged is to be able to narrate from the present a national scene of activity, accumulation, and reproduction that never becomes unintelligible, unmanageable: the wish of the dream cover is that American racial categories will have to be reinvented as tending toward whiteness or lightness, and whiteness will be reinvented as an ethnic minority (as in the story "III Cheers for the WASPS," which asserts that "Americanization has historically meant WASPification. It is the gift that keeps on giving"; moreover, it is the essence of America's "national character," which is in danger of "slipping into chronic malfunction"[26]).

Time, admitting the bad science of its imaging technologies, nonetheless makes a claim that crossbreeding, in the reproductive sense, will do the work of "melding" or "melting" that diverts energy from subcultural identification to what will be the newly embodied national scene. "For all the talk of cultural separatism," it argues, "the races that make the U.S. are now crossbreeding at unprecedented rates" such that "the huddled masses' have already given way to the muddled masses" (64–65). "Marriage is the main assimilator," says Karen Stephenson, an anthropologist at UCLA. "If you really want to effect change, it's through marriage and child rearing." Finally, "Those who intermarry have perhaps the strongest sense of what it will take to return America to an unhyphenated whole" (65). This ambition about what "the ultimate cultural immersion of interethnic marriage" will do for the nation is an ambition about the natural narrative of the national future (9): the promise of this collective narrative depends on a eugenic program, enacted in the collective performance of private, intimate acts, acts of sex, and everyday childrearing. The American future has nothing to do with vital national world-making activities, nor public life: just technologies of reproduction that are, like all eugenic programs, destructive in their aim.

Of course you wouldn't discover this violent desire in the tone of the special issue, which demonstrates an overarching optimism about the culturally enriching effects of all kinds of reproduction: the intimate private kind, and its opposite, from within the mass mediated public sphere. You will remember that the special issue begins with the morpher's fantasy of

cybersex with the fair lady's face he creates; it ends where "The Global Village Finally Arrives." *Time's* excitement about globality is very specific: if the new national world of America will be embodied in private, the new global world will be public and abstract:

> It would be easy, seeing all this, to say that the world is moving toward the *Raza Cósmica* (Cosmic Race), predicted by the Mexican thinker José Vasconcelos in the '20s—a glorious blend of mongrels and mestizos. It may be more relevant to suppose that more and more of the world may come to resemble Hong Kong, a stateless special economic zone full of expatriates and exiles linked by the lingua franca of English and the global marketplace. (87)

In other words, the melding of races sexually is not a property of the new world order, which *Time* describes as "a wide-open frontier of polyglot terms and post-national trends." This global scene is economic and linguistic, it has no narrative of identity, it is the base of capitalist and cultural expansion that supports the contraction of the intra-national narrative into a space covered over by a humanoid face.

It remains to be asked why this national image of immigration without actual immigrants is marketed now, in the 1990s, and in a way that elides the optimism and anxiety about immigrant assimilation of the previous decade. To partly answer this, one must look at the essay by William A. Henry III, "The Politics of Separation," which summarizes much in his subsequent book *In Defense of Elitism*.[27] This essay blames multiculturalism, political correctness, and identity politics for the national fantasy *Time* promotes in this issue: ". . . one must be pro-feminist, pro-gay rights, pro-minority studies, mistrustful of tradition, scornful of Dead White European Males, and deeply skeptical toward the very idea of a 'masterpiece,'" says Henry (74).

Henry equates the discord of identity politics and its pressures on the terms of cultural literacy and citizenship competence with something like an anti-assimilationist stance that might be taken by immigrants: indeed, he bemoans the ways the dominant narratives that marked competency at citizenship themselves have become "alien," thanks to the allegedly dominant fanatical multiculture that reduces the complexity of culture and power to authoritarian counter-cultural simplicities. As a result, "Patriotism and national pride are at stake," for "in effect, the movements demand that mainstream white Americans aged 35 and over clean out their personal psychic attics of nearly everything they were taught—and still fervently believe—about what made their country great" (75).

Henry's passionately committed essay is not merely cranky. It is also a symptomatic moment in the struggle that motivates the "new Face of America" to be born. This is a culture war over whose race will be the national one for the policy-driven near future, and according to what terms. For example, if whites must be racialized in the new national order, racial identity must be turned into a national family value. If race is to be turned into a national family value, then the non-familial populations, the ones, say, where fathers are more loosely identified with the health of the family form, or affective collectivities not organized around the family, must be removed from the national archive, which is here organized around a future race of cyborgs, or mixed-race but still white-enough children. It is in this sense that the defensive racialization of national culture in this issue is genocidal. It sacrifices the centrality of African-American history to American culture by predicting its demise. It sacrifices attention to the concrete lives of exploited immigrant and native people of color by fantasizing the future as what will happen when white people intermarry, thus linking racial mixing to the continued, but masked, hegemony of whiteness. It tacitly justifies the continued ejection of gays and lesbians and women from full citizenship, and deploys national heterosexuality to suppress the complex racial and class relations of exploitation and violence that have taken on the status of mere clichés—that is, accepted truths or facts of life too entrenched to imagine surpassing—by the panicked readership of *Time*. After all, the entire project of this issue is to teach citizens at the core culture to remain optimistic about the US future, and this requires the "new face" the nation already is becoming not to have a memory.

This epidemic of amnesia was sponsored by the Chrysler corporation, a company sure to benefit from the translation of the immigrant into an image of an immigrant's future racially mixed granddaughter from a nice family in a white American suburb. And it should not be surprising that the "new face of America" generated even more new faces: on the cover of the February 21, 1994, *National Review*, which shows a young African-American child running away from a graffiti mustache he has drawn on the "new face" of *Time*'s cover, accompanied by a story that blasts *Time*'s refusal to engage directly in the class and race war it is romancing away; on the cover of *Mirabella*, in which a picture of a morphed woman and a computer chip makes explicit the desire to love and aspire only to faces that have never existed, unlike one's pitiful own; and in at least two marketing magazines,[28] which were directly inspired by *Time*'s "new face" to think of new ethnic markets in cosmetics, so that "ethnic" women might learn how simultaneously to draw on and erase the lines on their faces that distinguish them as having lived historically in a way that threatens their chances of making it in the new future present of America.

VI. Making Up Nations (4): The New Face of the Old Race

In *Time* we have learned that the experience of the national future will be beautiful, will be administered by families, will involve intimate collective patriotic feelings, and will take place in the domestic private, or in foreign publics, places like Hong Kong or, say, CNN, the contemporary American post-nation. In reinventing the national icon, embodied but only as an abstraction, *Time* delinks its optimism about national culture from the negativity of contemporary public politics: in the abstract here and now of *Time*'s America, the rhetorics of victimhood and minority that identity politics and multiculturalism have deployed are given over to the previously unmarked or privileged sectors of the national population; in the abstract here and now of this America, people at the bottom are considered American only insofar as they identify with and desire the status of the unmarked.

In this light we can better see more motives for official America's embrace of heterosexuality for national culture. For one thing, *Time*'s fantasy logic of a tacitly white or white-ish national genetic system integrated by private acts of consensual sex that lead to reproduction provides a way of naturalizing its separation of especially African-American history and culture from the national future, and thus implicitly supports disinvestment in many contexts of African-American life in the present tense. In making the main established taxonomy of race in the U.S. an archaic formation with respect to the future it is projecting as already here or "new," the issue of *Time* makes core national subjectivity itself racial along the lines of scientific racism through images of what it calls "psychic genes" that mime the genes that splice during reproduction to produce new likenesses.

Second, heterosocial marriage is a model of assimilation like *e pluribus unum*, where sexual and individual "difference" is obscured through an ideology/ ethics of consensual "melding" that involves channelling one's world-making desires and energy into a family institution through which the future of one's personhood is supposed to unfold effortlessly. So too the new face of America, having been bred through virtual sex acts, projects an image of American individuals cross-breeding a new citizenship-form that will ensure the political future of the core national culture. In sum, the nationalist ideology of marriage and the couple is now a central vehicle for the privatization of citizenship: first, via moralized issues around privacy, sex and reproduction that serve as alibis for white racism and patriarchal power; but also in the discourse of a United States that is not an effect of states, institutions, ideologies, and memories, but an effect of the private citizen's acts. The expulsion of embodied public spheres from the national future/ present involves a process I have been describing as an orchestrated politics of nostalgia and sentimentality marketed by the official national culture industry, a politics that perfumes its cruelty in its claim to loathe the culture war it is waging, blaming social divisions in the U.S. on the peoples against whom the war is being conducted.

In itself, there is nothing cruel in using racial morphing to make up fantasy images of a new national identity, especially insofar as the purpose might be to counter the national/global traffic in stereotypes of nationality, race, sexuality, and gender. Indeed, this is what morphing was invented to do, to represent the unintelligibility of the visible body, and thus to subvert the formulaic visual economy of identity forms, which are almost always monuments to the negativity of national power. Yet the morphing technology *Time* uses to make its racial, sexual, economic, and national imaginary appear to be a visible reality is haunted by the process of amnesia/utopia that must accompany the seamlessness of these corporeal transformations. Nowhere is this haunting more manifest than in Michael Jackson's video for the song "Black or White." I say "haunted" because the ghosted forms of the bodies left behind by this mode of racial and sexual futurism are instructively and insistently visible in Jackson's fantasy. The visual scene of the video is at first located in public, collective, and historically-saturated spaces of dance and ends with Jackson's utter solitude: in this translation of space, this video seems to repeat the pattern of privatization I have been describing, which supports disinvesting in cultural, collective forms of personhood while promoting an image of the legitimate, authentic individual situated in the spaces of intimate privacy. Yet the video also disinvests in privatized citizenship, by representing in complicated and powerful ways the world of national, racial, sexual, and class injustice the politics of privacy ejects from the dominant national narrative.

The video is split into two. First, the song "Black or White," during which Jackson shuttles among a frenetic montage of national images. Neither the song's lyrics or its music refers to nationality: this mise en scène is invented for the visual text, which has its own narrative that meets up with, or morphs into, the song's love story in the section's final minutes. The story of the lyric is the story about love that modern sentimentality has long told: traditions of violence between people like us that might keep us apart do exist, but it doesn't matter, I can still love you; all the cruel forces of history could seek to hurt me for being with you and I would still love you. Absent the video, the pop lyric enters just enough into both the racial conflicts of contemporary US life and the self-esteem pedagogies of much pop music, to tell the absent lover that as far as Jackson's concerned, "It doesn't matter if you're black or white": history is "history" and conceivably anyone who wants to can be his "baby" or his "brother."

But the visual story reorganizes the song's emphasis on love's transcendence of the violence of racism, locating itself in the stereotypes and forms of intelligibility that characterize *national* cultures, as though the nation form is racism's opposite and the solution to the problem of "black or white," a racial taxonomy which the visuals reveal as ridiculously oversimple by virtue of the multicultural casting of the national scenes. Each national image Jackson encounters gets its own pseudo-authentic set, and each population is represented by the stereotyped version of itself that saturates the American popular cultural imaginary. National types from Africa, India, from Russia, from the Native American southwest, and from the US inner city dance national dances in open, public spaces, and as Jackson migrates transglobally through these scenes, he dances improvisations on the dances of the other national cultures.

But then every context for a national dance becomes subverted by shots of the video's production apparatus. There is, apparently, nothing authentic about the dances themselves: they are valued *because* they are invented traditions and joyous expressions of a desire for national form, especially for the artificiality of form. Michael Jackson himself wears no stereotyped national costume, although in wearing black pants and white shirts he starkly represents what doesn't "matter" in the song. His decision to sing the chorus "It don't matter if you're black or white" while standing on an artificial image of the Statue of Liberty, however, suggests that his absence of a stereotyped national body *is* his performance of being American. In addition, the US inner city scene is populated by the unmarked adult's symbolic other, a group of infantile citizens: and at a certain point, a black and a white baby in diapers sit atop the globe playing peacefully with a toy that contains and minimizes the hard history the song is telling. Indeed, as though it were advertising *Time*'s desire to eradicate multicultural citizenship politics, the video has the child actor Macaulay Culkin lip-synching, in the voice of an adult, male African-American rapper, the lines: "It's a turf war/on a global scale/I'd rather hear both sides of the tale; it's not about races, just places, faces. . . ."

The final segment of the video's first half takes literally the lyric's assertion "I'm not going to spend my life being a color," by performing through computer morphing technology what the lover would like to perform with his will: the end of racial and gender boundaries. The video moves through the space marked by a series of differently sexed and multiply-raced faces. Their bodies are naked, stripped of the national costume: absent any "cultural" boundaries, the faces happily turn into each other while singing the words "It's black, it's white, yeah, yeah, yeah." Despite the politically-saturated differences of race and gender in their faces, all of them have shining eyes, great hair, and beautiful teeth.

But countering the frenetic glossing of the stereotype with a lyric about a star's refusal to live his intimate life and his public life within the American-style color-scheme, Jackson choreographs another segment, which created such a scandal that Jackson cut it from the video directly after its television premiere on November 14, 1991. It is now available in its complete state in video stores. The uncut video, from Jackson's *Dangerous: The Short Films*, opens with a tabloid-style montage of the sensation the second part of the video created. The scandal was mainly provoked by Jackson's masturbatory self-groping and destruction of property in this scene, which people took to imply an advocacy of these kinds of acts. Jackson issued a public apology that said that he had meant no harm, and that he had not intended to promote either violence or masturbation.

In the suppressed segment, Jackson is alone in a city. There are no other persons there but himself—although it is not clear he *is* himself, for he enters the screen morphed into the body of a black panther—I mean the *Panthern pardus* kind. He enters the inner city scene as the panther, and his body emerges silently out of its body. Although this is part of the "Black and White" video, in this segment there is neither music nor song. There is no language either, but a series of screams, accompanied by dance. There is no happiness or optimism, but rage and destruction of property, property that displays the signs of white American racism by which Jackson, as a citizen, is always surrounded and endangered.

In the past, when Jackson has entered an imitation inner city—notably in the videos for "Beat It," "Thriller," and "The Way You Make Me Feel"—the inner city has been a place where a crumbling environment, a black public sphere, and heterosexual tension are entirely intertwined. The environment of "The Way You Make Me Feel" in particular predicts "Black or White" with its desolate and graffiti-laden surroundings: but the crisis "The Way You Make Me Feel" expresses is sexual. (In its first two lines someone says to Jackson, "You don't know about women. You don't have that kind of knowledge.") But in the suppressed segment of "Black or White" no one can question Jackson's sexual competence—he's a successful masturbator. Instead, the crisis here is racial.

On the walls and on the glass of the inner city he lives in we see the graffiti slogans "Nigger go home"; "No More Wet Backs"; "KKK Rules"; a swastika. Like the protest signs in *The Pelican Brief*, these epithets emanate from diverse sites and address different problems in American life: but if in *The Pelican Brief* slogans and rallies issue from the spaces of subordination, in "Black or White" the fighting words are uttered from the extremes of a contested racial/national privilege greedy for more domination. Screaming and dancing, Jackson breaks the windows that broadcast these messages. Amidst a cascade of sparks bursting in air from the sign of the "Royal Arms Hotel" that collapses from the sheer force of Jackson's rage, he howls a counter-national anthem beyond language and music. At one point he throws a trash can through a big generic storefront window. As when Mookie throws the trash can through the window of Sal's Famous Pizzeria to begin a riot in Spike Lee's *Do the Right Thing* (1989), Jackson's extraordinary violence performs the limit of what his or anyone's eloquence can do to change the routine violence of the core national culture. His act, isolated and symbolic, is almost as much a blow against a politically dissociated cultural studies.

One might say more about the films this segment quotes—*Singin' in the Rain*[29], *Do the Right Thing*, and *Risky Business*[30]. But I want to focus on the dominant

political intertext: the black panther, the animal that is Jackson's technological origin and end. By this single sign he signals the amnesiac optimism or the absolute falseness of the utopian performative "It don't matter if you're black or white."

Most importantly, the eloquent dance Jackson dances in the second segment, which refuses syntactic language in a hailstorm of howling, performs the violence of the traffic in US stereotypes, in order to show that *having an identity in the culture of the stereotype makes a citizen public, makes the citizen definitionally on the streets, not privileged by any privacy protections, constantly in danger*, and thus, here, for a minute, dangerous. In other words, life on the streets in this video reminds us that the fantasy of a private, protected national space is a fantasy only a non-stigmatized person, a privileged person, can realistically imagine living. This is the kind of person who can freely use the waste and stereotype-laden languages of national culture, like jokes, graffiti, and gossip, and who can, without thinking, keep coaxing the stereotype's reference away from the cartoon it should mean, back to the real it does mean, thereby making unsafe the contexts in which the stereotyped peoples live. As the last shot of the video proclaims in large type, "Prejudice is Ignorance."

"Black or White" seems to argue that the stigmatized person cannot use realism to imagine a world that will sustain her/him, for the materials of that world are saturated with a history of ordinary violence, violence so prosaic it would be possible to wield without knowing it, violence that feels like a fact of life. To break the frame of ordinariness, the stigmatized person seems to have two aesthetic choices: spare, howling, formalist minimalism, as in part two; or lush fantasy Diva activity, as in the broad oversimple wishfulness and technologically-supported impossibility of part one.[31]

And yet the processing of US racism in this video goes on. In 1995, Jackson released a greatest hits album of sorts, titled *History*. With it he released a greatest hits video collection, which claims that it includes "Black or White." However, *History* dramatically changes the story this video tells. While the re-released version follows *Dangerous* in returning the Black Panther segment to its rightful place next to

"Black or White," it also sanitizes this segment, but in ways that should not, by now, surprise.

In the expurgated version of the Black Panther portion, all the masturbatory images of Jackson remain. But all the racist graffiti has been cleansed from the scene: no KKK, no "nigger," no swastika, no "wet-back" anywhere. The clip of Jackson captioned by "Prejudice is Ignorance" is also edited out. The destruction of racism by fantasy solutions, refused by the video's first edition, is now completed in the video called *History*: and it requires the self-destruction of Jackson's own text, which has had to further bury its memories through a kind of horrifying mnemoplasty. These memories seem to have been digitally lifted, following the same logic that had Forrest Gump digitally edited into spaces he could not have historically experienced. That is, Jackson continues to revise history, and particularly the history of national racism, by revising what its images tell you about what it takes him to survive in America.

In the re-edited version, Jackson's destruction of property and his howling appear to be solely the expression of his physical and sexual power, frustration, and self-consolation. This shift from racial to sexual corporeality might be explained by the immediate context in which *History* was marketed: accused of sexually abusing children after so long identifying himself with advancing their happiness in the hard world, Jackson attempts to use *History* to make himself appear safe, and in several ways. He includes a brochure with the record that contains images of his abuse as a child, assertions of spiritual and not sexual feelings for children, and testimonials to his rectitude by mainstream American celebrities like Steven Spielberg and Elizabeth Taylor; he also draws attention to his very public heterosexual marriage to Lisa Marie Presley; and in the iconography of the *History* jacket cover, he casts himself as a heroic monument—to children and to "history." Thus in the re-edited version of "Black or White" Jackson attempts to assert conflicting views of himself: his safety to children, his self-contained sexuality, and his virile adult heterosexuality. To do this the signs of history, nationality, transnationality, racism, and the urban black public sphere are sacrificed from the Black Panther segment of "Black and White," remaining

only in their smudged traces in the song's happy lyric: his struggle for citizenship becomes fully sexual, and Jackson now appears animated by a desire for an infinitely expanding zone of privacy.

Imagine what kind of scandal the latter part of "Black or White" would have created were there were dozens or hundreds of angry black men screaming, destroying, dancing, groping. Before the revision, both segments expressed a wish for a public, a collective culture, perhaps a movement culture (of the Black Panther kind): one that supports a world that no longer polices the way one inhabits race, gender, or the isolations of ordinary privatized sexuality. Absent collective struggle, Jackson's own very public and painful relation to sexual anomaly, to racial ambivalence, to animals, and to bodily transformation is everywhere visible. Watching any version of "Black or White," it is impossible not to think of the compulsive self-morphing Jackson's own body has undergone to try to erase his vulnerability to the nationally-supported violence of race, gender, class, and sexuality—at least from his face. We can see the ravages of this violence in their incomplete effacement.

When *Time* magazine deploys the immigrant morph it is not to provide any kind of lens through which the most banal forms of national violence can be viewed and reexperienced painfully. Its essay on the morph takes us back to where we began, in the universe of *Forrest Gump*: the special issue is introduced by the headline "Rebirth of a nation." Can it be an accident that the new face of America is captioned with a citation of D. W. Griffith's racist nationality? (An answer: sure, racist citation can be unconscious or unintentional, that is what makes the simple pun and other cruel and popular forms of dominant cultural privilege so hard to contest.) When the magazine next participates in the logic of the morph, in the summer of 1994, it is to darken the face of O. J. Simpson, accused of killing his wife and a friend of hers. *Time* was saying many things in translating Simpson into darker hues: not only had the celebrity allegedly killed two people, but he had seemed to do it while passing as someone who had transcended his "origin," a word used broadly in the Simpson literature to denote poverty while screaming "race." Even now, passing is a crime against white people's desire to dominate race through fantasy scenes and fixed definitions. Simpson had seemed successfully to morph himself, but his arrest and the revelations of battery and drug use that quickly followed peeled away the new face to reveal a "darker" kid from the ghetto who was inassimilable to the "lighter" game face he used in his cross-over career.[32]

When a human morphs himself without a computer, through ambition or plastic surgery or assimilation to a putatively normal lifestyle or, say, through interracial marriage to a more racially and class-privileged person, that identification and that passing makes him more likely to be a member of the core national culture, according to the logic of normalization I have been describing. But when his passing up the hierarchy of value fails and falls into a narrative about the real trauma in which visible order is actually a screen over terrible misrule, he unsettles the visual discipline of the American identity form that makes white people feel comfortable, and thus fouls the space of abstract personhood, ostensibly the American ethical space. In Simpson, racial and class morphing comes to look like an abuse of the national privilege to be abstract, tacit, entitled, normal: or this is the view of *Time*, whose "optimistic" desire for the new face of America to create a post-historical future in which all acts take place in a private space of loving citizen discipline attempts and fails to screen out an ongoing race and class struggle of unbeautiful proportions; a sex war of outrageous exhibition; a global conflict about the ethics of labor and ideologies of freedom; and a political public sphere where adult citizens identify powerfully with living in the complex, jagged edges of a terrible and terribly national present tense.

Coda: A Scar across the Face of America

"There is a terrible scar across the face of America the beautiful," said Pat Buchanan in 1992, as he ran for President of the United States.[33] The scarred face to which Buchanan refers seems unrelated to the hypothetical forms—fetal, normal, cyborg—around which so much fantasy of a revived American way of life is now being invested. It is nothing like the face of America that *Time* produced, a prosthetic image

of a hopeful national future. It is nothing like the body of *Forrest Gump*, which transcends national trauma to produce beautiful children. And it is nothing like Michael Jackson's computer-generated (re)vision of a national body liberated from humiliation, strangeness, violence, and history. It is more like *Time*'s representation of the darkened face of O. J. Simpson, which is the current model moral image of what a damaged and veiled social subjectivity looks like, a once-beautiful thing whose degeneracy registers on the surface as a distortion, an eruption, a gash, or a scar, a brutal and unforgettable historicity that the body registers externally and eternally. Buchanan never represents what the face of America looked like before it was scarred; it was just beautiful, a luminous abstract image of the righteous body politic. It is as though the scar itself makes the face concrete, human, fallen, and representable. In any case, he argues, the once iconic face of American beauty has been scarred, and "terribly"—by "1.5 million abortions per year."

To Buchanan and many anti-abortion rhetoricians, the devastating violence of 1.5 million abortions per year by women in the United States destroys the natural beauty of America, a space which has nothing to do with anything remotely ecological. Instead, the beauty to which the presidential candidate alludes is an abstraction for a natural way of life that is also a specific version of American national culture. These days, identification with this natural, national way of life is cast as part of a holy nation-building project by much of the secular and religious right—in considerable pro-life material, and also in the three volumes of the Republican and Christian *Contract with America*.[34] In the image archives of these reactionary movements, the aborting or improperly sexual person is not only self-destructive, but destructive of nature, culture, and spirit as well. In Buchanan's rhetoric, the uterus is displaced to the unmarked face, and the abortion is a visible self-mutilation: this horrible image supports an allegory of wasted life, a wasted way of life, and a culture of degenerate citizenship in a declining nation.

As we have seen, one embodiment strategy of both the religious and the secular right, which has been adopted more fuzzily by the dominant media, is to produce a revitalized image of a future United States from the genetic material of what was dominant, and then to build a new national public sphere around this past/future image of the good life in the U.S. The pre-political child and other infantile and incipient citizens have become so important to public sphere politics partly because the image of futurity they convey helps to fend off more complex and troubling issues of equity and violence in the present. The recent book *Alien Nation* demonstrates this process, when the author, Peter Brimelow, explains his desire to bring into being a white, post-immigrant America: "My son, Alexander, is a white male with blue eyes and blond hair. He has never discriminated against anyone in his little life. . . . But public policy now discriminates against him" in favor of the " 'protected classes' that are now politically favored, such as Hispanics," a population he sees lamentably expanding, pushing his innocent son to the margins from his rightful place in the center (11, 274). Yet while inciting racialist and nationalist panic in the present through images of white pain in the future, national sentimentalists like Brimelow claim that their politics are superior to politics as usual. Driven by ethical and spiritual commitments to natural justice, common sense, and a generic good, long, intimate life, they promote a mode of being they think is at once sacred, ahistorical, and national.

The fantasy of an American dream is an important one to learn from. It has long been the public form of private history: it promises that if you invest your world-building energies in work and making a family, the nation will take care of the social and economic conditions in which this labor will allow you to live out your life with dignity. Yet this promise, which links personal lives to capitalist subjectivity and the cultural forms of national life, sets the stage for imagining a national people unmarked by public history. The fear of being saturated and scarred by the complexities of the present produces the kinds of vicious symbolic, optimistic, and banal politics I have been describing, a politics brimming over with images and faces.

One response to these politics among progressive writers has been to represent or put "faces" on members of the "protected classes" too, so that those

with prerogative in the formerly unmarked populations, those white, financially fixed, or heterosexually-identified people, for example, might recognize that people unlike them are humans worth full citizenship after all. Books in the important tradition of Studs Terkel's *Working*, Faye Ginsburg's *Contested Lives*, or Marilyn Davis's *Mexican Voices/American Dreams* might indeed teach the persons who read them to break with their own xenophobia, misogyny, racism, sex bigotry, or aversion to the relatively and absolutely poor. Likewise, every time someone who has suffered makes the pilgrimage to Washington to testify before Congress about the hard effects of the law, it is surely possible that someone else might see it and imagine millions of people so testifying in a way that changes the kinds of nationally-sanctioned prejudice and harm they are willing to support. But the nation has witnessed Anita Hill, and many others, testifying without making an irrevocable difference that counts: one person, one image, one face can only symbolize (but never meet) the need for the radical transformation of national culture, whose sanitary self-conception these days seems to require a constant cleansing of the non-normal populations—immigrant, gay, sexually non-conjugal, poor, Hispanic, African-American—from the fantasy scene of private, protected, and sanctified "American" life.

The changes that would make such testimony central to an undefensive democratic culture in the U.S. can only be effected in collective and public ways: not simply by changing your feelings about something to which you used to be averse. To effect such a transformation requires sustained, long-term, collaborative, multiply-mediated agitation against the narrow, privatized version of the American way of life everywhere: in the political public sphere, in the courts, in the middlebrow media, at work, in the labor of living everyday, in all the avant-gardes, sub-cultures, and normal spaces we can imagine. This means not killing off the family or intimacy, but inventing new scenes of sociality that take the pressure off of the family form to organize history for everything from individuals to national cultures. Only by taking the risk to make demands that will render people vulnerable (first, to changing their minds) will it be possible to make the culture here called "national" adequate to any of the things for which it ought to stand in this current state of emergency.

Notes

* Much thanks to Arjun Appadurai, Carol Breckenridge, Cary Nelson, and Candace Vogler for goading me on to do this competently; and to Roger Rouse for his archival help, vast knowledge, intensive debate, and heroic labor of reading.

1. Walter Benjamin, "Theses on the Philosophy of History," *Illuminations* (1969), 257.

2. See Michel Foucault, "Governmentality," in Graham Burchell (1991). esp. 100–104. Foucault argues that modern states substitute a relatively decentered economic model of population control for the familial model of the sovereign, pre-Enlightenment state, and at the same time become obsessed with maintaining intimacy and continuity with its governed populations, an obsession that results in a fetishism of the kinds of knowledge and feeling that support the security of the state. Thus the intimate identity form of national fantasy accompanies the increasing segmentation and dispersal of state force, violence, and capital.

3. The literature on the "culture wars" is extensive. Inspiration for the conservative war to make a core national culture continues to be derived from Allan Bloom (1987); its current figurehead is former Secretary of Education, Chairman of the National Endowment for the Humanities, and director of the Office of National Drug Control Policy, William J. Bennett. See Bennett (1992) and (1988), particularly the chapters "The Family as Teacher," 61–68; "Public Education and Moral Education," 69–76; and the section "In Defense of the West," 191–218. Some samples of the anti-core culture side of the struggle (mainly over the content of educational curricula and youth culture entertainment) are: Richard Bolton, ed. (1992); Henry Louis Gates (1992); Gerald Graff (1992); and Russell Jacoby (1994).

4. It is in this sense that this essay takes up the spirit of Ian Hacking's "Making up People," with its arguments about the mutual and dialectical constructedness of categories of identity and kinds of subjectivity, seeing nation-formation here as an institution of subjectification whose purpose is to install as a fact of life the verity of its own practice, and whose generation of *itself* as an area must always be a facet of understanding the motive force of its practice (Ian Hacking, 1986). See also Fredric Jameson (1988).

5. The literature on race, gender, migration, state formation, and transnational capital is extensive: for a start,

see Teresa L. Amott and Julie A. Matthaei (1991); Lena Dominelli (1991); Paul Gilroy (1987); Saskia Sassen (1988).

6. Newt Gingrich has recently claimed Republicans who oppose gays are "not representative of the future," and the GOP is open to homosexuals "in broad agreement with our effort to renew American civilization." This concession to queer American nationality is amazing. However, in the context of the radical right revitalization of the family as the nest for the future of national identity, it is clear that Gingrich has assimilated homosexuality to the project of reprivatizing sexual property in the person. See Gannett News Service wire report, "Gingrich: GOP must include Gays," (23 November, 1994).

7. A most succinct analysis of the violent state- and capital-prompted disinvestment in the city and the national poor can be found in a two-part essay by Mike Davis (1993). In addition, see the important anthology edited by Robert Gooding-Williams (1993), especially Ruth Wilson Gilmore, "Terror Austerity Race Gender Excess Theater"; Cedric J. Robinson, "Race, Capitalism and the Antidemocracy"; Rhonda M. Williams, "Accumulation as Evisceration: Urban Rebellion and the New Growth Dynamics"; Michael Omi and Howard Winant, "The Los Angeles 'Race Riot' and Contemporary U.S. Politics"; Meivin L. Oliver, James H. Johnson, Jr., and Walter C. Farrell, Jr., "Anatomy of a Rebellion: A Political-Economic Analysis"; *Covert Action Information Bulletin*, "An Interview with Mike Davis"; Thomas L. Dumm, "The New Enclosures: Racism in the Normalized Community"; and Elaine H. Kim, "Home is Where the *Han* Is: A Korean-American Perspective on the Los Angeles Upheavals."

8. Concepts of the protesting mass as a "mob" have even taken on Mafia-tones since the Supreme Court, at Clinton's behest, allowed RICO anti-mob statutes to be used against nonviolent pro-life protesters. See National Organization for Women Inc., et al. v. Joseph Scheidler, et al., 114 S.CT. 798. For discussions of the Court's decision to link organized protest to racketeering, see *The Connecticut Law Tribune* (12 June, 1995) and the *Chicago Daily Law Bulletin*, (7 February, 1995 and 25 July, 1995).

9. An apparent counter-example to the claim that public popular political activity has become a demonized and dominant form of containment for radical politics might be found in the *Washington Post* critique of *The New York Times* coverage of the 1994 Gay, Lesbian, and Bi-Sexual March on Washington, which, according to the *Post*, went out of its way to clean up the parade and edit out its powerfully sexual performances. But,

as often, the inversion into the opposite reinforces the Law: Queer complexity must be suppressed. See Howard Kurtz (1993).

10. This list of synonyms for "normal" is brought to you by the thesaurus of WordPerfect 5.1.

11. In a long commercially-sold preview for the film of *Forrest Gump*, titled *Through the Eyes of Forrest Gump*, director Robert Zemeckis and actor Tom Hanks very clearly state their desire to write the history of the recent U.S. in a post/pre-political vein of cultural memory (the screenplay was actually written by Eric Roth). Zemeckis says that "Forrest is a metaphor in the movie for a lot of what is constant and decent and good about America," and quite self-consciously goes on to show the film emerging from a revulsion at the culture of negativity that begins to mark the political public sphere in the sixties. Take what happens to Vietnam in *Forrest Gump*, for example. From the pilgrimage to Washington material we know that the director could have placed Hanks/Gump in newsreel footage from Vietnam. But in *Through the Eyes of Forrest Gump* Hanks says, "We wanted to capture the reality without playing the same images that we've seen over and over again. And what we don't want to do is make that be yet another editorial comment on how bad a place it was or why. It just was." Significantly, *Through the Eyes of Forrest Gump* shows an alternative take to Gump's speech at the anti-war March on Washington the film represents. In the unreleased version of the scene, Gump says "There's only one thing I can tell you about the war in Vietnam. In Vietnam your best good friend can get shot. That's all I have to say about that." This speech verbalizes the event from the novel: upset from thinking about his dead friend Bubba Blue, Forrest "heaves" his Congressional Medal of Honor at the crowd "as hard as he can" (Winston Groom, *Forrest Gump* [1986, 113]). In contrast, in the released film, Gump's speech against the war is silenced by a "pig" who sabotages his microphone: the one moment when Forrest's "virtue" might come into critical contact with the nation is deliberately expurgated by Zemeckis.

12. For a precise insider explanation of the technologies of corporeal transformation in the film of *Forrest Gump*, see Janine Pourroy (1994). Thanks much to Julian Bleeker for sending this to me.

13. See the chapter "*Ronald Reagan*, the Movie," in Rogin (1987). For another scene of infantile national politics that is a clear precedent both for Reagan and for *Forrest Gump*, see *Being There*. The novel is by Jerzy Kosinski (1970); the film was directed by Hal Ashby (1979).

14. While generally the novel of *Forrest Gump* is not nearly as reactionary as the film, it does predict the film's dismay at public political life. The novel represents the March against the War in Vietnam as "the most frightening thing I have seen since we was back at the rice paddy where Bubba was kilt" (78), and also describes a mass political movement for which Forrest is the political inspiration, called the "I Got To Pee" movement (Winston Groom [1986], 236).

15. Many examples of ridiculed protest representations against the left and the right abound at the present moment. Episodes from more liberal shows like *Roseanne*, *The Simpsons*, and *Murphy Brown*, for example, mock right-wing protest as the acts of yahoos. Cinematic instances tend to be more conservative and confused. A film less ambitious than the *Pelican Brief* and *Forrest Gump* reveals the sheer ordinariness of protest's debasement: *PCU* (dir. Hart Bochner; 1994), for example, looks at the plague of "cause-ism" on contemporary college campuses, and after much sarcastic and hyperbolic cataloguing of political activism by African-Americans, Gays and Lesbians, Vegetarians, Eco-radicals, and so on, the campus comes together in the end under the rubric "Americans," chanting "We won't protest! We won't protest!" The film *SFW* (dir. Jefery Levy, 1995) plays on three kinds of debased anti-normative social movement activity: a "terrorist" group, "Split Image," whose politics is never defined, takes over a convenience store and, in exchange for not killing its youthful hostages, puts them on national television for 36 days, where the nation learns to heroize them. Next, a political movement sweeps the mass-mediated country, inspired by the courage of the captives, especially the surviving ones, the working class Cliff Babb (Steven Dorff) and upper-crust Wendy Pfister (Reese Witherspoon). The movement's slogan is "SFW," for "So Fucking What!" Babb is at first alienated by the shallowness of this movement, but as his face and fame spread across television and the covers of many national magazines, and he comes to identify with his message, which is "that there is no message." Finally, Babb and Pfister are shot by a disgruntled leftist, "Babs" Wyler, whose slogan is "Everything Matters!" and who is very politically correct in the liberal way. The movie ends with Wyler becoming the national youth heroine of the moment; at the same "moment," the two stars agree to get married, and the movie ends. For yet a different set of contradictions, see the demonstration that introduces us to the fictional "Columbus College" in John Singleton's *Higher Learning* (1995). Starting with a shot of a crowd chanting "Fight! Fight! Fight!" and pointing their fists in the air, the film obscures whether this is a

sports event or a political rally. The person who leads the rally, standing in front of a large American flag that provides the backdrop for the extremely political events to follow, then asks the cheering crowd two questions: "How many people came here to change the world?" and "How many people came here to learn to make a lot of money?" The last shot of the film is the silent stark caption "Unlearn."

16. Archive: the 1970 ABC documentary on "women's liberation" (from the series *Now*); the 1993 25th Anniversary Special commemorating "1968" (Fox, 1993); footage from CNN throughout the 1980's; footage from Chicago television news broadcasts during the 1990's. For an impressive, if overoptimistic, general history of recent protest in the U.S. and police brutality during it, see Terry H. Anderson (1995).

17. In the contemporary US public sphere, the rhetoric of the "face" flourishes in discourses of social justice: currently issues of welfare, AIDS, wife abuse, crime, racism, violence, war, and sexuality invoke this logic. Its function is a classically sentimental one, an attempt to solicit mass sympathy for or commitment to difficult social changes via a logic of personal identification. Some examples, culled from many: on welfare, Jennifer Wolff (text) and Kristine Larsen (photo essay) (1995); Rachel Wildavsky and Daniel R. Levine (1995); on AIDS, Bettijane Levine (1995); Lisa Frazier (1995); Douglas Crimp (1992); and Stuart Marshall's video *Bright Eyes* (1984); on wife beating, Rheta Grimsley Johnson (1995); on race, Peter Watrous (1995) and Gilbert Price; on war, Catharine Reeve (1995); on the death penalty, Linnet Myers (1995).

Yet, as Gilles Deleuze and Félix Guattari argue, "Faces are not basically individual; they define zones of frequency or probability, delimit a field that neutralizes in advance any expressions of connections amenable to the appropriate significations." The face, in their view, is not evidence of the human, but a machine for producing tests for humanness at its limits. Likewise, this trend in the public sphere to put "faces" on social problems has the paradoxical effect of making the faces generic and not individual: thus the facializing gesture that promotes identification across the spaces of alterity is, in effect, an equivocal challenge to shift the political and cultural boundaries of what will count politically as human. Gilles Deleuze and Félix Guattari, "Year Zero: Faciality," in *A Thousand Plateaus: Capitalism and Schizophrenia* (1987, 168, 167–91).

18. See, for example, *Chicago Sun-Times* (28 August, 1993): 3 and (29 August, 1993): 3; *Cleveland Plain Dealer*

(29 August, 1993): sec. A:1; *The Los Angeles Times* (29 August, 1993): sec A: 1; *New York Times* (29 August, 1993): sec. 1:18; *The Washington Post* (29 August, 1993): 1.

19. *Gabriel Over the White House* comes from an anonymous novel of 1925, which reads American society as currently in a depression-style crisis mainly for the unemployed "forgotten men" who fought for the U.S. during World War I but reaped little prosperity from that sacrifice. The film of it takes bizarre twists. The President, an appetite-driven, politics-as-usual politician for the élite, drives too fast and dies in a car crash: but God, via the angel Gabriel, brings him back to life as an "ethical" person, in order to complete a short mission: the eradication of organized crime from the United States. To do this, he not only initiates a populist war on poverty by fiat but proclaims martial law, suspending the Constitution and all civil rights.

20. For the concept and the recent history of remasculinization, see Susan Jeffords (1989).

21. *Time* Magazine (8 July, 1985): 24, 36.

22. There continues to be a vociferous debate on the right as to whether the benefit the United States might receive from immigrant "blood" is not less than the cost their practices and histories pose to the maintenance of normal national culture. See, for example, Peter Brimelow (1995); the issue of *National Review* titled "Demystifying Multiculturalism," (21 February, 1994); and William F. Buckley and John O'Sullivan, "Why Kemp and Bennett are Wrong on Immigration" (1994), 36–45, 76, 78.

23. *Time*, Special Issue (Fall 1993), vol. 142, no. 21:5.

24. *Time* (8 July, 1985): 100; *Time* (Fall 1993): 3.

25. *Time*'s impulse to taxonomize and therefore to make firmer borders around racial types in the U.S. prior to their "melding" was evident in many places in the early 1990's: another parallel example of the graphic unconscious is in the *Newsweek* cover story responding carefully to Richard Herrnstein and Charles Murray's reinvigoration of scientific racism in *The Bell Curve*, titled "What Color is Black?" and illustrated by a 4x5 square of differently-shaded African American faces. As though randomly related, the three faces on the upper right hand corner are partly obscured by a yellow slash that reads "Bailing Out Mexico." *Newsweek* (13 February, 1995).

26. *Time*, Special Issue (Fall 1993): 79.

27. See also Henry's (1990) much less extreme prophecy of xenophobia to come.

28. See *Cosmetics and Toiletries*, vol. 109, no. 2:75; *Ethnic Marketing* (18 January, 1993): 11.

29. On *Singin' in the Rain* and "Black or White," see Carol Clover (1995).

30. "Black or White" cites *Risky Business* (dir. Paul Brickman, 1983) in its frame narrative, which is also a part of the recorded song. In this scene, Macaulay Culkin gyrates and plays air guitar in his bedroom, like Tom Cruise in *Risky Business*, to libidinously pulsating rock and roll. Berated by his father (George Wendt) for playing the music too loud, Culkin retaliates with an electric guitar blast so loud that his father explodes, still in his armchair, out of his house and to the other side of the world (Africa). The phrase Culkin uses as he blasts his father is "Eat this." Culkin's body is thus deployed here to link white, male pubescent rock and roll excess to masturbation, awakening masculine heterosexuality, Oedipal rage, generational identity, commodity attachment, and a desire to inhabit the publics in which he *feels* himself at his happiest.

31. These two aesthetic horizons of possibility for a nationally minor literature are predicted by Gilles Deleuze and Félix Guattari (1990).

32. A few weeks later, (18 July, 1994) *Time* no doubt unconsciously returned to the theme of racial/class passing in its cover story on "attention deficit disorder": it is illustrated by a caricature that looks uncannily like O.J.'s distorted icon, now the poster face both for distorted subjectivity and white despair over the alterity of darker faces.

33. Associated Press release, "Buchanan courts Michigan Baptists," *Chicago Sun-Times* (16 March, 1992): 14.

34. *Contract with America: The Bold Plan by Rep. Newt Gingrich, Rep. Dick Armey, and the House Republicans to Change the Nation*, ed. Ed Gillespie and Bob Schellhass (New York: Times Books, 1994); *Restoring the Dream: The Bold New Plan by House Republicans*, ed. Stephen Moore (New York: Times Books, 1995); *Contract with the American Family: A Bold Plan by the Christian Coalition to Strengthen the Family and Restore Common-Sense Values* (Nashville: Moorings, 1995).

References

Amott, Teresa L. and Julie A. Matthaei (1991) *Race, Gender, and Work: A Multicultural History of Women in the United States*. Boston: South End Press.

Anderson, Terry H. (1995) *The Movement and the Sixties: Protest in America from Greensboro to Wounded Knee*. New York: Oxford U.P.

Barthes, Roland (1981) *Camera Lucida*. New York: Hill and Wang.

Benjamin, Walter (1969) "Theses on the Philosophy of History." In *Illuminations*. Trans. H. Arendt. New York: Shocken Books.

Bennett, William J. (1992) *The De-Valuing of America: The Fight for Our Culture and Our Children*. New York: Simon and Schuster.

——— (1988) *Our Children and Our Country: Improving America's Schools and Affirming Our Common Culture*. New York: Simon and Schuster.

Berlant, Lauren (1995) " '68: or, the Revolution of Little Queers." In Diane Elam and Robyn Wiegman (eds) *Feminism Beside Itself*. New York: Routledge.

——— (1994) "America, 'Fat,' the Fetus." *boundary 2* (21)3, pp. 145–195.

——— (1993) "The Theory of Infantile Citizenship." *Public Culture* (5)3, pp. 395–410.

Bloom, Allan (1987) *The Closing of the American Mind*. New York: Simon and Schuster.

Bolton, Richard (ed) (1992) *Culture Wars: Documents from the Recent Controversies in the Arts*. New York: New Press.

Brimelow, Peter (1995) *Alien Nation: Common Sense About America's Immigration Disaster*. New York: Random House.

Buckley, William F. and John O'Sullivan (1994) "Why Kemp and Bennett are Wrong on Immigration." *National Review*, 21 Nov., pp. 36–45; 76; 78.

Clover, Carol (1995) "Dancin' in the Rain." *Critical Inquiry* 21, pp. 722–747.

Contract With the American Family: A Bold Plan by the Christian Coalition to Strengthen the Family and Restore Common Sense Values. (1995) Nashville: Mooring.

Coontz, Stephanie (1992) *The Way We Never Were: American Families and the Nostalgia Trap*. New York: Basic Books.

Covert Action Information Bulletin (1993) "An Interview With Mike Davis." In *Reading Rodney King/Reading Urban Uprising*. Ed. R. Gooding-Williams. New York: Routledge.

Crimp, Douglas (1992) "Portraits of People with AIDS." In Grossberg, Lawrence, Cary Nelson and Paula Treichler, Eds. *Cultural Studies*. New York: Routledge.

Davis, Marilyn (1990) *Mexican Voices/American Dreams: An Oral History of Mexican Immigration to the United States*. New York: Henry Holt.

Davis, Mike. (1993a) "Who Killed LA? A Political Autopsy." *New Left Review* 197: 3–28.

——— (1993b) "Who Killed Los Angeles? Part Two: The Verdict is Given." *New Left Review* 199: 29–54.

Deleuze, Gilles and Félix Guattari (1990) "What is a Minor Literature?" In Russell Ferguson, Martha Gever, Trinh T. Min-ha, and Cornel West, Eds. *Out There: Marginalization and Contemporary Cultures*. Cambridge: MIT Press.

——— (1987) "Year Zero: Faciality." In *A Thousand Plateaus: Capitalism and Schizophrenia*. Trans. Brian Massumi. Minnesota: University of Minnesota Press.

Dominelli, Lena (1991) *Women Across Continents: Feminist Comparative Social Policy.* New York: Harvester.

Dumm, Thomas L. (1993) "The New Enclosures: Racism in the Normalized Community." In *Reading Rodney King/Reading Urban Uprising,* Ed. R. Gooding-Williams. New York: Routledge.

Foucault, Michel (1991) "Governmentality." In G. Burchell, C. Gordon, and P. Miller, eds. *The Foucault Effect: Studies in Governmentality.* Chicago: University of Chicago Press.

Frazier, Lisa (1995) "The Face of AIDS is Changing." *Times-Picayune* (8 March): B:1.

Gates, Henry Louis (1992) *Loose Canons: Notes on the Culture Wars.* New York: Oxford University Press.

Gillespie, Ed and Bob Schellhass, Eds. (1994) *Contract With America: The Bold Plan by Rep. Newt Gingrich, Rep. Dick Armey, and the House Republicans to Change the Nation.* New York: Times Books.

Gilmore, Ruth Wilson (1993) "Terror Austerity Race Gender Excess Theater." In *Reading Rodney King/Reading Urban Uprising,* Ed. R. Gooding-Williams. New York: Routledge

Gilroy, Paul (1987) *There Ain't No Black in the Union Jack.* London: Hutchinson.

Ginsburg, Faye D. (1989) *Contested Lives: The Abortion Debate in an American Community.* Berkeley: University of California Press.

Gooding-Williams, Robert, Ed. (1993) *Reading Rodney King/Reading Urban Uprising.* New York: Routledge.

Graff, Gerald (1992) *Beyond the Culture Wars: How Teaching the Conflicts Can Revitalize American Education.* New York: Norton.

Grisham, John (1992) *The Pelican Brief.* New York: Dell.

Groom, Winston (1986) *Forrest Gump.* New York: Pocket Books.

Hacking, Ian (1986) "Making Up People." In T.C. Heller et al., Eds. *Reconstructing Individualism: Autonomy, Individuality, and the Self in Western Thought.* Stanford: Stanford University Press.

Henry III, William A. (1994) *In Defense of Elitism.* New York: Doubleday.

—— (1990) "America's Changing Colors." *Time* (9 April): 28–31.

Jameson, Fredric (1988) "Imaginary and Symbolic in Lacan." In *The Ideologies of Theory: Essays 1971–1986.* Vol. 1. Minneapolis: University of Minnesota Press.

Jacoby, Russell (1994) *Dogmatic Wisdom: How the Culture Wars Divert Education and Distract America.* New York: Doubleday.

Jeffords, Susan (1989) *The Remasculinization of America: Gender and the Vietnam War.* Bloomington: Indiana University Press.

Johnson, Rheta Grimsley (1995) "Nicole Has Given Wife Abuse a Face." *Atlanta Constitution* (15 May): C:1.

Kim, Elaine H. (1993) "Home Is Where the *Han* Is: A Korean Perspective on the Los Angeles Upheavals." In *Reading Rodney King/Reading Urban Uprising,* Ed. R. Gooding-Williams. New York: Routledge.

Kosinski, Jerzy (1970) *Being There.* New York: Harcourt, Brace, Jovanovich.

Kurtz, Howard (1993) "Don't Read All About It! What We Didn't Say About the Gay March—And Why." *Washington Post* (9 May): C:1.

Levine, Bettijane (1995) "The Changing Face of AIDS." *Los Angeles Times* (16 June): E:1.

Matsuda, Mari J., Charles R. Lawrence III, Richard Delgado, and Kimberlé Williams Crenshaw (1993) *Words That Wound: Critical Race Theory, Assaultive Speech, and the First Amendment.* Boulder CO: Westview Press.

Moore, Stephen (ed) (1995) *Restoring the Dream: The Bold New Plan by House Republicans.* New York: Times Books.

Myers, Linnet (1995) "Girl Puts Human Face on Death Penalty Debate." *Chicago Tribune* (5 February): 1:3.

Oliver, Melvin L., James H. Johnson, Jr. and Walter C. Farrell, Jr. (1993) "Anatomy of a Rebellion: A Political-Economic Analysis." In *Reading Rodney King/Reading Urban Uprising,* Ed. R. Gooding-Williams. New York: Routledge.

Omi, Michael and Howard Winant (1993) "The Los Angeles 'Race Riot' and Contemporary U.S. Politics." In *Reading Rodney King/Reading Urban Uprising,* Ed. R. Gooding-Williams. New York: Routledge.

Pourroy, Janine (1994) "Making Gump Happen." *Cinefex* #60: 90–106.

Price, Gilbert (1994) "Conservatism: A New Face." *Call and Post:* A:4.

Reeve, Catharine (1995) "The Face of War." *Chicago Tribune* (7 May): 6:3.

Robinson, Cedric J. (1993) "Race, Capitalism, and the Antidemocracy." In *Reading Rodney King/Reading Urban Uprising,* Ed. R. Gooding-Williams. New York: Routledge.

Rogin, Michael Paul (1987) *Ronald Reagan, The Movie: and Other Episodes in Political Demonology.* Berkeley: University of California Press.

Sassen, Saskia (1988) *The Mobility of Capital and Labor.* Cambridge: Cambridge University Press.

Terkel, Studs (1974) *Working: People Talk About What They Do All Day and How They Feel About What They Do.* New York: Pantheon.

Warner, Michael (1992) "The Mass Public and the Mass Subject." In C. Calhoun, Ed. *Habermas and the Public Sphere.* Cambridge: MIT Press.

Watrous, Peter (1995) "The loss of a star [Selena] who put a face on a people's hopes." *New York Times* (4 April): C:15.

West, Cornel (1990) "The New Cultural Politics of Difference." In Russell Ferguson, Martha Gever, Trinh T. Min-ha, and Cornel West, Eds. *Out There: Marginalization and Contemporary Cultures.* Cambridge: MIT Press.

Wildavsky, Rachel and David R. Levine (1995) "True Faces of Welfare." *Reader's Digest* (March): 49–60.

Williams, Rhonda M. (1993) "Accumulation as Evisceration: Urban Rebellion and the New Growth Dynamics." In *Reading Rodney King/Reading Urban Uprising*, Ed. R. Gooding-Williams. New York: Routledge.

Wolff, Jennifer (text) and Kristine Larsen (photo essay) (1995) "The Real Faces of Welfare." *Glamour* (September): 250–53.

34.
BURYING DON IMUS [SELECTIONS]
Michael Awkward

"What Evil Look Like"

For at least two weeks during April 2007, national attention was focused squarely on the question of what constituted appropriate punishment for John Donald Imus, who had used what was widely considered unforgivably racist and sexist language on his nationally syndicated radio program that was simulcast on MS-NBC. The wizened, perpetually impatient, and generally well-informed Imus has long been renowned for his cynicism, ribald wit, and the frequently crude, offensive, and self-absorbed jabs that he aimed at all sorts of figures who came within his sights, including his employers and employees, his wife, and his guests, who were, in the main, politicians, journalists, and book authors. He has used these traits to forge what has been, according to virtually any imaginable measure, a truly fascinating broadcasting career.

That career, spanning almost four decades, was propelled by his anti-authoritarian streak; biting, and at times mean-spirited, sense of humor; rapacious curiosity; and an impulse toward self-destructiveness that had led to his previously being fired during stints in New York, California, and Ohio, as well as to his energetic postmidlife pursuit of lasting moral, marital, and spiritual self-improvement. In the case of the nappy-headed hos incident, according to the most sympathetic commentators, the self-destructive streak of the phenomenally influential Imus, an originator of what came to be known as the "shock jock" formula who, in his more socially responsible late-life

manifestations, has swayed public opinion about presidential elections, autism research, and the medical treatment received by disabled soldiers returning to the United States from Iraq, had not so much resurfaced in his comments about the Rutgers women's basketball team as temporarily, but almost fatally, to have trumped his better nature.

During the first (six a.m. EST) hour of his show on April 4, as part of a skit for which the host ultimately proved grievously unprepared, Imus was speaking with the show's producer, Bernard McGuirk, who was also a major contributor to its comedic banter on political, cultural, social, athletic, and media topics. McGuirk commented on what he perceived as the "rough" appearance of the Rutgers team, whose improbable postseason run (widely reported in the northern New Jersey and greater New York City areas from which the show emanated) had ended the previous night with a resounding defeat in the NCAA championship game at the hands of a perennial powerhouse, the Lady Volunteers of the University of Tennessee. In response, Imus uttered the now-infamous line: "That's some nappy-headed hos."[1]

At the time, I was teaching a graduate course on contemporary black American novels at the University of Michigan. The works the class explored engage the psychological consequences of the systematic exploitation of blacks during slavery, Reconstruction, and Jim Crow, torturous epochs that constitute the bulk of our experiences in the world's self-described model democracy. Some of the class's most illuminating conversations were stimulated by Charles Johnson's *Oxherding Tale,* an irreverent, deeply philosophical rewriting of the genre of the slave narrative best represented by *Narrative of the Life of Frederick Douglass*; Edwin Jones's Pulitzer Prize–winning *The Known World,* which depicts the psychic consequences of black slave ownership in ways that challenge our understandings of race and America's peculiar institution; and the Nobel Prize laureate Toni Morrison's *Beloved,* an exquisitely crafted exploration of how traumatic events haunt survivors of slavery struggling to accommodate themselves to their barely manageable, almost unimaginable pain.

The text that perhaps best addresses the most abiding concern of the black American literary novel after the 1960s—slavery's impact on generations of its descendants—is Gayl Jones's 1975 work *Corregidora*. Its protagonist, the blues singer Ursa, is the last in a line of women whose oldest members, having been the property of and forced into prostitution by "a Portuguese seaman turned [Brazilian] plantation owner," dedicate themselves to keeping alive the memory of "what they . . . lived through." Besides their memories, distinctive features, and harrowing tales of their dehumanization, the only "evidence" they retain of those experiences is a photograph of the Brazilian slave master whom they insist is "what evil look like."[2] As Ursa tells her second husband, the owner of Happy's Café in which she plies her trade:

> I've got a photograph of him. One Great Gram smuggled out, I guess, so we'd know who to hate. Tall, white hair, white beard, white mustache, a old man with a cane and one of his feet turned outward, not inward, but outward. Neck bent forward like he was raging at something that wasn't there. . . . I take it out every now and then so I won't forget what he looked like.[3]

A confluence of events that dominated my attention that April—my course about fictional representations of black American trauma; television and newspaper accounts of both the women's college basketball tournament and Imus's history of making insensitive comments; *Time* and *Newsweek* cover stories devoted to the nappy-headed hos controversy in which the broadcaster was pilloried by, among others, people I'd seen yucking it up with him on his program—provided me with a way to understand both the event itself and the reactions to it by the media, corporate sponsors, and members of my race. As I looked at photographs of the beleaguered broadcaster on the covers of national newspapers and magazines and watched the troublesome clip of his show played on that endless television loop reserved for the currently disgraced and the recently deceased, I realized that Imus's lean, squinty-eyed, craggy, deeply-wrinkled face had become, for a nation as committed as Brazil in Jones's fictional representation to evading the most significant moral, psychic, and economic consequences of its mistreatment of blacks, "what evil look like."

Put simply, Imus was made to stand in for millions of well-known and faceless whites whom blacks (and liberal and progressive whites) want desperately to identify, put on trial, and excoriate because of incontrovertible—but to this point often easily dismissed—"evidence" of centuries of racially motivated sins. The US government's desire to forge a lasting reconciliation between the North and South following the War between the States compelled its elected leaders generally to neglect even the most basic needs of its freed slaves. That not-so-benign neglect was so pronounced that the tepidly pursued Reconstruction seems, in hindsight, to have morphed inevitably into a full century of intranational terrorism: lynching, unjust imprisonment, rapes, and murders that weren't deemed criminal acts, as well as state-sanctioned segregation and other forms of blatant discrimination, including the denial to blacks of basic civil liberties such as the right to vote. Coming on the heels of more than two centuries of slavery, an institution fundamentally at odds with the nation's vaunted ideals, Jim Crow, the intent of whose criminally unchecked reign of terror was to compel black Americans to accept perpetual second-class citizenship, placed them—placed us—in an even deeper "rut." Like the Corregidora women, we hope for a long-deferred hour of atonement when the legitimacy of our collective pain will finally be acknowledged and attended to. But, prior to that unforeseeable event, we seek—sometimes without even being aware of it—the satisfaction that comes from being able to identify "who to hate" and "what evil look like." In lieu of therapeutic rituals of confession, adjudication, and atonement similar to the ones used in South Africa after apartheid's end, scenes such as Imus's public excoriation are all that are available to fulfill this need for a people, the pain of whose historic oppression resurfaces in response to minor local episodes and especially to major national media events.

Also served by his expulsion were not only whites well aware of the depths of black pain and the fecklessness of the nation's efforts to ameliorate it but also major corporations, including his former sponsors such as General Motors, Staples, and Bigelow Tea, and CBS and NBC, the media outlets directly involved with his show, for which he had worked precisely because of the popularity of his insightful outrageousness and willingness to point out when others were manifesting "weasel[y]"[4] behavior.[5] Certainly, these sponsors, whose representatives had appeared on the show each year bearing gifts of thousands of dollars for the host's favorite charities, were saved the embarrassment of public ass-covering in the wake of protests by blacks in Chicago and New York City and those by feminist groups with which they surely would have had to contend had they continued to align themselves with the broadcaster. In addition, liberal and conservative whites alike received confirmation of the continued viability of the nation's system of moral checks and balances, albeit, in the case of potty-mouthed Imus, some of them claimed, much, much too late.

And MSNBC was spared a great deal of ignominy. It attempted to distance itself from the controversy by asserting that "'Imus in the Morning' is not a production of the cable network. . . . as Imus makes clear every day, his views are not those of MSNBC," and its spokespersons didn't have to explain why its Web site featured a raunchy Imus biography dated December 13, 2003. In addition to listing his accomplishments ("member of the Emerson Radio Hall of Fame, the National Broadcasters Hall of Fame, the Stolichnaya and Marlboro Halls of Fame") and confirming his cultural importance ("featured on NBC's 'Today' show, the ABC programs 'Prime Time Live'

and '20/20,' and on CBS' '48 Hours' and '60 Minutes' [, Imus has also] has been a guest of Charlie Rose, David Letterman, and of particular note, Larry King"),[6] this biography also makes comic use of his controversial 1996 address at the Radio and Television Correspondents' dinner in Washington, D.C.

In the address, Imus refers to rumors about President Clinton's peccadilloes:

> While at the podium, Don made some observations about Mr. Clinton that some felt were rude and upsetting to the President, and that tended to leave egg on Don's face. Little did we know then, that Mr. Clinton was already well into the business of leaving substances splattered on individuals with whom he might come in contact; that his discomfort that evening had its roots in his own wayward DNA, and that Don was Nostradamus.[7]

Could executives in the position of being aware of this not-so-subtle mention of "splattered" presidential semen and the sense of humor it bespeaks really have been surprised that Imus would use a phrase as relatively tame as "nappy-headed hos"? Certainly not the sage bosses at MSNBC, who now will never have to come up with an answer to an especially thorny question: why was one of these offensive utterances at least tacitly endorsed by the network through its appearance on the cable network's Web site, and the other, widely considered a sexist and race-inflected remark but containing no FCC-banned language, became grounds for swift termination? I am, however, more interested in another, equally perplexing question: in the long run, how much does it serve black Americans, who have been assaulted far too many times by language much more offensive than Imus's, to have positioned him as "what evil look like"?

Perhaps in response to such assaults and its achievement of mainstream popularity via the comedy of Richard Pryor, scores of black entertainers of the post-civil rights generation have turned verbal indecency into a highly lucrative form—often augmented by a synthesized beat—using, among other things, the very words and attitudes that a number of people have claimed inspired Imus. Rarely, if ever, have blacks been able figuratively to parade the head of such a potent figure around on a platter, and many of us, giddy with our newfound power, refused to entertain any doubt about the motives of those who had aided our efforts to ensnare an impressive white sacrifice. Certainly, the power to bring down an old, tart-tongued white man enamored of cowboy hats, country music, .357 Magnums, and caustic verbal abuse, to compel him to come begging for absolution from a frequent target of his comic derision, the Reverend Al Sharpton, our most visible (and most irredeemably compromised) grassroots leader, offered us a great deal of short-term satisfaction.

Once Imus was identified as the latest white scapegoat of the post-civil rights era to suffer for centuries of sins against our people, his employers suspended him for two weeks and then, just days later, summarily terminated him. Surely, for many blacks and members of other races, it was thrilling to have people's attention focused on what many— if not, as I suspect, virtually all—of us recognized as our relatively minimal collective harm, especially compared with the seemingly insoluble challenges confronting members of the black underclass. And we clearly reveled in exercising the power that was briefly entrusted to us, even if our victory hurts us in the long run. It allowed representatives of powerful sponsors, newspapers, newsmagazines, and multimedia corporations yet again to avoid reckoning with the soul-deep, centuries-old suffering that troubles our interactions with members of other races and with one another and haunts our dreams that feature dusty-faced ancestors with bloodstained clothes whose eternal rest—long deferred—is unsettled. Still, we let ourselves be placated by patronizing claims such as those offered by CBS president Les Moonves, whose network came under fire earlier in the television season for trying to improve the ratings of *Survivor* by dividing its rugged, win-at-any-cost campers into teams according by race. Moonves insisted that he was driven to fire Imus by his "deep" concern about "the effect language like this has on our young people, particularly young women of color trying to make their way in this society," and about "a culture that permits a certain level of objectionable expression that hurts and demeans a wide range of people."[8]

These issues motivate the argument that follows, which attempts to place the Imus skit in as broad and illuminating a context as possible. That effort is necessary if I am to examine precisely what I believe caused the vociferous public condemnation of Imus and the surprisingly swift termination of his influential show. In terms of sheer numbers of listeners, its reach was nowhere near as wide as that of Howard Stern or, for that matter, the shows of right-wing talk radio icons such as Rush Limbaugh, Sean Hannity, and Imus's former frequent guest Laura Ingraham. Still, *Imus in the Morning* penetrated at least as deeply as the programs of these figures into the consciences of its listeners and of the nation, whose print magazines frequently cited news developments connected to the show, including its interviews with politicians.

Watching Imus

I was a regular viewer of MSNBC's simulcast for the six and a half years prior to its being taken off the air. I found *Imus in the Morning* richly entertaining, informative, and even inspiring, partly because, while delving into many of the same subjects as the morning shows against which it competed, it offered a clearly demarcated and hence, for me, refreshingly both serious and satirical perspective on major political and social issues. Unlike its television competition, *Imus in the Morning* was not hostage to what has increasingly struck me as the incommensurability of the pursuit of both journalistic objectivity and massive ratings that translates into the largest possible commercial yield. Instead, it was driven by the whims, caustic wit, and deeply informed viewpoint of its alternately bitchily self-involved and empathetic host whose volcanic everyman persona always appeared no more than a perceived slight or insignificant annoyance away from erupting. While Matt Lauer and Katie Couric and, more recently, Meredith Vieira seem unnaturally good-natured and convivial, given the ungodly hour they awake to prepare for their interviews, cooking segments, and perfectly coiffed, fresh-faced close-ups, Imus often appeared bedraggled. Typically, it seemed as if he'd slept as fitfully as I had, that he hadn't combed his hair after he had gotten up on the wrong side of the bed, and that he would rather still be lying in it next to his attractive, impressive wife, Deirdre, or reading to their cherubic young son, Wyatt, than talking to his staff, guests, or, really, to his audience.

Rather than claim to be offering an objective take on the news or providing the sonic equivalent of a jolt of early morning cheer to help propel his audience through yet another day of what he called our "miserable lives," Imus railed against the slow, slogging, often grossly inhumane machines of government and media.

- Pissed off that citizens of the United States were being forced to endure another day of having to assess the horrendous consequences of allowing ourselves to be hoodwinked by the Bush administration into what he recognized early on was an unwinnable war in Iraq, Imus called the "awful" president, Vice President Cheney (whom he nicknamed "Pork Chop Butt"), and Secretary of Defense Don Rumsfeld "war criminals."[9]
- Incensed that government officials were not dealing more forthrightly with what he believes is a possibly preventable epidemic of autism in children, Imus begged, cajoled, implored, and, finally, helped shame members of the print and television media into addressing the topic.
- Livid about the conditions endured by disabled Iraq war veterans at Walter Reed Hospital in Washington, D.C., which he toured with Senator John McCain, his favorite political guest (whose charms were so utterly lost on me that eventually I began regularly to turn on ESPN's *Sports Center* the moment he came on the show), Imus helped inspire not only congressional investigation of this and other medical facilities to which injured soldiers were being sent but acknowledgments from politicians that they had not seriously considered what sort of medical care was being provided to young men and women they'd voted to put in harm's way.

In evidence for even his casual listeners and simulcast viewers, then, despite or perhaps because of his crusty demeanor, was his dedication to contributing to the alleviation of suffering, particularly that of terminally ill children and grievously injured young adults. His commitment to charity work included the Imus Ranch, whose mission is to buoy the spirits of children with cancer and other terminal illnesses (as well as members of their families). At the very least, he seemed to have developed a deeply empathetic soul and was quite willing to employ his bully pulpit, his far-reaching microphone, and the most biting, intimidating, and outrageous aspects of his personality to try to effect positive change. To achieve such ends, Imus concentrated on the areas that he knew could be influenced by the politicians and members of the media who flocked and listened attentively to, and were frequent targets of ridicule on, his show.

Once he himself was caught in the unforgiving media spotlight, he counted on broadcast and industry executives, faithful listeners, and casual onlookers factoring tangible evidence of his altruism into their portraits of him. That evidence, he seemed to believe, would lead Americans to conclude that his good deeds had come to define him and his show more suitably than misogynistic rants or naughty jokes whose bite sometimes relied on a tinge of racial and gender bias. And, indeed, while Imus's acts of philanthropy and aggressive advocacy are impressive, while his ongoing struggle to overcome the demons and genetic predispositions that compelled him to abuse booze, blow, and his body is admirable and, for me at least, fascinating, my concern here is gauging how viewing *Imus in the Morning* as what its host insisted it was—"a comedy show"—influences or, more to the point, could and should have tempered the nation's undoubtedly hysterical responses to the nappy-headed hos controversy.

Whatever else he is, whatever good he is able to do, whatever beneficial impact he was able to have on his audience and the nation, when he was on the air, Imus saw himself first and foremost as a rowdy entertainer overseeing a program whose governing impulse was the creation of well-informed laughter. His comedic gifts and willingness to approach the most difficult and complex issues with a caustic wit enabled members of his audience to endure, and even to enjoy,

- his rants about that damn book about Whittaker Chambers with which he was obsessed and for which Charles McCord memorably harangued him
- his interviews with insufferable twits like former Arizona representative J. D. Hayworth
- the excruciating appearances of the crass former New York City cop Bo Dietl and clueless Joe Lieberman, the latter of whom seemed unaware of the fact that his campaign to stamp out the coarsening elements of our entertainment culture was being waged on a program widely considered a major part of the problem
- his fits of prima donna entitlement
- his endless pursuit of the "finest doctors" to cure his innumerable ailments, including his recently diagnosed prostate cancer
- his railing against the "losers" who'd failed miserably in their attempts to recalibrate the studio equipment or, worse, to properly install or fix the high-tech gadgets he'd purchased for his home, including his computers and TiVo

Imus was able to communicate the humor he found in any number of his daily activities:

- his frustrating limousine rides around the greater metropolitan New York area being shepherded by his longtime chauffeur whom he claimed was bereft of both common sense and a sense of direction
- his encounters near his Westport, Connecticut, home with famous neighbors like Phil Donahue just after the pioneering daytime television talk show host had himself been fired from his own short-lived primetime MSNBC job
- his laborious efforts to find the perfect running shoes, Resistol hats, and tailored shirts, many of the latter of which were made for him by his frequent guest, the designer Joseph Abboud

And he found wonderfully satisfying ways to tweak guests who worked in the media and in politics:

- reveling in nice-guy Tim Russert's methodical vivisection of guests who were trying to weasel out of tight political spots on *Meet the Press* and teasing him incessantly about his nonstop promotion of *Big Russ,* the book he'd written about his working-class father
- insisting that the baldly ambitious NBC White House correspondent David Gregory (who succeeded fellow Imus favorite, the recently deceased Russert, as host of *Meet the Press*) wanted to sabotage the careers of colleagues such as Claire Shipman and Kelly O'Donnell, both of whom also covered that prestigious beat
- making fun of MSNBC colleague—and frequent guest—Chris Matthews's tendency to ask long, convoluted questions and to interrupt his guests as they tried to answer them
- implying that the objectivity of the NBC correspondent and devoted guest Andrea Mitchell's reports was compromised because she was married to longtime Federal Reserve chair Alan Greenspan
- deriding frequent guest Jack Welch for his marriage-ending affair with a prominent business journalist that began when she was interviewing him
- dressing-down presidential candidate John Kerry (I think in a tongue-in-cheek manner) for his failure to keep his promise to stop his campaign train near the Imus Ranch in Reader's Digest, New Mexico, so that he could visit with the sick kids waiting anxiously to meet him

Recognizing that he'd been positioned as an unregenerate sexist and racist before—and certainly after—his nappy-headed hos remark rather than as a comedic commentator on political, social, cultural, media, and athletic events, Imus turned to several tactics to try to clear his name. For example, on April 6, two days after the controversial skit, Imus offered a brief apology to the members of the Rutgers women's basketball team, their parents, and their coach, C. Vivian Stringer, the transcript of which Ryan Chiachiere of the liberal watchdog group Media Matters sent to members of the National Association of Black Journalists as the latest effort on the part of the group to convince others of the show's deeply offensive nature. This apology, Imus insisted, was not intended as an "excuse" for a skit that, in hindsight, he characterized as inexcusable. Three days later, after what he described as a "barrage . . . of newspaper articles" and television reports on the skit and calls by "a number of prominent people . . . for me to be fired," the host offered a more extensive apology, one that attempted to "provide a context briefly for them [the young women at Rutgers]—not as an excuse, not that this makes this okay, nothing makes this okay. But," he goes on to say, "there is a difference between premeditated murder and accident [homicide]. . . . I mean, somebody still gets shot, but the charges are dramatically different."[10]

Eventually, Imus came to realize that his earlier apology hadn't sufficiently "put into any sort of context what happens on this program, because [he] unwisely just assumed that everybody knows" the tenor and format of his long-running show that had recently been featured (among other places) in a fascinatingly self-deprecating cover story for *Vanity Fair* by the Pulitzer Prize–winning author Buzz Bissinger.[11] So he took pains to describe *Imus in the Morning* as a

program [that] has been, for 30 or 35 years, a program that makes fun of everybody. It makes fun of me, and it makes fun of everybody on the planet. And sometimes it makes fun of me to a vicious standpoint. Does that mean I get to say something about the Rutgers women? Of course not. But that's the context in which we operate here. Is it appropriate? Well, we will talk about that a little later, because that's got to change—some of that—because some people don't deserve to be made fun of, like these young women who played for the national championship in basketball. They played for the national championship, they beat Duke and then they played Tennessee in the national championship, [and] they don't need me to try to be funny about them.

But they don't know that I was trying to be funny. They don't know what this program is about. I mean, because I call my wife "the green ho," does that mean I can call [them nappy-headed hos]—of course not. I mean, that's a repugnant suggestion, to suggest that I think because

we make fun of everybody, or because I get made fun of, that it's okay to make fun of them, because it's not okay to make fun of them. But that's what we do and that's the context.[12]

What Imus fails to explain in this lengthy statement is precisely why, given the nature of his show, its status as the commercial anchor of both MSNBC and New York's sports radio station, WFAN, and the fact that Rutgers had just competed in a nationally televised, and broadly hyped, championship game, he came to feel that he had no right "to try to be funny about" or even, for that matter, "vicious" in his commentary on, "the Rutgers women." Feel-good stories about this team had flooded tristate area and national markets during its improbable string of Big East and NCAA tournament victories, and the team had been celebrated both for its fortitude (it began the season with several humiliating losses) and precocity (most of its core members were underclasswomen). Given what otherwise would surely have been a short-lived local and national celebrity, and ignoring, for the moment, the specific nature of the comments Imus offered in response to them, why do members of the Rutgers team fall into the category of "people [who] don't deserve to be made fun of"?

I agree with Marc Sheppard, who views Imus's explanation in this regard as "utter nonsense. The players on that team—regardless of sex or race—are no more satirically sacrosanct than President Bush, Nancy Pelosi, or any of the thousands of named or unnamed adult punch-line targets out there."[13] Rightly or wrongly, once previously unknown people such as Anita Hill, Monica Lewinsky, Donna Rice, and Joe the Plumber enter the national spotlight, they become fodder for comedians, talk show hosts, and members of the news media. That is the case even outside the political arena, because of which all of the aforementioned people gained notoriety. If the stakes are especially great in the world of politics, where reputations are made and besmirched seemingly in a heartbeat, they are not insignificant in the world in which the Rutgers team operated. That is the case because, as Welch Suggs argues in *A Place on the Team: The Triumph and Tragedy of Title IX*, while "women are still getting the short end of the stick when schools and colleges allocate resources," college women's basketball has evolved into a "hypercompetitive, highly commercialized" entity in which universities invest precisely because, like its infinitely more popular male equivalent, it serves exponentially to increase public awareness of their institutions.[14] Indeed, one athletic director whom Suggs cites indicates that "sports teams account for 80 to 85 percent of the times any college gets mentioned in newspapers and on television."[15] Certainly, a relatively small portion of this media attention can be attributed to women's college athletics. Still, even if we do not agree with the view articulated by less-than-fawning columnists that Coach Stringer used her team's post-Imus press conference as a recruiting tool, we cannot ignore the fact that college sports is "a nakedly commercial enterprise, whether it is to bring in millions of dollars at Miami or Michigan [or Rutgers] or to attract new students to MacMurray College or Mount Union College," and "that female athletes have been sucked into this mess."[16]

There are, of course, significant benefits connected to female participation in "this mess." These benefits include greater campus, regional, and national exposure, better training facilities and coaching salaries—after her successful postseason run, for example, Stringer was awarded a big raise and is now making more than $1,500,000 per year—and more assistant coaching positions and employment opportunities overall for women athletes following graduation, including, for a select few, spots on WNBA and European professional league rosters. And if women's college athletics are "nakedly commercial," if women's amateur sports generally, including teams that compete in various nationally televised and aggressively promoted NCAA, Olympics (especially gymnastics, softball, soccer, and basketball), and international tournaments, make claims on the attention of a sports-obsessed nation, how, then, does a Rutgers team playing for a national championship fall necessarily outside the purview of *Imus in the Morning*?

Consider the recent case of women's soccer. The star-studded national team, whose players had excelled in some of the country's most successful college programs, enjoyed massive exposure and a dramatic victory in the 1999 World Cup championship game. These events led, among other things, to the escalation of the reluctant superstar Mia Hamm's commercial marketability, to Brandi Chastain's meteoric rise (and subsequent, less spectacular fall) as a flesh-exposing spokeswoman following her game-winning goal and her celebratory jersey removal, and to the establishment of a short-lived professional women's league in the United States. Since women's sports have become big business, albeit on a significantly smaller scale than those of their male counterparts, their participants are frequently exposed to the sometimes complimentary, sometimes unflattering glare of that national spotlight.

Unfortunately, we live in a society that continues to evaluate young women less in terms of their accomplishments than in terms of their appearance. Consequently, the females who generally are the most successful in translating their athletic success into lucrative off-the-field recompense are those with traditional sex appeal (i.e., the leggy blonde tennis pro Maria Sharapova's outsized popularity with Madison Avenue advertisers despite her noticeable lack of charisma). In this context, it seems to me patently ridiculous to expect a Rutgers women's basketball team playing for the national championship to be protected from masculine—and, for that matter, misogynistic and racist—evaluation. For ours is a culture that rewarded Amanda Beard, Olympic gold medalist swimmer, for choosing, for what I assume was a substantial fee, to contribute her taut, muscular, but still traditionally feminine—and assiduously tanned—white body to the fantasy machines represented by the growing PG-13 men's magazine industry and, as a result, landing on the July 2007 cover of *Playboy.*

During his lengthy April 9 explanation, Imus failed to contextualize his barb in terms of the media hype the team received. (That being said, who among us doesn't sometimes become a bit cynical when faced with sports journalistic concoctions of heroes and heroines whose endeavors are manipulated to give us goose pimples, warm our collectively jaded hearts, and confirm the value of maniacal persistence, American or otherwise?) He also accepted his critics' faulty premise that "these young women at Rutgers" should have been exempt from his biting satire. Consequently, Imus was unable to articulate a convincing rationale for the skit and, ultimately, for a show that regularly ridiculed, among other things, our propensity to become enamored of manufactured sacred cows. Additionally, he failed to explain sufficiently how and why his offending phrase, "nappy-headed hos," was used in the context of a skit and to underscore that skit's satirical intentions.

Further, Imus's efforts to contextualize his remarks did not include a discussion of how comedy generally, and his brand of comedy in particular, can serve as effective social commentary. Instead, he emphasized what he had learned about the attitudes of black Americans regarding whites and the fact that his deep commitment to various charitable endeavors, some of which directly benefited blacks, evinced that he was not racist. His development of a greater understanding of the effects of racism and for why blacks had responded to his phrase with such fury resulted from extensive conversations he had with a number of people after his initial apology. For example, the Reverend De Forest Soaries, who both called for him to be fired and arranged for him to meet with the Rutgers team, told Imus that "every black person . . . believes that . . . white people don't like them [*sic*]" and that, "no matter how good a white person is . . . , at some point, it [whites' fundamental hatred of blacks] comes out . . . , [which] just confirms what they [blacks already] think."[17]

In referencing his charity work, Imus discussed in particular the Imus Ranch, an endeavor he oversees with Deirdre. This ranch, he told his listeners, has served hundreds of "kids who come . . . from minority groups, Native American, Hispanic, Asian American . . . , African American," the latter of which group—some of whom suffer from sickle cell anemia, an ailment that primarily affects people of African descent—comprises "ten percent of the kids who come."[18] His aim in discussing these matters was to get controversy-inspired listeners unfamiliar with his show, his general concern for mistreated American citizens, and his long-standing dedication to charitable enterprises to recognize him, as do his regular radio listeners and cable television viewers, as "a good person who said a bad thing."[19] But because

he did not attempt to examine precisely *why* he said this "bad thing," because he failed to explain his use of comedy generally or in this particular instance, he presented neither a defense for his remarks that might have helped sway already incensed and merely curious listeners nor a powerful condemnation of the shortsightedness of his harshest critics. These critics, of course, saw the "bad thing" he said not as part of a performance on his part but as a manifestation of deeply held racist and sexist attitudes.

My intention in the following pages is to continue what Imus himself started: to consider his skit in terms of the broad "context [of] what happens on this program." But I also look at the skit, and responses to it, in various other contexts. In particular, I evaluate the skit in terms of both informed discussions of the art of comedy, which consider the capacity of jokes and other forms of humor to offer potentially valuable contributions to the nation's cultural dialogue about contentious issues such as race and gender, and controversies that garnered national attention at whose core is the assumption that whites fundamentally "don't like" blacks. The issues that commentators regularly brought up in response to Imus's inflammatory skit—including the place of comedy that is considered sexually and racially offensive in an increasingly egalitarian society, and how listeners respond when members of empowered groups appear to use jokes to belittle the disempowered—constitute major emphases of contemporary assessments of the form. The analyses of comedy that I cite uniformly recognize that, as Ted Cohen argues, while "jokes and joke-telling are wonderful and can be very serious," there is potentially a "danger in too much joke-telling when it is out of place. Whether joking is in place or out of place may depend upon who is telling jokes to whom."[20] Drawing on, and offering my own perspectives on, analyses such as Cohen's, I hope to demonstrate that the conclusions at which people arrived about the nature of the nappy-headed hos skit reflect a failure to consider the comedic context in which Imus operated along with the other contributors to *Imus in the Morning*.

Perhaps most important, I also consider responses to this controversy, at least as they reflect deep-seated anxieties within the collective psyches of black Americans, as the inevitable consequences of the nation's historical failure to meet what others have discussed as its moral, economic, and spiritual obligation to atone for centuries of its shameful treatment of those who were the victims of slavery and Jim Crow. The election of Barack Obama notwithstanding, until the United States embraces the challenge of meaningful racial reconciliation on a large scale with at least as much zeal as it has approached its ill-fated ventures to achieve Middle East peace and the democratization of Iraq, until it offers something other than grudging recognition of the psychological, emotional, spiritual, and economic harm it has caused the vast majority of its African descendants, black Americans will continue, in moments of media-produced crisis when our disenfranchisement appears to be at issue and our psychic health seems threatened once again, to identify convenient targets as "what evil look like." And we will all continue to put off the more serious—and painful—task of examining, and seeking to repair, the tremendous damage caused by our model democracy's seemingly limitless capacity for expedient, racially motivated "evil."

However inspiring recent national electoral results prove, black Americans should not allow them to be viewed and used as an all-purpose racial panacea, as yet another turning point in our nation's history—like the Civil War, Reconstruction, the civil rights movement, the election of blacks to mayoral positions in major US cities, and, most recently, the official installment of Martin Luther King Jr. as a transcendent national hero—that enables a new bout of cultural amnesia about the impact of its legacy of brutal racism. Instead, we might more effectively view it as an occasion to demand accountability for physical, psychic, and spiritual violence that continues to cause us deep, grievous, and, often, vision-impairing pain.

[. . .]

Racial Violence and Collective Trauma

According to the literary theorist Cathy Caruth, an influential commentator of the phenomenon,

the term *trauma* is understood as a wound inflicted not upon the body but upon the mind. . . . the wound of the mind—the breach in the mind's experience of time, self, and the world—is not, like the wound of the body, a simple and healable event, but rather an event that . . . is experienced too soon, too unexpectedly, to be fully known and is therefore not available to consciousness until it imposes itself again, repeatedly, in the nightmares and repetitive actions of the survivor.[21]

In other words, trauma can be characterized as a "psychic bout" fought by an essentially debilitated survivor who does not see, and therefore cannot adequately guard against, the initial blows and whose pain "return[s] later in repeated flashbacks, nightmares, and other repetitive phenomena."[22] The survivor, engaged in a losing battle, comes to feel as if the force or entity that caused the wound is omnipresent. Possessed or haunted by an experience that she or he can neither fully process because of its shocking onset and intensity nor integrate into a vast store of recollections, the survivor is overwhelmed by the trauma, which comes to redefine her or him in a fundamental way. In other words, the unhealed survivor of trauma cannot construct a notion of self and a relationship to the external world that are not essentially determined by the throbbing wound. Consequently, she or he begins to operate on two independent psychological tracks: the prewounded course, marked by a requisite mixture of joy and heartache, and the course and attendant sensibility determined by the undigested trauma.

Descriptions of the traumatized or psychologically wounded self "torn asunder" by the strain of a double life are remarkably similar to W. E. B. Du Bois's depictions of black American "double consciousness." According to Du Bois, the fundamental task of the black citizen cursed with the "peculiar sensation" of "twoness"—"an American, a Negro; two souls, two thoughts, two unreconciled strivings, two warring ideals in one dark body"—is "to merge his double self into a better and truer self" to achieve an integrated New World self-consciousness that results from being "*both* a Negro and an American."[23] In the case of both the "Negro" and the trauma survivor, the moment of disruption—the Middle Passage and the "wound of the mind," respectively—results in a fragmentation of self so profound that the disconnected parts seem fundamentally disparate (African/American, pretraumatized/traumatized). Psychic unity, for Du Bois, requires not the "bleach[ing]" or eradication of one part of the self but a discovery of meaningful complementary features shared by the "double" selves or of the ability to forge a relatively peaceful coexistence between "warring ideals."[24] Similarly, the trauma survivor—a category that surely encompasses Du Bois's "Negro"—cannot achieve lasting psychic health by ignoring or attempting to repress either the former or the traumatized self. Instead, as Judith Herman suggests in her important book *Trauma and Recovery,* the survivor

> "draws upon those aspects of herself that she most values from the time before the trauma, from the experience of the trauma itself, and from the period of recovery. Integrating all of these elements, she creates a new self, both ideally and in actuality."[25]

Recently, scholars of Afro-American history, literature, and culture familiar both with Du Boisian double consciousness and with theories of trauma have begun to combine or "integrate" these formulations in persuasive discussions of black American identity.[26] For instance, in his examination of novels by such authors as Charles Johnson, Toni Morrison, and John Edgar Wideman, Keith Byerman insists that their

> narratives are trauma stories in that they tell of both tremendous loss and survival; they describe the psychological and social effects of suffering. More important, perhaps, they tell of the erasure of such history and, as a consequence, its continued power to shape black life. . . . The . . . tales are often represented as suppressed, hidden, forgotten, or distorted. Their tales . . . describe the compromised, the deformed, the criminal, [and] the disreputable.[27]

Byerman sees the concern with the past that dominates contemporary black literary narratives as a function of a painful irresolution whose cause is not merely "suffering." What makes the past linger for blacks, what forces its attendant pains to remain unresolved, is its "erasure" or suppression, is, in other words, the fact that slavery and Jim Crow are not incorporated in any discernible manner into the stories that the powerful whites who determined the meanings of our national past have chosen to communicate about it. Instead, blacks are "compromised," "deformed," "criminal[ized]," and rendered "disreputable" within a national discourse that deems their painful history what Byerman—echoing Morrison—describes as "unspeakable."[28]

The deformations caused by trauma cannot be resolved until survivors gain mastery over their psychically disruptive experiences, until they are able to unify their split—former and wounded—selves by creating what James Hillman calls "healing fictions" to effect what Farah Griffin terms "textual healing."[29] Because survivors are unable to incorporate their overwhelming experiences, and the pain they engender, into their understandings of the totality of their lives, they feel as if they are haunted by a loud, unsettled, and unsettling ghost that they need to help lay to rest. Efforts to silence that ghost prove largely unsuccessful, since the unconscious, struggling with unresolved urgings, is compelled to keep the experience of its wounding alive. In fact, laying the ghost of trauma to rest becomes possible only when the survivor, like the black American writer of historical novels, asserts mastery over that experience by combining the real and the fictional, the half-remembered and the half-imagined, in a manner that enables her or him to incorporate the wounding event or events into a larger personal and, hence, inevitably cultural narrative. For, as Judith Herman puts it, "The recreation of an ideal self involves the active exercise of imagination and fantasy."[30]

The sociologist Ron Eyerman identifies the experience of American slavery or, rather, its representation by succeeding generations of blacks as a wound that resulted in what he calls "cultural trauma."

> As cultural process, trauma is mediated through various forms of representation and linked to the reformation of collective identity and the

reworking of collective memory. The notion of a unique African American identity emerged in the post–Civil War period, after slavery had been abolished. The trauma of forced servitude and of nearly complete subordination to the will and whims of another . . . thus . . . came to be central to their attempts to forge a collective identity out of its remembrance. In this sense, slavery was traumatic in retrospect, and formed a "primal scene" which could, potentially, unite all "African Americans" in the United States.[31]

For Eyerman, then, descendants of slavery have strategically used it to construct a unifying cultural identity. That identity, whose fundamental feature is the effect of black "subordination to the will and whims" of whites, unifies and mobilizes black Americans into a collective force, one of whose major goals is to create and preserve an informed and informing version of blackness. Identifying epochs within black American history in terms of their distinct representations of that remembered "subordination," Eyerman suggests that generations construct healing fictions that unite their members, philosophically and otherwise, in terms of the presiding notions of black identity with which each black American must contend. They are further united by their participation in the struggles for social, political, and cultural power that constitute their eras' efforts to realize the national ideals of the United States.

The literary contributions of black American writers of the civil rights generation approach slavery in a manner that I think of as "reparative." That is to say, after situating slavery in terms of predominant features of trauma—specifically, the wound and its haunting repetition—their primary objective is to depict the wound's creation as a consequence of "nearly complete subordination" and to explore how it might be healed. In that regard, Morrison's *Beloved,* which investigates the ramifications of infanticide motivated by an escaped slave mother's determination to prevent her children from being subjected to the precise forms of subordination she herself had suffered, can be seen as thematically of a kind with the goals of the contemporary reparations movement. The aim of participants in this movement is to secure restorative forms of redress

from a nation whose white citizens, past and present, have profited greatly from uncompensated black labor.

Perhaps the most powerful presentation of the justifications undergirding the contemporary reparations movement I've encountered, besides Randall Robinson's lyrical book, *The Debt,* is the legal scholar Roy L. Brooks's more prosaic, more scholarly, and, as a consequence, potentially more broadly persuasive study, *Atonement and Forgiveness: A New Model for Black Reparations.* This "new model" is driven not by desires to seek revenge against people like Imus who can be positioned as "what evil look like" but by a greater national need for what Brooks calls "racial reconciliation." Brooks does not advocate that blacks struggle to achieve reparations primarily as a way to heal black American trauma, as Robinson does so eloquently. Nor does he focus solely on how their receipt might transform the perception of many that our current plight within the United States is essentially indistinguishable from that of our enslaved ancestors, an impression that belies, of course, the race's measurable sociopolitical, institutional, economic, and cultural progress. Instead, Brooks focuses on how reparations can benefit the nation and its citizens generally, on how, in other words, they can help effect a much-needed *national* healing:

Racial reconciliation should be the primary purpose of slave redress. It is what gives the idea of slave redress its forward-looking quality. When Americans embrace the idea of slave redress, they welcome the belief that we must go back in time and place to right a heavy wrong and to make the present and future more racially harmonious. They understand that there is a price to pay for collective amnesia, for that type of erasure. . . .

The federal government committed a horrific racial atrocity for which it has never apologized . . . [and] has little credibility on racial matters with the great majority of its black citizens, . . . [who] continue to suffer the lingering effects of slavery and Jim Crow. . . .

Redressing slavery and Jim Crow should be about honor, not alms. It should be about black pride and dignity, and, last but not least, it should be about commemorating and memorializing the slaves. These heroic men, women, and children were denied freedom so that all Americans might live in the freest and most prosperous nation humankind has ever known.[32]

Brooks suggests that the trauma of slavery, for subsequent generations, is largely the result of the "collective amnesia" the nation has exhibited vis-à-vis the suffering of black people from which it so exorbitantly profited. That "amnesia" is evinced, for example, in the nation's stunning refusal to construct a museum of the History of Slavery that tells what Susan Sontag calls "the whole story, starting with the slave trade in Africa itself, not just selected parts, such as the Underground Railroad." Sontag attributes the absence of such a site of commemoration, in a nation whose elected officials chose, for example, to house and helped finance the Holocaust Memorial Museum, to the fact that "this . . . memory [is] judged too dangerous to social stability to activate and to create." A national museum documenting the United States' participation in the barbarous institution of slavery would force its citizens to confront the gaps that it would create in the national narrative of "American exceptionalism." According to Sontag,

> To have a museum chronicling the great crime that was African slavery in the United States of America would be to acknowledge that the evil was here. Americans prefer to picture the evil that was there, and from which the United States—a unique nation, one without any certifiably wicked leaders throughout its entire history—is exempt.[33]

But if America's illusions of uniqueness and "social stability" are facilitated by its refusal to commemorate black enslavement, left largely unprotected as a result, both physically and, in the post-civil rights era, psychically, are its black citizens whose collective identity has been shaped by the very experiences the nation refuses officially to acknowledge. Brooks argues that the consequences of that refusal are catastrophic for blacks and include, among other things, a persistent lack of faith in the US government to exhibit heartfelt concern about their historic suffering

and contemporary needs. In the absence of "slave redress," Brooks insists, blacks will remain virtual outsiders within a nation whose fertile soil is stained with their ancestors' blood, a status that leads to the escalation of the antisocial behavior that marks and mars urban America.

According to Brooks, black Americans' lack of faith in the national government, however detrimental it is to us in some respects, is perfectly justified. He sees reparations as "essential to atonement, because they make apologies believable . . . [by] turn[ing] the rhetoric of apology into a meaningful, material reality and, thus, help to repair the damage caused by the atrocity and ensure that the atrocity will not be repeated."[34] In the absence of such measures, which he insists should include "a memorial honoring the lives of the dead victims" whose labor enabled "the socioeconomic development of this great country from which they [contemporary whites who believe they bear no responsibility for the nation's past sins] benefit," the "exceptional" nation will continue to confirm the veracity of blacks' views of its persistent "evil."[35]

Brooks goes on to insist that whites who refuse to recognize, along with the sacred national documents in which so many Americans take pride, the "past injustices committed in the name of Americans," ignore the fact that "where there is no room for [both] national pride [and] . . . national shame about the past, there can be no national soul."[36] Furthermore, they limit the possibility of ending blacks' bitterness and sense of marginalization, whose impact on the larger social fabric is great:

> In the absence of atonement, I am prepared to argue that forgiveness is *morally objectionable.* The indiscriminate forgiver disrespects herself. Her forgiveness manifests an unjustifiable abandonment of "the appropriate retributive responses to wrongdoing." The indiscriminate forgiver preserves an unhealthy relationship with her perpetrator. She, the victim, accepts the perpetrator "in his identity as offender."[37]

In other words, without atonement, blacks risk losing an already tenuous sense of racial self-respect and, hence, are justified in seeing figures like Don

Imus, whose behavior appeared of a kind with past wrongs for which there has been no national atonement, as "what evil look like." Brooks goes on to cite Ike Balbus's argument that "whites have an emotional interest in denying the fact that an American institution as horrific as slavery could have lingering effects in twenty-first century America." Hence they "are unlikely to be moved by principled arguments in favor of reparations if they have a deep psychological stake in resisting them" that manifests itself as "a 'powerful unconscious resistance' to slave reparations" because of "the 'depressive' anxiety and guilt that inevitably accompany the awareness that we have harmed . . . [an innocent people]."[38] Brooks himself believes that what could motivate officials within the US government to push for some form of redress is the knowledge that doing so might transform the perceptions of black Americans of the nation that, after centuries of denial, was finally willing to recognize that its historical treatment of members of their race was deplorable, if not unforgivably "evil."[39]

The wounds caused by the peculiarly American version of the institution of slavery, wounds that the nation has consistently refused to acknowledge are in need of careful treatment, distress both the blacks who bear them and the whites who claim, unconvincingly, to be unaware of their existence. In Brooks's view, the individual and collective interests of both groups and, indeed, of all citizens of the United States would be best served if immediate attention was paid to healing these long-festering wounds, an act that, in turn, could eventually obliterate the racial fissures that mark the nation and separate its citizens. At the very least, slave redress, which Brooks argues would "create . . . an *unconditional civic* obligation on the part of the victim to participate in the process of reconciliation," would enable black American

civil forgiveness[, which] is crucial for black progress in our society. . . . [I]f the federal government atones for slavery and Jim Crow, we must fully commit ourselves to a process of racial reconciliation. If the federal government's apology and reparations are substantial, then there is no reason for us to withhold forgiveness. . . . Atonement (apology plus reparations) and forgiveness

foster racial reconciliation. Viewed in this forward-looking way, slave redress provides Americans on both sides of the color line with a rare opportunity—a third Reconstruction—to finish building the palace of justice that the civil rights movement began.[40]

My goal is not to produce an extended justification for slave reparations; intellectuals infinitely more committed to the idea than I am, including Brooks, have already carefully outlined the arguments in favor of such a measure. Rather, I'm trying merely to underscore some of the consequences of the nation's long-standing refusal to consider the idea and the unwillingness of its presidents and congressional bodies to entertain the possibility of offering an official apology to blacks and their ancestors for their oppression in the United States. Perhaps inspired by the success of then Democratic Party nominee Barack Obama, the House of Representatives on July 29, 2008, issued a formal apology to black Americans for "enslavement and racial segregation." Still, it is impossible to believe that the effects of the government's long-term refusal to do so could dissipate immediately. Hence the Land of the Free continues to be seen by many black Americans as *the site* of collective trauma, as a fundamentally corrupt nation because, among other things, its officials have funded commemorative places for, and offered profuse apologies to, other groups of people grievously wronged on these and other shores.

If Brooks is persuasive in his assessment of the "morally objectionable" status of the "indiscriminate forgiver," black Americans are in an almost untenable position. To remain outsiders within the nation means to be trapped by the unrelieved experience of victimization. However, to seek a comfortable place within the cottony fabric of a nation that has traumatized our people and patently denied our just demands for an apology, acknowledgment of our historical suffering, and some form of redress is, according to Brooks, to enter into an "unhealthy" emotional terrain that may lead to forms of extreme self-loathing. As a result, it has seemed at times more reasonable to strike out, in a sometimes utterly unself-conscious manner, at people who, because of their words, looks, and apparent attitudes, resemble those who were responsible for that earlier and unending pain.

Through my contextualization of the Imus skit, I hope to demonstrate that the deep, festering fissures in the souls of black American folk have led us to react compulsively when we feel our humanity challenged by events and language we perceive of as indistinguishable from our experience of racism and the discourse used to buttress it as well as to justify slavery and Jim Crow. In such instances, our behavior indicates that our souls' wounds have metastasized and that our collective identities may be so thoroughly the product of our traumatized national status that we are unable to distinguish the real threats we face—such as the fact that in my own and the nation's birthplace, the City of Brotherly Love, black boys and young men kill each other indiscriminately and at an alarming rate—from cynically orchestrated events like the Imus controversy. Consequently, like Morrison's tortured, guilt-ridden, and hunger-addled Sethe, we sometimes respond to such events by striking out against shadowy white figures because, through the haze of our lengthy suffering, they sufficiently resemble the ones who have deeply injured us.

Notes

1. Chiachiere, "Imus Called Women's Basketball Team 'Nappy-Headed Hos.'"
2. Jones, *Corregidora,* 12.
3. Ibid., 10.
4. "Weasel" is one of Imus's favorite derogative terms. For a discussion of media and corporate withdrawal from *Imus in the Morning,* see, for example.
5. "Don Imus, Host."
6. Ibid.
7. Ibid.
8. Quoted in "CBS Fires Don Imus from Radio Show."
9. Soon after the start of the Iraq war, but especially during 2006 and 2007, when his disdain for the war grew increasingly more palpable, Imus frequently referred to Rumsfeld and Cheney in especially negative ways.
10. "Imus Puts Remarks into Context."
11. Bissinger, "Don Imus's Last Stand."
12. "Imus Puts Remarks into Context."
13. Sheppard, "Imus's Dishonest Apologies."
14. Suggs, *Place on the Team,* 3.
15. Ibid., 11.
16. Ibid., 175.
17. "Imus Puts Remarks into Context."
18. Ibid.
19. Ibid.
20. Cohen, *Jokes,* 69.
21. Caruth, *Unclaimed Experience,* 3–4.
22. Ibid., 91.
23. Du Bois, *Souls of Black Folk,* 45; emphasis added.
24. Ibid.
25. Herman, *Trauma and Recovery,* 202.
26. Byerman, *Remembering the Past,* 3.
27. Ibid.
28. Ibid.
29. Hillman, *Healing Fictions;* Griffin, "Textual Healing."
30. Herman, *Trauma and Recovery,* 202.
31. Eyerman, *Cultural Trauma,* 1.
32. Brooks, *Atonement and Forgiveness,* 141–42.
33. Sontag, *Regarding the Pain of Others,* 87–88.
34. Brooks, *Atonement and Forgiveness,* 143.
35. Ibid., 144, 149, 149.
36. Ibid., 154.
37. Ibid., 168.
38. Quoted in Brooks, *Atonement and Forgiveness,* 150–51.
39. Ibid., 168.
40. Ibid., 168–69.

References

Bissinger, Buzz. "Don Imus's Last Stand." *Vanity Fair,* February 2006, http://www.vanityfair.com/politics/features/2006.02/imus200602?printable=true&currentP (accessed May 27, 2007).

Brooks, Roy L. *Atonement and Forgiveness: A New Model for Black Reparations.* Berkeley: University of California Press, 2004.

Byerman, Keith. *Remembering the Past in Contemporary African American Fiction.* Chapel Hill: University of North Carolina Press, 2005.

Caruth, Cathy. *Unclaimed Experience: Trauma, Narrative, and History.* Baltimore: Johns Hopkins University Press, 1996.

Chiachiere, Ryan. "Imus Called Women's Basketball Team 'Nappy-Headed Hos.'" Media Matters transcript, April 4, 2007, http://mediamatters.org/items/printable/200704040011.

Cohen, Ted. *Jokes: Philosophical Thoughts on Joking Matters.* Chicago: University of Chicago Press, 1999.

"Don Imus, Host." Updates 1:04 a.m. ET, December 13, 2003. http://www.msnbc.msn.com/id/22070420.

"Don't Sack Me, I'm Suffering," April 7, 2007, http://www.smh.com.au/articles/2007/04/11/1175971179814.html.

Du Bois, W. E. B. *The Souls of Black Folk*. 1903; reprint, New York: Signet, 1969.

Eyerman, Ron. *Cultural Trauma: Slavery and the Formation of African American Identity*. New York: Cambridge University Press, 2002.

Herman, Judith. *Trauma and Recovery*. 1992; reprint, New York: Basic Books, 1997.

Hillman, James. *Healing Fictions*. New York: Continuum International, 1994.

"Imus Puts Remarks into Context." April 9, 2007. http://www.msnbc.msn.com/18022596.

Jones, Gayl. *Corregidora*. Boston: Beacon, 1975.

Sheppard, Marc. "With Imus's Dishonest Apologies to the Dishonest." April 12, 2007. http://mensnewsdaily.com/2007/04/12/with-imuss-dishonest-apologies-to-the-dishonest/ (accessed June 6, 2007).

Sontag, Susan. *Regarding the Pain of Others*. New York: Picador, 2004.

Suggs, Welch. *A Place on the Team: The Triumph and Tragedy of Title IX*. Princeton, NJ: Princeton University Press, 2005.

35.
INSIDE *INSIDE MAN*: SPIKE LEE AND POST-9/11 ENTERTAINMENT
Lori Harrison-Kahan

In his three decades as a filmmaker, Spike Lee has developed and sustained a reputation as an in-your-face provocateur. Just examine one of his signature cinematic techniques: the track-in close-up in which characters directly address the audience, a device unforgettably employed in the racial slur montage in his seminal *Do the Right Thing* (1989). Lee's self-declared "wake-up" calls have consistently taken on the hot-button issue of race in America, while allowing the director to make significant inroads in the landscape of American cinema in the process. Carving out a spot for himself in white-dominated Hollywood, Lee has helped pave the way for other filmmakers of color (even as critics have questioned the progress made by a so-called black film renaissance in which "gangsploitation" films have proved to be such a financially solvent genre). With a bold palette and political invectives etched in graffiti, Lee is not known for the subtlety with which he delivers his messages. In fact, his critics have accused him of sacrificing both art and entertainment for polemics, becoming, in the words of one reviewer, "predictably, and tiresomely, dogmatic."[1]

It is surprising, then, that when Lee's *Inside Man* was released in 2006, many reviewers reductively described the film as simply good old-fashioned entertainment. While a few critics expressed disappointment that Lee had left his moral concerns behind, most appeared to find the film's lack of a political agenda refreshing. "To judge from this precision-tooled amusement, Mr. Lee may have missed his calling . . . as a studio hire," wrote Manohla Dargis in the *New York Times,* aligning *Inside Man* with Richard Donner's *16 Blocks* (2006) as "another effective piece of genre showmanship."[2] Similarly, categorizing the film as a mildly innovative take on the heist genre, film critic Peter Rainer expressed relief at the "absence of any real social or racial bent" in *Inside Man,* declaring Lee "a better filmmaker, if not ideologue, when he's playing it straight."[3] With its bank-robbery-turned-hostage-crisis plot, *Inside Man* resembles the entertaining, gritty, New York–based 1970s thrillers such as *Dog Day Afternoon* (Sidney Lumet, 1975) and *Serpico* (Lumet, 1973) to which Lee's film self-consciously alludes. Even as the film achieved blockbuster status, earning Lee some of his biggest box-office returns in years, close analysis of *Inside Man* demonstrates that the director did not leave his politics behind.

Reviews of the film do nod to a few explicit moments in which Lee could not resist heavy-handed gestures, such as the oft-mentioned scene (one that Lee added to Russell Gewirtz's screenplay) between black detective Keith Frazier (Denzel Washington) and bank employee Vikram Walia (Waris Ahluwalia). Manhandled by the police under the suspicion that he is a perpetrator rather than a hostage, Walia desperately tries to convince them that he's a Sikh, not an Arab, as they claim. In the aftermath of his physical mistreatment, Walia refuses to respond to Frazier's questions until his turban, presumably removed in a search for explosives, is returned to him. As Walia rails against continual violations of his civil rights, Frazier responds, "I bet you can get a cab though." Walia resignedly concedes that this is one of the "perks" of being South Asian. Frazier's wry crack speaks to the social and economic discrimination experienced by racial minorities in contemporary Manhattan, referencing the racial profiling that makes it difficult for black men to hail cabs as well as the large number of Indian and Pakistani immigrants who make their livings as cabdrivers. As the scene suggests, in a post-9/11 racial climate, individuals of South Asian and Middle Eastern descent—those whose appearance, religious beliefs, regional backgrounds, or nationalities approximate that of the hijackers—may be in competition with African Americans for the role of the nation's most targeted outcasts within. In keeping with Lee's past treatments of race, the scene deflects its indictment of white authorities in order to cast an equally critical eye on interethnic conflict between African Americans and the nation's recent immigrants. Though seemingly confined to this scene, the film's commentary on twenty-first-century shifts in racial tensions turns out to be far from secondary to the narrative. On the DVD commentary, Lee reveals that he improvised the dialogue by telling Ahluwalia to "think of all the times since September 11 where you've been suspected of being bin Laden's brother and the treatment that you received. 'Cause that's what this script is about." The scene has drawn attention as an example of blatantly political content in *Inside Man,* content deemed marginal to the film's overall project, but the dialogue—improvised by two actors of color who are drawing on their personal experiences—also points us in the direction of Lee's masked political agenda.

In this essay, I examine *Inside Man*'s underlying critique of the shifts in racial politics that occurred after the terrorist attacks on the World Trade Center and Pentagon on September 11, 2001. Like David Gerstner, who argues that *Inside Man* can be understood in terms of contemporary theories of film authorship, I demonstrate how Lee's imprint as auteur pushes against the conventions of mainstream Hollywood and genre filmmaking.[4] Highlighting Lee's use of visual iconography, among other aesthetic and narrative techniques, this essay explores how the film

styles itself as star-powered, studio-backed entertainment while simultaneously encoding references to the events of 9/11 and its aftermath. It begins with a discussion of other post-9/11 films, including Lee's *25th Hour* (2002), which is often read as an elegy to New York City after the attacks. Contextualizing my reading of *Inside Man* with a brief overview of Hollywood's political engagements in the early twenty-first century, I argue that Lee maintains a socially conscious approach to filmmaking in his depictions of racial tensions and profiling in a globalized United States. In contrast, for example, to Mike Binder's *Reign over Me* (2007), which uses a renewed friendship between a white 9/11 widower and his black college roommate to assert racial harmony on the home front during the "war on terror," Lee does not back down from exposing the racial and economic rifts that threaten to divide the nation further in the aftermath of tragedy.

After the 25th Hour.   While rumors about a sequel to *Inside Man* abound, the 2006 thriller itself might be understood as a sequel to *25th Hour,* the 2002 release that earned Lee considerable critical acclaim. In contrast to *Inside Man,* critics readily identified *25th Hour* as a post-9/11 allegory despite the fact that it was based on a pre-9/11 novel by David Benioff, who also wrote the screenplay. While most directors filming in New York in the wake of the devastation in lower Manhattan went to great lengths to avoid any references to the tragedy, Lee was credited as being the first director to acknowledge the attacks, from the opening credits, which show the twin pillars of light commemorating the dead, to the shots of makeshift memorials throughout the city.[5]

While the backdrop of post-9/11 New York City sets *25th Hour*'s haunting mood, the film does not explicitly deal with these events. Instead, it follows a small-time Irish American drug dealer, Monty Brogan (Edward Norton). Sentenced to seven years in prison after a bust by the Drug Enforcement Administration (DEA), Monty spends his last twenty-four hours of freedom saying goodbye to friends, family, and the city. With Monty's farewell as metaphor, the film succeeds in evoking the city's grief and mourning and the sense that life will never be the same again. The pillars of light and Terence Blanchard's lush, mournful score for orchestra and voice fade as the opening credits come to a close and our first view of Monty after his sentencing takes place on the edge of Manhattan. Seated on a park bench, he gazes meditatively across the East River, the bars of the railing before him signifying his impending incarceration. The allegory becomes inescapable in a scene that has received both criticism and praise in which Monty's two best friends, English teacher Jacob Elinsky (Philip Seymour Hoffman) and Wall Street trader Francis Xavier Slaughtery (Barry Pepper), discuss his fate in front of a window in Francis's financial district apartment. As Francis tries to convince naïve Jacob that they might never again see their childhood friend, whose "pretty boy" good looks will make him a sexual target in jail, the soaring vocals from the credit sequence return, and a long take forces viewers to linger on the ruins of the towers below. Following the conversation, we hear military drumbeats as the camera cuts to an aerial shot offering a closer look at the excavation going on through the night at Ground Zero.

Building on reviews that took note of the film's deeper meanings, emergent scholarship on *25th Hour* has begun to examine the impact of 9/11 on Lee's filmmaking. In a *Sight and Sound* review, Ryan Gilbey equates Monty's fear of sodomization in jail to the emasculation experienced by the United States when the phallic towers crumbled to the ground; Gilbey reads the threat of same-sex rape in the film "as a metaphor for the brutalisation suffered by America."[6] In one of the few critical essays thus far published on the film, Patricia O'Neill argues that *25th Hour* interrogates the intersections of race and class by transposing global issues onto the local space of Lee's hometown: "By extending his critique of social injustice against the politically disadvantaged to the terrorist attacks of Osama bin Laden, by daring to film ground zero, and by subverting the myth of the American West as a viable escape from responsibility, personal or historical, Spike Lee's film offers us one of the very few meaningful American responses to globalization and the attack on the World Trade Center."[7] *Inside Man* further extends Lee's critique of social injustice after 9/11, and like many of Lee's films, takes aim at the ways that the nation's racial

inequalities are undergirded by the economic forces of capitalism—a critique that Lee extends to the film industry itself.

In the aftermath of 9/11, Hollywood feared that its standard fare of murder and mayhem might alienate American viewers, from those who directly witnessed, experienced, and lost loved ones in the attacks to those compelled to watch the towers fall over and over on their television screens, as the media endlessly replayed the footage. The Arnold Schwarzenegger vehicle *Collateral Damage* (Andrew Davis, 2002), for example, was pulled from its scheduled release shortly after the attacks, and its depictions of terrorism were reedited. In telling the story of a pusher whose ability to sustain his risky livelihood depends on the sadistic mobsters for whom he works, *25th Hour* could have easily included depictions of brutality that traditionally accompany films about the illegal drug trade. The Hollywood profile of drug dealing has historically featured black criminals and rarely refrained from glamorizing lifestyles on the edge, even as many of these films, especially those by black directors, contained underlying social critiques of the racist and economic forces affecting the inner city's residents of color.[8] Like *Clockers* (1995), Lee's film about the devastating effects of drug-related crime on black urban youth, *25th Hour* refuses to submit to the conventions of the blaxploitation and neo-blaxploitation genres, further flying in the face of media stereotypes by featuring a white ethnic narcotics peddler.

This refusal to play by Hollywood's rules is established from the film's prologue, in which we first hear the sound of a dog being beaten. Rather than allowing us to witness the attack visually, the film's initial image introduces Monty rescuing the bloody dog, who has been left for dead by unknown assailants. The dog becomes the protagonist's constant companion throughout the film, as Monty tries to find a home for the mutt before going to jail. This prologue prepares us for a later scene in the movie in which Monty, handed a gun by a Russian mob boss, rejects the opportunity to kill the man who has turned him in to the DEA. In the immediate post-9/11 context, when individuals and government officials called for revenge in the name of patriotism and national security, Monty's refusal to take the life of the man who destroyed his own life can be read as a prescription against vengeance. Over the course of his last twenty-four hours as a free man, Monty struggles to temper the rage he had expressed earlier in the film's notorious "Fuck You" montage, which occurs during his last supper at his father's Irish pub. In this sequence, Monty stares at himself in the bathroom mirror with the graffiti words "Fuck You" positioned next to a postcard of the Twin Towers superimposed over an American flag. Monty's mirror image engages in an extended verbal riff on the vandal's words accompanied by visual illustrations. His offensive "Fuck You" rant is directed at the various groups that make up New York City, from Sikhs and Pakistanis "bombing down the avenues in decrepit cabs . . . terrorists in fucking training," to African Americans "who blame everything on the white man"; from gay men, Puerto Ricans, "Dumbinicans," and Bensonhurst Italians, to upper–East Side white women, Hasidic jewelers, and even Jesus Christ. The rant extends, too, to "Osama bin Laden, Al Qaeda, and backward ass cave-dwelling fundamentalist assholes everywhere," whom Monty's image tells to "Kiss my royal Irish ass"—a quotation from the infamous Concert of New York benefit speech by New York firefighter Michael Moran, who lost his brother in the attempted rescue effort. While the tirade culminates in a wish for apocalyptic destruction of the city, the sequence concludes with Monty answering back to his own reflection: "No, fuck you, Montgomery Brogan. You had it all and you threw it away. You dumb fuck."

As this scene suggests, Monty will turn inward the violence and rage initially directed toward others. In one of the film's final scenes, he tries to convince and then actively provokes his best friend to beat him in order to damage the fine features that are likely to subject him to rape in jail. In light of Gilbey's reading of the film's obsession with homosexuality, we might understand this self-flagellation as a means of avoiding emasculation. In asking a friend to administer the violence against himself rather than shooting the man who betrayed him, Monty is forced to take responsibility for his actions, which the film views as the more "manly" alternative to revenge. As played by Norton, Monty is a morally ambiguous character

who becomes increasingly sympathetic in the act of acknowledging his own complicity in his fate. In equating Monty's loss (and the loss of Monty) to that of New York City, *25th Hour* advocates against the outward violence of "an eye for an eye," insisting instead that the nation take stock of itself by engaging in self-reflection.

The narrative of accountability, the imperative of facing up to the repercussions of one's actions and lifestyle, persists throughout the film. Although Monty and his friends contemplate admittedly bleak alternatives to prison (namely, suicide and escape), these options are not given serious weight, and the film ends with Monty's father driving his son to the upstate penitentiary. As Monty's battered face stares out the window of the car, the targets of his earlier "Fuck You" rant—Korean grocers, South Asian cabdrivers, black "brothers"—appear in a slow tracking shot, beneficently smiling goodbye. In owning up to his past indiscretions, Monty has won the city's compassion and forgiveness, and the mournful beauty of the sequence suggests that he has done the right thing.

At this point, it is not Monty but his father who fantasizes about driving westward and enabling his son to escape. Shots of Monty walking in the desert, getting a job as a bartender, and creating a new identity for himself are accompanied by his father's voiceover narration. The happy ending is supplied when the outlaw is joined by his Puerto Rican girlfriend, Naturelle Rivera (Rosario Dawson), and the two are depicted in gray-haired old age surrounded by their multiracial family. The idealized notion that one can shirk the past through reinvention is the norm of Hollywood cinema, persistent disseminator of the American dream. "The desert's for starting over," Monty's father says, but the fantasy sequence also shows the flags of our fathers tattered by the desert wind. The washed-out tones and all-white costuming of the modern-day pioneer family indicate that the dreamlike sequence remains irrevocably in the realm of imagination, and a final shot of the car heading up the Henry Hudson Parkway confirms that Monty's father does not take the left turn but continues to drive northward. Like the film's refusal of blaxploitation conventions, the westward fantasy sequence of *25th Hour* operates as a cinematic renunciation, this time of the Western, a genre similarly known for its depictions of racist violence. The film's ending raises and then rejects the father's frontier narrative of manifest destiny. The moral resolution of the film thus sounds a cautionary note against the imperialistic impulse spurred on by the events of 9/11, as the Bush administration pushed forward the frontier once again, declaring a "war on terror" in the service of spreading democracy to all.

Outside of *25th Hour* and Michael Moore's hugely successful 2004 documentary *Fahrenheit 9/11*, American cinema initially remained reluctant to confront the events of 9/11 and the ensuing wars in Afghanistan and Iraq. Bush's second term, however, brought with it the inevitable spate of films taking on the tragedies of 9/11 directly. In addition to *Reign over Me*, with its message of cross-racial reconciliation and healing in the face of insurmountable loss, films such as Oliver Stone's skeptically viewed *World Trade Center* (2006) and Paul Greengrass's better-received docudrama *United 93* (2006) tried to accentuate the positive by focusing on American heroes, whether or not they survived the attacks. The US campaign against terror has left an undeniable mark on a range of films, including comedies such as *Borat: Cultural Learnings of America for Make Benefit Glorious Nation of Kazakhstan* (Larry Charles, 2006) and *Harold and Kumar Escape from Guantanamo Bay* (Jon Hurwitz and Hayden Schlossberg, 2008); dramas such as *Munich* (Steven Spielberg, 2005), *In the Valley of Elah* (Paul Haggis, 2007), *Charlie Wilson's War* (Mike Nichols, 2007), and *Lions for Lambs* (Robert Redford, 2007); large-scale critiques of the oil industry in *Syriana* (Stephen Gaghan, 2005) and *There Will Be Blood* (Paul Thomas Anderson, 2007); war movies such as Clint Eastwood's 2006 Pacific-front World War II series *Flags of Our Fathers* and *Letters from Iwo Jima*; the science fiction–comic book formats of *V for Vendetta* (James McTeigue, 2005) and *Superman Returns* (Bryan Singer, 2006); and George A. Romero's allegorical *Land of the Dead* (2005).

In many of these films, and in the public discourse surrounding them, race plays a central role. While *Flags of Our Fathers*, for example, features a Native American character reluctant to assume the mantle of war hero, Eastwood's failure to include black soldiers in prominent roles came under attack by none other than Lee himself. The second installment in the *Harold and Kumar* series traces the evolution of Asian American model minorities, a stereotype comically skewered in the first film (*Harold and Kumar Go to White Castle* [Hurwitz and Schlossberg, 2004]), into new manifestations of the yellow peril. Indeed, domestic race relations became a preoccupation of Hollywood in 2006, when white director Paul Haggis's *Crash*, a post-9/11 look at racial strife in Los Angeles, took home the Oscar for Best Motion Picture. *Crash*'s multiple, intersecting plotlines include the story of a Persian family whose store is burglarized and vandalized in a racially motivated incident.

The unanticipated success of *Crash* and the initial, celebrity-fueled public outcry following Hurricane Katrina (the subject of Lee's 2006 HBO documentary *When the Levees Broke: A Requiem in Four Acts*) suggest that Americans may be more comfortable confronting racial tensions at home than dealing with the consequences of the nation's racist and imperialist policies abroad. Media pundits have recently called attention to the lack of audience for films dealing with the war in Iraq. "Iraq is to moviegoers what garlic is to vampires," wrote Frank Rich in his op-ed column on the topic, citing films such as *Standard Operating Procedure*, Errol Morris's 2008 Abu Ghraib exposé, and Kimberly Peirce's *Stop-Loss* (2008), about recent war veterans, which have failed utterly at the box office.[9] While early-twenty-first-century audiences flocked to high-profile documentaries like the agit-prop *Fahrenheit 9/11* and Al Gore's call to environmental reckoning, *An Inconvenient Truth* (Davis Guggenheim, 2006), the public did seem to grow reluctant to confront overt protest in the theater as the Bush administration waned. Taking the pulse of a nation increasingly uneasy with any marriage between entertainment and foreign policy statements (witness the hullabaloo that erupted after Dixie Chicks singer Natalie Maines condemned the war in Iraq and said she was "ashamed that the President of the United States is from Texas"), Lee not only transposes global issues onto local space, but also embeds most of his critique in the visual elements of *Inside Man,* thus inscribing political activism in his ostensibly escapist genre picture.

Location, Location, Location.

As in the scene in *25th Hour* in which Lee places the conversation between Monty's friends against the backdrop of Ground Zero, *Inside Man* strategically employs location to situate itself as a post-9/11 allegory. Its action taking place over the course of a single day, the film tells the story of a masterfully planned bank robbery at the fictional Manhattan Trust Bank. Like *25th Hour, Inside Man* was written by someone other than Lee, in this case screenwriting newcomer Russell Gewirtz. While filmmaking is without question a collaborative process, comparing Gewirtz's screenplay to the final product helps to shed light on Lee's methods as an auteur and the ways in which his signature techniques underscore the social and political undercurrents of the script. Under Lee's direction, for example, the bank was moved from West 23rd Street in Gewirtz's screenplay to 20 Exchange Place at the intersection of Broadway and Wall Street—a location established by the film's opening shots and dialogue. Lee thus turns the imposing structure of the Manhattan Trust Bank, located in the midst of Wall Street, into a metaphor for the towering global financial hub of the World Trade Center. As O'Neill points out in her reading of the meeting between globalization and localization in *25th Hour,* Lee's films represent the nation on a microcosmic scale by focusing on a confined sliver of geographic space that is broadened by the diversity of its residents. Substituting "Manhattan" for "World" and centering the action around a financial institution, *Inside Man* depicts New York as a global city dependent on the flow of transnational labor and controlled by capitalist exploitation. Lest we forget that we are situated within a post-9/11 world, a mural of an American flag, its stripes made up of the words "We Will Never Forget" and its blue square of stars replaced by a darkened image of the Towers and the Statue of Liberty, looms behind two main characters during a crucial confrontation.

To read the siege of the Manhattan Trust Bank as a metaphor for the attack on the World Trade Center is too easy, however. The film complicates such an understanding by blurring lines between good guys and bad, innocent and guilty, hostage and hostage-taker, victim and terrorist, through a number of devices, including casting, costuming, and disturbances in the linear framework of the narrative. The film's somewhat convoluted plot and extensive ensemble cast contribute to the narrative's defiance of a simple binary power struggle. On the inside of the bank, we have the hostages (both customers and employees) and the robbers, headed by Dalton Russell (Clive Owen), who establishes himself as the ringleader in an opening monologue. Russell and his cohorts are in a standoff with those outside the bank, whose ranks are divided between the NYPD, led by white Captain Darius (Willem Dafoe), and two maverick black detectives—Washington's Keith Frazier and sidekick, Bill Mitchell (Chiwetel Ejiofor)—who serve as hostage negotiators and whom the police view as incompetent. Into this already triangulated power structure, the film introduces a set of business suit–wearing power players. When fixer Madeleine White (Jodie Foster) is hired by the bank's president, Arthur Case (Christopher Plummer), to ensure that the robbers do not get to the carefully guarded secrets of his safe deposit box, she enlists the aid of none other than the New York City mayor, bribing him to gain access to the crime scene. As represented by the lethal Ms. White with her knifelike heels and stabbing smile of contempt, this last group—"the suits"—is the only one to materialize as unambiguously villainous. Their culpability is confirmed midway through the film when it is revealed that Case's bank was built with "blood money" he made while collaborating with the Nazis during World War II, a revelation that transforms the robbers/terrorists into ethically justified, if not completely heroic, characters.

A careful analysis of the opening credit sequence reveals the film's engagement with global cultural politics. Before attending to the visuals, though, it is worth noting the film's auditory prelude. Though the sound track of the film is composed by longtime Lee collaborator Terence Blanchard, the film opens with "Chaiyya Chaiyya," Indian composer

A. R. Rahman's hit from *Dil Se* (Mani Ratnam, 1998), a Bollywood film about a love affair between a female suicide bomber and a government servant. In an article on female playback singers in Hindi cinema, Pavitra Sundar expresses concern that *Inside Man*'s use of "Chaiyya Chaiyya" strips the song of its ethnic and nationalist context: "What matters [to Lee] is that 'Chaiyya Chaiyya' is a fast-paced song, appropriate for a crime thriller and the chaos of New York City. It also perhaps sounds exciting and vaguely mysterious to non-Indian ears."[10] Certainly, the high-energy "Chaiyya Chaiyya" effectively sets the stage for the suspense of *Inside Man,* but it is not at all clear that this is all that "matters" when we consider the role that language and polyvocality play in the rest of the film, as well as the fact that Lee is known for the messages he conveys via his careful musical selections.[11]

The fact that the first sounds we hear in *Inside Man* are Indian music and Hindi language is significant in light of both the film's representation of New York as a transnational Tower of Babel and Lee's contention that the script is about the mistreatment of South Asians after 9/11. To affirm the symbolic role that linguistic and auditory cues play in the film, we need to look at a series of scenes in which the robbers foil an attempt to bug the inside of the bank. The police grant the robbers' request for food by sending in boxes of pizza equipped with listening devices. Hearing a foreign language emanating from within the bank, Captain Darius incorrectly concludes that the hostage-takers are Russians, which increases his agitation. "If my guys got to shoot it out with those fucking savages . . ." he warns Frazier, in a throwback allusion to the cold war. When the police department experts fail to translate, let alone identify, the language being spoken, Frazier's solution is to broadcast it over the speakers, reasoning: "This is New York City. Someone on the street must know what it is. Probably the hotdog man." Like Frazier's pithy remark about the ethnic makeup of New York City cabdrivers, this quip is not just a throwaway line but instead a reminder of the realities of immigrant labor in a global economy. Indeed, a construction worker quickly identifies the language as Albanian, and his Albanian ex-wife is called in to translate, revealing

that the voice is a recorded speech by Enver Hoxha, Albania's late president.

The film's introductory juxtaposition of the seemingly localized setting with world music and languages similarly acknowledges the forces of transnational commerce and cultural exchange that define New York as a global city and its residents as global citizens. Contrary to Sundar's claims that *Inside Man* neglects the ethnic and nationalist specificity of "Chaiyya Chaiyya," it is exactly this specificity that makes it such a suitable preface to Lee's film. "Chaiyya Chaiyya" is temporarily interrupted by Russell's opening monologue, which also provides us with the film's first image: an extreme close-up of Clive Owen performing Lee's signature direct address. This monologue is initially delivered against a solid black backdrop, but slowly the background lightens to reveal the cinderblocks of what appears to be a prison cell. Russell informs us that he is not in jail, that "there's a vast difference between being stuck in a tiny cell and being in prison." One of the surprises of the film occurs later, when we learn that Russell's cell is in fact a self-imposed hideout that he and the other robbers created in the bank's supply closet. When the police infiltrate the bank, they find that no money has been taken; Russell emerges from his hiding place a week later with the contents of Case's safe deposit box, which includes diamonds and papers that incriminate the bank president as a Nazi collaborator. While the secret of Russell's location is one of the film's suspenseful twists, it is further significant that the opening refuses our knowledge of his location—a decontextualization of place that is repeated throughout the film in the interrogation scenes. From the mysterious-sounding music sung in a language not readily identifiable to most American ears, to Russell's cryptic monologue delivered from an unknown place, the opening of *Inside Man* unsettles and dislocates viewers.

Even when Lee appears to return to more conventional cinematic techniques after the monologue, however, he continues this process of dislocation by moving ethnic margins to the center. Viewers are denied the standard establishing shots of Manhattan with long shots of the skyline and close-ups of major landmarks such as the Empire State Building. Prior to

9/11, one of these landmarks would have inevitably been the Twin Towers, which created a conundrum for directors about to release their New York–based films when the attacks occurred. Although it does so more subtly than the credit sequence in *25th Hour,* the opening of *Inside Man* acknowledges how the events of 9/11 have transformed the cultural imaginary of Manhattan: the once-omnipotent city is now vulnerable to outside attack. The establishing shots use less recognizable landmarks in order to position us on the outskirts of Manhattan. Even the best known of these sites, the Statue of Liberty, does not dominate the screen; it is filmed from the perspective of the Brooklyn Heights promenade, a viewpoint clearly located outside of Manhattan. The first establishing shot is the Coney Island Cyclone, topped with the American flag; the camera lingers over the image of the roller coaster as we watch one of the robbers, in long shot, walk up to a van and begin driving. The Cyclone is, in part, a playful image, launching the thrill ride we are about to experience, but the Coney Island location also places us in a distinctly ethnic context since the seaside leisure area has historically catered to an immigrant working-class population. The subsequent establishing shots similarly place us in the ethnically diverse borough of Brooklyn (Lee's own hometown) and then, as the robbers' van traverses the Brooklyn Bridge, in the Lower East Side and Chinatown, past and present ghettos just north of the financial district.

Just as the opening credits decenter location, the introduction of the film's characters that occurs during this sequence similarly defies viewer expectations. Because they appear in either long shots or extreme partial close-ups, the robbers' identities are largely obscured; the fact that they are all dressed in identical white painters' coveralls, baseball caps, and sunglasses makes individuation nearly impossible. The suspense of the film depends on our not being entirely sure of the identities of the robbers, except for Russell. However, it is further remarkable that the members of the group emerge from different ethnic locales, even as their outward appearances are identically white. The interchangeability of the bank robbers and their lack of individualization are reinforced later when they call each other by variations on the same name: Stevie, Steve-O, Steven, and Steve. Even

the lone female member of the group (Kim Director) is identified with a seemingly masculine moniker, Stevie, though purposeful shots of her long hair and cleavage reveal her to be a woman. In dressing alike and calling each other by the same name, the robbers perform a mockery of Americanization. Their cleverly orchestrated performance of assimilation is a tactic that enables them to commit and get away with a crime. This narrative bears an eerie resemblance to the stories told of the 9/11 hijackers: members of sleeper cells, they made temporary homes in the United States, blending in with the American populace and taking advantage of the nation's freedoms, as they enrolled in flight lessons and prepared for the coordinated attacks. They became, in effect, "inside men," finding refuge in anonymity and in the very institutions that were the target of their aggression.

As the credits progress, the establishing shots showing the gathering of the bank robbers from outside Manhattan are crosscut with shots of the Manhattan Trust Bank, the robbers' destination. The gritty realism of the ethnic neighborhoods is juxtaposed with the façade of the bank, which is introduced in a series of fragmented medium shots and extreme close-ups. In the crosscutting sequence it is the bank, rather than the robbers, that appears ominous. The first shot of the bank is a gold plaque stating its name above an engraving of a ship, an icon of Western expansion. Other close-ups depict statues of fierce-looking animals, including an eagle. A low-angle shot of the equally menacing Wall Street bull and a high-angle shot of the New York Stock Exchange, prominently draped with American flags, confirm the financial district location and create a correspondence between Lee's fictional site and these national symbols of global financial dominance. The pristine image of the bank begins to erode with our first glimpse of human faces in military helmets, carved in white but stained with black by exposure to the elements. The color iconography of the bank façade is soon to be echoed on the interior when the hostages and robbers don matching black-and-white outfits.

While the exterior of the bank gives the impression of an impenetrable fortress, once the cameras take us inside we are offered a glimpse into the ethnic diversity of Manhattan that directly contrasts with the preternaturally whitened images of the robbers. The camera singles out people of color and members of immigrant groups to offer a cross section of this multiethnic urban space. The mise-en-scène includes African Americans (ranging from security guards and other employees to customers waiting in line, such as the father in suit and tie and his video game–playing son) and Latinos (including a Spanglish-speaking man named Paul who corrects the detectives when they insist on calling him Pablo during his interrogation). South and East Asians are represented by the Sikh employee previously discussed and by an iPod-wearing customer. An Orthodox Jew is identified by his black hat and later called "Rabbi" by Russell when he refuses to get down on the ground during the takeover. Other white characters are at some point identified as ethnic as well, often through linguistic markers. For example, an elderly man released by the hostages when he succumbs to respiratory problems tells a story involving his Polish grandmother who didn't know English; an elderly woman sprinkles her speech with Yiddish phrases. From the credit sequence that surveyed New York's often racially and ethnically segregated landscape, the camera has moved us into the space of the bank, where individuals from various backgrounds converge. Money may make the world go round, but according to the logic of global capitalism it also brings the world under one roof.

Black Suits, White Masks. The opening of
Inside Man thus sets the stage for an exploration of racial tensions in a multiethnic urban environment. As the narrative progresses, its messages in regard to the hypocrisies of American imperialism, the fear-mongering that produces racial profiling, and the dominance of white cultural capital in a global society are similarly shown to be integrated into the film's aesthetics. One element of the film that warrants special attention is the costuming of the hostages. Soon after Russell and his crew wrest control of the bank, they herd the customers and employees to the basement, where they instruct the hostages to strip to their underwear, supplying them with hooded black boiler suits and white face masks identical to the ones worn by the robbers. The contrast between the shots

of the hostages huddled together in the basement in identical attire and the earlier shots of them in the bank's lobby prior to the takeover is remarkable, yet it is also notable that we are still able to identify many of the individuals by their voices, marked by accents or the ethnic flavor of their speech.

When we next see the robbers after this scene, we discover that they too have put on black suits over their white painters' uniforms. Hostage-takers and hostages are now identical in appearance, save for the discrepancy between the dark sunglasses worn by the former and the black eye-masks that prevent the latter from seeing. The robbers' "genius plan," as one hostage calls it, involves a performative enactment of Stockholm syndrome, the psychological term coined in 1973 when, after a siege of a Swedish bank, it was discovered that many of the employees had come to identify with their captors and had tried to defend them. In its practical usage, the costuming functions as Stockholm syndrome in reverse, enabling the captors to embed themselves with their victims and thereby elude discovery. Instead of coming to see the hostage-takers as villains wielding power over helpless innocents, viewers are more likely to perceive them as sympathetic in their resemblance to the victims.

While the costuming appears to be first theatrical and then pragmatic on the part of the hostage-takers, it takes on a political valence also, as the film's iconography creates a web of allusions to recent events on the global and national stage. Again, it is worth noting that Lee has instituted a change from Gewirtz's script, in which hostages and robbers alike were dressed in white. In the film, the costumes have been altered to include black boiler suits with loose black hoods. The balaclavas may be suggestive of disguises worn by bank robbers, but in the climate of post-9/11 paranoia, they cannot help but also call to mind the garb of terrorists as well as Muslim head coverings. What makes the costume choice even more startling, however, is the similarity between the black hoods donned by the hostages and those that obscured the faces of the inmates at Abu Ghraib prison in the photographs taken by American soldiers as part of the systematic and sadistic humiliation of foreign prisoners. Supplying documentation of the physical, sexual, and psychological abuse suffered by detainees at the Iraqi prison, the appearance of these photographs in the press in 2004 instigated world-wide condemnations of and investigations into the US policies on torture and the maltreatment of suspected and confirmed terrorists in Iraq and Guantánamo Bay, Cuba. One scene in particular makes this allusion to Abu Ghraib vividly clear. When Madeleine White, wearing an oversized NYPD jacket over her tailored clothes, enters the bank to cut a deal with Russell, the film cuts abruptly to an aerial shot in which she is lying facedown, spread-eagled on the ground as she is frisked by one of his associates. In the dimly lit shot, the shadow of the alleged robber is cast over White, so that Jodie Foster's outstretched arms and the silhouette of the robber's black hood join together to form an emblematic facsimile of the nightmarish photograph in which a black-cloaked and hooded Abu Ghraib prisoner stands atop a crate with electrodes dangling from his hands.

Of course, the Iraq War Abu Ghraib prisoner abuse scandal was a crucial moment for undoing the patriotic discourse of a righteous America pitted against the dark forces of a strange and dangerous Islamic fundamentalism. As they circulated in the press, the photographs upended the established narrative of victim and perpetrator, hero and villain, opening up the United States to the same accusations of torture and terrorism it claimed to have set out to eradicate in the Arab world. Inducing Americans to recognize that there may be more than one enemy within, these photographs uncovered iniquity among those whose duty it was to defend the nation and its people. The costuming in *Inside Man* accomplishes a similar effect, confusing as it does the difference between hostage and terrorist, innocent and guilty, abused and abuser. This ambiguity enables the criminals to escape, not by disguising their guilt but by implicating everyone as suspects. Thus, at the same time that the costuming evokes international debate about the dangers of American imperialism abroad, it also allows the film to push forward a related component of its political agenda that is closer to home: racial profiling.

Inside Man's commentary on racial profiling was made evident in the scene between the black

detective and the Sikh bank employee, but it comes to a head in the film's dramatically filmed sequence in which the cloaked, hooded, and masked captives stream out of the bank in anticipation of a raid by the police. Installing their leader in his tiny cell, Russell's accomplices have embedded themselves among the hostages. With cries of "Don't shoot" and hands waving in the air, the hostages emerge amid smoke, rifles trained on them. In what turns out to be a hail of rubber bullets, one after another of the hostages falls to the ground before a cease-fire is called. In this scene, Lee uses forty-five-degree shutter speed to convey the panic and chaos that arise from the police's inability to differentiate the hostages from their captors. Following an aerial shot of the pandemonium, masks begin to come off and faces are revealed, but disclosure makes little difference. In most cases, the treatment the hostages receive at the hands of the police is worse than the robbers' treatment of them, especially for those with darker skins. The well-dressed African American customer who carries his son out in his arms is forced to the ground while grasping the young boy to him. As the hostages' names and mug shots are taken, a black security guard repeatedly insists, "I work in the bank," a direct echo of the words uttered by the Sikh hostage just before he was manhandled by the police. The scene depends upon a degree of dramatic irony, since the film's audience is privy to some knowledge of who is a criminal and who is not, but the jittery, disorienting subjective camerawork captures the paranoia of the authorities who, in the absence of other means of differentiation, turn to skin color to single out potentially dangerous suspects.

Unable to distinguish between guilty and innocent, the police are forced to take everyone into custody. As the Sikh employee earlier asserted about the lack of randomness in so-called random security checks, anyone who resembles a "terrorist" becomes a suspect; all the hostages have been made to resemble their captors. Handcuffed and forced to the ground, the bodies of the hostages are laid out like the dead and wounded—the black suits now resembling body bags more than anything else—before being herded onto a police bus. The camera cranes down and pans across the side of the bus to show us four faces in a row against the windows. As we find out later when the identities of all the robbers are revealed, the camera has identified the four culprits, their faces drawn and weary as if they too have barely survived the ordeal.

A powerful visual metaphor, the costuming works on multiple levels to critique the nation's prevailing racial ideologies and their devastating consequences at home and abroad. The identical uniforms are, on the one hand, symbols of compulsory assimilatory practices, especially in the imposition of white masks; the costumes deprive the bank's occupants of their ethnic and cultural specificity, forcing upon them a conformity to a dominant culture not their own, even as voice and accent often reveal the slippage in this ambivalent process of obligatory identification. On the other hand, the black outfits and hoods work in almost the opposite way, turning the captives into an undifferentiated sea of racial others in which darker outward appearance is the only determinant of guilt. Finally, in bringing the nation's abuses of power out of the shadows, the costumes serve as a painful reminder of how easily the threat of terrorism can transform the threatened from victim to villain.

In direct contradiction to the fundamental ideal of democratic justice, everyone inside the bank is guilty until proven otherwise, a perversion of the judicial system that is reinforced by the narrative's unusual chronology. Approximately twenty-five minutes into the film, Lee cuts from the unfolding action at the bank to an extreme close-up of an African American security guard who appears to be giving a talking-head interview; close to tears, he speaks movingly about how close he came to never seeing his family again. As the camera cuts to a reverse shot of Frazier and Mitchell, we realize that this is no media interview but the detectives' questioning of a man who is both witness and suspect. The narrative continues to defy strict linearity, interspersing increasingly hostile interrogations of the suspects with the crisis-in-progress, so that the two parts of the film—the events and their aftermath—operate as commentaries on and reflections of one another. In the course of the hostage situation, one hostage is beaten and another forcibly dragged from a room. Yet the gloomy cell where Mitchell and Frazier conduct

their interrogations bears more resemblance to a torture chamber than the basement of the bank where the hostages are held. The interrogation scenes are set apart cinematographically from the rest of the movie. Filmed in grainy tones with dim lighting against a greenish-gray backdrop, the suspects in the low-ceilinged room are shown in persistent close-ups that deny us any sense of the surrounding space; to heighten the effect of distortion, the suspects are occasionally shown in duplicate, blurrily reflected in a mirror behind the shoulders of the interrogators. While it quickly becomes clear that these interviews are taking place after the siege, the scenes also confirm that the hostages—many of whom we know to be innocent—remain suspects.

In stark contrast to the ways in which the film earlier used carefully constructed establishing shots to locate us in and out of Manhattan, these scenes take place in a dungeonlike no-man's-land suggestive of prison camps such as Guantánamo Bay. In an article asserting that the international debate about the treatment of suspected terrorists at Guantánamo has granted validity to the idea of an American Empire, once seen as a "contradiction in terms," Amy Kaplan describes the prison camp as "a liminal national space, in, yet not within Cuba . . . not clearly under the sovereignty of either nation, nor seemingly subject to national or international law."[12] As a site for the often antagonistic cross-examination of suspects who are never confirmed as criminals, the interrogation room is seemingly outside any legal jurisdiction. Circumscribed by its liminality, the depiction of this space contributes to the film's critique of American imperialism and misuses of power. A rare moment in the film addressing the objectification of women confirms this; told that she fits a physical description of one of the robbers, a large-busted woman (who turns out to be the aforementioned Stevie) sarcastically asks if she "violated section 34 double D."

In fact, much like the torture of suspected terrorists, the interrogations prove to be ineffective. "It's like the thing never happened," Frazier says when the suspects fail to implicate each other in the crime. Turning elsewhere for its villain, the plot thickens and unfurls in order to expose bank president Arthur Case as the real "bad guy." This facet of the plot is revealed to the audience approximately midway through the film, when Ms. White enters the bank to negotiate with the ringleader on behalf of her client, and Russell reveals her client's buried past. As Russell tells the story of a man who "used his position with the Nazis to enrich himself while all around him people were being stripped of everything they owned," a signature dolly shot of Case at his desk, surrounded by philanthropic awards, notably marked by Star of David and menorah, indicates that he attempted to atone for his sins through philanthropy to Jewish causes.

The profiling of suspects relies upon race—the suspicion that beneath every turban is an explosive and behind every black skin a criminal intent. But the film ultimately uncovers American capitalist greed and corruption as the true hidden evil. In the aftermath of Hurricane Katrina, as he was filming *When the Levees Broke,* Lee often spoke of class, in addition to race, as a great national divide. Critiquing the media's tendency to focus on African Americans of the Lower Ninth Ward and, in particular, the looting and violence that took place at the Superdome and the Ernst N. Morial Convention Center, Lee's documentary emphasized that poor white residents of New Orleans also suffered numerous fatalities and losses of property.[13] Even prior to this, Lee's films have remained attentive to the economic underpinnings of racial inequality. In *Do the Right Thing,* for example, the tensions in Bedford-Stuyvesant result from American capitalist ideologies coercing immigrants, whether Italian pizza parlor owners or Korean grocers, to participate in the economic exploitation of African Americans, thus diverting black-white conflict into an explosion of cross-ethnic resentment.[14] Tracing a trajectory from *Do the Right Thing* to *Inside Man,* Lee's DVD commentary for the latter film draws attention to a loaded intertextual reference: the pizza boxes sent in to the bank are from Sal's Pizzeria. In joking that "Sal's pizzeria burned down in Brooklyn and moved to Wall Street," Lee reiterates the codependency between capitalism and racism.

Clearly, race does not trump class when it comes to the gulfs in the nation. Instead, the conflation of white privilege with monetary power is figured in the aptly named Ms. White, *Inside Man*'s mysterious power broker, who is introduced to us in the process of assisting Osama bin Laden's nephew in purchasing a co-op on Park Avenue. While oil wealth allows bin Laden's nephew to circumvent the strictures of American racism, albeit by calling in the services of a fixer named White, African Americans remain firmly excluded from such access to illicit power. This is made evident in a series of confrontations between White and Frazier, whom she continually reminds of his low pay-grade and the fact that he cannot afford her services. (In an allusion to America's slave economy of the past, Frazier, in turn, must remind Ms. White that she doesn't "own" him.) Foster's character reveals the deeply entrenched corruptions of a class system in which the rich can purchase the privileges of operating outside the law. As the go-to woman for bank presidents and city mayors alike, Ms. White embodies the ease with which money sways the scales of justice.

Hollywood Insider.   In the opening and closing credits of *Inside Man,* a graphic circles the names of cast and crew. While at first appearing to be an abstract design, closer examination reveals that the circular image can be read as either the combination to a safe or the lens of a camera. A meta-cinematic device, the graphic serves to remind us of the director's presence in the construction of this narrative. Equating bank vault and camera lens, the symbol signals Lee's application of his critique to the Hollywood film industry itself. Like many of his other films, *Inside Man* protests the social injustices maintained by an American capitalist system and by a film industry in which directors of color are denied access to the same resources available to white filmmakers. Yet, as Marxist and feminist critics have been quick to point out, Lee's filmmaking is not as radical as it seems.[15] Even as Lee has engaged in guerrilla strategies, in looking for alternative avenues of funding outside the Hollywood studios, he has developed a reputation as a shameless self-promoter in collusion with the capitalist ethos, whether by filming Nike commercials or selling Malcolm X hats. As a studio picture, *Inside Man* provides evidence of Lee's ambivalent relationship to both capitalism and the Hollywood film industry, and the film's subtext actively acknowledges his complicit desire to "get paid" by aligning the director with mastermind bank robber Dalton Russell.

Although *Inside Man* contains numerous examples of Lee's unconventional aesthetic devices—devices often attributed to his sensibilities as a consciously black director—the film was viewed by many as his attempt to play nice with the film industry. This is evidenced by the reviews that cite him as capitulating to Hollywood's demands by downplaying his dogmatism. As my reading has established, though, this is far from the case; Lee's social consciousness is very much present, woven deeply into the film's texture and apparent in his visual metaphors. An analysis of the wordplay contained in the film's title suggests the multiple meanings circulating throughout. If we take the title at face value, it refers to a crime committed by someone on the inside (in this case, an ironic usage since Russell is not an employee but quite literally installs himself inside the bank). If we shift the accent to read "inside" not as an adjective but as a prepositional phrase, the title connotes instead the film's philosophical glimpse into the state of humanity. But the term "inside man" can just as aptly be applied to the director as to the film or its central figure. Once an "outside man" known for his independent guerrilla filmmaking, Lee has recently sustained a career *inside* Hollywood with films like *25th Hour* and *Inside Man*. I argue, however, that he only *appears* to be adhering to certain cinematic conventions while, like Russell, actually operating from the inside in order to subvert them. In fact, Lee ventriloquizes his position as film auteur through Russell's character, who, director-like, calls the shots, whether by dressing the hostages in costumes or instructing the police to train a camera on a window in order to stage a fake murder. Like Russell's, Lee's position within the Hollywood vault is misleading, for he is actually invested in hiding out in the storage closet until he can abscond with the goods.

Russell's complexity as a character comes from the revelation that he is a bank robber with ethics, a terrorist who inspires little terror. In one scene, he engages in moral debate with himself before deciding to beat a hostage; in another, he offers his supposed adversary a piece of gum (foreshadowing the fact that he later "pays" Frazier by slipping an unset

diamond into his pocket, which the detective discovers in the final scene of the film). Making off with the diamonds but leaving behind the Cartier ring so that Frazier can flush out the war criminal, Russell confesses in his voiceover narration: "I'm no martyr. I did it for the money, but it's not worth much if you can't face yourself in the mirror. Respect is the ultimate currency." Lee can be viewed in a similar light. His films certainly serve the purposes of entertainment and moneymaking. But his activist stance as a filmmaker, attuned to the aesthetic possibilities of cinema, simultaneously enables him to offer a meaningful message about global politics and racial and economic injustice in a post-9/11 world. In masking the difference between victims and perpetrators, *Inside Man* directs tough questions at viewers, if they are willing to look inside the film's deeper meanings and "pay strict attention" to what he has to say (to quote Russell's monologue). Yet, despite the didacticism of which Lee is often accused, the film refrains from supplying easy answers, maintaining the open-ended ambiguity that also characterizes *Do the Right Thing*. In interrogating a suspect who is hard of hearing, Frazier asks if the different colors of his hearing aids allow him to tell "right from wrong" as well as right from left. Lee's film may aid its audience in deciphering right from wrong, but it ultimately leaves its ethical conclusions, and the imperative to act upon them, up to us.

Thanks to Shilpa Davé and Kimberly Chabot Davis for their comments on this essay, as well as students in "Race and American Cinema" courses at Brandeis University and Connecticut College for fruitful discussions of Spike Lee's films.

Notes

1. Stephanie Zacharek, "Inside Man," *Salon*, March 24, 2006, http://www.salon.com/entertainment/movies/review/2006/03/24/inside_man/ (accessed June 8, 2009).
2. Manohla Dargis, " 'Inside Man,' a Crime Caper Starring Denzel Washington," *New York Times*, March 24, 2006.
3. Peter Rainer, "Spike Lee Thinks 'Inside' the Box," *Christian Science Monitor*, March 24, 2006.

4. Gerstner's essay, which interprets the film in the context of the "de-auteuring" of Hollywood, is one of the few pieces of film criticism on *Inside Man* to be published thus far. See David A. Gerstner, "De Profundis: A Love Letter from the Inside Man," in *The Spike Lee Reader,* ed. Paula J. Massood (Philadelphia: Temple University Press, 2008), 243–253.

5. See Manohla Dargis, "Two Movies Warring in One," *Los Angeles Times,* December 19, 2002; Anthony O. Scott, "*25th Hour* (2002)," *New York Times,* December 19, 2002; and "Monty's Wake," *The Economist,* March 15, 2003. Lee attributes *25th Hour*'s critical acclaim to the fact that it does not deal with African Americans explicitly. See Paula J. Massood, "The Quintessential New Yorker and Global Citizen: An Interview with Spike Lee," *Cineaste,* Summer 2003, 4–6. For an interview with Benioff discussing differences between novel and film, see Massood, "Doyle's Law: An Interview with David Benioff," *Cineaste,* Summer 2003, 8–10.

6. Ryan Gilbey, "25th Hour," *Sight and Sound,* March 2003, 58.

7. Patricia O'Neill, "Where Globalization and Localization Meet: Spike Lee's *The 25th Hour,*" *CineAction,* Spring 2004, 2.

8. See Eithne Quinn, "'Tryin' to Get Over': *Super Fly,* Black Politics, and Post–Civil Rights Film Enterprise," *Cinema Journal* 49, no. 2 (Winter 2010): 86–105.

9. Frank Rich, "The Petraeus-Crocker Show Gets the Hook," *New York Times,* April 13, 2008. See also "Speaking Documentary Truth to Power," *Cineaste,* Summer 2008, 6. 2010, however, appeared to mark a shift in popular and critical attitudes toward wartime dramas, as *The Hurt Locker* (Kathryn Bigelow, 2008) took home several Oscars, including Best Motion Picture and Best Directing. Other notable war movies released in the past year include *The Messenger* (Oren Moverman, 2008), which earned Academy Award nominations for screenwriters Moverman and Alessandro Camon as well as supporting actor Woody Harrelson, and *Brothers* (Jim Sheridan, 2009), adapted from a 2004 Danish film and with a screenplay by David Benioff.

10. Pavitra Sundar, "Meri Awaaz Suno: Women, Vocality, and Nation in Hindi Cinema," *Meridians* 8, no. 1 (2008): 171.

11. See, for example, Victoria E. Johnson, "Polyphony and Cultural Expression: Interpreting Musical Traditions in *Do the Right Thing,*" in *Spike Lee's Do the Right Thing,* ed. Mark A. Reid (Cambridge, UK: Cambridge University Press, 1997), 50–72.

12. Amy Kaplan, "Where is Guantanamo?" *American Quarterly* 57, no. 3 (September 2005): 832.

13. Spike Lee interviewed by Kaleem Aftab, "America's Greatest Disaster," *Sight and Sound,* January 2007, 45. See also Spike Lee interviewed by Jay Dixit, *San Francisco Chronicle,* August 21, 2006.

14. For more on Lee's capitalist critique, see Houston Baker, "Spike Lee and the Commerce of Culture," in *Black American Cinema,* ed. Manthia Diawara (New York: Routledge, 1993), 154–176.

15. See Amiri Baraka, "Spike Lee at the Movies," in *Black American Cinema,* 145–153; Wahneema Lubiano, "But Compared to What? Reading Realism, Representation, and Essentialism in *School Daze, Do the Right Thing,* and the Spike Lee Discourse," *Black American Literature Forum* 25, no. 2 (Summer 1991): 253–283; and William Lyne, "No Accident: From Black Power to Black Box Office," *African American Review* 34, no. 1 (2000): 39–59.

36.
DISPATCHES FROM THE TWENTY-FIRST CENTURY COLOR LINE
Catherine Squires

Conservatives changed the debate about race from an argument about how to best redress the economic and political injuries of racism to one that equates ending racism with eliminating racial reference within juridical discourse and public policy.

—Nikhil Pal Singh, *Black Is a Country*

Multiracialism does not lead to an invention of new human kinds but calls our attention to areas of overlap between different categories . . . [and] may challenge pernicious customs of differentially valuing human kinds in the following way: if a black person can be white and a white person black, then black and white persons cannot have different degrees of moral worth by virtue of being black or white.

—Laurie Shrage, "Ethnic Transgressions: Confessions of an Assimilated Jew"

At a time when Vin Diesel, Keanu Reeves, and Lenny Kravitz are the faces of pop culture cool, it's hard to remember that nary a generation ago the main symbols of multiracial identity were the "marginal man" and the "tragic mulatto," let alone that interracial relationships were either illegal or social suicide in most parts of the United States. Certainly, this shift in multiracial acceptance is cause for some celebration, albeit cautious celebration. Most people prefer to live in a society where a majority of Americans polled say they are not opposed to interracial marriage and legal barriers to it no longer exist. Many citizens enjoy the fruits of the legal victories of the civil rights movement that have made interracial romance a realistic possibility. But as multiracial celebrities and interracial families are touted as symbols of a new multicultural America of racial tolerance, what are media makers celebrating and what can we really say multiracial identity has brought us in terms of how we think about racial identity and public policy in the United States, and how the news media report race to the public?

The first three chapters of this book illustrated how news reports concerning multiracial people can easily be transformed into stories about Black/White biracial tensions. Before the press acknowledged the presence of the multiracial movement and/or the new label *multiracial*, the people of Black/White descent covered in these chapters were positioned as Black or non-White, but not multiracial. In the cases of Susie Phipps and Maria Hylton, mainstream journalists treated issues of race, racism, and racial labels as if they belonged to the past. Reporters and sources located the problem in arcane procedures of the state or in the minds of misguided Blacks and "politically correct" liberals. Only in the Malones' story did mainstream media begin to address more complex issues involved in how to classify people as Black, White, or otherwise. In addition, the Malone case prompted some journalists—particularly those who addressed African American opinions and experiences—to include and take seriously the claims of African Americans that race and racism still constrain the job market and affect their lives in subtle and non-subtle ways. This was also a case where a critique of Whiteness surfaced. The culpability of Whites in the Boston Fire Department made it harder to isolate African Americans as the problematic group in affirmative action, or as the group responsible for keeping race in the public eye. Thus, in the Malone case, White racial innocence was challenged implicitly, but a sense of a separate multiracial identity for "White-looking Black people" did not surface as an option, just as in the Phipps and Hylton cases. In all three cases, people of Black and White descent remained racial anomalies, awkwardly existing within a binary racial world.

In the last two chapters, which contrasted reports on the 2000 Census created by and for people of color with those of dominant media, differences in reporting reflect not only the policy preferences of each group; rather, we see opposing ideas about what race means in America. The writings of African American and Asian American journalists employed group-based frameworks of race to provide historicized analysis of present-day controversies. Rather than pushing race and racism into the past, writers of color used the racial past to reveal how history shapes the present. In the dominant media, however, the movement toward ever more privatized definitions of race continued. From the *New York Times* editorial that stated people such as Susie Phipps should be able to choose to be White if their "blood" is "51 percent White" to the *Washington Post*'s quiz on how to correctly label "hybrids" with hip racial lingo, there is a push toward seeing multiracial identity as a mere matter of choice. These news discourses communicate a strong desire to put racism in the past, to minimize racial identity by confining the issue to descriptions of individual choices, be they naming one's own racial identity or choosing to consume others' identities. The exuberant discourses surrounding the multiracial population smacks of the same conservative nostalgia[1] that excises Martin Luther King Jr.'s famous line from the Mall—judged by the content of their character, not the color of their skin—from the context of his vigorous fight to make economic and social justice part of the national program of racial reform.[2]

As described earlier in this book, news media frames promote particular solutions to public problems. In the dominant media, multiracial people and interracial marriage are proposed as a solution to the problem of the color line. In doing so, media are implicitly endorsing particular models for understanding the role of race in our society, in the public sphere. Citizens, thus, should think of race as a slowly dying social category, a nineteenth-century anachronism that will soon have less influence in our lives than eye color. Celebrating the fashion of multiracial identities, they hail demographers' predictions of increases in interracial marriage as a portent of good racial things to come, namely, a nation deracialized by virtue of race mixing. Thus, all of our cultural, political, and historical differences will be negated, and we will become one nation, out from under the shadow of race.

This Utopian—or I would say dystopian—vision of the impact of multiracial identity on the public is troublesome. It is still dependent on a myth of separate races; the only "positive" difference is the belief they can be joined through biological hybridity. However, this still leads us to asking biology—mating—to solve a problem that is political. Looking to Brazil, for example, we can surely see that majority mixed-race populations do not guarantee racial equality, or even uniformity of skin tone. Rather, a spectrum of peoples is arrayed on a light-to-dark hierarchy where lightness (if not Whiteness) is privileged. As multiracial identity is employed to reimagine and project an idealized multicultural nation, it is also prescribing how citizens should understand their own and others' racial identities in the public sphere, in public policy, and in private life. These discourses imagine how we citizens should "*do* race," how we should understand it and perform it in our own lives, and how to communicate our racial identity to our fellow Americans.

Theorist Robert Asen suggests that scholars reorient their "approaches to civic engagement from asking questions of what [citizens do] to asking questions of how" they do citizenship. He suggests we think of citizenship as consisting of "mode[s] of public engagement." Viewing citizenship as modalities, Asen asserts, helps us recognize citizenship as fluid and instructs us to look at the ways in which citizens engage each other, engage institutions, and produce communications. This theory of citizenship also recognizes that citizenship often entails risk, for in engaging other members of the public in, perhaps, creative or unapproved modes, one will risk rejection or even violence. Relatedly, this theory of "doing citizenship" sees engaged actors using discourse to draw lines; between public and private, for example, or between genders, races, or classes. As lines—of identification, perhaps—are drawn as citizens engage each other, "[s]ome participants will be better positioned to draw lines that better represent their interests."[3]

Using Asen's approach, I want to suggest that there are different modalities of *racial citizenship*, and that with their power to influence and set boundaries for public discourse, news media are major players in drawing lines between identity groups, and between acceptable ways of doing race, doing citizenship. For example, scholars have demonstrated how protestors are often framed as acting outside acceptable norms for public speech and citizen action. Likewise, others have demonstrated how "White," "male," "property-owner," and "citizen" have been yoked together from the founding of the country, when only White males were granted the rights and privileges of citizenship.[4] Being White in the public sphere means to do citizenship as an unmarked, raceless being. Being White in the eyes of the state has historically meant access to particular rights and privileges explicitly denied to other racial groups. To be Black or female in the public sphere has meant doing citizenship in a very risky manner: fighting for the right to name oneself a citizen in the face of legal, social, and economic barriers that denied that name.

Similarly, to be Asian American in the dominant public sphere has also been to be seen as an alien, noncitizen, to have to fight to be viewed as worthy of citizenship. As Lisa Lowe eloquently explains, immigration laws restricting or preventing particular Asian nationals from entering the country served to reinforce the connection between Whiteness, property, and citizenship.[5] In her work "Whiteness as Property," Cheryl Harris details how American property law structured a system that protected not only White property but implies Whiteness and its privileges to be "rights as legal property" to be protected by the state.[6] The connections between Whiteness, property, and citizenship are thrown into relief when those entities are denied to people of color. As Hong notes, Executive Order 9066, which forced Japanese Americans into internment camps, exposed the links as Japanese Americans' property was stolen by Whites with the permission of the state, and reparations were not to be had for decades. "Internment is thus arguably the most blatant demonstration that one must be white to have rights that are properly maintained and supported by the state. Indeed, it was the state itself that divested Japanese Americans of their property."[7] Thus, to be Black—or Asian or Native American or Latino—in the United States has often required a mode of citizenship engagement centered around risk, dissent, and creativity; and it has necessitated attention to the reality of race. If Singh is correct that the political lesson of the civil rights movement is indeed that we must encounter and reencounter race as we attempt to reshape our society, then the invisibility and privileges of Whiteness are the polar opposites of the racial experiences of citizens of color. That is, in prosecuting their case to be recognized as citizens, people of color have developed creative modes of engagement that center race and racial identities rather than covering them up or pretending they don't matter.

In the past, multiracial identity has engendered varied modes of enacting citizenship; under the antebellum one-drop rule, mixed race people of any iota African descent were enslaved, noncitizens. In nineteenth-century New Orleans, creoles of color often enjoyed certain political, economic, and social privileges, and were able to engage in limited expressions of citizenship. These expressions, of course, were bounded by the whims and strategies of White patrons. The modality of passing allowed the Whitest-looking multiracials to experience the privileges of citizenship close to that of Whites; however, because passers were beset by the fear of being unveiled, passing was a very risky mode of racial citizenship.

Today, multiracial citizenship is articulated with ideals of multicultural harmony and tolerance, imagined alongside color-blind visions of raceless citizens. The multiracial citizen is often described as a bridge, linking disparate racialized sections of the public. In exchange for sublimating the untoward (read: colored) aspects of his or her racial heritage, the multiracial individual is being offered a new way to be part of We the People. In the next section of this chapter, I explore this dynamic by sketching out the idealized ways of "doing race" exemplified by mainstream media portrayals of famous multiracial men. In these sketches, I show how restrictive and restricting these modes of racial citizenship can be, and how they feed on assumptions that continue to relegate other people of color outside racial norms.

Doing Race in the Twenty-First Century: Tiger Woods and Barack Obama

Two multiracial figures for whom racial autobiography has become part and parcel of their public appeal are Tiger Woods and Barack Obama. It is notable that both are male, and both share some African heritage. Gender is instructive here as it reflects the continued bias to see men as representative of racial groups. I do not mean to replicate that bias, but to point out that these two men have become prominent vis-à-vis multiracial politics in a time when Black leadership is still gendered male and where the experiences and images of multiracial women are relegated mostly to entertainment media and/or exotic exceptionalism.[8] Whereas pundits have dubbed these men "All-American," or "Son of the United States," women of multiracial descent, such as Halle Berry or Mariah Carey, are not described as such; they are celebrated (and in some circles, denigrated) for attracting White audiences and White male desire, but not for representing America.[9] The bodies of multiracial women are still coded as vehicles for illicit sex, illegitimate births, and hushed histories of sexual conquest;[10] thus, it is rare to find biracial women described as exemplary American citizens, as people who can stand for or represent *all* (White) Americans.

In mainstream media discourses, Tiger Woods and Barack Obama have represented two modes of racial citizenship:

• Tiger Woods's multiracial identity prescribes a multicultural consumer as the ultimate racial citizen. To create a more perfect union, we are encouraged to see figures of multiracial descent such as Woods as vehicles for understanding and experiencing the Other, and seeing some similarity in the Other. Multiracial figures like Woods solve the problem of an ever-fragmenting public sphere/marketplace by allowing each and all to safely project or find oneself in multiculturalism, where citizens can experience difference through purchases and media consumption. Watching Tiger win (and buying his Nike products), we are the world, and Tiger is us all. Racial difference need not be confronted or understood, only consumed.

• Barack Obama's biography is re-created by pundits as a space to deal with race without talking about it. This multiracial figure is, similar to Woods, a bridge between cultures, a cipher to fill with one's own racial desires—particularly the desire to avoid racial conflict. Although I argue that his own autobiography contradicts many of the hopes thrust upon him, when he was anointed the right kind of Black politician for the twenty-first century, his multiracial identity and class position were used to make clear distinctions about how race should and should not be articulated in politics and policy. In this vision of multiracial citizenship, Blacks are positioned as perpetual antagonists to national unity via their insistence on speaking out against racial injustice and utilization of cultural signifiers of Blackness.

We Are Tiger Woods? Consuming the Other to Make the Nation

It's also possible that multiracial individuals are more likely to inherit unusual combinations of traits. For example, Tiger Woods seems to combine the muscularity and masculine charisma of an African-American superstar with the self-discipline and focus of the finest Asian-American athlete.

—Steve Sailer, President of the Human Biodiversity Institute
http://www.isteve.com

498 Catherine Squires

Eldrick "Tiger" Woods is arguably the most famous multiracial person on the planet. Number one in the world golf rankings and beneficiary of the most lucrative endorsement contracts in sports, Woods's face is everywhere in the media and sports marketplace, often alongside those of his parents. Most recently, American Express has featured a loving portrait of Tiger embracing his Thai mother, Kulthilda. In a two-page classy black-and-white photo placed in top-selling national magazines, the picture with the slogan, "My life, my card," needs no explanation for the readers, for they know that this dark-skinned man hugging the lighter-skinned Asian woman is her son; we all already know the family history of the Woods clan, including Tiger's childhood term for his racial makeup, "Cablinasian."

Tiger's success as a spokesmodel for elite products and services (including luxury cars, platinum watches, and golf equipment) epitomizes the recent popularity of multiracial models in advertising. Prior to and since the 2000 Census, marketers recognized a new way to "do ethnicity" using ambiguous-looking multiracial models. And, since the Census data became available, advertisers are salivating over the potential multiracial youth market: 46 percent of people who chose more than one race are under eighteen, as compared to only 26 percent of the one-race population. This youthful profile, alongside the assumption that Generation Y is more tolerant of "mixing it up" as the mainstream press puts it, has made multiracial actors and models hot commodities. In a piece for American Demographics' *Forecast*, casting agents and advertising directors gushed over the popularity and utility of multiracial identity.

Paula Sindlinger, a partner in Godlove & Sindlinger Casting in New York City, says . . . "The blended look says 'we're all in this together' and that 'the world's getting smaller . . .'" Al Ries . . . also endorses the use of multiracial casts to advertise mainstream products. Ethnic casts, he says, are effective at targeting only one segment. A practice that may disappear along with single-race segments—if the trend toward multirace continues.[11]

Thus, it seems, multiracial people can do double duty: they are acceptable to both "mainstream" and "ethnic" consumers. However, as implied by Mr. Ries's paraphrased comment, neither ethnic nor multiracial casts are "mainstream" (read: White). The appeal of the multiracial model or cast, according to these experts, is that they communicate "current, youthful, and urban" in a flash with their ambiguous skin tones, wavy hair, and facial features. Hints of their multiracial parentage are believed to be simultaneously exotic and enticing as well as reassuring, as demonstrated by the "we're all in this together" remark.

Tiger Woods is often mentioned as a figure destined to bring us together as a nation of consumer-citizens. Not only did ad industry and sports pundits announce that part of his appeal to Nike and other firms was that he could be marketed to Black, Asian, and White middle- and upper-class consumers, but also the story of his family was cited as an inspirational example of racial progress. The sports audience was often conflated with the national public as columnists and commentators waxed rhapsodic over Woods's historic 1997 victory at the Masters Tournament. Journalists combined his Cablinasian heritage with his self-made athletic skills to shape a narrative of hope for a multicultural, harmonious future on and off the greens. Sports writer Jerelyn Eddings of *U.S. News & World Report* explained the Tiger phenomenon like this:

That's why the success of a Tiger Woods or a Jackie Robinson continues to have meaning beyond the individual's achievement. When such moments bring Americans of all races together in celebration of excellence, the process of coming together is as important as the values that inspire it.[12]

Although many commentators have ridiculed his father Earl's declaration that Tiger is "qualified through his ethnicity to accomplish miracles" to heal a racially divided world, time and again, as with Michael Jordan, sportswriters and politicians wax rhapsodic about Woods's ability to "transcend race." Although there is scant evidence that Tiger Woods desires such a role to change either the

White-dominated golf world or the course of racial politics, it is clear that he and other multiracial models are offered as symbols of national/racial unity via transcendence of race. This alleged transcendence, however, is not necessarily the model to which we should aspire when seeking ways to heal racial divides. Rather, "the rhetoric of transcendence is tied to notions of exceptionalism that appear to distance [celebrities] from the semiotic field that locates and positions other African American men," thereby erasing the particularities of race and power that shape both Tiger and the "other Blacks."[13]

Similarly, Woods's multiracial heritage and his mastery of an elite White sport—golf—further distance him from the "other" people of color. It is no mere coincidence that Woods has joined the three other men of color for whom, Dr. Ravi Dhar of Yale found, "the American public has broad, powerful associations: Bill Cosby, Colin Powell, and Michael Jordan."[14] According to Lauren Berlant, these men of African descent have become such familiar, likable figures for Whites because "these 'positive' icons of national minority represent both the minimum and the maximum of what the dominating cultures will sanction for circulation, exchange, and consumption." That is, the narratives crafted by and about these men adhere closely to the individualistic, patriarchal vision of the American Dream. Under the slogan, "Just Do It," itself a bootstrapping phrase, the icon of multiracial Tiger Woods works to personify and reinforce the myth of conquering race through hard work. But as D. L. Andrews succinctly put it, figures such as Woods don't transcend race, they "displace racial codes onto other black bodies."[15] Race does not and cannot so simply disappear into the ether.

The celebration of Tiger Woods and other multiracial celebrities as symbols of national integration via consumer choice is problematic on another level: it ignores the racial inequalities that limit certain groups' participation in the consumer economy. To acquire the products and participate in the leisure activities Woods promotes presupposes income levels and social status out of reach of many Americans of any color. Beyond that, the labor system that produces these goods depends on low-wage Black,

brown, and yellow female workers. The multiracial fantasy of consumptive citizenship erases the role of these citizens and would-be citizens of the United States. The sweatshops and factories where they work are a far cry from the idyllic golf courses and high-fiving multiracial school children who declare "I am Tiger Woods" in Nike's television commercials, which project an idealized vision of a White-dominated sporting world transformed by Tiger's mixed-race identity.

Another problem with the marketers' "we're all in this together" romanticized vision of multiracial identity is that it papers over the global and local politics that facilitate certain kinds of interracial relationships more than others. The Woods family is a perfect example of this phenomenon. Asian American women have the highest rates of out-marriage; the story of Earl and Kultilda Woods's marriage is not just a love story, but also a tale of the effects of the United States' military presence in Southeast Asia. Earl Woods spent two tours of duty in Viet Nam, and while stationed in Asia met Kultilda, who was working as a secretary at a US Army base. Their meeting was not chance; the movement of Black males to Southeast Asia in the 1960s was not for leisure travel, but to fight in a war. Asian women served, and continue to serve, many roles in and around US military bases.[16] Many became "war brides"; others were left behind with Amerasian children who were shamed for having American birth fathers. Retelling the Woods's story within the framework of American imperial and military might in the 1960s exposes a different set of reasons why Americans have "always been mixed" and why Asian-American mixing isn't so "new." As Lowe points out, the racialization and gendering of Asians as immigrants and imperial subjects in US law and custom sets the stage for contact with specific Asian subgroups.[17] It would have been highly unlikely for Earl Woods to have met Kultilda as a Black man in the 1960s outside the parameters of military occupation and immigration policies that made his passage to Asia possible.

Can we imagine other ways of interpreting Tiger's and other multiracial models' images and labels in ways that challenge the current trend? Could his multiracial identity be more than an object of commercial exploitation? Raquel Salgado's reading of his chosen moniker, "Cablinasian," suggests an alternative. Salgado says Woods's declaration of his Cablinasian identity, and his visible parents, offers us "a transmodern narrative, an imaginative political statement . . . demonstrating the limitations of words and the absurdity of categories that try to locate identity."[18] However, she contends that such demonstrations might not succeed without deliberations and actions that strive to dismantle racial hierarchies. Particularly, she contends that multiracial individuals such as Woods should

> challenge orthodoxies, realize that self cannot be separated from other, and work collectively for change. But too often, especially in this country that is built on imagined individuality, we often see individual well-being as a condition opposed to collective action—as if one negates the possibility of the other.[19]

However, even if only for a moment, "Cablinasian" excites the imagination and provides a glimpse of a novel discourse of race beyond the language we currently use.

How could we extend this moment beyond the catch of breath, exhaling it into a national discussion that has been choked by the rhetoric of racial realism and the primacy of the individual? One vehicle suggested by Salgado's musings on "Cablinasian" is for multiracial individuals and families to resist media typecasting of them as exceptional or transcendent. Rather, they should seek to explain their choices in a context that does not divide them from "other people of color" or valorize their multiracial existence as a function of colorblindness. Although some multiracial people surely hew to the racial realist paradigm, many do not, as evidenced by the prominent discussions of race privilege in the Asian American press. And, while individuals and organizations cannot control the entire framing process, they can endeavor to shift the balance by providing information about and characterizations of their identities in ways that emphasize collectivity and rejection of racial hierarchy. They can dispute the notion that the fight for inclusion on the 2000

Census was not a fight to erase race from the national lexicon, but to expand that lexicon in a way that forces us to confront the realities of pigmentocracy and racial inequalities. This kind of presentation of multiracial identity frames interracial intimacy as a starting point of new conversations rather than the end of talk about race.

Guess Who's Coming to the Senate: Barack Obama, Not a "Stereotypical Black"

> "My moment was a focus group," recalls Obama's campaign manager, Jim Cauley. "The moderator . . . asked the older [white female] group, 'Who do each of these [candidates] remind you of?' for Dan Hynes, a woman said, 'Dan Quayle,' . . . And she looked at Barack and the lady said, 'Sidney Poitier.' At that moment I was like, 'Shit, this is real.'"
>
> —Noam Scheiber, "Barack Obama's Miraculous Campaign"

Once Barack Obama lit up the 2004 Democratic National Convention with a rousing keynote speech, the whole country was talking about the senatorial candidate from Illinois. From declaring him the first Black politician to have a real shot at the presidency to anointing him the "de facto leader of the Black community"[20] should he win his Senate seat, the press ushered Obama into the sphere of political celebrity with great enthusiasm. The immediate embrace of this self-described "skinny guy with big ears"—by voices on the Right and the Left—is unprecedented for a politician of African descent. However, within this consensus of hope and excitement for a candidate of color are troubling discourses of race that resonate with those generated by and about Woods. Journalists, pundits, voters, and fellow politicians reacted to Obama with elements of the racial realism and liberal resignation about race described in the Introduction. When contrasted with Obama's own descriptions of his identity and connections to Black communities, their assessments of his interracial background clearly miss important aspects of the candidate's sensibilities about race in the United States.

In the afterglow of the keynote speech, journalists and commentators rushed to explain to the public why Obama was attractive to both White and Black voters. The merits of his rhetorical abilities are clear to anyone who has seen or read the now-famous speech; his dogged campaigning in all regions of Illinois clearly elevated his profile with rural and working-class Whites; and his connections to and endorsements from key Black politicians in Chicago and the Illinois legislature were crucial. But time and again, the press linked his popularity with Whites to his interracial—and implicitly, his middle-class—background. Scott Malcolmson of the *New York Times* wrote, "[S]ome political analysts have wondered whether white voters don't also find him attractive because while he is black, . . . *he is not black in the usual way.*"[21] The "usual way" being the tactics, mannerisms, and biographies of politicians such as Jesse Jackson or Al Sharpton, both of whom were compared unfavorably to Obama. For instance, the *Boston Globe* published a letter from reader Michael Johnson subtitled "It's time for Jackson to retire."

> [O]n the same day as [Obama's] unifying message, the Rev. Jesse Jackson was expressing his freedom of speech to further divide the races. Even if what Jackson says is the truth, his message almost always seems to come off as an attack on white people. . . . When Jackson speaks on race, the impressions many white people get is that he wants to raise black people up and tear white people down. Jackson will not get white people on his side by using that approach. . . . Obama's message was that we should all help each other, every race, to rise up![22]

In his letter, Johnson articulates a desire to assume a position of innocence in discussions of racial inequality. Whiteness theorists have emphasized that this desire has been an impediment to discussions of racial justice and equality.[23] Even if they recognize that racial inequalities still exist, the reluctance and refusal to acknowledge the historical and current role of white privilege in the maintenance of racial inequality continues to be a roadblock in discussions of race. Furthermore, the writer's letter suggested the idea that racial progress is a zero-sum game—that elevating the position of Blacks necessitates a lowering of Whites. His letter combines the Democrats' conventional wisdom that race loses white votes with the underlying fear of the loss of White privilege. Thus, any African American spokesperson or politician who talks about contemporary racism as a part of racial inequality is marked as someone trying to "bring down the whites."

Jonathan Tilove's article in the *New York Times* contained a similar assessment of Barack's appeal to Whites:

> The old model of the black protest leader making demands no longer makes sense in an age tapped out and tired of race, Professor [Angela] Dillard said. Obama can argue for policies virtually indistinguishable from Sharpton's in cooler, nonracial terms, *while still affirming a message of racial identity and uplift in his very being.*[24]

If the age is "tired of race," we can certainly imagine that the fatigue of Whites may be very different than that of people of color. Whites may be tired of hearing demands for racial equality and power sharing; Black, Hispanic, and Asian Americans may be tired of having their demands for equality construed as "special interests" or met with indifference. Furthermore, it seems a very interesting trick, to talk about race-based policies in nonracial terms. The key to this ability, it seems from reporters and commentators, is "[t]he power of Obama's exotic background" as Noam Scheiber put it.[25] Emphasizing his parents interracial marriage, his father's status as an immigrant from Kenya, and Obama's elite education at Harvard, journalists and interviewees surmised that Obama is not "stereotypically Black," but rather, "transcends race."

> The son of a Kenyan immigrant and Kansas native, Obama is the product of a interracial marriage. His Ivy League pedigree . . . belies his humble upbringing. . . . But on Tuesday, *he was simply a son of the United States*. He was us, all of us. . . . Time and again, Obama offered a vision

that transcended everything: race, creed, color, party politics, and social and economic strata.[26]

Interweaving his family story with lines from his speech calling for Americans to reach across the lines of Black and White, blue and red states, journalists made Obama a "son of the United States" who was the polar opposite of his Black predecessors. Class and parentage distance him from the alleged divisive old guard of Black leadership, as illustrated in this passage from Tilove's analysis:

Sharpton and Obama could not be more different in style and biography. Obama, the son of a white mother and Kenyan father he barely knew, was the first black president of the Harvard Law Review. Sharpton, who counts James Brown the closest thing to a father figure, was an ordained preacher while still a small child. Sharpton practices the politics of controversy and polarization. Obama listens, reasons, and calms.[27]

If we recognize the stylistic and biographical elements arrayed in this quote as proxies for both race and class differences between Sharpton and Obama, it is clear that Obama's sophisticated middle-class education and diverse background is deemed superior to Sharpton's working-class origins in the Black church. Especially telling is the parallel Tilove draws between their fathers: Obama's is absent, yet elevated due to his immigrant status; Sharpton occupies the space of the fatherless Black child, and Tilove's reference to James Brown has a mocking tone. The social capital and speaking style Obama accrued through his Ivy League education—indicated here by his ability to "reason and calm" rather than polarize—brings him much closer to the white middle-class aesthetic for political speech than Sharpton. Thus, part of Barack Obama's appeal is that he is seemingly not like "other Blacks." Writers made it clear that Whites are "tired" of racial politics and Black political leaders who make explicit demands for remedies to racism.

While Obama's exceptionalism works to include him as a son of the United States of America, it simultaneously "support[s] and obscure[s] the powerful naturalization and centrality of the White category"[28]

to his status as "All-American" and "presidential." The basis for comparisons between Sharpton and Obama are rooted in Anglo-American expectations for debate and decorum, in assumptions about how, when, and where race can be spoken of in public. Those black and brown leaders who do not display the "reasoning" style of Obama are not acceptable in the dominant public sphere. As the state and mass media recognize the demographic diversity of multiracial people like Obama, the privileged racial citizenship extended to them is still predicated on the continued denigration of other people of color. As such, this "positive" narrative about an interracial leader encourages people of color to "cover" the cultural and political traits that do not sit well with White majorities.[29] If one talks about race with its sharp edges and ugly past exposed, then one will be dismissed as an "old school" politician dealing in disunity. Thus, the narrative of interracial union promoted by these contrasting images of Obama and Jesse Jackson or Al Sharpton promotes a kinder, gentler assimilation ethic: bring us your difference, but only that which does not discomfit.

But the question remains, Can one talk about race without naming it and still solve the problems of race? The enthusiasm of the press for Obama's multiracial biography, like the hype surrounding multiracial models in the world of advertising, becomes a way of talking about race without talking about it. That is, speaking about multiracial individuals and trends provides a "race-specific technology" of discourse. I take the term *race-specific technology* from Dorothy Roberts's discussion of new race-specific pharmaceuticals that have recently entered the market.[30] Roberts argues that, as scientists have seesawed on the "biological realities" of race, these race-specific drugs may have opened the door for a "renewed acceptance of inherent racial differences" beyond the treatment of heart conditions or sickle cell anemia, partly because their emergence coincides with "intensified state surveillance of inner city communities: racial profiling, mass incarceration, welfare restructuring," and other policies that stigmatize particular racial groups. This return to discussions of the biological origins of race in the medical sphere, she fears, will spread to other arenas to provide "a ready rationale for . . . disfranchisement of black citizens and complement colorblind policies based on the claim that racism is no longer the cause of social equality."[31] Similarly, multiracial identity provides a technology—individual couplings—that can be extolled in mainstream media. The "positive" discourse of race mixing provides a language whereby we are explicitly talking about race and society, but the focus on individuals, style, and reproduction pushes discussions of social, political, and economic racial realities backstage. As such, the circulation of these discourses of racial biography dovetails with the racial technologies Roberts critiques, and furthers the racial project of colorblind policy that negatively impacts people of color. The "natural" progression toward interracial marriage becomes another aspect of the re-biologization of race; to eliminate racial disharmony, we must mate. People of color who do not participate in this genetic-level "integration" or engage in covering their differences are left out of the national equation.

But before we leave the new senator's story, we should ask, does the press's imagination of Barack Obama's transcendent racial identity match his actual approach to and opinions of racial politics? Looking at Obama's political career, he is very close to many movers and shakers in Black Chicago as well as African American power brokers in the Illinois senate. Furthermore, in his autobiography, his record in the state house and his campaign materials, it is clear that Obama's policy agenda runs to the left of the political spectrum. Beyond his articulation of his family story in front of the DNC, Obama wrote in his autobiography about race and the often torturous process someone of African descent must go through in the United States due to the continued effects of racism in our country. In *Dreams from My Father*, Obama conveys with deep-seated affection—as well as criticism—his relationships with Black communities in Chicago when he was a community organizer. Although he ultimately does not agree with the nationalist platform and ideology of the Nation of Islam (NOI), a strong presence on the South Side, he eloquently testifies to the appeal of NOI to African Americans in the context of continued racial stratification and oppression. He testifies to the need

for stronger Black political institutions and new Black political strategies, although not organized around an essential definition of Blackness. He writes of Black people not in terms of individualism, but collectivism. He calls for racial cohesion, but does not collapse into an easy single sense of who Black people are or must be:

> Black survival in this country had always been premised on a minimum of delusions. . . . The continuing struggle to align word with action, our heartfelt desires with a workable plan—didn't self-esteem finally depend on just this? It was that belief which had led me into organizing, and . . . which would lead me to conclude, perhaps for the final time, that notions of purity—of race or culture—could no more serve for the typical black American's self-esteem than it could for mine. Our sense of wholeness would have to arise from something more fine than the bloodlines we'd inherited. It would have to find root in Mrs. Crenshaw's story and Mr. Marshall's story, in Ruby's story and Rafiq's; in all the messy, contradictory details of our experience.[32]

After this moment of clarity, the author describes taking Ruby to a play featuring Black women telling their stories in song; he evokes the joy, beauty, and release the audience and performers experience together as Black men and women. He links his realization about race not to rejecting Blackness, but to embracing it in its collective contradictions. Obama's descriptions of his experience and revelation resonate with Singh's description of the political and cultural genius that has emanated from the Black public sphere in the long civil rights era. Singh reminds us that Black activists and scholars have long strained "at both the borders of the US nation-state and the boundaries of its liberal creed" as they fought the restrictions of racism within American democracy. Singh's framework challenges the conservative conception of the civil rights movement as

> the moment when black people emerged (at long last) as individual subjects of capitalist-liberalism and as formal participants in

democratic-nationalism. . . . What may be most remarkable about the long civil rights era is the emergence of black people as a distinct people and a
public—and the concomitant development of race
as a political space. There was no precedent for
this in the liberal-democratic narrative of nationhood that explained how they needed to progress.[33]

In this light, we might want to reframe Obama's call
for a new America, his appeal to our better angels
during the Democrats' convention, not as a simple
roll call for individuals, but a challenge to push the
boundaries of America and American identity yet
again. As he said in the speech, it is time to hold up
the dream of America "against a harsh reality and see
how we are measuring up" to it. That speech, when
placed in the context of his career in Black politics
and sense of Black identity, can be reread as an up-
dated version of King's charge to America to make
good on the bounced check of equality. Near the
end of his speech, Obama invokes the value of being our brother's keeper as central to Americanness.
This vision of nation as family is not consistent with
bootstrapping and colorblindness; one must be able
to see all aspects of her brothers and sisters in order
to communicate well and help keep us all from harm.

Rethinking Options for Racial Citizenship

What if the political lesson of the long civil rights
era is that we advance equality only by continually passing through a politics of race and by refusing the notion of a 'beyond' race? . . . The historic
denials of black voting rights, like today's racially
coded withdrawals of social welfare provision . . .
have disenfranchised and disempowered numeri-
cally far greater numbers of non-black citizens
and residents. Conversely, protections granted
under the Civil Rights Act of 1964 and affirmative
action programs have protected and enhanced
the life chances of broad majorities within the
society . . .

—Nikhil Pal Singh, *Black Is a County*

So what do these two men teach about the possibilities for multiracial identity in the news and public

discourse? One lesson is, as others have written, to
say that race is socially constructed cannot end the
conversation; rather, social construction allows us to
see how races are constructed in relation to one another, not in a vacuum. "Social and political power,
as well as the implications in social terms, must be
identified. There is no black without white, there is
no white without black,"[34] and so on. To return to Stuart Hall's question—What identities are working this
week?—this book testifies that the social construction of multiracial-identified individuals is occurring
in relation to devalued constructions of Blacks and
other people of color. Multiracial identity has been
working for neoconservatives precisely because they
have managed to cast multiracial identity in the mold
of individual choice and detach it from the racial
past. Multiracial identity works for Tiger Woods's
commercial partners because his image collapses
"multiculturalism into an easy pluralism that simply
adds what it constructs as the Other without upsetting the fundamental precepts and paradigms of
Western culture."[35]

We cannot celebrate the rise in interracial marriage as a simple indicator that the "last walls" of
racism are tumbling down; rather, there are new
cracks in the wall, but those flaws are not necessarily enough to bring the entire edifice down. Rather,
the kind of discourse being formed in response to
those cracks may be more likely to serve as mortar
for those fissures. Discourses of individual choice,
"best of both worlds," "colorblindness," and charges
of obsessive "reverse racism" or intransigence on
the part of other racial groups divert our attention
away from the continued strength of racial thinking
and entrenched racial inequalities in our society. The
use of the multiracial movement's attack on the one-
drop rule for conservative aims could silence many
other critiques and necessary innovations that could
spring from a serious meditation on the meanings
of multiracial identities in a racially stratified nation.
Look different, but don't act differently, is the message. Talk about your individual family's racial diversity, but not about how to achieve racial equality.

Salgado asserts that if the narrative of mixed-
race theory "is embodied in the tension, conflicts,
and deliberations that inhere in discursive genres like

the personal essay," then mixed-race theory is about the fluctuating moments of connection between self and other, across the racial lines that have been constructed.[36] The mainstream media, and at times, alternative media sources for people of color, often present a set of limiting choices and limited connections as they incorporate multiracial identity into existing racial frameworks. In their dispatches, there is colorblindness and the end of race, monoracial rules that define and delimit racial affiliations, honorary Whiteness, exotic multicultural playmates, and silence. But insisting that multiracial-identified people augur colorblindness or should adhere to prior models of racial identity are both invalid propositions. The engagement of self and other in productive, ongoing tension—at interpersonal and social levels— can inspire an ongoing dialogue that could lead to new questions, new consensus, or more dissent. For us to form multiracial society, this tension is to be expected, and the forming of a more perfect racial union may be too much to ask in the short term. But for people to share in the moments of possibility opened by a critical grasp of multiracial identity is not so hard to imagine, I think. To open up an honest, perhaps uncomfortable exchange of thoughts about what race has been, is, and will be with more diverse voices would be, perhaps, what President Clinton's abortive attempt at a national conversation on race was supposed to be.

Hapa Asian Americans interviewed in Asian American magazines embodied and performed Salgado's vision of this self/other confrontation and dialogue when they critiqued White assumptions about their race and questioned the viability of part-White privilege. As they critiqued Whiteness, they simultaneously entered into dialogue with Asian communities that desire their silence, asserting a role in both White and Asian American politics and cultures. We see the contextualization of racial identity dramatized in the Census results as well: Puerto Rican Americans in New York were nearly three times as likely to consider themselves Black and of Hispanic origin than Puerto Ricans in Puerto Rico, who were more likely to describe themselves as White and Hispanic. Those who did so demonstrate not only their desire to choose both/and, but also reveal the

continued relevance of and confrontations between the Black/White divide to their own lives.

In an earlier iteration of this project, I hesitantly threw out the statement that perhaps multiracial identity has ushered in the death of strategic essentialism. This concept has been batted about as a sort of compromise in a post-civil rights, postcolonial, postfeminist world where essential identities are rejected but still seem tactically necessary for women, people of color, gays and lesbians, and other marginalized social groups. Now I think I was too early to declare the end of this strategy, but I am also attracted to other theorists' alternative renderings of group identity and related interactions. The spatial metaphors of public spheres in particular draw my attention. If we imagine, as Arjun Appadurai has, that public spheres are made of scapes, or zones, we might reimagine the nation's projection of its identity as a zone, a zone of intersecting shifting planes of discourse and traffic of bodies. This zone in motion is a place where home is never guaranteed or completely safe from contradiction. What is home/nation, and who gets to claim and define membership is determined not only by the geography of this zone, but who moves in and out of the space. This set of intersecting zones— individuals, institutions, bodies, groups—that occupy and contest the space defines our sense of self, other, and nation.

Here I revisit the metaphor of the borderlands provided by Anzaldúa as exemplary of this zone: if multiracial people are, in and of themselves, products of intersection, then reading them as mobile subjects of multiple zones opens the door to discussion of what is happening in the moment of contact, or crossing, *now.* When we ask, *What identities are working today,* then, the first question we might want to ask is *Where are they and with whom are they colliding? How long do they remain in contact? What are their shared struggles? Conflicts?* This line of questioning asks us to be particular, yes, and perhaps that raises the fear of ever-fragmenting identities and publics. However, when one looks at the intersection of more than one group, then one must think in relational terms, to look for overlap as well as disjuncture, to work in tandem in order to get a sense of depth that honors all participants. This conception of racial identities could spark discourse that brings our sense of race to a new plane of specificity while still striving to develop communities of resistance.

Multiracial identities need not be a starting point on the journey to "one America, one race" but rather the beginning of a very rigorous debate, a contentious discussion, an often painful hearing of memories and histories buried under the scrim of official national identity and history. What state recognition of multiracial identity could prompt is a demand to end the quest for a common culture, and an end to the fiction that race did not structure our country. In other words, I argue we should reject mainstream framing of multiracial identity as the *end* of race, and attempt to interject the idea that multiracial identity can help us discuss the meaning of race in a society that is caught between the legacy and familiarity of a binary racial order and the demographic realities of a spectrum of racial identities. To do this, we have to imagine new modes of citizenship and interaction and sociality that go beyond consumption and facile labeling. I don't really know what this will entail, or what it will look like, but I know it is not a laissez-faire multiculturalism where anything goes; we can't tell people of color that their only place in society is in a static, cultural museum for others to tour or poach from to augment their own identities. If multiracial individuals explode the options for systems of racial and ethnic identification, then we must always remember to ask: Are all of the people within the state and society able to exercise the same freedom of choice, of perusal, of learning about identity—or rejecting identities? Are all of those identity choices afforded the same privileges of association and citizenship, and if not why? If the emergence of multiracial-identified people does not prompt us to ask these questions and to imagine a world where we can answer affirmatively, then our discourse on racial identity is truly idle talk.

How to Do Race and the News?

Although many of the minority news media outlets and practitioners represented in these chapters provide some stunning and promising examples of how to utilize multiracial identity as a way to open

discussions about white privilege, institutional racism, and the perils of colorblind ideology, the burden for reforming race reporting cannot fall solely on the shoulders of these small-circulation publications and their electronic counterparts. Due to the restricted scope of their circulation, it is unlikely that their frames will reach the majority White population. Furthermore, the "mainstream" media's lack of these frames and voices exemplifies the problem of race in general circulation publications: White news producers and White readers still set the parameters for an unstated norm against which people of color are measured. Thus, reforms within mainstream news media outlets—as well as academies of journalism instruction—need to occur.

Normalizing the Presence of Journalists of Color in Mainstream Newsrooms

Although some progress has been made in hiring more diverse staffs, the people of color who do join the ranks of elite and mainstream newsrooms are often under pressure to prove that they aren't "biased" toward their racial identity groups. As Pamela Newkirk's[37] and Clint Wilson's[38] studies of Black reporters revealed, African American reporters must often choose between career advancement and reporting on stories near and dear to their communities. They are often discouraged from investigating issues that would shed a different light on Black communities, and are wary of retaliation in the form of harassment or demotion. Nearly forty years after the Kerner Commission condemned the mainstream news media's coverage of Blacks, the American Society of Newspaper Editors (ASNE) is nowhere near its own goal of having 30 percent of its workforce composed of people of color.[39] Given that people of color still do not work in large numbers in dominant newsrooms—especially in editorial and managerial positions—it is crucial to maintain and enhance the presence of news media resources created by and/or for people of color. Because these alternative news media often strive to provide alternative framing of racial issues, dominant news media would do well to attend to the differences in coverage and evaluate their own practices to see where and how more diversity of viewpoints on racial matters could be created. Of course, there are very different stylistic and economic imperatives operating for mainstream and ethnic news media. Most ethnic news media were created primarily to make up for gaps and biases in mainstream news; they are first and foremost devoted to delivering information to their constituencies in a manner consonant with those cultures. Thus, with their community-centered imperatives, Asian and African American news publications take on racial news items and viewpoints we don't see in dominant news. In these newsrooms, Whiteness and White privilege do not operate to stifle journalists of color. As Gwyneth Mellinger summarizes:

> Diversity in newsroom employment, then, is not primarily a problem of economic inequity and class exploitation, as it would be in other workplace contexts, but an issue of cultural valuation and recognition as well; it is not just about who gets to be the boss but about who gets to mediate the messages that define racial reality within the dominant public sphere.[40]

While it may be crucial to maintain the presence of critical ethnic news media to continue to provide an alternative, it may be a heavy and unrealistic burden for these news outlets to spark wide-ranging conversations about race and transformations in dominant discourse on their own. Because minority audiences are smaller and valued less by advertisers, it is more difficult to sustain commercial media enterprises targeted at audiences of color. As Oscar Gandy notes in his overview of research on race and the market for ethnic audiences, current conditions make it difficult for Black-owned and/or oriented media to sustain news divisions due to lack of funds and commercial prejudices that favor lucrative entertainment media models.[41] Furthermore, given the influence of general audience news media, we cannot give a pass to the dominant news producers on racial issues. To say that race can only be done well (or at all) by racial minorities reinforces the myths that Whites are not affected by race and do not need to think about racial issues.

Changing Racial Narratives in the Mainstream News

A small number of journalism schools, private foundations, and professional organizations have been trying to address the interrelated issues of racial reporting and racial diversity in newsrooms. Most of their interventions currently focus on two goals: (1) increasing the number of journalists and editors of color in a variety of newsrooms, and (2) providing journalism students and practicing journalists with tools to improve the quality and quantity of race and ethnicity reporting. The former goal is usually pursued through mechanisms such as scholarships, internships, and seminars that provide students and up-and-coming journalists with opportunities to work with and learn from members of the profession. Other workplace-oriented programs invite seasoned journalists, managers, and editorial staff to participate in diversity seminars that provide guidance on how to seek and retain talented minority journalists. Predictably, many of these programs focus on socializing minority journalists into the existing newsroom culture; few concentrate on the ways in which newsroom cultures themselves need to change in order to truly integrate the "differences" minority journalists may bring. As such, many of these well-meaning programs may favor candidates who are willing to assimilate into the already-existing practices that mitigate against innovative reporting on racial issues.

A promising example of a program that directly confronts this dilemma is the Columbia Journalism School's "Let's Do It Better" awards and workshops. The central goal of the workshop is to encourage journalists, educators, and editors to view coverage of race and ethnicity "as an urgent journalistic duty." The program gives awards to journalists who produce exemplary articles and reports, which are judged by their candor about race and ethnicity, their creativity, and their attention to history and social factors that shape the issues and events being covered. These exemplars are then used as models for workshop participants to explore how race reporting can go beyond established norms. In the workshops, news "gatekeepers"—editors, journalism instructors, and journalists—are engaged in the process of improving race and ethnicity reporting, and are given tools to bring the lessons learned back to their classrooms and newsrooms. Importantly, this includes discussions of how to "improve the newsroom and classroom environment in which journalists and students of varying race and ethnicity function" so as to "deepen the multicultural dialogue and help retain talented young journalists in the profession."[42] While the workshops also provide advice about recruiting minority talent, they recognize that getting people in the door is just the beginning, and that changing the culture, not just the composition, of the newsroom is a necessary step in improving the overall quality of reporting on race and ethnicity.

Many scholars and critics of news media are quick to remind us, however, that market imperatives may work against integrating and transforming newsrooms. As summarized earlier, audiences of color are not highly valued by advertisers, particularly in the news industry. And, as competition between news providers increases across various media, and advertisers demand access to choice affluent segments of the audience, people of color and "their issues" may lose even more space to topics preferred by the desired audience. Even media outlets that are targeted at racial and ethnic minorities may not contain much, or any, news, as programming on BET (both before and after the Viacom takeover) suggests. However, I argue that the way in which media managers imagine the economically desirable audience and its news interests is linked to the dominant assumptions about race that make this market logic seem like common sense. If we conceptualize racial politics as a zero-sum game, or racial identity as an aspect only of the lives of people of color, not Whites, then it is hard to see race as anything but a "minority issue," not a "general market" interest.

I want to suggest that, in order to transform current practices of racial reporting and to curtail the negative impacts the dominant framing of race has on public discussion and opinion, journalists must endeavor to make clear how so-called minority issues impact the general public. Lani Guinier and Gerald Torres provide an extremely useful metaphor for us to discuss race across racial publics: the miner's canary.[43] In their book of the same title, these scholars explore how racial inequalities are indicative of broader social problems that, in fact, impact the majority of Americans, who will eventually pay hidden costs. That Whites and people of color share these problems can be seen best when one looks from the perspective of the canary in the coal mine. The canary, whose sensitivity to noxious gases tells all occupants of a mine that the environment is poisonous, will suffer first; if the miners and others see its suffering, the best course of action is to heed the warning and fix the problem rather than ignore the canary, blame it for getting sick, or tell the bird to shut up. Reports on racial controversies or specific racial groups should be similarly related to the condition of the general public. I recommend that we transport their canary metaphor for investigating and responding to racial inequality to discussions of how journalists craft discourses about race and ethnicity in both general- and specialty-market publications.

In their book, *The Black Image in the White Mind*, Robert Entman and Andrew Rojecki suggest that we need to see more news frames that support "racial comity" to encourage readers to see more commonalities between racialized groups than differences. Similarly, Amitai Etzioni reminds us that when one looks at poll results regarding "American virtues" such as hard work, Blacks, Whites, and Hispanics are closer in opinion than one would imagine given the prominence of racial discord in most reporting. I applaud these authors for calling on journalists and others to see and communicate how much closer we are to consensus on many political and cultural issues. But I am wary of the strategy of comity in the particular case of multiracial identity. More examples of people's commonalities are certainly needed to help break down color barriers, but looking at the current set of narratives involving multiracial people, frames of racial comity may also encourage racial amnesia. Certainly, the dominant articles analyzed in the previous two chapters reveal racial comity, but this agreement and comfort is built on "best of both worlds" mini-features that cast individual multiracial people as brave, special, and implicitly (or explicitly) better than other people of color in terms of their approach to racial identity. Racial comity, in these news reports, has been represented by profiles of interracial families "transcending race" and "bridging divides" to make relatives or neighbors see the light. Indeed, these stories are popular and circulate widely in the press, magazines, autobiographies, movies, and novels. But this thread of discourse can easily lead to colorblind conclusions that blind us to racial stratification.

What I would propose instead is the development of "racial courage" in addition to racial comity. By racial courage I mean producing reports that are complex but not esoteric; narratives that are not afraid to point out culpability or privilege; a narrative that tries to humanize participants not by playing to sympathy, but by taking a hard but nuanced look at how race is embedded in each person's life and what it means in broader context. This kind of reporting would acknowledge the influence of the past on not only current policies, but also on contemporary individuals' abilities to traverse racial boundaries, claim particular names or cultural objects. Racial courage would delineate the consequences of both social- and individual-level racial or racist acts. It recognizes that Black and White are important polarities in the racial system, but we ignore the realities of Native American, Asian, Latino/a, and Arab American experiences to our peril. Reporters who approach race with courage would discuss Whiteness as a social phenomenon that continues to exist as a benchmark for humanness. Racial courage would attempt to get away from simple quantifications of who suffers most and seek answers for the question: How might we, despite the fact that we are all implicated in the racial system, strive to work to end racism from our particular standpoint?

The kind of racial discussion I seek may seem impossible in a venue such as the commercial news media, yet some journalists and editors continue to reach for it. The "Let's Do It Better" awards have recognized eight classes of journalists who have covered race with courage. The *Akron-Beacon Journal's* year-long series on race relations, which grew into a public journalism project that involved and inspired the entire community to think about race is another example. The *New York Times* series "How Race Is Lived" also tried to provide a deeper and multifaceted portrait of race and racism in the United States.

Individual newsrooms, such as Georgia's *Savannah Morning News*, have opened their doors to African Americans and rural Whites in their city, training them in journalism and providing them with an outlet to write about their communities for the newspaper. Specialty magazines that straddle academic, activist, and lay audiences, such as *Color Lines*, *Ms.*, and *Race, Gender and Class*, publish insightful, progressive depictions of race and power that deserve larger audiences than each of these publications currently reaches. Outside of these topical periodicals, however, one of the greatest obstacles to changing the way race is done in the news is the fact that news values privilege coverage of sporadic and sensational racial events.

The kind of racial courage that we need to see in the news can only be developed through sustained coverage of social issues that have racial components. Today, if, say, a rash of shootings happen in an inner city neighborhood, it may spark a few articles on the economic depression of the area and the lack of educational resources, but then the coverage will dwindle as the shooting stops. Instead, we need regular coverage of the hypersegregated areas that delves into the history of how the area came to be hypersegregated; of how years of benign neglect and suburbanization contribute to failing schools at least as much as overworked and underpaid parents. Coverage of the role of race in the disaster wrought by Hurricane Katrina was to some a welcome change; reporters from some news outlets attended to structural and historical causes of the unequal impact of the storm on New Orleans' Black population. But as the story dwindles into the middle and back pages of mainstream newspapers, it remains to be seen if reporters will continue to include analysis of racial inequalities as they document the rebuilding and resettling of New Orleans and the Gulf Coast.

Beyond the news, there are other genres that certainly invite and provoke discussions that move beyond racial binaries and happy-go-lucky predictions of easy racial intermarriage. Recent documentaries, autobiographies, and fictional movies spark (often heated) conversations about what race means today. Independent journalists on the Internet and bloggers are credited by many with ensuring that race was part of the Katrina story. Many spaces can generate productive reports and dialogue about race. However, as the medium that purports to provide the salient descriptions of events in the real world, and to provide the preeminent vehicle for public information for political discussion, dominant news media have a special responsibility. We spend a lot of time debating the realities of race, and the contributions of the news media to our thoughts and discussions could certainly be improved.

Final Dispatch

If our society's vision of race is to be truly transformed, this process cannot only occur through the glacial pace of one-marriage-at-a-time. And even if this slow pace were the only road, all families have secrets, pain, and hard times; the stories of idyllic unions across racial lines that make up the majority of the dominant media's current coverage of the 2000 Census, multiracial celebrities, and their racial aftereffects do not tell the whole story. They cannot be but a beginning to a larger, more contentious and difficult set of "family conversations" about what race and race relations have been and are becoming.

Think, for instance, about the "multiracial state" of Brazil, or the "mestizo" nation of Mexico, or the territory of Puerto Rico: all three have officially embraced race mixing as part of the national heritage, but all three also exhibit troubling patterns of racial discrimination and stereotyping that have left the darkest-complected members of the multiracial family at the bottom of the socioeconomic ladder. In Mexico, President Vincente Fox's recent insensitive racial remarks about Black workers and the issuance of a stamp showcasing Black minstrel cartoon characters are indicative of the continued conflicts over the role of African heritage in the "national family." Thus, officially sanctioning mestizo/mixed racial identities, even celebrating them, is no guarantor for racial equality. If, as they say in many Latin American countries, "money whitens," then Blackness remains at the negative end of the color spectrum in most people's minds. The suppression and the return of the African influence in these nations demonstrates that the European/White elements of mixed heritage are still valued higher than Black contributions. The Cuban rejoinder, "where are you hiding grandma," is used to put people in their place, remind them of their Afro and Indian roots when they insist upon emphasizing only their "Spanish" lineage, an attempt to whitewash their history. Safely ensconced, allegedly, in only the most ancient roots of the family tree, Blackness (and often Indianness) is segmented off from the present day multiracial national persona.

This tension between public and private renderings of the racial/ethnic national family is also evident in a recent controversy over honoring participants in our national pastime, baseball. In the summer of 2005, fans were asked to vote for the "Latino Legends Team," sponsored by Major League Baseball and Chevrolet. Two notable absences on the ballot were Reginald Martinez Jackson, aka Reggie Jackson, Mr. October, and Ted Williams, both of whom are already enshrined in the Baseball Hall of Fame. These great players were not included, according to the organizers, because they did not have a public connection to Latino identity or community. Similar to the Malone brothers, then, being Latino was predicated on both family ties and community visibility. While some have said Jackson's middle name, prominently displayed on his Hall of Fame plaque, makes his Latino identity "public," others insist he is known as an African American player first and foremost, echoing the Latino law students' disqualification of Maria Hylton. Williams, most agree, did not do anything to acknowledge his Latino heritage while he lived, and by some accounts actively suppressed his mother's Mexican identity to avoid social embarrassment and discrimination as he came up in the leagues.

Will the Latino Legends controversy lead to calls for Ted Williams, *American* hero, to be recognized as Ted Williams, *Latino American* hero? Are we ready to remember him that way, or can we? Until we can wrestle with the contradictions that make the second incarnation of Ted Williams seem foreign and the former normal, then we have not dealt with the continued contradictions of looking at our racial world with binary blinders. If we cannot reimagine these people with a full view and reckoning of their racial and ethnic stories and how our society and state helped shape them, we will never embrace both the pain of Williams's Latino family and the excellence of their son's accomplishments. We can never fully recognize the triumph in the story of Mildred and Richard Loving, whose famous suit against the State of Virginia legalized interracial marriage, until we speak to the years they spent living in anxiety and danger as they waited for the judiciary to make their decision. If we do not chart our way to a future reckoning with these aspects of our mixed-up racial past, we will never let grandma out of the closet, and we can never form a more perfect union if we try to do it on the backs of individual couples and families, blending in an ever-distant future.

Notes

1. Houston Baker Jr. coined the term *conservative nostalgia* in "Critical Memory."
2. See Turner, "The Dangers of Misappropriation."
3. Asen, "A Discourse Theory," 199.
4. Harris, "Whiteness as Property." P. Williams, *Alchemy of Race and Rights.*
5. Lowe, "The International within the National."
6. Harris, "Whiteness as Property."
7. Hong, "Something Forgotten," 298.
8. See Streeter, "Hazards of Visibility"; Bost, *Mulattas and Mestizas.*
9. For example, Patricia Hill Collins notes in *Black Sexual Politics* how Halle Berry is able to "work her *Blackness*" (my italics) in her varied Hollywood film roles. She is light-skinned and "projects a kind of beauty that is not purely Black" and has been cast as an object of desire in roles that White or Latina actresses could also play (194–95).
10. See Bost, *Mulattas and Mestizas*; Zackodnik, *The Mulatta and the Politics of Race.*
11. Whelan, "Casting Tiger Woods."
12. Eddings, "Tiger's Triumph," 8.
13. Cole, "Nike's America/America's Michael Jordan," 91.
14. Quoted in Bamberger, "Mining Woods," 27.
15. Andrews, "The Fact(s) of Michael Jordan's Blackness," 128.
16. See Enloe, *Bananas, Beaches, and Bases.*
17. Lowe, "The International Within the National."
18. Salgado, "Misceg-narrations," 48.
19. Ibid., 50.
20. Scheiber, "Barack Obama's Miraculous Campaign."
21. Malcolmson, "Obama's Speech," (my italics).
22. Johnson, "Let's Hear More from Obama," D12.
23. See Fine, Weis, Pruitt and Burns, Eds., *Off White*; L. "Williams, *The Constraint of Race*; Frankenberg, *White Women, Race Matters.*
24. Tilove, "New Star Emerges," (my italics).
25. Scheiber, "Barack Obama's Miraculous Campaign," 26.
26. Hooper, "Speaker's Words Felt," (my italics).
27. Tilove.
28. Lowe, "The International Within the National," 32.
29. I take the term *to cover* from Kenji Yoshino's book, *Covering: The Hidden Assault on Our Civil Rights.* Yoshino claims there are overt and covert pressures on minority groups to "tone down" or not display cultural and behavioral differences in public settings. The pressure to "cover," he argues, masks important realms of discrimination and limits our ability to safely express our authentic selves. Yoshino identifies an "assimilationist bias" in American law and society wherein traits that are "mutable"—such as language or hairstyles—are not seen as realms of discrimination like "immutable traits"—such as skin color or gender.
30. Roberts, "A World Without Race," 33–34.
31. Roberts, 33.
32. Obama, *Dreams from My Father*, 204.
33. Singh, *Black Is a Country*, 214–15.
34. Powell, "The Colorblind Multiracial Dilemma," 158.
35. duCille, *Skin Trade*, 270.
36. Salgado, 53–54.
37. Newkirk, *Within the Veil.*
38. Wilson, *Black Journalists in Paradox.*
39. Mellinger, "Counting Color," 129–51.
40. Ibid., 145.
41. Gandy, *Communication and Race.*
42. "Let's Do It Better!" http://www.jrn.columbia.edu/events/race/about.asp.
43. Guinier and Torres, *The Miner's Canary.*

References

Andrews, David L. "The Fact(s) of Michael Jordan's Blackness: Excavating a Floating Racial Signifier." *Sociology of Sport Journal*, 12, (1996): 125–58.

Asen, Robert. "A Discourse Theory of Citizenship." *Quarterly Journal of Speech*, 90, (2004): 189–211.

Bamberger, Michael. "Mining Woods for Gold: Is Tiger Worth $100 Million to Nike? You Bet He Is." *Sports Illustrated*, September 25, 2000, 27.

Bost, Suzanne. *Mulattas and Mesitizas: Representing Mixed Identities in the Americas, 1850–2000.* Athens and London: University of Georgia Press, 2002.

Cole, C.L. "Nike's America/America's Michael Jordan." In *Michael Jordan, Inc.: Corporate Sport, Media, Culture, and Late Modern America*, ed. David L. Andrews, 65–106.

Collins, Patricia H. *Black Sexual Politics: African Americans, Gender, and the New Racism.* New York: Routledge, 2004.

duCille, Ann. *Skin Trade.* Cambridge: Harvard University Press, 1996.

Eddings, Jerelyn. "Tiger's Triumph, America's Gain." *U.S. News & World Report*, April 28, 1997, 8.

Enloe, Cynthia. *Bananas, Beaches and Bases: Making Feminist Sense of International Politics.* Berkeley: University of California Press, 1990.

Fine, Michelle, Lois Weis, Linda C. Powell, and L. Mun Wong (eds.) *Off White: Readings on Race, Power, and Society.* New York: Routledge, 1997.

Frankenberg, Ruth. *White Women, Race Matters: The Social Construction of Whiteness.* Minneapolis: University of Minnesota Press, 1993.

Gandy, Oscar H. *Communication and Race: A Structural Perspective.* London: Oxford University Press, 1993.

Guinier, Lani and Gerald Torres. *The Miner's Canary: Enlisting Race, Resisting Race, Transforming Democracy.* Cambridge: Harvard University Press, 2002.

Harris, Cheryl I. "Whiteness as Property." *Harvard Law Review*, 106 (June 1993): 1707–91.

Hong, Grace Kyungwon. "Something Forgotten Which Should Have Been Remembered: Private Property and Cross-Racial Solidarity in the Work of Hisaye Yamamoto." *American Literature* 71 (June 1999): 291–310.

Hooper, Ernest. "Speaker's Words Felt by Every American." *St. Petersburg Times*, July 29, 2004, 3B.

Johnson, Michael. "Let's Hear More from Obama: It's Time for Jackson to Retire." *Boston Globe*, August 1, 2004, D12.

Lowe, Lisa. "The International Within the National: American Studies and the Asian American Critique." *Cultural Critique* 40 (Autumn 1998): 29–47.

Malcolmson, Scott L. "Obama's Speech Says Much About Race Politics." *New York Times*, August 1, 2004, D3.

Mellinger, Gwyneth. "Counting Color: Ambivalence and Contradiction in the American Society of Newspaper Editors' Discourse of Diversity." *Journal of Communication Inquiry* 27 (2003): 129–51.

Newkirk, Pamela. *Within the Veil: Black Journalists, White Media.* New York: New York University Press, 2000.

Obama, Barack. *Dreams from My Father: A Story of Race and Inheritance.* New York: Three Rivers Press, 1995, 2004.

Powell, John A. "The Colorblind Multiracial Dilemma: Racial Categories Reconsidered." In *Race, Identity and Citizenship*, ed. R.D. Torres, 141–57.

Roberts, Dorothy. "A World Without Race: But Does Black Nationalism Have to Go Too?" *Boston Review*, May/June 2006, 33–34.

Salgado, Rachel Scherr. "Misceg-narrations." In *Mixing It Up: Multiracial Subjects*, eds. SanSan Kwan and Kenneth Speirs, 31–70. Austin: University of Texas Press, 2004.

Scheiber, Noam. "Barack Obama's Miraculous Campaign: Race Against History." *New Republic*, May 31, 2004, 21–26.

Singh, Nikhil P. *Black Is a Country: Race and the Unfinished Struggle for Democracy.* Cambridge: Harvard University Press, 2004.

Streeter, Carolyn. "The Hazards of Visibility: 'Biracial' Women, Media Images, and Narratives of Identity." In *New Faces in a Changing World*, eds. DuBose and Winters, 301–322.

Tilove, Jonathan. "New Star Emerges on Democratic Scene: Obama Speech Marks Race-Politics Watershed." *The Times-Picayune* (New Orleans), July 28, 2004, 1.

Turner, Ronald. "The Dangers of Misappropriation: Misusing Martin Luther King Jr.'s Legacy to Prove the Colorblind Thesis." *Michigan Journal of Race & Law* 2, no. 1 (1996): 101–30.

Whelan, David. "Casting Tiger Woods." *Forecast*, May 7, 2001, 1–4.

Williams, Linda Faye. *The Constraint of Race: Legacies of White Skin Privilege in America.* University Park: Penn State University Press, 2003.

Williams, Patricia J. *The Alchemy of Race and Rights: Diary of a Law Professor.* Cambridge: Harvard University Press, 1991.

Wilson, Clint III. *Black Journalists in Paradox: Historical Perspectives and Current Dilemmas.* New York: Greenwood Press, 1991.

Yoshino, Kenji. *Covering: The Hidden Assault on Our Civil Rights.* New York: Random House, 2006.

Zackodnik, Teresa C. *The Mulatta and the Politics of Race.* Jackson: University of Mississippi Press, 2004.

PERMISSIONS

The editor gratefully acknowledges permission to reproduce the following essays:

Section I: Concepts and Definitions

1. American Anthropological Association. "Statement on 'Race.'" Reprinted courtesy of the American Anthropological Association (http://www.aaanet.org/stmts/racepp.htm).
2. Michael Omi and Howard Winant. "Racial Formation," from *Racial Formation in the United States: From the 1960s to the 1980s*, 57–69. New York and London: Routledge, 1986. Reprinted courtesy of Taylor & Francis.
3. Beverly Daniel Tatum. "Defining Racism: 'Can We Talk?'" from *"Why Are All the Black Kids Sitting Together in the Cafeteria?": And Other Conversations about Race*, 3–17. New York: Basic Books, 1997. Copyright © 1997 by Beverly Tatum. Reprinted by permission of Basic Books, a member of the Perseus Books Group.
4. Peggy McIntosh. "White Privilege: Unpacking the Invisible Knapsack." *Peace and Freedom Magazine*, July/August, 1989. A publication of the Women's International League for Peace and Freedom. Copyright © 1989 by Peggy McIntosh. Anyone who wishes to reproduce this article must apply to the author, Dr. Peggy McIntosh, at mmcintosh@wellesley.edu. This article may not be electronically posted.
5. Stuart Hall. "The Whites of Their Eyes: Racist Ideologies and the Media," in *Silver Linings: Some Strategies for the Eighties*, edited by George Bridges and Rosalind Brunt, 28–52. London: Lawrence and Wishart, 1981. Reprinted by permission of the publisher.

Section II: Realities and Representations

6. Randy Ontiveros. "No Golden Age: Television News and the Chicano Civil Rights Movement." *American Quarterly* Vol. 62, No. 4 (December 2010): 897–923. Copyright © 2010 by The American Studies Association. Reprinted by permission of Johns Hopkins University Press.
7. George Lipsitz. "*Lean on Me*: Beyond Identity Politics," from *The Possessive Investment in Whiteness: How White People Profit from Identity Politics*, revised and expanded edition, 140–158. Philadelphia: Temple University Press, 2006. Copyright © 2006 by Temple University. Used by permission of Temple University Press. All rights reserved.
8. bell hooks. "Representing Whiteness in the Black Imagination," in *Cultural Studies*, edited by Lawrence Grossberg, Cary Nelson, and Paula A. Treichler, 338–346. New York: Routledge, 1992. Copyright © 1992 by Routledge, Taylor & Francis Inc. Reprinted courtesy of Taylor & Francis.
9. Kathy N. Newman. "The Forgotten Fifteen Million: Black Radio, Radicalism, and the Construction of the 'Negro Market,'" in *Communities of the Air: Radio Century, Radio Culture*, edited by Susan Merrill Squier, 105–121. Durham and London: Duke University Press, 2003. Copyright © 2003 by Duke University Press. All rights reserved. Republished by permission of the copyright holder. www.dukeupress.edu.
10. Sut Jhally and Justin Lewis. "White Responses: The Emergence of 'Enlightened' Racism," from *Enlightened Racism: The Cosby Show, Audiences, and the Myth of the American Dream*, 93–111. Boulder: Westview Press,

11. Tricia Rose. "'Fear of a Black Planet': Rap Music and Black Cultural Politics in the 1990s." *The Journal of Negro Education* Vol. 60, No. 3, Socialization Forces Affecting the Education of African American Youth in the 1990s (Summer 1991): 276–290. Reprinted by permission of Howard University.

Section III: Authenticities and Appropriations

12. Kembrew McLeod. "Copyright, Authorship and African-American Culture," from *Owning Culture: Authorship, Ownership, and Intellectual Property Law*, 71–108. New York: Peter Lang, 2001. Reprinted by permission of the publisher.
13. Arthur Jafa. "My Black Death," in *Everything but the Burden: What White People are Taking from Black Culture*, edited by Greg Tate, 244–257. New York: Random House, 2003. Copyright © 2003 by Greg Tate. Used by permission of Broadway Books, a division of Random House, Inc. Any third party use of this material, outside of this publication, is prohibited. Interested parties must apply directly to Random House, Inc. for permission.
14. Gilbert B. Rodman. "Race . . . and Other Four Letter Words: Eminem and the Cultural Politics of Authenticity." *Popular Communication* Vol. 4, No. 2 (2006): 95–121. Reprinted by permission of Taylor & Francis (http://www.tandfonline.com).
15. Karen Shimakawa. "Mind Yourself: On Soundwalking, Race and Gender," in *Staging International Feminisms*, edited by Elaine Aston and Sue-Ellen Case, 23–36. New York: Palgrave Macmillan, 2007. Reprinted by permission of the publisher.
16. S. Elizabeth Bird. "Imagining Indians: Negotiating Identity in a Media World," from *The Audience in Everyday Life: Living in a Media World*, 86–117. New York: Routledge, 2003. Reprinted courtesy of Taylor & Francis.
17. Peter A. Chvany. "'Do We Look Like Ferengi Capitalists to You?': *Star Trek*'s Klingons as Emergent Virtual American Ethnics," in *Hop on Pop: The Politics and Pleasures of Popular Culture*, edited by Henry Jenkins, Tara McPherson, and Jane Shattuc, 105–121. Durham and London: Duke University Press, 2002. Copyright © 2002 by Duke University Press. All rights reserved. Republished by permission of the copyright holder. www.dukeupress.edu.

Section IV: Technologies and Institutions

18. Richard Dyer. "The Light of the World," from *White*, 82–103. New York and London: Routledge, 1997. Copyright © 1997 by Richard Dyer. Reprinted courtesy of Taylor & Francis.
19. Herman S. Gray. "Jazz Tradition, Institutional Formation, and Cultural Practice," from *Cultural Moves: African Americans and the Politics of Representation*, 32–51. Berkeley: University of California Press, 2005. Copyright © 2005, The Regents of the University of California. Reprinted by permission of the publisher.
20. Grant Farred. "Introduction" and "Speaking for," from *Phantom Calls: Race and the Globalization of the NBA*, 1–64. Chicago: Prickly Paradigm Press, 2006. Reprinted by permission of the publisher.
21. Dwight A. McBride. "Why I Hate Abercrombie & Fitch," from *Why I Hate Abercrombie & Fitch: Essays on Race and Sexuality*, 59–87. New York: NYU Press, 2005. Copyright © 2005 by New York University. All rights reserved. Reprinted by permission of NYU Press.
22. Michael Eric Dyson. "Unnatural Disasters: Race and Poverty," from *Come Hell or High Water: Hurricane Katrina and the Color of Disaster*, 1–14. New York: Basic Civitas, 2007. Copyright © 2005 by Michael Eric Dyson. Reprinted by permission of Basic Civitas, a member of the Perseus Books Group.
23. George Lipsitz. "The Hip-Hop Hearings: The Hidden History of Deindustrialization," from *Footsteps in the Dark: The Hidden Histories of Popular Music*, 154–183. Minneapolis: University of Minnesota Press, 2007. An earlier version was published in *Generations of Youth: Youth Cultures and History in Twentieth-Century America*, edited by Joe Austin and Michael Nevin Willard, 395–411. New York: NYU Press, 1998. Reprinted by permission of NYU Press.
24. Carol Stabile. "Criminalizing Black Culture," from *White Victims, Black Villains: Gender, Race, and Crime News in US Culture*, 153–174. New York: Routledge, 2006. Copyright © 2006 by Carol Stabile. Reprinted courtesy of Taylor & Francis.

Section V: Identities and Globalizations

25. Stuart Hall. "Old and New Identities, Old and New Ethnicities," in *Culture, Globalization, and the World-System: Contemporary Conditions for the Representation of Identity*, edited by Anthony D. King, 41–68. Minneapolis: University of Minnesota Press, 2011. Copyright © 1997 by the Regents of the University of Minnesota. Reprinted by permission of the publisher.

INDEX

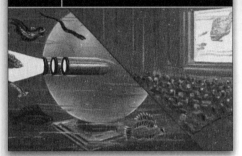
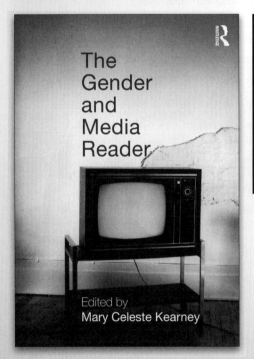